W9-CGN-619

UNIVERSITY ECONOMICS

UNIVERSITY ECONOMICS

ARMEN A. ALCHIAN
University of California, Los Angeles

WILLIAM R. ALLEN
University of California, Los Angeles

WADSWORTH PUBLISHING COMPANY, INC.
Belmont, California

L.C. Cat. Card No.: 64–18137

Printed in the United States of America

Preface

A test of any theory of science is its ability to explain the events of the real world in a coherent, consistent fashion. Economics passes that test. This book presents, at the introductory university level, an exposition of economic analysis, with persistent emphasis on its empirical meaningfulness and validity.

Although economics is often thought to be primarily concerned with national and international problems, it is in fact also germane to the everyday activities and situations that command our detailed attention. We have found, from some twenty years of experience in teaching, that students do not complain that economics is dull, dreary, or dismal. They show keen interest and even excitement in discovery of new understanding and interpretation—mainly because, we believe, the theory is made pertinent and convincing by repeated, hard-boiled, nonromantic applications in contexts that are familiar, relevant, and verifiable within their own range of experiences. At the same time, major national-policy questions are considered again and again without a loss of continuity of interest.

Of course, in any such book much must be left out; to cover all problems is to learn little about anything. But the fundamental principles and theorems of analysis are included and stressed and repeatedly applied. The propriety in stressing the few fundamentals is, we think, illustrated by the statement of an economist, Alain A. Enthoven, who has worked very successfully at the highest levels of national policy in the Department of Defense:

> . . . the tools of analysis that we [in Defense] use are the simplest, most fundamental concepts of economic theory, combined with the simplest quantitative methods. The requirements for success in this line of work are a thorough understanding of and, if you like, belief in the relevance of such concepts as marginal products and marginal costs, and an ability to discover the marginal products and costs in complex situations, combined with a good quantitative sense. The economic theory we are using is the theory most of us learned as sophomores. The reason Ph.D.'s are required is that many economists do not believe what they have learned until they have gone through graduate school and acquired a vested interest in marginal analysis ("Economic Analysis in the Department of Defense," *American Economic Review*, LIII [May 1963], 422).

The instructor will find that significant advances of the postwar years have been incorporated. The realm of the theory covering choice, demand, exchange, and supply has been extended to behavior beyond the old, narrow, wealth-maximizing behavior in simple private-property markets. The scope of costs, and their relation to various dimensions of outputs, has been enlarged to include mass-production economies of modern industrial techniques, so that economics now has replaced a former mere classification of mutually exclusive possibilities with a valid law of costs. Furthermore, advances in the theory of money and asset demands, and the recognition of the role of information and the costs of acquiring it, have enabled economists to discern a unified theory of economics valid for both individual behavior and for fluctuations in national aggregates of employment and income. No longer are economists condemned to reliance on schizophrenic assumptions about rigid and customary wages and prices, money illusions, liquidity traps, and fixed-input coefficients to explain the occurrence of significant fluctuations in employment and income.

A floodtide in recently revised textbooks to greater emphasis on price theory does not reflect a swing of fashions, or a correction of an excess departure, or fading memories of the deep depression of the 1930s. It is instead a result of these scientific advances in achieving a verified, unified, cohesive structure of analysis based on the broadened fundamental postulates of the behavior of individuals in the face of scarcity and uncertainty. For that reason, the exposition in this book reflects *primarily* a sequential development of principles and modes of analysis, rather than topics ordered according to social importance. This does not mean that topics or classes of problems are discussed at random. Instead, topics are taken up in the sequence that the development of the analysis permits most conveniently. The problems of aggregative income and general employment fluctuations are taken up in the second half. Instructors who find a topical sequence more congenial to their modes of teaching will find it more appropriate to jump from Chapter 1 to Chapter 31 and those following, returning later to pick up at Chapter 2. Although we personally prefer the order of presentation employed in this book, we see no overwhelming reason for recommending that others change their habits to conform to ours.

Though we have striven to make the book relatively unusual in its nonromantic emphasis on empirical meaningfulness and validity of the theory, perhaps the questions at the end of each chapter may be its most unusual feature. We think these questions are more akin to those typically found in mathematics, statistics, chemistry, and physics books. They are not cocktail conversation questions. They are designed (1) to repeat and reinforce the learning of concepts and principles, (2) to develop a familiarity and ease in applying economic theory, (3) to test the student's progress, and (4) to stimulate exploration in slightly more advanced aspects not covered in the text. Most unusual to economics, though not to texts in the other sciences, is the inclusion of answers (pp. 859–906) to half of the questions. (Questions that are answered are prefaced by a number in **boldface** type.) Answers serve two purposes: to guide and give the student confidence in his progress and to demonstrate that not all economic problems are answered merely with an expression of personal opinion, preference, or profound judgment. Instead, there is a right answer, an objectively or logically testable correct answer. Of course, some of the questions (mainly, those that ask for one's preferences or beliefs) admit of no uniquely correct answer. But our reason for asking the various classes of questions is precisely to emphasize the difference in the meaning of a correct answer. Unanswered, and answerable, questions are answered in an Instructor's Manual.

So great has been the aid of some of the following, all of whom we acknowledge for aid and comfort during this enterprise, that only with reluctance do we necessarily absolve them from blame for our errors: William Meckling, Norman Breckner, Russel Nichols, Robert Johnson, Donald Gordon, Karl Brunner, George Stigler, Jack Hirshleifer, Roland MacKean, Elmer Fagan, Joy Fort, and our employers at the University of California and the Rand Corporation.

In addition, we wish to thank the publishers of the *South Atlantic Quarterly*, the *Southern Economic Journal*, and *Oxford Economic Papers* for giving us permission to use material contained in articles they have published.

Although there are limits to the significance and usefulness of the formal study of economics (free societies and the free and open markets that have conspicuously characterized them admittedly have grown and prospered in the face of almost universal illiteracy regarding the academic discipline of economics), give it a fair try, anyway. Economics *does* deal with things important; and we believe a modicum of attention to the principles and analysis, along with a conscientious effort, can provide experience in analyzing problems and evaluating and utilizing evidence. Unless you fight it assiduously, it may well even be quite interesting.

April 23, 1964

Table of Contents

1

SCARCITY, COMPETITIVE BEHAVIOR, AND ECONOMICS

Inspiring allusions to an "economy of abundance" and intriguing references to an "affluent society" are fashionable today. To be sure, everyone realizes—or complains—that we do not actually have all we need. Indeed, those most inclined to speak of "abundance" and "affluence" are also those who most vigorously state that the community needs more schools, better housing, and additional highways (along with laws prohibiting billboards). The authors can add some needs of their own: Alchian needs longer vacations and a more luxurious house; Allen needs a hi-fi set and a second car.

How can we be rolling in abundance when we still have so many unfilled needs? One suggestion is that we *could* fill our needs if only we were more clever or worked harder or both. As one former government official put it: "We have not had enough of anything, because we have not used fully the fantastic productive power which could provide us with enough of everything." A second suggestion is that we *do* produce enough stuff in the aggregate, but—because of selfishness, bad planning, and poor taste—we turn out the wrong things: "silly gadgets" and cosmetics and overly large automobiles instead of symphony orchestras and art museums and lunar explorations.

Whether our frustration stems from failure fully to realize our productive potential or from imbalance in the particular lines of production or from still other factors, there is no doubt that (a) in most countries the absolute level of living has risen over time and (b) it would be physically feasible to produce still more and thus further increase per capita income.

EVER EXPANDING "NEEDS"

Although output and income per person have increased, are our current needs being filled more satisfactorily than they were a century or five centuries ago? Are people really more content and less anxious and frustrated now with their higher material well-being? The poor in this country today live better than the kings of yesterday, but do they feel like kings? Perhaps such questions suggest that our "needs" have not remained constant, but rather have grown, along with our means to satisfy them. Although our *absolute* standard of living has risen, it is not obvious that we have bettered our lot *relative* to our "needs." Possibly we should avoid speaking of "needs," for that term has connotations of constancy and of being a physiological imperative. A "need" is presumably something definite and unchanging; thus, finite means could satisfy the "need" fully. And ultimately, perhaps in Buck Rogers' time, we might be wealthy enough to satisfy *all* of our needs. But at present, so-called "needs" seem as numerous, varied, and pressing for this generation as for any in history.

Our frustrations from having insufficient worldly goods are best analyzed not in terms of "needs," but in terms of *desires, wants, preferences,* and *demands.* It is not analytically persuasive, however emotionally compelling it may be, to say that I "need" another automobile; but economics does have something coherent to say about my relative *desire* for another automobile, the implications of that desire with respect to my market behavior, and the repercussions of my behavior on economic decisions by numerous other people.

We could indeed satisfy more of our desires if we were willing to work harder and longer. Are we irrational, then, in toiling only 40 hours a week instead of 50 or 60 or 70? Obviously not; for leisure, too, has its worth. Similarly, we could have more over the long pull if we were to "save" and accumulate "capital," which could increase our productivity. Are we hopelessly confused in saving no more than we do? Obviously not; when saving diverts resources to capital accumulation, current consumption will be cut, and current consumption certainly has its value. In short, things—including leisure and consumption goods—are generally costly and not free. Typically, we must decide, if we want more of one item, how much of some other item we are willing to sacrifice. How much are we willing to pay or forego; what is our demand price?

Still another way to have more is to maintain "full employment." Short of actually destroying things, how could we be more inefficient in the use of our resources than to leave them involuntarily idle? It is one thing deliberately to decide on more leisure; it is another to be forced into idleness because supposedly no job is available. Thus, economics is concerned not only with how hard and how efficiently an employed person works, but whether all willing workers can find employment at all. But we shall see that the problem of "full employment"—like the issues of leisure and of saving and of resource use in general—involves making decisions and choosing among alternatives.

The moralists and the poets among us may find it convenient and satisfying to focus on our rising absolute standard of living, whether their particular emphasis be on stoking the productive fires even higher or on specifying to the community just what are the truly civilized uses of production. But economic analysis cannot ignore the fact that our demands have risen along with our material means; so it is as true today as it ever was that not all desires can be fully satisfied; that acquiring one thing generally involves giving up something else; that it thereby behooves us to use our resources as well as possible; that efficiency in use of resources is manifested in *minimizing* the sacrifice in getting what we want or, alternatively, in *maximizing* what we get in return for a given sacrifice (cost).

SCARCITY AND THE GENERAL PROBLEMS OF ECONOMICS

In the wide gamut of economic problems, there is a common, dominant element—one pervasive, inescapable, inevitable fact: *scarcity*. That is the starting point of our analysis, and behavioral implications and consequences stemming directly or indirectly from it is our subject matter.

Even in today's lands of milk and honey, few wants are wholly satisfied. We want more than we have, and—since the fiasco in the Garden of Eden—most of what we want must be acquired through sweat, strain, and anxiety. Since we cannot have *all* of *everything* we want, each of us must *choose* how best to use available resources. What things shall be made and in what proportions? How and with what resources? Who will consume which goods and how much? How much shall we direct from current to future consumption? We shall see that the problem of "efficient" production—which is only partly a technological, or engineering, problem—is intimately involved with appropriate exchange among people. To exchange implies specialization, with some people producing more than they consume of some things and less of others.

Just what is "efficient" production? Is it most likely to be achieved, or achieved in greater degree, under the direction of an all-powerful economic czar? Can it be achieved in any other way? What principles, if any, are there about exchange as a means of "efficient" utilization of existing goods? More succinctly, what is the nature and what are the sources of the "gains" from specialization and trade? Are the gains from international trade different from those of domestic commerce? What role is played by prices (the exchange ratios among goods and services) in coordinating and directing productive activities and in determining the distribution of wealth among people? What role is played by money? Finally, how will the alternative ways in which the preceding questions are resolved in the world affect the levels of wealth and the social, political, and cultural behavior and mores of people? These are the problems, in general form, of economics.

Economics, then, is concerned with some of the most fundamental and pervasive issues of society: What goods shall be produced? In what proportions? In what manner and over what time period? For whose consumption? With what social and cultural effects?

OUR ECONOMIC SYSTEM

The economic dimensions of American society are awesome: a population of 190,000,000 includes a labor force of 75,000,000 (one third of whom are women) and, through 11,000,000 business units (including 9,000,000 single proprietorships, 1,000,000 partnerships, and 1,000,000 corporations), annually produces goods and services valued at $600,000,000,000—some 30 percent of the world total. Who designed and who now directs this vast production-and-distribution machine? Surely, to solve the intricate problems of resource allocation in a vast economy, central guidance is needed. In small and intimate matters, willy-nilly individual decision making may be tolerable, but to resolve the vital, over-all, aggregate problems, obviously someone must be in charge.

In actuality, the American economy is *not* directed by an economic czar—governmental or private. No specified or specifiable person or group poses detailed questions of how the community is to use its resources, and no one imposes comprehensive answers to the questions. Yet, such problems—large and small—somehow *are* being solved daily. No particular person has been appointed to ensure that adequate food reaches the city each day and is allocated among competing claimants—and yet the people eat. No "big brother" oversees the multitudinous and infinitely varied operations of the economy and ensures that the essential functions are performed. But the alternative to "big brother" evidently is not chaos and anarchy. An economic order does exist; some sort of system or mechanism does operate. Moreover, this system allows individuals and business firms to be essentially autonomous—and self-interested—agents (though subject to the constraints that define private-property arrangements) and, at the same time, yields a high and seemingly maximum degree of economic efficiency.

To speak of an economic system or mechanism suggests that the efficient order which normally prevails rests on decisions that are not simply random. In a world of scarcity, it neither inevitably nor inexplicably "just happens" that millions of autonomous agents in the American economy are so reliably coordinated that they turn out $600,000,000,000 of goods and services in a year. But the requisite plans and corresponding decisions are, to one degree or another, of limited scope and objective. The individual person, far from wrestling with grandiose problems of the universe, must decide how much of his own wealth and income to expend on this article or that, what kind of work he personally may do to increase his wealth, how much to save from his income in order to acquire more wealth. No farmer adds up the total demands for food in a city, comparing the total with the amount being shipped to the city, to make sure that adequate supplies will be available. Instead, with his individual interest and perspective, he asks, "Would I personally be richer or poorer if I shipped more or less?" No czar resolves issues of the "big picture" of the economy; instead, millions of us make decisions on our own "little pictures."

Although many of us may successfully solve our personal problems, we may still be grossly ignorant about how our actions and those of other people interact so as to solve the large problems that every society solves somehow or other. Comprehension of these larger problems requires understanding of economic analysis. We can be sure that economic analysis is being ignored when any of the following fallacious arguments are presented: that the rationale of the capitalistic system rests on an essential assumption of a "harmony of interests"; that customers must take what producers offer them; that automation reduces available jobs; that tariffs protect domestic wage earners from foreign labor; that our otherwise unlimited productive capacity is curtailed by monopolistic capitalists who arbitrarily set prices high; that unions protect workers from greedy employers; that inflation hurts the wage earner and benefits the employer; that social-security payments contributed by employers to their employees are paid for by the employers; and that social conscience and civic sensitivity are or should be the main guides to business corporate behavior.

THREE ATTRIBUTES OF ECONOMIC ANALYSIS

To answer the various questions posed, three methodological attributes of economic analysis should be clarified at the outset. (1) Economic theory is "positive" or "non-normative." It cannot determine which consequence or type of behavior or economic policy or system is a good or better one—any more than physics can tell whether gases are a "better" state of being than solids, or any more than medicine can tell you whether or not you "ought" to smoke and drink. Economics can tell you only the consequences of certain conditions, policies, or choices. It is scarcely the proper role of the economist to sit on Mt. Olympus and decree whether you "should" consider a particular consequence desirable or preferable to another. (2) Economics cannot predict the future. It can merely explain what conditions will lead to what consequences. It yields only conditional "if-*A*-then-*B*" propositions; it does not predict that the *A* will occur—although some *economists* (as opposed to economics) may make such predictions. (3) There *is* a valid core of economic theory applicable to *all* economic systems and countries. There is *not* one special economic theory for capitalism and another for communism, although significant differences exist in the institutions and legal frameworks.

CAPITALISM AND SOCIALISM

Although economic theory is applicable to all economic systems, some portions of the theory are richer and more extensively instructive for a capitalistic system, and other aspects are more useful for socialistic institutions and arrangements. For the present, it is sufficiently accurate to define capitalism as a system of private-property rights in all goods, with the central government protecting and enforcing these rights. Private-property rights, in turn, can be defined as the rights of people to use their goods and resources (including labor and time) as they see fit. If a rock is my property and a piece of glass is yours, I have control over the use of my property and you over yours; but for me to throw my rock through your glass would violate your rights to use your glass as you see fit. However, mutually agreeable uses of property—e.g., exchange—are permissible.

Socialism, at the other extreme, is a system in which rights to the uses of a good are not assigned to specified individuals but instead are divided among various government agencies, who decide about uses and consequences to be borne. This system is usually called "government ownership."

The portion of economics comprising the theory of exchange is applicable to a wider class of problems in a capitalistic private-property economy than it is in a socialistic society. This does not mean there is no exchange in the latter; there is, of course, a great deal of it. However, the extent of and reliance on interpersonal exchange is greater in a capitalistic system. Capitalism is a system in which interpersonal exchange of private-property rights to goods plays a pervasive, extensive role. In a socialist system, on the other hand, political power and exchange of *non*private-property rights are used much more widely to solve the economic questions. If we were to devote primary attention to the socialist system, we would investigate much more fully the processes of political exchange and political decision making.

AN OVERVIEW OF THE CHAPTERS AHEAD

In the next chapter, we present the basic postulates of economics on the basis of which the theory of exchange can be formulated. As we shall see, these postulates have a wide set of implications. After pointing out some of the implications, we will, in Chapters 4 and 5, concentrate on developing an understanding of the rationale and consequences of simple exchange *per se*. Then, in Chapters 6–11, we will use that understanding to analyze the operation of marketplaces, which are institutions for facilitating the exchange process. The famous "demand and supply" analysis will be elaborated and applied to different types of exchange markets. Next, in Chapters 12–13, we shall investigate more fully the circumstances under which market exchange is restricted (even though we will have had in Chapter 5 a brief preview of some of these factors). Of course, when we analyze restrictions on market exchange, we shall have to consider other methods of competition; these other methods then become more influential in affecting the extent to which people can alter the mixture of goods they have. In other words, an inherent part of economics is an analysis of the form of competition, or discrimination, that determines the combinations of goods people can have. In fact, this analysis of competition is the subject of the first portion of the book. The first part concludes with a presentation and application of some economic concepts concerning the allocation of various scarce resources over *time*, rather than just among different people as if all goods were perishable and consumption had to take place now (Chapters 14–15). In short, in the first portion of the book, economic analysis is applied to the problem of allocating consumption goods among competing claimants; the problem of production of additional goods—which is the subject matter of the second portion—is not considered. Problems of producing more goods include changes in the aggregate level of productive activity as well as decisions by individual businesses and industries. Thus, the second portion includes "money and banking" and "national-income" analysis. The book concludes with a consideration of international economic relations and of growth problems of relatively poor countries.

In sum, at both the allocative and the aggregative levels, economics studies the competitive and cooperative behavior of people in resolving their conflicts of interest which arise from the fact that their wants exceed what is available.

Questions

1. A recent book tells us (partly in our paraphrase): "We are trapped by the 'dismal science'—economics, which is dominated by the belief that the achievement of abundance is impossible and that the economic problem is still the distribution of scarce resources. This is nonsense. Abundance has arrived! Look at our huge agricultural surpluses. Look at the fact that in America alone we have the ability to produce more than $600,000,000,000 in goods and services in a single year. The United States can produce beyond our needs. The basic problems are to see that the potential production is realized and distributed fairly and equitably." Are you inclined to agree or disagree? Why?

2. "If people were reasonable and acted with justice and good faith, there would be no strikes, no economic problems, and no wars." Do you agree? If so, why? If not, why not?

3. "A more equal distribution of wealth is socially preferred to a less equal distribution."

- a. Explain why you agree or disagree.
- b. What is meant by "socially preferred," as contrasted to "individually preferred"?
- c. How could you tell what is socially preferred?

d. Is "socially preferred" equivalent to "socially desirable"?

e. What are the criteria—and how are they determined, or how should they be determined, and by whom—of "social desirability"?

4. What do you think is meant by a fair share? Do you think other people will agree with your interpretation? How does your interpretation compare with the idea of students getting "fair" grades?

5. What is nonsensical about the proposition "A good economic system maximizes the welfare of the maximum number of people"?

6. Do you think employees and managers of publicly owned institutions (state colleges, post offices, bus lines) are more considerate of their patrons than are those of privately owned businesses? What evidence (other than your own experience) can you cite? Would you expect less attentive behavior to be more tolerated in one of these situations than in the other? Why?

7. Try to give a definition of "efficient" production, "scarcity," "shortage," "surplus," "needs." (Later, compare your definitions with those given in subsequent chapters.)

8. What is meant by specialization? Do you know anyone who does not specialize? Why do people specialize?

9. "The economy of the United States is directed by the capitalists concentrated in Wall Street." Evaluate this assertion now, and again when you have completed this course.

10. "Scarcity, competition, and discrimination are inextricably tied together. Any one implies the other two. Furthermore, to think of a society without these is to be a romantic dreamer." Do you agree? If so, why? If not, why not?

11. "Food is grown, harvested, sorted, processed, packed, transported, assembled in appropriately small bundles and offered to consumers every day by individuals operating in their own personal interests. No authority is responsible for seeing that these functions are performed and that the right amount is produced. Yet food is available every day. On the other hand, especially appointed authorities are responsible for seeing that certain goods, like water, education, and public housing, are made available. Is it not paradoxical that in the very areas where we consciously plan and control social output, we often find shortages and failure of service? References to classroom and water shortages are rife; but who has heard of a shortage of restaurants, churches, furniture, beer, shoes, or books? Even further, is it not surprising that privately owned businesses, operating for the private gain of the owners, provide as good, if not better, service to patrons and customers than does the post office, schools, and other publicly owned enterprises? Yet wouldn't you expect that publicly owned, not-for-profit organizations run explicitly for the people's benefit would provide better service than privately owned businesses operated for the profit of the owner? Furthermore, wouldn't you expect public agencies to be less discriminating according to race and creed than privately owned business? Yet the fact is that they are not." How do you explain these paradoxes?

12. Are scientific laws discovered or created? Explain why the correct answer is that they are created by man. Why do we seek scientific laws?

13. a. What is meant by the logical validity of a theory?

b. What is meant by the empirical validity?

c. Does either imply the other?

14. The economic ideals of the Middle Ages were influenced by Christianity and by Aristotle's doctrines. Among those ideals were the following:

"(1) The purpose of economic activity is to provide goods and services for the community and to enable each member of society to live in security and freedom from want. Its purpose is not to furnish opportunity for the few to get rich at the expense of the many. Men who engage in business with the object of making as much money as possible are no better than pirates or robbers.

"(2) Every commodity has its 'just price,' which is equal to its cost of production. No merchant has a right to sell any article for more than this price plus a small charge for the service he renders in making goods available to the community. To take advantage of scarcity to boost the price or to charge all that the traffic will bear is to commit a mortal sin.

"(3) No man is entitled to any larger share of this world's goods than is necessary for his reasonable needs. Any surplus that may come into his possession is not rightfully his but belongs to Society. St. Thomas Aquinas, the greatest of all medieval philosophers, taught that if a rich man refuses to share his wealth with the poor, it is entirely justifiable that his surplus should be taken from him.

"(4) No man has a right to financial reward unless he engages in useful labor or incurs some actual risk in an economic venture. The taking of interest on loans where no genuine risk is involved constitutes the sin of usury.

"It would be foolish, of course, to suppose that these lofty ideals of an economic system largely devoid of the profit motive were ever carried out to perfection." (E. M. Burns, *Western Civilizations, Their History and Culture,* 5th ed. New York: W. W. Norton, 1958.)

What do you think of these ideals? Do you approve of them? Which ones? If you disagree with any, how would you express your ideal? After completing this book, answer these questions again.

15. The *Statistical Abstract of the United States,* published annually by the U.S. Department of Commerce, Bureau of the Census, is a standard summary of statistics on the social, political, and economic organization of the United States. It presents a vast myriad of data and also reveals sources of data. Every college library has a copy. You are strongly urged to spend half an hour or so scanning the volume. For example, on page 136 of the 1963 edition you will find some data about faculty salaries. Do you think your instructor is underpaid or overpaid? After thinking about that for three minutes, compare faculty salaries with the information about earnings in other industries presented on pages 239–241 of that same edition.

16. Ask your parents what your family's income was last year, before income taxes. Then compare the answer with the data in the following table, showing the 1961 distribution of money income received by each tenth of all spending units, by lowest income in each tenth.

Spending Units	*Lowest Income within Tenth*
Lowest tenth	not available
Second "	$1,330
Third "	2,170

Spending Units	*Lowest Income within Tenth*
Fourth tenth	$3,160
Fifth "	4,180
Sixth "	5,000
Seventh "	5,820
Eighth "	6,930
Ninth "	8,410
Highest "	10,600

a. Probably most of the students in your class come from families in the top half. Guess what fraction of total national income goes to the lowest tenth, to the fifth tenth, and to the highest tenth.

b. Do you think the dispersion of *individual* incomes is less than for spending units? It is. Why?

c. If after-income-tax incomes were recorded instead of pretax incomes, how do you think the numbers in the above table would be changed? What would be the effect on the percentage of post-tax income available to each tenth?

d. Why is the post-tax measure of income better than the pretax as a measure of incomes to each spending unit? Explain in what respects it is a worse measure than pretax income.

2

SOME POSTULATES OF ECONOMICS

We now consider some of the basic postulates of economic theory—particularly, postulates about the behavior of people in the face of scarcity. These postulates provide a basis for and a beginning of analysis, and supply some of the elemental building blocks of theory. There is nothing presumptuous or absurd in basing analysis of human behavior on a few simple, idealized conceptual constructs. Indeed, there is no alternative. It is the essence of science that behavior and phenomena generally are comprehended and interpreted with, and only with, the aid of a limited number of mutually consistent postulates, propositions, and premises.

Postulate 1. The unit of analysis is the individual.

Groups, organizations, communities, nations, and societies are institutions whose operations can best be understood when we focus attention on the actions and choices of constituent members. When we speak of the goals and actions of the United States, we are really referring to the goals and actions of the individuals in the United States. A business, a union, or a family may be formed to further some common interest of the constituents; but the group actions are still the results of choices or decisions of individuals seeking to attain some jointly held individual goals. If we ask why a nation, family, union, or business behaves as it does, we must ask why individuals join or form such organizations and why they choose to act as they do within the organization. Here, therefore, we will not ask, "Why does the U.S. government make the decisions it does?" or "Why does General Motors do this or that?" or "Why does a union do what it does?" We ask instead, "Why does the individual who makes the decisions decide as he does?" The principles of economics are based on postulates or propositions about individual motives and responses to changes in the environment. Putting it disparagingly, the only tools for analysis offered by the study of economics are those based on the behavior of individuals.

Postulate 2. Each person seeks a multitude of goods.

Too often, it is incorrectly asserted that economics is based on the premise of the "economic man," whose sole interest is in making more money or getting wealthier. However, economics does *not* assume that men are motivated solely or even primarily by the desire to accumulate money or wealth. Instead, economic theory assumes that man—whether he lives in Karachi, Canton, or Kalamazoo—desires more of many other things as well: prestige, power, friends, love, respect, self-expression, talent, liberty, knowledge, good looks, leisure.

By and large, economists do not grandly claim that all choosing is part of practical economics. Day to day, economic theory is usually applied to the production, sale, and consumption of goods with money expenditures via the marketplace. Nevertheless, economic theory does not ignore, let alone deny, that man is motivated by cultural, social, and intellectual objectives, as well as material and monetary goods.

We will use the term "good" for any entity, or goal, that anyone desires. A "good," then, is anything that gives *utility* to someone. More rigorously, if having some of an entity is preferred to having none of it, then the entity is a "good." Your idea of "goods" may differ from other people's; maybe you think that cigarettes are not "goods" and that other persons would really be "better off" without them. Despite this possible difference of opinion, the term "goods" means no more than that some person—as *he* judges his situation—prefers to have some.

Postulate 3. For each person, some goods are scarce.

Economic goods is the technical name for *scarce goods*. A good is scarce if, and only if, one prefers to have *more* of it than he has. Fresh chicken eggs are quantitatively more plentiful than bad eggs; but good eggs are scarce, while bad eggs are not. If a good, however desirable, is so abundant that one need not sacrifice anything to get more of it, it will not be an economic good. Economic goods are those that command a price; the *price* is what must be given up to get a unit of the economic good. If nothing need be sacrificed, the item is a *free* good. Free goods have utility, of course. The classic case of a free good, to most of us most of the time, is air: we simply inhale, and there it is, without our sacrificing anything to obtain it; and, generally, for each of us to have more air than we now have would be of no value (although *fresh* air is an economic good to the astronaut, the deep-sea diver, and the city resident on a smoggy day).

A world without scarcity, in which nature profusely bestows on us all of the goods and services we could possibly desire, is not our world. Whether we would be happier in that world, we shall never know; for, despite our work and sacrifice of leisure, we are unable to produce enough to satisfy *all* the wants of any people *all* the time. In short, we live in a world of scarcity: there is not enough of everything to satiate our desires for more goods. Even for Americans, affluent as we may be, we are still a society of scarcity. *Choices* among available opportunities are still required. You cannot have all you want: better hi-fi equipment, wall-to-wall carpeting, walnut paneling, longer vacations, more golf courses. There are demands for more missiles, airplanes, hospitals, schools, highways, and houses—and more for foreign aid to buy peace and influence and to foster foreign economic growth. But nature simply has not provided enough to satiate the desires of every living being—not merely people, but also animals and plants, for they, too, are busily claiming all the earth. (We shall subordinate the struggle against plants, pests, and animals, while emphasizing the conflict of interest among people for more of the goods that exist or could be produced.)

Postulate 4. Substitution: a person is willing to sacrifice *some* of any good to obtain *more* of some other goods.

Among man's many goods, one is not more important than another. It is not true that man must first satisfy his hunger before he will seek play, love, artistic expression, or prestige; he does not wait until he has obtained some specific level of food before he begins to care at all about clothes or shelter or freedom. He simultaneously wants some of all these things. Even in the poorest and most primitive societies, a good deal of effort is devoted to art, music, play, self-expression, and status, as well as to food and shelter. Man strives for higher levels of realization in *all* these objectives. He does not satiate himself in one before seeking another. Furthermore, he is willing to sacrifice some of his food for the sake of more leisure or play or friendship or prestige or art. A bit of friendship or prestige or love will in turn be forsaken for more wealth or artistic accomplishment. There is no hierarchy of goods.

This postulate of substitutability can be stated more precisely: "For *some more* of any good, a person is willing to sacrifice *some* of any one, or group, of other goods." Or, in reverse, "A person is willing to sacrifice *some bit* of any desired thing if he can obtain a *sufficient* increase in the amount of some other desired goods." He will not necessarily sacrifice *all* of a good for some other good; but he will substitute *some* of a good for *some* more of other goods. Economics even has a measure of this substitutability. The *maximum* amount of some good which a person is willing to give up to get a *unit more* of some other specified good can be expressed as a ratio. For example, if you are willing to sacrifice a *maximum* of two bottles of Coke per month to get one more pack of cigarettes per month, the "consumption-substitution ratio" between Cokes and cigarettes is

$$\frac{\text{2 bottles of Coke per month}}{\text{1 pack of cigarettes per month}} = \text{2 Cokes per pack of cigarettes.}$$

This ratio reveals that you would *not* give up more than two bottles for one more pack; the *most* you would give up is just two bottles. If you did make an exchange at that rate, you would *not* reach a *more* preferred situation, because the sacrifice of the two Cokes exactly offsets the gain of one more pack of cigarettes. If you had been able to exchange *less* than two bottles for one more pack, you would have reached a more preferred situation. In the present instance, this ratio is formed by the *maximum* decrement you would tolerate for one more pack of cigarettes. That maximum, if sacrificed, would yield you no gain; anything less would. Therefore, sometimes the above-defined ratio is called the "indifference ratio," to indicate that any exchange at that ratio would not make any difference in the person's general state of satisfaction. That ratio, given the existing situation and state of preferences, is the *limiting* ratio of acceptable exchange among those goods as far as the person is concerned. Given an opportunity to exchange at that ratio, he would just barely be willing to do so; or, if you wish, he is indifferent to the substitution.

We shall not call this ratio the "substitution" ratio, because it concerns consumption; and, as we shall see later, it is also possible to substitute *production* of one good for another by *producing* less of one good in order to produce more of another. To avoid confusing these two different concepts, we will call one the "consumption-substitution ratio" and the other the "production-substitution ratio." For the present we are investigating the "consumption-substitution ratio."

Postulate 5. The consumption-substitution ratio depends upon the amount of each good available.

The rate at which a person is just willing to give up Cokes to get more cigarettes is not a random variable, nor is it a constant. It depends upon many things, such as past experience, exposure to ideas of other people, and inherent psychological traits. However, instead of investigating these influences, we shall concentrate on the effects of the particular mixture of various goods he happens to have at any time.

Suppose that a person has three Cokes and three packs of cigarettes available for consumption each week, and that he is willing to substitute more cigarettes for Cokes by giving up one Coke for one more pack. Now change his circumstances; suppose he has three Cokes and eight packs of cigarettes each week; that is, he has more cigarettes but no less of any other goods (here characterized by Cokes). His consumption-substitution ratio will change in a predictable way: he will not be satisfied with just one pack of cigarettes for one Coke; he will insist on more than one pack of cigarettes, say two. Or—making cigarettes (the good of increased amount) the unit of comparison—he will, for one more pack of cigarettes, now be willing to give up less than one Coke —say, half a Coke—per week (equivalent to one Coke every two weeks for one more pack each week). The consumption-substitution ratio of *X* for *Y* $(-\Delta y/\Delta x)$ decreases in absolute value as one has more *x* or less *y*.[1]

Restating the postulate: "As a person has a larger amount of any good, *X*, diminishing amounts of other goods will be given up to get another unit of *X*." For example, the more champagne I have available per year, the less I will pay in sacrifice of clothes, or food, or cars, or any other goods, to get one more bottle of champagne per year. The larger the amount of champagne I have per year, the lower the price I will pay to get still more. This interpretation suggests another description of this postulate: the principle of diminishing subjective value as one has larger amounts of any good.

Postulate 6. Not all people have identical consumption-substitution ratios for any given combination of goods.

Although everyone is alike in certain respects, no two people are alike in *all* characteristics. This diversity extends over talents, productive ability, attitudes toward various kinds of behavior, and *subjective valuations of various goods.* One man's tastes are another man's prejudices. One man's discrimination is another man's selectivity. Diversity extends over time; no person remains the same in all respects with the passing of time, even though certain characteristics common to all people persist—in particular, those specified by the preceding postulates. The particular diversity we shall emphasize is that among the substitution rates for different people and for different goods. Other differences in personal characteristics will also be relevant but need not be specified in detail here.

[1] This process is often called the principle of *diminishing marginal* (not total) *utility,* implying that extra units of any good add less and less to one's utility, the more of that good he has. Unfortunately, no one has yet demonstrated how to measure "utility" to the degree required. Therefore, instead of talking of diminishing marginal "utility," we shall refer to the increments in amounts of (changes in) a good that would suffice exactly to offset a unit change in the amount of some other good.

Postulate 7. The future is uncertain.

Not all outcomes are totally unpredictable, for laws of probability do predict the relative frequency of the outcome of a large series of trials. But, although probabilities may be computable or forecastable, foreknowledge of the outcome of specific trials or events escapes our ken. For the moment, it is helpful to note that a changing and unpredictable future means that the usefulness or value of resources will change. Unavoidably, some resources will become more valuable, and some will become less so. Just as a tornado or earthquake destroys some resources, so psychological variables such as tastes and fashions, or biological considerations such as age and health, destroy or create values in unexpected places and things. Gains and losses cannot be eliminated; they are inevitably thrust on somebody. If a city grows in one area and decays in another, who suffers the loss in usefulness and value of the declining areas, and who reaps the gains in the growing areas? Furthermore, upon whom should the gains and losses be thrust? The first question is one that economic theory can answer. The second is one that theory can help to answer by discerning (but not judging) some consequences of various methods of determining who does bear the unforeseen losses or gains. As long as uncertainty exists, both questions continue to demand answers.

Rationality of Analysis versus Rationality of People

You are not expected at this stage to foresee all the testable, real-world implications of these postulates. But their simplicity and generality should be appreciated. Indeed, they may seem so simple and trite as hardly to merit explicit, rigorous enunciation. Nevertheless, they form the bases of the economic analysis that we shall apply in deriving "explanations" of the real economic world. People may not be—and need not be—aware of these postulates, any more than parents are necessarily aware of the laws of genetics and sexual attraction. They still will behave according to certain laws and postulates. None of the present postulates requires that people perform some conscious mental calculation in determining their actions. The postulates assert simply that people *do* reveal regular, consistent, and predictable patterns of responses to specified choices or changes in the environment; they act *as if* they were purposeful.

For example, the third postulate says that people prefer more to less goods. But so do many animals. How can this be explained? In animals it is called the acquisitive *instinct*. In man we call it a rational process. In fact, it may be instinctive in both. Or possibly millions of centuries ago, very early in the evolutionary stream, some species of pre-man—for some inexplicable reason—manifested acquisitive behavior: collecting sticks, rocks, bones, food, or areas of land from which it kept out potential invaders. It may not have had any reason for doing so, but nevertheless that kind of behavior had high survival characteristics. Storing up food and territory enabled it to live longer and breed more prolifically. The survival value of that trait in the evolutionary selective process may have been a primary factor in the subsequent dominance of acquisitive species. Alternatively, you may believe that the acquisitive urge was instilled by God as punishment for man's fall from grace—a part of his original sinfulness. Man, by that acquisitive drive, has been condemned to greed, work, and conflict. According to this position, he should seek to suppress that urge in order to live a "better" life. Or you may believe that since man has the capacity to think and foresee consequences, he has consciously decided that acquiring more goods is "better" than having less. Therefore, his behavior displays the characteristic of seeking to have more. Just why he thinks it is better need not concern us here.

You are offered your choice among these three "explanations" of why people behave in a manner characterized by the listed postulates. It makes no difference which rationale you adopt—nor whether your interest be in simple understanding or in normative economic policy. But it will make a difference if you are seeking to influence people by exhorting them to deviate from those postulated characteristics.

Tolerant we can be with these three "reasons" for the validity of the postulates, but there is one that economic theory does not tolerate. Economic theory denies that these postulates represent drives, behavior, or traits that are taught and subtly imbued into people by the particular type of economic sytsem and institutions in which they live. These behavioral characteristics exist whether the economic system is capitalist, communist, or anarchist. You may choke at accepting this absolute denial; you may assert that economics is arrogant, stupid, or arbitrary in making such a denial. But if you want to learn how to apply existing economic theory to the real world, you should know the "preconceptions" of that theory. And this is one of them. Reject it at your peril; for if you do, you reject most of current economic theory. Reserve judgment, as we hope you will, until you can judiciously consider the ensuing applications of the analysis.

MEANING OF SELF-INTEREST

Where in the preceding set of postulates is the common belief that economic theory assumes an economic man who is greedy, egocentric, selfish, and interested only in his own wealth? It isn't there, and properly so. We did assume that man is greedy—meaning that he wants more rather than less goods. But a man may want control over more rather than less goods precisely in order to give some in charity to other people or to help other people. It was not assumed that he is oblivious to other people, that he is uncharitable or not solicitous of other people's welfare; nor is he assumed to be concerned only with more wealth (in the narrow sense of money wealth). If these assumptions had been made, the resultant theory would be immediately falsified by the fact that people do engage in charity, are solicitous of other people, and do consider the effects of their behavior on other people.

What *is* properly meant by "selfish economic man" is that he wants the right to choose among those options that will affect his ensuing state of affairs. In short, the *right to make choices* about the ensuing state of affairs is a desired thing, a "good," and an "economic good" to boot. However, like all other goods, the power to make choices among options that affect one's own and even other people's situations has its price. Raise the price, and less choice will be retained. Lower it, and more will be retained.[2]

UTILITY-MAXIMIZING BEHAVIOR

The preceding set of postulates is often called the "utility-maximizing theory of human nature." Why is it called "utility maximizing"? Is there something called "utility"—something like weight, height, wealth, or happiness—that people are really trying to maximize? No. The term originated during the early history of economic analysis. At that time it was popular to think that goods provide utility or usefulness in some objective, psychological, and measurable sense. But although that erroneous psychological conception has been abandoned, the name "utility" has struck. It is now simply an *indicator* for comparing options and showing preferences among them. Thus, it is now a matter of convention to say that if a person chooses option *A* rather than option *B*, option *A* has more utility for him.

Saying that a person "maximizes utility" may seem an elaborate camouflage of our ignorance; for it would appear that whenever a person voluntarily does anything, he can be said to be maximizing his utility. That charge would be correct if economics could not specify what entities are goods and goals, and if we could not classify some situations according to higher or lower costs of acquiring those goods. But, in fact, economics can make those specifications of goods and relative costs and therefore can provide a body of meaningful theorems.

Functional Analysis in Economics

A great deal of analysis in economics—and in other areas—is couched in terms of functional relationships. A *function* is a relationship between two or

[2] The proposition that man is motivated by, or values, the right to make choices about states of the world affecting other people's circumstances is often expressed by the proposition "Man loves power."

more entities. When we speak of a "function" or a "functional relationship," then, we mean that certain features of those entities can be meaningfully related. For example, a functional relationship is said to exist between caloric intake and weight, between force and speed, between height and weight, between age and baldness, between smoking and incidence of cardiovascular disease, and between wealth and higher education. Sometimes one entity is related to a group of other entities. For example, weight can be related to height and to girth and thus can be called a function of height and girth. To speak of weight as a function does not mean that there is necessarily a cause-and-effect relationship from height and girth to weight. A *functional relationship* implies merely that *knowledge about one set of variables or entities will yield more information about the magnitude of some other variable.* In some of the preceding illustrations, a cause-and-effect relationship may or may not be implicit. That will depend upon other information not inherent in or necessary for the use of a functional relationship. If one believes he is dealing with a causal relationship, he may identify some of the variables as the causal variables and the others as the determined variables. It is customary to refer to one set of the variables as the explanatory or independent variable and the remaining one as the dependent or explained variable. This terminology does not mean that the explained or dependent variable is presumed to be causally dependent, or that it is explained by the other variables. Thus, one could regard education as a variable dependent on wealth in the sense that we can estimate more accurately the extent of one's formal education if his wealth is known; it does not have to mean that the extent of his wealth determined how much education he did obtain. The extent of his education may, in fact, have determined how much wealth he later earned. In any event, regardless of whether the causation works in one direction or the other or even in both directions, to call one of the variables the independent, or explanatory, variable means only that a knowledge of the magnitude of that variable enables one to know the other variable with a greater degree of precision.

The functional relationship between the explained variable and an explanatory variable is said to be *positive* if similar magnitudes of each are associated (e.g., if an increase in one is accompanied by an increase in the other); it is a *negative* function if larger magnitudes of one are associated with smaller magnitudes of the other (e.g., if an increase in one accompanies a decrease in the other). Thus, weight and girth are positively related (form a positive function), while price and amount purchased are negatively related (form a negative function).

Use of a functional relationship between two variables does not mean that the explanatory variable is the only variable that affects the explained variable, or that other unspecified variables are assumed absent. An increase in caloric intake implies a gain in weight, even though an increase in caloric intake accompanied by increased physical activity may result in a weight decrease. There is still a positive relationship between caloric intake and weight, because—regardless of other factors—the weight will be greater than it would have been if caloric intake had not been increased. The expression "other things being the same" is merely a simple way of *concentrating attention* on the relationship between two particular variables, even though other explanatory variables may be pertinent and changing in magnitude. Thus, for example, the assertion "If I give you $10, you will be richer—other things being the same" is not falsified if other things change—for instance, if you lose $100 elsewhere. You are still richer than if I had not given you the $10.[3]

Questions

1. Explain the difference between the statements "People act in accord with certain fundamental propositions" and "People consult or refer to such propositions for guidance in choosing their behavior." Does either interpretation assume "free will" or independence from other people's behavior or tastes?

2. "The college football team has a goal."

    a. Is it the social goal of the "team," or is it the common individual goal of each member of the team?

    b. Are you sure that each member has only that goal and not also one of playing more of the game himself?

    c. Could these conflict?

    d. Is it helpful to talk of one goal's being preferred over another?

3. In trying to understand some policy enforced at your college, why is it misleading to ask why the college adopts that policy?

4. "All goods or goals are incompatible. And at the same time they are compatible." Can you make sense of that?

5. "People want wealth, power, and prestige." What is wealth? Power? Prestige?

6. Define "economic goods." How does an economic good differ from a "good"; from a "free" good?

7. As you use the words "scarcity" and "shortage," are they synonyms? If not, what is the difference?

8. If you don't smoke, is tobacco a good? Are purchase and sale necessary for an entity to be considered a "good"?

[3] In mathematical terminology, we are saying simply that partial derivatives are not to be confused with total differentials.

9. "A free good is an inconsistency of concepts, because what is free no one wants; otherwise it wouldn't be free. And if no one wants it, it can't be a good." Evaluate.

10. Explain or criticize the following statements and questions about the substitution postulate:

a. "Every student substitutes romance for grades when he dates rather than studying as much as he otherwise could have." Criticize.

b. "The substitution postulate says that a student does not seek the highest possible grades." Explain.

c. Does the substitution postulate deny that water, food, and clothing are more basic than music, art, and travel? Explain.

d. "There is no hierarchy of wants." What does that mean? Can you disprove it?

e. Is travel in Europe a substitute for formal academic education? For some food? For a bigger house or clothes or medical care? For what would it not be a substitute?

f. "I'd like to play some more poker with you again tomorrow night, but I don't think my wife would like it." Is this consistent with the substitution postulate? Is the wife's utility being compared with the husband's? Explain why not.

11. In testing a person's preference between two known options, it has been suggested that if a person agrees to let some unknown second party choose between the two options for him, then he is indifferent between the two options.

a. Do you think that is consistent with the postulates listed in the text?

b. Do you think that would apply to you in all cases?

12. Suppose that I am indifferent among the following three options of combinations of steaks and artichokes:

		Steaks		Artichokes
		pounds per year		
Options	*A*	100	and	30
	B	105	and	29
	C	109	and	28

a. What is the subjective substitution rate between *A* and *B*?

b. Which has the greater utility to me, *A* or *B*?

c. What is the subjective substitution rate between options *B* and *C*?

d. If the amount of meat in *A* were doubled to 200, what do you think might be the amount of meat required in *B* to make it of equal utility to *A*?

e. Using your answer to (d), compute the subjective substitution rate between the new *A* and the new *B*. Is your result consistent with the fourth postulate?

13. The following are combinations of *X* and *Y*, all of which are equally preferred by Mr. A.

Equal Utility Combinations	Goods X	and	Y
A	9	and	50
B	10	and	40
C	11	and	34
D	12	and	30
E	14	and	26
F	17	and	21
G	21	and	17
H	26	and	13
I	33	and	10
J	40	and	9
K	47	and	8
L	57	and	7

a. Plot each of these combinations as points on graph paper. (Y on vertical axis and X on horizontal.)

b. Connect the points with a smoothed line.

c. What postulate is expressed by the fact that there is more than one combination of the same utility to Mr. *A*?

d. Do these combinations conform to the postulates?

e. What postulate is expressed by the negative slope of the line connecting these combinations (the iso-utility line—sometimes also called an indifference curve, to connote that the person is indifferent among the combinations on this line)?

f. What postulate is reflected in the curvature (not the slope) of the iso-utility line?

14. If I regard each of the following combinations as equally preferred, does my behavior conform to the postulates of economic theory? If not, which postulate is denied?

Options		Goods X	and	Y
	A	100	and	70
	B	105	and	69
	C	110	and	68
	D	115	and	67

15. Suppose that Mr. *A* is indifferent between options *A* and *C*.

Options		X	and	Y
	A	100		200
	B	110		180
	C	120		160

If he is given a choice among the three options, prove that, according to the postulates, he will choose option *C* over either *A* or *B*. (The proof is easy—but it is *not* easy to discover that proof.)

16. What refutable proposition is revealed by the statement "*A* has more utility than *B* for me"?

17. Explain why the following statements are or are not consistent with the postulates.

a. Diminishing subjective value means that a person gets less satisfaction, the more he has of something.

b. Diminishing subjective value means that, as a person consumes some good, he gradually gets less satisfaction.

c. Diminishing subjective value means that, as a person acquires more of a good, he begins to value other goods more than this one.

18. How would you show graphically, on the diagram you drew for question 13, the meaning of postulate 3?

19. Many, if not all, of the postulates do not apply to some people. What happens to those people? Why?

20. Seven postulates were used to characterize some aspects of human nature and behavior.

a. Do you think any of them are also applicable to nonhuman animal life? For example, which of the postulates would give valid characterizations of behavior of monkeys, ants, bees, tigers, and birds?

b. Which postulates do you think serve to distinguish human from nonhuman behavior?

c. What evidence can you cite to support your answers?

21. Do you think the human race would survive if it lost the attribute described by postulate 2, while some other animals retained it?

22. "Economic theory is rational and logical, but man is not necessarily that way." What is the difference between a rational man and a rational theory?

23. "Don't be selfish, Jane," said Mother. What did Mother mean?

24. Would man be better off if he weren't selfish? How do you know?

25. In using the principle of utility maximization, does economic theory assume that man is maximizing some psychological entity? Explain why the answer is "No."

26. Answer the following questions concerning applications of functional analysis.

a. "Air density diminishes as altitude increases." If this is true, is density a positive or a negative function of altitude?

b. Do you think one's rate of use of gasoline is a positive or a negative function of his wealth? Of his family's size? Of his age?

c. In the relationship between gasoline consumption and wealth, which is the explanatory, predicting, or independent variable and which is the explained, predicted, or dependent variable? Can you suggest a situation for which the direction of explanation between these two variables is reversed?

d. In the functional relationship between the amount of a person's smoking and the state of his nervousness, which is the independent and which the dependent variable?

27. "Older people have more wealth than young people. Wealthier people eat more candy than poorer people. Therefore, older people eat more candy than younger people." What is the hidden assumption in that line of argument?

28. "Smoking shortens one's life." Does this mean that smoking is the only cause of death? That smoking is the only cause of a shorter life? That smoking is undesirable? That all people are alike except insofar as they smoke? That everyone who has ever smoked will surely die earlier than he otherwise would? That advertisements for tobacco should be prohibited?

29. Is "habitual behavior" consistent with the act of choice? Explain why it is.

30. A recently published book was entitled *Social Needs and Private Wants.* Would the title have suggested something different if it had been *Social Wants and Private Needs?* Why do you suppose the first title was chosen?

3

COMPETITION AND SURVIVAL TRAITS

A major implication of the postulates of economic theory is the existence of competition. Competition can take myriad forms, and these different modes have different personal and societal repercussions.

Competition

If there is scarcity and if there is more than one person in the world, then when one person obtains more of something, he generally leaves less for the others. You may have heard that "competition in the free-enterprise, private-property system promotes the worst antisocial, dog-eat-dog instincts in man. It provokes and rewards cheating and tawdriness, conformity and cowardice, while it destroys more genteel behavior. It breeds discrimination against people of a different religion, color, national origin, or sex." But competition—whether or not it has, or necessarily must, yield such dire consequences—is not at all unique to the free-enterprise, private-property system. Competition exists in every social system. Competition is a result of scarcity in a multiperson world having inherent conflicts of interest imposed by the physical world and by the nature of man—regardless of the social, cultural, or economic system within which he lives.

These strong statements should not be simply swallowed by the reader. Let him chew on them a bit before deciding whether to swallow them or spit them out. For example, let him inquire, "What do you mean by the 'nature of man'? What do you regard as his 'characteristic' or 'inherent' behavior? Are you asserting that human nature cannot change? After all, have not man's customs and behavior, codes and practices been evolved by a biological and cultural evolutionary process?" Our answer is that man's observed behavior, customs, and practices have indeed changed and evolved over time in response to cultural evolutionary forces. But by man's "nature" we mean the behavior postulates presented in the preceding chapter. And these postulates imply that competitive behavior resolves inherent conflicts of interests.

A sensible person, instead of futilely complaining about the existence of competition, will devote his attention to the way *alternative modes* of competition figure in economics. He will see that various types of competition imply various methods of ordering society or regulating the way people behave. It is not pertinent to ask, "How can we *eliminate* or *reduce* competition?" but instead: "What *kinds* of competition—or controls—are 'desirable' or 'undesirable'? What will make 'desirable' competition more viable, pervasive, and powerful; and what will make 'undesirable' competition ineffective?"

This question involves three phases: (1) understanding the effects of different kinds of competitive behavior; (2) choosing—on some basis not derivable from economics—a criterion of "desirability"; (3) knowing how alternative arrangements, laws, or institutions will affect the prevalence and effectiveness of each type of competition.

VIOLENCE AS A FORM OF COMPETITION

Violence is a type of competition for resolving interpersonal conflicts of interests. Thomas Hobbes, the seventeenth-century English political theorist, graphically analyzed such a state of anarchy: ". . . no place for industry; . . . no knowledge of the face of the earth; no account of time; no arts; no letters; no society; . . . continual fear, and danger of violent death; and the life of man, solitary, poore, nasty, brutish, and short." According to Hobbes, the problem of competition and order is resolved when each man gives up his right of governing himself: by "the foresight of their own preservation, and of a more contented life thereby," men escape "that miserable condition of Warre" by the establishment, under mutual covenant, of an absolute personal sovereign or "Common Power, to keep them in awe, and to direct their actions to the Common Benefit."

One may, of course, reject violence as an acceptable way of resolving the conflict of interests and still be dissatisfied with Hobbes's solution to the problem of societal order. But before rejecting the desirability of violence as a means of competition, the hard-headed student will observe that it has often been a highly respected and widely practiced technique—at least when it is applied on a nationwide scale and when it is successful. When Caesar conquered and took possession of Egypt, he was praised and honored by the Romans; had he instead roughed up a few people in Rome, he might have been damned as a ruffian and thief. When Alexander conquered the Near East, he was not regarded by the West as a gangster; neither was Charlemagne after he had conquered Europe. After the War of the Roses, kings of England did not lose the respect of the people. And the white man acquired America from the native inhabitants by force. Lenin and his successors were not universally regarded in Russia as a line of gangsters. Nor is Franco regarded by all in Spain as merely a successful gangster who seized power by violence. Nor Castro in Cuba, nor Ben Bella in Algeria.

Not all governments, of course, are founded on violence. However, this method is so effective that the application of violence is a jealously guarded monopoly of the main government—as a means of keeping itself in power and enforcing the use of *other* methods of competition in ordinary daily life. Thus, an apparently condemned method of competition is in fact a commonly used, often successful, and honored method; and, as we shall see, in certain areas of activity within a nation, violence is an accepted method of eliminating competitors.

"BRIBERY" AS A FORM OF COMPETITION

As an alternative to violence, competitive bribery is available as a partial solution—even though it, too, is generally classed as immoral. As a matter of fact, a free-enterprise economic system—a system in which the bulk of property is privately owned and in which most of the decisions affecting property and utility are made by the individuals themselves, in accord with their own perspectives and criteria—might be considered a system of competitive bribery. Let Adam Smith, the eighteenth-century British economist, comment:

> Man has almost constant occasion for the help of his brethren, and it is in vain for him to expect it from their benevolence only. He will be more likely to prevail if he can interest their self-love in his favor, and show them that it is for their own advantage to do for him what he requires of them. Whoever offers to another a bargain of any kind, proposes to do this: Give me that which I want, and you shall have this which you want, is the meaning of every such offer; and it is in this manner that we obtain from one another the far greater part of those good offices which we stand in need of. It is not from the benevolence of the butcher, the brewer, or the baker, that we expect our dinner, but from their regard to their own interest. We address ourselves not to their humanity but to their self-love.

OTHER TYPES OF COMPETITION

Violence and bribery—forceful imposition of will and inducement through offering gain—are only two of an enormous variety of interpersonal competitive techniques. The range and generality of other criteria for resolving interpersonal conflicts can be suggested by a few randomly selected criteria that are commonly used.

Suppose that you had to distribute 200 tickets to the Rose Bowl football game without selling them to the highest bidders. What forms of competition would you use in assigning priorities for deciding to whom to award the tickets? That is, what system of rationing or allocation would you use? If we, the authors of this book, could set the rules of the competition, we would ask all the applicants to send pictures, preferably in bathing suits. (Males need not apply.) We would select the prettiest 300—using our own standards of "prettiness"—and ask them to appear in our offices for interviews. Of these we would then select the most personable 200—using our own standards of "personality." Certainly this pleasant system is discriminatory. *All* competition is discriminatory. That, indeed, is its purpose: to discriminate among the various claimants in deciding who gets what. And beauty as a competitive, discriminatory factor is generally accepted and applied widely every day. Men and women allocate their wealth by selecting mates, in part at least, according to beauty and personality. You and I allocate our money to the prettiest women for letting us see them perform in the movies. In fact, it is difficult to find many situations in which beauty is not a source of competitive advantage.

If you think beauty is an improper criterion, you might use the "first come, first served" method; for instance, you could insist that all the applicants run a race and give the tickets to the first 200 to arrive at the finish line. Sounds silly. If you simply replace the words "finish line" by "box office at the Rose Bowl," it is now realistic, but is it less silly? The only difference is that for Rose Bowl tickets there is no uniform starting time or place, so that some wiseacres start out a lot earlier and then camp right at the finish line. In any case, we shall not find anything in economic theory saying that any particular form of competition is silly.

But is it fair? That depends on the circumstances and on what you mean by "fair"—which is simply another way of saying that it depends on the kind of competition *you* prefer. If you think "fair" means giving everyone an equal chance, would you want to give everyone an equal chance to operate on you for appendicitis, or to sing for you at a concert, or to teach you, or to be your wife, or to be the person you had to hire in your restaurant—or to whom you give Rose Bowl tickets? An equal chance could be provided by putting everyone's name (even those who did not take the time to apply for a ticket) on cards, then drawing 200 at random. That would be as equal a chance as possible, and nondiscriminatory. But, again, do you want to pick your mate that way? Do you want men selected for the armed forces that way? Obviously, "fair" or "preferred" does not mean "equal chance."

Before we leave this sampling of modes of competition, let us note that it is difficult to impose the competitive or selective criterion you would choose, even if you were given the opportunity to allocate some goods. Even after the resources (Rose Bowl tickets in our first example) are initially distributed and rationed, the problem of competitive criterion is not ended. Once your selected recipients get the tickets, what is to stop them in turn from handing them on to other people, with each initial recipient in effect treating the ticket as his *private property* and deciding to sell it to someone else, or re-allocating it according to his own preferred criterion? Apparently, the initial distribution is not necessarily the final one; each distribution can be followed by another one.

If I give the tickets to the prettiest girls, what is to prevent them in turn from handing the tickets to the handsomest boys? In other words, any person who has some resources to distribute will find it extremely difficult to ensure that his competitive selective criterion of who should get them will in fact be the only criterion followed—unless he tells all persons to whom he initially gives the tickets that they themselves must use the tickets in the way prescribed and not in any other way; that is, they must go to the game themselves and not re-allocate the tickets in exchange for money or love.

Competitive Criteria and Survival Traits

As mentioned, nothing in economic theory suggests that any particular form of competition is absurd. That particular judgment or evaluation rests on individual preferences about the different kinds of behavior and culture and allocation that are fostered by each variety of competition. For example, it is apparent that the first-come, first-served race to the box-office window, if used to parcel out food, would mean that the people best able to camp out or withstand the rigors of waiting in line will be those who have greater prospects of survival and prosperity. In accordance with the classic theory of evolution and selective survival of the fittest, that type of person will survive; and the institution of "camping out" will be characteristic of the economy. Instead, if food were parceled out to those who are the tallest, with short people getting the least, you can understand why the average height of the population would increase over time. And, alternatively, if beauty were rewarded, the beauty of women would increase—because women would make deliberate, conscious efforts to improve their beauty and because the more beautiful would be more likely to survive. Or one might propose to allocate goods on the basis of forensics and personality, somewhat as we parcel out votes for political office. Under that system, the society would become noted for its articulate and personable people. Or resources could be given to those with the most talent for deception and misrepresentation. The reader can imagine the mores and dominant types that would evolve in that society. Or resources could go mainly to those who are best able to create goods and services. In that kind of society, the more productive would be the wealthier and the dominant group.

These have been relatively simple and transparent examples of the relationship between forms of competition and simple survival traits. More complicated and subtle is an understanding of the kind of culture and the particular personality characteristics fostered in people by the various forms of competition implicit in different economic systems: in an economy where private property is authorized and encouraged, or where socialism is the rule, or where price controls are pervasive, or where monopoly is dominant, or where governments engage in heavy subsidization and control of various products. Although these forms of competition, as means of ordering our lives, are usually compared in terms of *productive* efficiency, we are concerned also with their cultural, social, and personality aspects.

Questions

1. "Government is the institution that holds the dominant power of coercive violence." "Government is a social agency for resolving interpersonal conflict."

a. Do you think those two propositions are correct and compatible statements of fact?

b. What evidence can you cite for your answer?

2. Name three famous, honored American statesmen who obtained that status by successfully competing in ability to use violence—whereas, had they failed, they would have been punished for treason or crimes against mankind.

3. Bribery, buying and selling, and threat of violence all are means of affecting other people's behavior. All involve an exchange of "this for that."

a. Why are some prohibited and others encouraged?

b. Try to identify the essential difference among those three forms of competition.

4. **a.** If you had the power to decide, what kinds of competition would you declare illegal?

b. What kinds of competition are made illegal by legal price ceilings, minimum-wage laws, fair-employment-practice laws, pure food and drug laws, private-property rights, socialism.

5. "Equality of opportunity" is widely advocated.

a. What does it mean?

b. How could you determine whether it exists?

c. Is there equality of opportunity to get an *A* in this course?

d. How would you make it equal, if it is not?

e. What is the difference between increasing and equalizing opportunity?

6. Defend competition for admission to colleges on the basis of mental ability, athletic ability, good looks, residence, willingness to pay, alumni status of parents, color, sex, religious belief. In fact, all are used to some extent. Why?

7. **a.** What kinds of competition are permissible in seeking political office but are not permissible in private business?

b. What kinds of competition are permissible in seeking admission to college but are not permissible in competition for grades in this course?

c. What kinds of competition are approved for business but not for admission to fraternities? Explain why.

8. Do you think politicians or businessmen or teachers are most honest? What is your evidence? Can you think of any reasons why dishonesty should be more surely punished in one of these professions? Is there any reason to suspect that dishonesty, if successful, would be more rewarding in one rather than the others?

9. "Under socialism, cooperation will replace competition."

a. What is the difference between cooperation and competition?

b. Do you believe the quoted proposition is correct?

c. What evidence can you cite to support your answer?

10. The economic system is alleged to have an effect on the types of social and cultural characteristics that will be viable in a society. Among these characteristics are the patterns of speech, expression, religion, travel, marriage, divorce, inheritance, education, legal trials, art, literature, and music.

a. Do you believe that these characteristics are in any way different under capitalism than under socialism? Why?

b. What evidence can you cite?

11. "The free-enterprise, capitalist system is free in the sense that it involves no imposition of force or compulsion." Do you agree? If so, why? If not, why not?

4

BASIS OF EXCHANGE

Another extremely important implication about the real world which can be derived from our postulates is that *trade,* or *exchange,* will occur. To expose that implication easily and clearly, we shall at first use "toy" problems, devoid of unessential, cluttering circumstances. After the principles of exchange and their method of application have been presented, real-world applications will be made in later chapters.

Mutually Advantageous Trade and the Middleman

CUBAN AND HUNGARIAN REFUGEE CAMP

Imagine a refugee camp in which Cuban and Hungarian refugees are temporarily housed. Weekly, each person receives a gift parcel containing, among other things, twenty bars of chocolate candy and twenty cigarettes. Into this camp a new refugee, for whom there are no gift parcels, arrives from an unknown country. Clever and knowledgeable about human nature, he cunningly begins to exploit the other inmates.

To a Cuban he suggests the possibility of a favor. The newcomer hints that he could arrange for the Cuban to have a gift parcel with thirty candy bars and thirteen cigarettes instead of twenty of each. "Merely give me seven of your twenty cigarettes," he says, "and I will give you in return ten bars of candy." The Cuban considers and accepts; he thinks to himself that he is taking advantage of the newcomer, because while he was prepared to give up at *most* eight cigarettes for ten more bars of candy, he is being asked to give up only seven. If he had given up that maximum of eight cigarettes for the ten extra bars of candy, his basket would be revised from twenty of each to thirty candy bars and twelve cigarettes. This revised basket would be no better and no worse—i.e., have no more or less utility—than the original one. True, it would contain more candy, but the additional candy would be just offset by the reduction of the fewer cigarettes.

The trader offered to change the Cuban's original consumption composition not merely to another composition just as good or equal in utility, but to a composition *better* (with "more utility") than the original one. Specifically, he magnanimously offered to enable the Cuban to change the composition from twenty each to thirty candy bars and as many as thirteen (instead of only twelve) cigarettes. The fact that the Cuban accepts this offer of ten candy bars for seven cigarettes means, by definition, that the Cuban prefers the new combination to the old. In other words, the sacrifice of seven cigarettes in order to get ten more candy bars is not so big a cigarette *price* for candy as to leave him worse off or indifferent. His acceptance of the offer of ten candy bars for seven cigarettes means that to him the ten extra candy bars are worth *more than* seven of his cigarettes.

Table 4–1 gives the composition of three consumption-combination "baskets": A, B_1, and B_2. The Cuban started with A and voluntarily accepted B_2 in preference to refusing the exchange opportunity. Now, consider basket B_1, which we shall assume has the *same* utility as basket A; although it is different in composition from A, it is no better or worse. The reduction in cigarettes, eight, is just enough to offset the increase of ten candy bars—which is another way of saying that ten more candy bars are worth exactly as much to the Cuban as eight cigarettes, given his present circumstances.

Table 4–1

EQUIVALENT AND PREFERRED BASKETS FOR CUBAN

	Component Goods	
	Candy	**Cigarettes**
Basket A	20	20
	(+10)	(−8)
Basket B_1	30	12
	(+10)	(−7)
Basket B_2	30	13

The ratio between the eight cigarettes given up and the ten candy bars gained, 8/10, is our old friend the consumption-substitution ratio of candy for cigarettes. Sometimes it is called the individual's *subjective value* of candy relative to cigarettes. It is simply that ratio of exchange to which a person is indifferent, or which leaves him at the same level of utility. This rate is also called the *indifference ratio* between candy and cigarettes for the individual concerned. (All of these names—and there are even more—for this same concept are commonly used in the economic literature. Here, we will usually use the terms "consumption-substitution ratio" and "subjective value.")

For one additional candy bar, then, the Cuban is indifferent to giving up 0.8 cigarette, assuming that he currently has a consumption pattern of twenty candy bars and twenty cigarettes. However, under the same conditions, he will regard the opportunity to receive ten more candy bars for only seven cigarettes as a utility-increasing opportunity—a trade that will put him in a more preferred position.

Thus the Cuban will accept an exchange that moves him from basket A to B_2. We would know that this exchange will increase his utility if we knew that he is willing to pay at most 0.8 cigarette for a bar of candy. But how do we know whether the opportunity rate of exchange presented to a person is in fact less or greater than his subjective value (or consumption rate of substitution)? We rarely know the latter rate; but, by assumption, "A person chooses to accept an opportunity only if he feels that it puts him in a more desired position—whatever may be the factors that he regards as relevant." We need not know his subjective value (consumption rate of substitution) for each possible situation. We need to know only that the person has had opportunities to engage in trade and that he has accepted some of these opportunities and refused others. For the moment, we assume that we know the numbers at which he would and would not trade—simply to help us expose the underlying ideas.

Where does the newcomer get the candy that he sells to the Cuban in exchange for the cigarettes? From some other refugee—say, a Hungarian. He offers the Hungarian five cigarettes in exchange for ten candy bars. Faced with this trading opportunity to substitute some cigarettes for some candy, the Hungarian, let us suppose, accepts the offer. In fact, he thinks the newcomer is a bit of a fool, since he would have been willing to trade the ten candy bars for as few as four cigarettes. The Hungarian's *subjective value* of cigarettes relative to candy (the *rate of consumption substitution* of cigarettes for candy) is 10/4 or 2.5. His subjective value of cigarettes (in units of candy), then, is 2.5 candy bars. (His marginal rate of consumption substitution *of candy* for cigarettes is 4/10; or, to say the same thing, his subjective value of one additional candy bar is 0.4 cigarette.)

The Hungarian moved from his basket A to his basket B_2. Basket B_2 is superior to B_1, for it contains more cigarettes and as much candy; and since basket B_1 is to the Hungarian just as desirable as basket A, the Hungarian has moved from A to a more preferred consumption basket, B_2, shown in Table 4–2.

And so—by the newcomer's transferring of candy from a Hungarian to a Cuban and of cigarettes to a Hungarian from a Cuban—the Cuban has achieved

Table 4–2

EQUIVALENT AND PREFERRED BASKETS FOR HUNGARIAN

	Component Goods	
	Candy	Cigarettes
Basket *A*	20	20
	(−10)	(+4)
Basket B_1	10	24
	(−10)	(+5)
Basket B_2	10	25

a preferred situation, and the Hungarian also has moved to an improved situation. They both hope that the newcomer will repeat his offer the next week.

However, we now have an amazing situation. The newcomer has two cigarettes left over for his own use. He has taken two cigarettes from the total stock of forty cigarettes previously held by the Cuban and Hungarian. Yet—although they have less goods in total—both say they are better off. How can they be better off with *less* goods? Hasn't the newcomer exploited them, when all the time they thought they were exploiting him? Suppose that the Hungarian and Cuban get together and find out they have between them lost two cigarettes? How can the newcomer explain or defend this odd result? Using our postulates, he could explain as follows:

"You have not been cheated. In fact, you both have been made better off. In return for the benefit you obtained by having revised the *pattern* of your consumption, you were able to reward me by giving me two cigarettes. The gain in utility to each of you from that shift in proportions was *more* than enough to compensate you for the payment to me of these two cigarettes. Consider an extreme example: If a person had lots of flour and only a little shortening, he would be willing to trade some flour for shortening. He would even be willing to pay someone for the service of making it possible for him to engage in such a revision of his possessions. And if someone else had lots of shortening and not much flour, he would be prepared to give up some shortening for more flour. This is like the situation in which I found you. Although, of course, you both could use all the candy and cigarettes that you had, each of you preferred a slightly different combination. I made it possible for you to shift to more preferred combinations. The cigarettes are payment for my helpful services.

"To be sure, I did not do all this with the intention of helping you. I helped you revise your baskets only because I was interested in myself. Indeed, each of you thought you were outwitting me, because you were each prepared to give up more (or receive less) than you did. But I knew that you had to be benefited, or else there would be no incentive for the trade. Certainly you would have been even more benefited if I had kept less than two cigarettes, but there is no denying that you *are* now better off than initially because of the revised proportions of candy and cigarettes.

"What makes feasible mutually beneficial trade," the newcomer generalizes, "is that the rates of consumption substitution (or subjective value or indifference ratios) differ among people. In general, whenever *these rates differ,* there is a basis for mutually preferred exchange."

To isolate that necessary or essential condition in which people gain from (i.e., prefer to) trade, even if they have to pay middlemen something to facilitate the trading, we compare the consumption-substitution rates between the "equally preferred or equal utility baskets" for the Cuban and for the Hungarian.

Table 4–3

RESULTS OF TRADE

	Cuban		Hungarian	
	Candy	Cigarettes	Candy	Cigarettes
Basket A	20	20	20	20
	(+10)	(−8)	(−10)	(+4)
Basket B_1	30	12	10	24
Basket after exchange	30	13	10	25

For the Cuban, as Table 4–3 shows, an additional candy bar is equivalent in utility to 0.8 cigarette. For the Hungarian, an additional 0.4 cigarette is equivalent in utility to one candy bar. The Cuban's subjective value of candy in cigarette units (*rate of consumption substitution* of candy for cigarettes) is 0.8, while for the Hungarian the subjective value of candy in cigarette units is 0.4. The Cuban is willing to give up (sell) cigarettes at the rate of *at most* 0.8 cigarette for one more candy bar, while the Hungarian is willing to give up (sell) one candy bar for *at least* 0.4 cigarette. The respective rates of substitution give the maximum price at which the Cuban will sell cigarettes and the minimum price at which the Hungarian will sell candy.

Again, we conclude, if *subjective values (rates of consumption substitution) differ between people, each person will have an opportunity to substitute goods (revise his consumption pattern) at exchange rates that will increase his utility.*

And, given the opportunity to trade, each person will act on this opportunity. Furthermore, the direction of trade will always be such that *commodity* X *moves from the person with the lower subjective value of* X *to the person with the higher subjective value of* X.

Because of the difference between subjective valuations, the newcomer could help the Cuban and the Hungarian reach more preferred positions by trade; at the same time, he himself, the middleman, could keep part of the difference as his reward for services performed. In summary, *whenever situations exist in which subjective values (rates of consumption substitution) differ, appropriate transfer of resources will result in a more preferred position for each person.* (We have here accounted for the *reasons* that trade takes place and the *direction* of trade. *To what extent* people will trade and revise their compositions will be studied later.)

This proposition about exchange is one of the most important in economics.[1] It will be applied again later in numerous different contexts: trade between two people, production, specialization of labor, speculative storing of crops from season to season, and interregional trade. Exactly the same kinds of numerical examples will illustrate the principle in these later applications.

Obviously, this "toy" example abstracts from many details, but that is precisely its purpose: to reveal the crucial aspects of the explanation of trade in bold, uncluttered fashion. For example, note that we did not compare the Cuban's value of candy relative to the Hungarian's value of candy; we did not ask whether the Cuban likes candy more than the Hungarian likes candy. Instead, we asked whether the Cuban values candy higher *relative to cigarettes* than the Hungarian values candy *relative to cigarettes.* No interpersonal comparison of absolute psychological level of desire for each good is involved. On an *absolute* scale, the Cuban may regard both candy and cigarettes as barely desirable goods, while the Hungarian literally drools, pants, and proclaims a passionate love for both candy and cigarettes. The Cuban may be a blasé old man who gets no joy out of life, whereas the Hungarian may be an eager, highly appreciative, sensitive, enthusiastic young man. Finally, the Hungarian may be a man of modest means, whereas the Cuban may be a very rich person with a basket not of twenty candy bars and twenty cigarettes but of one thousand candy bars and one thousand cigarettes. None of these personal characteristics is relevant here. As long as the Cuban subjectively values *more* candy relative to cigarettes at a rate different from that of the Hungarian, he will engage in trade with the Hungarian (via a middleman, if need be) to the benefit of each.

Just as we need not consider personal characteristics or attitudes, we need not consider the comparative importance of the individuals involved in an ex-

[1] The inequality of substitution rates among utility-producing inputs is a condition of "inefficient," and hence improvable, allocation. This is simply the standard first derivative condition for a constrained maximum—a problem familiar to all students in engineering and physical sciences.

change. This is a significant point; for sometimes people think that to determine how to allocate resources among various claimants, one must decide who performs the most important task. That kind of comparison may help one decide how *large* a basket of resources each person or agency should be assigned, but it has no bearing whatsoever in determining the most desirable *combination* of goods within the basket assigned to each. We can illustrate this point by considering the allocation of nuclear-energy material and men to the Army and to the Navy.

ARMY AND NAVY EXCHANGE

Let us assume that the Army and the Navy both have a certain amount of nuclear material and a specified number of men. Since the Army and the Navy have somewhat different tasks to perform, can the initial distribution of nuclear material and men be revised so as to increase the performance of both services —without necessitating an increase in the total amount of nuclear material and men? The feasibility of such a revision could be discovered if the Navy and the Army were each asked to indicate for some specified level of military capability how many more men they would require to make up for a decrease in the available amount of nuclear material, or how many less men they would require if they could get an additional unit of nuclear material. In other words, each service could determine its current consumption-substitution ratio, or subjective valuation, of nuclear material relative to men. The Navy and the Army would then compare their substitution ratios. As we know, if these subjective values differ, mutually advantageous trade of nuclear material and men will enable both services to reach a higher capability without increasing the total resources allotted to them jointly. Notice that we do not compare the *value* of the Navy's military performance with that of the Army. Such a comparison would have no bearing on the discovery of mutually advantageous exchanges of resources.

Marginal Values and Total Values

The *value* of a commodity is defined and measured only in terms of *one* unit more or less—that is, what a person will give up for one more unit or what he will insist on getting if he is to have one unit less. Prices of cigarettes (here expressed as so many units of candy to be exchanged per unit of cigarettes) are measures of values of *increments* in the stock of cigarettes for each person. Prices never enable us to measure the *total* value of the community's *total* stock of any good. The importance of the *total* stock of, say, wheat relative to *all* diamonds often seems to be opposite to their relative prices per pound. Diamonds, as compared to wheat, have a high value per pound or cubic centimeter, even though the "importance" of the community's *total* stock of diamonds is small compared to that of all the wheat. This latter comparison, the *total values* of the total stocks of each good, is a question completely different from that of *relative prices*. And for the questions we are trying to answer here, there is really no point in seeking a measure of the "total value of the total stock." Only the *marginal* values, or prices (the value of *one more* or *one less*), are involved in explaining the fact of trade and the way in which the desired mixes of various goods are determined for all the people in the society.

All this helps to explain a so-called "paradox of value"—namely, that diamonds are much more expensive per gram than wheat, but wheat is much more important than diamonds. The explanation is that *more* wheat is *not* more important than *more* diamonds. The relative prices of diamonds and wheat indicate that an *increment* of a gram of diamonds is more highly valued than another gram of wheat. There is no paradox, because the price simply is not a basis for a measure of the "total value of the entire stock of some resource"—not even when price per unit is multiplied by the number of units in the whole stock.

There still remain the questions "Why is a gram of diamonds more highly valued than a gram of wheat?" and "Why are prices what they are?" We will consider these questions later—not simply for the sake of seeing how prices are determined, but because certain inevitable social and individual problems of behavior are best understood by learning what determines prices.

Some Analytical and Ethical Aspects of Exchange

Before going further with the analysis of exchange, let us see how the preceding analysis can be helpful in appreciating (1) assertions about the reasons for trade, (2) the productivity of middlemen, (3) ethical arguments for and against free trade, and (4) criticisms of the method of analysis.

REASONS FOR TRADE

The statement is sometimes made that trade among two people rests on the fact that one of them has a "surplus" to dispose of. Even responsible social scientists have held this notion: "The development of cities rests ultimately on food surpluses obtained by agricultural producers above their own requirements." But nowhere in the preceding numerical example was there any need to refer to a "surplus" of cigarettes or candy. For trade to exist, one need not suppose that one party or both have "surpluses"; in light of the preceding analysis, it is clear that only *free* goods are in surplus supply. Surplus has nothing whatever to do with the possibility of exchange.

PRODUCTIVITY OF EXCHANGE

This analysis implies also that trade is productive. Middlemen (retailers, salesmen, brokers, wholesalers, transporters, to name a few) are productive in the only sense in which the word "production" has economic meaning. *Production* means an act that increases utility. When some act changes the shape or place or even the time of availability of something, the utility of people may be increased. Profit-making middlemen are not "mere parasitical intermediaries."

ETHICS AND FREE TRADE

Economic analysis does not *prove* that exchange makes people *better off* in some moral or objective sense or even that they should have the right to trade. If you believe that it is "good" for a person to get what he prefers, then you can believe that trade contributes to "goodness." But does a trader actually get what he prefers? The issue is not one of fraud or nonfulfillment of contract. One could insist on a guarantee or return privilege before completing a contract to exchange; and if the other party refuses to agree to some kind of inspection or test of goods, the buyer can always refuse to buy.

However, the trader may find that his chosen position is not as nice as he imagined it would be. Information before the act of exchange is sometimes inaccurate and inadequate; the assumption that he preferred to get what he actually did get is then open to doubt. But can a person find someone else who is better informed about the consequences of various choices *and* who is also well enough informed about other persons' preference patterns so that on net balance he can make a better choice for the individual than the individual can make for himself? In answer to this vexing question, one may hear it said that individuals know "well enough" what the consequences are. Or that although an individual is occasionally mistaken about outcomes of choices, so that other people may know more about consequences, their inferior knowledge of what each individual wants more than offsets the knowledge of consequences. Or one can take note of "brand names" as a means of assuring quality of product.

Another argument for individual choice is that people, as a moral duty, *ought* to make their own choices because this will produce in them the responsibility and self-reliance that *ought* to be characteristic of the "good" society. Finally, some believe that whether or not people *ought to,* they *do* in fact want the right to make their own choices. It is wrong, they say, to restrict the actions that other people can mutually agree upon, even if what they do doesn't accord with what we think is "for their own good." These various lines of argument all end up as defenses of exchange rights.

On the other hand, some humanitarian and thoughtful persons believe that certain people are not capable of proper understanding and therefore should be influenced or controlled "for their own good," much as with our children. We say that a child is not yet a "person"; that he is being trained to exercise choice with regard to the consequences—although after he has reached the age of eighteen, the parents must relinquish some of this control; and when he is twenty-one, they must relinquish all control. Why use the age of twenty-one as the method of defining a person to whom choice should be freely given? The answer is that this method is objective. Whether the adulthood stage be set at twelve, sixteen, or twenty-one is less critical than that it be unambiguously set, with no subsequent discretionary review by the parents. Otherwise, the parents would be able to keep the "child" in a dependent slave status, vitiating the fundamental moral precept of individual freedom and choice—which, to repeat, is not derived from anything in economic theory. But if the age of twenty-one, say, is used as a test of adequate maturity or adulthood, what do we do when a person of twenty-one has not reached maturity in an emotional or intellectual sense? People over twenty-one sometimes *are* confined to mental institutions; they *are* denied their rights of access to the free-exchange market. And in many other instances—e.g., for medical care, food, education—adults are prohibited from entering into mutually agreeable exchanges with whomever they please, not necessarily because their tastes are wrong but because, it is said, their knowledge is inadequate in certain areas, and therefore they would regret their actions. In these areas, the advice and control of experts is sometimes deemed better (by whom?).

The critics of free exchange are probably more impressed by, or attach more weight to, the regrettable consequences for those who make unfortunate choices; they are less impressed by, or attach less weight to, (a) the forsaken gains removed from those who would otherwise have made fortunate choices and (b) the desirability of individual choice *per se*. Those who favor enlarging the range of individual choice and responsibility probably make exactly the opposite evaluation. Neither group is necessarily more humanitarian or socially conscious than the other. They may differ simply in their valuation of the significance of the various forestalled errors and forsaken gains, and the kind of behavior that is fostered under the alternatives.

Very different from these two groups, both of which profess to be helping the individual realize an opportunity to lead a life that is more free (from error and/or undesirable and avoidable controls and constraints) and more individually expressive, are those who contend that other people's tastes and preferences are simply wrong or improper and that they should learn to have the right kinds of tastes and preferences. They *ought* to prefer classical music to jazz and modern music; realistic art to surrealistic and abstract art; clean, upright literature to immoral, decadent literature; wine to beer; opera, theater, and chamber music to bowling, golf, and skiing; compact, severe cars to chromium-fin cars; adult education to television Westerns, bridge, and poker; and study to football. If these critics had their way, they would rebuild the world in their own images. They might, for instance, try to reduce the scope of the free-exchange market (because access to that market enables people to realize their "cruder" preferences and odd tastes, just as the Cuban chose more fatness and the Hungarian more cigarette cough); or they might try to change tastes and preferences by educating, informing, persuading, or propagandizing.

This discussion may appear to be a digression from the scope of economics. That is precisely the impression that should be obtained. This whole ethical issue is raised here because too often people think that economic theory *justifies* trade among individuals. It does not. It simply presents an explanation of *why* trade occurs, and it shows how different kinds of behavior flow from alternative economic institutions and forms of competition. To ask whether trade, or some form of competition, *ought* to be allowed is like asking whether people ought to be allowed to see double-feature movies or to use fire. Physics explains the effects of fire and the conditions under which it occurs. The question of whether fire is desirable is beyond the realm of physics, just as the question of whether access to the open market *should* be allowed to each individual is beyond economics.

This evaluation of the right to voluntary exchange in the open market is a crucial issue; it is a major part of the clash between the capitalist culture and the socialist culture. We have advisedly not expressed the matter as "free versus unfree" or "democratic versus undemocratic." The socialist could say that people are freer in Russia, because they are free from the task or risk of making uninformed choices. They are freed from the danger of making certain kinds of later-regretted choices, just as you and I are "freed" (prevented) from the risk of hiring a complete quack to perform an operation or advise us about our illnesses, or from the possibility of buying whole milk with too low a cream content, or from all sorts of possibilities of acquiring inferior, undesirable things—substandard food, substandard airplane flights, substandard houses. In all these instances, we are supposed to be protected from our own folly; we are "freed" from doing things that someone thinks we do not *really* want to do or ought not to do. This may sound like an unusual meaning of "free," but it is a widely accepted meaning in Russian *and* in American life. It is easy to allege that one's preferred restrictions on other people are those that give them "more freedom," promote "good" and prevent "bad" consequences. Restraint from doing what is "bad" is, of course, no restraint on "true" freedom. But different individuals may have different notions of what is good and what is bad. Thus, to use the term "free" is to beg the question.

Nor do we speak of democratic versus undemocratic economic rights. Democracy is a way of allocating political power, not a criterion of what is done with it. A dictatorship, which is undemocratic, may enforce economic and legal rules that are conducive to what some might call a desirable society. A democracy can, by majority revision of various economic and legal rules, produce an undesirable society. Indeed, it is *not* perfectly self-evident that democracy as such is more conducive than *any* other system to the emergence or continuance of a society which many, but not all, would call "free," open," or "desirable."

CRITICISMS OF METHODOLOGY

A common objection to the foregoing economic analysis of exchange is that it assumes an unwarranted degree of rationality or of calculating behavior by each person. To this charge, there are several answers.

First, the charge misinterprets. Economic postulates, as we pointed out earlier, are formulated only on the basis of *observed* behavior. Similarly, the laws of physics are compact descriptions of what in fact does happen; they provide convenient ways of summarizing the measurable, observable characteristics of physical objects. Physics postulates a "force of gravity," or "attraction" between masses. Sticks and stones and birds behave according to the law of gravity, even though they do not know what it is; human beings obey this same law even before they have learned anything about it. "Gravity" or "attraction," like "preferences" and "decisions," is simply a convenient conception for ordering our analytical processes and observed events.

Second, despite the frequency of habit, custom, and erratic behavior, it can be argued that people do calculate and that habit itself is a form of purposeful behavior. People, in large part, resort to habitual patterns because they thereby avoid random, nonrational action and preserve what they have discovered to be desirable actions. If a person discovers that these habitual or conventional purchase patterns are less useful than other patterns, he forms a new habit pattern. Habits are also ways of avoiding unnecessary mental effort. Thinking, comparing, calculating, and deciding are difficult and costly activities. They take time away from other, more pleasant activities.

Third, a partially effective criticism of the preceding analysis of exchange is that one party to a potential exchange may dislike the other or fear his motives, and thus may refuse to engage in trade because the improvement thereby given to the second party may be turned against the first. Witness our ban on trading with Communist countries: we fear that their consequent gain in economic strength may ultimately be used against us; therefore, we forego our own possible gains and refuse to trade. This criticism is valid to a certain extent; that is, in our analysis, we did assume that each person's utility is independent of what other people own. More generally, we assumed that each person does not regard a more preferred position for the other person as undesirable (or desirable) in itself. If we were to consider motivations of envy or fear, then the analysis admittedly is made more complex; but it is not invalidated. We would then have to consider each person's attitude not only to the effect of exchange on his own "basket" but also to the relative effect on the other person's basket. With envy or interpersonal animosity, trade will still be implied, but to a lesser extent. The explanation and basic conditions will be unchanged (provided we explicitly include in the "goods" that enter into a person's utility situation those owned by the other person).

"This is all fine for simple baskets of candy and cigarettes," a fourth criticism runs, "but people don't always eat things in the same ratio. Some days they eat candy, and on others they may smoke. They vary their daily consumption mixture. Hence, the preceding concentration on a particular mixture that is supposed to be preferred over some other mixture is too artificial." Not at all. We said only that a person can in the course of a week consume candy and cigarettes. He is at liberty to eat all the candy at once or spread it out over time, any way he wants.

Questions

1. The left half of the table below shows the contents of three combinations of vegetables and meat among which Linus would have revealed indifference if he had been offered a choice; that is, all three are equally desirable to him. The right half shows three combinations of meat and vegetables among which Charlie would have revealed indifference.

LINUS				CHARLIE			
Options	Vegetables		Meat	Options	Vegetables		Meat
A	10	and	14	*A*	40	and	16
B	13	and	13	*B*	45	and	15
C	17	and	12	*C*	52	and	14

a. If Linus has combination *B*, approximately what is his consumption-substitution ratio between vegetables and meat?

b. If Charlie has combination *B*, what is his subjective value for vegetables?

c. Who likes vegetables more, Linus or Charlie? In what sense is it impossible to answer this question? In what sense is it possible?

d. If Linus's combination were 113 (instead of 13) vegetables and 13 meat, do you think the answer to (c) would be reversed? Why?

e. If Linus and Charlie are each with the combinations designated *B*, does any possible trade exist whereby each could reach a preferred combination? If so, give an example.

f. State the necessary consumption-substitution exchange-rate conditions that must hold if there is to be possibility of exchange between two people so as to move them to preferred positions, even though part of their goods might be lost in the process.

2. Suppose that Charlie and Linus have the same amount of meat and fruit. With these initial amounts, they have the following indifference consumption-substitution ratios:

Charlie: 3 meat = 1 fruit
Linus: 7 meat = 1 fruit

a. Compared to Linus, is Charlie more fond of fruit or meat?

b. If the government makes it illegal to trade fruit for meat, always assuming that any law is obeyed, who gains and who loses? Why?

c. Now, the government relents and allows trade, but makes it illegal for anyone to trade at any exchange ratio other than one meat for one fruit. Explain the likely consequences of this new ruling.

d. Next, suppose the government relents still more, but—in order to protect the "little people" who consume fruit—a price ceiling is put on fruit. The maximum meat price of one unit of fruit is set at four. Who is likely to gain, and who is likely to lose by this price control? Explain.

e. Finally, imagine that the government takes off all restrictions on the trade of meat and fruit. But introduce a middleman who conducts the trade between Charlie and Linus. What is the *maximum* cut the middleman can take in the form of meat? Or of fruit?

3. "The postulates of economics imply that to permit trade is better than to prohibit trade." Do they? Explain.

4. "The postulates of economics say that, when a person trades, he knows what he will get and that he will not regret it." Do the postulates say that? What *do* they say?

5. Suppose the Economics Department offers the Philosophy Department two faculty offices in exchange for one secretary. (Almost always, such independent trades are not allowed.) As president of the college, would you permit the departments to engage in exchanges of various facilities that you initially allotted to the departments? Why?

6. In some states it is illegal for a person to buy whiskey. Which of the postulates is denied as being applicable, or must a new one be added to explain such laws?

7. Your college allots some parking space for your car while a friend is allotted a desk in the library stacks. Suppose that you and he would each be better off if you were to trade him your parking space for his desk space.

a. This kind of trading is almost invariably prohibited by the college authorities. Why?

b. If you were the college president, why would you prohibit it?

c. Would you consider solving the whole problem by simply selling parking space to one and all at the market-clearing price, like a downtown parking garage? Why?

8. "Trade between the Mediterranean and the Baltic developed when each area produced a surplus of some good."

a. What do you think this quotation, taken from a widely used college history text, means?

b. Can you propose an alternative explanation?

9. A parent gives each of his two children some milk and meat. The two children then exchange with each other, one drinking most of the milk and the other eating most of the meat. As a parent, would you permit them to make that exchange? If you don't, then which of the postulates (if any) are you denying? Or does your explanation rest on some new postulate not made explicit in the text?

10. Can you explain how what is often called "impulse" buying is consistent with the postulates of choice? Can you explain why habitual buying is also consistent with the postulates of choice? Can you suggest some behavior that would not be consistent with the postulates?

11. "Economic theory is built on an idealization of man: that he has tremendous computational power, a detailed knowledge of his desires and wants, a thorough understanding of his environment and its causal relationships, a resistance to acting on impulse or by habit. It is difficult to bridge the gap between that model of economic man and the groping uncertain man of the real world." Does this statement correctly characterize the state of economic theory? Explain.

12. Upon reading an exposition (not in *this* book!) of allocation of resources by exchange, a professor of law at a distinguished university recently wrote: "One has the feeling that if it takes so much effort to explain, it just can't work." What do you think of the logic of that statement? If you read an elementary textbook on the physics of electromagnetic radiation (radio) and found it complex and difficult, would you conclude that it just can't work?

5

OPEN-MARKET EQUILIBRIUM

Up to this point, economics has shown *why* trade will occur and in what *direction* it will occur. We have not yet discovered implications about the *extent* to which people will revise their consumption patterns. That is, how much will the Cuban revise his consumption by taking more candy and giving up cigarettes before he says, "Stop; I have reached a most preferred combination of candy and cigarettes"? The answer requires the application of our fifth postulate: *The subjective value of a good will diminish as its available amount increases.* To see how this postulate gives a solution to the *extent* of trade, we continue with our refugee camp.

Diminishing Subjective Values

Our newcomer (middleman) has just completed his first trade with the Cuban. In that transaction, he bought seven cigarettes from the Cuban in exchange for ten candy bars and sold five of the cigarettes to the Hungarian in exchange for ten candy bars, with two cigarettes left for himself. True to the postulate that more profits are better than less, he then tries to expand the amount of trade. Why not buy twenty bars of candy from the Hungarian and sell them to the Cuban for a total gain of four cigarettes per week? He offers to provide the Cuban with ten more bars during *that same week* on the same terms of seven cigarettes. The Cuban agrees and awaits his candy. But when the trader tries to buy that additional candy from the Hungarian, he is in for a shock. He discovers that he cannot get more candy from the Hungarian at the old price. Although the Hungarian was happy to give up the first ten bars of candy for five cigarettes *when he had twenty of each,* he is not willing to give up ten additional bars for five more cigarettes. As he puts it, "Now that I have as little as ten candy bars and as many as twenty-five cigarettes per week, the candy becomes more valuable to me than it formerly was. It now takes more cigarettes to make up for the loss of a given amount of candy. Therefore, the price (in cigarettes) at which I will supply more candy is higher." Economic translation: "I will sell candy only at a price higher than my subjective value (consumption-substitution rate) of candy, and that value (or rate) has increased."

The middleman has run up against *diminishing* subjective values. Now that the Hungarian has revised his consumption pattern to less candy and more cigarettes, the amount of candy he will give up for still another cigarette has decreased; that is, the *maximum* candy price of cigarettes which he is willing to *pay* has *fallen.* To put it the other way around: With a smaller supply of candy relative to cigarettes, the value to him of each remaining candy bar has increased; that is, the *minimum* cigarette price of candy which he is willing to *receive* has *risen.* The middleman can induce the Hungarian to sell more candy only by paying him an ever increasing number of cigarettes per successive unit of candy. The Hungarian's consumption-substitution rate of cigarettes for candy diminishes as his consumption pattern is revised toward more cigarettes. This is our fifth postulate at work.

Thus, if the middleman wants to increase the extent of exchange, he will have to offer a greater number of cigarettes to the Hungarian in exchange for candy; and since the same force is at work for the Cuban, the middleman will have to offer more candy than before to the Cuban for the further purchase of more cigarettes. If the middleman wants to expand the amount of exchange each week between the Cuban and the Hungarian, he must offer a higher price for candy bought from the Hungarian and accept a lower price for candy sold to the Cuban; or, saying the same thing in reverse, he will have to ask a lower price for the cigarettes sold to the Hungarian and offer a higher price for the cigarettes he seeks to buy from the Cuban. No matter how the middleman looks at it, one thing is sure. Increasing the extent of trade will increase his profits, but the increment will diminish with each expansion of the extent of weekly exchange. The problem he faces is determining the optimal extent of exchange. How many cigarettes, in total, shall he buy each week from the Cuban and sell to the Hungarian, and conversely for candy—so as to yield for himself the maximum profits? That solution would be the equilibrium extent of exchange, *assuming that he is the only operating middleman.*

Competition between Middlemen

But before the middleman can figure out how much to revise prices to increase trade in order to increase his profits from the current two cigarettes per week to the blissful maximum, his wonderful world of profits is shattered by the appearance of another wily refugee, an old hand at the art of trading. This newly arrived dealer offers the Cuban ten units of candy for only six and a half, rather than seven, cigarettes.

Compared to the first middleman, the new dealer offers candy to the Cuban at a lower cigarette price or (what amounts to the same thing) bids a higher candy price for cigarettes. The Cuban, eager to make a better deal, accepts; and his situation has now changed to basket B_3. Basket B_3 is better than the old basket B_2, which contained only thirteen cigarettes.

Table 5–1

CUBAN

		Candy	Cigarettes
(Initial)	Basket A	20	20
(Old)	Basket B_2	30	13
(New)	Basket B_3	30	13.5

To the Hungarian, the new middleman offers to sell five and a half, rather than only five, cigarettes for ten bars of candy. This, too, is a better offer than that of the first middleman—who warns that the new middleman is unreliable and will not deliver; or, if he does, will deliver stale candy or dry, wrinkled cigarettes, and will not give service with a smile, and in any event cannot possibly continue to cover his costs with such prices. But if the Hungarian takes his chance and buys from the new trader, he will transfer to a new basket, B_3, which is better than his old basket, B_2.

Table 5–2

HUNGARIAN

		Candy	Cigarettes
(Initial)	Basket A	20	20
(Old)	Basket B_2	10	25
(New)	Basket B_3	10	25.5

The net proceeds to the *new* middleman is one cigarette per week (he sells candy for six and a half, and buys for five and a half cigarettes). If bigger baskets are better than smaller ones, the Cuban and the Hungarian are better off. And the new dealer has improved his own situation by one cigarette—not by two cigarettes, as had the old trader. But the old dealer, whose offers are now rejected by the Cuban and the Hungarian, can no longer get any gain. Thus, competition between the middlemen has reduced the profit spread between buying and selling prices; that is, the consumer now pays a lower price to the middleman and, in effect, sells his other commodity to the middleman at a higher price.

Both the Cuban and Hungarian prefer the new lower prices that they now pay for candy and cigarettes, respectively. The price at which the Cuban can now buy one candy bar is down to 0.65 (from .70) cigarette. The selling price available to the Hungarian from the middleman is up to 0.55 (from 0.50) cigarette for each bar of candy he sells. Buyers like lower prices, and sellers like higher prices. The spread between the buying and selling price for candy (and this will also be true for the other good, cigarettes) is down from 0.2 to 0.1 cigarette per candy traded. The profits to the middlemen are being eliminated. The competition that reduces profits is the competition of middleman against middleman, *not* consumer (or seller) against the middlemen. Middlemen do not compete with consumers; they compete with other middlemen.

Competition between the two middlemen will reduce the buying-selling price spread until it just covers the "costs" of providing the service at the quality level wanted by the consumers. If the spread were larger, more middlemen would be attracted; and they would shave the margin in order to get business. If the profits were negative, some middlemen would not survive as middlemen; and only those who could produce the middleman's service at lowest costs would be left in the business.

TWO FORCES OF EQUILIBRIUM

We must keep distinct two different kinds of convergences or equilibrating forces. One, to be discussed in the next chapter, is the force that causes market *price* to move to that level at which exchange opportunities are fully exploited —the exchange-equilibrium price. The second is the force that eliminates the source of *profit* to middlemen. In our example the market price of candy is really a twofold price: the cigarette price of candy to the consumer (0.65 to the Cuban) and the price to the supplier (0.55 to the Hungarian)—where "consumer" and "supplier" refer respectively to the person who buys to consume more and to the person who sells some to consume less (but more of other things). These two prices—variously called the buying and selling prices, or retail-wholesale prices, or simply price and cost—are brought closer together with the resultant elimination of the source of profits.

To say that neither of these equilibria can occur without the other's also occurring is to leap ahead of our current stage of analysis; but it is true, as we shall later be able to appreciate more fully.

COSTS OF CONDUCTING EXCHANGE IN OPEN MARKETS

A difference between the price at which the middleman buys candy from the Hungarian and the price at which he sells it to the Cuban does not necessarily indicate profits. Only if there were no costs involved in conducting the exchange transactions would that price spread be all profits. However, in the real world, there are many costs of conducting exchange: nuisance, foregone earnings elsewhere, time, labor, and risks; and these burdens are borne by middlemen. Every retailer or wholesaler is a middleman, and probably not much more than half of the costs are represented by payments for the goods sold. The rest involves the burdens of conducting the exchanges: rent for space in which transactions can be conducted and materials can be stored for inspection and immediate delivery; labor costs of record keeping; the cost of inventory, advertising, light, heat, and insurance—to name only a few items. Discount houses have lower costs, but they provide inferior service—although the lower price spread may be worth more than the better service sacrificed. But, in part, discount houses make the consumer bear part of the costs of exchange—e.g., collecting information about the item, return privileges, credit buying, delivery service, convenience of shopping conditions and location, speed of service by salesmen. All of these can be substantial portions of the total cost. Exchange costs could be reduced to zero only if everyone knew (without incurring any costs) all about the characteristics of what everyone else was willing to sell or buy, at what time, and at what price. But they don't, and so the cost of acquiring information is included in the price of the product purchased from brokers, real-estate agents, used-car dealers, etc.

The elimination of profits by the narrowing of the spread between buying and selling prices of the middlemen is a consequence of free-entry market competition or, as we shall call it, *open markets.* Open markets mean that access to markets is open to all people without legal or arbitrary barriers—*not* that there are no costs involved in using the market or in providing exchange-facilitating services. When there are no artificial barriers, the price paid by the buyer—say, the price paid by the Cuban in buying candy—will be revised until it is just high enough to cover the costs; that is, until it is just high enough to obtain the exchange services. As we saw from our earlier example, the initial selling-price–buying-price spread between the Cuban and Hungarian was more than enough; it therefore attracted an even greater offering of such services, as evidenced by the increase in the number of middlemen willing to perform the intermediary services. The increased supply of middlemen reduced the price to a level (0.5 cigarette) just high enough to induce and maintain the current amount of services, with no profit margin left over; the price now paid by the Cuban for candy and by the Hungarian for cigarettes is just enough to cover the costs of the services and goods that each gets.

Constraints on Open Markets

An open market is not a universal condition but an empirical condition that may or may not be present. It is not a postulate of economics that markets are always open for all goods, services, or professions. It is a fact that constraints are interposed—often at the urging of those already in the business, who expect that their wealth will thereby be increased by more than the costs of "closing" the market; they therefore ignore the consequences thrust upon the rest of society by these constraints on open markets. A brief description of a possible episode in the refugee camp will illustrate the major types of constraints that can be found. We look at these momentarily in order to appreciate their basic characteristics and role. Later we shall analyze and investigate their details more completely.

THREAT OF VIOLENCE

The original middleman thinks it unfair that he, who discovered this exchange possibility, should now find it taken away by someone else. The gains to the Cuban and to the Hungarian (and the profit to himself) were the result of his acuteness, and now someone else has stolen his discovery. To protect his interest, he therefore warns the new trader that any poaching will cost him his teeth. The Cuban and the Hungarian promise to protect the new trader from intimidation or harm by the old trader; they warn the old trader that he will regret it if he hinders the new trader from carrying on the trade.

CONTROL OF BUSINESS HOURS

To the continuing deaf ears of the refugees, the original trader goes on to argue that the refugees are trading with the new trader at unholy hours of the day, at nights, and even on Sundays. Arguing that it is improper to expect a person to work as a trader at night or on Sundays, he suggests that trading be prohibited except from 8 to 5 on weekdays. The camp manager, thinking that this will be conducive to order and proper life in the camp, agrees. Unfortunately, the new trader is so busy during the hours of 8 to 5 that he is unable to offer his services as a middleman to all his former customers. Furthermore, the schedules of some refugees would not permit them to negotiate with the middleman during the designated hours even if he were free. Thus, some who had formerly found it preferable to deal with the new trader after working hours are now restricted to dealing with the old trader, whose prices are not as favorable. Difficulties of enforcing this 8 to 5 restriction soon lead to its abandonment.

COALITION BY MERGER OR COLLUSION

Finally, as a last desperate tactic, the old trader approaches the new trader and offers to merge businesses. He points out that both have been forced to lower their selling prices and raise their buying prices to a very narrow spread; through joint agreement, they might increase their buying and selling spread back to two cigarettes per candy (with perhaps one going to the new trader and one to the old). This proposal appeals to the new trader, for it will give him a one-cigarette margin on *all* the candy trades at the new prices instead of one cigarette on only those exchanges that he himself would have conducted at the previous prices; the old trader will also get the same benefit. The profitability of this coalition immediately attracts new middlemen; because of the enhanced price spread, many others—who could not have afforded to act as middlemen at the narrow price spread—now have an opportunity to profit as traders. These new potential entrants either have to be bought off or let in on the group profits, or else the whole attempt to maintain high profits will collapse.

But no matter which of these profit divisions is followed, the profit will be spread over more and more new middlemen seeking the larger profit until the gains per middleman are brought back to what they would be with free entry—zero—a result achieved not necessarily by reducing price but by raising costs over a smaller volume of exchange per middleman.

COMPULSORY LICENSING

A means of preserving the profitability of the collusive (cartel) group would be the prohibition of new entrants. To this end, the two original middlemen persuade the camp manager to permit only camp-approved (that is, duly licensed, properly trained, ethical) traders to operate. The camp manager agrees that the best judges of "proper training, competence, and ethics" are those already in the business, who automatically get licenses; and they, of course, determine when "public necessity and convenience" calls for additional licensed middlemen. This arrangement, called self-regulation, is supposed to protect the unwary, unsophisticated customers from unscrupulous, incompetent, fly-by-night, quack middlemen. As it turns out, the "standards" of the two first middlemen are so high and their concern for consumer welfare is so great that they award no more licenses. The quality of middlemen must not be lowered; so the price spread is maintained at a level sufficient for respectable, qualified workingmen to enjoy the standard of living they think they deserve.

Furthermore, to make life easier for the middlemen, the cartel, composed of all licensed middlemen, permits trade only between the hours of 9 and 3, weekdays only. The traders say that longer hours would serve no purpose, since they can take care of everyone during that time. Customer convenience is somehow forgotten.

Yet, all is not tranquil. Every existing licensed member has an overwhelming temptation to get more customers by *secret* offers of better prices or by special gifts; thus, pains must be taken to prevent such competition. For example, for every exchange a written record of the prices paid by both parties must be posted in the Middlemen Association's office for the information of the buyers and sellers—and for the protection of the other members of the Middlemen Association, who can thus detect unethical price chiselers. As a result, since their licenses could be revoked by such practices, the licensed members do not cut their prices.

FRANCHISE FEES

All goes well with this licensing scheme until one day the camp manager realizes that he can collect from the dealers a "fee" for the right to license newcomers. He calls it a license or franchise fee. This fee happens to be almost but not quite equal to the anticipated future profits earned by the licensees in excess of what they would have earned if there were an open market. In this way, the camp manager transfers to himself the present and future monopoly-protected profit—in the interests of the refugees, whose welfare he is "protecting."

Before we can fully appreciate the problems of maintaining such constraints, or recognize the forces that operate in their absence—in short, before we can fully understand how consumers' goods (here illustrated by the exchange of candy and cigarettes between the Cuban and Hungarian) and productive resources (here illustrated by the services of middlemen) are allocated—we must do more than investigate two-person, two-good barter. We must use analytic devices that apply to real markets, wherein millions of people are involved with uncounted numbers of goods and services and money.

We can summarize our economic analysis as follows:

1. As long as there is a *revealed* disparity between the subjective values of goods for any two persons, the allocation of these goods can be revised by trade so that each person moves to a more preferred situation, provided the costs of revealing this disparity and negotiating the exchange contracts are not prohibitory.

2. Each party will shift toward *more* of the particular goods for which his subjective value exceeds the market-exchange rate (price).

3. Each party will increase (reduce) his stock of a good, relative to other goods, until the subjective value he places on it is reduced (increased) to equality with market price.

4. At equilibrium each party has the same subjective value of a good as every other party—a value that is also equaled by the market price at which exchange is available.

5. Every seller now in the market has an incentive to try to keep out other sellers. But in the absence of arbitrary obstacles or legal restrictions, the prospect of profits will entice new sellers to enter the market.

6. Existing sellers will have an incentive to reach agreements not to compete with each other in cutting price. But these agreements are more difficult to enforce, the more the prospective gain from the collusion, because the enticement to violate the agreements also increases with the size of the gain from the collusion.

7. The government will be appealed to as a means of keeping out new competitors—i.e., restricting the open market in order to maintain a larger buying-selling price spread, under the guise of protecting the consumer from unscrupulous sellers, who would undermine the quality of the product.

8. The legally protected "profits" can and often will be shared by the protected sellers and the government.

Such are some of the lessons from our refugee-camp exchange analysis. We used an extremely simple model of exchange precisely in order to separate these consequences from the background noise and cluttering details, idiosyncrasies and trivia of real-world market-exchange activities. Now that we have done so, we must also look at the way in which these results are brought about in the real-world markets. Thus, in the next chapter we shall dispense with the restriction that there are just two consumers and two goods in the exchange process.

Questions

1. "Competition is never 'buyer against seller' but always seller against other sellers and buyers against other buyers."

a. Is this true for you when you buy food? Automobiles? Shoes?

b. Can you give a case where it is not true?

c. If this is true, what gives a seller so much bargaining strength against the buyer of automobiles?

2. Upon graduation you will be shopping around for a job.

a. Against whom will you be competing?

b. Is your answer consistent with the proposition that labor competes against management? If your answer is "Yes," is that consistent with your answer to question 1.

3. According to economic principles of competition, if you were buying a new car, which tactic would be more likely to get you a lower price: going to just one dealer and acting like a tough and aggressive bargainer; or going to several dealers and mildly asking for their selling price while letting it be known that you really intended to buy a car? Explain why. Can you cite any evidence?

4. It is estimated that 25 percent of the price a housewife pays for a head of lettuce goes to the farmer, while the remaining portion is for middlemen and distribution costs.

a. Would you, as a farmer, necessarily prefer to have your percentage raised? Explain why not.

b. Would you, as a consumer, prefer to see his percentage raised? Explain.

5. "Middlemen and the do-it-yourself principle are incompatible." Explain.

6. Some discount stores advertise that they can sell for less because they buy directly from the manufacturer and sell to the consumer, thus eliminating many middlemen. What is the flaw in this reasoning?

7. "Equilibrium" prices exist in two different senses: exchange feasibility and profit levels.

a. What is meant by each?

b. Which one do you think is more commonly achieved?

8. It costs $2,000 to make an automobile; but to sell it, the producer must pay a tax of $100. What is the cost of access to the market?

9. Which of the following are compatible with open (or free) markets:

a. A new job applicant must get permission of present members of a trade before he can engage in that trade.

b. Medical doctors must pass a state examination before being allowed to sell medical services.

c. Banks must first obtain a license from the state before being allowed to operate —and not everyone can get a license merely for the asking.

d. Selling is prohibited on Sunday.

e. Pure food and drug laws restrict the sale of "impure" foods and drugs.

f. Consumption, manufacture, or sale of alcoholic beverages is prohibited.

g. Dealers and agents must be certified by the U.S. Securities and Exchange Commission before they can act as middlemen in buying and selling stocks and bonds; that is, before they can be security dealers.

10. Suppose you succeed in leading an army of liberation to rid Cuba of Castro Communists. Upon taking office as new dictator, you abolish all existing monopoly rights.

a. Would you then grant new monopoly rights?

b. If you did, how could you benefit the government (i.e., you)?

c. If you didn't think of doing that, who would suggest it to you?

11. You are campaigning for mayor or councilman in your home town, in which the taxi service (or, for that matter, garbage service, milk delivery, electric power, water, gas, etc.) is provided by anyone who wants to operate a taxi business or drive his own cab. In other words, the taxi service is provided by an open market. You campaign for more government control of taxi drivers in order to ensure better quality of service.

a. If elected, would you initiate a system of giving just one company the right to perform the service? Why?

b. If so, how would you decide which company?

c. Do you think that company would be one of your campaign financiers?

d. In California the right to sell liquor is restricted by the state government to a number far below that which would prevail otherwise. Would you be surprised to learn that the liquor dealers are a strong political "lobby" and source of "power" in state politics? Why?

e. What generalization does this suggest about a source of political power?

12. "Conakry, Guinea—Jan. 19, 1964: President Ahmed Toure has promised housewives that he will limit the profits of retail businessmen to 1 percent of the sale price. Toure's promise was made in reply to housewives' complaints about rising prices and food shortages. Toure warned the women to be on their guard against subversive influences and blamed storekeepers for the present erratic supplies, accusing them of trying to sabotage the state monopolies." Conjecture an interpretation of this news item.

13. "It is well to remind ourselves from time to time of the benefits we derive from the maintenance of a free-market system. The system rests on freedom of consumer choice, the profit motive, and vigorous competition for the buyer's dollar. By relying on these spontaneous economic forces, we secure these benefits: (a) Our system tends automatically to produce the kinds of goods that consumers want in the relative quantities in which people want them. (b) The system tends automatically to minimize waste. If one producer is making a product inefficiently, another will see an opportunity for profit by making the product at a lower cost. (c) The system encourages innovation and technological change. . . . I regard the preservation and strengthening of the free market as a cardinal objective of this or any Administration's policies." (Pres. J. F. Kennedy, September 1962, speaking to business magazine and newspaper publishers.)

Is it not surprising and confusing that while espousing the virtues of an open competitive economic system the businessmen and government officials proceed to hobble and restrict the open markets—e.g., by controlling allowable imports of sugar so as to maintain sugar prices in the United States at about twice the open-market level, and by limiting entry of some producers into markets in order to maintain larger wealth for incumbent businessmen and their employees? A confusion between freedom *of* competition in the open market and freedom *from* competition in the open market is suggested. What explains this espousal of the virtues of a system of private property and open markets with simultaneous attempts to suppress it?

6

DEMAND AND THE LAWS OF DEMAND

In the preceding chapters we have analyzed trade between two people. But in the real world, with millions of people, how can all of them compare their subjective values so that opportunities to trade can be exploited fully? Does a large community operate consistently with the two-person analysis? As we shall see, these questions involve a more general question: "What determines money prices, and what do money prices determine?" The answer rests on the use of money and of marketplaces.

Markets

Without a marketplace, how would you engage in trade? When considering the possibility of securing more meat and less milk, would you run from person to person at random, asking each whether he and you could agree on some barter trade? Imagine the required time and effort. But suppose there is a particular place where a person can go to compare his subjective valuations with those of other people. If he wanted to buy or sell a used car, for example, at such a place he could get information about potential exchange opportunities at less cost and effort than by other methods. This, obviously, is precisely the service that markets provide. Without them, a person might resort to advertising—publicly informing other people—as a cheaper means of finding potential buyers or sellers. And that, despite all the criticism of advertising, is its major role: to call people's attention to the fact that one is prepared to exchange certain described items. This way of identifying latent buyers and sellers reduces the cost of searching for information of exchange opportunities. Furthermore, another attribute of markets is the presence of brokers or specialized trading agents who serve primarily to provide a meeting place for potential buyers and sellers and furnish cheap access to information about particular goods and prices. Because a pooling of information generally means more information, buyers and sellers tend to go into one market rather than into many dispersed exchange locations.

A market is any place or institution in which people can negotiate exchanges. Usually markets are concentrated in well-defined geographical areas and times. A city or village is basically a market—a group of people living near each other to facilitate exchange of goods (as well as of productive services, which we shall investigate in the second portion of this book). So widely recognized are advantages of a market that "primitive" tribes in Africa have truces on market days. In the Bronx of New York City on a certain street at a certain day of the week there assemble people interested in buying and selling bakeries. In medieval times, some political leaders amassed fortunes by fostering marketplaces (fairs) in their favorite cities and permitting foreigners to enter the market —for a modest fee. Today, cheap telephonic and other means of communication and transportation have made markets larger and more efficient. Yet, at the same time, people have continued to restrict access of their competitors to the market, by devices and rationale we shall investigate later.

Money

It is easy for people to compare and respond to differences in their subjective valuations because money is usually involved in one side of the exchange. That is, the subjective value, or consumption-substitution ratio, is expressed in money units, so that all goods are subjectively "worth" some amount of money. Imagine the difficulty one would have in deciding upon his purchases if, when he went to the market, he found the price of shoes expressed in pounds of cotton, the price of shirts in pounds of iron, the price of meat in pounds of wool. Or imagine his even greater confusion if he found that different sellers used different commodities as the basis for the price of meat—for example, if one seller used cotton as his basis and another seller used pounds of iron; or if one seller expressed the price of shirts in pounds of meat and another seller priced shirts on the basis of gallons of gasoline.

Indeed, money is a wonderful invention that serves as a convenient *common denominator* for expressing exchange rates and facilitating comparisons of subjective values of various commodities. The use of money in fact makes pricing and purchasing decisions so easy for us that when we contemplate the prices of various items—say, of milk, margarine, butter, jam, and bread—we scarcely realize that we have implicitly included ten pairwise comparisons in these five money prices (or subjective values in money units). And in having some idea of the money prices of 100 different goods, we have summarized or dispensed with the necessity of 4,950 pairwise comparisons as a precondition to more effective trading.

But this is only part of the service of money. In addition to providing a common denominator or standard of value for expressing prices, it is a *common medium of exchange*. When we buy shoes, we pay money. When we sell labor services or a used car, we are paid money. We do not normally pay for shoes by giving up cigarettes, chocolate candy, or nails. Nor do we normally receive payment in such goods when we sell something. We buy with money and sell for money, because it is more economical and convenient. Imagine the problem we would have carrying around on our backs a sample of various goods that we would use to give to someone in exchange for goods. We would have to guess what particular goods the various people with whom we might trade would want at the time we considered an exchange. And since we don't know that, we would tie up a larger portion of our wealth (and time and energy) in various goods destined for trading purposes than if there were a common medium of exchange. A common medium of exchange—money—is used because it makes exchange less costly.

A person who holds some money is in nearly as appropriate a position as one who holds the particular combination of goods that he may later happen to want, because it is easy (cheap) to switch from money to other goods. If, instead of using money, a person held only nonmoney, then when he wanted different combinations of goods, he would find that as he tried to exchange some of his goods, he would end up with a smaller batch of goods than if he had used money. In effect, the retail-wholesale, or purchase-resale price spread of various goods is bigger than for money.

For present purposes, it is not necessary to investigate the question of which good will serve as money. It suffices to understand that the existence of money, as a common medium of exchange, reduces the costs of engaging in exchange. (Later chapters will present a more detailed investigation of money.) The cost-reducing property of money as a means of conducting exchanges of goods is generally described as lower "transaction costs." The buying and selling prices are more nearly the same. Nonmoney goods can be resold only with wider price spreads—like buying at retail and selling at wholesale—thus subjecting the purchaser to greater costs. Sometimes this attribute of money in being salable at the same price to all people is called "liquidity."

Although you can well imagine the considerable costs and difficulties of conducting exchanges by barter in the absence of money, people often overlook that great contribution of the invention and use of money in facilitating trade as well as the gains from enabling people to specialize in production instead of devoting so much time to barter.

The Demand Schedule

With the use of money, a person's choices can be characterized as choices between some good and money—with money being the intermediate, common medium of exchange. Whenever a person chooses to have more of some good, he will in the first instance give up money—and ultimately, of course, some of other goods that he might otherwise have had. A characteristic attribute of people's behavior in choosing goods is expressed by means of a *demand schedule* or general "state of demand" for a particular good. A demand schedule is a relationship between alternative possible money prices per unit of some good and the amount of that good that people will consume (or buy). An example of a demand schedule is given in Table 6–1.

Table 6–1

DEMAND SCHEDULE

Price (dollars)	Quantity (per year)	Price (dollars)	Quantity (per year)
2.00	0	.65	102.82
1.75	3.5	.60	110.67
1.50	14.2	.55	118.60
1.40	20.4	.50	127.01
1.30	27.7	.45	135.72
1.20	36.24	.40	144.48
1.10	45.97	.35	153.76
1.00	56.52	.30	163.07
.95	62.25	.25	172.92
.90	68.39	.20	182.79
.85	74.65	.15	193.21
.80	81.36	.10	203.92
.75	88.17	.05	214.62
.70	95.45		

The columns list various prices and their paired consumption rates. If price is $1, the rate of consumption is 56.52 (per week); if price is 50 cents, the rate of consumption is 127.01.

The demand given in Table 6–1 is portrayed as curve D_1D_1 (with some smoothing of the curve) in Figure 6–1. The negative slope of the curve (from

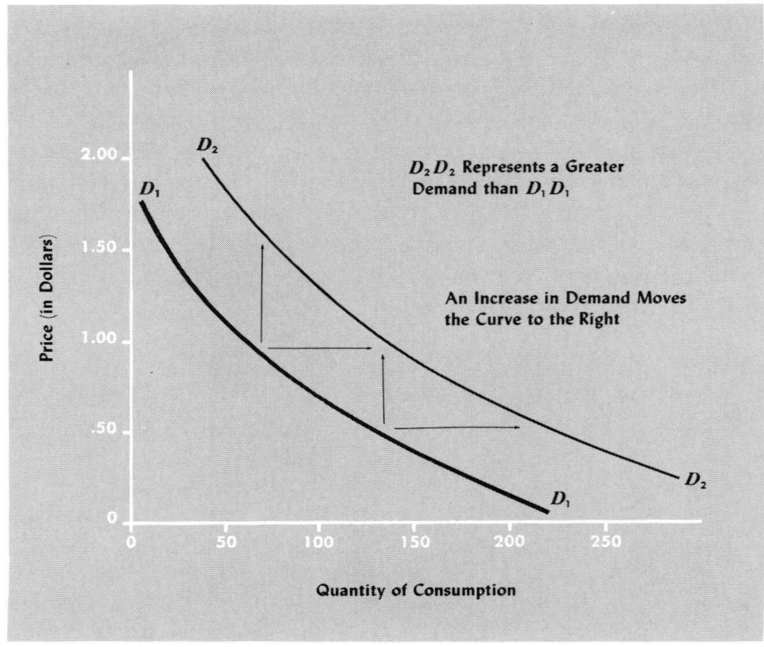

FIGURE 6–1. Demand curves. A demand curve shows the relationship between the price of the good and the amount of it that would be consumed. The farther the curve lies to the right, the more will be demanded at each possible price; the higher the curve, the greater the price for each quantity.

the upper left to the lower right) indicates larger consumption rates at lower prices. Curve D_2D_2 represents a bigger demand (schedule) than D_1D_1; that is, for any price, the particular quantity demanded is larger; and for any quantity, the maximum price at which that amount will be consumed is larger.

The expression "*increase* in demand" will always refer to increase in the rates of consumption *without* an initiating reduction in price. In the tabular schedule of demand it means that the quantities are all larger for the various prices. Graphically, an increase in demand is indicated by a shift of the demand curve to the right, as from D_1D_1 to D_2D_2.

Confusion can be avoided by a strict observance of the difference between the *amount demanded* at some price and the *state of demand.* The latter, usually simply called *demand,* is the whole schedule relating prices to amounts demanded. The former, the *amount demanded,* is the particular amount at a specified price; it is one of the price-quantity combinations rather than the whole set of quantity-price combinations that forms the state of *demand.* Having noted this important distinction, we must also strictly observe the corollary distinction between changes in the *amount demanded* and in the state of *demand.* A change in the *amount demanded* of some good is a change in the quantity that people want to buy in response to a change in its price. This is represented by a movement along a demand schedule from one price to another. On the other hand, the concept of a change in the state of *demand,* called simply a change in *demand,* refers to a change in the amount demanded without being in response to a change in the price. With a change in demand, the amounts demanded at each possible price are different than formerly. When demand increases, all the quantities shown in the quantity column of Table 6–1, for example, will increase (but not necessarily to the same extent). A change in demand can be the result of a change in wealth, population, or tastes, to mention only a few of the many factors; but a change in demand is not a result of a change in price. Thus, the demand for baby buggies will increase with an increase in the number of babies, or with the wealth of the parents. However, a lower price of baby buggies will not increase the *demand* for buggies; instead, it will increase the amount demanded, within the given demand. A change in the *amount demanded* is portrayed by sliding along the demand curve to the new price. Never confuse the two and never call one by the name of the other, if you wish to apply economic analysis correctly.

In the present analysis of demand, a change in price means that the price of a particular good—say, candy—has changed both *relatively* (relative to the prices of other goods) and *absolutely* (in terms of money). The simplest way to isolate a relative price change is to assume that no other price changes. This is an analytical isolation, not a statement of fact about the world. In the real world, many prices are changing at the same time—some upward and some downward. (The matter of *all* prices going up or down is covered in the later discussion of inflation and deflation.)

In Table 6–1, the quantity column refers to *rates* of consumption per year. It does not mean that a person buys or consumes that quantity at one time. He may buy them daily, weekly, or only when he eats. The fact that individuals do their shopping sporadically or at irregular intervals and do not consume goods at the moment of purchase causes no difficulty in the analysis, even if in the real world it makes a difference in shopping habits and affects the inventory problems of retailers and manufacturers. Do "durable" goods (automobiles, houses, pianos, appliances) create a problem in interpretation of the demand curve? That is, since most people have only one house, stove, and automobile, is there any sense in a demand schedule that indicates that a person will consume more when the price is lower? How can a person buy more cars if he owns only one at a time? The answer is that he can buy them more frequently, with a higher replacement rate; or he can buy a larger house, a bigger television set, a more awesome car, a more spacious and elaborate refrigerator; or he might possibly buy two cars if the price is lower.

In any event, whether we think of possessing more units at one time, or replacing them more frequently, or buying bigger ones, we have a schedule relating prices to amount demanded. Whether the quantity refers to amount owned, rate of consumption, rate of purchase, rate of replacement, or size of item owned, the principles of demand, to be presented shortly, still will hold true.

As a test of our understanding of the demand schedule, let's try a few interpretations. A person faced with a price of $1 per dozen eggs will—according to our data in Table 6–1—purchase about a dozen per week. Suppose that he has just purchased a dozen; while walking home, he notices that the price at a neighboring store is 80 cents. According to his demand schedule—which we assume we miraculously know—at this price he will buy about 1.5 dozen per week (81 dozen per year). Does he immediately go in and buy more? He might, but he need not. What he will probably do is keep the lower price in mind and consume the eggs he just bought at a slightly faster rate (1.5 dozen per week), knowing that he can replace them at the new lower price of 80 cents. Bygones are bygones, and the price *now* is 80 cents; so he immediately increases his consumption rate, in accordance with the new price, and uses up the dozen eggs in less than a week. Thus, *assuming that his state of demand as characterized by his demand schedule remains unchanged,* his *rates* of consumption and purchase rise when he sees that he can buy eggs for 80 cents instead of the $1 he has just paid; and as long as he thinks he can buy eggs at 80 cents per dozen, he will use eggs at a faster rate than when he thinks the price is $1 per dozen.

Similarly, if he discovers that the price has been raised, will he try to sell back some of the eggs he has purchased? No. He will consume them at a slower rate, purchase at a slower rate, and keep a smaller stock on the average. Why a smaller stock on the average? Because, given the higher price of eggs, he will prefer to have less of his wealth tied up in the form of consumer stocks of eggs and more in other goods.

The Fundamental Laws of Demand

A fundamental law of demand can now be stated: "The demand (schedule) for any good is a negative relationship between price and amount." Or, "The higher the price, the smaller the rate of consumption."[1] More elaborately: "Whatever the quantity of any good consumed at any particular price, a suffi-

[1] Mathematically, the demand function's derivative of the amount of a good consumed with respect to its price is negative.

ciently higher price will induce any person to consume less." Or: "Any person's consumption rate for any good will be increased (decreased) if the price is lowered (raised) sufficiently."

From whence comes this law? From the behavior of people in the real world. Just as our earlier postulates or propositions are justified or proved by their agreement with events in the real world, so the present proposition of demand is a law simply because it describes a universal, verified truth about people's consumption and market behavior.

ELASTICITY OF DEMAND AND TOTAL EXPENDITURE

The relative rate of change in the quantity demanded at different prices (*with the demand schedule unchanged*) is measured by the *elasticity* of demand. More precisely, the ratio of (a) the percentage change in quantity to (b) the associated percentage change in price is the measure of the elasticity of demand for any good. Usually, the price change is taken to be a small percentage change, because the relative response will depend upon the size of the price change. The demand schedule is said to be "elastic" where the percentage change in quantity demanded is numerically greater (and "inelastic" where the percentage change in quantity is less) than the percentage change in price.

In Table 6–1, a price fall of 5 percent from $1 to 95 cents would be accompanied by a quantity percentage change of almost 10 percent (from 56.52 to 62.25 pounds of candy per year). The demand schedule is elastic in that price region. On the other hand, in the region of prices around 50 cents, the demand is inelastic; a price decrease of 10 percent increases the quantity by less than 7 percent.[2]

The logical connection between demand *elasticity*, on the one hand, and the effect of price changes on *total receipts* (or expenditures), on the other, is quite simple. To say that price falls is to say that receipts per unit sold—i.e., *average revenue*—are smaller, and this in itself obviously tends to *reduce* total receipts. But at a lower price, the quantity demanded (not the demand) is larger, and the sale of more units tends to *increase* total receipts. The *net* change in receipts is determined by which effect, price or quantity, predominates. If the percentage increase in quantity is greater than the percentage reduction in price, total receipts rise—i.e., demand is elastic. We can summarize these definitions as follows:

1. "A price *fall* leads to an *increase* (decrease) in total receipts" means that the demand is elastic (inelastic).

2. "A price *rise* leads to a *decrease* (increase) in total receipts" means that the demand is elastic (inelastic).

[2] In mathematical terms, elasticity is usually defined for continuous functions as $dx/x \div dp/p$, of the demand function $x = f(p)$, and not as $\Delta x/x \div \Delta p/p$.

3. "A price *change*—fall or rise—leaves total receipts *unchanged*" means the demand has unitary elasticity.

Statistical studies have been made of several commodities, not merely to test the laws of demand but to measure the elasticity. Cigarettes, for example, seem to have an inelastic demand in the area of current price. The total community demand for beer and wine appears to be elastic. However, general classification of commodities is not very reliable; furthermore, the classification would depend upon the particular level of price at which the elasticity was being measured. There are no known general characteristics of goods from which economics can deduce the elasticity of any good in the real world. For example, what is the elasticity of demand for salt at the current price? For ice cream? For chocolate ice cream? We can only conjecture. We could talk around the point without saying much by asserting that the "closer the substitutes" for any good, the more will people change the rate of consumption in response to a change in its price. But the question is "Can we tell for which goods there are closer substitutes than for other goods?" Not for very many goods.

All is not lost, however. The second law of demand says something about elasticities: The longer any price change persists, the greater the elasticity. That is, although a price change for any good will have an immediate effect on the rate of consumption, the size of the effect will be greater after a week and still greater after a month, until eventually the full adjustment will be effective. *Elasticity of demand is greater in the longer run than in the shorter run.* Why? In the first place, more and more people will learn about the price change. Also, they often require time to adjust procedures in accordance with the price change. More accurately, the cost of revising consumption patterns or activities is less if done with less haste and with more economical side adjustments. For example, if the price of water were to be increased by 100 percent, the immediate rate of consumption would decrease—but it would decrease a great deal more within a few months, after people had made adjustments in associated activity and in water-using equipment.

"Demand," then, really refers to a host of demands, each applicable to a different lapse of time subsequent to any price change. If it were necessary for us to know all these curves and their exact paired price-quantities, we would be lost. Fortunately, because we know that these curves, whatever their location, are (1) negatively sloped with respect to price and (2) even more so for longer-persisting price changes, we have sufficient information from which to draw some important explanations or implications about the operation of economic systems.

Diagrammatically, the increase in elasticity with persistence of a new price is illustrated in Figure 6–2. Let the price change from P_1 to P_2. The different demand curves (1, 2, 3, etc.) show the greater amounts for the lower price at succeeding moments after the price change, with the ultimate rate being indi-

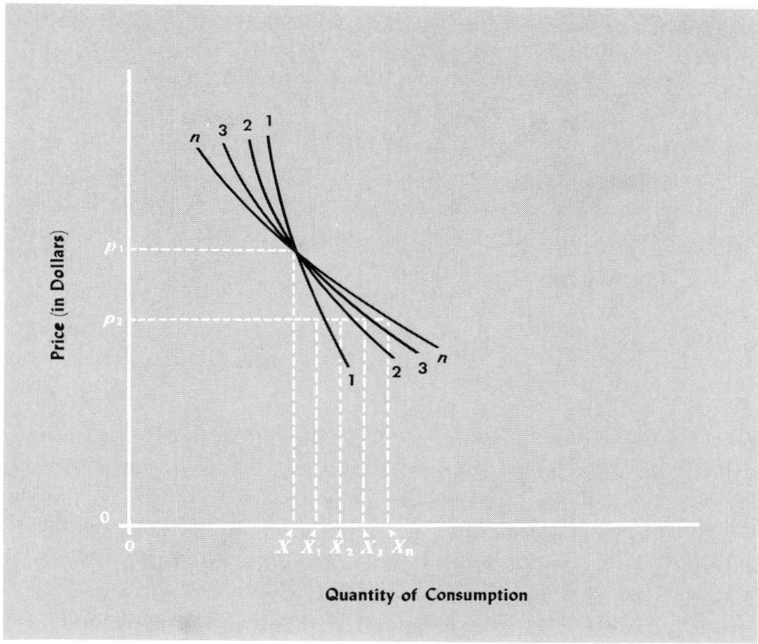

FIGURE 6–2. Effect of time on price-elasticity of demand. The longer the time after a price change, the greater the effect of that price change on the amount consumed—shown by the flatter curves for more elapsed time after a price change.

cated by the curve labeled n. After one "day" the rate is up to X_1, after two days it is X_2, etc., until at most it reaches X_n. The more time available, the flatter the curve (whether the price moves up or down from initial level)—up to some limiting demand curve when the full consumption adjustment to the new price will have occurred (or until price changes again, in which event the analysis starts over from the newly changed price).

SOME ILLUSTRATIONS OF THE LAWS OF DEMAND

The scope and meaning of the laws of demand can be illustrated by some special applications to specific commodities.

Demand for food. You should have no difficulty in seeing that a higher price of meat will induce people to economize on it—that is, to shift the pattern of their expenditure, buying less meat than before and more of other things. Alternative sources of protein—eggs, fish, cheese, and milk, to name but a few —are fairly obvious. Vegetables and even candy also substitute for meat. So do some drinks. Even more distantly, since some of us eat not solely for nutritional value but also for the pleasure of eating, we can reduce this source of pleasure and substitute more recreation, reading, or entertainment.

We do not speak of the "demand for food" as such, since no one buys "food" as such. He buys particular commodities, each of which is a part of his "food." For each of these, his total consumption is affected (or limited) by its price. But even if one insists on talking of the "demand for food," the law of demand asserts that the amount of food consumed is affected by the price of food. To deny this is to assert that one is *completely unconcerned* about what he could have if he gave up a little food, or that all he wants in life is food and there is simply no amount of other goods and services, *no matter how large,* which would induce him to consume a little less food. (Remember the postulates?)

Demand for wood. The law of demand applies to wood, too. If its price rises, we will be induced to substitute plaster, plastics, steel, aluminum, copper, glass, paper, coal, oil, and electricity; thus, less wood will be demanded at the higher price than at the old lower price. You and I may not respond very much, if at all, to a 10 percent rise in the price of wood. But since industrial engineers, product designers, and businessmen will shift in varying degrees to substitutes, the things we buy will have less wood in them and more of other things. Furthermore, since wooden furniture will rise in price relative to metal or plastic furniture, some of us will be induced to shift in some degree to the latter. It is not necessary that every person revise his purchase habits. There are always *some* people on the margin of choice between one and the other; and, as prices change, these marginal choices shift.

This phenomenon of marginal adjusters is common to all sciences. In physics or chemistry, for instance, some molecules will escape when a container of gas is opened. The fact that a majority did not escape does not mean that none escaped. When the price of a commodity rises, we (meaning "society") don't all have to reduce the use of the commodity in any *one* activity; instead, at least some withdraw it from its various uses. When the price of wood rises, we don't all abandon wooden houses, or wooden boxes, or wooden furniture. Rather, in all instances where we use wood, less is used than if its price had not risen. This is called the "marginal general-adjustment process" to distinguish it from an all-or-none adjustment by everyone.

Demand for water. An especially instructive example is the demand for water. Surely, since people cannot live without it, no one will reduce his use of water just because its price goes up. As a matter of fact, however, water is not an exceptional commodity. The amount of it that people will use depends upon its price. The amount used is not some technologically fixed necessity. We could all use more water than we do now, and we could all use less. The reason that people in the arid regions use less water is not that they couldn't use more but that they don't *want* more, given the *high* price of getting more water (say, by pumping it thousands of miles). Because the price of water is high, they choose to consume less and to use for other, more desired, purposes the resources that would otherwise have been used up in making more water available to that area.

In the United States the average per capita daily use of water varies among cities from, for example, 230 gallons in Chicago, to 150 in New York and Los Angeles, to 120 in San Diego and 110 in Boston. The quantities reflect, for one thing, differences in industrial uses. Chicago has steel- and oil-refining industries, which use a great deal of water; New York City businesses—finance, retail, apparel—are light water users.

A change in the cost of water will have a strong effect on the extent of various water-using activities. The law of demand says that *one* way to reduce consumption is to let the price of water rise to reflect its value in various uses. If water prices rise, water will be more worth saving. Reduction of waste is not costless and will be done more the higher the cost of water. In New York City, for instance, 10 percent of the total water consumption is estimated to be from leakages in street mains. As costs of water rise, it will pay to spend more money to reduce that loss. For example, at present water meters, which make people pay according to use, are not universally used. At a higher price of water, meters will be more economical; and when they are installed, people will have stronger incentives to waste less water (by repair and modification of faucets and water-using equipment).

Some waste-reducing activities are not so obvious and occur in an indirect way. With higher water prices, residential areas will have smaller gardens and lawns. Sprinkler systems will be used more because they waste less water. Gardeners will sweep, rather than wash off, lawns and sidewalks. Rock gardens, paved yard areas, and brick patios will become more common, relative to grass areas. Automobiles will be washed less often as the cost of a washing rises. Water will be softened to conserve on water use; already several cities partially soften the water to make it more effective. In sum, it has been estimated in studies of domestic water consumption that a doubling of water prices would within a year reduce domestic household water consumption by about 30 to 50 percent.

Still more ways of conserving water exist. Industrial users take about half the water in many cities. These users are probably even more responsive to price than are domestic users. For example, as shown in Table 6–2, there are great differences in the rate of use of water even within the same industry. The figures in the "maximum" column represent the amounts used in the most profligate plants in each industry, while the "minimum" column shows the least amount used per unit of output produced. Note the tremendous range in the first three industries, which happen also to be the heaviest industrial water users. Many industrial firms use large amounts of water for cooling purposes on a once-through basis without recirculation through cooling units. Some steel mills use 40,000 gallons of water per ton produced, but the Kaiser steel mill (in the Los

Table 6–2

VARIATIONS AMONG FIRMS AND PRODUCTS IN INDUSTRIAL CONSUMPTION OF WATER, PER UNIT OF OUTPUT

Product or User and Unit	Draft (in gallons)		
	Maximum	Typical	Minimum
Steam-electric power (kw-h)	170	80	1.3
Petroleum refining (gallon of crude oil)	44	18	1.7
Steel (finished ton)	65,000	40,000	1,400
Soaps, edible oils (pound)	7	. . .	1.5
Carbon black (pound)	14	4	0.25
Natural rubber (pound)	6	. . .	2.5
Butadiene (pound)	305	160	13
Glass containers (ton)	670	. . .	120
Automobiles (per car)	16,000	. . .	12,000
Trucks, buses (per unit)	20,000	. . .	15,000

Source: H. E. Hudson and Janet Abu-Lughod, "Water Requirements," in Jack B. Graham and Meredith F. Burrill (eds.), *Water for Industry* (Washington, D.C.: American Association for the Advancement of Science, 1956), Publication No. 45, pp. 19–21.

Angeles area) has reduced its use to 1,600 gallons. One soap plant in the same area has installed recirculatory cooling towers to reduce water consumption from about six million to less than half a million gallons per day. At higher water prices, the value of the water saved, appearing as savings to the firm, would make the cost of recycling worthwhile. Clearly, the amount of water "needed" is a variable depending upon various factors, one of which is the price of water.

But there are still more ways to adjust the uses of water in response to price. The largest user of water in Southern California is agriculture, which accounts for approximately 80 percent of the water usage. One reason it uses so much water is that water is sold to farmers for irrigation at prices much lower than those at which it is sold to urban dwellers, even after allowance for distribution and purification costs. What would the farmers do if the price of water were allowed to rise to reflect a reduced supply? Some of them would go out of business—a blunt way of saying that the water now used by farmers is *worth more in other uses* than in agriculture. The community communicates this fact via the impersonal indicator—higher water prices. Higher prices for water would indicate that some water now used to grow watermelons, lettuce, and celery, for example, would be more useful elsewhere. Less of these products would be grown in Southern California; they may be grown elsewhere where production is cheaper and shipped to Southern California, because this arrangement is cheaper than shipping in the water with which to grow them. Some areas or towns may decline as people find it preferable to move to places where water is cheaper or to tasks that use less water. That is, after all, the reason that the Western deserts are so sparsely populated.

How do people discover how to use less when the price of water (or any good) rises? Some people make a living precisely by giving just such advice and information. Business is constantly being sought by industrial engineers, architects, home-economist consultants, and commercial *salesmen* of water-recycling equipment, water softeners, automatic faucets, fertilizers, irrigation and sprinkling equipment, air-conditioning machinery, hard-top patios, chemicals that reduce evaporation, washing machines that use less water, steam generators, etc. Every rise in water costs provides them with more business prospects. Salesmen make it their business to detect situations in which their equipment is economical to use and to provide information and education by advertising and personal solicitation. As students, we may think that all worthwhile education and knowledge comes from schools, teachers, and books. The fact is that a very large portion of the information and knowledge of practical matters is provided by salesmen—not because they are interested in us, but because it is to their personal interest to see that potential customers are educated to particular facts of the world. We slurringly call this "advertising and propaganda," and indeed it is; but that does not change its educational value, assuming it is truthful. Even though no one can now imagine how the use of water, rubber, wheat, sugar, steel, or gasoline would respond to a change in price, the users of those goods would soon be swamped with information about new uses if the price changed.

We can classify these effects of price changes on quantity. Suppose that price falls. First, more of the item will be used in *current uses*. Second, *new uses* will be observed—uses that are valued too low to justify paying the former higher price. Third, *new users* will appear. People whose tastes were different or whose incomes were too low will now find at the lower price that they prefer to use the item. And the reverse holds for higher prices. As long as we think only of the first possibility (that is, using more or using less in the same old customary ways), we will underrate the effect of price on rate of use.

NEEDS VERSUS DEMAND

The law of demand is a denial of the idea of "needs." People often say that they need more water. What do they mean? That less than the "needed" amount would be absolutely intolerable? That even more would be useless? Of course not. Less water (not *none*) could be tolerated (although less is clearly not desirable). Statements that certain areas or people have water "requirements" suggest that they simply *must* have *that* amount of water. And to get that amount of water it is often proposed that water committees or boards be set up to assure that there is no unjustified competition for water and that all areas have their "needs" satisfied. But when they refer to "needs" in an absolute sense, people forget that the market price of water affects the amount used (the law of demand).

It is said that we "need" more highways. Does this mean that we should have them regardless of the cost—i.e., the value of the forsaken alternatives? If someone says that "we need" more teachers, does he mean that, if *he* had to pay the costs of getting more teachers, he would hire more? Or, to put matters in more transparent form, does he mean that other people should not prefer other things (which they must give up to get more teachers)? When someone says there is a "need" for something, he should always be asked, "In order to achieve what, at what cost of other goods or 'needs,' and at whose cost?"

If he says, "We need something," for whom is he speaking? When my wife says, "We need a new car" or "We need a larger house," if I want to object, I "agree" by saying, "Of course we need it. What shall we give up to get it? What do we need less?"

In sum, the word "needs" suggests that costs or prices are irrelevant. Whenever and wherever "needs" is used—whether it be prefaced by "urgent, critical, crying, vital, or essential"—you should immediately be alert to the danger of satisfying someone else's "worthy" demands regardless of the costs—as if the law of demand were completely false.

ALLEGED EXCEPTIONS TO THE LAW OF DEMAND

Some students may think that they know of some counter-examples that disprove the law of demand. The law of demand asserts that people *are* sensitive to costs or prices and that they buy *less* in response to a higher price. Someone might object to this assertion by pointing out that people *could* conceivably be insensitive to price or that they *could* buy more of some things when the price rises. Indeed, they *conceivably* could; but the law of demand says that *actually* they do not do so. Possibility or conceivability, therefore, cannot be regarded as an exception; for it is the *actuality* of such behavior that the law of demand denies. The pertinent question is "Does such denied, but conceivable, behavior actually occur?" Two cases bear examination.

An exception to the law of demand is alleged to occur when the price of, say, wheat falls and the buyers think to themselves, "Price is falling. It will fall further. If I wait, I can later buy more cheaply. Therefore, I will withdraw current orders to buy." This appears to mean that a lower price has resulted in less, not more, purchases. But wait. Has the price fallen? It is lower now than it was earlier. However, the relevant fact is that future prices are expected to be even lower. Therefore, *relative to expected future prices*, the present price has *increased*. People who have the alternatives of buying now or buying later transfer their purchases from relatively high-price times to relatively low-price times—exactly as implied by the law of demand.

Another alleged case is that of "prestige" goods—like Mumms champagne, Church shoes, Cavanaugh hats, Rolls Royce cars, Orrefors crystal, Dunlop furniture, Bristol Cream sherry, Countess Mara ties, Harvard degrees, or whatever you aspire to. The allegation is that the high price of these goods makes the demand higher than it otherwise would be. Presumably, people are motivated to buy high-priced goods because possession of such goods sheds prestige on the buyer. Undoubtedly the possession of such goods can enhance the "prestige" of the owner. But prestige goods do *not* produce a demand curve that is positively sloped with respect to price; they do *not* deny that the amount demanded will be smaller at higher prices and bigger at lower prices. Let the price of the "prestige" good be still higher, and less will be bought. Lower its price, and more people will be buying it. Otherwise, what would prevent the price from rising higher and higher without limit?

Perhaps the advocates of the prestige-good case have in mind the so-called "fashion" goods—items that experience violent fashion swings. But again fashions mean simply that demand schedules increase violently in response to a general shift in tastes; the new, higher demand curve still will have a negative slope. Mink stoles would be even more common if the price were lower. Perhaps when everyone has one, prestige will be enhanced by some other distinctive items. The continual pursuit of distinctiveness is in no way inconsistent with the law of demand.

And then there is the case in which a person offers to sell at a higher price and thus makes the buyer believe that the item is a better item. Similarly, anyone who proposes to sell something at a price far below its current market price will immediately stir doubts in the buyers' minds about the genuineness of the item being offered. But this attitude results from the fact that a higher price is an index of quality in open markets. If I offer to sell my new Plymouth for $1,000, a potential buyer will probably hesitate, suspecting that I don't really own the car or that its motor isn't really in good condition. If he can satisfy himself that the lower price is not the result of inferior quality, however, he will buy the car more readily than if I asked $3,000. Normally, an inferior-quality good is sold at a lower price because only then will anyone buy it; at the same price, everyone would prefer the better item. Fundamentally, then, the public's association of higher price with higher quality is a consequence, not a refutation, of the law of demand.

VALIDITY OF THE LAWS OF DEMAND

To some people, the empirical validity of the laws of demand is obvious, so that no formal, systematic empirical verification is required. In fact, some people think the theory is so obvious that it is hardly worth formalizing, just as some people think the law of gravity is so obvious that only people with nothing better to do would bother to formalize it. However, in the first place, the obvious sometimes is not true; and in the course of this book several things that may have seemed "obviously" correct will become "obviously" false. The danger in relying on the "obviousness" of a proposition is that people, ignoring embarrassing exceptional cases, collect and recollect only the favorable instances from their casual observation. In the second place, a formal rigorous, abstract statement induces one to seek or explain phenomena not otherwise noticed, as we shall shortly illustrate by suggesting some hidden indirect implications.

Therefore, even after the alleged exceptions are taken care of, there still remains the task of providing convincing evidence of the validity of the law. Merely showing that alleged exceptions are not exceptions does not prove the proposition correct (we call it a "proposition" until the evidence is overwhelming for it, after which it is called a "law"). We shall briefly hint at some of the evidence—both direct and indirect—for the validity of the law of demand.

Direct evidence of validity. Do merchants advertise a sale by announcing that they are temporarily raising prices? Have you noticed that prices of fruits and vegetables are lower when the crop is in season? The greater amount can be sold only at a lower price. If the law of demand were not true, prices would not change with seasons of perishable crops. If the law of demand were not true, there would be no limit to how high you could set prices, short of taking every bit of a person's wealth for one unit of whatever you seek to sell. If the law of demand were not true, poorer-quality goods would sell for the same price as better-quality goods (in those cases where everyone agrees in ranking of quality). Can you see why? Even more, there would be no point in charging prices so as to collect more from those who buy more, for that would have no effect on how much they buy, if amount demanded does not respond to price.

Indirect evidence of validity. Usually, it is in the corroboration of less direct, hidden implications that the power and validity of a law are made strikingly evident. For example, how does one explain the smaller proportion of good oranges sold in California than in New York? Why is a larger proportion of the good oranges shipped to New York? Is it because New York's population is richer or more discriminating? Possibly; but if so, then why are the oranges sold even in the poor districts of New York better oranges than those sold in California? The same question can be posed for other goods: Why do Asians import disproportionately more expensive American cars rather than cheaper models? Why are "luxuries" so disproportionately represented in international trade? Why do young parents with children go to expensive plays rather than movies *relatively* more often than do young couples without children? Why are "seconds" more heavily consumed near the place of manufacture than farther away? Why must a tourist be more careful in buying leather goods in Italy than in buying Italian leather goods in the United States? The answer is that these are implications of the law of demand. Let us see why.

Suppose that grapes are grown in California and that it costs 5 cents a pound to ship grapes to New York, whether the grapes are "choice" or "standard" (poorer), and that the total production of grapes is 50 percent "choice" and 50 percent "standard." Suppose further that in California the "choice" grapes sell for 10 cents a pound and the standard for 5 cents a pound; that is, in California 2 pounds of "standard" and 1 pound of "choice" grapes sell for the same price. If grapes are shipped to New York, the shipping costs will raise the cost of "choice" grapes to 15 cents and of "standard" grapes to 10 cents. In New York the costs of "choice" grapes are lower, *relative* to "standard" grapes (1.5 to 1), than in California (2 to 1). To buy 1 pound of "choice" grapes in New York would mean a sacrifice of 1.5 pounds of "standard," whereas in California it would cost 2 pounds of "standard." According to our law of demand, New Yorkers, faced with a lower price of "choice" relative to "standard," will consume *relatively* more "choice" grapes than Californians will. In California, where "standard" grapes are cheaper relative to "choice" grapes, a larger fraction of "standard" grapes will be consumed—and this is what actually happens.

Try the same analysis on choice versus commercial grades of meat in Alaska and Texas, or French wines in New York and France. A transport cost is added—a cost that is almost the same for the two classes of items; the price of the better item, relative to the poorer item, is lower after shipment than it is at the place of manufacture *before shipment.* Because the relative price of the higher-quality good is lower at the more distant places than at the place of origin, the more distant consumers will purchase a larger proportion of superior to second-grade items than will consumers at or near the place of manufacture. And, again, this is what indeed does happen. For instance, Italian producers will export their better items; the lower-quality goods are left at home, so that tourists have a greater chance of finding inferior goods in Italian markets than in the countries to which Italy exports goods.

What about the parents of young children? If they hire baby sitters at, say, 75 cents an hour, and are out for four hours, they will be paying $3 just to leave the house. Now, add the cost of two movie tickets at $1 each, and compare that total cost with the cost of going to the theater (at $4 per ticket). The theater costs a total of $11, and movies cost a total of $5. The theater, then, costs just slightly more than twice what a movie costs. But if a couple has no children and can avoid the baby-sitter fee, the movie will cost $2 and the theater $8—a ratio of 4 to 1: the theater now becomes relatively more expensive. In our original question, we did not assume that parents will go to the theater *more* than people who have no children; we said that, *when* baby-sitting parents go out, they will go to the theater a *larger fraction* of the time than childless couples will.

Questions

1. If one pair of shoes can be exchanged for four shirts, and one shirt trades for two pairs of socks, and if one pair of shoes trades for six pairs of socks, what series of trades could you make so as to get steadily richer? (This is known as "arbitraging" among markets for different goods.)

2. What are prices? Can there be prices without money?

3. For how many different goods do you think a person can estimate the current market price: 10, 100, 1,000? Defend the 1,000 answer.

4. What properties of a good do you think will enhance its chances of being used as money? To what extent are these properties attributes of gold, bricks, cigarettes, chewing gum, seashells, pearls, cattle, cotton cloth, rope, glass, spherical rocks, matches, diamonds, platinum?

5. Does "demand," as used in economic analysis, refer to a particular amount that someone wants, or does it refer to a whole schedule of various amounts at various prices?

6. To say that a person purchases and consumes water at a rate of 50 gallons per day, or 350 per week, is to say the same thing in two ways. What is the equivalent statement in terms of rates per year?

7. The following questions are intended to reveal clearly the difference between a total *stock* and a *rate*. (Thus, they ignore the argument of the woman who told the traffic policeman that she couldn't have been going at a speed of 60 miles per hour, since she had been traveling only ten minutes.)

   a. How many eggs does a person eat in one week at the *rate* of 365 per year?

   b. How many miles does a person walk in seven hours at a *rate* of 24 miles per day? At the rate of 1 mile an hour?

8. Mr. *A* currently uses water at a rate of 3,650 gallons per year at the present price. Suppose that his demand doubles, so that his rate increases to 7,300 gallons per year. How many more *gallons* of water will he consume during the first week of higher demand?

9. In Table 6–1 of the text, if price fell from $1 to 70 cents, the amount purchased would increase. Would that represent an increase in demand—in the jargon of economic analysis? What would have to happen to the data of Table 6–1 to portray an increase in demand?

10. If the price of candy rises from $1 to $1.25 a pound while the price of ice cream rises from 50 cents to 75 cents a gallon, in what sense is this a *fall* in the price of candy?

11. Can Table 6–1 be read as follows: "A person sees a price of $1 for one pound of candy, and he therefore buys 56.52 pounds. The next day he sees that the price of

candy has fallen to 90 cents; so he dashes out and buys 38.39 pounds. A couple of days later, the price rises to $1.10; so he buys 45.97 pounds." If it can't be interpreted that way, and it can't, then how is it to be interpreted?

12. **a.** Because we represent a demand curve with precise numbers, does that mean that people have these numerical schedules in their minds?

b. What essential property illustrated by the demand-schedule data does characterize their behavior?

13. "According to the law of demand, the lower the price of vacations, the more vacations I should take. Yet I take only one per year. Obviously the law of demand must be wrong." Is it?

14. Do you think the demand for children obeys the fundamental theorem of demand? The demand by immigrants for entry to the United States? The demand for divorces? The demand for pianos? The demand for beautiful women? The demand for a winning college football team? The demand for "A's" in this course? The demand for appendectomies?

15. "Elasticity is a measure of the percentage increase in demand for a one-cent change in price." There are two errors in that statement. Rewrite it correctly.

16. Are the following statements correct or incorrect? Explain your answer.

a. "A 1 percent rise in price that induces a 3 percent decrease in amount taken indicates elasticity of less than one." Correct?

b. "A 1 percent fall in price that induces a 3 percent increase in amount purchased indicates an elasticity of greater than one." Correct?

c. What is wrong with asking whether a 1 percent rise in price induces a 3 percent decrease in demand?

17. The price of first-class surface mail was increased from 4 cents to 5 cents; at the same time, the price of first-class airmail was increased from 7 cents to 8 cents. What effect do you think this will have on the amount of air service demanded relative to surface mail? Did you use the law of demand in your reasoning?

18. Suppose Mr. *A*'s demand should increase. What kinds of changes in the numbers of his demand schedule would indicate this?

19. An increase in demand is shown graphically by a demand curve (to the right of) (above) (below) (to the left of) the old demand curve. Select correct options.

20. A person purchases and consumes eggs at a rate equivalent to seven per week if the price of eggs is 5 cents each. Another person purchases and consumes eggs at the rate of 365 per year when the price of eggs is 4 cents. Who reflects a greater demand?

21. Sometimes luxuries are defined as goods whose demand is elastic, while necessities are those whose demand is inelastic. Evaluate the usefulness of that designation. How would you define a luxury and a necessity? For what problems is it useful to attempt a distinction between luxuries and necessities?

22. "If the price of gasoline fell by 10 percent, the average person would not change his rate of consumption." Explain why this does not refute the law of demand.

23. In the demand schedule of Table 6–1, at a price of $1 the annual consumption is 56.52. At a price of 95 cents the annual consumption is 5.77 units per year larger.

a. Can it be said that this person prefers to have *each* one of those 5.77 units annually, more than he prefers 95 cents' worth of annual expenditures on any other goods?

b. Note that at the price of $1, he spent annually $56.52 on this good; whereas, at a price of 95 cents, he spent $59.14 (= $.95 × 62.25), 2.62 (= $59.14 − 56.52) more than previously. Do you still say he values the extra 5.77 units at approximately 95 cents each, even though he spends only $2.62 more?

c. Explain why. In doing so, explain clearly what is meant by "value."

24. Can you think of a good for which the demand is absolutely inelastic (i.e., the amount demanded will not change, no matter how high the price)? If you name one, what would happen if its price were raised by a factor of 100? If cut by a factor of 100?

25. **a.** If the price of gasoline were 30 percent lower, would automobile manufacturers be induced to make changes in the designs or operating characteristics of automobiles?

b. What effect would they have on gasoline consumption?

c. Would those effects occur more completely within three months or within three years?

26. Which of the following do you think would increase a woman's demand for wigs?

a. A raise in her husband's salary.

b. Inheriting $50,000.

c. Higher price of hats.

d. Having a swimming pool.

e. Rise in cost of hair care.

f. Being older and grayer.

g. Getting divorced.

h. Number of other women who wear wigs.

i. Lower price of wigs.

27. Which do you think are more important: urgent, critical, crying, vital, basic, minimum, social, or private needs?

28. Explain wherein each of these is a denial of the law of demand and the basic postulates of economics:

a. "The budget of the Department of Defense covers only our basic needs and nothing more."

b. "Our children need more schools."

c. "Nothing is too good when it comes to education."

d. "America needs the atomic bomb."

29. "Economics does not admit of the concept of a 'need' or a 'necessary amount' of any good." Explain.

30. Diagnose and evaluate the following news report from the *Los Angeles Times:*

> Los Angeles needs 24 more golf courses, according to a report submitted to the City Recreation and Park Department by the National Golf Foundation. The survey discovered that there are 160,000 golfers in the Los Angeles area, and many of them do not play as often as they would like because of the lack of courses.

How does this differ from the situation of filet mignon steaks, champagne, and luxurious houses in the expensive part of town?

31. Does a prestige good *give* one prestige or *reflect* his prestige?

32. Let p_1 and p_2 be the domestic prices of two goods. Let T_1 and T_2 be the transport costs of these goods to a "foreign" market. Show that if $T_1/T_2 < p_1/p_2$, then relatively more of good "1" will be shipped; if the inequality is reversed, relatively more of good "2" will be shipped. "Relative" to what? In your answer, what do you assume about demand conditions in domestic and in "foreign" markets?

33. Economics asserts that people prefer more to less goods. Yet there are waiting lists of people seeking small apartments in slum areas while bigger, better apartments do not have a list of applicants at all. How can people want smaller, less luxurious apartments, rather than bigger apartments, without violating our postulates about people's preferring more economic goods?

7

MARKET DEMAND AND MARKET-EQUILIBRIUM PRICE

Demand in a Two-Person Market

The first application of demand analysis will be to a two-person market. Afterward, we shall examine the many-person market.

The demand of persons *A* and *B* for automobiles (one kind) is given in Table 7–1. Concentrate on two commodities, automobiles and money, with the latter representing all commodities other than automobiles. *A* already owns one automobile and $10,000 worth of other things (house, clothing, food, business properties, and money), while *B* owns three automobiles and $15,000 worth of other things, including money. Table 7–1 indicates the number of automobiles that *A* and *B* wish to possess at alternative prices. If the price is $1,000, *A* demands one automobile. We have assumed that he already owns one; therefore, at this price, he is content to stand pat and neither buy another nor sell the one he now has. But *B* puts a lower subjective value on automobiles; therefore, at a price of $1,000, he prefers not to own any. Since in fact he already has three, he will try to sell three.

If *A* were presented with the opportunity to get a car for $900, he would prefer to give up the money (i.e., whatever else he could buy with $900) and obtain another car. And if the price at which he could buy cars were as low as $600, he would prefer to own three cars—that is, a third car is worth more to him than is $600, and a fourth car is worth more to him than anything else he can do with $100. All of this is reflected in his demand schedule.

If the *present* price is $600, *A* will immediately buy two more cars. If the price were first $800 (at which point he buys one more car) and then $600 (at which point he buys still another car), *A* will have spent $1,400, or $200 more than in the first case. Surely, it may be objected, *A*'s demand for cars should be greater if he can buy *all* he wants for $600, because then he has $200 more wealth than in the "$800-and-then-$600" case. This consideration is correct (for the demand schedule lists *alternative,* not *sequential,* prices and corresponding quantities); but at present we can ignore this complication for two reasons. First, if the difference in wealth is a small enough proportion of a person's total wealth, it will have no perceptible effect on his demand for the item. Second, we could allow for this change in wealth by revising his demand schedule to accord with each sequence of price and level of his wealth. This would complicate the analysis, but since the *process* by which price is determined and the *nature* of the resulting pattern of consumption remain unchanged, we simplify the exposition and concentrate on the essential points by assuming this "wealth effect" to be trivial.

Table 7–1

CAR-OWNERSHIP DEMAND SCHEDULES OF *A* AND *B*

Price	Quantity of Good *A*	*B*	Total
$1,100	0	0	0
1,000	1	0	1
900	2	0	2
800	2	1	3
700	2	1	3
600	3	1	4
500	3	2	5
400	3	2	5
300	3	2	5
200	3	3	6
100	4	3	7

Similarly, *B*'s demand schedule tells us that *B* would prefer to have no automobiles if the price is $900 or more and only one car if the price is $600 to $800. He would prefer a second car more than $500, and a third car would be worth more than $200 to him.

A and *B* started, we have assumed, with one and three cars, respectively. *A* would be prepared to offer *B* at least $700 for a second car, and *B* would prefer $700 to a third car. Of course, if *A* knew *B*'s demand, he might initially offer *B* as little as $300 for a car; and *B* could, if he were well enough informed about *A*, demand a price as high as $900.

A trade will occur at some price between $300 and $900. Thereupon, *A* has two cars and *B* has two. Another trade is still open as an avenue of mutual benefit. *A* is prepared to pay as much as $600 to get a third car, while *B* prefers something over $500 to one of his two remaining cars. A trade will occur at, let us say, $600 (the only possible price if we think in hundred-dollar steps). These trades have re-allocated cars and claims to other goods so that no further trade can benefit both parties. At this price, $600, the total demand for cars is four, the number in existence; and after trade the distribution of cars conforms to the amount demanded by each person at that price.

To put it a bit differently, at the equilibrium price of $600, *A* wanted to buy two *more* cars, and *B* wanted to sell two. At no other price was the demand for additional cars equal to the amount offered for sale. The equilibrium price will always be a price at which the total amount demanded equals the total existing stock. The market price will converge to that $600 equilibrium price at which the demand to *buy more* cars equals the amount people are willing to sell, or—to say the same thing in terms of total stocks—at which the total demand to *own* cars equals the existing stock. The law of price determination by demand and supply implies that equilibrium price will result from the play of demand and supply in the open market. The free play of demand and supply is important not simply because it sets a price but because, in the process, it reveals relative consumption values; it thus enables people to exchange goods so as to achieve a preferred combination of goods. At this allocative equilibrium, no further revision of the pattern of ownership—with each person moving to what he regards as a preferred position—is possible. The market is "cleared."

It may be objected that no one knows any demand schedules with the accuracy specified here. But we have *not* assumed that anyone knows the demand schedules. We have merely described what happens when two people, whose behavior is characterized by the demand schedules, are not restricted in their opportunity to trade in an open market. Suppose that no one knows even his own demand schedule in the sense that he can write it out for you. All we require is that when faced with the opportunity to buy or sell a car at a price, *he can make a decision.* To this we add our law of demand: At a higher price he will buy less than he will at a lower price. Precisely *what* that larger or smaller amount is for each and every price is not necessary information. Our explicit use of numbers merely makes it easier to follow the analysis.

Even without the data, we can see that when people are given the opportunity to engage in trade, each will revise his pattern of consumption to what he thinks is a preferred position, if such a possibility exists. Furthermore, we can see that market-price bidding reveals to each person whether there are any further possible exchanges that will bring him to what he regards as a preferred pattern of goods. The process of bidding higher or lower prices, in accordance with each person's attempts to improve his situation as he sees it, is the essence of the operation of the law of demand.

Demand in a Four-Person Market

Let us now try a four-person situation: individuals *A, B, C,* and *D,* with the demand schedules given in Table 7–2.

Table 7–2

CAR-OWNERSHIP DEMANDS OF *A, B, C,* AND *D*

Price	Quantity of Good *A*	*B*	*C*	*D*	Total
$1,000	2	0	1	1	4
900	2	0	1	1	4
800	2	0	1	2	5
700	2	0	1	2	5
600	3	0	1	2	6
500	3	1	1	2	7
400	3	1	2	2	8
300	3	1	2	3	9
200	3	1	2	4	10
100	4	1	2	4	11

At first glance, one might think that *A* is rich and that *B* is poor. In fact, the contrary could be true. *B* might be a wealthy old man who rather regrets the invention of the internal-combustion engine; and *A* might be the head of a poor family, with everyone in the family working at places distant from home. We may reasonably suppose that a *given* individual's demand for automobiles will increase if his income increases, but the fact that *one* person's demand is greater than *another* person's demand is not reliable evidence that the first person is wealthier.

Since *A* is prepared to pay $600 to get a third car, we can conclude that he prefers having a third car to having $600. *B* would rather have one car than $500, but he would rather have $600 than one car. *C* and *D* would give up as much as $1,000 for one car; but *C* would give up only $100 to $400 for a second car, whereas *D* would give up as much as $800. The column labeled "Total" lists the total number demanded at each alternative possible price. The schedules for each person and for the total conform to our law of demand: greater amounts are demanded only at lower prices, and lesser amounts at higher prices.

Suppose that in this community there are seven cars and that three of them are owned by *A*, one by *B*, one by *C*, and two by *D*. It happens, as seen in the table, that this distribution of *ownership* is the same as the pattern of *demand* when the community wants to have a total of seven cars. In short, this is an *equilibrium distribution,* in that no one is willing to give up a car for what anyone else is willing to pay, and no one is willing to buy another car for what anyone else is asking. With the community holding seven cars and wanting seven cars, the equilibrium price is $500: no one would pay more than $500 to get another, and no one would be willing to sell a car for $500 or less. The market is cleared.

But fortuitous agreement between an initial and equilibrium distribution can't be counted on; so suppose that at first all seven cars are owned by A. And, as before, suppose that the stock of cars that any person may ultimately buy or sell is a proportionately small part of his wealth, so that these demand schedules are not changed perceptibly by the particular sequence of prices in the process of reaching an equilibrium. With seven cars, *A* would prefer to sell some if he could get even $100 per car. Suppose *C* and *D* each offer to buy a car for $900. *A* will sell. Then *B* offers $400 for a car; again, *A* sells.

These exchanges leave *A* with four cars, and *B, C,* and *D* with one car each. *C* offers to buy another car from *A* at $200. *A* is prepared to accept, because he would rather have $200 than a fourth car. *D* would be prepared to offer up to $800 for a second car; but suppose he doesn't learn that *A* is willing to sell until after *C* has bought the car from *A* for $200, leaving *A* with three cars. *D* now offers anyone $300 for a second car, but no one will sell a car at that price. *D* can complain that *A* sold a car to *C* for $200 and therefore ought to be prepared to sell another one to *D* for $300. *A* replies simply that he doesn't have any cars to "spare" now that he has only three. *A* does say, however, that he has a car to spare if *D* will pay him $800. As we know, *D* will pay this price rather than go without a second car; but he cleverly offers something less for a car—say, $600—thus trying to get a better price than from *A*. By this time, if *B* is alert to market offers, he will say that he will sell his car for $600, even though he just bought it. But *C*, being willing to sell his second car for anything over $400, will undercut *B*'s price by offering to sell at $500. At this price *A* will not sell, nor will *B*. That leaves only *C* as a seller, and *D* is prepared to pay that price. *C* cannot get a higher price, because *B* will also offer to sell at $600. *D* cannot get a car for less than $500. So he pays $500, and thereafter everyone is content with his *pattern* of goods, given his and everyone else's preferences and given the total *wealth* distribution.

As the cars are now distributed, *A* has three, *B* has one, *C* has one, and *D* has two. And, during every stage of the exchange process, each buyer and seller moved to a better (more preferred) position than he formerly had. There are several alternative possible sequences of trade that one could conjure from the illustrative data; but all lead to the same equilibrium pattern of distribution of goods, and in each case the price of the final transaction (equilibrium price) is $500, or the persisting bid-ask price spread is centered on $500.

With this final equilibrium allocation, there is *no further exchange of goods that would be mutually acceptable. This is a "market-clearing" situation.* In order to improve his situation further, a person would now have to take away some cars from someone else—i.e., without mutually acceptable exchange. The market-clearing result is not necessarily to be regarded as desirable. That judgment depends upon one's attitude toward individual responsibility (as well as some other, as yet unmentioned, implications of an "open market"). In other words, we have here simply demonstrated the *pattern* in which various goods are owned. We have not judged whether this distribution of the total wealth among various people is the best possible distribution or whether there should be a more or a less equal distribution of wealth or income.

If one person wanted to help another—say, by charity, he could give him some goods or money. And if this were done, the recipient might want to engage in further trade in order to revise his holdings to what he regards as a preferred *pattern* of possessions.

Market Supply and Demand: Graphic Interpretation

Graphic analysis of price and allocation with demand and supply curves is easier than using numerical tables. A graph of the demand and supply analysis is shown in Figure 7–1.

The individual demand curves *AA, BB, CC, DD* are added together horizontally to get the total demand, *TT*. The supply available, seven units, is shown by a supply curve, *SS;* it is vertical because, regardless of price, the stock of cars available is fixed at seven, no more and no less. The total demand and supply curves intersect at $500, and at that price the number of cars demanded by *A, B, C,* and *D* is three, one, one, and two, respectively, for a total of seven. Only the final equilibrium outcome is shown. The steps in the *process of adjustment* are not shown, but the net change from initial to final pattern for each person could be deduced.

Inspection of Figure 7–1 suggests that the community would want fewer cars than it actually has if the price somehow were held at $800, which is greater than the equilibrium price. Such a price might be set by a law stipulating that cars can be sold only for $800. There would be a *surplus* of cars, since at the legal price of $800 the people involved would want to own only five, but have seven instead. In particular, *A* and *B* would claim that they have a surplus of one car each. This means simply that each would prefer to have $800 rather than the car. But no one *has* to buy more cars; so *A* and *B* would continue to have the surplus.

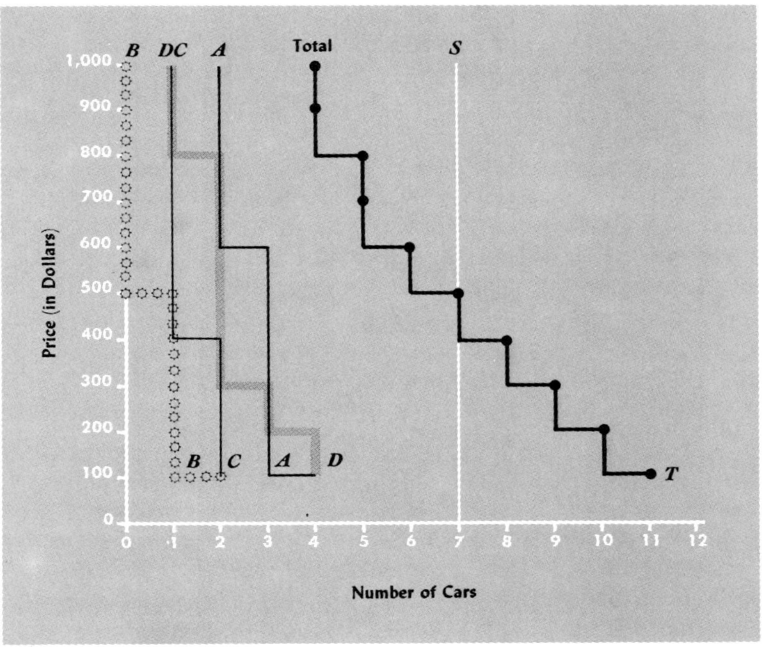

FIGURE 7–1. Individual and total community demand curves with existing stock of automobiles as the supply. The total demand curve is the sum of the horizontal distances of each of the individual demand curves at each possible price.

On the other hand, the surplus would instantly become a *shortage* if the maximum price somehow were set by law at $200, below the equilibrium price. Now, since everyone wants more cars at $200 than at $800, everyone asserts there is a shortage of cars; for, *at the price* of $200, not enough cars are available to satisfy the demand. *A* says that the one more car he "needs" would be used by his daughter in going to college. Currently she has no car and must use taxis and buses to come home. She "needs" a car. Of course, when the price of a car was $800, that "need" was less urgent than the "need" for what else one could get with the $800. Or, in more scientific language, "At $200 a car, *A* finds a car preferable to $200 worth of other things." And the same goes for everyone else.

At prices somehow held *above* the equilibrium price (the free, black-market price), there is a "surplus of supply" with respect to the amount people demand and, according to those who want to sell a car (*A* and *B*), a "shortage of demand" with respect to the supply. On the other hand, if the price were limited to $200, there would be a "shortage" of cars, according to those who want more cars (or, what is the same thing, "excess demand" with respect to supply).

How could these "surpluses" or "shortages" be eliminated? The equilibrium price of $500 would eliminate them. At that price, the amount that individuals want (or think they "need"), as reflected in the desired patterns of various goods, just matches the total available. This is what the intersection of the demand and supply curves means. This equilibrium price is a *market-clearing price*. There then remain no unexploited mutually agreeable exchange possibilities.

CHANGES IN SUPPLY

What happens if the total supply changes? Pretend a car belonging to *A* is destroyed by fire. Even if no one else knows of the loss, everyone will be affected. The total supply has decreased to six, as can be shown geometrically by shifting the supply curve to the left to six on the abscissa. (See Figure 7–2.)

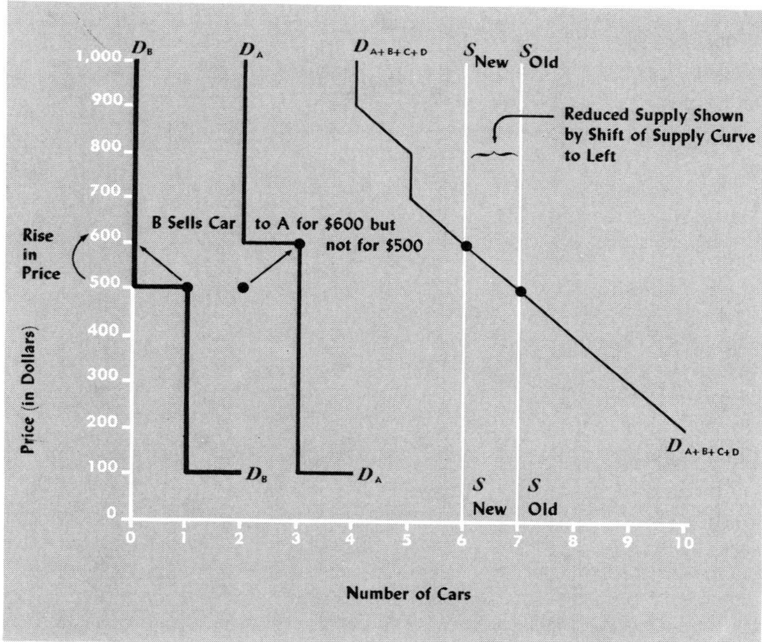

FIGURE 7–2. Rise in price with reduced supply. Price rise permits re-allocation of a car from *B* to *A* by an exchange of money. (Individual demands of *C* and *D* not shown.)

The intersection of demand and supply is now at a price of $600. This suggests that the price will rise. But how does a higher price come to pass? And what function does the higher price accomplish?

The reduced supply *is* an increased scarcity of cars. Who suffers? *A* has lost some wealth. If that loss of wealth is not great enough to affect his demand for cars perceptibly (as we assume in this example), *A* will try to buy another car at the old market price of $500 for a car. But no one wants to sell a car at $500. There is a "shortage of supply" or an "excessive demand" at that offer price. Everyone prefers his car to having $500. *A* prefers a third car even at $600; and if he offers $600, he will find that he can get a car. *B* would rather have $600 than a car, and so he sells. The offer is accepted. Initially, *A* was pushed to a less preferred position *by the burning of the car*, but now by the exchange he has moved to a higher level, although not to so high a level as before the fire. The fire brought a loss to *A*, part of which he has been able to offset by buying a car for $600. The opportunity to engage in trade even at the higher price enabled *A* to reach a position he preferred more than the one he found himself in immediately after the fire.

The fire brought a net benefit to *B* as he judges his position. It may seem "unfair" to have someone else, *B*, gain from *A*'s loss. But under the present system of private property, this can happen. However, don't overlook the fact that the gain to *B* occurred as he helped *A* to recoup part of his loss. By offering to improve *B*'s situation, *A* was also able to improve his own—again using the word "improve" to denote "improvement" as judged by *A* and *B* themselves.

Whether it was *A* or *B* or the reduced supply that raised the price is impossible to say and *irrelevant*. If price is not allowed to go up to reflect *A*'s and *B*'s demand for cars and the reduced supply, *A* will remain at the lowest post-fire position.[1] Because *A* can engage in trade at the best terms that he can negotiate with other people, he has an opportunity to move to what *he* regards as a preferred position. *B*, of course, is benefited because of the initial misfortune to *A*. The fact is that—*given* the disaster, which *B* did not cause—both can now move to more preferred positions, if *B* is allowed to trade with *A* at mutually agreeable prices.

One way to prevent this mutually agreeable change—given the disaster, about which nothing can be done now—is to prohibit trading of cars at any price over the pre-disaster price of $500. *B* is thus prevented from "gouging" *A*. We might think we were doing *A* a favor by authorizing him to buy cars at $500. But he *cannot* buy what he wants at that price. A *shortage* has been created—not by the burning of a car, which increased the *scarcity*, but instead by the prohibition against higher offers in order to raise prices. In *A*'s opinion, is he helped or hurt by a price ceiling at $500? In effect, the price ceiling at $500 prohibits full exploitation of mutually preferred exchange.

CHANGES IN DEMAND

Suppose that with the original situation of seven cars, a new person, *E*, joins the community. His demand schedule and the new market demand are shown on Table 7–3.

[1] Voluntary insurance is a method for distributing the loss over all co-insurers, rather than concentrating it on one person.

Table 7–3

CAR-OWNERSHIP DEMAND SCHEDULE OF *A, B, C, D,* AND *E*

Price	Quantity Demanded *A,B,C,D*	*E*	Total
$1,000	4	0	4
900	4	1	5
800	5	1	6
700	5	1	6
600	6	1	7
500	7	1	8
400	8	1	9
300	9	2	11
200	10	2	12
100	11	3	14

E would prefer a car to $500, but he finds he is unable to get one at that price. Why? Because now the community's demand curve for cars, including his own demand, has moved to the right; the demand for cars has increased. This *increase in demand* must clearly be understood to mean not that more is wanted because the price went down, but that at the *same* price more is wanted than formerly. And for other possible prices, more is wanted than formerly. In this instance, the demand has increased because a new member has joined the community. Increases for other reasons will be considered later.

What happens now? According to Figure 7–3, the equilibrium price will rise (in this case to $600) when demand increases—and fall when demand decreases. More pertinent is an understanding of what function is served when higher offers are permitted to raise price in the markets. A *re-allocation of the pattern* of ownership of various goods occurs, so that each member of the community can reach what *he* regards as a preferred pattern of consumption or combination of assets. *E* prefers a car to any amount of money up to $900. He will, therefore, rather pay $600 than not have a car. An offer of $600 would attract a car from *B*, who prefers a pattern of wealth consisting of $600 more and one car less over the pattern he now has. Exploration and discovery of opportunities are possible if *E* is allowed to offer whatever amount of money he chooses. The minimal possible successful exploratory offer is $600, which will be accepted by *B*.

This equilibrium price is at the intersection of the new demand and supply. If price is pushed to that equilibrium value, the resulting distribution of goods will give each person the pattern of goods he prefers at that relative value of

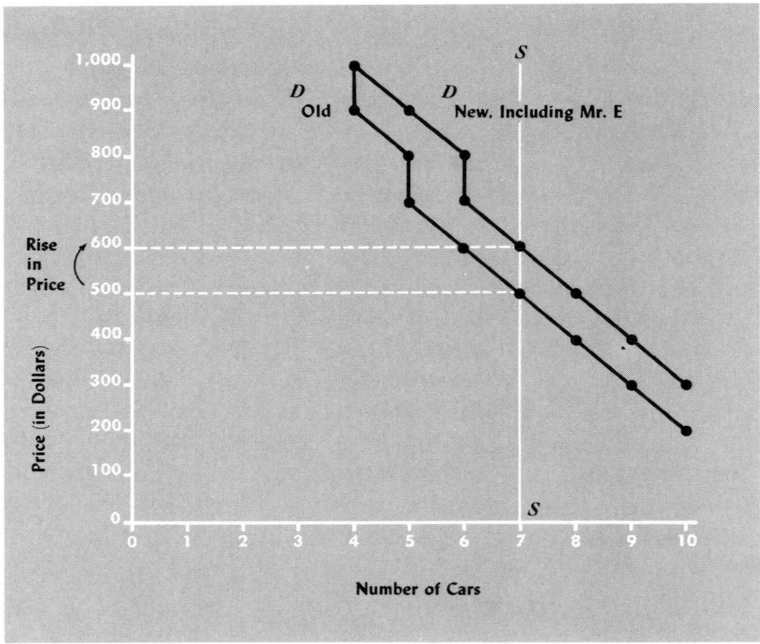

FIGURE 7–3. Higher-price effect of increased demand. Important conclusion is not merely that price is increased, but that the higher price permits a re-allocation of an automobile to *E* from *B*, who prefers $600 to an automobile.

each good; no further voluntary revision of the individual's patterns of consumption or goods is acceptable to *any* two persons (it takes two to trade), given the total stock of all goods and the wealth and income and the demand of each person. Obviously, however, still more wealth would be preferred.

Incidentally, if the exchange of cars had been conducted with the aid of intermediaries (used-car dealers), the buyers of cars would probably complain that the used-car dealers had unscrupulously hoisted prices. In truth, used-car dealers do raise prices scrupulously—and they must raise prices to replace the number being sold from their inventories. They attract cars from the rest of the public who prefer the greater amount of money to cars. And the reason the used-car dealers *can* offer more for these cars (and still stay in business) is that the demanders of more cars are offering more to get cars rather than go without. It makes no difference whether the higher bids first come from the potential buyer or are *suggested* by a used-car dealer. The willingness to pay more to get a car, combined with unchanged willingness of the rest of the public to sell cars, will result in a higher price—even without the used-car dealers as intermediaries. The one thing they do is make it easier for the buyers to get more cars and for the sellers of cars to get money instead.

Used-car dealers are not responsible for the higher equilibrium price. They can buy and sell only at prices between the "offer" and "asking" prices of the public. As people's ideas of what they want shift (as demands change), the dealers must move their prices to stay in that range; otherwise, used-car lots will either overflow or empty.

To let changing demands be reflected by "bids" and "asks" (offers), even when the supply is fixed and non-increasable, is *not* a matter of merely tolerating higher or lower prices for their own sakes. Instead, it is a matter of facilitating revisions in people's wealth or consumption patterns in conformity with their preferences.

CONCEPTS OF QUANTITY IN DEMAND AND SUPPLY

To conduct demand and supply analysis of pricing and allocation, the demand and supply concepts must be matched concepts. And there are two pairs of matched sets of demand and supply: (1) Demand may refer to the amount of a stock of a good a person wants to own. (2) Demand may measure the *additional* amount that a person wishes to have on hand; that is, it measures his demand to purchase. For example, if at a price of $1 I want a stock of ten golf balls, but in fact own only six, my *purchase* demand indicates four balls at a price of $1; while my demand to *own* (stock demand) is for ten at a price of $1. Paired with each of these demands (stock and purchase) is a supply. With the stock demand must be paired the supply schedule of the amount actually *in existence* at each price, regardless of who has it at the moment. Paired with the purchase demand must be the *selling* supply—the amounts, at each price, that current possessors will want to sell (in order to reduce their current stocks to the desired stock).

In our preceding five-person example, the demand and supply schedules were the *demand to own* and the *supply in existence.* An alternative pair of demand and supply curves, the *demand to purchase* and the *supply for sale,* can be derived from the same data. Use the *demand-to-hold* schedules for persons *A* to *D* in Table 7–2 and for *E* in Table 7–3. Assume that *A, B, C, D,* and *E* now possess two, zero, two, three, and zero units, respectively. Subtracting these amounts *actually* held, S_h, from the amounts each person *wants* to hold at each price, D_h, we get the numbers of Table 7–4, which indicates how much each person wants to *purchase* (plus numbers) and *sell* (minus numbers). *If, at each price, one sums only the plus numbers,* and ignores the minus numbers, he gets the community's *demand-to-purchase* schedules. On the other hand, the minus numbers in demand give for each person his *supply-for-sale* schedule; and these, when added at given prices, yield the community's *supply-for-sale* schedule (with the minus sign being ignored).[2]

[2] At any given price, let D_h be the amount of stock he wants to hold, and S_h be the amount he actually does hold in stock. Then the difference ($D_h - S_h$) will be the amount he wants to purchase, D_p; but if S_h is greater than D_h, the difference will be called S_p, the supply he will offer to other people for their purchase.

Table 7–4

CHANGES IN HOLDINGS, AND AGGREGATED PURCHASE DEMAND AND SALES SUPPLY CURVE

Price	Individuals					Aggregated	
	A	*B*	*C*	*D*	*E*	D_p	S_p *
$1,000	0	0	−1	−2	0	0	3
900	0	0	−1	−2	1	1	3
800	0	0	−1	−1	1	1	2
700	0	0	−1	−1	1	1	2
600	1	0	−1	−1	1	2	2
500	1	1	−1	−1	1	3	2
400	1	1	0	−1	1	3	1
300	1	1	0	0	2	4	0
200	1	1	0	1	2	5	0
100	2	2	0	1	3	8	0

* Minus sign omitted.

Table 7–4 presents the demand-to-purchase and the supply-for-purchase schedules for each person, derived from Tables 7–2 and 7–3, with the aggregated total demand and supply curves in the extreme right-hand columns. Notice that the D_p and the S_p schedules "intersect" at a price of $600—the same price at which the demand-to-hold schedule, D_h, intersects the total stock supply, S_h.

Figure 7–4 shows both pairs of demand and supply curves drawn to scale. Only the intersections of D_p and S_p, and that of the paired schedules, D_h and S_h, have meaning; and these two pairs of demand and supply *always* will intersect at the same price—simply because each pair of curves is defined in terms of the other pair for each person. The intersection of the D_p and S_h curves is meaningless; there is no "equality" of demand for *more* items and supply of stock in *existence.*

In analyzing the allocation and pricing of existing goods, we have seen that we could use two different kinds of demand analysis—a *stock* demand-and-supply analysis or an *exchange-flow* analysis, with attention devoted to the flow of goods (for instance, second-hand goods—houses, land, cars, paintings, common stocks) from one owner to another. For other durable goods in which sales from one owner to another are not significant (e.g., shoes, clothes, television sets, radios, tires), the exchange-flow analysis is not so convenient. The choice hinges on clarity and ease of interpretation, not on inherent accuracy or correctness.

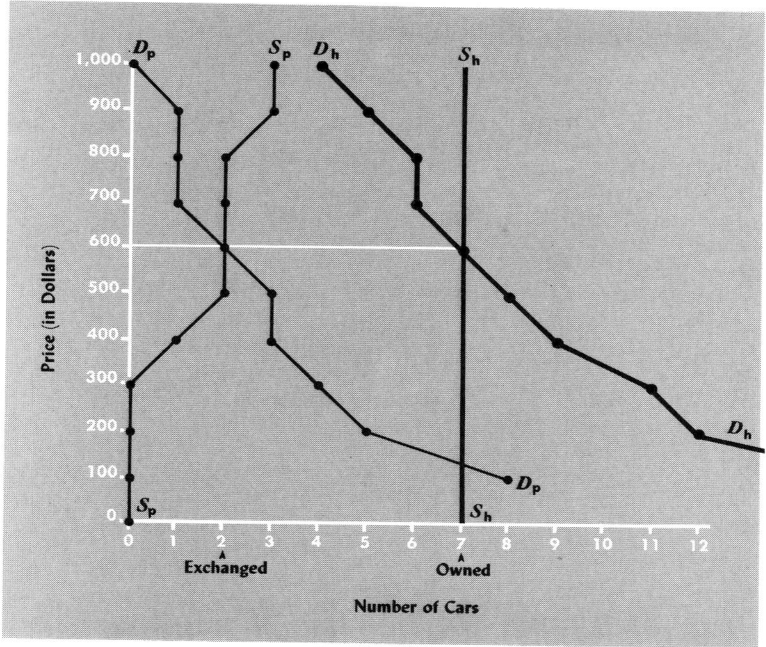

FIGURE 7–4. Demand-and-supply-to-purchase and demand-and-supply-to-own schedules. The horizontal difference between purchase curves is equal to the horizontal distance between owned demand and supply curves at each possible price.

INTERDEPENDENT DEMANDS

We conclude by noting that the two-variable demand function between the quantity and the price could be expanded to include other variables that affect the amount demanded. The demand schedule for butter depends upon the price of margarine, peanut butter, cheese, milk, and bread. The amount of gasoline purchased depends upon the prices of tires, automobiles, bus fares, and taxi rates, in addition to the price of gasoline. For almost every good, prices of other goods affect demand. Those events and prices that affect, but are largely unaffected by, events in the particular market under study are called "exogenous" factors. Those that affect, and also are in turn affected by, the particular market under study are called "endogenous," and they must be incorporated in a complete analysis in such a way as to allow for the reciprocal feedback effect. For example, if the price of margarine affects the demand for butter and hence the price of butter, and if events in the butter market affect the demand and hence the price of margarine, then this feedback interdependency between margarine and butter prices must be explicitly formulated in the complete analysis. Otherwise, we will have a "partial" analysis of how market-price competition allocates the available supplies of butter over the community's competing claimants.

This more general and explicit formulation is achieved by (1) letting the amount of butter demanded depend upon the price of butter, while (2) letting the butter demand—i.e., the whole demand schedule relating the amount of butter demanded to the price of butter—shift as the price of margarine changes. Hence, if the price of margarine should increase, the demand for butter would increase, in the sense that at an unchanged price of butter more butter is demanded. Graphically, the *position* of the demand curve for butter shifts as the price of margarine changes, but the position stays fixed as the price of butter changes. All other factors affecting the demand for butter are still taken as given or unchanged. For example, factors like wealth, age of the consumers, price of steel, population, and attitudes toward butter—which we presume to be essentially independent of the price of butter—are not explicitly specified in the analysis of the butter market. But after we recognize that the price of margarine is *dependent* upon what happens in the butter market and that it also *affects* what happens in the butter market, we must make a complete demand-and-supply analysis of the margarine market along with an analysis of the butter market. As a result of the simultaneous, joint analysis, we derive the implied process of clearing the markets for both butter and margarine rather than only one market.

In brief, an increase in demand for butter will raise the price of butter, which will increase the demand schedule for margarine, thereby raising the price of margarine. Since the demand schedule for butter depends in part on the price of margarine, a higher price of margarine will increase the demand schedule for butter—pushing butter prices still higher, which will raise margarine prices, and on and on. Where will the process end? The prices *converge* toward an equilibrium pair and do not rise indefinitely.

We can see that attempts to constrain one price will necessitate attempts to control other prices as well. Suppose, for example, that the price of butter were imposed at an abnormally high level. The effect would be to increase the amount of margarine demanded, and this would push up the price of margarine. The interrelationship among demands for commodities, and hence their prices, is so pervasive that attempts to raise or control particular prices quickly lead one into a much wider range of prices.

Questions

1. The demands by *A* and by *B* for good *X* are:

PRICE	DEMAND OF *A*	DEMAND OF *B*
10	0	0
9	1	0
8	2	0
7	3	1
6	4	2
5	5	3
4	6	3
3	7	4
2	8	5
1	9	6

a. What is the total market demand by *A* and *B*?

b. If six units of *X* are available, what allocation will there be between *A* and *B* if open-market exchange is used?

c. With six units available, if price were legally imposed at \$4, would there be a shortage, a surplus, or an exchange equilibrium?

d. If the price were legally imposed at \$9, would there be a shortage, a surplus, or exchange equilibrium?

e. How can there be a change from a shortage to a surplus without any change in supply or demand?

2. In problem 1 above, increase the amounts demanded by *B* uniformly by two more units at each price.

a. What will be the open-market price under the new demand situation?

b. What will be the allocation between *A* and *B*?

c. If price is held at the old level by law, will there be a surplus or a shortage?

d. How can that surplus or shortage be eliminated?

3. Return to the data of problem 1. Suppose that two units of *X* are stolen from *A*.

a. Will there be a shortage of *X*? Why?

b. How could this situation be converted to a surplus situation?

4. The following is characteristic of Mr. *A*'s market demand to own shoes. Each price is associated with the number of pairs of shoes he will own.

PRICE	QUANTITY	REVENUE TOTAL	REVENUE MARGINAL
10	1	$10	
9	2	18	+$8
8	3	24	+6
7	4	____	____
6	5	____	____
5	6	____	____
4	7	____	____
3	8	____	____
2	9	____	____
1	10	____	−8

a. Compute the total and marginal revenue.

b. At a price of $6 Mr. *A* wants to own five. At a price of $5 he wants to own six. At each of these two prices, he would have a total of $30 in shoes. Does this mean that he attaches no value to a sixth one? What value does he attach to a sixth one?

5. Using the demand-schedule data for Mr. *A* in problem 1, suppose that these refer to shares of common stock in a corporation and that he now owns four units of *X*.

a. How many units of *X* would he buy or sell at each possible price?

b. If the exchange-equilibrium price in the market turned out to be $3, how many would he want to buy or sell and how many would he then own?

6. "In analyzing the allocation of stocks of goods, like houses, we can refer to demand for a finite amount of houses or to the demand to have more (or less) houses. The latter gives a flow of houses through the exchange market—a set of sales or purchases—while the former does not. But neither of these has to be expressed in rates; both can be expressed as finite stocks or quantities." True or false?

7. Consumption is a rate concept, even though the good being consumed may be held as a stock or finite amount of goods. True or false?

8. For some goods, like shoes, a rise in price will reduce the number of pairs of shoes a person will want. Since the price at which he can sell used shoes is low relative to the new-shoe price, he will not sell some shoes in order to reduce his stock of shoes. How does he adjust his stock of shoes to the new, lasting, higher cost of shoes? (Hint: How does a person adjust his stock of clothes to his new demand after experiencing a reduction in demand consequent to a reduction of his income?)

9. Review the chapter, and you will find three *measures* of the amount demanded: (1) The *rate* of consumption or purchases; (2) the quantity of the good held or used at one time; (3) the quantity a person wants to buy in order to increase his current stock. As an example of each: (1) a person may consume eggs at the rate of $6/7$ per day (which does not necessarily mean he eats a fraction of an egg each day); (2) he may have an average of three eggs in his refrigerator; (3) and on Saturdays he buys a half-dozen eggs. Normally, explicit distinctions between rates of purchase and rate of consumption are not necessary since they are so highly related. We can use whichever demand is convenient; e.g., if one is analyzing a particular day's sales in the markets, the third is the relevant one to use. In each discussion the context will indicate whether it is the stock on hand, the rate of consumption, or a particular day's purchase that is the quantity demanded. Which of these three measures must be expressed as a rate of activity and which as a "stock"?

10. The demands for tires and gasoline are interrelated, somewhat in the sense that butter and margarine were related.

a. Derive with a demand-and-supply graphic analysis the effects of a reduced supply of gasoline on the prices and quantities of tires and gasoline. (Hint: Use two demand curves for tires: the demand before and after a reduced supply and higher price of gasoline.)

b. In what sense can one say butter and margarine are substitutes whereas tires and gasoline are not?

11. "With open-market pricing, housing units are scarce or expensive, whereas with rent control the housing market is characterized by shortages." Explain.

12. "If half the forests of the United States were destroyed, and if thereupon the price of lumber more than doubled, the value of the remaining forests would have increased. This shows how irrational economic value is: a smaller real stock of goods has a higher economic value than a larger stock! Something must be wrong with the measure of value." What is wrong?

13. A competitor to this text publishes a *Study Guide* as a supplement and asserts it is an "invaluable" guide. Does that sound consistent with good economics? Explain.

14. "A premise of economic theory is that economists know the demand schedule that is effective in the market and that each person has an explicit or implicit demand schedule in mind which he consults when making decisions." In fact, economics assumes none of those conditions. What does it presume?

8

APPLICATIONS OF THE ANALYSIS OF OPEN-MARKET PRICING AND ALLOCATION

To familiarize ourselves with demand analysis and to test our ability to apply it, let us try it out on a few simple market situations. We shall be especially interested in seeing how the market pricing process rations the existing supply over the claimants by discriminating among them according to the competitive criteria operative in the open market.

Prices of Common Stock

"Some 250,000,000 shares of American Telephone and Telegraph stock are owned by 2,500,000 people. Yet on any typical day only about 200,000 shares (less than 1/10 of 1 percent of the total owned) are bought and sold by 1,000 people (less than 1/20 of 1 percent of the owners)." From these figures, it is sometimes concluded that the remaining shares and their owners do not affect the price. It is said, "Clearly, this appears to be a case of the tail wagging the dog and illustrates the power of active stock traders." Or, in another context, it is said, "Used-car prices are determined by the few people who daily buy cars from the even fewer used-car dealers; the rest of the people don't affect the value of used cars unless they enter into the market to buy or sell their cars."

To check the logic of these allegations, let us apply the demand and supply concepts to see how the price of a share of American Telephone and Telegraph stock is determined. In doing so, we must keep the stock and flow schedules properly paired. At one time a share of this stock could be bought or sold for about $140. Why? The superficial answer is that demand and supply intersected at a price of $140. But why was the demand and supply intersection at $140? The supply part is not so hard to answer. The company had divided the total ownership into 250,000,000 shares. Had there been half as many shares, the price, it is plausible to believe, would have been about $280—just as a fourth interest in a car would sell for about twice what an eighth interest would sell for. But why is the demand such that people are willing to own the available shares at $140 a share? All we can say for given consumers' incomes, prices of other stocks, etc., is that beliefs about prospective future income induce a total demand-to-own schedule for this stock that intersects the existing supply at $140. This is diagrammed on the right-hand side of Figure 8–1. D_hD_h is the community's demand to hold (own) shares, and S_hS_h is the number of shares in existence.

Thousands of shares of this stock are exchanged daily because people's personal situations are changing. While some decide to sell their A.T.&T. stock at its current price, in order to buy something else, some other people are saving or have just received an increase in wealth or wish to hold more of their wealth in the form of ownership in A.T.&T. stock. Because of these various events, the *individual* demands to own shares change every day, even though the *net* effect on total demand to own may be unchanged. The increase in demand by those who want to hold more shares (i.e., buy) might just equal the decrease in demand by those who want to get rid of some (i.e., sell) at the current price. The community's demand to hold shares of A.T.&T. would be unchanged even though the individual demand curves of which it is the summation are fluctuating.

The effects are shown in Figure 8–1 with two pairs of lines. One pair is D_pD_p and S_pS_p. These curves apply, say, to each morning. Curve D_pD_p is the demand to *purchase more* shares by those who want more shares than they now have; and the S_pS_p curve is the schedule of offers to *sell* by those who have more shares than they would want to hold at alternative prices. When the price reaches a certain height—where the D_pD_p curve touches the price axis—no one wants to buy any more than he now has. Similarly, at a low enough price, no one will want to *sell* any shares. On the other hand, D_hD_h is the total demand, indicating for each possible price how many shares people want to *own* (not *buy*); and the S_hS_h curve indicates the constant supply in *existence* (not to *sell*).

At any price above the intersection of D_hD_h and S_hS_h, the horizontal distance between the curves is the amount by which the supply available exceeds the amount people want to hold; and this amount is the *same* as the amount people want to *sell* minus the amount other people want to *buy* (i.e., the net quantity offered to sell) in order to adjust their ownership of stocks. The distance between the D_pD_p and S_pS_p curves (buy and sell curves) at each possible price must, by definition of the concepts, equal exactly the distance between the D_hD_h and S_hS_h curves.

The price will, with competitive bidding of offers, be at the intersection of each of the pairs of curves. During the day, as exchanges are completed and people adjust their holdings to amounts desired, the D_pD_p and the S_pS_p curves will shift to the left. Since one person's purchase is someone else's sale, the D_pD_p and S_pS_p curves will jointly shift to the left whenever an exchange occurs, until

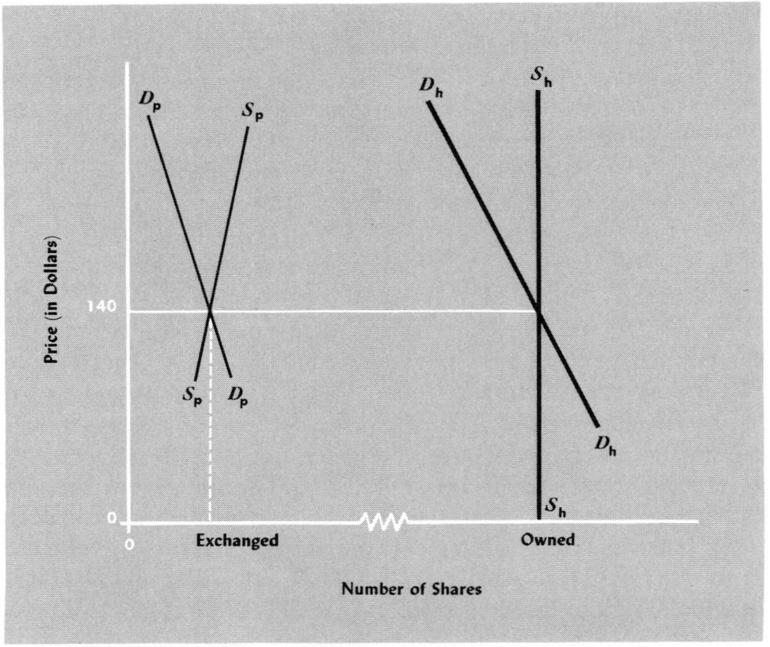

FIGURE 8–1. Effect of price on A.T.&T. demand and supply schedules. The same price simultaneously equilibrates (1) the demand and supply to purchase and (2) the demand and supply to own common stock in American Telephone and Telegraph.

all desired exchanges have occurred. At this moment, the D_pD_p and the S_pS_p curves will intersect at \$140 at a rate of sale of *zero,* indicating no further sales. None of these exchange transactions affects the position of the D_hD_h and S_hS_h curves.

Overnight, people's circumstances again change, so that some now want to buy shares and others want to sell some. This means that the D_pD_p and S_pS_p curves will have shifted to the right, but not necessarily by the same amounts. If the demand to buy additional shares has increased more than the willingness to sell, the D_pD_p curve will have moved farther to the right than the S_pS_p curve, so that the next morning's D_pD_p and S_pS_p curves will intersect at a higher price; so also will the new D_hD_h and S_hS_h curves intersect at that higher price, since the curve D_hD_h must move if the curve D_pD_p shifts to the right *more* than does the S_pS_p curve. Only if the shifts in the purchase demand and supply are exactly offsetting will there be no change in the price—even though many exchanges occur.

The question now can be answered: "If only a few thousand shares are being sold, does this mean that the price is set by these few thousand shares and that the other millions have no effect? Does the tail wag the dog?" No. Given the aggregate supply, S_hS_h, the price will rise if the demand to *hold more* shares, D_hD_h, increases; and D_hD_h increases if the demand to *purchase more* shares, D_pD_p, increases more than does the desire of other people to hold fewer shares (shown by a shift to the right of the curve S_pS_p). And the price will fall if the opposite is true. But not all 250,000,000 shares will be exchanged each day or even each decade. It suffices, insofar as the effect on price is concerned, that the owners want to continue to own their shares at the existing prices. Simply because they are held and not offered for sale at prices of $140 or less, these millions of shares contribute toward keeping the price where it is. That is why the price doesn't go lower than $140. And price doesn't go over $140 because then more shares would be offered by current owners than could be sold. This explains why the price of stock can make a tremendous jump or drop with just one share being sold. If the current owners' individual demands to own should increase greatly, the price would have to rise a lot to get any of them to sell even one share.

We can summarize: The *price* will change if there is a disparity between the total "demand to own" of all people and the supply of the whole community at that price. *Sales* (purchases) occur whenever the demand of *any* individual to hold stock changes relative to the total demand of other individuals. These exchanges will occur without a change in price if the total demand to own does not change. Otherwise, the exchanges will be accompanied by price changes. At the other extreme, if *every* individual's demand increases proportionally, there can be a rise in price even though no shares are exchanged.

When President Eisenhower had his heart attack (1955), the prices of most stocks immediately dropped because of the increased probability that government policies might change with a new president, and these might not be so favorable to profits. This caused a reduced demand to hold stocks. It was not the president's health *per se* that made the market prices fall; it was anticipated future events.

Another example occurred in 1962, when President Kennedy made an attack on U.S. Steel and businessmen's rights to sell their product at open-market prices; he so changed beliefs in the continuation of an open-market system that many people immediately reassessed downward the value of business assets. The reduced value placed on those ownership rights meant that people preferred to sell them at the existing prices rather than keep them. Other people, whether or not they owned stock, also placed lower values on the businesses, represented by the shares of stock; and so the demand to own stock fell, and the price fell immediately to levels low enough to reflect the new values.

Rental or Leasing Prices and Allocation

Demand-and-supply analysis is applicable not merely to purchases of goods but also to renting and leasing of goods, except that the allocative phenomena are a little different. A person renting a house will feel the effect of other people's increased demand for more housing space; the price (rent) rises. Since he does not own the house, he will not experience an offsetting gain in wealth from the higher price of the house. Instead, at the higher rent he will rent a smaller house or one of poorer quality, which is a way of saying that he has been induced to release housing to those whose demands have increased.

This situation, too, can be analyzed graphically. We shall use only the "demand-to-have" (not to have *more*) curve plotted against the total stock in existence, because we want to compare holdings of housing space before and after the demand change. In Figure 8–2 the curve $D_a + D_b$ represents the community's total demand for housing space, *before* the increase in demand. In the

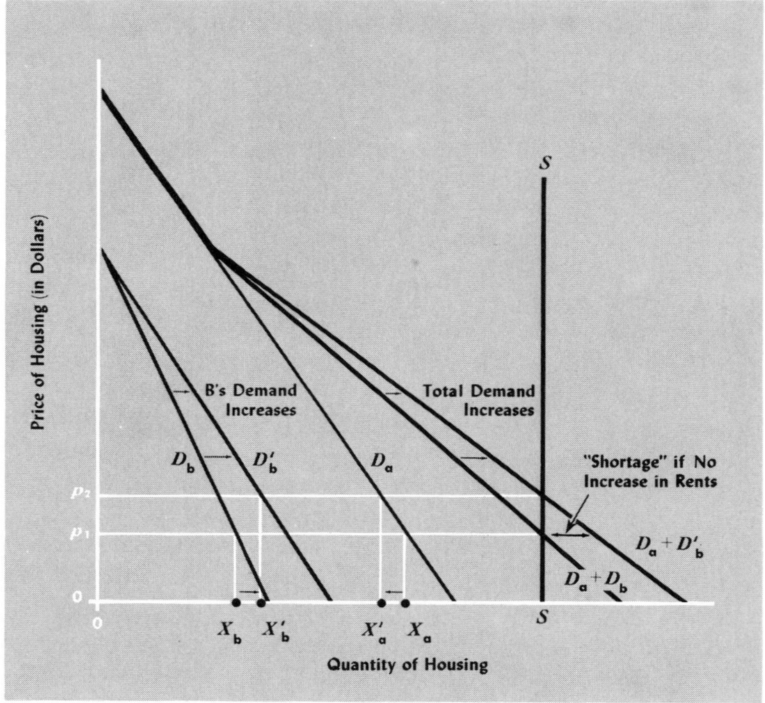

FIGURE 8–2. Price and amount of housing. Change in price of housing enables re-allocation of housing space among competing demanders, *A* and *B*.

two component demand portions, D_a represents the demand to have space by people who are not going to increase their demand for housing, and D_b is the "pre-increase" demand for housing space by those whose demand will increase. Initially, rental prices were p_1, and the space was divided with X_a and X_b held by group *A* and group *B*, respectively. After the increase in demand by group

B, their demand curve is shown by D'_b. The total demand, formed by summing the demand D_a and D'_b, is now $D_a + D'_b$. This demand intersects the existing housing supply at the price p_2, greater than p_1.

If rents do not rise from p_1 to p_2, the amount of housing space demanded will exceed the amount available. This excess is shown by the distance between the supply line and the new demand curve at all prices less than p_2. This excess amount demanded is commonly called a shortage; rarely is it called an excess of demand. At the prices below p_2 there simply is not enough supply to satisfy the demands or, as they are likely to be called, "housing needs." With open-market bidding for the available housing space, the price will be pushed up, toward p_2, as the frustrated demanders make higher offers to get more housing. The market for housing will be called "tight" or "strong." Vacancy rates that normally exist to facilitate the flow of movers, just as stores maintain inventories, will diminish. Houses will be "easy" to rent at the current prices. As the price rises toward p_2 in response to the increased demand (represented by the shift to the right of the market-demand curve), claimants for housing space will reduce the amount demanded—not because their demands have decreased, but because the price is higher. The higher price moves them, figuratively, back up along their demand schedules to smaller amounts demanded—on the current demand schedule. It is the shift in demand, in the sense of a shift in the demand schedule, that produces a shortage at the old price. And then when price rises, the people are induced to buy less as they are pushed back up their current demand curves. The excess amount demanded or the shortage of the amount available is eliminated by the rise in price.

If rental rates are allowed to rise from p_1 to p_2, as people in group *B* seek more housing for themselves by trying to outbid other people, what happens to the housing allocation? Group *B* obtains the amount X'_b instead of the former smaller amount, X_b. Members of group *A* end up with X'_a. The decrease, $X_a - X'_a$, for those whose demand did not increase is exactly equal to the increase available to group *B*. (At the present stage of analysis, we are concentrating on the market's re-allocation process, leaving the effect on production or supply for later; however, any increase in stock available as a result of a price increase would have offset part of the decrease imposed on group *A* and also reduced the price rise.)

Can we say anything about how the people feel about this process? The house owners are now wealthier—i.e., in a more preferred position than before the demand increase; they get more rent, and their houses are worth more. The members of the *A* group, whose demand did not increase, have to pay higher prices and use less than the amount of housing space they had earlier. The members of group *B* present a more complex result. Those whose demands increased most in that group are the ones who preferred to pay higher rents in order to get more space than they were getting at the lower price. So some of the members of group *B* reach more preferred situations. Other members of group *B*, those whose demands increased by only a very little, may end up paying higher rents and getting very little more or even less space than originally. Although their demand has increased, the higher price pushes them back up along their demand curve to smaller amounts than they wanted at the old price. Members of group *A* and *B* alike are forced by higher prices to slide back up their demand curve; those whose demands increased most will end up with increments in housing space, and those whose demands increased least or not at all will end up with less than formerly. To the *A*'s and the *B*'s, the trouble seems to be the higher rent for housing. The owners tell them they must pay more if they want to keep on renting. The tenants blame the owners for raising rents. But what enabled the owners to get higher prices? Who pushed the price up? The *increased demand* by tenants in group *B* pushed up the rent. Had their demand not increased and had they not offered to pay more, the owners would not have raised rents.

Competition among renters, starting with the increased demand by *B*, pushes up the price that everyone must now pay. The owners simply echoed the higher bids by the *B* people. The owners, in effect, told the *A* people to meet the competition of the *B*'s. Maybe the *B*'s are mutual friends and neighbors who complain to each other about the higher "exorbitant" rentals that the landlords are charging—never thinking to blame their competition against each other for the higher price.

Objections to the higher prices that reflect competitive offers are objections to the competitive superiority in providing offers that are more favorable to the owners than are the terms formerly offered by everyone else. These competitive offers vary from day to day. If anyone wants to gain from the possibility of trade, he must be prepared to face the fact that the *terms* of trade and hence the realizable *gains* from trade will vary from day to day. To put it differently, trade can, under commonly found circumstances, enable each party to move to a situation preferred to *no* trade at all; but the gains from *today's* available trade may be larger or smaller than the gains from *yesterday's* trade. Economics does *not* say that with every change in demand *everyone* moves from one exchange equilibrium to still more preferred exchange-equilibrium positions. It implies only that, with fully exploitable trade opportunities, any person can reach the most preferred of all the *possible* patterns, given other people's rights to compete in the same way.

The Cost-Price Illusion

The avenue from increased demand to higher exchange-equilibrium prices often is concealed by inventories in the distribution chain from producer to consumer. As a result, prices appear to be set by costs of production instead of competition among consumers. The cause of this illusion is illustrated in the following example of an increased demand for meat.

To start, pretend that for some reason people's desire for meat increases. As you can guess, this implies a rise in meat prices. How does this happen, and what does it accomplish?

Housewives express their increased desire for meat by increasing their market demand for meat. Market-demand schedules reflect what people do in the marketplace, not simply something they dream about doing at some later time. Housewives reveal an increased demand by buying more meat than formerly at the current prices in the meat markets. How can the prices remain unchanged? Retail butchers have inventories adequate for a day or two. As sales increase, that inventory is depleted more than expected. No single butcher knows that the demand has risen for the community as a whole. No single butcher knows that he could raise his price and make no fewer sales than earlier. All he knows is that *he* sells more meat at the existing price. But the increased demand takes its toll of inventories. Whether or not a butcher believes that the increased rate of sale is a temporary fluctuation, he will buy more meat than usual the next day in order to restore his inventory from its abnormally low level; and he will buy even more than that if he believes that the increase in sales will persist. If the demand for meat does increase so that one butcher's increase is not merely some other butcher's loss, the purchases by the aggregate of butchers from the packers will increase.

Just as butchers use inventories, so packers, on a larger scale, also rely on inventories to smooth out the effect of sales fluctuations on their pattern of purchases from cattlemen. We assume that the first day's change in demand was within that inventory limit and therefore was met without a price increase.

Packers restore inventories by instructing their cattle buyers (who travel around among the cattle raisers and fatteners and to the stockyards where cattlemen ship the steers for sale) to buy more cattle than usual. But with all the packers restoring their inventories in this manner, the numbers of cattle available for sale each day are inadequate to meet the increased total demand *at the old price*. There is not sufficient inventory in the stockyards to take care of this rise. Either some buyers for packers must report that they cannot get the number requested, or they must boost their offer prices in order to persuade cattlemen to sell the steers to them rather than to some other packers.

Rather than go without any increase in stock of meat, the buyers will begin to raise their offers in order to get more cattle. This rise in offer prices will occur nearly simultaneously, among the buyers, as if there was collusion among the cattlemen or buyers. The cattlemen simply let the buyers bid against each other until the price rises to a point where the packers will not want to buy more meat at the new higher price than they did at the old lower price; that is, the packers are induced by the higher price not to buy more than is available from the cattlemen.

In terms of our demand-and-supply apparatus, the supply curve of cattle is vertical. An increased demand by packers for cattle implies an intersection at a higher price. Each packer is therefore forced to slide or climb back up his new increased demand curve to a higher price, at which point he buys less than he had planned to at the old price. The total amount purchased is no greater than before, but the price of cattle is higher; at this high price, the amount wanted on the new demand curve equals the constant amount supplied. Each packer must pay a higher price for cattle in order to avoid getting less cattle and meat than he had before. Competition among the packers has raised the price of cattle during the immediate period when cattle production cannot be increased.[1]

The cattle raisers bask in the glow of higher receipts. Business for them is more profitable. But the packers, faced with a higher price of cattle, experience *a rise in costs.* Why did their costs rise? The costs of raising cattle did not increase. Nor did the costs of getting cattle to market, nor of slaughtering, nor of distributing meat. The price paid by packers to cattlemen was pushed up in response fundamentally to the increased demand by consumers—the housewives. Their demand, from butcher shops through packers, was met by depleting inventories. But the cattlemen did not have inventories that they could deplete and then restore quickly. Therefore, they simply let the buyers bid for the available amount brought to market (rather than allocating the cattle on some other principle).

Whether or not the packers are aware of the law of demand and supply, which says that a higher demand with the same old supply will permit higher prices, and whether or not they are aware that demand has increased, the higher price of cattle (higher costs to the packers) will mean that the packers must charge a higher price to butchers if they are to continue as profitable meat packers. In sum, a higher price occurs because the demand for meat has increased. The butchers, in turn, post higher prices to the housewives. When housewives complain about the higher price, the butcher in all innocence, honesty, and correctness says that it isn't his fault. The cost of meat has gone up. Cost, to him, is the cost of getting meat. The butcher can say, "I never raise prices until my costs go up." And the packers can honestly say the same thing. And if the housewife wants to know who is to blame for the higher costs and hence higher prices of meat, she can look in the mirror behind the butcher's counter and see her face and those of all her neighbors. She might then turn to each of them and say, "If you didn't want more meat, I could have more." But that observation and that tactless behavior is neither useful nor fostered by the competitive exchange system. The exchange system tends to conceal this fact of competition and make it appear as if the higher price of meat were caused by butchers' or packers' or farmers' greedy behavior—not that of ourselves or our neighbors.

[1] This "immediate" period in which cattle production cannot be increased is also called the "market" or the "very-short-run" period.

The consumers' own increased demand for meat, then, brought about a rise in the price of meat to consumers. This rise in price *appeared* to be the result of a rise in costs because the first price effect of the increased demand occurred at the cattle raisers' end of the line. The demand increase pulled up the price paid in the first stages of the production and distribution channels. The first rise in price could have occurred in the butcher shops and then have been transmitted back step by step to the farmers. But butchers' inventories are usually adequate to cushion the changes in demand temporarily until the impact of increased sales goes all the way through the productive processes. This explains why the illusion is so common that increases in costs are responsible for higher prices.

Pricing and Prices

The foregoing analysis and examples show how the pricing process allocates the existing supply of a good among the competing claimants. Putting the matter emotionally, it is an analysis of discrimination among competing claimants, in which some obtain more favorable treatment—get more goods—while others get less. The discrimination or competitive criterion is heavily weighted by the amount of money offered in exchange for the particular good at issue. The pricing process is a distributive, discriminatory process; our interest in pricing is not in whether prices are high or low, but instead in how prices solve the problem of deciding who gets what amount of particular goods.

The analysis does not say that this system of competition or discrimination among claimants is either a good one or a bad one. Under this system, people bid for some goods by offering others in exchange (via the intermediary of money). Sometimes it is said that under this system of allocation the goods go where there are the most votes or dollars. Thus, a rich man's dog may receive milk that a poor child needs to avoid rickets—not because demand and supply are working ineffectively but because they "are working effectively, putting goods in the hands of those who can pay the most or who have the money votes." But surely this interpretation is faulty. First and fundamentally, suppose everyone had the *same* amount of wealth. Some people still would feed dogs while other people would be able to use more food for children. Some simply prefer to feed their dogs rather than feed more to children. A cruel statement? Yes, but it is honest and nonromantic and avoids blaming some "system" for people's preferences.

In the second place, it seems misleading to say that the private-property exchange (price) system puts goods where the most dollar votes are. Rather, it puts *more* goods where there are *more* dollar votes and less where there are less. It is not an all-or-none allocation like a political election in which the winner takes all while the loser gets nothing. It is more akin to proportional representation than to majority rule. The exchange system puts some goods *wherever* there are some dollar votes *per unit* of the good, rather than only where the most votes are. A poorer person, by concentrating more of his money on some goods, can express a higher value *per unit* of the goods for which he bids. In this way he can match the per unit *price* of a rich bidder, if he wishes, by bidding for a proportionally smaller amount: thereby he will get *some* of the goods. This may seem a small solace to a poorer person, and indeed it is; but compare it with the case in which the person who is outvoted or outcompeted gets nothing, as would occur if the goods went only where the most "votes" were.

We are not saying that the price-exchange system for allocating goods is desirable or undesirable—only that it is easy to misinterpret its operation. This discussion, of course, suggests the desirability of investigating what determines how many dollar votes or how much wealth each person has, and we shall do that later. For the present analysis, we are taking the distribution of wealth as simply given—not as something granted by heaven or "naturally proper."

Economic Rent

Another misconception is one voiced about situations in which the supply is not augmentable even though price increases. It is complained that an increased demand and resultant higher price lead only to unjust enrichment of current owners without inducing increased production. Therefore, it is argued, higher prices should be prevented, for they serve no useful function. Holding in abeyance the question of the "unjustness" of the enrichment of current owners of the good, it is not true that higher prices serve no function. As we have seen, the process of bidding up prices in the face of an increased demand serves as a discriminating device to allocate the existing stock among the competing claimants. In saying that increased demand discriminates, we mean that it discriminates according to "proper" criteria. What is implied is that the higher price, like it or not, does serve the useful function of deciding who will get how much of which goods.

To avoid confusion between these two functions—the *allocation* of the existing supply and the control of the *production* of goods—the concept of economic rent has been developed. Although "rent" connotes a payment for housing space, the term here has a different meaning. "Economic rent" of a good is defined as that portion of the value of the good which does not influence the supply of that good. In our earlier automobile example, the existing number of cars was fixed and unchanging, regardless of price. Consequently, the payment received for, or value of, each car sold would be considered an "economic rent."

Consider the supply curve of good X in Figure 8–3. The price will depend upon where the demand curve is; but, at any price up to p_1, the amount of the

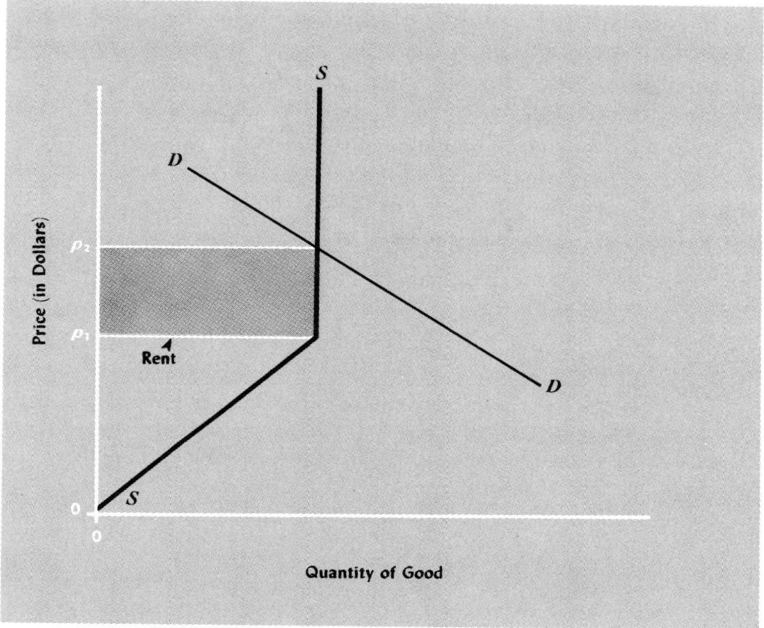

FIGURE 8–3. Rent. If demand intersects vertical supply schedule, rent occurs.

good made available will depend upon the price. At any price over p_1, the amount is unchanged; there is an economic rent—the difference in total receipts at that higher price and at p_1—because none of that extra payment changes the amount of X now available. There is a persuasive reason for calling this an economic rent rather than a surplus. It is not a surplus because it is a necessary valuation for the purpose of allocating the good to the highest-valued competing uses. Any lower valuation would fail to clear the market supply among all those who want some at its current price. Economics long realized that some payments, although not affecting the amount in existence, did affect the use to which a good was allocated. From the point of view of the *existence* of the good, the payment may be regarded as a surplus—i.e., a payment greater than necessary (insofar as affecting the amount in existence is concerned); but for another essential functional purpose—that of allocating among uses—it is effective.

In sum, economic rent is a "surplus" from the point of view of determining the amount in existence now. But it is not a surplus, nor unnecessary payment or value, from the point of view of determining the allocation among competing potential users; thus, economic rent serves a rationing function. From the point of view of any particular user, the payment made in order to get that resource is a cost. It is a cost to the user because, unless he pays that price per unit, he will not get to use any of that resource. The willingness to pay at least that price to get some of the good is his objective way of (1) asserting that the use he will make of the good yields greater value than other uses and (2) getting that good assigned to him for his use. The classic example of this kind of rent is the value of a piece of land. The value of the land (or the rent paid for it) is far in excess of the amount necessary to keep that land in existence or even to have gotten it produced. Yet for the important decision of determining the *use* of that land, the rent value is crucial. The renter or subsequent purchaser must pay that rent to obtain use of the land.

Quasi-rent

However, although economic rent does not affect the amount now in existence, it may affect the amount in existence in the future. In fact, a tough-minded logician could push us into a corner by asking, "Even for those goods that are produced by the sweat of brow, tears of thought, and blood of ulcers, the fact is that the currently available supply will be in existence no matter what its current price may be. Even at a zero price, the existing stock of goods would be in existence now. Therefore, does it not follow that any payment for any existing good is now an economic rent?" The answer is "Yes."

But beware of going too far. The existing price does have an effect on what will exist in the future, because expectations of future prices are not independent of current prices. Furthermore, very few goods are indestructible. If the present price is too low, the existing stock will diminish as goods wear out and are not maintained. To emphasize this impact on the future stock of goods, economics has developed the concept "quasi-rent" for analysis of the fact that while present payments are "economic rents" for creation (though not allocation) of some *existing* goods, they are not rents with respect to *maintaining* the existing amount of goods. The current payments are therefore only *quasi*-rents. For example, rental payments for a house serve two functions: (1) They determine the current allocation of the existing stock of housing among the competing claimants—and all prices of existing goods also are currently performing this function. (2) They also influence the maintenance and production of continuing output. For this purpose they do not possess the "economic rent" attribute. Hence, payments for current goods are, for that purpose, economic rents, and for another they are not. So, they are called "quasi-rents."

We can now dispose of two common misinterpretations:

1. Some people, having noticed that the price or receipts for some goods are unnecessary to create either the existing or future supply, have jumped to the conclusion that the receipts could be taxed away from those who get it, with

no effect on existing supply.[2] Indeed they could—but only for goods that are neither destructible nor producible, as allegedly is the case for land. And such a tax would diminish incentives to *use* or allocate goods via market processes in the most valuable ways. The rationing of existing supply among competing claimants would no longer be performed by competition via market values. However, many goods which at first sight seem to be imperishable and nonaugmentable are really not. What appears to be "economic rent" may be really "quasi-rent." For example, land has as one of its attributes fertility, which is perishable; also, land can be created by drainage and leveling and filling up of bodies of water.

2. Another argument advanced by those who have "discovered" the presence of true "economic rent" is that the receipt is "unearned." Since the good was not produced but was given by nature, the payment is "unearned" and therefore, they say, *undeserved*. This represents some big leaps in ethical judgments. Suppose the supply is given by nature and that the owner, in fact, does nothing to create its value—except preserve it! Would the owner then "deserve" the value? If not, then *no* one deserves it, and those who think it should belong to all the people or taxed away by the government will have difficulty in explaining why *everyone* deserves what *no one* deserves.

Questions

1. "The community's demand to own houses may remain unchanged; yet the demand to purchase houses may increase (or decrease) enormously." Explain why this is true. Give a numerical example of the demand to hold houses (in a two-person community) that stays constant, while the demand to purchase houses increases.

2. When prices on the stock market fall, the financial pages report a surge to sell stock; yet every share sold is bought by someone. Why don't they refer to a surge to buy?

3. "Higher prices cause higher costs." Explain why this is true.

4. "Allowing the prices of goods to rise in periods when none of the good is being produced is immoral, because the higher prices do not induce a larger output. They merely give unwarranted profits to those who are lucky enough to own the goods. Either prices should be prevented from rising, or the government should take over ownership in order to prevent unjust enrichment." Do you agree with this analysis? If so, why? If not, why not?

[2] Most prominent among these people are the "single-taxers"—followers of Henry George, who believed that only land rent is an economic rent and therefore that it should be taxed away. They blindly overlook economic rent to other resources—e.g., beautiful women. They also ignore the rationing function of economic rent in a private-property system.

5. "The rent paid for land in New York City is not a payment that is necessary to produce that land. Yet it is a necessary payment to obtain use of the land. From the first point of view, it is an economic rent; from the latter point of view, it is a cost." Do you agree? If so, why? If not, why not?

6. Which of the following do you think contain some economic rent? Insofar as any of them contains rent, for what is that rent unnecessary? For what is it necessary?

a. Sonny Liston's income.

b. The wealth of those who owned land in Palm Springs, California, from 1940 through 1950, when land values boomed.

c. Elizabeth Taylor's income.

d. The income of a genius.

e. The income of smart students.

f. The salary of the President of the United States.

7. Demand and supply is not simply a classification that is applicable only to private-property market exchange. Demand and supply is a categorization that is applicable to any problem of allocating scarce resources among competing uses. In any given possible use, the usefulness of the resource in that use is what is meant by its demand, while its usefulness in all alternative uses (against which this particular use must compete) is the supply. Do you agree? Explain.

9

EXCHANGE EFFECTS OF SUPPRESSING OPEN-MARKET PRICING

Controlled Prices

We can get a better understanding of an open-market pricing system if we investigate what happens when price controls restrict exchange negotiations, assuming that no one can legally contract at above the "maximum" price. What happens after the demand for some commodity—say, housing space—increases, if prices are not allowed to rise? The total amount wanted exceeds the supply available at the old, continuing, legal-limit price; a "shortage" or, what is the same thing, an "excessive demand" exists. Someone will be frustrated, because, despite the quoted price at which the commodity is for sale, he cannot get what he wants at that price.[1]

If rent controls prevent competing renters from bidding up the price of housing space, sellers will then rely more on nonpecuniary offers from the bidding buyers as the bases for discriminating among the claimants for that space. Formerly, with free bidding up of prices, the rents would have risen to a high enough level so that the amount of housing demanded would not exceed the supply, and everyone could get the amount he demanded at the higher money price. Poor people would pay the high prices *per unit* of space and accordingly take less than rich people. Poor families with children would get some space—even though, as everyone knows, landlords don't like children. With the higher price per unit of space, the landlords are induced to let the children occupy the house. And the amount demanded equals the available space.

[1] Although the legal maximum price of housing is deemed "fair," his demands are not met at that price. Any person caught in that situation could ask, "What is the meaning of a price at which I *can't* buy?"

Nonmoney Competition

The suppression of money bidding means that (1) more of the good is wanted than is available at the suppressed, controlled price; (2) other criteria will have to be used as the determining basis for discriminating among the claimants for the available good, and (3) the extent of re-allocation is reduced.

As the authors discovered during World War II, when meat prices were controlled at below market-clearing prices, their wives' extraordinary beauty suddenly began to count more heavily in the butcher's eyes when he decided to which customers to give the amount of meat demanded and which to disappoint. The butchers favored our wives, while the old, homely women were told there was no meat or only a little. Similarly, with controlled housing rentals, our beautiful wives were the ones we sent out to apply for an apartment that was going to be vacant. After all, as long as the landlord couldn't get a higher price as an inducement from the homely people, why should he ignore the virtues of delightful tenants? With uncontrolled rentals and meat prices, the butchers' and landlords' preferences for beautiful women as customers and tenants were dulled by the higher money offers from the "less desirable" types. These higher offers made everyone want less of the good than at the lower price, so that everyone could get the smaller amount he demanded at the higher price. Notice that the ability to offer a high price is not dependent upon one's money wealth. A poor person can offer just as high a price as a rich one for the finest meat, ounce per ounce. The poor person will get *some* meat, but of course he will get less. He can get *some* of almost any good, by taking a small enough amount of each. When not allowed to concentrate their offers of money wealth, handicapped people, rich or poor, are less able to induce others to overlook their "undesirable" features. The handicap is not, of course, eliminated or rendered ineffective by concentration of power; but it is easier to overcome a handicap when one is free to use all his competitive powers, including price competition, for exchange opportunities.

A difference between personal-characteristic competition and wealth-bidding competition is that a dollar of resources bid for one good necessarily means the bidder then has a dollar less for other goods. The amount of his biddable claims is some fixed total at any moment—given by the monetary value of his wealth. But the competition of "personal-characteristic wealth" does not involve this degree of interdependence among one's bids for various goods. More "beauty" as an advantage to get more meat does not mean that that much less beauty is available for vegetables. One can get more of "this" without having to take less of "that."

Competition by personal characteristics has elements of an all-or-nothing system, whereas competition by money-exchange inducements is a sharing or pro rata division. Money-wealth competition has characteristics of *proportional* representation; the minority gets representation proportional to its quantity of the total votes (dollar votes). Personal-characteristic competition is more like majority-decision rule, where the majority gets *all* the representation.

In other words, since scarcity, competition, and discrimination are inseparable, the basic economic question "For whom?" is merely a polite way of asking, "What will be the criteria for discriminating among the competing claimants?" With open-market prices to restrict the amount demanded to the amount available, less (not necessarily *no*) weight will be given to nonmonetary characteristics of the competing customers. Of course, in either event, poorer people will get less. But whatever your pecuniary wealth, you will get still less if you are poorer in the nonmonetary desirable characteristics—e.g., if you are a foreigner or a homely person. Price controls will reduce the ability to counteract these "undesirable" personal attributes by greater competition in pecuniary price offers—whatever your pecuniary wealth. In that case your nonmonetary, personal, disadvantageous traits are now even more effective in determining what you get because of your reduced ability to induce the seller to offer you more goods in return for the higher price. Of course, if you are beautiful and poor, you may prefer price controls for some goods, for then the homely rich will find they are restricted in their legal ability to offset homeliness with higher monetary offers.

This point should be kept in mind by "unpopular" people who believe that holding prices down below the free-market, demand-and-supply-equating price will necessarily help them in comparison with people who are richer in money. These "unpopular" people forget that the *other* forms of competitive power are then more relevant in choosing among customers. The disadvantageous personal characteristics, which they could more effectively make up for by a willingness to pay a higher money price, are no longer so effectively overcome.

The connection between rent controls and manifestation of greater discrimination by personal characteristics is exemplified in New York City, one of the few American cities still imposing rent controls. Perhaps no city is so beset with displays and complaints of racial discrimination in housing as in rent-controlled apartments and publicly subsidized housing—all involving rentals at less than exchange-equilibrium rates.

It is not clear which competitive systems give greater equality of distribution of all goods, even if equality were deemed desirable. If people's economic wealth were more disparate than their personal characteristics, it would not follow that the disparity of their share of goods would increase—because money bids help to offset the all-or-nothing feature of personal characteristics. The actual comparative outcome depends upon the degree to which people with inferior personal characteristics are also relatively inferior in other competitive characteristics as well, and upon their diversity of preference patterns and upon the society's attitudes toward personal characteristics. Little is known about this complex of factors. All we can conclude is that, whatever the amount of equality in economic goods, if you want to emphasize and give more importance to race, creed, religion, and other personal characteristics in allocating goods, you should seek to reduce the effectiveness of other types of competitive appeals—e.g., the money offer.

Rationing and Price Controls

At this point a perceptive student might ask, "Why not avoid nonmonetary personal discrimination by *rationing* the available stock—giving equal portions to everyone who wants some or allocating to each demander the same amount he got before?" Either procedure will eliminate nonmonetary and personal attributes, but each recipient will still be seeking to obtain a still more preferred *combination* of goods by a further exchange re-allocation with other people, exactly as were the Cuban and Hungarian in our refugee camp. Price controls restrict the realization of these more preferred combinations arrived at by exchanging the rationed goods.

This situation can now be analyzed with demand and supply curves as in Figure 9–1, a diagram basically the same as Figure 8–2. The demand curves of A and B are shown as they were before a demand increase by B and also after that increase. At the old price, p_1, the amount demanded is excessive. We suppose that, of the available supply, the amounts going to A and B after the demand increase—and with price controls keeping the price at p_1—is unchanged. What can we now deduce? Simply that B would prefer to buy some more, even at a higher price, and that he could buy some from A, who does not want more than he has at the existing price. At a higher price, A would prefer to sell some to B until the amount A has is reduced to X'_a and the amount B has is increased to X'_b. These two total to the amount in existence. Notice that these are precisely the amounts that A and B would have bought from the seller had prices been allowed to change without price controls.

The difference between this second, free-market price and the controlled price measures the wealth taken from the owner and given to A and B under price controls. This is represented by the rectangle $(p_2 - p_1)$ (X_1)—i.e., the change in price times the quantity. All of that is "saved" by A and B, as demanders, and divided between A and B, depending on who gets how much of the good in the first place and on how much A later sells to B at a higher price.

Now let's push the economic analysis a bit further. Under rent controls, some tenants, rich in other personal, competitive characteristics, are better off because they are able to get more housing space at the low controlled price than if rents were allowed to increase to a market-clearing level—for example, this is true of B in our diagram. The higher rents would reduce the amount of housing space B demanded; so on net he might be content with about the same space

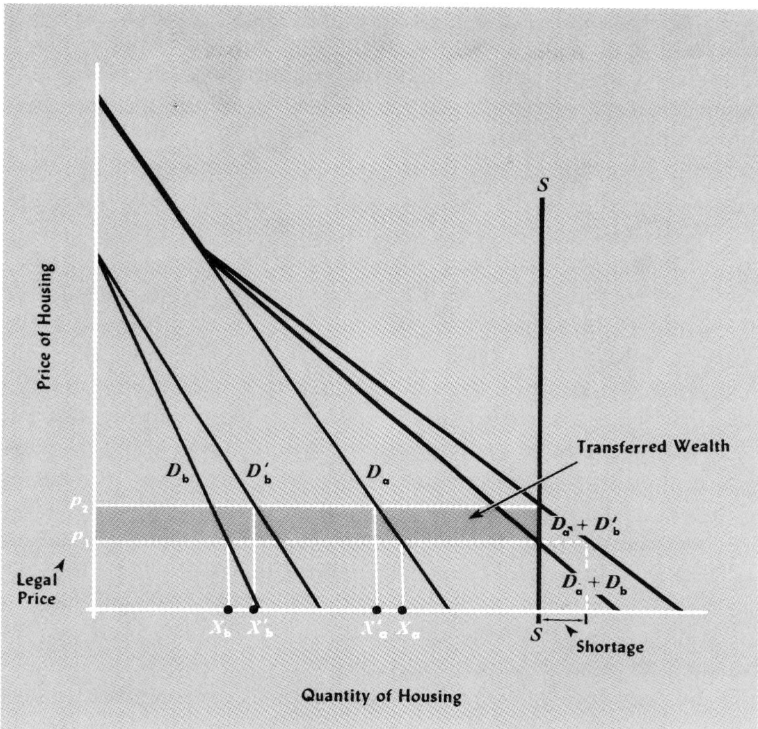

FIGURE 9–1. Effect of rent control. Shortages are created by rent controls, resulting in transferal of wealth.

he has now under price controls—and at a lower rent. Those who had all the housing space they wanted at the time controls were imposed, or who were lucky enough to have the right personal characteristics to get space when someone moved or died, can be better off under rent controls. Others who want more space, even at a higher rent, would be better off without rent controls; for by means of the higher rents they could offer, they would bid space away from current tenants.

Subleasing and the Transferal of Wealth

Now, the next step of the analysis is to note what would happen if a tenant were legally allowed to *sublease* his apartment at an open-market, exchange-equilibrium price, and to *keep all the higher rent for himself* while continuing to pay the apartment owner the old legal limit. Some original tenants may prefer to sublease, because they prefer the higher wealth to their particular apartment. And the new tenant who pays the higher rent is also "better off," because he could have stayed in his old apartment if he preferred it at the controlled rent. Everyone can move to a preferred position by this subleasing possibility, and no one is made worse off—as he judges his situation. The owners still get the legally limited rent, however.

In this subleasing case, wealth is being taken from the owners by the legal rent limit, and the original tenants are getting that wealth from the owners. Hardly anyone has proposed that under rent controls tenants really be allowed to sublease at market-clearing prices—despite the gains that would accrue. Is it because this would make the whole element of wealth appropriation or gift too transparent to be acceptable politically? Or is it that subleasing is in some other respect "bad"?

Whatever the position one takes on this question, the issue soon comes down to whether the apartment-house owners "deserve" the right to the value of their housing space at exchange-equilibrium free-market prices, or whether that wealth should, with rent controls, be transferred to the renters under the presumptuous doctrine that wealth should be taken from the rich (apartment-house owners) and given to the poor (tenants). Under rent controls, without subleasing at market prices, the same amount of wealth is being taken from the house owners. Since there is no free-market exchange-equilibrium value being openly expressed, wealth is transferred to the tenants, but not so obviously and not so efficiently.

We say "not so efficiently" because when tenants cannot sublease at higher rents, they gain only insofar as they take the extra wealth *in the form of housing space*. It is like a gift, given on the condition they use it for their personal living space instead of being allowed to exchange it for other, more preferred goods. Even if landlords were on the average richer than tenants—and the evidence does not support this widely held belief—wealth would be transferred from *landlords* to *tenants* and not generally from rich to poor. In any event, the ethics of such a purposeful wealth transfer lies beyond the scope of economics, which can indicate only the circumstances under which the wealth transfer occurs and some of its effects.

From the preceding, we discern three results of effective restrictions on free pricing as a means of inducing exchange.

1. The distribution of the various goods and services depends more heavily upon other utility-increasing (nonmoney) personal-characteristic preferences of the people whose supplies are being exchanged at less than the free-market exchange-equilibrium price.

2. The realized extent of mutually advantageous exchange is reduced.

3. Wealth is transferred from the owners of goods to those who get the goods.

Popularity of Price Controls

Given these consequences of price controls, or other restriction on exploitation of exchange, "Why are price controls imposed?" is an inevitable question. This question reflects the implicit judgment that these consequences are not desirable, but that is a gratuitous judgment. Yet students persistently decide that such consequences, if true, should make price controls unpopular. We offer the following conjectural explanations, which are consistent with economic analysis in general.

The popularity of price controls or any other devices that keep prices below the exchange-equilibrium level can be attributed to several factors. First, as we have just seen, wealth is transferred from the owners of the price-controlled resource to the users (renters or buyers). Those who expect to receive sufficient amounts of the good at that price will want price controls—unless they deem such action as improper. However, price controls bring about inefficient transfers of wealth. Always, those who get the wealth taken from the owners of price-controlled goods would in fact have been just as well off had they been given a cash gain in wealth. And this cash gain is less than the loss of wealth imposed on the owners—as we shall see in detail in Chapter 12. Nevertheless, one feature of price controls probably contributes to their viability; that is, they permit a transfer that is not readily apparent to all people, under the rationale of keeping prices "reasonable"—and who can object to "reasonable" prices? Furthermore, price controls are imposed by a political process; if the tenants far outnumber the owners, rent controls are probably even more likely. And in New York City, where tenants enormously outnumber owners, rent controls have continued since 1941.

Price controls occur for a second reason. Some people think others should be restricted in their choice of consumption patterns. They believe that some should be induced to consume at least specified amounts of certain goods. For example, on a national scale, if we wanted people to eat a specific amount of a certain kind of food or hear a certain amount of highbrow music, we would seek to keep the prices so low that everyone wanted at least as much of that food or music as we were prepared to allot to them. And then to keep them from re-exchanging rights to those goods among themselves, as they would do if they were allowed to compare their different subjective values via free-market price offers, we would prohibit any sales or offers at prices other than those low prices at which the initial allocation was made. The people would then have much less incentive to trade these goods among themselves and alter their consumption patterns. As can be seen, private property—which implies the right to buy and sell at any mutually agreeable prices—makes it harder for third parties to restrict the consumption patterns of people who have private-property rights in their goods. People who want to be paternalistic, dictatorial life-arrangers, and who want to impose their preferences on other people, will find that price controls or restrictions on trade will make their task less difficult.

Third, price controls are popular because they are erroneously believed to be an antidote for inflation. However, when inflation threatens, price controls prevent trading opportunities from being realized after demands have changed. The general increase in demands will push up prices and produce inflation, which can be defined as a general rise in most prices. But once demand increases, the price controls will merely suppress trade, not the demand.[2]

Another reason sometimes given for *rationing* applies in special circumstances of disasters accompanied by a *temporary* loss of production or goods. If people somehow could be kept alive, ultimately they would be able to produce enough to maintain a viable economy thereafter.

"But," it may be asked, "if these people will be productive again in the future, why don't they borrow against their future earnings to buy enough to survive in the interim? Or can't they find charity, relatives, or employers who will tide them over." That is certainly correct, and yet it does not deny that many people will starve because they can't negotiate loans—that is, because of their inability to convince potential lenders that the loan will be paid and not later dishonored. In times of catastrophe, the legal structure is not likely to be so well organized and reliable, nor is the loan market likely to be as efficient as it normally is. Loans therefore will be hard or impossible to negotiate because of defects in the enforcement of contracts. An alternative to this is a system of rationing and price controls. Rationing, yes, but why price controls? Isn't rationing sufficient, for people could then exchange particular kinds of food to reach higher utility levels? That would be more efficient than restricting each person to the rationed amount. Why then add price controls? Probably because free prices would rise high enough to make the suppliers of rationed goods and everyone else more keenly aware of the wealth confiscated from them. When the prices of "food" are held down, suppliers do not appear to lose wealth; hence, the confiscation of their wealth is easier on the public's conscience. In effect, the survival of some people is being financed (which is a technical way to say that the resources are being provided) by producers of the rationed goods. Alternatively, to get food at free-market prices, the government might have

[2] Resist mightily the temptation to reason erroneously as follows: "Increased demand is only *a* factor. Alternatively, demand could remain at a constant level for two years, while labor unions in the steel industry successfully struck for higher wages. It is realistic to assume that other unions in other industries would be spurred to successful efforts to get higher wages, too. So a number of industries are forced to grant wage increases, which when translated into higher costs and consumer prices means that in time there has been a general rise in prices. All this time demand has remained static, so that price controls help to restrain higher prices in other parts of the economy, thus restraining the inflationary spiral of costs." If this line of reasoning seems plausible to you, you can gain from a study of economics! (An explicit investigation of it is given in Chapter 38.)

taxed everyone and redistributed some of that wealth to the poorest. This is not done for at least two reasons: it is too open a redistribution of wealth, and it requires more time to initiate and bring to pass than do price controls and rationing. Whatever the facts, remember that this fourth reason is a reason essentially for rationing and applies only to those particular goods for which it is believed a free-market exchange-equilibrium price would lead to starvation of people who will subsequently become productive and who temporarily cannot obtain loans. As soon as any of these three circumstances end, this particular argument for rationing ends.[3]

Questions

1. When both are the same price, you choose a color television set over a black-and-white set; but when a black-and-white set costs half as much as a color set, you choose the black and white. In which case are you "discriminating"?

2. Which of the following choices involve discrimination?

a. Cadillac vs. Chrysler.

b. Van Gogh vs. Gauguin.

c. Blondes vs. brunettes.

d. Beautiful vs. homely women.

e. Chocolate vs. vanilla flavor.

f. Whites vs. Negroes.

g. Japanese vs. Koreans.

h. Filet mignon vs. hamburger.

3. "Under open-market, private-property pricing, a person is allowed to make any kind of appeal to a seller to get some of the good—even offering him money as a common medium of exchange for other goods. Under price controls, the buyer is told that there is one particular kind of appeal he cannot use—i.e., offer of a larger amount of other goods." True or false?

4. Do you think rent controls would be good or bad for each of the following:

a. Middle-aged couple who do not contemplate moving.

b. Young man moving to a new town.

c. Young married couple with two children moving to a new town.

d. Negro moving to a new town.

e. Young person receiving a raise in salary.

[3] This is not a complete analysis of price controls. *Production* effects have been ignored in order to concentrate the analysis on interpersonal allocation and exchange of existing goods.

f. Old person in retirement.

g. Person who likes to drink and smoke.

h. Beautiful young woman.

i. Homely immigrant.

j. Mormon in a Jewish community.

k. Jew in a Mormon community.

l. Rich.

m. Poor.

n. Excellent handyman who likes to work around the house and care for gardens.

o. Old couple who have saved wealth and invested in apartment house.

p. Dog and cat lover.

q. Old couple who are renting an apartment and living off of social security with no other wealth.

5. "Price controls are used in order to give adequate housing to those in the lower-income levels who would otherwise not be able to afford it." Subject this proposition to economic analysis.

6. In Figure 9–1, showing the demand for *X* by *A* and by *B* and the total demand, let price be held at p_1 by some legal authority. Suppose that one half the supply is sold to *A* and the other half to *B* at the legal price. Show that *B* would prefer to buy some more from *A*. How much would *B* be prepared to pay, and would *A* find this a desirable trade—if it weren't for the legal prohibition against sales at a price above p_1? What legal inducements do you think *A* and *B* could construct to consummate a sale at the legal price p_1?

7. The military draft of the U.S. government involves price control—in which the maximum price that can be paid by the military services is set by law. As a result, the number of personnel demanded exceeds the supply *at that price;* but the buyers, instead of letting the sellers provide the amount they are willing to provide at that proffered price, resort to a compulsory draft to satisfy their "excess" of demand. Graphically, in Figure 9–1, the price, military wages, is limited to p_1, at which the excess demand is $D_1 - S_1$, a difference that is obtained by the draft. Who gains what by this system of price controls? (Before presuming that military personnel could not be obtained by a wage system, note that the permanent military officers, the leaders, are obtained by a voluntary open-market wage system. So are policemen and firemen.)

8. News item (July 15, 1963): "Seoul, Korea (AP). The city government ordered the capital's 1,500 restaurants not to sell any meal containing rice during lunch hours. The measure is designed to encourage the customers to take other food. South Korea is experiencing a serious food shortage because of a poor rice crop." Would open-market prices achieve the same result? How effective will this measure be?

9. A distinguished professor of law has said: "Some people believe that every resource which is scarce should be controlled by the market. And since, in their view, all resources except free goods are scarce, all resources—even rights to radiate radio signals

—should be so controlled. But surely some resources are 'scarcer' than others, and thereby possibly merit different treatment. It doesn't advance the argument very much by placing a label of 'scarcity' on everything." Do you think economics should be studied by professors of law? Why?

10. "In the capitalistic system, only money or market values count in allocating productive resources." Evaluate.

11. "In capitalism, commercialism dominates and suppresses social, artistic, and cultural values." Evaluate.

10

VARIETIES OF DEMAND AND SUPPLY SITUATIONS: PRICE-TAKERS' MARKETS

The preceding chapter showed what would be observed in the real world if price were controlled below the intersection of the demand and supply schedules. If price is at the intersection, what should be observed in the real world? And is it observed? Obviously, if the price is at the intersection, buyers and sellers can buy and sell all they want at the existing price. No one can buy any at a lower price, and no one can sell any at a higher price.

The highest possible price for a seller is the lowest possible price for a buyer. If, then, we see queues or waiting lists of buyers or of sellers of some item, we can be sure that in this kind of market the price is not at the intersection; it is not a market-equilibrium price. Any farmer producing eggs, wool, spinach, meat, or fruits can sell *all* he can produce at the price at which he can sell *any*. He needn't have any unsold surplus at the highest market price for what he is selling. And similarly for buyers; if you look at the real world, you will notice that waiting lists and queues are quite rare. Any consumer can buy all the bread he wants at the lowest price at which he can get any; the same is true for meat, shoes, or clothes.

Nor would sellers advertise or carry inventories if they could sell all they had available at the existing price. Instead, it would pay them simply to sell all of their stock at the existing price. But advertising does occur, and sellers do carry inventories, hoping for customers. Also, in the real world there are queues and shortages. In such instances, as the preceding chapter suggests, one of the first things to suspect is legal restrictions on prices. However, although price controls do bring about shortages in many instances, they will not explain all the cases that do not agree with the implications of our demand-and-supply analysis. Even where there are no price controls, you can find queues of frustrated customers and frustrated *sellers* seeking or awaiting more customers, to whom they would be delighted to sell more than they are able to sell at current prices. Thus, manufacturers of Fords, Arrow shirts, Kellogg's Corn Flakes, Cokes, Luckies, Kodaks, Schlitz beer, *Life* magazine, and Texaco gasoline advertise and would be delighted to sell more at the current prices. Retailers of these items are "queued" in their shops with inventories, waiting for and seeking customers at the current prices. These observed events are flat refutations of the dictum that price is set by the intersection of demand and supply schedules.

Even more, you will observe that seats at the theater sell for the same price, with the superior seats going first as people stand in line at the box office to get the best seats. Similarly, at the restaurant, people stand in line awaiting tables, and at the night club the better tables cost the same as the inferior tables—at least to those who won't covertly "tip" the headwaiter. Again, you are probably aware of college classes with waiting lists or limited enrollments. And parking space on the campus is often allocated at the same price regardless of location or is not priced at all. College tuition fees have little relation to quality of education. Furthermore, queues of applicants are standard practice.

Clearly, something has gone wrong with the analysis—unless these observations in the real world are illusions or misinterpretations of fact. In the list of examples given above, however, the evidence is not an illusion or misinterpretation. Something is clearly wrong with the theory of price determination. But none of the evidence refutes the fundamental laws of demand. It does refute the implication that price is always set by the intersection of demand and supply. Either we have to junk the analysis or modify it. And we can modify it. The prior analysis was for price-takers in open markets. There are different classes of markets, and if we identify their essential differentiating characteristics, we can generalize the analysis to account for these characteristics so that they will no longer be unexpected. We do not mean merely to tack on another set of conditions under which the markets might or might not be cleared. Instead, the expanded theory will tell where queues and shortages are likely to be observed.

Types of Markets

We shall be investigating various types of markets. First, we shall discuss open markets, of which there are several subclasses: (1) In some markets each seller offers so small a part of the supply of the good that he has no effect on price. This is usually called a *price-takers' market.* (2) Where individual sellers can affect the price by varying the amount they offer, the market is called a *price-searchers' market.* (3) The costs of negotiating and policing the market-exchange agreement or contract may exceed the value of the good being exchanged, so that an exchange agreement or contract may not be profitable. For example, if one dollar is the cost for keeping track of and enforcing the contract of exchange for an hour of parking space, the cost of the contract would almost certainly be higher than the hour of parking space is worth—in most parking areas. If such parking space were therefore allocated on a nonprice basis, no one would be surprised. (4) Deliberate charity or philanthropy denies the use of exchange prices; this category includes those goods deemed immoral or undesirable to sell. (5) Private-property rights may be attenuated. For example, the goods may be under the control of nonprofit corporations, government agencies, or churches—none of which have the usual private-property rights.

Finally, certain markets are not open. Some people do not have access to them. Law or private coercion is enforced against outsiders who would enter the market to exchange on other than prescribed terms. Of course, real markets are not all or nothing. They are not completely open or completely closed. Between these two polar extremes, there are markets with various degrees and kinds of entry restraints. But we shall simplify the market range into open markets and closed, or legal-monopoly, markets.[1]

We haven't discussed *production* of goods in these market situations. We could at this point examine the conditions of production, but it seems preferable to continue with the investigation of types of markets and apply our economic tools immediately to some interesting problems.

Price-Takers' Open Markets

Markets differ in the way market demand appears to sellers; they differ in the way prices appear to be set; and they differ even in the extent to which exchange is facilitated. In some markets, the equilibrium price is so quickly and easily discovered that it seems to be set by an impersonal mechanism. In some others, the appearance is the opposite. One market in which prices converge to a unique, easily determined equilibrium price is a *price-takers' market,* where all the buyers and sellers act as if the price were impersonally set by market forces of demand and supply, independently of the demand and supply of individual buyers and sellers. And at the other extreme, called *price-searchers' markets,* it

[1] The sophisticated reader may be surprised at the omission of one class of markets—those in which the sellers collude among themselves to restrict their competitive actions, or in which buyers collude to prevent a bidding up of prices. Markets do differ in the extent to which participants compete independently or collusively. But analytical rigor requires that we distinguish between *attempts* to collude (including meetings, agreements, and detailed procedures) and the *actual* collusion. For convenience, we consider collusive behavior later, in the context of the closed-market classification.

appears (incorrectly) as if prices were arbitrarily set by sellers beyond the control of demand and supply.

In price-takers' markets there are so many sellers of an identical commodity (e.g., potatoes or lettuce) that no one contributes a significant part of the total supply. Everyone supplies only a small portion of the total. Any seller attempting to raise the price of his produce by withholding part of his supply from the market would only lose his sales to other sellers. For example, any lettuce farmer who held his own production off the market in an attempt to raise its price would find his supply too small to have a noticeable effect on price. As far as any one farmer is concerned, the price is set by the market; and there is nothing he can do but accept it. Of course, he could cut the price and sell his lettuce at a lower price; but if he did, he would lose wealth by selling below the highest price he could get—the market price. The market price is the highest price he can get, and still sell any; and he can also sell all he wants to. Therefore, he takes that price.

HORIZONTAL DEMAND AT MARKET PRICE

Graphically, the market demand facing each seller can be depicted by a horizontal straight line at the existing market price. At higher prices he can sell *nothing;* at the market price (and, of course, at any lower price) he can sell *all* that he can produce. From *his* point of view, the demand curve for *his* output is a *horizontal* line at the market price. This still conforms to the basic law of demand: If he asks a higher price, the amount demanded from him will be reduced—to zero.

If *every* producer of lettuce were to double his output, then—although the increase of any one of them would be insignificant—the total increase would be large enough to bring about a very noticeable drop in price. It would do this by increasing supply enough to represent a significant movement along the community's total demand curve for lettuce, as contrasted with the insignificant change attributable to any one producer.

When the total supply increases enough to require a lower price, some one producer or seller—we don't know which one—will suddenly find that, when he tries to sell his output at the last-quoted price, he has no buyers. He must lower his asking price if he wants to sell anything at all. And the level to which he must lower it is not something which he can control. He must lower his price until he finds some buyers, and at that price he can sell all he has. This is the equilibrium price. The equilibrium market price is easy to find, and he has to take it, like it or not. To say that he has to "take" it (or "find" it) means not that he *has* to sell at that price. It means instead that there is no higher price that he *can* obtain. He either sells at that price, or he sells none, for if he asked a higher price, he would lose all, or practically all, his customers.

No one knows exactly how small a portion of the total supply a seller has to provide in this analytically limiting case, where he sees demand for his goods as a horizontal line at the market price. The *highest* price at which he *can* sell is the only price he cares about; a *horizontal* demand curve for his goods serves as a *limit* and a very good approximation to that situation.[2]

The demand and supply situation can be diagrammed as in Figure 10–1. The curves *DD* and *SS* are the demand and supply totaled over *all* demanders and suppliers. The curve *SS* is drawn vertically, in order to continue concentrating on the allocation of *existing* supplies. Each supplier takes the price given by the market demand and supply. The supply from any one supplier, shown by *ss*, is so small that even if it were all withheld from the market the shift in the total supply along the total demand curve would be insignificant and hence would not affect price. Therefore, any one supplier can sell all he has at the market price—which is portrayed by a horizontal demand curve, *dd*, at the price p_1. The demand curve shown here is flat, at least until it passes beyond the range of supply of the individual supplier; the supplier can sell all his output at the one price, p_1, determined by the total market demand and supply. He could, if he would, sell all his goods at a lower price. Nothing prevents him from doing so—nothing except the force that we call the postulate of utility maximization. He could sell for less; but, since he prefers more wealth (as a source of greater utility) to less wealth, he takes the best price he can get.

WEALTH VERSUS UTILITY MAXIMIZATION

Have we been a little careless? How did *wealth*, or income, slip in to replace utility maximization? The explanation is simple. One way to increase a person's utility is by increasing his wealth, unless increments in wealth are obtainable only by certain actions that involve costs—i.e., the sacrifice of other sources of utility. For example, you could work sixteen hours a day and get more money wealth than if you worked ten hours a day. But you probably don't work sixteen hours a day because to do so you would have to sacrifice other activities like health and recreation—thereby, in your opinion, losing more utility than the utility gained in money wealth.

Sometimes, in certain situations, we can ignore these other nonmoney effects on utility simply because they are trivial. Suppose we are analyzing a

[2] In the literature of economics, this limiting market situation—where each seller is faced with a horizontal demand curve for his output—has been given another special name: "pure competition." This name, unfortunately, is misleading, since this market situation is neither more nor less competitive than many others. We use the term "price-takers' markets" to describe a class of markets where every supplier (and also every demander) provides so small a portion of the supply (or demand) that his output (or demand) has no significant effect on price; hence, he "takes" the market price as if it were given by outside forces. The name "price-taker" apparently was first used by T. Scitovsky in his textbook *Welfare and Competition* (Homewood, Ill., Richard D. Irwin, Inc., 1951).

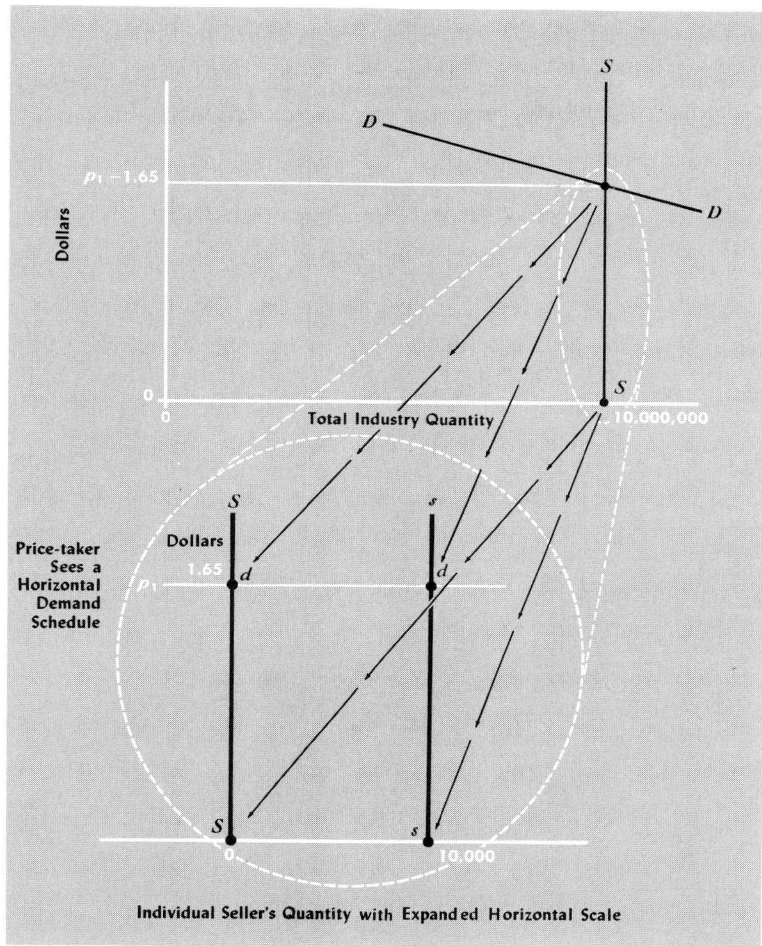

FIGURE 10–1. Price-takers' view of market demand.

businessman's pricing policy. If we assume that his decision to set a high or a low price involves no other factors affecting his utility, then we can concentrate solely on the wealth-maximizing effect of his pricing decision. He may devote a certain amount of resources to reaching a decision. Whether he sets a high or a low price, he will have to go through the same analysis and take just as much time and trouble. His choice of price will not change his nonmoney sources of utility; it will affect only his wealth. Therefore, he will pick the price that maximizes his wealth. In such cases we can simply assume he is a wealth maximizer, for that is now a special subcase of a utility maximizer. In other problems we shall not want to be limited in our perspective, and we will then revert to the more general case of utility maximizing, including wealth as only one component of the aggregate of entities that affects his decisions.

MARKET-EQUILIBRIUM PRICE

In price-takers' markets we have assumed that the price will be at the intersection of the aggregate-market total demand and supply curve. What is supposed to keep the price at the intersection of aggregate demand and supply? At prices below the intersection, some buyers would not be supplied with any. They prefer to bid a higher price to get some, rather than be faced with a lower price at which none is available. Similarly, at a higher price some sellers are unable to make sales. They prefer a lower price with actual sales to a higher price with none. Sellers will prefer to cut the price to sell their supply, thereby keeping price from rising above the intersection, while buyers will keep it at the intersection. This is the mode of operation of the price-takers' market, in which there are many sellers and buyers—many defined as a number sufficiently large to make *each* individual an insignificant portion of the total.

If the total community demand for this good should fall (meaning that the total amount that people want to have at any price is less than before), the equilibrium price will fall—as indicated by the intersection of the new lower demand and same supply at a lower price. In Figure 10–2, the demand has fallen

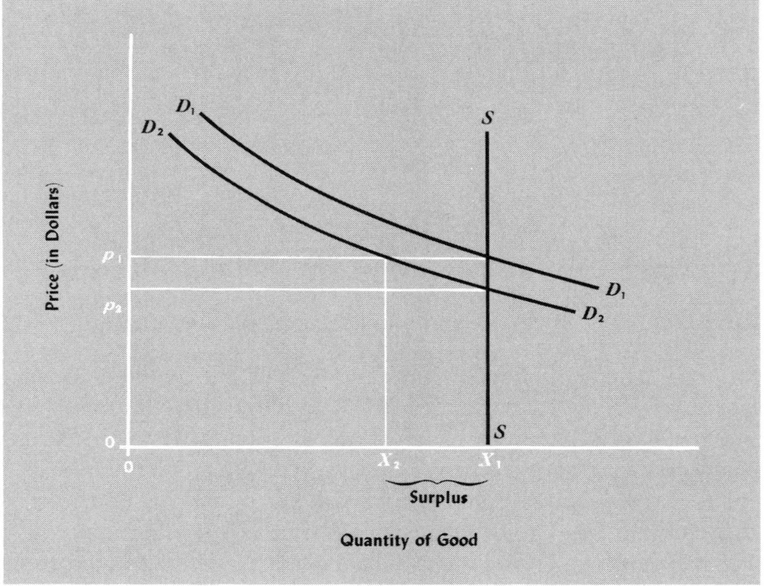

FIGURE 10–2. Equilibrium pricing, with market demand and supply for price-takers' markets.

from D_1D_1 to D_2D_2; and at the price p_1, which prevailed with demand D_1D_1, the amount of goods $X_1 - X_2$ will now be unsold. That unsold amount is a *surplus*. Some owners of those goods have the choice of selling nothing at the old price and holding the surplus, or of lowering the offering price until enough buyers can be induced to buy the existing supply, thus eliminating the surplus. That lower price which the sellers will find to be the feasible market-equilibrium price is p_2. Of course, those lucky sellers who might sell their stock at the former price even when demand declined would like to prevent other frustrated sellers from cutting the price. But the frustrated sellers prefer to cut price from p_1 to whatever level is necessary for existing stocks to be sold, p_2. The price-cutters can be thought of superficially as setting the lower price. Basically, however, the reduced demand and existing supply determine the only market price at which the entire supply can be sold. The frustrated sellers are *revealing* the new market-equilibrium price. They are neither "setting" nor "determining" it in their pricing activity. Price will be cut to the intersection of the new lower demand and supply curves, at which price every seller can sell all he wants and each buyer can buy all he wants. There is no incentive to lower price further.

Although no reason was given for the decrease in demand, we do know that the decrease means that people, in the aggregate, now demand less of the good at each price than before. This could result from a change in tastes, a reduction in wealth in the community, a reduction in the population, or a change in the condition of many people in other respects—e.g., getting older, with its attendant change in tastes. People are never static in their tastes, desires, and circumstances. Under the continual change of circumstances, demands for goods will be persistently shifting. People's attempts to adjust to their changed circumstances are facilitated by the change in price toward the intersection of the demand and supply curve.

We repeat an earlier warning. What is important is not merely that a change in demand indicates a changed intersection price in the demand and supply diagram, but instead that price will change *in order* to permit individuals to find and exploit mutually preferred exchange opportunities. If for some reason price were not allowed to change—because of legal or moral restraints on price changes—some buyers and sellers would be unable to reveal feasible, mutually preferred exchanges and to carry them out. This does not mean that price *should* be allowed to change to permit those exchanges to occur. That depends upon whether or not one "likes" the consequences of an individual-choice, voluntary-exchange system—called a capitalist system. And many of these consequences still remain to be more fully revealed.

EFFICIENCY OF EXTENT OF EXCHANGE

In price-takers' open markets, with equilibrium price at the intersection of demand and supply, the consumption-substitution ratio (subjective value) between any two goods is equal for all individuals. If any person values cigarettes more, relative to Cokes, he can purchase more cigarettes and fewer Cokes per week until the increased ratio of cigarettes to Cokes in his consumption pattern reduces his marginal valuation of cigarettes relative to Cokes. At the market-equilibrium price, for all persons with access to the market, there is no remaining unexploited opportunity of trade among them whereby they could reach still more preferred situations. Thus, a maximum of exchange occurs. In other words, the gains to individuals from trade, as they individually judge their own situations, are fully exploited in a price-takers' open market. Hence, there are no "shortages," queues, or waiting lists in those markets.

Questions

1. This question is designed to illustrate the demand situation facing an individual seller in a price-takers' market. Suppose the community demand for the particular product (say, wheat) is shown below, in the vicinity of the market price, $2 per bushel. (Conventionally, wheat prices are expressed to the nearest eighth of a cent per bushel.)

PRICE	QUANTITY
$2.01	9,986,000
2.00 7/8	9,987,000
2.00 6/8	9,988,000
2.00 5/8	9,990,000
2.00 4/8	9,992,000
2.00 3/8	9,994,000
2.00 2/8	9,996,000
2.00 1/8	9,998,000
2.00	10,000,000
1.99 7/8	10,002,000

You have 1,000 bushels. Could you affect the market price by withholding all of your supply from the market?

2. The rest of the suppliers provide the remaining 9,999,000 bushels.

a. If you tried to sell at a price of $2.00 1/8 while the market price was $2, would anyone buy wheat from you at the higher price you ask?

b. What does the demand curve for your wheat look like?

3. Suppose you had 6,000 bushels of wheat of the total of 10,000,000 bushels.

a. Could you sell *any* wheat at a higher price than the market price of $2? How much would you sell if you asked $2.00 1/8? If you asked $2.00 2/8? $2.00 3/8?

b. What does the demand curve facing you look like? Draw one on graph paper. Would you agree that it is, for all practical purposes, a horizontal line at the market price?

c. Would it pay you to ask for a price above the market price of $2 in view of the effect on the sales revenue?

4. Suppose you owned 1,000,000 bushels of the 10,000,000 bushels of wheat. Could you now affect the market price more? (We shall take up cases like this in the next chapter.)

5. You own 1,000 shares of General Electric common stock. If you try to sell some, you find you can get a price of $61½ per share for all 1,000 shares. If you offer only 500 shares, you can get a price of $61⅝ per share—12½ cents more per share. By reducing your amount sold by a half, you can get a price that is higher by about 1/500. And if you sought a price of $61¾, you would sell nothing. This is an insignificant rise in price as a result of withholding one's supply. Is this what is included in price-takers' markets?

6. A sugar-beet farmer produces and sells 300 tons of sugar beets at $80 per ton for total revenue of $24,000, in a price-takers' market; i.e., he cannot affect the price he gets by changing the amount he offers to sell. The demand for *his* product is therefore describable by the following table, in which you are to compute the data for the marginal-revenue column.

PRICE	QUANTITY	MARGINAL REVENUE
$81	0	______
80	1	______
80	2	______
80	3	______
80	4	______
.	.	
.	.	
.	.	
80	100	______
80	200	______
80	300	______
80	400	______

7. In a price-takers' market, does the marginal revenue of each seller equal the average revenue (price)? Why?

8. In a price-takers' market, is each seller's marginal revenue constant, or is it decreasing as a function of the amount he sells?

9. If price is set by demand and supply in an open market, then in price-takers' markets which of the following will not be observed?

a. Rationing by waiting lists.

b. Sellers who would like to sell more of their available supply at current prices.

c. Buyers who want to buy more at current prices but find no more available.

d. Queues.

e. Buyers told they must buy at least a certain quantity if they are to get any at all.

f. Tie-in sales, wherein to get one good you must buy some of another good.

g. Advertising.

h. Inventories.

10. At a price-takers' market-equilibrium price, every buyer can get all he wants at the price; and every seller can sell all he wants to at that price.

a. Do you know of any firms that do sell in price-takers' markets?

b. Try tentatively to classify the following as price-takers or as price-searchers.

(1) Egg producers.

(2) Chicken farmers.

(3) Tomato growers.

(4) Asparagus growers.

(5) Soybean producers.

(6) Crude-oil producers.

(7) Corner drug store.

(8) Local service station.

(9) Medical doctors.

(10) Music teachers.

11

VARIETIES OF DEMAND AND SUPPLY SITUATIONS: PRICE-SEARCHERS' MARKETS

Negative-Sloped Demand for Seller

Throughout the preceding exposition we assumed that none of the sellers provides enough of the supply to affect the selling price significantly. However, in many markets individual sellers *do* control enough of the supply to be able to shift the market supply a significant or perceptible amount along the demand curve. In these markets a seller faces a market-demand curve such that he can sell some of his product at a higher price and more at a lower price. The demand curve facing him for his product is a negatively sloping demand curve, with respect to price.

To see what difference the negative slope makes in the price-setting process, it will be convenient to use the concept of *marginal revenue,* the addition to total revenue by the sale of one more unit, as illustrated in the very simple demand schedule shown in Table 11–1. In that demand, a price of $10 per unit will induce daily sales of one unit. A price of $9 will induce daily sales of two units. Total daily revenue changes from $10 to $18, a change of +$8, when two units instead of one are sold daily. Although the second unit sells for $9, so does the first one sold each day, so that the increase in total revenue, compared to selling one at $10, is less than the price of the extra unit sold. The second unit alone does not bring in $8 more daily, but rather selling *both* units at $9 rather than just one at $10.

The fourth column in Table 11–1 shows the change in total revenue associated with unit changes in the rate of sale. For example, at a daily sale of five units, the total daily revenue is $30, which is $2 larger than the daily revenue when four units are sold daily at $7 each.

If the price were reduced from \$6 to \$5 while the demand curve did not change, total revenue would not increase at all. The marginal revenue for a sales increase of one unit from five to six per day is zero. This is expressed as a zero marginal revenue for six units (not for *the sixth*). And the marginal revenue is negative for an increase in sales to seven units; the total revenue decrease from \$30 per day to \$28. Marginal revenue is —\$2 when sales are at a level of seven, even though the seventh unit itself sells for \$4.

Table 11–1

ILLUSTRATIVE DEMAND SCHEDULE WITH MARGINAL-REVENUE DATA

Price	Daily Quantity Demanded	Total Daily Revenue	Marginal Daily Revenue
\$10	1	\$10	\$ 10
9	2	18	+8
8	3	24	+6
7	4	28	+4
6	5	30	+2
5	6	30	0
4	7	28	—2
3	8	24	—4
2	9	18	—6
1	10	10	—8

Because graphic techniques are convenient ways to express and analyze some economic problems, the simple data of Table 11–1 are plotted in Figure 11–1. The *area* of the rectangle, based on the quantity sold and the price (the average revenue), depicts the total revenue. Quantity times price, or base times height in area units, is the dollar revenue. If the price were lowered by just enough to sell one unit more per day, the new rectangle area may be larger (or smaller) than the old rectangle. If it is larger, total revenue is larger, which is to say that marginal revenue is positive: the *increase in sales* at the lower price was more than enough to compensate for the *lower price* on all the units. The marginal revenue at each rate of sales can be indicated by the height of the bar graph (labeled Marginal Revenue). For each rate of sales and associated price, the graph shows the change in total revenue (as compared to revenue at a sales rate of one unit less).

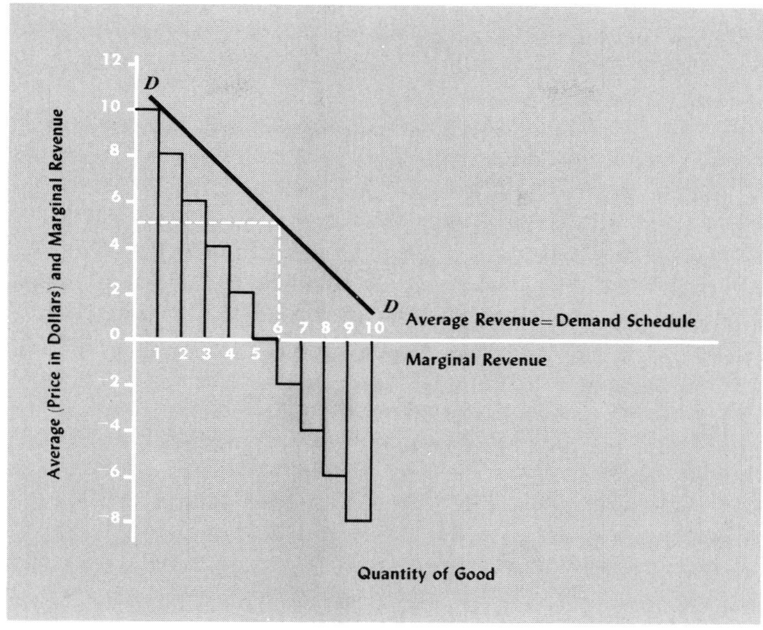

FIGURE 11–1. Average revenue and marginal revenue (demand schedule) seen by price-searcher.

The area of the marginal-revenue bars from the vertical axis out to the stated rate of sales is equal to the total revenue. For example, at a rate of sales of six units, the area under the *MR* curve gives a total value of $30; this is equal to the area subtended by the rectangle given by the *average-revenue curve* (equal to the rectangle indicated by 5 × $6), which is the demand curve.

EQUILIBRIUM (WEALTH-MAXIMIZING) PRICE

Suppose now that you are a seller faced with this demand curve for your product and that each day you have a total supply of ten units available at no cost whatsoever. In selling these units, what price should you charge to maximize your wealth? At a price of $6 per unit you will sell five, and at a price of $5 you will sell six. Either way your total daily revenue is $30. No other price gives so much. Notice also that between any other pair of prices the change in daily revenue is either positive (in the region where price is above $6) or negative (where price is less than $5). If you charge a price of $8, the positive marginal revenue indicates that you are forsaking greater available revenue by not lowering the price and increasing your sales more than in proportion to the cut in price. If you charge a price below \$5—say, \$3—the negative marginal revenue means that you are incurring negative changes in revenue by charging so low a price. If you raised the price up to \$5, you would reduce the rate of sales but not as much, proportionally, as the price rise. Although you would reduce sales, you would increase your *total* daily receipts.

Given this demand curve and your zero costs, the price that maximizes your wealth is either \$6 or \$5. These are your equilibrium prices. We shall continue to assume zero costs until we take up the problem of production; none of the basic results deduced here is affected by the presence of costs of production.

Now take up a more detailed demand schedule—one that gives more of the possible prices and for which the rate of sales does not increase in such simple unit amounts as in the preceding example. Table 11–2 gives the daily demand for water in a particular community. The columns give the price, total daily sales rate, daily total revenue, change in total daily revenue between two adjacent listed prices, and marginal revenue—the *change* in daily total revenue *per unit increase* in daily sales. At a price of \$1 total sales are 56.52 gallons of water daily, with daily total revenue of \$56.52. This is \$5.95 greater than the total daily revenue at a price of \$1.10, where 45.97 units are sold daily. The increase in rate of sales is 10.55 gallons of water daily. Dividing this into \$5.95 gives 56 cents, the marginal revenue—the increase in daily revenue for a one-unit increase in sales in the price range around \$1. This 56 cents is an approximation of how much total revenue changes if price varies just enough to alter the daily rate of sales by 1 gallon. As long as the marginal revenue is positive, a seller will do well to lower price until the marginal revenue is zero—if there are no costs of production.

In Table 11–2, marginal receipt is negative for all listed prices below 67 cents and positive for all prices above 67 cents. This means that 67 cents is the price that maximizes total revenue at 67 cents and higher per day. Since costs of production are zero, 67 cents is also the profit or wealth-maximizing price. As stated earlier, the demand schedule is the "average revenue curve," for it shows the average revenue per unit (or price) for each rate of sales. Remember that the *marginal* revenue is the *change* in total revenue that occurs when sales *change* by *one* unit in response to an appropriate reduction of price.[1]

The data of Table 11–2 are graphed (with graphic smoothing) in Figure 11–2. The curve *DD* is the demand curve for water in this particular market. The *MR* curve plots the marginal revenue. The height of the *MR* curve indicates how much larger total daily revenue is at various daily rates of sales, compared to the sale of one unit less per day at an appropriately higher price. The crucial idea is that with a negatively sloped demand curve, the marginal revenue at any rate of sales will always be less than the price. Notice that in both the pre-

[1] For those who know calculus, if $p = f(x)$, where x is rate of sales and p is price, marginal revenue is defined as the first derivative of total receipts, $xp = (x \cdot f[x])$, with respect to x.

ceding numerical examples (except for a price so high that only the smallest possible amount is sold) the marginal revenue is less than the price. This is understandable when it is remembered that the extra revenue from selling an extra unit is at least partly offset by the reduction in price on all units sold at the former rate of sales.

Table 11–2

DEMAND SCHEDULE FOR WATER

Price	Quantity Demanded Daily	Dollar Value of Daily Revenue: Total	Marginal	Marginal (for Unit Increment in Quantity)
$2.00	0	0	0	0
1.75	3.5	$ 6.13	$ 6.13	1.75
1.50	14.2	21.30	15.17	1.41
1.40	20.4	28.56	7.26	1.17
1.30	27.7	36.01	7.45	1.02
1.20	36.24	43.48	7.47	.87
1.10	45.97	50.57	7.08	.72
1.00	56.52	56.52	5.95	.56
.95	62.25	59.14	2.62	.46
.90	68.39	61.55	2.41	.41
.85	74.65	63.45	1.90	.30
.80	81.36	65.09	1.64	.24
.75	88.17	66.13	1.04	.15
.70	95.45	66.82	.69	.09
.67	100.00	67.00	.18	.03
.65	103.00	66.95	—.05	—.02
.60	110.67	66.40	—.43	—.05
.55	118.60	65.23	—1.17	—.15
.50	127.01	63.51	—1.72	—.18
.45	135.72	61.07	—2.44	—.28
.40	144.48	57.79	—3.28	—.37
.35	153.76	53.81	—3.98	—.43
.30	163.07	48.92	—4.89	—.53
.25	172.92	43.23	—5.69	—.58
.20	182.79	37.16	—6.07	—.61
.15	193.21	28.98	—8.18	—.78
.10	203.92	20.39	—8.59	—.81
.05	214.62	10.70	—9.69	—.91

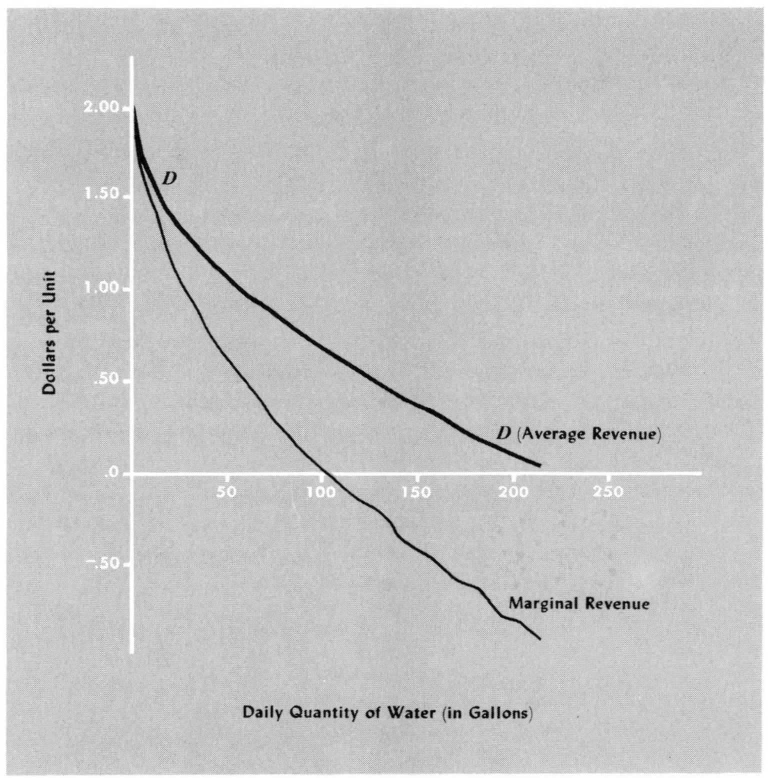

FIGURE 11–2. Demand for water (*DD*) and marginal-revenue curve (*MR*).

EFFECT OF DIFFERENCE BETWEEN MARGINAL REVENUE AND PRICE ON SELLER'S PRICING BEHAVIOR

This difference between marginal revenue and price of each unit sold implies a difference between the price-takers' and price-searchers' markets with respect to equilibrium price and sales.

Suppose that the existing supply of some fine drinking water comes from 200 different wells owned by 200 different owners, each of whom gets 1 gallon a day. Suppose also that *there are no costs* of producing the water and that only a total of 200 gallons is available per day. What will be the equilibrium market price of the water? *If we knew the market demand,* we could tell what that price would be in a *price-takers'* market. As indicated by the market-demand curve in Table 11–2 and shown in Figure 11–2, with the 200 different sellers competing for buyers and with no one of them able to affect the selling price, the price will be about 10 cents per gallon. At that price the amount demanded equals the amount available. The total receipts are $20, which is 10 cents per *seller*, since each one sells 1 gallon. This is the price-takers' market situation.

Now suppose that all the water wells were controlled by a single agency (leaving for later a discussion of how this can, in fact, be accomplished). By holding part of the supply from the market, the single controller could obtain a greater total of receipts. At 67 cents a gallon, 100 gallons would be sold, bringing in $67 instead of the former $20 when 200 gallons were sold at 10 cents a gallon.

The seller could sell some more water by lowering the price—say, to 50 cents. Some buyers would be happy to buy more at this price. And the seller would be happy to sell *them* some at this price—except that if he tried to do so, he would have to lower the price to *all* of his customers, and that loss of receipts from the lower price on all sales would more than offset the receipts from the extra sales.

The seller's receipts do not increase by the *value of the extra units* he sells. Instead, in a price-searchers' market, this *difference* between value to the buyer (price) and the gain to the seller (marginal revenue) is distributed to all the buyers when the price to all buyers is cut. This transfer of the reward from the seller to the buyer prevents the full realization of mutually preferred exchange opportunities. As long as the demand curve facing the seller has a negative slope, so that the seller must accept the lower price on all units sold, the marginal revenue to the seller will always be less than the price.

In the previously discussed *price-takers'* markets, each producer acting *independently* received 10 cents for his product. But *if* all the producers could get together and sell via a single agency, the income to each producer would be 33½ cents—the value of the half gallon of water sold each day. Why? Because at a price of 67 cents, 100 gallons are sold daily, which is equivalent to half a gallon and 33½ cents per individual supplier. Surely obvious is the wealth gain available *if* one could convert a price-takers' market into a price-searchers' market by coordinating or organizing all the price-takers into one agency or firm (and devoting attention to the group's marginal revenue). Beware of jumping to conclusions. It does not follow that price-searchers' markets are more profitable than price-takers' markets; entry into the open market will compete away those profits in both types of markets. The difference between price-takers' and price-searchers' markets is fundamentally a difference in the profit-maximizing *output and price program*, not in the amount of the profit. It is true that in the present example there is a difference in profits also, but we shall see later wherein the present comparison belies several other pertinent facts of life. For the moment we wish to concentrate attention on the pricing process as a facilitator of exchange.

Every seller, be he price-taker or price-searcher, seeks to increase his total wealth, which he can do by maximizing his daily receipts (costs being zero). The *price-taker* maximizes receipts by charging the highest possible price at which he can sell any at all; his extra receipt from selling more (marginal revenue) is equal to the price of each unit sold, simply because he doesn't have to lower price to sell at a higher rate. On the other hand, the *price-searcher* faces a demand situation in which he does have to lower price to sell more; therefore, as we have seen, his marginal revenue will be less than the selling price. At 67 cents he sells one hundred daily, and although people would be induced to buy more at a slightly lower price, he cannot be induced to sell more, even though unsold units are available to him at zero cost. The marginal revenue has fallen to the zero costs of those extra units (which can be sold only at a price below 67 cents). He will maintain the wealth-maximizing price of 67 cents per gallon and let the remaining water run down the creek, unsold, unexchanged, and unused.

In a price-searchers' market, less water is sold than in a price-takers' market —if the basic conditions of supply are the same. Although the equilibrium price is higher, *the equilibrium extent of exchange is less.* If we define as inefficient any situation in which resource use could be revised to increase the utility of some people without reducing that of anyone else, then price-searchers' markets can result in inefficient exchange. Here the inefficiency is the nonexchange (nonuse) of half the water.

Difference between Price-Takers' and Price-Searchers' Market

A buyer in either of these markets cannot tell which type of market condition prevails. In each case, *he* can buy all he wants at the going price. Of course, if many buyers were to increase their demand, the price would be affected; but no one buyer affects price by his own purchase rates. From his point of view, the buyer is in a price-takers' market, however the demand conditions may appear to the seller. For example, no one buyer of Chevrolets or Florsheim shoes affects the price by his demand.

The disparity between price (average revenue) and marginal revenue— the former determining the buyer's exchange decision and the latter the seller's exchange decision—is a consequence of the negatively sloped demand curve facing a seller. One warning: Although a price-takers' market was changed to a price-searchers' market by concentrating ownership of supply (which made the supplier so large, relative to the market, that he operated along a significantly large range of the demand curve for his product to have an effect on price), it does not follow that the only, or even the most important, source of price-searchers' markets is concentration of ownership. Even if it were, one could not justifiably recommend, on the basis of anything investigated so far, a policy of enforced dispersal of ownership in order to create price-takers' markets as a means of achieving market-exchange efficiency. In the first place, the recommendation would presume that efficiency is *better* than inefficiency. That is an ethical question; and though many readers might casually be prepared to *say* so, many other people advocate laws to prevent exchange "efficiency." For example, compulsory licensing of doctors, prescription of drugs, prohibition of alcoholic beverages, non-enforcement of contracts by minors, control of hours of business—all are examples of laws that restrict the extent to which exchange potentialities, and hence efficiency, are achieved. Perhaps, after all, exchange efficiency is not "good," especially if it means that people will be more able to trade and consume certain goods or services which you think, for their own good, they should not. Later we shall investigate this matter further; for the present, do not hastily accept *exchange efficiency* as an obviously desirable goal.

The second reason we cannot yet conclude that dispersal of ownership should be forcefully introduced is that even if efficiency were clearly good, the means of enforcing dispersal involves a denial of private-property rights, and one would have to examine the ancillary effects before concluding that simple dispersal to achieve efficiency is worth all the costs. We are not yet in a position to do that.

Multipart Discriminatory Pricing

Sellers do not always have to permit the buyer to buy all he wants at a particular price; yet that was the only kind of offer considered in the preceding discussion. A price-searcher seller, who is out to maximize his income, might do better with a price-quantity offer. We shall briefly explore some of these alternatives (called *multipart* and *discriminatory pricing*) and deduce some implications about the extent of exchange and the kinds of market behavior that should be observed in the real world.

Instead of allowing the buyer all he wants at the selling price, the seller might set up a schedule of prices with the buyer paying different prices, depending upon the amount taken. To see how this procedure can give an even greater income to the seller, imagine him to be faced with a demand schedule characterized by the data in Table 11–1. Suppose that the seller has ten units of a product available for the sale each day and that it costs him nothing to produce them. (This last assumption enables us again to isolate selling policy from production problems.) How can he maximize his daily income? A flat price of \$5 (or \$6) will bring in total receipts of \$30 daily, with sales of six (or five) units. And the remaining unsold units are wasted (insufficient exchange).

Our clever seller could tell the buyer that the price is not $5 a unit *for an unlimited quantity,* but only *for the first six* units; after purchasing six units, the buyer may, as a sort of quantity discount, buy more at $3 each. What will the buyer do? He will buy six at $5 each (paying $30) and then buy more at $3 each. Specifically, according to his demand schedule, he will buy eight per day at $3 each. From this it can be deduced that he will buy *some* additional units at $3 after buying six at $5; that indeed he will demand very nearly two more units, and that, for present purposes, he actually will demand exactly two more.[2] The buyer prefers buying the first six units at a price of $5 and two more at $3 to the former situation, in which he acquired a total of only six; and the seller, too, prefers the new pricing arrangement, which gives him greater income. And note that only two units are now left unsold—that is, the inefficiency of exchange is reduced.

Apply this kind of pricing to the water example. Our water seller could announce a price of 67 cents per gallon for the first gallon bought by each buyer—assuming now that there are 100 buyers represented in the aggregate demand schedule for water. Suppose, further, that each buyer will buy 1 gallon at 67 cents. If the seller announces a quantity discount whereby each buyer can buy a *second* gallon at only 10 cents per gallon, every buyer would buy a second gallon daily for 10 cents. As a result, the seller grosses $77 in daily receipts instead of $67, and all the water is sold. Each buyer prefers the new price-quantity discount to the old flat price.

The "inefficient" use or waste of water has disappeared. This remarkable result was achieved because the seller preferred more wealth, not because he was concerned with eliminating some "waste." Motivating causes and their effects are not always the same.

An even more clever seller can set up a more detailed schedule of discount prices and get still greater daily income from the sale of the water. Again, it will be simpler to use our earlier demand schedule of Table 11–1 to illustrate the range of possibilities. If you were the seller faced with that demand schedule, what could you do to maximize income? What does that schedule tell you? For

[2] We are comparing two alternative cases: (a) buy eight units at $3 each—which is indicated in the demand schedule; and (b) buy eight units, six of them at $5 and two at $3. Certainly, the alternatives are not identical: total expenditure in the first case is $24, and it is $36 in the second. In the first case, in which all units sell at the same price of $3, the eighth unit is worth $3 to the buyer; but in the second case, in which total expenditure is higher, the eighth unit may well be worth something less than $3. If the buyer has already acquired six units at $5 each, quite possibly either the *price* must be less than $3 in order to induce him to buy as many as two more, or the *quantity demanded* will be less than two at a price of $3. And the reason for this possible modification of demand may be labeled the "income (or wealth) effect"—i.e., the expenditure of $36 in the two-price case, compared to only $24 in the simpler case. But while the income effect *may* be sufficiently substantial to reduce demand at prices below $5, let us suppose for simplicity that it is not. And *if* the income effect is negligible, we may slide down an unmodified demand curve, with the buyer willing to buy two more units at $3 after buying six at $5, just as, of course, he is willing to buy two more at $3 after getting the first six also at $3.

one thing, the buyer regards having one unit per day as worth $10 more than having none. You know this because he prefers to pay $10 for one rather than to have none. Furthermore, if we continue to assume a negligible effect on wealth, he would rather pay $9 more to get a second one daily than be confined to only one daily at $10. How do we know? The schedule shows he would buy two at $9 each rather than just one; therefore, a second one daily must be worth to him at least $9, given his current total wealth and state of preferences. This means we could induce him to buy two units daily in either of two different ways. We could offer him all he wants at $9 each, or we could offer him one for $10 and then a second one for $9. In the one case he pays $10 for the first one and $9 for the second; and in the other he pays $9 for the first and $9 for the second.

What he pays for the first one presumably is *almost* irrelevant in his demand for a second one. If he pays $10 instead of $9 for the first one, that would not reduce the value of the second one to him by $1; for the effect of the $10 price for the first unit is to reduce by $1 his income available for *all* other things. This reduced-wealth effect will be spread over *all* his purchases. In fact, there *will* be a small effect on his demand for this article; and the amount he would be willing to pay for a second one, if he paid $10 for the first one, would be not $9 but, say, $8.90. A price of $10 for the first item and a price of $8.90 for the second would get two items sold for a total daily income of $18.90, compared with $18 for two units of a flat price of $9 each. As before, in order to avoid these minor adjustments, we continue as if the demand schedule stays unchanged, so that the seller can sell the first one for $10 and a second for $9.

As a seller you could offer the great bargain of "$10 for one or two for $19"—which is precisely the same thing as $10 for the first one and $9 for the second one. The buyer may think you are doing him a favor, and you are—compared to charging a flat price of $10. As a seller, you are interested in doing favors for other people only insofar as the favor also improves your situation.

Why not offer the buyer three for $27? Then he can buy three at a cost of only $8 more than for two. According to the demand schedule, he will prefer to buy three for $27 rather than only two for $19. There are two ways of expressing your sale offer: (1) "One for $10, 2 for $19, and 3 for $27." (2) "Ten dollars for the first one, $9 for the second, and $8 for the third one." Either way, you will sell three and get $27 daily.

If you now offer the buyer a fourth one for $7 (four for $34), he'll take the offer, because he would rather have a fourth one than $7. You now have total daily receipts of $34. Continue the process. Offer the buyer a fifth one daily for $6 (after he buys the first four on the preceding terms) or offer him a package of five for $40. He'll take the offer. The possibilities seem limited only by your daily supply of ten items. So extending the logic, offer him a sixth for $5 (or a package of six for $45); a seventh for $4 (or a package of seven for

\$49); an eighth for \$3 (or eight for \$52); a ninth for \$2 (or nine for \$54); and ultimately a tenth for \$1 (or a package of ten for \$55). He'll buy ten per day for a total outlay of \$55. The buyer prefers to take ten per day rather than anything less per day—given the offers you have made.

You have made offers to the buyer that are just sufficient to induce him to buy the items from you; you have squeezed from him approximately all they are worth to him.

Before seeing whether or not this kind of pricing is actually used in the real world, notice that it is equivalent, in extreme form, to what appears to be a still different kind of price. Suppose that, as the seller, you announce a flat daily *fee* of \$55, which entitles the buyer to have all he wants each day. He will take ten or eleven items per day. (An eleventh is worth zero, so that he is indifferent about whether or not he gets it; but in any event, aside from this marginal consideration, we can suppose we have eleven available each day if he wants eleven.) The buyer pays \$55 each day as a fee and then gets all the daily service he wants free (at no subsequent cost). This is in fact precisely the same kind of offer as the earlier graduated scale of multiprices and can be used if the demand curve is known with extraordinary precision.

In point of fact, no seller ever knows a demand curve exactly. We have used an extreme case of complete information to the seller (and we have ignored other sellers who might underprice him). This extreme example is designed merely to expose the basis for multipart, or fixed-fee, pricing in simplest fashion. If this theory is realistic, we should observe this kind of pricing in the real world. And it does occur in the real world, though usually in much cruder form.

EXAMPLES OF MULTIPART PRICING

Examples are available at the grocery store. Some goods are marked "15 cents, two for 25 cents." Some are marked simply two for 25 cents, it being understood that one would cost 13 cents. You may take the cynical view that quantity discounts make the price higher to those who buy only a few, or you may view them as a special favor to the customer who buys more. Whatever interpretation or motivation you wish to give, we see that quantity discounts are used because the seller wants to increase his income. But on second thought this does not mean that the seller must necessarily think of the device; actually, the *buyer* can suggest it. Reconsider our water seller faced with the demand data of Table 11–2. The buyer, seeing unsold units available, may suggest that the seller agree to sell the first six at \$5 each, and any additional units at a lower price—say, \$2 for each one the buyer takes in excess of six per day. Certainly the seller will accept that proposition rather than continue to sell only six at \$5 each. The seller will sell three more at \$2 each, according to the buyer's demand schedule, for a total daily receipt of \$30 + \$6 = \$36. Both buyer and seller prefer the new arrangement. Notice that the new arrangement can be viewed as a scheme whereby the seller squeezes the buyer, or one whereby the buyer gains over the flat price system that the price-searcher might otherwise use. In either event, the amount sold can, by multipart prices, be extended to the full amount available, so that none is left unused.

Electric power, water, and gas prices from public utilities are almost always sold on multipart-pricing schedules, where the unit price depends upon how much customers buy. Telephone service and sometimes water are sold for a fixed total fee of so much per month, with the buyer taking all he wants. Is the motive to reach a more extensive use of the available output, or is it to induce buyers to take more of the product for the benefit of the sellers? As we have seen, the motives are hard to isolate; several can operate together. All we have done is show that this kind of pricing will be viable to all parties concerned in certain circumstances—for instance, when the seller is a price-searcher. As we shall later see when investigating production costs, other conditions (such as costs of production that are lower for larger purchases by the buyer) will induce price to be lower for larger quantities. That, too, will induce multipart pricing.

OBSTACLES TO MULTIPART PRICING

Multipart pricing, although simple in concept, is difficult to achieve in open markets. *Buyers must be prevented from reselling to each other;* otherwise, one buyer will buy large amounts and resell to other buyers. If I can buy two items for 25 cents and resell to other people for 14 cents each to beat the 15 cents price they must pay for just one (assuming they would have bought only one themselves), I can undersell the original seller.

Effective in restricting resale opportunities is the cost of finding other buyers and convincing them of the quality of the product. If I, as an ordinary person and a stranger to you, offered to sell you a diamond, a new tire, a new car, or a fur coat, would you have confidence that what I offer is really the same as the item purchased in an established retail store? Certainly not for items that you cannot easily test prior to purchase. Even if you ignore the issue of whether the seller has proper legal title, you would buy little from a stranger, after brief inspection, because the quality of few items could be discovered in a five-minute inspection. In the real world some people have succeeded in spreading knowledge of the attributes of *their* products or services; these persisting retailers or manufacturers are not merely people from whom we can buy a known type of product, but also are people prepared to provide information on source of supplies. The mere knowledge that the local supermarket exists at a certain location and is available when you want to shop is no inconsequential matter. The casual, itinerant seller provides less service; and if sometimes he is able to sell for less, it is in part because he chooses not to bear the costs of maintaining the conventional retailer's greater availability of service. Furthermore, a stable location offers a greater incentive to sell items that are more likely to be what they purport to be, because of the higher frequency of repeat purchases.

As we can see, price differences among sellers often reflect differences in their services. Therefore, one should not expect to find people buying from lower-priced retailers and reselling to customers of higher-priced retailers.

Sometimes the original seller can get laws passed prohibiting his customers from reselling to other consumers. For example, in many states milk cannot be resold by one customer to other people at a price less than that in retail stores. The ostensible reason is to protect the purchasers from buying "impure" milk from those intermediate customers (who, it is alleged, will "water" the milk to make an even greater gain). Power and gas are sold more cheaply to large users, who by law cannot resell the power or gas to smaller users at prices under those charged by the power company to the smaller customers. Nor can one family purchase telephone service and then resell some service to a neighbor—say, by running an extension over to his house. Later, we shall investigate some of the reasons advanced for these legally imposed restrictions on resale.

Kinds of Market Pricing

We have now distinguished between price-takers' and price-searchers' markets; we have distinguished also between single-price offers and multipart-price offers by any one seller. Although we were not explicit in saying so earlier, the two kinds of price offers can be found only in price-searchers' markets. In a price-takers' market, the homogeneity of product and of sellers in the eyes of the buyers would enable a low-price buyer to resell to higher-price buyers, thereby undermining the multipart prices.

We are now in a position to compare in summary fashion three kinds of market pricing, all with legally free access to open markets: (1) price-takers' markets; (2a) price-searchers' markets with single price; and (2b) price-searchers' markets with multipart pricing. Case 1 yields efficient exploitation of all exchange opportunities. Case 2a does not. In Case 2b, exchange opportunities are more fully exploited, so that goods are directed to their higher-valued uses.

Case 2b also gives the *seller* a bigger income, although accompanied by greater efficiency of exchange. Case 2b differs from Case 1 less in the extent to which full exchange or use of goods is achieved, and more in the resultant distribution of income. In Case 2b the seller has more income than in Case 1. If we knew it was better for the seller of this good to be able to capture more of its value than for the buyer to capture more of the value, we would be able to tell whether Case 1 market pricing or Case 2b market pricing is "better." You may have an opinion about that, but you can't base it on any principles derived from economics. In any event, even if you understood some of the other implications (e.g., about effects on amount produced), there isn't much you can do about changing from one type of pricing to the other. Some fundamental conditions determining whether one or the other kind can and will be used are not subject to legislation or exhortation.

Questions

1. Answer the following questions concerning the demand schedule below.

a. Complete the total-revenue, marginal-revenue, and average-revenue data.

PRICE	QUANTITY	REVENUE TOTAL	REVENUE MARGINAL	REVENUE AVERAGE
20	2	40		20
			+17	
19	3	57		19
			+15	
18	4	72		18
			___	
17	5	___		___
			___	
16	6	___		___
			___	
15	7	___		___
			___	
14	8	___		___
			___	
13	9	___		___
			___	
12	10	___		___
			___	
11	11	___		___
			___	
10	12	___		___
			___	
9	13	___		___

b. What happens to the difference between selling price and marginal revenue? (It goes to purchasers as a lower price. For example, between a price of $18 and $19 with sales of four and three units, respectively, the marginal revenue, $15, is less than the average revenue, $18, by $3. This amount is distributed to buyers of the three units by a price that is $1 lower than formerly.)

c. How many units would you want to produce and sell if you could produce as many as you wanted at an average cost of $10 per unit and if you want to maximize your net receipts (revenue minus costs)?

d. What price would you charge?

e. Could you charge a price of $18 if you wanted to?

f. What would be the consequences?

g. What are the consequences of charging a price of $14?

2. a. How can a price-searcher be searching for a price, when in fact there is a wide range of prices—any of which he can charge?

b. What happens if he is not good at finding what he is searching for?

3. Most elementary-school arithmetic books contain the following type of question: "Mr. Black, who operates a grocery store, can buy bread for 15 cents a loaf. What price should he charge in order to make a profit of 50 percent?" Without worrying why Mr. Black should be content with a 50 percent profit instead of a 500 percent profit, wherein does this question ignore a basic economic fact of life? Do you think that question should be asked in arithmetic courses in grade schools? Suggest a sensible formulation of the problem that will enable students to learn how to manipulate percentage calculations without being taught erroneous economics.

4. Answer the following questions concerning the demand schedule below.

a. Complete the total-revenue and marginal-revenue data.

		REVENUE	
PRICE	QUANTITY	TOTAL	MARGINAL
$20	4	$ 80	
			+15
19	5	95	
			____
18	6	____	
			____
17	7	____	
			+9
16	8	128	
			+11
15	10	150	
			+9
14	12	168	
			+10.67
13	15	215	
			____
12	19	____	
			____
11	24	____	
			____
10	29	____	
			____
9	30	____	

b. Clearly, marginal revenue does not have to fall steadily. It can fluctuate; but it will be less than average revenue or price. Why?

c. If you could produce all you wanted at a cost of $10 per unit, what price would you charge in order to maximize your net revenue (revenue − costs)?

5. Let the demand schedule of Table 11–1 (page 136) represent the characteristics of the demand for your services as a gardener, and suppose you sell in a price-searchers' market.

a. What price should you charge per garden to maximize your daily net receipts if the "cost" of caring for a garden is zero?

b. If your time is worth the equivalent of $3 per garden maintained, what price would you charge?

c. Is this the "highest" price the traffic will bear, or the highest price possible, or the lowest price possible, or a "reasonable" price?

6. "A price-searcher does not have a supply curve. There is no schedule of amounts that he would offer at alternative possible prices, and which can be juxtaposed on a demand schedule." Explain why this is a correct statement.

7. You are buying trees to landscape your new residence. The following demand schedule characterizes your behavior as a buyer:

PRICE OF TREES	QUANTITY DEMANDED
$10	1
9	2
8	3
7	4
6	5
5	6
4	7
3	8
2	9
1	10

The price is quoted at $6. Accordingly, you buy five trees. Then, *after* you buy the five trees, the seller offers to sell you one more for $5.

a. Do you take it?

b. Suppose, strange as it may seem, he then offers you an opportunity to buy more trees (*after* you have already agreed to purchase five at $6 each and the one more for $5) at the price of $3. How many more do you buy?

c. If the price had been $3 initially, would you have bought more than eight trees?

d. Suppose you had to pay a membership fee of $5 to buy at this nursery, after which you could buy all the trees you wanted for your own garden at $3 each. How many would you buy?

e. If you could have bought trees at $3 each from some other store without a membership fee, would you still buy only eight trees—saving the $5 for use on *all* your consumption activities?

f. Now explain why, according to the demand schedule, your purchase of eight trees at \$3 each, at a total cost of \$24, is a consistent alternative to your purchase of eight trees under the former sequential offers, in which you pay a total of \$41 (five at \$6, one at \$5, and two at \$3).

The important lesson of this example is not that we can always slide down an unmodified demand curve, but that sometimes the modification required is slight and permits some of the kind of pricing illustrated in this extreme case example.

8. In the text, two kinds of pricing by a price-searcher were discussed: (1) uniform prices to all buyers, at which each *buyer* can buy all he wants; (2) multipart pricing, in which a buyer cannot buy all he wants at one price; instead the price he pays depends upon how many he buys. We now consider briefly a third type of pricing policy by a price-searcher: he charges *different* prices to *different* customers—called "price discrimination." Again within this third category there are two sub-cases: (a) "simple discrimination," where the price at which a buyer can buy all he wants is systematically different from the price to other buyers; (b) "multipart price discrimination," where multipart pricing is applied to *each* customer, with different sets of prices to each buyer.

We shall now by means of a series of questions explore these possibilities.

a. First, we see how simple price discrimination among different customers can give greater revenue to the seller than uniform prices.

Suppose you are a gardener and are faced with the following demand for your services from eight different garden owners:

PRICE PER GARDEN	NUMBER OF GARDENS
\$10	1
9	2
8	3
7	4
6	5
5	6
4	7
3	8

(1) In view of the fact that your gardening services to one customer cannot be resold to another customer by the first customer, can you think of some pricing technique that you could use to maximize your daily income without increasing your work, assuming that it always costs you \$3 in time and effort to care for another garden?

(2) What technique would you use and what prices would you charge?

(3) What would your income be?

b. An obstacle to this kind of *discriminatory* pricing is the ability of other gardeners to undercut your prices on the higher-priced sales. Other gardeners will find it profitable to underbid your higher prices. If you tried discriminatory pricing, one of them would offer to sell to your customers all they wanted at a slightly lower price than you charge on the "early" units. In this way several gardeners would, by competing for the higher prices, be led to a single price. To succeed with multipart pricing, you must prevent other gardeners from undercutting some of your prices to take your higher-priced sales. But with open access to the market, there is no way to prevent them from doing so. For this reason, discriminatory pricing is difficult to achieve where there are open markets. (We shall later investigate some cases where markets are "closed" by government action to all except a particular class of sellers.)

To discriminate successfully, sellers must prevent customers from reselling the good among themselves. The principle of keeping your customers separate (which is hard to do if they can buy from your competitors or if they easily buy and sell to each other) is illustrated by the following two demand schedules of two different customers.

	DEMAND OF		MARGINAL REVENUE	
PRICE	*A*	*B*	*A*	*B*
$10	1	0		
			$10	$0
9	2	0		
			8	0
8	3	1		
			6	8
7	4	2		
			4	6
6	5	3		
			2	4
5	6	4		
			0	2
4	7	5		
			−2	0
3	8	6		
			−4	−2
2	9	7		
			−6	−4
1	10	8		
			−8	−6

Suppose you have seven units of this good available. At the price you ask of *A*, you must let him buy all he wants, and you must permit *B* to have all he wants at the price you charge *B;* but the price charged *A* and *B* can be different.

(1) What price should you charge *A* and what should you charge *B*, given the demand schedules, if you want to maximize your revenue?

(2) If you charge the same price to both buyers, what is your best price and revenue?

(3) Suppose you can produce this good at a cost of $4 for each unit you make. How many should you make, and what price should you charge to *A* and what to *B*? How many will *A* buy, and how many will *B* buy? What will be your net revenue?

c. Assume that you are the seller with the data just given; construct an example of *multipart pricing* with *different* sets of price offers to each buyer, so as to get still more revenue than in the preceding example. Why do you think this kind of multipart plus discriminatory pricing is relatively uncommon? Can you give some examples of it? (Hint: Check the water, telephone, gas, and electric rates charged in your community. What prevents new sellers or customers from reselling to each other in all these cases?)

9. Consider another ingenious pricing policy: a seller who makes two different products and sells them to different customers. In particular, suppose that you are a movie producer and have made two movies: *A*, a social-problem-oriented drama, and *B*, a horror movie. You rent your pictures to various exhibitors, two of whom are "Roxy" and "Drivein." You know the amounts that Roxy and Drivein would pay for each movie rather than not get them:

	MOVIE	
	A	*B*
Roxy	$100	$20
Drivein	60	80

We now investigate three alternative price schedules you could set.

a. Set a price on *A*, with Roxy and Drivein each being allowed to rent at that price; and set another price on *B*, with each being allowed to rent *B* at that price. Under this arrangement the revenue-maximizing prices are $60 for *A* and $20 for *B*. Your revenue is $160.

b. Set a price on *A* for Roxy and a different price on *A* for Drivein. Also set different prices on *B* for Roxy and Drivein. You may have four different prices. What is the revenue-maximizing set of prices, and what is that revenue? ($260 is the total revenue.)

c. We come to the third alternative and the purpose of this problem. Suppose that you are not allowed to charge different prices to Roxy and Drivein. However, you do discover that you can engage in "block booking," whereby an exhibitor must buy both pictures if he is to buy any from you. What price (same to both exhibitors) would you set on the *pair* of pictures as one "block book," if you wish to maximize your revenue? What is the maximum revenue you can get this way? (Answer: $240.)

Explain how you determined the best block-booking price? (Answer: For each producer compute the sum of the highest amounts that would be offered by each producer for each picture. Charge the lowest of these two sums as the price of the "block." As a seller, it pays to engage in block booking only if your customers assign different relative values to the various products in the block. To show this, try to get a gain—over uniform prices for separate pictures—by block booking when both exhibitors rank the various pictures in the same way; e.g., both rank *A* as superior to *B*. Remember in "block booking" you charge the *same package price* to all exhibitors. You will see that block booking gives no advantage to the seller in this case—and no disadvantage either.)

d. The distributors Roxy and Drivein, who would prefer to prohibit block booking and discriminatory pricing, force you to sell the pictures at the same price to Roxy and Drivein, although permitting a different price for *A* than for *B*. (In this case, as we have seen, the best you could get would be $200.) In an effort to keep down their costs, Roxy and Drivein complain to the government that under block booking you the producer "really" are tying *B*, the poor picture, to *A*, the better picture, in order to get rid of your inferior picture. They complain they do not have freedom to buy what they want and that you are an unfair monopolist. Explain why the complaint is an error. Is the producer forcing the exhibitors to buy goods they do not want? Explain why or why not.

e. What open-market forces reduce your power to engage in block booking?

12

CONTRACT COSTS, ATTENUATION OF PRIVATE PROPERTY, AND PHILANTHROPY

Institutional arrangements and factors in addition to price-searchers' markets and price controls affect the extent to which price clears the market of all buyers and sellers. The capitalist open-market price system will operate as described in the preceding chapters only to the extent that contracting and enforcement costs are low relative to the value of the goods being allocated. Also, the more attenuated are the private-property rights in the goods being allocated, the less will market price determine the allocation. And finally, in some cases goods are deliberately being given away as gifts, in the sense that the allocator does not want them to be allocated by money exchange or market considerations. To these cases we now give our attention.

High Costs of Making and Enforcing Contracts

In Chapter 10 we noted that not all markets are characterized by conditions that lead to prices at which each buyer and seller can buy and sell all he wants at that price. Queues and shortages appear. One of those markets is the price-searchers' market, which we have already examined. A second circumstance is one in which the costs of negotiating exchanges are so high that market exchange is not as fully utilized as it otherwise would be. A practical example is provided by parking space. If a landowner must pay more to collect the money and police the transactions for a parking space than the value of the parking space, he has no reason to rent the space for parking. He might either give away parking rights or simply not let anyone park at all, depending upon the side effects of making the space available. Only when devices are invented (for example, parking meters with police enforcement) to economize on the costs of exchange will formal market exchange and prices be used.

Similarly, parking lots will be constructed and space rented if the costs of collecting payment from all space users is (sufficiently) lower than the value of the space itself. In some European countries, where labor is cheaper relative to land values than in the United States, the costs of having parking attendants in parking areas to collect charges is lower relative to the value of the space. Therefore, one should observe a greater use of such attendants than in the United States. And one does.

Another example is provided by theater seating. The variety (not absolute level) of prices of seats in one theater is affected by the costs of ushers and attendants who enforce multiple-sectioned seating. If ushers' wages are high relative to admission prices, fewer ushers will be used; and this will make it more difficult to ensure that those who pay premium prices are the only ones in the premium seats. In Europe, because of the lower wage rates *relative* to values of theater seats, there will be observed a greater segregation of seats by variety of price classes than in the United States. Seats of various quality will be priced more closely to the price that equilibrates demand with supply.

Development of cheap contracting devices has enlarged the scope of market demand and supply. Thus, a cheap parking meter permits more metering of street parking, so that more of the parking spaces on streets can be allocated by a formalized market system. Why doesn't the market control the allocation of *traffic lanes*? As yet no one has figured out a sufficiently economical way by which drivers who might want to use the parking lane as a traveling lane could bid away that space from those who want to park against the curb. Since the whole lane would have to be cleared before it could be effectively used as a traffic lane, an all-or-none sale of the whole lane would have to be negotiated. However, since each driver would use each strip for only a short interval of time, one can imagine the task involved in trying to buy up the right to a cleared traffic lane from people who might want to park. The costs of negotiating these exchanges would far exceed the value to the buyer.

Similarly—partly because of the high costs of negotiating exchanges—the market system has not been used for allocating radio and television programs of various types to various listeners. In the past, it was simply too costly to provide an electronic device whereby a receiver could pick up a program only if he had paid for it. However, economical devices for descrambling programs and negotiating exchange payments have now been developed, but so far the U.S. government has prohibited their use.

Other examples of economical ways of permitting market-exchange operations by means of coin vending machines are plentiful. Telescopes at viewpoints operate with coin-controlled machines; some airport waiting rooms have coin-operated turnstiles to allocate seats from which patrons can view airport operations; coin-operated devices control access to dormitory rooms and restroom facilities for travelers waiting between flights. We have coin-operated rental typewriters at libraries, coin-operated soft-drink and food vending machines, and coin-operated telephones.

Although difficult to prove definitively, an argument can be made that the principal class of goods and services that are *not* allocated via the market system at market prices are those *not subject to private ownership*. Two forces operate to make this argument true. One is a deliberate suppression of market-exchange price allocation through government ownership of such goods. Second, an administrator of goods has less incentive to use the marketplace and to get the best possible price if he is not responsible to someone who owns the goods as private property.

It is this second circumstance that we shall investigate next, leaving to a later chapter the problem of deliberate resort to government ownership and operation to take goods and services outside the nexus of the marketplace. Nor need we, at this time, enter into a detailed interpretation of the nuances of various forms of property rights. For the present, think of a private-property right as a person's right to use goods and services (called his private property) as he sees fits (without violating the same right for other people) and to sell or exchange such rights.

The preceding discussions of pricing and exchange were all based on an assumption of private property. Let us now consider behavior under some forms of property rights that are not what we ordinarily call private-property rights. We shall consider nonprofit institutions and state- and city-owned property as nonprivate property, even though private individuals are in control of the goods. As our first example, we shall consider a "not-for-profit" form of property right.

Nonprofit Institutions

In a *nonprofit* corporation, there is no group of individuals who can decide to distribute the net gains or profits to themselves as their own wealth, as can be done in a for-profit corporation. Any profits must be spent in the enterprise to further the purposes of that enterprise. Most private colleges are nonprofit institutions, and profits must be devoted to the educational aims of the institution, although precious few colleges cover their costs out of tuitions. Most charitable foundations—e.g., the Ford and Carnegie Foundations—are nonprofit organizations; all the profits of their investments are to be used not for the benefit of the trustees but to further the stated aims of the foundation. The Rose Bowl Association, the Metropolitan Opera Association, and in fact almost all symphony orchestras and religious and fraternal organizations are nonprofit institutions. Let us look at a sample case, the Rose Bowl Association, to see why queues, shortages, and "low" prices are likely to occur.

ROSE BOWL ASSOCIATION

Each New Year's Day, the Rose Bowl football game is held in the Rose Bowl in Pasadena, California. Every time, sure as fate, more tickets are wanted than are available at the price at which tickets are sold by the association. Some buyers are prepared to offer higher prices to get seats; and yet the Rose Bowl Association and the associated colleges refuse to accept those offers and persist in selling at a lower price to students, alumni, and Rose Bowl Association affiliates (and to 2,000 winners of a race to get to the Rose Bowl box office for a special "public" sale). Furthermore, the Rose Bowl Association and the universities declare it illegal for anyone to resell his ticket to some other person at a price higher than he originally paid for it. (The authors, from personal experience, know that many tickets *are* resold at premiums over the authorized sale price.)

Here is a case where a potential seller refuses to accept higher offers from frustrated buyers. Why does he refuse greater wealth? The Rose Bowl Association, sponsor of the annual Rose Bowl football game, is not *privately owned* in the conventional sense. One third of the gate receipts are used to finance its activities, such as providing the game, the Rose Bowl Parade, and other civic affairs. One third of the receipts goes to each of the participating universities and their athletic conferences. But no person can claim any part of the proceeds as being "his"; no one can spend the net proceeds in the way he could spend his privately owned wealth. In these circumstances, will the operator-members of this association—those who set its policies and determine the specific activities—behave as they would if they owned the association as private property?

Forget that there are a large number of people in the Rose Bowl Association management and assume that only one person (call him the manager) makes the decisions. At what price shall the tickets to the football game be sold? The answer, in accordance with our familiar principle, will be "at the price that maximizes the decider's utility." He could set too low a price, so that more seats are demanded than are available. He might then, by virtue of his position, secure tickets and resell some of them at market-clearing prices, thereby unethically diverting wealth to himself. But, being a moral person, he eschews *this* line of "gain." He can still gain utility by this "too low" price policy. First, by underpricing the tickets, he can buy tickets for himself more cheaply, thus releasing more of his own private wealth for other uses. Second, the excess demand for tickets enables him to grant favors to certain selected people in the allocation of tickets. This priority means that the "right" people can get tickets at a price less than they *and others* are willing to pay. Favorable treatment for certain people will enhance his utility. He will find that his prestige is increased: he is invited to the best places, clubs, and circles; and even when he buys a car or furniture, past favors are fondly and effectively recalled. This price policy will cost the association some of the wealth it might have earned. Although smaller receipts for the association reduce the manager's own utility, he must measure this reduction against his utility increase from being able to buy tickets cheaply and to favor certain individuals.

But what if the association were owned by someone, or if it were a privately owned corporation with private-property rights residing in the stockholders? Would he still prefer a low pricing policy? Yes, but the *owners* will have a stronger incentive to fire him or place him on a commission basis, to reduce this discrepancy between their gains and his.

Let's strain the analysis a bit further. If there are several qualities of seats, which seats will be underpriced? Primarily the kind that the manager wants to buy for himself and those that would be bought by the kinds of people he can favor in the queue. These are the best seats. We can always find a small set of especially good seats and charge less than they are worth to frustrated demanders, while charging market-clearing prices for the inferior seats that go to people who are neither students nor alumni.

There is still more to the situation, for the universities surely would want maximum receipts and therefore would oppose underpriced tickets. But the "universities" also are nonprofit, nonprivate-property institutions, and so the *individuals* who make the decisions on this matter are acting in the absence of private-property rights. The university administrators of athletic affairs are like the Rose Bowl administrator. Thus, the same story is repeated, with each university substituting for the Rose Bowl Association. If there were conventional private-profit-seeking ownership of the funds received, this incentive to price tickets below the market-clearing level would be much weaker, if not eliminated.

OTHER NONPROFIT ASSOCIATIONS

Similar implications should prevail with, for example, the Los Angeles (San Francisco, Philadelphia, Chicago, or New York) Civic Light Opera Association, another *nonprofit* association. Again, there is the same reason for prices to be below market-clearing levels, especially for the best seats, since these are the types of seats that the patrons or trustees of the association will purchase. The question is whether the saving to them personally is worth the few thousand dollars of smaller profits for the association. Again, the principle is the same: ownership rights in the receipts are absent, so that the incentive to seek market-equilibrium prices is reduced.

Both examples are implied by the general law of demand. The lower the cost of nonmonetary sources of utility (as they are in these cases, in which receipts are not "owned" by the allocator), the more those sources of utility will be utilized. And further, the lower the money price to the buyer, the more he can be induced to make nonmonetary payments to the allocator as an alternative mode of competing for the scarce goods.

As these two examples illustrate, economic theory implies that with *attenu-*

ated private-property rights the role of money market prices as an allocative device is weakened. These examples suggest that private-property rights provide a powerful and possibly necessary factor for the most effective use of market prices. In strict logic, the analysis implies that only with private property will market prices behave as equilibrium prices. However, notice that the *law of demand* holds, no matter what the form of property right and regardless of the extent to which formal market exchange is used.

Despite our switch in the preceding chapters from utility maximizing to wealth maximizing and back to utility maximizing, we have been consistent. In first moving to wealth maximizing, we noted that we were going to treat wealth as a source of utility and act as though the activities that increased one's wealth did not in other respects reduce any other sources of utility. Thus, the act of selling or buying was not regarded as onerous or immoral, and hence no utility was lost. Now, in considering nonprivate-property versus private-property rights, we see that there are institutional arrangements (e.g., nonprofit institutions) that change the terms of trade between (1) money income, as one source of utility, and (2) nonmoney sources of utility, more of which can be obtained if exchanges for money are restricted.

Philanthropy

Charity or philanthropy totals to billions of dollars annually. Charitable foundations and colleges are two prime examples—not to mention religious groups and extensive individual gifts. Musical concerts, museums, libraries, and art galleries are open to the public at prices far below those that would clear the market, precisely because the sponsor wants to be charitable. The Ford and Rockefeller Foundations, to name but two of the largest, are supposed to give away wealth—not sell it to the highest bidders. Almost every college provides services at less than market-equilibrium prices, because they are supported by people who want to give lower-cost educational opportunities to young people. In all of these cases, because the price is below the market-clearing or equilibrium level, there is a long list of applicants from which selections must be made on some other competitive basis. What form of competition is used to clear the market? How will the results differ from those in which market-price competition is allowed to help ration the demand? Economic analysis will shed some light on that question—perhaps with some surprises.

The economics of philanthropy, charity, or gifts may at first seem a contradiction in terms. If, according to economic theory, people seek to increase their own utility, how then can they be assumed to give gifts? Are these acts to be set aside from economics as simply unexplainable behavior? Not at all. Remember that the postulates of economic theory do not say that man is concerned only about his own situation. He was permitted to be concerned about other people's situations also. If he knows other people who are miserable, he may not himself have as high a level of utility as if they were less miserable. Other people's situation as well as his own can affect *his* utility—which means that *his choices* of what he does with resources at his command can depend, in part at least, upon the effects of such choices not only directly upon himself but upon other people.

This is perfectly consistent with the postulates of economics. They did not rule out the possibility that improvements in one person's utility might contribute to another's utility. From my point of view, increased wealth for you is a "good" thing (a source of increase of utility to me); similarly, an increase in my wealth is a source of increased utility for me. It is possible that a $1 decrease in my wealth could reduce my utility by *less* than a $1 increase in *your* wealth would increase *my* utility. If that is so, then I will contribute wealth to you. The likelihood of this happening is greater if my wealth is large and yours is small. This is consistent with all our other statements about various goods and "consumption-substitution" rates between them. As my wealth decreases relative to yours, my willingness to contribute to you will decrease, just as a decreasing amount of candy might decrease my willingness to give up additional candy for Cokes.

But the ingenuity of man must not be underestimated. Even if I were unwilling to sacrifice $1 in order for *you* to have $1 more, you—the recipient of charity—might propose that for every dollar I gave you, you could also get $1 from someone else. A *matching grant* would induce me to give still more, because now I know that each dollar I give up gets you more than $1. This implies that "matching grants" should be commonly observed in charity. And they are.[1]

We turn now to probe a bit into the question of who gains what from a gift, where a gift is defined as an allocation at a price intentionally set below the open-market price by those "giving away" the goods.

We shall develop the analysis more formally and generally by means of the following example. Suppose that I own a house that would rent for $100 at the open-market price; however, I offer it to you for only $40. Whether I do this because the price is controlled or simply out of the goodness of my heart is irrelevant. In any event, when deciding to *whom* to rent it for $40, I must have used personal considerations, which would not have been weighted so heavily if I had rented it for $100.

Look at the resulting situation from your point of view. Suppose that you would not have paid the open-market price of $100 for this particular house, but instead would have been prepared to pay $80 for it. We now have three valuations: *A*—the cost and market value of the house ($100), *B*—the price at which you *would* have been willing to rent the house ($80), and *C*—the actual

[1] Income-tax reductions for gifts are another way to reduce the costs of giving money to other people.

price of the house to you ($40). We want one more item of information: How much would you have spent for housing if I hadn't made you this special offer? Your answer we shall suppose to be $65, denoted by D; that is, you would have chosen a smaller or more inferior house than the one that costs $100 and which I offer you for $40 per month.

The following relationships can now be specified. The difference between A and C $(A - C)$ is the total wealth transferred *from* me. The house cost $100, and I get only $40 for it. In this transfer of $60 of wealth from me, what did you get? First, compare what you did pay, $40, with what you would have paid for some house ($65) had I not provided you with this unusual opportunity. This difference $(D - C)$ is $65 — $40, or $25—a measure of how much money you have had released every month from housing purchases and which you may now use in any way you would like. We call this an increase in your "money" wealth, which is just like a gift of $25 to you. Hence, one effect of the wealth transfer is to increase your general wealth by the amount $(D - C) =$ $25. You have got, in the form of money, $25 of my $60 wealth transfer.

The quantity $(D - C)$ could be negative, indicating that more would be spent by the recipient on this kind of good than if the subsidy had not been offered. If the giver stands ready to supply all the good the recipient wants to buy at this lower price, C can exceed D. By having sufficiently lowered the price to the recipient, the donor has induced the recipient to buy more of this good and to consume less of other things. If, on the other hand, the donor had provided only a fixed amount of this good, an amount no greater than the buyer formerly bought, the purchase price of more would still be the old price. In this case the recipient certainly spends less than formerly; so $(D - C)$ is positive.

Second, compare the cost of whatever housing you would have bought had this special offer not been made available to you and what you would have been willing to pay for the particular house that I made available to you. This difference $(B - D)$ is, in our example, $80 — $65 = $15. Fifteen dollars is the value to you of the extra housing space that my action has made available to you. You now have $15 more of wealth in the form of housing than you otherwise would have had. So we can say that $15 of my $60 wealth transfer reaches you in the form of that *specific* transferred kind of good. Of course, we should also add whatever portion of the released general-money wealth ($25) you would spend on housing. Since this $25 is distributable over all your possible purchases, we assume that only a small portion goes to housing. In any event, although this correction should be made, we omit it here for expository simplicity, and continue in the awareness that the preceding $15 is therefore a slight underestimate of the housing gain.

Of the $60 wealth transfer, we have accounted for $25 as a *general* (money) wealth increase to you and $15 more of a particular *specific* resource, housing; that leaves $20 unaccounted for. As far as *you* are concerned, that extra $20 is simply wasted: you have acquired for $40 a house that you value not at

$100 but at only $80. Although I have borne a cost of $60, the gift is worth only $40 to you. From your point of view, if I had given you $80 in money and let you spend it as you wished, you would have been just as well off. This "waste" of $20 is the third component of the $60 gift.

Don't forget *my* point of view. Is there really a waste of $20? If I am fully aware of these implications, and nevertheless choose to make the particular gift that I do, then from my point of view it is worth a sacrifice of $60 ($100 — $40) to give you the gain of $25 in cash and $15 in superior housing. It is worth it either because I think you don't really know what is good for yourself and you are wrong in thinking the $20 a waste, or because even if I admit that the $20 is a waste from your point of view, your having the extra housing is worth more than $20 to me. For example, by inducing you to live in a house that costs $100 (but which you think is worth only $80), I put you in an environment that I prefer for you. If it improves the view from my house (because I look past yours) or for whatever reason I may think relevant, then from *my* point of view the extra $20 expenditure is not a waste.

From *my* point of view, I have paid $100 to subsidize you (a gift is a subsidy, and a subsidy is a gift) to the extent of $60, of which $25 is released to you as a general increase in your wealth (exactly the same as from your point of view). I have induced you to consume more housing than you otherwise would have (worth $15 to you—at a cost of $35 to me). It is up to *me* to say whether or not it is worth it to *me* to spend $60 to induce you to utilize more housing.

We can summarize: For *every* instance in which goods are transferred from me to you at a price less than the free-market exchange-equilibrium price:

- $(A - C)$ is the net total cost to me of the resources transferred to you;
- $(D - C)$ is the general-purchasing-power wealth transfer to you;
- $(B - D)$ is the value to *you* of the extra specific resources made available to you;
- $(A - B)$ is the waste, from your (the receiver's) point of view, but not necessarily from mine (the giver's);

where,

- A is the market value of the transferred goods.
- B is the hypothetical price which, if existing, would have induced you to buy the good.
- C is the amount actually paid by you.
- D is the money you would have paid for whatever amount of the transferred good you otherwise would have purchased.

We have not mentioned the impact that *opportunities* to capture subsidies or gifts will have on the behavior of potential receivers in an attempt to get the subsidies. Prospects of competitive applicants can be improved if they spend money to get in a more advantageous position, as judged by the allocative criteria used by the donor. And each applicant will be induced to spend an amount, at the most, equal to the value of the subsidy as valued by the potential recipient. We shall, however, take up this matter in more detail in the next section of this chapter.

FOREIGN AID

The United States government gives economic aid (gifts) to some foreign governments, ostensibly for specific purposes. If the U.S. government gives $10,000,000 to the Egyptian government to build a dam, what has Egypt gained? What would the Egyptians have done had no gift been given? Suppose they intended to build the dam anyway, financing it by domestic saving. To that extent, a gift for the dam releases wealth for the Egyptian government to spend on other things. The gift purportedly "for a dam" is actually for general purposes —the Egyptian government now simply has $10,000,000 more than it otherwise would have. Conceivably it could lower taxes—thus giving the Egyptians that much more income for general consumption, or the government itself will spend the extra funds.

Why, then, do we give the money "for a dam"? One possible answer is that otherwise they really would not have built the dam, so that the gift does provide one more dam. The embarrassing implication of this answer is that this particular use of the money for the dam is so unproductive that the Egyptian government itself wouldn't have paid for the dam. Or, if they were too poor to have done so, then a simple gift of $10,000,000 to the Egyptians with no strings attached for its use would have enabled the Egyptians themselves to decide what were the most valuable uses of the extra $10,000,000 of wealth made available. Of course, government officials of both the United States and Egypt are aware of all this, and the "conditional" form of the grant is employed primarily to try to induce the Egyptian government to behave more in accord with the interests of the U.S. government.

BUSINESS DINNER DANCES FOR EMPLOYEES

A business sponsors a dinner dance for employees, with tickets available to each employee at $6 per person. The cost of the dinner dance is $14 per person, but the company subsidizes $8 of the cost per person. Question: Who gains what by this company gift? Again, the general proposition is applicable. "To the extent that the gift provides what a recipient would have purchased anyway, an increase in general wealth is gained." Consider employee *A*, who would have spent $14 for dinner dancing anyway. What does he get? The difference between what he would have spent and the price he does pay is $8; so he gains an increase in general wealth of $8—exactly equal to the subsidy. Employee *B* would otherwise have spent as much as $9 for a dinner dance. This is $3 more than the ticket price. Of the $8 subsidy ($14 — $6), $3 ($9 — $6) is an increase in his general wealth, and the remaining $5 buys him more dinner-dance activity than he otherwise would have had. Hence, his gain from the subsidy is in two components: general wealth of $3 and better dinner-dance activity, costing $5 but worth in his opinion less than $5. Employee *C* would have spent, let us say, $6 and no more for dinner dances. He gets no gain in general wealth; all of the $8 gift is in the form of more elaborate dinner-dance activity. (We know, in addition, that he would rather have the $8 than the dinner-dance activity that is costing the company $8. We know this because he was not willing to pay $14 for the $14 dinner-dance ticket. He may think the company has spent $8 wastefully because he could think of better uses for that gift to him.) Finally, consider employee *D*. He would have otherwise spent nothing for dinner dancing, and he doesn't want to spend even $6 for a $14 ticket. Therefore, he buys none at all. What does he get? Nothing.

Question: If you were the owner of the company, what would you think of partially subsidized dinner dances as a scheme to aid the employees to have a good time? Which employees?

Reconsider employee *B*, who would have paid $9 for a dinner-dance ticket. Why doesn't he play it smart? Why doesn't he buy a ticket for $6 and then sell it to some outsider for $14, thereby making an $8 gain in money? This is better for him than the alternative gain of $3 in money and $5 more (in *cost*) of dinner-dance activity (which is worth less than that to him). He doesn't buy and resell the ticket because the company prohibits him from doing so, probably because it doesn't want outsiders at the dance. Then, why doesn't he resell the ticket to some other employee? There are two cases to consider in answering this. On the one hand, if the supply of tickets provided by the company at $6 is large enough to provide all that the employees want at that price, no employee will be able to resell his ticket for more than he paid for it. But if the supply of tickets is not large enough for the demand at $6, and if the company does not increase the price, the lucky employees who get tickets could resell them at a higher price and take their gift entirely as generalized money gains, rather than as less valued dinner-dance activity.

Would reselling to a fellow employee thwart the intent of the company? Did it want to encourage dinner dancing by employees? If so, allowing employees to resell will not reduce the number who attend. If the company wants more dinner dancing, it has to subsidize more tickets. The effect of resale is to break the connection between dinner dancing and gifts, thereby allowing others than those who dinner dance to get some gift. The company's policy may not have been to encourage dinner dancing, but instead merely to make gifts to employees. Which employees? Permitting resale would have given the gift to those who got in line first and would have enabled them to take as much of it in the form of a money gain as they could. If the company prohibited resale, the first ticket getters would still receive a gift, except that now they would have to take at least part of it in the form of dinner-dance activity. With resale prohibited, the gift goes to those who get on the reservation list early *and* who like dinner dancing enough to engage in the dinner dancing themselves.

The implications can be summarized in a proposition: Allocation of resources below market-clearing prices implies allocations to those who are willing to engage in certain kinds of activity.

FREE SCHOOL TRANSPORTATION

Children in some public-school districts are given free bus rides to school. From this gift (subsidy) of bus rides to school children, who gains what? The answer should now be easy. The parents of the children must be classed according to those who would have purchased or provided transportation for their children and those who would have made their children walk. The first group receive all the subsidy as a general increase in their wealth. They can buy more of all things with the wealth which otherwise would have paid for their children's transportation. The other parents get no gain in general wealth, but take it all in the form of better transportation for the children. "Free bus rides" for school children turn out then to be composites of gifts of wealth to parents and of better transportation for children, with some families getting all of it in general wealth, some in mixtures, and some exclusively in transportation.

The corollary of our general proposition says that gifts might as well be resalable or given as money by the donors to the extent that the recipients already possess or use the services or resources given to them. If I am given a case of Coca-Cola each month by some kind-hearted person who thinks he is inducing me to drink more Cokes, he should note that already my family consumes a case a month. Therefore, I shall stop buying Cokes from the store and use the released wealth for other purposes. Whether he gives me Cokes (whether or not he lets me sell them) or gives me money is essentially irrelevant.

UNINTENTIONAL CHARITY

Intentional and unintentional gifts cannot always be distinguished. Nor, as we shall see, can we conclude that every allocation of resources made at less than a market-clearing price, even at a price as low as zero, involves a gift. Some gifts apparently occur *without* the intent of a gift. Fortunately, however, knowledge of intent is not necessary to discern what does in fact happen when market-clearing prices are not used for allocation.

Currently, if anyone wants to communicate or transmit by television, he must first obtain permission from the Federal Communications Commission

(FCC). Rights to transmit television programs—to operate a station—are valuable, and many applicants appeal to the FCC for authorization to operate a station in various cities on the as yet unassigned channels.[2] It is no wonder that in making his application, each applicant will try to show why he is just the proper person to get that right. How does an applicant show that he is the most deserving person? In sales of government-owned forests and oil lands, the right person is the one who will bid the most, with the proceeds going to the public treasuries. But the law creating the FCC forbids it to allocate channels on the basis of competitive prices. Nor is "first come, first served" the rule (although it was for radio in the early 1920s). Instead, the commission must "examine" the applicants and then in some manner decide which ones shall be assigned the right to broadcast television programs.

The applicant must show why the community "needs" another station—despite the protestations of the existing station owner, who proclaims that no more service is needed (and whose television station's value would fall if a new station were authorized). Once it is decided to authorize a new station, each applicant tries to appear as the applicant who best fulfills the commission's criteria of selection. Because there is no money-price competition of the open-marketplace variety, the competition in other attributes takes on even more significance and fierceness. Applicants pour money into a presentation of why they are the most "qualified" persons. Money that would have been paid to the government under price competition for that right or "property" will instead be devoted, at least in part, to "persuading" the commissioners. Since something worth millions is at stake, millions are spent in an effort to get the license.

On what criteria does the FCC decide who shall get these valuable rights? That, of course, is what the various applicants would like to know. They do know, however, that the applicant should be a man of respectability, good moral standing, public service, and high education (so that anyone now owning liquor stores or who has three ex-wives or has only a high-school degree had better think twice before spending much on lawyers, public-relations experts, and others to prepare his application). If he is a newspaper publisher or a radio-station operator, he has an advantage; for he is experienced in news collecting and dissemination. If he doesn't like to put on religious programs, if he likes only jazz and Western shows and intends to program few if any "cultural" programs, he will lose rank. He must detect the preferences, tastes, and kinds of shows that the commissioners think the public ought to be shown; then he must suggest that he will present that kind of program. If he lives outside of the town in which he proposes to operate a station, he will have to explain how he can still manage the station adequately. He must be careful not to offer explicit, de-

[2] The number of channels that could be used at one time is not a fixed technological fact. It depends upon the kind of receiving and transmitting equipment. With more expensive and sensitive receivers and transmitters, the number of available channels could be greatly increased.

tectable bribes to the commissioners, for that will embarrass them. On the other hand, if in the past he hired some of the FCC technical staff to operate his other radio or television stations, this indicates that he is the kind of person who recognizes able people when he sees them, and that he therefore must be the type of person who could successfully operate a television station. All the value of the rights to broadcast accrue neither to the federal taxpayers nor to the winning applicant; instead, part is consumed in legal fees, costs of publicity, and other expenses incurred to win the competition for the license. Thus, even though the nominal price of the license is zero, the costs of getting it are substantial—not to mention the costs of the losers' efforts.

The magnitude of the gift is suggested in the fact that the stock prices of companies jump when they receive a license to operate a station. Fortunately for the owners, this wealth gain *is* transferable; they can sell that stock to other people so they need not keep their gift in the form of enjoyment of ownership and operation of a television station. That increase in the value of the stock is in part a measure of the net value of the wealth given away by the federal taxpayers. Was it the intention of the government to make a gift? Presumably it is recognized that a gift (in some form to someone) is involved, but evidently the *motivation* of this rationing procedure is to "safeguard" the public and help to provide to the public what is "good" for it.

The preceding illustration does not imply that the Federal Communications Commission acts irresponsibly. The commissioners act just as anyone else would act in the same situation. The situation is different from a market process and hence seems peculiar only to one who thinks solely in terms of allocation of resources by market prices in a private-property context. Without judging the merits of the current allocative system for television stations, the present analysis reveals that in line with the implications of events in the absence of market-clearing prices, intentionally or not, gifts are involved. The form of the gifts and the conditions determining who gets them and the extent to which they can be converted to generalized wealth can be ascertained by an analysis of the pertinent circumstances.

More examples could be investigated. Market-clearing prices are not used initially to allocate licenses to operate (a) passenger airplanes between certain cities in scheduled passenger service, (b) liquor stores (in many states), (c) taxis (most cities), and (d) banks (most states), but these rights are salable once they have been initially allocated. For example, the right to operate one taxi in New York City sells for about $20,000 (which at 6 percent is worth $1,200 income per year in perpetuity). The preceding analysis is applicable to all these cases and many more that could be mentioned. The student is advised to apply the analysis to each case to see whether he can detect who gets what gain under what conditions.

We now inspect a second class of possibly unintended gifts where the allocated goods *cannot be resold* after they are initially allocated. Rights to enter college, obtain a medical training, enter the United States, join some unions, adopt a child, play golf on a publicly owned golf course, camp in a national park—these rights often are allocated at zero prices or at prices below those which would clear the market. (Consequently, there are "shortages" and allocation by methods discussed in the earlier examples.) Whether or not the allocated item is subsequently resalable at free-market prices does not destroy the fact of gift. However, that can affect the extent to which the gift can be realized as an increase in the recipient's general wealth, instead of only as a gain in a particular kind of good. For example, when a municipally owned golf course underprices its services and has a waiting list and "shortage" of playing space, those "lucky" enough to get access receive a gain—if they haven't had to pay other costs to get on the reservation list.

Nothing in economic analysis warrants the judgment that these allocative methods are good or bad; such a judgment must be based on criteria derived from other sources. But economic analysis does expose an error in a commonly advanced defense of these allocative methods. Sometimes it is contended that the open-market price is being deliberately bypassed in order to help the poor people. But if it is really desirable to help the poorer people at the expense of the richer, it is pertinent to consider (1) whether this allocative method helps the poor people in general to acquire a greater share for whatever use they deem most appropriate, or (2) whether it helps only those poor (and rich) people who can succeed in the more limited kinds of competition that are fostered in enhancing one's prospects of getting more of this *particular good*. Whichever objective you may think is preferred, if any, the fact is that only the second one is achieved.

Questions

1. Distinguish between the law of demand and the law of price that equates supply and demand. Which holds more generally?

2. "A diamond ring selling for $10,000 is an example of high negotiation costs." True or false?

3. If a cheap enough method could be invented for metering the extent to which each motorist uses a street, would use of streets be rationed more with a price system? Do you know of any such cases now in use? Name two.

4. Explain how the coin vending machine, by reducing the cost of exchange, has increased the extent to which resources are allocated by exchange.

5. Churches are typically nonprofit institutions. Can you think of a problem in allocation of church facilities that is solved without use of the price system?

6. The college you now attend is almost certainly a not-for-profit institution. Are any of its resources allocated at less than market-clearing prices? (Hint: Library facilities? Athletic facilities? Counseling? Course admission? Campus space?)

7. "To the extent that nonprofit private institutions do not use the price-exchange system to allocate resources, they are operated inefficiently." True or False? Explain.

8. News item: "Lake Crowley's rental boats were put on the block for opening day of trout season. Here are the three simple rules which must be followed by applicants for boat rental: (1) Letters must be postmarked after midnight, March 17. (2) Letters must be clearly marked on the outside, "Boat Rental." No unmarked letter will be considered. (3) Checks covering the full amount of the rental for the number of days requested must be included with the application for reservation. The fee for boats is $4 per day. Approximately seventy boats will be available, and every effort will be made to allocate them on a first-come, first-served basis."

Who do you think owns the lake and the boats? Why do you think so?

9. Camping fees in almost all state and national parks are so low that people want more space than is available.

a. Why is the market price not at a market-clearing level?

b. How much space would people want at a market-clearing price?

10. Government-owned housing is typically rented below the market-clearing price.

a. Is this a result of deliberate aid to those who live there, or is it a result of non-private ownership?

b. Regardless of the answer to (a), who gains what?

c. Would you classify this as intentional or unintentional charity?

11. In Los Angeles two golf courses, one privately owned and one publicly owned, are near each other and both are open to the public.

a. Which do you think charges the higher price of play, and which one do you think requires less or no advance reservation? Give reasons for your prediction.

b. Who is benefited in what respects by each golf course's policy?

c. As land values rise around the course, which one do you think will first be converted to housing or business? Why?

12. The U.S. Food Stamp plan is a system whereby poorer people are permitted to buy certain foods deemed to be in surplus supply at "low" prices—with the difference being made up by government payments to the seller of the food. Who gains what? Who loses what?

13. There are reputed to be over 100,000 voluntary health and welfare organizations soliciting contributions from the general public, in addition to hundreds of individual hospital-support groups, as well as about 100,000 fraternal, civic, and veteran's organizations and 300,000 churches which sponsor a variety of charitable activities, not to mention individual charities or gifts. A professor of public-health administration says, "It should not take over 100,000 voluntary agencies to provide private health and welfare services in the U.S." How many do you think it should take? Why?

14. "Charity in any form other than money always involves a 'waste.'" Does it follow that nonmoney charity is undesirable?

15. The *New York Times* sponsors a charity appeal each Christmas and gives cash gifts to selected poorer families. The *Los Angeles Times* sponsors a charity appeal each summer to send children of poorer families to summer camp. If you had your choice of contributing to these forms of charity, to which would you contribute more? Why? Do you think people who choose the other way are mistaken?

16. In early 1950 many public-welfare and charitable aid organizations refused to give aid to poorer families that owned a television set—no matter how poor the family might be. The welfare workers claimed they were not supposed to finance luxury. What would have been your policy if you were dispensing the aid?

17. Suppose you are running a university and the faculty is asking for higher salaries, some of which you will have to grant at the sacrifice of buildings and other alternative activities. Now, the Ford Foundation gives you $1,000,000, the income of which is to be allocated exclusively to faculty salaries. Who gains what?

18. States collect taxes from cities to help pay for education in the rural districts. The federal government is being urged to levy taxes and then to redistribute the proceeds to states to aid education. Under these systems, who gains what? Who loses what?

19. A parent spends 50 cents for his child's school lunch. Subsequently, the school initiates a low-cost subsidized school lunch program, so that now the parent spends only 40 cents for the same lunch.

a. Who gains what?

b. Suppose the new lunch is a better one that costs 60 cents but is provided at a subsidized price of 40 cents. Who gains what?

c. Suppose the school lunch is still better and costs 75 cents and is sold to students for 55 cents, so that the parent who formerly spent 50 cents now gives his child 55 cents to buy the bigger lunch. Who gains what?

20. Let your current college education involve a true annual cost of $1,000, of which you are required to pay $200, and for which you would have been willing to pay $700. If you had to pay the full costs of $1,000, you would not have purchased your present level of education; instead, you would have purchased a lower level of training costing $400.

a. What do you gain by being able to get the $1,000 education for $200?

b. If the above quantities refer to the amount your parents are willing to spend for your tuition, who gains what?

21. University faculty often apply to "foundations" for grants of money to finance travel expenses for trips to Europe to help pursue some "study." Grants are usually awarded for the payment of travel but not for food, recreation, or the family. In fact, what does the "grant" subsidize?

22. Students are awarded fellowships to finance college tuition. In fact, who gains what by such grants?

23. Some colleges charge high tuitions, but at the same time they give a large number of tuition fellowships ranging from full tuition payment down to practically nothing. If you apply the principles of discriminatory-pricing techniques of an earlier chapter, can you show that tuition grants are a form of discriminatory pricing of education? Does that make them undesirable?

24. Who gains what from the availability of "free" parking space in an area where parking space is an economic good?

25. The faculty of many colleges are given free parking space even in areas where parking space is not a "free good."

a. Who gains what?

b. What would be the effect if the faculty could sell their space to students?

26. Publishers usually give faculty members 15 percent discounts. Ignoring the reason for doing so, what do the faculty or their families gain?

27. In the state of Washington rights to kill some kinds of deer are periodically allocated by a lottery.

a. Why aren't rights sold to highest bidders?

b. Who gains what under the present system, and who loses what?

28. The state of Washington permits a person to collect twenty-four razor clams a day from its beaches.

a. Why is the right to collect clams given free, and why does the state limit the number to twenty-four instead of permitting more if a higher fee is paid?

b. Who gains what under the present system?

29. Immigration-quota rights to the United States are priced at "zero" instead of being sold at a market-clearing price to "acceptable" types of people. Who gains what? Why are these rights not sold at the highest price to acceptable people?

30. In 1963 the right of Northeast Airlines to offer commercial air service between New York City and Miami was rescinded by decision of the Civil Aeronautical Board, the U.S. government agency that allocates such rights.

a. What do you think happened to the value of the stock of Northeast Airlines upon news of that decision?

b. At the same time the price of the common stock of two other airlines remaining in service on that route, Eastern and National Airlines, jumped about 25 percent. Why was Northeast Airlines not allowed to sell its right to that route to National and to Eastern instead of having the right taken away from it?

c. Who gained what by the decision to take that right away from Northeast Airlines and let National and Eastern remain as the two carriers?

d. As a final twist, after losing that right, Northeast Airlines reverted to a status of a "local-regional" airline, serving now only the New England area and as such became entitled to federal subsidies to help cover its costs. Who lost what by the transfer of flight rights being accomplished by authority rather than by sale to other airlines?

31. In some states, the government, when disposing of its property, sells the property at auction to the highest bidder. In many states, the right to form and operate a bank, a liquor store, a race track, or a savings and loan bank is not sold at auction to the highest bidder among a set of "acceptable" businessmen. Instead, the "winner" is selected by a board, much as judges choose the winner in a beauty contest.

a. What is your explanation for not letting the highest bidder win?

b. Who gains what?

c. Which system do you think increases the wealth of lawyers? Of the politicians?

d. Explain why such a system of controlled entry is conducive to creating a strong political lobbying group.

32. In California the cost incurred by the winner of a competition for the right to form and operate a new savings and loan bank is about $50,000 to $100,000.

a. What kinds of activities do you think are paid for by that cost?

b. How could much of that be diverted to other uses?

c. Why would a group be willing to pay that amount for the right to enter, as distinct from investing in, the business?

d. Do you think this industry is a strong political lobby group? Why?

33. "Californians are crazy. Near a beautiful California beach, there is a luxurious motel and a state-owned camping area. Despite the greater luxury of the motel facilities, scores of cars are lined up for hours each morning seeking camping sites, whereas at the motel there is hardly a day that rooms are all taken. This shows that Californians prefer outdoor, dusty camps to the luxuries of a motel with pool, TV, room service, and private bath." Do you agree? Explain.

34. "Economic theory is applicable only to a capitalist society." Evaluate.

13

COLLUSION AMONG BUYERS

Not all buyers or sellers compete independently. Some coordinate their bids or offers to keep prices down or up. The success of buyers in keeping prices below the market-clearing demand-and-supply intersection is evidenced by queues, shortages, and nonprice rationing criteria. Prices can be below the intersection in the absence of any of the institutional circumstances discussed in the preceding chapters. The large potential gain from successful collusion among buyers on the one hand, or among sellers on the other hand, is a persistent force inducing them to seek to collude. From this observation it is then sometimes concluded that competitive open markets would be undermined unless there were laws against collusions.

In this chapter we shall apply economic analysis to test the logic of this conclusion. We shall investigate the incentive and the obstacles to successful collusions among buyers, leaving sellers for a later chapter after we have investigated production conditions. We shall see that although many attempts are made to collude, the obstacles are formidable, even in the absence of legal prohibitions against collusions. As we shall see, some effective and significantly successful collusions are supported by government sanctions that penalize those who refuse to obey the conditions of the collusive agreement. In fact, in a capitalist open-market system, successful and effective collusions may be trivial without government support or aid. It may be surprising that governments should support collusive agreements while laws exist against collusions, but governments have strong reasons for aiding collusion and closing markets to those who will not act in accord with the collusion. (Later, in Chapter 25, we shall see what some of these are.)

Buyers' Incentives to Seek Effective Collusion

Buyers like a lower price as long as they can get the amount they want at that price. And even if they can't, they may prefer to get *some* at that low price rather than pay a higher price for the privilege of getting all they want at the higher price. For example, suppose that (a) the price of Cokes is 10 cents and that at that price I can get as many as I want, 30 per month. On the other hand, suppose that (b) the price of Coke is kept down to 5 cents by an agreement among buyers not to bid more. At that price I want 60 per month. Will I be able to get them? No, for the supply is no greater. How many will I be able to get? As we know from earlier considerations, I may still get the 30 I used to get at 10 cents each or I may get more or less, depending upon the relatively greater influence of the other nonmonetary factors I can offer the seller. Of course, if the buyers could still get the amount they used to get at 10 cents, it would clearly be better for them if they could keep the price down to 5 cents. But since they will not get the same amount as formerly, they will have to decide who will now get how many Cokes before they can reach a collusive agreement. We now begin to see what some of these obstacles are and how they might be overcome.

Obstacles to Successful Price Collusion

Each buyer will claim that others are getting more than their "fair" share, or more than they "deserve," and that he should get more. Even if every member were getting the same number of Cokes, some would claim that because they have bigger families or are younger or because of some other consideration they "ought" to have more than they are now getting. Whether or not they make a big fuss depends upon how susceptible other members are to nagging, threats, and complaints, and how costly such activities are—and also upon how much difference in utility or wealth the extra Cokes will make. If a raw material required in a business is involved, instead of merely Cokes, one's major source of wealth may be at stake. Then the complaints are strong.

This conflict and difference of opinion is implied by the postulates: People are not identical; not all of them regard equal sharing as "correct," so that there is the inevitable problem of an "equitable" division of the supply among the eager buyers. Attempts to form collusive price agreements often flounder on this rock; although the buyers all desire a lower price, they often disagree about how much lower the price should be and how the supply available at that price should be allocated. The more buyers who must be included in the agreement about price and shares, a greater variety of situations must be reconciled, the greater the source of disputes, and the higher the costs of policing the agreement.

Imagine that somehow these enormous problems are resolved, so that agreement is reached under which each buyer feels he will be better off with an effective price collusion than without one. But agreement is *not* reached once and for all. Every day the colluding group must continue to keep all the members placated with their shares and convinced that they should continue to collude to keep prices down. This placating may involve more costs and loss of utility than are gained by the lower price. There may have been long discussions and meetings to arrange for a compromise and settlement of all these allocative conflicts, and such an agreement may actually be reached, but on the very next day some of the participants may immediately break it with *secret* violations because *enforcement* is ineffective.

So a second problem—one that must be solved continuously—becomes apparent. It will always be in the interest of *every* member to violate the agreement *secretly* by offering a slightly higher price for Cokes in order to get more than his collusive share. How can the group supervise *all* the sales of *every one* of its members? How can it police the collusion? How can it make sure that each member is ethical in observing the gentlemen's agreement or the code of proper behavior? How can it detect chiselers; rotten apples; dishonest, unethical, and unreliable members? An effective collusion provides for access to each member's records to discover what he is doing. Spies, agents, or commissioners representing the collusion must constantly inspect the activities and books of each member.

Even if the costs of detecting such behavior are worth bearing, can errant members be punished without destroying the collusion? If punished too severely, they will find it preferable to leave the collusion rather than pay, thus wrecking the whole scheme. If each violator is not punished enough to make secret evasions a losing proposition, secret evasions will flourish and destroy the collusion. Exhorting each member not to break the agreement is insufficient. Although *every* member really wants every *other* member to abide by the rules, it still pays every member secretly to break the agreement. The greater the gains from secret violations, the greater the temptation to break it; hence, the greater the costs of enforcing the agreement. Incidentally, if the gains from secret violations are very large, it may pay each to try to reach an agreement simply in the hope that he can secretly (and he hopes *alone*) violate the agreement.

There is yet a third bar to effective collusion—a sort of parasitic disease. Not all buyers of the product can be cheaply induced to join the collusion. If anyone is left out, he will reap the advantage of the lower price at which *he* can get all *he* wants, because an outsider merely has to beat the collusion's price by a wee bit to drain the supply away from the colluders. The wealth advantage of openly staying outside an effective collusion is enormous. But outsiders tend to kill the collusion.

Finally, even if every present buyer were induced to join an effective price collusion, *new* buyers would be attracted by the profits of the lower price. And the greater the effectiveness of the collusion in reducing price, the greater the incentive to new buyers to enter the market and take away the existing supply.

Should the buyers succeed in pushing the price down, they must be prepared to face the seller's decision to reduce production of the particular item. But for the present we are analyzing the incentives and obstacles to buyers' collusions, on the temporary supposition that the supply will not be eliminated or reduced as a consequence. None of the mentioned hazards or flaws to a collusion depends upon the sellers' responses. We have assumed that the sellers passively allow the collusion to occur and merely respond to the blandishments and inducements by members for secret favorable treatment. However, one can readily see how an aggressive seller could solicit secret payments for special favors to certain members, especially to those who have least to gain by staying in the collusion and most to gain by secret violations.

In summary, there may be a great deal of activity among competing buyers *seeking* to reach collusive price agreements, to agree on shares, and to find methods of enforcing the collusive agreement against secret violations. But the road to a successful collusion is beset by obstacles created by the buyers themselves, not even counting the protective action of sellers. First, the members must constantly be resolving the conflict of interests among themselves, all of whom want more at the low price. The collusion merely shifts the conflict of interest from the marketplace, where the allocation problem can be solved more impersonally by prices, into the clublike atmosphere of meetings and discussions of the colluding buyers, where it will be solved more personally, with recriminations and ill feelings. Secondly, the inducement to secret violations increases as price is lowered. And detection of violations is expensive, conjectural, and incomplete. Third, penalties must be imposed to dissuade "cheating" without persuading subsequent departure from the collusion. Fourth, outsiders will benefit from the collusion and attract supply away from the colluding buyers. Fifth, if there are no outsiders initially, the lower price will attract them. If kept out, they erode the collusion's effectiveness; if allowed to enter, they reduce the supply of the good to each of the incumbent members.

We cannot conclude, therefore, that large potential gains from collusion for lower than market-clearing prices will induce effective collusion. The costs of collusion—costs resulting from natural economic behavior, and not only from special laws—are heavy. In addition, collusion contains self-destructive forces—sometimes so strong as to prevent a collusive agreement from even being sought by the various buyers. Consequently, *successful* collusion to keep down prices is probably uncommon.[1]

Successful Price Collusions

The following cases provide some understanding of how obstacles to successful price collusion can be overcome. Two cases have a remarkable and unusual longevity. One is the hospitals' practice of paying low salaries to interns, and the other is the colleges' practice of paying low salaries to student football players. Perhaps even more remarkable is the general opinion that both practices are desirable.

HOSPITAL INTERNS

Compulsory licensing in all the states is a prerequisite to practicing as a doctor, with the American Medical Association or its members being the legal administrator of the licensing law. Also, membership in the American Medical Association is, for all intents and purposes, necessary if a doctor is to realize the greater income available from practice in a first-class hospital (other than at a medical school). Now suppose that the association, in order to keep down medical or hospital costs or permit higher profits, were to restrain the hospitals from paying more than $300 a month for interns, whereas with open competition among hospitals the rate would be higher—say, $500 a month. Any hospital that violated the agreement could be punished by having its "class-A" certification withdrawn or its doctors expelled from the medical association if they continued to practice at the "unethical" "non-class-A" hospital. The power to *enforce* the price agreement is now established. The gains from secret violation are small in comparison to the possible punishment, and secret violations will very likely be detected.

Notice how all the hazards and obstacles mentioned earlier have been conquered. All the buyers (class-A hospitals) of this service (interns) are forced into the agreement. Outsiders can be killed with a *state-enforced* power of licensing or certifying hospitals and doctors. The organization (the American Medical Association) wielding the power to enforce the price collusion was formed not simply to keep interns' wages down, but for other more valuable purposes, so that denial of membership means a greater loss of wealth than is to

[1] A most spectacular and well-publicized case of successful collusion is that among the *sellers* of heavy electrical generating and switching equipment to the *government* or government-regulated firms. The reasons these agreements were successful will be examined in a later chapter on *sellers'* collusions. Suffice it to say here that this case does not refute anything stated in this chapter.

be gained by violating the intern wage agreement. Private persuasion of recalcitrants or of secret violators to stop violations is made effective by the laws giving to the organization the control of certification of hospitals and licensing of doctors.

One conclusion stands out: It is sufficient to get the power of the *law* on the side of the collusive organization so that persons who do not agree to abide by the price collusion can be *legally* prohibited from buying any of the "service" at all, at any price. Without this *legal* constraint, secret violators could go their way, independently taking advantage of the price agreement by paying slightly more and getting a larger supply.

COLLEGE FOOTBALL PLAYERS

An effective collusion with which college students are relatively familiar is the collusion by colleges to hold down wages of college football players. Not long after intercollegiate football games became a substantial source of income to many colleges, the best football players were being sought with money inducements—hereafter called "wages" in our discussion. Some college administrators were opposed to any money payments to athletes, because that was professionalism, and they believed amateurism had some inherent virtue or that a professional would be attending college only to play football. (Of course, today colleges have departments for physical education in which football players can major and retain status as bona fide students.) Other administrators, with an eye on the football profits, were dismayed that the wage competition among schools was reducing profits.

Without worrying about which of these motivations dominated, it is easy to see that both gave a strong inducement for college administrators to seek to curtail wages for the student football players. An agreement among the colleges to pay no wages was reached; but, not surprisingly, it broke down as colleges switched to offers of athletic fellowships, free food and board, travel to college, sinecures, easy jobs for relatives, free clothes, etc. These other methods of competition were also brought under a general ban, but this agreement could be obtained only by permitting wages up to $2 an hour; for not all colleges could be induced to refrain from making offers. At identical offers, the most distinguished colleges would get the best football players, while the less distinguished colleges would be left with the poorer players. With uniform offers, the incentive was stronger for the less distinguished colleges in metropolitan areas (with large potential gate receipts) to resort to covert offers, and they did so more than the distinguished colleges—as evidenced by the frequency with which their violations were detected and punished. Choosing from hundreds of examples, two Southern California colleges were caught violating the code. They were punished with $100,000 fines and prohibited from playing in post-season (the most profitable) Bowl games. Even the tennis, basketball, track, and baseball teams—members of which had received no "unethical" payments—also were banned from national tournaments.

Why did these colleges agree to pay fines and accept the punishment? How could the collusion to restrict wages survive in the face of the great advantages of "cheating," especially when colleges that stayed outside the agreement could get the better football players at just slightly higher wages than the artificially low wages that the rest were maintaining? Why would all the colleges agree to observe this collusion most of the time? After all, if all existing television and radio networks tried to suppress performers' wages, other networks could profitably be organized to take advantage of the reduced wages. Somehow newcomers must be induced to agree to the terms of the collusive agreement as a condition of operating at all. The National Professional Football League tried this trick but soon found itself faced with two other leagues that wouldn't abide by its pay scales. Similarly, the National Baseball League was faced with a new American League. How, then, did the colleges prevent the formation of new leagues of college football? Or, to put the question in more analytic terms, what rewards or advantages of membership in the collusion are greater than the advantages obtainable by not belonging? If the advantages of membership are greater than the gains from breaking the agreement or not even belonging to the agreement, then membership cancelation can be effective in enforcing the terms of the agreement—on the assumption that violations can be detected without prohibitive detection costs. (In this connection it is interesting that the various athletic conferences—all members of the collusion—hired private detectives and investigators to spy on recruiting activities of students, coaches, and alumni.)

The answer can be found in the fact that prior to the time of the rise of collusion all the colleges belonged to the National Collegiate Athletic Association (NCAA) or to related associations. These conferences supervised the rules of the games. When the collusive wage agreement was formulated, the NCAA then acted as the supreme authority in assessing fines and punishment. But, more important, it indicated that any college placed on probation or expelled for violations of the athletic "code" would find its academic accreditation threatened. The colleges that belonged to the NCAA would support actions of the college-accreditation group—composed of these same colleges that were in the NCAA—to place violators of the athletic wage code on probation or to expell them. Any college placed on probation or expelled would find it much more expensive to recruit faculty, and students would be dissuaded from attending. (Even Phi Beta Kappa refused to authorize chapters at colleges that gave "disproportionate" amounts of money to athletic scholarships, regardless of the academic qualities of the college.) In sum, expulsion from NCAA or its related organizations would mean not merely loss of intercollegiate athletics; it would mean loss of academic standing. The survival of the college could be threatened.

But we can't stop here. After all, why don't some colleges that want to hire football players form their own accreditation group? Why does the present accreditation group have so much power that it can prevent formation of new colleges with their own accreditation system? A very important reason is that colleges do not operate on a self-supporting basis. The profits from football are not enough to offset the losses from the low tuition fees at state or endowed colleges. A new college could not expect to survive from football profits if it had to charge competitive tuition to students. No new school could get subsidies from the state or major philanthropic foundations without recognition by the present accreditation group—which is powerful in influencing the government and the foundations. We have finally arrived at the source of the value of membership in the NCAA and related organizations: subsidized education. Since the value of the subsidy exceeds the potential football profits, and since control over the subsidy lies partly in the hands of the NCAA via influence on accreditation, the wrath of the NCAA can mean the difference between a college's life or death. We emphasize that the NCAA was not created to restrict pay of football players. It was set up for other purposes, but once its greater value for these other purposes could be denied to a nonmember, it became the enforcement agency for various rules against certain kinds of competition.

This and the preceding chapter investigated allocations of goods and resources in contexts other than the demand and supply market-equilibrium price. In the preceding chapter, we saw that the costs or incentives prevented price from being at the equilibrium level that would be implied by the analysis of still earlier chapters. Yet that demand-and-supply analysis could be used without implying that the allocative price was set as in the price-takers' markets at the intersection of demand and supply. Again, use of demand-and-supply analysis did not imply that the allocative price was set as in the price-searchers' market at the clearing price, where no buyer was willing to offer a higher price to get more than he was then getting, and no seller was willing to take a lower price in order to sell more. In the preceding chapter, buyers were willing to offer a higher price to get more, but for some reasons (which we investigated) the sellers would not or could not be brought into an agreement or contract to take a higher price as an inducement to give the higher bidder a greater amount of the good being allocated. In this chapter we analyzed cases where buyers successfully managed to enforce a self-imposed agreement not to bid up price in order to get the available supply from the sellers at less than a market-clearing price. The situations analyzed in these last two chapters are often regarded as examples of defects in the market or capitalist system. In fact, they are neither defects nor imperfections of a market system nor characteristics of capitalism. They simply are consequences or attributes of different types of property rights, institutions, or costs of keeping track of goods. Some are consequences of certain laws and public policy, but that does not necessarily make them good or bad, for economic analysis cannot reveal whether these consequences were the desired or possibly undesired side effects.

Questions

1. When the supply of a commodity such as coffee decreases, and prices rise, some housewives propose to initiate a buyers' strike. That is, they propose to buy no coffee in order to drive the price down.

a. Would you advise your wife or only other wives to join?

b. If the strike is successful, which housewives gain?

c. What gain goes to the housewives who strike?

2. Suppose Harvard, Stanford, Notre Dame, Southern California, Miami, and Chico State College agreed not to pay any football player over $1,000 for a year's football service.

a. Which of the mentioned colleges do you think would have an advantage in attracting better football players at that wage? Why?

b. Suppose that the colleges agreed that graduate students serving as teaching assistants should not be paid more than $500 per year. Which college would be least hurt by that agreement?

3. The University of California, whose current president is a distinguished labor economist and arbitrator, has an agreement with other colleges in California that none of them will recruit or negotiate with faculty men from another college without first notifying and getting the approval of the president of his college.

a. Does this kind of buyers' collusion help *all* the colleges in California?

b. Do you think it is effective in restraining competition among buyers?

c. What do you suppose would be the legal status of such an agreement if made among the private movie producers of California?

d. Do you think all private employers would be willing to enter into and abide by such an agreement even if there were no law against it?

e. Why can colleges legally make such an agreement?

f. Do you think the form of ownership of the colleges, which are *not*-for-profit institutions, has anything to do with the possibility of reaching such agreement?

4. The president of Stanford University stated that it is improper for a university to condone dishonorable conduct by its students in enticing or permitting them to accept money for playing football at above the wages sanctioned by the accepted athletic conference "code."

a. Do you think a "code," which is an agreement among prospective employers not to pay competitive wages, is an honorable kind of code and that it is dishonorable to break it?

b. If General Electric and Westinghouse agreed not to pay competitive wages to engineers and tried to avoid *money-wage* competition with each other in the open market for you as an engineer, would you feel dishonorable in accepting money wages from one of them at above the wage specified in the collusive agreement?

c. How about other kinds of favors?

d. Is the situation different when colleges make such agreement not to compete? Why?

5. a. Could you interpret the military draft as a buyers' collusion among the majority of the voters of the United States against the young men of military-service age? How?

b. Or as a collusion by parents of girls against parents of men?

6. a. Could you interpret the laws against explicit buying of votes as a collusion among the major political parties?

b. When a politician promises to pass a law giving you more education, or a subsidy, is he buying your vote with someone else's money?

c. Reconcile that with the illegality of explicit purchase of votes.

7. Do you know of any successful collusions among buyers that effectively keep down the price of what they are buying—and are not supported by legal sanctions against anyone who violates the terms of the agreement?

8. a. Would you prefer to have gasoline prices cut 25 percent and get what gasoline you can by waiting in line or waiting on reservation lists, or would you prefer to pay the market-clearing price?

b. How did you make your decision?

9. You and all the other customers of the local dairies agree to tell the milk dairies that hereafter you will pay only 80 percent of what you formerly paid. Suppose the agreement is 100 percent effective and price is cut to 80 percent. (To concentrate attention on the allocation problem, let us assume that the milk producers have no alternative work to which they could turn and that they produce just as much milk as ever.)

a. What problems will still have to be solved by you and your neighbors?

b. Might these be sufficient to break up the coalition?

10. If wages of interns are held down below open-market levels, is it not possible that the high income they will earn later as practicing doctors is only partly an offset to that earlier low income—so that, on net, young men now entering the profession of medicine will not have more income over their lifetime than do those in other professions?

11. Do all-Americans or the less able players suffer more from the athletic code restricting football salaries in colleges?

12. "A high school athlete cannot be visited by a college football coach and asked to go to that coach's college. A high school student, upon deciding to attend a certain college (in view of what they offer him), must sign a "letter of intent" to attend; if—before the school year starts, or even before getting any of the compensation offered for the letter of intent—he changes his mind and decides to go to some other college, he will not be allowed to play football. Furthermore, any student transferring from one college to another loses a year of athletic eligibility." Why are these rules applied to athletes when they are not applied to members of the debate team, band, college newspaper, or honor students?

14

ALLOCATION OF CONSUMABLE GOODS OVER TIME: SPECULATION

The allocation of goods among people, the problem we have studied in the preceding chapters, is not the only economic problem. There is also the task of allocating consumption between people *today* and people *tomorrow.* What we eat today, we cannot eat tomorrow. The choice from today's menu affects tomorrow's menu. After the crop of wheat is harvested in the summer, how is it decided what amount will be eaten in the fall, in the winter, and next spring? Does a governmental agency set quotas for how much can be consumed today, tomorrow, and next month until the next crop is harvested? If no central agency does this, how do we avoid running out of wheat in midwinter? In the United States no agency makes these decisions. No group of people is charged with the responsibility of seeing that we don't consume too much now and have too little later. Yet some people, without any such delegated responsibility, devote their major activity to checking on this problem. In a capitalist system these individuals are private citizens acting in the interests of their own wealth; yet, in some mysterious way, their decisions influence the allocation of consumable goods over the year. In this chapter we shall study the way these actions affect allocation. A very simplified example, the allocation of a wheat crop from harvest to harvest, will bring out all the essential details. Although we discuss wheat, note that this problem applies to *all* goods, whether agricultural or manufactured; next year's manufactured good has to be produced, just as next year's crop has to be produced. Both rely on the productive effort of people in determining output. For all goods this question must be faced; for many agricultural goods and for a few others, formal "speculative" futures commodity markets facilitate this task.

The Risk-Taker in Commodity Markets

The wheat crop (consisting of only one type of wheat) has just been harvested. What do the farmers do with the wheat? They could accept the task of storing it, gradually selling a bit each month until the next harvest. However, most farmers do not want to hold so much of their wealth in the form of wheat, because farmers are experts in growing and harvesting wheat, rather than in storing and rationing it. The value of the stock of wheat will fluctuate over the year in response to changing demands, and the farmer would be bearing that additional risk of changes in the value of his wealth if he held the wheat. Farmers, in general, prefer not to mix growing and harvesting of wheat with the extra tasks of storing and of speculating in the value of existing wheat between harvests.

How does the farmer separate these tasks? He can offer to sell the wheat as soon as harvested, so that someone else stores it and bears the risks of changes in value of the wheat stock and decides how much to sell to consumers each month so as to ration the supply out over the year. By offering to sell his harvest, the farmer is unintentionally seeking other people for these tasks. Like the rest of us, he seeks the best price he can get. He is in a price-takers' market, so he charges what the market will bear—provided he can sell *all* his wheat. If we momentarily retain this assumption that each farmer sells all his wheat, rather than keeping any of it for himself or for later sale, the *total supply schedule* for wheat aggregated over all farmers is a vertical line on a price-quantity diagram.

The intersection of this curve with the community's market demand sets a price at which the stock of wheat now held by farmers will be transferred to new owners. Who are these other people who buy the harvested wheat? The millers, who grind the wheat grain into flour, don't want to store up a year's supply of wheat in advance. Their job is grinding and distributing wheat, not storing it for the coming year and deciding how much to release for consumers each month. Even the housewives refuse to take on this duty. One would think that housewives should be required to buy a year's supply at the end of the harvest period and then live on the supply. But they refuse to do this, because they do not want to make commitments so far in advance.

Even though farmers, millers, and housewives don't want to store a year's supply, there is a very simple device to induce someone else to store the wheat until it is demanded. When farmers refuse to store all the wheat, the price of wheat falls until someone thinks he can make a profit by buying the wheat at the "ridiculously" low price and selling it later as the available wheat is gradually consumed. Who first thought of this profit possibility? Maybe back in pre-Sumerian civilization some opportunistic person remembered that in preceding years the price had fallen just after the harvest and then had later risen greatly before the next harvest. Had he bought wheat in the fall, he could have sold it before the following spring at an enormous profit. This little fact of life has been handed on from generation to generation through thousands of years and, like much of the information of the world, is taught not in schoolbooks but in the marketplace.

To pick up our story again, when the farmers offer their harvest for sale, the price of wheat will fall because of the greatly increased supply. But something prevents the price from falling very far. If, as we have supposed, this decrease of price is the result of the increased supply at harvest, there is an increased prospect of profit in buying wheat at the lower price, storing it, and selling it later at a higher price after some of the wheat is consumed. This is called speculation. In a capitalist system, anyone may buy wheat at harvest time in a "self-centered" endeavor to make profit by selling it later at a higher price. This is known as a speculative demand for wheat.

Except for these *speculators* who buy the wheat, the price would fall still lower until the less venturesome, less perceptive people were induced to buy the wheat. After all, at a *sufficiently* low price of wheat, the millers (and even housewives) could be induced to buy a year's stock of wheat, because the prospects for profits now look so sure that they, too, are willing to take on the diminished risk of loss and increased costs of storing with an enhanced chance of profit. The differences among people in the willingness to bear risk, in their talents and facilities for storing wheat, in the profit prospects that will induce them to risk buying wheat—all these differences determine how low the price of wheat will have to be after the harvest.

Permitting *any* or all persons to buy stocks of wheat for speculative purposes keeps the price from falling so far at harvest and gives the farmers a higher price for their crop than if some of these buyers were not allowed to buy the harvested wheat for speculation. It also reduces speculators' actually realized profits below what they would otherwise have been. In the United States, anyone who wants to buy and store wheat can do so by telephoning a commodity-market broker. He can arrange at the same time to have wheat stored in rented facilities and even get insurance against theft or spoilage while he owns it.

Any farmer who prefers the chance of profits (or losses) from the fluctuating value of the wheat held during the winter can refuse to sell some of his wheat. For each farmer there is a price below which he will prefer to keep some of his wheat for speculation. More accurately, as the price gets lower and lower, each farmer will keep more of his stock of wheat—hoping to make some speculative profit himself by selling it later at a higher price. He will reserve more and more for himself as the available price at harvest time is lower *relative* to anticipated future prices. In other words, he has a list of "reservation" prices and amounts. This means the farmer can also be one of those speculators who may—under sufficiently attractive prospects of profits—hold wheat in storage (withhold it from consumption) and gradually sell it off during the winter and spring.

In summary, we have an answer to our question of who holds the wheat from the existing harvests. Under the incentive of increased wealth (buying low and selling later at a higher price) anyone can shoulder this task—not because he *intends* to perform some socially useful function (storing and rationing wheat from harvest to harvest) but because he wants to increase his wealth. Private interest provides a method of accomplishing this task—a method not consciously designed or motivated by the social storage purpose but one discovered by a trial-and-error selective process and not widely understood by the members of society, not even by many of the speculators.

Control of the Rate of Consumption out of Stocks

So far, we have explained how people are induced to store the crop and incidentally provide for a continuing supply between harvests. But we have not explained the determination of the *rate* at which the stored-up stock of wheat is gradually allocated to consumption. Who tells speculators how much wheat to sell each month for consumption? No one. Some *thing* does, and that thing is the current price of wheat relative to expected future prices.

Past experience, that prime source of knowledge, provides the basis for *expectations* of what the price of wheat will do between harvests. The lower the current harvest price relative to expectations about what the price will be before the next harvest, the greater are the prospects of profits by holding more of the wheat away from current consumption. And the higher is the current price relative to future price expectations, the more will sellers be willing to sell for current consumption, because profit prospects of continuing to hold wheat are diminished.

The present (*spot*) price of wheat is affected by both the consumption demand and the supply of wheat coming into consumption channels from storage. If current consumption demands should increase, the *current* spot price of wheat will rise and reduce profit prospects, thus inducing storers of wheat to sell more wheat to consumption channels. *The relationship between the current "spot" price for wheat and the price that is expected in the future affects the rate at which wheat will be released from storage into consumption.* So important is information about expected future prices of wheat that special markets have long existed as means of forecasting the prices that will exist in the future. These are "*futures* markets," where "future supplies" of wheat are bought and sold. People now make contracts to deliver or to accept delivery in the *future* and to pay in the future at *presently* agreed-upon prices. This means that the prices now agreed upon for future delivery are predictions of what the price will be in the future when the wheat is delivered. No one would make a contract today, at a price higher than he thought the price would be in six months, to buy wheat to be delivered and paid for in six months. Nor would anyone sell wheat *forward* (i.e., for future delivery) if the price were less than he thought it would be in the future. Therefore, the prices of these current contracts for future deliveries of wheat reflect beliefs and predictions about the future price.

"Futures" Prices and Spot Prices

Suppose that it is now the month of September, and you can buy a bushel of wheat (in 5,000-bushel lots) for $2 a bushel for delivery immediately. The *spot* price of wheat is $2. Today, you also can make a forward contract for delivery of wheat and payment of $2.10 per bushel *next May*. The price of $2.10 agreed to now, but to be paid in May, is called the *May futures price* (formed in September). The difference between the two prices (spot and futures) usually converges to a spread covering the storage, insurance, and interest costs of holding wheat in the interim. This is called an equilibrium relationship. The forces bringing about that equilibrium will be explored.

Markets for Futures Prices

The prices in the commodity *futures* markets are reported in the financial section of major newspapers. You will find in September of year 1900 something like the following for the wheat futures market (Chicago is the place of the market).

Wheat Futures Prices

September 1900 (new harvest)	$2.00
December 1900	2.04
March 1901	2.07
May 1901	2.10
September 1901 (new harvest)	2.02
December 1901	2.06

The interval covered extends from one crop year into the next. Unless next year's harvest is anticipated to be unusually small, at least smaller than the current year's harvest, the September 1901 price presumably will be lower than the May 1901 price. The September harvest cannot be used in the *preceding* May to increase the amount available for consumption; if it could, the May price would be pushed down and the September price raised.[1]

[1] There is some downward pressure on May prices, for consumers will reduce current consumption in the expectation of buying and consuming more wheat at a lower price after the new crop is harvested.

These *futures prices* in today's futures markets provide the best predictions of what the spot price will be in the future. If anyone can make a better prediction of next May's spot price of wheat (i.e., one that in fact turns out to be a more accurate prediction), he can quickly reap a fortune. All he must do is take his better prediction to this marketplace and "put his money where his mouth is." For example, suppose the present (in September 1900) May (1901) futures price in the futures market is $2, a price lower than he believes will actually exist in May of 1901. He could place a bet in this futures market that the presently quoted *May futures* price is too low and that the spot price next May will actually be higher. The process for placing this bet is to buy now a *futures contract* for, say, 5,000 bushels of May 1901 wheat at $2 a bushel—to be delivered to him and paid for next May. He agrees to this contract now in September at the presently quoted *May futures price* of $2 per bushel. Then he nervously waits until May; *if* the spot price next May is in fact higher than $2, he can take delivery of the wheat and sell it at the then higher price, reaping the difference as a profit. If, regrettably, the price is lower, he suffers a loss.

An important consequence of this activity is that increased demand for wheat for future delivery pushes up the current "futures price" of future wheat from $2 toward that predicted May price. In this way beliefs that the current "futures" price of future wheat is too low will increase the current "futures" price and reveal to the world the new expectations of future spot prices.

Of course, for every buyer of a contract for future wheat, there must be someone who sells him the promise to deliver wheat in the future. That other person believes the future spot price will be lower than the current futures price, and, if *he* is correct, later he can buy wheat at the lower future spot price and deliver it to the buyer for the currently agreed-to higher futures price.

If the demand for current wheat consumption increases so that the spot (present) price of wheat rises, continued storage will be less profitable unless it is also expected that the price in the future will be correspondingly higher. A faster rate of consumption will leave smaller stocks and higher prices in the future. Currently, therefore, futures prices now in the futures markets will be pushed up. What will push them up? First, the knowledge of the faster rate of consumption of current stocks of wheat will induce speculators to anticipate higher prices in the future, and they will act accordingly in making current futures contracts. Second, there is a sort of automatic force in the sense that this force does not require any general knowledge of a faster rate of reduction of the stock of wheat. This second force is the result of *hedging*.

A *hedge* is a temporary use of futures contracts to protect a person from changes in the value of stocks of goods he owns or has contracted to acquire. Suppose an expert at storage techniques or a flour miller owns inventories of wheat in anticipation of future customers. The stored stocks and inventories may fluctuate in value, downward as well as upward. To protect his wealth, the storage specialist and the miller can, in the futures markets, find someone who will guarantee him a price (say, \$2) at which he can sell wheat or its converted product, flour, next May: he *sells* a May futures contract now in October for \$2. If the price of wheat and flour goes down in the interim, the reduced value of his existing inventories is a loss of wealth; but, at the same time, he will be able to buy wheat at a lower price and make a profit by exercising his right to deliver wheat for the promised \$2 per bushel. That profit offsets the loss on the inventories of wheat he was holding when he entered the futures contract. In this way an interim fall in wheat prices gives him a profit on his futures contract at the same time and to the same extent that it imposed a loss on his milling inventories.

The larger the existing inventories of wheat, the more wheat that is hedged by such guarantees against adverse price changes (by selling "futures contracts"). The increased supply of futures contracts (reflecting large stocks) lowers the futures prices. In other words, the greater the inventory of wheat, the greater the supply of futures contracts—and the lower their price.

We are now in a position to see how a higher demand, higher spot price, and consequent faster rate of consumption out of inventories has an effect on futures prices. As the hedging inventory holders sell their wheat for the current consumption at a more rapid rate, they have less wheat to hedge, so that there is an increased demand (to buy back) for futures contracts (promising delivery of wheat in the future). The increased demand to buy back futures contracts, as hedgers reduce their inventories, raises futures prices.

Illustrative Application: Coffee Futures Markets

Having completed the logical analysis of the interrelationships of prices and stocks and speculative decisions, we turn now to an application of those principles in a real situation. In particular, we shall examine how it is decided at what rate to consume this year's crop during the months prior to the next harvest and also how much of this year's crop to save for use along with next year's crop. We shall inquire into market functions with a "scenario" of public reaction to the movements of the coffee futures markets; the scenario is only semi-imaginary, being based on recent actual events.[2]

The news spreads that the next coffee crop now blossoming in Brazil has been nipped by unseasonably cold weather. During these snaps, no one really knows how much the buds are affected, but there is an increased probability that next year's yield will be reduced. The same doubt arises with drought, frost,

[2] Coffee can be replaced by some other good for which there are organized futures commodity markets. For example, today there are organized open futures markets for at least the following goods: wheat, soybeans, oats, corn, cotton, barley, sorghum, sugar, cottonseed oil, soybean oil, hides, lard, eggs (frozen, powdered, and shell), potatoes, frozen chickens and turkeys, silver, tin, rubber, cocoa, platinum, pepper, flaxseed, copper, lead, zinc, and wool.

pests, etc. No economist has to tell people that a reduced supply implies a higher price next year. In turn, this implies greater (or surer prospects of) profits for those who own coffee today and who store it for next year's prospective higher prices. Immediately, the flow of coffee out of current stocks to consumption is reduced. Immediately, people try to buy existing stocks (before prices rise) to get that profit of storing this year's supply over to next year. Therefore, the current spot price of coffee to consumers will rise as less coffee is made available for current consumption. There is, of course, just as much coffee as there was before the news about a potential shorter crop. And yet the present (spot) price has risen. With the rise in the price of coffee, congressmen, responding to housewives' protests, begin publicly to demand investigations of the rise in coffee prices. Sure enough, the fact is discovered that there is just as much coffee in existence *now* as before the rise, but that greedy, antisocial speculators have driven up the price. Speculators are criticized; when called upon to explain their activities, they fail miserably to make a defensible case for themselves. They reluctantly admit to speculating with the sole intent of personal profit. They are forced to confess that since there is still as much coffee as ever, they are responsible for the higher-priced coffee.

If you were a speculator—and they're people of all types: dentists, carpenters, doctors, salesmen—what would you tell the complaining congressmen? What, according to economic analysis, was the source and the effects of the current price rise? Could you defend yourself by saying that you deserve not censure but a medal for having benefited *all* mankind; or where you working against the interests of other people? But without answering the questions of whether or not the results are *good* or *bad*, your defense might run something like this:

"Yes, it is true that news of the cold weather suggested that the coffee buds would be nipped and the coffee harvest reduced. This would mean higher prices *next* year. Being a clever fellow, I believed that if I bought some of this year's currently stored crop at present spot prices, I could store it and sell it at next year's higher prices, thereby making a quick, tidy profit. Fortunately, I was one of the first who believed the crop damage was severe and was able to buy coffee from other holders of current stocks who did not happen to believe the future supply looked smaller. But I was not alone; many people were competing for current stocks of coffee. Soon, those who had coffee were not willing to sell at the former prices. They, too, looked forward to selling the coffee next year rather than this year. Less coffee was released from stocks for consumption. No one would sell existing stocks to consumers at a price less than he could get by holding until next year (allowing for the costs of storage, insurance, and interest). The current price, therefore, rose almost to the expected future prices as reflected in "futures prices" of coffee. This higher price was necessary to draw coffee out of storage and to induce consumers to decrease consumption to match the reduced flow of coffee. All this is summarized in the first fundamental law of economics, which states that less will be consumed as price increases.

"That is why I bought coffee as a speculator. However, quite incidentally and unintentionally, my action—like those of the many other similarly motivated, foresighted, informed persons—augmented the supply of coffee for next year, by adding part of this year's stored stocks to next year's reduced harvest. The consumer next year will have more coffee to consume and at prices lower than if we speculators had not carried more coffee from this year over to next year. For that, the consumers should thank us.

"We speculators did not cause the reduced supply of coffee next year. Nature did that. The fact is that there simply *is* going to be *less* coffee next year. The choice facing people therefore is: 'Shall we continue to consume coffee today *as if* there were not going to be less next year, and then reduce consumption next year by the full reduction in the harvest; or shall we reduce consumption a bit this year in order not to have to reduce it so much next year?' The choice is *not* more coffee rather than less, nor is it lower prices rather than higher prices.

"If I must *defend* my actions rather than merely *explain* them, I would say that, like the middlemen in the refugee camp, we speculators enabled people to obtain greater levels of utility than they otherwise would have obtained, despite their protestations about the currently higher price of coffee. From the fact that prices are predicted to be higher next year than now, I know that people *prefer* to give up a pound now in order to have one more next year. This is precisely what the higher futures price for next year's coffee means, relative to the present price this year. And if we are right in that forecast, we will make a profit; if wrong, a loss. The profitability of our activity is an acid test that people did want coffee shifted to the future. Because more coffee is stored for the future, the price is reduced next year below what it would have been.

"As speculators, what we have done has been to convey immediately to people the predicted fact of scarcity of future coffee relative to other goods next year. We are not responsible for that *bad event,* but we are responsible for anticipating the effects of impending unfavorable events so that people can more fully or quickly adjust to them—so as to keep their utility from being reduced as much as it would have been had the news of the coming crop failure been hidden until even more of the current crop was eaten up. We speculators are blamed for bad events because people either confuse *news* of the event with the *event,* or because they sometimes think that news of bad future events is worse than not knowing about it.

"You say, 'But what if your predictions were wrong? Suppose coffee buds were *not* frozen? Instead, only a few buds on each tree were damaged, while the hardier undamaged buds produced even bigger coffee beans—more than enough to compensate for the reduced number, so that the crop next year was going to be even larger! Or suppose the cold snap did no damage at all. Or maybe the news about cold weather was simply false. After all, South American governments have been known to issue false bad news about an impending coffee crop precisely to drive up the price of coffee now, so that they could sell some of their existing stock at higher prices. What then?'

"The answer is simple. If speculators are wrong and if anyone else thinks he knows better or can predict better, all he has to do is out-predict the present speculators, and his fortune is made. Moreover, if speculators or people who store coffee make *perverse* mistakes in foresight, they will suffer a loss of wealth, which, in part, pays the rest of the community for the error. Speculators will have paid more for the coffee than they will get when they sell it.

"I will not go so far as to say that the losses of the speculators fully compensate the rest of society for the damage done in shifting coffee stocks in the wrong direction. It has sometimes been said that any damage done to other people by our erroneous forecasts is made up to them by the losses we incur—a transfer of some of our wealth to the rest of society. In part this is correct, but our perverse forecasts do more damage than our loss of wealth to the rest of society can offset. They do damage in the sense that if our forecasts had been more correct, everyone else could have achieved a more desirable adjustment in his consumption patterns over time than he did achieve. Obviously, the more accurate our forecasts, the better for us and for everyone else. The less accurate they are, the worse for us, and the worse for everyone else. However, the results are not as bad for everyone else as they would be if everyone had to do his own forecasting and storing of stocks for his own consumption, thereby bearing the full consequences of his own forecasts—right or wrong.

"Clearly, then, the issue is not whether the forecasts of speculators are correct or incorrect. The issues are instead: (a) What systems exist for making and acting on better forecasts? (b) What systems exist for allocating coffee among people over time *and* for allocating the risks and consequences of the erroneous forecasts? Any system will have to rely on erroneous forecasts. Which one will have fewer erroneous forecasts? Which will bear the major burden of the consequences of erroneous forecasts?"

And so our scenario ends. While it answered one question, it ended up by posing two new ones, to which we turn in the next section.

Allocation of Risks in Futures Markets

Do the speculative markets to which everyone has access predict future prices more accurately than some other possible scheme? If we compare situations in which the speculative markets are open to everyone with situations in which such markets are prohibited, we do get an unambiguous answer. When organized and open futures commodity markets are prohibited, speculative holdings of crops are concentrated in the hands of people more intimately connected with distributing the physical stocks of the goods. They do not have to reveal their forecasts by open-market contracts, and they form a more restricted set of bidders for farmers' crops. Fortunately for this analysis, but not necessarily for those who produce onions or consume them, the open, organized futures market in onions has been closed by federal law since 1959. This has provided an opportunity to compare the behavior of prices of onions—with and without open markets. The record is clear. With the organized open futures markets for onions, the forecasts were more accurate than when they were closed. In particular, spot prices varied less during the interval between crops with open speculative markets than without them. In other words, the forecasts of future prices—the futures prices—influenced spot prices more accurately toward what was going to happen, avoiding large fluctuations when spot price responds to unforeseen events. It is not often that we have a controlled experiment to compare two systems for resolving economic problems.[3]

How should consequences of forecasting errors be borne? Sometimes it is contended that only experts should be allowed to make speculative decisions, and then we would eliminate the errors made by less informed people. To this there are several replies. First, if experts are now better informed than the consensus of the markets, they could easily get wealthy very rapidly by speculating. Furthermore, experts' superior information would help move the present spot and future prices in the "correct" directions. Second, there is the problem of discovering who these experts are. When the government employs a group of specialists in this matter, the specialists are not automatically superior forecasters. The predictions of "experts" differ. It is just as easy to form two groups of experts as one group, but disagreement between two groups about forecasts would be even more dismaying than disagreements within one group. If, despite these inherent difficulties, a group of experts is responsible for making forecasts and controlling the storage rates, who is to finance that activity? Who is to bear the losses when the forecasts are erroneous? In other words, how are the consequences of ignorance about future events to be allocated among people? Shall we require that all people, whether they individually want to or not, shall bear, in proportion to their taxes, the changing wealth values of the stocks of stored commodities? If the speculative activity were a voluntary arrangement with open futures markets, those who want to bear more of the risk can hold more of their wealth in the form of goods to be stored, and those who want to be relieved of those risks can own other forms of wealth. This points up one fundamental attribute of a capitalist system. It permits individuals to adjust their patterns of

[3] Why was the onion futures market closed? Since this was done by federal legislation, one would have to ask congressmen why they voted to prohibit the market. However, among those who wanted the market closed were distributors, who would thereby have a more exclusive access to information and opportunities to buy and sell onions. How they managed to induce enough congressmen to vote for that legislation is a question we leave to political science.

risk exposure. If you wish to avoid the wealth changes of certain types of goods, you can choose to own some other kinds of goods. You can concentrate your risks on a few particular goods or on a large class of goods, by appropriate patterns of ownership of goods. Complete avoidance of risks is not possible, but selectivity and choice of types of risks are possible with open markets and private-property rights.

Speculative holding of goods is inevitable. A person who buys goods now, with the intent of consuming just that amount before the next harvest, speculates that he can estimate accurately his own demands and prices in the future. If he doesn't buy now for future consumption, someone else holds wheat for sale to him later—in the expectation that the price will have risen enough to make risks worthwhile.

But people differ in their attitude or willingness to bear the risks of losses of wealth consequent to the prices that do emerge. Given these differences, each individual can move to a preferred position, as he sees it, if he will let the risks be borne by those who are sure about a price rise, or more willing to bear risks inherent in the uncertainty of future prices. Of course, he will have to pay them to bear those risks, but if they regard carrying such risks as less burdensome than he regards them, the cost will be less than if he bore the risks. Abolishing futures markets would raise the costs of performing the storage function, because it would prevent those who are more willing to bear these risks from doing so, and force the less willing persons to bear these risks.

Having chosen not to bear the risk of wealth changes of a certain good, a person should not complain later if its price rises. His complaints would amount to the assertion that "hindsight is wonderful" and that insurance is wasted if the insured-against disaster doesn't happen! (In this case, by not holding stocks in advance of use, he has insured against decreases in their value.)

Sometimes it is mistakenly believed that speculation can be avoided by legally imposing fixed prices on commodities. This is identical to painting the thermometer to avoid a fever. Price controls do not prevent shifts in demand as subjective valuations change. What they do prevent is the opportunity of people to adjust to differences in interpersonal subjective values, thereby restricting the realized extent of exchange potentialities.

Speculative Markets under Different Economic Systems

Our lengthy and detailed investigation of the principles underlying the speculative markets in a capitalist system reveals clearly the issues that must be faced in every society when bearing the risks of changes in values of goods. In every society, someone will have to receive less (reflecting the lower value of some goods), and someone will have more (reflecting the higher value of other goods). Who will bear the profits and who the losses is an issue in all societies, and it cannot be avoided by abandoning a capitalist system. From system to system, only the method of allocation changes. In a capitalist system, individuals can negotiate among themselves, offering to exchange "this" risk of loss or gain for "that" risk. Just as people can negotiate for the particular pattern of consumption goods they shall have, so they can negotiate about the pattern of risks they shall bear. Although the option of bearing no risk at all is open to *no* man, what is available in a capitalist society is the option of exchanging risks for other risks or kinds of wealth. In a socialist system, the risks of value changes for state-owned goods—or those owned by the people as a whole—are borne by everyone in accord with tax liabilities and access to state services. The risk patterns are not individually negotiable with other people.

If you believe that people individually should have less choice of risk patterns and if you think that risks should be separated from the people who control the use of goods, you will prefer to reduce the scope of private property. But if you prefer a wider class of choice of risk patterns and a closer correlation between risk bearing and control of use, you will prefer a greater range of private property. However, you may, in fact, not have much choice about the system under which you live, unless you move from one country to another.

Questions

1. The following was reported in the *New York Times* on July 26, 1963:

PRICES OF WHEAT FUTURES (CHICAGO)
JULY 25, 1963

September	1963	$1.78
December	1963	1.84
March	1964	1.87½
May	1964	1.79½
July	1964	1.55
September	1964	1.56

a. In what months does it appear that the new crop is harvested?

b. Explain the basis of your answer.

c. Approximately how much does it cost to store a bushel of wheat for one month?

2. Does storage from one crop season to the next season occur because people are far-sighted and contemplate their own future demands, or is it done because people think they can make a profit?

3. Which good will have a greater fall in its price as the crop is more fully harvested: one that will store readily or one that is more perishable? Why?

4. What is the difference between a "futures" price and a "future" price?

5. "A futures price is a price of a contract in the future." True or false?

6. "A current price differs from a futures price in that the former is a price agreed to now while the latter is a price that will be agreed to in the future." True or false?

7. Today you can buy 100 bushels of wheat to be delivered today and paid for today. Does this involve a spot or a futures price?

8. Today you make a contract for delivery of wheat next year with payment to be made now. Is this a futures contract? Why not?

9. In May, what is the September futures price an estimate of?

10. What is meant by "risk"? How is it measured?

11. I own wealth of $1,000, while your wealth is $500. Who bears the greater risk?

12. I own $1,000, and tomorrow I will own either $2,000 or nothing depending upon whether an oil well I am drilling strikes oil. You own $1,000 in wealth, and it is all in cash. Who bears the greater risk for the next twenty-four hours?

13. Suppose I strike oil and my wealth jumps to $5,000. I sell out and buy some stock in a new electronics company. Who bears the greater risk?

14. Explain how markets in which people can bet with each other can result in (a) exchanges of risk, (b) reductions in risk, or (c) increases in risk. If such a market increases risk, is it bad? Why or why not?

15. I am worth $1 today. Tomorrow I shall be worth either $1.50 or 50 cents, with a probability that I believe to be 50/50. You are also worth $1 today. Tomorrow you will be worth $1.50 with probability ¼, or 50 cents with probability ¼, or still worth $1 with probability ½. Who would you say faces the greater risk?

16. The Los Angeles Dodgers and New York "Mets" are tied for the National League baseball title. They are to have a play-off game in a neutral stadium. The winning team will then be host for the World Series, with consequent receipts to the owners of neighboring parking lots. I own a parking lot near the Dodgers' stadium, and you own one near the Mets' stadium. If the Mets win the play-off, you gain; if the Dodgers win, I gain.

a. Into what kind of contract can we enter so as to reduce the risk each of us bears?

b. Have we exchanged or reduced risk? Can you construct a kind of "futures contract" that would accomplish the same effect?

17. "That speculators push up the price of a good is evidenced by the fact that the price often rises before there is any change either in the rate of consumption or the existing supply." Do you agree? If so, why? If not, why not?

18. A soybean processor, who extracts soybean oil, buys in March 50,000 pounds of soybeans at $2.35 per 100 pounds. He expects to crush the beans and sell the soybean oil in about two months. He sells "futures" in soybeans at the same time he buys soybeans, hoping to obtain some protection from wealth changes resulting from changes in the price of soybeans and soybean oil. He sells futures in soybeans—say, May futures—to the extent of 50,000 pounds. Suppose that the price of soybeans falls to $2 per 100 pounds in the interim and that therefore the price of soybean oil also falls. How will this enable the processor partially to avoid wealth changes caused by fluctuations in soybean prices?

19. A silverware fabricator usually holds large stocks of silver. To concentrate his energies on the design and fabrication of silverware and to avoid the big changes in wealth resulting from swings in the price of his silver inventories, a silverware manufacturer can hedge in the silver futures market. How would a silver fabricator hedge against changes in the value of his silver inventory?

20. In what sense is insurance a one-sided hedge?

21. "If forecasts are correct, some speculators will reap a profit. Also, they will have pushed up present prices, which will reduce current consumption and give a larger carryover to next season, so that prices in the future will be lower than they otherwise would be; but current prices are higher than they would have been had foresight been less perfect." In what sense can it be argued that this is "preferable" to a higher price later and lower price now?

22. As the next crop is planted, news suggests that it will be smaller than usual and that prices will be higher when it is harvested. Immediately, futures prices rise in response to speculative demands for futures contracts. People have a greater desire to buy futures contracts at present futures prices because they believe the higher prices during the next harvest will give them a profit. When futures prices rise, how does this make current prices rise, even though the present stock of goods is not affected?

23. "When speculators' foresight is good, they make a profit and perform a service to society. When it is bad, they incur losses and thus compensate the rest of society for the maldistribution of goods they induced." Do you agree? If so, why? If not, why not?

24. There are no speculative futures markets in some countries. Does that mean there is no speculation? Explain.

25. "If the speculative commodity markets were closed, there would be less speculation and smaller fluctuations in the prices of goods. Farmers could more reliably know what their crop would be worth, and consumers would be spared the price swings that are initiated in the speculative futures markets." Do you agree? If so, why? If not, why not? Can you cite any evidence?

26. In 1963 a U.S. Senate Agriculture Committee recommended the prohibition of futures trading in potatoes in formal speculative markets.

a. If prohibited, would that stop speculation in potatoes?

b. What would be its effect?

c. Why do you think congressmen were induced to advocate the prohibition of futures markets in potatoes?

27. News item dated August 5, 1963: "The New York Sugar Exchange, where sugar

futures prices soared and then dived in May 1963, will have to be placed under government supervision according to Rep. Leonor K. Sullivan (Democrat—Missouri), chairman of the Consumer Affairs subcommittee of the House of Representatives. Her report said in part, 'It was excessive speculation in futures rather than manipulation that stimulated the price advance and the subsequent price break. The investigation did not show indications of price manipulation on the part of any individual or groups of traders.' Mrs. Sullivan said the interest of consumers—'who are still paying higher prices for sugar and products containing sugar because of the market behavior'—requires some measures to dampen speculation. 'My own opinion is that this exchange will have to come under government supervision. I am not at all convinced that the self-regulation there is effective or adequate in a period of market disorder and abnormal pressures.' In New York, President Erle MacHardy of the Sugar Exchange said, 'Sure, there has been speculation—this is the nature of our competitive system to speculate on things.' "

The news story listed the occupations of the 1,694 speculators who were holding sugar future contracts on May 23. Sixty-two were connected with the sugar industry, 137 were professional speculators belonging to the exchange, while 95 were housewives; also, there were 117 retired people, 88 engineers, 82 retail proprietors, 278 other proprietors, 13 teachers, and 12 students. The list also included chemists, bankers, dentists, salesmen, realtors, and insurance men.

a. What do you think of Representative Sullivan's economic analysis? Explain.

b. Of Mr. MacHardy's? Explain.

c. What do you think of Representative Sullivan's *political* acuity?

28. "Short selling" consists of selling promises to deliver at a specified date in the future some goods that the seller does not now own. Newspapers sell short when they take subscriptions with advance payment. A house buyer sells short when he borrows money, for he is promising to pay money in the future—money that he does not now have. A college that charges tuition and room and board in advance is engaged in short selling; it sells something it has yet to produce. I sell short if I sell a promise to deliver 1,000 bushels of wheat to you next year for a price currently agreed upon and in receipt for payment now from you. Why is short selling often regarded as immoral, improper, or bad?

29. The Chairman of the U.S. Securities and Exchange Commission proposes to prohibit or restrict short selling at times when the market prices are under "temporary pressure or distress." The presumption is that short selling destabilizes the market and induces larger downward swings than are justifiable in times of temporary distress. Suppose you were appointed by the President to decide when to restrict short selling in order to prevent it from pushing prices down lower.

a. How would you decide when a drop in prices was temporary and unjustified?

b. Who would decide when a drop in prices was "justified"?

30. Futures markets exist for stocks and bonds. These are known as the markets for "Puts" and "Calls." A "Call" is a right to purchase a stock within the next six months at a prespecified price, regardless of how high the price of that stock may rise in the next six months. A Call is guaranteed or sold by a party who, in effect, has sold "short." He is betting that the stock price will fall in the interim. If it does, he will not have to fulfill his promise to sell at the higher specified price, since the buyer of the Call can buy more cheaply on the market. If the stock rises, the guarantor of the Call will have to buy the stock on the market at the higher price and deliver it to the holder of the Call for the lower contract price in the "Call" contract.

The buyer of a "Put" buys the right to sell a stock at a prespecified price within some agreed-upon period of time regardless of how low the price may have fallen in that interval. The other party to the agreement (the seller of the Put) enters into the agreement in consideration of a payment inducing him to undertake the commitment to buy later at the specified price. Thus, a person owning A.T.&T. common stock can guarantee himself against a serious decline in the value by purchasing a Put. If it falls, he exercises his right to sell to the seller of the Put.

On August 1, 1963, you could have purchased a Put for Chrysler stock giving you a guaranteed price of $60, at which the seller of the Put will purchase 100 shares of Chrysler stock from you at any time during the next six months. That Put would have cost you $600. How far would Chrysler stock have to fall for you to have saved or made money by purchasing that Put?

31. The following was the set of futures prices of wool on August 1, 1963:

October	1963	133.4
December	1963	132.7
March	1964	131.8
May	1964	130.8
July	1964	129.7
October	1964	129.3
December	1964	128.8

What explanation consistent with economic analysis can you give for this "reverse" sequence of futures prices?

32. Russian farm officials when visiting the United States persisted in asking how we controlled the flow of wheat out of existing stocks so as to ensure an appropriate supply over the year. When they were told that no one made that decision, they insisted we were naïvely trying to keep secrets from them. What was our "secret"?

33. "Open speculative markets are defended on the premise that it is better to be aware of impending events than to be unaware of them. But for events like impending crop disasters, earlier news merely shifts forward and thereby spreads the effects over a longer interval to no one's benefit. People might prefer to experience a short, intense period of less coffee in the future rather than have an earlier, longer-lasting though less intense reduction in consumption." What does economic theory say about this?

34. There are no organized speculative exchanges or futures markets for orange juice, wine, raisins, dried peaches, coal, oil, gasoline, whiskey, or olive oil.

a. Does that mean there is no speculating in these commodities?

b. Who does the speculating?

35. How many different goods have futures markets? (Check the financial pages of newspapers or business publications.)

15

CAPITAL VALUES AND INTEREST RATES

People are interested in the future as well as the present, a fact attested to by the existence of the commodity futures market discussed in the preceding chapter. Utility at any moment depends not only upon present consumption but also upon expected future consumption. In our terminology and postulates, both present and future consumption are *goods*, and, as with all goods, a person is willing to substitute among them. He is willing to consider giving up *some* present for *more* future consumption. This kind of trade is called "saving." The reverse direction of substitution is known as "dissaving." Usually, but not necessarily, it involves "borrowing," so that a person consumes more today and less tomorrow when he repays.

All this is extremely simple; yet adequate analysis of its implications requires careful use of some new concepts. Just as we have analyzed exchange of present goods between people, we can analyze exchange of rights to present and future consumption. Earlier, each person had a subjective value (rate of substitution in exchange) of one current good for another. Now we have a subjective value (acceptable rate of exchange) of present consumption for future consumption. Instead of asking how much candy a person would give up now for one more cigarette now, we ask how much candy a person would give up now in order to get one candy, say, a month *later*.

At first one might think, "Candy is candy; therefore, I would give up one candy now for the right to one candy a month from now." But second thoughts suggest if you give up candy now, you also will have given up the right to eat or otherwise use the candy any time during the next month. The candy you will get at the *end* of the month will not give back the right to use or eat candy *during* the month. You will have accepted a reduced range of possible actions—and you will have obtained nothing in return. On the principle that more is preferred to less, you are not willing to accept such an exchange. Candy now is preferred to candy available only at a later date: candy now and candy available a month from now are simply not the same commodity. The former, in our jargon, has more "utility." Therefore, *less*—even if not much less—than one candy now will be traded for one candy a month from now.

Rate of Interest

Suppose you were just barely willing to give up only 0.9 candy today for the right to one a year from now (with no uncertainty or doubt about the payment). The *present* price of one candy *now* is, of course, one candy, while the *present* price of one candy available in a *year* is 0.9 candy. The relative price or exchange rate between present and future candy can be expressed as a ratio, 1/.9, which equals 1.11. A present candy sells for a price premium, or higher price, of 11 percent over the current price of a right to one candy deferred a year. In other words, one year's later availability reduces the *present* value of something, by 11 percent in our numerical example. The value of earlier availability is 11 percent for one year; in technical jargon, the *rate of interest* is 11 percent per year.

Express this generally in money. If you were to ask me, "How much money would you give up today for the right to get $1 a year from now?" my reply would be, "I would today pay 90 cents." I would give up 90 cents now for the right to $1 a year later; I regard the loss of one year's availability of opportunity to use goods as equal to 11 percent of the value of current goods. For every good I can buy with money, earlier availability of *any* (and all) goods is worth 11 percent per year.

Because money is the commonly used medium of exchange, thus dispensing with much barter, it is customary to speak of the rate of interest on present and future *money* rather than in terms of commodities.

Although interest rates are expressed almost exclusively in terms of money loans, they represent the value (price) of earlier rather than later availability of nonmoney commodities, just as *money prices* for ordinary exchanges reveal the value of alternative purchases that must be forsaken. The fact that interest rates usually apply to *money* loans does *not* mean that interest is a monetary, financial distortion or exaction that financiers and bankers have somehow managed to impose on ordinary people. We point this out because often engineers and technicians in the physical sciences believe that the rate of interest on loans for financing building projects should be ignored (set at zero) in order to get at the "real" costs or to avoid being misled by superficial financial considerations. This is an error and amounts to saying there is no preference for earlier over later availability—a proposition that no one would defend once he realized he was saying it.

Economics does not say that people prefer to have something now rather than later because they are impatient or shortsighted. They may or may not be. It makes no difference for deducing a lower present value for deferred relative to nondeferred goods. Nor does a positive rate of interest exist to anticipate inflation. Regardless of inflation, the rate of interest is positive.

Some other considerations do imply a lower present value of deferred goods. The certainty of death—the certainty that we shall some day *not* be able to enjoy some postponed goods—makes us unwilling to give up 1 gallon of gasoline (or anything) today for just 1 gallon in the future, when we may not be alive. Another factor is the productivity of capital. Even if you don't die during the period in question, you could be using the resources given up now to earn more income.[1]

The rate of interest, then, reflects: (a) convenience of earlier availability, (b) preference for assured consumption over contingent consumption, and (c) ability to use resources to increase total output. *Any* society—capitalist, communist, advanced, primitive, industrial, agrarian, democratic, totalitarian—in which these elements are present will have a *positive rate of interest*—i.e., a rate greater than zero. Some of these societies may have an official dogma which denounces this fact or which tries to hide it—but it is nevertheless present in all of them, so long as there is scarcity.

So far, we have shown that (1) earlier availability has a value, as an implication of the postulate that more is preferred to less; (2) this higher value of earlier availability, expressible as a percentage of the present value of a current good, is called the "interest rate"; and finally (3) the interest rate applies to *all* goods as well as to money.

METHODS OF EXPRESSING OR MEASURING RATE OF INTEREST

There are several ways to express or measure the rate of interest. All are really the same, looked at from different points of view.

1. Suppose you give up an amount of money today, p_1, in return for an amount, A, to be received in one year; p_1 is the *present* price of that *future amount* A. The rate of interest for that year can be expressed as

$$\frac{(A - p_1)}{p_1} = \text{annual rate of interest.}$$

[1] The "productivity of capital" will be discussed later, in Chapter 29.

For example, if A represents \$1 to be obtained in one year, and if the present price, p_1, of that future dollar is 90 cents, the rate of interest works out to

$$(\$1 - \$0.90)/\$0.90 = 0.11.$$

This can be related to the goods one can buy with money. If the price for a gallon of gasoline available today is 30 cents, and if you could make an agreement to pay 27 cents today to get a gallon one year later (presumably selling at that time for 30 cents), then the rate of interest implied is

$$(\$.30 - \$.27)/\$.27 = 11\%.$$

Few of us ever have occasion to make this kind of arrangement, because we find it cheaper and more convenient to make commitments for money rather than for specific goods; barter is less convenient for exchanges involving the present and future just as it is less convenient for exchange of current goods. So we shall persistently use money rates of interest, even though underlying the use of money are the specific goods and services.

2. Most of us are familiar with a slightly different way of measuring the interest rate. Suppose you can lend 90 cents today and get \$1 a year later. We say that the rate of interest is 11 percent, because 90 cents today "grew" into \$1, or required a repayment of 11 percent more than was initially lent. "If I lend 90 cents today, I can get back \$1 in a year—I get 11 percent interest per year." Or, "I can today purchase for 90 cents a \$1 payment deferred one year." Or, "Since I pay the 90 cents (lend it) for your promissory note as evidence of the right to a deferred payment of \$1, I have bought today for 90 cents your promissory note for \$1 to be paid a year hence." That promissory note may say that you will pay me 90 cents plus 11 percent interest per year, or simply that you will pay me \$1 in a year with no explicit reference to interest. That makes no difference—except possibly in the eyes of the law, which is sometimes blind to certain economic facts of life. But the total repayment is composed of repayment of the money loaned, plus interest.

This way of interpreting the rate of interest can be expressed

$$p_1(1 + r) = A,$$

which is to say that the present payment, p_1, will grow in one year at the annual rate of interest, r, to A. In our present example, 90 cents will grow at 11.1 percent to \$1.

$$\$.90\,(1 + .111) = \$.999 = \$1.$$

The equation

$$p_1(1 + r) = A$$

can be rearranged and solved for r, in which case we get the formula of the preceding section:

$$(A - p_1)/p_1 = r.$$

3. The present price, p_1, of something deferred a year is sometimes known as a *discounted* value. The term "discounting" is suggested by the fact that, at positive rates of interest, $1 due in a year (deferred for a year) has a present value less than $1. The *lower* present price of a future amount due is the "discounted" value of the future amount due. This way of looking at the problem means simply that we solve the preceding equation for p_1 as the key variable, in which case we get

$$p_1 = \frac{A}{(1+r)}.$$

If A is $1 and the rate of interest is 11 percent,

$$\$.90 = \frac{\$1.00}{(1+.11)}.$$

So the amount deferred one year is worth 0.90 of that amount now, at the rate of interest of 11 percent. Or, 90 cents will grow at the annual rate of interest of 11 percent to $1 in one year. Or, if $1 deferred one year has a price now of 90 cents, the implied rate of interest is 11 percent. These three different ways of saying the same thing correspond to the three alternative expressions discussed in the preceding paragraphs.

4. A fourth alternative is to express the interest rate as a relationship between the present price of some good available now and the present price of its availability deferred a year. Call that present price of a good available now (deferred zero years) p_0. Obviously, the present price, p_0, is equal to that amount itself. You can buy $1 *available now* for $1 now. However, the present price of $1 to be available next year is, let us say, 90 cents. The rate of interest can be interpreted—in fact, defined—as the relative premium of the present price of *present* goods over the price of the same goods *deferred* a year. This can be expressed as

$$\frac{(p_0 - p_1)}{p_1} = r.$$ [2]

For example, if the present price of a gallon of gasoline to be delivered now is 30 cents, and if the present price to be paid now for a gallon of the same gasoline

[2] This equation is identical to an earlier one, with p_0 replacing A. A little reflection will indicate that the numerical magnitude of A will always be the same as p_0.

to be delivered a year from now is 27 cents, then the rate of interest is 11.1 percent, from the expression

$$\frac{\$.30 - \$.27}{\$.27} = .111 = 11.1\%.$$

Consider a more common illustration. The U.S. government, almost every month, seeks to borrow money for short periods—say, one year. It does so by selling its one-year promissory notes to pay \$1,000 in one year to the buyer at a zero interest rate. Thus, no interest rate is explicitly specified. These notes are then sold to the highest bidders. Suppose the highest bidder offers only \$900 for one of these notes. What is the implicit rate of interest? By what percent of \$900 will the \$1,000 repayment exceed the amount actually loaned (paid for the note) to the U.S. government? The \$100 difference is 11.1 percent of \$900. Therefore, the annual interest rate is 11.1 percent. (Actually, the price for the last several years for such notes has been around \$970, implying an interest rate of about 3 percent.) Even though no interest rate is stated on the note, there is actually a positive rate as long as the present price or amount borrowed is less than the total amount to be repaid. This is a legal and orthodox arrangement; it is a convenient way to find the best possible terms at which the government can borrow.

INTEREST—THE PRICE OF MONEY?

The interest rate is often called the price of money. This "nickname" is misleading, for the price of \$1 right now is, of course, simply \$1. More accurately, the rate of interest is the price of earlier rather than later *availability* —sometimes also carelessly referred to as the price of time. The term "price of money" has become popular because people usually borrow or lend money rather than specific goods. Lenders buy future money in exchange for present money; they buy deferred-availability money; they pay out less now than the future amount received. That excess *future* amount (interest) is the *price* paid for *present* money, but the emphasis is on the *present time* element rather than on the money element. Rigorously speaking, interest is the price of earlier availability of rights to use goods rather than later availability.

To digress momentarily, our present purpose is not to see how interest rates are determined by the demand for present relative to future goods. We shall take this up later. Here we are concerned with the implications of the facts that (1) people can and do evaluate and exchange present for deferred goods and services (i.e., there *is* a rate of interest); and (2) future deferred goods are less valuable than the same amount of goods and services available now (i.e., the rate of interest is *positive*).

We observe in the real world that people lend money only if they can get a positive rate of interest in one form or another. There is little need to present formal evidence here that a positive interest rate does exist in the real world. Just try to borrow money at a zero rate of interest! True, in some areas and in some times, there have been laws against "usury"—another word for interest. The Catholic Church, for example, from almost its beginning has considered interest as improper, unjust, and unsanctioned. Similarly, Communist doctrine regards interest as a capitalist tool of exploitation (although *recent* Communist economists have "rediscovered" the presence and role of the interest rate). And when William the Conqueror ruled England, interest was illegal—except if collected by Jews—a convenience to William, who allowed Jews to live in England so that people (especially William and his nobles) could borrow from them. It is impossible to give a satisfactory economic reason for the Christian and Communist opposition to interest—when one understands that interest is merely a manifestation of individuals' preferences for earlier rather than later availability. We can only conjecture that perhaps the stricture against interest reflects the Church doctrine that people *should not* be the way they are; they *should* be neutral as between earlier and later availability. Why do the Communists object to this fact of life? In truth, they really do not if you judge by their actions rather than their words. The Russian government borrows money and pays interest, and its investment policy recognizes the advantage of early over later availability. Perhaps its façade of objection is a carry-over of typical Marxian confusions about economic fundamentals.

THE FARTHER IN THE FUTURE, THE LOWER THE PRESENT VALUE

The *more distant* the deferred money (or income, or goods), the *lower* its present price. A dollar deferred two years is worth less today than a dollar deferred one year, if the rate of interest is positive and the same for both periods. At an interest rate of 15 percent, the current price of $1 deferred a year is 87 cents—the amount that will grow at 15 percent in one year to $1. This is given by the formula

$$p_1 = \frac{A}{(1 + r)}$$

or

$$\$.87 = \frac{\$1.00}{(1 + .15)}$$

To get the present price for $1 deferred two years, simply repeat the above operation. If $1 deferred one year from now is now worth 87 cents, then deferring the dollar an additional year again reduces its present value by the same proportion.

For two years, this is $.87 \times .87 = .756$. A dollar due in two years is worth today 75.6 cents.

This same relationship can be expressed by noting that at 15 percent per year 75.6 cents will grow in one year to 87 cents, and then in the second year the 87 cents will grow to exactly \$1. This can be expressed in the form

$$p_2\,(1+r)(1+r) = A,$$

where p_2 represents the amount now that will grow at the 15 percent annual rate of interest to \$1, the amount A, at the end of the two-year period. Solving for p_2, we get

$$p_2 = \frac{A}{(1+r)(1+r)} = \frac{A}{(1+r)^2} = \frac{\$1.00}{(1.15)^2} = \$.756.$$

Two years' discounting is measured by the factor $1/(1 + .15)^2 = .756$; three years of discounting is obtained by multiplying the future amount due in three years by $1/(1.15)^3 = .658$. The present value of \$1 deferred t years from today is obtained by use of the factor $1/(1.15)^t$. Multiplying the amount due at the end of t years by this present-value factor gives the present value (or present price, or discounted value) of the deferred amount, A, due in t years. A set of these present-value factors is given in Table 15–1 for various rates of interest and years of deferment. The present-value factor decreases as t is larger; the farther into the future the amount due is deferred, the lower is its *present* value.

Present Capital Value for Series of Future Amounts

If there is a sequence of amounts due at future times, we can find a present value for this series of amounts. Just as we add up the costs of individual items in a market basket of groceries, we add up the present values of each of the future amounts due. That sum is the present value of the whole stream (series, sequence, or set) of amounts due at various future dates.

This can be illustrated with the following example. Imagine having an oil well that each year on December 31 spurts out 1 gallon of oil that sells for \$1. To simplify the problem, suppose that it will do this for exactly two years. If the interest rate is 15 percent, the present value of \$1 deferred one year is 87 cents (see Table 15–1, column of .15 rate of interest for one year); and the present value of \$1 due in two years is 75.6 cents (see the same table, same column, but now read the entry for two years). The sum of the present capital values of both amounts due, the one in one year and the other in two years, is the sum of 87 cents and 75.6 cents, which is \$1.63. To say that the rate of interest is 15 percent per year is equivalent to saying that you can exchange in the market

Table 15–1

PRESENT VALUE OF $1

WHAT A DOLLAR AT END OF SPECIFIED FUTURE YEAR IS WORTH TODAY

Year	4%	6%	8%	10%	12%	15%	20%
1	.962	.943	.926	.909	.893	.870	.833
2	.925	.890	.857	.826	.797	.756	.694
3	.890	.839	.794	.751	.711	.658	.578
4	.855	.792	.735	.683	.636	.572	.482
5	.823	.747	.681	.620	.567	.497	.402
6	.790	.705	.630	.564	.507	.432	.335
7	.760	.665	.583	.513	.452	.376	.279
8	.731	.627	.540	.466	.404	.326	.233
9	.703	.591	.500	.424	.360	.284	.194
10	.676	.558	.463	.385	.322	.247	.162
11	.650	.526	.429	.350	.287	.215	.134
12	.625	.497	.397	.318	.257	.187	.112
13	.601	.468	.368	.289	.229	.162	.0935
14	.577	.442	.340	.263	.204	.141	.0779
15	.555	.417	.315	.239	.183	.122	.0649
16	.534	.393	.292	.217	.163	.107	.0541
17	.513	.371	.270	.197	.146	.093	.0451
18	.494	.350	.250	.179	.130	.0808	.0376
19	.475	.330	.232	.163	.116	.0703	.0313
20	.456	.311	.215	.148	.104	.0611	.0261
25	.375	.232	.146	.0923	.0588	.0304	.0105
30	.308	.174	.0994	.0573	.0334	.0151	.00421
40	.208	.0972	.0460	.0221	.0107	.00373	.000680
50	.141	.0543	.0213	.00852	.00346	.000922	.000109

$1.63 today for the right to receive $1 in one year *and* an additional $1 in two years.

As the preceding example shows, we can express as a *single* price the present capital value of a *sequence* or *series* of several future payments. The capital value, or present price, is *less* than the sum of those undiscounted amounts due. The sum of the undiscounted amounts due in our example is $2; yet the present or capital value is $1.63 (which implies a 15 percent rate of interest).

Suppose that this same sequence is to last three years, with three $1 receipts. The aggregate present value is augmented by the present value of the dollar due in the third year. At a 15 percent rate of interest, this extra dollar has a present value of 65.8 cents; therefore, the present value of the three-year series is $2.28. We have noted that this present value of a series of amounts due may be called the *capital value* of the future receipts. *Capital value* is a single value at a moment (usually the present moment), whereas the thing being capitalized is a stream or series of expenditures or receipts extending over time. Capital value is the current *price,* or market value, of the rights to the stream of receipts.

Some technical jargon will be convenient for subsequent analyses. The sequence of future amounts due is called an *annuity,* suggesting amounts once a year. A two-year sequence is a two-year annuity. The term "annuity" denotes the series of annual amounts for a specified number of years. A person who has purchased the right to a stream of future annuities or amounts due—for example, his pension benefits—is sometimes called an *annuitant.*

How about a four-year annuity? The fourth year's $1 has a present value of 57.2 cents, which, when added to the present value of a three-year annuity of $1 a year, gives $2.86. A five-year annuity would have a present value of $3.35, because the dollar received at the end of the fifth year is now worth 49.7 cents. Proceed to the end of ten years, and you will find that the present capital value of a ten-year annuity of $1 each year is $5.02.

If we extended the series to twenty years (still with $1 at the end of each year) at 15 percent per year, the present capital value would increase to $6.23. Notice that the *present* value of the *last half* of that series (the ten amounts due in the eleventh through the twentieth years) is only $1.21 (= $6.23 – $5.02). At a 15 percent interest rate, $1.21 *today* will buy you $1 a year for ten years, beginning at the end of the eleventh year from now. But this should no longer be surprising. If people value earlier availability at 15 percent a year, then the current value of availability after eleven years should be relatively low.

Table 15–1 gives the present value of each separate future payment in the annuity. For convenience, Table 15–2 gives the present value of annuities of various lengths, where the payment *at the end* of each year is $1. Looking at that table under the 15 percent interest rate, you will find that the present capital values for the *sum* of the discounted amounts due in the preceding examples are the entries in the rows for one, two, three, four, five, ten, and twenty years. (This table saves the trouble of sequentially adding up the entries in the columns of Table 15–1.) Look at the entry for two years at 15 percent. It is the sum of .870 and .756, based on the data of Table 15–1. For an annuity lasting fifty years, the entry is $6.66—which says that a fifty-year annuity of $1 per year, with the first payment coming at the end of one year, has a present capital value of only $6.66 (at 15 percent).

Even an annuity that lasted forever, or for as long as you and your heirs desire, would have a finite capital value—namely, $6.67, only a penny more than

Table 15–2

PRESENT VALUE OF ANNUITY OF $1, RECEIVED AT END OF EACH YEAR

Year	4%	6%	8%	10%	12%	15%	20%
1	0.960	0.943	0.926	0.909	0.890	0.870	0.833
2	1.89	1.83	1.78	1.73	1.69	1.63	1.53
3	2.78	2.67	2.58	2.48	2.40	2.28	2.11
4	3.63	3.46	3.31	3.16	3.04	2.86	2.59
5	4.45	4.21	3.99	3.79	3.60	3.35	2.99
6	5.24	4.91	4.62	4.35	4.11	3.78	3.33
7	6.00	5.58	5.21	4.86	4.56	4.16	3.60
8	6.73	6.20	5.75	5.33	4.97	4.49	3.84
9	7.44	6.80	6.25	5.75	5.33	4.78	4.03
10	8.11	7.36	6.71	6.14	5.65	5.02	4.19
11	8.76	7.88	7.14	6.49	5.94	5.23	4.33
12	9.39	8.38	7.54	6.81	6.19	5.41	4.44
13	9.99	8.85	7.90	7.10	6.42	5.65	4.53
14	10.6	9.29	8.24	7.36	6.63	5.76	4.61
15	11.1	9.71	8.56	7.60	6.81	5.87	4.68
16	11.6	10.1	8.85	7.82	6.97	5.96	4.73
17	12.2	10.4	9.12	8.02	7.12	6.03	4.77
18	12.7	10.8	9.37	8.20	7.25	6.10	4.81
19	13.1	11.1	9.60	8.36	7.37	6.17	4.84
20	13.6	11.4	9.82	8.51	7.47	6.23	4.87
25	15.6	12.8	10.7	9.08	7.84	6.46	4.95
30	17.3	13.8	11.3	9.43	8.06	6.57	4.98
40	19.8	15.0	11.9	9.78	8.24	6.64	5.00
50	21.5	15.8	12.2	9.91	8.30	6.66	5.00

a fifty-year annuity. This means also that the present capital value for $1 at the end of each year forever, *but beginning after fifty years,* is very small indeed. For only 1 cent today you could buy (at 15 percent) a *perpetuity* retirement payment of $1 per year, beginning *after fifty* years. A perpetuity is a perpetual annuity. A deferred (for fifty years) perpetuity is one that begins after an interim of fifty years. A student who is not yet twenty years old can ponder this implication: a cent put aside now at 15 percent per year will bring you and your heirs forever, after fifty years, $1 a year.

A second thought will remove the mystery from the fact that an infinitely long series of amounts due has a *finite* (limited) *price today*. To get a perpetual series of payments of $1.50 *every* year, all one has to do is keep on deposit in a bank, if he can get 15 percent, the amount of $10. Every year the interest payment of $1.50 can be taken out, and this can be done forever. In effect you pay $10 today to *purchase* a sequence of annual receipts of $1.50 for as long as you or your heirs like.

Future Amounts Corresponding to Given Present Values

Instead of deriving present values of future amounts, we can derive for any annual rate of interest the future amount that will be exchangeable for any present value. How much will $1 paid now purchase if the future amount is due in one year, or in two years, or in three years? At 15 percent per year, $1 will be worth $1.15 in one year. And at 15 percent for the next year, that $1.15 will in turn grow to $1.32. Hence, $1 today is the present price or value of $1.32 in two years. In terms of our formula, this can be expressed

$$p_2(1+r)(1+r) = A$$

$$\$1(1.15)(1.15) = \$1(1.32) = \$1.32.$$

If the future amount is deferred three years, the term (1.15) enters three times, and if deferred t years, it enters t times. For three years, the quantity (1.15) is multiplied together three times, denoted $(1.15)^3$, and equals 1.52. Therefore, in three years $1 will grow to $1.52. In general, the formula is

$$p_t(1+r)^t = A$$

for any present payment, p_t, that is paid for an amount A available t years later. The multiplicative factor $(1+r)^t$ is called the *future-value* (or *amount*) *factor*. Values of this future-amount factor for different combinations of t and r are given in Table 15–3. For example, at 6 percent in five years, the future-amount factor is 1.34, which means that a present payment of $1 will buy, or grow to, the future amount $1.34 at the end of five years. Notice that the entries in Table 15–3 are simply the reciprocals of the entries in Table 15–1. The factor that multiplies a present amount to some future amount in t years $(1+r)^t$ must be the reciprocal of the factor that converts the future amount back to a present amount. Table 15–3 lists $(1+r)^t$, while Table 15–1 lists $1/(1+r)^t$.

To avoid getting lost in details, let us again note what we are discussing. In earlier chapters we discussed choices among alternative consumption patterns *via* exchange in the marketplace. We saw that, in comparing two different patterns, a person could make choices if he knew what each basket would cost

Table 15–3

COMPOUND AMOUNT OF $1

AMOUNT TO WHICH $1 NOW WILL GROW BY END OF SPECIFIED YEAR AT COMPOUNDED INTEREST

Year	4%	6%	8%	10%	12%	15%	20%
1	1.04	1.06	1.08	1.10	1.12	1.15	1.20
2	1.08	1.12	1.17	1.21	1.25	1.32	1.44
3	1.12	1.19	1.26	1.33	1.40	1.52	1.73
4	1.17	1.26	1.36	1.46	1.57	1.74	2.07
5	1.22	1.34	1.47	1.61	1.76	2.01	2.49
6	1.27	1.41	1.59	1.77	1.97	2.31	2.99
7	1.32	1.50	1.71	1.94	2.21	2.66	3.58
8	1.37	1.59	1.85	2.14	2.48	3.05	4.30
9	1.42	1.68	2.00	2.35	2.77	3.52	5.16
10	1.48	1.79	2.16	2.59	3.11	4.05	6.19
11	1.54	1.89	2.33	2.85	3.48	4.66	7.43
12	1.60	2.01	2.52	3.13	3.90	5.30	8.92
13	1.67	2.13	2.72	3.45	4.36	6.10	10.7
14	1.73	2.26	2.94	3.79	4.89	7.00	12.8
15	1.80	2.39	3.17	4.17	5.47	8.13	15.4
16	1.87	2.54	3.43	4.59	6.13	9.40	18.5
17	1.95	2.69	3.70	5.05	6.87	10.6	22.2
18	2.03	2.85	4.00	5.55	7.70	12.5	26.6
19	2.11	3.02	4.32	6.11	8.61	14.0	31.9
20	2.19	3.20	4.66	6.72	9.65	16.1	38.3
25	2.67	4.29	6.85	10.8	17.0	32.9	95.4
30	3.24	5.74	10.0	17.4	30.0	66.2	237
40	4.80	10.3	21.7	45.3	93.1	267.0	1470
50	7.11	18.4	46.9	117	289	1080	9100

him. The cost was simply the sum of the products of the quantity of each good multiplied by its price. But often decisions involve purchases of goods that are not always available at the same time. Furthermore, and this is the crucial point for present purposes, the purchase price is not always expressed as an amount to be paid now, but possibly a year or so later—or even as a sequence of installments over several years.

The present-value concept, also called the *present capital value,* is a basic economic measurement, because it provides a basis for comparing different time-patterns of future receipts and expenditures. The present-capital-value measure is a valid measure of cost, for it correctly indicates which choice will cost him least—i.e., result in the least reduction in wealth.

Income, Saving, Consumption, Wealth, and Profits

Rigorous definitions of income, wealth, consumption, saving, and profits can now be considered. Something that will be worth \$110 in one year will today be worth \$100 (at a 10 percent rate of interest). It follows that the wealth will rise from \$100 to \$110 in one year. This change is predictable and foreseeable and represents the interest that is said to accumulate, or which was subtracted in getting the present value of \$100 from the year-hence value of \$110. This predictable increase in value is called *income* (sometimes, *net* income) available from the economic goods. A person could consume some of his wealth (or sell it and spend the proceeds) and still end the year with exactly the same amount of wealth with which he started. He would be consuming all his income. *Income* is defined to be a *predictable* maximum absolute rate of growth in wealth, which can be consumed and still leave the owner with an unreduced amount of wealth. If he saves (does not consume) any part of that income, he will increase his wealth; that nonconsumption of his income is defined as an *investment* or *saving* of the income.

If present wealth is \$100 and the rate of interest is 10 percent, then annual income is at the rate of \$10 per year in perpetuity (as long as wealth stays at \$100); that is, income $= r \times W$, where r is the rate of interest and W is wealth. The \$10 per year is the interest; it is the income; it is the uniform maximum foreseeable consumption of wealth that is possible each year without reducing the wealth.

Wealth, the existing interest rate, and income are locked together. If any two are known, the other can be determined. Which of these three are objectively observable quantities in the market? The first two: wealth and the rate of interest. With the market measure of wealth and interest rates, we can compute an income by multiplying wealth by the rate of interest.

Although the *measure* of income is derived from the market measure of wealth and the rate of interest, in a basic sense the value of wealth is a reflection of future expected flow of services. Therefore, the future flow of services is the basic variable, with the present observed market value of wealth really a derived concept. Yet this is not inconsistent; the only directly, objectively measurable magnitude is the present market value of the goods yielding those future services. The wealth value may be based on those future yields, but the future yields are not now directly measurable or observable. What is measured now is the present capital value—wealth—of the rights to those future services.

Regardless of what the time profile of actually received future receipts may be, the peak periods can be flattened out by storage and the troughs filled by withdrawal from stocks. As long as those peaks and troughs are predictable, we do not refer to them as over- or underconsumption, since we know the future will provide replenishments. We do not say we overconsume on Saturday and Sunday and underspend on work days, just because the expenditures on those days exceed receipts. For purposes of planning consumption, the *maintainable rate* is the useful reference point. Again, with seasonal variations in crops, we do not speak of overconsuming wheat in January as long as we are consuming it at a maintainable rate in anticipation of the next crop.

Yet income can change. How? Suppose that wealth today is $100, with a rate of interest of 10 percent. Suppose that foresight or predictions are changed, and it is now believed that consumption rates can be increased in the future. Current market measures of wealth suddenly rise. The market value of wealth rises to $120 (while the interest rate, we shall suppose, stays at 10 percent). If this revision in values occurs on January 1, what is the predicted annual income thereafter? Is it $20, the rise in the present-wealth value plus the interest, $12, that will accumulate (10 percent of $120) to a total of $32? No. The revision of future prospects instantaneously adjusted wealth upward to $120. That $20 rise was a previously unforeseen rise in wealth. That unforeseen, unanticipated, unexpected rise is called *profits* (*losses* if negative). On January 1, a profit of $20 was realized; and thereby the uniform, maximum foreseeable annual rate of consumption (without reducing wealth) is increased to 10 percent of $120, or $12 per year. There has occurred an unanticipated wealth change (profit) of $20 in wealth, and an income change of $2; but each is merely a measure of the other. The $20 increase in wealth is the present value of the $2 per year increase in income perpetuity.

To say, then, that "a person consumes all his income" means the same thing as "a person chooses to save nothing." "All the foreseeable maximal available growth in wealth is consumed." "A person's income is $1,000 a year" is an equivalent statement to "the maximal foreseeable available growth he could have experienced, had he consumed nothing, is $1,000." And "A person saves or invests annually $500 of his $5,000 income" is equivalent to "He chooses to end the year with $500 more wealth rather than with all of the $5,000 of maximal foreseeable increment."

In the earlier example, in which the unforeseen increase in wealth (profit) of $20 occurred, it is tempting to say that the person must have decided also to save the $20 increase in wealth rather than to consume it. However, this would be inconsistent with our definition of the term "saving." There is no need to do any saving to get that $20 profit, any more than there is a need to save every day all of one's wealth in order not to consume it. Saving, as we have defined it, is not simply any nonconsumption; it is a special kind of nonconsumption. It is nonconsumption of *income*. The nonconsumption of wealth is not an act of saving.

In sum, if a person consumes none of his income, he saves all of his income, and he can't possibly save more than that. If he consumes part of his income, he saves the remainder. If he consumes all of his income, he saves nothing. And if he consumes more than his income and thereby destroys part of his wealth, he is dissaving. Since income is the maximum foreseeable steady (constant percentage) rate of growth of potential wealth, a person who consumes is to that extent preventing a growth of wealth. And by saving, he is permitting an increase in wealth. However, wealth *can* increase without saving, but only if there are profits.

The analysis of this chapter shows how anticipations of future events affect prices of assets, even without any other changes in the current situation. It is sufficient that expectations change. In the stock exchange these revisions are made especially apparent, for the price of a share of common stock—a share of ownership in a business corporation—is interpreted as the capitalized present worth of the expected future net receipts. A firm may have negative net receipts this year; but if it is expected to have positive net receipts thereafter, the present worth of that entire conjectured future-net-receipt sequence is capitalized into a present-wealth value. If it is suddenly expected that higher taxes will be placed on cars, the present capital value of General Motors stock will drop now, imposing a loss of wealth on the *current* owners.

Do not miss the implication. Both private-property rights and capital-goods markets, in which ownership of assets can be bought and sold, are essential institutional foundations of the capitalist system. If either is suppressed, the system will lead to actions that appear to be "wasteful or shortsighted," especially in the maintenance of and investment in durable goods with future yields. A houseowner will maintain and repair the house even though the repairs do not give him better housing now. The market anticipates lower maintenance expenditures consequent to present repair expenditures. The houseowner may, in fact, sacrifice some current heating and lighting to save money for that repair and maintenance. If, instead, the owner had spent the money for current services—such as a warmer, brighter house—the value of the house would have fallen.

This suggests that a *renter-tenant* responsible for maintenance and expenditure would divert less funds from current heat and light to repair and maintenance and improvement than would an owner. The owner will experience larger changes in his wealth as the anticipated future consequences of present actions are capitalized into his present wealth. On the other hand, a tenant who does not have these wealth consequences capitalized into his wealth will be more prone to use funds for current "heating and lighting" pleasures.

An illustration of this divergence between concern for long-run effects—measured by the present value of the wealth of the organization and the short-run current sources of satisfaction—can be found in the modern firm. The owner is influenced by all effects—present and future—that change the wealth of the firm. Future developments will be capitalized more into the ownership value of the firm than onto the current employees, who will be motivated more by what happens now and less by what happens to the firm in the more distant future. To direct the employees' actions more toward increases in the wealth of the firm, two kinds of pay systems are sometimes annexed to the wage system. One is a stock-option scheme, in which employees have rights to buy shares of stock at pre-assigned values. Because the wealth effects of their actions will be reflected in the value of the shares of stock, employees will pay more heed to the long-run effects than they would without the stock-option scheme. Another scheme —called "profit sharing," in which employees share the annual "earnings" of the firm—misses the mark because "earnings" do not measure the true profits of the firm. The true profits are the changes in the capital value of the business revealed by the price of the common stock. Instead, "earnings" are computed more in terms of current net receipts, with inadequate attention to expenditures that are inherently investments in the future. The computed current "earnings" are less responsive to the longer-run implications of present events and fail to call as much attention to the wealth-changing factors. Of the two, the stock-option plan is more effective in encouraging subordinates to make decisions according to the wealth-maximizing criterion, because employees share in the ownership of the firm. They are more responsive to the capitalization process, in which future consequences of present actions are capitalized into present wealth of the owners.

Definitions and Relationships Summarized

1. Present prices, or values, can be attached to a sequence or series of future receipts or services. Economic analysis is not restricted to one-shot services or goods used up immediately.

2. Earlier availability is more valuable than later availability—i.e., the rate of interest is positive. This is an implication of the postulate that more is preferred to less (and that storage costs are trivial).

3. The rate of interest is: (a) a measure of the relationship between present amounts and the future amounts for which they can be exchanged; (b) a measure of the relationship between the current and future prices of a good; (c) a measure of the maximal growth rate of wealth; (d) a measure of the price of earlier availability of a good; and (e) the time premium paid for borrowed wealth.

4. Failing to allow for interest rates—i.e., assuming a zero rate of interest —is equivalent to assuming there is no scarcity in society. Assuming a zero rate

of interest will mislead people about the costs of alternative future consumption choices.

5. The higher the rate of interest, the lower the present value of any future good.

6. By means of present capital values, different future sequences of services or receipts can be made comparable.

7. Present capital values react immediately to revisions about beliefs of future events.

8. Income is the maximum foreseeable rate of consumption that can be maintained for an indefinitely long time.

9. Income is equal to the product of wealth and the rate of interest.

10. Saving is the unconsumed portion of income.

11. Profits (or losses) are the unanticipated changes in wealth.

12. Under the influence of a capital market and private-property owners, decisions will be affected by the fact that future consequences of present actions are capitalized in present wealth.

Practical Applications of Capital-Value Concepts

Ten applications of the principles of capitalization will now be explored. These will familiarize you with the purposes and uses of the concepts in this chapter, and give you an understanding of some pertinent everyday economic choices.

1. Two salesmen want to sell you a book for $1. Salesman *A* says that if you pay him when you order the book, he will give you a nickel discount, so that he asks 95 cents. Salesman *B* charges the full $1 but gives you one year to pay. If you can get 10 percent interest, which is the cheaper offer? How much would it take now to accumulate $1 in one year at 10 percent, in order to pay salesman *B*?

Answer: 90.9 cents. Salesman *A* requires 95 cents. Buy from salesman *B*. You will save $.950 — $.909 = $.041, which you may use for something else in the meantime.

2. You can rent a car for $800 a year, excluding the operating, insurance, and tax costs; this rent is to be paid at the *end* of each year. You can buy a car by paying $3,000 *now*. The car, if purchased, is to be kept five years, at the end of which time it is to be junked with no value. Which is cheaper—to rent or to buy?

If the yearly rental were only $600, it would clearly be cheaper to rent at *any* positive rate of interest; five annual payments of $600 is certainly less than $3,000. But is the present value of five annual rentals of $800 less than $3,000?

That depends upon the rate of interest. From Table 15–2, in the 10 percent column, we see that the present value of an annuity of $1, at the end of each of the next five years, is $3.79. Therefore, for $800, the present value is ($800 × 3.79 =) $3,032. Since this is more than the price of the new car, you should buy instead of rent. You can obtain a new car now for $3,000, whereas at 10 percent interest you now would have to pay $3,032 to purchase an annuity providing $800 at the end of each of the next five years.

At sufficiently higher interest rates, it is cheaper to rent than to buy. For example, if the interest rate is 11 percent, the five-year $800 annuity has a present value of $2,980.

3. You own a house that you are renting for a net income of $1,000 a year, after allowing for all costs (maintenance, insurance, taxes, etc.). At 10 percent annual rate of interest, that house will have a present capital value of $10,000. (Be sure you can see why!) Suppose this house is in some South American country, and you are told that housing will be nationalized after five years, with all subsequent rental receipts going to the government. The government offers you $4,000 now for the house or nothing in five years. At 10 percent rate of interest, would you sell now or keep the house? (Use Table 15–2 to see that your wealth is larger if you sell now. Refer to entry for 10 percent, five years, and obtain $3,790 as present capital value of remaining five $1,000 rentals to be received.)

How much would it be worth to "bribe" the government officials to delay confiscation until after eight years—if you were naïve enough to trust them? (Table 15–2, entry for $r = .10$, $t = 8$, gives $5,330. This is $1,330 over $4,000.)

4. Your parents, having reached age 70 with a small fortune of $50,000, now plan to live on that fund. They want to use up this wealth at a rate that permits them to draw out a fixed amount each year for fifteen years. After that, if they are still alive, you will shoulder your moral responsibility. How much can they spend each year for fifteen years? Rephrased, the question is the following: "What annuity for fifteen years has a present value of $50,000?" If you can invest the fund with safety at 10 percent, we can read the answer from Table 15–2 under column headed 10 percent. The entry in the fifteen-year line is $7.60. That is the present capital value of a fifteen-year $1 annuity. Since there is now $50,000 in the fund, $50,000/7.60 = $6,570 is the available amount of each annuity payment for the next fifteen years. This is an approximation, since $6,570 is really the amount that could be spent at the *end* of each of fifteen years (not during each year), but the difference is slight.

If they want to use up the fund in ten years, they can get $8,140 (= $50,000/6.14) at the end of each year. If they invest at 4 percent, they will get a fifteen-year annuity of $4,500 (= $50,000/11.1).

Do not be astonished by rates around 10 to 15 percent. The stock market gave at least 15 percent per year (based on *any* thirty-year period taken from the twentieth century, and after allowing for inflation). For some thirty-year periods, the market did much better. For some five- to ten-year episodes, it gave less or a great deal more. This average of the performance of all listed stocks is higher than one can get by lending money in bonds, if one is willing to accept a *variable* annuity with an average of 10 to 15 percent. In bonds and other securities in which no variation in year-to-year receipts is to be allowed, the steady state rate of yield is about 5 to 6 percent.

5. If I wanted to sell you a service that would give you $100 at the end of each year for the next thirty years, would I, for the purpose of trying to persuade you to buy it, use a high or low rate of interest to indicate its value? If I used 10 percent, the present value from Table 15–2 would work out to $942, but with 3 percent, it would work out to $1,960. If the service could be purchased now for $1,500, I would be tempted to use some relatively low rate of interest to suggest that you would get your money's worth. Always be on the alert to detect the incentive to use a "biasing" rate of interest. For example, advocates of the California Feather River project, an immense endeavor to supply additional water to Southern California, held it to be an excellent investment—as it may well be at rates of interest of 2 to 4 percent. But if the relevant alternative earning power of money is, say, 6 to 10 percent, then the resources would be more valuable if used for other things. And in the public pre-election debate on whether the state government should finance this project, virtually no publicity was given to the question of the appropriate interest rate.

6. Consider a more private question. Suppose that when you enter college you can borrow money (say $1,000) without *any* interest, but you must repay the $1,000 eight years from the date you first get it. Should you borrow? You could at least take the money and put it in a savings bank, where you will earn at least 4 percent per year. Each year you can draw out the $40 interest and throw a big party. Finally, at the end of eight years, you can draw out the $1,000, plus the last year's interest; repay the $1,000; and have $40 for a last party.

Another way to look at this is to see that you are being given free a $40 eight-year annuity beginning in one year. Even at so low a rate as 4 percent, the present value is $\$40 \times 6.73 = \$269.20$. (See Table 15–2.) The possibility of borrowing $1,000 at zero interest rates is equivalent to a gift of $269.20 upon entrance to college. Any parent who fails to encourage his children to borrow for their college education is throwing away a gift.

Question: How many college students who get interest-free or low-interest loans thereby enable parents to withhold money from college expenses and divert them to personal uses? It is no answer to say that no parent *intends* to act that way. The fact that he is *enabled* to do so is sufficient.

Apparently, in most colleges a student can arrange for at least a low-interest loan (as a gift of an annuity). For example, if a college offers to lend you $1,000 for eight years at 3 percent, and if money were worth 4 percent to you (either as a borrower or lender), the college would be giving you an annuity of $40 − $30 = $10 a year (the interest you can earn minus the interest you must pay). In fact, since the lender could just as well have invested the money himself at 4 percent, he could have simplified matters enormously by investing the money at 4 percent and then (out of the $40 interest payments he receives) hand over to you $10 a year for eight years. The present value of $10 a year for eight years at 4 percent is $67.30 ($10 × 6.73); as far as you are concerned, a gift of $67.30, or an eight-year annuity of $10, or a 3 percent loan of $1,000 when money is worth 4 percent are all equally satisfactory, in that they all have the same present value—although the student loan involves more red tape.

In blunt language, a loan at a rate of interest below the market rate is a gift of the amount of interest saving. You can see why low-interest government loans are so eagerly sought by people who at the same time claim they are not being "supported" by the government.

Similar examples are becoming more common. Today, many land developers offer home sites to home builders on the condition that any house still on the land in fifty years is to become the landowner's property. The landowner is really charging a lower rent for the use of the land, and that lower rental charge is his way of paying for the title to the house, which he ultimately gets. Consider the fact that at 10 percent an annuity of $429.50 each year for fifty years will pay for, accumulate to, or be equivalent to $50,000 in fifty years. This means that the landowner who gets title to a $50,000 house in fifty years must be renting out his land at an annual rent of $429.50 less than he could get if he did not insist on title to the house. One reason a landowner makes this kind of leasing arrangement is to take advantage of certain tax provisions. Use Table 15–4 for periodic installments that will grow to a specified future amount.

7. The Empire State Building in New York City stands on land *leased* by the owner of the building for 99 years (until about the year 2050). What will happen in 99 years if the landowner tells the building owner to remove the building? The building owner will simply give the building to the landowner! In fact, the terms of the land lease actually in force today specify that in 99 years the building title *will* be "given" to the landowner. This is not crazy. The landowner is really buying the building over a 99-year term, by charging an appropriately lower rent in the interim. The annual difference between the rent actually paid and the rental otherwise available is the amount of an annuity which if invested at, say, 10 percent for 99 years will amount *in 99 years* to a sum sufficient to buy the building *at that time*. In other words, the landowner has sold an annuity to the building owner in exchange for ownership of the building at the end of the 99-year period. Taxes and other factors dictate this roundabout method instead of the landowner's charging full rent and at the same time explicitly agreeing to buy the building and paying for it over a 99-year period.

Table 15–4

END OF EACH YEAR PERIODIC DEPOSIT THAT WILL GROW TO $1 BY END OF SPECIFIED YEAR

Year	4%	6%	8%	10%	12%	15%	20%
1	1.00	1.00	1.00	1.00	1.00	1.00	1.00
2	.490	.485	.481	.476	.472	.465	.454
3	.320	.314	.308	.302	.296	.288	.275
4	.235	.229	.222	.215	.209	.200	.187
5	.184	.177	.170	.164	.157	.148	.134
6	.150	.143	.136	.130	.123	.114	.101
7	.127	.119	.112	.105	.0991	.0904	.0774
8	.109	.101	.0940	.0874	.0813	.0729	.0606
9	.0945	.0870	.0800	.0736	.0677	.0596	.0481
10	.0833	.0759	.0690	.0627	.0570	.0493	.0385
11	.0741	.0668	.0601	.0539	.0484	.0411	.0311
12	.0666	.0592	.0527	.0467	.0414	.0345	.0253
13	.0601	.0530	.0465	.0408	.0357	.0291	.0206
14	.0547	.0476	.0412	.0357	.0308	.0247	.0169
15	.0499	.0430	.0368	.0315	.0267	.0210	.0139
16	.0458	.0390	.0329	.0278	.0234	.0179	.0114
17	.0422	.0354	.0296	.0247	.0205	.0154	.00944
18	.0390	.0324	.0267	.0219	.0179	.0132	.00781
19	.0361	.0300	.0241	.0195	.0158	.0113	.00646
20	.0336	.0272	.0219	.0174	.0139	.00976	.00536
25	.0240	.0182	.0137	.0102	.00750	.00470	.00212
30	.0178	.0126	.00883	.00608	.00414	.00230	.000846
40	.0105	.00646	.00386	.00226	.00130	.000562	.000136
50	.00655	.00344	.00174	.000859	.000417	.000138	.0000219

8. You own a factory in which you make plastic parts. You earn net income each year of $10,000, and you and your heirs expect to continue at that rate for, say, twenty years. What is the business worth now? In other words, what is the present value of a twenty-year annuity of $10,000 a year with a payment coming at the end of each year? At 10 percent the present worth is $85,100. Suppose, now, that a tax is levied on this business in such a manner that the "after-tax" net income is expected to fall to $5,000. What will happen to the present value of the business? It will fall immediately to half its value—$42,500. Now suppose that some new person comes along, and you accept his $43,000 offer for the

business. The effect of the continuing tax is on *you,* the owner at the time the tax was *announced.* You lost when the price fell—even though the decreased net receipts were in the future.

If in four years the tax is unexpectedly removed, the value of the business will jump to $78,200—assuming sixteen years of business remain (and 10 percent rate of interest). The owner at that time will receive the benefit of the jump in capital value. Of course, if it had been believed initially that the tax would only be temporary, the value would not have fallen as far as $43,000.

9. Why is land so expensive in Southern California? Per acre it is not more populated than many other areas, and yet the value is high. Population is expected to increase in California at a rate greater than in many other places. The value of the land in ten years will be higher than in some other areas that are even more populated now. If you knew something would be worth $100,000 in ten years, how much would you be willing to pay for it right now? Even if the land were completely useless (not *worthless*) right now, you couldn't buy it for $1,000 now, because at 10 percent $1,000 now will grow in ten years to only $2,590. Any person who could get the land now for $1,000 would in ten years reap a gain of $100,000 − $2,590 = $97,410! That is such a good deal that other people also would try to seize it; they would bid up the present price of the land. If the best they can do with money (resources) in the meantime is 10 percent a year, then they will pay that amount now which in ten years will grow at 10 percent to $100,000. In our jargon, this can be expressed as follows: What is the present capital value of $100,000 due in ten years at 10 percent rate of interest? Reference to Table 15–1 in the 10 percent column shows that $1 ten years from now is worth today $.385. Therefore, $100,000 ten years from now has a present value of $100,000 × .385 = $38,500. That is the price today of that land, if the rate of interest is 10 percent, and if the future value in ten years is expected to be $100,000.

If the expected population growth of Southern California were suddenly revised downward, the anticipated value of that land in ten years would be revised downward, too. Right now, the present value of the land will fall. Thus, slight variations in the *expected* rate of growth of population have substantial effects on land values.

Finally, if one thinks that land is therefore a good investment, let him note that he will have to pay now a sufficiently high price so that if future events do in fact match the present forecasts, he will make only a "normal" 10 percent annual rate of interest growth in his wealth. What it takes for him to make a greater gain in wealth is for the expectations about the future to be *revised still further upward.* If those revisions in expectations occur, the price of land at that moment will change—to "capitalize those future events into present values."

10. We conclude with a practical problem that will probably face everyone at one time or another. After ten years of working for an employer, you

decide to transfer to a new job. Your old employer reminds you that for the past ten years he has contributed (i.e., he has diverted from your wages)[3] $1,000 each year to an account for your retirement, and you have contributed the same amount each year. The fund was invested at 4 percent during that time; the total value of your account now stands at $24,000. See Table 15–4 (4 percent column, ten years, $2,000/.0833 = $24,000). Two options are open to you. (a) You may leave both contributions in that fund until retirement in thirty years when you will get the total value of this amount now credited to your account plus 4 percent per year interest. (b) Your other possibility is to take out the present value of "your" accumulated contributions, which is $12,000 (one half of the present value of $24,000). You can do as you wish with the money you take out, but the other half will be lost as far as you are concerned. In other words, you can give up $12,000 today for the sake of getting now the other $12,000, with which you may do as you like. Otherwise, you must wait thirty years more to get the accumulated value at 4 percent of the entire fund. Which shall you choose?

One of the issues upon which the answer depends is the rate at which you can invest your own funds. Suppose you believe that you can invest the amount of your contribution at 10 percent per year. Should you sacrifice half of $24,000 now for the opportunity to get 10 percent on the other $12,000 rather than 4 percent on $24,000 for thirty years?

$12,000 invested at 10 percent will be worth $90,600 in thirty more years. (See Table 15–3, 10 percent column, thirty years.) If you leave your money in the fund at 4 percent, the $24,000 fund will have grown to only $77,700 in thirty years. (See Table 15–3, 4 percent, thirty years.) Shocked?

Only if you failed to earn over 6½ percent would your own $12,000 fund have been smaller at the end of thirty years than the whole $24,000 fund at 4 percent. The interesting fact is that today most pension investment funds credit the accounts with barely 4 percent a year, while the rates of return available on the stock market just by random investing, including interest and profits, was nearly 15 percent a year, for *any* thirty-year period you care to pick between 1915 and 1960, and averaged over 18 percent over the whole period.

But suppose you had just twenty years to wait before retiring. Would it then pay you to take out your own contribution? Look in Table 15–3 (10 percent column for twenty years). The amount to which $1 will grow is $6.72. And at 4 percent the dollars in the fund will grow in twenty years to $2.19. Each of your own dollars at 10 percent will grow to *more* than twice the amount that the amount credited to you in the fund will grow at 4 percent. Even for twenty years a 10 percent growth rate will overtake the slower (4 percent) growing fund that is initially twice as large. What rate of interest is the rate that makes the two funds grow to the same amount in twenty years? (Answer: about 7.5 percent for the smaller fund, if the total pension fund accumulates interest at 4 percent.)

[3] The part of your wages he diverts is called a "fringe" benefit.

The kind of choice discussed here faces you not only with your old employer, but also at the new job. If the new employer offers to create a retirement fund for you, in which he will match your annual contribution, and the pension fund so created is credited with interest at 4 percent, what should be your choice? Should you invest in that fund for the sake of his matching contribution? In part it depends upon the rate that you think you can earn with your own investment elsewhere.

Questions

1. You invest $350 today. At the end of the year, you get back $370. What is the implied rate of interest?

2. To how much will $250 grow at 7 percent compounded annually in three years?

3. At the end of a year you will get $220. At 10 percent rate of interest, what is the present amount that will grow to that amount? In other words, what is the present value of $220 deferred one year, at 10 percent?

4. What is the present value of $2,500 due in five years at 4 percent?

5. In what sense is interest the price of money? In what sense is it not the price of money?

6. What present amount is equivalent to $1,000 paid at the end of each of the next three years, at 6 percent interest?

7. If you can borrow money from your college at a zero rate of interest for six years, and if you borrow $1,000 now, what is the present value of the "gift" to you, at 5 percent rate of interest? (Hint: Each year you earn $50 interest by investing that money now at 5 percent. What is the present value of that six-year annuity of $60?) Which would you rather have—an outright gift of $250 or that loan?

8. Your wealth today is $1,000. At 10 percent rate of interest, what is your income?

9. If your income from non-business wealth is $500 a year, what is your wealth, at a 10 percent rate of interest?

10. Your wealth today is $1,000. You can expect, at 5 percent, what perpetuity rate of income per year?

11. If you spend that income every year, what will your wealth be?

12. If you consume none of your income for two years, what will be your wealth at the end of two years, if it is $1,000 now with 5 percent interest?

13. If you announce today that you intend to save all your income for the next year, what will happen to the value of your wealth now? In one year?

14. If you announce that you are going to consume all your income during the coming year, what will happen to your wealth now? What will it be in one year?

15. You borrow $1,000 today and agree to pay the loan in five annual equal installments at 6 percent rate of interest. Use Table 15–3 and determine amount of each payment, the first due in one year.

16. You buy a house by borrowing the full price of the house, $20,000. Your annual installments in repaying the loan are $1,744 for twenty years at 6 percent. (Do you agree?)

a. At the end of the first year, how much of the house's value is yours—i.e., what is your equity? (Hint: On $20,000, the interest for one year at 6 percent is $1,200. You paid $1,754 at the end of the first year.)

b. At the end of the second year, what is your equity?

c. At the end of twenty years, assuming the house is still worth $20,000, what is your equity?

17. You are a building contractor. The rate of interest rises.

a. What happens to the value of buildings that you may build?

b. What do you suppose the effect will be on your business?

18. If the value of your buildings or common stock should fall, how can you tell whether there has been a rise in the rate of interest or a fall in anticipated future net receipts? (Hint: Look at the bond market. How will this help give an answer?)

19. You own a building worth $10,000. You receive word that the value of your building has fallen to $5,000. One possibility is that the rate of interest has risen to twice its former level. A second possibility is that the building has been damaged by a fire. In either event your wealth is now $5,000. Do you care which factor caused a decrease in your wealth? Why?

20. Mr. A has an income of $10,000 per year. At Christmas his rich uncle gives him $5,000 in cash.

a. What is his income during that year?

b. Is the $5,000 gift a part of his income?

c. How much is his annual rate of income increased as a result of the gift of $5,000 (at interest rates of 10 percent)?

21. Which do you think will have a bigger influence in revising your consumption rate over the future—an unexpected gift of $1,000 or an unexpected salary increase of $50 per month? (Hint: What is the present value of each at, say, 6 percent per year?)

16

PRODUCTION, EXCHANGE, SPECIALIZATION, AND EFFICIENCY

To this point, the production of goods has been ignored. Our analysis has been confined to what is typically called the "rationing" problem. But man can create goods and services, even if not in amounts sufficient to make them free goods. As a result, people will disagree about which goods should be produced, how they should be produced, and who should produce them.

As with the rationing problem, there are many ways to resolve these questions: a dictator can use slaves; people can work as coowners in a communal-ownership society; they can act within a private-property market system—to mention a few. Economic analysis is applicable to all of the systems.

Earlier we spoke of a system characterized by private property in goods and services, in which the owner has the right to decide how those goods shall be used or to whom he will pass that title (right to use). Furthermore, a person's labor services were included in his own private property. To the extent that private-property rights are restricted by threats of violence, anarchy intrudes. To the extent that the government enforces legal restrictions on the choice of use or of exchange, socialism replaces private-property systems (capitalism). Socialism is a system in which decisions about the use of economic goods and services are exercised via governmental political processes. Every society is a mixture of capitalism and socialism; furthermore, the composition of the mixture varies over time, partly in response to changing attitudes toward risk, degrees of tolerance for idiosyncratic behavior, and ease with which certain groups can acquire government power.

Regardless of which system is used, certain key concepts are essential to its analysis

—e.g., *production, efficient production,* and *specialization.* After defining and interrelating these concepts, we shall apply economic theory to see how the production problems mentioned earlier are answered in a private-property system; that is, the "production logic" of that system will be derived. We concentrate on that system because it is the dominant system for controlling production in the United States—not because it can be shown to be the "best" system. However, if one feels he must make judgments, the analysis provides a better understanding of the operation of that and other systems and thus permits a more informed (less arbitrary) judgment.

Production and Exchange

In the broadest sense, production is the act of increasing one's utility. *Exchange* of existing goods is *productive* because, as we have seen, it increases one's utility. Production also can occur when the physical attributes of resources —including their time of availability, place, or form—are changed. However, we shall bow to convention and restrict the label of production to the changing or creating of goods and services—i.e., wealth. Moving water from a well into a house is productive; carrying coal from the mine to the furnace is productive; tilling the soil, planting seeds, or caring for the crop is productive; so is harvesting, cleaning, grading, transporting, preserving, and distributing the crop of retail stores; so is advertising, wrapping, and delivery to the consumer's home. Production consists also of play and of entertainment. For example, any activity that I offer to pay a person to do (to increase my utility) is productive from *my* point of view. If he accepts my offer, the activity is productive from *his* point of view.

Economic theory analyzes ways in which given states of distribution of technical knowledge, effort, and resources can be organized or coordinated so that production can be achieved. Economic theory implies that people will increase their utility through exchanges of existing stocks of consumer goods; theory implies also that production of goods will increase when people appropriately "exchange" their productive activity. We now direct our attention to this latter feature. The basic principle was used nearly two hundred years ago (in 1776) by the first "economist," Adam Smith. In his famous book *An Inquiry into the Nature and Causes of the Wealth of Nations,* he called the principle "division of labor" or "specialization"; it is now generally labeled "comparative advantage."[1]

[1] Had Smith lived today, he might have called it the "*Don't*-do-it-yourself" principle. It is interesting that Smith's book did not contain a logically correct exposition; instead it contained a masterfully persuasive statement of the results of free exchange. It was David Ricardo who, nearly fifty years after the idea had been "sold," demonstrated its logical validity. We conjecture that had Smith tried to give a logically air tight demonstration, instead of a suggestive plausible interpretation, he would never have made his "point" popular.

We can hardly do better than let Smith speak in his own words:

> This division of labor, from which so many advantages are derived, is not originally the effect of any human wisdom which foresees and intends that general opulence to which it gives occasion. It is the necessary, though very slow and gradual consequence of a certain propensity in human nature which has in view no such extensive utility: the propensity to truck, barter, and exchange one thing for another.
>
> Whether this propensity be one of those original principles in human nature, of which no further account can be given; or whether, as seems more probable, it be the necessary consequence of the faculties of reason and speech, it belongs not to our present subject to enquire.

The student will note that this "propensity" to exchange was shown in earlier chapters to be an implication of the postulates about human nature, in which more is preferred to less, and substitution is possible.

In the same way that *exchange of goods for consumption* was numerically illustrated in the first portion of this book, we will show how *exchange* in *production* can yield a greater total physical output with higher utility to each person than if no exchange in production were permitted. We shall first deduce that appropriate specialization and exchange in productive activity can yield a bigger *physical* basket of output. Then we shall investigate some methods for inducing that appropriate exchange and specialization—one method relying on the free marketplace with individual incentives and private-property rights.

Specialization and Enlarged Output

The existence of large corporations, labor unions, credit buying, suburban shopping centers, trading stamps, discount houses, factories, and all the other institutions through which economic activity is conducted tends to obscure the basic principles that underlie the organization of production in a capitalist system. A television set is a complicated mechanism; yet it is built up with a chain of relatively simple principles. Once these principles are grasped, the method by which a set operates is said to be understood. Even though one doesn't know how to make a television tube, resistor, capacitor, or transformer, he can understand the function of each and even assemble them into a working system. From the surface, the system looks enormously complicated and confusing. And, without a theory, it is. But if one has a valid theory, bewilderment is replaced by confidence, complexity by sequences of simplicity, and confusion by order.

What assurance do you have that the economic theory and principles to be presented are valid? At the present moment, you have none—just as you have none when you take a physics or chemistry course. The experiments in a physics course illustrate the principles and provide tests in special experimental circumstances. In precisely the same way, the principles stated in economics can *here* be only illustrated. How does one know that these principles will apply to the rest of the world, which the student cannot yet observe? He doesn't know; and he doesn't know that the principles of physics will always work, either. He simply has to wait until he has had time to observe real events; in that way he tests, observes, and decides for himself whether to continue to believe in these principles and act accordingly, or whether to reject them. At present, we do tell the reader that overwhelming evidence supports the validity of the economic principles. With this prologue, we shall now explain the principles of specialization in production, in the context of a simple five-man society with two alternative producible goods.

PRINCIPLES OF SPECIALIZATION IN PRODUCTION

Upon entering this society, we first meet Mr. *A*, whose currently relevant distinguishing attribute is not his sex, color, age, religion, height, weight, marital status, eye color, blood type, political affiliation, or personality, but is instead his *production-possibility set* for two goods, here called *X* and *Y*. Given the resources that he represents or owns (including his capital goods, state of knowledge, and training), how much *X* can he produce if he produces *X* instead of *Y*? How much *Y* can be produced if he produces some *Y* instead of nothing but *X*? (If he produces neither *X* nor *Y*, he takes all of his time in leisure, which he could but, we suppose, does not prefer to working.)

We suppose that Mr. *A* can, with a given amount of time, energy, and resources, produce daily six units of *X*, *or* three units of *Y*, *or* any linearly interpolated combination of *X* and *Y*. For example, if he devoted half a day to *X* and the other half to *Y*, he could produce daily three units of *X* and one and a half units of *Y*. Or he could devote all of his working day and resources to *Y*, producing three *Y* and no *X*. Table 16–1 shows part of the set of possible daily output combinations of *X* and *Y*.

Table 16–1

SOME DAILY COMBINATIONS FROM MR. *A*'s PRODUCTION-POSSIBILITY SET

X	and	Y
6	and	0
5	"	0.5
4	"	1.0
3	"	1.5
2	"	2.0
1	"	2.5
0	"	3.0

For each unit increment of X, he must forsake production of $.5Y$ (or, conversely, for each extra Y he must forsake $2X$). His *production marginal rate of transformation* (substitution by production) between X and Y, the ratio of the possible change in output of X consequent to a unit change in output of Y, is always $2X = 1Y$, or $.5Y = 1X$. This can be expressed also by the statement that his production cost of $1Y$ is $2X$, and his production cost of $1X$ is $.5Y$.

Mr. *A*'s production-possibility set can be easily graphed. In Figure 16–1, all the possible output combinations he can produce are represented by the points

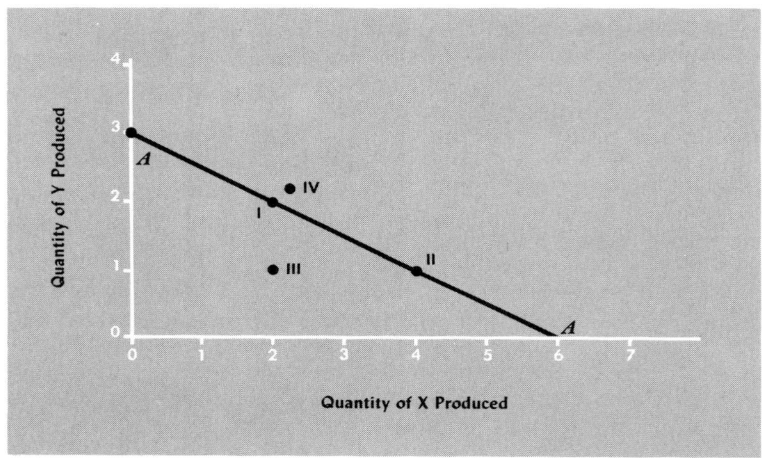

FIGURE 16–1. Mr. *A*'s production-possibility boundary.

that lie on the straight line; if he produces less than is possible, his actual production is represented by a point inside the triangular area bounded by that line and the horizontal axis. The daily rate of production of X is measured along the horizontal axis, and the daily quantity of Y is measured along the vertical axis. The extreme upper-left point on the production-possibility boundary denotes an output of all Y (3) and no X, while the lower-right-hand extreme point denotes a maximum possible output of $6X$. Point I denotes an output combination of $2X$ and $2Y$. Point II denotes $4X$ and $1Y$. Mr. *A*'s production technique will be called *efficient* if he is producing outputs *on* the production-possibility boundary at points like I or II, but not III *inside* the boundary. A production technique is "efficient," by definition, as long as the output of *both* X and Y cannot be increased. To be efficient means that the only remaining way he can increase the output of any product, X, is by giving up some output, Y (or conversely). Any point on his production-possibility boundary is defined as an efficient *production* point.

An output of 2.25 of X and of Y is portrayed by Point IV in Figure 16–1. This point is *outside* his production frontier. According to Mr. *A*'s production possibilities, it is impossible for him to produce 2.25 units of X and 2.25 units of *Y*. If he produces 2.25 units of *X*, he can produce also a maximum of 1.875 of *Y*; if he produces as much as 2.25*Y*, he can produce only 1.5*X*. Unless Mr. *A* sacrifices leisure or gets extra productive resources or learns better methods of production, he cannot get outside his production-possibility boundary, *AA*.

Which particular efficient point is best (i.e., gives him the greatest utility) cannot be detected from just these data. But the best point is one of the efficient points.

For the moment, we will suppose that Mr. *A* is producing two units of *X* and two units of *Y* per day and contentedly consuming them. He cannot get a bigger output of both.

Mr. *B* is a second person in our community, and his production-possibility set is indicated in Table 16–2 and Figure 16–2.

Table 16–2

SOME DAILY COMBINATIONS FROM MR. *B*'s PRODUCTION-POSSIBILITY SET

X	and	*Y*
3	and	0
2.5	"	0.5
2.0	"	1.0
1.5	"	1.5
1.0	"	2.0
0.5	"	2.5
0	"	3.0

Mr. *B* can produce any of these (or linearly interpolated) combinations he wishes. If he decides to produce the biggest daily output, subject to the condition of producing an equal number of each of *X* and *Y*, he can produce 1.5 of each. And he can't produce more than 1.5 of each. He could produce 2*X* and 1*Y*, giving up .5*Y* in order to get .5 more *X*. In other words, his production marginal rate of substitution in *production* is 1*X* = 1*Y*, which differs from Mr. *A*'s marginal rate of substitution in *production* of 2*X* = 1*Y*. We shall see that this difference in production marginal rates of substitution—portrayed by the differences in the *slopes* of the two production boundary lines, *AA* and *BB*—is a crucially important feature. Mr. *B*'s line, *BB*, has a slope of "minus one"; for with every increase of one unit in output of *X*, he has a decrease of one unit in *Y*. Mr. *A*'s slope is minus ½, because for every increase of one unit in *X*, he incurs a decrease of a half unit of *Y*. The *marginal cost* in producing *X* is the amount of *Y* that must be forsaken to produce a unit more of *X*. The steeper the slope of the

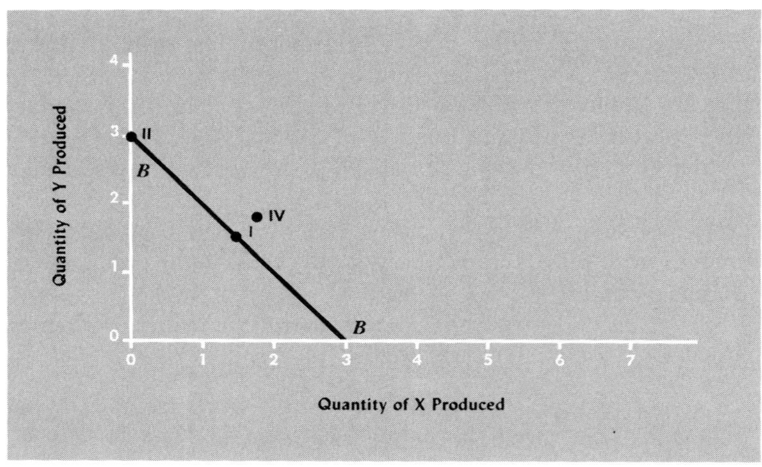

FIGURE 16–2. Mr. *B*'s production-possibility boundary.

production-possibility boundary, the greater the amount of *Y* that must be sacrificed to get an increase of one unit in *X*. Mr. *B* has the steeper slope; therefore, he has higher costs for producing *X*. Conversely, he must be the lower marginal-cost producer of *Y*.

A *straight-line* production-possibility boundary for each person reflects our supposition that the marginal cost of production for each person is *constant* regardless of how much he happens to be producing. (Later we shall investigate a less special case.)

Temporarily, suppose that Mr. *A* wants his own consumption mix to be such that for each *X* he has one *Y*. Also assume that Mr. *B* wants the same ratio of *X* to *Y*. In this event, Mr. *A* would be producing and consuming 2*X* and 2*Y*, while Mr. *B* would be producing and consuming 1.5 of each—each combination being portrayed by points "I" on the respective graphs of the production possibilities. The top half of Table 16–3 (p. 235) shows that the *total* "national" output of *X* is 3.5, and the total "national" output of *Y* is also 3.5. At best, *A* can have 2*X* and 2*Y*; Mr. *B* can have 1.5 of each—*if we prohibit production specialization.* But if specialization (and exchange) is allowed, then—without exceeding either person's production-possibility boundary—it *is* possible to get an output of *more* than 2*X* and 2*Y* for Mr. *A* and also *more* than 1.5 of each for Mr. *B*. How can this "magical" increase in total output be achieved? Answer: By use of the principle of *specialization,* which rests on the fact of *comparative advantage*—a name for differences in marginal costs of production. To see how the principle of production according to comparative advantage leads to efficient allocation of productive resources and thus to efficient production, we shall resort to a parable.

In the community we are visiting, a dictatorship exists, and the dictator is responsible for all production control. At the present moment he finds that Mr. *A* is producing 2 each of *X* and *Y*, while M. *B* is producing 1.5*X* and 1.5*Y*. By a clever reassignment of tasks, the dictator will be able to get a bigger total output. The dictator tells Mr. *A* to reduce his output of *Y* by one unit and increase his output of *X* by two units, which he can do. His output mix changes from 2*X* and 2*Y* to 1*Y* and 4*X* (represented by point II of his production-feasibility frontier of Figure 16–1). At the same time, the dictator orders Mr. *B* to reduce his output of *X* by 1.5 units, down to zero, and to increase his production of *Y* by 1.5 units to three units. This moves him from point I to point II on his production-feasibility frontier (Figure 16–2).

The total output of *both* persons is four units of *X* (4*X* from Mr. *A*) and four units of *Y* (1*Y* from Mr. *A* and 3*Y* from Mr. *B*). The total national output has "miraculously" increased from 3.5 units to four units for both *X* and *Y*! Before "explaining" how this miracle occurred, we note that for Mr. A and Mr. *B* *each* to have *more* *X* and *Y* than before, the dictator may take 1.75 units of *X* (or anything less than two units and more than 1.5) from Mr. *A* and give them to Mr. *B* in return for 1.25 units of *Y* (or any amount less than 1.5 units and more than one) which he transfers from Mr. *B* to Mr. A. This will leave Mr. *A* with 2.25 units of *X* *and* also 2.25 of *Y*, which is exactly .25 units more of *X* and of *Y* than he was able to produce alone without the dictator's instructions. On the other side, Mr. *B* will have 1.75 units of *X* and of *Y*, or .25 more of each than he is able to produce. Table 16–3 gives a summary of the operation.

Table 16–3

BEFORE SPECIALIZATION
PRODUCTION AND CONSUMPTION

	X	Y
Mr. *A*	2	2
Mr. *B*	1.5	1.5
	3.5	3.5

AFTER SPECIALIZATION (AND TRADE)
PRODUCTION (AND CONSUMPTION)

	X	Y
Mr. *A*	4 (2.25)	1 (2.25)
Mr. *B*	0 (1.75)	3 (1.75)
	4 (4.0)	4 (4.0)

What has happened can be summarized by saying that Mr. *A specializes* in the production of *X*, while Mr. *B specializes* in the production of *Y*. To specialize means that a person *produces more of some commodity than he consumes.* It does *not* mean he produces only *one* thing; rather, he produces *more* of some things, and less of others, than *he* consumes. It most certainly does not imply "surplus" production of *X* by Mr. *A*, nor of *Y* by Mr. *B*. Except for the work involved in the dictator's instructions and actions, neither *A* nor *B* works any harder than before. Both were originally working on their production possibility before the revision; so they were *individually* efficient. Now neither person has violated his production-possibility boundary—yet the total output has increased. The explanation is that formerly, although each was *individually* efficient in his production, there was "inefficient" *social* production. As long as the marginal rate of transformation between *X* and *Y* for Mr. *A* is different from the rate for Mr. *B*, it will always pay them to specialize.

Mr. *A* can produce two more *X* at a cost of 1*Y*, while Mr. *B* produces only one more *X* at a cost of 1*Y*. If Mr. *A* reduces his output of *Y* by one unit, his output of *X* could be increased by two, and to offset this Mr. *B* could be instructed to produce one more *Y* at a marginal cost of only 1*X*. This gives a net gain of 1*X* (and no decline in *Y*). We can now see that the "production marginal rate of substitution" is a measure of the "cost of production." And we have the logical proposition: Output can be maximized if goods are produced by the lower-cost producers rather than by the higher-cost producers, via specialization and exchange. Mr. *A* can produce one more *X* at a "cost" of only .5*Y*, but Mr. *B* can produce one more *X* only at a higher cost of 1*Y*. Mr. *A* is the lower-cost producer of *X*. Who is the lower-cost producer of *Y*? Mr. *B*. He can produce another *Y* at a cost of only 1*X*, whereas Mr. *A* has to sacrifice 2*X*. Table 16–4 shows the new production possibilities. This represents the output potential from the most efficient production assignments of Mr. *A* and Mr. *B*. It is impossible to get more *X* (or more *Y*), with each indicated amount of *Y* (or *X*), than given in this table.

When seeking most efficient production, then, one should use the cheapest methods of production. If *X* and *Y* are to be produced efficiently, the cheapest (marginal cost) producers of *X* should be assigned to *X*, and the cheapest (marginal cost) producers of *Y* to *Y*. The principle of comparative advantage says the same thing as follows: Efficient production of *X* is obtained if it is produced by those with the greater comparative advantage (or lower marginal cost) in production of *X*, while resources with less comparative advantage in production of *X* should be used in production of non-*X*.[2]

[2] A proof of the logical validity of this proposition requires a bit more complicated mathematics than our simple arithmetic example. For those who have had at least a year of calculus, this proposition is a verbal translation of some of the conditions (marginal equalities or inequalities) for a constrained maximum—i.e., for a specified output of *Y*, maximize the output of *X*, subject to the constraints of all the individual production-possibility conditions.

Table 16–4

TOTAL DAILY PRODUCTION POSSIBILITY
OF *X* AND *Y* BY MR. *A* AND *B*

Output *X* and *Y*
9 and 0
8 " 1
7 " 2
6 " 3
5 " 3.5
4 " 4
3 " 4.5
2 " 5
1 " 5.5
0 " 6

THREE RULES OF PRODUCTION CONTROL

Results of some other production assignments of Mr. *A* and Mr. *B* can be illustrated by Figure 16–3. In that figure are plotted the production-possibility boundaries of Mr. *A* and Mr. *B* individually, and the total community or national-output boundaries for three different rules of production control.

I. Let both Mr. *A* and Mr. *B* produce *Y*, and then if any *X* is wanted, first have Mr. *B*, the higher-marginal-cost producer of *X*, divert some resources toward producing the desired amount of *X*. If even more *X* is wanted than Mr. *B* can produce, then let Mr. *A* also divert from *Y* toward *X*. Line I gives the total set of production possibilities yielded when Mr. *A* and Mr. *B* are assigned to production of *X* and *Y* according to this pattern.

II. Line II is obtained by telling Mr. *A* and Mr. *B* always to produce *X* and *Y* in the same proportion as the other; i.e., each produces the same proportion of the total output. If more *X* is wanted, everyone is told to increase his output of *X* by that desired percentage.

III. Line III is the achievable set of outputs if the rule for line I is revised: let both Mr. *A* and Mr. *B* produce *Y* if only *Y* is wanted; but if some *X* is wanted, assign first to its production Mr. *A*, the lower-marginal-cost producer. If even more *X* is wanted than he can produce, assign the next higher-marginal-cost producer, Mr. *B*. The resulting set of production possibilities is indicated by line III, the outermost, and hence most efficient, boundary. This is a graph of the data in Table 16–4.

In effect, we first move down along Mr. *A*'s production-possibility boundary from all *Y* toward more *X*, while keeping *B* fixed at all *Y* and no *X;* and we move down *B*'s boundary only after *A* has moved to the point of all *X* and no *Y*.

Illustrating the earlier numerical example: Point III_{a+b} on boundary III is obtained by assigning Mr. *B* to production of *Y* only (represented by his being at the upper-left-hand point, *b*, where his production line cuts the *Y* axis) and by assigning Mr. *A* to the point *a* on his boundary. The sum of the outputs of *Y* from Mr. *A* and Mr. *B* is represented by the height of the point III_{a+b}, while the sum of these outputs of *X* gives the horizontal position of the point III_{a+b}.

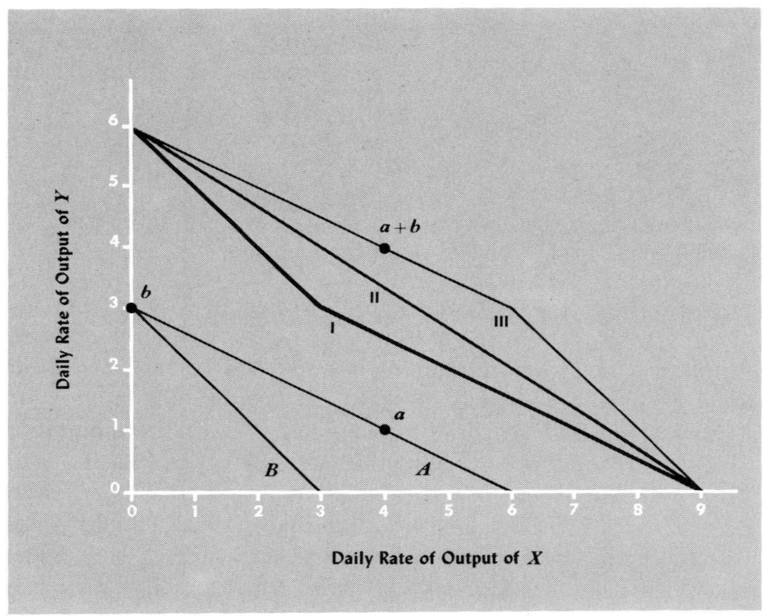

FIGURE 16–3. Production possibilities for different production rules.

OTHER ASPECTS OF SPECIALIZATION

Assembly-line production, in which everyone produces only a particular, special part of some final consumers' goods, is also called specialization. Someone specializes in digging coal, someone in making coke, someone in operating blast furnaces, and someone in operating a crane to handle the hot steel, etc. People specialize in components. This is, of course, consistent with our definition of specialization, because the specialists sell their products to get other goods for themselves. Specialization need not involve this kind of decomposition into special parts made by "specialists." Specialization, or the division of labor, requires only that a person makes something that he intends to sell to others rather than consume himself.

The principle of specialization is carried further if the components of a final product are produced more by component specialists than by final-product specialists. If one product is now being produced separately by ten different producers, all at equal costs, it may be possible to decompose the production of that good into ten different components or subtasks, in which each person performs his task at a different cost. Then, if the lower-cost man concentrates on the one subtask at which he is the lowest-cost producer, the total output can be increased. The search for more detailed production steps, "concentration" or "specialization," is merely the search for more effective realization of lower-cost production (i.e., bigger output). Increased differentiation in production (with a wider scope of specialization) is more productive than decreased specialization, as long as the attendant costs of communication and exchange do not exceed the differences in other costs.

The more cheaply that people can communicate and exchange, the greater are the possibilities of discerning and exploiting differences among their relative productive abilities, and therefore the greater the output of the entire group. In the words of Adam Smith, the gains from specialization depend upon the "extent of the market." Even with only two people and two products, specialization and its gains are made possible if people have access to a common marketplace to negotiate (i.e., exchange information) for exchange of their products.

DISADVANTAGES OF SPECIALIZATION

Despite its gains, specialization is not without its disadvantages. One of these is the monotonous and tedious repetition of tasks day in and day out; a person who chooses variety and jack-of-all-trade activity must be willing to pay the cost in smaller wealth. Another consequence of specialization is interdependence; what is supposed to be bad about interdependence is that the wealth a person can get from specialization is dependent upon other people's tastes and abilities.

Specialization usually involves making advance investments in wealth. Later, if demands of other people should shift to other products, some producers will lose some of the value of their investment. They will be poorer. The imperfection of foresight may involve losses of investments that exceed the short-lived gains from specialization. However, people know that their forecasts are fallible, and they correspondingly make smaller long-term investments in particular products. Less expensive, less durable equipment is purchased. In part, this reduces the losses of imperfect foresight and "premature" obsolescence, even though it also reduces the extent of specialization. But, on closer examination, the losses of overinvestment or of job changes in the face of demand shifts are *not* consequences of specialization, nor consequences of dependence on other people via specialization. Without specialization it would still pay to make long-term investments even for one's own use of the product. But our own demands and talents will change unpredictably. Foresight of our own situation is not made perfect merely by producing for ourselves. In a market exchange and specialization economy, losses from changes in our own demands and talents would still occur.

Achievement of Efficient Production

If the output decisions are dictated by an all-wise dictator who knows all the production possibilities of each person, presumably efficiency can be achieved—ignoring questions of how the dictator will get his orders enforced and how he will distribute the resulting product.

But in the event of a successful revolt and disposal of the dictator, is an efficient allocation of productive resources possible? How can people tell what to produce? And if they know, what induces them to do so? What signals and incentives will be effective? One possibility is that after the revolt a system of private property is instituted in each person's rights to his labor services. He is a "free man"; he can work where and at what he wishes. He can sell his goods or services to others if both parties can find a mutually acceptable price (wage).

In a private-property system, the new "dictator" is the rule of law of private property. The government enforces that rule against all people, even those who do not like private-property systems. The new dictator constrains each person's ambitions for the sake of everyone else's property rights. What will each person do? Suppose, at first, each subsists off his own production; that is, each person is self-sufficient. He will produce whatever mixture of X and Y that he most prefers of those that he can produce. If Mr. A is producing a mixture of X and Y such that he values (subjectively) one more X as equal to $1Y$, he will note that he *can* produce one more X if he forsakes only $.5Y$. Therefore, he will shift production toward more X and away from Y, for he is *willing* (in consumption) to forego as much as $1Y$ to obtain one more X, whereas he *must* (in production) sacrifice only $.5Y$. He will continue to shift toward more X until he values one more X as equivalent to only $.5Y$. In this way he is led to a consumption pattern at which he *values* $1X$ at $.5Y$, the same ratio as his *production*-transformation ratio. Let us suppose this situation is reached when he is producing (and consuming) $2X$ and $2Y$.

Look at Mr. B. His production-transformation ratio is $1X = 1Y$. He, too, adjusts his production mixture until he has a consumption mixture such that he values one more X the same as one more Y. Let us suppose that his output mixture is then 1.5 of each X and Y. Each person is a *subsistence* producer. He does not specialize, he engages in no exchange, he is independent, he is his own boss—or so he likes to think. But each has a different cost of production and a different subjective value of X relative to Y.

Now we can analyze the effect of opening up the possibility of exchange. We know from the preceding discussion that, with proper organization, Mr. A and Mr. B could jointly produce more than the total of $3.5X$ and $3.5Y$. With proper (efficient) organization, they could achieve $4X$ and $4Y$—with no harder work. How can they be led to that preferred situation without a central, all-wise control center?

The answer should be obvious. We could introduce another middleman, who cleverly buys goods from one person and sells them to the other. We know that trade is feasible, since each has a consumption pattern that gives them different subjective valuations of X relative to Y. Since we have already investigated how the middleman facilitates interpersonal comparisons of subjective values, we can now simply note that he also facilitates a comparison of marginal costs of production among producers. The disparities in these costs enable the middleman to act profitably in facilitating trade *and in inducing each producer to revise his production toward more efficient combinations.* We shall ignore the middleman here, because we already appreciate his function, and let Mr. A and Mr. B deal directly with each other—to avoid cluttering the basic plot with extra characters. In effect, Mr. A and Mr. B will be their own (unrealistically costless) middlemen.

Mr. A discovers that Mr. B is willing to buy an X at any price less than $1Y$, since Mr. B currently produces X's for himself at a cost of $1Y$. Mr. A values, and *can produce,* an X for only $.5Y$. Therefore, Mr. A will be willing to produce another X to sell to Mr. B at any price over $.5Y$. Suppose that he gets a price of $.71Y$. Mr. A and Mr. B each will reach more preferred situations. The daily amount of trade at that exchange rate will increase until Mr. A sells $1.75X$ and gets $1.25Y$; that is, when Mr. A has 2.25 each of X and Y, with 1.75 of each for Mr. B—compared to 2.00 and 1.50 without trade. Table 16–4 again shows the situation. The first part shows the outputs and distribution prior to exchange; i.e., when each person was self-sufficient. The second part shows the new production ratio, with the resulting consumption rates in parentheses, when each person is no longer "self-sufficient" but is "dependent" on other people for his preferred situation. Production differs from consumption for each person; that is, there is specialization and exchange, with a bigger total output and a bigger consumption.

Each is specializing on his product of comparative advantage, *without a dictator.* Such specialization was induced by the compulsion, desire, or drive of each person to benefit himself by getting more goods, and a chance to negotiate acceptable exchange with other people. Even though this driving force is not imposed by other people, it is pervasive, persistent, and powerful. It is a response to the compulsive desire for more.

PROFITS AND LOWER COST OF LIVING

The increased output of .5 units of *X* and of *Y* is distributed in the form of (1) profits and (2) reduced consumers' prices. Mr. *A* produced more *X*'s and sold them at a price (.71*Y*) above his costs (5*Y*). And in turn Mr. *B* bought *X*'s more cheaply (for only .71*Y*, instead of 1*Y*). Reducing the cost of *X* to the consumer and increasing the producer's profits are ways of distributing the increased output of *X* to *A* and *B*. (A similar division can be made for product *Y*.) Profits are part of the increases in product, *not* the exploitation of consumers.

THE UNSEEN HAND AND LAISSEZ FAIRE

Production resources (human or physical) are guided toward an efficient allocation as if by an "Unseen Hand." The "Hand" is (1) the desire of each person to achieve a more preferred situation, in this case via increased profits and lower costs of getting goods; (2) the right of free access to a marketplace where exchanges can be negotiated; and (3) private-property rights in goods and services so that there is something to exchange in the market. This is often called a *laissez-faire* ("let-it-do" by itself) system, because no one has to intervene to control the system, *assuming* in the first place a system of private-property enforcement and a marketplace where exchanges can be negotiated at mutually agreed upon prices.

Compared to a subsistence or self-sufficiency system in which each person produces what he consumes, appropriate concentration yields a larger aggregate output. If this is then allocated between Mr. *A* and Mr. *B* by exchange, each person can have a bigger consumption than when on a self-sufficiency basis. And it is a bigger output than if there are restrictions imposed on either Mr. *A*'s or Mr. *B*'s rights to produce. Restrictions that prevent Mr. *A* or Mr. *B* from producing and selling private-property goods will prevent the community from realizing the efficient output that would otherwise be possible. In our current example, for instance, if Mr. *A* was told he could not produce any of product *X*—because, say, production and sale of *X* is reserved exclusively for Mr. *B* as a legal monopoly—then the aggregate feasible output in our example could *not* be achieved. The smaller output is a result of "monopoly restraints" or of restrictions on "open markets" or "free enterprise." This is why it is said that "legal monopoly" or restrictions on "free enterprise" or "entry" are inefficient in a production sense. Later we shall see how legal restrictions help *some* people, despite the generally smaller total output.

Although the preceding example uses a Mr. *A* and a Mr. *B*, we could generally think of them as America and *B*ritain—and thus explain the basis of and incentives to international trade; or as New York and Nebraska, implying interregional or intercity trade; or as the U.S. Steel Corporation and the Pennsylvania Railroad, explaining the specialization by businesses. The essence of all exchange among producers—whether they be viewed as members of different nations, regions, businesses, or simply as individuals—is captured by our simple "two-person" example.

IS EFFICIENT PRODUCTION GOOD?

A warning: "Efficiency in production" is desirable in the sense that more economic goods are preferred to less. But are you sure that the produced "economic good" is a "good" economic good? For example, the authors do not allow their minor children unrestricted access to the market, because the children would probably buy economic goods that we believe they should not. We don't accept their judgment of what is "good." Similarly, if someone believes that other people do not know what is good for themselves—as evidenced by differences of opinion about the use of tobacco, alcohol, opium, heroin, gambling, low-brow television programs, comic books, lewd literature—then he may deem it appropriate to prohibit the production of such goods. Many highly educated, socially conscious people are prepared to take the position just suggested. To them, the standard of efficiency is useful only insofar as the "right" goods are wanted by the public. They feel they know better than other people what is good for other people. And therefore "efficient production of undesirable goods" is not desirable. Are they justified in their opinion? That depends upon whom you set up as the ultimate judge. Economics is neutral or amoral; it does not say that such and such motivation or result is "good" or "bad." It merely develops the implications of whatever people regard as good. "Efficiency in production" is "good" in your opinion only insofar as you admit it is "good" that individuals should make and bear more of the consequences of their choices. And not all of us are willing to admit that.

Questions

1. *A* steals from *B* successfully.

a. Is that "production"? Why?

b. If you say "No, because someone is hurt," what would you say about the case in which a new invention displaces some other producers?

c. Are there some kinds of production which you think should not be allowed?

d. Name six that in fact are not legal.

2. Smith's production possibilities are indicated by the following table:

ALTERNATIVE DAILY PRODUCTION POSSIBILITIES
BY SMITH

OATS		SOYBEANS
10	and	0
9	and	.2
8	and	.4
7	and	____
6	"	____
5	"	____
4	"	____
3	"	____
2	"	____
1	"	____
0	"	2

a. Compute the missing data, assuming linear interpolation gives his production possibilities.

b. For each increment of oats, he incurs a uniform sacrifice of an amount of soybeans. The ratio between these two changes is called the marginal rate of transformation between oats and soybeans. This rate also yields his marginal cost of oats (in terms of soybeans). What is the marginal cost of a bushel of oats?

c. Of a bushel of soybeans?

d. If that marginal cost is constant for all combinations, then production is said to involve constant costs. Does this example reveal constant costs?

e. Graph Smith's production possibility. Put oats on horizontal scale.

f. On the graph, label, as point *I*, the output that has an equal number of bushels of oats and of soybeans.

g. What is the number of bushels of each?

h. Which is the larger output—1.67 bushels of each, or 5 bushels of oats and 1 of soybeans?

3. On the graph of the preceding question, plot the production possibility of Mr. *B* (call him Black) taken from Table 16–2. Let *X* denote oats and *Y* denote soybeans.

a. Label this line *BB* and mark the point of equal numbers of bushels of oats and soybeans. (That is, 1.5 of each.)

b. What is the maximum amount of oats that Mr. Smith and Mr. Black jointly can produce if they produce only oats?

c. Only soybeans?

d. What is the maximum amount of soybeans and oats they can produce if each person produces as many bushels of oats as he does of soybeans?

e. What is the total output of each if they divide their time and resources equally between oats and soybeans?

f. Which output is larger—the one where (i) each divides his time equally among the two products or (ii) where each produces as many bushels of oats as of soybeans?

g. Which output is better?

h. Would it be efficient for them to produce either of these two combinations?

4. On the graph for question 2, plot the outputs of soybeans and oats that represent the "efficient" total production-possibility set for Smith and Black.

a. Plot also the set of possible outputs obtained if Smith and Black use identical ratios when dividing their time between oats and soybeans.

b. Does this give the same production-possibility set as the preceding question?

5. **a.** If the price of a bushel of soybeans is $1 and the price of a bushel of oats is 50 cents, which good should Smith produce if he wants to maximize his wealth? Which should Black produce?

b. If the price of a bushel of oats rises above $1 while soybeans stay at $1, what should Black do if he wants to maximize his wealth.

c. At what ratio of prices would Smith be induced to produce soybeans?

6. What is meant by efficient production? Give two different versions of the definition.

7. In a non-centrally dictated economy, how did private property serve as an inducement to efficient production?

8. What is meant by a subsistence, self-sufficient economy as contrasted to a specialized, interdependent economy?

9. Increased output resulting from more efficient specialization is distributed via what two means in a capitalist open-market system?

10. An open-market system presumes enforcement of certain institutions or rules. What are they?

11. **a.** Do you think specialization will be carried to greater extent in a large city or a small one?

b. Why?

c. Give examples of what you mean by greater specialization.

12. "It's wrong to profit from someone else's needs."

a. Explain why, if that were taken literally, we would *all* be poorer.

b. Does the doctor profit from your illness? The farmer from your hunger? The shoemaker from your tender feet? The teacher from your ignorance? The preacher from your sinfulness?

c. How are their earnings different from those of the liquor producer, the race-track owner, the burlesque strip-teaser, and the dope peddler?

13. The following remark is commonly made about some rich people: "He is an inde-dependently wealthy man."

a. From what is he independent?

b. Does his wealth not depend upon other people's demands?

14. A premier or prime minister of a new "emerging" country bragged that he was going to make his country self-sufficient and independent of foreigners. Do the principles of this chapter suggest anything about how you as a native of that country might be affected? Explain.

15. "Laissez faire means the government should do nothing." Evaluate.

17

PRODUCTION IN A MULTI-GOOD, MULTI-PERSON SOCIETY

Money Measure of Costs

Analysis of a many-person, many-good economy is basically the same as analysis of a two-person economy—despite the fact that with millions of people and millions of goods, exchange and specialization are even more extensive. And none of us has to carry in his head all the possible exchange rates among all the existing goods and people; for the information necessary to coordinate a many-person, many-goods society can be distilled to a *few* understandable, pervasive measures. All the many-person comparisons of transformation rates and exchange values among the vast array of goods are reduced to a relatively few measures—money prices and costs. To explain this, we shall first elaborate the meaning of costs where there are not just two alternative goods, but a very large number (still with just two people). Then we shall see how to make the many-person case manageable by using prices in a common marketplace to which all people have access.

Which of the many alternative goods is the relevant measure of forsaken output, or cost of producing a unit of whatever is produced? All the alternatives are compared for their potential contribution to more preferred situations (increase of utility). If these alternatives are products that can be exchanged in the market, then the *highest market value* of the forsaken outputs is the measure of cost.

In any event, whether or not an exchange market exists, exchanges between possible outputs can be achieved by revising production. Therefore, market or no market, the cost of any good is the highest value alternative that could otherwise have been realized; costs are forsaken opportunities.

The resort to prices—or dollar market values—as a measure of costs reflects not a worship of dollars but rather a concern for comparing desirabilities of different possible situations *via market exchange*. Dollars serve merely as a convenient medium of exchange, but money values and market prices reflect individual subjective valuations. As we saw in the earlier analysis of exchange, each person with access to the market adjusts his mixture of consumption until market prices and individual subjective values of various goods are equal. Market prices, therefore, depend upon the amounts of each good in existence, the preference patterns of individuals, and the distribution of wealth. But still the measure of costs is an exchange measure, whether there are markets or not. Costs of a good are always the highest valued of the alternative possible outputs that must be forsaken to have the good.

Under this more general "value interpretation," the idea of relative productivity is still reflected in marginal cost of production. And "comparative advantage in production" still means "lower marginal costs." The principle of allocation according to comparative advantage still is the principle of allocation according to lower marginal costs. In the ensuing analysis of a five-person community, we continue to talk of two goods, X and Y; but Y is here treated as some particular good, and X stands for alternatives to Y. The numerical value assigned to X is the highest market-valued alternative output.

Inherent in the *allocation* of resources among competing uses is the concept of *costs*. As a device for influencing allocation, costs must reflect values of alternative uses. In choosing between A and anything else, we ask what is the value of A and what are the values of the other opportunities—one of which could be taken if A is not. We can assume that the highest valued of the alternative possibilities would otherwise have been realized; that value of the forsaken opportunity is called the cost of A. And it follows that A should be chosen if and only if its value exceeds its cost. But whether or not A is chosen and regardless of its value, A's cost is defined as the highest-valued forsaken ouput if A is selected. This is the rationale for using costs in making allocative decisions. If a person does not *want* to heed cost, other people will refuse to let him use resources unless he can pay at least what could have been realized in the highest-valued alternative.

Probably none of the preceding is surprising. But what may be surprising is that no reference is made to "labor, toil, trouble, and pain" as costs. Costs are *not* defined as the *undesirable* consequences of having A, even though A may contain "undesirable consequences." All these annoyances are weighed when one evaluates A. For example, a swimming pool yields the pleasures of swimming and keeping cool, but it also involves the undesirable consequences of maintenance, heating, cleaning, loss of yard space, neighbors' children splashing up the yard. Taking the desirable and undesirable into account, a (net) value is assigned to having a pool; this value is measured in terms of some other equivalent good—usually money, the common denominator of exchange value.

If one subdivides the attributes of some activity or good into desirable and undesirable features, he *could* call the former the value and the latter the costs; however, this is *not* the concept of cost inherent in allocative decisions. Costs are the forsaken opportunity, not the undesirable consequences. When undesirable consequences are included in the cost concept, the result is intellectual error and confused social policy. Classic examples of error are the attempts to measure costs on the basis of labor or pain. Almost everyone knows that discomfort is great in digging ditches and that teaching in college is almost a pleasure; yet neither costs nor value of output nor salaries are correlated with labor or pain. Exactly how labor, toil, and trouble do enter into valuation is something we shall take up later, after hinting here only that they have some effect on the relative amounts of goods produced.

Production-Possibility Boundary as Supply Schedule

Table 17–1 gives the production possibilities of five people, Messrs. *A*, *B*, *C*, *D*, and *E*.

Table 17–1

DAILY PRODUCTION-POSSIBILITY FUNCTIONS AND PRODUCTION MARGINAL TRANSFORMATION RATES

Person	Goods $X	Or	Y		Production Marginal Transformation Rates
A	6	or	3	or all linear combinations	$2X = 1Y$
B	3	"	3	" " " "	$1X = 1Y$
C	1	"	2	" " " "	$5X = 1Y$
D	9	"	6	" " " "	$1.5X = 1Y$
E	6	"	10	" " " "	$.6X = 1Y$

These data are interpreted as before. Mr. *A* can produce daily at most $6 worth of goods, called *X* (excluding *Y*), if he devotes all his productive resources to *X*; *or* he can produce 3*Y* if he devotes all resources to *Y*. If he devotes .1 of his resources to *X* and .9 to *Y*, he can produce $.6 worth of *X* and $(.9)(3) = 2.7Y$. If he devotes half of his resources to each, he can produce $.5(6) =$ $3 worth of *X* and $.5(3) = 1.5$ of *Y* in one day. These mixed combinations are called linear combinations. Similar interpretations and computations are possible for all the other people.

Mr. C is the least productive person of all, on an *absolute* scale. Maybe he is lazy, slow-witted, physically weak, poor in productive resources, very young or very old, or just doesn't want to work much. Mr. D and Mr. E are more productive. Mr. D can produce more X daily than anyone else, while nobody can outproduce Mr. E at Y.

In this community, who will (not necessarily "should") produce what? In what amounts? How are they induced to do so? One possible set of answers to these questions is the following. Let each person's production possibilities be reported to a dictator (other than these five people). If only X is desired, A, B, C, D, and E are told to produce only X, for a total of $25 worth of X. On the other hand, if only Y is wanted, then all will produce Y, with a total of 24 units.

Now make the dictator's task a little harder. If he wants precisely one of Y and as many X's as possible, whom should he order to produce the Y? At first sight, it appears that E is the man. He can produce daily more X's than can anyone else. In just one tenth of a day, he can produce $1X$, whereas poor C requires half a day. E is "absolutely" the most productive producer of Y, while C is "absolutely" the poorest producer of Y. Yet the truth is that the dictator should reverse the assignments! Absolute productivity is completely irrelevant for determining efficient production allocations. Poor little C is the person to assign first to the production of Y! E is the *second* person to put to work on Y. And the reason is simply that C is the *lowest-cost* producer of Y. Cost is not the amount of labor or time it takes to produce a Y; cost, as we have seen, is what is sacrificed when labor or time is used to produce a Y. After all, no one can "save" time; it is used, like marriage, for better or for worse. What *can* be saved is sacrificed output. C sacrifices only $.5X$ when he devotes half a day to producing a Y. C's marginal cost is $.5X$ for $1Y$, while E's is $.6X$ for $1Y$. With C producing $1Y$, and the rest of the people producing X's, the total output will be $1Y$ and $24.5X$. But if E had produced the $1Y$, total output would have been $1Y$ and only $24.4X$. (If B had first been assigned to Y, the total mix would have been $1Y$ and only $24X$. Can you determine which person would have been the worst to assign? Had he been assigned, the total output would have been $1Y$ and only $23X$.)

C, the lowest marginal-cost producer of Y, should be directed to produce the first and second units of Y. If the dictator desires more than two units, E is the next worker to assign to Y production. If the dictator wants more than twelve units of Y (two from C and ten from E), he will assign B, whose marginal cost of Y is $1X$. If C, E, and B produce Y, and D and A produce X, the total output will be $15Y$ and $15X$. No other assignment can produce more than $15X$, given that $15Y$ are produced; other assignments *will* result in *less* than $15X$ being produced. Conversely, if $15X$ are to be produced, the maximum output of Y is 15.

We can summarize the principle of efficient allocation. Workers, or any productive resources, should be ranked according to their marginal costs before assigning them to production. Then assign first those workers who have the lowest cost for the particular good and then, as a larger output rate is desired, gradually divert to that task those with successively higher costs.

The community's total production-possibility frontier is given in Table 17–2.

Table 17–2

COMMUNITY'S TOTAL PRODUCTION POSSIBILITY

Producers of *X*	Feasible Production *X*	and *Y*	Producers of *Y*	Marginal Cost of *Y* in Terms of *X*
ABCDE	25.0	0	—	.5
ABCDE	24.5	1	C	.5
AB DE	24.0	2	C	.5
AB DE	23.4	3	C E	.6
AB DE	22.8	4	C E	.6
AB DE	22.2	5	C E	.6
AB DE	21.6	6	C E	.6
AB DE	21.0	7	C E	.6
AB DE	20.4	8	C E	.6
AB DE	19.8	9	C E	.6
AB DE	19.2	10	C E	.6
AB DE	18.6	11	C E	.6
AB D	18.0	12	C E	.6
AB D	17.0	13	BC E	1.0
AB D	16.0	14	BC E	1.0
A D	15.0	15	BC E	1.0
A D	13.5	16	BCDE	1.5
A D	12.0	17	BCDE	1.5
A D	10.5	18	BCDE	1.5
A D	9.0	19	BCDE	1.5
A D	7.5	20	BCDE	1.5
A	6.0	21	BCDE	1.5
A	4.0	22	ABCDE	2.0
A	2.0	23	ABCDE	2.0
—	0	24	ABCDE	2.0

On the left side are listed the names of the people assigned to producing *X*, and on the right side those assigned to producing *Y*. When a man's name appears on both sides, he is producing some of each. It is impossible to alter the pattern of assignments without sacrificing production efficiency.

Graphs of every person's production-possibility boundary are superimposed in Figure 17–1. Lying beyond all these lines, as a summation of them, is the

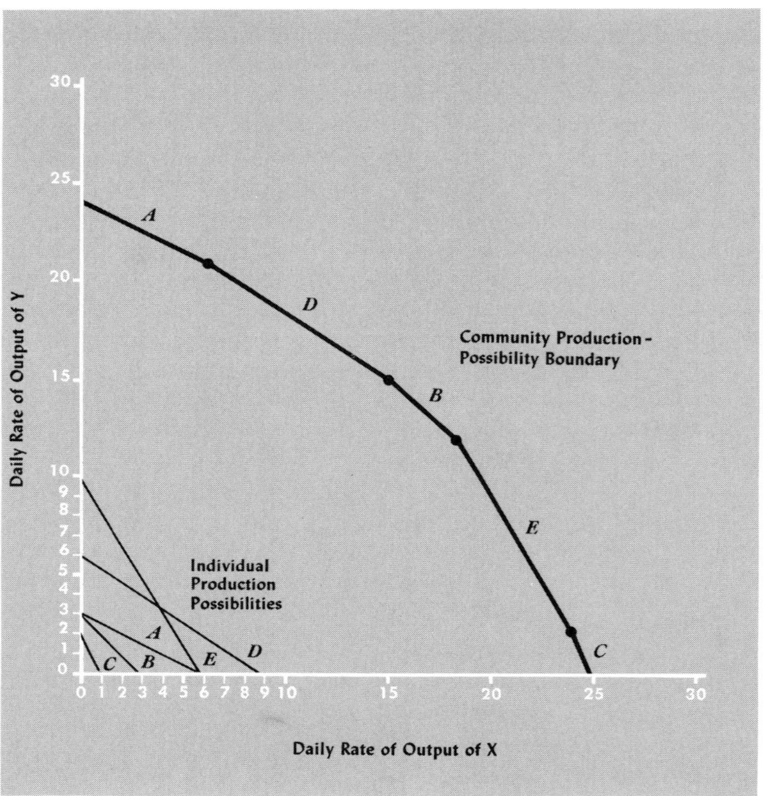

FIGURE 17–1. Total production possibility of community and of each person alone.

community's total or aggregate production-possibility boundary. An inefficient assignment of producers will result in an output, indicated by a point, inside the boundary. Note that the community's production-possibility boundary starts at the lower right with the steepest slope (the same as that of *C*'s boundary line) and then moves upward to the left along lines that are successively flatter and flatter. The slope of that boundary with respect to the vertical axis is a measure of the marginal cost of producing *Y* (and the slope with respect to the horizontal axis is the marginal cost of *X*). Failure to follow the principle of increasing order of slope will give a boundary that lies inside the portrayed and "efficient" boundary. The steepest boundary line (least loss of *X* for producing *Y*) is *C*'s; the next is *E*'s; and so on, until at last there is brought into the production of *Y* the producer with the least relative productivity of *Y* (in terms of *X*)—namely, *A*.

On each straight-line segment is the name of a person. When the point of production (showing the combination of *X* and *Y* produced by the whole economy) is on a given segment—say, *E*'s segment—each of the other workers is producing a single good; *C* is producing 1*Y*; and *A*, *B*, and *D* are producing only *X*. *E* also produces solely one good if the production point is at one end or the other of his segment; he is producing *X* if the point is at the lower end and *Y* if it is at the upper end. If the point of production is at some intermediate position of *E*'s segment, he is producing both commodities.

In the extreme right column of Table 17–2 are the marginal costs of producing *Y*, starting at .5*X* and increasing to 2*X* at higher production rates. These marginal costs are the comparative productivities of the last person reassigned. Implied by this is the principle of *increasing* marginal costs. As the daily-output rate of any good is increased, marginal costs for producing it are also increased —if production is efficient. If we can interpret *X* as the dollar value of all sacrificed outputs necessary to produce *Y*, the marginal costs of producing *Y* increase from 50 cents at an output of 1*Y* per day, up to $2 at an output rate of 24*Y* per day. Figure 17–2 shows marginal costs for each output rate.

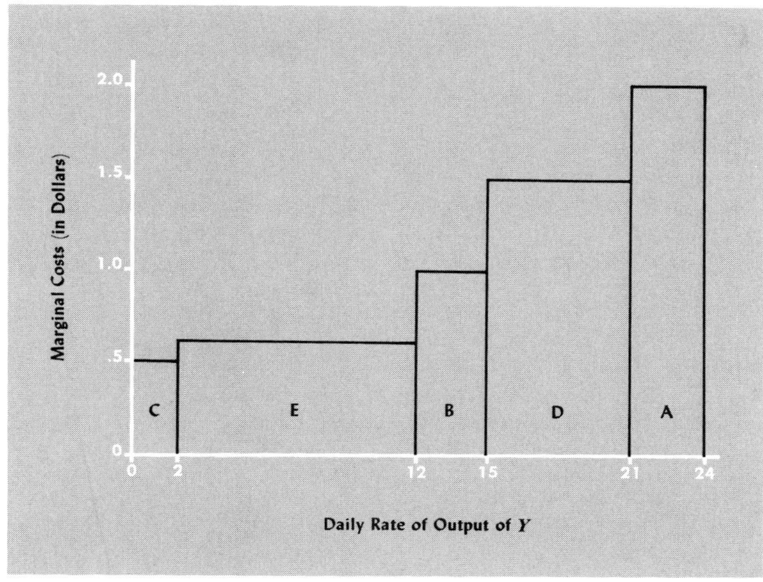

FIGURE 17–2. Daily marginal costs as function of rate of daily output of *Y*.

Production Controls under Private-Property System

Let us once again trace out the production assignments in a capitalist system, in which each person is a free agent with private-property rights, can choose what to produce, and has free access to a market.

INCENTIVES TO EFFICIENT PRODUCTION

While everyone is producing *X*, so that the daily total output of *X* is 25 ($25) and no *Y*, let Mr. *B* decide whether he would like some *Y*, even if it does cost as much as 1*X* to produce it himself. If he reveals that 1*Y* is worth up to 1*X* to him, as he can by expressing a willingness to buy 1*Y* for as much as 1*X*, some people will be induced to switch to production of *X*. For example, Mr. *E*, who can produce a *Y* for only .6*X* (60 cents), can sell the *Y* he produces to Mr. *B* for, say, .9*X* (90 cents). This transaction leaves Mr. *B* with $2.10 of *X* and 1*Y*, which is a bigger basket than if Mr. *B* produced the 1*Y* himself. Mr. *E* ends up with $6.30 instead of the $6 of *X* he had formerly, for he produced the *Y* at a cost of 60 cents and sold it for 90 cents.

Other people are allowed access to the marketplace, and they too may try to make a profit. If Mr. *C* discovers that Mr. *B* is paying 90 cents for a *Y*, it may occur to him that he can produce a *Y* and sell it for, say, 80 cents (taking the business away from Mr. *E*) and earn a net gain of 30 cents.

Only Mr. *E* and Mr. *C* can produce a *Y*, sell it for as little as 80 cents (.8*X*), and make a net gain. If Mr. *A* and Mr. *D*, however, think *they* are lower-cost producers than *C* and *E* in the production of *Y*, they can test their belief. If they do, they will incur losses and thereby discover their error.

The issue is now between Mr. *E* and Mr. *C*. Rather than lose all the business to Mr. *C*, Mr. *E* will cut his price below 80 cents, even as far as 61 cents if necessary. And it is necessary, because Mr. *C* can gain by producing some *Y* as long as he can get anything over 50 cents for 1*Y*. The end result is clear. Mr. *C* will drive Mr. *E* out of the business of producing *Y*. Only Mr. *C* will specialize in *Y*, if the community wants just 1*Y*, because Mr. *C* is the lowest-cost producer of 1*Y* or even of 2*Y*. And the price that Mr. *C* gets for the *Y* is at most 60 cents.

In our illustration, just what is the increase in product? And how is this gain distributed? Mr. *B* wanted a unit of *Y*; producing it himself would have cost $1. But it is actually produced by Mr. *C* and priced at, let us suppose, 60 cents, with the production cost to Mr. *C* being 50 cents. Then, Mr. *B* enjoys a convenient gain of 40 cents from the lower price, and Mr. *C* obtains a producer profit of 10 cents; the total gain of 50 cents is the gain of specialization over no specialization.

Free competition (i.e., open markets) for Mr. *B*'s business has resulted in only Mr. *C*'s specializing in the production of *Y*. "Greed," which induced Mr. *C* and Mr. *E* to make competitive offers in the marketplace, resulted in an increase of utility for Mr. *B*—although neither Mr. *C* nor Mr. *E* entered the market with that motivation.

In the preceding example, each person was induced to submit his marginal costs of producing *Y* to a market test, and the lowest-cost producer survived as a specializer in *Y*. The person with the greatest comparative advantage (lowest marginal cost) in production of *Y* was discovered and allowed to continue to specialize in production of *Y*. Personal interest and market competition brought about efficient allocation of productive resources. With Mr. *C*'s survival in production of *Y*, the total output is 1*Y* and $24.50 (24.50*X*)—precisely as large as under an all-wise planner. Apparently, central planning can be replaced by the private-property, free-enterprise market system.

If anyone wants more *Y*, he will have to offer the independent, private-resource owners a price at least equal to what they could get from producing other things. And that, of course, is measured by the marginal costs of producing the extra *Y*. The marginal costs of *Y* rise as the daily-output *rate* of *Y* is increased by efficient production assignments; this phenomenon is the *law of increasing marginal costs with higher or faster output rates.* Not only does the *total* cost of *Y* increase as the output rate increases, but the total daily cost increases by *larger increments:* the larger the output rate of *Y*, the greater the marginal cost. This rise is a consequence of efficient resource use.

CONTROL OF PRODUCTION RATE

At what rate will *Y* be produced and sold in the market? To get a specific numerical answer, let us use the demand for *Y* given in Table 17–3.

Table 17–3

DAILY COMMUNITY DEMAND FOR Y

Price in $X	Y
$1.50	1
1.30	2
1.10	3
.90	4
.70	5
.50	6
.40	7

According to this table, the daily sale of Y is one if the price is set at $1.50; it is two per day at a price of $1.30; and so on. It will be most profitable for Mr. C to produce all the Y he can ($2Y$) and for Mr. E to produce $3Y$ daily. This total of five per day can be sold at 70 cents each, and it would not be more profitable for Mr. E to produce a fourth one each day (because that would cost him 60 cents, but he could sell it only if the price were dropped to 50 cents). Our equilibrium result is that, with this demand, five units of Y will be produced and sold daily at a free-market price of 70 cents.

Figure 17–3 is obtained by drawing the demand curve on the preceding graph of the marginal costs for the community of producing Y (Figure 17–2).

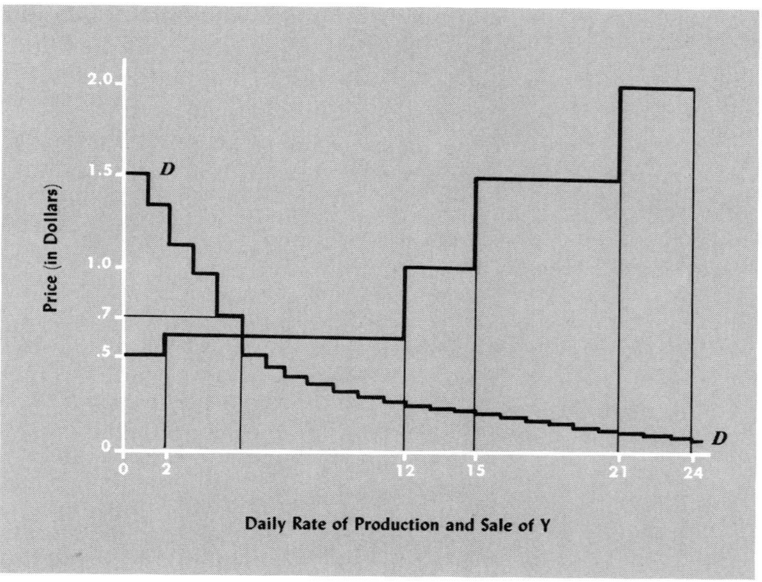

FIGURE 17–3. Community demand and supply for Y.

The curves in the two graphs would intersect at an output of five units of Y per day, with a demand price of 70 cents. Our community's *supply* schedule has turned out to be the *marginal-costs* schedule of Y for all the members of the community added together. We have a demand-and-supply-curve intersection like that used in the first chapters—except that the supply curve, instead of being vertical, slopes from lower left (low prices and low daily rate of output) to the upper right (higher prices and higher daily rates of output). Higher prices on the market will elicit a higher daily rate of output, while lower market prices will reduce the daily rate.

Productive Efficiency and Wealth Maximizing

Let us see whether the efficient allocation of productive resources does maximize each individual's personal wealth, given the market prices at which trade is possible. In the earlier example, where we had achieved an efficient allocation, the market price of Y was 70 cents (where an X was by definition equal to \$1) and daily output of Y was five units. In one day Mr. A can produce \$6 if he produces X, or 70 cents $\times$ 3 $=$ \$2.10 if he produces only Y. His maximum-valued output is obtained if he specializes in X. And he does. Similarly, B will maximize his wealth if he produces only X—which gives him \$3. And he does. Mr. C earns \$1.40 if he produces Y, whereas he earns only \$1 if he concentrates on X. So he produces Y. Mr. D—who earns \$9 from producing X, compared to \$4.20 if he produces Y—will maximize his earnings by concentrating on X. And he does. Mr. E can earn \$6 if he produces only X, whereas he can earn \$7 if he produces and sells only Y. But the most Y he can sell, according to our demand schedule, is three; therefore, he will produce that many and devote the rest of his resources to producing X. His daily earnings would be the value of $3Y$ at 70 cents each, plus $4.2X$ at \$1 each—a total value of \$6.30.

Test other output combinations; for this market demand, no combination gives anyone a bigger wealth. If the demand for Y should increase so that its price rises relative to that of other goods, some producers will be induced to revise output to maximize their wealth. Resources will be directed toward a new efficient allocation with production of more Y. For example, if the demand for Y increases so that it will support a sales rate of $14Y$ per day at a price of \$1.10 (with $1X$ equaling \$1), you should be able to show that individual wealths will be maximized if Messrs. A and D concentrate on X, with Messrs. C, B, and E concentrating on Y. Also note that this allocation is efficient, in addition to being the result of each person's efforts to maximize his wealth. Thus, a private-property, open-market system is conducive to efficient resource allocation.

RESTRICTED MARKET ACCESS: A SOURCE OF PRODUCTION INEFFICIENCY

Not every activity designed to increase one's wealth will lead to efficiency. Thievery, violence, and restricted market access for one's competitors will obstruct efficiency. Although few capitalists would encourage theft and violence, many people who have benefited from capitalism advocate socialism and restrictions on access to the market—not necessarily because they like socialism or dislike capitalism, but simply because their own wealth will be increased. A common example is the legally instituted and enforced restriction on rights of access to the market. Such restrictions are socialistic (which does not make them bad) because they reduce the realm of private-property rights and increase the realm of control over resources exercised via the government. Examples of legal restrictions on access to the market are laws controlling hours of business, Sunday closing, quality standards, apprenticeship, prices, usury, tariffs, minimum wages, and professional licensing, to name but a very few. Support for these laws can be found among many presently successful businessmen, and is not confined to so-called callous, cynical, unscrupulous people. Some of our most thoughtful humanitarians advocate them. The Supreme Court of the United States deems them not only constitutional but proper. The medical profession regards them as essential. Obviously, the support does not reflect an anticapitalist bias *per se*, but something else.

Our five-man economy will illustrate some of the motives nicely. Everyone had the right to produce and to sell whatever he could. Mr. *C* entered the market to sell some *Y*, even though Mr. *E* was already producing and selling *Y*. Mr. *C*'s entry cut the wealth of Mr. *E*; yet Mr. *C* and his property were legally protected from any threat of violence from Mr. *E*. There were no contrived legal barriers to anyone's access to the market—i.e., the market was open.

Suppose, however, that Mr. *E* had been able to keep all other people from producing and selling *Y*. Then Mr. *E* would produce (if we stick with our earlier numerical illustration) exactly 3*Y* per day and sell them for $1.10 each. To see why, examine the market demand for *Y* (Table 17–3). If Mr. *E* produces 1*Y* per day, he will have daily sales receipts of $1.50. If he produces and sells 2*Y*, he will take in $2.60, an *increase* in receipts of $1.10 (called, it will be remembered from Chapter 11, the marginal revenue). If he produces and sells 3*Y*, he will get a gross revenue of $3.30 daily, with a marginal revenue of 70 cents. To produce 3*Y* will cost him each day 60 cents more than if he produces just 2*Y*; the marginal cost of a daily output rate of 3*Y* is therefore 60 cents, while the marginal revenue is 70 cents. He will increase his profit by 10 cents if he produces and sells 3*Y* rather than 2*Y*. Total daily revenue will be $3.30, while his total cost will be $1.80, giving a total daily profit of $1.50 (compared with the smaller profit of $1.40 if he produces and sells 2*Y* per day). If he produces 4*Y* daily, total revenue will rise to $3.60 from $3.30 daily (when he produced 3*Y* per day), but his total cost will increase from $1.80 to $2.40 daily, for a marginal cost of 60 cents. His profits will fall to ($3.60 − $2.40 =) $1.20, since daily receipts increase less than the costs do. In our jargon, marginal revenue for 4*Y* is less than marginal cost. Mr. *E* will set daily production at 3*Y* because that will maximize his profits at $1.50 per day.

Although some consumers are prepared to pay a price more than the marginal cost (60 cents) of producing more *Y*, Mr. *E* will not produce more because he would have to lower his price on *all* his daily sales to sell more, and this would affect his total daily receipts and lower his profits. Mr. *C*, however, would be eager to produce and sell *Y*, because he would increase his wealth by producing *Y* at a cost of 50 cents and selling for more than that. Yet prohibiting

C's entry to the market eliminates his incentives for switching resources into *Y* and away from *X*, even though he and the other people in the community, *except for Mr. E*, would be "better off" if *C* could produce and sell *Y*.

Contrast the situation with what it was when we assumed that Mr. *C* did have access to the market. The output of 5*Y* per day (3*Y* produced by Mr. *E* and 2*Y* by Mr. *C*) was sold at a price of 70 cents. With contrived restrictions on entry, the output of *Y* is only three units (all produced by Mr. *E*) and a price of $1.10 (but the output of other goods is larger). The daily output of the restricted product, *Y*, is smaller and its price higher, while the resources that could be employed in *Y* must remain in other activities, where they are worth less. The excluded producers have to keep using resources in less useful activities, where they produce less wealth than they otherwise could have earned. In other words, the members of the community have more *X* than they want and less *Y* than they want and could have—given the true costs and subjective values of *Y* relative to *X*. By restricting Mr. *C* from entry to the market, Mr. *E* has increased his own wealth; but the restriction imposes an even greater reduction of wealth on the rest of the community, since Mr. *E* produces *Y* at a higher cost (sacrifice of *X*) than if the lowest-cost producer were allowed access to the market. That cost difference is a measure of the total wealth reduction in the whole community because of the restriction on entry.

Is this bad? Not if you are Mr. *E*. You get a daily income of $1.50; if expressed as dollars, this income (at 10 percent) has a present capital value of about $5,000. ($1.50 per day is about $500 per year. If that is expected to continue into the indefinite future, the present value is about $5,000.) If the restriction on entry were removed, Mr. *E*'s income would fall to 30 cents per day (producing 3*Y* daily at a total cost of $1.80 and selling them for $2.10). The daily income rate of 30 cents is worth only about one fifth as much; his wealth, in present-value terms, would be about $1,000. If entry had been unrestricted, the rest of *E*'s wealth would have been competed away in the form of lower prices of *Y* to the consumers. The portion remaining represents part of the gain arising from specialization and superior productive ability.

If you were Mr. *E*, how much would you be willing to spend to help pass a law to restrict market-access rights of other people. Close to $4,000. No *one* else would find it profitable to try to outbid you in an attempt *to prevent* such laws. (It can be shown that *if* every person were to join in a campaign and contribute a small amount, total contribution could exceed your $4,000. The difficulty in the real world is effectively to organize consumer counter-pressure groups against *every* case in which restrictions on entry are sought.)

Do laws restricting entry of some competitors to the market involve political chicanery and immorality or bribery when the protected parties pay part of their monopoly gains to the powers that be? No. The most noble monarchs of England accepted these "taxes." Most of our states and cities in the United States do, too. The modern way is not to reward a particular official by paying him personally, but rather to be willing to "accept" a larger tax burden or pay a larger license fee for the privilege of being a monopolist or, as it is euphemistically put, a public utility—e.g., water, light, power, gas, or taxi companies that have obtained operating franchises to eliminate competitors or raise their costs of getting into the market.

Various techniques for passing laws to restrict entry are moral, politically encouraged, and openly utilized. Later we shall examine some. For the moment, it suffices to indicate that government power can be used to protect free access or to deny it. For example, the government can help to ensure access by protecting entrants from private threats of violence and physical harm; it can restrict access by failing to grant such protection and by enforcing laws that prohibit access.

ACTUAL ATTAINMENT OF EFFICIENCY?

Nothing *guarantees* that the most efficient producer—the lowest marginal-cost producer—will be induced to produce Y. If any of a host of things interferes with his opportunity or willingness to risk wealth in the hope of greater wealth by producing Y, inefficient production will continue. The efficient producers will be discovered more easily if access to the market is easier (i.e., cheaper), if more people desire wealth, and if the people are willing to take a chance for wealth. But also, the trial-and-error costs incurred by hopeful but overconfident people are greater.

Which feature dominates? Over-entry into activities in which people lose wealth or under-entry into activities in which they would have increased their wealth? The answer, however, is not really so simple to determine. For example, I *believe* that my costs would far exceed my market value in the following activities: professional football player, music composer, musician, steel welder, farmer, doctor, lawyer, architect, electronic technician, stonecutter, watchmaker, shoemaker, coal miner, lumberjack, etc., etc., etc. I may be wrong in this belief. Maybe, for instance, I *could* operate a wine-grape farm at a cost less than the market price of grapes. My productivity as a grape farmer might really exceed the wages I get for teaching. Rather than run the risks and costs of an experiment to find out whether my relative productivity is higher in grape farming than in teaching, I may prefer to continue as a teacher—simply because the "discovery" costs are too high to induce me to try the experiment. Therefore, I shall continue working as a teacher, with the result that my utility (and wealth) is lower than it otherwise would have been. The allocation of my productive efforts would be inefficient and my wealth smaller than it would be if I were a grape farmer. That smaller wealth is said to be a reflection of the reduction in total output resulting from my misallocation of productive resources. Too many resources (mine) are in teaching instead of in grape growing.

The more pertinent questions are: (1) Is the dispersed knowledge utilized efficiently? (2) Is there incentive for a person to increase his knowledge of what he can do?

To both, the answer is: Wider access to the market increases the likelihood of a "yes" answer.

The market-exchange system, with its prices, provides more than a place to exchange goods. It is a place where information is collated and compared.

A restriction on price and exchange negotiation among interested parties would restrict not only the exchange of existing goods but also the transfer of productive resources from lower-value to higher-value uses.

It is easy to see why. First, market prices reflect consumers' demands and values of goods and services. They also reflect producers' costs of production. Each potential and actual producer, by looking at the selling prices, indirectly compares his estimated and realized costs with those of other producers, and with the values that consumers place on his product. If his (marginal) costs exceed prices, he will reduce or eliminate his production and move to something else that he can produce unless he is willing to sustain a continuously falling wealth. The fact that his marginal costs are greater than prices indicates that other people can produce this good more cheaply than he can, and that consumers value his product less than other things he could do.

Second, specialization in production is in large part specialization and coordination of dispersed knowledge. Specialization of production does not mean simply that one person produces a pencil while someone else produces paper. It means also that different people produce the various component parts of goods and that different people perform the various special tasks that have evolved in making goods. In fact, in a modern society *no one* knows how to produce all of any one thing. Take, for example, the simple common pencil, which represents the culmination of the joint efforts and knowledge of millions of people. One person knows something about the paint; another about the graphite—how it is mined, transported, processed, shaped, and inserted in a pencil; others are knowledgeable in growing timber, cutting it, shaping the wood, and painting it; others make the steel holder for the eraser; and still others are involved in making the rubber eraser. Activities of thousands or possibly millions of people are coordinated to produce pencils at lower rather than at higher costs. Exchange prices among people in the market guide coordination, and each person strives to increase his wealth while being constrained by competitive suppliers, and by consumers' desires.

Implications of Specialization under Capitalism

What has our economic analysis revealed about production specialization in a capitalist system?

1. Specialization brings about greater output and enables individuals to

attain more preferred situations than under "do-it-yourself" or "self-sufficiency" systems of individual production.

2. Specialization yields more efficient production if increases in the output rate of any good are provided by the lowest-cost producers.

3. The principle of specialization relies on relative, not absolute, productivity.

4. A person does not need to understand the principle of specialization in order to specialize in accord with that principle.

5. Unless all people are identical in productive ability, *every* person will *always* find some goods or services for which his marginal costs are less than or equal to the market price; he can therefore produce these goods or services as a means of increasing his utility above what it would have been had he acted self-sufficiently—unless his access to the market is prohibited.

6. The cheaper the cost of access to the market, the greater the extent of specialization.

7. Cost of a specified output is defined as the *highest* valued of the alternative opportunities.

8. The measure of that cost is the market-exchange value of the forsaken output.

9. Property rights and access to a market in which any mutually acceptable opportunity can be exploited provide incentives and means to specialize efficiently.

10. The increased total output brought about by increased efficiency is distributed (a) via profits to the owners of the productive resources and (b) via lower prices to consumers. Together, these two absorb all the increased output.

11. As market demand for any good increases, and as the market price of that good rises, higher-cost producers will switch to that product.

12. Individual wealth-maximizing behavior in the face of market-equilibrating prices is conducive to efficient resource allocation.

13. No economic system can guarantee continual realization of productive efficiency.

Questions

1. "Costs are an opportunity concept." Explain.

2. Are costs the same thing as the undesirable consequences of some action? Explain why not.

3. a. If there is more than one opportunity to be forsaken, which forsaken opportunity is the cost?

b. How are opportunities made comparable so that one can determine which one is the cost?

c. Can there be production without costs?

4. A lower-cost producer can produce more than a higher-cost producer. Do you agree? If so, why? If not, why not?

5. "The slope of the production-possibility curve is a measure of costs." Explain.

6. "An implication of efficient production is that marginal costs increase as the rate of output becomes larger." Explain.

7. Why are costs not measured in terms of labor hours?

8. *A* and *B* can produce according to the following:

	DAILY RATE OF OUTPUT OF			
	X	or	*Y*	
Mr. *A*	10	or	15	(or any linearly interpolated combination)
Mr. *B*	5	or	10	(or any linearly interpolated combination)

a. Who can profitably produce *Y* at the lowest cost and price of *Y*?

b. Who can profitably produce *X* at the lowest cost and price of *X*?

c. If Mr. *C* is allowed to trade with Mr. *A* and *B* and if *C*'s production possibilities are 4*X* or 4*Y* (or any linearly interpolated combination), who now is the lowest-cost producer of *X*? Of *Y*?

d. Who is not the lowest-cost producer of either *X* or *Y*? Does this mean he will have nothing to gain by specializing and trade? Explain.

9. The following questions involve the production data of the five people given in Tables 17–1 and 17–2.

a. If the selling price of an *X* were $1 and the selling price of a *Y* were also $1, what should each person produce in order to maximize his wealth?

b. Would the resulting assignment of tasks be an efficient one?

c. What should each person produce in order to maximize his wealth if the selling price of an *X* is $1 and the selling price of a *Y* is $1.60?

d. Is the resulting job allocation an efficient one?

e. If the price of an *X* is $3 and the price of a *Y* is $3.20, what should each produce in order to maximize his wealth?

f. If the price of an *X* falls to $2 and the price of a *Y* is still $3.20, what should each produce to maximize his wealth?

g. Is the allocation of labor efficient?

h. Is it absolute prices or relative prices of *X* and *Y* that guide allocation?

10. The following questions are based on data in Table 17–3.

a. If all the prices in Table 17–3 were to be doubled (while the price of an *X* stayed fixed at $1), which would happen to output?

b. Is this the result of an increased demand for *Y* or of a reduced demand for *X*?

c. Suppose a tax were to be collected from each producer of *Y*—a tax of 50 cents for each unit of *Y* produced. If, before the tax, the prices of an *X* and of a *Y* were both $1, what effect would this tax have on job allocation and output?

11. The following questions are based on data in Tables 17–1 and 17–2.

a. What are the dimensions of the output of *X* and *Y*? That is, are they measured in units of total output or in rate (speed) of output?

b. If the output is 15 per day, does this mean that 15 will be produced? (Hint: What if price changes at midday?)

c. What would be the total volume of output of *X* in five days if *C* and *E* produced *Y* exclusively and the other three specialized in *X*?

d. What would be the rate of output per hour for a ten-hour day.

12. "The increased output of increased specialization is distributed as profits and as a lower price to consumers." What determines the portion of each?

13. "Every profit represents the gain from moving resources to higher-valued uses." Do you agree? If so, why? If not, why not?

14. In the discussion on pages 258–260, let Mr. *C* be a resident of Japan, while the others are residents of the United States. Mr. *E* is a tuna-boat owner and fisherman, and *A*, *B*, and *D* are American workers in other American industries. Let *Y* be "tuna" and *X* be "other products." Mr. *E* persuades his congressman to induce other congressmen to pass a law prohibiting the importing of Japanese tuna—which in this problem is product *Y* produced by Mr. *C*. Who gains and who loses by a tariff or embargo on Japanese tuna? (This example captures the essence of the purposes and effects of tariffs and embargoes.)

15. The five-person problem in this chapter can also be interpreted as a case in which all producers of *Y* must be members of an organization, and Mr. *C* is denied membership in this organization. Who gains and who loses? Can you give some actual examples of this situation in the real world?

16. The five-person problem can also be interpreted as a case in which admission to the market for sale of one's production of *Y* requires a license from the state, and this license is given only if the current output from those now in the production of *Y* is deemed "inadequate to meet current demands." Who gains and who loses? Can you give some real examples of this situation?

17. Would the problem also serve as an example of the effect of apprenticeship laws that prohibit a person from acting as a "qualified" carpenter, meat cutter, etc., until he has served a specified number of years as an apprentice? Explain.

18. Does efficient production assume that perfect knowledge exists? Explain.

19. "Someone always has a comparative advantage in the production of some good." Explain.

20. The production-possibility schedule for Mr. *A* is:

X	and	*Y*
5		0
4		1.5
3		2.9
2		3.8
1		4.5
0		5

For Mr. *B* the possibilities are:

X	and	*Y*
3		0
2		1
1		2
0		3

a. Add these two production possibilities together for the efficient, combined production possibility. (Hint: Notice that Mr. *A*'s production possibilities involve *increasing*, rather than constant, marginal cost of *X*. Use the condition that must hold between each person's marginal cost at an efficient allocation of productive inputs.)

b. Who would be first to produce profitably some *X* at a low price of *X*? Who would be last?

c. Who would be first to produce profitably some *Y* at a low price of *Y*?

d. Why is the answer to "b" and "c" the same?

e. At what ratio of prices of *X* to price of *Y* would Mr. *B* switch from production of *X* to production of *Y*?

21. Think of the five men *A, B, C, D, E* as being the five employees in a manufacturing company.

a. Can you think of any reason why the output data could be different if the five men were to work together rather than specialize separately with exchange of individual products? Do you think the output would be larger or smaller?

b. Why?

18

THE BUSINESS FIRM

How do output and use of resources respond to demand? This basic question was answered earlier in a five-person economy, where we were concerned primarily with the principle of efficient resource allocation and the principle of comparative advantage in production. Now we must investigate the issue in the more complex context of business firms, with various types of production changes (rates, volumes, and date), different types of markets (price-takers' or price-searchers'), degrees of constraints on market access, etc.

A business firm is a legal form of ownership of assets and contractual relationships; a business produces and sells goods to increase the wealth of owners. Basically, it is an institution through which people (employers and employees) seek to increase their utility by increasing their wealth. Of course, job-related "goods"—like working conditions, congeniality of associates, and nervous strain of management—affect one's utility. For some people, the business may be a hobby, as some owners of baseball teams or racing stables contend. In every business and work, there are elements of excitement and sources of utility aside from the wealth obtained; still, the less the wealth available or the higher the wealth costs of the hobby, the less likely will a business be sustained for hobby purposes. In any event, without denying the relevance and impact of these nonpecuniary sources of utility, we shall concentrate on the business firm as a wealth-producing institution.

Proprietorships, Partnerships, and Corporations

Business firms commonly take one of three legal forms: individual proprietorship, partnership, or corporation. A proprietorship is owned by one person, who is also responsible for all debts to the full extent of whatever wealth he owns; that is, he has *unlimited liability*. A partnership is jointly owned by two or more people, each of whom has unlimited liability for the entire firm and can individually make contracts binding the other partners. A corporation is a form of ownership usually with limited liability; that is, limited to the existing financial investment in the firm. Almost always, several people share in the ownership of a corporation. One person might have an interest of 30 percent of the ownership; his legal title would be evidenced by ownership of 30 percent of the shares of "common stock"—each share denoting a minimal share of ownership.

FORMATION OF CORPORATIONS

One might think that by mutual agreement a group of individuals could organize a corporation, issue common stock as evidence thereof, and engage in business—just as one can with a proprietorship or partnership. But historically the state has not recognized the right of people to form a corporate contract with other people (i.e., form a corporation); indeed, any persons who try to form a corporation will be restrained by law from doing so. They must first obtain "permission" from the state, which "incorporates" the corporation. The reasons for this are not entirely clear, although the English crown once sold *monopoly* rights to organize a corporation in order to engage in a certain business venture—for instance, to engage in trade with the East Indies—and thus captured some of the monopoly value. (Remember our earlier discussion of the middlemen in the refugee camp?) Monopoly rights are no longer automatic in the act of incorporation; however, government authorization is still required before a corporation can be formed. In every one of the United States, incorporation must first be authorized by state officials. In some instances, the approval is pro forma; in others, substantial fees and conditions are imposed.

FEATURES OF CORPORATIONS

What are some of the features of corporations?

Limited liability. Only the wealth of the corporation itself can be held as security or for payment of corporation debts. Other wealth of the owners cannot be legally attached for payment of liabilities in the event of bankruptcy. In contrast, a proprietor or a set of partners is personally liable for all debts of the proprietorship or partnership. Their other wealth may be attached by creditors in the event of default on debt. In England, the name of the corporation is usually followed by the abbreviation "Ltd." ("Simpsons, Ltd."), to indicate the corporate limited liabilities. The attraction of limited liability to a potential investor-owner is that liability is limited to specified portions of the owner's wealth. Because of limited liability, lenders may regard corporations as higher risks and thus charge them higher rates of interest; but limited liability is so attractive from the investor's standpoint that corporations usually have little difficulty in collecting large sums to finance ventures.

Continuity. Death or withdrawal of any owner does not terminate a corporation's existence, whereas in a partnership these changes require more expensive reorganization procedures. Corporate continuity is achieved by the right of owners to transfer their shares by sale, gift, or inheritance to other people without permission of the other current owners; in a partnership, permission must first be obtained. Sales of shares of many large, widely owned corporations are usually negotiated in a stock market, a formal marketplace where shares of certain corporations are listed and sold by brokers for those wishing to sell and to buy shares. Some corporations are not so well known, and the shares are sold so infrequently that they are not listed on the formal stock exchanges. These lesser-known corporation shares are bought and sold by private negotiation through a dispersed set of independent stock-brokerage agencies known as the "over-the-counter" market.

Capital accumulation. Relatively large amounts of capital can be accumulated if many individuals can each contribute small portions of the total cost of the investment in some venture. Given limited liability, the prospect of continuity, and the transferability of shares of ownership, it is not surprising that the corporate form of enterprise thrives as an institution for financing expensive or even riskier production ventures.

Despite these advantages, the corporate form of doing business is subject to special burdens imposed by law. For example, it is taxed more heavily, probably because corporation taxes do not alienate as many votes as do some other forms of taxation. Nearly one fourth of the federal tax receipts are from taxes on the corporate forms of business; it is difficult to find another source of so much revenue for the government with fewer complaints from voters. Also, prior to public sale of corporation stock, approval must be received from a state regulatory agency as well as from a federal agency called the Securities and Exchange Commission. To obtain that approval, the corporation must reveal about its assets and liabilities certain information that might be useful to any prudent investor. But if the regulatory commission thinks the corporation is not "strong enough," it can in some states prohibit existing owners from selling stock to the public.

Ownership and control. Stockholders elect directors on a one-vote-per-share basis; directors are authorized to make contracts (i.e., to conduct the business) in the name of the corporation. As a result, stockholders who own only a small portion of the shares have an insignificant effect on the voting outcome. In fact, in many large corporations no single owner owns enough stock to control a majority of stock. Hence, it is said that directors, in effect, control the wealth of the corporation (while stockholders bear the ultimate risk of changes in the value of the corporation). This kind of statement is easy to make but harder to interpret and still harder to substantiate. Actually, though, do only a portion or even a minority of the shareholders (the director-managers) run the corporation while the rest of the shareholders hold the bag? A little thought may suggest a different interpretation. Many people want to invest wealth in ventures operated by especially skilled persons and to share in the profits. The money they provide enables skilled managers to operate on a larger scale; in turn, buying stock gives them a share in the consequences brought about by those who operate the business. Whether one calls this process "holding the bag," or "submitting to control of others," or "being duped by those who use your money," or "investing in the skills of other people" is largely a matter of words.

But there *are* genuine conflicts of interest within the corporate ownership structure. Sometimes directors and managers use the corporation in order to throw especially profitable opportunities to a second corporation in which they have a substantial interest—against the interests of the stockholders of the first corporation. Or majority-interest directors can vote especially high salaries to themselves, leaving smaller profits to be distributed to the minority interests. These dangers are not novel, and they are not free of counter-pressures. For example, this last-mentioned practice will reduce the price of the shares of stock and make it easier for the minority group to purchase more shares and become the majority group. Nevertheless, despite inherent disadvantages and higher taxes, the corporation has become an increasingly important form of business venture.

The Population of Business Firms

In sales value of output, the corporation, with approximately 65 to 75 percent of the total, is by far the dominant form. Proprietorships account for about 15 to 20 percent. But in numbers of business firms, the proportions are almost reversed. Almost half of the five million business firms are in wholesaling and retailing proprietorships; if we include agricultural and professional activity, the number of firms would be larger by about another five million, most of which are unincorporated proprietorships.

In absolute size, the largest corporations have nearly a million employees each. The one hundred largest industrial corporations employ almost six million people, or about 10 percent of all employees. They also average over a billion dollars in sales annually for each firm, with assets of about the same value. Often, when hearing that the size of business firms today is much larger than thirty years ago, we are tempted to conclude that it is harder to organize a new business. In fact, however, people are getting wealthier, so that organizing a $50,000 fund of capital for an initial business venture is probably easier than getting $10,000 fifty years ago. Each year for the past fifty years, new firms have been organized at a ratio of about one for each ten existing firms.

Of new firms, half die in five to ten years. Relatively large size may not *cause* or *assure* success; actually, larger size may be a *result* of efficient operation. Bigger firms are more efficient because efficiency increases the growth rate, while the inefficient are killed off before they can grow large or get old. The higher survival prospects of a big, old firm must not be attributed simply to size and age. And small, new firms are not necessarily handicapped compared to big, old firms; newcomers *can* effectively compete. Small, new firms may effectively compete for business and grow faster than bigger, older firms, but they will need phenomenal growth rates for a long time to surpass some of the giants. A few hundred large corporations produce nearly half the total value of industrial output. But what does that signify? General Motors buys from thousands of smaller firms; when all these products are assembled in a Chevrolet, it can be said that General Motors produced the Chevrolet; yet, thousands of firms were involved in providing parts and equipment to that giant assembly line known as General Motors. If we count only the last assembler, then we can say that General Motors "produces" 50 percent of the cars. If we count all of its suppliers, then over one thousand firms "produce" half of the cars.

Does General Motors "dominate" the automobile industry in the sense of setting prices, styles, quality, and employment policies for other producers, or merely in the share of cars produced? Is General Motors less responsive to consumer demands than if there were several firms in place of one General Motors? Does General Motors' "dominance" mean that its employees are paid lower wages? Or that style changes occur less often or more rapidly? Or that General Motors' decisions about its production play a bigger role in affecting the economy than if there were a hundred firms replacing it? The answers to some of these questions will be suggested in the succeeding analysis. For the moment we note that the corporate form of business organization is far and away the major form and that some corporations are of enormous size.

Why Do Business Firms Exist?

Is the existence of a business firm consistent with market-exchange principles outlined earlier? Why don't people in the firm individually engage in direct market exchange? If resource uses are directed and coordinated by prices and market exchange without conscious direction, then why are centrally directed organizations—business firms with employees—in existence? Why are there "islands of conscious power in this ocean of unconscious cooperation like lumps of butter coagulating in a pail of buttermilk"? [1]

In truth, the existence of a business firm with employees does not deny voluntary exchange specialization under control of market prices. In the first place, the firm—with its employee-employer relationship—facilitates such exchange by avoiding the higher costs of the inconvenient continual negotiation, contracting, and record keeping involved in repetitive purchases and sales. For many goods and services, demands are so regular and stable that people prefer to perform the same tasks for the same customers for long periods or sometimes even for a lifetime. Employees regularly and repetitively sell labor services to the same buyer, the employer. This employee-employer relationship does not eliminate the role of market exchange and pricing.

In the second place, the employee-employer relationship economizes on transactions costs between cooperating producers. If you were working on the assembly line in my factory, you could, in principle, buy the partly completed item you get from a worker next to you and then sell it to the next worker after you. The price you get is higher than the price you pay because of the improvement you have made on the item while you had it. If I, the employer, paid you just that difference between the two prices, your income will be the same as if you bought at one price and then sold at a higher price the item you worked on. That difference, or payment to you, is called *wages;* it reflects the value of your services. In a repetitive process, that difference does not vary much from day to day or among "similar" people. When the difference is expressed as "so much" per day, hour, or month, the payment is called a wage.[2]

A result of this employee-employer relationship is that whereas we formerly derived implications about each person's income and wealth from the simple direct sale of his produce to a consumer, we now must explain his income in terms of prices per unit of labor service—that is, as wages. Each person sells his services to purchasers (employers) by "working for" an "employer" for "wages." Rather than a host of individuals buying and selling to each other, we now have a host of individuals selling to a common buyer, their employer, in return for a time-related price, called a "wage." We shall later see that this does not change any of the principles of control of production by market-exchange prices, despite common belief to the contrary.

[1] D. H. Robertson, *Control of Industry* (Cambridge: Nisbet & Co., 1923), p. 85.

[2] If the management problem becomes too formidable, the firm will stop "hiring" its "own" employees and resort to purchase of services from other firms—that is, subcontracting or purchasing materials from other firms.

Questions

1. The purpose of this question is to explain how to read business financial statements. Most business firms periodically (commonly every three or six months) issue financial reports of their activities and current status. Reproduced below is the balance sheet issued by the United Nuclear Corporation for March 31, 1963. A balance sheet presents a listing and valuation, according to the company's books, of its assets, liabilities, and ownership structure. Assets, as we know, are the property owned and used by this corporation. The rights of the proprietors to these assets are called proprietorship, capital, or net worth. If there are no outsiders with legal claims against the assets, other than those of the proprietors, the net worth of the ownership is then equal to the asset total. However, if there are claims held by other people against this business, these liabilities reduce the net proprietorship or ownership claims. The basic principle is

$$\text{Assets} - \text{Liabilities} = \text{Ownership},$$

which can be rewritten as

$$\text{Assets} = \text{Liabilities} + \text{Ownership}.$$

The financial situation is then presented in the form of a balance sheet.

The following is an example of a corporation balance sheet.

UNITED NUCLEAR CORPORATION
March 31, 1963

ASSETS		(thousands of dollars) $000
Cash		$ 3,352
Receivables		4,261
Unbilled costs		2,487
Inventories		12,986
Prepaid expenses		455
Investments		1,274
Property, plant, and equipment		67,781
Depreciation		−16,630
Long-term leases		1,954
Goodwill		75
		$77,995
LIABILITIES		
Current		
Accounts payable	$ 1,948	
Notes payable	6,504	
Accrued liabilities	4,185	
		$12,637
Long-term		
Long-term debt	$33,489	
Long-term leases	1,954	
Minority interest	5,512	
		40,954

EQUITY	
Common stock (par 20¢)	
4,104,476 shares outstanding	821
Additional paid-in capital	21,883
Retained earnings (Surplus)	1,700
	$77,995

What do these items mean?

ASSETS

Cash. This is the amount of money held in bank accounts.

Receivables. The corporation has sold nuclear materials, which it produces, to various customers. This records the amount of purchases yet to be paid for by the customers. In a sense, these are the charge accounts or credit extended to its customers, allowing them usually thirty days to pay.

Unbilled costs. The corporation is making nuclear reactors to custom order; and, as the reactor is gradually completed, the corporation records the amount of claims accruing against the customer, for which a bill will be submitted upon completion. In a sense, these are the incurred costs of products produced to customer order but not yet delivered because they are not completed.

Inventories. The corporation refines uranium ores. This is the value of the ore it has removed from its mines and has not yet sold.

Prepaid expenses. The corporation has paid in advance for goods and services to be delivered. These are rights against other people who have contracted to deliver goods and services for which the corporation has already paid. This is an asset. For example, when you prepay a magazine subscription (say, for *Life*), you would record that asset as a prepaid expense in your personal balance sheet.

Investments. The corporation has purchased some stock in some other company, or it has purchased some U.S. bonds, rather than hold so much cash. Usually, sufficient information is given along with the balance sheet to identify the particular investment.

Property, plant, and equipment. This is the amount paid for the physical property, mines, mills, etc., of the corporation. Sometimes this is recorded as the "cost of replacing" it, especially if there have been drastic changes in costs of purchasing this equipment now.

Depreciation. The property, plant, and equipment have been used and worn out in part. An estimate of the portion of the plant so consumed is "depreciation." Subtracting this from the cost figure gives the net book value of that property, equipment, and plant.

Long-term leases. This corporation has leased housing facilities for its mining employees. The recorded amount is the discounted or present value of housing space (as measured by the future rental payments due). This measures the right the corporation has against the houseowners.

Goodwill. Patents and trademarks are often given some conservative estimate of value and called goodwill. Sometimes, successful companies represent the result of certain intangible attributes. This may be recorded as a goodwill item. Usually the item is not a significantly large amount, precisely because it is so subject to discretionary opinion.

LIABILITIES

Liabilities are conventionally divided into current and long-term liabilities, with the former usually representing claims that must be paid within a year.

Accounts payable. The corporation has purchased goods and equipment which it has received and for which it must yet pay the price. The amount still due is the amount recorded.

Notes payable. The corporation has borrowed cash for a short period of time, and the amount due is shown. This item may also include the amounts of long-term debt that are falling due within the year.

Accrued liabilities. At the present moment, the corporation has accrued obligations to pay taxes or wages at some near future date. For example, if wages are paid on the 15th of the month, then at the end of the month it will have about half a month's wages accrued and to be paid in two weeks.

Long-term debt. The corporation has borrowed funds and issued bonds. In the present instance, these will run until about 1970 before falling due.

Long-term leases. The corporation, in leasing houses for its employees, is obligated to pay the rents when due. The present value of that rental sequence is recorded as the amount of the long-term-lease liability. (Notice that the asset value of this claim is explicitly identified on the asset side of the balance sheet.)

Minority interest. The corporation is the primary owner of a mine, the purchase price of which along with equipment has been recorded among the assets. However, since United Nuclear Corporation is not the sole owner, it has recorded here the pro-rata ownership rights of the other owners of this subsidiary mining company. This recorded minority interest offsets part of the asset value shown on the asset side. In other words, of the total recorded value of the subsidiary company, $5,500,000 is the share of the other owners. Usually every balance sheet has an appended list of footnotes or additional information giving further details. In this case the report happens to tell us in a footnote that the subsidiary company has a recorded value of about $14,700,000 included in United Nuclear's reported property, plant, and equipment on the asset side.

Equity. This is the ownership or proprietorship item. After the assets are totaled and the total liabilities subtracted, a difference of $24,400,000 is obtained. This is broken up into three parts. For official, legal, and tax purposes (involving considerations that are irrelevant here) *common-stock* shares are each recorded at a par value of 20 cents. Since the corporation has issued 4,104,476 shares, this totals to $822,329. For all present intents and purposes the par-value figure is irrelevant and useless. Some companies record it at zero par value.

Additional paid-in capital. This, along with the par-value amount, is the amount paid to the corporation by the people who first bought common stock from the company. This total of $21,800,000, plus the $820,895, is the amount paid in to the company by the owners. What has happened to that money (and the proceeds from loans)? It has been spent for property, wages, equipment, etc.; and, at the moment, the results of that expenditure are what are shown on the asset side, along with other incurred obligations in the liabilities.

Retained earnings. During its history the corporation has had net earnings which it has kept in the company as new equipment and facilities. This amounts to $1,700,000. It may have paid out some as cash dividends to stockholders, but we can't tell this from the balance-sheet data.

Such is what the historical records of the United Nuclear Corporation indicate. If we take the recorded *book value* of the ownership, we see that there is a recorded "book value" of $24,400,000, which, when divided by the 4,104,476 shares outstanding, comes to almost exactly $6 a share.

It is tempting to conclude that a share of common stock is worth $6; but don't yield to that temptation, or else you are rejecting everything you have learned in this book, and especially in Chapter 15. Why? Because the figures in the balance sheet's asset items are the historical costs of the equipment (adjusted for wear and tear). They do not tell us what the company will be able to do in the future. How do we know that the uranium mine—which *cost*, say, $1,000,000 to find and mine—is not going to yield $100,000,000 in receipts, or maybe nothing?

None of this is revealed by the balance sheet's asset records. None—unless the corporation directors decide to make a prognosis of that future receipt stream and discount it into a present value and record it under "Goodwill" or "Profits." But they don't do this, simply because they know how unreliable that is. Instead, with their balance sheet they issue a report of operations and events. For example, United Nuclear Corporation reported in its annual report: "The outlook for widespread civilian and military use of nuclear energy for both power and propulsion improved greatly during the past year. The capability of the industry in the free world countries, based on presently known ore-reserve information, is estimated to be about 20,000 tons annually. This in the face of a projected annual amount demanded during the early 1970s of 40,000 tons, excluding military purchases." But the directors did not foresee that within a year the decision to build another nuclear-powered airplane carrier would be in the negative. All the directors could do was report what was then known and make some clearly labeled forecasts, which other people can accept, reject, or revise at their volition.

Try to guess what a share of common stock in United Nuclear Corporation was purchasable for in April 1963. Probably not less than $6, except that maybe the mines are all mined out and depleted, in which case the stock is not worth what it *cost* to dig holes in the ground. But if the mines are rich in ore, beyond the cost of discovering, running, and refining the uranium concentrate, the stock may be worth more than $6. As it happened, the stock was selling for about $12 a share at that time—twice the cost of the assets (net of liabilities). Some would say the stock was "watered" (as cattle sellers were accused of encouraging their stock to drink water prior to weighing for sales) because clearly the price is far above the cost of those assets. (And so, of course, is the price of an early Picasso above the cost of the canvas, paint, and labor.) That does not mean that the company will not in fact obtain a future net receipt stream whose present value is far in excess of $6 book figure. In fact, the owners expected it to earn a stream of net earnings with a present capital value of about $12 a share.

At the time that annual balance sheet was revealed, the corportion also reported the results of its operations during the preceding year. It published an *income statement* chronicling its operating activities.

INCOME STATEMENT, UNITED NUCLEAR CORPORATION
(Year ended March 31, 1963)

Sales		$45,400,000
Costs and expenses		
Costs of goods sold (labor, materials, power)	$29,500,000	
Depreciation of equipment (wear and tear and depletion of ore)	5,000,000	
Selling and administrative expenses	3,100,000	37,600,000
Operating net income		$ 7,800,000
Interest on debt	$ 600,000	
Abandonment of depleted mines	200,000	
Miscellaneous charges	200,000	1,000,000
Share belonging to minority interests of subsidiary company		3,000,000

Federal income tax
(No provision was made for federal income tax because the company has substantial deductible losses from prior year which may be carried forward to the current year.)

Net earnings	$ 3,800,000
	Per share of common stock $.93

A share could be purchased for $15 with reported earnings of 93 cents per year. Of course, if the future develops an even rosier hue, the price of stock may go still higher—or lower if the future deteriorates. That's the risk you take if you buy a share.

a. Look up the price of a share of stock in United Nuclear Corporation now.

b. Get its latest balance sheet and income statement. (Ask your librarian for aid. You may be referred to *Moody's Manuals of Industrials.* Or ask a stockbroker.)

c. Compare the most recent balance sheet with that of 1963 and try to explain what has happened in the interval.

2. "A corporation owned by one person is the same as a proprietorship." Do you agree? If so, why? If not, why not?

3. "Limited liability means that a corporation is limited in the amount of liability it can create against itself." Do you agree? If so, why? If not, why not?

4. "Continuity of a corporation means that if any or all of the current owners of the corporation die, the corporation continues as a unit of ownership." Do you agree?

5. Why is the corporation the dominant form of ownership of very large conglomerations of wealth?

6. Is it a disadvantage of the corporation that not every stockholder can make the controlling decisions? That the control is dispersed? That some people who own less than half of the corporation can make controlling decisions?

7. "Very few corporations lose wealth, and still fewer go broke." Do you agree? What evidence can you cite?

8. "Business firms exist in order to permit some method of coordinating the work of cooperating employees, who otherwise would not know how to cooperate with other workers." Criticize.

9. "The employer is called the boss because he is able to tell people what to do." Evaluate.

10. "Business firms exist because some people do not have enough wealth to own the capital equipment and machinery with which they can work more efficiently." Evaluate.

11. A friend of yours, a brilliant engineer and administrator, is operating a business. You propose to bet on his success and offer him some money to expand his operations.

A corporation is formed in which you will have 40 and he 60 percent of the common stock. You invest $30,000. This is often described as separation of ownership from control, since he now has the majority controlling vote. Would you ever be willing to invest wealth in such a fashion—that is, give up control while retaining ownership in certain property rights? Why?

12. A criticism of the modern corporation is that the management or directors, by virtue of their central position, are able to collect proxies (rights to cast votes of stockholders) from the existing stockholders; and as a result the management is in a powerful position and cannot be easily dislodged. It has been said that "the typical small stockholder can do nothing about changing management and that under ordinary circumstances management can count on remaining in office; and often the proxy battle is fought to determine which minority group shall control." Take the factual assertions as being correct.

a. Does it follow that stability of management in "ordinary circumstances" reveals some kind of weakness of stockholders?

b. Does it follow that a typical small stockholder "should" be able to turn out management?

c. If a minority group succeeds in getting a majority of stock votes, does this mean that a minority controls or that a majority controls through the medium of a minority group? Is this to be interpreted in the same way that political parties consisting of a group of organized politicians have elections to see which minority group shall control the government? Why or why not?

13. **a.** In analyzing the behavior of corporation management and directors, why is it pertinent to distinguish among nonprofit or publicly regulated, profit-limited corporations on the one hand, and private-property, for-profit business corporations on the other?

b. Which do you think would be more marked by self-perpetuating management and stockholder lethargy? Why?

c. Which do you think would show more discrimination in employment practices according to race and religion? Why?

14. Joseph Thagworthy has a stable of race horses. He also has a breeding farm. The two, although operated as a business, lose him over $50,000 annually. Yet he continues year after year because he enjoys the activity more than if he spent a similar sum for travel or conventional types of consumption activities.

a. Would it be correct to say that he is maximizing his wealth in that business?

b. Would it be correct to say he is maximizing his utility?

c. Do you think an increase in the losses would induce an increase in that kind of activity? What does economic theory postulate about that?

19

MEASURES OF COSTS, REVENUE, AND PROFITS

Estimation and computation of costs is not as simple as was suggested by the easy illustrations in earlier chapters. We assumed that all forsaken alternatives are coincident with the present action; yet, in almost every real situation, any decision today results in a series of future consequences or sacrifices. Furthermore, although we assumed earlier that we knew the forsaken values, these values actually are not known and must be forecast or estimated. As a result, we must modify the preceding exposition to allow for future consequences of present actions and of inaccurate forecasts.

Cost concepts enable people to make choices among *present* alternative actions. In choosing among presently available alternative actions, a person, we assume, wants to know what opportunities are forsaken. Hence, to each possible present action he attaches a measure of the present and future forsaken opportunities. That measure is "cost." The sacrifice is made inevitable when the present action is taken. In that sense the present action involves a present cost.[1]

Capital-Value Measure of Costs

Because goods are substitutable sources of utility, and because substitution is facilitated by exchange via money rather than barter, it is possible to *measure* the *value* of a forsaken option in money terms. This value we call "cost." *The money-cost measure of some event is useful* because if, among various ways of performing some task, we choose

[1] In a deeper sense, no sacrifice really occurs only in the future. A reduction in command over future services is a current reduction and hence is a currently experienced cost.

the method with the lowest *present-capital-value* measure of cost, we achieve the most preferred situation possible (in the sense that a greater value of other goods is left). As shown in Chapter 15, a series of money payments or values at different times can be made commensurable and added to get a single capital value. For that reason, *capital values* serve as the basic *measure* of costs.

The calculations in the estimation of cost can be illustrated by a simple numerical example, in which we first ask what it costs to obtain ownership of a Ford car and keep it for, say, two years. The price is $2,000; so the cost of *obtaining* ownership is obviously $2,000. Since we are not yet asking what it costs to own *and operate* the car, we momentarily ignore all operating costs and assume that the car is not going to be used at all. What will the owner sacrifice for *two years of ownership*? He pays $2,000 now for title to the car. At the end of two years, he terminates ownership—not by dumping the car in the ocean, but by selling it for the highest available resale value, $1,400. However, $1,400 two years from now is not the same thing as $1,400 *now*. At a 10 percent rate of interest, the present value of $1,400 deferred two years is .826 × $1,400 = $1,-156.40. The present-capital-value measure of the cost of owning the car is equal to the initial purchase expenditure minus the present value of the resale proceeds two years later: $2,000 — $1,156.40 = $843.60.

The decrease in value of the car from the $2,000 purchase price to the $1,400 resale value could be called a "loss," but since that "loss" is expected, the conventional name is "depreciation."[2]

Suppose there are other outlays, like taxes and insurance, of $100 for each year. For the first year, these expenses are paid at the time of the purchase of the car; the taxes and insurance for the second year are to be paid at the *beginning* of the second year. The expenses of $100 at the beginning of the second year are discounted back to the present (through one year); at 10 percent rates of interest, this gives a present value of $90.90.

Collecting all the data, we have (in present-value units):

$2,000.00	purchase price
100.00	first year's tax and insurance
90.90	second year's tax and insurance, present value
—1,156.40	resale value, present value
$1,034.50	present-value measure of cost of two-year ownership.

The cost of purchasing and owning this car for *two* years is $1,034.50 in present-capital-value measure (including taxes and insurance).

[2] "Unexpected depreciation," called obsolescence, is discussed in some detail in the final section of this chapter.

We can rearrange the data as follows:

$2,000.00	purchase price
—1,156.40	resale value
$ 843.60	depreciation
100.00	first year's tax and insurance
90.90	second year's tax and insurance
$1,034.50	present-capital-value cost of two-year ownership.

In this way costs are expressed as the sum of *depreciation* and all other attendant costs.

What does it cost to own and use a car at the rate of 10,000 miles per year for two years for a total mileage of 20,000 miles? Suppose that the outlays (for gasoline, lubrication, etc.) for 10,000 miles in the first year are estimated at $300. To avoid tedious but precise interest-rate discounting for every payment during the year, simply suppose that the payments are made at the *end* of the year (as if the user paid all his bills by credit card at the end of the year). At 10 percent, the present value of the first year's operating costs of $300 is .909 × $300 = $272.70.

During the second year outlays for gas, oil, lubrication, repairs, and other maintenance are estimated at $350. Discounting this back two years to a present capital value gives .826 × $350 = $289.10. The resale value of the car will be lower than if it had not been used, despite the maintenance expenditures; it is estimated to be $1,300 instead of $1,400. The present value of $1,300 deferred two years is .826 × $1,300 = $1,073.80.

Collecting the data, all in present-value measure:

$2,000.00	purchase price
100.00	first year's tax and insurance
272.70	first year's operating outlays
90.90	second year's tax and insurance
289.10	second year's operating outlays
—1,073.80	resale value
$1,678.90	capital-value measure of cost of two-year ownership and operation at 10,000 miles per year for a total mileage of 20,000.

Alternative Numerical Expressions of Costs

The present-capital-value measure, once computed, can be converted into a variety of measures of costs, as we saw in Chapter 15. For example, it can be expressed as a value for some future moment. Or it can be expressed as present-value costs per unit of output. Another alternative is simply to convert the present-capital-value measure into a constant, continuous annuity sequence—called a *rate of costs.* For example, if one rents a machine for 60 cents an hour, the rate of cost will accrue to $1.20 in two hours (if we forget the interest rate for so short a time) or, equivalently, at the rate of 1 cent per minute, or 1/60 cent per second. Thus, any "cost" can be measured by a single capital-value total, or it can be expressed in terms of a steady *rate of accrual* of costs *over some specified time interval,* as if costs were accruing at some continuous rate —even though in reality costs may occur in discrete lumps at various times. For example, if we rent equipment for one hour on one day, and for two hours on a second day, and for four hours on a third day, the capital-value measure of cost (ignoring interest) is $4.20 for seven hours at 60 cents per hour.

We can now re-express the $4.20 cost as equivalent to a continuous accrual of costs at the rate (speed) of $2.10 per day for two days, or a rate of $1.05 per day for four days, or 1 cent an hour for 420 hours. All of these have the same present-capital-*value* measure of costs—even though the time patterns of cost accrual differ.

For an individual, payment of costs need not be concurrent with either service or incurring of costs. There is no reason why a person couldn't buy a car for two years' use and yet pay for it over ten years. He could borrow the purchase price and repay in later installments. Reference to our capital-value tables indicates, at 10 percent, an annual payment or accrual of 16 cents per year for ten years for each dollar of present capital value that he borrows. He would be making payments for it long after he had used it, but he would be paying less while he had it. There is nothing "wrong," "inefficient," or "irrational" in selecting various lengths of time over which to pay—some longer and some shorter than that over which the particular service is involved. As long as all have the same *present capital value* at the relevant rate of interest, the only difference is in the distribution of the sacrifice of consumption over time. To save before one gets some service or to save afterward is equally sensible. If one expects a larger flow of money receipts now and a smaller one later, paying earlier may be preferable; but if one expects larger receipts later, paying later may be preferable.

Another way to express the measure of cost is in terms of cost per units of the output. In the automobile case, we could ask what the costs are for each mile of travel. Divide the present-capital-value measure of cost by the expected number of miles of distance to be traveled in the two-year period: $1,678.90/20,000 = $.0839, the *present-value* measure of cost averaged over each unit of product. This is how much we must be paid *now* (at the beginning of the two-year run of this car) for each mile that we plan to drive in the next two years, if the receipts are to cover the total costs—since that average-cost figure was obtained simply by dividing the present-value total cost by the total mileage.

A similar question is: "What measure of cost can be imputed to each mile *at the time each mile is traveled*?" In other words, if at the time each mile is traveled a payment is received, what must be the receipt per mile of the expected 20,000 miles if all costs are to be covered? The answer is *not* $.0839; that was the payment if made *in advance* at the beginning of the two-year interval. What we want now is a uniform payment for each mile *at the time of the output* (or, let us suppose, at the end of each year of service). That cost will be larger because of the deferred date. This can be computed as follows: Convert the total present-capital-value measure, $1,678.90, to a two-year annuity allowing for 10 percent rate of interest, and divide *each* year's amount by the mileage of that year. This gives $969 as the annual rate of accrual of costs for the 10,000 miles each year, or 9.69 cents per mile of annual travel.[3]

This figure of 9.69 cents per mile means that if at the time of each mile of service (or, more accurately, at the end of each year) we collected 9.69 cents, the total costs would just be covered. The difference between this figure of 9.69 cents and 8.39 cents reflects the difference in timing of payments.

Costs, then, are measurable sums of all the "interest-discounted" outlays minus the "discounted" value of materials left over. Since outlays occur at different times, they are made comparable by discounting at the appropriate

[3] Another, more generally applicable way to get this same answer involves what may appear to be a bit of trickery, because it is a simplification of an involved algebraic formula that applies also to cases where the rate of output varies from year to year. Instead of converting the present capital value to an annuity type of rate of accrual of costs, convert the annual output to a single "present-capital-value output," as it were. In other words, "discount" each of the future miles of travel by the interest-rate discount factor back to equivalent "present-time" miles.

The present-value-equivalent number of miles for the first year's mileage, 10,000 miles, is .909 × 10,000. The second year's mileage must be discounted two years to the present moment. At a 10 percent rate of interest, this is done by multiplying the 10,000 miles of the second year by .826 (the present-value factor for two years at 10 percent). The two-year total mileage in present-value equivalent is:

9,090	(1st year: 10,000 × .909)
8,260	(2nd year: 10,000 × .826)
17,350	("present-value" miles)

If this is divided into the present-value cost of the 20,000 miles, the result is 9.7 cents per mile, precisely the same cost we obtained when we used the alternative procedure of converting the cost to a two-year annuity. This figure is how much should be charged for each mile at the end of the year in which the mileage is obtained, if the total costs are to be covered. This is equivalent to computing a "variable" annuity—one that varies in proportion to the rate of output.

rate of interest into a *present-capital-value* measure of cost. Once computed, the capital-value measure of costs can be converted to alternative expressions of costs—for example, (a) rate of costs for periods of time, (b) cost per unit of service, depending upon whether the cost is to be paid now or at the time of service.

Fixed and Variable Costs

We have classified costs as (a) the costs of purchase and possession of some productive equipment and (b) the costs of production by use of that equipment with other associated services and materials. For some other purposes, a different way of classifying costs may be useful. It may be interesting to know how much of the costs of some output program one has already incurred and would have to pay even if he were to abandon the output program. If he proceeds with the decision to produce, he will then incur the remainder of the contemplated costs involved in the program. In our automobile example, if he purchases a car in preparation for operation of a taxi service, at the moment of purchase he will have incurred some loss of resale value, even if he should abandon his plan to operate the taxi service. That cost is fixed upon him; it is a "sunk, bygone" cost; and, as we shall see, it should play no role in any possible subsequent decision to revoke his plans and abandon production or to go ahead and produce the taxi service. For ensuing decisions, only the subsequently avoidable or *variable* costs would be relevant. (We shall use this classification later, when discussing decisions to revise output programs.)

"Fixed" and "variable" costs are also used in a different sense from that just given in the preceding paragraph. Sometimes "fixed" refers to costs that are *constant and common* to several alternative actions. For example, suppose that, regardless of the rate of operation of my factory, I shall pay for night watchmen, advertising, insurance, etc. Since those costs will occur no matter which of the choices I make, it is conventional to refer to them as "fixed" costs. This kind of "fixed" cost, however, is very different from the former kind, which has been incurred and cannot be avoided, *no matter what* one does. The present "fixed" costs are avoidable; one can, if he wishes, hire no night watchmen, take out no insurance, do no advertising, and shut down completely. Perhaps confusion between the two concepts of "fixed" cost would be avoided if the first were called "sunk" costs and if the second were called "common and constant" costs of a specified limited set of options. Obviously, to each of these concepts of fixed costs there is the corresponding concept of variable costs, the difference between the total cost and the particular "fixed" cost.

Revenues and Profits

Now we introduce sales receipts or revenue from the use of a car if I operate it as a taxi. The wage I could have earned at some other job is estimated at $4,000 per year. Suppose I believe I shall obtain sales of $6,500 in the first year and $5,500 in the second year, with the receipts presumed to come at the end of the year—on a sort of credit-card system.

Collecting all estimated expenditure and receipt data in Table 19–1, where each column lists the receipts (+) and expenditures (−) as of January 1, 1970, January 1, 1971, and January 1, 1972, we estimate the aggregate profit collected over the two years as $2,450 and the *present* value of the business as $1,833.

Table 19–1

RECEIPTS AND EXPENDITURES

	1/1/1970	1/1/1971	1/1/1972
Purchase of car	−$2,000		
Tax, insurance	− 100	−$ 100	
Operating and repair		− 300	−$ 350
Wages and salary		− 4,000	− 4,000
Receipts		+ 6,500	+ 5,500
Sale of car			+ 1,300
Net receipts	−$2,100	+$2,100	+$2,450
Present-value factor (10%)	(1.000)	(.909)	(.826)
Profit (capital value) $1,833 =	−$2,100	+$1,909	+$2,024

The cost of the taxi service, including the wages, is $8,619—the present value of the two annual $4,000 outlays ($6,940) added to the $1,679 present-value cost of owning and using the car. The present value of the service receipts ($6,500 and $5,500), $10,452, exceeds the cost by $1,833 ($10,452 − $8,619). My wealth will be $1,833 larger if I buy and operate the taxi service for the next two years than if I work for wages of $4,000 per year. If, in effect, I pay myself "wages" of $4,000 per year to drive the cab, my "profits" in the taxi business will be $1,833.

We can clarify the meaning of all these data by assuming that on the first day of operating the taxi, business is so good that people perceive what a splendid idea I had. Suppose, for reasons we shall investigate later, it will be two years before other people enter competition sufficiently to eliminate subsequent net earnings. But anyone who wants to enter the business immediately can do so by buying the business from me. The total resources in the business the day of opening consist of the car and the tax and insurance prepayments for the rest of the first year; these total $2,100. The present value of all the assets of the business is now $3,933, which is equal to the capital value of profits plus the initial investment. I invested $2,100 and I find my wealth is now $3,933, a profit of $1,833. Before answering the question of why I am able to get a profit, we should look at another commonly used measure and expression of profits.

If I had incorporated the taxi company and hold stock in it, the stock price would have risen. For example, if I had issued 100 shares of stock for the $2,100 to raise the money to buy a car and pay the first year's tax and insurance, the value of each share initially would have been $21. Now, upon perception of what the future promises, the price of the stock rises to $39.33, for a profit of $18.33 per share.

When that higher market value is revealed, my wealth is higher. I have at that moment realized a profit. Although people often call this profit a "paper profit" because I have not yet "cashed" it, it *is* a genuine increase in my wealth. The only question is whether to convert the form of the greater wealth into other assets or whether to keep it in the present form of business assets.

When the value of the taxi business is revised upward from $2,100 to $3,933, I can ask what *income* I now have. In other words, at what rate can I consume my wealth and still not have it decrease—because I consume it just as fast as it grows at the rate of interest. The answer is $393.30 per year. If I consume wealth at that rate, with the rate of interest 10 percent per year, I can consume that much annually forever and always have wealth of $3,933.

A principal point of this analysis is that the present value of a business depends upon the expectations of the future, not simply on how much was paid in the past to create the particular assets. One reason that reports by business firms of annual net earnings or profits are so important is that they serve as an indicator of the extent to which earlier forecasts are being fulfilled. For example, some business firms with rapid growth rates, like International Business Machines and Xerox, have a present price of their stock (wealth) that is nearly one hundred times greater than the annual reported net earnings. The market expects the future net earnings to increase rapidly, and the high present price of the stock relative to *current* net earnings, reflects that future growth expectation. Those future net earnings are capitalized into current values of assets—that is, stock prices. Other companies (for example, U.S. Steel) have low prices for the common stocks, only ten to fifteen times as great as current annual net earnings. If the reported net earnings for IBM in any year should merely equal the prior year's, instead of being 10 to 25 percent higher, the price of IBM stock will fall. If earnings fail to increase, expectations are disappointed and revised downward.

On the other hand, if the net earnings of U.S. Steel are reported as unchanged from a prior year, the price of U.S. Steel stock will not fall—that is, the expectation that U.S. Steel does *not* have substantial growth facing it will not be upset. Evidence for these statements of fact is available from the behavior of stock-market prices.

These examples provide a good opportunity to explain another much misunderstood term, "watered" stock. Suppose that on the day I started my taxi business with the $2,100 investment, I offered to sell you one of the one hundred shares of stock in the company for $30. At first, you might think I was selling you something worth only $21. You might say I was selling you a share at an inflated value or that the stock was "watered." [4] In fact, however, the share of taxi stock is worth more than $30, if the foresight we have is accurate. For this reason, investors often pay more for a share of stock than the costs of the resources in the business. What they are buying is part of the higher value of those resources—the profits. As long as you can get a share of my taxi stock for less than $39.33, you will have made a profit, too—assuming we have forecast future events accurately.

NET EARNINGS

Instead of concentrating on the wealth change (a capital-value concept), we could look at the future sequence or flow of *net earnings*. What is that flow? Is it the sequence of net receipts: —$2,100, $1,909, and $2,024? No, for that would suggest negative earnings in the first year and would in the last year include the resale value of the automobile. That final value is not earnings. Also, the first year's expenditures include purchase of a car; this purchase is primarily a change in form, not amount, of wealth.

The clue to the meaning of net earnings was given earlier in our discussion of costs. There we first obtained the present capital value of all expenditures —a value we converted to (or expressed in terms of) an annuity of uniform amount in each year or, alternatively, of uniform amount per mile. On page 282 will be found the figure of $969 as the annual "cost" for the car. If we add to this the imputed labor costs for driving the taxi, $4,000, we get a cost of $4,969 for each year. The receipts in the first year are $6,500 and in the second they are $5,500, which gives $1,531 and $531 for the first and second year respectively. The present value of those two amounts is ($1,531 × .909) + ($531 × .826) = $1,833 (which checks with the present value of profits, formerly obtained, indicating merely that our computations are arithmetically accurate, not that our *estimates* are accurate forecasts).

We now have three different value measures for the same event. The event

[4] The expression comes from the fact that cattle—stock—take on weight when fed water, as the seller is tempted to do before selling his cattle for their live weight.

is the purchase of a car and operation of it as a taxi for two years with sale of the cab at the end of the period. The operation can be described by (1) a sequence of "net receipts" (—$2,100; $2,100; and $2,450); (2) the *present capital value* of those net receipts ($1,833); or (3) a constructed, logically implied sequence of "net earnings" ($1,531 and $531) designed to measure the difference between (a) the "using" of resources during the year, called a "cost" sequence ($4,969 for each year) and (b) the values of services thereby created, called the "gross-earnings" sequence ($6,500 and $5,500).

Sequence 1 is called the *net receipts*, and sequence 3 is called the *net earnings*. Both have the same present value as concept 2, called the *capital value of profits*. The fact that 2 and 3 are both called "profits" is somewhat confusing, unless you remember that the term "profits" can be used consistently in various ways as long as the relationships among the uses are kept in mind. To call sequence 3 the profits is not to deny that 2 also can be called the profits; one is the "flow" or annuity type of measure, and the other is the capital value. Each implies the other. Don't make the error of adding them together or of speaking of one without making clear from the context which measure is being used.[5]

Of these three gages of wealth changes, only the capital-value (wealth) measure is directly measurable in the market. The current price of any resource is the measure of its present value. Therefore, if upon opening a taxi business I were to solicit bids for its sale, the price I could get would be a measure of the wealth value of profits. If other people now appreciate the possibilities and estimate them consistently with our data, the market value of the business will have jumped by $1,833.

Business accountants would report, as the profits and net earnings of each period, the amounts of $1,531 and $531, if the events materialized as predicted and if they reckon $4,000 each year as the implicit wages of my own time—as we did in our numerical calculations. However, accountants normally do not enter a cost item for the time of the owner. Failing that, the accountant's reported "net earnings" (not counting my implicit wages in costs) would be reported as $5,531 and $4,531. This differs from what we call profit because it includes a foreseeable value of my labor services.

ACCOUNTING RECORDS OF EARNINGS

Business-accounting records are designed to keep a clear record of the company's financial activities, such as the amounts of money spent, amounts committed to future payment, and the goods and services obtained in exchange. A record is kept of actual expenditures and receipts, but *not* of all the foreseen and predictable receipts and expenditures. More accurately, although all past expenditures and receipts are accounted for, only *some* of the future commit-

[5] Tax authorities usually call our profit concept, 2, a "capital gain or loss."

ments for expenditure and foreseeable future receipts are included in the accounts. Noncontractual future receipts or expenditures are excluded. To see why accountants have been led to exclude noncontractual *prospects* of future receipts and expenditures from their valuation processes and data, consider the following example.

Starting with $36,000, I buy land for $1,000, and oil-drilling equipment for $10,000. Also, I pay out $20,000 for wages and related services during the year. All these expenditures will be recorded by the accountant. More important, "costs" of the current year's activities will be interpreted and measured as follows: $20,000 for wages and services, plus the decrease ("depreciation") in value of the oil-drilling equipment during the year. If at the end of the year the oil-drilling equipment itself is estimated to be salable for $6,000, its loss of value (depreciation) would be $4,000. Labor, related services, and depreciation total to "costs" of $24,000. Since it is not always possible to assess the resale value of the equipment one owns and uses, accountants have adopted "rules or conventions"; otherwise, an accountant, by using his own discretion, could very easily select a rate of depreciation reflecting his personal bias and emotions. If a known rule is followed, anyone analyzing the accountant's report can make his own subsequent adjustments or evaluation.

There is room for enormous differences of valuation in still another part of the picture. Suppose that we strike oil. What should the accountant do? Should he make an entry designed to show the present value of the oil, which as yet is an unknown amount, uncaptured, and unsold? If the market values the oil field at $100,000, our wealth will amount to $100,000 plus $6,000 oil equipment plus $5,000 cash, for a total of $111,000. We have no liabilities. Hence, our net wealth or equity is $111,000. At the start of the year, it was $46,000 (composed of $1,000 in land, $25,000 in cash, and $20,000 in equipment). Our profit or "unforeseen" increase in wealth is $111,000 − $46,000 = $65,000. If he were bold and foolish enough to enter into the record his estimate of the value of the oil reserve, the accountant would report this profit of $65,000. Instead, he officially records *no* value for the oil field and reports a loss.

The accounting records say we lost $24,000 during the year. (We used up $4,000 of oil-well equipment and $20,000 for wages and related services and have sold no oil.) But we *are* wealthier. Why was the accountant unwilling to record a value on the amount to be received from the future oil sales? Because it is not yet a legally obligated, objectively measurable future receipt. No one knows how much oil is there or what further expenditures will be involved in getting it, and when it will be sold or for how much.

If the oil reservoir is to be valued, we could say that we spent $24,000 to find it; this $24,000 is the "book" value of the oil reservoir. As long as we know the convention, we can ignore it when deciding what we think the company is worth. But if we didn't know the convention, we might think the $24,000 represented an estimate of what the oil field is worth on the market. An alternative accounting convention is that of not recording any value at all, or a formal $1, until there is a clear-cut market for that asset, in which its value can be and *has been* measured by actual sales.

The zero or $1 value procedure is adopted frequently when the asset is not a physical tangible thing but an idea, design, patent, new product, trademark, or personality. An advertising campaign and a reliable product built up the name "Kodak" so much that the name "Kodak" serves as a symbol of reliability, thereby attracting sales. How should that asset, the name "Kodak," be valued? At the advertising costs? At zero? Or at some estimated value? Convention prefers the zero value, unless an overwhelming case with objective measurement can be made for the market value.

Earlier, we commented that the accountant usually ignores the implicit $4,000 annual wages that I, as owner, could have earned if I did not operate the taxi business. You can now see why the accountant does so. How would anyone know that the accountant is reporting an unbiased estimate rather than a figure to make the net earnings look good or bad as suits his whim?

Regardless of what the accountant does, *we* must not take his final figure for "profits or net earnings" to be a measure of the actual change in value of wealth. We must recognize that the prospect of future sales is an integral part of the value of a good. The local grocer has absolutely no assurance or guarantee that he will sell any goods next year. No retailer or manufacturer has any warranty that the public will continue to buy his product. He has no contract or commitment with consumers in which consumers bind themselves to future purchases. And yet we can be "sure" that sales will occur. To be "sure" means only that we are prepared to "bet" on it. I am prepared to bet that the local grocer will have lots of sales next year, and I am prepared to back my bet by *buying* some share of ownership (common stock) in that grocery. I pay for (bet on) the *prospect* of successful future operations. In fact, the value of almost *every* good rests on a present bet about *prospects*. The present price or value rarely rests on a contract that someone will buy something in the future. About the only commodity for which there is legal commitment of that nature is a debt contract (bond) or money which can be so used for the legal payment of debts. The accountant knows this and refuses to register a value that he cannot take from some objectively revealed market exchange. Subject to the conventions indicated, the accountant presents what would otherwise be the change in value of the firm as a result of the year's actions. These are reported as the "net earnings" or "profits" of the year. They do not correspond to his predictions of future events. His reported data are nevertheless important in influencing people's judgments about what they are willing to pay for the business or for shares of ownership in it.

Meaning and Measure of Obsolescence

Obsolescence occurs when the value of assets decreases in excess of depreciation. Values decrease either because the demand for the asset's services has fallen more than expected or because new and unexpected superior methods of production have become available. For example, suppose machine *A* is available at a purchase price of $100 and will produce one thousand units of *X* before it "falls apart." Suppose further that the machine's value will decline in proportion to its use—that is, at the rate of 10 cents per unit. This means the machine depreciates at the rate of 10 cents per unit produced by the machine. Suppose also that this machine has associated costs for materials and labor of 20 cents per unit, so that the total cost per unit is 30 cents. Finally, suppose that the product sells for 30 cents per unit. In this case, the receipts will just cover the costs of purchase of machine and associated materials. The value of the machine at time of purchase is $100.

Immediately after purchase, as luck would have it, a new machine is introduced for the same price; the new machine, *B*, will produce one thousand units before it falls apart, but the associated costs are only 16 cents per unit, instead of 20 cents as with machine *A*. What will happen to the value of machine *A*? Nothing—if the number of new machines of type *B* is not large enough to increase the output of the good being produced so that the price of the good falls below 30 cents per unit before machine *A* can produce one thousand units. Instead, the value of machine *B* will be $140; and if anyone can buy one for less than $140, he will make a profit.

Machine *A* will not be left idle. It will be used until the price of the item it produces falls to below 20 cents per unit. As the price of the item falls from 30 cents, under the impact of an increased supply as the new machine is more commonly used, the value of machine *A* will fall. The value imputed to machine *A* is the difference between the price of the item produced and the associated costs of producing the item, 20 cents. At a price of 30 cents the machine can be used for one thousand items; therefore, the machine's value will be $100 (equal to one thousand units times the difference between 30 cents and 20 cents). When the price of an item of product falls *to* 20 cents, that difference is wiped out; and machine *A* is then worthless. The machine will be retired from use if the price falls *below* 20 cents. As we said, this decrease in value because of the reduced price of the product is called obsolescence.

Only unexpected, unfavorable developments cause obsolescence to become a "loss" to the machine owner. If buyers anticipate future developments when considering the purchase of a machine, they will offer a price low enough to avoid subsequent loss of value. If purchasers do not anticipate future developments, obsolescence (reduction in value of the asset) does not necessarily mean that the asset is idled. Instead, the reduction in value is just sufficient to permit successful competition with the newcomer. This is why today old DC-3 airplanes are still flying, despite the existence of superior aircraft. Not until the value of the old asset falls to zero will the asset be idled. That is, the old item will be abandoned only when savings in costs of use (or gains in revenue) of a new item are greater than the purchase price of the new item.

Questions

1. "The expression 'to incur a cost' is equivalent to saying that one has committed certain acts that will involve sacrifices of opportunities that could have been realized had the act not been taken." Do you agree? If so, why? If not, why not?

2. Why are capital values used as a measure of costs?

3. Why cannot money expenditures be identified with costs?

4. A house can be purchased for $20,000. At the end of a year it could be resold for $21,000 if you had also spent $1,000 for a concrete fence, $300 for landscaping, $800 for air conditioning, and $1,200 for carpeting; otherwise, the house could have been resold for $19,000. Taxes of $300 must be paid in any event. Assume that all these expenditures—except for the taxes, which are to be paid at the end of a year—are paid at the moment you buy the house. The interest rate is 10 percent.

a. What is the cost of owning a house for one year—if you do not install fence, landscaping, air conditioning, and carpeting?

b. What is the cost of owning the house if you do install those improvements?

c. What is the year's depreciation on the house without the proposed improvements?

d. Express this cost of ownership of the improved house for one year, as a constant two-year annuity.

e. Express the cost as a perpetuity.

f. Express the cost as a five-year annuity.

g. Which of these is the correct way to express cost?

5. You operate a cleaning establishment. A new cleaning machine has a price of $5,000. You estimate its resale value at the end of the first year to be $3,000 and $1,500 at the end of the second year. The rate of interest is 10 percent.

a. What will it cost to purchase and own the machine for one year?

b. For two years?

c. What is the depreciation on the machine in the first year?

d. In the second year?

e. If you use the machine, you will incur expenses during the first year of $6,000 for labor, power, and repairs; and the machine will still have a resale value of $3,000 at the end of the first year. The same expenses will be involved in the second year, and the resale value will be $1,500 at the end of the second year. Assume that all expenditures are payable at the end of the year in which they are experienced. What is the cost of having and using the machine for one year?

f. For two years?

g. What is the cost of the second year of possession and operation?

h. If, immediately after buying the machine, you should reconsider and decide to sell it, the resale value would be $4,000. What cost would the purchase of the machine "fix" upon you? This is called "fixed," "sunk," or irrecoverable cost.

i. After purchasing the machine, you can either keep it idle or use it with the attendant expenditures indicated earlier (in "e" above). As between these two alternative actions, what is the fixed cost?

j. What are the variable costs; that is, the costs incurred over and above the "fixed" costs?

6. Suppose you expect to obtain $8,000 revenue from use of the cleaning machine during the first year. (Assume you receive all of it at the end of the first year.) Also you expect to receive $15,000 during the second year. (Again assume all revenue is received at the end of that year.)

a. What is the profit implied by your expectations?

b. Suppose that within a month after you have installed the machine, other people form expectations consistent with yours; however, despite their efforts to open similar cleaning establishments, your revenue forecast will still be accurate (since it was in part based on anticipations that other people would soon copy your techniques). At that time the capital value of your business will have been revised upward with a profit equal to that profit of $5,491. When do you realize that profit?

7. What is the sequence of *net* receipts as of the beginning of year one? Compute missing data.

	BEGINNING OF 1ST YEAR	END OF 1ST YEAR	END OF 2ND YEAR	
Purchase	$5,000	0	0	
Expenses	0	$6,000	$ 6,000	
Resale	0	0	1,500	
Receipts	0	8,000	15,000	
Net Receipts	______	______	______	
Present Values	______ +	______ +	______ =	______ (Profit)

8. Suppose that within a month after you open your cleaning establishment, people revise their expectations to conform to the data and forecasts given in the problem. Your wealth increases by the profit, $5,491, at the time the market revaluation occurs. If you had issued 1,000 shares of common stock for $5 each at the time you organized your business, each share would now be worth approximately $10.50. Formerly you were worth $5,000; now you are worth approximately $10,500. How much larger is your income than before?

9. In the cleaning-establishment problem, suppose that within two years other people will have time to buy a machine and establish a similar business, and that this has been anticipated in the forecast data. Suppose the only way someone else can realize the higher value by buying a cleaning machine and opening a cleaning firm is by hiring you to operate it—because of special skills you have in operating the establishment.

a. What asset rises in value—the physical assets or you as a personal owner of labor services?

b. Do you realize a profit in this second case; or are profits present only in the first case, when physical, inanimate goods rise in capital value?

10. "Don't buy your business cars. Lease them from the A and A Leasing Company. You can lease a Chevy for $60 a month. Avoid the loss of depreciation and necessity of tying up capital funds in the purchase of capital items." This is an accurate paraphrase of leasing advertising. What errors of analysis does it contain? Would the reasons given provide any advantage to a businessman? Explain why not.

11. "New business firms can underprice older firms, because the newer firms can buy the latest equipment and are not burdened with the older, less economical equipment which older firms must retire before they can economically adopt the new. This is why continued technological progress contributes to maintaining a competitive economic system." Explain the errors in both sentences.

12. Why are the airlines still flying piston-engine propeller planes when more economical and better-performing jet-driven planes are available? Is it because of lack of competition among airlines?

20

FORESIGHT, PROFITS, AND PROPERTY RIGHTS

Fundamental Sources of Profits

Because foresight is imperfect, unforeseen changes in values will inevitably occur; profits and losses will be realized. Profits and losses occur in all economic systems. A change from a private-property to a communist or socialist or feudal society will not eliminate profits and losses; it will not even hide them. It will only change the determination of who bears the profits and losses. Only if uncertainty is eliminated will the situation be different; and in all probability no revolution or earthly change will remove uncertainty.

It is convenient for subsequent analysis to group the sources of uncertainty into two polar classes, one consisting of extraneous, uncontrollable events and the other of deliberate innovative activity by resource owners.

EXTRANEOUS EVENTS

Changes in demand serve as an excellent example of extraneous, uncontrollable events. For example, the value and usefulness of a dress or suit of clothes falls because of changes in styles. You may think a dress will still keep the wearer as neat, warm, and modest as ever, but the dress simply does not give all the usefulness it formerly did. It no longer gives the wearer a feeling of stylishness, attractiveness, or sense of belonging. And neither you nor I can say that these are irrelevant, improper, or merely superficial attributes that shouldn't count in usefulness or value. The simple fact is that they do.

Some of us may think that basic values really do not change; we may think that people so concerned with style are extravagant and that the prices of their clothes, for example, bear little relationship to real values. We have every right to *say* that, but we should realize that we are saying that we know better than other people what the properly desired things are in this world and that, therefore, the market values that reflect *their* preferences are not true values. Maybe other people *ought* to behave in accord with our opinion, but they choose not to, and hence values will reflect preferences that you, or I, may think are senseless. And if people shift their preferences unpredictably, values will change unpredictably, with profits or losses as the result.

Changes in value occur because some people change their beliefs about the future desirability of various assets (whether because of physical loss or change in preference patterns or changes in distribution of wealth among people is irrelevant). Some event may produce, say, a fall in demand for one asset relative to others—and hence change the present price of the asset. Society then finds itself with a good no longer as valuable as formerly; that good will not command as much of other goods in exchange.

INNOVATIVE ACTIVITY

The other, or opposite, source of profits or losses is deliberate innovative activity, in which owners try to use resources in ways not heretofore evaluated by the community. Their hope, ambition, gamble, or speculation is that their wealth will be more highly valued by the market after innovation. Anyone who seeks to do this must own some resources, the value changes in which will accrue to him as a result of innovation. While he is the owner, *any change* in value of resources, regardless of the cause, will have to be borne by him, at least according to laws of ownership and responsibility in a private-property economy.

All the changes in value of resources (at a rate greater than the rate of interest) are profits or losses. If I increase the value of a house by painting it, so that the new house value is equal to the former value plus that of the paint and labor, then the change in value is merely the sum of the former values of a changed set of goods. But if the value of some newly combined set of resources is greater than the sum of their former values, there is a profit, an *unexpected increase in value.*

Deliberate innovative activity can lead to a higher amount of profits. For this reason it is often said that the prospects of profits serve as the motivating force for innovative activity. Yet one man's innovation and resultant profits may be another man's losses. For example, the invention of the automobile reduced the value of buggy whips, and the innovation of television reduced the value of theater buildings. The loss in value of the theater building—in the sense that it will no longer be as useful to other people—is more than offset by the gain from television. But the theater owner who bears that loss, if he is not somehow compensated, is no better off than if a fire damaged the theater. When losses are the result of "improvement" elsewhere, is the bearer of this loss compensated, even if in principle it were possible to do so? As we shall see, in every social and economic system the answer is "No." Still another question is whether or not one should try to compensate him; but that is a question of normative policy, and we shall postpone it.

Profits, Ownership, and Management

Although he may hire a manager to run his business, the owner still owns the resources and still bears profits or losses. The owner may seem to be passive, abiding by the manager's decisions and advice; yet the so-called "passive" owner is the one who has decided to permit this use of his resources. And even though the manager makes all the decisions after the owner decides to submit his wealth to the venture, and even though the manager seems to be doing all the work, the owner still bears the wealth consequences.

If an owner operates his business as his own manager, he counts wages for his labor services. Some owner-managers make the mistake of combining into one total their wages of management and their profit—calling the whole thing "profit" or calling it all "wages." In the earlier taxi example, in which profit was $1,831, wages for driving the cab (and let us assume also for managing the firm) were $4,000. The former is profit, a value change in wealth; the latter is wages or payment for labor services. Even though the profit could be measured or expressed in terms of an equivalent present valuation, to add the two together or to call them both either profit or management wages would still be to mix two different economic concepts. However, in the language of the layman, you will often find this confusing practice. You will, in each instance, simply have to reinterpret the situation for yourself, if you want to keep your analysis consistent.

Profits of Labor

A distinction between profits and wages of management, or between profits and wages in general, does not mean that labor or personal service is not a source of value to a person. Wages are payments or receipts going to a person for his personal services, while "rent" is the name for the payment to the owner of inanimate goods. Both wages and rentals have present values (wealth), reflecting anticipated future receipts. The present value of my future wages may be $200,000. If I have an accident and fracture my skull, I will suffer a reduced prospective future series of receipts; and the present value of my wages will fall, say, to $150,000. The accident will cost me $50,000.

We see and measure profit of nonhuman wealth more clearly because inanimate goods can be bought and sold, whereas a person does not sell himself; he sells only the current services as they are performed. If he could literally sell his future services now, he could convert (or "cash in") his profit to other forms of wealth. But he cannot, and so he must keep that wealth tied up in the form of his labor services. Labor profits are not salable, like the profits of discovering an oil field, which the owner can sell immediately on realization rather than waiting until the oil is pumped out and sold.

Even though there is no marketplace where a person can sell his future services now, he can borrow now against his future wages. He resorts to the loan markets, where he can sell his promissory note in exchange for present goods. Thus, he can approximate some of the results he would have achieved if he could actually have sold his future services.

Another device to approximate the results of a sale of one's future services is the long-term contract. In Western societies, people may make long-term contracts to sell their future services at specified future wages. For example, movie and television stars, baseball players and some other professional athletes make "exclusive-service" contracts with certain employers. The employee cannot be forced to render specific performance if he should change his mind, but he cannot legally do such work for any other person; and he may have to pay for damages sustained by the employer who made expenditures or commitments in anticipation of employee performance. These kinds of contracts are relatively minor in the American economy and will not be investigated further.

In a sense, all profits—or values—are values of people rather than of inanimate goods. Goods are valuable only because of the way in which people use them. People with superior talents know how to use resources to make them more valuable. If, for example, General Motors hires a superior designer to design a car of greater value, the increased value shows up as a profit. But if we keep our analysis correct, we must first recognize that the designer was obtained for a salary less than his worth proved to be to GM. No one *knew*, in advance, just how valuable his services would be. When hiring him, GM had to accept the initially uncertain value of his services. GM's ability to hire him for less than his ultimately revealed worth reflected differences in opinion about that worth among General Motors, other potential employers, and the employee himself. GM cannot continue to purchase his services at less than they are revealed to be worth unless *all* other potential employers remain ignorant of his ability—and he will not let his ability stay hidden. The high value of his services will accrue to him as other employers bid for his work, driving up his wages and raising costs to all who thereafter use him.

None of this means that GM or any other employer intentionally makes profits by paying less for resources than they are worth. What resources are paid is what the rest of the market thinks they are worth *at the time* they are bought or hired. Who knows before a horse race what a bet on each horse is worth? Always, too little is bet on the winner and too much on the losers. If anyone makes a profit, it follows, by definition, that the price paid for the resource was initially too low. In that sense, profits are the result of underpaying resources—with hindsight to tell us what underpaying is. And losses result from overpaying.

Profits, Losses, and Insurance

To avoid the risks of "losses" from physical damage (fire, flood, etc.) or theft, people "insure." Thereby, they modify the pattern of risks and incidence of losses. By joint voluntary insurance, a group of people can agree to share such losses by spreading them over the group, in the form of premium or insurance fees paid by each member. Out of these fees, compensation is paid to those who suffer the contingent misfortune. This pooling of risk of losses does not necessarily reduce the total losses. It spreads them over the insurees, as each one pays a fixed fee for the insurance. The aggregate of the fixed fees is (hopefully) enough to cover the losses incurred. In general, the insurance converts the risk of a possible large loss into the certainty of a small loss—the payment of the premium for the insurance.

Even though, as a condition of getting insurance, the insuring group may require that the insured take special precautions, the remaining precautionary incentives are reduced. Without insurance, we may devote more resources and care and anxiety to protection than with it. Nevertheless, even if total losses were greater with insurance than without (as they may well be), the savings in resource use and anxiety in providing security and safety may be of greater value than the losses avoided.

Some losses are not insurable. For example, insurance by a retailer against bad business or loss of customers would mean (if it were somehow available) that the retailer could try less hard to provide consumers with desirable products—relying on the insurance company to indemnify him for the lost sales. The resultant claims for indemnifying the insurees against the "losses" will exceed the amount of wealth that the insurance company can get from voluntary insurees as premiums for insurance. For this reason, insurance on business failure because of loss of customers, or on crop failures for farmers, or on unemployment is not actuarily sound.

There are still a very large number of other uninsurable hazards. For example, you can't get insurance against having your oil well dry up, or *not* finding gold on your land, or having other people's tastes and demands shift against your services or goods, or against divorce, or against dull children, or against marital infidelity. And yet in a sense you can insure against some of these events. The risk of your oil well's drying up unexpectedly can be transferred to someone else. Just sell the asset to him and hold money. When you sell your oil-well land, you get the present value of that land as judged by other people on an expectational basis (weighing some odds that it will dry up against odds that it won't). If the oil well does dry up, the buyer bears the loss.

In this way—by choosing not to hold certain goods—you can escape the hazards of loss of those goods (and chance of profit from those goods). In a private-property system, those losses or profits are imposed on the person who is the owner of the particular goods.

This modification of hazard of loss is a form of insurance and is available in a private-property system, in which people can exchange ownership and choose which risks to bear. By shifting private-property rights to various goods and buying one kind of good rather than another, people can obtain "insurance" against certain kinds of risks and losses. More precisely, private property is not insurance in the sense that one takes a small but sure loss (premium) in order to avoid a large contingent loss; rather, it is a selective, discretionary, risk-bearing institution.

A rental arrangement is also a risk-shifting system. By renting a house on a month-to-month basis, instead of owning one, you can "own" only one month's value of the house and thereby avoid having so much of your wealth in a particular house. A renter will not suffer the entire loss of value of a house if its value changes. By renting those goods a person wants to use, he can diversify his ownership of goods or he can concentrate on one good, independently of his consumption patterns.

It is worth noting that in some countries farmers cannot sell the land they "own." They can use it for themselves or sell the crop for their own wealth, but they cannot sell the land or borrow against it as security. (If they could borrow against the land, they would borrow its current value and then let the lender take the land when they refuse to repay the loan—thus circumventing the intended ban on sale of the land.) This is a modified form of private-property rights, but it does not provide the extent of risk sharing and re-allocation that is provided by a system of full private-property rights. Obviously, the incentive to invest in land is weakened, since the risks of value changes cannot be shifted to those most willing to bear the risks of changes in the value of the land. A person who "owns" land under these restricted conditions will invest more of his wealth in forms of property with more transferable property rights. This is part of the explanation for the unwillingness of people in so-called "backward" countries to invest in farming land.

Attitudes toward various systems of property rights should, in part, be based on attitudes toward the *way* of determining the distribution of profits and losses. Since profits and losses occur regardless of the form of property rights, the issue is not whether one is for or against profits and losses but whether one is for or against this or that system of distributing them over various people. Who shall bear the joy of profits and the despair of losses? Laws might be passed to impose losses on brunettes and profits upon blondes, by an appropriate system of taxes. Profits and losses could be owned by the people as a whole, with each person's use rights determined by a lottery or his taxes or by his standing in line, as it is with public parks and rights to hunt deer in some states.

Profits and losses could be assigned by the political decision system, in which case the assignments will depend on one's power of affecting political decisions. Socialism is an example of this form of profit-and-loss risk-bearing system. Part of the issue between a capitalist, private-property system and a socialist system is over the kind of risk-bearing mechanism or institution used. Although both systems have profits and losses, the distribution and extent of value changes will be different. And under the private-property system, those who decide about the use of resources are more likely to be the ones to bear the effects of resulting value changes. As a result, under the private-property system the resources are more likely to be used where the profit potential is highest. But proponents of socialism believe that market values should not be so influential in determining resource uses and that individuals should not be able to specialize in bearing various kinds of risks.

Profits, Monopoly Rents, and Changes in Monopoly Rights

Not every occurrence of profits reflects a transfer of resources from lower-valued to higher-valued uses. Suppose I managed *unexpectedly* to have a law passed preventing other people from producing goods that compete with mine. The reduced supply from a reduced number of competitors will raise the price of my goods, giving me a profit. This kind of profit can be created by the levying of special taxes on my competitors; for example, interstate tariffs on produced goods in other states that compete with mine in domestic sales.

The profit that results when greater restraint is placed on competitors' access to the market is called a "monopoly rent." The higher rate of "earnings" on which that monopoly rent rests is also called a monopoly rent—here measured in the sense of the flow of higher earnings that are capitalized into the present wealth measure of "monopoly rent." The wealth gain is called *monopoly* rent because of the legal restriction on market access; it is called monopoly *rent* because it is not allowed to induce an increase in supply.

The legal-monopoly restriction on entry will raise the market valuation of assets in the protected industry. The restriction prevents more resources from being transferred to higher-valued uses sufficiently to bring values down to costs. The result, from the consumers' point of view, is the same as would occur if costs were higher than they really are. The "privileged" or "licensed" resources earn their owners a higher value, while the excluded resources receive a lower value.

How much of the current value of a resource is "monopoly rent"? This is an interesting, important, but unanswered question. We have some estimates and evidence on tobacco acreage, ranging up to $3,000 for an acre of land on which tobacco can be grown and sold in the market without a special tax. This is nearly 50 percent of the total value of that acre of land. In New York City the monopoly rent of one taxi is about $20,000. In California the monopoly rent of a liquor license ranges from $10,000 to $40,000. In most states the present value of banks, insurance companies, airlines, and all public utilities reflects a monopoly rent of various amounts, depending upon the extent to which entry is restricted. Value also depends on the extent to which the monopoly rent is taxed away by the government, or prices are kept down by law so that the legal monopolists cannot realize the maximum market value of their monopoly situation.

Monopoly rents depend on legal restraints on market access, but we must be careful not to confuse monopolists in this situation with price-searchers, who are also called "monopolists" in the technical economic literature. Both are called monopolists because both face negative-sloping demand curves for their products. Almost all retailers and manufacturers, large and small, are called "monopolists" because they face a negative-sloped demand curve for their products. We have in this book used the name "price-searchers" for such sellers who operate in *open* markets, where there are no restraints on entry. The reason for calling them "price-searchers" rather than "monopolists" is simply to keep the two situations distinct. There is nothing about price-searchers' markets to suggest monopoly rents resulting from protected competition. In a price-searchers' market, anyone can open a business to make a new kind of cornflake, and anyone can open another drugstore, but the fact that they will be facing negatively sloped demand curves for their products does not mean they can produce the product profitably. Anyone can be a monopolist with respect to some unique resource; but if the demand for the services of that unique resource is not high enough, he will have no wealth advantage. It is easy to identify many firms that are losing wealth despite a negatively sloping demand curve for their services. Yet economic folklore about the American economy would have us believe that the large price-searcher firms make most of the profits.

Where does the myth arise? Probably from two sources. One is the failure to distinguish between the two types of monopoly. The second is the failure to distinguish between large and small firms, and even here the confusion is compounded by the notion that big firms make bigger profits because they are big, rather than that firms making big profits will become big firms. Being big is in itself no assurance of a higher probability of making profits. That, at least, is what economic theory indicates, and the evidence is consistent. It is easy to think that one can refute this evidence by pointing out a big firm like General Motors, which has earned profits in the capital-value sense during many years (and had losses during many years in that same sense—for example, in 1962: see question 9 at end of chapter for evidence). But some very large firms have lost wealth in many years (Chrysler, Ward's), and some very small firms have had spectacular growth (Varian, Texas Instruments, Zenith, Control Data, Mc-

Donnell Aircraft). The total evidence falls into the predicted pattern—namely, that the probability that any firm will in the next interval of time experience a profit (unforeseen capital-value gain in its wealth) is the same for big and small firms, for price-takers and price-searchers, and even whether the resources of the firm have free or restricted access to the market. All the foreseeable events have been capitalized into the present valuations; only the unforeseen ones remain to be revealed. There is no way of knowing which firms will experience the new unpredictable favorable events.

The idea that it is possible to know which firm or class of firms is more likely to earn profits is self-defeating. If they were detectable in advance, then it would pay to buy the firms immediately, thus pushing up their values *now*. Consequently, any statements about which class of firms will in the future experience unusual wealth increases, as profits, is a statement with which the general public (and especially the wealth-holding portion of it) is in disagreement. It is in disagreement because the statement implies that there is today a class of firms whose assets or resources (stock prices) are systematically undervalued. If you know of that class, you have a good road to profits for yourself; but beware, for you are betting against the judgment of the rest of the community.

Other Definitions of Profits

DIFFERENCE BETWEEN WHOLESALE AND RETAIL PRICE

"Profits" as used by the ordinary businessman does not always correspond exactly to "profits" as defined here. No one has a copyright on the term "profit," and anyone can use it as he likes. The definition in economic analysis is used to describe an observed economic phenomenon, the unpredicted changes in values of goods. But the term is also sometimes used to describe a wide variety of relationships between expenditures and receipts. Sometimes the difference between the price for which a retailer buys goods and the price at which he sells them is called "profit." More normally, that difference is called "markup," as an indication of how much above the purchase price the selling price must be if all the other attendant costs are to be met. To ignore those other costs is to forget about space, shelter, management, sales clerks, inventory for display and immediate delivery, record-keeping, safeguarding, insurance, advertising, taxes, light, heat, fixtures, breakage, pilferage, packaging, returns, employee training, and many other costly activities. "Overhead costs" commonly refers to some of those costs. Some say that a markup of 100 percent (above the wholesale purchase price, or 50 percent of the retail price) represents a profit of 100 percent—if he sells at that price. Even U.S. congressional reports have used that expression, for example, in reporting drug-industry profits.

PROFITS BEFORE TAXES

Another error is to omit taxes as a cost and calculate "profits before taxes"—although allowing for all other costs. For example, Figure 20–1 shows "profits

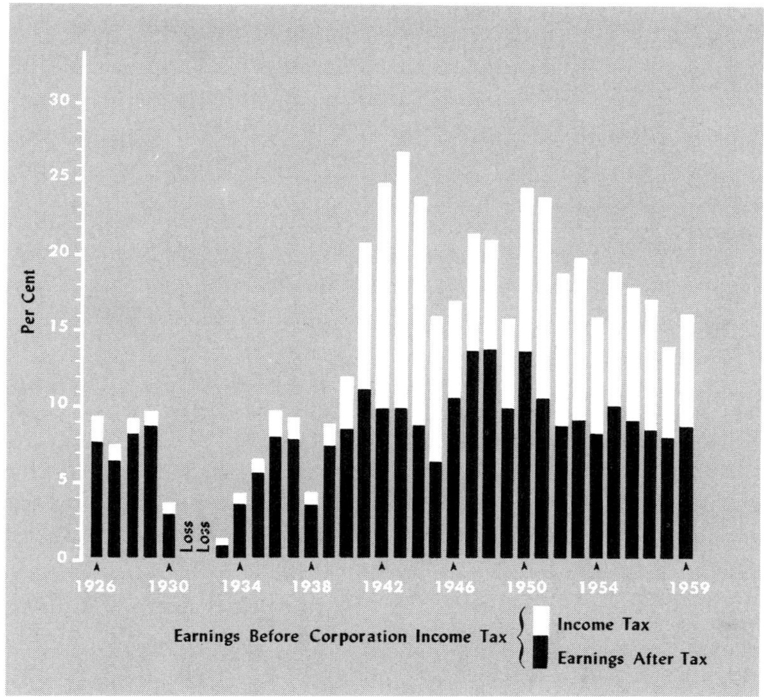

FIGURE 20–1. Taxable earnings of all American manufacturing corporations as percentages of recorded amount of investment. (Source: *Statistics of Income.*)

before taxes." Remarkably, this graph was used by a government agency apparently unaware of its implications, for when initially presented no reference was made to profits after taxes. Does it not suggest that taxes are really not a part of costs—that they are payments for no service? It is difficult to believe that the government agency would want to suggest that taxes are merely tribute collected from those obtaining profits. One would hardly be more surprised if a labor union published a graph of "profits before wages" as if to assert, falsely, that wages are not a part of costs.

Figure 20–1 deserves some further attention. The taxes imposed on business firms were increased about 1941 to help finance the war. The profits before and after the imposition of the tax bear about the same ratio to net worth (net worth is a measure of the amount invested in the company). The impression given by the graph is that the business firms have simply passed on the tax to consumers or employees. This impression is not supported by economic analysis; as we shall see later, the result is a decrease in wealth to business firms, a decrease in the value of resources used in the firms, and a higher price and smaller output of goods produced by the business subjected to the tax.

GROSS PROFITS

"Our wholesale costs are $5 per unit, but we sell each unit for $9, with a gross profit of $4 each." But from that *gross profit* must be subtracted the outlays for labor, taxes, space, etc., ending up possibly with a loss of 50 cents per unit. Clearly, "gross profits" in that sense—and it is a commonly used one—have little to do with the real phenomena causing gains in wealth.

EXPECTED CURRENT LOSSES

If you examine the annual reports of business firms, you will find assertions like: "We have started production on a very promising new product and are currently operating at a loss, but we expect that in a year we shall be covering costs and making profits." If that statement were taken literally, one would wonder why they hadn't waited until next year to start operations. In our terms what was meant is: "At the present time the rate of receipts is less than current expenditures, but the present outlays will bring about larger future receipts and lower future outlays. We believed the new product will promise a net flow of actual receipts in the future that would increase our wealth. The investing public is now of the same opinion, and the market value of our shares of common stock has increased during the current year, so we have had a profit. Hooray!"

THE QUICK PAY-OFF PERIOD

"It takes three years for us to recover our investment before we can start making a profit." This type of statement, implying some "payout" or "cost-recovery" period, means merely that money outlays exceed the money receipts during the first three years and that only in the fourth year do total receipts begin to overtake the total expenditures. But who cares, if the important thing is that the *present wealth value* of the receipts should exceed that of the outlays? To worry or be concerned about the length of that period is to be worried about whether or not the expected or hoped-for receipts will really materialize. The virtue of a short "payout" or "recovery" period is not that it increases that probability, but instead that it reduces the time one has to wait to find out whether the new venture really does as well as hoped.

In this chapter we have investigated sources of profits and losses and methods of allocating the risks of profits and losses among the members of the community, with particular attention to how this is done in a private-property system. Even if those who receive profits are no smarter, no more clever, no more productive, no more virtuous, and no more foresighted than those who do not get profits or who get losses, it does not follow that the profit receivers performed no economic function. They voluntarily bore risks of value changes, and they won the gamble. Those who incur losses obviously are those who lost. The possibility of getting rich by bearing these risks could be eliminated if individuals were prohibited from concentrating their wealth on certain forms of property. One way to do this is to prohibit private property and replace it with socialism; another way is to prohibit people from deciding for themselves what kinds of wealth they shall own. Still another way is to tax away the profits of those who win the gambles; for if people knew their profits were going to be taxed, they would not be so willing to bear the risks that the rest of us wish to avoid.

Questions

1. "Under a socialist system, profits and losses are eliminated." Comment.

2. "Private property permits selective, discretionary risk bearing." Comment.

3. Contrast socialism and private property as means of distributing risks of profits and losses.

4. What is the relationship between the right to buy and sell and the distribution of profits and losses?

5. For what events is the distribution of risk the same in socialist and capitalist systems? (Hint: How about divorce, cancer, baldness, homeliness, having only female children, being left-handed?)

6. Our laws and customs reflect the assignments of risk bearing. A person who owns land as private property must bear the consequences of changes in the value of that land if people move away or no longer value that location so highly. Similarly, if he catches cold or breaks his leg or becomes hard of hearing and can no longer earn so large an income, he must bear the consequences.

   a. Would you advocate that people bear the wealth losses to their private property regardless of cause (aside from legal recourse to violators of property rights)?

   b. Would you want a homeowner to bear the consequences of a meteorite's falling on his house? Fire from using gasoline in the house? Flood damage to houses near rivers? Income loss from cancer? Blindness?

   c. Whom do you think should bear the loss if the individual does not?

d. Why would you draw the line differently in different cases? What is the criterion you used?

e. In each case, do you think people's behavior would be affected according to the risk bearing involved?

f. Would you allow people to agree to take on certain risks in exchange for not bearing other risks, if two people could make a mutually agreeable partition and exchange of such risks? How would that differ from a system of private-property rights?

7. "It is better to buy from a firm that is losing money than from one that is making a profit, because the former firm is charging too low a price while the latter is charging more than costs." Evaluate.

8. A grade-school arithmetic book poses the following question: "Chairs cost the manufacturer $15 each. What price should he charge in order to make a profit of 20 percent on each chair?" Why is it impossible to answer this question? The answer involves *economics*, not arithmetic.

9. On July 15 the Chrysler Corporation president announced that earnings for the past quarter year (April–June) were up 20 percent over the preceding quarter and 50 percent over the similar quarter last year. At the beginning of the quarter reported on, April 1, the price of Chrysler common stock was $70. On June 30 it was $65, and on the day this news was reported the stock *fell* from $64 to $60 because investors expected an even bigger earning. Did the owners of the company have any profits during the quarter from April 1 to June 30?

10. You buy some stock for $100. A month later it has risen to a high of $150. Another month later it is down to $125. Have you had a profit or a loss?

11. A young beginning college teacher hits upon a sparkling teaching style and is rewarded with a higher salary. Has he had a profit? Explain.

12. An actress, after years in the movies, suddenly hits it big and obtains an enormously larger salary. Has she a profit? Three months later she begins to get fat, and in a year her contracts are canceled. Has she experienced a loss in any sense different from that suffered by Ford when it introduced the Edsel?

13. Estimate the present value of your future earnings. Project your earnings until age 65. Then obtain the present value of that projection, using a 10 percent rate of interest. Can you promise your fiancée that you are now worth over $100,000?

14. "Paper profits and losses are not real profits or losses." Do you agree? If so, why? If not, why not?

15. "I bought some stock at $70 a share. It has fallen to $55, but I'm going to hold it until it rises to $70 so I can avoid taking a loss." What is wrong with that reasoning —even assuming that the stock price does shortly thereafter rise to $75?

16. A liquor-retailing license in California recently was sold for over $40,000. The seller was the person who initially got the license from the state at a cost of $6,000. Did the

subsequent buyer get a profit in the form of a monopoly rent? Did the initial licensee get a profit in the form of a monopoly rent?

17. a. Which of the following represent some wealth based on monopoly rents?

TV station in New York City

Radio station in Rapid City, Iowa

United Air Lines

General Motors

Teamsters in Teamsters' Union

General Electric Company

American Telephone and Telegraph Company

Frank Sinatra

U.S. Post Office

Local electric company

Aluminum Company of America

Savings and loan banks

b. In each case in which you think wealth based on monopoly rent is present, how would you test for its presence? And how would you measure the amount of monopoly rent?

c. In each case where you think it is present, who gets it?

18. International Business Machines common stock sells at a price one hundred times as great as the accountants' reported current annual earnings. The stock of Allegheny Ludlum Corporation, a steel producer, sells at about ten times its accountants' reported "earnings." Assume that the same accounting principles are used in each firm. What do you think will happen to the price of each firm's stock if in the next reporting period each firm reports earnings that are *unchanged* from the preceding period? Explain.

19. Suppose it were true that the rich people got rich exclusively from profits. Suppose further that those who received the profits were no smarter, no more foresighted, no nicer, no harder working, no more productive than other people. Does this mean that their profits are "undeserved" and that the rich people perform no service? Would you advocate taxing away those profits? Why or why not?

20. "Rio de Janeiro—Jan. 19, 1964. President Goulart's executive decree limiting remittance of profits to foreigners brought joy to Communists and Nationalists and apprehension to American businessmen. The decree, a political swap for extreme leftist support in Goulart's drive to restore full powers to the presidency, limits the profit a foreigner may remit to his home country to 10 percent a year of his registered investment in Brazil. Any profits above that amount must be reinvested in Brazil in government-approved projects, but no profits on this reinvested capital can be removed from Brazil. Any firm desiring to close out its investment may take out 20 percent of the registered investment in five years. Eighty-two other restrictions are placed on payments to foreigners." Which Brazilians do you think will benefit from this decree? Who will be hurt?

21

COSTS AND OUTPUT PROGRAMS

Cost depends upon what is produced or, more generally, upon the output program selected. Three important characteristics, aside from the particular product, usually affect the costs of an output program. One is the total *volume,* or amount, of the good to be produced. A second is the *rate,* or speed, at which that volume is produced once it is under way. A third is the *date* of the output (for example, date it is to be completed). In making refrigerators, the manufacturer can plan a volume of 150,000 refrigerators at the rate of 15,000 per month (for ten months), with the first completed item to appear six months from the date of decision to produce. The *volume* is 150,000 items, the *rate* is 15,000 per month, and the *date* is six to sixteen months hence.

Cost Effect of Volume

A larger volume of output for some given initial date and constant rate of output will cost more than a smaller volume of output. More resources are required to produce more. In our automobile example, the mileage put on the car is the volume. If the car is to be driven 40,000 miles in *four* years rather than 20,000 in two years (constant *rate* of 10,000 miles per year), the total cost will be greater for the whole output. But although the volume (40,000 miles) is twice as large, the total cost will not necessarily be doubled. The exact amount of increase cannot be determined in advance, but generally the cost increase will be less than in proportion to the increase in the volume (keeping the *rate* unchanged). This is illustrated in Table 21–1, which, for different miles of *distance* (volume), gives the present-capital-value measure of costs. For example, transportation is often measured

Table 21–1

TOTAL COST (PRESENT CAPITAL VALUE) OF MILES OF SERVICE (AT CONSTANT RATE OF 10,000 MILES PER YEAR)

Distance (Miles)	Total Cost	Marginal Cost
5,000	$ 750	$750
10,000	1,100	350
15,000	1,400	300
20,000	1,679	270
25,000	1,940	261
30,000	2,200	260
35,000	2,420	220
40,000	2,600	180
45,000	2,760	160
50,000	2,900	140

in passenger-miles of service rather than as the speed at which some number of passenger-miles of service is provided.

This schedule of total costs and output programs is a schedule for *alternative programs*, only *one* of which can be undertaken. This table is not a list of *sequential* output programs wherein, for instance, one plans for an output volume of 20,000 miles (in two years) and then later, part way through that program, decides to shift to a planned total volume of 60,000 miles (in six years) and then part way through that (or even after that is completed) again adopts some other program. All these cost-associated programs are *alternatives*, among which, as of any given moment, one may choose—the choice made implying the total costs indicated. Once a choice is made and action taken, new circumstances exist (with different legacies, stocks of equipment, and production situations). As of that new moment, there applies a new schedule of costs for various output alternatives. Nevertheless, at whatever moment one contemplates such a list of alternatives, certain general relationships characterize the way costs are related to volume, rate, and the timing of output. It is these general relationships that we are summarizing.

As Table 21–1 shows, when the planned volume is increased by steps of 10,000 miles, cost increases—but by diminishing increments. Also, the average cost per planned mile (unit of volume) decreases for larger volumes. A larger volume takes a longer time to produce because the rate of production of the mileage is assumed constant at 10,000 miles per year. Conversely, if the planned volume (distance) is kept constant but had been produced more quickly (i.e., at a higher rate), the total cost of that volume (distance) is higher.

In our illustrative automobile problem, with miles of service as the volume dimension, we may use a different kind of car for a planned mileage of 20,000 miles in two years than for 100,000 in ten years. It might be cheaper to use two cars sequentially for the 100,000-mile case than to use one car. Or it might be cheaper to buy a different kind of car, depending upon the total mileage contemplated. For very small distances renting a car may be the cheapest procedure. In any case, the relevant cost is the *cheapest* cost method of obtaining the volume contemplated. If it turns out that one kind of car is most economical for 20,000 miles in two years, perhaps a different kind of car is most economical for 100,000 in ten years. If we assumed use of the same technique or car for all alternative output programs, the schedule of estimated costs for output programs would be higher—except for that one program for which that technique happened to be most economical.

Figure 21–1 shows the costs of various mileages for each of several differ-

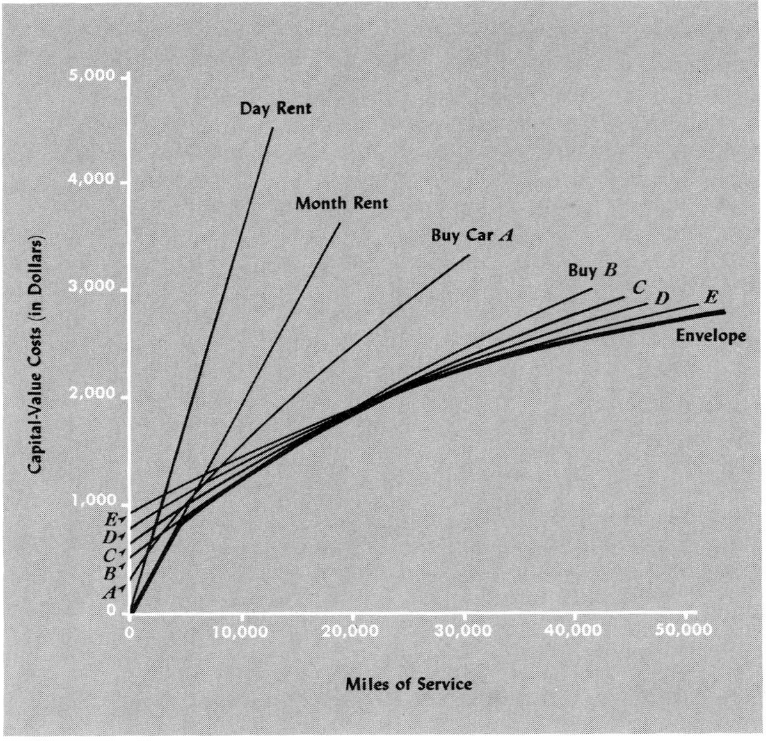

FIGURE 21–1. Total cost as function of miles of service (at constant rate of 10,000 miles per year), indicated for various techniques.

ent techniques of getting car services for some hypothetical situation. The vertical scale measures the present value of the costs of the whole output program, while the horizontal scale measures the volume of output (in this case distance), given some rate of service and initial date of service. Each technique portrayed is most efficient for some particular range of mileage. Specify the particular mileage, and the most efficient technique is determined. An envelope curve under all these curves, consisting of the lowest of the specialized curves at any given output, indicates the lowest cost of achieving each of the various alternative output programs (here differing in mileage but all for the same speed of 10,000 miles per year).

INCREASING TOTAL COSTS

The envelope cost curve rises out of the lower-left corner (since a zero volume of output program can be had at zero cost) and ascends for larger volumes. The cost line *rises* at a *decreasing slope*. The *marginal* cost of volume is the *change* in total cost consequent to a unit *change* in the volume. Graphically, the *slope* of the total cost line shows the increase in cost with larger volume. Since the slope gradually gets flatter (or smaller), it means that the marginal cost of volume, although always positive, is gradually diminishing.

The way in which the total cost changes with changes in the projected volume can be made clearer by another graph. In Figure 21–2, the height of the curve *MC* measures the *addition* to total present value of cost for successive unit increases in volume. This is a graph of the "marginal cost of volume." If the curve were a straight horizontal line, it would mean that a unit increase in the volume increases total costs by a constant amount. But a *downward*-sloping line indicates that extra units of volume can be produced at decreasing increments to total cost.

Furthermore, the *average* cost per unit of volume of different programs can be shown. For larger volumes the cost per unit decreases, possibly to some ultimate lowest value. This is often expressed as the *economy of mass* or *volume production.*

Briefly, the present-value measure of cost increases with larger programmed volume, but at a decreasing rate of increase; that is, marginal cost of volume is positive but decreases as volume is larger, and average cost per unit decreases with larger volume. The increase in volume is obtained by lengthening the run of production while holding the rate of production constant.

The relationship between costs and output given earlier, in Chapter 17, showed a rising, not a falling, marginal and average cost as output was increased. Can this be reconciled with the present decreasing marginal and average costs as output increases? Yes, and the answer lies in the ambiguity of the word "output." In earlier chapters we were increasing the *rate* of output; here, we are increasing the *volume* while holding the rate constant. One can produce one

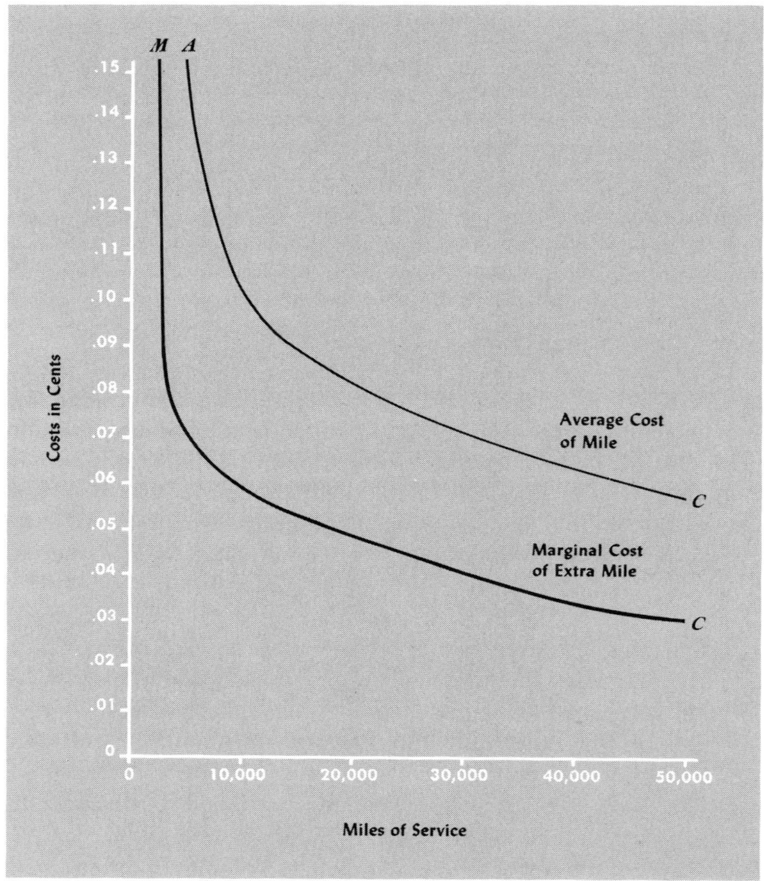

FIGURE 21–2. Marginal and average cost of service at rate of 10,000 miles per year.

thousand houses in one year or in ten years; in this case, volume is given, but the rates differ. And one can produce one house in three months or ten in thirty months; here, the rate of production is constant, but the volumes differ.

For which goods is the *volume* effect important in reducing average and marginal cost? Mass-produced, large-volume-of-output goods, like automobiles, radios, typewriters, electric motors, refrigerators, and tires are produced at a lower cost *per unit* precisely because the volume of output is large.

If you ask a printer to print some personal letterheads, or circulars, you will be told that the price *per unit* is lower, the more you buy. Aircraft companies know that the average cost of a jet plane is cheaper if they can produce one hundred than if they produce only ten. Ford knows that the average cost of some model is lower if it produces half a million than if it produces one hundred.

Polaroid cameras are cheaper to produce if several thousands are produced rather than merely a hundred. Different techniques of production are used for large outputs, and the result is a lower cost per unit. Who hasn't heard that "when production runs get larger, the average cost will be reduced"?

If large-volume production is cheaper *per unit* than small-volume production, *standardization* of products is implied. This is why people who want individually styled or custom-built goods must pay more than for mass-produced goods. We should expect to see many people using the cheaper standardized goods, as they in fact do with automobiles, shirts, shoes, watches, airplanes, etc., because of the cost-reducing effect of a larger volume. A country with a large population can take greater advantage of this cost-reducing effect since it can produce in larger *volume*. This effect of a large market in reducing costs is one of the major advantages of the United States over smaller countries.

The lower cost of larger volumes of output of some item does not eliminate the desirability of smaller volumes of output. For example, a change in automobile models annually prevents costs from falling for that *particular* kind of model. Then why change models every year, if that is more expensive than keeping the same model for a larger scheduled volume? There are two reasons: (1) The percentage decrease in costs is related to the *percentage* change in output volume; therefore, the cost reductions are very small for further unit increases to an already very large scheduled volume. Another 10,000-unit increase over 100,000 is only a 10 percent increase, whereas it is a 100 percent increase over 10,000. (2) Tastes change, new ideas occur, improvements in technique must be incorporated if a producer is to continue to have a profitable business. This suggests that there should be a high correlation between the extent of technical progress and the frequency with which new models occur. Such is the case.

INCREASING TOTAL VOLUME

Why, to consider the volume effect a bit more, does the increased volume (with constant rate) result in decreasing marginal and average costs per unit of volume? Perhaps the major factors fall into two general classes: (a) variety of techniques and (b) learning by doing.

Variety of techniques. One unit can be made either by hand or by some complicated machine and assembly technique. Suppose the latter is more expensive for making only *one* unit of the product. Then "hand" methods will be used. We assume that we could make one thousand units by hand at just about one thousand times the cost as for one. But if the machine method will do it at less than one thousand times the cost, it will pay to use the machine. If we now grant that it may be impossible to divide that complicated machine into a small productive facility that would produce just one item at 1/1000 the total cost, we can see that what can be used economically for large volume may not be economical for small volume. On the other hand, what is possible with small volumes can always simply be repeated (at the same *rate*) to get the bigger volume. We can multiply upward the economic techniques for small techniques, but we can't miniaturize or subdivide in the opposite direction. Thus, if any new technique results in lower costs for larger volume, there is no way to use this technique at lower volumes.

A case in point is the "initial setup" cost. For a large volume, these can be very large; if that same technique were used for only a small output, the costs would be catastrophically high. Therefore, large initial or investment cost will be observed only with large volumes. An example is the transport of oil from wells to refineries. If the well owner believes the well will produce about 100,000 gallons before exhaustion, he might ship the oil by truck—shipping, say, 1,000 gallons a day for one hundred days. But if he thinks he will get 1,000,000 gallons, at the same rate of 1,000 per day he can ship either by truck or pipeline. Suppose the pipeline is cheaper if it is used for one thousand days (at the rate of 1,000 gallons per day) but more expensive than a truck if it is used for only one hundred days. Depending upon the volume (not the rate) of oil to be transported, the selected method of production will be different, with the larger volume having less cost per gallon transported.

Learning by doing. The other general explanation of reduced unit costs with larger volume is called the "learning" factor. Improvement by experience is evident in managerial functions, production scheduling, job layouts, material-flow control, on-the-job learning, and physical skills.[1] The rate of learning may be greatest at first and then reach a plateau; but, in any event, the larger the volume of output, the more opportunity for learning and hence the lower the unit costs of larger outputs.

EXCEPTIONS TO THE AVERAGE COST-REDUCING EFFECT OF LARGER VOLUME: EXHAUSTION OF RAW MATERIALS

Not for every good does a larger volume yield lower unit costs. Sometimes as a larger volume is contemplated, more cheaply available raw materials are used up, and resort must be had to more expensive ores and raw materials. For

[1] The fact that there is increased productivity from learning on the job led Adam Smith to believe that specialization gives a bigger product *because* people get more practice at specific tasks and hence become more productive. Unfortunately, "learning" is *not* the reason for a larger product via *specialization*. Whether or not one specializes, he will learn to do better whatever he is doing. Even a jack-of-all-trades will improve in everything, instead of in only one thing. The gain from specialization is a gain from more efficient *allocation of varied* productive talents, no matter how those talents are acquired. Credit for explaining the gains of specialization in terms of (a) the difference in productive talents (comparative advantage is illustrated in Chapter 16) rather than by (b) the improvements resulting from practice must go to David Ricardo, who lived in England a generation after Smith. Ricardo applied the crucial principle of comparative advantage to international, rather than merely interpersonal, specialization; but the principle is the same regardless of whether we think of countries or individual people as the producers.

example, the production of oil is now characterized by deeper drilling, in more remote areas. Fortunately, however, technological progress and growth of our wealth has more than offset that exhaustion of easily available raw materials—in part precisely because men were sensible enough to use the easily available materials first. Had they instead been worried about "conservation," they would have used resources at a lower rate, with the result that income would have been lower; and hence not so much could have been devoted to investment, technology, and research.

The advance in technology and supply of capital goods has meant that, despite the relative decrease in availability of some raw materials (iron ore, coal, wood), many goods are producible at lower costs than formerly, when cheaper materials but poorer technology and less wealth were available. Perhaps man has been lucky in the race between technological knowledge and depletion of natural resources, but, whatever the reason, the fact remains that technology and growth of stock of capital from saving and investment have more than offset the increased difficulty of obtaining some raw materials and have increased the stock of existing man-made wealth by a more than offsetting amount. It is *investment* and *growth*—rather than conservation—that aids future generations. Conservation, as we shall see more clearly later, means merely less income today.

Rate of Production and Cost

The faster the rate or speed at which a given volume is produced, the greater the total cost. To do a job more rapidly involves more workers, more overtime, and more reliance on less efficient workers in a given time (relative to their efficiency in other jobs).[2] This is simply what was illustrated in our earlier examples of a five-people, two-goods world. A larger *rate* of output of Y involved a greater rate of sacrificed X. One might have thought that since the same volume of output is being produced, the same stock of materials will be used up, whether it be produced quickly or slowly; but, in fact, a higher rate of production involves bringing in more resources at the same time, thus requiring resort to relatively less efficient resources. Furthermore, the most efficient resources insist on higher pay for overtime because the sacrifice of leisure is increased. And the task of coordination is more difficult.

It is important to note that reference here is only to a situation in which the rate or speed of output is increased, while the volume is held constant. If, for example, both the rate and the volume are increased so that we are comparing both a low rate and small volume, on the one hand, with both a high rate and large volume, on the other, the marginal and average costs are subjected to opposing forces.

[2] Remember the analysis of Chapters 16 and 17 and the reason given there for the rising marginal costs of higher rates of output.

The higher-cost effect of higher rates of service is portrayed in Figure 21–3, which shows a different curve for each of three different rates of output. The

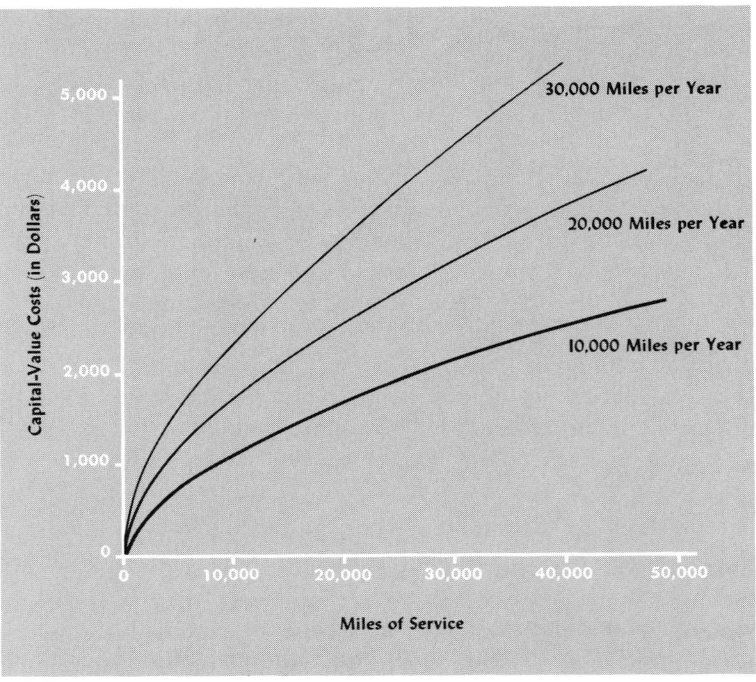

FIGURE 21–3. Total cost as function of miles of service (mileage) for three different rates (10,000, 20,000, and 30,000 miles per year).

same information is presented in different form in Figure 21–4, which shows rate of output along the horizontal axis and a different curve for each of three different volumes. Each curve shows how costs increase for higher rates of output, with a given volume. These curves rise at an increasing slope, which means increasing increments in costs associated with an increase in the output rate. The middle curve shows the costs for various rates of production of the specified volume of 20,000 miles of distance. Any increase in *rate* induces a more than proportional increase in costs. In contrast, Figures 21–1 and 21–3 show that if *volumes* were doubled—with constant rate—the costs would not be twice as high; for the laws of costs relating to volume indicate that total costs do not rise proportionally with volume.

From the curves, we note that to produce 20,000 miles of service at the rate of 20,000 miles per year would cost $2,400, compared to $1,700 for the same mileage at the slower rate of 10,000 miles per year (in 24 months). Would the customer be willing to pay at least $700 more to get delivery of the service that much quicker? If so, it will pay to produce at the faster rate.

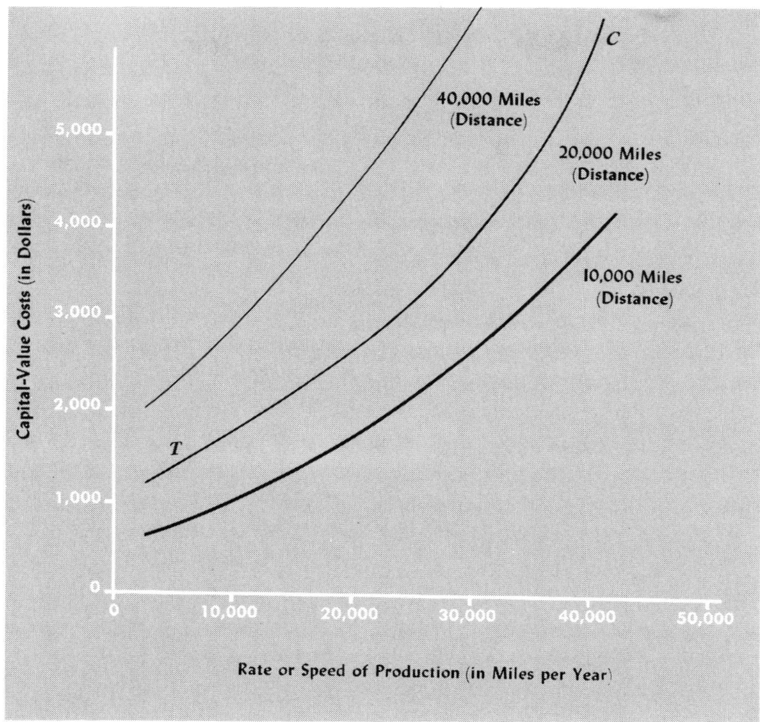

FIGURE 21–4. Present value of cost as function of speed for fixed service mileage (20,000 miles).

Since the total cost of the output of 20,000 miles of service increases as the rate of service (speed) is increased, it is obvious that the cost per unit of distance (not of speed) will increase for higher speeds of production. Figure 21–5 shows the rising average cost per *mile* of service as a function of the speed of production. At a rate of service of 20,000 miles per year, the average cost of a mile of service is 12 cents, while it is only 10 cents at 15,000 miles per year rate of production. Higher speeds of production involve higher average costs per unit of product, whereas the earlier sections showed that for a given speed a larger volume of output can be produced at a lower cost per unit.

Proportionate Increases in Both Rate and Volume

For many goods, a common feature of production is a joint increase—indeed, the same proportional increase—in both the rate and volume of an output program. For example, *if the length of the production run is constant,* say one year, then a higher rate for that period will mean proportionally larger volume. An automobile manufacturer can contemplate *rates* of output from 1,000 a

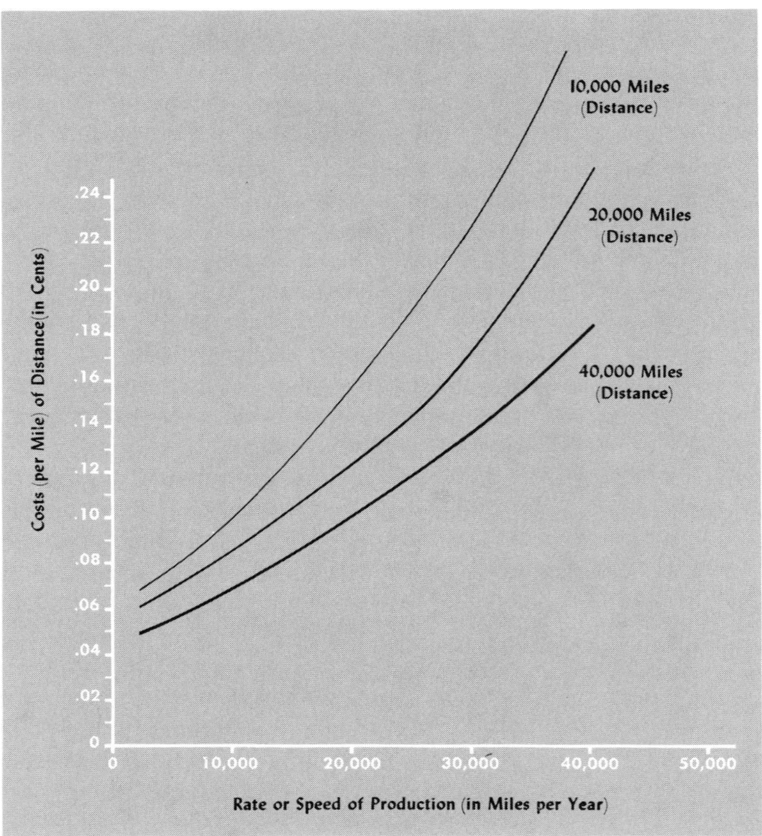

FIGURE 21–5. Cost per mile of service for various speeds of service (distance fixed at 20,000 miles).

month to 50,000 a month for one year. If any of these rates persists for a full year, the range of volumes implied is from 12,000 to 600,000 cars. In such cases, one can speak of either the annual rate (*lasting for a year*) or of the volume of a program.

Increases in the rate of output and in the volume both increase total costs, but they have opposite effects on average cost per unit of volume of output. Larger volumes reduce average costs, while the higher rates raise average costs per unit of any volume produced at the higher rates. Which effect dominates when both the rate and the volume increase in the same proportion—i.e., when the total volume is increased but is produced in the same interval of time? For "low" rates of output the average cost may fall as the rate is increased; but increases in the rate of output, even though accompanied by a proportionate increase in the volume, will ultimately dominate and cause higher average costs.

In any particular situation one must have actual data to know where average costs start to rise.

As an example of the behavior of costs, we can pick the costs off Figure 21–6, which presents the same kinds of cost curves as Figure 21–3. Each curve of Figure 21–6 indicates the total costs for alternative volumes of output—

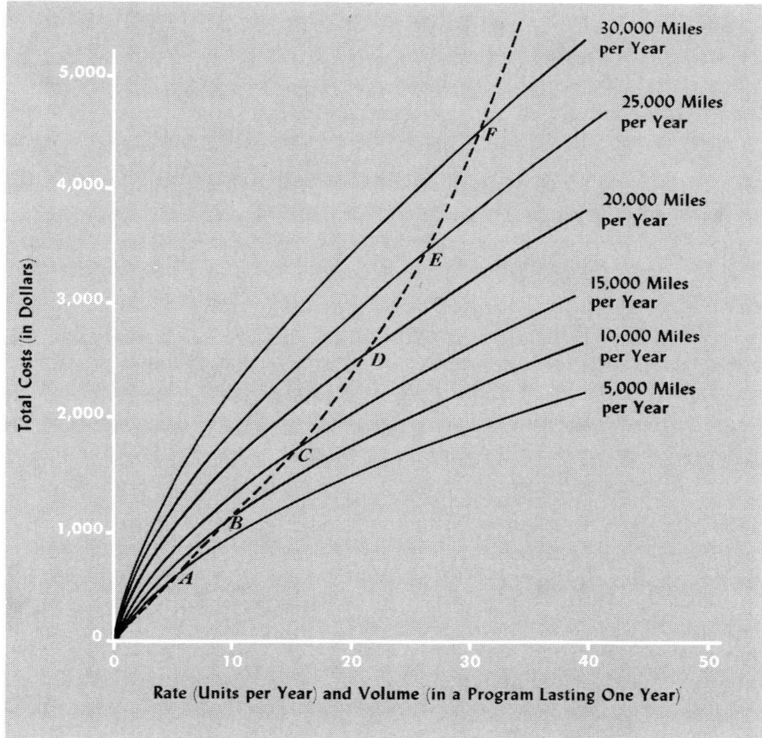

FIGURE 21–6. Total cost as function of volume *and* rate of output.

measured on the horizontal scale—with each curve being identified with a particular rate of output. If we consider alternative output programs—where each differs from the other in both rate of output and volume, with the two varying proportionally together—the costs will be indicated by the height of the appropriate curve at each volume, here exampled by the points *A*, *B*, *C*, *D*, *E*, and *F*. *A* represents the cost of 5,000 miles at 5,000 per year. *B* is the cost of 10,000 miles at 10,000 per year. *C* is the cost of 15,000 miles at 15,000 per year. Connecting these points by the dashed line, by interpolating we assume we can approximate the costs of various combinations of outputs with proportional changes in both rate and volume.

Notice the characteristic shape of the total-cost curve. Total costs start at zero—for zero output, naturally—and rise at a decreasing rate (reflecting the dominance of the volume effect) until the slope straightens out and rises at a constant rate, to be superseded by an increasing slope, or rate of rise of costs—reflecting the dominance of the *rate* of output effect. Ultimately, at greater rates of output, the total costs increase more and more rapidly until there is some limiting rate of output using all the available resources of the community.

We can illustrate this with numbers. Table 21–2 lists the total costs, portrayed by the height of the line *AF* (in column 2). Column 1 gives the volume and rate of output—both of which can be represented by the same number, since both rate and volume are here assumed to increase proportionately. Column 3 lists the average total cost per unit of volume of output. At first, for small rates and volumes, average cost decreases; it then levels off and finally starts to rise for larger outputs.

Column 4 gives the marginal cost of each extra unit of volume of output—the calculation of which is considered in the next chapter. However, the interpretation of the marginal costs is as follows: If the output program is made larger by one unit of volume, the total cost will be larger by the amount of marginal costs. The marginal cost also falls at first, but levels off and then starts to rise. For those output programs where marginal costs are less than average costs, it is apparent that an increase in that program by one unit of volume would increase total costs by less than the average and hence would yield a still lower average cost per unit of volume. However, if the output considered is in the range where marginal cost is greater than average cost, a still larger (by one unit of volume) output program would entail an increase in costs greater than the existing average cost. As a result, the increased output program would imply higher average costs.

Table 21–2

COSTS OF ALTERNATIVE OUTPUT PROGRAMS

	Costs		
Output *	Total	Average	Marginal
500	$ 650	13.0¢	11.0¢
1,000	1,100	11.0	10.0
1,500	1,620	10.8	13.8
2,000	2,400	12.0	17.0
2,500	3,280	13.1	21.0
3,000	4,400	14.6	25.1

* Output is in miles of distance and in miles per year—i.e., output is yielded in exactly one year.

This means that the average total-cost (per unit of volume) curve will always slope downward in that output range where marginal costs are less than the average cost, and will slope upward where the marginal cost exceeds the average cost. An implication of this is that the marginal-cost curve will, as it slopes upward, intersect the average-cost curve at the minimum average-cost output, "pulling it up" for larger outputs and "pulling it down" for smaller output programs.

Drawing the average and marginal-cost curves for the various alternative output programs, we get Figure 21–7.

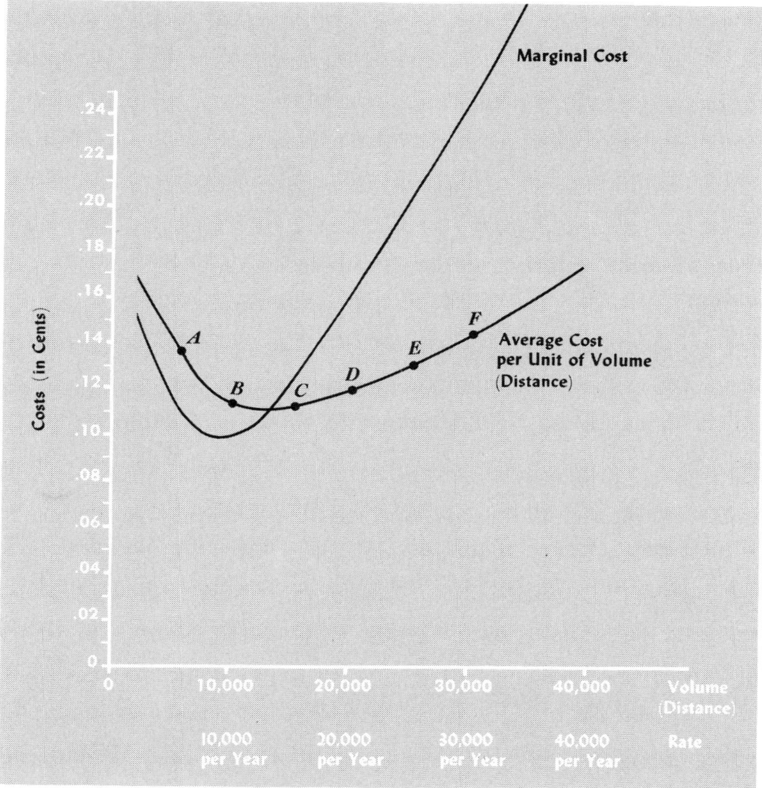

FIGURE 21–7. Average cost as function of program with joint volume and rate (volume in one year's output at specified rate).

Dates of Programmed Output

Another important characteristic of any program of output is the date of the output. The earlier the output is to start, the greater will be the cost. "Haste makes waste" suggests the principle at work, although it would be an error to conclude that haste is never worth the price. Hasty (though not reckless) preparations and changes, whether made with existing equipment or with equipment newly acquired for the purpose, are more expensive—the first because of less appropriate available techniques and equipment, and the second because changes to more appropriate techniques are more expensive when they are completed more quickly. In other words, for a specified cost, the inputs are less variable in a shorter than in a longer interval. Turned around this means the physical constraints are more binding in the short period than in the longer period. In general, because higher rates of production of a given volume are more costly, and because higher rates of use of resources are involved in accomplishing production earlier, the cost of earlier output is greater than a later output.

The relationship between cost and time from decision to actual output varies with the technique of production to be used. Some techniques involve higher costs of preparation than do others if all techniques are to be made ready at the same time, although the order of costs depends upon the length of the interval to production. Some techniques of production which are the more expensive ones if only one week's preparation were allowed may be the lower-cost techniques if three months' preparation time is allowed.

Shelters can be built relatively fast from tents or wood; concrete or steel buildings are economical only if a longer preparation period is allowed (leaving aside the question of how long the shelter will be used after it is created). The longer the adjustment interval, the lower the cost of switching to more appropriate techniques, at least for all those methods or techniques that involve the use of material that is not already on hand in the right amount. In summary: (1) For any other output program than the one for which a person's existing production equipment is already optimal, the cheapest technique will depend upon the amount of time available. (2) Whatever the cheapest technique may be, any output program will be less costly the longer the time for preparation and adjustment that is allowed.[3]

Joint Products with Common Costs

"JOINT AND VARIABLE" OUTPUTS

Production processes do not always yield only one product. Many give several *joint* products. Wool and mutton are joint products of a sheep. Cotton and cottonseed oil, kerosene and gasoline, leather and meat are samples of joint

[3] There is one obstacle to the possibility that if one allows a long enough adjustment period and thereby defers the output into the distant future, he can reduce the present-value measure of costs to as low a figure as he likes: A person is producing to increase his wealth, and deferment of output reduces the present value of the receipts.

products. They are interdependent in supply; generally, more of one involves more of the other. More wool also yields more mutton. More cotton yields more cottonseed oil. In fact, a higher price of one of the outputs will, by inducing a larger output, also lead to an increased output of the other good. Thus, the supply of a good is dependent upon not only its own price, but that of other goods—especially of joint-product goods.

Yet we mustn't overdo this jointness; even for these joint products, more of one may involve less of the other. Wool and mutton, although joint products in that both are yielded by a sheep, are substitutes in that there are different breeds of sheep, yielding different ratios of wool to mutton. One could increase the ratio of wool to meat and, in fact, get more wool and less meat, by selecting different breeds and slaughtering ages. The *ratio* in which joint products are produced is variable; that is why they are also substitutable at the same time they are joint. Although an increase in one will normally mean an increase in the other, a change in breed may mean a larger increase in wool with a smaller increase (if not actual decrease) in meat. These propositions hold for gasoline and kerosene, both of which are obtained by refining crude oil. Different refining methods yield different ratios of output. Cotton and cottonseed are also variable, though joint, products. Depending upon which of the joint products one is interested in, the other is often called the by-product.

IMPOSSIBILITY OF IMPUTATION OF COMMON COSTS

The determination of market-clearing prices for joint products poses no new problems. The general implications about allocation of supply and control of rates of output are unchanged. Yet one problem often seems to rise and plague observers. If two products are produced jointly from some "common" input, how does one allocate the costs of the common resource to each of the joint products? If, for example, hides and meat are produced from one steer, and if the feed and care of the steer is a common input or a common cost to both products, what portion is the cost of the hide and what portion is the cost of the meat? If an airplane carries passengers and freight cargo, what portion of the common costs of gasoline, labor, and facilities is assigned to each? Can a "common" cost be allocated among joint products?

Depending upon which product is treated as a residual or by-product, a different allocation of costs may be obtained. In effect, by calling one product the by-product, one is implicitly assigning all the "common costs" to the other, the "basic," product. But this, of course, is merely an arbitrary allocation, depending upon which product one calls the basic product. There is a temptation to leap to the unwarranted proposition that something must be incomplete or faulty with the analysis or with the economic system. If costs can't be allocated, how can one tell what prices to charge? How can a producer tell whether he is making a profit on each item? How can he tell how much to produce? Things seem to fall apart at the seams (or at the joints). In fact, however, the presence of costs which cannot be allocated uniquely to the joint products does not upset anything.

PRICING AND OUTPUT DECISONS INDEPENDENT OF ASSIGNMENT OF COMMON COSTS

One purpose of prices is to allocate the existing supply of product among the competing claimants, and another purpose is to provide a source of revenue to induce the output to be produced. But both tasks can be performed by the same market price, even if there are common costs that cannot be allocated. The "rationing" price, as we have seen, does not depend upon costs. It depends solely upon the demand and the supply offered on the market. What about the second function—that of inducing production of goods in the "appropriate" amounts? Again there is no necessity to allocate the common costs to the joint products. All that is necessary is a comparison of the total costs of the whole set of joint products with the total revenue from their sale. If the total revenue does not cover the total costs, some producers will be induced, by a loss of wealth, to stop production, leaving a smaller output and resultant higher prices of the various joint products, until the price is high enough to cover the total costs of the entire set of joint products.

Still unsolved is the question of the appropriate rates of output by those firms that are profitable. Accepting the wealth-maximizing output rate as the appropriate rate, the producer still does not have any use for an average cost of each joint product based on some allocation of the common costs. He requires a measure of incremental costs for an increase in each of the joint products. If he expands the output rate of any of the joint products, either singly or jointly, how much do total costs increase? If that incremental cost is observed to be less than the incremental, or marginal, revenue from that extra output, the output will be expanded, if the producer is interested in increasing his wealth. Otherwise, the output will be contracted. In either event, equality of the incremental cost and revenue is the wealth-maximizing clue to rate-of-output decisions. None of these decisions—pricing or output, or even combinations of inputs—depended upon separability or bookkeeping allocation of the common costs of any input shared by the joint products. This is a crucial point. Pricing and output decisions can be made even though one cannot assign portions of costs of a common production input to the products that are jointly produced. Nothing is lost, except an answer to an irrelevant, pointless question: "What is *the* cost of production of *one* of the joint products when allowing for proper assignment of its due portion of the common costs?"

To say that the question is pointless doesn't mean it won't frequently be asked. If we wonder why people should be asking such a meaningless question, we shall see that they have a different objective in mind. Essentially, they are objecting to some market price and are seeking to show that the price is not a "fair" or "appropriate" price.

UNFAIR DISCRIMINATION?

One of the classic examples of such "unfair" prices are those in which a railroad charged more to ship goods from New York to Denver than to San Francisco. Naturally, this seems "unfair, unreasonable, and unjustly discriminatory" against people in Denver. Why did those rates exist? The railroads from New York to San Francisco compete with transport by water *via* the Panama Canal. There was no such low-cost alternative competition to Denver. The rates charged to San Francisco had to be high enough to cover the *extra* costs of a shipment to San Francisco to make it worthwhile to carry the freight. Any higher rate was, of course, better if the demand would support it. The higher rates to Denver were set high not in order to permit the lower rates to San Francisco. The crucial conditions were: (a) together the two services jointly had to realize sufficient proceeds to cover total costs; and (b) no matter what the Denver rates were, the rates to San Francisco had to be low enough to compete with the water route.

The prices set for rail services to San Francisco and Denver are market-rationing rates, and must meet competition of other sources of services. The roads then charged the rates that maximized their wealth, net of the total costs. It seems "unjust" to charge more to Denver, since it certainly costs more to ship to San Francisco by rail than to Denver. But again this statement implies that the price must be such as to collect at least as much as some prorated portion of total costs. And that is a fallacy. Price rations the existing supply, *and* it provides revenue to induce the output. The idea that, for joint products, each price should also cover some specific or equal pro-rata portion of total costs is the source of the fallacy in the charge of an "unfair" price discrimination.

The fact that it costs more to ship goods by rail to San Francisco than to Denver from New York neither *justifies* nor *permits* a higher price for rail shipments to San Francisco. What one can get for what he produces depends not upon what it costs *him* to produce, but upon what the supply will sell for when confronted with market demand and upon other goods that are offered for sale. In transportation to San Francisco, the supply of available transport was much larger than to Denver at any given price.

The source of the "discrimination" is that San Francisco is located on an excellent harbor with cheap sources of transportation, whereas Denver is located in a landlocked area to which transportation is more expensive. To correct this "injustice," the law has compelled the railroads to charge not less to San Francisco than to Denver. So, rather than raise the San Francisco rate on the much larger volume of shipments to San Francisco, the rails lowered the rate to Denver (and thereby did not realize the maximum possible wealth from service to

Denver). Had Denver been the major terminal of most of the freight, the rate would not have been cut. Instead, the San Francisco rate would have been raised, since the railroads would prefer to lose that smaller service income rather than the large Denver service revenue. In that event, things would again be "fair," with San Francisco suffering in the *name* of "equality."

Sometimes, joint products that seem to cost the same sell for very different prices. For example, long-distance telephone service in the day is higher than night service. Yet the costs are essentially the same and are primarily composed of the common costs of the physical facilities, even though there is no way to allocate the common-facility costs to night and to day service except in some arbitrary way. Of course, there is no point in doing so. Given the fact that the facilities exist, the phone company charges a lower night rate simply because the demand is smaller at night. It does not follow that the night rates are lower because the day rates are higher. If the night demand were stronger, the night rates would be higher than the day rates. The relative level of rates depends upon the relative demands which must be rationed by a price. If those seem "unfair," one is making a personal judgment that people ought not to be so "irrational" as to have different demands for day and night service.

Is it "fair" to the day people that people who work at night should be able to make long-distance calls more cheaply? That theaters should charge less for matinees than for evening performances? That paintings involving the same costs should sell for different prices? That beautiful girls should get higher salaries than homelier girls, even if both spend the same amount in trying to be more beautiful? All these "disparities" arise because of some differences in the demand for the good or service, reflecting differences in availability and convenience or, in the eyes of demander, in quality—regardless of production costs.

The person paying a higher price wishes he, too, could buy in the lower-priced market. Then why doesn't he shift to the lower-priced market? Because the lower-priced market is not worth all the sacrifices he must make in order to do so (like moving to Denver from San Francisco or working nights rather than days in order to save on long-distance telephone calls or learning to ignore superficial beauty). It should now be apparent that the jointness of products in using some common resources with costs which cannot be uniquely apportioned to the individual outputs has nothing whatever to do with determination of pricing or output. Nor is it pertinent to any economic criterion of appropriateness or "justice" of possible prices.

There is nothing in economic analysis that permits any propositions about what is fair or not fair. In fact "fair," "just," or "reasonable" simply have no objective content—Aristotle, Aquinas, the Council of Christian Churches, the President of the United States, or anyone else to the contrary notwithstanding. Except, possibly, one meaning—"The fair price is what *I* think it should be."

We may summarize as follows:

1. For output programs with larger volumes, the total cost is greater; but

the marginal cost decreases, and the average cost per unit of volume falls. (See Figures 21–1 and 21–2.)

2. For higher rates of output, the total cost increases, the marginal cost increases (i.e., the marginal cost of an increase in the *rate* of output), and the average cost per unit of volume increases. (See Figures 21–3, 21–4, and 21–5.)

3. For nearer dates of initial output, the total costs increase; the marginal costs (with respect to either increments of volume or rates of output) increase; and the average cost per unit of volume increases.

4. For output programs that are larger by proportional increases in both the rate and the planned volume, the total cost increases; but the average costs can decrease for a range of output after which for larger outputs average costs will rise persistently. Marginal cost (of a rise in both the volume and the rate of output) at first may fall, but it will begin to rise persistently at larger volume-rate outputs. (See Figures 21–6 and 21–7.)

Questions

1. Output has at least two dimensions. What are two of them that have a bearing on total costs of some output programs?

2. A firm plans to produce 2,000,000 cameras in the next six months. What is the volume and what is the rate of output?

3. If that rate is continued for one year, what will be the volume?

4. What happens to total cost of production for larger volumes of planned output?

5. What happens to total cost as the rate or speed of output is made larger, while the volume is kept constant?

6. What happens to average cost per unit of volume for larger planned volumes with unchanged rates of output?

7. What happens to average cost per unit of volume for larger rates of output with constant volume?

8. What is the behavior of marginal cost as a function of volume (for a fixed rate of output)?

9. What is the behavior of marginal cost as a function of rate of output for a fixed volume of output?

10. Are the answers to the preceding questions implied by comparative advantage and efficient means of production?

11. One of the first things an economist learns is to distinguish between total, average, and marginal cost. What is the difference in meaning?

12. If it were illegal to sell automobiles in any state other than in which they were made, would cars be cheaper or more expensive in the United States? Give two reasons for your answer.

13. Why do manufacturers produce a few standardized models rather than a much larger variety of custom-made, custom-designed models?

14. Suppose that total cost changes with total volume so that every doubling of volume (100 percent increase) increases total cost by 90 percent. Suppose further that the cost of producing just one hundred items would be $1.00. Compute the missing data.

VOLUME	TOTAL COST	AVERAGE COST
100	$ 1.00	$1.00
200	1.90	.95
400	3.61	.90
800	6.86	.86
1,600	13.03	____
3,200	24.76	____
6,400	47.05	____
12,800	89.39	____
25,600	169.84	____
51,200	322.69	____
102,400	612.00	____
204,800	1,164.00	____
400,000	2,212.00	____
800,000	4,204.00	____
1,600,000	7,988.00	____
3,200,000	____	____
6,400,000	____	____

15. Give some examples, if you can, of average costs being lower with large-volume production. Can you cite from personal memory the price history of television sets, transistor radios, surfboards, aluminum, penicillin, Polaroid cameras, ball-point pens?

16. Telephone a local printing company and ask the price for 100 letterheads on bond paper. Also get a price for 10,000 letterheads. Which has the lower cost per unit? Ask for the expected delivery date. Then ask how much it would cost to get the letterheads in half that time—even if it means setting up a night shift and overtime work. What do you expect will happen to the quoted price?

17. Telephone a local building contractor and tell him you want to build a garage at your apartment house. After getting his price, see what he charges if you insist on getting it in half the promised time. Also ask how much he would charge if you have five garages to build. Do you predict it will be five times as much?

18. The British Aircraft Corporation is now manufacturing a two-engined jet plane for intermediate-distance flights. Airlines now placing orders are quoted a price of $2,500,000 with delivery in one year. What do you predict the price would be if you requested to have one delivered in six months? Do you think there would be any connection between the price of quicker delivery and the price you would have to pay to buy such a plane from someone who already has one; e.g., from Braniff Air Lines?

19. If a business firm finds its selling price and output so related that larger output is associated with lower selling price, is this evidence that it has lower costs with larger volume or that the demand is such that more can be sold only if the price is lower?

20. Do you know of any products that have become more expensive (aside from inflation) over the past several decades or centuries because of the exhaustion of cheaper ores or resources from which that product is obtained? (One answer is "oysters.") Is it true for copper, iron, oil, tin, diamonds, coal?

21. Give some examples of how the selected technique of production will depend upon the *volume* to be produced. For example, what about methods of producing letterheads, cookies, holes for fence posts, dresses, airplanes?

22. Give some examples of goods for which you think the selected technique of production will depend upon the *rate* at which items are produced—for fixed volume.

23. Do economics of mass production refer to a high rate or a large volume?

24. "A bigger output means lower unit costs. Therefore, a bigger output lowers prices." On a true-false questionnaire this should be marked False. Why?

25. Heat and light are joint products of an electric light bulb. The bulb uses electric power at the rate of 1,000 watts. In one hour the cost of the power is 5 cents.

a. How much does the light cost? How much does the heat cost? How much do the light and the heat together cost?

b. If you were selling the heat to someone, how much would you charge him? And if, at the same time, you were selling the light to someone else, how much would you charge him?

c. Suppose that you are getting 4 cents for the light and 2 cents for the heat. You discover a new light bulb that gives more light and less heat, but this costs 6 cents per hour to operate. You can sell the extra light for 3 cents more, but you get a total of only 1 cent for the available heat. Should you use the new device? (Forget the cost of the new bulb—to simplify the arithmetic.)

d. But now the *light* buyer complains that you are charging him a total of 7 cents, which is more than enough to cover all the costs, while formerly you charged him only 4 cents, which did not cover the whole costs. He contends that the price should be lower and that the buyer of heat should pay part of the costs. What is your reply?

e. Having told him to take it or leave it, you find he leaves it! Why? (Answer: Because someone else can duplicate your service and charge him a lower price to get his business. The price will, with open markets, be cut to where the total receipts from the joint products are just sufficient to cover the cost of production. And the total amount produced will be of such size that another joint increment would not quite bring in enough new receipts to cover the marginal cost of producing that joint increment of output.)

26. Meat, wool, and hides are joint products of sheep.

a. What assurance do you have that the prices paid for meat, for wool, and for sheepskin are just adequate to cover their cost of production?

b. What assurance do you have that meat users are not paying a disproportionate share of the common costs?

27. You purchase a car. It will depreciate by $500, we shall assume, regardless of whether you use it for recreation or business, and regardless of whether you drive it 5,000 or 10,000 miles. Each mile you drive it, you will also pay 8 cents for gasoline, oil, tires, repair, etc. (not counting the depreciation). If you drive the car 10,000 miles, the depreciation cost amounts to $500/10,000 = 5 cents per mile. If you drive it 5,000 miles, the depreciation cost is 10 cents a mile. Suppose you drive it 5,000 miles for recreation and 5,000 miles for business.

a. What is the cost for the recreation mileage, and what is the cost for the business mileage?

b. Should you allocate half of the depreciation to the recreation?

28. The air fare from Los Angeles to San Francisco is $12, compared to over $20 from Los Angeles to Phoenix, although both distances are the same. Pacific Southwest Airlines, the local intrastate airline that first cut the San Francisco fare so low, is exempt from fare-regulating activities of the Civil Aviation Board, a federal regulatory agency that controls fares of *inter*state airlines and which prohibits price cutting or new airlines on the Los Angeles-Phoenix (Arizona) run.

a. Explain why the price differential exists.

b. Explain why the Civil Aviation Board, which is supposed to protect the consumer from "monopolistic" airline fares, follows its current fare policy? (This is not a joint-product or common-cost problem.)

29. The air fare from New York to Paris is cheaper than from New York to Los Angeles, although the latter is a shorter distance. Can you guess why the differential exists?

22

PRODUCTION RESPONSE TO DEMAND: PRICE-TAKERS' MARKET

Earlier chapters on production explained the organization of productive effort in terms of individual productive resources. In this chapter we examine the same question via the decisions of a business firm as they are affected by its cost and revenue considerations. The basic unit of analysis or decision is the operator of a business firm, rather than the owner of some particular single kind of productive resource. We shall adapt the relationships between costs and rates of output derived in earlier chapters and use them in summary form for the business firm. But first it is appropriate that we state the context within which the exposition will be presented and applied.

It is well to notice that there are two problems in the allocation of resources to production. (1) How is the decision of the amount of each good to produce related to market demand? (2) How is it decided, given the fact that productive resources are not all identical, which resources (which workers, which materials, etc.) to use? You will recall that both these problems were solved in our simple two-product, five-person economy. The first problem is investigated in this and the next three chapters: "How is the amount of production of each good (rate, volume, and timing) controlled?" In other words, how is the amount of resources to be allocated to the production of each good, from among the competing end-uses, determined via decisions of business firms?

In this chapter the response of production to demand changes will be investigated in price-takers' markets with free access to the market for all potential buyers and sellers. In the next chapter price-searchers' production responses will be studied. In contrast to our earlier analysis of these markets, when production problems were ignored in order to concentrate attention on the problem of allocating existing output, the present chapters will incorporate the production response.

We shall not conduct a whole series of analyses, each designed to tell what happens one day, one week, one month, one year, two years, and so on, after an initial demand change. Instead, for convenience of exposition, the analysis of the supply reaction will be in terms of the response of *existing* firms. Then, adjustments in the number of firms are introduced. This division is solely for analytic convenience and does not require that no new firms enter into production until the existing firms have had all the time they want to adjust their production. The usual presumption is that production changes within existing production.[1]

The output response depends upon the kind of increase in market demand. A change in demand could mean a change in (a) the *rate* at which the demanders wish to purchase or (b) the total *volume* the community will want to purchase. For example, an electric-power company may place an order for 120 generators to be delivered at the monthly rate of five for twenty-four months; shortly thereafter, it modifies that decision and increases its demand by ordering sixty more to be delivered in the third year at the same rate of five per month. Only the *volume* dimension of demand, not the rate, has increased. At the other extreme, the buyer may increase his *rate* demand from 120 in two years to 120 in one year. Or he may increase his demand for *both* rate and volume—from five per month for two years, to ten per month for two years. While these various demand increases could be investigated, examination of the third alternative—a joint, proportional increase in both rate and volume over a given time period—is sufficient here to elucidate principles.[2]

Influence of Demand Changes on Output

As we know from our earlier analysis of price-takers' markets (see Chapter 10), an increase in demand is revealed by an increase in market price. Now let us suppose that some producers believe that a particular increase in demand and price will last for some time—say, at least a year. Each producer will plan to produce more (both a larger rate and a larger volume) during the coming year,

[1] And this opens up a new issue: "What if the output program is only tentative because one knows that in a short time he will have to revise his program in the light of changed demand-and-supply conditions?" Instead of picking a single output plan, he is worried about a method that will give him flexibility in shifting from plan to plan as conditions change. We merely indicate what is meant by lowest costs of whatever program one wants to contemplate—whether or not it be a program of steady rate and foreseen volume.

[2] In our earlier discussion of production problems, we could, without causing confusion, treat the increase as an increase in the demand for either or both the volume and rate. But now that production can be changed in rate and volume, with different effects on costs, the kind of demand change will have to be made explicit.

because, as we shall see, this would increase his wealth. Our supposition is tantamount to an assumption that producers have great foresight—an assumption we shall later abandon. In addition, we shall temporarily assume that each producer knows the costs for different output programs that he could undertake, in order more readily to see the direction of his response to price changes. Afterward, we shall see how these responses are induced when information is less complete.

COSTS OF OUTPUT PROGRAMS

Temporarily, suppose the producer knows the costs of alternative one-year programs, as given in the cost and output data of Table 22–1. Use of a one-year program permits simple capital-value measures of costs. The definition or measure of output must be the same as that used in market demand. Since the demand quantities are measured both in units of annual *rate* and *volume* of purchase in one year, the output programs are also identified in terms of *volumes* produced in one year at indicated annual *rates*. Furthermore, it is assumed that there is a three-month interval between decision to enter production and the first unit of the completed product.

The costs are plotted in Figure 22–1. The curve labeled *MC* shows the marginal costs, while the curve labeled *AC* gives the average costs per unit of output. Both curves are U-shaped for this special kind of output program in which both rate and volume are increased jointly.

OUTPUT PROGRAMS AND WEALTH MAXIMIZATION

Survival in business is greater the greater are profits. Which of the various output programs will maximize the wealth of the owners of this firm? The answer, given these costs of production, will depend upon the price at which the output can be sold. Suppose the market price is $1.10; this producer, being a price-taker, can sell all he wants at that price. What rate and volume should he produce and sell if he is to maximize his wealth? The answer is ten (or eleven) at the rate of ten per year. At ten, the total costs will be $10, and the total receipts will be $11, giving a wealth increase (profit) of $1. The same profit will be obtained at eleven units of output, but at all other outputs the profit will be smaller.

Suppose the demand were greater (for both rate and volume), so that the market price for this good is $2. What is the wealth-maximizing output rate now? Answer: Eighteen units per year, with a profit of $14.55. Any other rate would give the producer smaller wealth. A larger demand in this case induced a larger rate of output. Can we generalize and say that a larger demand implies a larger rate of output? Yes. To see why, examine the marginal-cost data in column 3. These marginal costs tell how much costs increase for a one-unit larger rate of

Table 22–1

COSTS OF ONE YEAR'S OUTPUT

INDICATED RATE PER YEAR AND VOLUME FOR ONE YEAR BEGINNING IN THREE MONTHS

(1)	(2)	(3)	(4)	(5)	(6)	(7)	(8)	(9)	(10)
1	$ 2.00	$2.00	$2.00	$ 1.10	$1.10	$ —.90	$2.00	$ 2.00	$ .00
2	2.90	.90	1.45	2.20	1.10	—.70	2.00	4.00	1.10
3	3.70	.80	1.23	3.30	1.10	—.40	2.00	6.00	2.30
4	4.45	.75	1.11	4.40	1.10	—.05	2.00	8.00	3.55
5	5.25	.80	1.05	5.50	1.10	+.25	2.00	10.00	4.75
6	6.10	.85	1.02	6.60	1.10	+.50	2.00	12.00	5.90
7	7.00	.90	1.00	7.70	1.10	+.70	2.00	14.00	7.00
8	7.95	.95	.99	8.80	1.10	+.85	2.00	16.00	8.05
9	8.95	1.00	.99	9.90	1.10	+.95	2.00	18.00	9.05
10	10.00	1.05	1.00	11.00	1.10	+1.00 *	2.00	20.00	10.00
11	11.10	1.10	1.01	12.10	1.10	+1.00 *	2.00	22.00	10.80
12	12.25	1.15	1.02	13.20	1.10	+.95	2.00	24.00	11.75
13	13.50	1.25	1.04	14.30	1.10	+.80	2.00	26.00	12.50
14	14.85	1.35	1.06	15.40	1.10	+.65	2.00	28.00	13.15
15	16.30	1.45	1.09	16.50	1.10	+.20	2.00	30.00	13.70
16	17.85	1.55	1.12	17.60	1.10	—.25	2.00	32.00	14.15
17	19.55	1.70	1.15	18.70	1.10	—.85	2.00	34.00	14.45
18	21.45	1.90	1.19	19.80	1.10	—1.65	2.00	36.00	14.55 *
19	23.55	2.10	1.23	20.90	1.10	—2.65	2.00	38.00	14.45
20	25.95	2.40	1.29	22.00	1.10	—3.95	2.00	40.00	14.05
21	28.75	2.80	1.37	23.10	1.10	—5.65	2.00	42.00	13.25
22	32.05	3.30	1.46	24.20	1.10	—7.85	2.00	44.00	11.95
23	35.95	3.90	1.56	25.30	1.10	—10.65	2.00	46.00	10.05
24	40.55	4.60	1.69	26.40	1.10	—14.15	2.00	48.00	7.45
25	46.00	5.45	1.83	27.50	1.10	—18.50	2.00	50.00	4.00

(1) Annual rate *and* volume
(2) Capital value measure of cost
(3) Marginal cost (for one-unit increment in annual rate *and* volume of output)
(4) Average cost per unit of *volume* of output
(5) Total receipts before demand increase
(6) Marginal receipts (at price of $1.10)
(7) Profits (at price of $1.10)
(8) Marginal receipts (at price of $2)
(9) Total receipts (at price of $2)
(10) Profits (at price of $2)
* Maximum-profit programs

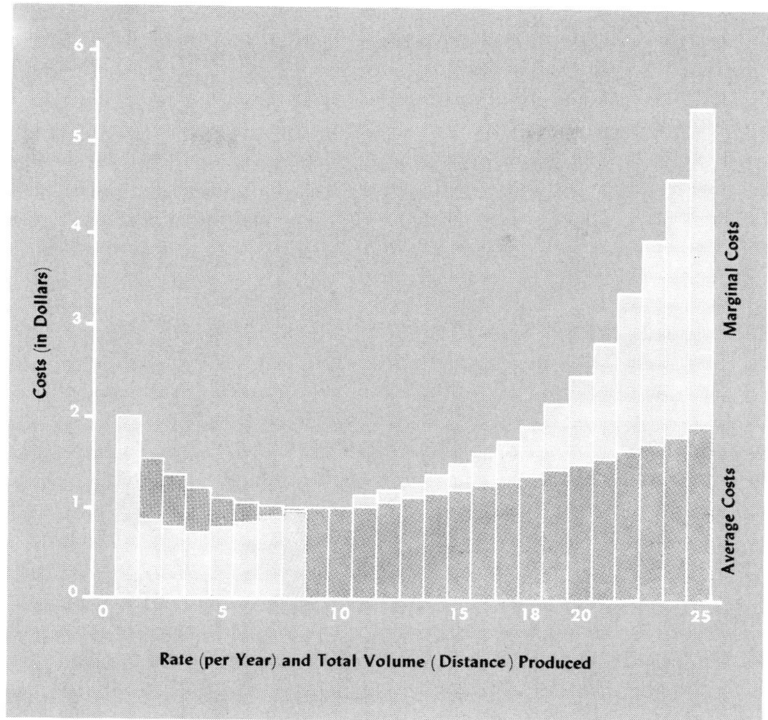

FIGURE 22–1. Marginal and average cost for output program of one year.

output. It will be profitable to increase the rate of output as long as the larger rate results in a larger increment of receipts than costs. The increment in receipts is simply the marginal revenue. Since this producer can sell all he wants to produce at the going price, the marginal revenue is, for each increment of output, equal to the price. His marginal costs, despite an initial decrease for small rates, increase with larger rates and, at some rate of output, will rise to a height equaling or exceeding the marginal revenue. To produce more would increase costs more than the increase in receipts—and his profit would be reduced. The conclusion is that, in a price-takers' market, profit-maximizing output is one at which the marginal cost equals marginal revenue. It follows that a higher price caused by a larger demand will induce a larger output.[3]

The preceding ideas are shown graphically in Figure 22–2. The marginal- and average-cost data are the same as those in Figure 22–1. The horizontal line from the price axis indicates the market price at which the firm can sell all it

[3] Because of discrete unit steps in our measure of the rate of output, and the possibility that the marginal cost exactly equals marginal revenue for some unit, there may be two adjacent rates of output with the maximum rate of profit.

produces. This horizontal line is the demand curve as seen by the price-taker firm for its products. And it is also the marginal revenue; for, with each extra unit sold, the revenue increases by the amount received (i.e., the price).

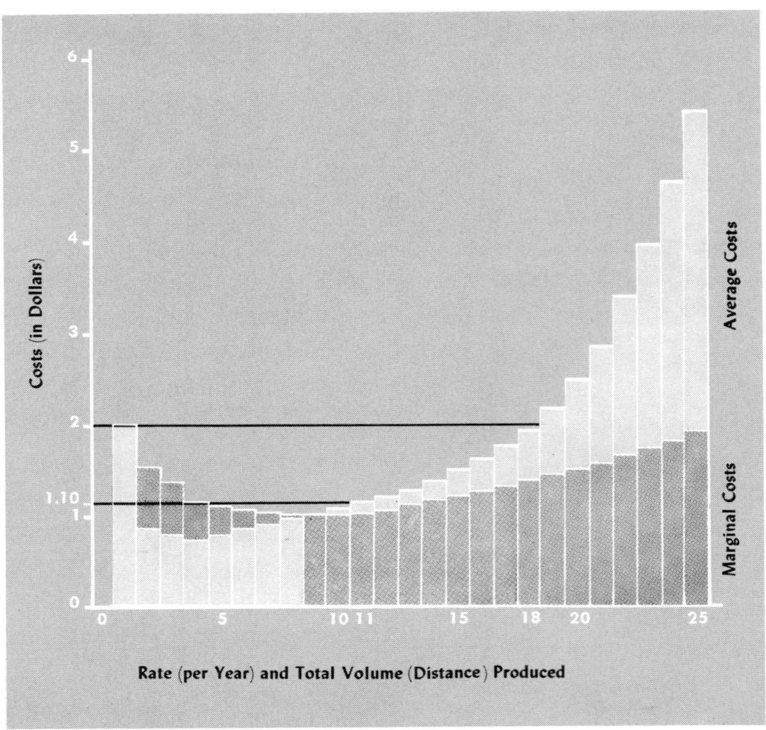

FIGURE 22–2. Marginal and average cost for output program of one year.

The marginal-revenue curve intersects the marginal-cost curve, at an output of ten units in rate and volume. This output can be sold at a price of $1.10, a figure that is indicated by the price line (the average-revenue curve for this firm). For any larger output rate, the marginal-cost curve, *MC*, is above the marginal-revenue curve, *MR*, showing that costs would be increased more than revenue. Similarly, at smaller outputs the marginal revenue exceeds the marginal cost, showing that an increase of output would yield a greater increase in revenue than in costs; clearly, then, an output of ten (or eleven) would give a bigger profit.

Since each unit is sold at a price indicated by the average-revenue curve, and since this average-revenue line is above the average-cost curve, the difference in heights of these lines at any output is a measure of the profit *per unit* of output. At an output of ten, the average cost per unit of volume is $1, while the average revenue (price) is $1.10. The difference is 10 cents per unit, which gives

$1 for ten units of output—the maximum *total* (not average per unit) profit output.

All this may seem a roundabout way to detect the output that maximizes wealth. But whether it is roundabout depends upon how the producer does his figuring. He can first compute total costs (column 1) and compare them with total receipts (column 5); or he can compare output programs, gradually creeping upward—all the while weighing marginal costs and marginal receipts until the two are equal. If thereafter marginal costs rise above marginal receipts and stay above them, there is no gain in considering higher-output programs, for they all have smaller profits. At any given price in the market, the wealth-maximizing one-year output program will be that at which marginal cost equals the price. Either way of ascertaining the maximum-wealth program—maximizing the gap of total revenue over total cost or equating marginal revenue with marginal cost—is logically equivalent. In any case, a higher demand and higher price induces a larger output.

Now, to show the effects of an increase in demand, suppose the demand (rate and volume) had been larger, so that price was $2. The maximum-profit program is eighteen units, with a profit of $14.55. At still larger outputs, the marginal cost is at least $2.10, while the marginal receipt (price) is only $2. Had demand and price been lower, the maximum-wealth output would have been smaller. This positive relationship between higher price from our increased demand and the wealth-maximizing output can be read directly from the marginal-cost data, and that is why we have directed attention to the marginal costs. At any specific price the wealth-maximizing output is the biggest output program for which marginal cost does not exceed marginal revenue.[4]

A higher (lower) price caused by increased (decreased) demand will increase (reduce) a producer's wealth, whether or not he responds by expanding his output program, but the important implication is that he can make bigger profits if he does adjust output. A higher price means that the profit-maximizing output is bigger, and a lower price implies a lower output.

For example, faced with the costs of these possible production programs given in Table 22–1, no one would *enter* the business unless he expected to sell at least eight units at a price of over 99 cents. But not all production decisions are those of entering a business. Many business firms already exist, and what is important is that they have already incurred "entry" costs. Thus, when equip-

[4] However, one side condition must be added. At any price below 99 cents, our producer will not produce any of these outputs, even though the marginal cost of joint rate and volume changes is less than that at the output program of three, four, or five units of volume. The side condition is that price must be greater than average cost; else total receipts will be less than total costs, and losses would be incurred if he produced anything. This side condition implies that the marginal-cost schedule can be interpreted as a supply schedule *only* for all prices higher than that at which marginal costs rise above average costs. (And this lowest price of the production supply schedule always is equal to the lowest average cost of the average-cost curve—by force of mathematical logic.)

ment is purchased, there is an immediate cost (loss of wealth) that occurs because the equipment suffers an initial loss of resale value as soon as it is purchased by the firm. This value decline is an example of what we can call a "cost of entry into production": It is a cost that is borne as soon as equipment is purchased. A person who buys a car or who constructs a manufacturing building will find that its resale value is not as great as its cost—even when still unused. (See Chapter 19, pages 279–280.) Once he has entered a business and purchased the equipment, that cost has been fixed on him; they are, in another sense, "sunk, irrevocable, bygone" costs. They will be unaffected by subsequent decisions; for, no matter what he does next, those costs have occurred. Only future reductions in value of assets are costs for present operating decisions. These are the costs he can control, or decide to accept, depending upon what output program he chooses. Thus, it is only these variable or avoidable costs, by definition, that are relevant in choosing among alternative output programs or actions.

This fixed or sunk cost can be illustrated with some examples, using Table 22–1. We see that the total cost of *entering the business and producing* eight units in one year is $7.95. Now suppose that in the production program a machine purchased for $5 can be resold at the end of the year for $4.50 (ignoring the interest-rate discount effect). Depreciation of the capital good during the year, then, is 50 cents. This 50-cent cost is included in the total cost of entry *and* operation, which amounts to $7.95.

But suppose that *immediately* after entry into the business, we had computed the costs only of subsequent operation. If, at the moment after purchase of equipment, the resale value of the purchased machinery is $4.60, then an immediate loss of wealth (depreciation) of 40 cents has been incurred. Subsequent operation for one year would *then* incur the remaining 10 cents of the 50-cent depreciation (of entry *and* production). In effect, 40 cents is a "sunk, fixed, bygone, irrevocable" cost, while 10 cents remains as the variable or avoidable cost depending upon output. This means that costs of subsequent production would be $7.55 instead of $7.95, because 40 cents of those costs do not enter into the costs of subsequent operation. *Given* that the firm has already incurred costs of entry, like the initial depreciation on purchase of equipment, these sunk costs (in our example, 40 cents) should not be counted as the costs of subsequent output for deciding which output program to produce.

What are the costs he will incur for the output decisions he may now make—*given* that he has entered business and purchased some equipment appropriate for the intended output program of eight per year? As seen in the preceding paragraph, the costs of production (excluding the "sunk" costs he has already incurred) are now for an output program of eight per year—$7.55, or 40 cents lower than before (or $.945 per unit). If he decides to abandon production and shut down, he will have incurred only those sunk costs of 40 cents. He can, if he wishes, avoid the costs of $7.55 inherent in subsequent production decisions. These costs of $7.55 are called variable costs, to indicate that they are not invariant regardless of what he does next, but are variable in that he can yet determine what costs to incur.

We see, then, that we have two costs. First, the total cost of $7.95 is the cost of entry *and* subsequent production. The second, $7.55, is the cost only of subsequent production, assuming entry and equipment has already been purchased, with initial depreciation amounting to 40 cents. The first cost reflects what is called a long-run decision—i.e., a decision to enter production or at least to renew productive equipment. The latter is called a shorter-run decision; some equipment already is on hand and will be used up without intention to replace or renew equipment for subsequent long-term production.

For whatever output program that was initially selected and for which equipment was purchased, the variable costs of *that* program subsequent to the purchase and the incurred initial depreciation will be lower than the cost of initial-entry purchase *and* production (by the amount of that sunk cost). This suggests that once a firm is in business, if price should fall below the average total costs of production (including entry of new equipment), the firm that is already in production will continue to produce until equipment is used up to an extent requiring new equipment of a nature equivalent to new entry into business.[5]

The implication of our analysis is that the price of a product may fall below the long-run average total costs per unit (the costs incurred by entry *and* production of the good) without inducing all existing producers to close down output immediately. As long as the lower price covers the continuing variable costs, output will continue. But in time, if price stays low, successive firms will close up when they have to replace old equipment or to incur even higher costs by continuing to repair and use it. In the long run, after some existing firms will

[5] At first thought one would think he could subtract this 40 cents of incurred cost from the costs of each of the *other* possible output programs listed in Table 22–1, letting the difference be the costs that will then be incurred by the subsequent decision about *revised production* from the existing plant and equipment. We could do this legitimately if it were not for the fact that the data of Table 22–1 are based on the initial purchase of different kinds of equipment for the different output programs. But if a person purchases equipment which is best for an output program of, say, ten per year, and then revises his output program to twenty a year, his total costs will be greater than shown in the table for twenty a year. For example, his total costs may not be $25.95, as indicated in Table 22–1, but $30 if he tries to produce twenty a year for a year with his existing equipment designed for ten a year for a year. It might even pay him to sell his old equipment and buy some new equipment, such as he would have bought initially if he knew earlier that he would later want to produce twenty a year. If he does not insist on immediately raising his output rate to twenty a year, he may have sufficient time to purchase new equipment in not too hasty a fashion so as to have costs that are not much different than if he had initially planned for twenty a year—except for the sunk costs of 40 cents inherent in his initial purchase decision, illustrated in the preceding example. If, however, he tries to move to that higher output immediately, he will find it more expensive to bring in new equipment so quickly; as a result, he may stick with his old equipment. The less hastily he insists on revising the output rate, the less costly that new output will be. (But this behavior of costs as a function of different output programs has been discussed already in Chapter 21.)

abandon production, the supply will be reduced enough to push price back up along the existing market-demand curve to a sufficiently high price to sustain continued long-run production with the replacement of equipment of surviving firms.

Large-Volume Effects in Price-Takers' Markets

In the preceding, the rate of output was assumed to last a year after it started, so that the volume was produced in *one* year. A longer length of production could have been used. For longer planned volumes of output, the producers might make more extensive production-method changes or buy more new equipment or more land than would be done for a shorter-length run or with smaller volume; as a result, the relevant costs would be different. In particular, the cost per unit would be lower for larger planned *volumes* at a given rate of output. Recall that the volume effect may dominate the rate effect, so that although the marginal cost must be *positive* for programs with increased rate and volume, the marginal cost may *decrease* for joint increases in rate and volume. However, marginal costs ultimately do increase at greater rates of output whether or not the volume is also increased. And for goods produced and sold in price-takers' markets, the output of each firm must be in the range of *increasing* marginal cost with larger output (in rate as well as in volume). Otherwise, if higher outputs gave lower marginal costs, it would be more profitable for the producer to increase his output rate to larger and larger rates—until the marginal cost began to rise or until he became so large a part of the total supply that his output affected price—thus destroying the conditions of a price-takers' market.

Market Supply: Aggregated Output of All Firms

The preceding discussion concentrated on the output adjustment of one firm. However, the market supply of a good is usually provided by many firms—called an industry. The proposition that an increased demand induces a larger output from a *firm* is easily converted into an industry proposition: The higher the price, the greater the output supplied. At a specified price, the output of each firm is added, and the total is called the industry output. The schedule of prices and associated outputs is the industry supply schedule.

To illustrate, the marginal-cost data like those of Table 22–1 are drawn in Figure 22–3 as a smooth line labeled MC_a, the marginal costs of Firm *A*. Also on that graph is a marginal-cost schedule (MC_b) for Firm *B*, which produces less at any given price. The total output of this industry, here illustrated with the output of just these two firms, is obtained by *adding the output (horizontal distance) of each firm's marginal-cost curve at any specified price* above the low-

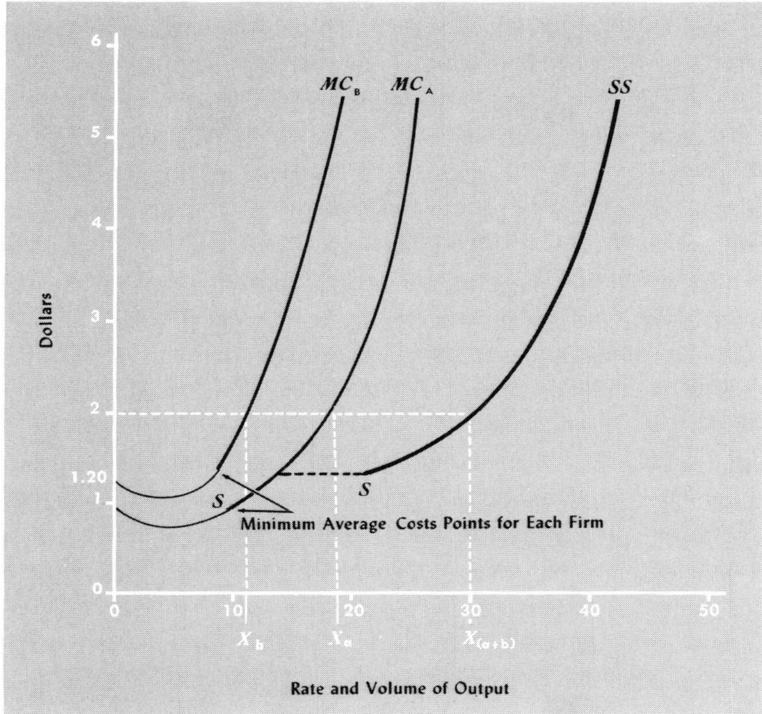

FIGURE 22–3. Marginal-cost curves as basis of supply of industry under price-takers' market conditions.

est average-cost output for each firm. The summed curve, SS, shows the industry's output at each possible price.

If the price were $2, Firm *A* would have its maximum wealth output at X_a, and Firm *B* would have its maximum wealth output at X_b. The total output at this price is the sum of these outputs. At prices below $1.35 (but not less than 99 cents), only the output for Firm A is in the long-run SS curve—because at any price below the minimum *average* cost for a firm, the firm will eventually go out of business. At higher market prices, with larger demand, each firm is induced to produce a larger output; therefore (as signified by the upward-sloping SS curve), an increased output of this good is offered to the market.[6]

Figure 22–4 is the same as Figure 22–3, with the addition of a demand

[6] We emphasize our special assumption that these marginal costs are for output changes *jointly* in both rate and volume. In the present example, production is expected to last for one year, so that a unit increase in annual rate corresponds to a unit increase in the volume of output. Costs of less conveniently correlated rate and volume changes can, with more complex computations, be converted to marginal and average costs per unit of rate *or* volume increase; but the principles elucidated here are unchanged.

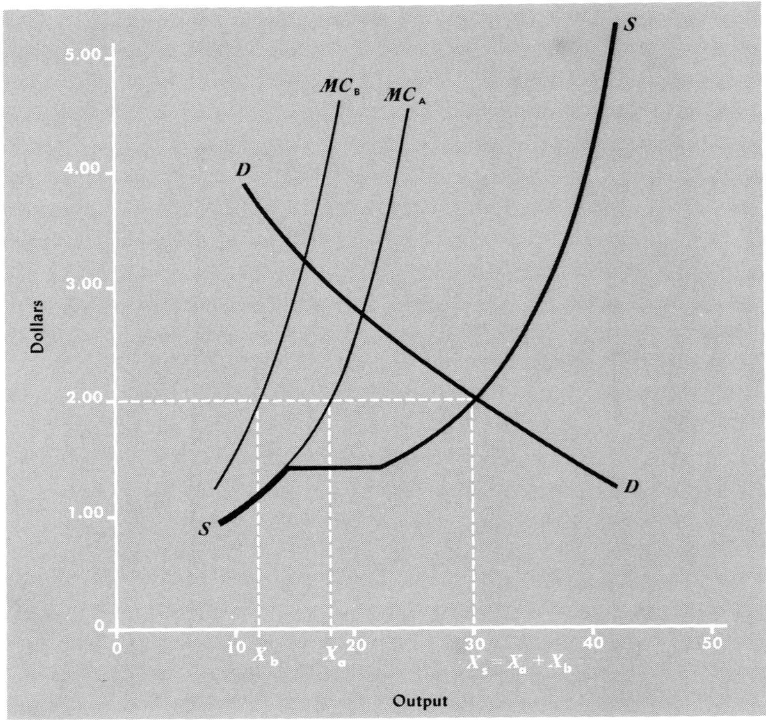

FIGURE 22–4. Demand and supply and output determination in price-takers' markets.

curve and the intersection price. A demand curve, *DD,* intersects the supply curve at the price of $2. According to the price-determination process outlined earlier, the price will be $2, and the total output will be produced by Firm *A* and Firm *B*. The portions of the total output produced by Firms *A* and *B* are indicated by the distances $0X_a$ and $0X_b$, which total to $0X_s$. In earlier chapters, we saw how price rationed the existing stock among the competing claimants; here we see that price also affects the production by each firm. Price allocates in the sense that it both rations existing output and assigns production.

This demand and supply "intersection" price is the price at which each producer can sell all that he wants to produce at that price, and each consumer can buy all he wants at that price. In that sense, it is an *equilibrium* or *equilibrating* price. Price is in "equilibrium" because price has moved to the level necessary to make the amount demanded equal the amount of production evoked by that price. A higher price would reduce the amount demanded to less than the amount of production induced by that higher price; a lower price would mean that the amount demanded exceeds the amount produced.

If demand increases (i.e., if the demand schedule, *DD,* shifts to the right), price will be bid up—in the absence of effective laws, customs, or conventions preventing price changes. The higher price induces producers to increase output—as indicated by the SS curve, which shows larger output at higher prices (and marginal costs). Conversely, a reduced demand would, under the stipulated conditions, yield lower prices and thereby a reduced output. Every firm would be induced to expand or to contract.

When demand and hence price change, not all firms will respond to the same extent, because the response of marginal cost differs among the firms. For some firms, the marginal cost increases considerably with a given change in output, while for others it rises only a little. The former firms will change their output less in response to price changes. Furthermore, as demand decreases and price is lowered, fewer firms will remain in production. As price falls to lower levels, the average cost of production for fewer firms will be covered, and some firms will shut down until, they hope, demand increases. If demand increases so that price rises, existing firms will expand output and higher-cost firms will be attracted into the business. These higher-cost firms can operate only when price and demand are high; they appear as "marginal," "fringe" firms.

Supply Response by Entry of New Firms

Firms that produce only when price and demand are high are typically higher-cost firms; they cannot survive unless price is high. This fact is not indicated by their marginal costs (for every firm adjusts its output until the marginal cost has increased to the higher price) but is instead indicated by their average costs.

At low prices with low demand, only a few firms will be able to operate without incurring losses. If price is higher, a new firm will enter. This firm will probably be regarded as one of the "marginal," "fringe" firms; for if demand falls, the lower price will induce it to shut down. There always are potential firms on the "margin," ready to appear if demand and price should rise sufficiently. If demand rises and stays high, then these firms become recognized as "established" firms, and in turn look on still higher-cost firms as constituting the new fringe of marginal, unreliable firms.

Equilibrium in the number of firms is achieved when the price is reduced to the minimum average cost of the firm with the highest average costs in the industry. If we suppose all firms in the industry to be alike with respect to costs, the number of firms will increase and so will the total industry output until price falls to the lowest average cost of each firm, thereby eliminating further incentive for new firms to enter or for the number of firms to increase. If all firms had the same cost conditions as in Table 22–1, the price would be 99 cents at the long-run equilibrium. In fact, of course, not all firms are alike. Nevertheless, even though some firms will be larger and some smaller, in an equilibrium with respect to both number of firms in the industry and with respect to the aggregate output, the average cost of production in each firm will be equal to price.

How will this cost-price equality be accomplished? If any firm has a special talent or resource that enables it to produce at lower average per unit cost than other firms, the value of that special resource will be bid up as other firms compete for its use. Its value will rise until at that higher price it no longer yields a lower cost to the firm. The firm now using that resource must reckon with that higher value; i.e., cost of using the resource. We shall discuss this revaluation process more fully a bit later; for the moment we first note some examples of entry of firms in commonplace activities.

A homely but practical example is that of parking-lot operators near a stadium. For big crowds, the parking fees are higher, and there are more high-cost parking lots available as some residents sell parking space in their driveways and yards. These "fly-by-night," fringe, temporary operators are disliked by the "established" operators, for they take away some business. More accurately, these "fly by nights," who appear when demand and price are high, manage to keep prices lower than if they did not appear. No wonder the established firms do not like them.

However, the thoughtful student may note that the established firms often do not raise their prices when demand increases temporarily and that it is the fringe sellers who seize the opportunity to sell at the higher prices. How do the fringe operators, who do not hesitate to take a higher price, contribute to *lower* prices—if they are the ones who in fact charge the higher price? There are two answers. First, the established firms sometimes *do* raise their prices, so that the fringe operators, by providing an increased supply, prevent the price from rising as far as it otherwise would. Second, remember that "price" or consumer cost includes more than the monetary payment. People who cannot park in the "standard" lots overflow to surrounding areas. The price they must then pay is "walking farther." If the fringe operators do not spring up and provide parking space at the higher price, the people will have to park farther away. The cost imposed on the patrons of parking farther away and walking is greater than the parking fee of the fringe operators. How do we know? Simply because some people do prefer to pay more and walk less; they seize the opportunity provided by the fringe operators. No one *has* to pay the higher price asked by the fringe operator; those who do pay think the fees are worth the saving in time and effort. And this saving in time and effort is provided by the increased supply of the fringe operators, despite (or in response to) the higher prices. Without their services, the costs (pecuniary and nonpecuniary) imposed on patrons would be even higher—especially on those who do not get to park in the standard, established parking lots.

Some more examples are provided by the influx of people into the building and contracting business or into farming or into taxi driving at rush hours.

When demand for building or farm products increases, the number of contractors and builders increases, and the number of farmers increases. Later, when demand falls (in terms of rate of annual output), the lower price makes it impossible to maintain so high a rate of production and still cover costs. Therefore, many firms withdraw from the business, and the resources (labor services) used there must now regretfully and complainingly revert to their next-best sources of income (which served as a measure of their costs when used in building or farming). In Washington, D.C., hundreds of people become taxi operators during "rush" hours, but during the rest of the day they work at other jobs. Still other examples are available. Steel mills have blast furnaces they operate only during peak demands. Barber shops have chairs that are "idle" most but *not* all the time; at peak demand periods they are used. They represent high-cost, rather than excessive, capacity. Some firms use second and third shifts when demand warrants it, even though or, more accurately, because they are higher-cost ways of production.

Timing of Supply Responses

Not all producers respond equally rapidly in output adjustments. Some adjust their programs in a slower, economical way and have lower total costs and also lower marginal costs for their output. At any price, a larger output will be produced, or for any specified output the cost will be lower, if the output is produced later and less hastily rather than earlier. The producer of the more deferred output programs can say to the more immediate or earlier-date producer, "Anything you can do, I can do better—if I do it later or in less haste."

Suppose, as we did, that the data given in Table 22–1 refer to alternative contemplated output programs, all to yield their first production beginning three months hence. If the output selected now were to be forthcoming in six months, the costs would be lower. This deferred output is often referred to as a "longer-run" output—not in the sense that the production run is long but in the sense that the run of time prior to the output is longer.

That costs are lower is a direct implication of the fundamental cost proposition that higher rates of production are more expensive. More immediate production requires a higher rate of use of existing resources for preparation. Overtime, premium delivery prices, greater use of higher-cost resources to hasten output are only a few of the cost-increasing factors involved. It will not pay to defer indefinitely in order to get lower costs, since that also defers and reduces the value of the output. We shall assume some lower limit of costs, below which they will not be reduced by any practical deferment of output initiation. These lowest-cost, or long-run output, programs represent the ultimate adjustment of inputs.

The production and market-price effects of an increase in demand can be generalized in summary form. Starting in a long-run equilibrium price and output position, the rate of output can be instantly increased only at very high costs, but with time the output rate can be increased more cheaply. With more time, an even larger output can be produced at a given total cost. Graphically, this relationship of costs and time of output can be portrayed by two supply curves: one for the moment, and one for the extreme limiting output rate for any given cost. Figure 22–5, along with two demand curves, shows a "before-and-after" situation. Demand, initially at D_1 with price at p_1, has increased to D_2. As it did, price rose and then fell along a path suggested by the dotted line as the larger output was forthcoming—to the long-run equilibrium at p_n. There is no point in trying to indicate the exact course of the price. All that can be deduced is that, depending upon how much and how rapidly the demand increases, price will move up somewhat higher than the long-run equilibrium at which it settles eventually as the output adjustment takes place.

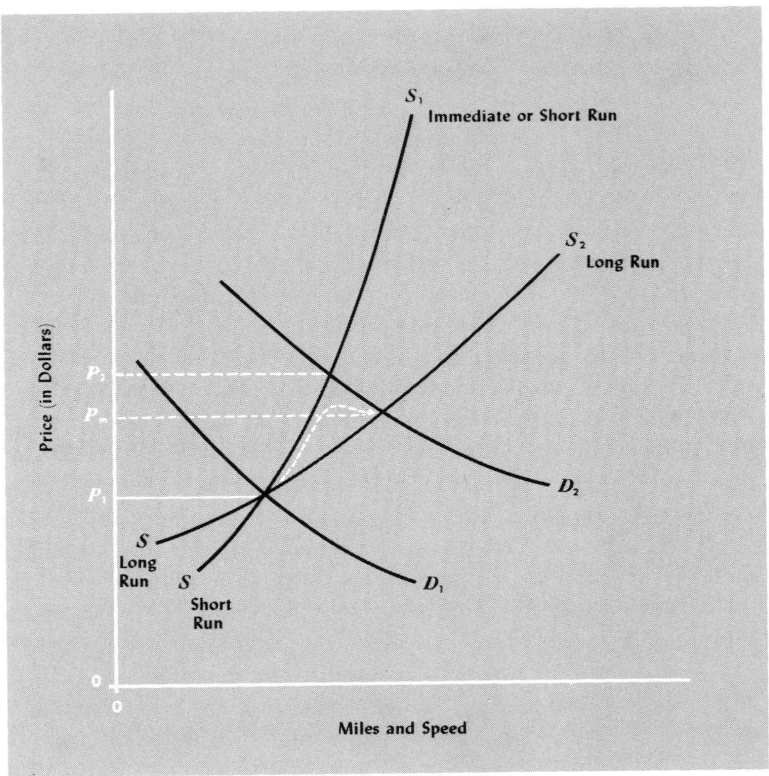

FIGURE 22–5. Supply curves for various adjustment dates for specified volume and rate-of-output programs.

The lower costs associated with less hasty output adjustments also permit an increase in the number of producers. The ultimate equilibrium cost of production toward which competitive free-market forces tend is one in which birth and death rates of firms in the industry are pushed toward equality. By definition, the long-run equilibrium involves an equality of price and average costs and no net change in output either from individual expansion or number of firms. We refer to a *net* change, for while some firms are expanding, others are contracting (e.g., the owner is aging, the firm has lost its special abilities, population is shifting). At any one time, then, though there is no change in the average characteristic of the aggregate of firms in the industry equilibrium situation, individual firms are experiencing changes.

Resource Valuation as a Director of Resource Uses

The foregoing analysis has concentrated on the response of output to demand changes, but it did not clearly indicate the process whereby resource revaluations induce owners and users to re-allocate resources. If we tie the lessons of the preceding chapter on costs and profits to this chapter, we can see the elements of the process.

The market demands of people change unpredictably (e.g., sports cars, compacts, short skirts, natural shoulders, wigs, polyunsaturated fats), so that prices of goods also change. Or the prices may be revised because someone discovers how to use resources in "better" ways than foreseen. In either event, the earlier value placed on resources, as forecasts of their highest use value, proves erroneous. Producers then are faced with a choice: whether blindly to retain the old valuations or to accept the new information about values and revise the allocation of their resources so as to achieve a higher aggregate wealth. Anyone who ignores the new valuations sacrifices the gain or takes a loss of wealth.

This higher value potential in a certain productive activity will increase the demand for the responsible resources, leading to a change in their prices, supplies, and allocations. The revised demand for other resources used in the production of these resources will in turn revise the values imputed to the other resources in a lengthening chain of repercussions.

The market's revaluation of resources in the light of the new higher value (profit) of their use results in an imputation of that profit back to higher values of the responsible goods. The cost of using these resources—i.e., their highest alternative use value—is revised upward, which means the profit has been amalgamated into higher costs. The new revised costs are reflections of the new use values. It is not a contradiction that a profit is both a gain in wealth and also an increase in cost. Profits are unforeseen gains in wealth, and the higher value of resources means that costs of their use are now greater. To say that profits imply higher costs is to say both that the output is of greater value and that the cost of getting it is higher. These increases are the two sides of the same "profit."

As an example of this duality, suppose I discover oil on my land. I can then sell the land with the oil rights to you and convert my wealth (including the profit) to cash. You will certainly count what you paid for the land and oil rights (and that includes my profit) in your subsequent costs of operation. If, alternatively, I do not sell my land and oil rights, *I* should count the cost of subsequent operation at the same high figure that *you* would. The costs of use are higher than before the increased value of the resources was recognized, and the costs do not depend upon *who* uses them.

This duality means that any firm that succeeds in putting resources to higher-valued uses than any other firm did will immediately revise the value of those resources—which revaluation appears to the owner as a profit and to the user (whether or not he is also the owner) as a higher cost of *use*. Profits and losses in the real world, therefore, not only reveal increased wealth value of particular resources but also direct those resources to their higher-valued uses (as judged ultimately by the consumers' market).[7] The quicker and less constrained the revaluation of assets and recalculation of costs, the more quickly will resources be directed in accord with highest-valued uses, whatever may be the value criterion used for this purpose.

The redirection of resources in response to a change in demand extends through a long chain of resources. If, for example, as a result of an increased demand, more wheat is to be produced, resources must be released from production of some other goods. Only if resources were wasted or idle could the output of wheat be increased without reduction elsewhere. With an increased demand for wheat, resources are transferred into wheat production as their owners seek greater utility (via greater wealth). Land transferred to wheat is taken from oats, corn, and building sites, and thus their supply will fall and their price increase. Other land will now be used for corn and oats—land formerly used for, say, cotton, barley, grazing land, parks, and potential housing or industrial sites. Not only land but also labor and other resources are diverted to wheat. Some laborers who would otherwise work as barbers, carpenters, or gasoline-station attendants switch to wheat production. And their places are partly filled by resources from still other occupations. The long chain of ramifications and substitutions and shifting or resources is so broad and extensive that ultimately each one of the many effects on output of other final consumers' goods may be so slight that the

[7] In Chapter 16, we defined the cost of a given use of resources as the highest *alternative* sacrificed value of output of those resources, seeming to exclude the value of their *present* use. But we now see that a more general conception of costs consists of imputing to a given resource a market value which reflects its highest possible value in *any* line of activity, including the present one. Costs of resources in a particular occupation stem not only from *alternative uses,* but also from alternative *users.* Even if my land is good only for oil production (i.e., it has no alternative uses) it still has a value, which must be taken into account, because other people are willing to bid for it.

reduction is hardly noticeable over the perturbation of the many other everyday events. For this reason we are sometimes misled into thinking that some more of a good can always be produced without producing less of some other.

Desirability of Basing Output on Wealth Maximizing

According to the data in Table 22–1, although the wealth-maximizing output program at a market price of $2 is eighteen units of volume at a rate of eighteen per year, this producer could produce twenty-five at a rate of twenty-five per year and make profits of $4. But in the interests of his own wealth, he does not produce that much. There is a temptation to indulge in the ethical judgment that this restriction is socially wasteful, because there appears to be under-production of this particular product. However, although the price does exceed *average* costs, it does not exceed *marginal* costs. Consequently, if this producer were to expand his output beyond eighteen units, he would use resources worth more than $2 (that is what marginal costs measure), and he would be selling to people who value the extra output at only $2—which is *less* than the costs of the extra output. A larger output would *not* be preferred by consumers. Therefore, the price-taking producer, by holding his output rate to eighteen units per year in order to maximize his wealth, is not "under-producing," even though he could produce more without wiping out all his profit.

Ironically, this implication of wealth-maximizing producers with free access to a price-takers' market was developed by socialists. Socialists asked what "should" be the output, and when they used the criterion that resources should provide the greatest value as judged by consumers, they noticed the implication that a private-property system of wealth maximizers with free access to a price-takers' market gave precisely that result. Everyone was embarrassed—the socialists because this provided an "argument" for capitalism and the capitalists because, much as they would have liked this "justification" of their activity, not all of them could validly claim to be selling where there was free access to markets or even defending open markets. Although some discussion and argumentation about each system hinges on this kind of criterion of productive efficiency, there are other considerations: freedom, culture, and social behavior. And in the opinion of many people, these latter are more weighty considerations.

Adjustments without Full Information

With market-expressed values of productive goods, there is no necessity for anyone to have *full* information about all possible costs of various programs in order for a higher demand and price to induce a greater output in a price-takers' market. There are forces inducing a larger output if demand increases—and a smaller output if demand decreases—in a private-property, market-valuation economy. We shall examine some of them now.

In the first place, many producers do keep records and compile data with which to estimate costs. They have adequate data with which to increase their probability of being near the wealth-maximizing output. They know that when demand rises and takes price up with it, an expanded output becomes more profitable than formerly. If their output was less than the wealth-maximizing amount, the incentive to an increased output is now even stronger. If the output was too large, the incentive is again to increase it; but, at the same time, the wealth-maximizing output also increases, whether or not each producer knows what that output is. All the forces are now more strongly for a larger output.

Second, even for those who may not compute costs in an endeavor to find the wealth-maximizing output, the increase in demand means that the set of profitable, viable, sustainable output programs is larger than formerly. Even if every firm picked outputs at random, those that picked larger outputs would themselves be more profitable than those that picked smaller output programs. The observed or revealed profits will be greater for the producers of the larger output program. Larger-output producers will find their profits increasing more relatively to smaller-output producers. Imitation of more profitable producers will induce expanded output.

Third, a powerful force pushing output toward the wealth-maximizing output is the competitive actions of people. If the demand for wheat should increase, a corn farmer ultimately will probably shift his land into wheat production. This would *not* be done by exhortations or appeals invoking the national or social interest. Instead, other people offer to rent the land from him and pay him more than it is worth to him as a source of corn. The inducement to transfer to wheat, then, is the prospect of greater personal wealth, which he can realize either by his changing production in the greater wealth direction or by renting or selling his farm land and wheat-producing resources to others who think they can use the wheat land in more valuable ways. Demand and price of productive resources reflect a valuation not merely by the owner but by other people, who can offer to buy or rent the resources. They will try to get those resources from the current owner if he doesn't use them in as profitable ways as they think possible. If he is willing to entertain offers from other people for his resources, they will bid the price up. By being the owner at the time that other people think its use value has risen in response to higher demands for its potential products, he thus captures the present capital value of that future product (along the principles of valuation explained in the earlier chapter on capital values). But the important point is that resources are thereby transferred to higher-valued uses as people seek greater wealth—if the resources are salable as private property.

Illustrative Application: Effects of a Tax

An excellent and important exercise in applying the principles so far presented is provided by an analysis of the effects of levying a tax on a good. Suppose that the manufacturers of, say, playing cards are taxed 50 cents for each deck produced. This tax will increase each firm's marginal cost by 50 cents at each possible output, and it will add 50 cents to the average cost of each deck. Summing the new higher marginal-cost curves over all the firms of the industry yields a smaller supply curve, as illustrated in Figure 22–6. Before the tax, the price was 75 cents. Each firm, now operating on a higher marginal-cost curve, will be induced to reduce its output *at the initial price*. The reduced output offered on the market will push up price, which will induce each firm to restore *part* of the output cut. Our first conclusion is that the higher tax raised costs but that price rose only *because the supply decreased*. The effect on price is through the effect on supply, and only because the higher tax decreased the supply did it lead to a higher price.

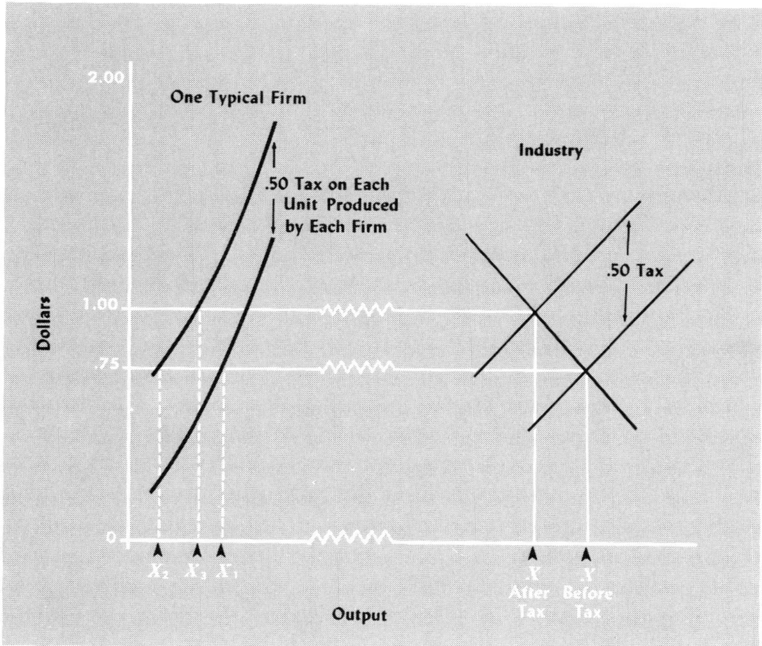

FIGURE 22–6. Price and output effect of tax on each unit produced or sold and levied on all firms.

Suppose the tax had been levied on just *one* of the producers. His wealth-maximizing output rate at any given price would be smaller. Could *he* therefore raise his price? No. Without a similar tax on the other producers, the supply curve of the industry does not shift by a perceptible amount. In this case, *his* output and wealth fall more than if the tax had been levied against all producers. And he has no way to recoup part of his wealth by a higher price. If he tried to raise price, all his buyers would simply shift to other sellers, who provide perfect substitutes.

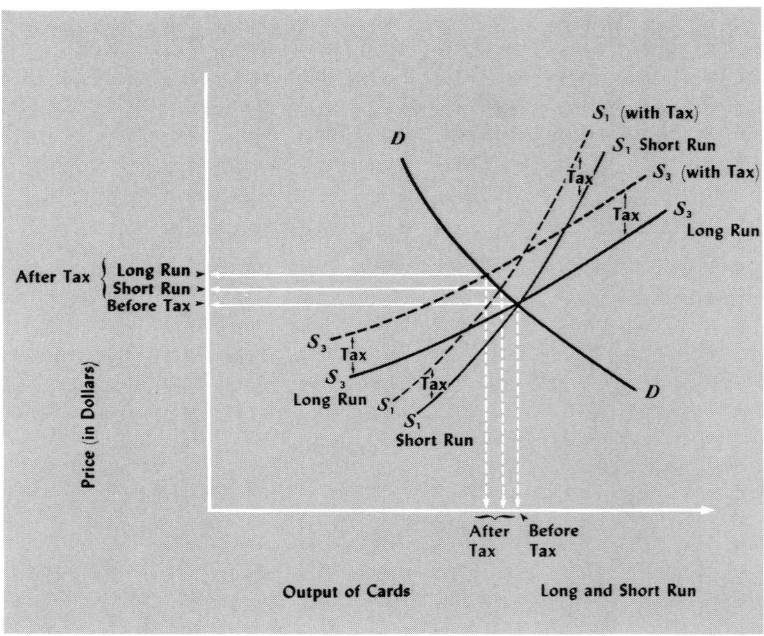

FIGURE 22–7. Price and output effects, long and short run, of a per unit tax on playing cards.

Inspection of Figure 22–7 shows that the price is increased by less than the tax on each deck—namely, to $1 from 75 cents. Part of the tax cost is countered by reducing the rate of output, so that the output is at a lower point on the marginal-cost curve. But this also means that part of the resources used in producing playing cards are no longer as valuable to the firm. This decrease in their worth reflects the smaller value of the final product, the playing cards, after deduction of the tax that must be paid. Thus, we see that the total tax receipts (tax per deck times number now produced) are accounted for, in part, by a higher price to consumers and in part by a lower income or value of resources of the manufacturers of the taxed good. If someone says that taxes are ultimately borne by the consumer, we can see the error in that statement. Instead, part of the tax is borne by consumers in the form of higher prices, and part is borne by the producers whose wealth fell at the time the tax was announced. Be careful not to confuse the effect on the wealth of those who own resources useful in card production at the time the tax is announced with that of those who purchase those resources afterward. All new buyers will make offers that are reflective only of the lower capital value of the future receipts *net* of the taxes that must be paid; this imposes the wealth loss on the owners of resources at the time of the announcement of the tax.

But this is not the end of the adjustment. As was illustrated in Figure 22–7, the first impact on output and on prices occurred with the existing productive equipment then devoted to card making. The reduced value of these resources devoted to card making means that it will not pay to replace them as they wear out—despite the higher price of the cards, including tax. In time—the long run —the stock of resources devoted to card making will be reduced, and the output will be smaller than the immediate or short-run response. The longer-run adjustment in price and output includes the adjustment in the stock of all the resources in all the firms making cards. When this final adjustment is achieved, the price of cards will be high enough so that the price net of tax will be high enough to cover the costs of maintaining and replacing the smaller stock of resources.

The reduction in output of cards is not all a loss, because some resources that would have produced those cards are now redirected to other goods. But these other goods are less valuable, in the opinion of consumers, than that of the "unproduced" cards. We know this because, without the tax, the cards were preferred; that is why they were formerly being produced. However, before we conclude that the tax on cards is therefore undesirable, there are two further considerations. First, it is sometimes argued that the tax is imposed on a good that should not be produced so extensively, because card playing is undesirable. A tax will reduce the extent of that activity. Thus, some people argue for taxes on alcoholic drinks, gambling, night clubs, and tobacco. Second, it is alleged, the tax proceeds are spent by the government for goods that are "more important" than the playing cards that would otherwise have been produced. Educators and parents of young children commonly can be found in the ranks of advocates of taxes on cigarettes, alcohol, etc., in order to permit more educational expenditure.

This analysis of the response of price, output, and wealth to a tax is very similar to that for a change in the price, unaccompanied by any change in productive power, of some resource used in making cards. It is also applicable to the case of a change in demand, for a tax is equivalent to a reduction from the demand for playing cards, where the demand schedule is shifted vertically downward by an amount equal to the tax per unit of output. Thus, Figure 22–7 shows the results for price and output of playing cards; the same tax as in the preceding example is here treated as a deduction from or reduction in demand to the producer of playing cards (after allowing for the tax). It will be seen that the same price and output effects are again implied. (Unfortunately, neither Figure 22–6 nor 22–7 shows the wealth effects; hence, when using these diagrammatic techniques, one must avoid the error of thinking that they describe all the consequences.)

"Sick" Industries

Another useful application of the preceding economic analysis is provided by the study of what are commonly called "sick" industries—"sick" because they are alleged to have an "excessive" number of firms; "excessive" because most of the firms do such a small volume of business that they steadily lose wealth. And as rapidly as old ones lose out and leave, new ones enter—only to experience a similar fate. There seems to be no long-run adjustment that restores the industry to a profitable or at least a non-loss balance. The more commonly cited examples of "sick" industries are retail groceries, bars, restaurants, night clubs, coal mines, gasoline stations, textile manufacturers, and farming.

People who try to explain why so many firms enter these industries usually point to foolish gambling, overestimation of one's ability, plain ignorance, or the low cost of entering into the business. But upon closer study these explanations fall to the ground, primarily because the whole idea of a "sick" industry is a "sick" idea. In the first place, all firms in an industry could be losing wealth when demand is falling unexpectedly. But to call this a sickness is to confuse the cure with the malady. In the second place, all firms could be losing wealth if the business has a sufficiently large amount of nonpecuniary satisfaction, as is said to be the case for horse racing or novel writing or acting or owning baseball clubs. One man grows orchids and makes money and considers it a business; another grows orchids and loses money but regards it as a hobby or consumption activity like being the best-dressed man or buying drinks and hi-fi equipment. Everyone could lose money in some business if the fun of the business operation were great enough to be worth the losses. But although these considerations might explain why some industries or occupations always run at a loss and seem never to reach a long-run adjustment to profitable operations, on the average, for the surviving firms, they will not apply.

In some industries the profits may be large for only a few winners, with the rest of the members losing money. Acting, writing, painting, and sports are classic examples wherein only a few seem to make a big success while the vast majority never make enough to make the effort worthwhile, in retrospect. Nothing in economic analysis says that an industry in which only a few make vast fortunes or even as much as they could have made elsewhere should not have a vast number of "failures." These failures (or is it more accurate to call them non-successes?) entered in the hope that they might be one of the favored few, and they often remain despite years of frustration and disappointment.

Finally, there is the contention that an industry is sick because it has excess capacity that is almost never fully utilized (e.g., barber shops and service stations). Only a naïve observer would believe they should be constantly "fully" utilized. Customers do not come in predictable unchanging rates and amounts. Some barber shops have chairs or barbers that are not utilized most of the time; but when demand hits its peaks, they are utilized, and it is precisely the peak demand that is served by this "apparent" overcapacity. How would you like to live in a community in which there were just enough barbers to cut everyone's hair if the barbers were always "fully" employed? Would you like to have to plan your purchases on some schedule that allowed you no opportunity to adjust to unexpected events? Would anyone argue that Palm Desert or Palm Beach has too many hotel rooms because most of them are empty during the summer and that there are too many ski resorts because they are idle most of the time, or that there are too many churches because all of them are empty almost all the time? If you think there are too many service stations, would you be prepared to let me assert that the one you happen to buy from is the one that should be abolished? Does Sak's Fifth Avenue have too many salesgirls because many or most of them are "idle" most of the time? Would you say two-bathroom houses are uneconomic because neither bathroom is fully utilized at all times? To ask these questions is to answer them.

This rather extensive analysis of production response of the firm to demand changes in price-takers' markets has touched on the basic principles, leaving more of the details for advanced study. Had we discussed demand changes involving only the volume with the speed of that output unchanged, we would have had to delve into principles beyond the scope of this elementary survey. Nevertheless, the principles of resource guidance and adjustment developed in the more restricted range of cases carry over generally to the entire range of market behavior.

Questions

1. Do the data in Table 22–1 yield constant costs for the firm?

2. What is the wealth-maximizing output program if the selling price is $1.50? What is the profit? What is the wealth-maximizing output program if price is $5?

3. Explain why part of the marginal-cost schedule (that is, for outputs at which marginal costs are at least equal to average, or variable, costs) is the supply schedule of the firm in a price-takers' market.

4. A producer with the costs given in Table 22–1 could produce *more* than twenty units at a price of $2.50, but he would be penalized with reduced profits.

a. In what sense is it good that he does not produce more?

b. In what sense is it bad that he does not produce more?

5. You are a public employee operating a publicly owned golf course, or swimming pool, or taxi service, or gun factory; and you have the costs indicated by the data of Table 22–1. Furthermore, you are selling the product in a price-takers' market.

a. At a price of $1.80 you choose to produce not 17 units but about 25 units. Why do we predict you would produce about 25 units? (Hint: How do the rewards and punishment meted out to you as an operator of a nonprivate-property firm depend on, or vary with, the selected output program? Compare this with a privately owned business.)

b. Suppose that you are *told* to maximize the profits. Would you? Why?

6. If, in some industry, there were 100 firms exactly like the one whose cost data are given in Table 22–1, what would be the supply schedule—assuming a price-takers' market? Plot that industry's (100 firms) supply curve on graph paper.

7. The following describes the state of market demand in the price-takers' market in which there are the hundred firms assumed in the preceding question.

DEMAND SCHEDULE

PRICE	QUANTITY
$5.00	450
4.50	500
4.00	560
3.75	610
3.50	660
3.25	710
3.00	770
2.80	810
2.60	850
2.40	900
2.20	950
2.00	1000
1.80	1100
1.60	1200
1.40	1400
1.20	1700
1.00	2100
.90	2400
.80	2800
.70	3300
.60	3900

a. Draw this demand curve on the diagram of the preceding question.

b. What will be the equilibrium price?

c. What will be the rate of output at that price?

d. At that price what will be observed in the market?

e. To each seller what will appear to be the shape of the demand curve of his products?

f. If price is somehow kept from that equilibrium, what will be observed in the marketplace?

g. At the equilibrium price of the current problem, will new firms be attracted into producing this good?

h. Would the attraction be more pronounced and more effective if the demand were twice as great, with the supply schedule being what it is? Explain why.

i. If new firms can enter this business, each one having the same cost conditions as firms already in the business, to what value will the market price move? (Hint: You must first determine the long-run supply curve, including entry of new firms, in order to get the answer.)

j. When plotted on graph paper, what kind of shape or position will the new supply curve have relative to the older one?

k. As new firms enter, what will happen to the output of the existing firms?

l. What will be the total long-run equilibrium rate of output? (You should be able to read the answer from the chart you have graphed or compute it from the tabled data.)

m. Will all the firms that enter survive in the business? Why?

n. If all the new firms are not identical, in that some have higher minimum average costs, to what level will the long-run equilibrium price move?

o. What will happen to the costs of the firms whose minimum average costs were lower? (Hint: What happens to the profits of those lower-cost firms?)

8. Why don't adjustments in the number of firms and in the rate of output from existing firms occur instantly?

9. "Marginal costs serve as a guide as to how much of a good to produce, while average costs help indicate whether to produce the good at all." Explain.

10. The process whereby secret information is revealed by the stock market is exemplified by the following episode: On March 7, 1954, the *New York Times* reported a test in which a new bomb of enormous force had been exploded on March 1, 1954. On March 31, 1954, Atomic Energy Commissioner Strauss reported publicly for the first time the nature of the new bomb and its dependence on lithium. Weeks prior to his announcement, the price of the stock of Lithium Corporation of America, one of the producers of lithium, increased substantially. How is this rise in price consistent with the fact that everyone connected with the corporation and the test really kept the secret?

11. A tax of 1 cent is levied on each pound of peanuts grown by farmers.

a. What effect will this have on the output of peanuts?

b. How will it induce that effect?

c. What will happen to the price of peanuts?

d. Will the land on which peanuts are grown fall in value—in view of the facts (i) that peanuts are grown from plants that must be seeded every year, and (ii) that the land can be used for other crops?

e. What will happen to the value of *existing* machines used for harvesting, shelling, roasting, packaging, and crushing peanuts? Why?

f. Explain why these changes in value of those kinds of goods will not be permanent even though the tax is permanent.

g. Does the temporary drop in value mean that the wealth-reduction effect of the tax is only temporary? Why or why not?

h. The proceeds of the peanuts tax is used to finance purchases of this book for free distribution to college students. Who is paying for the books so distributed? (The answer is *not* that those who lost wealth from the revised valuation of existing resources are paying for the books. That loss of wealth is not offset as a gain to anyone else.)

i. Who gains what as a result of the tax and expenditure of the proceeds?

12. Suppose that the tax in the preceding problem is levied against only *one* producer of peanuts.

a. What will happen to the price of peanuts?

b. To the output?

c. To the wealth of the various peanut producers?

d. Whose wealth will be affected by this tax?

13. Stradivarius violins are rated as about the best in the world. Yet there is evidence that at the time they were built (1700) other violin makers were making even more costly violins. Those more costly violins did not, at that time, sell for as much as the Stradivarius violins, nor do they even today sell for as much. How can you reconcile this with the statement that prices depend upon, or are affected by, costs?

14. The average cost of the resources used in producing X is \$5, where cost is interpreted as the highest sacrificed use value. On the other hand, if these resources were to be used elsewhere, their sacrificed value of output here, \$6, is their cost. What will make these two different "costs" of the same resources converge to the same value?

15. "The free-enterprise, capitalist system is a system of consumer sovereignty. Consumer preferences determine what shall be produced and how much shall be produced." Evaluate.

23

PRICING AND PRODUCTION IN PRICE-SEARCHERS' MARKETS

Earlier, in Chapter 11, the price-searchers' market classification was introduced to augment the range of market-exchange behavior explainable by demand and supply. The extent to which sellers could sell all they wanted at the equilibrium price differed from that of price-takers' markets. In price-searchers' markets, sellers were willing to sell more than buyers would purchase even at the equilibrium price. Furthermore, in a price-takers' market, price seemed to be set by an impersonal market mechanism, and the sellers and buyers had no alternative but to take that price. In price-searchers' markets, the sellers were faced with a negatively sloped demand schedule and had the task of setting or administering the price—not, however, independently of the forces of market demand and supply. The purpose of introducing these two types of markets was to show how demand analysis explained pricing tactics of price-searchers in their efforts to expand the range of sale of goods. This avoided the erroneous impression that demand-and-supply analysis applies only to impersonal price-takers' markets in which price is set by forces beyond the control of any single seller.

Price-searchers differ from price-takers not only in that the former administer or set prices via various pricing strategies, but also in that they advertise and hold inventories. These and other differences in behavior can be explained by postulating that price-searchers are faced with a negatively sloping demand curve of their products. We have already shown how a negative functional relationship between amount sold and price charged would require firms to search for the wealth-maximizing price instead of finding it ready made in the market. General Motors announces the prices of its cars; Parker Pen

Company does the same for its pens. The local restaurant sets its prices, and so does the local druggist and grocer. Each could have charged a higher price without losing all its sales, and each could have charged a lower price as a means of increasing the amount demanded (not of increasing the demand schedule). It seems as if each could set prices arbitrarily and without regard to market demand and production conditions. Yet they cannot get by with *any* price; some prices will yield bigger profits than others. Which price will make the most profits for the business, and by what strategy can it be found? What restrictions are placed on the permissible prices by the conditions and costs of production? These are some of the questions we shall investigate.

Two Types of Monopolies

Price-searchers' markets are often called monopolistic markets because the seller has the power to change price. But, if we are to avoid analytic error, we must draw a distinction between two different situations, both of which are commonly called monopolistic. Perhaps less confusion would have been engendered if one had been called monopoly "type 1" and the other "type 2."

TYPE-1 MONOPOLY

Historically, monopoly referred to a grant of government power to restrict certain sellers from the market. The "type-1" monopolists were those who were given access to the market (and protected from the competition of those who were denied free access). In this sense, type-1 monopoly is the negation of free access to the market—i.e., of open markets. We shall call sellers who are protected from open-market competition of other sellers type-1 or legal monopolists.[1]

Any of the following, if true, would be examples of type-1 monopoly—legal restriction on competitors' access to exchange markets: Du Pont persuades the U.S. government to prohibit one of Du Pont's competitors (e.g., the Stauffer Chemical Company) from selling a certain good that Du Pont now sells or from selling below some specified minimum price; or Du Pont uses the law to prevent Stauffer from exceeding some sales quota; or General Motors, by law or privately administered threats, prohibits the sale of Fords, Valiants, or Ramblers at prices

[1] Type-1 monopoly has had a colorful and persisting history. Elizabeth I, to mention a most honorable monarch, granted Essex a monopoly on the importation and sale of white wines, and Raleigh possessed the monopoly rights to sale of playing cards. The French crown retained the monopoly for itself of the sale of salt. Reasons for monopolies should not be hard to deduce. We have, in fact, already seen in the preceding chapter how in price-takers' markets the threat of losses from demand reductions or entry of more efficient producers is used as a reason for erecting legal barriers to market access.

below those to be determined by General Motors; or a labor group prevents other workers from offering to work for lower wages.

TYPE-2 MONOPOLY

Any seller facing a negatively sloped demand curve will be called a type-2 monopolist—no matter why he is faced with that kind of demand. This means that a type-2 monopolist may or may not be a type-1 monopolist at the same time. In this chapter we shall assume no type-1 monopoly situations. In other words, entry to the market is open to all, given their talents and productive abilities. Yet type-2 monopoly can exist for other reasons. What are some of these other reasons for a price-searchers' market (type-2 monopoly)?

Oligopoly. There may be many producers of a *homogeneous* product, but some may produce so much that variations in their output will shift the aggregate supply a perceptible amount along the market-demand schedule. Thus, although steel is produced by over one hundred companies in the United States, many are big enough so that if any of them cut production in half, the output of the industry would be reduced enough to cause a rise in price—even though all firms produced identical steel and sold it under identical sales conditions. U.S. Steel Corporation certainly has the power to raise the price of steel if it is willing to reduce its output and suffer the consequences. Standard Oil of New Jersey could boost the price of gasoline if it reduced its output. Although gasoline may be the same among different producers (and we do not insist that it is), a seller could still have a large enough portion of supply to affect price. Economics has a classificatory name for this situation: oligopoly, meaning a few sellers (from Greek *oligi* for "few" and *polein* for "sell").

A question we shall pose but *not* answer is, "Why are some goods produced under conditions of oligopoly instead of with so many small sellers as to have a price-takers' market?" Except in the case for which special laws are passed to prohibit the entry of new firms, we can give no satisfactory reason other than the question-begging remark that it depends upon the technological characteristics of the product or the production process—e.g., large complexes of productive equipment are sometimes more efficient, so not enough small firms can coexist to make each of them "insignificant."

Product differentiation. Some people think that most product differentiation is silly. Are Chesterfields not the same as Lucky Strikes, Cokes the same as Pepsis, and Palmolive the same as Lux? However, although the physical differences may be trivial, in the minds of some customers they exist and are significant. All men are created equal; yet women are disconcertingly choosy about them. Palmolive is green, and Lux is white. Some girls are blondes, and some are brunettes. The difference between women's clothes is in large part merely a matter of looks or some other "trivial" differences. The difference between mink and rabbit fur is slight, except perhaps to minks and rabbits. Yet the public's preference among them is enormous, even if it is all a matter of looks and feel. The difference between two gasoline stations may be in their location, some hundred feet apart. Yet that is enough to give one a preference. Ridiculous? Not in the eyes of the customer. The attendant may be more pleasant and cordial. Irrelevant? Not in the opinion of real people. How many marital mates are chosen on more substantial grounds? That is, differences that do not "matter" to us will matter to others—and *they* may think that what matters to *us* is of no matter. You may think it really of no matter whether you eat meat or fish on Friday, or pork rather than beef, or meat rather than vegetables, or walk to the left or right of your lady, or rest or work on Sunday; but many other people do and have killed people over such "trivial" issues. You could declare them to be prejudiced, ignorant, or discriminatory, but all you mean is that their tastes or preferences differ from yours.

Can you be sure that steel, coal, gasoline, oil, aluminum, copper, etc., are really homogeneous among different producers? Steel comes in thousands of varieties, grades, qualities, and specifications. Firms specialize in various types of steel. Similarly, manufacturers of corn flakes, milk, and bread turn out different products. The differences among these products may appear to be "trivial" and not "fundamental"—just as the differences among women may be trivial and not fundamental; but to young men there is a detectable difference, even if only in the superficial appearance. And this should give us reason to pause before confidently asserting that buyers who discriminate among brands of cigarettes, aspirin, paper tissues, soap, corn flakes, or canned milk are irrational or uninformed.

Trivial features can make an enormous difference in sales if the two items sell at the same price. The difference between two cola drinks, Coke and Pepsi, is indeed trivial in my opinion; yet if the former were priced 25 percent higher, I would still take Coke. But at a 100 percent difference in price, Pepsi would capture a dominant if not entire portion of my cola purchase. (Are your preferences as discriminatory?) The smaller the difference between prices of goods, the greater is the influence of any other difference on the purchase decision. Let the price difference increase, and the trivial differences are dominated by the increased pecuniary differences; this is, of course, merely an application of our old friend the law of demand.

Much product differentiation is "natural," and no one else, try as hard as he can, can duplicate the product or service. Bing Crosby, Elizabeth Taylor, Bob Hope, and Arnold Palmer have attributes that no other person can duplicate. Each is a monopolist with respect to the service he renders. Crosby can raise his fees and still perform, even if less frequently. There is no legal restriction against anyone else's trying to sing like Bing Crosby, but the consumer can tell the differences even without trademarks or copyrights.

Some of these differences in preferences may result from ignorance (not stupidity) of some people. You may not know that the portable electric typewriter sold by Sears is precisely the same as the Smith typewriter, except for the shape of the exterior shell. The price of the two is different, if you don't shop around for special sales or discounts. Some people do not know this, and hence they pay a higher price for some "identical" item (assuming that the value of the superficial design difference is less than the price difference). However, to point out that such behavior reflects ignorance is to say nothing useful, since everything we do reflects a lack of perfect knowledge. To say that buying behavior is based on ignorance would be more meaningful if by that one meant that it is based on the high cost of acquiring more information—usually because the extra cost is expected to exceed the value of the extra information. For example, why do I persist in buying gasoline from the local distributor when it happens to be selling today at a lower price three blocks farther down the street? Simply because I don't know it is cheaper there. You may know it, but how am I supposed to know that if I drive around those three blocks I'll find a station selling gasoline at a cheaper price—let alone considerations of convenience, speed, and quality of service.

But elimination of ignorance, if you knew how to do it, would not eliminate preferences. People would still not think that all goods of all sellers are very much alike, so that a seller of a preferred product would be able to raise his price relative to that of any other seller without losing all his sales. If every person evaluated all the various goods precisely in the same way that all other people did, *and* if there were enough sellers so that no one supplied enough to shift the supply up or down along the community's demand, then, and only then, could price-searchers' markets be avoided. But such a revision of the world is simply impossible.

A price-searchers' market based on product differentiation is called "monopolistic competition." The term "monopolistic" concentrates attention on the "uniqueness" or single-seller aspect of a differentiated product, and "competition" emphasizes the context of open markets. But it is not entirely a felicitous expression, because it obscures the difference between (1) natural differences that persist despite free access to open markets and (2) legal, contrived, or extra-legal barriers to access to the market—i.e., a closed market.

Price and Output in Price-Searchers' Markets with Full Knowledge of Demand and Cost

If the price-searcher has full knowledge of demand and of costs of alternative output programs, he can easily ascertain his maximum-wealth price and production program. To illustrate this, assume the contemplated output program is for one year, so that an increase in the rate implies also a proportionate increase in the planned volume.

The costs of alternative output programs (different annual rates and planned volumes for one year) are assumed to be those given in Table 22–1 of Chapter 22 and graphed here in Figure 23–1. The average costs and the marginal costs are graphed and labeled as *AC* and *MC*. The demand conditions are given in Table 23–1 and are portrayed in Figure 23–1 as the demand curve (average

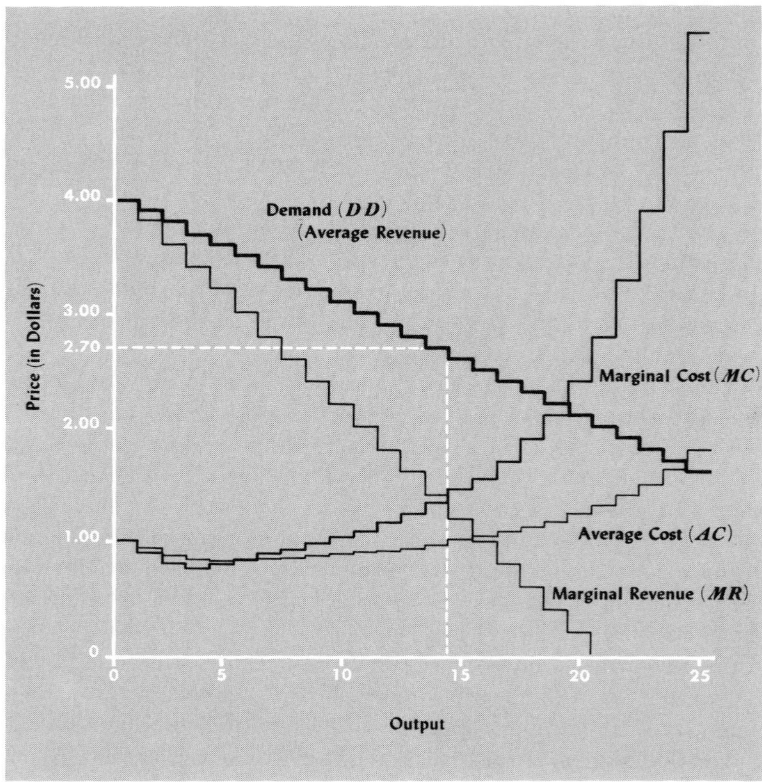

FIGURE 23–1. Costs and demand for price-searcher with profit-maximizing output program and price.

revenue) and the marginal-revenue curve, labeled respectively *DD* and *MR*. The output program that maximizes the firm's wealth is the program of fourteen units. These can be sold at a price of \$2.70, with an average cost of 99 cents. The profit is \$23.95. If a larger output (for instance, fifteen units) were to be sold, the price would have to be lower (i.e., \$2.60) and the average cost would be greater (\$1.02, compared to 99 cents). However—since the marginal revenue at fifteen units is \$1.20, which is less than the marginal cost, \$1.55—the extra sale is not enough to compensate for the reduced gain on each unit sold. Therefore, since marginal revenue falls below marginal cost beyond fourteen units, the output program of fourteen units is the profit-maximizing output.

Table 23–1

DEMAND FOR PRICE-SEARCHERS' PRODUCT

Price	Quantity Purchased In One Year	Total Revenue	Marginal Revenue
$4.00	1	$ 4.00	$4.00
3.90	2	7.80	3.80
3.80	3	11.40	3.60
3.70	4	14.80	3.40
3.60	5	18.00	3.20
3.50	6	21.00	3.00
3.40	7	23.80	2.80
3.30	8	26.40	2.60
3.20	9	28.80	2.40
3.10	10	31.00	2.20
3.00	11	33.00	2.00
2.90	12	34.80	1.80
2.80	13	36.40	1.60
2.70	14	37.80	1.40
2.60	15	39.00	1.20
2.50	16	40.00	1.00
2.40	17	40.80	.80
2.30	18	41.40	.60
2.20	19	41.80	.40
2.10	20	42.00	.20
2.00	21	42.00	.00
1.90	22	41.80	—.20
1.80	23	41.40	—.40
1.70	24	40.80	—.60
1.60	25	40.00	—.80
1.50	26	39.00	—1.00
1.40	27	37.80	—1.20
1.30	28	36.40	—1.40
1.20	29	34.80	—1.60

The seller could, instead, have set any price he wants to if he is prepared to bear the consequences. At $1.60 he will sell twenty-five units and lose $5. At a price of $3 he can sell eleven units, but he will gain only $22.90, compared to $23.95 at a price of $2.70. His market demand and cost conditions, along with the desire for more wealth, constrain him toward the price of $2.70.

The Search for Wealth-Maximizing Price and Output with Incomplete Information

If it were true that businessmen had knowledge of the demand curve facing them, and *if* they knew what it would be in the future, and *if* they knew their cost conditions for various possible output programs, then the preceding analysis would be sufficient to show *how* people would shift resources toward or to wealth-maximizing points (with due allowance for the possible sacrifices in other sources of utility that may accompany the revised price-output program).

In fact, however, the search for the price-output programs of greater wealth is done by people who do *not* have perfect foresight and who therefore do not have cost or demand data as explicit as those in our earlier numerical examples. They may know all the laws of economics; they may know that an increased demand indicates greater wealth for higher-price–larger-output programs. But how do they know which demand, if any, has really increased and how much? Perhaps an observed increase in sales is merely a transient, random fluctuation. How do businessmen know when they are charging the wealth-maximizing price?

With complete information, it is a trivial task to find the wealth-maximizing price. But with incomplete information the businessman's task is very difficult. The task of the economist or student of economic affairs is slightly different; his is to ascertain the direction in which specified changes in demand and cost conditions will modify the wealth-maximizing price-output programs. The economist can postulate changes in these external conditions; and then, with his principles of demand and cost conditions, he can deduce the direction in which the new wealth-maximizing price-output programs are shifted. But that is not all that the economist should do; he should also show how businessmen, even in a state of incomplete knowledge about demand and cost conditions, are induced by changes in demand and cost conditions to adjust their price-output programs in the directions indicated by economic theory.

To see how the real world responds to actual but not fully known demand and cost conditions, we abandon the fiction of full knowledge and work in a context of partial ignorance—which is *not* to be identified with stupidity or irrationality. The price-searching seller must feel like a gambler at the racetrack: there is *a* horse that will provide his biggest returns if he bets on it, but *which* one is it? If you told him to bet on the *winning* horse, he would say, "What kind of prescription or rule of behavior is that? What good does it do to formalize a rule for maximizing my wealth if I do not know how to implement the rule?" Of course, the seller would like to announce a price that, given the market demand and supply, is his wealth-maximizing price. But he can only search for it.

Consider the problem faced by an airplane company. It has just designed a plane which it believes will make a good replacement for the DC-3—the Douglas two-engine piston-prop plane that was the Model-T Ford of the airplane industry. What price should it announce, and what scale of production should it plan? This is precisely the kind of question faced by Douglas when it started to make the DC-8 jet, and by Boeing with its 707, and by Convair with its 880. Only Boeing guessed right. The demand curve for the Boeing 707 did lie above the cost curve for a region that Boeing managed to find, whereas if the demand curve for Douglas and Convair commercial jets ever did lie above their cost curves, they weren't able to find out. If they had known where it was, before they decided to produce, they would have saved the stockholders scores of millions of dollars.

Similarly, when Ford decided to produce the Edsel, he clearly misjudged the location of the demand curve for Edsel cars—to his loss of millions. Packard Bell Electronics also badly misjudged—not where the demand curve was for an important electrical item which it sold to the government, but instead the costs; the cost curve was above the demand curve for the price-output program it selected. Philco Electronics produced a "futuristic model" television set in 1960, for which the directors estimated the demand curve was above the average-cost curve at the planned output program. They were wrong—but they didn't find out until they had lost considerable wealth. Chrysler designed an automobile in 1958 for which it "misplaced" the demand curve. As it was, the demand curve was under the average-cost curve. Chrysler lost millions, and this was evidenced by the decrease in the value of its stock during that year.

But there is no need to talk of the giants to demonstrate uncertainty, ignorance, and fallibility. A corner restaurant must decide what prices to set and what volume to plan for. And the same goes for the local gasoline-station operator, the drug store, grocery store, discount house, automobile repair shop, as well as for General Motors, U.S. Steel, General Electric, and Du Pont. All are in the same boat. We don't hear much about those who lose wealth in this task compared to those who succeed. Success enables one to grow and become well known. Failure possesses other attributes. There are no magazines called *Death* or *Misfortune*.

Output and Price Response to Demand Changes

Let us first see how changes in demand for existing goods are revealed to existing producers and how their production programs are revised.

Buyers shop sporadically and accumulate goods for subsequent consumption. Sellers know that there is a difference between mere fluctuations in sales and fundamental changes in demand (where a fundamental change can be considered as a change in the average around which the sales rates fluctuate). They could handle these transient fluctuations by letting price rise or fall at each instant so as to balance out demand with existing supply, much as stock-market prices match momentary demand and supply. However, *it will pay sellers to maintain an inventory of buffer stocks to meet these transient fluctuations in daily market demands rather than lose sales or try to produce to order instantly.* Inventories make the current *momentary* supply schedule a horizontal line at the selling price, out to the limits of the existing inventory. This is in sharp contrast to the price-takers' markets, where the momentary supply is represented by a vertical line—and each seller sees a horizontal demand curve for his goods. However, it is only for the transient demand fluctuations that inventories serve as a buffer stock. Should demand increase, the sales rate increase would deplete inventories and require higher replacement rates to accommodate larger rates of sales, the costs will rise for higher production rates, and the new momentary supply curve will be horizontal at a higher price.

An increase in demand will mean a larger average rate of sales. Inventories will have to be replenished at a higher rate of production. The higher persisting demand will involve higher marginal costs of production at a higher rate. To maintain a higher rate, a higher price will have to be available. The higher price will be maintainable because of the increased demand. The sequence of effects from increased demand to inventory depletion, to replenishment of inventories by higher rates of production, and to higher costs and then prices is identical with that explained earlier, in Chapter 8, when tracing the demand-increase effects on the price of meat.[2]

Price-takers' markets have more frequently changing prices within a narrow range than do price-searchers' markets. But prices in price-takers' markets are not necessarily more responsive, less rigid, or more adaptive to changed market conditions than are prices in price-searchers' markets. Because of the economy of inventory availability, price-searchers can provide the transient changes in amounts wanted by demanders without having to change price. This kind of stability is not a reflection of price rigidity or power of seller to control price. It reflects instead the horizontal momentary supply out of inventory in the current market.

If demand falls, the theory and the evidence are that the price falls and is accompanied by a reduction in purchases and consumption. In other words, the preceding adjustment process is applicable to decreases in demand. *Changes*

[2] If the larger output is larger in *volume* as well as rate, and *if* unit costs fall sufficiently with larger volume, then prices, which may first have risen before output increased, will again fall, possibly to lower levels than originally. In any event, the increased demand is translated into an increased output.

in demand and cost conditions are effective in inducing output changes even though firms do not know the precise demand and cost conditions or the new wealth-maximizing output and price program. A trial-and-error search process is used and will induce convergence toward that wealth-maximizing program. The farther the actual output program is from the optimal, the smaller are profits or the greater are losses—both of which will increase the probability of the firm's having to quit production or change its tactics.

Entry of New Firms in Response to Demand Changes

The preceding analysis has concentrated on the price and output response of firms already in this "industry." There is also an adjustment as people switch jobs and as firms switch to new products. Output of particular goods expands with higher demand, both because existing producers increase output and because new firms enter into production.

Increased wealth of an existing firm cannot be concealed. Its expansion, the behavior of the owners, and the larger number of customers are visible. If the firm enlarges, if the owners drive more expensive cars and their homes become more expensive, you have telltale indicators. Salesmen of competing firms know who is getting the sales. In various ways, the word gets around. As a result, other firms try to copy this firm. Perhaps employees leave and organize their own company, taking part of the company's "know how"; for example, hundreds of firms have been created by former employees of the earliest electronic-computer companies.

Other firms will find it profitable to shift production toward closer substitutes for the good whose demand has increased. If the production of steel, Cokes, Fords, or Arrow shirts becomes more profitable, other producers will produce close, if not perfect, substitutes and reduce the profits of the first producer as some customers switch part of their purchases to other products and sellers. Goods are substitutable in one degree or another, and a higher demand for steel can be attenuated by an increased use of wood or brick. Or an increased demand for a certain kind of Ford will within a year bring close substitutes from General Motors, Chrysler, American Motors, or foreign producers.

Under the competitive open-market pressures, other producers will enter the market for this and related goods. These other producers will bid away the resources that the price-searcher has been using. His assemblers, supervisors, designers, production engineers, salesmen, managers, and research staff will find competitors making offers for their services. The cost of keeping resources rises. Even the cost of having the owner stay in his business must be valued at a higher figure; the more others are willing to offer for his services, the higher are the costs he must impute to continuing in his own business.

Both of these competitive market forces—(1) on the product side, taking away sales; and (2) on the resource side, raising the costs of a business—operate until the prospect of further increase in wealth disappears. The effect here is the same as in the situation, discussed earlier, of middlemen eroding away each other's profits. Prices to consumers are reduced after the initial prices increase, and the rise in prices of the productive resources gives resource owners a higher income. With open markets to other firms, the gains from modifying production in the directions more demanded by the public are distributed via lower prices to consumers and higher earnings to the productive resources. Whether it be a price-takers' market or a price-searchers' market, the same forces operate. Only a price-searchers' market based on legal monopoly (type 1), with imposed or contrived barriers to entry, will reduce or thwart that revision of production and redistribution of the gains from revised production.

If demand falls, the analysis is reversed. A reduced demand implies a lower price and output. The value imputed to resources used to produce that product falls as the product prices and output are reduced. Resources currently devoted to this particular good will be shifted to other activities, where they can earn more than their reduced value here. Existing producers will reduce output, and in time some will leave the industry.

By selective differential survival, growth, and imitation by competitors, the population of business firms converges toward the maximum-wealth output and price programs. Add to these factors the activities of "raiders" who think they know how to run a business better than the present owner and offer to buy the firm in an effort to test their superiority. The new owner pays less than he thinks he can earn with the firm, while the old owner gets more than he thinks he could earn. The resources are shifted toward higher-valued uses—if these forecasts or conjectures are correct. If not, the new buyer discovers his error and can sell out, but only by bearing the loss. The more accurate forecasts *yield* higher gains and enable the higher-valued uses to displace less appropriate uses of resources.

The simple, unemotional statements of the preceding paragraph are full of heartbreak and drama. When demand falls for any good, some people find their current services no longer so valuable. They cannot keep their jobs at the current rate of pay. Substantial wage cuts or movements to new jobs are indicated. Business owners experience changes in the value of their plant and equipment. Either they revalue their resources downward and accept the lower value they can get by staying in the particular business, or they sell the assets at the lower price.

The fundamental institutional feature of the preceding adjustment process is private property, not price-takers' versus price-searchers' markets. In both market situations, the resource owners bear the wealth changes and are induced to make revisions in the uses to which the resources are put. In a nonprivate-property system, there is less specialization and voluntary choice of the kinds of resources whose value changes a person must bear; and resource-use decisions are less influenced by the market-value changes in resources, since each person's wealth is less identified with value effects of the way each resource is used.

Some Confusions about Price-Searchers' Markets

ARBITRARY ADMINISTRATION OF PRICES

The fact that prices in price-searchers' markets are relatively stable, that they all change at about the same time, and that one firm usually acts as a price leader has supported what we shall call the modern folklore and mythology that in such markets dominant firms arbitrarily administer or set prices.[3] Therefore, it is alleged, unless price-searchers administer their prices with responsible, enlightened self-restraint, government must be ready to intervene in price-searchers' markets to protect the overriding public interest. It is difficult to conjure more confused, misleading, and erroneous propositions than the assertions and conclusions in the two preceding sentences. Insofar as they have meaning at all, neither is correct. Usually the conclusions are related to "administered" prices, as if these were something different from prices in any other market. Most of the discussion about "administered" prices is nonsense. For example, it has been said that U.S. Steel, General Motors, and large drug companies set the price of their products by administrative decision without regard to public interest. Such sellers do, indeed, set their prices. They do not find or take them in the market the way wheat sellers do. The Aluminum Company of America announces the price of aluminum; R.C.A. sets the price of its radios and television sets.

Price-setting versus equilibrium-price search. What does all this reflect? Simply that each seller must search for the wealth-maximizing price.[4] But everyone does this, even the lettuce farmer, the commonest laborer, and the steel company. It's just easier to find that price in price-takers' markets. The lettuce farmer "sets" his price at the level that will maximize his wealth. All lettuce farmers in the area, for a given quality of lettuce, will find that price is the same for all of them. Yet each one *could* have sold his product at a *lower* price. But his selfish disregard of "public interest" made him "set" the price at which his income would be greatest—in this case the highest price possible, since he can

[3] "Folklore and mythology" is admittedly name-calling and simply is a way of indicating which theory you think best explains observed economic events. There are people who regard the economic analysis presented here as mythology and folklore. What is the truth? As we said at the beginning, that must be judged in the light of both the internal logical consistency of the whole theory and the conformity of actual empirical facts with its implications. We first presented what economic theory says because we believe the evidence provides overwhelming support for it in all its implications.

[4] To avoid the impression that we are assuming businessmen have no goals other than maximum wealth, reread pages 128–130.

sell all he has at that price. At a higher price he would sell none. He has a wide range of prices he can set, from zero up to the highest price at which he can sell any. This highest possible price is determined by the market and the total supply of competitors (including other commodities).

The situation is no different for the "price-searcher," who "sets" his price. His best price, the one that maximizes his wealth, also depends upon the demand and supply conditions. Neither self-restraint nor concern for interests of other people prevents him from raising prices. It is the effect on his wealth that restrains him; higher prices may lower his net receipts.

That same motive keeps price up to where it is in *every* market. The poorest common laborer or retail clerk or employee *could* charge a lower price and be poorer; but because he, too, is greedy and wants more wealth for himself, he charges whatever price will give him the maximum of income. Thus, Du Pont "sets" *a* price of nylon. Although it does *not* charge the highest possible price at which it could sell *any* of its output, it seeks the wealth-maximizing price determined (but not readily disclosed) by the market. It might charge less or more. But the price it sets is the one it hopes is the wealth-maximizing price inherent in the market demand and supply conditions. It cannot discover this price as easily as the price-taker can; it has to resort to trial and error, never being sure it has found it. Because of this exploratory charging of prices above or below the "best" price the market will tolerate, some people are misled into thinking that Du Pont, U.S. Steel, or other sellers can *set* or *administer* any price it pleases in a monopolistic, noncompetitive sense.

We have been considering sellers who are trying to maximize wealth, whether they be price-takers (i.e., highest price-taker competitors) or monopolistic, price-searching competitors. *All* of them seek the wealth-maximizing price *allowed* by the market. Whether sellers are described as "setting" prices or merely searching for the best price the market will allow them to set, consistent with their desire to maximize their wealth, is all a matter of semantics. Call them "monopolist-administered prices" if you want to make the seller look like a powerful, selfish, noncompeting, economic royalist. Call them "market-revealed, market-demand-and-supply-determined prices" if you wish to de-emphasize individual motivation for more wealth. All prices in all markets are administered in the sense that each person decides at which price he shall sell (from the range of prices that the market will tolerate). But the parenthetical clause reminds us that all prices depend upon consumers' demand and prices and costs of production of all other goods.

Price-searchers and price increases. One complaint should be forestalled immediately. You may some day hear that price-searcher firms restrict or limit output *in order to increase prices.* Despite the superficial appeal of that allegation, a little thought should expose its foolishness. If the price-searcher were interested in *raising* price, he could always raise it *still* higher and sell less until he sells just one unit—or none at all. But his total profits or wealth would be reduced, because the reduction in sales more than offsets the higher price. What he does is restrict his output to match the sales at prices that maximize his wealth.

Does the price-taker, who has no power over prices by varying his output, restrict output in order to raise prices? No. But, as we shall see, the price-taker does in fact restrict *his* output—in order to maximize his wealth. He could produce more than he does, but it would add more to his cost than to his receipts. The marginal costs of producing more would be greater than the marginal revenue; hence, his profits or wealth would decrease. Therefore, he decides to adjust his output so as to avoid reducing his wealth. And this is precisely what the price-searcher does. He adjusts his output to maximize his wealth. No bigger and no smaller rate of output is desired. He does not restrict his output simply to raise price. Like everyone else, he selects the output that he hopes will maximize his wealth. So, of course, do all firms. And the prices and sales of firms are interdependent. Hence, they watch each other closely and, like dogs chasing a rabbit, move together, even in those cases where there is no central director or real leader, simply because they seek the same quarry.

Justifiable price changes. Compounding the confusion are the excuses and public utterances made by price-searchers who seek to "justify" their actions, as if they really did have the power to raise prices and get more income whenever they wanted to or whenever they thought they had a "justifiable" reason to want larger profits—justifiable in the eyes of public opinion rather than in the market-demand and cost conditions. Instructive in this respect is the U.S. Steel price-rise episode of 1962.

Roger Blough, President of the United States Steel Corporation, announced an increase in prices, and he attempted to "justify" it by asserting that costs were higher and that more income was needed to finance new investment. In the first place, the *use* he intended to make of the increased wealth (if the price rise increased it) is irrelevant to the *ability* to get it. Whether Mr. Blough intended to spend more money for a fancy office or new steel mills has nothing to do with the ability of U.S. Steel to raise prices and thereby get greater profits. In the second place, the fact that his costs had risen does not mean that he could thereby raise prices and get a higher income. Obviously, if that were true, he could let costs mount without limit and simply raise prices to cover them. What he might have said is that costs of all steel producers were rising and that the new wealth-maximizing price had changed, and that U.S. Steel, in the interest of maximizing its wealth, intended to move its selling price to that new equilibrium price. Or possibly the demand for steel had increased in the meantime. If the market demand and *industry-wide* cost conditions had changed, a higher price would result in larger profits than if the price had not been changed. That new price would succeed in the sense that other producers would also find it more profitable to raise their prices.

If Mr. Blough had said simply that U.S. Steel, like other firms, was seeking the wealth-maximizing output and price program and that demand and cost conditions had changed so that the "equilibrium" price was now a higher price, would President Kennedy have been misled into so strong an application of governmental pressures to prevent the price increase? Would he have said that U.S. Steel owners should not seek to maximize their wealth—that they should be different from other businessmen, teachers, writers, engineers, or common laborers and that they, in particular, ought to sacrifice wealth in order to keep down the price of steel temporarily?

Unfortunately, Mr. Blough's statement fostered the impression that he really did have the power to raise price higher to get more income whenever he wanted more, and that only his noble, statesmanlike restraint from seeking maximum profits because of a concern for some amorphous "public interest" had kept prices down theretofore. We do not say it is unfortunate that he lacks that power; but it is unfortunate that he talked as if he did have that power, because he does not have it. The income-maximizing price is controlled by competition in market demand and costs. The steel companies want to find and quote that new wealth-maximizing price when demand and supply conditions change. But U.S. Steel hasn't the power to get more revenue simply by raising prices *whenever* it wants more wealth.

Dependence upon market conditions was appreciated by Mr. Blough. At the time he announced higher prices by U.S. Steel, he realized that unless other companies also raised their prices and *thereby had greater profits* (than if they did not raise them), the price rise would not succeed. Most other companies in fact concluded that higher prices would not give them greater wealth, simply because market conditions of demand and costs had not changed in that direction; they did not follow the lead of U.S. Steel. This suggestion of leadership in price setting again reminds one of the leadership of the first dog in a pack of hounds in pursuit of a rabbit. That dog is the leader in the sense that all are pursuing a common objective, and therefore they will be observed to move together—if and only if the lead dog follows the rabbit. Many of the dogs may even conduct their chase not only by trying to keep the rabbit in sight but also by using the movements of other dogs as clues to the prey's position. If the leader moves in the wrong direction, the rest will leave him alone as soon as they detect his error. Therefore, the fact that the same firm is almost always the first to make a change and that others almost always follow does not mean that the leader dictates prices to other firms, nor does it imply some tacit agreement not to compete with prices. It can attest to the greater acuity and knowledge of market conditions by the lead firm. If that firm keeps more careful check on cost conditions and on sales rates and general economic conditions, it should be able to detect more reliably the shifts in market conditions. Other firms watch its behavior and then follow, thereby avoiding the costs of maintaining a research staff. If the price change turns out to be a money loser, then "follower" firms will return to the original prices. Then they are the leaders in that return movement.

If Mr. Blough's rationale for higher prices—that price had to be raised in order to get more income—were valid, one could wonder why the price of steel was what it was in the first place. Why not keep on raising price and increasing income indefinitely? Because Mr. Blough used a fallacious argument as a defense of U.S. Steel's pricing policy, the presumption is created that political pressures are necessary in order to prevent prices from being raised inordinately, unreasonably, unjustifiably, and possibly without limit, even to the extent of setting off that modern bogeyman—the "inflationary spiral." [5]

In summary, we are saying that in price-searchers' open markets, the wealth-maximizing price sought by sellers is determined by competitive market demand and cost conditions; that sellers are probing interdependently for that price because it gives a greater income; that price-searchers do not set prices in an act of self-abnegation and change them only when they justifiably need more income; that, in a world of uncertainty and lack of complete knowledge about the equilibrium price, the process of search by trial and error for that equilibrium price will sometimes give the appearance of arbitrary administration and setting of prices by price leaders or market dominators, who in fact can be viewed as analogous to the hound that is the best pursuer of the rabbit.

PRICE RIGIDITY

Charges that price-searchers administer prices regardless of demand and supply—or that the more concentrated the output of an industry in a few large firms, the more inflexible the price—are refuted by all the available evidence. The number or size of firms in an industry has no statistical connection with the frequency or magnitude of price change. Yet to this day, some Congressional committees are duped by publicity-seeking economic mythologists who repeat in solemn testimony an old wives' tale that was born some thirty years ago as a result of careless and naïve statistical analysis. The myth is that administered prices are set and kept rigid in industries characterized by high degrees of concentration of output in a few firms. Also it is asserted that output fluctuates more in those rigid price industries than where prices are not so administered. The myth lives on and on, sometimes buttressed with the same errors of statistical methods applied to more recent data.

What are the early data that were so naïvely interpreted? Initially, price

[5] Interesting enough, in 1963, a year later, the price of steel was raised immediately after the U.S. Tariff Commission announced it would open hearings to decide whether to impose higher taxes on imports of foreign steel—and to impose them retroactively on all prior imports at prices deemed too low. That simple announcement immediately induced foreigners to reduce shipments to the United States. For government officials to protest the rise in the market price of steel would have been somewhat awkward, since the government had granted domestic steel producers (type-1) monopoly protection from continued foreign imports.

data were collected for goods like automobiles. The price of automobiles was reported to be stable and invariant because the list—or recommended—price announced by the automobile companies stayed unchanged throughout the year. One of the first things a person learns in shopping for a car is that the list price is not the selling price, except at the beginning of the new-car season. Immediately thereafter, the salesmen's pencils are sharpened, and the serious shopper is offered "special" deals—which in fact are offered to everyone who says he is going to shop around. Yet, the U.S. government's Cost of Living Index at one time used the list price as the actual price.

Despite overwhelming evidence that list prices are not the prices at which purchases occur, prices taken from catalogues and price lists are still collected and reported as *the* prices. For example, the official quoted price of certain kinds of steel does not change for many months. Yet the actual transaction price at which the steel is sold is quite different. Sometimes it is lower and sometimes higher. Discounts for cash vary; speed of delivery and special services vary from week to week; quantity discounts are common. A steel purchase is a complex transaction. Extensive studies of actual contract transaction prices of steel show that the actual prices are highly variable from week to week, despite an apparent stability of the official quoted price. Furthermore, even if one firm's actual prices were its list prices, one would have to observe *all* the firms all the time to know what was happening to price.

The current assessment of the price-rigidity allegation has been summarized characteristically by a president of the American Economic Association:

> Economists have long struggled to find a rational explanation for prolonged price rigidity, which is in general as inadvisable for profit maximizing monopolists as it is impossible for "price-taker" industries. Putting aside minor or special circumstances (the cost of a price change; the procedural delays in cartel or public regulation), they have failed to discover any such explanation. It appears that the real world has been equally remiss in supplying the phenomena they were seeking to explain.[6]

EXCESSIVE ADVERTISING

Price-takers do not advertise, since they can sell all they have available at the current price. Nor would advertising by any seller enable him to get a higher price, for other sellers would provide the increased amount demanded. Only if the price-takers advertised so as to raise the demand for the whole industry's product would a higher price be possible. On the other hand, price-searchers are faced with limited sales at existing prices; each is eager to sell more at the current price but will not cut price below the wealth-maximizing price in order to sell more. Advertising his product informs potential customers of his existence

[6] George J. Stigler, "Administered Prices and Oligopolistic Inflation," *The Journal of Business of the University of Chicago,* 35, No. 1 (January 1962), 8.

and goods. Information about possible sources of goods is a scarce resource, as anyone knows who enters a strange town and wonders about accommodations and restaurants. Often we forget this when we see advertising that tells *us* nothing we didn't already know. If a seller wants to sell one thousand items and decides to advertise, how does he know which thousand persons are most likely to buy? He doesn't. So he advertises over a wide group of people, hoping thereby to inform those currently interested in his type of product. When I see ads for ladies' clothes in the magazine I get, there has been a waste of paper and of the advertiser's money. Is the advertising therefore wasted? Not at all. The advertiser would be delighted to advertise in selective ways not noticed by people who would not possibly be interested in the product. But that is more expensive and uses more resources than some methods of general advertising. Much criticism of advertising reflects failure to take account of this lack of ability to identify in advance each potential buyer or to advertise in ways that will be noticed only by them. If we knew which people were going to have flat tires at which times, repair cars would be at the spot ready to give service, and that would be less expensive than carrying around fifth tires. The fire-escape sign is useless on many nights, but should the light be turned off when it is not needed? Similarly, in school are we not taught several things that some of us will never use again later? Was there a waste of resources in that act of "indiscriminate" teaching? In exactly the same sense, some advertising is "wasteful"—which means only that if we all knew more, we could save resources.

Some advertising is wastefully "duplicative" in that it consists of unsubstantiated ours-is-better-than-theirs exhortation. Cigarette and soap advertising is uninformative, and there is obviously too much of it on our television and radio. Billboards are unslightly and block the views. Billions are spent to no benefit of the consumer.

Is this true? Many people think so. But there are reasons to doubt the validity of the charges. In the first place, the amount of advertising on radio and television is the result of the way in which radio and television are paid for. Movie theaters do not show commercials the way television does, because the patron pays for what he wants and thus rewards or punishes producers and guides the pictures produced. On the other hand, illegality of pay television has prevented the viewer from such direct control over the programs shown. It is not surprising that television and radio programs are tied to advertising. One can readily imagine the kinds of programs one would see in movie theaters if patrons could come in free of charge. Special programs appealing to a smaller group would be overruled by mass-media programs because a minority could not concentrate its "dollar votes" on preferred programs; diversity of preferences yield to majority tastes.

Pay television and radio stations now exist, and the advertising is almost completely absent, and the programs of a different quality. If newspapers could not be sold, they would have even more advertising, as is evidenced by the ratio of advertising to news in neighborhood throw-away newspapers. The criticism of advertising on television is not a criticism of advertising; it is a criticism of the system of paying for television and radio programs.

Similarly, the criticism of billboard advertising as obscuring and making the area unsightly is equally appropriate for buildings. The problem is not created by advertising, but by the difficulty of constructing any building without changing the view in ways that some people don't like. To build an apartment to house people and thereby obstruct a view is no different from putting up a sign that obstructs the same view.

Another issue is the uninformative, duplicative, competitive nature of advertising. Camels advertises, and in self-defense Chesterfield has to advertise. The net effect is no gain to anyone except the advertising people. Is there any interpretation other than waste? The charge of waste implies that customers who buy one brand rather than another simply because of that uninformative advertising do so for no *good* reason. When I see people being influenced by inane, tasteless, or substantially empty advertising, I am tempted to regard that advertising as wasteful or harmful. But in doing so, either I fail to comprehend why anyone should be influenced by that kind of advertising, or I think he should not be influenced by it; therefore, I consider it wasteful and bad. However, if I took a less authoritarian, less paternalistic attitude, with more humility and recognition of differences in tastes, I might be willing to entertain the possibility that customers prefer—perhaps for reasons which they have never articulated, could not now readily specify, and leave us wholly unpersuaded—to buy the cigarette that does that advertising rather than the one that does not.

Finally, we consider the situation that is regarded as the clearest use of wasteful advertising: the customer is supposed to be uninformed about various goods, and, as a result, the seller deliberately *misleads* him with advertising. This is, unhappily, a real-world event. There is no dispute that dishonesty is not a trait our society wants to reward. But it is dishonesty that is bad, not advertising. We should not condemn advertising for its dishonesty any more than we condemn political speeches because of dishonest statements. Rival suitors for a maiden's hand are dishonest in their claims of superiority. People are dishonest in daily conversation, in part, by being excessively tactful. As far as dishonesty is concerned, is it as fruitful in advertising as in private conversation? Open advertisements can be seen by competitors, and dishonest statements will more surely be refuted in advertisements.

This excursion into advertising is not designed to show that it is in everyone's eyes a desirable activity, any more than horse racing, gambling, drinking, smoking, modern music, and art are desirable activities. The crux of the defense of advertising is the same as for any other economic activity. The defense of what seems to be wasteful advertising is that to others who pay for it, it does succeed somehow in affecting their utility or that of other people. Those who are affected by it may be unwitting dupes or captives of an environment in which they cannot escape the persistent propaganda that molds their behavior. Like children, their behavior patterns are partly molded by advertising and unhidden persuasion. This may be a correct charge. But what is it proposed therefore to do? The answer to this question reveals the degree to which one is prepared to assert his preferences by use of compulsion in arranging the life and actions of other people. We can be less humble and believe that it is possible to find people and charge them with the responsibility of deciding what can and what cannot be publicly said in advertising and the kinds of consumption that can be tolerated, or we can believe that it is not possible to find such people with any more assurance of lesser consequent "evils."

Do Producers Produce What Is Wanted by Consumers?

This is an appropriate place to examine a pair of complaints about the response of production to demand.

Some consumers believe that they can buy only what producers decide to offer them. To some producers the opposite seems to be true: producers must produce only what the public is willing to buy at prices that will at least equal costs. In fact, neither of these exclusive positions is completely correct, although both contain truths.

One, but not the only, source of incompleteness of the two views is that no one knows exactly what goods people will want to buy. They don't carry placards announcing everything they would be prepared to buy at all possible prices. Furthermore, some goods aren't thought of until seen by the customer, so that some demands are revealed, as it were, only by the appearance on the market of new goods. The development of transistor radios found the market demand ready and waiting for it. No consumer had gone around expressing a desire to buy it; but, once it appeared, the demand was effectively revealed. How many of us who now have stereo records "demanded" them before 1955? New products, varieties, and methods of satisfying consumers are continuously being tested for market demand: power steering, automatic transmissions, television, instant coffee, supermarkets, consumer credit buying, frozen foods, credit cards, electric wrist watches, cordless electric shavers, no-iron fabrics, synthetic fibers, stretch clothes, electric toothbrushes, coin-operated dry-cleaning machines, water-based paints, zippers, hula hoops, etc. In what sense did these represent a response to demand? The hope of increasing wealth provoked someone to invest some of his wealth into producing some new item to test the market demand. The assurance of profit need not be demonstrated in advance. It is enough that there are foolhardy, gambling, venturesome, greedy, optimistic individuals willing to use some of their wealth to produce new goods for which they hope demand will be great enough to yield them profits.

People seek out and respond to market demands and produce what is wanted if the price exceeds the cost unless (and often even if) laws prohibit it. But, and this is the second complaint about the response of production, it is alleged that some goods won't be produced because they must be used jointly with some other as yet unproduced good. For example, Congress, with the support of the President, enacted a law requiring, after 1963, any producer and seller of television sets to sell *only* television sets that can receive all 83 television channels, from channel 2 to 84. Presumably that law was passed because there allegedly was not enough incentive to make all-channel sets, and until sets were made to receive all 83 channels there would be insufficient incentive to telecast on the higher-channel stations, and until the telecasts occurred there was no incentive to make the sets. A "vicious circle" was alleged and apparently believed in Congress. What are the analytical implications and empirical evidence about this "vicious circle"?

Historical facts do not support it. Did automobiles fail to be produced because there were no gasoline stations—or vice versa? Did movie makers not make movies until theaters were built? Did suburban shopping areas not develop at all until everyone moved into the area at once? Did radios wait for radio stations? Did FM receivers fail to be developed because they required transmitters to send FM first? In fact, they developed despite laws restricting FM broadcasting. Did stereo records await stereo record players? Did FM multiplex stereo programs and FM multiplex stereo receivers "bottleneck" each other? Did automobile repair shops and automobiles "bottleneck" each other? Did frozen foods and freezers for home use "bottleneck" each other? Did color television require a law compelling all manufacturers of television sets to include color capabilities?

The examples of FM radio and color television provide direct refutations of the presumed necessity for a law compelling all-channel television receivers. No law required radio manufacturers to make only FM-AM combination radios. They could make any kind. As the design technology improved in the 1950s, FM sets became easier to tune and keep tuned, cheaper, and more reliable. The public demand was evident. FM broadcasters, however, were allowed to use pay FM. They could broadcast music via closed circuits to business and institutions for a monthly fee. The prospect of capturing a profit in FM broadcasting was enhanced by the station owners' opportunity to "own" and sell the broadcast via pay FM. In color television, on the contrary, for a long time the Federal Communications Commission *prohibited* color broadcasts until it could decide on the "best" kind of color system. And when it first decided, it chose wrong. Fortunately, the Korean war forestalled production until the better system became more obvious. The development of color television did not require a law compelling people to buy only television sets with color *and* black-and-white capability.

There is no bottleneck joint-product effect which must be legally broken; there is much evidence from other goods and products refuting that proposition.

The pace of development of joint-use goods depends upon the present wealth value of the prospects of profitable production of all necessary items. *If* the prospect is reduced by prohibiting, threatening, or attenuating ownership and sales rights on any of the jointly used items, their joint development will be inhibited. For example, if stereo record players could not be produced by "wealth-seeking producers," the motivations to produce stereo records would be reduced by the denial of the incentive of a prospective profit, not by an alleged, spurious "bottle-neck-interdependence" effect.

What happened to the alleged vicious circle of new-product interdependence? It never was there in the first place. Perhaps a better question is, "Why should anyone have expected a blockage of development of joint products if the economic analysis given in the preceding chapters is valid?" Specialization of production is the rule in an economy in which exchange and access to the market are permitted. Specialization implies reliance on other people to produce jointly used products as they seek opportunities to increase their wealth. The search for profits is the tie that connects the production of jointly used products. Only if one forgets the incentives and exchange opportunities in a marketplace will he fail to see the coordinated activity of other people. A visitor from Mars might contend that the real world is a much too complicated place for a capitalistic system to operate. He would be surprised that exchange prices and self-interest in a private-property context are capable of organizing a system as complex and productive as those he would see in Western countries. The strongest evidence that can be cited for the validity of economic theory is precisely the observed events in the capitalist economic system. At the most rudimentary level, the theory implies that jointly used products will be produced "independently" even though each assumes the presence of the other. And they are produced by independent producers. Specialization does not imply a lack of coordination, nor does it imply that joint-product profit opportunities will be ignored. In fact, it implies that jointly used goods will be more effectively produced if specialization *is* permitted rather than if one person or firm must do the whole task.

In truth, the vicious circle, bottleneck-product interdependence among jointly used products is a delusion arising from the belief that current output must be carried out on a large scale initially, that people don't have any foresight and are unwilling to invest now in anticipation of future receipts (implying that present capital values are irrelevant), that jointly used products must be produced by the same person because no one can expect other producers to respond to the profit lure of producing anything except the entire package. All these suppositions are disproved by events in the real world.

Questions

1. "If some firms producing *X* have unsold output potential that they would like to use to produce more *X* at current selling prices, if only the market demand were great enough, then the good *X* is not being sold in a price-takers' market." Explain why that conclusion can be drawn.

2. The difference (for pricing and output behavior) between price-takers' and price-searchers' markets can be characterized by a difference in the demand curve facing each seller. Describe the difference in the demand curve.

3. Type-1 monopolies are those resulting from closure, in one degree or another, of the open market to other sellers. In earlier chapters, examples of restrictions on access to the market were given. Can you identify some market closures or restrictions in the field of education? Labor? Agriculture? Business?

4. Market closures need not result in price-searchers' markets, especially if the existing number of sellers is very large. Can you identify or suggest cases where market entry is restricted and yet a price-takers' market exists? (Hint: How about agriculture—e.g., wheat, tobacco, milk producers? Teachers?)

5. Tentatively classify the following, on the basis of your present information, into (a) price-takers, (b) type-1 monopolists, or (c) type-2 monopolists. (Remember, market closure does not necessarily convert a price-takers' to a price-searchers' market.)

Electric company
Railroad
City bus line
Airlines
General Motors Corporation
Corner drug store
Prescription pharmacist
Tobacco producers
Standard Oil Company
U.S. Steel Corporation
Lettuce grower
Carpenter
Electrician
Elizabeth Taylor

6. Is it possible for an economy to be one in which everyone is a type-1 monopolist, and yet everyone is poorer than if there were no restrictions on the open market and with everyone being a price-taker? Explain.

7. a. Can you suggest some good for which the differences among various brands are insignificant? (Hint: Sugar, flour, aspirin, tires, dog foods, bread, milk, soap, corn flakes, cigarettes, canned peaches, banks at which you can have a checking account, beer.)

   b. Obviously you will not agree that *all* these are examples of goods whose brands are of insignificant differences. Are any? If so, does this mean that when you buy this kind of good, you purchase at random without regard to brand?

c. If not, what do you mean by an insignificant difference?

d. What is it that makes you prefer to buy one brand rather than the other at the same price?

e. Can you name any good and two of its brands for which you believe no one in his right mind could have a "good" reason for preferring one over the other?

8. Change the data in Table 23–1 as follows: From every indicated "quantity purchased" at each price, subtract 5. If the new number is negative, simply call it zero.

a. Recompute the total and marginal revenue.

b. What is the new wealth-maximizing output for this producer?

9. Using the cost and revenue data of Tables 22–1 and 23–1, suppose a $5 tax is levied on your business—an annual license tax of a flat $5 regardless of how much you produce.

a. What will be your price and output?

b. What is the amount of your profits?

c. Suppose that a $25 tax is levied. What will be your new price and output?

10. Again using the data of Tables 22–1 and 23–1, suppose that your costs of production are changed by a rise in the cost of materials or labor so that at every output your costs are 30 cents greater per unit of output.

a. What will this do to the marginal-cost schedule?

b. What will be your new wealth-maximizing price and output?

c. What are your profits now?

11. As a superior student you provide a tutoring service. The higher the price you decide to charge, the fewer the hours of work you get.

a. Are you a price-taker or a price-searcher?

b. Assume that your time, when you are not tutoring, is worth an equivalent of $2 an hour. The daily demand for your tutor services is not perfectly predictable; it varies at "random" around a mean rate of daily demand which depends on the price you can charge. If, at the price you charge, you find that all your available time is always used, and there are occasional applicants whom you must reject because you are fully booked up, do you think you are charging the wealth-maximizing price? Explain.

c. If you are charging a price at which you occasionally have idle time, are you charging too low a price?

d. Given a fluctuating demand, how can you be sure that you have charged the "right" price?

12. You are constructing an apartment building. You can construct one with many units and have vacancies sometimes, or you can construct a smaller apartment building and have a waiting list and a no-vacancy sign all the time.

a. If the latter behavior (low prices and waiting list) is profitable, can the procedure of charging more and having vacancies sometimes be even more profitable?

b. Would you interpret an average vacancy rate on apartments of 5 or 10 percent as evidence that they are oversupplied, overpriced, or neither?

13. "General Electric announces a new 11-inch, 12-pound portable television for $99.50." "Parker '45' Pens are sold at an announced price of $5." "Sunbeam appliances are sold at retail prices set by the manufacturer." Explain why the above statements do not imply price setting by the seller. That is, explain why the prices were not all three times as high as they are.

14. Does U.S. Steel have the power to raise the price of steel? Does it have power to raise the price of steel in order to make more profits?

15. In question 9 above, higher costs induced the firm to reduce output and raise price.

a. Is this to be interpreted as an example of the power of the price-searcher to raise price?

b. If your answer is "No," how do you reconcile your answer with the Council of Economic Advisors (to the President of the United States), who regard the attempt of U.S. Steel to raise its prices as an "unjustified" use of the power to set prices?

16. In France, Italy, Spain, and Germany individual bargaining over the price of a good is commonplace.

a. Would you prefer that custom to the more common one in the United States of not bargaining?

b. But on second thought, can you name three goods that are commonly purchased in the United States by bargaining?

c. How would you explain the simultaneous presence of two different customs?

17. You are collecting data for a cost-of-living survey. For each of the cases below, which "price" would you report as *the* price? Why?

"Special one-hour sale! $10 items for $6.99!"
"Regular price $1.—Today only, 89¢."
"$100 dresses; marked down to $60."
"List price, $125. Special discount to $90!"
"35¢ box of Kleenex for 29¢."

18. When collecting prices for your cost-of-living survey, you discover that not all customers can buy a good advertised on sale because the limited stock was sold out in the first hour.

a. Would that have introduced any error into your cost-of-living data?

b. Continuing with your cost-of-living survey, in New York City the rents are controlled; but at the controlled rents apartments are not available to many who would pay the legal price. Would you use that legal price as the cost of housing? Why?

19. "Advertising by savings banks is wasteful. It doesn't induce any more saving. All it does is attract depositors away from one bank and to another. Since all banks are guaranteed and regulated, there is no difference among the banks. Hence, advertising that merely attracts depositors away from other banks does not a whit of good." Do you agree? If so, why? If not, why not?

20. "Much advertising is deceitful, dishonest, misleading, fraudulent, and disingenuous. Therefore, it should be subjected to government regulation." If you accept that conclusion, would you accept the same conclusion for daily conversation, political talks, lovers' pleadings—which are subject to the same charges? Explain why or why not.

21. Is it true that for some brands and for some products you prefer one brand over the other if both have the same price, but if there is any price difference between them you will take the lower-priced one?

a. If this is true for some goods, does it suggest something about the basis for or "strength" of your preference?

b. Would you say that you "discriminate" among brands?

c. Is that "justifiable" discrimination?

22. Are there any products that are not being produced today because complementary, jointly used products are not being produced, so that each is waiting for more of the other—with a resultant stalemate of underproduction of both items?

23. In the spring of 1963, a year after the steel-price hassle of 1962, the federal government, in response to complaints from domestic steel producers about low-priced imported foreign steel, initiated hearings to determine whether foreign imports were being provided at less than the foreign costs—with nothing explicit as to what is meant by costs. If the hearing determines that imported steel is being sold at prices below cost (below whose cost?), taxes can be imposed on the imported steel. Within a month, the domestic steel companies began raising the price of steel, in a discreet manner, with only lip-service complaint from politicians.

a. Do you think it likely that the higher prices proved to be more profitable?

b. Why did the government at one time object to higher prices of steel and then within a year take action to reduce the imports of steel, thereby enabling a higher domestic price?

24

SELLERS' COLLUSIONS AND TYPE-1 MONOPOLY

Sellers, faced with decreasing demand for their productive goods, do not always docilely submit to open-market competition. Instead, some try to restrict the scope of open-market competition. Some do not even wait for "hard" times; they try to form coalitions with other sellers in the hope that such coalitions will protect them from open-market competition. Some go further and try to restrict new producers, or possibly all other producers, from access to the markets, usually by getting the government to exercise its police power to that end.

If we ignored these activities, we would leave two false impressions: first, that such activity does not occur and, second, that economic theory does not imply or explain it. In fact, it does occur, and economic theory is applicable. Therefore, this and the next chapter diagnose examples of activities intended to circumvent or restrict the scope of open-market competition. As we shall see, the restrictive intention, even when backed with activity, is not synonymous with success; in particular, without government-enforced restraints on market access, prospects of success are dim. This chapter will discuss efforts by existing sellers to collude voluntarily. We will start with an investigation of efforts by existing sellers to collude with each other to prevent market competition, and then will be led to consider government-enforced restrictions on market access—earlier called type-1 monopolies.

Collusions: Objectives and Obstacles

The source of potential gains from effective collusion can be illustrated very easily by means of our earlier water-demand example.[1] The individual competitive price happened to be 10 cents. *If* the firms selling this product could agree to charge a price of 67 cents, the total income for the whole group of sellers would be increased, and each would have a larger profit and wealth—or so it might seem.

But consider the series of obstacles to organizing an effective collusion, even if, contrary to fact, it were legal.

(1) Who are your competitors? If you were trying to organize doctors, what would you do about interns, chiropractors, registered nurses, druggists, dentists, and drug companies? All of them are substitutes in one form or another for some medical service. If doctors raise their fees, some people will ask more aid of their druggists and self-prescribed drugs. Or suppose you are a steel producer. What would you do about aluminum, brass, plastics, wood, paper, and concrete? They are all close substitutes. Would your "collusive" group be able to raise steel prices without intolerable sales losses if these other competitor producers do not join? And what are you going to do about firms that make their own steel? If you collude and raise price, they will begin to sell some of their steel output to other steel users; their steel production becomes more profitable, and thereby a new producer appears to take away your sales.

(2) Suppose, however, that you decide to include only the steel companies and not those who produce aluminum or other substitutes. You may be dismayed to discover that more than one hundred companies produce steel in the United States. But since ten of them produce 90 percent of all the steel, you plan to get just the big ten together. The rest will not be important enough to upset your plan too quickly, you hope. All ten companies send representatives to the first meeting of the "Committee to Stabilize the Steel Industry," where you present plans to raise prices of steel products. You tell the companies that all they have to do is follow your leadership. You say that at the higher price, of course, sales of steel will be lower. Some buyers will shift to other products, some will shift to the non-member fringe producers, and a very few buyers will begin to make their own steel. But, you believe, total value of sales will be larger. Of course, each of the ten producers wants someone else to bear the major share of the reduction in output; each wants the lion's share of the gain in sales value. Your answer could be that all of them will let the buyers decide from which company they will buy. Not all sellers may agree, for some may contend that at a higher price the relative shares will change and the effect on profits will not be equal. The same percentage change in sales can mean very different changes in total profits, depending upon how responsive each firm's costs are to changes in its output. Many attempts to collude never pass this obstacle of reaching agreement on how much each firm is to reduce its output and how the wealth gain is to be divided. But some do pass it, and suppose that ours is one of them: all ten steel-

[1] See Table 11–2, page 139.

company representatives agree to some proposal and immediately initiate the price rise.

(3) What happens next is easily predicted if we remember the first chapters, wherein we discussed collusion among middlemen. Each producer now finds that customers complain—as they always do—about prices. But this time each steel producer can increase his profits if he *and only he* secretly cuts prices and attracts customers from the other colluding members. That would be a "double-cross," of course. However, a steel company can ethically get new customers from the other companies—without cutting explicit prices; it merely has to offer quicker delivery, longer time to pay, lower credit charges, more trial purchases with return privilege, lower freight costs, and many other more technical devices that any steel producer or buyer can easily describe. Competition in these special services will raise costs to steel producers, but with their higher price-cost margin there is more room for it; therefore, they will engage in it until the extra costs match the extra gain.[2]

(4) In the meantime, customers also are wide awake. At least one of them will suggest that since different suppliers have quoted the same price, he will choose at random—unless the seller is willing to grant a secret price cut in the form of a rebate. Soon all the companies know what is happening, and the collusion is destroyed, if it ever was effective. If something could be done to tie each customer to a specific steel company (e.g., requiring customers to buy from local producers only, analogous to the way elementary schools assign students), they can't play one against the other.

(5) Another problem is that not all competitors (actual or potential) can be induced to join: excluded firms are delighted at the opportunity to capture customers who shy from the higher price. These firms will grow in size and wealth—at the expense of the colluding members. The fraction of sales remaining with the colluding group becomes smaller and smaller.

(6) The economic costs of quick creation of new facilities may be large enough to dissuade many new potential competitors from soon entering the business. This delay in entry would appear to make at least short-lived effective collusion more likely; but there is another side to this coin. If expensive facilities are involved, the colluders will suffer a loss of their own large investment if new entrants do appear—an effect that will continue after the effectiveness of the collusion has ended. High initial outlays of entry *into production* (as distinct from entry into a market to sell something) will make a collusion more likely to be effective or to last longer. But this is countered by the threat of the greater loss imposed on the existing producers by the induced entry of new producers.

Such are some of the inherent contradictions, obstacles, and hazards to

[2] The elaborate service in first-class air travel is an especially spectacular example of diversion of competition from prices to other service adjuncts.

effective collusion. We emphasize *effective* because many exploratory attempts to collude simply never come to fruition. Proposals are discussed, agreements are reached only to be dashed on the hard realities just mentioned.

Simultaneity of price action or "dominance" by one firm is not evidence *for or against* the existence of effective collusive agreements. The fewness of numbers of sellers and the coordinated price-search process, whether it be simultaneous or lagging behind some apparent "price leader," is also irrelevant as evidence for or against the fact of effective collusion. Then what is good evidence? The best evidence is to the presence and use of an *enforcement* technique. If costs are being incurred to enforce concurrence in competitors' actions, there is strong evidence that an *effective* collusion exists—one effective enough to make it worth the costs of enforcement. Legal restrictions on entry to the market by newcomers or outsiders and legal penalties for noncompliance with the terms of the collusion by the members provide an effective enforcement device. Self-regulation or legally authorized self-policing by members of an industry provides a weapon of enforcement. Members who do not comply can be denied the right to do business because their licenses or special privileges granted to those who do behave "properly" can be revoked for "unethical" behavior. The special privileges can include exemption from special taxes or fees; it can include the right to do business with the government. Sometimes enforcement costs are very low because the nature of the buyer makes it easier to detect secret violations. One example is that in which the government is the buyer, and we shall briefly explore this case, before investigating collusion by "merger."

Sealed-bid government buying reduces costs of enforcement of collusions. The government solicits bids from several sellers and opens them all at one time, with the lowest bid winning the competition. All the proffered bids are publicly revealed, and there is no rebidding by higher bidders in a subsequent attempt to win the contract. Secret offers of price cuts to government officials are illegal under this system (in sharp contrast to the purchase of a car by a private party who solicits bids from various sellers, giving each a chance to undercut the others). Therefore, the incentive for sellers to engage in collusion against the government (or public utilities—which are government regulated—with public records of their activities) is stronger, because the buyer is less able to play one seller against the other. If any of the colluding sellers does not bid as he agreed to, the others will find out immediately. It is not entirely accidental that most of the cases of established effective collusion that have been prosecuted in the courts have been against the government or government-regulated public utilities.[3] The government contracting system, then, involving public announcement

[3] An alternative explanation of the observed predominance of cases of collusion against the government is that the government is more willing to take cases to court, and hence reveal the collusion, whereas a private firm is less willing to resort to court costs. This sounds like a good alternative explanation if we forget that the greater facility of legal prosecution by the government should serve to inhibit attempts to collude against the government.

of all final bids facilitates the private policing and hence effectiveness of the collusive agreement—by enhancing detection of violation.

Collusion by Common Ownership or Merger of Producers

If collusion among independent firms is so costly, why not bypass the problem of enforcement of the agreement by merging all the companies into one big company? But the merging of several firms is not so easy either. In the first place, it will forsake the advantages of separate management and specialization. In the second place, before one can merge with his competitors, he must have an *identifiable* set of competitors. But if a firm produces more than just one kind of product, then its competitors for a particular product will not be the same as for its other products. If an electronics company makes television sets, radios, computers, transistors, traveling-wave tubes, to name a few, it will have a separate set of firms as competitors for each product. It would have to merge with an enormous number of firms, and each of these would in turn have to make sure that all *its* competitors were brought in. Therefore, if a firm believes that a collusion with respect to a particular product is profitable, it will seek to *collude* only with respect to that particular item rather than *merge*. Making such collusions and abandoning them quickly in order to reduce attraction to new entrants is cheaper if done by explicit agreement rather than by merger.

However, supposing that one company intends to buy its competitors to make itself the sole company in order to achieve a greater profit, how much must it pay for each of its competitors? Not all will sell at a sufficiently low price, because each understands that as more firms are merged and prices raised it can, by remaining outside, capture more customers from the bigger company and make more wealth. This extra wealth potential will enable the outsider to insist on a higher price for selling out to the merging company.

As a counter-force to this, some people think that the buying firm can—by cutting product prices and threatening insufferable losses—buy up the other firms at distress prices. Easier said than done! Consider some of the obstacles to such an action: (a) The big firm with more sales will have to accept a lower price on the greater sales, so that its loss is heavier than that borne by the smaller firm. (b) The smaller firm can and often does shut down to await the return of prices to profitable levels. The predator must continue with his low-price policy for a long time—until the attacked firm's resources wear out. Predatory price cutting to impose losses on other sellers is not as simple and as smart a policy as it may seem at first sight.[4]

[4] Warning: What appears to be a predatory policy is often in reality something entirely different. For one thing, it can be competition by more efficient lower-cost producers. Or when demand falls, producers who therefore cut prices may appear to be "predators"; but these producers are merely adjusting to the new situation by trying to minimize their wealth losses (i.e., maximize their wealth at the lower attainable levels).

Suppose, however, that a firm is successful and buys up all the *existing* competitors at costs that still leave it in a position to reap a net gain by now raising selling price, along its enlarged market-demand curve. Whatever success any group or person may have in buying up competitors, the rock on which such schemes must avoid foundering is the difficulty of raising and maintaining price above the open-market level, for there is nothing to prevent other firms from bringing *new* resources into the industry and undercutting the higher price.

Ethics or Desirability of Collusion

An interesting ethical question is involved in collusions. Insofar as they are voluntary, with no compulsion placed on outsiders who do not want to join, what ethical precepts, if any, do they violate? Why should the law prohibit collusions?[5] If firms do collude effectively to raise prices and reduce output, they do not differ from any price-searcher, who, faced with a negative-sloped demand curve, charges the wealth-maximizing price. For example, Mickey Mantle, Arnold Palmer, and Elizabeth Taylor hire an agent to sell their services. In fact, each could hire several agents who would compete with each other. Each agent would look only at the amount of Mantle's services *he* could sell. He would cut the proffered price of Mantle's services below the offer of the other agents (of Mantle's services), driving down Mantle's income. To avoid this, Mantle hires *one* agent (possibly himself) and prevents "ruinous" competition among sellers of Mantle's services. Similarly, Elizabeth Taylor does not let her several agents compete with each other in selling her services. No one seems to complain. Similarly, why should one complain if the diamond mines are owned by one person who acts in the same way? Is it that, in the one case, diamonds will be produced in smaller amount? But so will Taylor performances. In each case, from the point of view of the rest of us, a natural talent is not "fully" used. In the Taylor case, it is even worse, since the talent ages, whereas the diamonds are still there.

The fundamental ethical question is what "right" the rest of the public has to require by *law* that Taylor or Mantle or Palmer perform more frequently than they do at lower wages? That is exactly what the crucial issue comes down to. Are private-property rights to be repudiated if people use their resources in ways

[5] If there is something bad about voluntary collusion, is there not also something bad whenever people voluntarily pool their private wealth to form a corporation that is big enough to affect the market price by its offerings of some good? Every corporation and partnership is a collusion to use jointly owned resources in wealth-maximizing ways. Why is effective collusive agreement among several businesses different from merger or new creation of a large business? It isn't. Then why have we devoted the past several pages to a discussion of interfirm collusion, as if it were different from the formation of a corporation or partnership? Simply to understand the obstacles to any group's controlling of market behavior, either by collusion or by buying up firms until only one firm is left—*in the absence* of legal compulsions requiring producers to join a collusion and obey its policies as a condition of access to the market. The second half of this chapter and the next chapter are devoted to restrictions on access to the market.

that they prefer rather than in ways that we prefer? If an author decides not to publish a novel he has written, by what ethical principle does it follow that such "waste" should not be tolerated? If the author prefers to play golf instead of writing or doing other things that are more helpful to other people, by what "right" is it deemed proper to prohibit him from doing so?

Economics gives no judgment about this. The case against effective collusion comes down to the same point earlier raised in connection with price-searchers' markets—"inefficiency" in the allocation of resource uses.[6] Granted, for the sake of the argument, that there is a misdirection of resources, a proposal to prevent voluntary pooling of private wealth is a denial of private-property rights. Pooling wealth does not in any way reduce anyone else's right of free access to market exchange nor his right to use his own resources. This point is particularly relevant because the criterion of "misdirected" or inefficient use of resources is itself dependent on the normative premise that individuals should have the right to make choices about use of private property. If, for that purpose, we accept a criterion of efficiency relying on revelation of values based on access to the open market to trade private property, we cannot in logical consistency propose to deny private-property rights in order to achieve a kind of efficiency that is meaningful only for private-property rights.[7] Yet that is what a refusal to allow pooling and mergers amounts to. Of course, there may be grounds *other* than economic efficiency for objecting to collusions and mergers; furthermore, private property and individual choice may not be socially desirable institutions. In addition, there may be other causes of inefficiency, such as restrictions on entry to the market. In fact, in the next chapter we shall investigate several kinds of restrictions on market access.

Legality of Collusion

We have investigated the common belief that collusion is something that all sellers will seek and, in the absence of special prohibitory laws, will in fact be successful enough to raise prices and earn extra wealth. As we have seen, the implications of economic analysis are that there are potent forces working against the successful attainment of extra wealth *via* collusive sellers' arrangements. Nevertheless, though we can recognize some of the potent counter-forces, we cannot say that *all* collusions are unsuccessful. A commonly cited piece of evidence of the success of collusion in the absence of prohibitory laws has been the frequency of cartels and collusive agreements in European nations, where such

[6] See pages 142–145.

[7] Individual freedom of choice is the ultimate test of value or "proper" direction of resource use in this efficiency criterion. This will be evident if you recall that the measure of value is derived from "individual preference" as revealed in choice of use or exchange of goods.

laws were rare or weak. Unfortunately, this does not enable us to draw any conclusions, because in instances where successful collusions have been carefully investigated, their existence has been facilitated by special laws, favors, or government controls that enabled the colluding group to "police" recalcitrant members and keep out new producers. The available evidence as to the relative power of forces for and against successful collusions in the absence of special prohibitory laws is simply not good enough to permit any confident conclusion. Nevertheless, the fact is that in the United States laws have been enacted against such collusion and "restraints on competition."

Late in the nineteenth century, public apprehension about the possibility of a weakening of open-market competitive forces in the American economy reached a stage sufficient to induce enactment of the Sherman Antitrust Act in 1890. This law prohibited "monopolies" and "combination or conspiracy to restrain" trade. Since it did not define "monopoly" or "restraint of trade," the act, as enforced, was and still is dependent upon ad hoc arguments in individual law suits against companies accused of such action. At the turn of the century, the Standard Oil Trust (organized by Rockefeller), the U.S. Sugar Trust, and the American Tobacco Trust were prosecuted by the U.S. government's antitrust division and were split into smaller companies. It is still a moot point whether these "trusts" did charge higher prices than would have been charged by a larger number of smaller firms and, if they did, whether or not the power to do so was a result of laws denying other competitors the right to enter the market. In any event, the Sherman Antitrust law exists and is intended to dissuade further growth of some firms. For example, in 1961 the Du Pont Company was compelled to divest itself of ownership of a substantial portion of General Motors. Bethlehem and Youngstown steel companies (two of the larger steel companies) were dissuaded from merging when told by the antitrust division of the Justice Department that the proposed merger would be prosecuted in court as a violation of the Sherman Act. More recently, a large shoe company (U.S. Shoe Company) was forced by court order to divest itself of ownership of a former competitor. All of these were results of judicial opinion or belief that these mergers reduced competition. In fact, the judicial interpretation is even stronger; in order for a firm to be deemed illegally large, it is now sufficient to show that competition "might probably" be reduced. No great understanding of economics is required to perceive that the law is ambiguous, vague, and subject to individual interpretation, preference, and opinion. By 1914 confusion had reached the stage that the U.S. Supreme Court was able, with a straight face, to declare that only "unreasonable" restraints of trade were illegal.

In an effort to achieve greater precision in concepts, the Clayton Act was passed in 1914. The act prohibited both "price discrimination" and mergers "reducing competition." As we have already seen, price discrimination sometimes increases the efficiency of resource use, and mergers can enhance the competitive status of some firms in the market. Experience suggests that the Clayton

Act has not removed ambiguity of interpretation, except that after 25 years it did exempt labor unions from the provisions of "anti-monopoly" laws. Also in 1914, the Federal Trade Commission Act established a commission to dissuade firms from "unfair" competition by issuing orders to "cease and desist" from actions that the commissioners deem unfair. Most of these orders are the result of investigations initiated upon receipt of complaints of some aggrieved business firms.

To what extent these laws and their subsequent amendments have maintained, enlarged, or reduced market competition in the American economy is impossible to determine. But their other effects should not be ignored. Dissuasion of mergers and restrictions on growth of efficient firms mean higher prices to consumers. Attenuation of private-property rights is involved, but if one regards socialism or government-regulated use of resources as preferable, this attenuation is desirable.

One of the principal "undesired" effects of this kind of legislation is that it opens the door to special protection from open-market competition. Confusion between protection *of* competition and protection *from* competition of the open market is easy to generate. For example, the Federal Trade Commission relies heavily on complaints of one business against another in deciding which actions to investigate. Complainants will try to protect their wealth from market competition rather than to preserve open-market competition. They complain of "unfair," "de-stabilizing," "disorderly," and "cut-throat" competition —which is a way of saying that one's competitors are more successfully catering to the buyers' preferences. A competitor whose costs are lower or who is willing to provide the service for less is selling below costs—your costs. Therefore, you contend that he is driving you out of business and "tending to reduce" competition. If you say it fast, loud, and often, it may sound good.

An especially common example is the so-called gasoline price war. Sometimes a sudden and dramatic break in gasoline prices occurs. Occasionally these are the result of greater seasonal variations in gasoline demand than were predicted, so that prices are cut to move extra-large inventories out of refinery storage facilities. Shutting down refineries quickly is sometimes less economical than reducing inventories by temporary price reductions. On other occasions a few stations find that demand has fallen, so that they do not believe they can survive at existing prices and rates of sales. The reduced income lowers the value of the filling station's facilities, with a consequent unprofitability of maintaining it in first-class condition. It will be economic to run it down gradually by not investing in repair and maintenance until later, when possibly the demand may increase again. The costs of selling gasoline at that station are lower by the amount no longer used for maintenance and repair of facilities. That station will find it economic to cut prices to sell more gasoline, at least until it or enough stations have shut down or reduced hours of business. Many of the surrounding stations will have to match the price cuts. Later, after the readjustment in number of stations, hours of business, or demand—or after station owners revise their estimates of the desirability of investing in facilities—prices will return to levels covering also the costs of long-term replacement and maintenance of the existing number of stations.

The preceding discussion of gasoline wars is only a sketch of events; it is not intended to be a complete explanation of pricing in the gasoline industry. Rather, it is designed to forestall a leap to the conclusion that some big operator is trying to drive out a bunch of small sellers in order to raise price later, or that such "wars" call for laws to maintain prices to protect "legitimate" service-station operators and preserve "orderly" competition.

Our discussion has been couched in terms that may suggest these laws are undesirable. However, we have merely tried to point out some of their effects, superficialities, and costs. A naïve belief that the American economy has been kept competitive because of these laws cannot be supported by the available evidence. More fundamental attributes of the market system are responsible. In the ensuing section we shall explore some devices that have been used to reduce the effects of those fundamental forces of an open market.

Restrictions on Sellers' Access to Markets

In many markets, laws restrict access to the markets in order to increase or protect the wealth of existing producers, rather than to ensure open-market competition.[8] Before we examine how these laws operate to protect the wealth of incumbent producers, let us first distinguish between restrictions on access to open markets and high investment costs of production. It is true that some goods are best produced with large amounts of capital equipment, and consequently a person who would produce that kind of good will incur large initial expenditures; but restrictions on access to the market are different. High costs of production or of initial investment restrain production without any interference in the market process. By restrictions on access to the market we mean restrictions and costs imposed on people (consumers or producers) as a condition of engaging in exchange of goods that they may have available for exchange. Examples of restrictions on access to the market are special taxes imposed as a condition of doing business in the market; requirements that the sellers pass qualifying examinations in addition to the judgment of the market customer; special apprenticeship and training laws in addition to those inherent in the judgment and choice of customers; legally imposed maximum (or minimum) prices; tariffs that prohibit or tax goods that foreigners would like to sell in our markets; prohibition of sales on certain days or hours; prohibition of sale of certain kinds of goods; necessity of having

[8] That other reasons may exist for restriction of access to markets is not denied. The next chapter is devoted exclusively to some of those reasons.

a certain race, creed, or residence as a condition of buying or selling. Some of these may be trivial, but most are effective in one degree or another.

We can best start by investigating the reactions to a fall in demand, in a price-takers' market in agriculture—say, for wheat. Rather than take their losses and reduce or stop output in submitting to the forces of the free market, distressed wheat producers frequently resort to political procedures they would not normally condone in others. But now "times are not normal," "this is a special case," and, besides, "everyone else does it." And they have been so successful in their political action that much has been said in solemn and statesmanlike terms about the "great farm-surplus" problem. Most of these statements are nonsense, at best, and plain wrong, at worst. They ignore the first fundamental law of demand: more will be consumed at a lower price, and less at a higher price. The simple fact of the matter is that the price of many farm goods has, by law, been kept above the market-clearing level; as a result, the amount the public demanded is less than the amount available. There is no truth whatever to the popular allegation that farm production exceeds consumption demand, for demand is not a fixed amount. The amount demanded varies with price—a fact possibly embarrassing or tedious to the reader, but necessary to repeat again and again and again. The American public (not to count the enormous foreign population) would happily consume all the current farm output if prices of those "surplus" farm goods were not kept up by political controls. The genesis of the farm problem is the post-war relative decline in demands for food (a move of the demand curve to the left) with a consequent necessary decline in price—if the output were to be purchased and consumed. Rather than submit to the reduced wealth resulting from decreases in demand for their products, the farmers sought to adjust—not by transferring their resources to other uses where they were more highly demanded, but instead by forcing the consumer to pay a higher price. But when prices were kept above free-market levels (by devices we shall investigate in a moment), the amount demanded was reduced and the amount produced was increased. Hence, the so-called surplus. If price were allowed to fall, the amount demanded would increase and the amount produced would fall, until a balance was restored. The problem of the farmer is not the existence of the "surplus"; nor is the problem a result of the unwillingness of farmers to submit to free-market revision of the value of their resources and re-allocation to other productive uses. This unwillingness to submit to the market discipline is not unique to the farmers. The problem arises because the farmers have successfully obtained sufficient political competitive power, by use of the government's police and taxation power, to escape some of the market's discipline.

If these seem harsh words of condemnation, reread them; there is no suggestion of impropriety on the part of the farmers. We examine the agricultural case simply because it is a particularly instructive example of efforts to protect wealth from the effects of competitors' open access to the market. We shall select tactics used in different farm commodities, each representing a different stage in the degree of political control over access to the market.

A convenient starting point is provided by the experience of lemon growers, who at first sought voluntarily to withhold part of their output from the market in an endeavor to keep up prices. Their hopes of higher prices were thwarted by the refusal of some producers to reduce output, for it would pay any grower to stay out of the agreement and sell *all* his crop at the higher price while the other producers reduced their offerings. Furthermore, even if the scheme were successful, some superior producers preferred not to join because they could make more wealth for themselves if there were no such agreement at all than if there were an effective one in which they were an abiding member. How can they and other producers be induced to join? One way is compulsion. How can they be forced? They can be accused of standing in the way of those who are "voluntarily" willing to reduce output, and threatened with private violence.

The threat of violence, however, is not as reliable as a law—if it can be passed. Labor unions have succeeded in some use of private violence—e.g., on the picket and strike lines; but the lemon growers, along with many other groups, were able to get laws passed to compel joint action. This is sometimes called "self-policing" by the industry itself—i.e., use of "police" power to force nonconforming producers into line.

In 1941, a law was enacted permitting a majority of the lemon growers to compel *all* lemon growers to withhold part of their crop from the market. Any grower who refused to reduce his offering in accord with majority rule could not legally sell *any* fresh lemons in the American market. This replaced the threat of coercive private violence by coercion via police power. Still, as we know, even 100 percent membership does not solve all the problems facing the sellers. How much of each producer's output is to be sold? Who is to get the lion's share of the sales? Will the share depend at all upon the relative costs of each producer? Whatever the share, how can the group know that the pro rata quota assigned to each producer is observed and that not more than that quota is sold by a producer. One way to police the "pro rata quota" scheme is to have the group act as the only permissible sales agency. That is what the lemon growers did.

This authority determined what part of each producer's output could be sold as fresh fruit in domestic markets and what part would be sold as concentrates or flavorings in domestic and foreign markets. Domestic fresh-lemon prices were raised. But in order to keep fresh-fruit prices high, the proportion of lemons authorized for sale had to be steadily reduced over the years—from 90 percent in 1942, when the sales-control scheme went into effect, until now, when over half of the crop is barred from the fresh-fruit market.

Diverting unsold output to other markets in order to keep up prices of lemons will result in larger supply and lower prices elsewhere than would have prevailed. In effect, fresh-fruit consumers are subsidizing the output of frozen juices and concentrates. The success in raising prices and incomes to lemon growers induced a larger output by each producer and increased the number of producers. Without the scheme there would have been fewer producers, each of whom would have been on the average more efficient and with a lower price per unit of product sold.

There are still more weapons in the political arsenal that producers can exploit in the interest of their wealth. Why not pass laws forcing the market to buy *all* that is produced at the proposed high price? For example, let the government buy (out of taxes) whatever part of the crop the consumers refuse to buy voluntarily in the market. This denies *consumers* the right of free access or withdrawal from markets. But that kind of law has been passed for producers of wheat, cotton, tobacco, peanuts, rice, and corn, and it is proposed for more.

But we exaggerate—slightly. The government *or* the taxpayers do not *buy* the unsold crop. They only *lend* money to the farmer, using the crop as security. If the farmers don't repay the loan, the government keeps the unsold crop—which is, after all, no different from selling the crop to the government. But after borrowing money on the unsold ("surplus") wheat, a farmer can always repay the loan and get back the wheat—which he will do if the demand should later unexpectedly increase so that price rises above the amount he borrowed per bushel. The farmer is thus assured of a minimum price, but the maximum is open. Unfortunately for appearances, since the government is usually left holding the deteriorating "surplus" product, there will be *visible* signs that this storage scheme is wasteful. In 1962, the total accumulated crops in government-held stocks had cost the taxpayers about $5,500,000,000, with an annual cost of about $1,000,000,000 to keep them stored.

An alternative scheme is to avoid these wasteful "surpluses" by government or by majority decision of producers about production, rather than about sales or prices directly, so that only as much will be produced as can be sold at the desired price. If that is done successfully, the entire crop will be small enough to be sold to voluntary purchasers at that "minimum" price, and there will be no "surplus." This kind of crop control, if effective, is very tidy and solves the problem in the sense that there will be no "surpluses" around to embarrass anyone and no low price to the producers.

One way to obtain effective crop controls or "management" is to assure each producer who agrees to reduce acreage of a particular crop by at least 20 percent (obviously he will pick the poorest 20 percent of his land), that he will be guaranteed a price at the "parity" price for all he produces of that crop, and that he will even be paid something for the released land if he keeps it idle—a payment called a "conservation" payment. Those who do not agree to restrict their acreage will not be able to get "loans" on their output and must sell what they produce at the free-market price, which is almost certainly going to be lower than the support "parity" price. In fact, in the case of tobacco not only must you sell the "excess" acreage product at the open market, but in addition you must pay a prohibitive "fine" of 75 percent of the value of that excess product. To get such a program into effect requires a majority vote of the current producers—which usually is not hard once the law permits such an arrangement.

Under this acreage-control scheme, efficiency in production will *not* be the criterion for deciding which land will be licensed for tobacco (or whatever crop is being "protected"). One procedure is simply to require all existing producers to eliminate the same percentage of land. But percentage of what total amount of land used by each producer? The amount he planned to use this year? Or the amount he used last year? Or five, ten, or twenty years ago? This comical question is indeed a serious one. Acreage in any product is always changing. New areas develop. Cotton production has swept westward to more efficient lands—e.g., the San Joaquin Valley of California, where cotton can be produced at a lower average cost than in the southeastern United States. In no small part, it is because of this new cheaper source, rather than a decreased demand, that cotton prices have fallen; the older, higher-cost producers are using the government taxing power to help protect them from the new competitors, who are often hurt by the crop-control plan, as we shall see.

The open-market forces toward efficiency are modified because the use of land is affected by a political voting process. The selection of acreage is partly removed from the marketplace—*because* of the desire to avoid the efficiency criterion with its adverse effect on inefficient producers. Therefore, the government authorizes someone (either some government employees or an industry representative group) to decide on the land allocation. The decision must be such as to induce a voting majority of the growers to accede; else the whole acreage-reduction scheme will be jeopardized. In cotton growing, the most efficient lands are in the western United States, and the farms are larger. Therefore, the more efficient producers are outnumbered. A proposal to cut back the use of older, less efficient lands before that of the newer ones is obviously not acceptable to a majority. A proposal to cut everyone back by the same percentage is used instead. But it is ingeniously effective in reducing the newer, more efficient acreage by a bigger percentage than the old. How? Suppose you decide to cut all acreage back to 75 percent of former use. Should it be 75 percent of last year? If so, then those who happened to expand their acreage last year would have an advantage over those who happened to reduce theirs last year. Then how about making it 75 percent of the past two-year or the past five-year average? The farther back into the past one goes for his base, the greater the cut for the newly expanding areas; for some of them may have had no land in cotton five years ago. And conversely for older areas that are *declining*. Finally, if there are more old farms than new ones, the new ones are outvoted in the decision. Anticipating this kind of restriction, some farmers will vote against such a scheme if they are the newer, more efficient, expanding producers. They vote against it because, while they will get a higher price, it is on such a greatly reduced output that they would make smaller profits than if they were permitted to produce more for sale at lower prices. If one examines the voting records of cotton landowners, he will see that the percentage of votes for acreage-restriction schemes falls off dramatically as one moves into the more efficient western lands.[9]

Acreage control, combined with a guaranteed high price of output, promotes large increases in use of fertilizer and other jointly productive resources. Production becomes more intensive, and the output per acre skyrockets. If output is to be reduced, acreage must be cut back more than appeared necessary at first sight.

Acreage controls have been most effectively and rigorously used in tobacco production. Acres that are licensed as tobacco-growing lands are carefully marked and policed. The type of output control used in tobacco production has been publicly extolled by recent Presidents as very successful and deserving application to other crops. In tobacco, the control is via *licensing* to grow tobacco on specific plots of land and to sell the crop on the free market. Unlicensed producers must pay a prohibitive 75 percent tax on the value of the output. In effect, the tobacco license is an exemption of the production of *only* that land from the tax. No one could afford to produce without a "license"—unless tobacco growing were a hobby. Since the licenses are for so few acres, the untaxed output is small enough to yield a high price. There is no tobacco surplus because the price goes to whatever level will clear the market *of the licensed* (untaxed) output. Although consumers pay less taxes than in the wheat case, here they pay via higher prices for the reduced amount.

Monopoly Rents: Creation and Disposition

The concept of "monopoly rent" (as distinct from economic rent) will make further analysis easier. (Here, monopoly refers to type-1 monopoly only.) In all the preceding cases wherein legal barriers were placed on open access to the market, the effect, and often the purpose, was to increase the wealth of those who were allowed to enter the market. This excess of wealth is called *monopoly rent* —"monoply" because it is the result of legalized monopoly, and "rent" because it is

[9] We interject an ironic and humorous note. Although we have been calling the western lands more efficient, some of these lands are more efficient only because the costs of irrigation are not borne by the farm landowners who use that water. Some of the water is provided to the farmers by federal irrigation projects at prices substantially below the costs—the difference being made up by taxes on the rest of the country. Thus, we see farmers in southeastern United States paying taxes to enable water to be sold to cotton growers in the western desert areas at less than cost in order to compete with the cotton from the southeast. And to protect themselves from the consequent lower prices, they appeal for more taxes on the city consumers to finance "loans on unsold cotton"; finally, they appeal for federal regulations restricting production of cotton on those very same western lands for which they have paid taxes to help irrigate at less than cost.

an amount of wealth in excess of that which would in an open market attract the amount of output that is in fact produced.

This monopoly rent is achieved by *restricting* the transference of resources, so that a difference between value of product and costs is maintained or created. Monopoly rent is not achieved by transferring resources from lower- to higher-valued uses but, rather, by restrictions on that transfer. Regardless of whether the differences in values of use were caused by an unexpected increase in demand or by an enterprising person who discovered a new higher-valued use for resources, that difference in value would be eroded away by a subsequent transfer of more resources from lower-valued uses. That subsequent shift of resources can be impeded by the legal restriction on the right of other people to transfer resources to this market—a monopoly grant to the person who can. The value difference that is created or preserved beyond what it would have been in the absence of such legal restriction is the "monopoly rent." The more effective the restriction on access to markets, the greater that monopoly rent.

What happens to the "monopoly rent" that results from the agricultural crop-control scheme? It goes to the *landowners* who owned the land at the time the scheme was first revealed, regardless of whether they be rich or poor, efficient or inefficient. Thus, the value of the particular land on which the authorization, or license, to grow tobacco is granted is the value of the tobacco crop after all other costs of production (labor, equipment, fertilizer, insecticides, management, taxes, etc.) are subtracted. Suppose that net revenue amounts to $400 an acre for each crop year. Recall from the earlier capital-value analysis that if it has a new income of $400 per year, the licensed land would have a value of about $4,000 if the interest rate were about 10 percent. Taking that as a simple assumption, suppose that land of the same kind, without the "license for tax exemption," has a value of $1,000. This difference of $3,000 is the capital value of the monopoly rent resulting from the acreage-licensing scheme. As soon as the licensing scheme is revealed, the favored tax-exempt acre rises in value, and anyone who then owns it can capture the higher income. Land not authorized for tobacco production will not rise in value. The difference, $3,000, goes to the landowner. He can sell the land (with the license for exemption from the crop tax) and use the wealth for other kinds of consumption (vacations in Florida); he can keep the land and the annual higher-income stream; he can rent the land out for the higher annual value. In any event, the owner of the tax-exempt land gets the wealth gain provided by the tobacco-production scheme. Incidentally, our numbers are representative of the actually available monopoly rent to landowners in tobacco-growing areas.

A *new* owner gets no monopoly-rent *gain*. The high monopoly-rent income from tobacco production is merely, to him, a normal competitive return on *his* $4,000 purchase price. The person whose wealth increases by the amount of the monopoly rent is the owner at the time it became known that such controls or licenses would be effectively authorized.

Since not all licensed (tax-exempt) tobacco land is equally good, licensed land will rise in value by different amounts. If the license to grow an acre of untaxed tobacco could be sold separately from an acre of land, it would be profitable and more efficient to have the landowners of less efficient lands transfer their licenses, acre for acre, to the more efficient lands. Just as each landowner will use the most efficient of his acres for tobacco growing, withdrawing first from his less efficient lands, so it will be profitable and efficient for less efficient landowners to sell licenses to owners of more efficient lands. A bigger crop, or a lesser-cost crop, could thereby be grown; and the owners of more efficient lands would compete among themselves to buy the licenses from the owners of less efficient lands. As a result, the owners of the less efficient lands could sell the "bare" license rather than the land itself and capture some of the value of the crop which could be grown on the more efficient lands. Regardless of who captures that monopoly-rent gain, the total costs of the produced tobacco would be lower if transfers to better land were legal. This general increase in achieved level of efficiency is not permitted under the law. Why? An alleged reason is that the total tobacco output would be larger for the same cost of production, and that would involve a lower selling price. An appropriate further restriction of licensed acreage could offset that increase in yield per acre. Some political observers have suggested that the outright sale of these bare licenses would expose the monopoly rents provided to the tobacco landowners—just as it would be exposed in the sale of bare liquor-store licenses, taxi franchises, and radio and television station licenses.

The effects of the tobacco price-support program—widely regarded as politically "good" because there is no "surplus"—are (a) reduction of consumption compared to what it would have been had the price been allowed to reflect a free-market demand and supply, (b) wealth gains in the form of monopoly rent to those who are able to get their tobacco-producing land designated as licensed tobacco land, (c) political protection of the wealth of tobacco landowners (as distinct from tobacco growers), (d) reduced level of achieved efficiency in tobacco production as more efficient lands are retired while less efficient lands are used with more expensive resources (e.g., fertilizer) being substituted for more efficient land, (e) reduced range of choice of occupation and consumption for producers and consumers.

As we saw in Chapter 5, there are ways to make the monopolist pay for his monopoly rent. In some cases, the monopolist must pay a price to get that legal monopoly right. Outright bribes, political contributions, higher taxes as a payment for monopoly rights, costs of public-relations men and lawyers to obtain "rights, licenses, franchises, or authorizations" are sometimes large enough to match the monopoly rent. If there were restrictions on entry into some business, so that in each year only selected people were admitted, candidates for admission would be prepared to spend money to obtain admission rights. They would each seek to buy whatever qualities the candidate believes the authorities will use in their criterion of admission. For example, a young man setting out to enter the medical profession might find that by the time he had paid the "costs" of being admitted, educated, and permitted to practice, he would be so old that the high but short-lived income he eventually gets has a capital value, as seen from date of application to medical school, no greater than the average of all college students. In other words, the monopoly rent is consumed by these entry costs.

In California and many other states, liquor licenses—right to sell bottled liquors at retail—have sold for as much as $40,000. Tobacco-growing rights—which are assigned to particular parcels of land—are worth about $3,000 an acre. Cotton allotments are worth over $500 per acre—if we judge by the prices paid in certain illegal transfers in Texas in 1961. In Virginia, milk farmers must have a license to produce and sell milk. Entry into the savings-and-loan banks in many states is subject to the approval of the state-government officials. The value of permission to open a bank has often exceeded $50,000 in California, as evidenced and measured by the immediate rise in price of stock of groups obtaining permission. Radio and television stations are also protected from new entrants, and *not* because there is no more radiation space, for in fact there is lots of it. Radio and television stations are "requested" to provide free coverage of political campaigns, especially at the national level, for the major parties. They are also required to broadcast the kinds of programs that the federal-government authorities think they should broadcast. (Notice the contrast with newspapers, which have less government control because they do not have to apply for a license. They act in ways that radio and television cannot; they needn't fear retaliation by the Congress or by the Federal Communications Commission.) Part of the "monopoly rent" to radio and television is extracted from the station owners, not necessarily in the form of money payments, but by being used to pay for the kinds of programs that the authorities prefer.

Conclusion

What do we learn from this application of economic analysis to attempts to reduce open-market competition?

1. Voluntary collusion among existing sellers in an effort to avoid price or quality competition faces several formidable obstacles. Clearly, many attempts founder on these obstacles; yet the conclusion must be avoided that all have so foundered. Unfortunately, we still have only biased evidence; and successful conspiracies—those that eliminate an excessive amount of price cutting, which would lead to collapse of the agreement—are less likely to be reported or detected. On the other hand, there is a bias in the other direction. Enforcement of current anti-collusion laws reveals many instances in which collusion was attempted but without success; as a result, the observer is tempted to conclude

that *effective* collusions are widespread. At the moment, however, there is no evidence to support the contention that the competitive open-market system would not survive without laws against collusion; nor is there evidence that the open market's obstacles to collusion prevent all collusions from being effective. We cannot jump to either conclusion.

2. Legal protection of collusions, via restrictions on open markets, does enable collusions to be effective, and several instances of these were discussed. We saw that it is not sufficient for producers to contend simply that their activities are legal or policed by a rule of law, for laws can close the markets to potential or actual sellers. The issue, insofar as a capitalist, free-enterprise system is concerned, is "What rule of law shall be enforced by the state in economic matters: (a) open access or restricted access to market exchange and (b) private- or nonprivate-property rights?" As usual, the answer is not one that economics can reveal. Economics can reveal only the differences in the consequences of each. The answer depends in part upon the preferences of the people of the society, but ultimately it depends on the ability of a society operating under those laws to survive in the face of competition from societies operating under other rules. Ultimately, we cannot determine even our own policies to accord with our own preferences if other societies adopt rules that enable them to "dominate" ours.

Questions

1. Suppose that there are ten identical producers of the goods being sold in the market characterized by the demand schedule of Table 11–2. Each has *zero* costs of production and can produce up to twenty units each.

a. If all are selling in a price-takers' market, what is the price and output?

b. If all sellers could reach an effective agreement to restrict output and raise price, what price should they select?

c. What will be each seller's output and revenue?

d. How much would each seller gain by the effective agreement?

e. How much would it be worth paying to seek means of reaching and enforcing that effective agreement?

f. How much would you gain if you as *one* seller succeeded in staying outside the agreement or in secretly breaking it while all others raised the price and reduced their output?

2. An old firm approaches a new firm and suggests they collude to keep prices up. Each firm will, of course, have to be content with smaller physical sales than it otherwise would have.

a. How will they decide how much each is to restrict his output?

b. Why are past sales not likely to be acceptable to the smaller or new firm?

3. Ten concrete-block companies in a certain community were accused by the city attorney of colluding to restrain output and fix the prices of concrete blocks. The accusation stated that the ten producers accounted for 85 percent of the output of concrete blocks in the community. What do you think was meant by "colluding": Meeting and talking in an effort to reach an agreement? Or reaching of an agreement? Or a restriction of output and higher price by those ten firms? Or a higher price by all firms?

4. Assume that all existing firms producing a commodity were successfully and effectively to collude to restrict output and raise prices.

a. What open-market forces would operate to obstruct the effectiveness of the collusion?

b. How can those forces be restrained from operating? Illustrate in the context of the behavior of lemon growers, wheat producers, tobacco growers, longshoremen, carpenters, doctors, retail liquor stores, and steel producers.

c. What devices are used in each instance to keep the supply below the open-market supply?

d. Are these regarded as "proper"?

5. The first case prosecuted under the federal laws against collusion to raise prices involved collusion to raise prices on steel pipe sold to the U.S. government. More recently, an electrical-equipment industry's collusion, which sent some business leaders to jail, was also against the government. In fact, a majority of prosecuted proven cases involve collusion against the government. What explanations are there for this evidence of bias toward collusion against the government?

6. As determined by Congressional action, radio and television networks are not required to give "equal-time" rights to any political parties other than the Republican and Democratic parties.

a. Would you consider this a collusion by the two major political parties against the many smaller political parties? Explain.

b. Why are newspapers not required to give equal-space rights to the two major political parties? (Hint: The answer is *not* that radio space is limited or a natural resource that "belongs to the people.")

7. Six supermarkets in a city decide to merge into one company and become a chain of stores operated by one company. If, on the other hand, they did not merge but acted in concert with agreement via collusion, they could be prosecuted for anti-competitive devices. Why is the former legal, whereas the latter is not?

8. The eight campuses of the University of California are managed by one board of regents and a president. Competition among the eight campuses is controlled by the top authorities. If the eight campuses were eight different businesses and if they agreed to one central-control agency, they would be accused of undesirable collusion. Why are the colleges not so accused?

9. The National Baseball League, a league of ten "independently" owned teams, attempts to prevent competition among the team owners in hiring baseball players. No team owner can transfer his team to another city without permission of the owners of other teams. The U.S. Supreme Court declared this policy to be legal on the grounds that baseball is a sport, not a business. Suppose the teams were all owned by one person much like ten different retail outlets—which is legal, even for a "business." Would it be less or more desirable, according to your criteria of proper kinds of behavior?

10. What is the difference between collusion, cooperation, and competition? How would you define collusion between two people so as to exclude partnerships and corporate joint ownership from the concept of collusion? Why is collusion considered undesirable?

11. Do you think Congress will abolish price supports for tobacco as a means of discouraging smoking? Why?

12. European coal producers sell their coal through a central sales agency.

a. Why is that essential for an effective policing of the collusion agreement among the producers?

b. Why haven't some coal producers stayed out of the agreement and taken advantage of the opportunity to sell more coal at the price maintained by the "cartel" as it is called?

13. Why, despite so much political campaigning against "monopolies," do politicians create type-1 monopolies?

25

MARKET-ENTRY RESTRAINTS

In a society that desires the types of freedoms and consequences dependent upon a free-enterprise, private-property system, the police power of the state will be used to restrict entry to the market only if very strong reasons can be advanced. In the preceding chapter, we looked at some laws designed primarily to increase or preserve the wealth of politically strong groups by protecting them from open-market competition and even by forcing consumers to purchase a "satisfactory" amount of the product. However, there are other reasons for restricting access to the market, reasons often deemed worth the price. These objectives, and some consequences of pursuing them by restricting open markets, will be considered in this chapter.

Types of Restraints

TRADEMARKS AND TRADE NAMES

Trademarks and trade names cannot be copied. Even though I were to manufacture an item physically identical to Morton salt or Bayer aspirin, I could not legally sell it if I inscribed on it their trademark. Trademark laws prevent someone from trying to sell something in the pretense that it is made by someone else. Is this a restriction on access to the market, or is it instead really an affirmation of private-property rights? If identification of the maker is part of private-property rights, then trademarks and trade names are private property. Anyone can enter the market with his own goods; free access to the market does not include the right to sell something belonging to someone else—where the name or identification of the product is part of the thing owned. Some countries do not recognize trademarks and trade names, and they do not prohibit imitation of trademarks, just as we do not prohibit imitation of the good itself. However, trademarks and trade names are included in the spectrum of property rights of the maker in the United States.

PATENTS AND COPYRIGHTS

Patents and copyrights are grants of exclusive rights to use commercially (i.e., sell) certain goods or ideas. A patent is what a *monopoly* used to be called. Today a patent is a monopoly to market certain ideas.[1] The principle of the zipper is patented; this means that the inventor is given ownership rights in it and can sell rights to others to produce and sell zippers. The patent is given for a period of years, usually seventeen, and is occasionally renewable for another seventeen years. Patents and copyrights are intended to induce people to discover and reveal useful techniques and knowledge. If a person invents a way to kill flies, show three-dimensional television, or cure the common cold, everyone else could quickly copy the idea without paying him anything. Even though many people try to invent or do research without that incentive, the prospect of a gain will attract more people and resources into such activity. We should not be surprised that the price charged by the patentee for the use of the idea is not zero. The purpose of the patent or copyright was to enable him to get a reward by charging a price. But if he charges a price, the use of the idea is restricted. He may—like a price-searcher—withhold it from some useful applications, so that he can charge a price that will increase his wealth. Having given a patent as a monopoly right, we should not be surprised when the patentee uses that monopoly right.

Still absent is the criterion as to the right amount of reward and inducement for an invention. One might conjecture that the right amount should not exceed the "value" of the resources the invention saves or the gain it gives society. If an invention reduces the costs of production by $1,000,000, then presumably the inventor should not be paid over $1,000,000. But who knows how much each invention is worth? And who is to pay the inventor? Because these questions are impossible to answer, people have resorted to the grant of a patent whereby the inventor will get some gain, and the most direct beneficiaries, those who use the idea, will pay for it out of the benefits received. The absence of a clear-cut criterion for "proper" inducement leaves room for considerable dispute or doubt as to how long a patent should be protected and what kind of pricing and use of the patent should be allowed the patentee.

Several misapprehensions exist about uses and effects of patents.

[1] Patents do not prevent other people from using some idea or device if they use it for themselves and not to produce something for *sale* to other people; only commercial use is forbidden.

Suppression of new ideas. Sometimes an inventor discovers a new idea that will make obsolete what he currently owns. If I owned a pay-television system using wires from station to home and then discovered a means to eliminate the wires, would I use the wireless system? Often it is contended that I would suppress the wireless system because it would destroy the value of my wire system. Actually, what I would do depends upon the relative costs. Since the wires are already installed, their continued use is free to me (until they must be replaced). If it would cost me less to produce and install the new equipment than to continue the old system—allowing for the fact that the wires are already installed—I would immediately abandon the old system and use the new one. But if the older system were cheaper, I would not use the new system until the old wires had to be replaced or repaired. Only then would I introduce the new method. This delay in introducing a new idea is sometimes regarded as "unjustified," but instead, in fact, it may reflect the efficiency of using up existing equipment first. Whether it pays to switch immediately to the new technique depends upon how much the new idea reduces costs.

One of the tales in modern folklore is the legend that the gasoline or automobile producers have discovered a new kind of fuel, or carburetor, or something that will enormously reduce the demand for gasoline. In order to protect their wealth, they withhold the device from use. What are the facts? If any *one* company had such an invention, its value would exceed the value of the company's gasoline equipment and inventories. Then the new fuel or device could be sold for a higher value, and the oil or gasoline company would be wealthier. If the invention were known by all the companies but not patented, then a person who knew about it could take a new job with other people and manufacture the device and make an enormous fortune—more than the existing companies would find it worth their while to pay him in order to induce him not to sell the secret. And if the device or idea were patented, it would be public knowledge, since patents are publicly recorded; but there is no patented evidence or record of any such device.

Non-patentable research and development. It is relevant to note that much research and development are carried on without the incentive of patents or copyrights. Most businessmen who develop new ideas have to rely on their being first and being able to make enough profit before competitors come in and erode the profit prospects. For example, the supermarket, the double-pump arrangement in gasoline service stations, drive-in banks, colored soaps, open-all-night stores, discount houses, and a host of other business innovations might be considered patentable on the grounds that they contribute to cost reductions or quality improvements. Yet they are not subject to copyright nor patents. There is no good objective rule as to what range of exploratory activity should or should not be given the special protection of patent and copyright monopolies.

Alleged extension of patent monopoly to other goods. Another feature, related to the *use* of some patents or copyrights, is widely misunderstood: the use of discriminatory pricing, wherein the different licensees of a patent pay different prices for the right to use the patented idea. This discriminatory pricing is often misinterpreted by the law courts as an attempt to extend one's monopoly (in the patented item) to other kinds of items in which he does not have a monopoly by law. For example, the International Business Machines Corporation owned the patent to punched-card computer machinery. It told users of its machines that they had to buy the *cards* from IBM only. This appeared to be a clear-cut case of an attempt to extend one's monopoly over the machinery into the area of card production. Another example would be provided by Christian Dior, who might give retailers the right to sell his dress "creations" (which he can copyright) *only* if they also agreed to buy handkerchiefs from him. Would Dior be trying to extend his monopoly by copyright into the handkerchief areas? It appears so. Yet there is another interpretation (more consistent with economic theory) that fits all the facts more closely.

Recall our water monopolist in Chapter 11.[2] He was selling water at the wealth-maximizing uniform price to all buyers, who could buy all the water they wanted at that price. We saw also that he could have employed two other kinds of pricing policies, each of which would get him more wealth and would also involve less waste of water. In one case, he could have used a multipart price system; that is, each buyer who bought a certain amount at one price could then purchase more at a still lower price.[3] The IBM company, as patentee—assuming that it has a negatively sloping demand curve and that *no one else can legally enter the market* for providing computers—would like to use a multipart pricing system to get all the wealth it can from the use of the machines. However, to use this multipart, discriminatory pricing procedure in the real world with *many* different buyers, IBM people would have to know each buyer's demand curve and set a different rental rate for each renter of business-machine equipment. Is there a method it could employ both to detect who would pay more and to collect that amount? Yes.

Suppose that it costs IBM $2 to produce or maintain an hour of rental service by the machine. It should charge a fixed minimum daily *fee* (facing a demand schedule of $10 + $9 + $8 + $7 + $6 + $5 + $4 + $3 + $2 = $54) for the right to rent a machine for nine hours per day. The renter would get *no*

[2] See pages 143–148.

[3] Ideally, we saw how he was charged a price of $10 for the first unit, with the right then to buy a second one at $9; and then, *given* that he agrees to buy a second one for $9, he is allowed to buy one more at $8, and so on down until he can buy a tenth one at $1 for that tenth unit. In this way, the water seller collected $55 for the ten units of water, whereas the best he could have gotten with a uniform, constant price per unit—take all you want at that price—was only $30 (having sold six) with four being left unsold. This multipart pricing (wherein the "price" changes for each possible amount) has the "advantage" that inefficiency in use is eliminated. Nothing is wasted. There is no misdirection of resources. And it also gives the water seller a bigger wealth, leaving the consumer with little gain from exchange.

machine at all unless he paid \$54 each day. If the company offered to rent machines simply at a *price* of \$2 an hour, it would make no profits; and if it asked \$5 an hour, it would take in \$30 for a daily profit of \$30 — \$12 (six hours at \$2 each) giving a daily profit of \$18. But if IBM charged a daily *fee* of \$54, with the renter being able to use the machine up to nine hours a day, it would earn a profit of \$54 — \$18 = \$36 per day. The machines are produced and used up to the extent that their marginal cost of \$2 per hour is equated with the *extra* value of an hour's extra machine availability, \$2, as indicated by the demand curve (which shows that nine hours' use would be wanted at \$2 per hour).

However, if customers differ, the rental *fee* (not price per hour) should be different for each, depending on their demand conditions. How can IBM, as patentee, detect the renter's demand curves and charge different fees to each user? One piece of information is provided by the fact that the number of IBM *cards* the customer uses is related to his demand for the use of the machine. IBM could simply count the number of cards used per day and charge a fee for the machines based on that number of cards—say, 1 cent per card per day. A big user of cards (and hence big demander of machines) would thereby be detected and charged a higher rent than a smaller user of cards. And, in effect, that was the system IBM used, except that it did not count daily or monthly use of cards. Instead it charged a higher price for the purchase of cards than the customer would have to pay if he bought the cards from someone other than IBM. If a user could rent machines from IBM and then buy cards from some other source, IBM would have no measure of demand nor any method for collecting indirectly through the higher price for each card (since the user would rather buy from a cheaper source). And so IBM insisted that, as a condition of using the machines, the renter had to use IBM-made cards (even though their price was higher), ostensibly because any other cards would be inferior and likely to jam the machines. If any machine jammed and IBM-made cards were not being used at the time, the service guarantee would be voided and the renter charged the repair costs; by guaranteeing to service and maintain the machines (under the rental scheme), IBM could also check to see that its cards were being used. Thus, the insistence on tie-in of IBM cards (sold at higher than competitive price) was not in order to *extend* IBM's machine monopoly into the card area. Instead, the tie-in enabled IBM to use the cards as a meter device—not only to collect the monopoly-rent value of its machine patent but also to get still more wealth from the area under the demand curve. This discriminatory-pricing arrangement has the "desirable" effect of more fully utilizing resources, just as in the water case; the so-called "inefficiency" of price-searchers' markets in resource allocation is reduced to the extent that discriminatory pricing can be charged.

The federal and state governments and the courts have attacked these tie-in and restrictive arrangements, alleging that they represent attempts to enlarge the area of monopoly or to restrict competition. However, according to the implications of economic analysis, they are metering devices to measure demand to determine the discriminatory price or fee for the patented item.

The implications of our discussion of patents as a source of legal monopoly are that (1) patents, as legal-monopoly restraints on entry, are used to encourage research and invention and new ideas by rewarding successful inventors with more wealth than they could get without patents and copyrights; (2) monopoly involves misdirection of resources unless discriminatory or multipart pricing can be used; (3) patents and copyrights are often involved in tie-in sales and other restrictive conditions of licensing, which seem to be attempts to extend the monopoly into other areas, whereas they can more consistently be considered as devices designed to discriminate among customers with a multipart price system.

DECREASING-COST INDUSTRIES

If a product is produced under cost conditions such that larger rates (and volumes) mean lower average cost per unit, it is called a decreasing-cost product. In this case, only one firm could survive; if there were two firms, one could expand to reduce costs and selling price and thereby eliminate the other. In view of the impossibility of more than one firm's being profitable, two is too many. But if there is only one, that incumbent firm may be able to set prices above free-entry costs for a long time. Either resources are wasted because too many are in the industry, or there is just one firm, which will be able to charge monopoly prices. The preceding line of reasoning often serves as a rationalization for government regulation of a single authorized firm in this industry—often called a public utility.

Government action controls the market in two essential respects: (1) Only one firm is allowed to produce for the market, all others being prohibited by law; i.e., a legal monopoly is created. (2) The monopoly firm is regulated in the profits it earns, the prices it can charge, the amount and kind of service it is supposed to provide, the costs it can incur, and in many many other details. The only assurance the monopoly has of making profits is its own efficiency *and protection from new entrants.* If it fails to make money, the private owners must bear the losses. The owners will then sell out at a loss to new buyers who expect to do better, or the service will come to an end (railroad passenger service, street cars) or will be paid for out of tax-supported subsidies (city bus lines, subways, airlines), or the government will buy and operate the firm.

Examples of public utilities are electric, gas, water, telephone, railroad, and airline companies. Other products are sometimes monopolized by law, although not because of the decreasing-cost technicality. These, too, are sometimes called public utilities, even to the extent of including every monopoly that is regulated by the government—e.g., taxi, radio, television, and municipal garbage-collection services.

In the late nineteenth century, the development of railroads, which is believed to be as close to a decreasing-cost industry as one could expect to find, brought about the charging of rates for services which seemed too high to some shippers and too low to others, partly because the railroads were using discriminatory pricing in order to obtain as much utilization (and wealth) of their railroads as was possible. To control the "interstate" rates charged and to prevent "excessive" profits and bring greater "uniformity" of rates, Congress in 1887 established the Interstate Commerce Commission as a regulatory agency.

By now the commission is also authorized to approve rates charged by highway transport, waterways, pipelines, and telephone and communication companies. If companies want to change services or routes of services, they must obtain permission from the commission. Its control authority is extensive, but it is used primarily as a policing agency rather than as a directing agency administering details. Additional federal regulatory commissions deal with other public utilities. The airlines are controlled by the Civil Aeronautics Board, which allocates routes and authorizes rates, types of service, mergers, etc. The Federal Communications Commission controls radio- and television-station ownership and programming. The proposition that open-market competition is feasible for these activities is challenged by the existence of these regulatory commissions. In fact, all these regulatory boards were set up because Congress reflected the belief that open-market competition in providing such services was inappropriate.

The creation of a legal monopoly for a decreasing-cost product imposes some serious costs on consumers.

(a) Granted that the product is truly one for which decreasing costs exist, does this mean that entry should be prohibited if there is already one firm in existence that is selling at a price no higher than costs? The answer depends upon beliefs about the possibility of new firms introducing improved products or lower-cost methods of production. Decreasing costs for larger output does not mean that all possible producers have the *same* costs. New entrants may have lower costs and drive out the old producer. Although it might then raise price afterward, it does not follow that this would involve higher prices for consumers than if the old monopoly had been protected and controlled by the regulating commission.

(b) Prohibiting new entrants is not conducive to development and an application of new lower-cost methods of production or new products. The reason for this is not merely that the incumbent firm refuses to use known lower-cost techniques; instead, the incumbent firm does not know everything. Other firms, other people, have different ideas about how to produce. These firms are blocked out by prohibition on entry. The incumbent firm is dilatory in introducing even known lower-cost innovations—not because it is a monopolist but because its *profits are limited* by the regulatory commission. Cost-reducing devices would be introduced if the firm could garner the profits; however, if the firm is already making its maximum allowable profits, incentives to reduce costs are blunted.

Nor would the members of the regulatory commission force the firm to introduce new techniques to bring about lower prices; they cannot capture the net gain of lower costs, so they, too, will be less motivated. It's not that regulators are indolent or lazy; it is just that the incentives in the form of rewards for instituting cost-reduction techniques are lower than for the new entrants to open markets. Consequently, the industry will be less acute and energetic than it would be if its customers could shop among competitors.[4]

In summary, the public-utility regulatory commission avoids the "waste" of duplicate facilities by several competitors where only one can survive; and it negates the possibility that an excessively high price might be charged by the one legal monopolist. But the other side of the coin is that the restriction against new entrants reduces the opportunity and incentive to use lower-cost methods of production and improvements in service and quality. The net effect on prices and quality cannot be discerned from analytical comparison, and the empirical factual evidence also is not conclusive, but what evidence is available suggests that prices are not lower in regulated public utilities than where there is no government regulation of those same kinds of goods.

ORDERLY MARKETS

The "orderly-market" argument asserts that unless an industry is controlled so as to ensure adequate prices and profits during hard times, some of the firms will go out of business, and then when demand increases there will not be enough firms to take care of the higher demand. Prices will gyrate from extremely low to extremely high levels. Output will swing from extreme to extreme like an unstable pendulum. Thus, for highly seasonal products like milk (peak supply comes in June and the low point in November), it is argued that prices must be stabilized during all seasons in order to ensure an adequate supply at all seasons. Presumably, if price fluctuated from troughs in June to peaks in November, the farmers would be driven out in June and wouldn't be available in November to provide adequate milk. The contention also is that when demand is good and prices are high, fly-by-night producers will enter and skim the cream, only to leave when prices and demand fall. The responsible, long-lived producers will not be able to survive. Therefore, controls should be placed on entry so that the irresponsible short-term producers cannot enter and undermine the long-term stability of the industry.

Can the reader spot the holes in these arguments? For one thing, all the

[4] Remember the earlier discussion (on page 389) of the likelihood of successful collusions against governments. The same analysis is applicable here in the case of sales to public utilities, since they are "profit limited" and regulated by the government. Because of the restricted incentives or rewards available to public utilities, collusion among sellers of items bought by public utilities is more viable. In fact, and as an illustration of this implication, the 1960 indictment of the major electric-power-equipment companies involved collusion of items sold almost exclusively to public utilities and governments.

arguments fail to recognize that the amount demanded depends upon price and that "adequate" supply is an empty expression. Any supply is adequate if the price is high enough. Any supply is inadequate if the price is low enough. For goods with seasonal swings in production, a *stable* price over the year will certainly imply too large an output at peak periods and too low a supply at low-output months—unless storage costs are low enough so that the output can be stored from peak-production to low-production months and thereby obtain relative price uniformity. But to *impose* price uniformity without somehow eliminating the costs of storing the output from peak to low periods is to create excess supplies in peak periods and inadequate supplies in low-production periods. Seasonal variation of prices over a year is a predictable phenomenon, and no business person will be pushed out of business by low prices in peak periods if he recognizes the seasonality phenomenon. Retail stores do about half their business in the Christmas season, but they are not pushed out of business by the summer low-sales months. The fact is that they are not—just as stores are not pushed out of business by low sales on Sunday. As long as seasonality is predictable, it can be adjusted for in counting income and costs. Yet the milk industry has obtained strong control over entry to the market by alleging that seasonality requires such controls in order to assure "adequate" supplies at all seasons —with a uniform year-round price despite prohibitively high storage costs. The storage is achieved by maintaining enough cows for periods of low production (per cow) and too many for the rest of the time. Instead of letting the price fall in peak-production periods, the milk in excess of the amount wanted as fresh milk at that high price is diverted into cheese, ice cream, and processed foods. Essentially, what is achieved is a higher income for the milk producers, *less* fresh milk over the year, but more ice cream and cheese, and a prohibition on entry by new farmers who would provide more milk at the peak period when prices are maintained at levels above cost.

The fluctuation argument is also carried over into business fluctuations of a nonseasonal nature. In depressions, the elimination of some producers from some industries is alleged to mean that "when prosperity returns there won't be enough producers to ensure an adequate supply. Therefore, existing producers must be protected during bad times to ensure their survival into good times. Furthermore, during good times too many new firms might enter the business, so that, when demand falls off, all firms will lose money. So many might be eliminated that, when demand increases, the supply will not be adequate. The excessive number of entrants will dilute profits so that some firms will not be able to earn enough to carry them over the subsequent harder times. As a result, there will be extreme variations in output."

This argument is full of internal inconsistencies. On the one hand, it says that too few firms will survive the depression, so that the *prosperity* output will be too small because of too few firms. But on the other hand, it alleges that too many new firms will enter during prosperity. Both of these things can't be true;

there can't be both too many and too few producers during prosperity. Furthermore, when business falls off, new resources should withdraw or fail to enter; and when business revives, there should be an increase—if market valuations are to be effective in directing resources. We cannot avoid the suspicion that the orderly-market argument simply seeks to deny free access to the markets by competitors in order to keep wealth and production more "orderly" for incumbent producers.

The "orderly-market" rationale has an almost unlimited number of candidates. Farm price-support laws, for example, control entry of new producers to the market, thus reducing competition in ways already discussed. Farm marketing boards for grapes, peaches, cantaloupes, oranges, and lemons, to name a few, control the salable output of those crops in the interest of greater wealth for the producers, but in the name of preserving orderly competition. Domestic sugar producers have been able to pass a law permitting control of sugar imports, so that the domestic sugar price will be high enough to increase the market value of resources in the domestic sugar industry. And the examples could be extended.

PRESERVATION OF PUBLIC HEALTH AND MORALS

Standards of sanitation. The Federal Food and Drug Acts prohibit sale of foods that the Federal Food and Drug employees deem unfit for human consumption. Foods manufactured under conditions deemed insufficiently sanitary can be banned from commercial use. Surely no one could object to this, and the advantages hardly need be listed. Consumers rely on a government agency to enforce some standard of cleanliness; time and resources are saved for them. But on reflection, there are some clear "costs" of this law. For example, some consumers prefer the right to buy cheaper goods (e.g., imported dates), even though they are produced in less sanitary conditions (cleanliness is not a costless "good"). This right may seem silly for anyone to want—if costs are ignored. As another example, consider the fact that at the present time the Food and Drug Administration refuses to allow the sale of a cheap, high-protein, biologically sterile food sold in powdered form (like powdered milk) and made from whole fish. Although this is a cheap source of nutrition, it has been banned because the Food and Drug employees say it is a filthy food—being made from *whole* fish. People eat whole oysters, sardines (except for heads), shrimps; pigs and chickens are converters of garbage, insects, and worms. The point, of course, is that the people who make decisions to restrict certain items do not necessarily have the same preferences as those for whom they are thought to be acting. It may be captious to emphasize that such constraints have their "costs," but we believe these costs are too often overlooked or ignored by proponents of restrictive or protective legislation. No one can object to cleanliness, if the *degree* of it is not excessive in view of the costs. But a high-priced barbershop that uses a new protective apron for *every* customer will find itself underpriced by one that reuses the apron with a new piece of paper around each customer's neck. The higher-priced shop would do well to insist on equal standards of cleanliness as a restrictive and protective means of keeping out lower-cost competitors. Clearly, a requirement that all sellers maintain at least the same high standards is a restriction on those buyers who prefer less sanitary but cheaper service.

Quality protection. Until about 1950, margarine could not be sold in some states—ostensibly because it was considered a "low-quality" substitute for butter. And in many areas where it could be sold, it could not be sold except as a *white* spread. To color it yellow—even though butter is also artificially colored and flavored—was illegal. Again, the publicly espoused rationale was that margarine is an inferior substitute and that consumers would be misled into thinking they were buying butter. In fact, however, the laws protected milk producers from new market competition—as is evidenced by the fact that major milk-producing states had the strongest bans on margarine. Even mayonnaise was at one time similarly protected from competition from the "inferior" (and cheaper) substitute, salad dressing.

In many states, it is illegal to sell milk if the butterfat content is less than some specified level—even though it is clearly marked on the container. The ostensible reason is protection of the consumer from watered milk; but in those same areas the sale of skim milk is legal.

In almost every city, building codes restrict the right of people to buy homes built with "inferior" materials. The subsequent buyer is protected from his ignorance, and the building is stronger. But that is not all that happens. If one compares building standards in different cities, he will find that some permit cheaper but equally fire-resistant materials and techniques; in others, no option is provided for the use of the cheaper method. Many of the regulations have nothing to do with fire, but refer simply to consumer comfort—e.g., size of rooms, number of windows, number of required electrical outlets. A householder who wants a cheaper and inferior product can't buy it new; he will have to settle for an old house built before these restrictions. Or he may live in a trailer, whose low cost is in part attributable to its exemption from archaic building-code restrictions.

When television sets were first being built, some of the manufacturers—those who used expensive, high-quality materials and techniques—proposed a law prohibiting lower-quality television sets. If the law had passed, the inferior, cheaper sets, which are currently available, would not be available. Speakers would be larger. Picture quality would be better. Tuning would be easier, repairs less frequent. But over-all, the set would have cost more. High-quality sets are still manufactured, but they are so expensive that only a few are produced.

We have all heard the aphorism "Bad goods drive out the good." Cheap champagne drives out good champagne. Cheap music drives out good. Cheap cars drive out good. The complaint always arouses the urge to save other people from inferiority by passing laws prohibiting inferior items. Unfortunately, the aphorism is in error; it confuses inferiority with cheapness. A less costly item will probably be inferior, just as cotton is inferior to silk, Fords to Rolls-Royces, Macy's to Dior's. But the lower cost more than offsets the lower quality, in the opinion of the buyer. Low quality does not drive out high quality. Everyone prefers higher quality to lower quality *at the same price*. But when both quality and price are lowered, we can no longer say that bad drives out good. Instead, the better drives out the worse—when both price and quality are taken into account. Often, a seller may seek laws prohibiting consumers from buying lower-quality goods so that he will not be undersold by lower-cost competitors—whose products may be as good or worse but whose price is enough lower to make them preferred items, just as Volkswagens are worse cars than Porsches, Fords worse than Lincolns, and Sam's Cafe worse than the Hilton Escoffier Room.

The medical profession restricts entry to the market for medical aid except by those that the present incumbents in the profession authorize—by state licensing laws administered by the licensed doctors. This procedure is supposed to assure the public of higher-quality medical attention, given the current state of medical knowledge. If a law permitted the sale of only Rolls-Royces, Cadillacs, and Lincolns, we could certainly say we had the best-*quality* automobile service in the world, as well as the most pedestrians. The medical profession emphasizes that it has brought the United States the highest-quality medical care in the world. But not the same can be said for the quantity. Without such laws, there would be many more doctors of a lower quality. It can be contended that there would be *fewer* deaths if lower-quality *and* hence more medical aid were available, because at the present time even worse substitutes are used—nurses, druggists, books, self-medication, faith-healers, friends, hearsay, phone calls instead of personal inspection, not to mention *no* medical attention at all for many people.

Sometimes it is hard to draw the line between sincerity and satire in this desire to protect other people. For example, would you regard the remainder of this paragraph as sincere or facetious? Economists are members of a profession that has not been able to obtain licensing and compulsory certification similar to that of the medical doctors. An excellent case could be made for such licensing. "Like health, one's wealth can be ruined by carelessness. If a person breaks his leg, it can be reset. If he breaks his budget, it can't be reset by anyone. The loss is gone. Wealth, like health, must be protected. If a person wants to spend $1,000 in some business, how can he be sure that it is a safe investment? If he loses it, not only he but his family suffers. Investments are far riskier and more subject to vagaries than is health. Therefore, before making *any* investment every person ought to be required to consult a licensed, certified economist, who will prescribe how his money should be invested. He can then take the prescription to the seller or the stockbroker and buy or invest according to the prescription. Without this safeguard, millions of people every day make foolish investments and irrevocably lose their wealth and harm their families. As it is today, many people are taking the advice of economic quacks—stockbrokers, politicians, friends, and tip sheets. They buy houses without consulting economists, who can prevent their going too far into debt or buying in the wrong area, or taking the wrong job or the wrong kind of insurance. Today the public is economically uninformed; even worse, people have no protection from the irresponsible, uneducated, untrained, quack advisers. Certainly any economic advice about how to spend and invest wealth should not be provided except by licensed, certified economists. The case for the medical doctors and for economists is completely parallel and equally strong. It is out of greater solicitude for public welfare that the medical profession has been more responsive to the humanitarian, selfless instinct than have the economists." [5]

Protection of employees, morals, and service standards. Laws are enacted prohibiting sales during evenings and Sundays. Again, these laws ostensibly are passed to protect the health of employees, the morals of the community, and the quality of the service. Selling at all hours is hard on employees; they get tired and give inferior service. Sunday selling diverts people away from a restful day and violates the stricture of the Sabbath. The United States Supreme Court says so. However, the facts are that although stores may be open 24 hours every day, the employees don't work 24 hours. There is no reason for a second-shift employee to be more exhausted than a first-shift employee. Sunday and evening buying is a great convenience to many shoppers. Of course, consumers *could* do all their shopping between 9 and 5 on weekdays. They *could* do it between 1 and 4 each Monday, Wednesday, and Friday only. Any store able to reduce costs enough by such hours could survive with the business it managed to get from consumers who prefer the lower prices at those days and hours. But apparently there aren't enough people with such preferences, for those store hours are exceptional. If we probe a bit, we shall find that these laws are often supported by employers rather than by employees. In particular, conventional retail stores are aided by a ban on evening and Sunday shopping. But some stores find that by providing poorer service (less labor per unit of floor space and per item sold),

[5] Or is it the other way around? After this was written, the Securities and Exchange Commission issued a report evaluating the securities and stock-market dealers' practices. In the covering letter written by Mr. Cary, the chairman of the committee, is the following pregnant passage: "Under existing Federal law there is a right of free access and unlimited entry into the securities business for anyone, regardless of qualifications, except those excluded on the basis of prior securities violations. The steady growth in the very numbers of investors and participants, according to the report, has made this concept obsolete. Neither the industry nor the Government nor the investing public can afford the burden of policemen at every transaction; the gateway to the industry (i.e., entry into the securities dealers' business) is the point where Government and industry should look first for the solution." And it also said: "Greater emphasis should be given by the Securities and Exchange Commission and the exchanges and associations of security dealers to the concept of suitability of particular securities for particular customers."

they can stay open on evenings and Sundays at a lower extra cost than conventional stores, whose costs involve a greater share of labor costs. Because conventional retail stores are designed to provide a larger amount of labor service than the evening-Sunday discount houses, the extra hours add more to total labor costs for conventional retail department stores than for discount houses or for "Sears" or "Ward's."

Protection of consumer from unethical sellers. Commonest of all attempts to restrict entry to the market in the name of consumer welfare are those aimed at "unethical" operators who promise a spectacular bargain, special prices, etc. These competitors take business from the established, better-quality, higher-cost, more reliable sellers. Surely, no one could object to the elimination of "unreliable" sellers—no one except those who think that they are clever enough not to be fooled or who can recognize a bargain, or are willing to risk inferior service, inferior guarantee, or less reliable delivery date for a sufficiently lower price. Anyone can buy his new car from the old, well-established dealer who is a pillar of the local chamber of commerce. He can be surer that any squeaks, defects, scratches will be given quicker, better attention than if he buys from the fast-dealing seller on the edge of town who sells at 10 percent less but can't be counted on to give such service. Yet the 10 percent lower price may be worth more than the extra assurance of that "free" service.

Any buyer who wants greater assurance can buy from the well-known retailer, and anyone wanting to try to get a better deal with all the attendant risks and possible problems can choose the bargain dealer. Laws prohibiting these "bargains" provide protection to the unwary, but they impose costs on those who prefer the lower-quality bargains; the cost is the lost opportunity for a buyer to have more of other goods by accepting a lower level of quality or a greater degree of risk.

The foregoing discussion of laws designed to protect the welfare of other people by restricting entry to the market by competitors has been negatively critical. Our judgment, obviously, is that most people are sufficiently exposed to the well-publicized protective effects of such laws but that the restrictive side effects are not usually presented so vigorously; therefore, we have intentionally emphasized some of the "shadow costs," thereby hoping to provide a more complete understanding.

Indirect Restraints on Entry

Laws directly prohibiting entry except on satisfaction of certain conditions are not the only means of obstructing the market. Bans on advertising, restrictions on price cutting, taxes on new entrants, subsidies to incumbent firms already in the market, and threats of privately inflicted violence upon new entrants are also effective. As we shall see, all of these also require support by the government.

ADVERTISING RESTRICTIONS

Although a person may have a legal right to enter the market, any obstacle to providing information about himself or his offers will protect those sellers already in the market, about whom buyers are better informed. Advertising is primarily a means of informing potential buyers of the presence of a seller and his goods. To appreciate advertising, imagine trying to shop in a community with no signs proclaiming one's business, with no directories of location of firms, and with no idea where sellers are located. Most of us quickly learn about some sellers, and we then assume that their advertising is of no further use. But to strangers it is valuable. Furthermore, any change in the seller's offerings can be expressed cheaply and effectively by advertising—as one learns if he travels in a foreign country and cannot read the advertisements; his sense of ignorance about opportunities is made profoundly clear.

Institutions or arrangements facilitating the flow of information about sellers to buyers are important, even though they are frequently ignored. If you wanted to keep your competitors at a disadvantage, what would you do about their advertising? How should General Motors act with respect to advertising if it wanted to restrain the growth possibility of American Motors (makers of Rambler) or Volkswagen? One way would be to prohibit advertising. Since GM is already better known than newcomers, a ban or reduction of advertising would make it more difficult for them to call attention to their presence and offerings. And since the newcomer often has to demonstrate and establish the quality of his service, a prohibition on price cutting would be especially helpful to GM. Price cuts are a way for competitors to attract buyers; at a lower price some customers will be tempted to try new products, risky though it may be. A ban on advertising would make it more difficult for a new seller to announce his presence and availability, as well as his lower price. This double-edged effect—the reduced publicity of a newcomer's presence and the reduced knowledge of lower prices—is very convenient for the well-established, reliable (higher-priced?) seller. In this connection it is interesting to note that the American Medical Association prohibits advertising. Examine the yellow pages of the telephone directory and compare the advertising of various professions. Whatever business you may enter as a young man, would you regard restrictions on advertising as helpful to your ability to attract customers? After you are well established, what would be your attitude?

TAXES AND SUBSIDIES

Taxes on imports of goods from a foreign country are legally imposed barriers to the market that enable domestic producers to produce what otherwise would not have been so profitably salable. Often, taxes or tariffs are defended, erroneously, on the ground that domestic labor is protected from cheap foreign labor.[6]

Taxes or extra costs imposed on foreigners or on new domestic producers are not the only ways to shelter incumbent firms and resources. Subsidies to existing firms, but not to new firms, enable the old firms to underprice the new. Examples are provided by our mode of financing the public schools, which are subsidized, thereby making it less likely that private nonsubsidized schools can survive in competition—unless the private nonsubsidized school is capable of offering not merely a higher quality of education, but one that is better by a margin sufficient to offset the whole private tuition fee.

Subsidies are granted to firms to perform some service that otherwise could not be performed because the sales price of the service or output would be less than the costs. This is true for the post office (in rural mail delivery and third- and fourth-class materials) and public golf courses, to name two. At this point, however, it is well to recall the earlier discussion of gifts and their effects, presented earlier, in Chapter 12. (We mention subsidies as a form of restriction on entry, even though they are normally extended to encourage more production. However, they enable those firms getting the subsidy to keep out new potential entrants who cannot get a subsidy.)

STRIKES

The right to strike and to strike effectively is currently an accepted part of our economic institutions. A strike by the employees of a firm is an attempt to prevent other people from offering to sell their services at rates (or working conditions) lower than those sought by the striking employees. Access to the labor market is restrained by threat of violence to person and property of any would-be strike breakers.

If the preceding two sentences seem harsh or anti-labor, the reader is injecting his own interpretation. They are no more critical or disapproving than the statement that hydrogen is lighter than nitrogen. They do not say that employees ought not to engage in strikes. But where they do differ from common folklore is in their explicit recognition of a fact which strikers prefer not to bring out in the open, probably because some strikers have the impression that by and large the use of violence or intimidation by threat of violence is generally regarded by the public as undesirable. But our federal and state laws permit employees to strike. While the laws do not authorize strikers to engage in violence or physically to restrain workers from crossing a picket line, the police of many cities and the national guard discourage workers from crossing the picket line, because to cross the line would provoke a fight. Therefore, to prevent violence

[6] The fallacy in this argument will be explained later, in Chapter 42. Other effects of the tax can be deduced by using the tax analysis of Chapter 22.

at the strikers' picket line, anyone who tries to cross a picket line and thereby provokes violence may be jailed for contributing to a disturbance of the peace. Both the strike breaker and striker are declared guilty. In few areas will the police sweep aside the strikers and permit the strike breakers free access to the market for work (at lower terms than those sought by the strikers), for that usually leads to violence.

That the union acquires legal (type-1) "monopoly" power when allowed to strike is widely recognized. Our courts decreed this in 1940 when unions were specifically exempted from the Sherman Antitrust laws, in order that they could achieve legal-monopoly status. Furthermore, the Norris-LaGuardia Act of 1932 legalized group picketing and boycotts. The Wagner Act of 1935 required that employers deal with unions and that employees not be prevented from forming or joining the union of their (majority) choice. And the National Labor Relations Board was created to enforce the conditions of those acts.

Some people think it necessary to conceal the essential purpose of strikes because they believe, probably mistakenly, that society would not tolerate strikes if their intent and effect were well perceived. Instead, they advance alternative interpretations of the essential function of the strike: (a) The bargaining position of the worker must be equated to that of the employer. Unfortunately, this statement has no meaning; it suggests that in some sense the worker is at a disadvantage compared to the employer—not merely that the employer may be wealthier, but in some other sense as yet undefined. (b) Wages would be cut to a minimum level in the absence of the right to strike. But what is the "minimum" level? It is not a level of wages that will just keep a man alive. Rather, it is the minimum required to attract workers, and that minimum may be very high or very low. Later we shall present a more complete analysis of the factors affecting wages.

Do not be shocked or incredulous at the preceding statements, lest you reveal a romantic illusion. Is there any reason why the people who seek to eliminate competitors should be only, for example, businessmen, doctors, teachers, radio and television station owners, and not ordinary employees like teamsters, carpenters, mechanics, retail clerks, or dock workers? What one can do, others can try. If one group can resort to legal tax-supported violence via laws (the state police power), it should not be surprising that others would resort to some private violence (thugs, gangsters) to deny access to the market. None of the foregoing is *necessarily* tied to unions. Employees need not be in a union in order to strike. A closely knit group of employees can utilize the strike. As can easily be understood, however, the probability that the many employees of a firm or group of firms could get together and reach effective agreements to strike is increased if the employees already belong to an employee "interest-group" organization such as a labor union. Another reason a union is tied to the strike is that our laws permit legally recognized unions to strike; in that case, the government will be solicitous of the strikers' interest and will seek to prevent violence at the picket line. If the striking employees are not part of a legally recognized union with exclusive rights to negotiate for the collective group (collective bargaining), the employees will probably be ordered not to strike—that is, they will be "enjoined" from striking by issuance of a judicial decree called an "injunction."

To indicate that a strike attempts to restrict entry to the market by other workers who would work at lower wages than those sought by the strikers is not to condemn it. For example, if by such a restraint some people are able to get work at higher wages than otherwise, even though others who are prevented from this market will have to take lower wages, who is to say this is "bad"? The answer depends upon one's judgment of the particular system of competition with which he prefers to see society face the issues raised by scarcity.

We summarize these two chapters on restrictions to market access by noting that they encourage forms of competitive behavior different than where there are open markets. Open-market competition does not always bless everyone. New competitors make more attractive offers and displace former sellers whose products are no longer so highly valued. This does not deny that the market opportunity to exchange will help every person compared to his not having *any* right to negotiate exchanges in the market. But it does assert that restraint on the right of some *other* people to enter the market can be beneficial to some of the sellers who already are in the market. Competition among existing and potential sellers over the terms of trade can take two forms: (a) competition in offers to buyers, and (b) competition in acquiring political power (law) to restrain other potential sellers from competing in the free market.

We emphasize that none of the examples of restraints on rights of some sellers or buyers to free access to the market (i.e., closure of the market) is automatically to be considered "bad" or "good." Each can be judged by its effects on your basic criteria of the good society. In the good society, should the individual have the right to make whatever exchanges he deems desirable? Some people think not. They believe, for example, that people should be protected from open-market competition of unlicensed doctors, since the latter will not do as good a job as will a certified doctor. Essentially, they believe that people cannot be trusted to make the right decisions for themselves. Or some may think that voluntary-exchange competition breeds behavior that they would like to see used less in meeting the issues of scarcity. The presumption of the authors of this book is that the reader, not sure what kind he prefers, wants more information about the operating characteristics and consequences of different systems of competition before forming judgment. But even with perfect knowledge of those consequences, it is not certain that people would agree on the preferred forms of competition.

Questions

1. The judicial council of the American Medical Association recommended that it be considered unethical for a doctor to own a drug store in the area in which he practices medicine. It also recommended similarly for ophthalmologists who dispense eyeglasses for a profit. "Any arrangement by which the physician profits from the remedy he prescribes is unethical," in the opinion of the council.

   a. Who do you think would benefit if this recommendation were adopted by the American Medical Association and made effective?

   b. If it is unethical for a surgeon to profit from the remedy he prescribes, should any surgeon diagnosing a patient be allowed to perform the recommended operation? Should any diagnostician be allowed to collect money for treatment that he gives following diagnosis?

   c. Should a building contractor be allowed to have any interest in a lumber company? Should any teacher be allowed to use his own textbook? Should a doctor be allowed to be an owner of a hospital? Or own an undertaking business?

   d. As a patient, would you prefer to deal with doctors who are prohibited from ownership of drug stores? How would this help you or hurt you?

2. Diagnose and explain the various features reported in the following news story:
"An attractive brunette seated in a rear row gave an excited whoop when her name was called Wednesday during a drawing at the County Building. She had good reason to be elated. For $6,000 she had picked up an on-sale liquor license with a market value of about $9,500. She was one of 54 persons who had applied for the 25 new on-sale licenses to be issued in the county this year by the Alcoholic Beverage Control Board. A drawing was used to determine who would get the new on-sale licenses, which permit sale of drinks on the premises. An applicant must have had a premise available and must operate the business for two years before he can sell the license."

3. Suppose you could live in a society in which trademarks were not protected by law and anyone could imitate the trademark.

   a. As a consumer, do you think you would prefer to live in that world or one in which trademarks were exclusively reserved for a particular manufacturer as part of his property? Why?

   b. As a producer, which would you prefer?

4. You invent a photocopy machine. You know that the average cost of making the machine is $1,000 and that its operating costs are 1 cent each time the machine is used. You could sell the machine to users for, say, $2,000, letting them pay the 1-cent operating costs. On the other hand, if you can discriminate among customers, and charge some a higher price than others, you can make still more money. In order to make discriminatory pricing effective, you must not sell machines to the users, for they could then resell them from the "low-priced" to the "higher-prieed" customers, and

undermine your attempt to charge "discriminatory" prices. A scheme that will discriminate is to rent a machine to each user for a nominal fee, and then charge him a high fee for each use of the machine—say, 3 cents a time. (Remember, the cost is only 1 cent per use.) In this way the "high-use–high-demand" customers pay more for the machine than the lower-use–low-demand customers; and there is no resale from one user to the other. It is illegal for International Business Machines to do this with its computing machines, but it is legal for Haloid Xerox Company to do this with its photocopy machines.

Would you favor changing the law to prohibit such rental of Xerox copying machines, or would you favor changing the law to permit IBM to rent machines, or would you favor continuance of the present mixed situation? Why?

5. Charles Pfizer Company, the patent holder of the drug tetracycline, used in various forms as a general antibiotic (Aureomycin is an example), has licensed other firms to produce and sell the drug. In doing so, it has set certain conditions as to price and amounts each licensed producer can make and sell. This practice has been attacked by the Federal Trade Commission as "illegal." The patent holder does not have to license any other firms at all, and instead could produce the drug only itself as it was entitled to do under the patent terms.

a. As a potential consumer of drugs, which arrangement would you prefer to exist?

b. Do you think this kind of licensing would explain why this drug is sold for a lower price in foreign countries than in the United States?

c. Is that kind of price discrimination bad? Why?

6. Milk delivery is sometimes called inefficient because several firms deliver milk to homes, with duplication of delivery trucks and labor.

a. For so standard an item as milk, would you prefer to live in a community with one centralized milk-delivery service controlled by a regulatory commission to ensure low prices and adequate quality, or one in which anyone who wants to deliver milk can enter the market? Why?

b. Apply your analysis in the preceding problem to the case in which garbage collecting, instead of milk delivery, is involved. Would you feel differently about that?

c. How about mail service? Newspapers? Electric power?

d. If your answers differ, what is the factor that makes you change your preference?

7. European countries import inspected frozen fresh meat from Argentina. But the United States limits the imports of fresh meat from other countries, because some other countries have hoof and mouth disease (a particularly virulent, rapidly spreading disease that kills cattle, although it does not endanger human consumption). Whom does it benefit and whom does it hurt? How?

8. The stock exchanges, with the sanction of the U.S. Securities and Exchange Commission, occasionally prohibit (suspend) all trading in certain common stocks, especially when some spectacular news about that company suddenly is heard. For example, if the president of a corporation is sued for fraud by some government agency, with a consequent rush of sell orders by current common stockholders, the exchange suspends trading to permit time for the full news to be digested and to prevent wild swings in the price of stock. The defense of the suspension is that it protects some stockholders from selling in panic at the developing, but as yet unsubstantiated and unweighed news. These sellers would later find the price had recovered—with the result that they had sold at exceptionally low transient prices.

Does that reasoning—as a defense of suspension of trading of the stock—convince you that it would be better for you to be in a situation in which the exchange could stop trading in common stocks you happened to own any time it decides that new developments are so unnerving as to panic some owners of corporation common stock? In making your decision, consider the risks that the news will turn out to be accurate and the swing will not be temporary. Consider also the effect on the new potential buyers who are restrained from buying. (Incidentally, trading can always go on elsewhere than in the formal exchange markets—whether or not the exchange suspends its trading.)

9. Gasoline price "wars" have induced many gasoline-station owners to propose a regulatory agency to establish orderly marketing conditions in gasoline markets. Also, they propose that no service station be allowed to charge a price less than costs, and further that no new stations be opened unless the convenience and necessity of the area warrants more stations.

a. Who would benefit and who would be hurt by these proposals, if carried out?

b. If the proposals were carried out, how should the commission decide who got to open a new service station?

c. What would be your preferences about this kind of regulation if you were a Negro, immigrant, or young gasoline-station operator?

10. Read the first quotation in footnote 5, page 419.

a. Why has the growth in numbers of investors made open markets for security dealers and for investors an obsolete concept?

b. If you were a Negro, a Jew, or an immigrant, would you find this development to your advantage? Why?

11. Refer to the last passage in footnote 5, page 419.

a. Restate the proposition of that passage in terms analogous to the control of medication by prescriptions from doctors.

b. Do you think economists should campaign for laws to prohibit any person from buying a security, land, or a house without a prescription from an economist certifying the suitability of that particular purchase by the particular person involved? Why or why not?

12. Probably it is safe to say that a majority of the faculty at any college contends that students are not competent to judge the quality of the instruction in various courses and hence should not be relied upon as evaluators of instructor competence.

a. What do you think?

b. At the same time, it is probably safe to say that a majority of the faculty thinks its students have come to that college because the students can tell good from bad colleges. Do you see any inconsistency in this pair of beliefs? Explain.

13. To protect and maintain standards of education, many states provide state-approved textbooks paid for by tax receipts. Imagine that system were used at your college.

a. Would you prefer to have the textbooks selected by a state board and provided by tax funds, or would you prefer to have them selected by the instructor and bought at your own expense? (In answering, consider the effect on the variety of texts and types of classes from which you might choose.)

b. Do you suspect the author of a textbook would prefer that state, free-text system—recognizing that if his text were adopted by a state, he would obtain substantial royalties? On what do you base your conjectured answer?

14. If state schools (primary through university) are financed by taxes, while private schools must rely on tuition and gifts, will the private schools be able to survive by providing an equally good quality of education? At the collegiate level most state universities are progressing toward higher entrance requirements. As they move to higher requirements, what types of students will constitute an increasing proportion of the private colleges? Explain.

15. Texas, which has the legal right to subdivide itself into seven states, surprises us by doing so. One of the new states, Texaseven, with no college in its boundaries, decides to give to every high-school student a four-year annual grant of $1,500 to be applied to education costs at the college of his choice anywhere in the world.

a. Would you consider that new state to have the finest or the worst educational system in the world?

b. Why is that method not used more widely, despite its temporary wide use immediately after World War II as an aid to veterans?

c. Why is it bitterly opposed by the officials of the University of California (and most state universities)?

16. The U.S. postal system is a monopoly. No one else may institute a competitive system of transporting personal messages for pay.

a. Why do you think it has remained a monopoly?

b. The prices charged are uniform despite vast differences in costs of service to different patrons. Why is this kind of discriminatory pricing practiced for mail but not for food, clothes, or dancing lessons?

17. **a.** Do you know of any instances where inferior goods have driven out superior goods?

b. Would any of the following be such cases: compact vs. larger cars; margarine vs. butter, salad dressing vs. mayonnaise; blended vs. straight whiskey; plastic cartons vs. milk bottles; frozen vs. fresh orange juice; ready-made vs. custom clothes; office vs. home visits of the doctor. Would you consider any of these to be unfortunate developments? Why?

18. Almost every team in the two baseball leagues is subsidized by the city governments

in providing stadium facilities. If new leagues cannot be assured of access to those facilities, will this have any effect on the income of the existing teams?

19. Why don't instructors at your college advertise their courses in the college newspaper? Is it because they think advertising is ineffective? Or do they have a gentlemen's agreement not to advertise? Or is it professionally demeaning?

20. Why do union officials bitterly object to admitting that their power rests on a type-1 monopoly, while at the same time bitterly opposing any legislation that would destroy that monopoly power? Answer the same question when applied to the American Medical Association.

21. The University of California, with eight campuses and an upper limit of 27,500 students decreed for each campus, already has reached that number at two campuses.

a. What rationing system is going to be used in deciding which students to admit to Los Angeles and Berkeley and which ones to "redirect" to the less populated campuses?

b. Which system do you conjecture the majority of the faculty will prefer at Berkeley and Los Angeles?

c. What will the faculty at Santa Barbara, Davis, Riverside, Santa Cruz, Newport Beach, and San Diego say?

d. What system would you propose if you were a high-school student planning to attend college?

e. What would you propose if you were a taxpayer in the state of California? Which taxpayer?

22. **a.** Why will a person who has salable property rights in an enterprise for which he is making decisions be more influenced by the longer-run effects of his decisions than if he did not have salable property rights in the enterprise?

b. Does this difference in type of property right induce a systematic difference in the kinds of decisions made by government employees, as contrasted to employees of a privately owned enterprise—even if both are engaged in the same kind of activity (e.g., production of power)? Explain why the influence of the salable capital value of property rights will or will not make a difference in decisions.

23. "Capitalism encourages deceitful advertising, dishonesty, and faithlessness." Do you agree? If so, why? If not, why not?

26

THEORY OF ALLOCATION OF PRODUCTIVE RESOURCES

Heretofore interest has centered on the first two of the following four decisions: (1) allocating available consumption goods among competing claimants, (2) determining how much of each possible type of consumers' goods to produce, (3) deciding how goods shall be produced, and (4) selecting the producers of each. The first two decisions were investigated via a market of householders buying consumers' goods from business firms in exchange for money—usually called the market for consumers' goods. Next we shall take up the third and fourth questions. We shall look at the channels of communication and the system of incentives that monitor choices in the market for producers' goods. Again the focus will be on a market for exchange between business firms and households—this time, the householders selling productive services to business firms who pay in money. In talking of householders and business firms, we do not mean that people who buy productive services are different people from those who make household decisions. Almost everyone acts in both capacities.

We can portray the relationship between these two markets and between households and business firms and between goods and money by the circular-flow diagram of Figure 26–1. The top half represents the consumers' goods markets, with money flowing from householders to business firms from left to right and consumers' goods going in the opposite direction. At the bottom half of the circle, money flows from business firms to householders (right to left), while services go in the opposite direction. The bottom half represents the market in which households earn income by allocating their productive services to various possible tasks, the producers' goods markets.

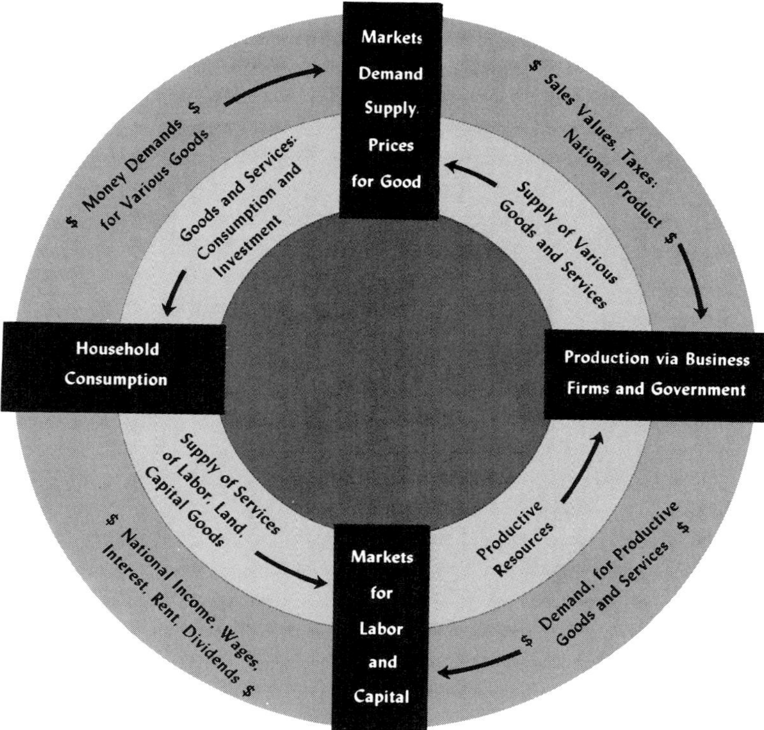

FIGURE 26–1. This chart is solely a visual classificatory aid by which the flow of goods and incomes are related to some of the problems analyzed in economics; it is not an analytical device. Chapters 4–14 discussed issues of allocation of existing goods (the upper-left quarter of the circle)—with Chapter 15 covering the meaning of the market-revealed magnitudes: prices, income, and wealth. The amount and mixtures of goods and services produced (the upper-right-hand quarter-circle) were covered in Chapters 16–25. Methods of determining how goods shall be produced and by whom and for whom (the bottom half of the circle) are discussed in Chapters 26–30. These chapters also cover determination of individual incomes and wealth. For each case, in the capitalist system the communications and controls are channeled via market prices and incomes.

Chapters 31–38 will investigate factors that reduce and increase the total flow of services and values "around the economy"—called problems of aggregate employment and national-income fluctuations. Some functions of governments are analyzed in Chapter 30. Although governments rely primarily on markets in determining how to spend money for resources (lower half), a substantial portion of expenditures—for example, welfare aid and the military draft—are not market controlled. In the allocation of government output and services (upper half), receipts are channeled to the government primarily by nonmarket forces—i.e., by taxes. Finally, Chapters 40–45 analyze the effects of connecting several nations via international trade.

Money flows around the circle in a clockwise direction, while goods and services flow in the opposite direction. The diagram is less of an analytical tool and more of a pictorial device to keep order among the various problems and decisions. Within each of the markets represented by segments or arcs of this circle, we used the concepts of demand and supply in order to see how prices were affected and how prices in turn affected the allocative decisions. The flow of money and of goods around this circle is thought of as the summation of those individual decisions in each market. We have analyzed the factors affecting householders' demand and the supply of goods from producers—both in the top half of the circle. We now redirect our attention to the bottom half. In making this analysis we shall see how the system determines which productive goods shall be used to make which consumers' goods; for this is the question the business firm will be solving in expressing its demands for productive services. We shall also be seeing how incomes of people are determined, for the prices of the services they offer and the quantity of those services sold determine their income. This all means that the exposition with which we started when we simply accepted each individual's wealth and income as a given datum in analyzing consumers' market behavior is now a closed circle.

The circle of our exposition just matches the circular flow of money from households to business firms and back to households, with the flow of goods and services going to the opposite direction. On the other hand, the logic of the analysis involves no circularity. The analysis relies on a simultaneous determination of interdependent outputs of various goods—along the lines of the simultaneous solution of a set of equations. Not surprisingly, the analysis will be based on demand for and supply of productive services. In this chapter, we investigate the general conditions of demand for productive resources as derived from the uses to which the resources can be put.

Demand for Productive Services

If producers were to sell their products directly to consumers, the production-process decision would be simple; the value of a producer's good is the value of what it produces in the form of consumers' goods—just as in our earlier five-man economy. What is meant by the expression "what it produces"? If two or more producer goods are jointly or simultaneously used as productive "inputs," what part is produced by each? If I mow a lawn *with* a lawn mower, how much did I produce, and how much did the mower produce? If three people jointly move a box, how much did each person move? When a carpenter builds a house, does he produce it, or is it produced by the people who make the nails, lumber, etc.? With jointly used productive resources, it is impossible to measure or even define what part of the item is produced by a jointly used input. Thus, no identifiable value of product can be imputed to the joint, cooperating productive resource.

This question of "what it produces" has been raised here simply because it is really a "red herring," after all. You may have heard it said that in the Communist society each will be paid not according to what he produces but according to what he deserves or needs. Whatever may be the emotional worth of that statement, it is analytically meaningless. And if it is said of the capitalist system that people are paid according to their product, that, too, is a meaningless statement. Instead of asking the meaningless question of whether some input gets what it produces, we ask, "What determines what it gets—i.e., its price?"

Labor and Capital as Standard Names of Inputs

To facilitate derivation of a generally applicable answer, we shall find it convenient to speak of just two general kinds of inputs, even though there is in reality an infinite variety of types. Rather than identify the particular inputs in each case, we could call them inputs *A* and *B*. More commonly, the standard names given to the two broadest classes of inputs are *labor* and *capital,* although the inputs in any real situation may be different types of labor, or different types of nonhuman goods.

Every person except the one at death's door is a form of capital good. And almost every physical good is a form of labor, in the sense that someone's labor was involved in making it as valuable as it is now. Choices among productive inputs, although commonly expressed by the pair "labor" and "capital," must be clearly understood to be choices among two different varieties of inputs —both of which may be types of labor services or both of which may be current physical goods. We shall for present purposes arbitrarily call one input labor and the other capital—letting the exact goods be identified by the details of each real situation.

Variety of Productive Techniques

There are alternative production techniques for every good, and a choice among them must be made. One technique differs from another if they use different proportions of productive inputs. One technique may use more water and less cooling equipment; another may use more laborers on the site of production and less equipment made earlier by laborers elsewhere. One technique may use more electric power, while another uses more hand power. Houses can be built with varying combinations of power tools, pre-cut lumber, on-the-site assembly, and common-laborer assistants. In the operation of a grocery store, the variety of available techniques is enormous. You can hire fewer butchers if you have them devote their time only to cutting, while women clerks sell the cuts of meat to customers. Refrigeration enables the store to display arrays of cuts of meat wrapped in plastic. The butchers can be provided with power cutting equipment and elaborate facilities, or these can be dispensed with by the use of more butchers. At the checking stand an expert cash-register operator can concentrate on checking items purchased by the customer, with an automatic machine to deliver "change" to the customer, plus a moving belt to convey the groceries past the checker and on to a high-school boy who bags and boxes the groceries for the customer. Alternatively, the grocer could use more clerks and less equipment and still sell the same amount of groceries at the same rate.

That there is an unlimited variety of ways of doing something often escapes our notice simply because we usually see very similar ways used in our own neighborhood of experience. But if you travel to other countries or regions and look for these differences, you will see them. The alert businessman watches competitors and other producers; he subscribes to trade journals that tell about ways to improve his operation. Salesmen for equipment tell him of different ways of doing things, and seek to show why their way is better. Labor-union representatives suggest that things are done differently in other firms. Business consultants are hired; employees are hired away from other firms to facilitate copying their techniques.

The Law of Variable Proportions

The fundamental pervasive properties of the "production function"—the relationship between alternative combinations of inputs and the resulting product—can be illustrated by the data in Table 26–1. The table presents amounts of outputs produced by different combinations of two inputs, *L* and *C*—each considered to be a homogeneous resource.

In Table 26–1, increasing *rates* of use of *L* are involved as one moves horizontally from left to right, while the rate of use of *C* increases as one moves vertically. The inputs of *L* and *C* are measured in rates of use of physical units, while the output of *X* is given in the rates of physical output. If the selling price of *X* is a constant $1 for different rates of output (price-takers' market in sale of *X*), the output data can be considered as value data. Within each cell (intersection of a column and row) is given the value of the output produced with the production "technique" or "process" identified by the input combination of *L* and *C* associated with that cell's column and row. For example, the technique using one unit of *L* and six units of *C* yields an output of $246 of *X*. A bigger output of *X* cannot be produced with known methods except by using more *L* or *C*. You can get less with the same amount of *L* and *C* if you are technologically inefficient, but the data presented here all represent *technologically efficient* techniques—i.e., the output of X is in each cell the maximum producible with the specified amounts of inputs and existing technology.

Table 26–1

PRODUCTION OF X AS FUNCTION OF INPUTS OF L AND C

Inputs of Capital		Output of X					
	6	246	304	340	372	395	416
	5	224	277	310	340	360	376
	4	200	246	277	302	321	333
	3	171	210	237	259	277	285
	2	141	172	194	214	228	234
	1	100	121	138	152	162	165
		1	2	3	4	5	6
		Inputs of Labor					

All this discussion of substitutability and variability of combinations of inputs can be summarized in a *law of variable proportions*—"the proportions or combinations in which productive inputs can be used in producing any specified output is not a fixed, invariant proportion."

Technological Efficiency

Examination of Table 26–1 reveals several ways to produce, say, 277 units of X. It can be done with $5C$ and $2L$, with $4C$ and $3L$, or with $3C$ and $5L$. Other combinations are available if we consider non-integral amounts of C and L; thus, something between $3C$ and $4C$ along with $4L$, or about $4.5C$ and $4.5L$, will produce $277X$. All these combinations are technologically efficient in that it is impossible to produce $277X$ with less inputs. If there were no law of variable proportions (no substitutability among inputs), only one combination of L and C could produce $277X$. However, there always is more than one technologically efficient way to produce any specified output. And this introduces the question of *economic* efficiency in production: Which of the technologically efficient processes shall be used? Or, which is the *economically* efficient method?

Economic Efficiency

Should the selected process be the simplest, or the most recently discovered, the most reliable, the most commonly used, or the one that uses the least amount of scarce, critical materials? Or should you select the technique that involves large expenditures now but only small ones later? Should you pick the techniques that maximize the output per unit of labor? Or per unit of raw materials purchased? (Which raw material?) Or per unit of power used? Or per unit of floor space in the factory? Actually, none of these would be encouraged by the capitalist market system.[1]

Will society penalize you for using an inappropriate criterion? It will, indeed. But what is the appropriate criterion? The answer depends in part upon the economic system used—i.e., upon the property right enforced. In a capitalistic system, the criterion imposed on users of productive resources is that they achieve the highest known market value of the output obtainable with those resources, or—what is the same thing—achieve a given output at minimum cost. Failure to do that will impose a loss of wealth on the user. Any individual who does not use resources in line with that objective will find that other people will bid away those resources in ways that will increase their wealth. He sacrifices that potential increase in his own wealth. Market competition for resources will make it expensive to persist in using resources inefficiently. He will find himself less able to retain command over the use of productive resources, which will be diverted to other users who are more successful at discerning the wealth-maximizing techniques of production. His personal desire for more wealth rather than less will "force" him to choose the higher-valued, or lower-cost, techniques. Whether you judge that to be a desirable solution depends upon your evaluation of the social, cultural, and economic consequences. At any rate, it is an *accurate and valid* explanation of the incentive system that operates in the private-property economy.

Efficient Production Techniques and Relative Prices of Inputs

Returning to our numerical example, we know that there are different ways to produce an output of 277 units of X. The table shows three ways (if we, for

[1] From one point of view, the question of the appropriate combination of inputs may seem pointless. After all, at any moment there is a certain amount of each productive resource in the community and hence a given over-all ratio of inputs. With full use of resources the community can't help but use the resources in that given ratio. That is true for the community *as a whole,* but consistent with that over-all total ratio of inputs is an unlimited set of different sub-combinations of use by the producers of various goods. The question is not, then, to select the average ratio for the economy, but the specific allocation among the many members of the community competing for those resources. Upon what criterion shall it be decided for each person, and resource, how much to allocate to each productive task?

simplicity of computation, look only at the ways involving integral units of input). Thus, five units of capital and two units of labor, or four units of capital and three units of labor, or three units of capital and five of labor will do the trick. All are equally efficient in a *technological* sense, but only one is *economically* efficient. Which one? It depends upon the prices of labor and capital. Suppose that a unit of capital costs $35 and a unit of labor costs $30. Then, the lowest-cost, or economically efficient, method happens to be the one with four capital and three labor. The cost is $(4 \times \$35) + (3 \times \$30) = \$230$. The costs for the other combinations at these prices are shown in the middle column of Table 26–2. This table also shows the costs of production if the input prices are different.

Table 26–2

COSTS OF PRODUCING 277 UNITS OF *X* AT DIFFERENT PRICES AND INPUT COMBINATIONS OF CAPITAL AND LABOR

			Prices		
	Capital		$30	$35	$45
		Labor	$50	$30	$15
Quantity	5	2	$250	$235	$255
	4	3	340	255	210
	3	5	270	230	225

Suppose the price of capital had been higher (say, $45) and the price of labor lower ($15). Now which of these alternative techniques, all equally efficient technologically, is the economically efficient one—i.e., the lowest-cost technique? Recomputing costs gives the results entered in the right-hand column of Table 26–2. The economically efficient combination has moved to one with more labor and less capital. This is not surprising, since capital is now more expensive than formerly, while labor is cheaper.

Conversely, if the price of labor had increased to $50 and the price of capital had fallen to $30, the costs would be those given in the first column in Table 26–2. This shifts the economic technique to five capital and two labor. As would be expected, the lower price of capital moves the efficient technique to a combination with more capital relative to labor.

The Law of Diminishing Marginal Returns

The direction of shift in the economically efficient combination of inputs implied by a change of input prices can be derived from the fundamental laws of production. To illustrate the procedure, reconsider the data of Table 26–1.

Look at the output data along one horizontal row; for example, the row with three units of capital shows outputs of 171, 210, 237, 259, 277, and 285 as the input of labor increases from one to six units. Each unit increase of labor used jointly with the fixed amount of capital yields a larger output. The output increases from 171 to 210 (an increase of 39) as a second unit of labor is applied to three units of capital. The increment of output with the third unit of labor is 27 units of X (237 — 210). The increment for the fourth unit added of labor is 22 units of X. The increments in total output with increases of X are shown in Table 26–3, which must be read along the *rows;* each *row* is for fixed amount of capital and unit increments of labor. The increments in output with one more unit of labor are called *marginal* products of labor.

Table 26–3

INCREMENTS IN OUTPUT FOR UNIT INCREMENTS OF LABOR WITH VARIOUS FIXED AMOUNTS OF CAPITAL

		Marginal Products of Labor						
Fixed Amounts of Capital	6	246	58	36	32	23	19	....
	5	224	53	33	30	20	16	....
	4	200	46	31	25	19	12	....
	3	171	39	27	22	18	8	....
	2	141	31	22	20	14	6	....
	1	100	21	17	14	10	3	....
		1	2	3	4	5	6	....
		Imputs of Labor						

Two cautioning remarks against misinterpretations are warranted. First, these increments are obtained by the use of one additional unit of labor with the same amount of capital. In adjusting inputs to this larger amount of labor, one can rearrange the physical form of the capital so that it is most effectively used with the larger amount of labor.

The second remark concerns the meaning of "product." When four units of labor and three of capital are used, the total product is 259 units of X. How much of that is due to the capital and how much to the labor? As we said earlier, there can be no answer to that question. All we can know is that when four units of labor and three of capital are used jointly, the total output is 259. Take away either all the labor or all the capital, and the output is zero.

Nor does the marginal-product concept give an answer to the question of

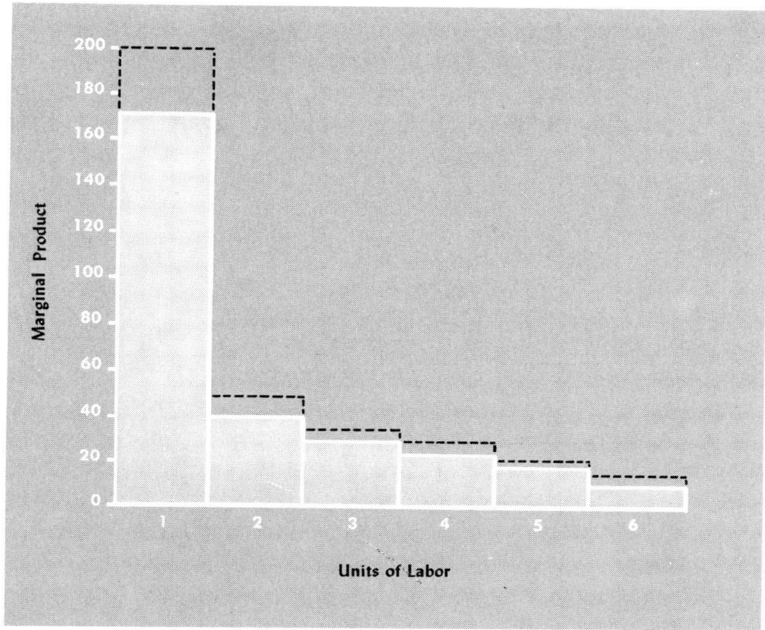

FIGURE 26–2. Marginal products of labor: with three units of capital (———); with four units of capital (– – –).

"how much a unit of input produces." According to Table 26–3, the marginal product of four units of labor (as compared to three units of labor) used jointly with three units of capital is 22 units of X. Twenty-two units of X are not produced by the fourth unit of labor. Instead, that is the increase in the total product when four units of labor are used instead of three units, along with three units of capital. If a basketball team used six men instead of five, would the sixth man say that *he* produced the larger score? If he did, he would be at least wrong and possibly immodest, since all the men are responsible. Each can validly claim that six of them produce more than do five, by the amounts of the marginal product for six people. Instead of referring to the marginal product *of the sixth worker,* then, we should speak of the marginal product *of labor* when the number of workers is six.

DIMINISHING MARGINAL RETURNS AND DEMAND FOR INPUTS

A graph of the diminishing marginal products of labor, for capital fixed at three units, is shown in Figure 26–2. Also shown (with dashed lines) is the diminishing marginal product of labor, for capital fixed at four units. The data for this graph are obtained from Table 26–3.

The marginal products in Table 26–3 diminish as one reads a row from left to right. These are the marginal products of labor. Although the productive process is adjusted to take full advantage of greater amounts of L, each increment in L yields *diminishing* increments in output. This can be generalized: "In any production process, as the amount of the inputs is increased, with fixed amounts of other inputs, the marginal products resulting from increments of the input *decrease*, after reaching a maximum—called the point of diminishing marginal returns." This law holds whether output be measured as rate or volume. Note that it is not the *total* output but the *marginal* product of an increasing input that reaches a maximum; and then, as more input is added, the *increment* is *positive* but successively *decreasing*. Table 26–3 illustrates this law, wherein the data given are all beyond the point of diminishing marginal returns.

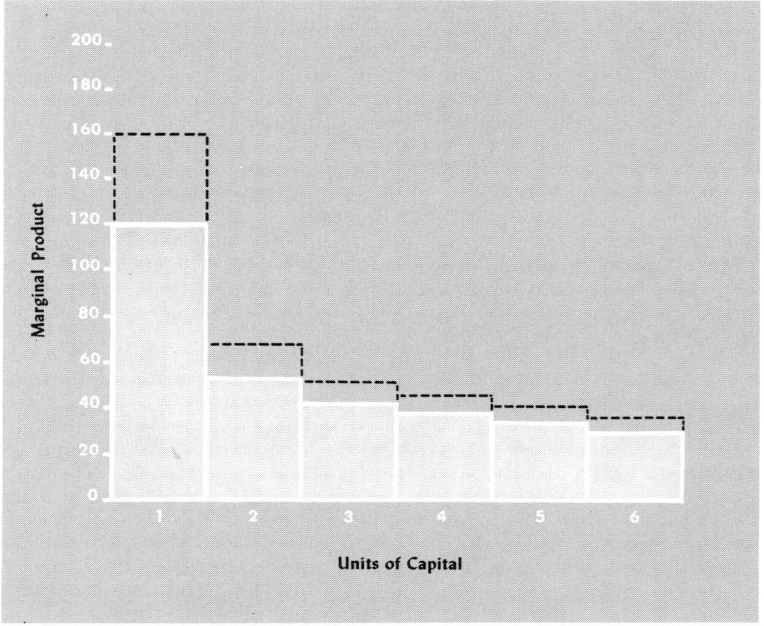

FIGURE 26–3. Marginal products of capital: with two units of labor (———); with five units of labor (– – –).

Capital can just as well be treated as the variable input. Again, the law of diminishing marginal returns will hold; that law holds for every productive resource. Table 26–4 shows diminishing marginal products of capital, for alternative fixed amounts of labor. The data are to be read up along *columns*. As one progresses up a column, the marginal product of capital diminishes. Figure 26–3 is a graph of the marginal products with labor set at five units. Also shown is the marginal-product curve for capital with labor set at two units. The latter (with fewer jointly used inputs) lies under the former curve.

Table 26–4

MARGINAL PRODUCT OF CAPITAL FOR FIXED AMOUNTS OF JOINTLY USED LABOR

Variable Inputs of Capital		Marginal Products of Capital					
	.	.	.	.	.	.	.
	6	22	27	30	32	35	40
	5	24	31	33	38	39	43
	4	29	36	40	43	45	48
	3	30	42	43	45	49	55
	2	41	51	56	62	66	69
	1	100	121	138	152	162	165
		1	2	3	4	5	6
		Fixed Amounts of Labor					

This law of diminishing marginal product implies the uniqueness of the direction in which cost-minimizing input combinations will shift in response to changes in input prices. To see this, we use a mathematical truism that is satisfied at any cost-minimizing combination of inputs that yields a specified output. This condition can be expressed as follows:

At the lowest-cost combination of inputs for any specified output, the *ratio of the marginal products* of the inputs equals the ratio of the marginal costs (or prices) of the inputs. Thus,

$$MPL/MPC = P_L/P_C,$$

where MPL and MPC denote the marginal product of labor and of capital, and P_L and P_C denote the marginal cost or price of labor and of capital. This condition can be re-expressed as

$$MPL/P_L = MPC/P_C.$$

That is, the marginal product from an extra dollar spent for labor should equal the marginal product of an extra dollar spent for capital. If these two ratios are not equal, costs can be reduced by using more of the input with the higher ratio of marginal value product per dollar of extra cost and less of the others.

A numerical illustration is provided in Tables 26–5 and 26–6, which show three different combinations of labor and capital yielding 277 units of X and the marginal products and their ratios at each combination. When the price of capital is $35 and the price of labor is $30, the combination with the ratio of marginal products nearest the price ratio, 35/30, is the combination of four units of capital and three units of labor. It is therefore the lowest-cost combination of those listed for the output of 277X. (An exact equality between the ratios of marginal products and prices could be achieved if interpolation with small adjustments in amounts of input were considered.)

Table 26–5

RATIOS OF MARGINAL PRODUCTS OF REPRESENTATIVE INPUT COMBINATIONS FOR AN OUTPUT OF 277X

(PRICE OF CAPITAL = $35; PRICE OF LABOR = $30)

Quantity of		Marginal Product of		Ratio of Marginal Products	Price Ratio	Total Costs
Capital	Labor	Capital	Labor			
5	2	31	53	31/52 = .6	$35/$30 = 1.16	$235
4	3	40	31	40/31 = 1.3	1.16	230
3	5	49	18	49/18 = 2.7	1.16	255

If the prices of the inputs were $30 for labor and $50 for capital, the results would be those in Table 26–6. The change in relative prices has shifted the low-cost combination toward one with a ratio of marginal products of 0.6, which is equal to the new input-price ratio.

This numerical example illustrates that the lower the price of capital relative to labor, the greater the amount of capital that will be employed. For if the price of capital is lower, the ratio of marginal product of capital must be lowered relative to the marginal product of labor. This ratio can be lowered by increasing the amount of capital employed. A minimum-cost method of production, combined with the law of diminishing marginal returns, implies a demand that involves greater use of inputs at lower prices. Again we find our old friend the law of demand applicable here to the demand for productive services by busi-

Table 26–6

RATIOS OF MARGINAL PRODUCTS OF REPRESENTATIVE INPUT COMBINATIONS FOR AN OUTPUT OF 277X

(PRICE OF CAPITAL = $30; PRICE OF LABOR = $50)

Quantity of Capital	Quantity of Labor	*MPC/MPL*	P_C/P_L	Total Costs
5	2	.6	.6	$250
4	3	1.3	.6	270
3	5	2.7	.6	340

ness firms, just as it applied to the demand by consumers for consumers' goods: The lower the price, the greater the amount demanded—whether it be for bread, shoes, or labor services.

INTERPRETATIONS OF THE LAW OF DIMINISHING RETURNS

The law of diminishing marginal returns is much misunderstood and misused. It is not a law foreboding a declining future of the world. It does not say that the rate of growth of output will diminish. It does not deny that increases of knowledge with time will enable man to improve his technology and increase the output from a given set of available resources. Nor does it say that the *total* output decreases with greater amounts of some inputs or productive factors. Yet the law is an accurate characterization of what happens in the real world.

What would you observe if the law of diminishing marginal productivity did *not* hold? That would mean that with a pot of soil one could add successive increments of capital to that soil and feed the world. But we don't see all the wheat being grown on the one acre of best wheat land. Suppose you were a farmer with 100 acres of land and your neighbor offered to let you have the use of his land (just as good as yours) for one year for free. To use it would require some resources. But you could use those extra resources on your land and get as much as you could on his land, since your land is just as good. There would be no gain from use of more land. You would never consider using any land except the very best single acre you had. In fact, however, farmers do cultivate inferior qualities of land by putting some resources on the inferior land, even though they have to divert those resources from the superior land. Why don't they concentrate solely on the superior land? Because of diminishing marginal returns to increments of resources on any fixed amount of other resource.

A grocery store, a manufacturing plant, a trucking company—all of them would delightedly accept more resources at a zero price, even if their use required some diversion of other resources. Why would anyone be willing to divert resources? Because those resources will produce a larger total product if some are diverted to uses with the newly available resources than if their more intensive use is continued solely with the presently available resources.

In *no* production activity do we observe only the single most superior unit of some resource being used while the slightly inferior units are left idle, even though available at a zero price. That *would* happen if the law of diminishing marginal returns were false.

In summary, a given amount of resources will be allocated over other resources of varying quality until the marginal product of the given resource is equal in all its uses. Labor will be applied to superior land *and* to inferior land. The greater, more *intensive* use of labor on the superior land brings its marginal product down to the same marginal product as the less intensive use on the inferior land.[2]

Although the marginal productivities of any given homogeneous input are pushed toward equality in all its alternative uses, the equalizing marginal productivity of one homogeneous input need not equal the marginal productivity of some *other input*. What controls the particular equalized value of achieved marginal product of any resource? That is the question for the next section.

Marginal Value of Output with Larger Rate of Output

The basis for the demand relationship between price of input and the amount demanded in any use relies on a *substitution* effect, wherein more is used of the lower-priced input and less of the more expensive *without changing the total output*. We must now examine the effect of a lower price of an input in

[2] Recognition of various intensive margins, at which the marginal products of an input are equated by varying the allocation of the input, is important because it generalizes the earlier simplified analysis of production (in Chapter 17), which was based on only one unit of each of several different qualities of productive inputs. That chapter explained only the assignment of different *kinds* or qualities of resources on the oversimplified principle that each input had a constant marginal product no matter how much it was used to produce *Y* rather than *X*. That assumption appeared as the constant marginal cost of producing *X* by one of the people, *A*, *B*, etc., regardless of how much *Y* the person produced. There we had decreasing marginal products (or increasing marginal costs) only by bringing in inferior producers, after first utilizing the lower-cost producers of *Y*. However, the present law says that there is a diminishing marginal product for applications of increasing amounts of each input as it is used more intensively with any specified amount of other resources. Therefore, now, for efficient production an input should be increased wherever its marginal product exceeds its marginal product in other directions of use (where it should be decreased). We can thereby apply our analysis to the assignments of *amounts* of different, but homogeneous, inputs, as well as to assignments of different kinds of inputs.

lowering production costs and increasing production by an increased employment of the lower-priced input. This input response to lower prices can be illustrated with the production data given in Tables 26–3 and 26–4. Suppose each unit of X produced will sell in the market for \$1, regardless of the amount this particular producer offers for sale (i.e., he is in a price-takers' market). Suppose he has three units of capital. How many units of labor should he use if the price of a unit of labor is \$20? If he hires one, the value of product is \$171, as compared to hiring none and producing nothing. If he hires two units of labor, the marginal value of the product is \$39—which is more than the extra cost of a second unit of labor. The marginal value of the product exceeds the marginal cost of a second unit of labor. If he hires a third unit, the marginal value of output, or marginal revenue, is \$27—which exceeds the wage rate, or marginal cost, of labor. If he employs four units of labor, the marginal product will exceed the marginal cost. His earnings will increase by the excess of the marginal value of product over the marginal cost of labor—\$2 = (\$22 − \$20). But if he were to use a fifth unit of labor (with three units of capital), the marginal value of product would be only \$18, which is \$2 less than the marginal cost, leaving him with a loss on this extra output. He achieves maximum earnings if he hires four units of labor (*given* that he uses three units of capital—an assumption we shall later abandon).

A little reflection will indicate that the diminishing marginal value of product provides another force for buying more at a lower price—in particular, for determining how much to buy at each price. Whatever the market price for employing labor, the employer will hire units of labor up to the point beyond which the marginal value of product is less than the marginal cost of the input —if he has free access to the markets for this particular input. Both the increased output effect and the substitution effect induce an increased use of the input at a lower price.

Maximum-Profit Output-Input Combination and Demand for Inputs

Let us now apply marginal-productivity analysis and simultaneously review what it implies about both the combination of inputs *and* the amount of output for a producer interested in maximizing his wealth—assuming his production possibilities are given by the data of Table 26–1. Start at a level of two units of capital, although any starting point would do. How many units of labor should he use if the price of X is \$1 and the price of labor and capital are \$30 and \$35, respectively? The answer will be found by using the marginal-product data in Tables 26–3 and 26–4. Looking first at Table 26–3, showing the marginal product of labor, we see in the row of two units of capital that it will pay to employ two units of labor. A third one would yield a marginal product less than the costs of hiring it. But now that the producer has two units of labor and two capital, he should inquire if it would pay to increase capital.

Looking at the marginal products of capital in Table 26–4, and reading up the column identified with two units of labor, we see that it will pay to increase the capital to four units. A fifth unit would yield a marginal product of \$31, less than its cost of \$35. Having expanded the use of capital and *also the output,* he will again ask whether it would pay to revise the amount of labor, since he earlier computed the appropriate labor input when he had only two units of capital. Returning to Table 26–3, we read along the row associated with four units of capital and find that it will pay him to employ a total of three labor, one more than he now has. A fourth unit of labor will yield a marginal product less than its cost. At four units of capital and three units of labor, the output has increased to \$277 of X. No further application of capital or labor is profitable.

Where has this producer arrived? At the maximum-profit, or wealth, output and *also* at the minimum-cost method of producing that particular output. To check this, we can compute total receipts for each of the combinations of Table 26–1 (multiply the output by the \$1 selling price per unit) and then, by subtracting the total costs (the sum of the products of price and quantity of each input), we get the differences, which are the profits or losses. The output with the maximum profit is 277 units of X if it is produced by the input combination of four units of capital and three units of labor. The output value is \$277, and the costs are \$230 $=(4 \times \$35)+(3 \times \$30)$, yielding a profit of \$47. No other input combination and associated output yields a bigger profit (unless you resort to interpolation between the integral amounts of each cell).

Furthermore, he will always be led to this selection of the maximum-profit output and technique of production that is economically efficient. The maximum-profit output and the lowest-cost method of producing it can be identified, even though one looks only at the behavior of the marginal products of the inputs.

The general condition holding true at that combination which yields the output with the greatest wealth is: "The marginal value-product of an extra dollar's worth of each and every input is equal to a dollar." If any further increment of any input would yield a return greater than the increment in cost, profits could be increased. Possibilities of increasing profits are exhausted when the amount of each input is such that the marginal value-product of increments of any input has been reduced to equality with the marginal cost of that input. This condition includes as a special case the condition indicated earlier for a minimum-cost method of production of whatever amount of output is produced; i.e., the former condition of

$$MPC/MPL = P_C/P_L$$

is replaced by a more restrictive pair of conditions,

$$MPC = P_C$$

and

$$MPL = P_L.$$

When these are satisfied, the former certainly is. But the former could be satisfied—indicating that the output, whatever it was, was being produced in the lowest-cost way known—even though the present conditions are not satisfied. The present conditions say not only that the output produced is produced in the lowest-cost way known for producing it, but also that this output yields the maximum profits.

From this stronger condition, the achievement of which rests on market competition and the desire for profit-maximizing outputs, we have even stronger reason to conclude that the market demand for inputs is a negative function of their prices. If the price of capital falls, the marginal product of capital will be adjusted downward by increasing the amount of capital, both to substitute some of it for labor and also to increase the output, which at a lower cost can be profitably sold in greater amount.

Position of Demand Function

Not only is the market-demand schedule for a resource a negative function of its price, but its position (the amounts demanded at various specified prices) depends upon (1) the quantity (and hence price) of other jointly used inputs and (2) the price of the output. Inspection of Table 26–3 shows that the marginal value-product of labor depends upon which row you read. The more capital (the higher the row), the greater the marginal products of labor. In that table, a larger amount of capital causes a higher demand for labor. The two resources are said to be *complementary*. The opposite effect could have occurred: larger amounts of capital might have caused small marginal products for labor. They then are called substitutes. Unfortunately, this is very misleading terminology. The two inputs are *substitutes* for each other even though they are complements in the sense just indicated. One can always use more labor and less capital. The term "substitutes" has two different meanings: (1) It means that it is possible to produce some specified rate of output with less of one input and more of another. (2) It means that more of one input causes a lower marginal product for the existing amount of the other resource. It is in the former sense that the term "substitutable" is ordinarily used. A more precise term for the second effect would be "negative cross-marginal productivity," suggesting that the effect of increasing one resource "crosses over" to another resource and lowers its marginal product, too. In our Table 26–1, there is positive cross-marginal productivity, and negative self-marginal productivity (called the law of *diminishing* marginal returns).

Not enough is known to tell in advance whether the interaction between two joint inputs will raise or lower the marginal productive schedule of the other as the amount of one of them is increased. But whatever the effect on the position of the marginal value-productivity schedule, the implied demand schedule retains its negative slope with respect to its price relative to prices of other inputs.

It is difficult to overstress that the marginal product of any worker is a function not merely of his own inherent and acquired talents and education but also of the quality and quantity of other goods with which he can work jointly. To "work jointly" does not mean merely to work hand in hand with other goods, as a carpenter works with a hammer, a seamstress with a needle, or a driver with a truck. It means also the equipment and resources of the whole economy. The transportation system, power costs, the education and technology of other workers, the effectiveness of the market in facilitating specialization and exchange, the amount of theft, the extent to which contracts are honored—all these are examples of "joint cooperative resources."

Take all the carpenters in any small city in the United States to India, Morocco, Brazil, or Indonesia. The wages they would get are lower simply because there is less jointly available "capital." A richer country with lots of capital equipment is a better place for a given amount of labor. While the productivity of the American carpenters would be less in those other countries than in the United States, the productivity would be greater than for natives of those countries—a reflection of the greater technology or education of the Americans.

Inter-firm Input Substitution

The demand relationship between the price of an input and the amount of its use is not dependent upon only the purposive adjustment of each producer. Even if no producer were to shift toward the more efficient combination, each would experience a change in his profits. Those firms nearer the new, more efficient combination—whatever the reason they happened to be there—will have a greater increase in their profits than will those firms whose input techniques are now less efficient. The efficiency of any utilized technique is changed not merely by adjustment of the producer in his utilized inputs but also by the shift in relative prices of inputs. Profits and losses will be different as a result of the revised price structure, with the bigger rewards going to the possibly inadvertently lucky firms that happened to have the input combination nearest the most appropriate. Less favored firms with less efficient techniques will experience bigger losses or smaller profits and will soon be dominated by the more rapid growth and proliferation of the more efficient combinations.

The changing environment *adopts* the more appropriate existing techniques by rewarding them with greater profits and growth whether or not the individual producers themselves *adapt* to the new price situation. We need not go to the extreme and assert that people, like nonmotivated plants, will not adapt to circumstances. Productive techniques of the more successful firms will be copied. The imitating firm, emulating the successful firm, may not know the marginal productivities of various inputs. All it knows is what tested techniques did succeed best. Not even the initially successful firm has to know the marginal products. All it has to do is simply be nearest the "right" combination. Whether it got there by calculating marginal productivities via an extensive research and testing program, by sheer accident, astrologers, or consulting economists is irrelevant. The fact of success is sufficient.

Competition among firms with different productive techniques is a selective discriminating force, just as is purposive, knowledgeable discrimination by one producer among alternative available production techniques. To the extent that individuals are protected in their right to offer their wares in an open market, inter-firm market competition adds its force to the intra-firm selectivity of production techniques in generating and strengthening the observed demand relationship between price and rate of use of inputs.

Input Substitution by Output Substitution

There is still another way in which the lower price of an input induces bigger employment. Even if there were no possible substitution between jointly used inputs of a given product, the lower price of some inputs leads to lower costs of those goods in which it is a cost item, and this increases the amount of the input used. Consumer goods that use more of the now relatively more expensive inputs will be relatively more costly, and their sales or profits will decrease. Therefore, substitution among inputs also occurs *via* substitution among the goods they produce, as well as by the previously mentioned shifting of inputs within the production processes of a good. If the price of plastics falls relative to glass, the supply schedule of plastic containers increases relative to that of glass bottles; the price of plastic containers falls; the consumer buys more plastic containers; and plastics are thereby substituted for glass. This effect, operating through the consumer's substitution of different consumer goods, is called inter-product substitution.

Speed of Substitution and Adjustment of Production Techniques

Making substitutions and changing the rates of employment of inputs are costly activities. One doesn't change a production technique merely by a wave of the hand. He must learn of new ways. He must administer his decision; he must rearrange the inputs; and he must schedule the arrival of the new inputs so as to ensure efficient coordination. In other words, the amount of substitution carried out in response to a new price situation depends upon how much time has elapsed since the price change. The longer the time, the more the amount of substitution or revision of employment of inputs that will have taken place. In terms of demand schedules, the demand response for an input is more elastic with respect to a price change, the longer the time since the price change. This same proposition also holds for demands for consumers' goods. And it can be portrayed graphically by showing different demand curves for different times after the price changes from that level at which the curves are all shown intersecting each other—as in Figure 6–2 back in Chapter 6.

The relatively inelastic demand for an input in the immediate period, when changes can be made at relatively high adjustment costs, sometimes misleads people into thinking that the price change has no effect on the amount demanded. But in the ensuing days, or weeks, the adjustments can be made at a more economic pace. Since they are made after a substantial interval, the changes often are not identified as consequences of the price change. Of course, the employer need not announce to the inputs that he no longer will buy so much of their services because their price is too high. He simply has to say that his sales aren't big enough to warrant their employment.

As an illustrative example, we cite the rise in wages of elevator boys in Chicago. Formerly, wages were $1 to $1.25 an hour. The elevator-operator union imposed a minimum wage of $2.40 an hour for operators in downtown (not suburban) Chicago buildings. Owners of buildings are thereby induced to install additional automatic elevators, which can be done for an extra annual cost of about $8,000. With two shifts of operators, the higher wage cost of $2.40 per hour raises the cost of manually operated elevators by about $10,000 per year. Clearly, it pays the owner to "automate." This process takes several months. When the elevator operators are discharged several months later, after having been paid $2.40 an hour for the intervening time, they are not likely to believe that it was a result of the higher wage, since that was "initiated" a long time ago. They blame it on "automation." This is not to say that all introduction of automatic equipment is a response to higher wages (as we shall see in the next chapters) nor does it imply that higher than open-market wages are "wrong."

Pricing of Productive Resources

If the price of an input is not set by administrative fiat, decree, law, or inviolate custom, employers will be able legally to bid higher or lower prices in the open market for inputs, according to whether they want more or less inputs than they can get at the present price. If at its present price there are not enough inputs of L available to bring its marginal product down to that price, some employers will find it profitable to bid a higher price for more inputs of *L*, rather than leave demand unsatisfied. The higher price will reduce the amount of that input demanded. The higher price bid will attract inputs from other uses, which raises the price they must be offered in order to be kept at former tasks. In this way, the prices paid for this resource by buyers in various industries are correlated and brought together. The differences in prices that will not be competitively erased reflect nonpecuniary offers by buyers—better working conditions or more pleasant and congenial employers.

The determination of prices of productive goods and rates of employment is the determination of wealth of their owners. This formally completes our expository circle. From given wealth and preference patterns of people, reflected in their market demands for consumers' goods, we have gone via derived demands for inputs to the prices of resources and hence to income and wealth of those who provide or own the resources. Prices and outputs of consumers' goods, the wealth of individuals, and the allocation of productive goods have been analyzed primarily in the context of a market-exchange, private-property system—although we have occasionally considered these questions under other systems. If access to an open market is restricted, or limitations are imposed on permissible bids or offers, the extent of adjustment of output to consumers' market demands is reduced; the efficient allocation of inputs is weakened, and the wealth of owners of productive goods is made less dependent upon satisfaction of consumers' market-revealed preferences.

Nothing in this analysis implies that such attenuation of efficiency in production or composition of output is undesirable. That depends upon whether or not one prefers the economic, cultural, and political implications of a free-market, private-property exchange system. Those who dislike that system (because they think they could achieve what they regard as a better way of life with a differently weighted mix of types of competition for resolving conflicts of interests in the presence of scarcity) will, of course, try to reduce the scope of that system. For example, people with certain kinds of personalities may find "vote-getting," political competition more favorable to them than market competition. They will prefer political competition and will expect to gain from extension of this realm of government activity. Socialists express that preference and intent. Some capitalists express a different preference; and yet some seek government limitation on their market competitors. By this stage of this book, it should be obvious that although some of the differences in cultural, political, and economic consequences of various economic systems are discernible with the aid of economic theory, economic theory cannot evaluate their propriety.

Generality of Marginal-Productivity Theory

Before summarizing the analysis of this chapter, a few precautionary comments may forestall some erroneous inferences.

(1) The payment to each productive input is its price. The rate of employment of that kind of input and of others is so adjusted that the marginal product of a unit is moved toward equality with its price. If we multiply the number of employed units by the marginal product, which equals its price in equilibrium, we should get the total income to that kind of resource. For example, suppose that in our Table 26–1 we were employing three units of labor and one unit of capital, because the price of labor was $17 while the price of capital was $138. We now compute the total income to capital and labor from our firm. Three units of labor at $17 each is $54 income, while the one unit of capital gets $138. The total payments to the productive resources are $54 + $138 = $192, an amount that *exceeds* the total value of the output produced, $138. How can a producer continue in this situation? How could a whole economy pay a wage equal to marginal product if that would exceed the total output? Has something gone wrong with our theory? How can inputs be paid more than the total product? This is not impossible, for awhile at least. What it means is that the employer of these productive inputs must make up the difference out of his past accumulated wealth. And this is something he can't do for a very long period. He will lose wealth and will stop hiring or using those inputs in that way.

Abandoned will be the "loss-resulting" production. As resources are released from that business, their supply price to all other potential employers is pushed down. Other employers who were just breaking even or losing money will now be able to get profits or break even by employing the released resources. The situation is saved. No inconsistency is inherent in the open-market equilibrium.

(2) The present analysis does not require the assumption that there be sets of different but internally homogeneous and infinitely divisible resources. They can all be discrete, different items, so that interpolation such as we used in our illustrative example might be impossible, and so that equality between marginal value-product and prices may not be achievable. Instead of equality of marginal value-product and price, an *in*equality condition suffices. Inputs will be employed up to the point beyond which the marginal value-product of the input would be smaller than the marginal cost of the input.

An economist, Senator Paul H. Douglas (Illinois), once wrote a book entitled *The Theory of Wages*, in which he examined in great detail many assumptions and suppositions commonly used in marginal-productivity principles of the demand for productive resources. He showed conclusively that many of the assumptions were oversimplifications of reality, and that some were not true. Many readers concluded that a theory built on those assumptions must therefore be false in its implications about observable events. Do not fall into that error. Every theory abstracts from details and considerations that it is not seeking to explain. All theories make redundant, overly strong assumptions for ease of logical analysis. They assume away certain idiosyncrasies in the interest of concentrating on other phenomena. For example, a theory relating caloric intake to body weight can assume, as a means of abstracting from tangential detail, that all people are alike (for a given age and sex); then certain consequences are implied if caloric intake is increased. It is doubtful that you would challenge the validity of that implication by challenging the validity of the assumption that people are alike or the assumption that when caloric intake is increased, no other events impinge on the individuals—such as their getting sick for other coincident causes. Actually the complexities could be assumed; but then the theory would be cumbersome in having to use more complex methods of notation, logic, mathematics, etc., in deriving and expressing its results. And there is an opposite error. Do not presume that one theory is better than another simply because it is more detailed or realistic in its premises, assumptions, and number of variables considered in its premises. This is a common error, especially among people who are fascinated with the internal logic and number of variables included in a theory rather than with its scope of empirical validity.

(3) Is the marginal-productivity principle of demand applicable only to capitalist economies? No, the marginal-productivity theory of demand is valid in every economy. In the capitalist economy, the increase in wealth belongs to an identifiable *private* owner, or *private* group of owners. If, however, a property holder were not able to keep the profits (or did not have to pay the losses) of his business, he would more heavily weight the other sources affecting his utility. He would be more disposed to employ pretty girls if he weren't able to retain the profits of hiring lower-cost labor that was equally productive of pecuniary value of marketable goods. If the economic rules of surviving in business only mildly punish people for not increasing profits when possible, and if the business owners cannot keep the profits achieved, then neither they nor their employed agents will be influenced by the sources of profits but instead will look more toward the nonmonetary, nonmarketable sources of utility. This, it should be noticed, is implied by the *generalized* marginal-productivity theory of demand. The lower the price of any source of utility, the more it will be used. Market wealth is only one source of utility.

To prohibit or make it more difficult for one to keep and use the profits that he generates by his production decisions raises the cost of increasing his wealth. A rise in the price of keeping personal wealth means that the costs of other sources of personal utility are *relatively* lower than before—in terms of the costs of personal wealth. The only thing changed is the relative costs of sources of "goods" that increase the production of nonmonetary sources of utility. Now that the costs of obtaining pecuniary benefits are higher and the nonpecuniary are lower, he will increase his purchase of goods more heavily loaded with nonpecuniary sources of utility. A lower cost of that nonpecuniary source of utility implies he will purchase more of it. And this he does by looking at the marginal productivity of inputs less in terms of their pecuniary products and more in terms of the nonpecuniary products to him—good looks, racial and religious characteristics, friends, prestige, relaxation, etc. Nonpecuniary discrimination is cheaper and will be more common. Production will be less closely oriented to market demands and values. Less likely also is it that market prices will be sufficiently high to clear the market—for reasons discussed in Chapter 12. The detailed implications of the theory are different only because the relative costs of various sources of production of utility differ. The marginal-productivity principle still stands, as long as one incorporates the various ways of "producing" utility—of which wealth is one.

Our investigation of the selection of productive techniques and uses of productive resources is incomplete in that the *supply conditions of productive resources* were not investigated. The supply of produced inanimate goods is, really, already covered by the earlier discussion of output determination. But the supply of laborers, who are not produced by business firms nor bought and sold like slaves, merits special investigation—something we shall try to provide in the next two chapters.

We summarize the propositions and principles expounded in this chapter.

1. Substitutability among all inputs is pervasive in production.

2. Efficient, wealth-maximizing producers reveal a market-demand curve for inputs that is inversely related to the price of each input. The inverse (or negative) relationship with price of the input results from (a) substitutability among inputs, (b) diminishing marginal value-productivity (which reflects both a decreasing marginal physical product and a lower price of the output as more is sold), (c) substitution by consumers among outputs.

3. A longer-period demand is more elastic than short-period demand. The effect of a price change will be less pronounced immediately than with the passing of some time.

4. Since an increased supply of any resource in the market implies a lower price, the observed response is a shift to techniques employing more of that now lower-priced input. The technique of production is revised toward those that use more of the now more plentiful and cheaper input—all without central direction or planning.

5. The wealth-maximizing activity and market competition among producers lead them toward an economically efficient technique of production—without central direction or dictatorial planning. An "unseen hand" (as Adam Smith called it) is at work—provided, of course, that producers are not constrained by law to use inputs in proportions other than those which they choose in the light of market prices—i.e., to the extent that there is open-market competition.

6. Since the income (or wealth) of any productive resource is determined by its selling price, the incomes of owners of various productive goods, be they labor or nonlabor forms of services, are determined in a free market by the forces of demand and supply. The demand for resources reflects their marginal productivities in various tested highest-valued uses. For this reason, this analysis is often erroneously called the marginal-productivity theory of *pricing* of productive resources. More accurately, it is the marginal-productivity theory of

demand for productive resources—which is to say that it is the basis of demand for productive resources. The marginal-productivity concept is merely an analytic expression for the premise that the demand for resources is derived from the actions of people who are seeking to increase their utility.

7. The marginal-productivity basis for demand applies to all types of economies. Economies based on different systems of property rights differ in the costs imposed on various types of decisions. They do not destroy the validity of the marginal-productivity theory of demand—whether it be demand for consumer goods or for pecuniary or nonpecuniary productive resources, in a capitalist or in a socialist economy. Nor does it have any bearing on how prices are set. They may be set by decree or custom. But the theory is invalid as an explanation of rates of use of inputs if the allocations are also controlled by decree or custom.

Questions

1. Why is economic efficiency a more general test than technical efficiency?

2. There are two kinds of economic efficiency—one of cost minimization and one of profit maximization.

a. In what sense is profit maximization a more general criterion of efficiency?

b. In what sense could it be considered a less desirable criterion?

3. A jet plane can fly across the United States three hours faster than a propeller plane. Which is the more efficient?

4. In Iowa the yield of wheat is 30 bushels per acre compared to 50 bushels per acre in Washington. Which is better?

5. Jet engines are given an efficiency rating according to the thrust generated per pound of engine weight. Explain why that is an inadequate measure of efficiency.

6. Steers can be bred with such superb qualities that they will sell for about 50 percent more per pound than the standard steers raised for meat. Which type should the farmer raise? Give the answer in terms of technological versus economic efficiency.

7. A high-fidelity stereo sound system is called an efficient one if it uses a low amount of electric power per decibel of sound generated. Why is that technical efficiency not an adequate efficiency criterion for choosing among sound systems, even if the quality of the sound were the same?

8. A dam is to be built, and engineers are asked for advice about it. They propose a dam and attest to its efficiency.

a. If they attest to its technical efficiency, does that still leave open the question of its economic efficiency? For example, if they propose to build a dam to store water at a certain site, but if the value of that water is less than the cost of impounding and distributing it, is the dam, though it may be technically efficient, an economically efficient one?

b. This problem extends the notion of economic efficiency beyond the selection of the cheapest way of doing something. Economic efficiency is extended to include what?

9. An American organization may use a communication satellite system to communicate with its branch offices in Europe. But it is cheaper to communicate by cable. Both systems may be used with perfect technical efficiency, but which one is the more efficient in an economic sense?

10. The United States Federal Communication Commission, charged with assigning rights to use of the radio spectrum, says the radio-frequency spectrum should be assigned so as to permit maximum usage.

a. Explain why that statement as it stands is meaningless and useless.

b. Would it have been meaningful to say it should be assigned so as to achieve efficient use?

11. After adding 100 to all the output data in Table 26–1, recompute the marginal products of labor and the marginal products of capital. (This is not as hard and long a problem as it may at first seem.)

12. In Table 26–2, the data are *values* of output, where, for simplicity, each physical unit was assumed to be salable for $1. Suppose instead that the output can be sold for $2 each.

a. Recompute the "marginal value-products" for labor and for capital.

b. What is the effect of a rise in price of the product on the marginal value productivity of inputs?

13. Use the data of Table 26–1 to answer the following questions:

a. Defining efficient production as the lowest-cost method of production, which method is the efficient method for producing 277 units of X if the price of labor is $60 and if the price of capital is $70?

b. If the price of capital is $20 per unit and if labor is $10 per unit, which is the cheaper way to produce 228 units of X: with 2 capital and 5 labor or 5.1 capital and 1 labor?

c. Which is cheaper if the prices are $2 and $1 respectively?

d. $60 and $30 respectively?

e. So long as the prices bear the same ratios to each other, will the same method remain the cheaper method?

14. The law of diminishing returns is a law of diminishing *marginal* returns. What is the difference between diminishing *total* returns and diminishing *marginal* returns?

15. a. In Table 26–3, is the law of diminishing marginal returns illustrated by the decreasing values as one reads a row from right to left, or as one reads a column from bottom to top?

b. Explain the meaning of each method of reading the table.

c. Is Table 26–4 interpreted in the same direction? Why not?

16. Let a particular elevator system be represented by the combination of 3 labor and 4 capital. A change in the elevator is made to permit self-operation. In what direction does this shift the process—as measured by the ratio of labor to capital?

17. "Chicago, August 10, 1962. A federal judge blocked today the firing of thousands of workers on the nation's railroads pending final court ruling on the legality of the drastic economy. Prior to the decision five unions representing the men were ready to order a nation-wide walkout. Today's U.S. District Court action, technically, granted the unions a court order barring the railroads from applying new work rules pending a union appeal to the U.S. Circuit Court of Appeals. Judge Perry said, 'I have preserved and protected the right of appeal,' adding that he felt an interim decision affecting both jobs and capital must be resolved 'in favor of jobs and men.'" In what sense can it be contended instead that the issue is one between jobs *and jobs,* rather than between jobs and capital?

18. Who is substituted for whom when a firm uses one typist, an electric typewriter, and a copying machine rather than two typists and two nonelectric typewriters? This is called a substitution of capital for labor. Why is that misleading?

19. "The advent of the one-man bus involved more capital equipment: an automatically operated coin box and a door control device—to name two of the capital goods that replaced the conductor."

a. Is this a case of capital replacing labor? Where?

b. Is it a case of labor replacing labor? Where?

c. Is it a case of no substitution for labor at all, but instead a job revision with a greater total output? Where?

20. "Invention and the lower cost of power in the home have replaced the domestic servant by capital equipment. Without that machinery more people would be working in homes as 'servants.' But the replacement of domestic employees by capital has not led to the replacement of labor. The released labor is used elsewhere."

a. Can you suggest where?

b. What other goods are more plentiful because of the advent of domestic machinery?

c. Who was aided and who was hurt by the use of the vacuum cleaner, washing machine, water heater, forced-air furnace, garbage disposal, automatic oven, electric mixer, and refrigerator?

21. The electric refrigerator replaced the iceman with capital. By eliminating (i.e., making other means cheaper) the job of the iceman, was the total number of jobs reduced? Explain why not.

22. "Automation does not mean there will be more people than jobs available. It does not mean less jobs for unskilled people—in fact a person can be less skilled if all he has to do is punch buttons, pull triggers, and turn steering wheels, compared to driving a

team of horses, shooting a bow and arrow, or wielding a chisel." Do you agree? If so, why? If not, why not?

23. You operate a factory and discover that some resource used obtains *increasing* marginal returns.

a. What would you do?

b. Does this suggest that we will never find any firm using an amount of resources involving increasing marginal returns?

24. "A molecule of sugar is composed of a fixed ratio of atoms of hydrogen, carbon, and oxygen; it follows that there is no substitutability of inputs in the manufacture of sugar."

a. Do you agree? If so, why? If not, why not?

b. Is the reasoning in the preceding question applicable to every other kind of good that can be manufactured—whether or not the good is composed of a fixed ratio of components? For example, is the reasoning applicable to making gasoline, running a railroad, operating a bus, building a house, or selling groceries?

25. "Even if for each good only one combination of productive inputs could be used to produce that good, there would still be substitution among productive resources in response to changes in their prices." Explain what that substitution is and how it would be induced.

26. According to the analyses developed in this chapter, resources will be employed in open markets in amounts at which marginal value-product is not less than price. That also determines their earnings (price times the number of units employed).

a. What ensures that the total earnings will not exceed the value of the total output of the community?

b. Who makes up the difference if payments exceed the value of output?

c. If the payments are less than the total value of output, who gets the difference?

d. In each case, what forces revise payments toward equality with value of output?

27. "If the ratio of the prices of two kinds of resources differ from the ratio of their marginal products for the amounts being employed, a change in the amounts employed can increase the total output without any increase in costs, or can reduce costs without reducing output." Explain why.

28. "If the ratio of the price of resource *A* to the price of resource *B* exceeds the ratio of the marginal value-products of *A* to *B*, it will be efficient to decrease the employment of *A* relative to *B*." Explain why.

29. "If a firm uses resources efficiently, a change in their prices will induce a change in the relative amounts employed." What will induce that change—some directive from a central planning agency, the social consciousness of the employer, or what?

30. Adjustments in the amount of resources used so as to equate the *absolute* prices of each resource with its marginal value productivity imply more than does the equality

of the *ratios* of prices to the ratios of marginal productivities. What is the stronger implication?

31. Suppose you operate a factory that is not privately owned or in which profits could not be retained by owners.

a. What would be your criterion of resource use in production?

b. What would induce you to act in accord with that criterion?

c. Would you have any incentive to adjust the use of resources so as to preserve the equality of the ratios of prices and marginal productivities—i.e., to minimize the cost of the output? Explain.

32. "In a socialist state it is difficult for the state to own the producers' goods that are involved in artistic creativity—the human brain and body. Consequently musicians, artists, authors, and poets will be more able to behave in deviant, unorthodox, nonnationalistic ways than those whose earnings are more dependent upon state-owned resources—machines, factories, land, etc. In a capitalistic system this difference would not be present."

a. What premises underlie the propositions?

b. Would your preference for one system over another be influenced by the validity of those propositions? Why?

33. In Russia and China, two socialist states in which most producers' goods (i.e., goods with which you can earn a living) are owned by the government, targets are assigned to factories in terms of the total value of the output (not profits) they are supposed to produce. Plant managers are told to accomplish and overfulfill targets as much as possible. Prices are set by law.

a. Is it desirable to have these targets overfulfilled?

b. Is it more desirable to state a target in terms of total value of output or in terms of profits? What are the differences in performance that will be induced?

c. Which criteria are more likely to provide a stronger incentive for the manager to conform?

34. Assume that you are a member of a minority group in some country and have reason to doubt that your private-property rights would be enforced and respected in that community.

a. In what forms of capital would you invest?

b. What kinds of skills (as forms of accumulations of wealth) would you encourage for your children?

c. Do you know of any evidence of actual behavior of such minority groups?

35. When Defense Secretary MacNamara recommended against building nuclear rather than oil-fueled airplane carriers because the nuclear system was more expensive, Congressman Pastore of New Jersey is reported to have said that if we looked at economics we would never have shifted from wooden sailing ships to steel, oil-fueled ships. Whatever the Congressman may have said, is the asserted remark correct? Explain.

27

WAGES AND LABOR

Labor Service as a Commodity

"Labor is not a commodity" is the battle cry of some labor groups. The assertion even appears in some laws. Whatever its propaganda and romantic value, the assertion is misleading at best and false at worst. Labor service is bought and sold daily, because that is a convenient way to obtain the advantages of specialization and exchange. To deny that labor is a commodity is to deny that it is a good exchanged in the market.

What *is* different about labor is the general prohibition against buying and selling *people;* however, human *services* are bought and sold. For example, when you work for someone, you sell him your physical and intellectual labor.[1] In some countries, slavery still exists; people are bought and sold by other people—or are "owned" by governments. They do not have private-property rights in themselves or their services. Even where no one is a slave, private property in one's own labor is denied if he is prohibited by law from exchanging his services for goods or money with any other person at mutually satisfactory terms, or if he cannot migrate to another area to sell his labor services there. Once upon a time, not more than a few hundred years ago, Englishmen could not work where they pleased, for whom they pleased, on whatever terms they found mutually agreeable. Nor was entry into occupations unrestricted. And this is true today in many countries in varying degree, even in the United States. For example,

[1] Fortunately, the ban against selling all one's future services for a single advance payment, as he could sell other things, does not prevent a person from converting some of his future earnings into present wealth values. If he has just obtained a higher salary, he can borrow more money now to buy a

even if mutually agreeable, I could not legally sell to you psychiatric, medical, or dental services. The law often dictates qualifications, permissible wages, hours of work per day, and working conditions; other deviant terms, although mutually agreeable between employer and employee, are not legal. These restrictions on market competition and sale of labor do not thereby mean that labor is not a marketable commodity.

Furthermore, the fact that labor services cannot be dissociated from personalities and from social relationships does not deny the market forces. What is changed, as we shall see later, is the contracting and negotiatory procedure. But before exploring those changes, we shall concentrate on the basic factors affecting wages and allocations of labor services via market competition—using again the analytic concepts of demand and supply.

Demand for Labor

The basis of demand for any productive input was investigated in the preceding chapter, where we saw that market demand for inputs reflects the anticipated marginal value-product of that input and that the marginal value-product depends upon the amount of other jointly used inputs. Our main demand proposition was that the lower the price of the input, the greater the amount of the input that will be demanded. And this holds for labor services as well as for all other productive inputs. In this chapter we shall explore the supply factors of labor and then put demand and supply together to see what can be said about wage rates and the allocation of labor to various jobs.

Supply of Labor

The supply of labor obviously is a reflection of the total population. The portion of the population seeking to increase its wealth by work is, in the United States, usually the adult male population and part of the female population. Males of about 14 or over are usually considered to be members of the labor force, even though some of them are in school. If we were a poorer country, youths of an even younger age would enter the work force.[2]

The population increases as the country's wealth increases; over the centuries, part of the increase in wealth has been utilized to support a larger popu-

---

house and car and repay out of the greater future income. In this way, he has exchanged part of his future earnings and obtained goods. Without the right to borrow or to mortgage wealth as security or to buy on the installment plan, laborers would be at a greater disadvantage in adjusting consumption to present wealth value of future earnings.

[2] This suggests that child labor exists not merely because the adults are greedy, cruel, and inconsiderate, but because the parents regard the extra earnings of children as more important to those children than the other uses of their time.

lation. Furthermore, increased knowledge of techniques of birth control seems to have destroyed the old generalization that poorer people have larger families. At the present time, with adjustments for level of education of the parents, their wealth, and agricultural versus city status, the evidence is that higher education and higher wealth are associated with *higher* net reproduction rates. Agricultural areas (after adjustment for education and wealth) have a higher reproduction rate. Whether that relationship will change at random or in some systematic way is still a question with no answer. In any event, although the introduction of birth-control techniques will lower the population growth rate—as of some level of wealth—the increase in wealth will induce an absolute population growth.

As wealth increases, what is the effect on the proportion of the population seeking work? In considering this question, be sure to distinguish between the wealth of people and the rate of pay per unit of work performed. The first factor, wealth, may imply a reduction in the proportion of the population working; the second, the rate of pay per hour of work, may induce a larger proportion (given some level of wealth) to work.

Labor Force and Rate of Wages

What is the relationship between the rate of earnings available and the portion of the population engaged in work? Since leisure and work can be viewed as alternatives, it follows that *more* work will require a *greater* inducement. The less the extra reward for extra work, the less willing a person is to provide the work. Let us hasten to allay a common misinterpretation of this statement. Can it not be, it is sometimes asked, that as a person is offered higher and higher wages per hour of work, the rise in his income will make him want to work fewer hours? At $1 an hour I would work 50 hours a week, but at $3 an hour I might prefer to work only 40. In graphic form, a supply curve of hours of labor offered by a person would look like that in Figure 27–1. At the wage W_1 per hour, the maximum number of hours of work per week would be offered. The wealth effect and the wage-rate effect are working against each other. At wages above W_1, the wealth effect on the demand for more leisure is strong enough to more than offset the higher wage-rate effect. The supply schedule is backward bending. But, strangely enough, the implication is *not* that less than Q_1 units of labor will be available if wages are higher than W_1. To see why, we must reckon with two kinds of supply curves. One indicates the number of hours of labor offered at each wage rate, *in a situation where the employee (or seller) can choose how many hours* he will sell at that wage rate. A different supply curve shows the wage that must be offered to induce the employee to work *at least* a specified number of hours.

Suppose an employee prefers to work not over 60 hours a week during summer vacation if he gets $2.50 per hour (which is $150 per week). Suppose

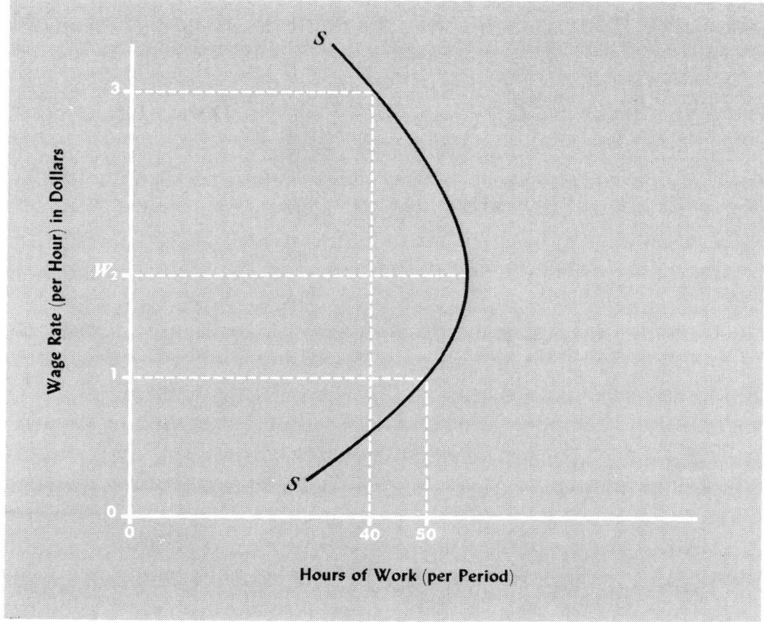

FIGURE 27–1. Supply curve of hours of labor.

also that he would prefer to reduce the hours to 54 if offered $3 per hour. That reduction implies the backward-bending supply, where the employee can choose the number of hours. However, an employer might decide to offer what he had to pay in order to induce laborers to work *at least* 66 hours every week. Now suppose he offered $208 for a 66-hour week and told them they would get that amount *if and only if* they worked 66 hours per week. By successively raising the offer for *a stated amount of time,* he could get more labor. This supply curve facing an employer involves higher wage for more labor (despite the other backward-bending curve). A wage of $208 for a 66-hour week is equivalent to $2.50 per hour for the first 60 hours, *plus $9.67 for the next six hours;* no wonder the laborers are willing to work six more hours. Higher overtime wage rates can be used to counter the backward-bending supply curve of labor (i.e., where the laborer is offered a set wage rate per hour and allowed to choose the number of hours). If you recall the discussion of "all-or-none" pricing by the monopolist seller of water, you will see the similarity; the *buyer* offers a fixed payment on the condition that at least a specified number of hours is sold to him. Although in this example the employer makes the special offer to get more labor, the employee could have told the employer that he would work if and only if the employer would pay at least $208 for a work week of 66 hours. Who happens to think of the arrangement and first suggests it is irrelevant.

The resulting generalization is that employers can obtain greater amounts of labor only by offering higher wages. The supply-of-labor curve is positively sloped with respect to wages, throughout its range, despite the backward-bending type of supply schedule (where a laborer is given the sole control of choosing how many hours to work). The relevant supply curve indicates for various amounts of work how much must be paid to induce that output. For this function, the relationship between offers of work and total (or even hourly average) wage is a "positive" one.

WAGE RATES

The demand-and-supply analysis in the open-market determination of wages and employment is similar in principle to that for any other good. Suppose that demand increases. How are wages affected? Underlying the market's operation is the assumption that people are free agents and can quit or change jobs when they wish, and that at least some will change jobs when knowledge of more attractive openings is available. Employees who are willing to entertain offers or to look for opportunities elsewhere will also permit their current employers to make a counter-bid.

An employer, then, if he is to retain his employees, must be prepared to offset offers of other employers. The employer who detects the competing wage rates and at least matches them (through periodic wage and salary reviews and raises), without forcing his employees to seek offers and then ask for a raise, will have to pay no higher wages than if he waited for each employee to initiate negotiations. This kind of searching is costly for employees; so the employer who takes the initiative in anticipating or matching market offers will find more employees willing to work for an employer with his reputation than for one who erroneously thinks he can impose all the costs of this kind of activity on employees.

Because many employers periodically review wages and give raises without an employee's obtaining a competing offer, it is sometimes alleged that wages are not set by market competition, so that instead, wages are adjusted simply because it is conventional or proper to do so or because of some internal employee pressure. But, according to economic analysis, market competition *is* present; and the employer is meeting it by "rehiring" or keeping his existing employees from going elsewhere, as they would if he did not provide competitive wages.

CHANGES IN LABOR FORCE

It is instructive to consider an example in which the supply of labor changes. How does the employment of labor adjust to the changed (say, smaller) amount? We have already answered this question, in principle at least, in the preceding chapter.

Suppose that the labor force in some occupation *decreases* as some of the laborers go off to other jobs or communities. The smaller remaining supply will result in a rise in wage rates. Employers who lose employees will prefer to bid up wages to replace some of the employees they have lost, rather than continue with unfilled jobs (and less wealth). Competition among employers for employees will pull up wages—especially for those who are willing to move to new employers. Not all employees must move to get higher wages; present employers will bid up wages to retain employees. If they do not, they will lose workers and suffer some loss of business. And if they do, fewer workers will be demanded than initially at the old lower wages. In this way, the amount now demanded will have been made equal to the smaller amount available.

The higher wage rate, consequent to the reduced supply, will induce substitution of some other types of labor or productive inputs, according to the formal theory explained in the preceding chapter. Against this implication, it is often objected that if the employer could have managed with fewer employees, he already would have done so. Those he still employs, he really "needs." This is said of every kind of occupation. And it is wrong in every case.

Consider, for example, a decrease in the supply of carpenters. A higher wage resulting from fewer carpenters will induce more standardization of types of woodwork, for standardization involves less carpentering service. The number of wood-paneled walls will decrease, and there will be more plaster and glass windows, with steel and aluminum window frames. There are thousands of ways to reduce the amount of carpenters' services by using other goods.

Another example is that of retail clerks. At higher wages, employers will seek to preserve their wealth position by providing the cashier in a supermarket with elaborate capital goods, which are expensive but permit servicing of more customers per employee: a cash register that records each item, the amount paid, and the change; a motorized turntable; young assistants who handle and package the purchases and thus economize on the more expensive retail clerk.

The more time allowed after a change in wages, the more will the substitution and re-allocation possibilities be exploited and the less will wage rates have to rise for any given reduction in the size of the work force available. Within a week little change may occur, except that employers may not replace those who quit. But in a month, two months, six months, very great changes can occur. In that time, the employer can more cheaply revise the layout of his store or more economically get new equipment to replace some of the formerly used but now more expensive labor.

Wage Differences

We have been investigating wages of groups of laborers as if everyone were equal in ability and personal characteristics. But people are not equal, and it is time that we examined some of the factors that make for differences in wages among, as well as within, occupations.

God may have started out to create all men equal, but our parents intervened. No amount of effort will give you a mental capacity equal to that of some people with photographic memories and brains that operate like logic machines. No amount of preening can make me as handsome as Rock Hudson, or my wife as beautiful as one or two other women I have seen. I just haven't got it. No amount of resources will change an Indian into an Italian, or a Chinese into a Russian, or short people into tall people. People simply have innate differences. And, for better or for worse, these affect our preferences about other people. Within the same occupation, be it carpentry, medicine, professional golfing, taxi driving, cooking, breeding children, barbering, or singing, there are differences in marginal productivity among people, even those who have had the same amount of education and training. Some doctors get $100,000 a year, and some get only $10,000. Some students get *A*'s easily, and some barely get *D*'s with enormous work. Some football players make the first squad, while others never are seen in action. Natural differences in abilities, attributes, and tastes are not eliminated by education or propaganda.

Some sense of proportion of differences in wages can easily be obtained from available data. First, however, Table 27–1 presents the distribution of the labor force by types of work. The largest category in 1963 was machine operatives, constituting about 18 percent of the work force. The fastest-growing category is that of professional and technical workers, followed closely by clerical workers, with farm labor showing the greatest decline over the past several decades.

Table 27–1

PERCENTAGE DISTRIBUTION OF CIVILIAN EMPLOYEES IN VARIOUS TASKS, 1963, SUBCLASSIFIED BY COLOR

Major Occupation Group	Nonwhite	White
Professional, technical	6	13
Farmers and farm managers	3	4
Managers, proprietors	3	11
Clerical	7	16
Sales	2	7
Craftsmen	6	14
Machine operatives	20	18
Private-household services	15	2
Service workers, except household	19	9
Farm laborers	5	3
Laborers, nonfarm	13	4

Source: U.S. Department of Labor, *Monthly Bulletin of Labor Statistics*, 1963.

Table 27–2 presents estimates of annual wages of nonsupervisory employees in various industries in 1963. The average annual wages within each industry for nonsupervisory employees range from about $2,600 for personal-service employees (hotels, motels) to over $7,000 in petroleum refining. If we include professional workers (engineers, managers, chemists, teachers, supervisors, dentists, and physicians), the average annual wages would extend to almost $20,000.

Table 27–2

AVERAGE OF ANNUAL WAGES OF NONSUPERVISORY EMPLOYEES BY SELECTED INDUSTRIES, 1963

Personal services	$ 2,600
Apparel	3,300
Leather goods	3,500
Textiles	3,600
Assembly (toys, sporting goods, jewelry)	4,200
Furniture	4,400
Lumber	4,500
Electrical	5,200
Local bus	5,200
All manufacturing	5,200
Chemical	5,900
Mining	6,100
Bituminous coal	6,600
Motor vehicles	6,800
Contract construction	6,900
Motion pictures	6,900
Petroleum refining	7,000
College professors	10,000

Source: U.S. Department of Labor, *Monthly Bulletin of Labor Statistics*, 1963.

Even within the same general class of skill, a substantial range of annual earnings is present, as illustrated by the data of Table 27–3 for department stores, groceries, automobile dealers, and gasoline service stations. The range shown there is basically dependent upon the differences in hours of work per week. Note, however, that automobile salesmen, who are primarily on a commission earnings basis, show earnings that do not conform as closely to hours of work as in the other sampled industries.

Do not conclude that the range of wages in an occupation reflects just hours

Table 27–3

PERCENTAGE DISTRIBUTION OF AVERAGE WEEKLY EARNINGS OF NONSUPERVISORY EMPLOYEES IN SELECTED LINES OF RETAIL BUSINESS, 1961, BY HOURS

	Dept. Stores		Groceries		Motorcar Sales		Service Stations	
Hours per Week	% of Employees	$	% of Employees	$	% of Employees	$	% of Employees	$
1–14	8	12	9	12	1	14	8	11
15–34	21	32	26	33	4	47	20	29
35–39	13	53	6	59	4	76	3	49
40	43	67	25	83	16	100	11	61
41–48	13	73	23	78	45	100	18	70
Over 48	2	86	12	76	30	93	40	70

Source: U.S. Department of Labor, *Monthly Bulletin of Labor Statistics*, 1963.

of work. Table 27–4 illustrates a typical range of wages reflecting incentive and skill, in this case for women sewing-machine operators in New York City. About 10 percent earn over $3.50 an hour, and almost 10 percent earn less than $1.50 an hour on a piecework pay system.

Table 27–4

PERCENT DISTRIBUTION OF INCENTIVE, PIECEWORK WAGES PER HOUR FOR WOMEN SEWING-MACHINE OPERATORS, IN NEW YORK CITY, 1963

Hourly Average Wage	Percent of Employees
Under $1.50	8
$1.50 and under $2.00	24
$2.00 and under $2.50	25
$2.50 and under $3.00	20
$3.00 and under $3.50	11
$3.50 and under $4.00	6
$4.00 and over	3

Source: U.S. Department of Labor, *Monthly Bulletin of Labor Statistics*, 1963.

Even the size of the firm is a factor that affects wages. Larger firms pay more on the average than smaller ones. Employees may prefer small firms and therefore obtain higher wages in large firms as a pecuniary offset to the non-pecuniary advantages in a small firm. Or possibly the large firm employs a higher general quality of labor. In retail trade, the average hourly earnings in 1963 for nonsupervisory employees were $1.74 for firms of over $1,000,000 in annual sales, $1.40 for firms with less than $250,000 in annual sales. Table 27–5 shows the distribution of hourly wage rates of nonsupervisory employees in retail trade in 1963, subclassified by geographical areas.

Table 27–5

HOURLY WAGE RATES OF NONSUPERVISORY EMPLOYEES IN RETAIL TRADE, 1963, CUMULATIVE IN REGIONS

	% of Employees by Regions			
Wage Rates	Northeast	South	North Central	West
Under $ .75	1%	13%	3%	1%
" 1.00	3	31	12	3
" 1.25	29	57	34	17
" 1.50	49	72	54	35
" 2.00	74	88	77	60
" 2.50	88	94	89	77
Average	$1.74	$1.32	$1.65	$2.00

Eating and drinking places excluded.

Source: U.S. Department of Labor, *Monthly Bulletin of Labor Statistics*, 1963.

Table 27–5 serves the double duty of revealing geographical differences in wage rates. Thus, the percentage of employees earning less than $1.25, the current legal minimum-wage rate, is 29 percent in the Northeast, 57 percent in the South, and 17 percent in the West. This means not that the West is more law abiding; the minimum-wage law exempts a large number of employees in various trades. However, the variation reflects productivity of employees, type of industry, and cost of living. To pin down a bit more the effect of geography, Table 27–6 presents wage rates for "common unskilled" laborers in the labor contract of Swift and Co. for various states. Again notice the lower wages in the South and the higher wages in the West.

Table 27–6

SWIFT AND CO. COMMON UNSKILLED LABOR BEGINNING WAGE RATE PER HOUR, 1963 *

$2.14	$2.47	$2.54	$2.70
Texas	New York	Pennsylvania	California
Mississippi	Illinois	Kansas	
Alabama	Pennsylvania	New York	
Georgia	Oregon	Michigan	
Florida	Nebraska		
Tennessee	Minnesota		
	Connecticut		

* Rates depend upon cities; therefore, some states have two rates.

Source: U.S. Department of Labor, *Monthly Bulletin of Labor Statistics,* 1963.

WAGE DIFFERENCES AMONG AND WITHIN OCCUPATIONS

If the talent to be a first-class musician were very widely available and the talent (strong back) to be a ditchdigger were relatively rare, some ditchdiggers would get a higher salary than fine musicians. If the talent it takes to fly an airplane were less common than it is, pilots would command even higher wages, but if anyone could fly a plane as safely as anyone else, pilots would command trivial pay. A large supply of some talent will intersect the community's demand way out where the wage rate is low. It's just the old law of demand and supply in open markets. The larger the supply, with given demand, the lower will wages be.

Wages of window washers are lower than those of lawyers because the supply of lawyers is small enough *relative to its demand* to maintain a higher wage. And it is smaller because of the relative scarcity of the kind of talent that is wanted in lawyers as compared to window washers. Consequently, given the demand, wage differentials reflect the relative differences in supply of acceptable talent, resulting from heredity and training. If an extra dollar's worth of education and training increases a person's estimated productivity, it will pay him to buy the education, whether it be for a brain surgeon or for a cotton picker. The amount of training sought responds to its marginal cost relative to the increase it provides in marginal productivity.

The amount spent in training to be a surgeon presumably yields an even bigger increase in the present capitalized value of his future productivity. And if a smaller amount is spent in training cotton pickers, the presumption is that the costs of that education exceed the gains. But suppose that any cotton picker could be educated to be a brain surgeon at some cost. The supply of cotton pickers would decrease until cotton picking yielded as much as brain surgery —net of the costs of acquiring the education. Actually, however, the costs of training some people to be surgeons would be so great that it simply wouldn't pay them to go to medical school.

Suppose a person could borrow now against the clearly perceived higher future earnings he will be able to have as a result of education. Then a poor man, by borrowing against his prospective future earnings, could buy education as readily as a rich one. Notice, we do not say that the opportunity to buy education will equalize wealth among all people, but that they have the opportunity to exploit their potential talents by borrowing against their future, clearly perceived potential increase in earning power.

But, in fact, not everyone who wants to exploit his profitable education opportunities by paying for it out of the increased future earnings can do so—and for at least two reasons: (1) The future is uncertain. If I wanted to borrow $10,000 from you to buy an education for myself, you would check into the evidence and form your own judgment as to whether the education really will enhance my earning power as much as I predict. It's easy to see that there is going to be disagreement about prospective earnings. Then, what will happen if the future earnings aren't as big as I expected? Will I repay and be poorer than if I had not borrowed so much money, or will I plead bankruptcy, or undue duress, when my creditor demands repayment? (2) Significant also is that a large part of one's education is obtained before he reaches 21. Our legal system and courts will not enforce rigorously the debts incurred by a young man before he was 21. And when some borrowers fail to fulfill their expectations, the courts are not inclined to enforce repayment out of current earnings. No wonder lenders are wary of educational loans to young people.

A factor conducive to wage differences among people is the difference in their venturesomeness. Some are more willing to try new applications or techniques, giving up relatively sure prospective wages in the hope of getting a higher wage. An architect who gives up a secure job designing conventional buildings and risks coming up with desirable new designs may end up very much richer or poorer. Some choose the risk of ending up poorer for the prospect of being richer, with awareness of the contingencies. In this sense, rather than to be denied the chance to be rich, they prefer to have had the chance even though they may fail. And their choices produce a wider spread of realized wages.

Finally, we note that wage differences within an occupation are as great as among occupations. The spread of actors' incomes is greater than the difference between the averages of doctors' and actors' incomes. Better a good actor than an average doctor. Better a good ball player than an average lawyer.

WAGE DIFFERENCES AND NONPECUNIARY FACTORS

Employment conditions differ in nonpecuniary respects: employer personality, size of firm, prestige, climate, type of work, location, congeniality of fellow workers. The higher pay offered to overcome nonpecuniary disadvantages is called an "equalizing" wage difference; it helps equate the totality of rewards to labor in different working conditions. These conditions can persist indefinitely if the cost of getting rid of them exceeds the equilibrating or "equalizing" difference in wages. For example, people may be willing to work in the hot sun only at premium wages; if the equilibrating premium is less than the cost of erecting sunshades, sunny work will continue.

Nonpecuniary productivity of *employees* differs. Those who are better looking, more courteous, pleasant, uncomplaining, cooperative, and congenial provide the employer with nonpecuniary sources of utility. Both the pecuniary product and the nonpecuniary product to the employer affect the employer's utility. Therefore, just as an employer discriminates among potential employees by selecting, at any given wage, employees who are more productive of pecuniary wealth to the employer, he also discriminates with respect to nonpecuniary attributes as well. If two stenographers have equal pecuniary productivity, but one is more beautiful, pleasant, well dressed, with a better-modulated voice, then, at equal wages, she would be preferred. Therefore, her nonpecuniary qualities, in addition to the pecuniary productivity, will enable her to get a higher wage than the inferior (in a nonpecuniary sense) stenographer. The higher wage to the superior stenographer is the same thing as lower pay for inferior people. And that lower pay enables inferior people to get jobs. Equalizing wage differences, then, provide employment opportunities for employees who are inferior, just as equalizing differences induce people to work in inferior environmental conditions. However, although people recognize and admit differences in working conditions and environment as valid reasons for discriminating in choice of place to work by employees, there seems to be some resentment about job choices on the basis of personal characteristics. Employees should not be concerned with whether the employer is Jewish, Catholic, immigrant, Negro, female, a midget, or an ex-convict; at least, that is what some employers would like. Similarly, it is sometimes argued that employers should not care whether the employee is Jewish, fat, homely, Catholic, immigrant, Negro, female, a midget, or an ex-convict; that is what some employees would like.

Preferences and discrimination are revealed by "compensating" or "equalizing" wage and price differences, if markets are open to all types. Poor paintings sell for less than superb paintings; otherwise, the poor paintings would not be sold. Because Chevrolets sell for less than Cadillacs, Chevrolets can survive in competition against Cadillacs. At the same price, fewer would want Chevies. The Negro in dominantly white countries can get jobs as readily as the white man if he will shade his price, just as housewives are willing to pay more for brown eggs than for white ones (though in some areas the preference is reversed). Minority groups and homely people can offset their "inferiority" in the eyes of other people to whom they desire to sell services by charging a lower price than that charged by orthodox, beautiful people. You buy round steak rather than filet mignon only because the price of round steak is sufficiently lower, thus compensating you for the inferior tenderness and flavor of round steak, even though the food value of the two is the same.

People have such preferences, and discrimination will occur *either* in wages paid or in extent and kinds of employment. At the same wage rate, the less preferred people will get less employment in good jobs. At lower wage rates, they can get more employment. But the less preferred will *not* receive *both* the same wage and the same amount or kind of employment—for the same reason that high-quality goods get a higher price or women of 35 get fewer jobs in a chorus line than girls of 25. The *customers* are discriminating. So is an employer, even though he may be the only one who sees some of the employees. He discriminates among people in order to maintain morale, productivity, and cooperation of employees—that is, to satisfy the nontechnical aspects of employment. This interest in personal attributes explains why employees and employers both place so much reliance on personal channels of recruitment and job finding.

Effect of Technological Progress on Job Allocation and Wages

Although viewed with alarm and fought by various labor groups, automation (which has been progressing since man first learned to wield a stick) is a major source of increased wealth, new and easier jobs, higher real incomes, and a larger population. The plough drawn by horses (rather than people) was a great technological advance. What happened to the displaced people who lost their jobs in front of the plough? They turned to what were formerly less important tasks like collecting wood and building stone fences. And when the tractor replaced the horse and several plowmen, what did the workers do? They went to work producing other things. With the advent of the new machines labor services in the old jobs became less valuable than in jobs to which the workers turned (and which formerly were too costly). Today, after millenniums of technological progress people still worry about the mechanical, self-controlled machine because it induces labor re-allocation. And that is a valid reason for concern, though not of the kind most commonly talked about—i.e., a lack of jobs.

INVENTION AND JOB RE-ALLOCATION

It is tempting to say to those concerned about job effects of automation or technological progress that new jobs in far greater amount and variety have been created. But that really is an irrelevant fact, despite overwhelming talk to the contrary. To see why, suppose that *no* new jobs were created by new inventions. But these permit a larger output, and some workers will find the demand for their services reduced in their old jobs. They must now turn to other jobs, which formerly were left unfilled or unperformed simply because the cost of filling them was too high. The sacrificed output was even more valuable than that to be had from the unfilled jobs. But now the formerly unperformed jobs or unavailable output can be produced by those whose services are no longer so valuable in the old jobs. Therefore, whether or not the new invention or technique creates new jobs or increases the demand for workers in that new industry, there still will be plenty of jobs—in fact, more than can ever be filled. The problem is not one of too few jobs, but of too many jobs; the problem is deciding which jobs or tasks to perform and which jobs to leave unperformed because they would yield a less valuable product. That is the persisting problem of labor allocation. Inventions, automation, and progress do not eliminate it.

From the preceding analysis it should be apparent that the underlying cause of concern is that some people whose services in their current jobs are outcompeted by new methods must shift to new jobs—presumably to jobs that pay less well than the current jobs formerly did. We must therefore distinguish among three groups of people. (1) Some people get higher wages because they are able to work with the new techniques or because they are demanded to produce the new equipment. They benefit doubly: they gain from the higher income and from the lower prices of the increased output of goods. (2) Some people find their old jobs being displaced by the new techniques. They must transfer to new jobs, jobs that pay less than they formerly earned. Their reduced income completely offsets the lower prices of the new enlarged output, so that it is small consolation to these people to be told that output is larger. (3) Some people do not experience any perceptible impact on the value of their jobs or on their working conditions. They benefit from the lower prices of goods now produced in larger amounts or more cheaply, and they suffer no loss of income.

Obviously it is preferable to be a member of group 1. But the particular group in which a person finds himself depends upon the characteristics of new inventions and techniques. All of us fall in group 3 with respect to most inventions, but all of us sometimes fall in group 1 or 2 with respect to some inventions. Clearly, we will be prone to favor cases 1 and 3 and resist those inventions that place us in category 2. And it is probably safe to say that since the beginning of time people who at any moment fall in category 2 will vocalize louder and more often than those in groups 1 and 3.

Perhaps the relevance of these three classes can be illustrated helpfully if we consider in some detail a very spectacular recent case—that of the introduction of television.

Some people shifted from radio and movies to the manufacture of television programs and equipment and earned larger incomes. Some people had to transfer to other jobs at less pay than they formerly got or had to take a bigger cut to stay in the old jobs. They didn't find *as good* a job as they formerly filled in radio or movies. This class can be further classified in three sub-categories: (i) Some nevertheless were better off on net, after considering the gains of their being able to use television as a consumer. (ii) Of the remainder who did not reap a gain even after considering all the effects of this particular innovation, some were nevertheless better off than if they had been able to keep their old income but had to forsake *all* progress since television started. They gained through the general dispersal of improvements *via* lower prices and quality improvements to consumers—despite their income loss from the displaced product. (iii) Some employees and owners of equipment suffered such severe reductions in demand for their services that, even after taking into account the gains from television and from all other technological improvements during the rest of their life, they were still worse off. This category is more characteristic of older people than younger, who have more years of progress to look forward to in their lifetime.

Examples other than television can be cited. A new material for shoe soles might wear so long that the demand for shoe-repair men will fall. Half the existing number would suffice to resole shoes, since they would be resoled half as often. The displaced workers could be retained in shoe-repair work only if shoes are resoled for a third, fourth, or fifth time; but the diminishing marginal product of the extra repairs would mean lower wages. Hence, wages would fall, or some of the workers would shift to other jobs that promised more than the now lower wages they would get if they stayed in shoe-repair work. On the other hand, because of the improved quality and consequent reduced costs of shoes, other people may buy many more shoes.

As yet, economic theory has been unable to tell in advance for any invention how many people (let alone which ones) will fall in each class. Even afterward it is often impossible to tell, because subsequent changes impinge on the situation and obscure the effects of each earlier change. For example, did the invention of the typewriter increase or decrease the demand for secretaries? Demand may have increased enough so that more people obtain jobs as typists than formerly obtained jobs as scriveners and at higher wages, to boot. The discovery of oil may have attracted labor from coal mines into oil-well drilling, refining, and pipeline work, so that the wages of coal miners increased despite a relative decrease in the demand for coal. New inventions not only affect the schedule of marginal value productivity of workers in the affected jobs; but they can also attract workers away from other jobs, thus raising wages elsewhere, too.

It is true that the new machines sometimes reduce the cost of some products so much that the increased amount of output demanded raises the demand for labor in that job; consequently, wages are raised. Spectacular examples are the railroad and the automobile. They substantially lowered the costs of transport; as a result, the amount of transport services increased, as did the demand for workers to provide materials for transportation. Yet even that involved a job shift. The old canalmen, livery-stable operators, and buggy-whip makers shifted to new, better-paying jobs in the new transportation industry. Also, sometimes the increased productivity of new machines, ideas, or inventions and the demand for workers to make them are so great that workers are able to shift to more lucrative jobs created by the new inventions before they are no longer demanded in their old jobs.

COMPENSATION PRINCIPLE

Employees whose present wages or jobs are threatened have argued that since the new inventions increase the total output, the whole community ought to pay out of the net gain an amount sufficient to compensate re-allocated workers for their lost income. This is a logically airtight possibility *in principle,* because the increased value of output exceeds the losses of the displaced factors. However, one difficulty with this proposal is that innovations occur so extensively that it is impossible to identify each case and to determine who loses how much. How would we know how much to pay a person who claims to be hurt by the introduction of electronic computers, or of stainless-steel razors? How could we be sure that he has not taken some easy, low-paying job—in the expectation that he will be given a payment large enough to make up the difference? Obviously, if a person knows that he will be compensated for every loss of job (or for the difference between the wages of the former job and the one he takes), he will have less incentive to shift to new jobs and may claim that every loss of job or wage cut is the result of socially beneficial innovation. Only *if* people's incentives were not changed by the compensation principle, and *if* there were *no* costs in discovering who gained or lost how much, would some kind of compensation system be feasible; when information is costly and incentives are affected, such a system becomes impossible.

Nevertheless, the compensation principle is not ignored in our governmental policy. Today the federal government is financing (by taxing other people) a program whereby workers who must relocate to new jobs (or whose wages would be reduced to retain their jobs) can receive federal aid or training in new occupations.[3] This aid is proposed, however, not only for those whose incomes are cut by competition of new, more productive equipment, but for any laborer who lives in an area where there is general decline in demand for services—whatever the reason. A displaced worker in a prosperous area is not eligible. There must be a "large number" of such workers in some region, not because the damage suffered by each individual is greater when there are large numbers involved,

[3] The Trade Expansion Act of 1962 gives the President additional powers to negotiate for tariff reductions and provides for "trade adjustment assistance" for both business firms (through technical assistance, loans, tax relief) and workers (through special unemployment benefits, retraining, loans for moving to jobs in different communities) when injury from increased imports can be demonstrated.

but because the political power of a group is greater. For example, consider the "disaster-area" relief programs. If your house alone burns down because of a nearby grass fire, you will get no special financial aid from the government. But if your house is one of many houses that burn in some area (for the same reason), then the political process will work. Fire, storm, flood, drought—all are causes for federal disaster-area relief, but only if there are large numbers of people in the one area.[4]

A more fundamental problem inherent in the compensation proposal is that not only labor but also existing capital goods lose productive value as they are outcompeted by new innovations. The owners of these assets lose wealth. If one compensates injured labor, he should, in simple justice, also compensate injured owners of nonhuman assets. Yet if compensation is paid for every change in value resulting from innovation, the *owners* of productive resources, human and nonhuman, do not bear the risks of unforeseeable future consequences; instead, the general public is the risk bearer according to the tax load. The fundamental problem posed by the compensation principle is that it conflicts with a basic purpose of a private-property capitalist society: to enable people to escape the necessity of common bearing of all risks of future values of all resources. If I don't want to bear the risks of the future value of some building, I simply choose not to be an owner of it; in that way I neither capture any gain nor suffer any loss of value. I free myself of *that* risk, if I wish to, by letting other people own the item. If I wish to bear the risk, I can buy a share of ownership in it or in like resources. Risk bearing is selective and adjustable. Suppose I were to agree that I am prepared to bear all the losses of value of my services, whatever the cause, and that in exchange I have the right to keep whatever gains might occur in the value of my resources. That is the kind of agreement that is implicitly made by a private-property owner. The compensation principle denies him the privilege of making such an agreement with the rest of society.

ADJUSTMENT TO INNOVATION

The shift from jobs where demand has fallen to a new job that pays more than one could get by remaining in the old job, but less than he formerly got, is a poignant problem of human readjustment to circumstances. A move to a new area, to a new kind of job, to a lower standard of living, to a new set of colleagues and social circles can be a traumatic experience, especially for older people. Economic analysis may be scientific, impersonal, and unemotional, but the subjects are people with emotions and desires. Even if, in the overwhelming

[4] But if an equal number of houses are burned or flooded, or farms abandoned, in separate parts of the country, they get no relief. The cost of all these people banding together to exert political pressure is prohibitively high. The moral is that if you buy property especially exposed to a certain kind of risk, make sure there are a lot of other people in the same area exposed to the same risk, so that if one suffers all will suffer.

majority of cases, the job displacement caused by new innovations in technology shifted people to better and higher-paying jobs, the hardship for some is not avoided. These hardship cases are the ones most likely to be remembered.

A few adults never outgrow childhood romanticism and fantasy; they believe scarcity is merely a result of some plot or failure to exploit our allegedly unlimited production potential. They assert that new machines and modern scientific methods have brought us to the stage where we can produce more than we can consume and that there aren't enough jobs to keep everyone employed. They go on to say that all that is lacking is the will or the knowledge of how to revise our economic institutions so as to achieve that unlimited production and thus assure everyone of a high standard of living—presumably a level of unlimited satisfaction of everyone's fondest dreams.

The fact is that technological advance has raised the over-all level of productivity of human labor so that the real earnings and real output of society are much larger. As a result, more people are alive today because we are not trying to survive with the technology of 1860 or 1760 or 1560. More are alive because they have knowledge and capital to enable them to yield a high enough marginal product in the jobs they perform. But there is no prospect that man will ever be so fortunate as to have all his wants fulfilled, with no jobs any longer worth doing. Until that unforeseeable day he will be plagued by the task of allocating his productive energies to the most valuable jobs—an allocation that will be persistently changing with new inventions and resources and changing demands. And until that day we shall see people resisting the effects of those changes. Those experiencing a reduced market value of output of their current jobs (because others are outcompeting them in the market) can and will resort to nonmarket competitive behavior to try to offset market competition. Political competitive power may be directed toward changing the results of, or to restrict, market competition. It is a very safe prediction that whenever one's wealth is being competed away in the market by new inventions, changing tastes, or new products, his attempts to restrict that market competition will increase. In the next chapter, we study some tactics and the effects of attempts to constrain market competition for labor.

Questions

1. Minors are not "free" individuals; for example, they cannot own property (a guardian oversees them) and they cannot make legally binding contracts. Their legal status is not far removed from temporary slavery. Because of the conflict of interest between parents and minor, legal restrictions (e.g., compulsory education and prohibition of child employment, both of which are nineteenth-century developments) are imposed to increase the probability that the parent will make decisions of the kind the minor would presumably make if he were "of age and sensible." Is there an alternative

and not necessarily incompatible force at work that would bring about an increase in academic education and a decrease in child employment even if no laws had been passed?

2. A 20-year-old man with an earning expectancy of 45 years (beginning at \$3,000 per year and increasing annually at the rate of 6 percent to about \$13,000 per year at the end of twenty years and then holding constant thereafter to retirement at 65) has a present capital value of his future earnings of about \$100,000 at 6 percent rate of interest. If he expects continued salary increases after age 40, his present value will be even greater. It has been estimated, on the basis of projections of wage earnings of college graduates, that the "time-of-graduation capital value" of a college graduate's future income is on the average about \$150,000 at 6 percent rate of interest. This means that if he could sell his future wages (and not affect his willingness to work!), he could "sell" himself for approximately \$150,000 at graduation. A woman who marries him gets ownership of half his wages; by marrying him she "purchases" a wealth of about \$75,000. Is there any other way "in effect" to sell off those future earnings? What method do most people use to spend now some of that capital value?

3. "Overtime premium wages are a device to restrain employers from working employees overtime." "Overtime premium wages are means whereby employers induce employees to work overtime more than they otherwise would." Which of these two propositions is correct? Explain.

4. "The birth rate is controlled by custom and emotion, not by economic calculations. Certainly, it is not reasonable to expect more children, the wealthier the parents." Yet the fact is that in communities with relatively widespread knowledge of contraceptive methods, there is a positive correlation between number of children and wealth of parents (after allowing for other factors like education, occupation, and location). For purposes of testing the above propositions, would you define "number of children" as number of pregnancies, of live births, of children surviving to age 1 month, or to 1 year, or to 6 years, or what?

5. Assume that wage rates of gardeners were to double, despite an unchanged demand.

a. Would people go on hiring the same amount of gardener services and pay more?

b. What would happen to gardens?

c. What substitution for gardeners would occur?

d. Where or from whom could you learn about the available substitution techniques?

6. "The higher the wage rate, the higher the wages." Explain the error in this statement.

7. "Different workers receive different wages because the workers are different, the jobs are different, and workers can't move to another job easily." On the other hand, "Workers are different but get the same pay in many jobs; many different jobs pay the same wages; and it is just as 'easy' to move across the country as it is to move next door." Obviously the first quoted statement is either wrong or ambiguous. Rewrite it so as to make it sensible and correct.

8. "The population of Arizona is increasing at a record rate. Special effort must be made to create new jobs to provide employment for the increased labor force." Explain why this is wrong.

9. "Automation is a threat to employment." Explain why this is erroneous.

10. "Automation is destroying 300,000 jobs a month." Accepting this as a fact, explain why it does not mean that anyone will be left without jobs.

11. "Automation, like any change in demand or supply of labor, leads to changes in jobs and wage rates—not to increased unemployables." Explain why that is a true statement.

12. "Automation can create unemployment. It can cause severe problems for those who lose their current jobs." Explain why that is a true statement, without being inconsistent with your answers to the preceding questions.

13. "A substantial number of relatively unskilled persons report that they are unemployed. At the same time, there are many unfilled jobs for relatively skilled people. Apparently, the problem is that there are more unskilled people than unskilled jobs." What is wrong with the reasoning?

14. "My doctor charges me a high fee because he has to cover the high cost of his education and equipment. On the other hand, my golfing teacher also charges me a high fee, even though his education is practically absent." Is either one cheating or fooling me? Explain.

15. "Elizabeth Taylor was paid over $5,000,000 for making the film *Cleopatra* (half of that goes to her former husband, Eddie Fisher). Yet Audrey Hepburn could have taken her place for, say, $1,000,000. There must be something wrong with the movie industry. Certainly, Taylor is not worth that much more to 20th Century-Fox than Audrey Hepburn would be." Explain, using marginal-productivity theory, how it can be sensible to pay Taylor that much, even though Hepburn might have been available for one fifth as much.

16. "The presidents of some big corporations are paid as much as $500,000 in one year. All they do is make the kinds of decisions that are made in thousands of other companies by much lower-paid people who are as intelligent, but who just haven't had a chance to get those fancy jobs and who aren't as well known or don't have the reputation. Clearly, salaries are based more on past experience, reputation, and pull. Therefore, marginal productivity—which is an academic, unrealistic abstraction of an imaginary world—is useless at best and false at worst." Explain why the last sentence is not implied by the preceding sentences.

17. In deciding who is an unemployed person, would you consider the following:

a. Is he now working for someone else as an employee? If his answer is Yes, would you classify him as unemployed or as employed?

b. He answers "Yes" to the preceding question, but answers "No" to the question "Is your current job your usual kind of work?" He reports that he is working at a service station, while looking for a job as a lathe operator. Would you change the classification?

c. Next he is asked, "Are you willing to take an available job as a lathe operator at a wage of $2 an hour?" He answers, "No, I used to work for $6 an hour and I'm an experienced operator, not a novice." Is your classification of him still the same? Why?

d. Another person is not now employed and says he is unemployed. He says he is looking for a job as a bank president at $50,000 a year. Do you classify him as unemployed, or as not in the labor force?

e. How would you categorize a person who refuses to take a job because the job is not to his liking or the wage is too low to satisfy him. (Unemployed? Not in the work force? Employed?)

f. If you do not call him unemployed in the preceding question, then how can you call anyone unemployed; for there are always jobs available at some sufficiently low wage—i.e., a wage he would call "ridiculous," "un-American," or "below standard"?

18. The usual criterion of an unemployed person is "not employed for someone else and actively looking for a job." It says nothing about the range of jobs or wages he refuses to consider. What do you think the criterion implicitly assumes, in order to avoid being completely useless?

19. "Unemployment is a wonderful privilege. Without it we would all be slaves to tyrants."

a. Can you interpret this "ridiculous" statement so as to make it not ridiculous? (Hint: There is no unemployment in the military forces. There is none in Russia either, according to the Russians.)

b. Would you prefer to live in a community in which unemployment is forbidden? Why? (We shall later analyze other ways of reducing unemployment without forbidding it.)

20. In feudal England (in the eleventh–fourteenth centuries, when peasants were "tied" to the soil and could not transfer allegiance from one lord to another or move from one community to another and did not work for money wages) there was no unemployment —only work and leisure. Employment for wages was rare. Even rarer were market-negotiated wages. But the rise of the commercial system introduced markets for labor services and induced peasants to break away from their feudal ties and to sacrifice their feudal security for the hazards of private contractual employment and unemployment. By the sixteenth century employment for money wages was well established (but maximum wage rates were imposed by government, and potential employers were exhorted not to offer more and were punished if caught).

a. What devices do you think developed as a means of circumventing the maximum-wage restrictions?

b. Why would the government impose *maximum* limits to wages whereas today minimum limits are commonly imposed?

21. America was founded partly on "slavery" of white men. In colonial days immigrants "indentured" themselves, pledging to work for the benefit of a master for 7 (or some specified number of) years if the master would finance their way to America. Today, this is illegal.

a. Why?

b. Who gains and who loses if such contracts are prohibited?

22. "In the open market, wages are driven down to the subsistence level." That is the iron law of wages. What is meant by "the subsistence level"?

23. "A man who loses his job through no fault of his own should not have to bear the losses of unemployment. The government must see to it that he does not." This is a quotation from a campaign speech of a major candidate for governor of California.

a. Is the candidate proposing that there be no unemployment or that anyone not currently employed should be given an income equivalent to what he was formerly getting?

b. How can either of these be accomplished?

24. Is a person who loses his job through no fault of his own also unemployed thereafter through no fault of his own? Explain.

25. In what sense does the range of wealth and income of people reflect their own preferences?

28

LABOR MARKETS

As we have seen in earlier chapters, buyers and sellers in all markets occasionally seek to restrict the ability of other people to enter the market as competitors. And the market for labor services is no exception. Labor markets do differ, however, in the degree to which personal relationships, legal restrictions, and group action affect negotiations between buyer and seller. In the present chapter, some of the constraints on labor markets will be analyzed in an effort to detect and disentangle the effects from the avowed motives.

Employee-Employer Bargaining Power

First, however, we should explore a fallacious motive. Restrictions on the play of the open market are often advocated as a means of protecting the employee from the superior bargaining power of the employer. Proponents of such restrictions usually say that individual workers have limited bargaining power and hence are helpless against the powerful employer. The average worker, acting alone, can readily be replaced if he asks for higher pay; his alternatives are limited. Therefore, to protect the laborer it is proposed that minimum-wage, fair-employment, and working-condition laws be passed. Employees are urged to unite in group action to prevent the employer from playing one against the other.

Whatever one's impression about the deserts of employees relative to employers, the fact is that the preceding argument is at best meaningless and at worst misleading or dead wrong. In the first place, everyone has only limited bargaining power; he is limited in the price he can get by the offers made to him by all potential buyers. General Motors has limited bargaining power. To see this, one need merely ask what limits its ability to keep wages down. The answer is that if General Motors offers less pay than is offered by other employers, employees will not work for General Motors. The reason any employee gets as high a salary as he does is that his services are worth that much to at least some other employer. The reason his wages are not any lower than they are is that he could quit and work for someone else rather than take a lower wage.

The authors of this book are employees of the state of California; yet they have enormous bargaining power against the state of California—which presumably has even greater bargaining power. Any time we feel like it, we can quit and take a job elsewhere, at slightly less desirable salary and working conditions; that is what forces the state of California to pay as much as it does if it wants to keep us. That it is willing to do so means that our services are worth at least that much to the purchaser. What bargaining power may mean, therefore, is simply the highest salary one can get from *other* jobs. If that is a great deal less than he is now getting, the employee will be reluctant to press for higher wages and may even accept some impositions rather than quit.

It may be said that the employer who loses an employee loses only one employee while the employee who loses his job loses his entire source of income. In fact, the employee does not lose his entire source of income; he loses the premium he was getting in his former job over the next best alternative adjusted for moving and job-exploration costs. Of course, the losses suffered by an employee who loses his job can be greater than those imposed on the employer when one employee quits; but such a comparison is totally irrelevant. It does not follow that the employer is therefore more willing to let an employee quit or fire him rather than pay at least what the employee can earn elsewhere (if he is worth that much to the current employer). Employers hire employees because the employer gains by doing so, not because the employee gains less or gains more. To fire someone because that hurts the employee more than it hurts the employer would impose a loss on the employer. It is a form of business suicide. It is his own loss that the employer wants to avoid; whether the employee suffers a large or small loss or even a gain is irrelevant.

The idea that the big rich employer has more bargaining power or can tolerate more losses is irrelevant for determining wages in the *open* market. Where it *is* relevant is in situations in which markets are *closed* to newcomers; for example, when a strike occurs, the issue becomes in part how long each party is willing to continue without any income. During a strike the employer cannot get other labor, and the striker usually does not take other jobs—although there is nothing to prevent him from doing so, since the employer does not picket the employees who take other jobs during a strike. In this kind of situation, involving a restriction on purchases and sales, what counts is not the amount of wealth one starts with, but the rate at which it disappears when neither party is allowed to continue productive work.

Restrictions on Open Markets for Labor

We leave this digression on bargaining power and turn to our main problem—restrictions on open markets for labor.

If one wants a higher wage than is compatible with open-market competition, a restriction on open markets is necessary. There are several ways to accomplish this.

MINIMUM-WAGE LAWS

Minimum-wage laws prohibit anyone from offering to work at less than some stated wage per hour. These laws are passed by states as well as by the federal government. Currently the minimum legal wage rates vary among the several states that have such laws. Federal law specifies currently that the minimum wage shall be $1.25 an hour. This means that no person will be allowed to seek work by offering to work for less than $1.25 an hour and that no employer will be allowed to pay any employee less than $1.25 an hour.[1] The implication of economic analysis is that a minimum wage rate above the current market rate will lead to unemployment. At the minimum legal wage rate the quantity of labor demanded will be less than the quantity of labor services supplied—if the minimum wage is above the open-market wage level.

When minimum-wage laws are imposed, usually several months' advance notice is given, so that employers can let their work force gradually be reduced through normal attrition (deaths, illness, retirements, and voluntary quits). When the law is put into effect, the employer either will have gone out of business or will have adjusted his work force to about what he wants it to be at the higher wage rate. No one seems to have lost his job. But newcomers, seeking jobs at the higher minimum wage, will not be able to get a job.

The unemployed, who cannot get jobs because of prohibitions on their seeking work at lower wages than those being paid incumbent workers, can and do resort to working as private, independent contractors to their former employer, taking a lower income by means of a low contract price rather than as a reduced wage rate. For example, a person seeking a job as a taxi or a truck driver, at the stipulated rate of, say, $100 a week, could rent a vehicle from someone else and drive as an independent subcontractor, or independent driver, making a net of perhaps $80. In effect, he has cut his wages by renting the taxi from his "employer"

[1] The law usually specifies several exceptions—usually for those employees or types of work that provide so much less value per hour than the legal minimum that the particular kind of employment would be very much reduced; e.g., farm workers, hotel workers, restaurant workers, and employees in firms with less than about five employees. It is a challenging problem to analyze why these exceptions are granted if the effects of the law are desirable.

for a weekly fee of, say, $20 a week (above the free-market car rentals—a sort of secret rebate). This kind of independent contracting is common practice in the trucking industry, where teamsters' union rates have been raised above open-market competitive levels. The small independent businessman, whether he drives his own or a rented vehicle, may be a displaced employee effectively cutting the controlled wage rate. On the average, he earns less as an independent operator than he would have earned as an employee in a free market. When minimum wages were imposed on lumber-mill employees, the discharged employees turned to operating as independent tree-cutting contractors. They were again able to work, this time by taking low wages under the guise of low "profits."

EQUAL PAY FOR EQUAL WORK

As we know, because of different relative demands and supplies, wage differences exist among different occupations and even within the same occupation. In some instances, the differences in demand reflect not only pecuniary marginal productivity but also nonpecuniary productivity. As a result, there are equalizing or compensating differences in wages. These compensating differences are not always welcomed. One of the classic methods of trying to eliminate them is to advocate "equal pay for equal work"—on the presumption that equal work is easy to identify and that nonpecuniary differences among services of employees or employers should not count.

Proponents of imposed wage uniformities. All employees (superior and inferior) seem to dislike "equalizing differences." The inferior person dislikes the idea of being paid less for the "same" work. However, the "equalizing difference" enables him to offset his "disadvantage" where employment is concerned. It is a competitive device, like the lower price that a seller offers in order to sell his inferior product. The source of his lower income is not the equalizing wage difference but other people's preferences about these traits.

"Superior" people complain about the equalizing difference because it allows "inferior" people to compete for jobs that would otherwise have yielded a still higher wage to superior people. In many jobs (e.g., teaching) where both men and women might do equally well, men usually are hired because of employer preference for male employees. But that preference is in part overcome by the lower-wage competition of women. Rather than try to prohibit women from access to these jobs in order to preserve the jobs for men, the men will advocate "equal pay for equal work"—at, of course, the wages now being paid to the men. Then the employer's incentive to employ women is reduced. Men can profess to be doing this for the benefit of women. Whatever the motivation, the effect is to protect men's jobs by reducing opportunity for women teachers to replace men by taking a lower salary.

This analysis extends even to geographical differences in pay. Wages for the same kind of labor are lower in the South than in the North. Also, wages are lower in Puerto Rico than in the United States. How can a Northern employee protect his wage level from the competition of lower-wage Southern labor? And how can a laborer in the United States protect his job (and higher wage rate) from Puerto Rican labor? One device would be to advocate "equal pay for equal work" in the United States, *including* Puerto Rico, by a minimum-wage law above the prevailing level in the South and Puerto Rico. If Southern and Puerto Rican labor have to be paid a higher wage, they cannot compete so effectively against Northern laborers. It should come as no surprise to learn that in the United States, Congress's support for minimum-wage laws comes primarily from Northern congressmen, who profess to be trying to help the poorer Southern laborers.

Opponents of imposed wage uniformities. Who can object to equal pay for equal work? First, it is opposed by those inferior people who understand that their source of market power lies in their accepting a compensating wage difference, however much they may regret their inferiority. Second, employers might object; but if they do, they will be confessing to a "greedy" desire for more wealth by employing inferior labor, as well as confessing to "prejudice" and discrimination in hiring. A third objection to these laws rests on the general ethic that they interfere with freedom of voluntary contract; this objection presumes that freedom of contract in the market is of some inherent merit.

FAIR-EMPLOYMENT LAWS

If a uniform or minimum-wage law is effective in raising anyone's wages, discrimination will be transferred from wages to employment rates. Fewer "inferior" people will get jobs. Therefore, pressure mounts for "fair-employment laws," prohibiting employers from choosing employees on the basis of any criterion ruled unethical—usually race, creed, color, age, and sex. These laws probably reduce the extent of observable discrimination among employers. But they are incredibly difficult to enforce. How can one tell whether an employer is hiring as many "inferior" workers as he would if he really didn't think them inferior, or if his customers didn't think their services were inferior? Furthermore, the employer will be even more reluctant to observe the spirit of the law when he knows it will be more difficult to fire those whose services are unsatisfactory.

Fair-employment laws also impose other burdens on some employees. If a class of people want to work together, the fair-employment laws prohibit that. If Armenians prefer to work with Armenians, or Catholics with Catholics, or a Negro with Negroes, or a Mormon with Mormons, these laws make that illegal, for the employer would be susceptible to legal prosecution for "discrimination."

Labor Unions

"The high standard of wages of the American worker is a result of a strong labor-union movement." Would, perhaps, that it were true. For then the path to higher income for all workers in poor countries would be open. Simply organize labor unions and strike for higher wages. However, neither economic reasoning nor factual evidence supports that prescription. Do you believe that the people of India, Iran, Egypt, Mexico, or Japan could achieve American wage levels simply by organizing into labor unions and striking for higher wages? Not even the English or Germans could do it. It is the high marginal-productivity schedules of labor for the amount of labor available that explains high wage and employment levels. If a community has abundant natural resources and capital equipment, high educational levels, skilled workers, and a system for organizing productive activity, then the marginal productivity of the existing supply of labor will be high. The foundation of high wages and large incomes is precisely there and no place else. What the union can do in that respect is help that system organize diverse talents more efficiently by smoothing grievance procedures, providing increased information about job opportunities, and helping workers improve their skills.

In addition, laborers can seek to limit entry into the country via immigration laws; and this, too, has been done, beginning in the mid-nineteenth century. While it is somewhat "impolitic" to admit to the desire to create barriers against competition from one's fellow "Americans," it is not impolitic to bar entry to "foreigners." It has been often urged that not only foreign workers but also the *products* of foreign workers be largely excluded; the alleged fear of "pauper labor" abroad has been perhaps the most persistent argument by American high-tariff protectionists.

It is a tribute to the intelligence and economic analysis of the union leaders that they fought hard for the restriction of immigration and for the right to use the strike in domestic industry and that they correctly insist the right to strike effectively is crucial to a strong and effective union. It is a tribute to their political skill in concealing that fact behind the façade of double talk about the "equating of bargaining power" as a means of protecting the standard of "labor's" wages in America. It would not be a tribute to the intelligence of the reader to let that distinction pass unnoticed. Therefore, in the remainder of this chapter we shall apply economic analysis to the role of the union in affecting wages and employment allocation.

Unions are agencies whereby employees can resort to coordinated group action to get more favorable contracts or to modify the results of open-market competition for labor. The association is voluntary in the sense that no one has to join a union, as he does have to pay taxes; but it is often compulsory in the sense that access to the market for sale of labor in some occupations depends on union membership. Basic to the union as an effective instrument in affecting labor market conditions is the union's ability to strike.

THE STRIKE AS A BASIS OF UNION POWER

A strike is an action wherein two things happen: (1) incumbent employees stop work for their existing employer *and* (2) other laborers are prevented from competing for those jobs on terms inferior to those sought by the striking incumbents (e.g., lower wages, longer hours). Without the ability to prevent other applicants from negotiating for these jobs, the strike would merely be a mass resignation. Take away *that* power, and you take away *effective* strike power; the union as we know it today would be destroyed.

Legislation concerning strikes. In England and in France in the early part of the nineteenth century, labor or trade unions were prohibited as "conspiracies." They were conspiracies of groups of laborers to modify market negotiations and competition by resort to threat of violence against other laborers who undercut their desired higher wages. The threat of violence against competitors via the strike was basically what nineteenth-century anti-conspiracy laws aimed to stop; but they tried to do it by abolishing the right to form a union—which is a very different thing from a strike. To unite voluntarily is a right of free men, as defined in most concepts of freedom. Hence, the anti-conspiracy laws were objected to both by employees who had their eye on the right to strike and by people who had their eye on the ideal of freedom. By 1830, the English anti-conspiracy laws had been repealed and the right to strike tacitly granted—with the forlorn hope that no violence or coercion would ensue.

The right to strike has had its subsequent ups and downs. At times, it was prohibited as an interference with a non-striker's freedom of access to labor markets. Even when legalized, it has sometimes been tolerated only if strikers did not interfere with non-union people who continued to work at less than the wages demanded by the strikers. At other times, the state has so leniently recognized the right to strike that violence was inevitable if non-union employees tried to cross the picket line. The police have at times permitted pickets to block entry and have refused to help non-union employees in crossing the line, because that would mean a breach of the peace—which means that the picket line was supported by the police.

Today, practice and law differ among cities and nations. Some countries (Russia and Spain, to name but two) prohibit strikes; anyone can quit his job, or the whole group can quit. In some other countries, tolerance for the strike ranges from strict restrictions against any interference with non-striking employees and job seekers to support of the strikers by preventing non-union job seekers (strike breakers) from accepting employment in a "struck" firm.

In the United States, the right to strike was legally recognized by the United States Supreme Court in 1842 in the case of *Commonwealth* v. *Hunt,* but the law has not always permitted that crucial feature wherein non-members are intimidated or prevented from working for the "struck" employer. In 1914, unions were exempted from anti-monopoly laws and permitted to strike to establish a labor monopoly insofar as any one employer's use of a certain class of labor was concerned. Then, in 1932, as part of the reaction to the depression, the federal government passed the Norris-LaGuardia Act, which reduced the power of the judiciary to issue "injunctions," court decrees prohibiting a strike. And in 1935, the Wagner Act passed by Congress proclaimed that union agents should be the sole collective-bargaining agents of the employees; to enforce this, it declared that employers must recognize the union as the employees' representative if two thirds of some class of employees desired to have a union. Employers were denied the liberty of refusing employment to any person solely because he was a union member. A National Labor Relations Board was created to administer the law and to determine when the requisite majority of employees in some occupation desired to have a union as the sole collective-bargaining agent and to determine "unfair labor practices by management." Subsequently, the Taft-Hartley Act of 1947 declared illegal certain union strike tactics and permitted employees to refuse to become union members even against the wish of a majority of the firm's employees. It also prohibited Communists from holding certain offices in a union, although it did not deny the right of a Communist to be either an employer or an employee.

Compulsory arbitration. To prevent strikes, the employer and union sometimes hire an outsider to suggest or even arbitrate terms that might be mutually acceptable, though neither party publicly admits in advance that it will accept intermediate terms. The outside mediator may be a private specialist in this kind of service, a government employee, or a distinguished, disinterested person such as a university president or professor. Presently, no law requires employers and unions to submit disputes to an arbitrator for a binding settlement, but about 90 percent of labor contracts provide for arbitration of grievances. Federal law gives the President authority to prohibit strikes in any situation in which he asserts that the strike would "imperil national health or safety." Though it is impossible to tell what is meant by imperiling national health or safety, the President merely has to *proclaim* that the strike would do so, and a strike is forbidden for the next eighty days. After that, the strike can occur.

Some people want compulsory arbitration wherein a governmental agency could declare the terms of the new contract. Whether new contracts would be more like those that would prevail in a situation with open markets for labor or would result in even greater monopoly restriction is impossible to say. Often it is thought that the new contract's wage and work conditions can be most sensibly determined by criteria like the "ability" of an employer to pay—as judged by his income, the cost of living, or the change in productivity. None of these, of course, would reproduce the free market's wage and work conditions. But, of course, they aren't supposed to. That is precisely what the union is trying to avoid by its threat to strike effectively.

MAINTENANCE OF EFFECTIVE STRIKE POWER

Unions lose power if a number of the existing employees refuse to join the union, for they may refuse to join in the strike. The simplest way of overcoming this latent membership weakness is to insist on a "union shop," wherein all employees must become union members. Furthermore, all members with a given skill should belong to the same union. If two unions represented, say, musicians, the two groups would try to dominate each other; and the employer could play one against the other—just as he lets one employee bid against another in the free market, and also just as each employee lets one potential employer bid against the other in a free market. The single union (exclusive bargaining agent) and the union shop then become the "silent" rallying cry for unions, because they increase the effectiveness of a strike.

It is easy to see why many union members and especially union officials dislike "right-to-work" laws; these misnamed laws are not for the right to work, but instead for the right to work without having to join a union. These laws declare it illegal for an employer to agree to hire only employees who belong to a union, and they exempt non-union members from having to pay a fee to the union. Such laws do not, *in logic,* necessarily increase the workers' freedom or range of choice. For example, even if some employer and *all* his employees want a union shop, a "right-to-work" law would prevent them from establishing one. On the other hand, it prevents one group of employees from forcing other employees to join a union if the other employees and the employer do not want a union shop.

Once the power to strike effectively is sanctioned, better working conditions can be sought for *some* members of the striking unions—better than if other people were free to compete in the same market. Higher wages, shorter hours, easier working conditions, and increased job security against layoffs are ways in which *some* union members can increase their wealth and utility.

However, the fact that union bargaining is associated with increases in wages is not conclusive evidence that it achieves higher wages than are obtained in a free market. Suppose, for instance, that a wage contract were signed two years ago for specified wage rates, and since that time wages in general have risen by 15 percent. The employer is ready to grant a pay raise of 15 percent. In fact, he may be eager to do so in order to retain, as well as improve, his work force in the face of better wages elsewhere. Union officials, however, might demand a 20 percent increase. After a ritual of negotiation and bargaining, the terms come out to be 15 percent; and the union claims it has raised wages. However, neither the employer nor the union sets the wage rate; instead, both accept, adopt, or adjust to wages in the free market—the employer offering that amount because he has to in order to get employees, and the union negotiators accepting it unless they are prepared to face a noticeable loss of job opportunities from this employer. In the absence of a union, the wages would have risen anyway—maybe even earlier, since employer and employee had to wait for a formal union-contract negotiation.

Entirely different is the case in which wages and working conditions really are improved by the presence of a union. To achieve these improvements, the union must require that competing employees, who would have undercut the union's terms of work, be denied access to the market for these jobs. Compulsory union membership, laws, fines, and threats of privately administered violence are devices for restricting the competing supply in order to compel employers to agree to better terms. This interpretation—reliance on restriction of right to free access to the job market—is often publicly denied by union officials. Some of them say that higher wages can be paid by employers out of profits or greater efficiency when the employer is spurred to greater effort. But they overlook the fact that employers would not have to pay higher wages if other employees would work for less; and employers, like employees, regard more wealth as preferable to less. Even though the employer *could* pay more, just as the employee could work for less, the fact is that neither wants to. Employees will receive higher wages and better working conditions than can be had in a free market only if they can keep other employees from successfully offering to work for free-market wage rates. A test of their success in raising wages is the extent to which the union has to engage in activities designed to keep out wage cutters and to ration out the available jobs at wages above the open-market competitive level.

UNIONS AND WAGES

No one knows exactly how much some unions have succeeded in raising wages. Aside from unions of doctors, teamsters, coal miners, musicians, and longshoremen, for which it seems clear that wages are above free competitive levels, it is difficult to draw up a complete list. The best available data suggest that unions on the average have raised union members' wages to nearly 5 percent above those of non-union workers. To what extent there are fewer workers in union jobs and more elsewhere is impossible to determine, but examples are easy to find. Thus, when wages were increased during the reign of John L. Lewis in the coal miners' union, employment in the coal industry fell off dramatically.

If unions are effective in controlling market competition so as to put wages higher than they would be in a free market, who gains and who loses? Usually it is claimed that the gains come out of the profits of the employers. But, according to economic analysis, the consequences are spread more widely over the community. Some employers who cannot survive at the new higher costs sell their assets at correspondingly lower prices or take a write-down in the value of their assets. Output contracts until prices are high enough to cover the higher wage costs, or a growing industry does not grow quite so much.

People who would have been employed here had wages not been raised work elsewhere with smaller incomes. Output of products of the higher-wage labor is smaller, and output of other goods is larger. The resources transferred to the other good would have produced a greater value of output in the first good if all labor could compete freely for highest-valued markets. Consumers get a less preferred output mix.

NON-WAGE RATIONING OF EMPLOYMENT

When any group succeeds in getting an employer to pay a higher wage than the open-market level, the increased number of qualified job applicants will, by definition of an open market, exceed the reduced number of jobs available at that wage rate.[2]

[2] Except in one special kind of labor-market situation, a "wage-searchers'" market. That market is one in which the employer is such a significant part of the total demand that to increase his number of employees he must offer higher wages than before. He is a "wage-searcher" in the buying market, analogous to a seller in a price-searchers' market.

This analysis can be graphed. Figure 28–1 shows the labor-supply curve to the firm. Above it is the marginal-wage-cost curve (*MWC*), the height of which shows the *increase* in the total wage bill per unit increase in the number of employees. It lies *above* the average-wage curve, *WW*, because each new employee increases the wage bill by his wage and also increases the wage rate paid to all the existing employees. Also drawn is the marginal-value-product, or demand, curve for labor, *DD*. The intersection of this curve with the marginal-cost-of-labor curve indicates the wealth-maximizing rate of employment, E_0, at which the wages paid each person is W_0, indicated by the height of the average-wage curve at the profit-maximizing employment rate. The employer would not hire more employees because the increase in cost, shown by the height of the curve *MWC*, exceeds the marginal value-product of one more employee.

Now we are prepared to see what would happen if the wage were raised to W_1 *and* if the employer must pay only that fixed wage rate, *no matter how many employees he hires.* In effect, he is now faced with a horizontal supply of labor along the straight line W_1 out to where it hits the *WW* line.

The employer will hire as many employees as yields a marginal value-product of labor no less than the average wage, W_1—at level of employment E_1. E_1 is the maximum amount of employment at any wage rate that can be imposed. If the wage were imposed at a level of W_2, the quantity of employment would be the same as at a level of W_0; at wages higher than W_2, employment would be less.

Once the employee group enforces a fixed wage rate above the level W_1, any subsequent increase above the level W_1 will induce employment reductions—with qualified employees exceeding the number demanded at that wage rate.

How important is this case? Does it characterize the typical market for labor? Available evidence suggests that few if any employers are large enough to have significant long-time effects on wage rates by individually varying their rates of employment. Over a longer period, with a flow of workers from other employers and areas, the supply of labor is highly elastic to individual firms, so that this case is of little significance. Nevertheless, we take note of it, for it represents the one possibility for imposing a higher wage rate without reducing employment. But remember this is a once-and-for-all effect of converting the market; a subsequent imposed wage increase will reduce employment in that market, once the level of W_1 has been achieved.

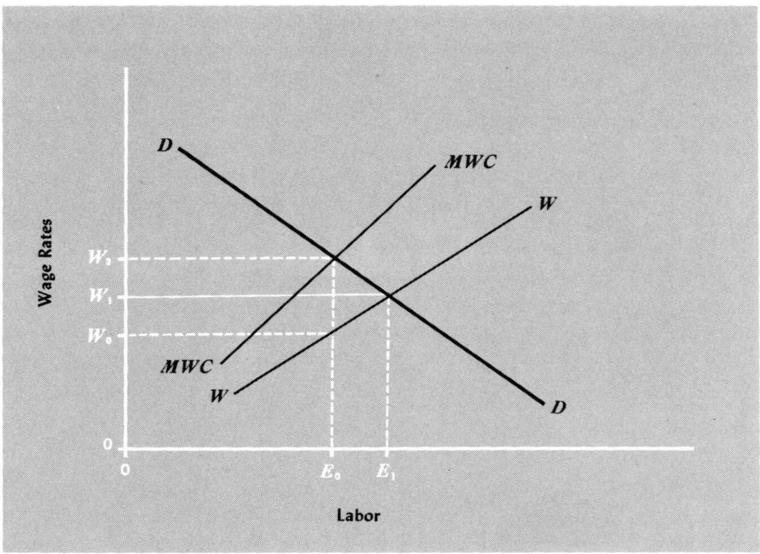

FIGURE 28–1. Wage-searchers' market for labor: effects of imposed wage rate.

An imposed higher wage, with reduced jobs and increased applicants for union membership, creates a task of rationing available jobs. This task is thrust on the union and the employer. Non-wage rationing of jobs occurs both by intra-union non-wage competition for jobs and by restriction of entry into the union.

Within the union (and the firm), seniority rules protect some employees from the intra-union competition of unemployed union members. The intra-union (or firm) battle is usually resolved in accord with the relative political power of various members. If the union is dominated by old people, or by men, or by whites, the answer to the rationing problem should not be hard to miss. Another common procedure is to hire a class of probationary members for temporary and seasonal jobs. When an employer's demand increases, these employees are used; later, when demand falls, they will be the first to go. The use of apprentices and probationary members serves, whatever its other purposes, as an employment-rationing device.

If the reduction in employment is particularly severe, so that some "seniority" men also are without jobs, explicit work sharing is likely to emerge, with limitations on the number of hours a week any one person can have. Frequent and compulsory attendance at union meetings as a condition of good standing will help to reduce "excessive membership," because the hope of getting a job is less of an incentive to payment of dues and attendance at meetings than is keeping a present job. In time, therefore, some of the "hopefuls" will drop out, thus reducing explicit unemployment in this union. In addition, jobs may be rationed through restriction of union entry (through larger initiation fees and more rigid standards: color, age, personality, sex, education, experience, probationary membership periods). Unethical job-seeking conduct prejudicial to the employed members of the union (whether it be the American Medical Association, the American Bar Association, the teamsters, or the longshoremen) can warrant expulsions; thus, advertising or secret price cutting is unethical conduct. Probationary membership periods also help to inculcate a sense of "proper" conduct and to weed out those who are prone to violate the standards. They also restrict entry into the union. One publicized reason for these restrictions is protection of the employer and consumer from shoddy work. Whatever the intention, one effect is certainly to strengthen the union's ability to maintain wage rates above the free market, because the more the unemployed *members*, the more difficult to preserve union cohesion.

Pervasive and creative of social conflict is the control of entry to occupations on the basis of color. Today, a person who wants to become a carpenter, plumber, electrician, studio projectionist, mason, plasterer, to name only a few examples, cannot enter the occupation of his choice by also joining the union. He must first obtain admission to the union as an apprentice. In some instances, he must first be nominated by three members in good standing, much in the fashion of entry to a country club. Negroes have long been excluded from many unions, as a means of restricting numbers in order to maintain wages above the free-market level. At the maintained wages, many Negroes would enter these occupations, and wages would fall but still be higher than in alternative jobs now available to Negroes. Even though a union charter states there is to be no discrimination, some criterion must be used to ration entrants as long as entry is not open to all who wish to join at existing wages.

Recent Negro demonstrations and replies by union officials have elicited public admissions of the fact of union discrimination by color. After meetings with the President of the United States, union officials have promised to try to change the situation; but substantial changes probably cannot be made. Union locals make their own decisions about admissions; and, as long as union membership is limited, discrimination is necessary in deciding who shall be admitted. The only question is what form of competition shall be weighted in granting membership—which returns us to the earlier discussion of principles of rationing when open-market pecuniary offers are not allowed as a competitive device to every potential employee and employer.

If the union is strong enough, it can impose work rules, known as "featherbedding," whereby an employer must employ laborers whether or not he wants them. Teachers decry the use of television; hod carriers once refused to carry premixed concrete; newspaper typesetters require the publisher to set duplicate sets of type if preset type forms are submitted by advertisers; railroads must carry firemen on diesel engines; building codes specify unnecessarily expensive and old-fashioned labor-using techniques; standby local musicians must be hired when visiting touring orchestras perform locally. All these are examples, taken from various cities, of make-work practices. All are legal, and all rest on the continued monopoly power deriving from the power to strike effectively. The railroads have perhaps the most publicized featherbedding provisions; and this should not be surprising, because the railroads were themselves in a *legal* monopoly position. Their rates were controlled; consequently, the companies had a protected income and could therefore pay higher wages than in firms that were not legal monopolies. In effect, higher wages were paid out of the monopoly-rent potential. However, the growth of competition from trucks for freight and airplanes for passengers has bankrupt several railroads and practically eliminated inter-city passenger service by rail. Threatened with complete loss of business, the railroad owners went to court and won prohibition against the union's striking for such contracts. Fully effective featherbedding rules are difficult to enforce. After all, the employer cannot be forced to continue in business if he is losing money. Higher wages raise costs and lead to a higher business mortality of employers.

MONOPOLY-RENT ACQUISITION

Restriction on entry into the union may be so effective that death, retirement, and normal attrition will reduce the membership. Entry might be completely closed for years (as with longshoremen's unions). Because the union has this power to limit supply to employers by restricting union membership, current members can keep wages up; all they have to do is maintain the restriction on entry and then let the employers bid up the wages of the union workers.

Limited membership in the union with higher than free-market wage rates permits "unusual" behavior. First, and without regard to relative importance, the union agent or officer will be tempted to keep wages *down*, so that the available workers must be rationed to the competing employers—who, at the repressed (although above free-market) wage, want more workers than he has available. If the wage rate would have been $5 an hour under the contrived scarcity of members, and if the agent can hold the wages to $4 an hour, then the employer would be prepared to pay an additional $1 per hour per worker to get more work; and he needn't pay it to the worker, but to the person responsible for assigning workers to various job opportunities. As a condition for giving preference in assigning as many workers to an employer as the employer desires at that wage rate, the agent can demand or be willing to accept a "side" favor or "under-the-table" payment from the favored employer. In effect, the cost ends up being just as high to the employer, but it is paid not entirely in the form of wages to the workers. Reluctant employers can be penalized without a strike; they simply don't get many employees. Secret payments to union officials are fundamentally a payment for laborers—with the payment going to the union officials rather than to the member employees.

Considerations of equity and morality of the "sharing" by union officials are not so simple as may seem at first sight. The union organizers can say that they were the ones who developed, directed, organized, and accomplished the contrived (i.e., type-1) monopoly for the union. Why shouldn't they be rewarded with larger salaries, expense accounts, and vacation resorts and homes, rather than the union members, who really had little to do with the development of the organization—in fact, no more than the employees of a successful businessman who builds a greater enterprise? Economics gives no ethical criteria by which to judge this. It merely "explains."

Utilization of monopoly power. Employ*ers* are quick to exploit opportunities inherent in the contrived labor monopoly. Some employers will propose to pay the union a special reward if it will withhold workers from competitor firms. If the output of competitors is reduced, the favored firm will be able to command higher prices for its services. The increased profit, or "monopoly rent" (because it is obtained by restricting market access to competitors), can be shared among the owners of the protected firm, its workers, and even all the union members, if adequate payment is made to the union. This form of agreement is known as a "sweetheart" contract. Whether it is first suggested by the employer or by the union official is immaterial; nor is it important who gets the special "bribe." The union official might share it with the union members or keep it as a secret income or personally benefit from being able to administer extra-large pension funds set up by the employers for the benefit of the union.

Difficulty of maintaining long-lasting monopoly rent. The right to exclude competitors from the market does not give one unbridled economic power. Competition facing a union carpenter, for example, cannot be excluded merely by prohibiting non-union carpenters from offering services to *his* employer. Other employers will hire non-union carpenters and sell their products at lower prices. Even if all carpenters joined forces and forced all employers of carpenters to hire only the members of the carpenters' union, product competition in the market would be effective. Plaster, steel, cement, glass, and other building materials can partially displace carpenters. Even doctors' attempts to raise fees are partly restrained by the availability of brand or proprietary drugs, advice of friends, Christian Science, do-it-yourself care, faith healers, etc. As any organization—be it a business firm, union, or group of professional men—acquires greater power to restrict direct competitors from the market and thus can make effective the higher prices it wants for its services, the rest of the society is more likely to object to such use of power. Whether it is objecting primarily to the higher prices or to the denial of freedom of others to compete in the market or to the interference with production during strikes is an open question.

Some people object to the interference with the right of individuals to seek jobs in the open market. They believe that the right to participate in voluntary market transactions should not be prevented by anyone, let alone one's direct competitors. These critics do not object to unions as voluntary associations of employees for negotiating with employers, but they do object to the strike as a coercive method of controlling working conditions. It is not clear whether these critics are aware to what extent a union would lose power if strikes (as distinct from voluntary group decisions to quit a job) were prohibited. Unions could still exist and negotiate with employers, but their power to get working conditions above the free-market level, by preventing free access to the market for jobs, would be reduced. When the President of the United States says that unions are basic institutions in a free society, the relevant question is still to be faced: "Unions with what kinds of power over rights of access to the market for jobs?" And on that issue "reasonable" men differ.

What is the difference between a labor union that keeps non-union workers from working at wages less than those sought by the union, and a medical profession which prevents a free market for medical services? Both result in higher wages for the "incumbents." The differences are that the medical profession has defended its actions not so much in the name of higher wages, but in the name of raising the quality of medical service. This is an enormously persuasive argument. That it also enables doctors to get higher wages is obvious, and presumably irrelevant. The second difference is that the medical profession does not have to rely on strikes and intimidation against competitors who would sell services at "substandard" prices; instead, it has obtained a licensing law, and, rather than strike against any seller or buyer of "substandard" service at "substandard" wages, it merely telephones the government to send a policeman and restrain the competitor. In effect, the police department acts as the "strike picket." If labor unions could get laws passed prohibiting the sale of workers' services by anyone except a "licensed" (union) person, then, by controlling the licensing and certification, the union could keep the supply small enough so that wages would have to be higher in order to clear the market demand.

Until laws are passed enabling the union to call upon the state to enforce the exclusion of non-union members from the particular job market, the union will probably continue with its accepted procedure of engaging in private threats of violence and intimidation of non-union members. Were the public police force available, gangsters and hoodlums—the specialists in intimidation—would be of less value. Then union officials would all be as free of the "undesirable elements" and as respectable as are the officers of medical and legal associations and public utilities.

Employee union monopoly vs. employer monopoly. Union monopoly power is often said to be necessary to match the monopoly power of the industry. This is a superficially plausible, but invalid, generalization. Consider the steel industry, the industry most often said to be a "monopoly." The steel industry is a group of independently owned firms—just as a union is a group of independent workers. The firms are "price-searchers"; consequently, their search for the wealth-maximizing price contains all the façade of "price-setting and administering," though, as we have seen, market demand and supply conditions control the price that will maximize wealth of the sellers. The union is also a "price-searcher"; for it, too, is desirous of seeking wage rates that will give its employed members a higher income. Yet there is a fundamental difference between the industry and the union. A union, to be effective in pushing wages above the competitive level, must prevent non-union members from taking jobs by wage cutting. Analogously, it is sometimes said that the firms, on their part, can engage in a lock-out; they can all shut down and thus try to force the employees to accept terms more favorable to the firms. But the firms cannot force wages below the open-market levels by a collusion, simply because the individual firms will find it profitable not to do so, for reasons already discussed: access to the market is open to existing and to new employers. In this one crucial difference lies the error of thinking that a group of price-searching employers who have joined together for negotiation with the union constitutes a "monopoly," which requires a countervailing union monopoly. Not even for purposes of negotiating with a common "antagonist" is it possible for the steel companies to avoid open-market competition. Some firm always breaks the industry "front." The industry simply is not a type-1 monopoly. This bilateral-monopoly-bargaining thesis is empty unless (1) the employers are a "legal" monopoly or (2) the union and certain employers make a "sweetheart" contract, wherein the union agrees to provide no employees to any other firms, in order to protect the favored firms and thus convert them into a monopoly that will cooperate with the union—which can happen only if the union already has type-1 monopoly power.

Questions

1. You are an immigrant. Would you prefer laws insisting on equal pay for equal work, minimum-wage laws, apprentice laws, or strong unions that have been effective in raising wages above the open-market level? Explain.

2. The federal government is taxing and paying for job retraining for those who lose a job.

   a. Do you think it should provide an apartment-renovation service for people whose apartments become vacant?

   b. What is the difference between the two forms of aid?

   c. Why would you support one and not the other, if you would?

3. "Long ago we stated the reason for labor organizations. We said that they were organized out of the necessities of the situation; that a single employee was helpless in dealing with an employer; that he was dependent ordinarily on his daily wage for the maintenance of himself and family; that if the employer refused to pay him the wages that he thought fair, he was nevertheless unable to leave the employer and resist arbi-

trary and unfair treatment; that a union was essential to give laborers opportunity to deal on an equality with their employer." (Charles Evans Hughes, Chief Justice, Supreme Court of the United States, from the decision in the case of the United States vs. Jones and Laughlin, 1937.) Evaluate the above propositions for their meaning.

4. "In a society where there has not been an adjustment of wages to the savings of time afforded by the use of new techniques, and where such savings may result in an oversupply of labor, an agreement among laborers to prevent such conditions has a lawful labor objective." (Decision by Superior Court Judge Martin Coughlin, San Bernardino, California, in case of Orange Belt Chapter of Painting and Decorating Contractors vs. AFL-CIO Painters District Council 48, July 1958.) Suppose the introduction of spray and roller painting methods reduced the amount of man hours in painting a house to 50 percent of its former level.

a. Does the above decision mean that wages should be doubled? Or that if not doubled, the laborers can force the houseowner to hire as many hours of labor with the new technique as with the old?

b. What does it mean?

5. As a beginning lawyer, would you benefit if fees for the following were set by the Bar Association: drawing up someone's will, serving as an executor of an estate, arranging for a divorce?

6. As a summer-job-seeking college student, are your chances of getting a job increased or decreased if the wages you can get in a cannery, summer resort, factory, etc., are set by a union comprised of current full-time employees? Why?

7. As a college-aged baby sitter, would you be benefited if an association of baby sitters were organized and a minimum wage of $1.50 an hour enforced? Why?

8. "A man's labor is perishable. If he isn't employed, he loses forever that potential earning. Therefore, labor has a special disadvantage compared to nonhuman goods, which can be stored and used later." Is that correct? (Hint: Suppose labor were storable. What do you suppose would be the effect?)

9. "The higher the legally constrained minimum-wage rate, the greater the amount of unemployment of unskilled workers." Is this correct? Explain.

10. A representative of the Congress of Racial Equality advocated raising the minimum legal wage to $2 an hour in order to help Negroes get higher wages.

a. Would Negroes benefit from a higher minimum wage?

b. Would it reduce or increase discriminatory hiring?

11. A law is passed requiring each employer to provide hospitalization and premature retirement benefits for his employees who have "heart attacks."

a. Who will be benefited by such a law?

b. Who will be hurt?

c. Who will pay the costs? (In answering, first try answering the same questions if a law were passed requiring employers to pay for all the housing costs of red-haired employees. Explain why if you were a redhead you would be smart to dye your hair black. Similarly, if you had a heart condition, why would you try to keep it a secret? Does the employer pay for these services—in the sense that his wealth is lower as a consequence of the law? If he doesn't, who does?)

12. The National Teachers Federation, a teachers' union, advocates as a basic proposition a single salary scale—wherein every teacher, regardless of speciality, gets the same salary in his first year of teaching, with salary thereafter tied strictly to years of service. Who will benefit and who will suffer if that were made universal: Men or women? Negroes or whites? Superior or inferior teachers? Mathematics or physical-education teachers?

13. An employer seeks an employee to operate an electronic computer.

a. Will the employer take into account anything other than the applicant's ability to operate the machine? What other factors will be considered?

b. Which "should" not? Why do you think so?

c. In the event the employer disagrees with you about what factors to take into account, whose opinion should be binding?

d. Would you change your opinion if the employee were being considered for a job as a secretary or welder or truck driver or nurse or baby sitter or maid? Explain.

14. If in some town the minimum wage rate for taxi-driver employees was raised to $5 an hour, what would happen to the ratio of cabs driven by the owners to the number of cabs driven by employees of cab owners? Why?

15. The higher above the open-market wage rate the plumbers may set the minimum *wage* payable for plumbers, what will happen to the size of plumbing establishments in terms of the number of employees per shop? Why?

16. "If an enterprise cannot survive except by paying wages of 75 cents or $1 an hour, I am perfectly willing for it to go out of business. I do not believe that such an enterprise is worth saving at that price. It does more harm than good, socially and economically. It is not an asset; it is a liability. So if this kind of business is killed by a minimum wage of $1.25, I for one will not be sorry." (George Meany, Hearings before Subcommittee on Labor Standards, 86th Congress, 2nd Session, 1960, p. 36 of Part 1 of printed hearings.)

a. How does this statement differ from one that says, "Any person who cannot produce a product worth at least $1.25 an hour should not be allowed to work as an employee"?

b. Explain why Meany did not suggest that a business that paid wages of $5 an hour was an even greater liability to the community?

17. "Technically speaking, any labor union is a monopoly in the limited sense that it eliminates competition between workingmen for the available jobs in a particular plant or industry. After all, all unions are combinations of workingmen to increase, by concerted economic action, their wages, i.e., the price at which the employer will be able to purchase their labor." (Arthur Goldberg, Justice, Supreme Court of the United States, and formerly Secretary of the Department of Labor and counsel for the United

Steelworkers; quoted from *AFL-CIO: Labor United,* New York, McGraw-Hill, 1956, p. 157.) Why did he write "*technically* speaking" and "in the *limited* sense"? Is there some other mode of speaking and is there an unlimited sense of monopoly? Does a monopoly eliminate competition? What does it eliminate and how?

18. "The strike is an attempt to deny some people the ability to sell their services at open-market prices." Explain why this is a true statement. For which people?

19. "The union that utilizes or threatens to use the strike is a type-1 monopoly." If true, does that make unions bad?

20. A union strikes against some employer. The strike is unsuccessful if the employer is able to get sufficient other laborers. In order to prevent his successful operation with these other workers, the union initiates a "boycott," urging the public not to buy this employer's products. If that maneuver is successful, the employer will lose sales and close down, unless he is willing to hire only the union men at the wage they request. Thus, boycotts are devices to prevent the employer from being able profitably to employ other workers than those on strike. Sometimes the union will also engage in a secondary strike—a strike against anyone who buys that employer's products. Whether the union is striking and refusing to work for the employer, or picketing the employer as a means of urging customers to boycott products made by non-strikers, or using secondary strikes against any other producer who buys this employer's products (made with non-striking labor), the tactics are designed to remove from the open market one particular group of people. Who? Explain.

21. In strike or labor-dispute negotiations, the government sometimes appoints an investigating panel composed of representatives from the union, the employers, and the consuming public. Which especially affected group is *not* represented on these panels? Can you explain why?

22. You are the leader of a strong, closed union that has obtained wages above the open-market rate for the union supply of employees.

a. At next contract negotiations, at which it is clear a still higher wage can be obtained in view of increased demand or reduced union supply relative to the demand, what incentives are there for you, the union officer, to seek to get that higher wage not in the form of higher explicit money wages for the union members but instead in the form of fringe benefits—such as retirement pensions, medical insurance, vacation resorts, provision of workers' uniforms—which are dispensed and controlled by the union?

b. Would a greater portion of the "wage" being diverted to the control of the union leaders increase the utility of the union leaders? How?

c. Does the income tax on *money* income also produce a "bias" toward nonmonetary fringe benefits?

23. Construct the analogue to the preceding problem for a situation in which the state, instead of paying money to students and letting them buy their education, pays the money to the schools and lets them give the education to the students. Does financing schools directly rather than giving money to students to spend for schooling operate to increase the "utility" of school administrators and faculty relative to the students—along the lines of "fringe" benefits and the union leaders relative to the employees (students)? Which schools? Which faculty members?

24. "The steelworkers' union and the U.S. Steel Corporation are both monopolies." In terms of the type-1 and type-2 monopoly distinction, is that correct?

25. You work for a television manufacturer as a welder, and two unions contend for recognition as the sole bargaining unit for welders. One union, a "craft" union, would be composed only of welders; the other, an "industrial" union, would admit all employees who work for television manufacturers.

a. In which type of union do you think you will be able more effectively to raise your wages by imposing apprenticeship conditions and other devices to restrict the number of people who can seek jobs in competition with you?

b. Which union do you think will be more able to impose a wage-rate increase upon the employer without first restricting union membership? Explain why.

c. If the craft union successfully restricts entry to the union, in time the reduced supply of welders will enable those who are union welders to get a higher wage than if markets were open to all comers. What effect do you think a successful restriction on entry will have on the composition of the union membership in terms of race, religion, age, kinship, nationality, and personality? Explain.

26. The National Association for the Advancement of Colored People contends that the building-trade craft unions (among others) discriminate against Negroes. The national-headquarter officials of each union reply that the local unions in each city are autonomous and determine membership. The charter provides that there will be no discrimination. The unions reply variously that no qualified Negroes have applied, that a new member must be nominated by three members in good standing, that they do have some Negroes, that they use a quota system to ensure that all groups are equally represented, and that the present time, when even the white members are unemployed, is not a feasible time to increase entry rates. Given that the craft union has the power to determine who and how many may join the union, some system of choice is necessary —if the number is to be restricted in order to maintain wages above the open-market level.

a. What criteria for selection do you think should be used and declared defensible? Explain why.

b. Would you recommend a quota system? Why?

27. Unemployment among the self-employed normally runs less than 1 percent, compared to 3–5 percent for employees. What explanation can you suggest?

28. a. Labor groups were strong advocates of raising barriers to immigration in the nineteenth century. Employers objected. Why?

b. Labor groups were less enthusiastic for tariffs (taxes on imported goods), but some employers were in favor of them. Why?

c. In what sense do immigration barriers and tariffs make the people of the United States type-1 monopolists against the rest of the world?

d. Would you therefore advocate abolition of tariffs and immigration restrictions? Why?

29. Walter Reuther, head of the auto workers' union, contends that the automobile producers should lower their prices to benefit the public.

a. Why does he not propose that the current tax (tariff) of 12 percent on importation of foreign cars be abolished as a means of increasing domestic supply?

b. Why do you think Reuther says he wants lower prices for products produced by members of his union?

30. Union members constituted less than 10 percent of employment in 1930. In the 1930s federal laws favoring union organizations aided the growth to about 30 percent of the employment in 1945. Since then the proportion has fallen slightly with about 18,000,000 members. Almost half of them are in manufacturing work. About half are in ten unions (teamsters, steel, auto, machinists, carpenters, electricians, miners, ladies' garments, hotels, and hodcarriers). Of these, all except the teamsters and miners are American Federation of Labor–Congress of Industrial Organization (AFL-CIO) affiliates. Over 43 unions report at least 100,000 members each. Some employers welcome the growth of powerful unions that will be able to raise wages and control number of employees admitted to the union. Why? In answering, show why some employers would be hurt by the elimination of effective unions (even ignoring the conflict in trying to eliminate the union).

31. Laws have been passed designed to prohibit employers from discriminating among potential employees according to race, religion, and, in some instances, age. Why are there no laws prohibiting employees from similarly discriminating among employers for whom they choose to work?

32. Some employment contracts provide the employee with the following: paid time off for jury duty, funerals of relatives, voting, sickness, and vacations; free parking space and work clothes; retirement; two weeks' severance pay; seniority rights over new employees; no discharge for union activities; no discharge if job is displaced by new machinery.

a. Suppose you were to offer to work for some employer who did not give any of these provisions and who insisted on the right to fire or discharge you at any time for any reason whatsoever. Would you consider working for him at the same take-home pay as for the other employer?

b. Would the employer be willing to pay you a higher take-home salary for an employment contract without all those provisions listed earlier?

c. In the light of your answers to the preceding questions, who do you think pays for those fringe benefits listed earlier?

33. "Plumbers' and steamfitters' union local 2 of New York has no Negroes, and 80–95 percent of the members are the sons of existing or former members." News story from *New York Times,* August 2, 1963. What explanation can you offer for this?

34. "Any craft union that has to resort to the strike to get higher wages is not being operated efficiently. It should instead concentrate on control of apprenticeship rules and admissions in order to assure high-quality, reliable, skilled union members. And it will incidentally thereby achieve its higher wages in a peaceful, democratic way." Explain what the speaker, a highly successful union leader, meant.

29

INTEREST RATES, SAVINGS, AND GROWTH OF WEALTH

Since Eve and the fall from grace, man has wanted more wealth. There is no doubt that we *can* have more wealth by consuming less and saving more; the question is whether we *want* a faster growth of wealth in view of the necessary greater sacrifice of current consumption. Paralleling the earlier analysis of consumer choice among goods, choices about production of more wealth are influenced by the available opportunities for exchange between present consumption and growth of wealth. Think not of wealth and capital goods as merely inanimate piles of machinery, buildings, fertile land, sheltered harbors, rivers, and a fine climate. *People* are wealth, too; skills, talents, knowledge, initiative, manners, and customs contribute to our productive prowess. The historical accident that people do not sell themselves like capital goods, even though they sell their services, means that market valuations of the wealth of people, as people, are not readily available. Yet, as we saw in Chapter 27, labor does have means of capitalizing its value and accordingly of modifying its consumption patterns.[1] To be told, then, that the total stock of wealth of the United States is about $3,000,000,000,000 in terms of inanimate goods is to be told the value of only part of our wealth. Our stability of government, the reliability of the judicial and legal system, and the certainty of property rights also are parts of our wealth. They contribute to our income and utility. None of these are free goods given by God for the asking. They have evolved from centuries of testing and adaptation. They have been accumulated from the past endeavors of man.

In the preceding chapters, we took the level of wealth in its various forms as being given, and analyzed the other factors affect-

[1] See pages 460–461.

ing wages in various occupations. In doing so, we imagined labor on one side and capital goods on the other; for example, we spoke of labor and capital in Chapter 26 as generalized categories of resources. A better classification might have been human and nonhuman resources, because human beings contain a large amount of capital. People are capital goods—in the sense that at any time a person represents an asset capable of producing future services and also in the sense that at any moment his productive ability is what it is partly because of past investment in his training. Every student is sacrificing consumption for future increments of productive power. He acquires knowledge and skills, and these are "embodied" in him. Your son can be trained as a mathematician, or the resources to train him could be spent for a machine with which he could produce other valuable forms of services—say, a factory. A parent can spend for his son's education, or he can build a business for him. Both constitute capital goods—one inherent in the person's talents and knowledge and the other in the form of physical capital goods. Depending upon your son's revealed aptitudes, you may invest in one or the other form of capital.

But we did not use the terms human and nonhuman goods because that is not the fundamental distinction. At any one job location, we do seem to substitute machinery for labor; but viewed more generally the machine is produced by some other labor, and it is that other labor that we are substituting for this labor via the product of that other labor. Fundamentally, it is one person or one task that is substituted for another, not inanimate goods for people. And that is why the terms labor and capital are used to denote the broadest and simplest classes of alternative types of resources, with respect to any particular product. Labor used elsewhere to make a computer is used earlier to produce a good that will later be used to yield its output jointly with the operator (labor) of the machine. When computers are installed, the *producers* of the computer are replacing those who were replaced by the computer. Those who are replaced see only the physical electronic computer and think that machines are doing away with people. In fact, it is other people doing other tasks (making electronic computers) who are replacing these workers in this task.

Why are the machine producers called capital instead of indirect or off-site labor? The answer is that the machine producers worked earlier and produced an item that would yield its services later over a period of time. The user of the machinery must pay for the machine in advance of all its future services if he is to own the machine. That is, the owner must have paid the laborers when they produced the machine; he must wait for his future payments as the machine is used. And so he is called a capitalist. The machine is called capital or a capital good. The labor working with the machine is said to be working with capital, and the labor thereby avoided at the later date when the machine is used is said to be displaced by the capital good—even if really displaced by the earlier-used labor.

The accumulation of wealth in all its forms is not entirely a happenstance affair. Whether it is accumulated in the form of physical equipment, buildings, soil, graded lands, intellectual skills, knowledge, customs, stable governments, or "good" laws depends upon many factors and forces that have so far escaped our ken. Some factors, however, have been discerned; and the way in which they are manifested in the economic system is the problem to which we turn now. The problem can be put as a question. "Whatever the form in which capital is accumulated, what incentives and economic controls coordinate the investment activity of the society?"

Rate of Exchange between Present Consumption and Future Income

The rate of interest reflects the rate of exchange of present consumption rights for future income rights (wealth), no matter in what form those rights may be held. Usually the rate of interest is thought of as the price of a loan of present money in return for future money; however, that is only one manifestation of the rate of interest. It enters into *every* evaluation of *every* possible form of exchange between present and future consumption rights—and of these there are many.

In a capitalistic society, a person can save and can invest in several forms. (1) He can sell current consumption for future income rights (wealth). The form of the rights can be (a) promissory notes or (b) particular goods that he can have in the future. If he gets promissory notes as evidence of his rights, he is said to be lending. He can get more money in the future by not spending and by lending now what is paid him for current services. Or he can exchange relatively perishable goods for more durable goods. (2) He can use his productive powers to produce goods that are more efficient for future income than for present consumption—which is to say he invests in making "capital goods" for future consumption. These "capital goods" include knowledge and skills by education and training. All of these actions constitute saving and investing. They differ in the form in which the savings are used. And they differ in the particular markets in which the production or exchanges are conducted. But for all of them the rate of interest is influential, and, as we shall see, activity in all of them is interdependent and correlated.

In some markets, the rate of interest is explicit, and the way it facilitates exchange and affects decisions about current relative to future goods is transparent and direct. In others, it is implicit and operates to facilitate exchange and modify decisions in a more subtle, though no less powerful, way.

LENDING OR BORROWING: BOND MARKETS

Anyone can lend part of his wealth today for the right to more goods in the future. Lending wealth is giving up rights to current consumption. The lender usually gets a promissory note or a bond as evidence of his legal claim to future consumption. In fact, what he has done is sell rights to consume now for the right to consumable wealth in the future. The rate of interest involved is usually explicitly stated in the loan transaction.

Sometimes, when people invest their own income, as compared to borrowing from other people, there is a temptation to say that they make their choice independently of market rate of interest. This interpretation runs the danger of implying that a person uses what he owns without any regard to their alternative use values. It suggests, erroneously, that when I occupy my own house or office building, I do so regardless of the rent I could get by renting to someone else. But it would be more accurate to say that I took those "opportunity" costs into account. If I could rent my present house for $1,000 a month, or sell it for $100,000, I would indeed rent or sell. But at a price of $40,000, I continue to occupy it. People who use their own income or wealth to build goods for future income do not thereby ignore the rate of interest. To ignore it, they would have to ignore all their other opportunities for use of their wealth. The evidence does not support the proposition that people act so blindly.

CAPITAL-GOODS MARKETS

The time profile of present and future consumption can be revised by altering one's combination of goods *via* market exchange. To convert current income to the future (i.e., to wealth), one buys more capital goods that yield more future income relative to present consumption sacrificed. Not everyone can do this simultaneously, since we buy and sell existing goods from each other. Only a change in production of current consumption services could alter the composition of the total stock of goods. But the interpersonal exchanges of present and future consumption rights by loans or by purchases of specific existing goods can reshuffle current consumption among people in accord with their revised preferences. A shift in demand between present and future consumption will be manifest in a revision of prices of existing assets. Changes in relative prices of consumption and capital goods, in turn, will affect the rate at which these types of goods are consumed. In the course of that exchange, if preferences for future consumption have increased, prices of steel and concrete buildings will rise relative to those of wood; young, rapidly growing trees or animals will rise in value relative to older and slower-growing ones. A yearling grows at a faster percentage rate than an old steer. Every pound of a yearling now represents a greater relative increase of future beef than does that of older, slower-growing steers. The demand (and price) of yearlings will rise relative to steers; the price of veal will rise relative to beef.

Recalling the analysis of capital values and interest rates (Chapter 15), it will be apparent that the rise in the price of long-lived goods relative to the price of short-lived goods (e.g., yearlings relative to steers) means that the interest rate has fallen. Therefore, the interest rate shows up also in markets other than simply the bond market for lending and borrowing. We shall draw upon the ideas of Chapter 15 to demonstrate briefly the connection of the rate of interest with present prices and future yields.

Suppose we have two alternative annuity investments, which differ in their pay-off patterns. One yields \$100 at the end of each year for the next nine years, and the other yields \$200 annually for four years. Which of these annuities has the higher present value? As the acute and assiduous reader immediately recognizes, the answer turns on the interest rate. A \$1 annuity has a present value equal to

$$\frac{1-\dfrac{1}{(1+i)^n}}{i}.$$

These are the entries in Table 15–3, where i is the interest rate and n is the number of years. There is an interest rate which equates the two present values—namely, 5 percent. That is, if we round off a little here and there,

$$100\times\left[\frac{1-\dfrac{1}{(1+.05)^9}}{.05}\right]=200\times\left[\frac{1-\dfrac{1}{(1+.05)^4}}{.05}\right]=\$710.$$

Thus, \$710 invested at 5 percent will produce either \$100 yearly for nine years or \$200 yearly for four years.

If the rate (which is a *discount* rate) were to fall to 3 percent, the present values of both yield streams naturally rise, but by different amounts. We then have:

$$\frac{100\left(1-\dfrac{1}{(1.03)^9}\right)}{.03}=\$779,\text{ and }\frac{200\left(1-\dfrac{1}{(1.03)^4}\right)}{.03}=\$743.$$

Reducing the interest rate increases the present value of the nine-year annuity more than the value of the four-year annuity; and if the interest rate were to be increased to 7 percent, both present values would fall—the fall in the value of the nine-year annuity being greater: from \$710 to \$677 for the shorter annuity and to \$652 for the longer. Changes in the interest rate have greater (proportional) effects on annuities of longer periods.[2]

[2] To illustrate more generally the *proportionality* effects, begin with two annuities of *different* present values. Suppose that each annuity—one for four years and other for nine—pays \$100; at an interest rate of 5 percent, the nine-year annuity is presently valued at \$710 and the four-year annuity at \$355. Now, if the interest rate falls to 3 percent, the nine-year annuity rises to \$779, an increase of 9.7 percent; the shorter-termed annuity value becomes \$372, an increase of only 4.8 percent.

We have gone from a change in the interest rate to a change in present values. We can reverse the relationship or line of causation: a change in present values of given future-income streams changes the interest rate. In fact, a change in the relative present values *is* a change in the rate of interest in the capital-goods markets. Suppose that the community initially places the same value (of $710) on each of our two annuities—i.e., $100 for nine years and $200 for four. Now, for some reason, the community's preference changes at the margin in favor of the longer annuity; people prefer to forego consumption of some amount of present and near-term income in favor of more long-term or delayed income. The nine-year annuity will now be valued more highly than the four-year annuity. The shift of the community toward more future returns lowers the interest rate. For given the initial equality in the present values of the two annuities, and holding to the constraint that at any given time there is a common rate of interest in any market, the only way the present value of the nine-year annuity can now rise relative to the four-year is for both to rise absolutely in different, appropriate amounts. For example, the present value of the nine-year stream can rise to $779 and the four-year stream to $743, both from $710, in which case the interest is 3 percent, down from 5 percent.

All this is not restricted to "purely financial" transactions. Instead of considering the purchase of an annuity from an insurance company which will pay annual dollar sums, we could apply the analysis to any current commitment of resources which is expected to yield future returns. We might construct a relatively small but relatively long-lived concrete building to bring in $100 rent every December for nine years, or we might use wood to build a larger but shorter-lived building that will return $200 annually for four years. With an interest rate of 5 percent, we may invest $710 in either one. If the interest rate now falls, say, to 3 percent in response to a shift in demands toward more distant consumption rights relative to nearer consumption, there will be a shift in preferences toward concrete buildings, the price of which will rise relative to that of wooden buildings or current consumption assets.

The lending and capital-goods market prices are interdependent. For example, if the explicit rate of interest in the lending market were still 5 percent, there would be disequilibrium between this exchange and the lending market. A person who owned the long-lived good would be getting only 3 percent on his wealth, now valued at about $780. If he sold the goods and lent the $780 at 5 percent in the loan market, instead of $100 he would get $110 a year for nine years. The offer of his goods would tend to lower its price (thereby raising the exchange-market interest rate), and lending the proceeds would tend to lower the explicit rate in the lending market. This "arbitrage" between markets by selling in one and lending in another would bring back into equality the present values of the two assets and also the interest rates.

The effects would spread even further. The rise in the price of some goods relative to others affects the relative profitability of production. In the present example the relative rise in concrete buildings would present enhanced prospects of profits for producers of concrete buildings. The output of such buildings would increase, thereby diverting current income from current consumption more to future income (i.e., to wealth). But before we go into this matter, a more systematic exploration of principles of capital-goods production is desirable.

FUTURE CONSUMPTION THROUGH SAVING AND INVESTING

Any person can convert present consumption power to wealth simply by saving. Goods that are relatively imperishable will more likely be the type saved. Some goods can be physically changed to reduce the cost of storage. Sometimes the new good is preferred to the original form; for example, we convert fresh milk to cheese, apples to cider, pork to bacon, beef to sausage, grain to whiskey, grapes to wine, olives to olive oil. Often it is possible to divert present consumption power to other goods that will make feasible a *bigger* future consumption, in a physical (whether or not in a value) sense, than the current consumption sacrifice. The laws of nature enable us to plant (forego present consumption of) seeds and end up with even more seeds in the future. But merely saving current goods will not do. We must know enough to plant them. The more we "understand" the laws of nature, the more we seem to be able to increase future output. The discovery of the principle of the wheel and axle permitted an enormous increase in future production. The time taken to make a wheel and axle required a sacrifice of consumption output, but the increase in future consumption power thereby obtained exceeded the cost.

This increased productivity is "economic" productivity. The law of the conservation of energy is not denied; instead, energy, or material, is converted to more desired forms.

Since capital goods usually involve the intermediate step of making a tool or a good that is then used to produce consumption services, this process is often referred to as a "roundabout, indirect" method of production. Man has been using roundabout capital goods from time immemorial. Because we are accustomed to seeing future output increased by use of capital goods, we easily but erroneously conclude that all durable goods or tools are more productive of future income than their current cost. However, although it is no trick to make tools or capital goods that are worthless for purposes of future production, obviously "wasteful" production or investment is avoided where possible, so that the only capital goods we commonly see are those that have proved productive.

Some goods that can be produced today are more effective than are others in yielding an output further in the future. Compare production of buildings of concrete, steel, aluminum, and plastic with wood; canned and frozen foods with fresh food; concrete with blacktop roads; aluminum sidings with paint; diamond with metal-tipped record needles; Omega with Timex watches; and pipelines with trucks or boats. All these involve a greater diversion from present consumption to future consumption. Of course, constructing two wooden houses is more diversion of current income than one wooden house, but we are interested here in comparing ways of getting different amounts of future services *per unit* of present consumption sacrificed. A steel building, at the same sacrificed present consumption as two wooden buildings will yield a larger or longer stream of future services. The greater durability of steel relative to wood is relevant only in so far as it means that, *per unit of current* consumption, it yields a longer sequence of future services.

The rate of interest affects this decision to produce capital goods in the same way it does the decision to buy them. In deciding whether to produce capital goods, one estimates the current costs and compares them with the present value of the future net income thereby made available. One can estimate the value of capital goods that will be produced by current investment activity by forecasting the future income derived from the good and then discounting that to a present value, which it is believed or hoped the capital good will command in the market upon its production. If that present value exceeds the current costs, the investment in production of those capital goods will be profitable. This means that, according to the market-revealed valuation of current and future consumption rights, the available future consumption rights are preferred to the present sacrificed consumption.

The classic example of this relationship between the rate of growth of future yield, the interest rate, and present value is illustrated by the growth of a tree. In Figure 29–1 the value of usable board feet of lumber in a tree for different ages of the tree is shown by line *LL*. The right-hand vertical scale indicates the amount of wood in the tree. The tree grows rapidly at first, but at a declining percentage rate. If we keep the value of a cubic foot of lumber constant, then the right-hand scale also measures the value of the lumber in the tree *at the time the tree is cut*. The value of the lumber in the tree would grow according to the curve of the diagram. Young trees grow faster than old trees, and at some age, T_n, the tree—and hence the value of the lumber—grows at a rate equal to the rate of interest. Thereafter, the value of the lumber in the tree increases by less than the rate of interest.

What is the tree worth as a *live, growing tree* at each age? Not the value of the cut lumber in the tree at that moment; for if the tree's lumber value will grow during the coming year by more than the rate of interest, the present value of the *live tree* will be greater than the present value of the *lumber now* in the tree. In other words, the value of the living tree is the capitalized present valuation of the future lumber available from the tree. Anyone would be foolish to cut a tree prior to the age 12; for, if it is allowed to stand, it grows in *value of lumber* by more than the rate of interest. That is why its value as a live tree exceeds the value of the lumber of the felled tree until age 12.

In Figure 29–1 we can measure on the left-hand scale the present value of a tree scheduled to be cut at some future date and age. From each point of the *LL* line (the height of which measures the value of the lumber in the tree at the time it is cut) draw back a line, *RR*, to the left-hand axis to indicate the present value of that future (*n* years later) lumber. Figure 29–1 shows two such lines, RR_1 and RR_2, the intercepts of which on the left-hand scale indicate the present value of the lumber in the tree at the age at which the *RR* curves touch the *LL* line using a 4 percent rate of interest. RR_2 indicates the maximum present value achievable ($100) by planning to cut the tree at the age of 12 years (when its lumber value will be $160). Cutting the tree earlier or later, say, at age 8 or age 19, would imply the present value ($88) given by the left-hand intercept of the line RR_1, which touches the *LL* line at age 8 and 19.[3]

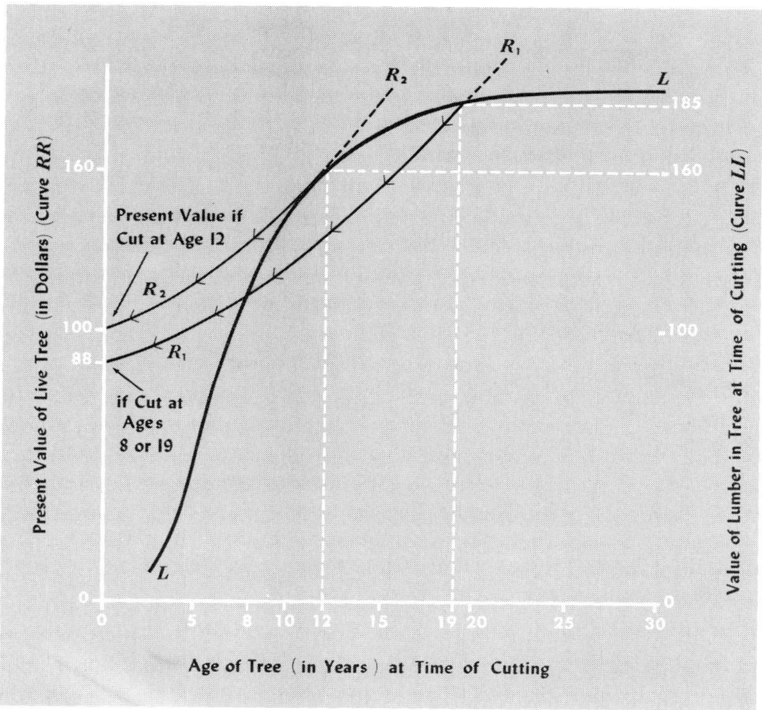

FIGURE 29–1. Present value of live trees at 4 percent is maximized if intended age of cutting is 12 years.

The relative rate of growth of the line *RR* reflects the rate of interest. The higher the rate of interest, the greater the relative growth of the *RR* line. In

[3] The *RR* lines can be computed by using the entries of Table 15–1 as discount factors with which to multiply the height of the *LL* curve as indicated on the right-hand scale. An *RR* line indicates all the various future values, one for each future date, that have the same present value—indicated by the left-hand intercept of the *RR* curve.

Figure 29–2 the same *LL* curve is drawn but with steeper *RR* lines to indicate the presence of a higher (e.g., 10 percent) rate of interest. Notice that the highest present value of the live tree ($48.40) is smaller and is now associated with an earlier age of cutting, 8 years.

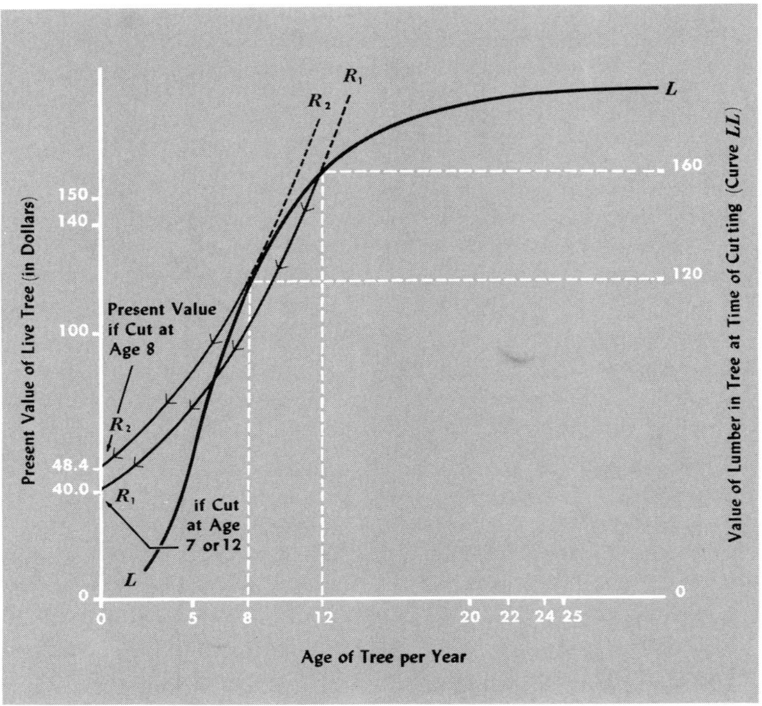

FIGURE 29–2. Present value of live trees, at 10 percent rate of interest, is maximized if intended age of cutting is 8 years.

In Figure 29–2, the present value ($40.00) of a live tree to be cut at age 12 is *less* than the live-tree value ($48.40) of the tree to be cut at age 8. The relative present values are reversed from the former figure, when interest rates were lower. This change in values is expressible also as a change in the rate of interest, or equivalently as a change in relative values of capital goods that differ in their rates of yield of future services. Conventionally, this revision in values is called a change in the rate of interest. The assets that change in relative values are those that are different in their time patterns of actual or potential yields of services; e.g., a 12-year-old tree would fall in value relative to an 8-year-old tree, because their future growths are different: The lower the rate of interest, the longer the tree will be kept alive.

Incidentally, this example explains why it is *not* true that the private-property system tends to cut trees too fast. It does "conserve" them by capitalizing the future lumber values to present values to determine when their live value is greater than their felled value. It is not self-sacrificing people who preserve our forests; it is wealth seekers who can obtain greater wealth by keeping trees growing rather than cutting them. But there are circumstances in which people will be induced to cut the trees even though their felled value is less than their standing value. Suppose no one owns the trees and the only way to capture the value of the tree is to cut it down and take the wood. Then no one will have wealth incentive—or legal power—to preserve the tree from those who would change it to lumber. This is why the forests in many parts of England and China were prematurely cut. They were community property. First come, first served. No one had any rights in the live value of the tree. Anyone who cut the tree could claim its value. It is lack of ownership, not personal greed and lack of foresight, that is responsible for this "wasteful" use of resources.

Savings and Growth of Wealth

You will hear about high-interest-rate versus low-interest-rate policies. (The former is also called a "tight-money" policy.) How can low interest rates be achieved, if that means keeping the interest rate lower than it otherwise would have been? It might be attempted by encouraging people to refrain from consumption—e.g., to save and lend more as a means of lowering the market interest rate. If successful, that would increase both the supply of lending through the loan markets and people's willingness to own assets that give more of their consumption yield in the future. The increased demand for bonds would lower the rate of interest. More savings would permit a faster growth rate of the wealth of the economy.

ACHIEVING A FASTER GROWTH RATE

Whatever the reason for wanting more saving, investing, and a greater growth of wealth, how can it be achieved? First, we might try to persuade people to save more of their income—if we knew who should pay for costs of the persuasion. A second way is to make people less fearful of theft or expropriation of the wealth they accumulate. An unwillingness to strengthen private-property rights is one of the major obstacles to rapid growth in many poorer, undeveloped countries of the world. Some countries (for instance, Switzerland) have reputations for observing private-property rights. Others (such as Brazil, Chile, Mexico, Iran, Egypt, Cuba, Algeria, India, and Indonesia) have reputations for not protecting private-property rights; they are ready to convert private wealth to government wealth or simply are not ready to enforce private property.

Third, private investment can be supplemented by tax-financed government investment, on the basis of the contention that private wealth owners refuse to invest enough in "vital" projects. One way for the government to act is to tax private wealth and use the proceeds to redirect current income toward the kind of investment activity deemed more appropriate. One counter effect of this is to reduce the rate of saving out of the reduced disposable income. Furthermore, private investments will be directed more in the direction of wealth that yields nontaxable income or wealth. Individuals, to escape the tax, will use savings more to create goods that yield more nonpecuniary income, since nonpecuniary income is rarely taxed as heavily as pecuniary income. (An example of this is evident in the United States, where homeowners are not taxed on the nonpecuniary income from owning their own home, whereas an investment in machine or business tools yields a taxable money income.) More drastically, the state may acquire the wealth by nationalizing private wealth and promising to compensate former owners at some distant future date at a low rate of interest, if any interest or payment is given at all. Cuba, Cambodia, Mexico, Egypt, Algeria, and Brazil, to name a few, have recently used this approach. This is not always done to increase investment; frequently Socialism or government control itself is desired.

Fourth, leaving aside techniques for increasing saving and investment in general, the government may seek to increase investment in one particular kind of wealth—namely, knowledge from research and invention. Such action is considered necessary because people who invest in discovering new knowledge will find that other people can use it at practically no cost—which reduces the exchange value of the discovered knowledge to the initial discoverer; therefore, the incentive to invest in this kind of intellectual capital is less than for private-property goods. How much income should be diverted by governmental authority to research activity in the hope of discovering new principles and ideas that will enhance wealth (at a rate greater than the rate of interest per dollar spent for research)? If some investment in research seems to be wasted, the researcher can always claim that the real gains simply aren't perceived by the critic. They are dispersed and not objectively measured. But the person footing the bill may just as honestly contend that the investment is really not investment but consumption under the guise of employment in research. There is as yet no generally accepted test against which the value of research can be assessed.

CONSERVATION, GROWTH, AND PROPERTY RIGHTS

A popular misconception of how to increase our wealth at a faster pace is inherent in the "conservationist" proposals, which would restrict exploitation of many of our natural resources. Conservationists assume that, for the sake of future wealth, we should not use up forests, fertile lands, and iron ore, for example. In so assuming, however, they fail to comprehend the meaning of capital values of resources and to understand that "using" goods can mean converting them into even more valuable forms of wealth. We have already seen that if a tree is more valuable for the future than are the current goods that can be made with the lumber, the present capital value of the live tree will exceed the value of the lumber in the felled tree; consequently, the trees will not be cut so fast. The capital goods that can be made from current use of the lumber will give a smaller future income than the standing trees; otherwise, the tree would be cut. People can save by saving trees, or they can save by cutting trees and saving wealth in the form of products made from the trees. Comparison of present values indicates which of the two will give the future greater wealth.

The conservationists have three contentions. First, even though the use of trees now will give a more valuable form of wealth for the future, they contend the actual rate of saving "should" be larger. One way to increase saving is simply to force people to save by not letting the goods be used. Clearly, this contention assumes that other people prefer more present consumption than the conservationists think desirable.

Second, it is argued that other people have the wrong idea about the most valuable *kinds* of goods to preserve for the future. As things are now, people would use up the forests and commercialize the wilderness, and, although we would have more buildings and other real capital goods, we would have "too few" trees, which "should" be preserved as natural wilderness. Wildlife and natural-wilderness advocates disagree with other people in wanting to close off certain areas from use as residences or as resort and ski areas. This kind of conflict really has nothing to do with conservation or growth of wealth; it is instead an argument as to which people will have their preferences more satisfied. This issue is the one with which this book started, the question of allocation of an existing stock of goods among competing claimants. Here "conservation" means to use goods in the ways that suit conservationists' tastes rather than someone else's.

Third, an examination of the particular classes of goods that conservationists propose to conserve will reveal that many of them are goods in which private-property rights do not exist or, under the laws, can be obtained only by "using" the goods. Oil, water, timber provide examples. Once upon a time timber was available for cutting, and only for cutting. No one could claim ownership of a standing tree. Hence, the race to cut trees as a means of establishing rights to the lumber. Similarly, at one time and even yet in some states, oil belonged not to the person under whose land it lies, but to him who first pumped it up and "controlled" it. Hence, the race to pump oil out of the ground, rather than letting it stay in discovered pools. Water is today generally, though not universally, owned by the person who "uses" it. Thus, today people build aqueducts to sources of water even though the water, if currently used, would not justify the present costs. The construction of the aqueduct and taking of the water now is simply an expensive way of establishing rights to use the water, often far in excess of currently economical amounts.

To prevent such excessively rapid and uneconomic depletion, the conservationists propose to control the rate of use with government planning boards. However, as we know, there is another solution: to establish salable property rights in these resources, rather than let them be claimed by the first person who makes use of the resources. Then like the tree it will be left standing until its use is economic, rather than being cut down to keep someone else from cutting it down first. It is not the capitalist private-property system that is responsible for what appears to be a wasteful use of resources; it is instead an absence of a system of salable property rights. If that system were instituted, the conservationist proposals would lose much of their force.

SOURCES OF GREATER WEALTH

The source of greater income is higher productivity and efficiency of use of labor and non-labor resources in exploiting profitable investment options. The mere existence of natural resources is not sufficient. Many countries (for example, a number of South American countries) rich in natural resources have not succeeded in exploiting them by efficiently organizing economic activity. Others (European countries) have fewer natural resources but have effectively exploited them.

Natural resources are defective in being "natural"; they have to be converted to useful form. In this country, the prairie was a forbidding area until man with the plough sweated over it. The Western areas are dry, and require irrigation. New England's soil is rocky, its winters severe and summers short. Natural resources are not "free" resources. They were available to the Indians for centuries, but still the Indians were poor. Resources must be worked on with skill and energy. In other words, people are a part of the natural resources. America was fortunate in being populated by a biased sample of mankind. Those who came were harassed into leaving Europe because they possessed unusual attributes. Many of the criminals who were "transported" to Georgia and Australia from England were guilty of strange crimes—disagreement with the crown, religious heresy, bankruptcy, evasion of economic restrictions on market competition in England. Murderers and thieves were more likely to be dealt with at home by capital punishment—which is not to assert that none of them were transported. In general, those who came were escaping regimentation; they had to be self-reliant and dependent upon their energy in a community of open-market competition. The law of selective survival of the fittest according to market-valued productivity was more effective.

Private property was the standard property-right system. The advance to the West occurred when people who occupied and cleared the land could regard it as private property; they could sell it or borrow against it. They weren't tied to it; they didn't have to stay on it in order to obtain the value of the income of the land they had created, as one must today in many foreign countries—e.g., Mexico, Iran, Egypt, and India.

Just as the pioneers pushed back the frontiers of land and today we are pushing back the frontiers of knowledge, so we have here reached a frontier of economics. The question of what policy or political actions will give a higher rate of growth is one to which a definitive answer cannot be given. The first comprehensive book in economics, by Adam Smith, was called *An Inquiry into the Nature and Causes of the Wealth of Nations.* Smith pointed out the suppressive effects of restraints to access of the market. But there is another school of opinion that a socialized economy can achieve a higher rate of growth by government control, rather than leaving the rate and kind of investment to be determined by the voluntary market-coordinated decisions of individuals. Undoubtedly, a higher proportion of income can be diverted to saving by government action. The issue is whether a higher rate is desirable on those terms, and whether the higher proportion of savings can be invested successfully with as high a gain in future yield. The debate waxes hot, and the evidence is conclusive only to the adherents of each position.

Questions

1. If you were a Jew in an Arab country, or an Asian in Africa, or an Englishman in Indonesia, or an American in Argentina, or a Moslem in India, would you invest for your son in personal human capital or in physical capital? Why?

2. A tape-recording machine displaces a telephone-answering girl. Who or what has displaced whom? Explain why the displacement of labor by capital reflects a displacement of labor by labor.

3. By giving up $100 of present income for $105 of consumption rights available in one year, a person gets what rate of interest per year?

4. A farmer who dries grapes to convert them to raisins is investing. Why is this investing, since it merely changes one form of consumption good to another form of a consumption good?

5. Instead of playing bridge, a man works around the house painting and refinishing the walls. Explain why this is a form of investment.

6. Changes in the rate of interest are detectable in the changes in the structure of relative prices of various types of goods.

a. If the price of raisins (relative to grapes), of prunes (relative to plums), of whiskey (relative to corn), of cider (relative to apples) should rise, would that mean a change in the rate of interest? In what direction?

b. What effect would that have on the profitability of producing raisins, prunes, whiskey, etc?

c. Ultimately, what effect would the revised production have on the relative values (e.g., of raisins and grapes)? What effect would that have on the rate of interest?

7. Suppose the world was going to last for just two years. You have wealth of $100.

a. If the interest rate is zero, what is the income available in each of the next two years?

b. If the interest rate is 10 percent, what is the income of each period (again assuming a two-year life to the world)?

c. If the interest rate is 10 percent but the world is going to last for an indefinitely long period, what is the maximum annual maintainable rate of consumption?

d. If the interest rate is 5 percent, what is the rate of income—assuming wealth is $100?

e. If your wealth unexpectedly increases from $100 to $120, what happens to income with an interest rate of 10 percent?

f. What was the amount of your profit when that wealth increase occurred?

8. Goods differ in their rate of yield of consumption services, or in their "durability." Pine lumber naturally deteriorates more rapidly than redwood. If demand for future consumption rights should *rise relative* to present consumption rights, would pine or redwood experience the greater rise in present price? Show why this is expressible as a fall in the rate of interest. (Hint: The interest rate is the exchange rate between present and future consumption rights.)

9. You are a visitor in some underdeveloped country in which all lending and borrowing are effectively prohibited.

a. Is there a rate of interest?

b. If so, where could you get data to compute it?

c. How could you tell when it changes?

10. "Roundabout, more capitalistic methods of production are always more productive than direct methods using less capital equipment. Therefore, any country that wants to develop should start increasing the amount of capital goods it has." Evaluate.

11. A man plants a seed for a tree. Assume for simplicity that there are no subsequent expenses. The tree, if cut and converted to lumber at the end of any of the ages indicated in the table below, will yield lumber worth the amount indicated in the second column. The third column gives the *present* value of that future potential lumber, at 10 percent rate of interest. Some of the entries are not presented.

(1) CUTTING AGE	(2) LUMBER VALUE	(3) PRESENT CAPITAL VALUE OF LUMBER	(4) PRESENT VALUE OF COSTS	(5) PROFIT IF CUT AT AGE INDICATED
0	$ 0	$ 0	$5.00	$−5.00
5	1	0.38	5.70	−5.32
10	4	1.54	6.20	−4.66
15	11	2.63	6.50	−3.87
20	25.0	——	6.60	——
25	60.0	5.52	6.80	−1.28
30	140.0	——	6.82	——
35	260.0	——	6.95	——
40	450.0	10.00	6.96	+3.04
45	650.0	——	6.97	——
50	800.0	6.80	6.98	−0.18

a. Compute the missing values and find the age at which the tree should be planned to be cut to promise the maximum *present* value of that tree.

b. What is that maximum present value?

c. How much is a newly planted tree worth?

d. Suppose now that the rent for the land on which the seed is planted is 50 cents per year. Suppose that, in addition to that cost, there are other costs—spraying, watering, fire protection, taxes—to be paid over the years. The present value of those future costs for various lengths of time is indicated in column 4. Column 5 gives the present value net of these costs. Compute the data for that column.

e. Suppose that the value of the trees rises relative to current lumber prices. What would this imply about the rate of interest?

f. If no one owned the tree, and it could be cut by anyone who wanted to use the lumber, when would it be cut?

12. Some whiskies improve with age. The following table lists the consumption value of a barrel of whiskey, if the whiskey is removed and sold at that time. For example, if the whiskey is removed from its aging vat and sold now to consumers for current consumption, it will sell for $100. If sold in ten years, it will fetch $250 for *consumption.*

a. How much will the vat of whiskey be worth right now (at 10 percent) if it is to be held until the end of the second year before being bottled and sold?

b. For what length of time should one expect to keep the whiskey in the vat for a maximum present value? (Hint: How much is it worth paying for the whiskey now if it is to be held for five years? For ten years?)

c. If no one owned the vat of whiskey, how long would it be kept unconsumed?

d. Suppose it were owned but could not be sold; how long would it be kept before consumption?

CONSUMPTION DATE	CONSUMPTION VALUE
Now	$100
1 year	120
2	140
3	160
4	175
5	190
6	205
7	220
8	230
9	240
10	250

13. In a public park an apple tree yields excellent apples. These may be picked by the public, but not more than one apple per person at a time. When will apples be picked? Why?

14. The following is a quotation from the *Scientific American,* 1963:

"Recently a number of steelmaking organizations in Western Europe and the U.S.S.R. have eliminated several costly steps in the manufacture of steel by advancing the technique known as continuous casting. U.S. steel firms, which account for about a third of the world output, were for the most part content to observe these developments. They were inhibited by a paradox of industrial supremacy: the huge sums already invested in established methods made experimentation with the new technique seem impractical. The smaller producers, whose competitive position might have been enhanced by continuous casting, could least afford to build the pilot plants."

Assume that the facts stated in the first sentence are correct. The second sentence describes the alleged behavior of U.S. steel firms in response to these facts; and the remaining sentences strive to explain that behavior. Do you agree that the last two sentences present an economically acceptable explanation of the events in the second sentence? Explain why they do not.

15. A further quote from the same article in the *Scientific American:*

"The ideal time for a producer to consider the use of a continuous-casting machine is when he is building an entirely new steel mill, from melting furnace on through to milled products. In such a situation the mill can be designed around the known limitations of the continuous-casting process, and there will be no costly overlap between conventional and continuous equipment. Unfortunately, U.S. firms are not planning to build many new steel mills. Therefore, many U.S. producers are 'not ready' for continuous casting, whereas small producers in India, Venezuela, and Peru, for example, have already obtained plant designs. The producers in these countries will avoid the large cost of primary mills. If there is any solace in underdevelopment, it is this 'advantage.'"

Note that the writer did put the last word in quotation marks, as if to admit there really was no advantage as he seemed to suggest. Comment on the reasoning in the quotation; but first note whether or not the quotation says that *no* U.S. firms are now using continuous casting or merely that *not all* are; and whether *no* firms or *not all* firms plan to introduce it. In evaluating this quotation, consider: If you already have an old-model car, would you be more or less likely to buy a new-model car that is more economical than an "old" model?

16. If the American buffalo had been owned by someone, do you think the buffalo would now be so nearly exterminated? Why?

17. Do you think seals and whales would be faced with extinction if some person or group were able to buy, as private property, the right to catch whales and seals? Why?

18. A large lake is stocked with excellent fish, but no one owns the fish or the lake. Only by catching the fish can you acquire ownership in the fish.

a. What do you think will be the average age of fish caught as compared to the age of fish in a privately owned lake?

b. Which system will induce overfishing in the sense that more resources will be devoted to catching fish than is worth the extra fish thereby caught? Why?

19. You are an unborn spirit; you are offered your choice of country in which to be born. In country *A* all land is owned by its users; absentee landlordism is forbidden by a progressive government. The land cannot be mortgaged by the owner or rented to a highest-bidding tenant farmer. Everyone is born with rights to use certain parcels of land and these cannot be taken away or contracted to others. In country *B*, absentee landlordism is common and legal. All land is privately owned and either used by the owner or rented to the highest-paying tenants. Land can be sold or mortgaged. Private-property rights are strictly enforced for everyone. Many people do not own land at all. Into which country will you request that you be born? Why?

30

INTEREST RATES AND THE LENDING MARKETS

Interest Rates and Saving and Investing

Still unexplained is the determination of the rate of interest and investment. We can shed some light on this if we note that an isolated person is in a utility-maximizing equilibrium with respect to choice between present consumption and future income if he has adjusted his activity so that a further increment to future income rights is worth to him just what it costs him to get it. For example, if he values a $1 change in current consumption at $1.05 of next year's consumption, and if he can produce or transform current into future income at the rate of more than $1.05 of next year's services for each $1 of current consumption forsaken, it will increase his utility to make some of those conversions or transformations.

However, the greater the rate of devoting current income to investing in the growth of wealth, the less is the marginal increment of wealth gained for each increment in the rate of current consumption given up. This reflects a law of diminishing marginal productivity. We postulate that the more wealth he has relative to current income (i.e., the lower the rate of interest), the less he will be willing to sacrifice current consumption for increments of wealth; for it follows that the lower the rate of interest, the less of his income he will be willing to save.

We can portray ideas more generally diagrammatically. The *DD* curve in Figure 30–1 shows the rates of current income a person thinks he could invest profitably in the production of new capital goods, or wealth. It is important to know what is meant by "invest profitably." We shall explain with an example. Start on January 1 to convert cur-

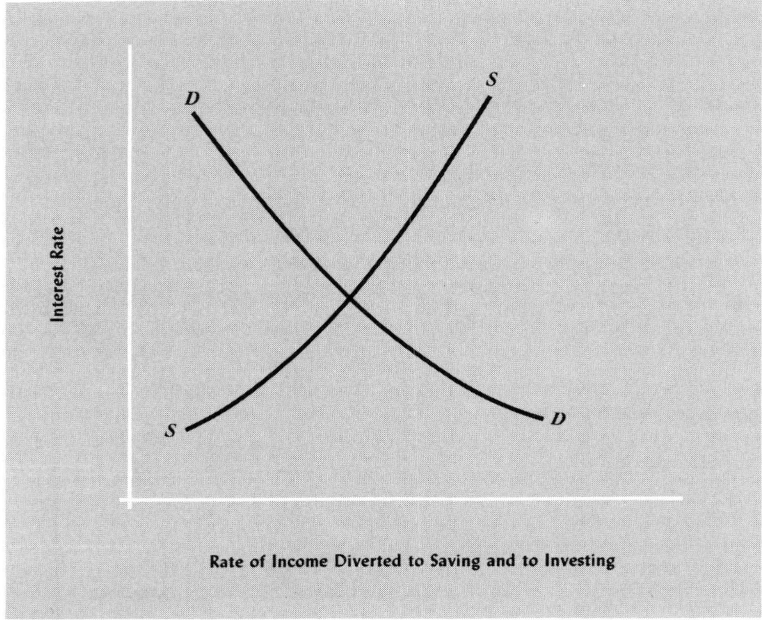

FIGURE 30–1. Demand for investing and supply of savings are related to interest rate.

rent income from consumption to the creation of wealth. Convert current income at the rate of $1,000 per year. At the end of the year, we will have converted the amount of $1,000—just as a person traveling at the speed of 1,000 miles per year would at the end of a year of continuous travel have covered a distance of 1,000 miles. While we have diverted income at the rate of $1,000 a year to the creation of wealth, what is the value of wealth that we have acquired by the end of the year? If it is only $1,000, we have lost interest. We have deferred consumption with no compensation for the deferral. So we have sacrificed earlier consumption opportunities for the *same* amount of later consumption. This is consistent only with a *zero* rate of interest. With a *positive* interest rate, we would be willing to sacrifice current consumption only for a *greater* amount of future income; if the community rate of interest is 10 percent per year, we should require an investment at the rate of $1,000 per year for a year to grow to at least $1,100, if we are to consider the investment to be profitable.

Investment at the rate of $1,000 a year for a year, then, must yield a growth of wealth of $1,100 at the end of the year if the investment is to be considered profitable, at 10 percent interest. For a 5 percent rate of interest the wealth increment at the end of the year must be at least 5 percent larger than the year's cumulated income devoted to investment. When the investment or production of the good is completed, it must be worth at least what was invested, multiplied by $(1 + r)$, with r the rate of interest, if it is to be deemed profitable.[1]

The *DD* curve indicates the highest rate of investment of current income a person thinks (or bets) he *can* invest profitably, at each indicated rate of interest. The lower the rate of interest, the greater the rate of income that he thinks can be profitably diverted to wealth creation—because the necessary rate of wealth growth per dollar of extra investment is smaller. And the higher the rate at which a person converts current income to wealth, the more costly it will be to do so; he must bring in successively less appropriate resources as he steps up the rate of current investment activity. Therefore, he can profitably invest at higher rates if the rate of interest is lower.

Although we have said that the rate of interest has an effect on the rate of investment for a given investment demand, we do not mean that the rate of investment is unaffected by any other factors. Indeed, anything that will affect expectations about future values of future goods or relative productive transformation possibilities will affect the rate of interest and the rate of investment.

The *SS* curve is the schedule of the rates of saving—that is, the rates at which a person would be *willing* to divert current income to production of wealth if he could realize the rate of growth of wealth (indicated on the vertical axis) on the marginal dollar of investment. The *SS* curve reflects the *willingness* to divert present income to future wealth, while the *DD* curve reflects beliefs about the *ability* to divert it *successfully* at the indicated profitability rate. We might all be willing to save at the rate of $3,000 a year out of our annual income of $10,000 if we could experience a growth of wealth of 15 percent per year, but we might be able to do that successfully at a rate of 15 percent for only $1,000. We simply may not know how to invest at the rate of $3,000 and get a rate of return as high as 15 percent, although we would be willing to invest that much if we could get that rate of 15 percent.

We digress momentarily to warn against a slightly different meaning to the terms savings and investment. Sometimes *both* terms are used to describe the same thing—diversion of present income from present consumption to accumulate wealth. Unless a distinction is made between (a) the amount of current income that the community "bets" *can* be invested successfully in increasing wealth by a rate equal to at least the rate of interest and (b) the amount that the community would be *willing* to divert to wealth increments if offered that rate of increment (measured by the rate of interest), the terms savings and

[1] If we divert present income at the rate of $1,000 a year for one year and end up with an increment of wealth of, say, $900, what is the rate of investment? $1,000 a year or $900 a year? We shall say it is $1,000, but that it was not profitable. And we shall say also that there was a loss of $200, the difference between the $1,100 (counting interest at 10 percent per year) and the realized $900. Another way to express a profitable investment is in terms of investing in goods that will yield perpetuities. Then $1 of investment per year yields a stock of wealth capable of yielding 10 cents of income per year in perpetuity, if the investment is to be considered profitable at 10 percent rates of interest.

investment are likely to be different words for the same thing. However, here they have very different meanings. And only in equilibrium are the measures or amount of the two different activities brought to equality.[2]

The effect of a lower rate of interest is not to be conceived of as merely a reduction in the amount of interest costs one pays when borrowing. Many people, having observed that interest costs on borrowed funds are only a small portion of the total costs (presumably no costs at all if the investor doesn't borrow!), have jumped erroneously to the conclusion that interest-rate changes have little effect on the rate of investment. But this ignores the fact that interest-rate changes involve changes in the relative *values* of different kinds of goods. As we saw earlier, a rise in the rate of interest changes the prices of longer-lived annuities relative to shorter-lived annuities. Though both fall in value, the longer-lived one falls by a greater proportion. Conversely, a fall in the rate of interest implies a larger proportionate rise in the value of longer-lived annuities or goods that yield longer series of services. A fall in interest rates implies a rise in the price of buildings relative to automobiles, shoes, wage rates, and food. The prices of capital goods rise relative to present consumption types of goods and services.

Demand for Investment and Supply of Savings and the Market-Equilibrium Interest Rate

Every *person* is considered to have a *DD* curve and an *SS* curve, summarizing his own investment and his own savings proclivities. But each person may have a different personal equilibrative interest rate. However, if people can trade with each other via a marketplace, the personal interest rates will converge toward the same value, just as marginal costs of production of various goods by different people will in the market converge.

Figure 30–1 can be used as the *community DD* and *SS* curves simply by summing the individual curves over all the individuals exactly as we did for ordinary demand curves earlier in Chapter 7. For the community as a whole, the interest rates of all people are pushed to that equilibrium value at which the total rate of investment the people believe they can invest profitably is equal to the rate of savings they are willing to provide. But it would be a mistake to think of this adjustment of all individuals' actions and personal interest rates to a common equilibrating rate as occurring in some unique market for savings and investment.

[2] Do not make the careless error of thinking that the difference between our concepts of investment demand and saving supply reflects a presumption that people who invest are different from those who save. That is an error equivalent to assuming that people who demand wheat produce *no* wheat, while those who supply wheat consume *no* wheat. The basis for the distinction between demand and supply is not that they are decisions of different people, for they are not; some people enter on both sides.

There is no market for savings and investment per se. Instead, those activities are guided in the lending and borrowing markets, the exchange markets, and production activity. Therefore, it is to these several markets, and particularly *loanable* funds markets (i.e., lending and borrowing, rather than saving and investing), that we look to observe the effects of changes in the more basic investment opportunities and preference patterns for present consumption relative to more wealth.

We have seen that people adjust saving and investing in three ways: They can lend to and borrow from each other. They can buy and sell existing capital goods and services. They can engage in production of capital goods; but since this is done most efficiently by specialization and exchange via the marketplace, this third process is also a market phenomenon. Furthermore, if people have different individual equilibrium subjective interest rates (i.e., if they differ in their marginal valuation of increments of future wealth relative to present consumption), it will pay those with higher subjective interest rates (i.e., those who place a higher value on present consumption) (1) to borrow from the lower-interest-rate people, (2) to sell more of their existing capital goods to the lower-interest-rate people and own instead goods that yield more current consumption services, and (3) to invest more in the production of capital goods in order to sell these to the lower-interest-rate people—and to do all these things until everyone's internal rates of interest are equalized with each other.

For example, if a high-interest person were a housebuilder, (1) he would borrow more, (2) he would build more houses to sell to other people, and (3) he would sell more of the houses he currently owns and hold other forms of wealth. The second of these enables him to increase his wealth, whereas the first and third involve a revision of his asset holdings, whatever his wealth may be. This adjustment activity can be illustrated even for two countries. (1) The higher-interest-rate economy will borrow from the lower-interest-rate economy. (2) It will divert more of its current income to production of good-yielding future services (in order to sell them to the lower-interest-rate country where they are valued high relative to consumption services—which we know to be true because that is what a lower interest rate means). (3) It will sell some of its existing future-service-yielding types of goods to the lower-interest-rate country and in exchange take more current-consumption-yielding goods or resources.

The important point is that the internal individual saving and investing adjustments via (1) lending and borrowing, (2) exchanges of assets held (and changes in their prices), and (3) productive activity are correlated by the opportunity to exchange in the market, and there are three markets (and their interest rates) in which the adjustment toward a common rate of interest takes place. *The* interest rate is "determined" in all three of these markets, and it affects all three forms of adjustments of present and future options. It is tempting, but incomplete, to say that the interest rate is set by savings and investment, as if there were only isolated individuals who couldn't lend-borrow or trade specialized goods and services. And it is incomplete to say that the rate of interest is determined in (as distinct from manifested or affected by) the lending-borrowing marketplace, because that would ignore the other forms of savings-investment activity. And it is wrong, because incomplete, to say the rate of interest is set (as distinct from being manifested and affected by) the demand and supply for existing capital goods relative to current consumption. Forces in all three markets determine the interest rate, and the possibility of acting in all three markets keeps them correlated and interdependent.

The interrelationships among these markets can be illustrated and perhaps better understood with a few examples.

INCREASE IN SAVINGS PROPENSITY

If preferences should change so that increments of wealth are desired more relative to present consumption, this would imply an increase in the supply of savings—i.e., a shift in the *SS* curve to the right. This would be manifested or revealed in real-world markets by an increase in the supply of loanable funds—i.e., an increase in the supply of funds offered for claims to future consumption rights. In the bond market, an increased supply of funds for lending would increase the rate at which bonds could be sold at each price. The rate of interest in this market would fall. An offer to sell a bond is the same thing as an offer to buy present consumption rights—in the convenient form of money; and an increased willingness to save implies an increased demand for bonds—i.e., claims to future income. An increased demand for bonds raises the price of bonds, which means that the rate of interest is lowered. That change in price, or interest rate, allocates the increased savings over the competing claimants—the same old rationing problem investigated in earlier sections for all "consumption" goods.

An increased desire to trade current consumption for more future income will be revealed also by an increased demand for those assets that are relatively more effective than other goods in yielding future consumption if they are not used for current consumption. Goods that are more effective in this way are called "capital" goods, as if goods could be classified into just two classes—i.e., those used for either current or future consumption and those used only for current consumption (consumers' goods). In reality, there is a whole range of possibilities in the extent to which goods can yield future consumption rights relative to abstinence from their current consumption. Houses, steel buildings, automobiles, lathes, bridges are usually considered as "capital goods," while lettuce, fresh meat, milk, and most commodities that are consumed in the immediate period are called consumers' goods. Sometimes "capital goods" or "investment goods" or "investment" is used to mean not only goods or activity designed to yield future consumption but also goods that are expected to be sold with a profit. The term "consumers' goods," then, means goods bought by individuals for personal non-wealth-augmenting purposes (clothes, pianos, shoes, swimming pools, houses, etc.). It is apparent that some goods can be consumers' goods in one sense and capital goods in the other sense. Thus a good may be used for personal consumption purposes by one person and by someone else as a source of income, as when the pianist uses his piano professionally, the swimming teacher uses the pool, and the owner rents his house to a tenant. For some purposes a house is a consumers' good, for others a capital good. For some purposes house building is a consumption activity; for others it is investment activity. For the analysis of how a society reaches and implements decisions about the amount of current income to devote to future consumption rights, the construction of a house is most usefully defined as an investment activity in producing a capital good.

Returning to our main line of analysis, an increase in desire for wealth relative to current consumption—i.e., an increase in the supply of savings—is revealed as people shift their market demands toward "more capitalistic" goods relative to consumption-type goods and services. The prices of equipment, buildings, and "producers'" goods rise relative to labor services and food, for example—which means the interest rate falls. Investment activity in producing more of those goods increases because their increased demand and price increase the profitability of making them.

In all markets, the rate of interest is the ratio of exchange between present consumption and future income. The rate of interest cannot be one rate in one market and another in some other market without inducing people to switch their exchange activities from one market to the other, just as people would switch their buying and selling among automobile dealers if the prices of similar cars differed among dealers. If the explicit interest rate in the lending market is lower than the interest rate in the capital markets (implied by the price relationships among goods of different durability), people will lend less. What will they do with their savings? They will buy more long-lived goods at the relatively low prices of the capital goods. They will do so because current prices of such goods are low relative to their future receipts; that is, the interest rate is higher than in the loan market. When the price of those goods is bid up, the interest rate in the capital-goods market is driven down.

INCREASE IN PRODUCTIVITY OF INVESTMENT

Instead of an increased preference for more wealth relative to present consumption rights, we can suppose that there is an increase in the *possibilities* of producing wealth relative to its costs in present consumption. New inventions are useful in enabling us not only to get more current consumption from existing resources but also to get more future income. Cheaper refrigeration, more durable and rust-resisting metals—which are examples of ways to create more future consumption per dollar of present income diverted—will induce more investment.

The *DD* curve (of Figure 30–1) shifts to the right, and the rate of interest increases. This is revealed in the lending and borrowing markets as an increased demand for borrowed money. (In terms of the demand and supply of bonds, the supply of bonds offered increases. The price of bonds falls, which is another way of saying that the rate of interest rises.) That the rate of interest rises is important not in itself; it is pertinent in that it facilitates rationing among the many demanders of claims to the presently available supply of savings offered on the loan market. Failing a rise in the rate of interest, for whatever reason, non-price rationing would occur. The allocation would be more heavily influenced by non-marketable wealth-exchange offers—something we shall later investigate in the specific context of lending markets.

An increase in technology or new inventions enabling conversion of current income into greater amounts of wealth than formerly will raise interest rates in the capital-goods markets. For example, the development of jet engines provided a means of making a more productive capital good (jet planes) from current income. The increased demand for current income to make new jet planes and the reduced demand for older piston-type planes implied that the price of existing capital goods fell relative to current services. As we know from our earlier discussion in this chapter and in Chapter 15, this revaluation of various types of capital goods relative to values of current services used for production of new goods is a change in the rate of interest. This increased profitability, and increased production of the new types of capital goods, is revealed and effected in the production markets.

INCREASED STOCK OF CAPITAL GOODS

What would happen if there were an increase in the stock of capital goods, possibly by a gift from a foreign country or by the accumulation of capital goods over the years? Don't jump to the conclusion that the rate of interest will be lower because the increased stock of capital goods means an increase in the potential future income. Even though it does mean that, it also means an increase in the present income. A larger stock of capital goods, once realized, provides an increase in the present and future income. If the increase in wealth is more heavily weighted by that type of good that yields greater future-service potential relative to the present, the rate of interest would be higher than it otherwise would be. Why? With a larger ratio of future relative to present consumption rights, people will be willing to pay a higher price in terms of giving up some of that future consumption for present consumption rights. The analogy of the person who learns he will in the future inherit a fortune is apt; he immediately borrows against his future. On the other hand, a different proportion of future relative to present consumption potentialities inherent in the increased stock of capital goods can have the opposite effect. Thus, nothing can be said about whether a country that is rich in capital goods will have a higher or lower rate than if it were poorer; nor can it be concluded that as a country accumulates more capital it experiences a decreasing rate of interest.

Operation of the Lending Market

VARIETIES OF BORROWERS

The loan market is a vast variety of institutions and marketplaces. Why are there so many? Again, the answer is "because of gains from exchange of specialized services." Since potential borrowers differ, lenders specialize; through detailed knowledge of each kind of borrower, lenders can more cheaply channel savings to the most profitable or most rewarding investment activities after allowance for risks. Just as producers specialize in the products they make, so lenders will specialize in the borrowers to whom they lend.

One reason for the variety of borrowers can be illustrated by a few of the stages in making, selling, and using an automobile. A firm's employees and suppliers are glad to make a car if someone else is willing to wait for the future services of the car. They want to be paid so that they can consume now. If the owner of the business were to "finance" the work, he would have to defer his consumption to the future. But he wants to specialize in production activity, not in saving and deferring of consumption. So he looks for someone else to do the saving. The lender "finances" the current production; that is, he transfers current consumption rights to producers in exchange for later repayment of consumption rights.

Automobile manufacturers can borrow by selling bonds to the public or to institutions that channel public savings (e.g., insurance companies). Producers also borrow for short periods to carry them over seasonally active periods, and for this they rely heavily on commercial banks. Car retailers also rely on commercial banks. In addition, they borrow from finance companies and commercial-credit companies. The ordinary consumer has little occasion to deal directly with these firms. Yet, because they exist, the car dealer can carry a bigger inventory. Thereby the consumer can inspect a larger variety of cars in showrooms and get quicker delivery.

The consumer will often borrow to pay for the car. He is likely to deal with a consumer-credit company directly or indirectly via the car dealer, who attends to details of the loan. The consumer may borrow from a credit union at his place of work, because the credit union is relatively well acquainted with his personal situation and prospects of repayment. He may even borrow directly from a neighborhood bank or from an insurance company in which he has a policy. As goods pass along the line from producers to final consumer, a series of different lenders sequentially succeed each other in financing the next owner, with each lender specializing in knowledge about each successive participant.

Specialization occurs also in the collection of savings. Savings banks solicit savings from savers; so do commercial banks. Insurance companies are an especially important collection agency for savings; in turn, they lend to businessmen and home buyers, for example. All of these "money-market" institutions are interrelated by the rate of interest via a complex chain of exchanges and flows of funds from one to another. Few of us negotiate with more than the institutions in which we deposit our savings and those from which we borrow. But between them there are scores of financial intermediaries specializing in facilitating a flow of information and funds from suppliers to demanders.

Some debts reflect a very high assurance that the borrower will pay interest and principal promptly. Currently, U.S. government bonds are as high in quality as any available, but not because government officials are more honest or reliable than private individuals. Instead, the government can use the armed forces to collect taxes. (Also, as we shall see later, it has power to create money.) Private bonds sometimes can be repaid only if the borrower is able to induce people to purchase his products.[3] The bonds issued by private firms like General Motors, American Telephone and Telegraph, and Santa Fe Railroad are of very high quality because they are almost certain to be paid when due. Bonds of other strong firms promise an indicated yield of about 5 percent, with some running up to 10 percent. And then there is a vast range of riskier bonds that promise even higher yields.[4]

You will notice that we have referred to "yields" and not to the rate of interest. Superficially, riskier bonds appear to pay a higher rate of interest. That interpretation is not consistent with economic analysis. The rate of interest is the same for all bonds of the same loan interval; the difference in yields reflects a risk premium. For example, if someone seeks to borrow money and offers to repay in one year with 5 percent interest per year, you may regard the chances of repayment as being only a half. What you are getting for your money now is a .5 probability of payment plus interest in one year. To make that an attractive proposition, you would offer to lend him only $50 for the promise to repay $105 in one year, if the interest rate is 5 percent. Under this arrangement you will get $105 with a probability of .5 and nothing with a probability of .5. On the average you would expect to get $52.50, which would be equivalent to 5 percent on your loan of $50. The yield is 110 percent on a loan of $50, if we ignore the risk of repayment.[5]

A test of the validity of the preceding interpretation is provided by events

[3] Evidence of the importance of the ability to collect taxes is that government bonds that are repayable only from receipts of particular projects (i.e., toll roads) are regarded as being of lower quality.

[4] For example, Chilean government 3 percent bonds can be purchased for about $400, Boston and Maine RR 4½ percent bonds at about $200, and Estonian government 7 percent bonds for about $50. All promise to pay $1,000 at maturity.

[5] This is like reporting the yield on the *winning* ticket in a lottery.

in the bonds markets. If the risk premium accounts for the differences in promised yield, then when a business firm has increased earnings that improve its prospects of being able to meet its debt obligations promptly, the price of its outstanding bonds should rise. And they do.

Differences in the quality of the bonds or promissory notes reflect the power to collect funds to repay the debt, and the willingness of the borrower to repay when able. Most of us are strongly tempted to complain when lenders express doubts about our ability to repay a loan when due. I may know that I will repay the debt when due, but I cannot expect the lender to know it. In fact, some people complain that the loan markets are imperfect because *they* cannot borrow at the same promised rate of interest as their neighbor; and some complain that they cannot borrow at all. This complaint is analogous to a seller of automobiles complaining that people are buying his competitor's cars instead of his cars, when his are just as good. If they were just as good, he would sell his cars; but there is a difference in the eyes of the buyer.

Similarly, the lender of money (i.e., the buyer of bonds and promissory notes) sees differences in the prospects that the borrower will repay promptly and with extra costs being imposed on the lender. You should not expect the lender to tell you that your promises are too risky, especially if he can use a less offensive way of expressing the matter. Thus, a banker says, in refusing to lend to you, "I'm sorry, we just don't have any funds to lend now." You should (we hope) wonder how the supply could be inadequate if the interest rate were really high enough to ration out the existing supply so that all who want to borrow at that rate of interest can do so. Is there something wrong in the capital markets? Actually, however, the banker is merely being tactful—and misleading. If he were tactless and completely honest in his reply to your request for a loan, he could have said, "We think the prospect of your repaying is not quite high enough. We specialize in loans to people with better credit prospects. To lend to you, we feel we should ask not 6 percent, but 15 percent. And then we would have to be prepared to have a staff to take care of the harder collection problems and other activities involved in defaulted loans. We prefer not to engage in that kind of business. You should go to other lenders who specialize in activities related to higher risks and are prepared to handle the problem of defaults."

NEGOTIABILITY OF BONDS

Suppose that a lender wanted to change his mind about his commitment to defer consumption until a bond is repaid. He could do so by selling the bond to someone else, who will act as his substitute to continue to defer consumption rights. The right to sell an outstanding bond to someone else is known as "negotiability." Access to markets where negotiable bonds and notes can be resold reduces the costs of negotiability. The lender would then be willing to accept a lower rate in exchange for the greater "liquidity." [6] Nevertheless, a borrower may prefer not to have his debts transferable. The borrower may believe that the original lender, from whom he first borrowed, would be more considerate and lenient in pressing for legal action against him in the event of difficulty in repaying a debt. Because of the agreement not to sell the bond to someone else, non-negotiable notes usually carry a slightly higher rate of interest.

Negotiability of bonds is facilitated by the existence of the New York Bond Exchange, a formal, privately owned marketplace where the bonds of well-known, strong American corporations can be bought (and sold)—not from the corporation itself but from people who lent money to the corporation, or from those who have subsequently bought the bond from the original lender.[7] A large portion of bond resales takes place elsewhere via bond brokers or dealers—much in the fashion of used-car dealers. They maintain small inventories of bonds, but they know other dealers or people from whom any particular bond can be bought to satisfy customers' demands—at a price. These bond brokers are known as "over-the-counter" security dealers, since they do not operate in a formal, physically compact exchange like the New York Bond Exchange.

Because none of these bond-market transactions transfers money to the original borrower, some people erroneously think no useful purpose is served by these markets in facilitating borrowing and lending. However, new bond buyers will more easily be able to transfer the bond to some other buyer if they wish to stop deferring consumption. Used-bond markets are as important in the production and sale of new bonds (saving and lending) as the used-car market is for production and sale of new cars. How many people would buy cars if they were told they could never sell them, but had to keep them until they were junked? Because these markets facilitate the transfer of bonds, more people are willing to hold bonds. Negotiability of bonds also permits people to be more selective. Some will buy "seasoned" bonds only of blue-ribbon companies—which may have issued their bonds long ago when they were relatively unknown and less secure.

Legal Restraints on Access to Loan Market

The fact of a positive rate of interest has been much denied, rejected, condemned, and legally "prohibited." Even Aristotle asserted that money is "sterile," so that no interest should be paid for money loans. Christian theology also used

[6] As we shall see later, much of our money is a form of debt of commercial banks, a debt payable on demand. Holders of this debt, because it is repayable immediately *on demand* at the option of the holder, will get a lower rate of interest *per year* than on a debt payable only after some time.

[7] Reports of prices and amounts of bonds exchanged on the major organized exchanges (e.g., the New York Bond Exchange) are given in the financial pages of major periodicals and newspapers and stock brokers' offices.

this erroneous conception; until about the sixteenth century it "officially" banned interest as a venal sin. But neither philosophical nor theological contemplations harmonized with the circumstances of earthly life. Interest was paid long before Aristotle and continued thereafter—despite theology, protestations, and dogma. It was paid because the borrower offered to pay it rather than not get the loan. And he had to pay it because the demand for savings was greater than the supply at a zero price. Some rationing criterion had to be used.

Christians, who regarded taking interest as a venal sin, conveniently permitted Jews, whose religion placed no severe ban on interest taking, to lend to them. Christians could then borrow with a clear conscience, blaming the Jews for the interest. As a matter of fact, however, the Papacy itself engaged in charging a positive interest—though under the name of "fees," "gratuities," or anything but "interest" or "usury." Interest is inherent in prices of goods. In medieval times, lords had claims to payments from users of land. Sometimes the lord wanted to sell to the church his rights to the future rents. Suppose an annuity of rents was expected to run for at least fifty years. For what price could it be sold? A fifty-year annuity of $1 a year would be sold only for far less than $50—because the rate of interest was positive. In buying lands, the Church was charging a positive rate of interest—unless it paid a price equal to the expected *undiscounted* sum of the future annuity payments. And it never did that.

Economic facts of life have insidious ways of circumventing laws or decrees designed to ban them. With man's usual speedy perception, it took only about 1,000 years to abolish the ban against interest on loans—and then it was replaced with a ban on unreasonably high rates of interest. In modern times, the state government, having replaced the church as the secular and moral authority, also decrees that "unreasonably" high—usurious—rates of interest are illegal. For example, commercial (not savings and loan) banks in this country are not allowed (by government administrative edict) to pay over 4 percent interest on the funds deposited as time or savings accounts.

Lenders who make riskier loans at a higher rate of interest in the hope of averaging out at an acceptable return usually must resort to legal fictions. For example, pawn shops can lend to strangers of dubious credit at a rate of 30 percent per year—not by a "loan," but by a purchase and repurchase agreement. You may sell your camera for $100 (less than its market value) and simultaneously obtain the right to buy it back in one year for $130; then when, and if, you buy it back, you have paid 30 percent to cover the risk and higher costs, under the façade of a capital gain to the lender. To effectively prohibit high rates of interest would be to prohibit borrowers of more dubious credit from borrowing at all. Almost every law designed to prevent some particular agency from lending money to risky borrowers leaves open the opportunity for other lenders to create new agencies not restricted by regulations imposed on the former lenders.

Legal barriers, of course, are not necessarily undesirable. That depends upon one's attitudes toward the consequences of "free contracting" and free access to markets for lending. Restrictions on the access of commercial banks to the market for certain types of loans (e.g., long-term loans, second mortgages, and stock-exchange loans in excess of certain amounts) are defended as attempts to prevent a bank owner from making "too risky" loans in the hope of earning bigger profits; if such loans turn out to be riskier than believed, the bank may not be able to honor its debts to its depositors. For their "own best interests" and the safety of their depositors' accounts, then, commercial bank owners are severely restricted by laws—also with respect to the rates of interest they can offer to depositors or charge borrowers. The laws controlling financial institutions may have been enacted just to be on the safe side; however, a bank prevented from lending on certain *types* of loans can still make risky loans within the authorized class of business borrowers; and a law restricting the class of borrowers to whom banks can lend does not prevent banks from competing with each other in other cost-incurring services in order to get more money to lend.

The result of restrictions on bank activities is that depositors are not allowed to negotiate freely with commercial banks. To get a higher rate of return on slightly riskier loans, people therefore lend to financial intermediaries other than commercial banks. As yet, there is no law that prevents a private individual from directly making risky loans—for instance, to institutions that (like second-mortgage and consumer-finance companies) specialize in riskier loans. It is difficult to protect people from their own desire for a riskier, possibly higher rate of return. Even though such protection may be called an invasion of their "freedom," the rationale advanced for restrictive laws is that this loss of "freedom" for some people is a "small" price to pay for more secure commercial banks.

Some laws restricting lending negotiations are directed at the borrowers. For example, laws control consumers' installment purchases of furniture, appliances, cars, vacations. The principle behind these laws apparently is that since some consumers can't avoid the error of going "too far" into debt, everyone should be prohibited from going "too far" into debt. Furthermore, although it's all right to buy a house with a mortgage or to go into debt to meet doctor bills, or to buy business equipment, to go into debt "merely to enjoy consumption before one has earned all the costs" is bad. A generation ago there was considerable publicity and legislation about the evil of consumer installment loans. But the insidious convenience of earlier over later consumption, and of consuming while earning, won out over the virtue of consumption in one's old age. Today, despite many laws trying to limit the rate of interest and amount of borrowing, installment buying is an accepted modern convenience—which has, for better or worse, brought the specialized loan market to the young man as well as to the older.

Still, the U.S. government has a law that enables the Board of Governors of the Federal Reserve to place limits on installment purchases. It once prohibited installment credit for more than 50 percent of the value of the item purchased. A 50 percent "down-payment requirement" is a prohibition against going into debt for more than 50 percent of the price of the item purchased. What is the purpose of this particular restriction? Three reasons have been advanced. (a) First, as said earlier, it prevents the consumer from "excessive" debt. (b) A second reason is that the total amount of consumer credit is deemed too large for the "good of the economy," and must be curtailed to prevent "too rapid" an expansion of credit and "too vigorous" a growth of output of the items being purchased. (c) A third reason alleged by *opponents* of the law was that the Federal Reserve Board, which also keeps its eye on the U.S. government's borrowing problems, wanted to channel more of the available savings to the government. By establishing borrowing limits for private consumers, the government was left with less competition for loans and hence could borrow at lower interest. These cynical analysts do not believe that government borrowing is "more important" than private borrowing, even though the former is always said to be in the national public interest whereas the latter is in the private selfish interest.

What are the effects? Do higher minimum down-payment regulations reduce the amount of installment debt? Yes. But they increase other kinds of debt. Frustrated consumers are induced to increase or maintain mortgaged debt on their houses or land in order to cover down payments on the consumers' goods purchased. The inconvenience and costs of increasing such debts are often more than the costs involved in installment loans. In addition, these loan restrictions certainly have different impacts on people: older, richer, more informed capital-good owners are not restricted as much as are younger, poorer, less informed (in terms of costs of knowledge of and access to other sources and means of borrowing).

Not only as consumers but also as business investors, individuals are prevented from "excessive" indebtedness. At the present time, the Federal Reserve Board has the power to limit the amount of money a person may borrow against the stocks and bonds he owns in companies whose stock is sold on the organized stock exchanges. Anyone who owns a share of stock in a corporation such as American Telephone and Telegraph can borrow up to 30 percent of its market value on the security of that share of stock. Why is the lender prohibited from lending more than 70 percent? Not to protect him from loss of security value if the stock should fall, but instead to prevent stock prices from being bid up higher—as they allegedly would be if people could buy shares with lower down payments—and to reduce the extent of price declines. This grant of power to control credit assumes the Federal Reserve Board is better able to judge what the general level of prices of stocks should be at any moment than are investors in a free market.

Of the two rationales advanced—prevention of individuals from excessive indebtedness and prevention of "excessively" high prices of stocks—how well does this "margin requirement" operate? It seems to have only a momentary impact on stock prices. Furthermore, there are many ways to get around the debt limit. Instead of borrowing from your stock broker, borrow from your banker, using the stock as the pledged security. Your banker can lend more if he wants to, but not for the express purpose of buying stock. That restriction means very little, because you can take the money you get from the banker and use it to pay some other bills, while the money you otherwise would have used to pay these bills is released for other uses. Money is fungible.

In most countries, there are strong restrictions on access to security markets. Unless the person proposing to sell new bonds or new common stock satisfies the law in giving out certain information and in not holding out gleaming promises, he can be prevented from selling the securities via the mails. Turning it around, buyers-lenders-investors can be prevented from buying his bonds and stocks. In some states, the law prevents the sale of stocks or bonds of existing companies located in other states if the state authority deems the business too risky for its residents to own.

If there are no controls on open-market solicitation and sale of investment securities, there will be more "suckers" in the get-rich quest. Instead of putting savings only in the sounder schemes, some people will divert savings to bad, risky ones. Established business firms will find it more difficult to borrow if new, unproved firms can compete for funds. Open markets do enable the market *testing* of investment options, but that requires actually making the investment. If it is believed that some people can select among investments better than can other people, and if these people can be identified in advance, then giving them power to control the kinds of investments for which funds can be solicited in the market will lead to less waste of resources.

The issue of the propriety of controls on the stock market cannot be settled by simply weighing their effects on the extent of profitable or unprofitable investments nor on the extent to which "unethical" security dealers are detected. It concerns also the right of a person to make whatever investment choice he would like to make, through whatever agency he chooses, as long as he pays for the resources used. Whether he invests his savings foolishly or consumes them in eating too much chocolate cake is a decision he might consider his own. If someone else wants to help him make a wise decision, he will listen to the advice unless it takes too much time; but to prohibit him from taking a one-in-a-thousand gamble simply because someone else thinks he is too gullible is an invasion of his basic rights. So *he* may think. Who is right? It depends upon what you conceive to be the desirable basic rights of a person.

Measure and Determination of Rate of Interest

We conclude this discussion of interest and the growth of capital with two comments on the measure and the determination of the rate of interest.

THE COMMODITY AND THE MONEY RATE OF INTEREST

As long as there remain opportunities to *invest* current income so as to obtain a future yield greater than the current sacrifice, the rate of interest will be positive. Furthermore, as long as people are willing to give up current *consumption* rights only if they can get more consumption rights in the future than given up now, the rate of interest will be positive. All available evidence indicates that at least one or both of these conditions have been true since the beginning of man.

In another and superficial sense, the "effective" rate of interest has not been and need not always be positive, even though the above conditions are satisfied. This qualification results from the possibility of a price change of the commodity in terms of which the interest is to be paid. Usually it is money, because of the exchange convenience of money. If I borrow $40 from you now and agree to repay you with 10 percent interest, or $44, in one year, what is the rate of interest *in terms of, say, onions?* It depends upon the present and future price of onions. If I repay you next year $44 worth of onions, I will have paid you 10 percent interest in terms of *money* units. But suppose that although the present price of onions is $40 per ton it will double to $80 next year. Next year $44 of onions will be 1,100 pounds of onions. I repay you 45 percent *less* onions than I borrowed from you, since I borrowed $40 or the equivalent of 2,000 pounds of onions. The interest rate for one year was a *minus 45 percent in terms of onions.*

This suggests that the rate of interest in money units could be *negative* if a fall in the general price level were *anticipated.* If the price level were expected to be only half as high next year as it is now, how much interest in money would you pay next year for a loan today, if the rate of interest were 10 percent in money units for a stable price level? The amounts $100 today and $50 next year are equivalent in buying power at their respective times. An interest rate of 10 percent would call for $55 to be repaid next year for a loan of $100 now, which would imply an interest rate in money of *negative* 45 percent per year. On the other hand, if the price level were expected to double, a rate of interest of 120 percent for a one-year loan would be equivalent to a 10 percent stable-price money rate of interest.[8] All of our previous discussion of the rate of interest has been based on the assumption that the money-price level is stable. If it is not, and if the rate at which the price level is going to change is foreseen, then the rate of interest on money loans can be adjusted to give the lender and borrower the same net result in real goods as if there were no change in the price level.

[8] The relationship between the rate of interest, r, in money units for a stable price level, and the adjusted rate of interest, R, in money units, if the price level is changing at the rate of p percent a year, is: $R = (1 + r)(1 + p) - 1$.

DETERMINATION OF RATE OF INTEREST AND OF INVESTMENT

It is tempting to think that we have outlined an analysis of the determination of the rate of interest and how it serves to equilibrate demands with supplies—that is, to ration scarce resources among competing claimants. One is led to believe that the rate of interest varies so as to equilibrate demands and supplies in the markets for lending, production, and capital goods. Unfortunately, there is one further important fact. It is not true that a shift in the supply (or demand) curve in one of these markets will leave the demand (or supply) curve unchanged. The two are not independent.

For example, suppose that a portion of the community increases its desires for future relative to present consumption. They start to save more of current money income and spend less on consumption goods. The reduced demand for consumption goods will make the production of such goods less profitable and will affect the demand for equipment used to make those goods. This can lead to a reduced demand for capital goods. Contrary to our earlier assumption of an increase in savings and no change in the expected selling prices of future output, the reduced consumption that attends increased savings can affect the investment demand curve. Furthermore, the increased savings may not immediately be spent elsewhere to offset the reduced consumption-goods demand. The general decline in demand will imply a decline in income, prices, and wealth, and a reduced expectation about salability of future consumption-goods output.

We tread warily here because a more rigorous, detailed investigation would take us into employment and income theory—a subject we shall start to study in the next chapter. For the moment it suffices to note that shifts in the savings schedule cannot generally be assumed to be without transient effect on the investment demand. Income and wealth will undergo transient change in the process of adjusting to the changed savings schedule. Hence, we cannot say that when the supply of savings changes, the interest rate simply adjusts without any attendant transient changes in other important economic factors like prices, employment, and income. However, these feedback effects via wealth and income will work themselves out in time as income and employment are restored to their normal equilibrium levels. But transient effects are important; after all, after a temporary illness, one never regains the lost days of activity, even though he may regain his health.

We avoid the temptation to say that the rate of interest simply equilibrates savings with investment. Changes in prices, income, and wealth are also involved. Therefore, it is the rate of interest, prices, income, and wealth that equilibrate "savings and investment." Further, whatever affects the savings and investment functions will affect the rate of interest, income, and wealth. We are reminded of the relationships among the prices and quantities of butter and margarine. The price of butter is affected by the demand for and supply of butter, but so is the price of margarine; and the price of margarine also affects the demand for and supply of butter and hence the price of butter.

In summary, instead of saying the rate of interest is determined by, or equilibrates, savings and investment, we recognize that the rate of interest, income, and wealth all change in equilibrating the savings and investment functions and in turn are partly determined by those functions. In this and the preceding chapters, we explored only the role of the rate of interest in this equilibrating task, and we saw how that rate of interest depends upon the savings-investment functions and how it affects the growth of wealth. In the next several chapters, we pursue an investigation of how income and wealth depend upon the savings and investment functions.

Questions

1. **a.** "If savings is defined as an increase in wealth and if investment is defined as an increase in wealth, then savings by definition is always equal to investment; for it is merely the same thing looked at from the point of view of two different people." Correct or incorrect?

   b. Since the preceding statement is correct, how is it possible to speak of equilibrating the rate of investment and the rate of savings?

2. Define the demand for investment; define the supply of savings and do so in such a way that the two are not synonymous.

3. "The most important fact about saving and investment is that they are done by different people and for different reasons."

   a. Is that why savings must be equilibrated to investment via a demand for investment and a supply for savings function? Why not?

   b. Suppose that everyone who invested had to do his own savings and could not lend or borrow or buy capital goods from other people. Would that destroy the principles of demand-and-supply analysis for growth of wealth? Why?

4. If a person saves all his increase in wealth, how much does he save?

5. The interest rate is 10 percent per year. A person uses $100 of current wealth so as to make his wealth grow to $105 at the end of a year.

   a. Has he maximized his wealth?

   b. In what sense has he not even maintained his wealth, despite the fact that he has $105 at the end of the year compared to $100 at the beginning. (Hint: When his wealth was $100 at the beginning of the year, with an interest rate of 10 percent, how much could he consume during the year and still end up with $100? Could he not have consumed any amount up to $5 and still ended up with $105?)

6. In a certain country the only productive goods are "rabbits." Either the rabbits are eaten or the rabbits grow at the rate of 20 percent per year.

a. If there are 1,000,000 rabbits in the community at the first of the year, what is the income of the community (measuring the income in rabbit units)?

b. What will be the rate of interest in that community?

c. What is the maximum possible growth rate of the wealth of that country—barring new discoveries in rabbit growth?

7. If the rate of interest is 10 percent in the New York bond markets and 5 percent in the Boston bond market, describe the adjustments you think will ensue.

8. Someone discovers how to reduce refrigeration costs to almost zero, and tells everyone about it.

a. What will this new improved technology do to the rate of interest?

b. What price shifts are implied?

9. The propositions on costs in Chapter 2 imply that the demand curve for investment is negatively sloped with respect to the rate of interest—that is, that higher *rates* of investment will be less profitable. Why is this implied by the earlier propositions on behavior of costs?

10. "Debtors are exploited by creditors, because a person who has to borrow is usually in distress and is willing to pay a very high price to get the loan. Unless laws were passed controlling the rate of interest, debtors would be forced to pay unreasonable rates of interest." Is the analysis correct? Explain why.

11. Savings and loan banks in the Far West offer 5 percent on guaranteed savings deposits against 4 percent from Eastern banks. As a result, "brokers" entered the business of advertising in Eastern papers so that they could arrange for transfer of deposits to Western banks. The brokers received a payment from the Western banks; the Eastern depositors got a higher interest; Western banks got more funds and could lend more in the West, thus helping to lower the Western rate; the Eastern banks lost a supply of savings, and their profitability suffered. That was a few years ago. Now there are no brokers, but the interest-rate difference still persists. According to a president of one of the largest groups of Western banks, the federal government's Home Loan Bank Administration prohibits payments of commission by Western banks to these brokers. Can you guess what reason the Home Loan Administration gave for its actions?

12. "Five states—Arkansas, California, Oklahoma, Tennessee, and Texas—have constitutional provisions restricting the maximum contract rate of interest. All other states, except Colorado, Maine, Massachusetts and New Hampshire, have general statutory restrictions upon the rate of interest that may be contracted for in the absence of special statutory authorization for higher rates. The most common maximum contract rates are 6 percent and 8 percent a year, but a few states permit contract rates as high as 12 percent. Loans to corporations are generally exempt." So says the *World-Telegram Almanac* of 1962.

a. What is the difference between the "contract" rate and the rate paid?

b. Who is helped and who is hurt by these laws if they are effective?

c. Do you think they have any effect on the rate of interest?

d. What effect do they have on borrowing activity?

13. You propose to buy a house for $20,000. You have $3,000 in cash now. So you seek to borrow $17,000 from a lender at 5 percent rate of interest. We say 5 percent because the government of the state in which you live has agreed to guarantee the loan on your house since you are a veteran (and the community feels a bit guilty about having drafted your military services, or else your group of veterans has a strong voting bloc). The law will guarantee your loan so long as the lender will lend at not over 5 percent. Unfortunately, no one will lend to you at that rate because 6 percent is available elsewhere. But you are clever enough to find a lender who will lend to you at 5 percent, *after* you make the following proposal: If he will lend you $17,000 at 5 percent (which is, let's say, 1 percent less than the 6 percent rate he could get elsewhere—and thereby costs him $170 a year interest otherwise available; i.e., 1 percent of $17,000 is $170 per year), you will buy from him insurance on the house and on your car and life. In doing this, you may or may not realize that you could have bought the same insurance at a lower rate or more conveniently elsewhere.

a. Why do you make this agreement with him?

b. Is he being "unfair" or "unscrupulous" or "unethical"? Are you?

c. Who is aided or hurt if such tie-in agreements are prohibited?

d. Do you think they can really be totally prohibited by laws? Why?

14. Diagnose and evaluate the following news story from the *New York Times* (Feb. 7, 1959, p. 30): "Earl B. Schwulst, chairman of the Bowery Savings Bank, said he would be greatly distressed if other savings banks moved soon to increase their dividend rate to depositors. Most New York City institutions are paying 3¼ percent. There have been some rumors that some institutions would announce soon an increase to 3½ percent. Mr. Schwulst said that the Bowery, the largest savings bank in the nation, was as well qualified as any other institution to pay the higher rate. But, he said, the Bowery would not lead the way because of a number of reasons he described as 'in the long-run interest of our depositors.'"

15. If overnight you received a gift of $10,000 in cash, in what forms would you hold your wealth in the ensuing time? Suppose you decided to convert it to some intermediate kind of claim or goods (like bonds and savings-bank deposits) before finally holding more stocks and personal or business goods directly? Trace out the sequence of effects on the interest rate if you follow the sequence suggested in the preceding sentence.

16. Tonight the government prints twice as much money as there now is and sprinkles it from the skies as a sort of Fourth of July celebration and reward to all the people.

a. The next day, when the money is found, what do you think will happen to prices?

b. What will happen to the rate of interest? (Hint: How will the demand and supply of various goods be affected? How will the current demand for bonds be affected relative to the demand for other goods?)

c. Instead of sprinkling the money from the skies, suppose the government uses the money to buy up existing government or existing privately issued bonds. What will happen to the rate of interest?

d. Why does this give a different result, even though it involved an increase in the stock of money?

17. The rate of interest helps to equilibrate investment and savings and the demand for borrowing and the supply of savings; it is the premium price of current consumption rights over future consumption rights; it is the price of money; and it equates the demand and supply of assets. Explain wherein it is all these things at the same time.

18. The President of the United States government, in order to prevent a loss of gold, decides to take governmental action to increase the rate of interest. If he can successfully do this, he believes foreigners will leave gold on loan in the United States for that higher interest rate rather than take the gold home. Suppose that belief is correct and suppose the interest rate is increased.

a. What do you think the effect will be on the rate of building and housing construction? Why?

b. Will the higher interest rate affect all kinds of business activity equally? Why?

c. Why do you think the businessmen are so concerned about the policy that may be taken by the President and Congress if those officials decide to try to prevent a further outflow of gold? (We shall discuss the gold "problem" later in Chapters 43 and 44.)

19. "Havana: Oct. 15, 1961: All renters in the towns and cities of Cuba became property (building—not land) owners this morning when the Castro government approved a long-awaited reform law. However, renters must pay the Cuban government for their newly acquired property during the next five to twenty years at the same monthly rate as their present rents. In addition, they must pay the government the taxes formerly paid by the owners. The former owners will receive a "life monthly indemnity" of from 200 to 600 pesos without regard to the amount of property they owned. Heirs will receive nothing. Any buildings now in construction will be turned over to renters selected by the government. If the owner (up to today) refuses to complete the building, the state will seize the existing building with no compensation at all. Holders of mortgages on residences and apartment houses will receive 50 percent of the amount paid by the tenants to the state until the loan is paid, but no interest will be allowed."

Why do people in many foreign countries "foolishly" hoard gold instead of using their wealth to develop the country?

20. "Where total investment is concerned, the economic system is in the lap of the gods." Do you agree? If so, why? If not, why not?

31

FLUCTUATIONS IN RESOURCE USE AND INCOME

If all people were alike, if all kinds of work and working conditions were the same, if all resources were identical, then people and resources could transfer from job to job instantly. But such is not the case. Learning, shifting, and experimenting are costly. The costs of comparing opportunities and capabilities in new situations must be borne in one way or another. Although it is easy to talk of a world in which full knowledge of all circumstances is immediately available at no cost, the fact is that information is hard to get, communicate, and digest.

Re-allocation of productive resources involves some "unemployment" or "wasted" productive capacity. This may seem both strange and unfortunate because other phenomena also are called "unemployment"; but this kind of unemployment is not necessarily wasteful or undesirable given the fact of changing tastes, desires, and costs of information and movement. Unemployment and "idle" goods and services will be inevitable and, as we shall see, will be convenient ways to adapt to those changes in preferences and costs.

In the United States over 80,000,000 people had gainful employment of one kind or another in 1963. Some 55,000,000 worked full time, and 25,000,000 worked part time. Approximately 10,000,000 changed jobs or took on new jobs during the year. Every month approximately one in twenty employees quit, was laid off, or terminated a job for one reason or another; the same proportion took on new jobs or returned to an old job. In this process, over 15,000,000 reported themselves as "unemployed" during the year, although at any one time the number averaged about 4,000,000. Of those 15,000,000, some 2,000,000 were unemployed all through the year; 1,000,000 between one and three months; and a little less than 3,000,000 each between four and six months and more than six months. Over 5,000,000 of these people had at least two spells of unemployment, the total time of which is the basis of their classification in the above categories. Clearly, there is a persistent and extensive flow of people from job to job and between jobs and unemployment, along with constant reassessment of old jobs and consideration of possible new occupations. Such unemployment of people and resources—and even widespread and prolonged unemployment—is consistent with the economic analysis presented in earlier chapters. So far, we have ignored these phenomena in our endeavor to concentrate on the distinctive features of the exchange economy.

To facilitate analysis of unemployment on this broader aggregative level, it is convenient to consider first the meaning of unemployment (of labor and of goods)—a term generally applied quite indiscriminately to very different phenomena, not all of which are bad and to be avoided.

Some Sources and Kinds of Unemployment

One kind of unemployment or idle or excess supply of some resource is caused by a restraint on access to the market, perhaps because of imposed prices below which the resource cannot legally be offered for employment. To call people "unemployable" because the value of their services is less than some maintained minimum wage is to confuse the issue. They are employable; but they are not employed because of the constraints placed on their right to seek employment in an open market at terms that are mutually acceptable to buyer and seller.

A similar group of "unemployed" are those excluded from particular jobs because of apprenticeship or licensing laws. These people will call themselves unemployed "electricians," "meat cutters," "projectionists," or "bricklayers" while taking less desired jobs elsewhere on what is, they presume, a temporary basis.

If there are levels of prices and wages below which sales and employment are illegal, some people will be prevented from selling their services at prices acceptable to buyers. If the wage rate is legally set at a minimum of $1, some less productive people will be unable to provide services worth $1 an hour. Some could do something worth, say, 80 cents, but they cannot be employed at that wage. We presented a more detailed discussion of this in Chapter 28. Suffice it to note that some of these people will constitute members of the "unemployed" until they shift to "independent" owner-operator status. How many people are in this situation is not known.

Another group of the "unemployed" are workers who entered into employment when demand was, but is no longer, high enough to warrant higher wages. For example, some housewives work during seasonally high demands for certain types of labor—in fruit-packing houses or dress shops. During the rest of the year, when demand is lower, they prefer not to work at the lower wages they would have to take. During these seasonal lulls they are often counted as unemployed, especially if they can thereby collect unemployment benefits. People working in jobs that involve separate projects, like movies, plays, or construction, are commonly found in the ranks of the unemployed between projects—again especially if they have qualified for unemployment benefits.

Sometimes it is asserted that there are not enough jobs available. This assertion is simply unacceptable if reality is to be recognized rather than romantically wished away. There are always jobs available, but the wage offer may be unacceptably low in view of alternative prospects or uses of leisure. To ask a former steel-mill employee to work at 50 cents an hour as a gardener, handyman, farm hand, clerk, or machine-tool operator is "ridiculous"—which means only that the steel-mill employee deems it preferable not to work at those jobs for those wages or that he believes he can get a better job by continued search for job information. In other words, he believes the time spent waiting or seeking information is worth more than 50 cents an hour.

There are also people who at times are out of a job and who would be happy to continue at their *old* job *at the old wage* if *that* job were still available. But they will refuse to accept a wage cut sufficient to keep them at work in their former jobs, because they believe there are other job opportunities at approximately the same wages—or certainly at better terms than those available in the old job. After all, those other opportunities are what kept their wages up to the level at which they were in their recent jobs. They will therefore look for these other opportunities—as long as the expected cost of discovering them is less than the loss of wealth from accepting a wage cut in the previous job. When demand for a product falls, then, do the productive inputs simply shift to other tasks at which they can get better pay? If they did, there would be no unemployment and no idle resources, for prices would adjust so as to re-allocate resources—just as in earlier chapters we re-allocated cars and candy and cigarettes. But such shifts are not always possible, because of one crucial element in that re-allocation process—the costs of finding the various buyers and sellers and bringing them together, so that each can realize his best trading opportunities. Putting the matter more succinctly, acquiring *information* about bid-and-offer possibilities and about the characteristics of the goods is not costless. And this will explain a wide class of unemployment, as we shall see. To this end, we shall first explore the relevance and the costs of acquiring information, and we shall see how people behave when they have incomplete information. Having done so, we will be in a position to see why there are periods of mass unemployment.

Information about Employment Opportunities

If information about everyone else's offer and asking prices, their current interests, and their potential buying and selling plans were instantly and costlessly available to everyone, then indeed we would be hard put to explain the phenomenon of "unemployment" and "idle" resources. Furthermore, the marketplace would appear to be simply a place for exchange of goods and services. But actually it is also a device whereby people can collect and exchange information about the various goods and whereby potential sellers can find potential buyers. Information about the sellers of goods and the location and characteristics of available goods is valuable—not obtained at zero cost. Information about various tracts of land or houses is irrelevant or useless for most of us, but to people interested in using land it is valuable information. Similarly, the names and addresses of local retailers or wholesalers, the particular products they sell, the kinds of goods they use, the possibility of openings for more employees, working conditions in the many firms, location of distant sources of supplies of various goods, the freight rates from here to there, the special talents of employee *A* relative to employee *B*—all are valuable information to *some* people.

Now, recognizing that information is not free and instead can be obtained only with some effort and expenditure of time, we should expect to see substantial resources devoted to information collecting about exchange possibilities in the market. And we do. Real-estate agents, retailers, salesmen, brokers, wholesalers act not only as sellers of goods but as providers of information about various goods and services and potential buyers and sellers. Housewives devote substantial time to window shopping and inspection of goods—i.e., to collecting information about purchase possibilities. That a retail store performs the function of providing information about goods as well as providing goods themselves is made painfully obvious to those who try to buy only by mail order.

The young student just completing his formal academic education discovers that there are costs of collecting information about the grubby details of working conditions and wages of various potential employers. He spends hours and money in learning about different possible employers; information about more distant employers is so costly that often he simply doesn't try to get it. Similarly, employers devote large sums of money to telling students about working conditions and to discovering the attributes of various potential employees.

In other words, housewives, employees, and employers do not take the first offer of goods, jobs, or employees they see. If complete information about all job possibilities and all workers and all goods were free and instantly available, there would be no point to shopping or waiting for better offers. One would instead instantly take the best one. But information is neither free nor complete. And it is valuable; consequently, people will devote resources to collecting more information so as to make better purchase and sale decisions. A failure to grasp this has led to much confusion and misinterpretation of the role of certain kinds of economic activity—especially much of that which is called "idleness" or "unemployment."

Before investigating some of the actions consequent to the recognition of the cost of information collecting, we state two central propositions.

(a) *Information is not free*—a point which it is now sufficient simply to state. (b) *The more rapidly it is obtained, the greater the cost of the information.* Try to find out what is on sale at a local store in the next 30 seconds. Would it be cheaper to find out in the course of the next day in a more convenient way? Or if you are looking for and comparing various possible jobs, is it cheaper to get information about wages and working conditions in the next hour or in the next week? The simple fact is that "production" of information, as with any other good, conforms to the general laws of production. More rapid production or acquisition of information is more costly than less hasty production, and more rapid acquisition of information may or may not be worth the extra cost.

Given these facts about the costs of information, how do people react to changes in demand for their services? How do they collect information? What use of resources is economical in the face of the costs of getting information? The behavior implied by the answers often gives rise to what is called "unemployment" and "idle" resources—with a consequent misinterpretation of the purpose being served by this apparently undesirable state of affairs. Without implying that all forms of behavior that are called unemployment are economic adjustments to the higher costs of acquiring information more rapidly, we nevertheless will see that many forms of it are. Even in mass unemployment during depression, uncertainty and the cost of acquiring information play a vital role. But before we can conveniently apply economic analysis to mass unemployment during depressions, we must appreciate the importance of information about jobs, the costs of acquiring information, the higher costs of hastier adjustments, and the means of economizing on these costs.

Actions That Economize Information and Adjustment Costs

(1) *Buffer stocks are held and sometimes called excess capacity.* When information-collecting costs are recognized, extra stocks of goods are held in inventory, even though these may appear to be "idle" or "unemployed." Yet they are not wasteful. What may appear to be wasted or unemployed is more accurately identified as economical "information-collecting" uses of resources. Consider, as a simple example, the problem facing a newsboy who expects to sell an average of one hundred copies of each edition of a local paper—but not exactly one hundred each day. He has several options. He could spend a lot of money to find out who was going to buy copies each day. He could stock less than one hundred and rarely have any unsold copies. He could stock more and have copies left over. He could stock one copy, and each time he sold one he could order another one, getting special-delivery service. The first and last options are very costly. The more accurately he tries to predict or the more quickly he tries to adjust to demand fluctuations, the more expensive the process. The customers prefer to have him stock an excessive number on the average in order

to have instant availability out of inventories, despite a slightly higher cost of the newspaper (implied by each seller's ending up with extra copies). The higher cost to customers need not appear as a higher money price; it may appear as a smaller newspaper or as fewer retailers. But this cost of extra copies will be less than if the newspaper sellers attempted to obtain complete information or make instantaneous adjustments in the number of papers.

Similarly, an apartment owner will build more apartments than he expects on the average to have fully occupied. Exactly like the paper seller, it will pay him to build more apartments in order to satisfy the unpredictable vagaries of demand. The apartment-house owner can always keep the apartments fully rented at a lower rental; or at a higher rental he can have some vacancies part of the time. In providing some occasional vacancies, he is catering to renters' desires to move when they want rather than having to make plans and reservations far in advance. The situation is exactly analogous to a person's building a home with enough bathrooms and dining space to seat more visitors than he will ordinarily have. To say that he has "wasted" or "idle" or "unemployed" bathroom or dining-room capacity is to consider only the cost of that extra capacity and to misunderstand its value and to overlook the higher costs of alternative ways of obtaining equally high convenience or utility.

Empty apartments *per se* are not a test of waste. They are a method of production to economize on the high costs of predicting the future and also of the high costs of *immediately* producing whatever a person wants. If it costs no more to produce instantly than in less haste, we would carry no inventories and produce whatever a person wanted when he wanted it. However, the costs of immediate production are excessive. By producing in advance at a less hasty, more economical rate and holding resources available for contingent demands, we economize in having more housing services at a cost that is worth paying, taking into account the value of being able to move without long, advance, "reservation-type" planning. We could reduce housing costs by more advance planning of people's activities and refusals to allow them to change their minds, but this would also reduce housing services and convenience.

In a given community, then, there will be more houses or apartments than people want at any moment to occupy. There will also be an "extra supply" of service stations, barber shops, dress shops, real-estate agencies, insurance salesmen, and car dealers. The extra supply is really an inspection supply or a convenience supply. Imagine what it would be like trying to move in a community that had as many apartments as families and every apartment was now rented. "Costs" would be imposed on tenants who wanted to move. Vacant apartments are like left-overs at dinner. They would be "waste" only in an imaginary world of perfect predictability at zero cost or in a world where instant production to every moment's demand is no more costly or troublesome than cooking in advance of dinner time.

Moreover, the buildings will be provided with fire escapes, and residential areas with fire hydrants; first-aid kits will be located in homes and fire extinguishers in strategic places in buildings. Such provisions would not be necessary if information about the future were free and available immediately; for everyone could know early enough how to avoid catastrophes. Or if information were not free, but it were just as cheap to make instant physical adjustments as slow ones, then upon word of fire the building could immediately be altered to have fire escapes, or water lines could be laid to the site of the fire. This suggestion is absurdly fanciful, precisely because it rests on a denial of higher costs for both more rapid acquisition of information and more rapid subsequent physical adjustments. If "instant production," like instant coffee, could be achieved at no more cost than less hasty production, if instant information were as cheap as less rapidly obtained answers, there would be no "idle," "excess," "unemployed" resources. But instant adjustments *do* cost more than less hasty adjustments. We therefore expect to observe what might carelessly be called "idle" resources.

(2) *Some "unemployed" resources are employed in information seeking.* Effects of higher costs of acquiring information and making more rapid adjustments are evident not only in the production of new goods but also in the re-allocation of existing goods. In earlier chapters, we indicated that prices re-allocate goods among competing claimants. But how rapidly do they re-allocate in response to changes in demands? How rapidly and accurately are new alternatives revealed? Information about changing demands and supplies is not free. An essential function of the market is to make that information more readily (cheaply) accessible. And it costs more to collect or to spread information more rapidly than less rapidly. Although it takes no time to announce a higher price offer or a changed demand, it does take resources to communicate that change to other people; and the more people to whom it is communicated the more it costs—as any advertiser can verify.

Consider the implications of this for an apartment owner who loses a tenant. Should he lower the rents of the empty unit far enough to induce anyone to occupy it *immediately?* That probably would involve a greater cut than if he waits a few days for information to be made available to potential occupants. If he cuts immediately, at least he will be getting some income in the interim; then, when he finds a higher-paying tenant, he can raise the rent. However, any tenant will usually want a lease or a month's agreement, exactly because he would otherwise have to incur the risks of having to move. Attracting new tenants with the understanding that they can be evicted *immediately* will require the landlord to accept a lower rent than if a longer notice of eviction or rent adjustment is promised.

If moving were a costless operation in both a pecuniary and nonpecuniary sense, rents would be altered immediately to keep apartments always rented, at the highest available rent. But moves are not costless, and hastier moves are more costly than slower moves. The gains from immediate price changes and moves are exceeded by the costs. In effect, the apartment owner achieves a lower cost of less hasty adjustments by sustaining some vacant housing. Not all apartments or houses should be occupied at all times in a changing world. Vacancies are not a sign of inefficiency, nor of a defective operation of either a capitalist or a socialist system.

When a person decides to move and sell his house, does he cut price low enough to sell to the first person he sees? Generally not. He knows that information about his house is not completely dispersed over the whole society. Wider, more rapid dissemination is costly. He can save some of those costs by taking time and "sampling" potential buyers until he thinks he has found the highest-bidding buyer or until he thinks the cost of waiting longer will probably exceed the gains of awaiting contact with still higher-bidding buyers. Heterogeneity among buyers and kinds of houses and a higher cost of more rapid acquisition of information both imply that house sellers will, on the average, keep their houses "on the market" for awhile. During the time the house is unsold or unoccupied, there is a temptation to call it an idle resource. But it is as idle as the housewife who idles away time shopping and comparing goods before making a purchase.

Similarly, although it may seem strange, labor "unemployment" is consistent with efficiency. Consider the costs that would be imposed on you if you were *never* allowed to be unemployed regardless of changing demand and supply conditions. Suppose you were dissatisfied with your present job and wanted another job. You could not quit and spend a week or a month looking for a new job, because you would then be "unemployed." It is unlikely that you could find the *best* alternative job with an instant search of no cost or while working at the old job in order to avoid "unemployment." The activity in question is not *job* seeking, it is *job-information* seeking. Many jobs are available, but information is being sought about still other jobs in the belief that the other jobs will be superior. The currently known jobs do not pay enough to induce a person to stop looking for *better* job opportunities. Some "unemployment" is preferred even from the point of view of the "unemployed," given the greater costs of more rapid acquisition of knowledge and adjustment in response to changes in demands, tastes, and talents. If an employer should experience a decrease in demand, so that he wants to employ fewer employees at the existing wage, he will drop employees. This is equivalent to the case in which a renter terminates his renting and leaves the apartment empty. Like the apartment owner, the employee now has the option of cutting his wages immediately by a relatively large amount to get a job quickly, or he can invest in a hunt for information about various alternative jobs. Exactly as the apartment owner did, he will not accept a cut in wages to whatever level is necessary to find another employer immediately. The cost of the search is in large part the loss of interim wages he could have had by accepting whatever employment he could get immediately. A job is always immediately available at *some* lower wage, but he wants a better job. And if he believes that the sacrifices and costs he incurs in the search yield a greater increase in the present value of his wealth, then he will engage in some information hunting, an activity called job hunting.

A transparent example of such activity is provided by new college graduates who spend much time and other resources investigating alternative potential employers. No student knows everything about each potential employer, nor does each employer know everything about each potential college graduate. Wage offers differ among employers, in part reflecting nonpecuniary features that are in turn evaluated differently by various people. Offers obtained by college graduates for the "same" kind of work will differ by 5 to 10 percent of the average offer. Accepting the first offer reduces the probability of getting the highest-paid job and lowers one's *wealth* compared to what it would be if he took longer to find more offers. The more firms that are contacted, the greater will be the probability of finding higher wage offers or better jobs. The greater the difference in actual wage offers and working conditions, the greater the amount of search that it will be profitable to perform.

A person will search for and explore other wage offers until the expected marginal gain (in present value of anticipated future income) equals the incremental cost of continued search. The increment of *gain* from *extra* search time diminishes the longer the time devoted to information collecting. Hence, there is a limit to the length of search. Although very few persons may make any detailed calculations, their observed behavior conforms to this explanation.

Search by employees (and employers also) would eliminate all the dispersion among offers *if* there were unchanging conditions of demand and supply and tastes of employers and employees. The greater the rate of change of tastes and demands, the greater the differences among worker talents and employer's working conditions, and the greater the costs of movement, the greater will be that dispersion among discerned job opportunities and the greater the gain in wealth by more extended search.

The fact that employment agencies exist and charge fees for their services is evidence of the costs of search. As one would expect, it will pay some people to specialize in obtaining and disseminating this kind of information, just as it pays to specialize in obtaining knowledge of medicine, accounting, and news reporting.

When a person is engaged in this process of acquiring information for better jobs, he is said to be "frictionally unemployed." Frictional unemployment, referring to stand-by, reserve, better-job information-hunting activity, is applicable to labor, houses, capital goods, or any good whatsoever. It is the efficient way to adjust to unpredictable demand and supply changes. Perhaps it should be called "frictional *use*" to indicate that the resources are being used to *overcome* "frictions" in the operation of any economic system—much as oil is used in a mechanical device—rather than being a source or cause of trouble.

This kind of frictional unemployment of resources is therefore not to be thought of as serving the function often attributed to it: "The capitalist system requires and has a pool of unemployed people in order to keep wages low enough to give profits to the capitalists. Because there is a group of unemployed in reserve, those who have jobs can be dissuaded from asking for higher wages, for then the unemployed would get their jobs." We leave it as a simple exercise in economic analysis for the student to expose the fallacy in that allegation.

Another facet of this process is the presence of "unfilled" jobs. Some employers would like more employees, and, if information and transfer costs were zero, they would instantly hire the right people at the appropriate wage and never have unfilled jobs. But again, the higher costs of more rapid acquisition of information makes it uneconomic for an employer to fill a job immediately. Filling jobs immediately is more expensive in that it will take a higher wage to get the right person immediately; or, if the employer takes the first available person, he will have a smaller probability of getting the "best" person.

Mass Unemployment and Declines in General Demand

People who leave a job rather than accept a lower wage have expectations about the opportunities that exist elsewhere, as explained in the preceding paragraphs. If now there should be a decrease in *general* demand, and if people do not realize it, many will refuse to lower their offer or asking prices in existing jobs before, or without, engaging in a search for better options elsewhere. After all, they formerly could get about the same wage elsewhere. But, with a *general* decrease in demand, they will be unable to do so. However, they will discover this only in the course of the information acquiring, and it will take a good deal of information to detect the *generally* lower state of demand. For example, when sellers sample bids from a distribution of potential buyers, the lower observed offers will at first appear as unrepresentative, and for a time it will be expected that better opportunities will shortly be found. It takes *additional* acquisition of information to discover that the *general* state of demand and opportunities has indeed declined. The period of "unemployment" or information acquisition will be extended and beset with disappointment. After a period of search, the resources will be employed in the "best" new uses. The splurge of "unemployment and excess capacity" will diminish as the information-hunting process is completed.

The extent of unemployment from a general demand decrease will be even more spectacular if the decrease in demand is not simply a once-and-for-all drop but a persisting decrease extending over several months or years. This requires more extensive information collecting, since the state of beliefs about opportunities elsewhere must be *continuously revised downward* with a continuous flow of new information. By the time a person became convinced that alternatives elsewhere were no better than here, they would have deteriorated even more.

Acquisition, evaluation, and comprehension of information lags behind the event, because instantaneous information is prohibitively expensive, and a continuing fall is even more costly to detect. Prolonged periods of unemployment and slowly falling "asking and offer" prices are implied if there is some factor causing a continuing decrease in general demand. (Not only employees but employers, too, find it harder to get good information about the current state of demands.)

It is tempting to jump to the conclusion that after a fairly long period of falling demand and unemployment—say, several weeks—people will catch on and anticipate the situation. But this is easier said than done. To find out what has been happening is one thing; to predict what will happen next is a far different thing. Even though one learns with a lag that demand has been decreasing for some several months, should he extrapolate that into the future? For example, it is folly to conclude that the longer the time the average of prices of stocks in the stock market has been falling, the more likely it is to continue to fall. There is no reason and no evidence for any belief that one can extrapolate past downward or upward moves in prices, production, or employment to predict subsequent developments. Fortunes would await those who could. People are not blind or stupid in refusing to forecast that a long observed downswing will continue.

Information, then, is a scarce good. To obtain more of it is costly; and the more rapidly it is collected, the higher the cost. Furthermore, more rapid physical adjustments in resources are more expensive than slower adjustments. People shift their demands among goods; their actions are not perfectly forecast at zero cost; they change in their tastes, abilities, and demands, so that they want to move their residence or adjust their production and wealth activities to changing conditions. Therefore, "idle," "unemployed," "excess" capacity will be observed in the real world. However, nonromantic terminology would not call it "idle, unemployed, or excess," for it literally is none of these. Yet, to the layman, who sees resources not "employed" *by someone else*, but instead employed by the owner to obtain information or to provide a buffer to demand shifts, this economizing search for information appears as "idle" resources. Economists also have been prone to use the term in writing for laymen—with the result that much confusion about the operation of the economic system has resulted. But this again proves our point: information is costly—about economics, as well as about medicine, chemistry, horse races, and psychology. The economist's premise is that people are not completely informed. It is *not* that they are stupid or thoughtless. They do the best they can with the information available and in view of the costs of getting more. They will "look" stupid to us only if we forget that it costs them something to get information.

Economic theory does *not* imply that all resources will always be fully "employed" in a conventional sense. It shows that some capital goods will not be fully rented at all times, that some people will be searching for employment, and that inventories will be larger than necessary to handle realized sales. And none of these are inefficiencies, because to eliminate them would involve a cost that exceeds the gain. Unemployment is an inherent part of an open-market system of exchange, in which people are entitled to select their work and produce at their own volition at open-market prices rather than being tied to jobs as serfs or assigned them by dictators.

In the military, there are never unemployed people. Everyone always has *a* job. However, it is not clear that this is more efficient or preferable to an "idle" search for other *better* jobs. Authorities will always regard an "idle" person as inefficient, since *they* know something he could do that is *absolutely* useful, even if not the most useful. Furthermore, if less attention is paid to seeking overall efficient assignments of workers—as distinct from their producing *some* thing rather than nothing—it is easier to keep everyone busy, even though a more valuable total output could be achieved as a result of some "unemployment" in order to conduct a successful search for better jobs. Concealing or avoiding such unemployment by arbitrary work assignments is called "disguised unemployment" in the economic literature.

No place in this analysis is there any reliance upon inflexible or legal minimum wages and prices, union wage controls, or customary, conventional prices and wages. In the analysis, every seller or buyer has completely flexible prices and wages in the sense that anyone can instantly adjust his prices or wages without any interference or obeisance to convention or outside pressures. Yet he refuses to adjust this price as much as our earlier analysis would appear to have suggested. He does not cut prices and wages that much because he believes that he can sell his goods or services elsewhere at terms better than those being offered by the current employer.

The fact that the analysis we have employed did not rely on wage and price rigidities does not mean that there are none in the real world. There are indeed wage and price controls that prevent adjustments so as to maintain employment, output, and sales to consumers. But it is not possible to attribute all of the unemployment observed to restraints on the open market—convenient and simple as that explanation might have been.

Correlated Fluctuations in Employment

Normally the unemployment of labor explainable by the information costs associated with changing demands for various products, changing tastes, new products, etc., seems to run about 3 to 5 percent of the labor force, or about 4,000,000 people at present. However, at times the rate of unemployment, as evidenced by data taken from people eligible for unemployment pay or who report in labor force surveys that they are "out of work and seeking work," rises to substantially higher levels. In what we commonly call recessions, the rate runs up to above 5 percent and approaches 10 percent. In the deep depression of the 1930s, it is believed to have reached 25 percent. But if the preceding analysis is valid, why should it ever get so high as 5 percent or more?

It is possible that the demands for goods might shift about so rapidly that many people have to shift jobs and that therefore the job-information searching and comparison activity increases—and is characterized as unemployment. However, the evidence suggests that this is not the responsible factor. Instead, there seems to be large, long-lived, simultaneous decreases in demand for *many* goods, without offsetting transfers of demand to other goods. Certainly it is true that some firms experience an increase in demand for their products while others are experiencing a decrease. Industries also differ. Some show increasing output for months at a time while others show decreases. For example, Table 31–1 shows the directions of monthly changes in the value of new orders in manufacturing

Table 31–1

DIRECTION OF CHANGE IN VALUE OF MANUFACTURERS' NEW ORDERS

Industry	One-Month Spans 1962						1963											
	Jun–Jul	Jul–Aug	Aug–Sep	Sep–Oct	Oct–Nov	Nov–Dec	Dec–Jan	Jan–Feb	Feb–Mar	Mar–Apr	Apr–May	May–Jun	Jun–Jul	Jul–Aug	Aug–Sep	Sep–Oct	Oct–Nov	Nov–Dec
Percent rising	81	33	33	71	55	38	57	62	57	57	69	40	67	38	67	48		
Iron and steel	+	+	–	+	–	+	+	+	+	+	–	–	+	–	+	+		
Primary nonferrous metals	–	+	–	+	–	–	+	+	+	–	–	+	–	–	+	+		
Other primary metals	+	+	–	+	+	–	+	–	+	+	o	–	+	–	+	–		
Electrical generator apparatus	–	–	+	–	+	+	–	–	–	+	+	o	–	+	+	–		
Radio, television, and equipment	+	+	–	+	–	+	+	–	–	+	+	–	–	+	–	–		
Other electrical equipment	+	–	+	–	+	+	–	+	+	–	+	+	+	–	–	+		
Motor vehicles	+	–	+	–	–	+	+	+	–	+	+	+	+	–	+	+		
Motor vehicle parts	+	–	+	+	–	+	–	+	–	–	–	+	+	+	–	+		
Aircraft	+	+	–	+	–	–	+	+	+	–	+	–	+	+	+	–		
Other transportation equipment	–	–	+	–	+	–	+	+	–	+	+	–	–	+	+	–		
Stone, clay, and glass products	+	–	–	+	+	–	–	–	+	+	+	–	+	–	+	–		
Metalworking machinery	+	–	+	–	+	+	–	+	–	+	+	–	–	+	+	–		
Special industrial machinery	+	+	–	+	+	–	–	+	–	+	+	–	+	–	+	+		
General industrial machinery	+	+	–	–	–	+	+	–	+	–	+	–	+	–	–	+		
Engines and turbines	+	–	–	+	–	–	+	–	+	–	+	+	+	–	+	–		
Agricultural implements	–	–	–	+	+	–	–	+	+	–	+	–	+	–	+	–		
Construction machinery	+	–	–	+	+	–	–	+	+	–	–	+	+	+	+	–		
Office machines	+	–	–	+	o	–	–	–	–	+	+	+	–	+	–	+		
Household appliances	+	–	+	+	–	–	+	+	+	–	+	–	+	–	–	+		
Other machinery	+	–	–	+	+	–	+	–	+	+	–	–	+	–	+	–		
Fabricated metal products	+	–	–	+	+	–	+	+	–	+	–	+	–	–	–	+		

+ = rising; o = unchanged; — = falling. Series components are seasonally adjusted.

Source: U.S. Department of Commerce, Bureau of Census, *Business Cycle Developments*, November 1963.

establishments over a representative interval. In the monthly change from June to July of 1962, new orders increased in seventeen industries and decreased in four. Further, as one looks across the columns each industry shows noticeable fluctuations. For example, iron and steel showed 11 increases and 5 decreases in the sixteen-month interval.

Within each industry a similar variety of behavior among firms comprising that industry would also be observable.

A more extensive index of the diffusion of productive activity is shown in Figure 31–1. In that figure the rate of *employment* is the variable whose expansion in thirty different industries is plotted. In particular, the percentage of those thirty industries experiencing an expansion in any given month is indicated by the height of the curve. The curve fluctuates up and down, rarely reaching 100 percent or zero. In other words, not all industries are expanding at the same time, nor are all contracting at the same time. The curve usually oscillates within the limits of about 20 to 80 percent. A perfectly steady line at 50 percent would mean that there are always as many expanding as contracting industries. Obviously, that is not what happens.

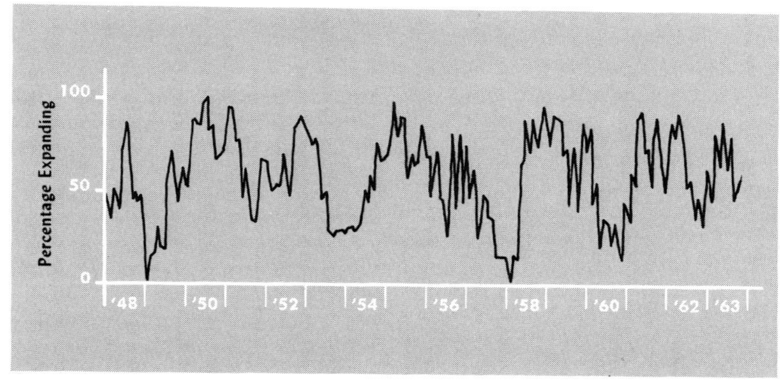

FIGURE 31–1. Percentage of employment-expanding industries (thirty industries, one-month interval of expansion). Source: U.S. Department of Commerce, *Business Cycle Developments,* November 1963.

Similarly, *industrial production* in various industries shows the same general pattern of diffusion of expansions and contractions, as is evident from Figure 31–2. As one would expect, when the curve runs along near the bottom—indicating that most industries are experiencing a contraction—that is called a recession, while when the curve runs along on the upper side, the period is called a recovery or entry to prosperity.

If the lines in Figures 31–1 and 31–2 ran along steadily at about 50 percent, it would mean that there is a relatively steady state of demand, with roughly offsetting shifts occurring among various goods. However, the diffusion index fluctuates over a wide span, suggesting that the growths and declines in

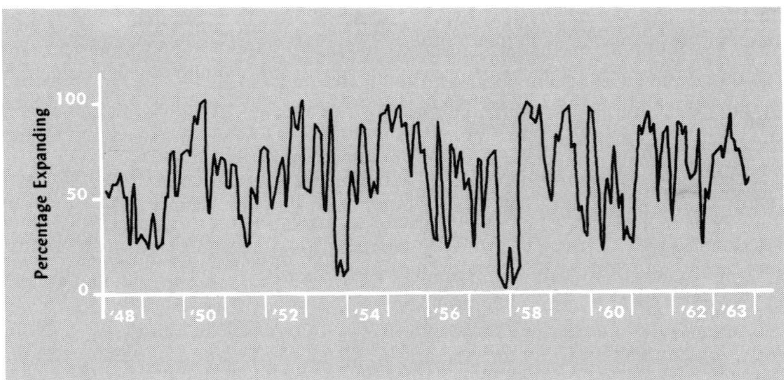

FIGURE 31–2. Percentage of production-expanding industries (twenty-four industries, one-month interval of expansion). Source: U.S. Department of Commerce, *Business Cycle Developments,* November 1963.

various industries are not simply offsetting shiftings of demand from product to product. The fluctuations do not seem to be the sum of a large number of independent random deviations. Instead, there seems to be a swing upward to a condition in which most industries are expanding more than enough to offset contractions elsewhere; and at other times total demand summed over all goods seems to be decreasing. Fluctuations in demand for the products of various industries seem to be correlated rather than independent or mutually offsetting.

Fluctuations in total employment and total industrial production are closely correlated with what are known as prosperities and depressions. In fact, depressions and prosperity are practically definable by the levels of total output and employment. Figure 31–3 shows the index of industrial production from

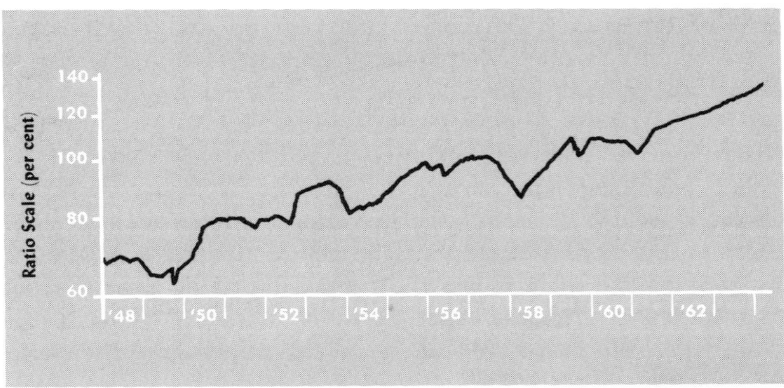

FIGURE 31–3. Industrial production (index based on physical volume, adjusted for seasonal variation, 1957 = 100). Source: Board of Governors of the Federal Reserve System, *Monthly Bulletin.*

1948 through 1963, while Figures 31–4, and 31–5 show the number of employed and the percentage of unemployment since 1948. It is evident that in about the years 1949, 1954, 1958, and 1961 there were recessions.

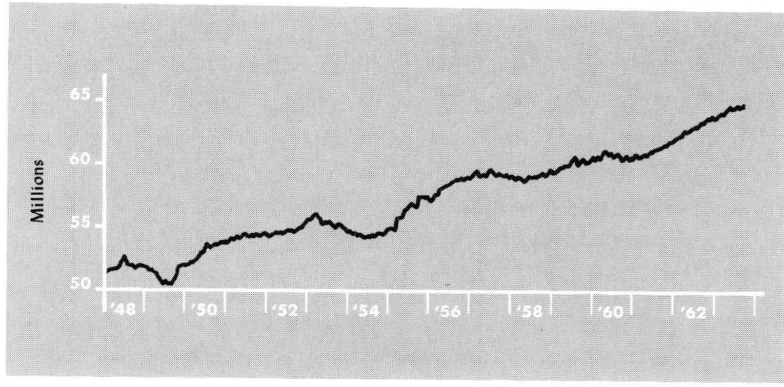

FIGURE 31–4. Total nonagricultural employment.

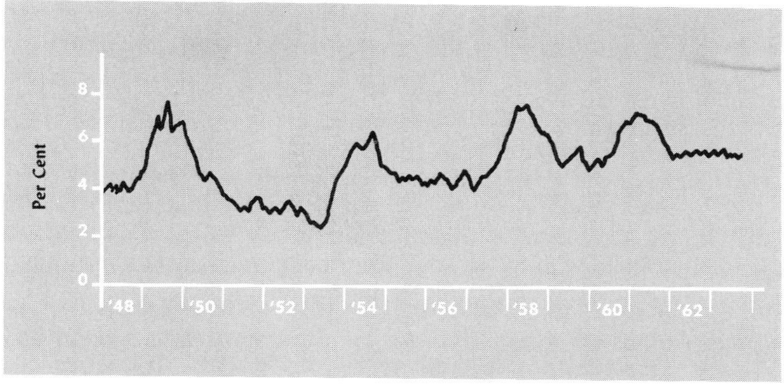

FIGURE 31–5. Unemployment percentage (nonagricultural employees).

What makes demand in general fluctuate instead of being constant with mere offsetting shifts from one product to another? What ties the demand for the products of various industries together, if they are; or are they all independent of each other in the sense that what one does has no effect on others? Are their fortunes correlated by a common factor that operates to increase demand for all of them at the same time? As we know, there is a mechanism or connection among them, so that expansions in one industry or sector set up forces for expansion in other sectors. Specialization in production means that some firms buy their inputs from other firms. Thus, an increased output of final goods in one industry will increase the inputs bought from supplier industries; for example, an increased demand for cars will increase the demand for steel and a whole host of auxiliary services with consequent feedback on the demand for cars. One firm's input is another firm's output. The web of linkage spreads through the economy. That several sectors expand and contract in close step should not be surprising. But this does not explain the fact of relatively large fluctuations in these mutually interrelated industries. Although correlated, why should they experience such large persisting swings in general demand for the aggregate of their products? It is to these general questions—the interconnection and the size and duration of fluctuations in output and employment in general in the economy—that the next few chapters are devoted. Several useful concepts for that investigation—national income and its components—will be presented in the next chapter, to be followed by a framework for organizing the analysis of the factors leading to fluctuations in wealth, income, money, employment, prices, and production.

Questions

1. How would you define "unemployed resources"? Does it apply to both people and physical goods?

2. How useful is the following definition of an unemployed person: "A person not now at work but seeking work"?

3. "Mass unemployment exists because there simply are no jobs available." True or false?

4. You are employed now at $2 an hour. Your employer says he must drop you because of poor business unless you are willing to take a wage cut to $1.50. If you refuse, why did you refuse—in view of the fact that employment at $1.50 is certainly better than no work at all?

5. How long and how much do you think it will cost you to search out all employment opportunities for students in your college area? Would you take the first job offered? How many would you search out for comparison before you took a job as an employee? Or before you went to an employment agency?

6. It has been estimated that carrying a spare tire on automobiles costs the public about $150,000,000 or about $5 per year per car. Is this a wasted, idle resource? What do you think it would cost if that cost were cut to zero by not carrying spare tires at all? Do you think it would be cheaper to make tires more durable and to devote more resources to handling emergency "flats"? What evidence can you cite?

7. You are planning to build an apartment with eight units. You are told you can add a ninth unit for an extra cost of $10,000; and, if the extra unit is occupied all the time, it will be worth $15,000. If occupied three fourths of the time, it will be a breakeven proposition.

a. Would you then consider building more apartments than you could expect to keep always rented?

b. Would you consider that apartment to be unemployed when not occupied?

c. Would you consider every unemployed person as a "waste"?

d. Why?

e. Is there any distinction between unfortunate and wasteful?

8. a. Can you make an estimate of the fraction of your wealth tied up in resources designed to ease the consequences of your own unforeseeable changing demands or circumstances?

b. How about the amount of money you hold; items in the medicine cabinet; waiting time for a haircut in the barber shop; food kept at home in the refrigerator, freezer, and in canned goods: Are these idle, unemployed resources?

9. On the average, the cost increment of each extra job investigated increases. Also, on the average, the gain in wages from another job investigated diminishes. If these two propositions are true, then what must be the relation between the increment of gain and the increment of cost in order to conclude that it will pay to take the first job investigated?

10. Employment agencies charge about 50–60 percent of one month's salary for their services for jobs paying about $400 per month. For jobs paying about $800, the fee is one month's salary. If this is paid to the employment agency by the employer, does it mean the employer bears the costs? Do you think this fee is too large? Why?

11. a. What different kinds of unemployment (with respect to why unemployment exists) do you think it is relevant to distinguish?

b. Why?

12. Suppose the daily sales of each of fifty firms are determined by a process simulated by the turn of a roulette wheel with numbers from 0 through 30. Further, suppose that the firm will on the next day seek to hire as many employees as the sales of the preceding day. Thus, if sales are 20 on the first day, the firm will seek to hire twenty people on the second day—given the wages of $25 per person per day. If there were fifty firms, the average number of employed people would be $50 \times 15 = 45$.

a. Would that employment rate stay constant day after day despite the independent additive random process for determining the number of employees demanded at that wage rate?

b. If those who were laid off by one employer took a day to select a new job, would there always be some unemployed?

c. Would there always be some unfilled vacancies?

d. Would these be equal to each other?

e. What would happen to the number of job seekers and to the number of vacancies if the top five numbers on the roulette wheels were erased?

f. What would happen if all the numbers had been increased by 5?

g. The change from day to day in the totals of the fifty firms, with an unchanged roulette wheel, and the change from day to day when the roulette wheel is changed are two different kinds of changes. Which is the change that is consistent with the independent additive random fluctuations?

h. Which would correspond to a correlated decrease in general aggregate market demand for goods?

i. What could cause a general aggregate decrease?

j. How quickly do you think a person would detect the occurrence of a general demand change?

k. What does all this have to do with the real world?

32

NATIONAL INCOME: COMPOSITION AND MEASUREMENT

In the preceding chapter, "general" or "aggregate" demand changes were seen to affect the total output of the community. In short, we are now concerned with "national income": what it is and how it may be measured, how it has fluctuated over time, and how it may be affected by governmental fiscal and monetary policies.

Basic Theme and First Approximation

Money national *income* created over a time period is the market value of real national *output* during that period. That is, money national income *is* spending on domestic output. Put a bit more fully, money national income is equal to, and consists of, *spending* (or the receipt of spending) on *domestic current final output.*

Factors of production (otherwise known as agents, inputs, and resources) produce things; the things are sold, actually or in effect; payment is made by the buyers and received by the sellers; the money received is money income. The *real* income of the community is the basis for the standard of living and derives from *real* output, but the mass of variegated output can best be measured in *money* terms and distributed through *money* flows. And, in the "circular-flow" expenditures, *money* income stems from *spending* on the output.

We have spoken of real output, which is the real income of the community, and spending on output, which provides (and, indeed, is) money income. We shall see, shortly and briefly, that the collectors of such data —the national-income accountants and statisticians—generally speak of "product" rather than "output" (gross national product, net national product); and they have a number of "income" measures (national income, personal income, disposable income), none of which is identical to the product categories. Do not be dismayed, at least do not be overwhelmed, by the busyness, ingenuity, and arbitrariness of the accountants and statisticians. Our main focus in this section will be on *money income*. Our dominant theme, therefore, will relate to the volume of, and fluctuations in, *aggregate spending on output*.

Gross National Product

Over a period of time (say, a year), an economy produces a collection of goods and services. Whether or not each item produced is actually sold in the period (for some probably will be held in inventory at the close of the period), everything in this heterogeneous bundle has a salable market price, so that we can measure the total flow of output in dollar terms. The market value of the aggregate domestic final output may be called gross national product (*GNP*).

We are here interested in the *nation's* aggregate economic activity—income, output, employment; so we will consider all spending on *domestic* output. This includes spending by foreigners ("exports") on home production; by contrast, spending by domestic residents on foreign-produced goods ("imports") contributes to foreign, not domestic, money income. (Does it follow that exports are "good" and imports are "bad"?)

We refer to spending on "current" output simply to indicate that we are analyzing production, income generation, and income disposal in some finite period of time or as a current rate of income. The usual income-accounting period is one year, but no law precludes shorter or longer periods, and, indeed, data is commonly presented on a quarterly (i.e., three-month) basis.

And our concern is with "final output." We are dealing with *production* and *income*, not with *all market transactions*. *All* transactions include, for one thing, inter-firm buying and selling of "intermediate," as opposed to "final," outputs. Final outputs are not resold: they are purchased by their final user, whether an individual (consumer goods) or a business firm (investment, or capital, goods); intermediate products are resold in some form. For example, steel bought from U.S. Steel by General Motors is not thereby bought by the final user, for General Motors now resells the steel as embodied in automobiles; the purchase is, indeed, a market transaction, but it is not a "final" transaction. In measuring the national output, we must not "double count" by including intermediate products: to add together the total output of U.S. Steel and of General Motors would mean counting the value of steel twice. That is, the market value of General Motors' merchandise is not attributable completely to the productive activity of General Motors, for some of the inputs utilized by General Motors were the outputs of U.S. Steel and other suppliers. Similarly, U.S. Steel bought supplies from still other firms. Each firm along the line buys some inputs from others and then adds to the value of those inputs. The national output is, then, the sum of the *values added* by all of the firms.[1]

All transactions include, for another thing, buying and selling not immediately associated with, or a reflection of, "productive activity" at all. Perhaps the stock market provides the most obvious illustration. If, in a burst of reckless speculation, we purchase a share of common stock of American Telephone and Telegraph, the transaction simply shifts ownership of *already existing* wealth. Typically, the stock is bought not as issued immediately by A.T.&T., but from another individual; the stock probably was issued by the corporation long ago, and A.T.&T. does not obtain funds from this current purchase. Even the purchase of stock directly from the corporation does not in itself contribute to *GNP*. A.T.&T. may later spend the proceeds to obtain use of real resources. But the sale of a share of stock for money is simply a "financial" transaction (rather than genuine "investment," as we shall use the term), involving the shuffling around of claims—A.T.&T. obtaining a monetary asset and the other party obtaining a nonmonetary (corporate-ownership) claim. Similarly, the buying and selling of used cars and old houses does not constitute an addition to the flow of national output.[2] To be sure, presumably both parties to the transaction have moved to positions of asset holding which they respectively prefer. The transaction is, therefore, productive of utility, which is the ultimate criterion; but to the national-income accountant, the shifting of claims to *existing* wealth, as opposed to the creation of additional wealth, is nothing more—indeed, it is less—than neighbors taking in each other's washing.[3]

This stream of output—this summation of final outputs, or of values added —is, when valued in terms of market prices, *GNP*. *GNP* thus is the sum of the products of (a) the quantities of all the goods produced by the nation's resources during the time period (b) multiplied by the prices of the respective

[1] Consider an arithmetic illustration. A farmer producers wheat at a zero money cost and sells it to a miller for 5 cents; the miller works the wheat into flour, which he sells to a baker for 9 cents; the baker uses the flour to produce bread, which is sold to a customer for 15 cents. The value of the final *output*, which is the sum of all the *values added* by the respective producers and is measured by the consumer's expenditure, is 15 cents; also, 15 cents is the total of *incomes* earned by the value-adders: the farmer receives income of 5 cents, the miller receives $9 - 5 = 4$ cents, and the baker receives $15 - 9 = 6$ cents. While expenditure on final output is 15 cents, expenditures in *all* transactions, including the buying and selling of "intermediate" products in inter-firm transactions, is $5 + 9 + 15 = 29$ cents.

[2] There may be salesmen or lawyers or others who render services in connection with the transaction, and these services are part of the economy's output stream, their value contributing to *GNP*. But the value of the old asset itself is not included in current *GNP*.

[3] If person *A* buys a share of A.T.&T. from person *B*, presumably they both feel that they have gained, but *GNP* does not rise. By contrast, if *A* washes *B*'s clothes and *B* washes *A*'s clothes, it could be that neither gains utility (they might even prefer washing their own clothes, so working for each other diminishes utility for each); but *GNP* rises, for the market transaction is counted in *GNP*, and "housewifely" activities (such as washing the family's clothes) are not.

goods. Thus, $GNP = PQ$, where $PQ = p_1q_1 + p_2q_2 + \ldots$, with p_1q_1 being price times quantity for commodity 1 and similarly for the other commodities designated by numerical subscripts. While it is convenient and suggestive to refer to P and Q respectively as "the price level" and "output," more accurately, as we shall explore below, P is the "implicit price index" (or "price deflator"), and Q is "*GNP* in constant dollars (prices)." Obviously, *GNP* of one period may be different from *GNP* of an earlier period, because either the physical collection of production has changed or because at least some prices have changed; actually, we may be sure that over any substantial (or even perceptible) period there have been both kinds of change. Both of these variables, outputs and prices, give difficult problems (and employment) to the keepers of the national-income records.[4]

Changes in the output stream can stem from changes in the "proportionate" composition of the stream. Is basket *A*, consisting of 5 trucks, 40,000 haircuts, and 100,000 toothpicks, bigger or smaller than basket *B*, made up of 6 trucks, 1,000 haircuts, and 89,000 toothpicks? Or there may be a change in the "absolute" composition. How does basket *A* or *B* compare with basket *C*, which contains 4 trucks, 41,000 haircuts, and 50 *radios?* In both these cases, we obviously have a problem of *weighting* the respective components; and there are alternative methods of weighting. Or, still more subtly, there may be a significant change, especially over longer and longer time periods, in the "quality" composition. Compare basket *A* of 1934 with basket *D* of 1964. Basket *D*, like *A*, contains 5 trucks, 40,000 haircuts, and 100,000 toothpicks; but suppose that 1964 trucks are better than 1934 trucks, 1964 haircuts are worse, and toothpicks in the two years are indistinguishable. We can rely on the accountants and the statisticians in the back room to come up with *GNP* figures for 1934 and 1964. But what do the figures measure? Even if prices are the same for all commodities in the two years, what would a larger figure for 1964 mean? That the 1964 basket is "better"? Hard-headed number counters are likely to shy away from an evaluation smacking of subjectiveness. Do the figures show clearly even that the 1964 basket is

[4] It is approximately the case that a percentage change in a product (*GNP*) equals the sum of the percentage changes of the respective factors (P and Q):

$$\begin{aligned} GNP &= PQ, \\ GNP + \Delta GNP &= (P + \Delta P)(Q + \Delta Q), \\ \Delta GNP &= (P + \Delta P)(Q + \Delta Q) - PQ, \\ &= Q\Delta P + P\Delta Q + \Delta P\Delta Q, \\ \frac{\Delta GNP}{GNP} &= \frac{Q\Delta P}{PQ} + \frac{P\Delta Q}{PQ} + \frac{\Delta P\Delta Q}{PQ}, \\ &= \frac{\Delta P}{P} + \frac{\Delta Q}{Q} + \frac{\Delta P\Delta Q}{PQ}. \end{aligned}$$

Generally (unless the time period is very substantial), changes in P and in Q are sufficiently small that the last term on the right side $\left(\frac{\Delta P\Delta Q}{PQ}\right)$ can be conveniently dropped for purposes of approximation.

"bigger"? When one component of the 1964 basket is worse than the corresponding component of the 1934 basket and another component is better, we again have a weighting problem, a particularly delicate one.

In addition to the quantitative and qualitative changes in composition of the output stream, there are changes over time in the price tags on the goods. *GNP* is sometimes presented in terms of "current" dollar prices; for instance, 1934 output is measured in 1934 prices, and 1964 output is measured in 1964 prices. But in an effort to measure *output* (i.e., real) changes rather than simply *value* (i.e., price) changes, *GNP* may be calculated in terms of "constant" price dollars: both 1934 and 1964 outputs are weighted by prices of a single year—which may be 1934, 1964, or some other year. (The use of "constant" price calculations is to make allowance for price changes and thereby to provide a measure of physical output. But in the case of trucks, comparing 1934 and 1964, how much allowance for price changes should be made? Indeed, in what *direction* should the allowance be made? Is $9,000 for a 1964 truck more or less—and by how much—than $3,500 for a 1934 truck?)

We thus have two types of *GNP* measures: (a) we may derive the *GNP* value for a given year by using prices of that *same* year, which may be called *GNP* in "current" dollars (GNP_{cur}), or (b) we may compute *GNP* for a given year by weighting with prices of some *other* year, which is *GNP* in "constant" dollars as of some base period (GNP_{con}). In short, with subscripts indicating the years, we have:

$$P_{64} \times Q_{64} = GNP_{cur64},$$
$$P_{34} \times Q_{64} = GNP_{con64}.$$

Now, divide the first equation by the second:

$$\frac{P_{64}Q_{64}}{P_{34}Q_{64}} = \frac{GNP_{cur64},}{GNP_{con64}}$$

$$\frac{P_{64}}{P_{34}} = \frac{GNP_{cur64}.}{GNP_{con64}}$$

Let the ratio of the current price level to the price level of the base period, which equals the ratio of current-dollar *GNP* to constant-dollar *GNP*, be designated as *P*. Thus:

$$\frac{P_{64}}{P_{34}} = P = \frac{GNP_{cur64},}{GNP_{con64}}$$

and:

$$P(GNP_{con64}) = GNP_{cur64},$$

that is, *GNP* in current dollars equals GPN_{con} (which is an indicator of real output) weighted by *P* (which is a price indicator). The price ratio, *P*, is the "price index" in columns 4 and 5 of Table 32–1 and, as we have noted earlier, is often referred to as the "implicit price index" or "*GNP* price deflator." The table gives price indices of two different base years, 1929 and 1954, along with two corresponding sets of calculations of *GNP* in constant dollars.[5]

The foregoing discussion of temporal changes in the composition of output and in prices does not exhaust the difficulties in using *GNP* as a measure of the flow of final goods and services. Awareness of the existence of difficulties and deficiencies should make us reluctant to say more than can reasonably be said. But, inadequate though *GNP* is as a measure, one can reasonably suppose that, for example, a fall from $104,000,000,000 in 1929 to $56,000,000,000 in 1933 reflects an actual great decline—probably in the neighborhood of 50 percent—in aggregate spending on final output; and a fall, in the same period, from $104,-000,000,000 to $74,000,000,000 in 1929 prices would scarcely be camouflage of an *increase* in the physical volume of output.

GNP, OUTPUT, EMPLOYMENT, AND PRICES

The young scholar may feel a bit uneasy about the promised concentration on spending on output. Even granted that the emphasis on spending may be, in one way or another, most convenient, is not the convenience purchased

[5] To elucidate the basic notion that $GNP = PQ$, consider a basket of two goods, commodities 1 and 2, distinguished by subscripts; and we have base period o and current period t, indicated by superscripts. For example, p_1^o is the price of commodity 1 in period o. And $p_1^o q_1^t$ is the quantity of commodity 1 in period t multiplied by the price in period o. Now, for the two commodities together, $p_1^o q_1^t + p_2^o q_2^t = GNP_{con} = Q$.

Next, p_1^t/p_1^o is a "price relative" for commodity 1, comparing the price in the current period with the price in the base period. If we weight the constant-dollar values of the respective commodities by their price ratios, we convert GNP_{con} into GNP_{cur}; i.e.,

$$GNP_{cur} = \left(\frac{p_1^t}{p_1^o}\right) p_1^o q_1^t + \left(\frac{p_2^t}{p_2^o}\right) p_2^o q_2^t.$$

Since, as indicated in the text, the price deflator $P = GNP_{cur}/GNP_{con}$, we have:

$$P = \frac{\left(\frac{p_1^t}{p_1^o}\right) p_1^o q_1^t + \left(\frac{p_2^t}{p_2^o}\right) p_2^o q_2^t}{p_1^o q_1^t + p_2^o q_2^t}.$$

In light of this expression, we can say that P is the sum of the price ratios as weighted according to expenditures (in constant dollars) on the respective goods as proportions of total expenditures (in constant dollars).

Finally, multiplying the aggregate price and quantity variables together:

$$\begin{aligned} PQ &= \frac{\left(\frac{p_1^t}{p_1^o}\right) p_1^o q_1^t + \left(\frac{p_2^t}{p_2^o}\right) p_2^o q_2^t}{p_1^o q_1^t + p_2^o q_2^t} (p_1^o q_1^t + p_2^o q_2^t), \\ &= \left(\frac{p_1^t}{p_1^o}\right) p_1^o q_1^t + \left(\frac{p_2^t}{p_2^o}\right) p_2^o q_2^t, \\ &= p_1^t q_1^t + p_2^t q_2^t, \end{aligned}$$

which is just what we said it was!

at a very high price? After all, more "basic" than mere *spending* is the real *output* itself and the *employment* of resources (particularly labor). Also, changes in the *price level*—the question of inflation and deflation—may be deemed more vital than just the dollar size of *GNP*.

How many of these more interesting things do we miss in focusing on spending? How do output, employment, and prices fluctuate in comparison to changes in *GNP*? Table 32–1 gives annual data for the period beginning 1919. In Table 32–2, comparisons are made between pairs of these variables. The correlation is simply in terms of the *direction* of change. If each of the variables of a pair moves in the same direction (up *or* down), a + is entered in the table; if the changes are inverse, rather than direct, there is a —; a 0 indicates that one of the variables did not change.

There are 43 year-to-year rows. *GNP and real output* (given by *GNP* in "constant dollars" in columns 2 and 3 in Table 32–1) moved in the same direction, as did *employment and output,* over 85 percent of the time. *GNP and employment* moved in the same direction nearly 90 percent of the time; *GNP and the price level,* almost 85 percent; and *output and the price level,* over 75 percent. So, over a period approaching half a century, encompassing peace and war, boom and depression, inflation and deflation, a rise (fall) in *GNP*, expressed in current dollars, was accompanied by a rise (fall) in employment and in output in the vast bulk of the cases and by a rise (fall) in the price level in a very large majority of cases; also employment and output regularly moved in the same direction, as did output and the price level about three fourths of the time.

For the 17 cases (out of 123) in the first three columns in which there is either a — or a 0, the percentage change, if any, in *GNP* is noted in parentheses. In 11 of the 17, *GNP* changed by 1.7 percent or less. To put it the other way around, in only six instances did *GNP* change substantially when output or employment or prices failed to move in the same direction. In only one case, 1921–22, did all three of these variables fail to move in the same direction as did *GNP*—and in that case, *GNP* itself was unchanged. In only two cases, 1944–45 and 1957–58, did two of the variables move inversely to *GNP*.

Comparing only the *directions* of change does not give a very refined measure of correlation. Even when two variables move in the same direction in two periods, the relative *proportions* of change may differ considerably. In Table 32–3, two six-year periods are reviewed. 1933 was, according to almost any index, the bottom of the Great Depression. Beginning with substantial unemployment, one would normally expect that a large increase in *GNP* would have proportionately greater impact on output and employment than on prices; and, partly because the average number of hours worked per week was unusually low, one would expect also that output would rise even faster than employment. This is the picture suggested by the figures: a 63 percent increase in *GNP* was accompanied by a 50 percent rise in output, an 18 percent rise in employment, and only a 9 percent rise in the price level.

Table 32–1

PRICES, PRODUCT, AND EMPLOYMENT, 1919–62

	GNP: Current Prices (Billions of dollars)	*GNP:* 1929 Prices	*GNP:* 1954 Prices	Price Index: 1929 = 100	Price Index: 1954 = 100	Employed (000)	Unemployed: % of Civilian Labor Force
	(1)	(2)	(3)	(4)	(5)	(6)	(7)
1919	78.9	74.2		106		41304	2.3
1920	88.9	73.3		121		41750	4.0
1921	74.0	71.6		103		42101	11.9
1922	74.0	75.8		98		42368	7.6
1923	86.1	85.8		100		43125	3.2
1924	87.6	88.4		99		44364	5.5
1925	91.3	90.5		100.8		45000	4.0
1926	97.7	96.4		101.3		46316	1.9
1927	96.3	97.3		99		46098	4.1
1928	98.2	98.5		99.7		47273	4.4
1929	104.4	104.4	181.8	100	57.4	47630	3.2
1930	91.1	95.1	164.5	96	55.4	45480	8.7
1931	76.3	89.5	153.0	85	49.9	42400	15.9
1932	58.5	76.4	130.1	77	45.0	38940	23.6
1933	56.0	74.2	126.6	75	44.2	38760	24.9
1934	65.0	80.8	138.5	80	46.9	40890	21.7
1935	72.5	91.4	152.9	79	47.4	42260	20.1
1936	82.7	100.9	173.3	82	47.7	44410	16.9
1937	90.8	109.1	183.3	83.2	49.5	46300	14.3
1938	85.2	103.2	175.1	82.6	48.7	44220	19.0
1939	91.1	111.0	189.3	82.1	48.1	45750	17.2
1940	100.6	121.0	205.8	83	48.9	47520	14.6
1941	125.8	138.7	238.1	91	52.8	50350	9.9
1942	159.1	154.7	266.9	103	59.6	53750	4.7
1943	192.5	170.2	296.7	113	64.9	54470	1.9
1944	211.4	183.6	317.9	115	66.5	53960	1.2
1945	213.6	180.9	314.0	118	68.0	52820	1.9
1946	210.7		282.5		74.6	55250	3.9
1947	234.3		282.3		83.0	58027	3.6

Table 32–1—Continued

PRICES, PRODUCT, AND EMPLOYMENT, 1919–62

	GNP: Current Prices (Billions of dollars)	*GNP:* 1929 Prices (Billions of dollars)	*GNP:* 1954 Prices (Billions of dollars)	Price Index: 1929 = 100	Price Index: 1954 = 100	Employed (000)	Unemployed: % of Civilian Labor Force
	(1)	(2)	(3)	(4)	(5)	(6)	(7)
1948	259.4		293.1		88.5	59378	3.4
1949	258.1		292.7		88.2	58710	5.5
1950	284.6		318.1		89.5	59957	5.0
1951	329.0		341.8		96.2	61005	3.0
1952	347.0		353.5		98.1	61293	2.7
1953	365.4		369.0		99.0	62213	2.5
1954	363.1		363.1		100.0	61238	5.0
1955	397.5		392.7		101.2	63193	4.0
1956	419.2		400.9		104.6	64979	3.8
1957	442.8		408.6		108.4	65011	4.3
1958	444.5		401.3		110.8	63966	6.8
1959	482.7		428.6		112.6	65581	5.5
1960	502.6		439.9		114.2	66681	5.6
1961	518.2		447.7		115.7	66796	6.7
1962	554.9		474.8		116.9	67846	5.6

SOURCES

Column 1: 1919–1957, U.S. Bureau of the Census, *Historical Statistics of the United States, Colonial Times to 1957* (Washington, D.C., 1960), p. 139.
1958–1962, Department of Commerce, *Survey of Current Business,* July 1963, p. 12.

Column 2: *Historical Statistics,* p. 139.

Column 3: 1929–1957, Department of Commerce, *U.S. Income and Output* (Washington, D.C., 1958), pp. 118–19.
1958–1962, *Survey of Current Business,* July 1963, p. 14.

Column 4: *Historical Statistics,* p. 139. Calculations to first decimal place in selected years made on basis of data in columns 1 and 2.

Column 5: 1929–1957, *Income and Output,* pp. 220–221.
1958–1962, *Survey of Current Business,* July 1963, p. 14.

Column 6: 1919–1928, calculated on basis of column 7 and unemployment data in *Historical Statistics,* p. 73.
1929–1957, *Historical Statistics,* p. 70.
1958–1962, Board of Governors, *Federal Reserve Bulletin,* October 1963, p. 1452.

Column 7: 1919–1957, *Historical Statistics,* p. 73.
1958–1962, *Federal Reserve Bulletin,* October 1963, p. 1452.

Table 32–2

RELATED CHANGES IN PRICES, PRODUCT, AND EMPLOYMENT, 1919–62

	GNP and Employment	*GNP* and Output	*GNP* and Price Level	Employment and Output	Output and Price Level
1919–20	+	– (+13%)	+	–	–
1920–21	– (–17%)	+	+	–	+
1921–22	0 (0%)	0 (0%)	0 (0%)	+	–
1922–23	+	+	+	+	+
1923–24	+	+	– (+1.7%)	+	+
1924–25	+	+	+	+	+
1925–26	+	+	+	+	+
1926–27	+	– (–1.4%)	+	–	–
1927–28	+	+	+	+	+
1928–29	+	+	+	+	+
1929–30	+	+	+	+	+
1930–31	+	+	+	+	+
1931–32	+	+	+	+	+
1932–33	+	+	+	+	+
1933–34	+	+	+	+	+
1934–35	+	+	0* (+12%)	+	–
1935–36	+	+	+	+	+
1936–37	+	+	+	+	+
1937–38	+	+	+	+	+
1938–39	+	+	– (+7%)	+	–
1939–40	+	+	+	+	+
1940–41	+	+	+	+	+
1941–42	+	+	+	+	+
1942–43	+	+	+	+	+
1943–44	– (+10%)	+	+	–	+
1944–45	– (+1%)	– (+1%)	+	+	–
1945–46	+	+	– (–1.4%)	–	–
1946–47	+	– (+11%)	+	–	–
1947–48	+	+	+	+	+
1948–49	+	+	+	+	+
1949–50	+	+	+	+	+
1950–51	+	+	+	+	+

Table 32-2—Continued

RELATED CHANGES IN PRICES, PRODUCT, AND EMPLOYMENT, 1919–62

	GNP and Employment	*GNP* and Output	*GNP* and Price Level	Employment and Output	Output and Price Level
1951–52	+	+	+	+	+
1952–53	+	+	+	+	+
1953–54	+	+	− (−.6%)	+	−
1954–55	+	+	+	+	+
1955–56	+	+	+	+	+
1956–57	+	+	+	+	+
1957–58	− (+.4%)	− (+.4%)	+	+	−
1958–59	+	+	+	+	+
1959–60	+	+	+	+	+
1960–61	+	+	+	+	+
1961–62	+	+	+	+	+

* Using 1929 as the base, the price level fell slightly; using 1954, it rose minutely. The table compromises by indicating "no change."

Compared to 1933, 1954 was rather a different sort of year. The rate of unemployment was appreciably greater than in the preceding three years and somewhat higher than in the three following years. But 5 percent unemployment (in 1954) is smaller than 25 percent (in 1933). The proportionate rise in *GNP* was considerably less than in 1954–60 than in 1933–39; and it is, therefore, not surprising that output and employment also rose less in the later period. But the interesting point is that output and employment in 1954–60 rose at a slower pace *relative to GNP;* most notably, the proportionate increase in output is 79 percent of the proportionate increase in *GNP* for 1933–39 and only 54 percent for 1954–60. By contrast, in 1954–60, the price level actually rose appreciably more than in 1933–39, despite the relatively small expansion of *GNP*.

GNP, NNP, AND ABSORPTION

Only by coincidence will *GNP* be exactly equal to the goods and services currently available to, and utilized by, the national community for its consumption and investment purposes. We may designate by *A* the goods and services

Table 32-3

CHANGES IN PRICES, PRODUCT, AND EMPLOYMENT, 1933–39 AND 1954–60

	GNP: % Change	Output: % Change	Output/ *GNP*	Employment: % Change	Employment/ *GNP*	Prices: % Change	Prices/ *GNP*
1933–39	63	50	79	18	29	9	14
1954–60	39	21	54	9	23	14	36

actually "absorbed." *GNP* is the measure of total *current* production; *A* represents *current* use of *current and past* production.

One reason for discrepancy between *GNP* and *A* is that the national economy is a member of the world economy. *GNP* is larger than *A* if the nation sells, lends, and gives more output to foreigners than it acquires from abroad, for output is then greater than the quantity of goods and services domestically available; a net inflow of goods and services from foreigners makes *A* larger than *GNP*. (Does this consideration alter your earlier view of the "goodness" and "badness" of imports and exports?)

Even if we envisage a "closed" economy (one not engaging in international trade and finance), there will be a difference between current *gross output* and *net output,* because of "capital consumption." There will be some wearing out of the nation's equipment and plant during the period. Some machinery may be junked and not replaced. Presumably, part of the current output will be devoted to repairing and replacing (some) capital goods. Whatever is done (if anything) to maintain the capital which existed at the start of the period, the depreciation itself means that net output is less than gross output. We can define so-called net national product (*NNP*) as equal to *GNP* minus capital consumption.

But neither gross nor net *output* is necessarily equal to *absorption* even for a closed economy. An economy could, for some time, absorb during a period in which *GNP* is *zero* and *NNP* is either *zero* or *negative*. If there is no current flow of output, *GNP* equals 0, but the nation could absorb previously accumulated inventories and capital. Absorption without production necessitates the drawing down of inventories or the depreciation of capital or both (e.g., automobile travel would eat into inventories of gasoline and wear out both vehicles and highways). The *reduction of inventories* is not included by the statisticians in "capital consumption," so the non-producing economy which lives off inventories would have $GNP = NNP = 0$ and $A > 0$. And the nonproducing economy which *depreciates capital* would have $GNP = 0$, $NNP < 0$, and $A > 0$.

Thus, absorption is equal to output modified by inventory reductions,[6] depreciation of capital, and the foreign-trade balance:

$$A = NNP + \text{capital consumption} + \text{inventory decrease} + \text{imports} - \text{exports}$$
$$= GNP + \text{inventory decrease} + \text{imports} - \text{exports}.$$

NATIONAL INCOME, PERSONAL INCOME, AND DISPOSABLE INCOME

We have seen that *GNP* is the market value of the final *total* output produced by the economy over a time period and that *NNP* is the market value of the *net* output, making (probably quite inaccurate) allowance for depreciation and capital consumption.

Three further measures of "aggregate economic activity"—concentrating on *income* rather than *output*—are commonly used. National income (*NI*) consists of the total earnings of the productive agents of the economy: wages and salaries, rents, profits, and interest. *NI*, which is actually disbursed to workers and property holders, is smaller than *NNP;* for some of the spending on *NNP* goes immediately to the government in the form of "indirect business taxes" and thus is not income for anyone. "Indirect business taxes" are business taxes not based upon profits, the chief ones being federal excise (especially liquor and tobacco) taxes, state sales (especially general and gasoline) taxes, and local property taxes. Most conspicuously excluded are personal-income and corporate-profits taxes; being taxes on income, they are considered to be part of income, first disbursed to income recipients and then collected by government.

Personal income (*PI*) is the income which finally finds its way to individuals (and to nonprofit institutions and to private funds). Some portions of *NI* are not in *PI*: corporate profits which are not distributed, corporate-profits taxes, and contributions for social insurance. However, *PI* does include some things that are not part of *NI*: net interest paid by government, and government and business transfer payments (i.e., payments, such as veterans' benefits, *not* made in compensation for current productive activity).

Not all of *PI* is available for private expenditure, for personal taxes must be paid. What remains of *PI* after payment of such taxes is disposable personal income (*DI*)—some of which is expended on personal consumption and the rest of which is, by definition, saved.

Figure 32–1 illustrates the relations among the five "product" and "income" measures. *GNP* is subdivided into the four output (or purchase) categories—discussed below—of personal-consumption expenditures, private domestic investment, net exports of goods and services, and government purchases, as well as

[6] Inventory *increases* are not listed separately, for they form a part of current output and are thereby included in *NNP* and *GNP*; that is, the community absorbs part of its current production by investing it in larger inventories.

noting *GNP* as equal to *NNP* plus capital-consumption allowances. In addition, *NI* is subdivided into the four major income categories, with wages and salaries and supplements to them making up over 70 percent of the total and proprietors' income plus corporate profits being more than 20 percent. The data, in billions of dollars, are for 1962.

Henceforth, when we consider national income, we shall not worry much about the five distinctions between the different measures. When reference is made to "national income," we shall have in mind *GNP* or *NNP*. (For our purposes, there is no point in fretting about whether *GNP* or *NNP* is most appropriate. Especially when dealing with *changes*, there is little basis for choosing; for the ratio *NNP/GNP* changes only minutely from year to year, ranging from .87 to .95 since 1929 and from .91 to .95 since 1946.) In our later discussion of fiscal policy, we shall make use of "disposable income," defined simply as "national income" minus "tax collections." However, we shall make no further mention of the national-income accounting categories of *NI* and *PI*; aside from expositional comprehensiveness, the only excuse for noting them at all is that they are sometimes referred to on financial pages of newspapers and the like.

GNP AND DOMESTIC SPENDING

Thus far we have looked mainly at the *output* flow and various categories of *income distribution*. But national-income accounting, like national-income theory, can be approached from the view of *spending* on output.

GNP and *NNP* have a market value because of spending (both literal spending in market purchases and inventory valuation of things not yet sold) on output. The spending can be broken down into categories. Three of these components are "domestic": consumption (C), investment—including changes in inventories (I), and government expenditures (G); one is "foreign": exports (X). If I is gross investment, inclusive of capital consumption, the sum of C, I, G, and X is *GNP;* if I is net investment, the sum is *NNP*. In the discussion to follow, we shall not make use of the distinction. Instead, we shall speak of the sum of the spending categories as adding up to "national income," designated by Y. Thus:

$$Y = C + I + G + X, \text{ from the standpoint of income } \textit{creation}.$$

The (money) income thus generated by spending is allocated in various ways. Suppose momentarily that government and foreign trade are omitted from the model: then there is no G and X, nor would there be tax collections (T) and imports (M). In that case, income is conceived to be disposed of in two ways: some is spent on consumption, and the rest is *not* spent on consumption. Income which is not consumed—whether it goes into the sugar bowl, the bank, or

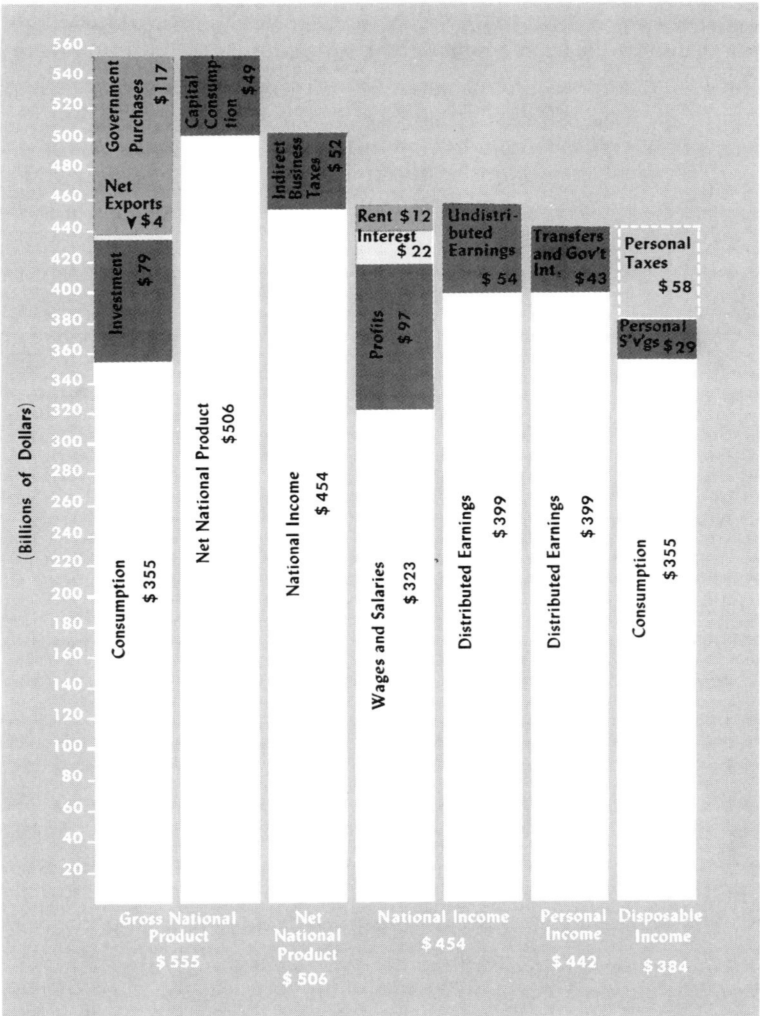

FIGURE 32–1. The national-income accounts, 1962.

the purchase of A.T.&T. stock—is "saved." If now we bring government and foreign trade back into the picture, the definition of saving must be modified: saving (S) is income which is not spent on domestic consumption goods (C) *or* taxes (T) *or* imports (M). Thus:

$Y = C + S + T + M$, from the standpoint of income *disposal.*

The national-income-data collectors provide us with figures for the income-*creation* equation, in a somewhat different form. For 1962, we have (in billions of dollars):

Personal-consumption expenditures		355.4
Gross private domestic investment		78.8
Government purchases of goods and services		117.0
Net exports of goods and services		3.8
Exports	28.9	
Imports	25.1	
GNP		555.0

Put into equational form, we can write:

$$\begin{array}{ccccccccc} Y & = & C & + & I & + & G & + & (X-M) \\ 555.0 & = & 355.4 & + & 78.8 & + & 117.0 & + & 3.8 \end{array}$$

And by appropriate selection and rearrangement of available data, as summarized in Table 32–4 we can write the income-*disposal* equation with 1962 figures.

$$\begin{array}{ccccccc} Y & = & C & + & S & + & T \\ 555.0 & = & 355.4 & + & 85.0 & + & 114.6 \end{array}$$

But obviously a change has been made in the equations; here we have subtracted M from both equations, eliminating it from the income-disposal equation and converting X into $(X—M)$ in the income-creation equation. *Conceptually,* X (not *net* X) is what we want in the income-creation equation, for in that equation we want to include only the components of spending on *domestic output.* X is one of the components, and M is not; X is one of the "creators" or "generators" of domestic income; X is an "*injection* into the domestic income stream." By contrast, M is spending on *foreign* output of domestic income already created; it is a "*leakage* (to foreigners) out of the income stream," and it should appear (only) in the income-disposal equation.

Then why did we modify, in inserting the 1962 data, what is conceptually so clear-cut? The answer is simply that that is the way the dispensers of the data give out the information. Actually, the C, I, G, and X figures announced by the national-income statisticians are misleading for our purposes. For example, the consumption figure we want is, of course, the consumption expenditure on *domestic* goods and services; what we get, however, is the total expenditure on *all* consumption goods and services—including *foreign* output. That is, the C figure of $355,400,000,000 includes consumption imports. Similarly, the I and G figures include import expenditures and thus are larger than the expenditures

Table 32–4

INCOME DISPOSAL, 1962

Consumption	355.4		
Saving		**Taxes**	
Personal saving	29.1	Personal tax and non-tax payments	57.7
Undistributed profits	8.1	Contributions for social insurance	23.9
Inventory valuation adjustment	.2	Corporate-profits tax liability	22.2
Capital consumption allowances	49.4	Indirect business tax and non-tax liability	53.0
	86.8		156.8
Statistical discrepancy	1.8	**Minus:**	
	85.0	Government transfer payments	32.5
		Net interest paid by government	8.0
		Subsidies less current surplus of government enterprises	1.7
			114.6

solely on domestic output. Even the *X* figure of $28,900,000,000 is bloated, for our exports include some imported raw materials, so that not all of the $28,900,000,000 is spent on U.S. output. In short, the import expenditure of $25,100,000,000 has been scattered through *C*, *I*, *G*, and *X*; we must then subtract it in order to leave us with just the spending on domestic output. Aggregate spending, including spending on *foreign* output, is 355.4 + 78.8 + 117.0 + 28.9 = 580.1 billion; by subtracting import expenditures, we have the market value of *domestic* output: 580.1 − 25.1 = 555.0 billion.

With the aid of an assumption, we can insert empirical (as opposed to hypothetical) data into our conceptual equations. Assume—surely contrary, in some degree, to the actual facts—that the import spending, *M*, of $25,100,000,000 is scattered *proportionately* through the *C*, *I*, *G*, and *X* categories. For example, total consumption as a proportion of total spending is 355.4/580.1 = 61.27

percent; on the basis of our assumption, then, 61.27 percent of the import spending is included under C; 61.27 percent of 25.1 is \$15,400,000,000; this consumption-import spending must be subtracted from total consumption spending in order to obtain consumption spending on domestic output: 355.4 — 15.4 = 340.0 billion. I, G, and X are similarly reduced, giving us the income-creation equation:

$$\begin{array}{ccccccccc} Y & = & C & + & I & + & G & + & X \\ 555.0 & = & 340.0 & + & 75.4 & + & 112.0 & + & 27.6 \end{array}$$

M is thus eliminated from the income-creation equation to get domestic income creation; but it must be put back into the income-disposal equation. We use the same C figure in both equations; presumably the tax-collection figure is unchanged; the S figure is adjusted as a residual: [7]

$$\begin{array}{ccccccccc} Y & = & C & + & S & + & T & + & M \\ 555.0 & = & 340.0 & + & 75.3 & + & 114.6 & + & 25.1 \end{array}$$

Finally, reverting back to the form of the income-creation equation utilized by compilers of the data (i.e., $Y = C + I + G + [X - M]$), we may note that in 1962 consumption expenditures made up 64 percent of gross national product, investment was about 14 percent of the total, government purchases were about 21 percent, and net exports were under 1 percent. These proportions have remained remarkably stable since the early 1950s, in contrast to the preceding period back to 1929, as may be determined in Table 32–5. Consumption hit a proportional peak of over 84 percent of *GNP* in 1932 as income fell in the depression at a greater rate than did consumption, and consumption declined to a low of 52 percent of *GNP* in 1943 and 1944 during World War II. Investment has seen wide fluctuations, hitting bottom in 1932 when it was only 1.5 percent of *GNP* and reaching a high of nearly 18 percent in 1950. Government purchases were just over 8 percent of *GNP* in 1929, then rose steadily during the 1930s, reached 46 percent of the total in 1943 and 1944, and fell to a postwar low of 12 percent in 1947 before leveling out in the last dozen years at 20–21 percent. Net exports typically are a minute proportion of *GNP*—which scarcely reflects the total importance of the economy's foreign trade and finance sector, as we

[7] If, as we have supposed, some imports are nonconsumption goods and services, then C cannot be deflated by the entire \$25,100,000,000. Therefore, $S + T$ must fall by the value of non-C imports. But since it is difficult to envisage an "import content" of T, the entire remaining adjustment must be in S. The rationale for reducing S—other than arithmetic convenience—may be illustrated by considering an import of machinery. The value of the machinery was initially included in the \$78,800,000,000 figure for I, but it has now been subtracted in the income-creation equation. This import expenditure is a *nonconsumption disposal* of income; that is, it is a form of *saving*—when M is not listed in the income-disposal equation. Now that M has been moved to its proper place, the S figure is reduced, so that S now represents only the non-C, non-T, and non-M disposal of income.

shall see in due course; after hitting almost 4 percent in 1947, they generally have been less than 1 percent.

National Income or Wealth?

A motive for measuring national income is to find out whether a nation is becoming "better off." And is a nation with a smaller but more rapidly growing national income better off than one with a larger but slower-growing income? Many people apparently think so. First, the question is nonsense. It does not say what is meant by a nation's being "better off." It does not say how one would evaluate changes in situations in which some people in a nation are now "better off" while others are "worse off." Second, even if those questions could be settled, for groups as well as for individuals, it is *not* the *rate of change* of wealth or income that is relevant. It is the *absolute amount* of wealth that provides a measure of economic capabilities.

To illustrate, suppose two young men of 21 years had wealths of $1,000 and $30,000, respectively. At 10 percent interest rates, their annual incomes are $100 and $3,000. Now, suppose the poorer man saves half of his income each year and invests it, while the richer person consumes all his income and keeps his wealth constant. A little calculation on the basis of principles explained in Chapter 15 will indicate that, at 10 percent interest, the poorer man will experience growths of income and of wealth of 5 percent per year, and he will have a wealth of about $30,000 by the time he reaches age 57. If he continues his higher rate of saving, his wealth will then increase beyond that of the formerly richer person. Given that prognosis, which of the two young men would I rather be: the poor one, who will have the rising income stream as he saves more; or the richer one, who will have a constant income which will be surpassed in wealth 36 years later?

The answer is obvious. If I had $30,000 and wanted my wealth to grow, I could save some of my income and still do more than the poor man with $1,000 could have done. The question actually asked two questions: Is it better to be rich *and* to keep a constant wealth? There is no necessity to tie them together. The correct procedure puts the two questions separately. "Is it better to be rich?" "Is it better to have a rising level of wealth?" The answer to the first is, Yes. The answer to the second depends upon what time pattern of consumption you want.

There is a strong temptation to think that the person who is following a pattern of rising wealth is clearly better off—and probably smarter or more energetic or more progressive—than the one who is now richer and only maintaining his wealth. However, the growing one is sacrificing current for future consumption. Is it necessarily "better" to give up consumption now in order to have more in the future? Even though the poorer person ultimately becomes

Table 32–5

GROSS NATIONAL PRODUCT AND ITS COMPONENTS ANNUALLY, 1929–62; SEASONALLY ADJUSTED QUARTERLY AT ANNUAL RATES, 1939–63 (BILLIONS OF DOLLARS)

	Gross National Product	Personal Consumption Expenditures	Gross Private Domestic Investment	Government Purchases	Net Exports
1929	104.4	79.0	16.2	8.5	.8
1930	91.1	71.0	10.3	9.2	.7
1931	76.3	61.3	5.5	9.2	.2
1932	58.5	49.3	.9	8.1	.2
1933	56.0	46.4	1.4	8.0	.2
1934	65.0	51.9	2.9	9.8	.4
1935	72.5	56.3	6.3	10.0	—.1
1936	82.7	62.6	8.4	11.8	—.1
1937	90.8	67.3	11.7	11.7	.1
1938	85.2	64.6	6.7	12.8	1.1
1939	91.1	67.6	9.3	13.3	.9
I	88.8	65.5	9.1	13.5	.7
II	89.1	67.3	7.8	13.4	.6
III	92.6	68.3	10.4	12.9	1.0
IV	93.9	69.2	10.0	13.4	1.2
1940	100.6	71.9	13.2	14.1	1.5
I	97.3	70.1	11.9	13.6	1.8
II	98.5	71.7	11.9	13.4	1.6
III	101.7	72.2	14.6	13.5	1.4
IV	104.9	73.5	14.3	15.8	1.3
1941	125.8	81.9	18.1	24.8	1.1
I	112.5	76.8	15.7	18.8	1.1
II	122.8	81.2	19.5	21.4	.7
III	129.3	84.5	18.2	25.9	.6
IV	138.7	84.9	18.8	32.9	2.1
1942	159.1	89.7	9.9	59.7	—.2
I	141.7	86.4	15.4	39.2	.6
II	153.6	87.8	12.8	53.6	—.6

Table 32–5—Continued

GROSS NATIONAL PRODUCT AND ITS COMPONENTS ANNUALLY, 1929–62; SEASONALLY ADJUSTED QUARTERLY AT ANNUAL RATES, 1939–63 (BILLIONS OF DOLLARS)

	Gross National Product	Personal Consumption Expenditures	Gross Private Domestic Investment	Government Purchases	Net Exports
III	163.6	90.4	4.8	68.2	.2
IV	177.6	94.3	6.4	77.9	—1.0
1943	192.5	100.5	5.6	88.6	—2.2
I	182.6	97.2	1.9	85.1	—1.7
II	191.3	99.9	5.4	88.5	—2.5
III	194.9	101.5	6.9	88.7	—2.2
IV	201.3	103.6	8.2	92.1	—2.7
1944	211.4	109.8	7.1	96.5	—2.1
I	205.6	105.3	8.0	95.0	—2.7
II	209.4	108.4	7.6	96.2	—2.9
III	214.1	111.4	7.0	96.9	—1.2
IV	216.5	114.1	5.9	98.1	—1.6
1945	213.6	121.7	10.4	82.9	—1.4
I	221.2	117.4	8.0	98.6	—2.7
II	223.7	118.8	10.2	97.4	—2.7
III	212.2	122.2	10.7	80.2	—1.0
IV	197.1	128.4	12.9	55.2	.6
1946	210.7	147.1	28.1	30.5	4.9
I	198.0	137.3	22.1	34.9	3.8
II	206.3	143.0	29.0	29.7	4.5
III	217.1	152.7	29.6	28.3	6.5
IV	221.2	155.4	31.8	29.1	4.9
1947	234.3	165.4	31.5	28.4	9.0
I	226.0	159.4	29.8	27.8	9.0
II	230.0	163.9	29.2	27.5	9.4
III	235.6	167.2	29.6	28.8	9.9
IV	245.1	171.2	36.7	29.4	7.9

Table 32–5—Continued

GROSS NATIONAL PRODUCT AND ITS COMPONENTS ANNUALLY, 1929–62; SEASONALLY ADJUSTED QUARTERLY AT ANNUAL RATES, 1939–63 (BILLIONS OF DOLLARS)

	Gross National Product	Personal Consumption Expenditures	Gross Private Domestic Investment	Government Purchases	Net Exports
1948	259.4	178.3	43.1	34.5	3.5
I	249.5	174.7	39.9	30.1	4.8
II	257.7	177.5	43.2	33.7	5.3
III	264.0	180.2	45.2	35.8	2.8
IV	265.9	180.8	43.9	38.2	3.0
1949	258.1	181.2	33.0	40.2	3.8
I	259.8	179.0	36.8	39.5	4.6
II	256.4	181.1	30.8	39.9	4.6
III	258.8	180.5	33.7	40.9	3.7
IV	257.0	184.0	30.6	40.3	2.1
1950	284.6	195.0	50.0	39.0	.6
I	265.8	185.7	39.8	38.4	2.0
II	274.4	189.9	46.9	36.5	1.1
III	293.2	204.4	51.1	38.2	—.6
IV	304.3	200.1	61.4	43.0	—.2
1951	329.0	209.8	56.3	60.5	2.4
I	317.8	211.5	56.9	49.5	—.2
II	326.4	205.5	61.6	57.7	1.7
III	333.8	208.8	56.3	64.9	3.9
IV	338.1	213.4	51.0	69.5	4.2
1952	347.0	219.8	49.9	76.0	1.3
I	341.0	214.6	52.2	71.1	3.1
II	341.3	217.7	45.6	75.2	2.8
III	347.0	219.6	49.1	78.2	.1
IV	358.6	227.2	52.6	79.5	—.7
1953	365.4	232.6	50.3	82.8	—.4
I	364.5	230.9	52.0	81.8	—.3
II	368.8	233.3	52.9	83.3	—.7

Table 32–5—Continued

GROSS NATIONAL PRODUCT AND ITS COMPONENTS ANNUALLY, 1929–62; SEASONALLY ADJUSTED QUARTERLY AT ANNUAL RATES, 1939–63 (BILLIONS OF DOLLARS)

	Gross National Product	Personal Consumption Expenditures	Gross Private Domestic Investment	Government Purchases	Net Exports
III	367.1	234.1	51.1	82.7	—.8
IV	361.0	232.3	45.2	83.5	.0
1954	363.1	238.0	48.9	75.3	1.0
I	360.0	233.7	46.6	79.4	.3
II	358.9	236.5	47.2	74.4	.8
III	362.0	238.7	48.8	74.1	.4
IV	370.8	243.2	52.3	73.0	2.3
1955	397.5	256.9	63.8	75.6	1.1
I	384.3	249.4	58.8	74.6	1.5
II	393.0	254.3	63.1	74.9	.7
III	403.4	260.9	65.4	75.8	1.3
IV	408.9	263.3	67.6	77.1	.9
1956	419.2	269.9	67.4	79.0	2.9
I	410.6	265.6	67.1	76.6	1.4
II	415.0	268.2	66.9	77.3	2.6
III	421.0	270.4	67.3	79.8	3.5
IV	430.0	275.6	68.1	82.0	4.3
1957	442.8	285.2	66.1	86.5	4.9
I	438.5	280.1	67.1	85.3	6.0
II	442.1	283.3	67.3	86.4	5.1
III	448.3	288.7	67.6	86.9	5.1
IV	442.3	288.6	62.4	87.7	3.5
1958	444.5	293.2	56.6	93.5	1.2
I	432.9	287.4	53.9	89.8	1.7
II	437.2	290.9	53.0	92.0	1.3
III	447.0	294.5	55.8	95.1	1.6
IV	460.6	299.8	63.6	96.7	.4

Table 32-5—Continued

GROSS NATIONAL PRODUCT AND ITS COMPONENTS ANNUALLY, 1929–62; SEASONALLY ADJUSTED QUARTERLY AT ANNUAL RATES, 1939–63 (BILLIONS OF DOLLARS)

	Gross National Product	Personal Consumption Expenditures	Gross Private Domestic Investment	Government Purchases	Net Exports
1959	482.7	313.5	72.7	97.2	—.8
I	472.0	305.7	69.8	97.2	—.8
II	487.8	313.0	79.0	97.5	—1.7
III	482.7	316.7	68.8	97.8	—.5
IV	488.5	318.8	73.2	96.5	.0
1960	502.6	328.2	71.8	99.6	3.0
I	500.4	324.2	77.6	97.2	1.5
II	504.1	329.7	73.3	98.9	2.3
III	503.5	328.7	70.9	100.5	3.3
IV	502.1	330.3	65.3	101.6	4.9
1961	518.2	336.8	69.0	107.9	4.5
I	500.4	330.7	59.6	104.7	5.4
II	512.5	334.9	66.6	106.8	4.3
III	521.9	337.9	72.0	107.9	4.1
IV	537.8	343.8	77.6	112.3	4.0
1962	554.9	355.4	78.8	117.0	3.8
I	544.5	348.8	77.3	115.1	3.3
II	552.4	352.9	79.6	115.5	4.4
III	556.8	356.7	78.9	117.0	4.1
IV	565.2	362.9	78.8	120.2	3.3
1963					
I	571.8	367.4	77.8	123.0	3.6
II	579.6	370.4	80.7	123.8	4.8
III	588.7	374.9	83.7	125.7	4.3

SOURCES

1929–1938, Department of Commerce, *U.S. Income and Output* (Washington, D.C., 1958), p. 118.

1939–1945, Department of Commerce, *National Income, 1954 Edition* (Washington, D.C., 1954), pp. 224–225.

1946–1955, *U.S. Income and Output*, pp. 120–121.

1956–1963, Department of Commerce, *Survey of Current Business*, July 1962, p. 7; July 1963, p. 13; November 1963, p. 3.

richer and thereafter can do more than the initially richer person can do, it does not follow that the increase in wealth was worth the earlier sacrifice in consumption. That is a matter for each person's own choice, and there is no obvious objective answer.

The implication that does come through is that the *level of wealth* is the pertinent index of choice of alternative situations. *How* that wealth is used is another question and should not be allowed to detract from the relevance of the *amount* of current wealth.

For national comparisons, concern about present and future levels of wealth arises because of a presumption that one nation may use its wealth to take away the wealth of the other. Our discussions have presumed a continuance of a system of private property; if one believes that system is threatened by the rise in wealth of some other person or nation, then the concern about future wealths or rates of increase of wealth, such as permeates comparisons of Russia and the United States, becomes pertinent.

Whether the sobering presumption about the use to which the other party will put his wealth is well founded cannot be answered here. But it should be noted that a nation (or an individual) obviously need not wait for superiority in either wealth or income, per capita or absolute, before muscle flexing is undertaken. The level of wealth constitutes a constraint on what can be done in the aggregate, but more can be undertaken in one activity by curtailing other activities. Devoting half of relatively meager resources to a selected, crucial endeavor (armaments) may carry the day over a competitor who commits only 10 percent of greater resources to that endeavor.

Surely, in light of the foregoing considerations, there should be measurements of national wealth as well as of national income. In fact, there are very few such measurements. The principal reason is that a major portion of our wealth is human wealth, and people are not bought and sold as capital goods. Only their *current flow* of services is sold. Hence, not human wealth but a sort of measure of income from current use of human resources is available in wages measurements. To be sure, nonhuman wealth (even though produced by human effort) is bought and sold as capital goods, and a measure of the market value of that wealth is available. Still, the absence of wealth measures for human labor precludes the availability of market values of the total stock of all forms of wealth. As a result, measures of income are used instead for all goods. Insofar as these income-flow measures are accurate, they provide an indirect measure of wealth via the interest-rate relationship between wealth and income.

National-income measures are not good indicators of changes in wealth, because the data are based primarily on current market value sales of services from current use of resources. Thus, if a building should be vacant for a year and yield no service sales, the record would report no rental receipts even though the capital value of the building would not thereby have fallen to zero. Similarly, if a person were unemployed for a period, so that he reported no wage income, this would not mean that the wealth value he represents has fallen to zero.

Since there are periods in which sales of services of economic goods fluctuate, recorded flows of market values of resource use would exaggerate the relative changes in wealth—if the national-income data were to be treated as proportional to national wealth. Although real national income fell by about 30 percent from 1929 to 1933, it does not follow that national wealth was 30 percent smaller in the latter year. Instead, it was not being used as efficiently. Nor when income rose by about 40 percent from 1933 to 1937 did it mean that our stock of real wealth increased by that percentage. Again it implies that there was some increase in wealth and also in the efficiency with which the stock was being used.

Questions

1. Two cases of misplaced and misleading emphasis are (i) concentration on money national income rather than real income and (ii) concentration on income rather than wealth. Defend this contention; oppose this contention.

2. Distinguish between *all* market transactions and so-called *final* transactions. Which is the better measure of the economy's "productive activity"? What is the relation between final transactions and the sum of values added?

3. Label each of the following statements True or False, and briefly defend your evaluation.

   a. "If we added the total amounts of goods and services sold by every individual and business firm in the United States in 1964, this sum would be *GNP* for 1964."

   b. "Inventory investment can never be negative, because purchases of goods for inventory cannot fall below zero."

   c. "Every money payment from one individual or firm to another increases *GNP*."

   d. "An increase in *GNP*, expressed in current prices, necessarily reflects a proportionately greater outflow of goods and services."

4. What are the inadequacies of *GNP* as a measure of aggregate productive activity? Distinguish between *GNP* in current dollars and *GNP* in constant dollars. Does the calculation of *GNP* in constant dollars resolve all of the deficiencies in the *GNP* measure?

5. What is the relation between "absorption" and *GNP*? And *NNP*? And inventory changes?

6. What is the "*GNP* price deflator" or "implicit price index"? For what purpose is it used?

7. From 1929 to 1930, *GNP* fell from $104,400,000,000 to $91,100,000,000. What proportion of this fall can be attributed to a change in real output and what proportion to a change in prices?

8. Based on data for the periods of 1933–39 and 1954–60, what generalizations can you suggest with respect to various repercussions of an increase in aggregate final expenditure when the increased spending comes in (a) a depression and (b) a generally prosperous period. Does your jungle instinct suggest any explanations for these different sets of repercussions?

9. For the following questions, use the data of Table 32–5:

   a. Which variable (among *C*, *I*, and *G*) is most closely correlated with annual and quarterly *directions* of change of *GNP*? Which moves least consistently with *GNP*?

   b. Generally, which component of *GNP* (other than net exports) shows the greatest percentage variation? Which shows the least variation? Which components varied most and which varied least from 1929–1933? 1933–1940? 1940–1944? Do these comparisons suggest any hypotheses to you?

   c. How often does *G* "compensate" or "counter" (i.e., move *oppositely* to) *GNP*? Does *G* compensate *GNP* more when *GNP* is falling or when it is rising?

   d. Particularly with the quarterly data, can you discern any pattern of "turning points" (i.e., sequence of peaks and troughs) in the *GNP* components?

33

NATIONAL-INCOME THEORY: THE BASIC KEYNESIAN MODEL

We have seen that, from the standpoint of income determination or income creation, money income is equal to—and, indeed, consists of—spending on currently produced final domestic output. Spending constitutes, or generates, money income; income equals spending. We have seen further that total spending is composed of several elements: consumption expenditure, investment expenditure, government expenditure, and foreign expenditure.

To understand how various factors affect the value of national income, we must have more than definitions of income and its components. An analytical structure relating the way in which each component depends on or affects others is necessary. To this end we shall use the formal analytical constructs and model of income determination known as the Keynesian model.[1] As we shall see, this model uses two relationships, one relating consumption (and saving) decisions to income and wealth, and another relating investment decisions to income. These two relationships are the consumption and investment functions. It will become evident that shifts in the "positions" of these functions (like demand and supply schedules in a supply-and-demand diagram) serve as the basic means of analyzing how various factors or events affect income.

Left to later chapters is discussion of some of the factors that induce shifts in these functions and hence in the level of national income. However, we may anticipate that discussion by noting that some of the factors are government policy actions on taxes, spend-

[1] John M. Keynes (1883–1946) was an English economist and government adviser. Since he frequently dealt with crucial matters of public economic policy, it was well-nigh inevitable that he became highly controversial. Some have regarded him as a virtual messiah; in the eyes of others, he was—if not

ing, and borrowing. Also crucial is the community's total stock of money, changes in which, as we shall see, have an important effect on national income. Still another factor is the community's willingness to invest out of current income for the future—a decision sensitively dependent upon individual expectations and confidence in future profit prospects. In order to facilitate an analysis of how these factors or policy actions can affect national income, we present in this chapter the simple Keynesian income model, along with a few embellishments.

The Consumption Function

Suppose for the moment that consumption is the only form of spending. Then money income in a given time period will be equal to whatever is the amount of consumption spending in that period.[2] In tabular form, we can give illustrative dollar figures, with consumption in a given period (C_1) creating income in that same period (Y_1):

Table 33–1

CONSUMPTION EXPENDITURE AND INCOME

C_1	Y_1
0	0
50	50
100	100
200	200

And in algebraic notation:

$$(1) \qquad Y_1 = C_1.$$

the devil himself—at least the first lieutenant of the fallen angel. Our purpose here is not to discuss in detail the particular policy recommendations of Keynes; rather, we investigate a simple mode of income analysis that stems from his work (in particular, *The General Theory of Employment, Interest and Money* of 1936).

[2] A bit of elaborative modification is in order. Money income is a manifestation of spending on *currently* produced output, but not each spending component of income is spending solely on current output. For example, consumption expenditure is expenditure simply on consumption goods, whether produced currently *or* in the past. Suppose that the economy is producing nothing, and therefore no income is being generated; nevertheless, the community is consuming. If, in a simple economy with no government transactions or foreign trade, $Y = C + I$, and if $C > 0$, how can $Y = 0$? Answer: Current consumption in the absence of current production is feasible only though reducing inventories, and a decrease of inventories is negative investment (i.e., "disinvestment"); thus, the positive C is balanced by the negative I, and Y remains zero.

To present the relationship still differently, consider Figure 33–1. On both the horizontal and the vertical axes, we measure in terms of *money units* (dollars). Furthermore, let us use the *same scale* on both axes: a given distance measures x dollars on either axis. Therefore, if we construct a straight line from the origin, rising to the right at an angle of 45 degrees, any point on the line will have equal coordinates. Thus, if consumption (measured vertically) is 50, income (measured horizontally) is 50, and the equal vertical and horizontal measurements locate a point on the 45-degree line; or, to put the matter the other way around, if we are at a point on the 45-degree line, the point measures equal vertical and horizontal distances from the origin. Since income always equals expenditure (here taken to be only consumption), we *must* always be some place on the 45-degree line.

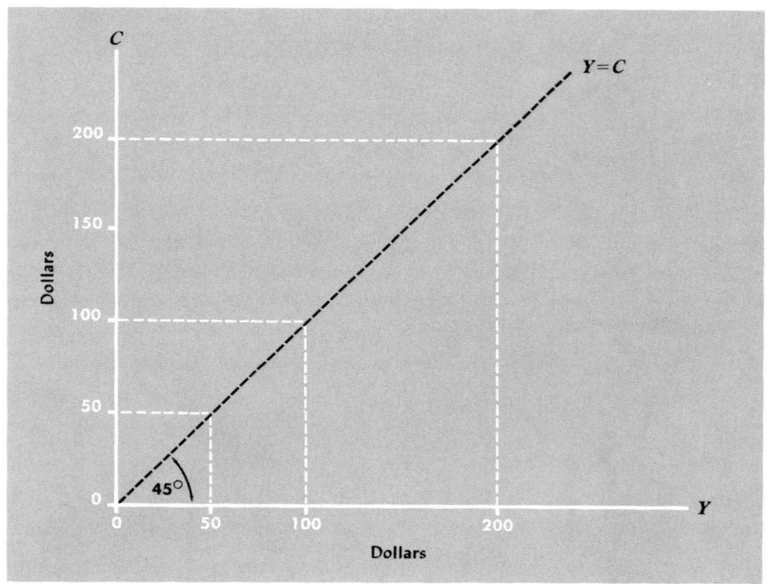

FIGURE 33–1. The 45-degree diagram: income equals expenditure.

If there is consumption expenditure of 50 and no other form of spending, income will be 50. But what determines the level of consumption expenditure? Our answer is: income! Consumption not only constitutes income, but is a function of income. We avoid confusion in exposition by using different time periods, with consumption lagging a period behind the income which determines it. Income *created* by consumption in *one* period is *disposed of* through consumption and nonconsumption (i.e., saving) in the *following* period. What the community desires to consume in period 2 is determined by its income in period 1—and it may not desire to spend on consumption exactly all its income. Assume the following schedule of desired consumption at selected alternative levels of income:

Table 33–2

THE CONSUMPTION SCHEDULE

Y_1	C_2
0	50
50	87.5
100	125
200	200
300	275

If income is at a level of 200, the community wishes to spend 200 on consumption; but, at lower levels of income, desired consumption is less than 200 although greater than income; and with income greater than 200, the consumption figure rises but is less than income.

Why should the amount of consumption expenditure not rise proportionally with income? Why should the portion of income spent on consumption fall as income becomes larger? Reconsider remarks about the measurement of income *and* of wealth in the preceding chapter. We noted that the measured income does not serve as a perfect measure of wealth; measured income fluctuates more than wealth. If a real estate salesman does not sell any houses in one month, he does not assume that his wealth has fallen to zero. If a businessman's net receipts decline during some period, he does not conclude that they will necessarily stay as low in the future. A wage earner who loses his job does not suppose that his wealth and all future earning power have fallen to zero. Nor when he gets overtime pay does he assume his income will stay that high permanently. All receivers of income, as measured by sales value of current services, learn to recognize that over short periods measured income from sales of services undergoes transient fluctuations. Therefore, people do not assume that their wealth or "basic" or "permanent" income has changed proportionally with every fluctuation in current earnings. They do not gear their consumption rigidly to transient income. Instead, they relate it in large measure to long-run income or to wealth.

A drop of $100 in transient or money income will induce a smaller drop in consumption than if permanent long-run income (wealth) had fallen that much. Whereas a decline in long-run income might have induced a decrease in consumption of $80 (and a drop in saving of $20), a decline of transient income would be associated with a decrease of consumption of, say, only \$60. Conversely, if transient income should increase by \$100 in some period, consumption would increase by, say, \$60, whereas an equal increase in permanent income would have increased consumption by \$80. Consumption may be a nearly constant proportion (perhaps .8) of the permanent or long-run average rate of income, so that rich and poor people alike may save about .2 of their permanent income. Furthermore, if people get richer over the decades, their rate of saving as a proportion of their wealth or permanent income may remain quite stable. This is, in fact, what seems to have happened in the United States.

Yet, if we relate consumption to transient income, as measured by current money income, rather than to permanent income as measured by wealth, we find that consumption has been more stable than money income. When measured money incomes fell, consumption fell by a smaller proportion. When transient money income rose, consumption rose by a smaller proportion.

Consumption evidently is related basically to permanent income or wealth by a simple proportionality and is related indirectly to transient income in a slightly more complicated form. Nevertheless, we shall use the relationship that relates consumption to transient measured national income in current-money flows, for we are interested in transient variations in the rates of production of goods and services—variations more conventionally indicated by the measured monetary income instead of by wealth or permanent income.

It will be useful to state the current-money-income–consumption relationship of Table 33–2 algebraically. What is the equation of the *consumption function*? How can we express C in terms of Y? If $Y_1 = 0$, then $C_2 = 50$; if $Y_1 = 50$, then $C_2 = 87.5$. Thus, C increases from 50 to 87.5—a change of 37.5—as Y goes from 0 to 50; the ratio of the *change* in consumption to the *change* in income is $\Delta C/\Delta Y = 37.5/50 = .75$. A little doodling with the data in the table will demonstrate that for any change in income, $\Delta C/\Delta Y = .75$. It follows that our equation for consumption is:

$$(2) \qquad C = 50 + .75Y.$$

That is, consumption is equal to 50 plus three fourths of whatever Y is. If, for example, $Y = 300$, then $C = 50 + .75(300) = 275$.

In Figure 33–2, the data (which give the equation) are plotted. The arithmetic table, the algebraic equation, and the geometric curve are alternative representations of the consumption function. The consumption function tells us that we *wish* to be some place on the C curve, the *desired* amount of consumption spending being determined by the level of income.

Consider equations (1) and (2) together: Y is equal to C, and C is a function of Y. We have noted that this situation is not circular; rather, it is a situation of *mutual determination*. We have the two unknowns, Y and C, stated in two equations. Both equations must be simultaneously satisfied. Simultaneous

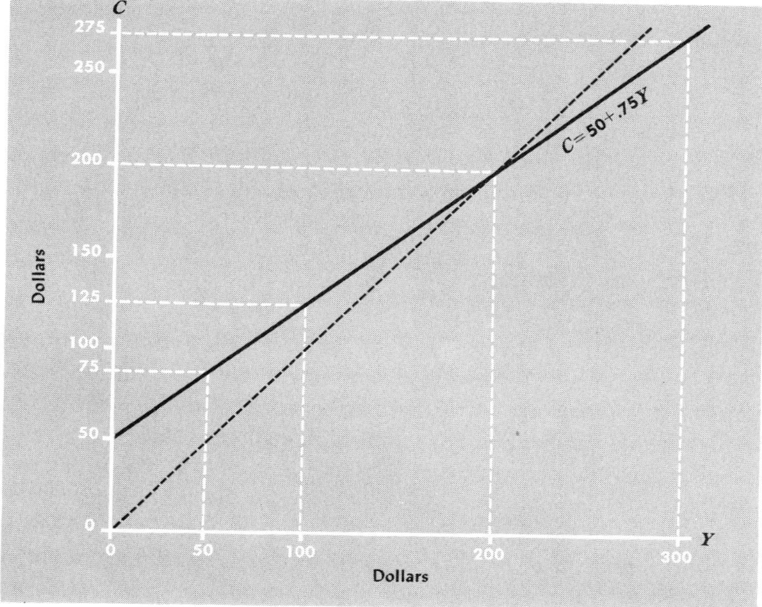

FIGURE 33–2. The consumption function.

solution of the equations will give us the value of income and the corresponding level of consumption.

$$(1) \qquad Y = C,$$
$$(2) \qquad C = 50 + .75Y.$$

Substituting the equivalent of C in equation (2) into equation (1):

$$Y = 50 + .75Y,$$
$$Y - .75Y = 50,$$
$$Y = 200.$$

And since, from equation (1), $Y = C$:

$$C = 200.$$

When $C = 200$, $Y = 200$, according to equation (1); and if $Y = 200$, then $C = 200$, according to equation (2). No other values of Y and C will thus satisfy both equations.

To put the matter in terms of the diagrams, we have already established that we *must* be some place on the 45-degree line (income equals *actual* consumption); and also we *wish* to be some place on the *C* curve (*desired* consumption is determined by income). Obviously, we can meet both of these conditions only by being at the point of intersection of the two curves—that is, by being on both curves simultaneously; and, as indicated in Figure 33–2, they intersect at an income level of 200 and at a consumption level of 200.

Equilibrium Income

This intersection value of income is also called the equilibrium value of income. It equilibrates the level of income in all the relationships comprising the income-determination model. In other words, by the "equilibrium" income we mean the level of income that simultaneously satisfies the equations of that model. As long as the consumption function (as well as the investment function, which will be introduced later) does not change, the equilibrium level of income will be unchanged. We conclude that *the equilibrium level of income is determined by the intersection of the total expenditure curve with the 45-degree line.* That income level may be "high" or "low," "good" or "bad," according to some historical or ideal standard. The mathematics (grade-school algebra and geometry) are easy. The computation of the equilibrium level of income can be illustrated by investigating the arithmetic and economic repercussions of a shift in the consumption function.

Suppose that the whole consumption curve shifts upward from its initial C position to C'. For convenience, we keep C' parallel to C, raising it simply by 50 at every income level, thereby making the new consumption equation $C = 100 + .75Y$. Now, at the original income level of 200, the new desired rate of consumer spending is 250, rather than 200.

Before continuing, pause to note that people wish to spend more at the initial (and every other) level of income. The increase in spending is *not induced* by a prior rise in income. Rather, it is a result of the *autonomous* increase in the *C* curve. We are not here *moving along a C curve in response to an income change;* instead, we *shift the entire curve of demand for consumption at every rate of income.* We shall call a change in a variable in response to a prior change in income an "induced" change; any change that occurs for any reason other than a prior change in income is "autonomous."

At the point where we left Figure 33–3 (call it point 1), consumption is 250 while income seemingly is only 200: we are on the new *C* curve, but apparently not on the 45-degree curve. Is this really the case? Once the 250 consumption has been made, income no longer is 250: spending constitutes income; therefore, the 250 consumption immediately moves the income level to 250 (to point 2). But this is still not the end of the matter, for, having once created income of 250, the community is not content to spend only 250: according to the new consumption function, at an income level of 250, desired consumption

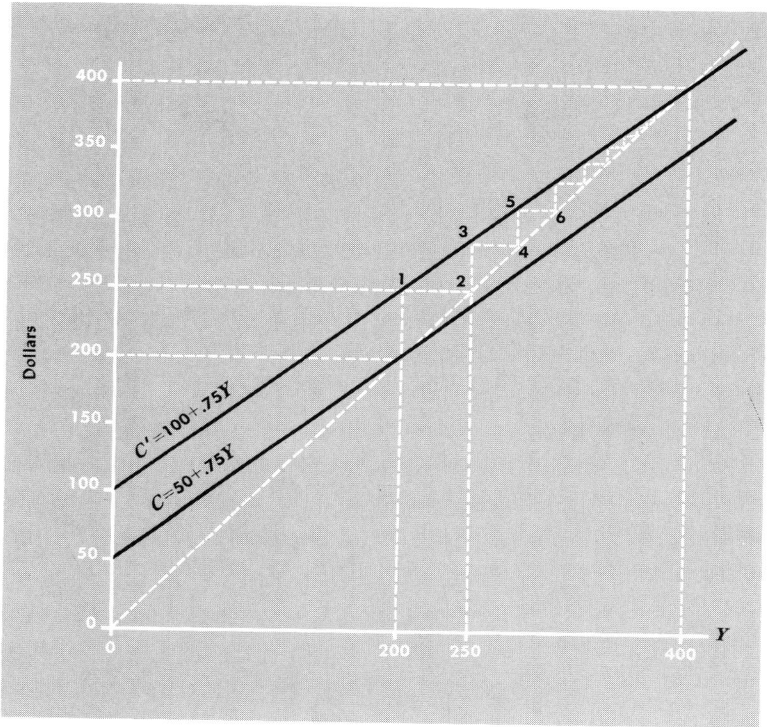

FIGURE 33–3. Increase in consumption function increases equilibrium income.

in the next time period will be 287.5, moving us to point 3. But the act of spending 287.5 means creating income of the same amount, moving us to point 4. After we have reached point 4, new consumption soon takes us to point 5, which actually means going immediately to point 6. And so it goes, with each new spending level raising income, and with each new income level inducing more spending, until finally we reach the new intersection where $Y = C = 400$. (We shall discuss later how this new level of income and consumption is computed to be precisely 400.)

We see that "autonomous" changes can operate via changes in the consumption *function.* If the amount of consumption at any given level of income were to be larger, the whole consumption function would be represented as having shifted upward—also called an increase in the consumption *function*; and an increase in the function determines a higher level of income.

THE MARGINAL PROPENSITY TO CONSUME AND EQUILIBRIUM INCOME

The "marginal propensity to consume" (*MPC*) expresses the response of consumption to changes in income when the consumption function itself (i.e., the

C curve in Figure 33–2) is constant. This relationship of consumption *changes* and income *changes* along a given consumption function may be stated as a ratio: $MPC = \Delta C/\Delta Y$.

Table 33–3

MARGINAL PROPENSITIES TO CONSUME AND TO SAVE

Y_1	C_2	$MPC = \Delta C/\Delta Y$	S_2	$MPS = \Delta S/\Delta Y = 1 - MPC$
0	50		−50	
		37.5/50 = .75		12.5/50 = .25
50	87.5		−37.5	
		37.5/50 = .75		12.5/50 = .25
100	125		−25	
		75/100 = .75		25/100 = .25
200	200		0	
		75/100 = .75		25/100 = .25
300	275		25	

Table 33–3 elaborates Table 33–2. In the *MPC* column, differences in successive consumption figures are divided by the corresponding changes in income. Recalling the income-disposal equation, $Y_1 = C_2 + S_2$, it obviously follows that $S_2 = Y_1 - C_2$. And *MPS* is figured in the same manner as *MPC*. But note that $MPS = 1 - MPC$. Is this only a coincidence in this particular illustration? If $Y_1 = C_2 + S_2$, then $\Delta Y_1 = \Delta C_2 + \Delta S_2$; if both sides of this equation are divided by Y_1, we have $1 = \Delta C_2/\Delta Y_1 + \Delta S_2/\Delta Y_1$, which is simply $1 = MPC + MPS$, and thus $1 - MPC = MPS$.

Observe that $MPC = .75$, which is also the coefficient of the *Y* variable in the consumption function, $C = 50 + .75Y$. The coefficient measures *MPC*; for, as we have seen, we can calculate the values of *C* corresponding to alternative values of *Y* by means of the coefficient.

Finally, note that *MPC* is reflected in the *slope* of the *C* curve. The "slope" of a curve is defined as the vertical change divided by the corresponding horizontal change. But in the 45-degree diagram (vertical change)/(horizontal change) is (consumption change)/(income change). Thus, slope of the consumption curve $= \Delta C/\Delta Y = MPC$.

Now, let us again pick up our problem (illustrated in Figure 33–3) of what happens when initial equilibrium is upset by a shift in the consumption curve. But this time we shall use an arithmetic "period" analysis of iterated approximations.

We can imagine that income in a given period is generated by expenditure in that *same* time period ($Y_1 = C_1$), and the income thus created in *one* period is disposed of in the *following* period ($Y_1 = C_2 + S_2$).[3] In Table 33–4, continue the assumption that $MPC = .75$ and $MPS = .25$.

Table 33–4

INCOME CHANGE WITH AN AUTONOMOUS INCREASE IN CONSUMPTION

Period		C		S	Y	
1		200		0	200	
2		200		0	200	$\Delta Y = 50$
3	$\Delta C = 37.5$	250	$\Delta S = 12.5$	−50	250	
4		287.5		−37.5	287.5	
5		315.625		−28.125	315.625	
6		336.719		−20.094	336.719	
		.		.	.	
		.		.	.	
		.		.	.	
*		400		0	400	

Periods 1 and 2 correspond to the initial situation in Figure 33–3, where the original C curve cut the 45-degree line. The community is creating income by consumption spending of 200 per time period, and people want to consume 200 when income is 200; thus, income does not change—that is, income is at an equilibrium level. Now, in period 3, consumption rises to 250: this is an *autonomous* change (i.e., a change not induced by a prior change in income) and corresponds to the movement to point 1 in Figure 33–3, resulting from a shift in the consumption function. Since $C_3 = 250$ while $Y_2 = 200$, and assuming that consumption and saving in one period are always dispositions of income created and received in the preceding period, it follows that the autonomous increase in consumption is accompanied by an equal autonomous fall in saving (or "dissaving"). The consumption expenditure of 250 in period 3 creates income of 250 in period 3—as in moving to point 2 in Figure 33–3. There is thus a change in income of 50, from period 2 to period 3, which will increase income disposed of in period 4 over that in period 3. Specifically, since $MPC = .75$, the increase in consumption is 37.5; since $C_3 = 250$, then $C_4 = 250 + 37.5 = 287.5$. Similarly, saving increases by $.25(50) = 12.5$, from −50 in period 3 to −37.5 in period 4.

[3] In strict logic, the income computed by the income-generating equation (1) replaces the trial value of income in equation (2); and each trial is called a "period." By iteration, the generated income converges to the equilibrium income.

Consumption in period 4 creates income of 287.5, which is 37.5 more than in period 3; this increases consumption by .75(37.5) = 28.125 to 315.625 and saving by 9.375 to —28.125 in period 5; and so on and on.

The increases in income (and thus in consumption and saving) become smaller and smaller: 50 from period 2 to 3, 37.5 from period 3 to 4, 28.125 from period 4 to 5, etc. It is apparent that income is increasing at a decreasing rate, tending ultimately to "flatten out" at a new equilibrium level. At a level of 400, people wish to consume 400 (and thereby again to save nothing).

CONSUMPTION, INVESTMENT, AND EQUILIBRIUM INCOME

Previously (p. 597) we utilized a model of two equations, in which consumption was the only form of expenditure, and deduced that the equilibrium level of income was 200. Now, we may retain the same consumption function and add an *investment* function. In particular, we assume that the rate of investment is constant at a rate of 50, regardless of what the income is. Later we shall relax this assumption and let investment depend upon the income.

But be careful about the meaning of *investment* here. In Chapter 15, we defined savings as that portion of income that was not consumed and which was diverted to future income—i.e., invested. Savings and investment, *there,* were just two ways of describing the same event. But here we use the word *investment* in a slightly, but fundamentally, different sense; we use it in the same sense as in Chapter 29, where investment refers to the portion of current income which people think can *profitably* be diverted to the future as an accumulation of wealth; that is, diverting a dollar of income will result in more than a "dollar of wealth plus interest."

On the other hand, the savings schedule indicates, for each possible income rate, how much of that current income people would be *willing* to divert to future accumulation of wealth at the proffered current rate of interest. There is, of course, no reason why at every rate of income the rate of savings or desired nonconsumption of current income by the aggregate of the community should equal the rate at which people think it is possible *profitably* to divert (invest) income from current consumption. We shall discover that the rate of income at which these two magnitudes are equal is the equilibrium rate of income.

To see this more clearly and to discover the equilibrium rate of income, we first express our fundamental analytic relationships in algebraic form as follows:

$$(1) \qquad Y = C + I,$$
$$(2) \qquad C = 50 + .75Y,$$
$$(3) \qquad I = 50.$$

Equation (1) has been expanded to include the investment-spending component. Equation (2) is unchanged from the earlier model. Equation (3) tells us that, in the absence of autonomous changes, investment spending is always 50, regardless of income. By substituting (2) and (3) in (1), we can readily solve for the *equilibrium* values of income and consumption:

$$\begin{aligned} Y &= 50 + .75Y + 50, \\ Y - .75Y &= 100, \\ .25Y &= 100, \\ Y &= 400, \\ C &= 350. \end{aligned}$$

Also, $S = Y - C = 50$, which is equal in equilibrium to the constant I.

Geometrically, introducing the investment element involves simply superimposing the I schedule on Figure 33–2. The C curve is the same in Figure 33–4 as in Figures 33–2 and 33–3. The I curve is horizontal at a level of 50 (only by coincidence do the C and I curves have a common intercept on the vertical axis). Now, to obtain a total-expenditure (E) curve, we add the C and I curves: the E curve is parallel to the C curve, being greater by the amount of investment (50) at every level of income. The intersection of the total-expenditure ($E = C + I$) curve with the 45-degree line locates the equilibrium level of income.

Thus far, how does the income analysis illustrated in Figure 33–4 differ from that in Figure 33–3? Essentially, not at all. In the earlier case, we began with a C function that yielded an equilibrium income of 200 and then autonomously increased consumption at every income level by 50, thereby raising equilibrium income to 400. In Figure 33–4, we began with the same C function and then added investment of 50 at every income level; investment increased autonomously from zero to a level of 50, and again the new equilibrium income is 400. The alternative autonomous injections of new expenditure, consumption in the first case and investment in the second, had the same effect on income.

Also in Figure 33–4, we have drawn the S curve. As illustrated in Table 33–3, the saving schedule is derivable from the consumption function. Geometrically, the amount of saving at any given income is a vertical distance (positive or negative) equal to the gap between the C curve and the 45-degree line. At the income level where the two curves intersect, saving is zero, and the S curve thus crosses the horizontal axis.

Having introduced investment both algebraically and geometrically, let us see how to handle the arithmetic computation by means of a period-analysis table. We must expand Table 33–4 to include a column for investment. Starting with an equilibrium level of income (200) and no investment, in period 3 we autonomously insert investment of 50, which is repeated for each subsequent period. As in Table 33–4, the computed income ultimately converges to a new equilibrium value of 400.

THE CONDITIONS OF "EQUILIBRIUM" INCOME

Before taking up in detail the question of just why the autonomous increase in spending of 50 raises the equilibrium level of income by 200, let us take another look at the conditions of "equilibrium" income. The economic content of the conditions may be more apparent in the 45-degree diagram. In Figure 33–4, there are two ways of expressing the conditions of equilibrium income: (a) the intersection of the total-expenditure $(C + I)$ curve and the 45-degree line, and (b) the intersection of the S and I curves.

Consideration of the rationale of these two methods of solving for equilibrium income in the diagram leads us to the basic conditions of equilibrium. We may focus first on the relation between income and spending: income equals spending, and at least some components of spending are functions of income. Income will be constant from one time period to another—that is, income will be at an equilibrium level—when spending is constant; and spending will be constant when the community *wishes to spend* at the same rate that it is *receiving income*. This is reflected in the crossing of the E curve and the 45-degree line: income is 400, and people wish to spend 400.

Or we can reach the same result with respect to income by thinking in terms of the saving "leakage" and the investment "injection." Saving is a variable in the income-*disposal* equation; saving is income received and not consumed; saving is a leakage out of the income stream. Investment is a variable in the income-*creation* equation; investment is a form of spending on output; investment is an injection into the income stream. If the rate of leakage out of the stream of income expenditures is exactly equal to (offset by) the injection

Table 33–5

INCOME CHANGE AND AN AUTONOMOUS INCREASE IN INVESTMENT

Period	*C*	*S*	*I*	*Y*
1	200	0	0	200
2	200	0	0	200
3	200	0	50	250
4	237.5	12.5	50	287.5
5	265.625	21.875	50	315.625
6	286.719	28.906	50	336.719
.	.	.	.	.
.	.	.	.	.
.	.	.	.	.
*	350	50	50	400

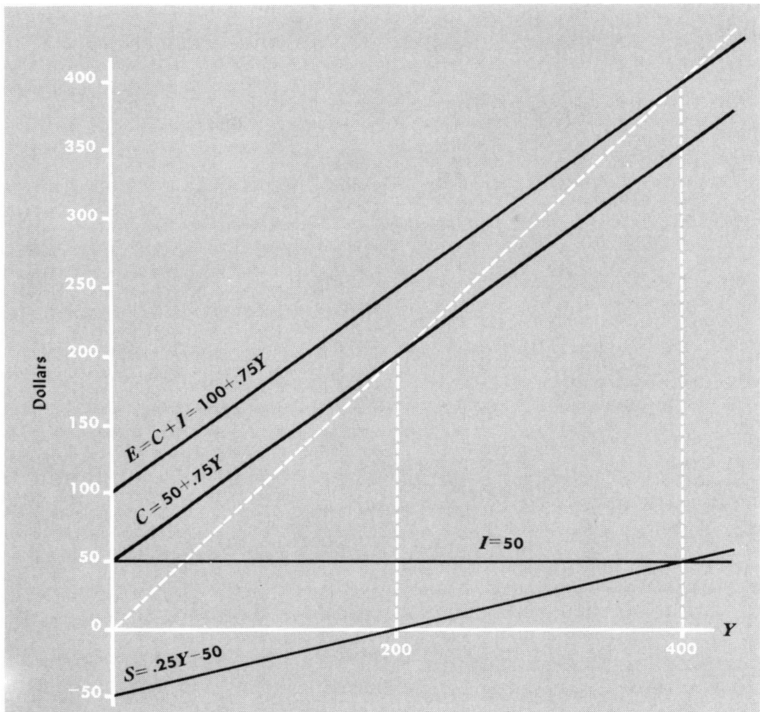

FIGURE 33–4. Effect of investment on equilibrium income.

into the stream, the stream continues at a constant volume. This equality is represented by the intersection of the *S* and *I* curves.

Unsurprisingly, these two approaches have counterparts in the period-analysis tables, represented by Table 33–5. It is an old story by now that the income of a given period (whether or not that is the equilibrium income) is created by spending in that period. Thus:

$$Y_1 = C_1 + I_1,$$
$$Y_2 = C_2 + I_2.$$

But in equilibrium, income is the same in each period:

$$Y_1 = Y_2.$$

Thus, by substitution, in equilibrium:

$$Y_1 = C_2 + I_2.$$

That is, income is at an *equilibrium* level ($Y_1 = Y_2$) when *total spending in one period* ($C_2 + I_2$) *equals income created and received in the preceding period* (Y_1).

With respect to the second approach, recall that

$$Y_1 = C_2 + S_2.$$

Since, in equilibrium, $Y_1 = Y_2$, it follows that

$$Y_2 = C_2 + S_2.$$

And since it is always the case that $Y_2 = C_2 + I_2$, then in equilibrium

$$S_2 = I_2.$$

In short, an alternative way of stating the condition of equilibrium income is that *saving equals investment in a given period.* If $I > S$ in a given period (see Table 33–5), income rises; if $I < S$ in a given period, income falls.

THE MULTIPLIER AND EQUILIBRIUM INCOME

In our previous illustration, the initial equilibrium level of income was 200, with income consisting solely of consumption spending and with saving and investment both zero. Then we autonomously increased spending—consumption in one alternative case, and investment in the other—by 50. The autonomous injection of additional spending (for convenience, call it investment) triggered a series of spending rounds, with income rising period after period, but rising ever more slowly and ultimately reaching a new equilibrium level of 400. The autonomous injection of 50 increased the equilibrium level of income by 200. Why?

One proper, even if not wholly satisfying, answer is that these results are simply algebraic. Given our model of equations in the variables Y, C, I, and S, and given $\Delta I = 50$, simultaneous solution of the equations indicated that the new equilibrium value of Y must be 400.

The simultaneous solution of the equations deduced the new equilibrium income level, but the *process* of determining that new level from the initial equilibrium level was illustrated both in a diagram (Figure 33–3) and in period tables (Tables 33–4 and 33–5). Such illustrative detail helps to fill out and make more readily understandable the austere algebra, but, even so, our discussion has been quite formal. What, then, is the *common sense* of the proposition that an autonomous injection of new spending (investment) will lead to an increase in income which is a multiple of the injection?

Begin, as before, with income in equilibrium at a level of 200. Income is

200 because (consumption) expenditure is 200, and consumption is 200 because that is how much the community wishes to spend when income is 200. There is no investment spending, and, with consumption equal to income, there is no saving.

Now, we introduce positive investment, which rises autonomously from zero to 50. Income rises, for investment is a determinant of income—but how far?

We can concentrate on the saving-investment relationship. We have seen that income equilibrium is characterized by equality of saving and investment in a given period—that is, at a given income level (see, for example, periods 1 and 2 of Table 33–5). At the moment that investment rises autonomously, saving is as yet unchanged; therefore, in the period of the investment increase, there is a gap of investment over saving of 50 (period 3 of Table 33–5). If equilibrium is to be regained (at some level), the investment-saving gap must be closed.

Since it is assumed that investment will henceforth remain at 50 each period, income will not again be in equilibrium until saving rises by 50. But what will cause an increase in saving? An increase in income; for, in our model, saving is a function of income alone. How great an increase in income is required to induce a rise in saving of 50? The marginal propensity to save, in our illustration, is .25; that is, saving will rise by $1 for every $4 that income goes up. Therefore, if saving is to rise by a total of $50, income must rise by $200. At the initial income level of $200, the community preferred to save nothing; if income is $400, it prefers to save $50. When income reaches $400, the saving-investment gap is closed, and thus income is again at an equilibrium level.

Or consider the common sense of the spending-income approach. Again, there is a gap to be closed—namely, the gap of consumption plus investment ($C_2 + I_2$) over income created in the preceding period (Y_1). To revert to Table 33–5, in period 3, consumption plus the new, higher investment is greater than the equilibrium income of period 2 by 50. Whereas the saving-investment gap was closed by bringing saving up to the *constant* investment level, the expenditure-income gap is closed by rising income catching the *increasing* total expenditure. At what level of income is the gap eliminated?

Income rises immediately, in period 3, by $50. However, the gap is not closed; for the income rise itself increases consumption (and thus the sum of consumption and investment) by $37.50 in period 4. But at least the rise in income of $50 has reduced the gap by $12.50 (i.e., from $50 to $37.50). Since the gap is narrowed by $1 for every $4 that income increases, income must rise a total of $200 to close the entire initial gap of $50.

Whether we speak of closing the gap of investment over saving or the gap of expenditure over income, income must rise by $200 to close a gap of $50. But this ratio of 4:1 reflects the value of the marginal propensity to save (.25). A little doodling will summarize and pinpoint this relationship.

We are here concerned with the relationship between an autonomous change in spending (represented by investment) and the resulting ultimate change in income. This relationship is often expressed as a ratio, $\Delta Y/\Delta I$, and labeled the "multiplier" (k). Thus, $k = \Delta Y/\Delta I$. Since $\Delta Y = \Delta C + \Delta I$ and therefore $\Delta I = \Delta Y - \Delta C$, we may substitute for ΔI: $k = \frac{\Delta Y}{\Delta Y - \Delta C}$. Dividing numerator and denominator by ΔY, we have: $k = \frac{1}{1 - \frac{\Delta C}{\Delta Y}}$; i.e., $k = \frac{1}{1 - MPC}$, and $k = \frac{1}{MPS}$. So the multiplier (in this simple model which omits governmental and international transactions) equals the *reciprocal of the marginal propensity to save.*

Since $k = \Delta Y/\Delta I$, it follows that $k\Delta I = \Delta Y$. To apply this in our previous illustration, $k = 200/50 = 4$; and $4(50) = 200$. Or, to derive the multiplier from the marginal propensities, $k = \frac{1}{1 - .75} = \frac{1}{.25} = 4$.

It is apparent, since $k = \frac{1}{1 - MPC} = \frac{1}{MPS}$, that the larger is MPC (and thus the smaller is MPS), the larger is the multiplier. This is to be expected: the larger is the absolute response of consumption to given income changes, the greater will be the ultimate repercussion on income of an autonomous injection. In addition to the algebra and the common sense of the matter, the point can be easily illustrated geometrically.

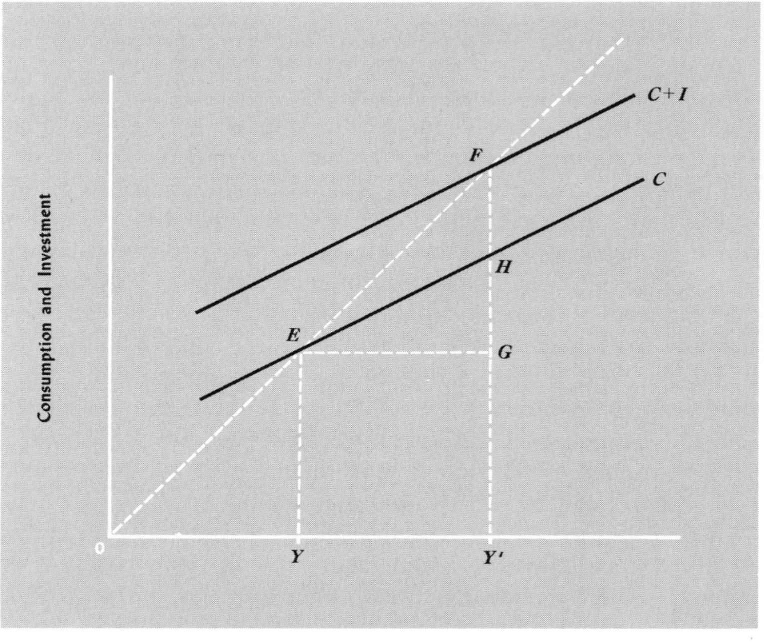

FIGURE 33–5a. The multiplier with a positive marginal propensity to consume.

In Figure 33–5a, suppose that initially consumption is the only form of spending, in which case equilibrium income is $0Y$. Now, we add investment with $C + I$ parallel to C, and equilibrium income moves to $0Y'$. EG, which equals the change in income, YY', is the same distance as GF. (Why?) The GF change in income is larger than the HF injection of investment: the value of the multiplier, GF/HF, is greater than unity. Compare this with Figure 33–5b, where the slope of the C curve (which measures the marginal propensity to consume) is zero. In this case, the change in income ($YY' = EG = GF$) is equal to the injection responsible for the income change (GF), and thus $k = 1$. It appears that the multiplier is greater than unity if the marginal propensity to consume is greater than zero, and the multiplier will vary in the same direction with the marginal propensity to consume.

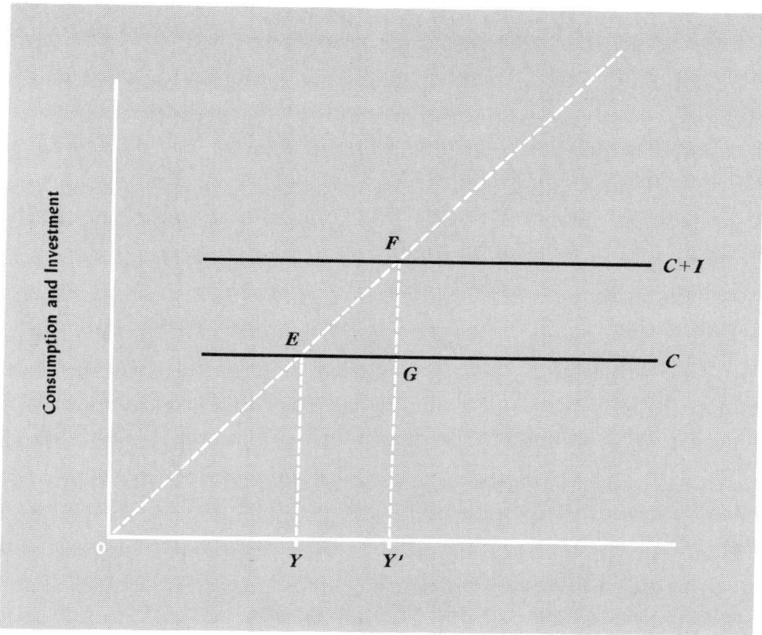

FIGURE 33–5b. The multiplier with a zero marginal propensity to consume.

Single versus Continuous Injections

Our discussion has been predicated on a *permanent* shift in some spending schedule. In terms of period analysis, as illustrated in Table 33–5, this means that investment autonomously increases and *stays* at the new level in succeeding periods. The result of the higher *level* of investment is that income rises at a decreasing rate to a higher equilibrium *level.* The income path over time is plotted in Figure 33–6a.

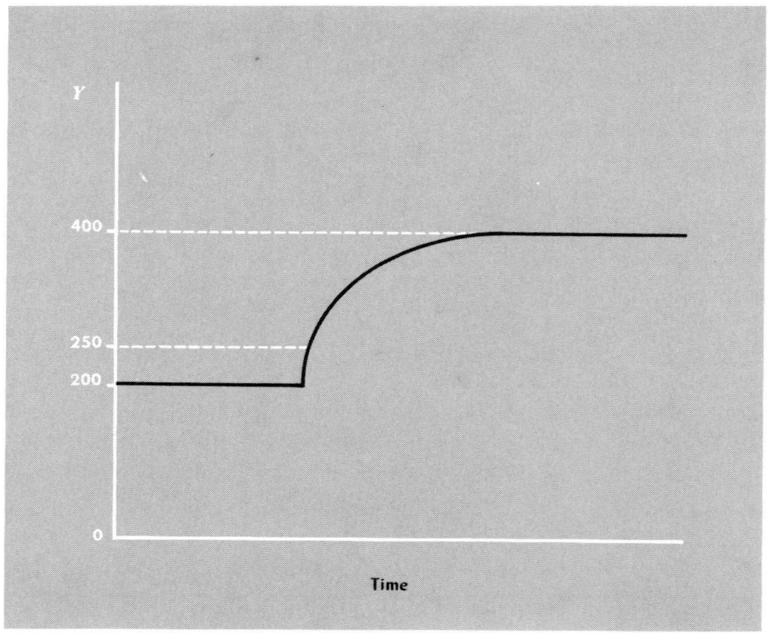

FIGURE 33–6a. Income with continuous injections.

This case of continuous, or repeated, injections period after period should be contrasted with the case of a single injection. Suppose that we begin the period analysis as before and again upset the initial equilibrium by an autonomous increase of investment. The first three periods of Table 33–6 are identical

Table 33–6

MULTIPLIER PROCESS WITH SINGLE INJECTION

Period	C	S	I	Y
1	200	0	0	200
2	200	0	0	200
3	200	0	50	250
4	237.5	12.5	0	237.5
5	228.125	9.375	0	228.125
6	221.094	7.031	0	221.094
	.	.	.	.
	.	.	.	.
	.	.	.	.
*	200	0	0	200

to those of Table 33–5 (and the marginal propensity to consume is .75 in both cases). But the investment injection is not repeated. In period 4, consumption rises to 237.5, as in Table 33–5; but here investment has fallen back to zero, so that income is equal to consumption alone. From the peak of 250, income declines. From period 3 to period 4, income falls by 12.5; therefore, from period 4 to period 5, consumption falls by 9.375, and saving falls by 3.125. Declining at a decreasing rate, income approaches an equilibrium. In this equilibrium, the 12.5 gap of saving over investment must be closed. With a marginal propensity to save of .25, income must fall (from 250) by 50 in order to reduce saving by 12.5 to zero.

It appears, then, that an unrepeated injection will not change the equilibrium *level* of income: the initial equilibrium level was 200, and, after the multiplier mechanism has worked itself out fully, the equilibrium is still 200. In the absence of other changes—notably, in the absence of raising the consumption schedule or of introducing a new spending component (government or exports) —the single injection did not "prime the pump," leading to a new, higher equilibrium income. The income time pattern is plotted in Figure 33–6b.[4]

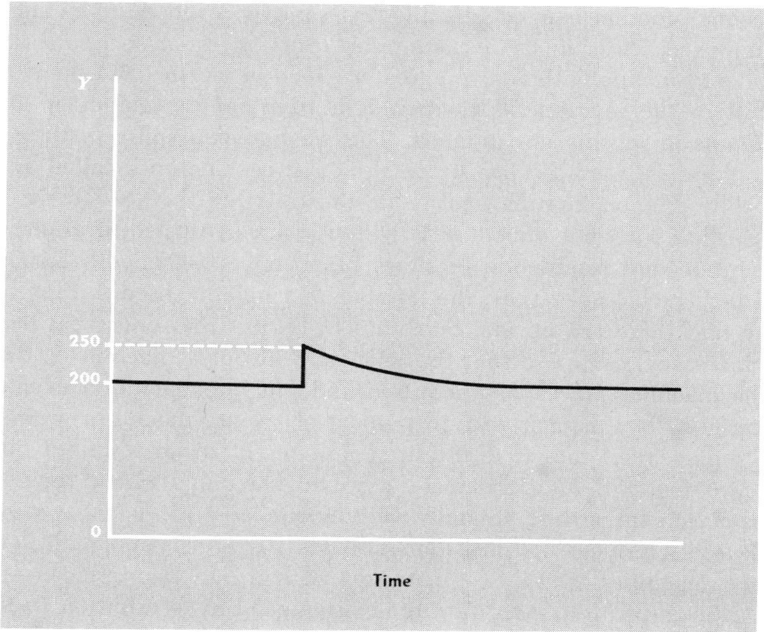

FIGURE 33–6b. Income with single injection.

[4] It was sometimes argued in the 1930s that the economy had stalled at an underemployment equilibrium and that one way of jarring it off dead center was to have a massive but brief injection of governmental spending. This, it was hoped, would "prime the pump," and a continued rise in income would be self-generating. But, in order to obtain this happy result,

In this case of the single injection, is the multiplier process and relationship inoperative? After all, $\Delta Y = \Delta I = 0$—if ΔY and ΔI refer to changes in the the *equilibrium levels* of income and investment. But we may somewhat differently interpret ΔY and ΔI—namely, as changes in the *aggregate* income created and the *aggregate* investment expenditures over time.

As for ΔI, obviously there has been 50 more investment in Table 33–6 as a result of the injection in period 3 than if there had been no injection. And as for ΔY, there is 50 more of income in period 3 than if there had been no injection, 37.5 more in period 4, 28.125 more in period 5, etc. Therefore, even though income ultimately resettles at the old equilibrium level, while the injection of 50 is being gradually "absorbed" into saving $(12.5 + 9.375 + 7.031 + \ldots = 50)$, 200 extra income is created in the aggregate $(50 + 37.5 + 28.125 + \ldots = 200)$.

The Accelerator Effect

So far, we have seen that changes in the consumption function and in the investment function can be identified as sources of changes in income. As we shall now see, shifts in the consumption function can also induce shifts in the investment function with an even greater effect on income. But more significantly, the shift in the investment function is a *transient* or temporary shift, so that *fluctuations* in income are induced. This tie between shifts in the consumption function and shifts in the investment function is sometimes called an accelerator effect. The phenomenon can easily be illustrated with the data in Table 33–7. Suppose that for some time (at least ten years in this illustration) the annual consumption and production of shoes has been 100,000; with 5,000 being produced per machine per year, the number of machines used is thus twenty (and assume that there are no idle machines to be put into operation if demand for shoes increases); suppose that the economic life of a machine is ten years *and* that the machines have been acquired and put into operation evenly over time in years gone by, so each year 10 percent of twenty machines wears out, which is the replacement rate if the desired number of machines does not fall. In a static situation, with annual demand constant, the only demand for new machines is for replacement of the 2 annually wearing out.

But now in year 21, shoe demand rises 10 percent and with it the demand for shoe machines. Only two machines still are to be replaced—namely, the two machines put into operation ten years ago. But in addition to the replaced

---

there must be more in the picture than is assumed in Table 33–6. The advocates of governmental pump-priming could argue that such a policy will autonomously raise the C and I curves: people will be willing to spend more at every income level, for the government's action will inspire confidence and improve economic expectations. Others, however, could suggest that the community might react negatively to such "wild-eyed," possibly deliberately "subversive fiscal irresponsibility," with investment thereby falling and equilibrium income being lower.

Table 33–7

ACCELERATOR EFFECT

Year	Shoe Sales	Shoes per Machine	Machines in Production of Shoes	Depreciation (10 years, 10%)	Replacement Demand	Net Investment in New Machines	Gross Investment in Machines
(1)	(2)	(3)	(4)	(5)	(6)	(7)	(8)
20	100,000	5,000	20	2	2	0	2
21	110,000	5,000	22	2	2	2	4
22	130,000	5,000	26	2	2	4	6
23	150,000	5,000	30	2	2	4	6
24	155,000	5,000	31	2	2	1	3
25	155,000	5,000	31	2	2	0	2
26	145,000	5,000	29	2	0	0	0
27	140,000	5,000	28	2	1	0	1
28	140,000	5,000	28	2	2	0	2

machines, there is a net increase of two machines, so that "replacement" plus "expansion" add up to a total machine demand of four in this year. And so it goes: the data of column 2 are assumed; column 3 is constant; column 4 equals 2 divided by 3; column 5 is given; column 6 reflects the sum of the total machinery purchases with a ten-year lag and *decreases* in the current number of machines required (for example, in going from year 25 to year 26, required machines fall by two, and exactly two are wearing out; so none is replaced); column 7 equals an *increase* over the preceding year in desired machines; column 8 equals 6 plus 7.

The table illustrates two aspects of the accelerator relationship. (a) The *percentage* amplitude of gross investment changes is greater than the swings in consumption: from year 20 to year 23, column 8 rises 200 percent while column 2 rises only 50 percent, and from year 23 (or year 25) to year 26, investment falls 100 percent while from year 25 to year 26 consumption falls less than 7 percent. The number of machines used (column 4) maintains a constant relation to shoe sales, but gross investment in machinery (column 8) varies proportionately more than does consumption. As the reader can verify with his own numbers, the more durable the machinery—that is, the smaller the depreciation rate—the greater is the percentage movement in investment in connection with a given consumption change.

(b) Although changes in consumption are the initiating factor (that is, the line of causation runs from consumption to investment), the *turning points* of investment precede those of consumption; for example, investment reaches its peak in year 22 and starts down after year 23, while consumption continues to rise through year 24 and does not fall until year 26. Why? Obviously, investment does not always move in the same direction as consumption. Rather, the relationship is that increases or decreases in investment are determined by the *rate* (not simply the *direction*) of change in consumption. As long as consumption increased by larger amounts each year (i.e., from year 20 to 21 and from year 21 to 22), investment rose; when consumption rose by a constant amount (i.e., the increase from year 21 to 22 equals the increase from year 22 to 23), investment was constant; when consumption rose by decreasing amounts (i.e., the increase from year 23 to 24 is smaller than the increase from year 22 to 23), investment fell. Similarly, investment falls when consumption goes down at an increasing rate, is constant when consumption falls at a constant rate, and increases when consumption falls at a decreasing rate.

The accelerator effect is not a rigid technological effect. Machines do not have to be purchased according to the inflexible assumptions in the preceding illustration. Some machines can be worked overtime, depreciation replacement can be deferred for a time, inventories can be used as buffer stocks to absorb fluctuations in consumption rates. A more general exposition allowing for flexibility in the assumed relationships would require advanced mathematical techniques and would yield a much greater variety of patterns of fluctuations of income, employment, and output. The basic result of a shift in consumption and consequent induced shifts of a transient nature in the investment function still would be present. We in fact do not know at any given time how much a given shift in the consumption function would lead to a similar or opposite-direction shift in the investment function. In one case the investment effect would reinforce the consumption effect on income, and in the other it would partially offset the effect of the consumption-function shift. In sum, we do not know at any moment whether the consumption function and the investment function will shift together in the same direction or independently or in exactly offsetting amounts and directions. What we do think we know is that the relationship between the two is not necessarily always the same; and a decrease in the consumption function can occur while the investment function stays unchanged. In this case, an apparent paradox results, the paradox of thrift.

The Paradox of Thrift

The "paradox" is: If the community as a whole tries to save *more*, it may well end up saving only the *same* number of dollars per time period or even *fewer* dollars, and with a lower national income in either case. Thus, the effort to save more results simply in saving a larger percentage of a smaller income, the absolute amount of saving in the new income equilibrium at best remaining unchanged.

The consequences of the paradox are especially significant in light of the fact that increased saving (and subsequently reduced income) appears most likely just when it is most unwelcome—in a depression. If it is desired that money income be maintained or increased, then spending must be maintained or increased. Consumption expenditure represents the major part of total spending. But can we reasonably expect consumers to spend *more* (i.e., save less) out of any given income as income tends to *fall*? If the man on your left lost his job two weeks ago and the man on your right lost his last week, with the odds dismally high that you soon will join them on the relief rolls, it would scarcely seem to be prudent behavior to go out on a spending spree.

But you may decide to increase your personal propensity to save for reasons other than a depression. It may be simply that you take Benjamin Franklin's "Poor Richard" seriously and decide to save more out of your current income. What are the repercussions?

Assuming that you succeed in screwing up your courage to the sticking point, your program of increased asceticism is successful: you save a larger proportion of a presumably unchanged income, and so you save more dollars per time period now than before. To be sure, the incomes of *other* people will not be unchanged. If you buy less chewing gum each week, the distributors and producers of gum will have smaller incomes, other things remaining the same; your dentist also may lose some business, if dental services and chewing gum are complementary goods. And if you put the saved money into a checking account, the bank, with its excess reserves thereby enlarged, may expand loans and make a greater income; the borrower from the bank likewise can produce a larger income with the loan than he could without it. The repercussions of your cutting back on chewing-gum consumption can spread widely, with some people surely hurt and quite possibly some being helped.

In an economy with a *GNP* in the neighborhood of $600,000,000,000, we may suppose that the repercussions of an individual's saving an extra 20 cents a week out of his chewing-gum account, while wide, will not be quantitatively momentous—either to the chewing-gum industry specifically or to the economy as a whole. Even if the amount of saving involved were much larger, it is not certain that the income of the chewing-gum industry itself, much less the income of the community generally, will be adversely affected. For your reduced purchases of gum may be offset, or more than offset, by increased purchases by the banker and others whose incomes have risen. (In addition, although we conveniently assumed earlier in the book that a person buys less of *everything* when his income falls, it is conceivable that an individual whose income has been reduced by your greater saving will, in his anxiety, chew more gum.)

The "saving paradox," however, relates, not to an *individual's* increasing his percentage of income saved, but to the *community's* shifting upward the aggregate saving schedule. Some people may be willing to save more at any given income level and some save less, but suppose that on balance the saving propensity for the economy shifts from S to S' in Figure 33–7a. Assume further that the investment schedule remains constant; the I curve is not only unchanged it is also horizontal.

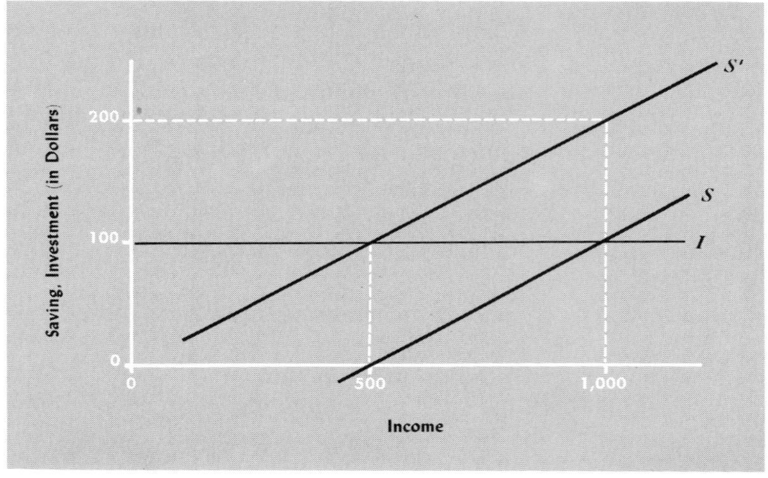

FIGURE 33–7a. The "paradox of thrift" with a horizontal investment schedule.

The initial income, determined by the intersection of the S and I curves, was 1,000. But with the propensity to save now being S', 1,000 is no longer the equilibrium level of income; at this income level, the community wishes (intends) to save more than it wishes to invest ($200 > 100$). The fact that the I curve is horizontal tells us that investment will be 100 irrespective of the value of income. Therefore, the adjustment required in bringing saving and investment back into equality falls entirely on saving. Saving must be reduced; so income must fall. In the diagram, when income has fallen as low as 500, the community has reduced its desired saving again to a level of 100. The results of the increased propensity to save are: (a) equilibrium income falls from 1,000 to 500; (b) the increase in the absolute amount of saving is only transitory during the period of income change, and in the new equilibrium, saving is just equal to what it was initially; and (c) therefore, the community now is saving a higher percentage of a smaller income—i.e., the *average* propensity to save (S/Y) has increased from .1 to .2.

It should be useful to interpret this case with Table 33–8a. In period 1, there exists an income equilibrium. (What is the evidence?) In period 2, there is an *autonomous increase in saving*. But the income of period 1 is disposed of in period 2 through consumption and saving, so that if saving in period 2 rises to 200, there must be an accompanying *autonomous fall in consumption* to 800.

Table 33–8a

PARADOX OF THRIFT WITH CONSTANT INVESTMENT

Period	*C*	*S*	*I*	*Y*
1	900	100	100	1,000
2	800	200	100	900
3	720	180	100	820
4	656	164	100	756
5	604.8	151.2	100	704.8
	.	.	.	.
	.	.	.	.
	.	.	.	.
*	400	100	100	500

The autonomus fall in consumption of 100, from period 1 to period 2, triggers the multiplier mechanism; we have here a "consumption multiplier" (in contrast to the "investment multiplier" in most earlier problems). The fall in income of 100 from period 1 to period 2 *induces* a further fall in consumption of 80 from period 2 to period 3, the marginal propensity to consume evidently being .8.

A gap of saving over investment of 100 appears in period 2. Income will reach a new equilibrium when it has fallen enough to induce saving to fall back to 100. If the change in saving must be —100, and if $MPS = .2$, it follows that the change in income must be —500, falling from the initial equilibrium value of 1,000 (at which level intended saving is 200) to the new equilibrium level of 500 (at which desired saving is 100). And the 500 fall in income induces a 400 fall in consumption, from 800 to 400. That is the "common sense" of the adjustment to the autonomous changes in consumption and saving. We can, of course, employ the multiplier formula: $k = \frac{1}{MPS} = \frac{1}{.2} = 5$; and $\Delta Y = k \times$ (autonomous change in spending). The "autonomous change in spending" in this case is the —100 change in consumption. Therefore, $\Delta Y = 5(-100) = -500$.

Consider an alternative case. In Figure 33–7b, the *I* curve has a positive slope. Beginning with the same initial income, saving, and investment as before, and with the same *MPS* and the same shift in the saving function, in this case of a positive marginal propensity to invest ($MPI = \Delta I/\Delta Y$), the fall in the equilibrium level of income is greater.

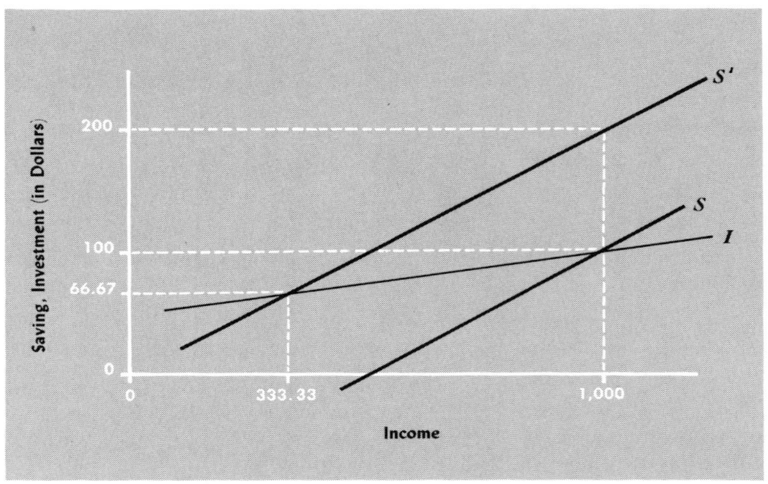

FIGURE 33–7b. The "paradox of thrift" with a positive marginal propensity to invest.

In Table 33–8b, we begin as before with the first two periods, and in period 3, the table is still the same as previously through the S column. But with an *MPI* greater than zero, investment falls as income falls. Suppose that $MPI = .05$. Then, the fall in income of 100 from periods 1 to 2 induces a fall in investment of 5 from periods 2 to 3. In each period, $Y = C + I$, as before; but now I as well as C is smaller with each succeeding period. (And, of course, $MPC + MPS = 1$, regardless of the value of *MPI*. Why?)

How far does the multiplier process take us before we reach a new income equilibrium? Whereas in Table 33–8a saving fell to equal a *constant* investment, in this second case, S is chasing a *diminishing* I. Since $MPS = .2$ and $MPI = .05$, the saving-investment gap is being closed at the rate of $20 - 5 = 15$ per 100 change in income. That is, $\Delta S - \Delta I = .15\Delta Y$. Since the total gap to be closed is 100, we can rewrite: $100 = .15\Delta Y$; therefore, $\Delta Y = 666.67$, which is a negative change.

Since income falls 666.67 as an ultimate result of consumption autonomously falling by 100, the apparent multiplier is 6.67. We can easily derive this from the basic equation of income change, in which is noted the two consumption components, autonomous (ΔC_a) and induced (ΔC_i):

$$\Delta Y = \Delta C_a + \Delta C_i + \Delta I$$

Rearranging:

$$\Delta C_a = \Delta Y - \Delta C_i - \Delta I$$

By definition:

$$k = \Delta Y / \Delta C_a$$

Substituting:

$$k = \frac{\Delta Y}{\Delta Y - \Delta C_i - \Delta I}$$

Dividing numerator and denominator by ΔY:

$$k = \frac{1}{1 - MPC - MPI} = \frac{1}{MPS - MPI}$$

$$k = \frac{1}{1 - .8 - .05} = \frac{1}{.2 - .05} = 6.67$$

Table 33–8b

PARADOX OF THRIFT WITH POSITIVE MARGINAL PROPENSITY TO INVEST

Period	C	S	I	Y
1	900	100	100	1,000
2	800	200	100	900
3	720	180	95	815
4	652	163	90.75	742.75
5	549.200	148.550	87.137	681.337
	.	.	.	.
	.	.	.	.
	.	.	.	.
*	266.666	66.667	66.667	333.333

The foregoing discussions of the accelerator and the paradox of thrift show that there is no unique relationship between shifts in the consumption and the investment functions. From one extreme of opposite and exactly offsetting shifts (with no consequent change in income) to independent shifts (as illustrated with the paradox of thrift case, wherein the consumption function alone falls) to the other extreme in which shifts in one function induce or are correlated with similar direction shifts in the other function, there is a very wide class of possible situations. The fact is that we know only that none of these is necessarily out of the question at any moment. Economists may differ about what is happening at any moment in terms of shifts in these functions; at times, they differ also as to the effects on the positions of these functions of general governmental policy (e.g., changes in taxes and government expenditures). Until better information is collected—and no one is sure just how that knowledge could be acquired—we must admit of a range of possible effects, rather than insist that one particular relationship always holds.

However, economic theory is not helpless. Some policy actions do have relatively clear-cut effects on the functions, and we shall investigate some of these. In the next chapter we look at some governmental fiscal-policy effects. And in later chapters we investigate a particularly powerful factor that almost invariably shifts both functions in the same predictable direction—the quantity of money in the community.

Questions

1. How can consumption be both a *function* of income and a *determinant* of income? Isn't it inconsistent to posit a "line of causation" between C and Y running in *both* directions?

2. "Consumption is a function of income." But what kind of income: "transient" (measured money) income or "permanent" income (wealth)? What is the distinction between these two kinds of income? In our analysis of income determination, why do we generally relate consumption to one kind of income rather than the other?

3. Distinguish between *autonomous* changes and *induced* changes in a variable (e.g., consumption). In the earlier discussion of supply and demand, was there an analogous distinction?

4. "One would scarcely hope for a *disequilibrium* level of national income, and no community would strive for disequilibrium. So far as national income is concerned, the great objective is to achieve an *equilibrium* level." Concur or dissent, with stated reasons.

5. Study the following graph.

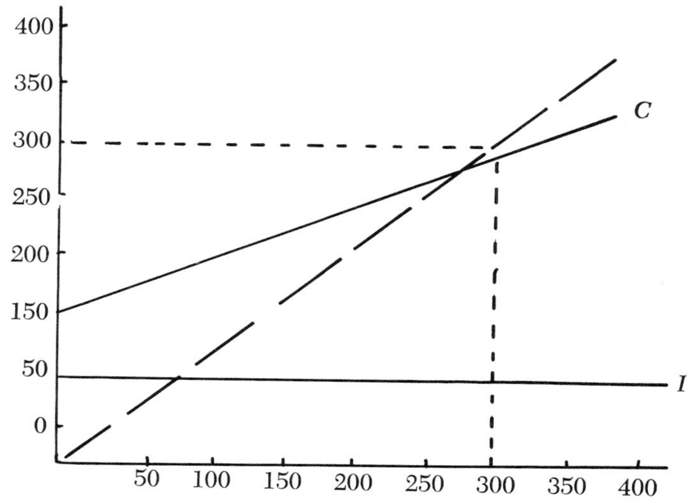

a. Carefully construct the propensity-to-save schedule.

b. In this example, what is the equation for the propensity to save?

c. In this example, what is the equation for the propensity to consume?

d. Define "marginal propensity to consume."

e. In this example, what is the numerical value of *MPC*?

f. With $I = 50$ at all income levels, what are the equilibrium values of income; consumption; saving?

g. If investment were to fall to zero at all income levels, would this be an induced or an autonomous change?

h. If investment were to fall by 50 at all income levels, then what would be the equilibrium values of income; consumption; saving?

i. Define "multiplier."

j. In this example, what is the numerical value of the multiplier?

For the remaining questions, suppose that the figure were redrawn, leaving the *C* curve unchanged but rotating the *I* curve around the point of "300 income and 50 investment," so that it goes through the origin.

k. Define "marginal propensity to invest."

l. In this example, what is the numerical value of *MPI*?

m. What are the equilibrium values of income; consumption; saving?

n. If investment were to fall by 50 at all income levels, what would be the equilibrium values of income; consumption; saving?

6. We have discussed two modes of determining equilibrium income or two approaches to characterizing the condition of equilibrium income: (a) the expenditure-income ap-

proach and (b) the saving-investment approach. Distinguish these alternative expositions; illustrate them both in the 45-degree diagram and in the arithmetic period table. How is it that they necessarily give the same answer?

7. "In income equilibrium, $S = I$. Therefore, the larger is S, the larger will be I; and the larger is I, the larger is income. Therefore, an autonomous increase in S leads, through a larger I, to a greater income." Right?

8. "Of course, $MPC + MPS = 1$, whether MPI equals 0 or .05 or any other value." Why?

9. In the latter part of the chapter, we discussed a case in which $MPC = .8$, $MPS = .2$, and $MPI = .05$; thus, $MPS > MPI$, and $MPC + MPI < 1$ (with $MPC + MPI$ being the "marginal propensity to *spend*"); and with autonomous changes in C and S, income moved from the initial equilibrium level to another equilibrium level. Now, redo Table 86, starting with all the same data as before *except* that $MPI = .25$. Also, try Table 86 with $MPI = .25$ and everything else as before *except* that the autonomous change in consumption is an increase instead of a decrease. Can you make any generalizations on the basis of these experiments?

10. The theory of income presented in this chapter hinges on the shapes, positions, and changes in position of certain schedules (or functions). In particular, the analysis has run largely in terms of *savings* and *investment* schedules. In the first part of the book, we analyzed frequently in terms of *supply* and *demand* schedules. Are the (income) relationships between savings and investment at all analogous to the (price) relationships between supply and demand? If so, is the analogy perfect, or can you distinguish the two sets of relationships from each other?

11. In the theory of the accelerator, how can it be that the line of causation runs from changes in consumption to changes in investment and yet the turning points in investment precede the turning points in consumption? Is this not a case of the result's preceding the cause?

12. Two eighteenth-century giants assure us that saving is splendid. Benjamin Franklin counsels that "a penny saved is a penny earned," and Adam Smith concludes that "every prodigal" is "a public enemy," while "every frugal man" is "a public benefactor." Does the "paradox of thrift" demolish this ancient wisdom—or turn it on its head?

13. Prepare two alternative versions of the table on page 613, in which the first four columns are the same as in the original table, but with the life of a machine being five years in one case and twenty years in the other. The original table, plus these two alternative versions, illustrates what characteristic of the accelerator?

34

NATIONAL-INCOME THEORY: FISCAL POLICY

Aside from fleeting references to the governmental and foreign-trade sectors of the economy, our attention has been directed to the other components of national income: consumption, investment, and saving. Still leaving until later the effects of changes in the quantity of money and of foreign trade, we now incorporate government into the income model. Thus, in the income-creation equation, we shall have government spending—$Y = C + I + G$; and in the income-disposal equation, tax collections—$Y = C + S + T$.

This expansion of the equations is not made just for the sake of adding additional details. Rather, these variables have a special significance because they are subject to fairly close determination by government agencies exercising *discretionary* authority. In the awesome machinery of government—and the emphasis here is on the federal government—it is impossible to point to a particular person or even to a department or agency exercising sole spending or taxing discretion. Nor can government spokesmen foretell precisely just what will be the dollar values of government spending and taxing over the next year or two. (It is using very gentle language to suggest that forecasts of government expenditures and receipts are "imprecise." They may each turn out to be five or ten billion dollars different from what was predicted a year or so earlier.) Nevertheless, these spending and taxation figures (especially the spending figures) are subject to governmental decisions which are determinable to a considerable degree in isolation from the rest of the economy.

Because government action is relatively autonomous, government spending and taxing can be used consciously and deliberately for the purpose of influencing national income. Governmental spending and taxing (and borrowing) for the purpose of influencing national income is "fiscal policy." The government can affect income *directly* by varying the rate of government spending and *indirectly* by varying tax collections and thereby affecting the levels of consumption and investment.

Suppose that we have the following situation:

C	*S*	*G*	*I*	*Y*	*T*	*D*
720	180	100	180	1,000	100	900

(All symbols should be familiar except the last: $D = Y - T =$ "disposable" income—i.e., income net of tax.) Income of 1,000 is at an equilibrium level, for in that period total injections $(G + I)$ equal total leakages $(S + T)$. But while income is at an *equilibrium* level, it may not be at a *full-employment* level (where "full employment" is consistent with "frictional unemployment," as discussed in Chapter 31).

Imagine that government officials (perhaps the President, with the compliance of Congressional leaders, on the advice of a few economists and many lawyers scattered through various departments) decide to raise income to 1,200, an increase of 200. How was the figure of 1,200 determined? There are a number of infallible guides, including a wetted finger to the breeze and a Ouija board. Now, some recalcitrants may deny the infallibility of such sources: some suggest an increase of 93 and others an increase of 469; some want an expansionary policy but prefer to rely wholly on monetary policy, leaving government spending and tax rates unchanged; others desire some judicious mixture of monetary and fiscal policy; and a few even deny that expansion is the right *direction* in which to move. The fact is, of course, that even if all of the governmental advisers and officials decide that (a) an expansionary policy is desirable and (b) reliance is to be placed on fiscal policy, no one *knows* just how big a change in income is required for full employment—or just how much production will increase if full employment is achieved. And (c) even if all agree on an increase of 200 in income through fiscal policy, no one *knows* just how big a change in government spending and/or tax rates is required to achieve the desired income increase. Finally, (d) there will be considerable heartburn over the question of relative emphasis on the two tools of fiscal policy, with some favoring a tax cut (which taxes?) and others an increase in government expenditures (on what goods?) and still others some combination.

There are still other things which are unknown but which it would be nice to know (e.g., how much price inflation, if any, would be generated by increasing income by 200). But enough has been said to warn the reader that the world is neither so easily predictable nor so readily described as the following mechanical discussion might suggest. Still, if not taken as being either comprehensive or literally descriptive, the mechanics are useful.

To return to our illustration, the *objective* is to raise the equilibrium level of income from 1,000 to 1,200; and there are two *policy variables* available, to be used either singly or together: government spending and the tax rate (r). An infinite number of combinations of ΔG and Δr will meet the income objective, but they fall into the following categories:

1. Increase G; r unchanged.
2. G unchanged; r reduced.
3. Increase G; r reduced.
4. Increase G and increase r with budget balanced.
5. Increase G and increase r with budget deficit.
6. Increase G and increase r with budget surplus.
7. Decrease G and decrease r with budget deficit.

This list of alternative "routes to full employment" is asymmetrical. Specifically, first, there is no analogue to route 3; we cannot decrease G and increase r in order to raise income. Second, whereas we can increase G and increase r with a deficit, a surplus, or a balanced budget, if G and r are decreased, there must be a deficit.

Route 1

The first policy—increasing government spending and holding the tax *rate* (not tax *collections*) constant—is illustrated in Table 34–1. The autonomous increase in G triggers the multiplier mechanism.[1] Table 34–1 provides the first five periods plus the new equilibrium values. Tax collections increase as income rises, but in the new income equilibrium a budget deficit still prevails: G (156) $>$ T (120). Saving also increases; and, in equilibrium, S (216) $+$ T (120) $=$ I (180) $+$ G (156).

While we here filled in the table by first deducing ΔG through a bit of

[1] It requires a little manipulating to determine that $\Delta G = 56$. One procedure is to use the following model, in terms of *changes* in the variables:

$$\Delta Y = \Delta C + \Delta G$$
$$\Delta C = c\Delta D$$
(where c is the marginal propensity to consume with respect to *disposable* income—i.e., $c = \Delta C/\Delta D$)
$$\Delta D = \Delta Y - \Delta T$$
$$\Delta T = r\Delta Y$$

Therefore, by substituting:

$$\begin{aligned}\Delta C &= c(\Delta Y - \Delta T)\\ &= c\Delta Y(1 - r)\\ \Delta Y &= c\Delta Y(1 - r) + \Delta G\\ &= \frac{\Delta G}{1 - c + cr}\\ \Delta G &= \Delta Y(1 - c + cr)\end{aligned}$$

The policy calls for $\Delta Y = 200$; and if we take $c = .8$ and $r = .1$, then $\Delta G = 56$.

algebraic doodling, we could have done so in "commonsensical" fashion. Begin with the final equilibrium row. We know the value of Y, for that is the specified objective; since, in this first route, $\Delta r = 0$, we thereby can calculate T and then D; with the value of D (and thus ΔD), we can determine C and S. I is assumed constant; and, since $Y = C + I + G$, we can infer G. Having obtained G and ΔG, we can then go back to period 2 and proceed to fill in as many periods as are desired.

Table 34–1

GOVERNMENT SPENDING INCREASED, TAX RATE UNCHANGED

($\Delta G = 56$; $\Delta r = 0$)

C	S	G	I	Y	T	D
720	180	100	180	1,000	100	900
720	180	156	180	1,056	105.600	950.400
760.320	190.080	156	180	1,096.320	109.632	986.688
789.350	197.338	156	180	1,125.350	112.535	1,012.815
810.252	202.563	156	180	1,146.252	114.625	1,031.627
.	.	.	.	.	.	.
.	.	.	.	.	.	.
.	.	.	.	.	.	.
864	216	156	180	1,200	120	1,080

Route II

An equation can be deduced for calculating directly the necessary decrease in the tax rate. However, we can fill in the new equilibrium values without the Δr equation. We know, by assumed objective, that $Y = 1{,}200$; and we know, by assumption, that $G = 100$ and $I = 180$; since $C = Y - (G + I)$, then $C = 920$. But if $\Delta C = 920 - 720 = 200$, it follows that $\Delta D = 250$. (Why?) And since $T = Y - D$, then $T = 1{,}200 - 1{,}150 = 50$. Finally, $r = T/Y = 50/1{,}200 = .04167$. Having thereby found r, we can fill in the entire table. Thus the multiplier mechanism which ultimately yields a new equilibrium income of 1,200 is triggered by an autonomous fall in tax collections of 58.333 ($= 100 - 41.667$) in the second period—compared to an autonomous increase in government spending of 56 in Route I.

Table 34–2

GOVERNMENT SPENDING UNCHANGED, TAX RATE REDUCED

($\Delta G = 0$; $\Delta r = -.05833$)

C	*S*	*G*	*I*	*Y*	*T*	*D*
720	180	100	180	1,000	100	900
720	180	100	180	1,000	41.667	958.333
766.666	191.667	100	180	1,046.666	43.615	1,003.051
802.441	200.610	100	180	1,082.441	45.105	1,037.336
829.869	207.467	100	180	1,109.869	46.248	1,063.621
.	.	.	.	.	.	.
.	.	.	.	.	.	.
.	.	.	.	.	.	.
920	230	100	180	1,200	50	1,150

Route III

We can "combine" the first two routes, increasing G by less than 56 and reducing r by less than .05833. If we decide arbitrarily on a new value for either of these variables, the value of the other is implied. If, on the one hand, we designate that $\Delta G = 50$, we can (as in Route II) immediately determine the new equilibrium value of C, and this implies the new D and then the new T and r. On the other hand, if we decide that $r = -.00625$ and therefore that the new $r = .09375$, we can calculate T and therefore D; the change in D implies the change in C and thus the necessary value of G.

Route IV

In each of the preceding alternatives, a budget deficit ($G > T$) was created with the inception of the policy, and a deficit (of smaller magnitude) still existed even when the new equilibrium income was attained. It might be supposed that *any* income-expansionary policy *must* be characterized by a deficit. After all, how could it be expansionary for the government to relieve the community of as many dollars through collecting taxes as it pumps into the income stream through spending? And yet, as Table 34–4 illustrates, even though the budget was bal-

Table 34–3

GOVERNMENT SPENDING INCREASED, TAX RATE REDUCED

($\Delta G = 50$; $\Delta r = -.00625$)

C	*S*	*G*	*I*	*Y*	*T*	*D*
720	180	100	180	1,000	100	900
720	180	150	180	1,050	98.438	951.562
761.250	190.312	150	180	1,091.250	102.305	988.945
791.156	197.789	150	180	1,121.156	105.108	1,016.048
812.838	203.210	150	180	1,142.838	107.141	1,035.697
.	.	.	.	.	.	.
.	.	.	.	.	.	.
.	.	.	.	.	.	.
870	217.500	150	180	1,200	112.500	1,087.500

anced initially and is balanced in the new equilibrium (at a higher level of spending and taxing), income has again increased to 1,200.[2]

Income rises by 200 simply because the *spending* components which constitute income have increased in the aggregate by 200. The important point with respect to income creation is *not* the government deficit (or, more generally, the government budget) per se; rather, it is the matter of *aggregate spending*. In our illustration, investment spending is assumed, as before, to be unchanged; consumption spending is held unchanged (actually lower during the transition) by the curtailment of disposable income as a result of the increased tax rate and consequently the increased tax collection; so income rises, dollar for dollar, by the increase in government spending.[3] Indeed, income increases by the increase in

[2] The basic answer to the puzzle does *not* lie in the fact that a deficit exists throughout the transition from the initial equilibrium to the new, beginning with the third period. For, as the reader can verify with his own table, it would be possible to maintain a budget *surplus* all through the transition, either by increasing G only gradually to 300 instead of jumping directly to that figure or by initially raising r to more than .25 and then gradually reducing it to that figure. As a third variant on the "balanced-budget route," we could eliminate the transition entirely, by increasing G to 300 in the *same* period as r is increased to .25 instead of increasing G in the *following* period, as in the table.

[3] Initially, in a given time period, $G = T$, and—with a balanced-budget route—$G = T$ in the new equilibrium. Therefore, since total leakages necessarily equal total injections in equilibrium, $S = I$ when the multiplier mechanism has worked itself out; and since I is unchanged, S also is unchanged. But if $\Delta S = 0$, then $\Delta D = \Delta C = 0$. And if $\Delta C = \Delta I = 0$, then $\Delta G = \Delta Y$.

Table 34–4

INCREASED GOVERNMENT SPENDING AND TAX RATE, BUDGET BALANCED

($\Delta G = 200$; $\Delta r = .15$)

C	*S*	*G*	*I*	*Y*	*T*	*D*
720	180	100	180	1,000	100	900
720	180	100	180	1,000	250	750
600	150	300	180	1,080	270	810
648	162	300	180	1,128	282	846
676.8	169.2	300	180	1,156.8	289.2	867.6
.	.	.	.	.	.	.
.	.	.	.	.	.	.
.	.	.	.	.	.	.
720	180	300	180	1,200	300	900

aggregate spending even if the government has a budget *surplus*—as we shall see in Route VI.

It may be objected that if disposable income is not increased (and even is decreased during the transition), this balanced-budget policy is scarcely worthwhile. The objection seems to gain force if the increase in money income is accompanied by increased employment; for if a given disposable income is divided among more employees, the *average* disposable income per *employed* worker actually falls. While a previously unemployed person who now has a job is better off (i.e., some income is better than none), those who already had jobs and who now have a lower income are worse off.

What can we say about the "goodness" of this policy? Two types of evaluation can be suggested. First, while aggregate disposable income is not increased, total output may well be larger. Presumably it will be larger if employment has gone up; if there has been no price inflation, the entire increase in money income represents an equivalent increase in real income. (Of course, if there *is* some degree of inflation, one consequence is that *real* disposable income is actually *less* as a result of the fiscal policy.) With disposable income unchanged, the entire increase in real output (income) goes to, and is disposed of by, the government. This enlarged "communal" income can take the form of, say, more parks and missiles. So those (previously employed) workers who now have smaller incomes may be mollified by the availability of more public parks, where they can sit in the evenings and happily contemplate the nation's growing military strength.

Some workers, however, may feel that their enjoyment of the communal income does not fully compensate them for their loss of private income. And if some members of the community are hurt by a policy, even though others gain, it is not clear that the policy has increased over-all "social welfare." At least in abstract principle, there is a possible solution to this "welfare" problem. Give *no* private income to the newly employed, and continue to split up the unchanged aggregate disposable income among the originally employed; the originally employed thus have as much private (money) income as before, in addition to greater communal income; and the newly employed have no less private income than before, but they do gain in communal income. With the aid of some supporting—and perhaps heroic—assumptions (notably, that the utility of increased communal income to the newly employed is greater than the disutility of work and the disutility of receiving no private income when others are being paid), we can conclude that social welfare is unambiguously increased: *everyone* is better off!

This favorable evaluation of the balanced-budget policy may appear unconvincing. Some may deem the constancy of disposable income to be a fatal objection. But consider another evaluative approach, one in which it is considered actually *desirable* to curtail disposable income. Suppose it to be 1939 or 1940. There is a substantial amount of unemployed resources; there is also a growing and serious threat of war. Therefore, we have a twofold objective: (a) increase national income to 1,200, and (b) prevent private consumption (and investment) from rising, thereby permitting all of the increased output of the economy to flow to the government for the war effort. Route IV meets both conditions—and Route VI, below, gains the first objective while actually *reducing* the consumption "absorption" of the national output.

Route V

If Y is to be raised to 1,200 by increasing both G and r in such manner as to have a budget deficit in the new equilibrium, ΔG must be greater than 56 and Δr greater than 0 (as in Route I), and ΔG must be less than 200 and Δr less than .15 (as in Route IV). Table 34–5 is based on arbitrarily choosing $\Delta G = 100$, thereby implying $\Delta r = .04583$, or choosing the value for Δr, thereby implying the value for ΔG. For brevity, only the initial and the new equilibrium data are given.

Route VI

A policy of greater G and r with a budget surplus calls for increasing both variables by more than they were raised in Route IV. One possible case is given in Table 34–6.

Table 34–5

INCREASED GOVERNMENT SPENDING AND TAX RATE, BUDGET DEFICIT

($\Delta G = 100$; $\Delta r = .04583$)

C	*S*	*G*	*I*	*Y*	*T*	*D*
720	180	100	180	1,000	100	900
820	205	200	180	1,200	175	1,025

Table 34–6

INCREASED GOVERNMENT SPENDING AND TAX RATE, BUDGET SURPLUS

($\Delta G = 300$; $\Delta r = .25417$)

C	*S*	*G*	*I*	*Y*	*T*	*D*
720	180	100	180	1,000	100	900
620	155	400	180	1,200	425	775

Route VII

If the income objective is to be attained by reducing both *G* and *r* (necessarily with a budget deficit), *r* must fall by more than in Route II. For example:

Table 34–7

INCREASED GOVERNMENT SPENDING AND TAX RATE, BUDGET DEFICIT

($\Delta G = -20$; $\Delta r = -.07917$)

C	*S*	*G*	*I*	*Y*	*T*	*D*
720	180	100	180	1,000	100	900
940	235	80	180	1,200	25	1,175

Which Route?

There are, then, these seven types of combinations of ΔG and Δr, each of which results in a ΔY of 200; and each type has variations of one sort or another. Which of the infinity of alternatives is best? Or, since each can affect income by the same amount, are they all equally good?

What are some of the possible criteria that may be used in evaluating the alternative routes? First of all, probably almost everyone would agree that the smaller the tax collections, the better. Even if one desires certain consequences of greater taxes (e.g., to curtail disposable income, as in Route IV), few people rejoice in higher taxes as such. Other things being equal, we presumably want T to be smaller rather than larger.

A second criterion relates to the size of government spending. Some would prefer G, considered in isolation, to be as small as possible. Some would be pleased to have G larger within a broad and indefinite limit. Perhaps others might be content to see G rise to, say, 50 percent higher than initially (i.e., from 100 to 150) in order better to fulfill its "obligations."

The size of disposable income provides a third criterion. Whereas one might expect a majority of the community to prefer a greater D to a smaller, at times, as in girding for war, a smaller D is preferred. Furthermore, just as some may prefer a larger G on grounds, say, that government uses resources more "efficiently" and "equitably" than do households and business firms, so a reduction in private income may be desired.

Still another criterion is the status of the government budget. One might feel that the smaller the deficit or the larger the surplus, the better. Or perhaps a zero balance is judged to be ideal, with any surplus deemed better than any deficit, but with smaller surpluses preferred to larger and smaller deficits preferred to larger.

Even this brief and incomplete review is enough to indicate (a) that there are various criteria and (b) that no route is best according to all criteria. These conclusions are illustrated in Table 34–8. The table lists the criteria we have mentioned; the *original* data for T, G, D, and $G - T$ are noted in parentheses at the top. The numbers outside parentheses in the various columns are the *new* equilibrium data for the alternative routes. And the numbers in parentheses in the columns indicate the preference ranking of the specified route with respect to the criterion in question. For example, initially $T = 100$; and, in the new equilibrium achieved by Route I, $T = 120$—which makes Route I the fourth best of the seven routes according to the criterion of minimizing tax collections.

There are, then, fiscal ways and ways to get income up to 1,200. And in trying to determine the best way, we are faced, first, with the problem of *identifying* the possible criteria and, second, with the problem of *weighting* the several

Table 34–8

SUMMARY EVALUATION OF ALTERNATIVE FISCAL POLICIES WITH ALTERNATIVE CRITERIA

	Tax Collections (100):	Government Expenditures (100):			Disposable Income (900):		Government Budget (0):	
	Small *T*	Large *G*	Small *G*	Ideal *G* = 150	Large *D*	Small *D*	Small Deficit or Large Surplus	Balance, Surplus, or Deficit
I	120 (4)	156 (4)	(4)	(2)	1,080 (4)	(4)	—36 (4)	(4)
II	50 (2)	100 (6)	(2)	(3 tie)	1,150 (2)	(6)	—50 (6)	(6)
III	112.5 (3)	150 (5)	(3)	(1)	1,087.5 (3)	(5)	—37.5 (5)	(5)
IV	300 (6)	300 (2)	(6)	(6)	900 (6)	(2)	0 (2)	(1)
V	175 (5)	200 (3)	(5)	(3 tie)	1,025 (5)	(3)	—25 (3)	(3)
VI	425 (7)	400 (1)	(7)	(7)	775 (7)	(1)	25 (1)	(2)
VII	25 (1)	80 (7)	(1)	(5)	1,175 (1)	(7)	—55 (7)	(7)

criteria. Route VII, for example, is ranked first according to some of the criteria and last according to others. What is the weighted average of these rankings?

A Variation: Increase G with Y Constant

We have considered cases in which Y was raised to 1,200 while D and C were held constant (Route IV) or reduced (Route VI). It was suggested that such cases might represent a situation of unemployed resources in which for military reasons it was important to raise G; all of the increased income could then be directed to the government. Now, suppose that there are no substantial idle resources to draw upon, so that real income cannot be appreciably increased. The only way for the government to acquire more of the total output is to curtail the output going to the rest of the economy. One way to do this is to raise taxes and thereby reduce disposable income, thus inducing a fall in consumption. (*Some* forms of investment also may be curtailed, but while fewer bowling alleys are built, General Motors will build a Willow Run plant to turn out tanks. Aggregate investment could well increase, even though its composition is changed. For convenience, in the table below, we continue the assumption that I remains constant.)

Suppose that G is increased to 300. With I held at 180 and with the stipulation that Y remains 1,000 (for, with full employment, an increase in money income is a reflection of inflation, not of increased output), it follows that C must be cut to 520. The fall in C requires that D be reduced to 650; thus, T is raised to 350, giving a new $r = 350/1{,}000 = .35$.

Table 34–9

GOVERNMENT SPENDING INCREASED WITH INCOME CONSTANT

($\Delta G = 200$; $\Delta r = .25$)

C	S	G	I	Y	T	D
720	180	100	180	1,000	100	900
520	130	300	180	1,000	350	650

If an increase in money income is to be avoided, it is not sufficient to raise T simply by the amount of raising G. It is not enough to "pay our way" by matching government spending with tax collections, dollar for dollar, keeping the budget balanced. To avoid inflation, taxes must be raised by *more* than government spending; we must generate a *surplus*.[4]

On this criterion, the U.S. record of war financing is not very good, but improving. In the Civil War period, 1861–65, federal government receipts (other than receipts from borrowing) were equal to only 24 percent of expenditures; in the World War I period, 1917–19, receipts were 30 percent of expenditures; for World War II, 1941–46, receipts were 45 percent of expenditures; and for the Korean War, 1950–53, receipts were 94 percent of expenditures.[5] Except for the latter case, receipts (from taxes and other sources) did not even closely approach expenditures, much less exceed them. But progress has been made: the percentage gets bigger with each war. After a few more tries, we'll get the hang of it.

Automatic Stabilizers

In the first part of this chapter, we investigated alternative *discretionary fiscal policies* for the raising of national income. In addition to deliberate changing of government spending and of the tax rate, the *fiscal system* itself "automatically" acts to modify fluctuations in income. So-called automatic, or built-in, stabilizers cannot hold the income level constant (indeed, the stabilizers operate only as income varies), but they act to dampen the income effects of autonomous changes in spending components.

Of the several stabilizers, the most obvious is the income tax. The existence of a tax rate (and thus of tax collections) in the income model we have used served the purpose of "stabilizing" income—that is, reducing the size of income fluctuations—even though we employed a "proportional" rate, and a "progressive" rate would have been even more effective.[6]

[4] If there is initially a sufficiently large deficit, in the new equilibrium the budget must be *balanced.* (For example, if tax collections in Table 34–9 had been only 50, giving a deficit of $100 - 50 = 50$, G could be raised from 100 to 300 without raising the equilibrium level of income if the budget is balanced in the final equilibrium—that is, if T is raised from 50 to 300. Try it.) And if the budget is in even larger deficit, then a *deficit* (of reduced magnitude) is required. But in any case, it is necessary that $\Delta T > \Delta G$.

[5] Calculated from data in U.S. Bureau of the Census, *Historical Statistics of the United States, Colonial Times to 1957* (Washington, D.C., 1960), p. 711.

[6] With a "proportional" tax, collections change with income by the same percentage, and "progressive" tax collections change by a larger percentage. To put the distinction differently, with a proportional tax, the marginal tax rate ($\Delta T/\Delta Y$) *equals* the average rate (T/Y): $T = rY$, and the schedule of tax collections is a straight line through the origin of the 45-degree diagram; with a progressive tax, the marginal rate *exceeds* the average rate: $T = a + rY$, where a is the (negative) vertical-axis intercept of the tax-collection schedule. In the figure, T_1 reflects a proportional tax and T_2 a progressive tax ($a = -50$), with $100 collected under each alternative at the assumed initial income level of $1,000. Obviously, the marginal tax rate, measured by the slope of the T curve, is greater with T_2 than with T_1 (with the slope of T_1 measuring also the average rate in both cases at the initial income level): $r_1 = .1$, and $r_2 = .15$.

In Table 34–10 we have three alternative cases involving an autonomous fall of investment by 30. Basically, all cases begin with the same equilibrium situation—although, in the first case, in which there is no taxation leakage, saving is correspondingly higher. In Case B, the marginal tax rate equals the average, so that Y and T move together proportionately. The result is that income falls substantially less than in Case A. The autonomous change in investment is the same in both instances, but the effect of introducing the (proportionate) tax rate into the model is to reduce the multiplier from $\frac{1}{1-c}$ to $\frac{1}{1-c+cr}$ and thus to reduce the repercussion on income of the fall in investment.[7] The new equilibrium will be attained when total leakages are induced to fall to the new lower level of total injections, and in Case B we have a second leakage, taxes, to supplement saving, so a relatively small change in income is required to bring leakages and injections in a given period back into equality.

In Case C, beginning with the same average tax rate ($100/1000 = .1$) as in Case B, the marginal rate ($r = .15$) is greater. As income falls, the tax leakage falls more rapidly than in Case B, thereby reducing $(S + T)$ to the new level of $(G + I)$ before income has been reduced so far. It is apparent that, other things the same, the more responsive is T to changes in Y, i.e., the greater

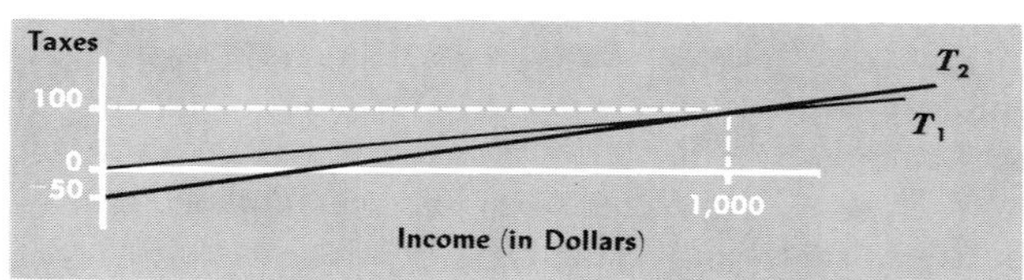

[7] The latter multiplier was derived in footnote 1 of this chapter by means of variables couched in terms of *changes*. Let us now obtain the equilibrium-income equation in the following manner:

$$Y = C + I + G,$$
$$C = cD,$$
$$D = Y - T$$
$$T = rY$$
$$I = \bar{I}$$
$$G = \bar{G} \qquad \text{where } I \text{ and } G \text{ are constant (i.e., nonfunctional) values;}$$

by substituting and rearranging:

$$Y = c(Y - rY) + \bar{I} + \bar{G}$$
$$Y - cY(1 - r) = \bar{I} + \bar{G}$$
$$Y = \frac{\bar{I} + \bar{G}}{1 - c + cr}$$
$$= \frac{150 + 100}{1 - .2 + .08} = 892.857$$

Table 34–10

EFFECTS OF AUTONOMOUS FALL IN INVESTMENT

(A) AUTONOMOUS FALL IN INVESTMENT WITH NO TAX

C	*S*	*G*	*I*	*Y*
720	280	100	180	1,000
720	280	100	150	970
696	274	100	150	946
.	.	.	.	.
.	.	.	.	.
.	.	.	.	.
600	250	100	150	850

(B) AUTONOMOUS FALL IN INVESTMENT WITH PROPORTIONAL TAXATION ($r = .1$)

C	*S*	*G*	*I*	*Y*	*T*	*D*
720	180	100	180	1,000	100	900
720	180	100	150	970	97	873
698.4	174.6	100	150	948.4	94.84	853.56
.	.	.	.	.	.	.
.	.	.	.	.	.	.
.	.	.	.	.	.	.
642.857	160.714	100	150	892.857	89.286	803.571

(C) AUTONOMOUS FALL IN INVESTMENT WITH PROGRESSIVE TAXATION ($r = .15$)

C	*S*	*G*	*I*	*Y*	*T*	*D*
720	180	100	180	1,000	100	900
720	180	100	150	970	95.5	874.5
699.6	174.9	100	150	949.6	92.44	857.16
.	.	.	.	.	.	.
.	.	.	.	.	.	.
.	.	.	.	.	.	.
656.250	164.062	100	150	906.250	85.938	820.312

is the marginal tax rate and thus the more "progressive" is the tax, the smaller need be the change in income in order to equate leakages with injections.[8]

While a progressive tax-rate structure provides a more powerful "automatically stabilizing" effect than does a proportional rate structure, the progressivity of personal-income-tax rates in the United States actually means little in terms of government revenue and thus adds little to stabilization—however desirable it may seem to some on the (non-economic) criterion of egalitarian equity.[9] Some four fifths of taxpayers have incomes in the first (that is, 20 percent) tax

[8] Let us make explicit the income equation for the "progressive" Case C:

$$Y = C + I + G$$
$$C = cD$$
$$D = Y - T$$
$$T = a + rY \qquad \text{(In our illustration, } T = -50 + .15Y.\text{)}$$
$$I = \bar{I}$$
$$G = \bar{G};$$

thus:

$$Y = c(Y - a - rY) + \bar{I} + \bar{G}$$
$$Y - cY + crY = \bar{I} + \bar{G} - ca$$
$$Y = \frac{\bar{I} + \bar{G} - ca}{1 - c + cr}$$
$$= \frac{150 + 100 + 40}{1 - .8 + .12} = 906.25.$$

[9] The (marginal) tax rates in the various brackets of taxable income—that is, the rates which apply only to those parts of income falling within the respective brackets—range from 20 percent to 91 percent. The *average* tax rate for people with income beyond the lowest tax bracket is naturally smaller than the marginal, for the marginal rises from the outset. In addition to the rate being higher in each succeeding income bracket, other features depress the average well below the marginal, including the filing of joint returns by married couples and the relatively low maximum rate applied to capital gains. The *average* effective rates for joint returns in 1956 were as follows:

Returns with adjusted gross income of:	Actual tax as percent of adjusted gross income:
$600– 2,500	4
2,500– 5,000	7
5,000– 10,000	11
10,000– 15,000	15
15,000– 20,000	17
20,000– 25,000	20
25,000– 50,000	25
50,000– 100,000	35
100,000– 150,000	41
150,000– 200,000	44
200,000– 500,000	47
500,000–1,000,000	49
1,000,000 or more	49

SOURCE: Richard A. Musgrave, "How Progressive Is the Income Tax?" *Tax Revision Compendium* (Washington, D.C.: House Committee on Ways and Means, 1959), p. 2226.

bracket (taxable incomes up to $2,000 for single persons and $4,000 for married couples). Over three fifths of taxable income is in the first bracket; another fifth of taxable income is in the second (that is, 22 percent) bracket ($2,000 up to $4,000 for single persons and $4,000 up to $8,000 for married couples). More precisely, 83 percent of taxable income is found in only the first two tax brackets—and the tax collections from this income amount to 73 percent of total income-tax collections. To indicate in another way the modest significance of progressivity, if the entire taxable income were taxed at the basic 20 percent, tax collections would be 86 percent of actual collections. And if all taxable income were taxed at a rate of 23 percent—between the actual rates of the second and third brackets—collections would equal the actual collections under the law existing at the end of 1963.[10]

Taxes—in particular, the progressive personal income tax—are not the only stabilizer. All automatic government-transfer payments and nondiscretionary government expenditures which "run counter" to income fluctuations and thus modify those changes can be classed as stabilizers. Such, for example, is unemployment-compensation payments (and taxes): as income falls and unemployment rises, payments would increase (and tax collections for the program would fall), thus tending to support disposable income and spending. While our discussion and illustrations have been related to modifying decreases in income, the stabilizers tend also to dampen increases in income—although the symmetry of operation of the stabilizers is not always matched by the attitudes of observers; for some people, while rejoicing in the alleviation of recessions, take a dimmer view of restraints on expansions.

The quantitative importance of automatic stabilizers is not trivial: in the four postwar recessions, the federal government's budget moved in the direction of bigger deficits or smaller surpluses for "automatic" reasons by an average of about $6,500,000,000, and in the recoveries, the change in the budget toward larger surpluses or smaller deficits was over $11,000,000,000. Indeed, generally and on the average, the magnitudes of automatic budget changes were much larger than those of discretionary changes. Furthermore, the automatic changes were always countercyclical, whereas discretionary moves sometimes leaned perversely with the wind rather than against it.[11]

[10] Calculations are from 1963 data supplied by the Office of the Secretary of the Treasury, reprinted in Committee on Federal Tax Policy, *Financing America's Future: Taxes, Economic Stability and Growth* (New York, September 1963), p. 46.

[11] See Wilfred Lewis, Jr., *Federal Fiscal Policy in the Postwar Recessions* (Washington, D.C.: The Brookings Institution, 1962).

Questions

1. Evaluate the following quoted statements.

a. "A disadvantage of using public works as a counter-cyclical policy is that tax collections would have to be raised in depressions in order to finance the government expenditures."

b. In 1947, a year of "full" employment, President Truman vetoed a tax-reduction bill, and a financial columnist commented: "Perhaps the most curious argument in the tax message [of the President] was that when business is active and employment high, it is unwise to reduce taxes. In other words, we must not cut taxes when there is a lot of money coming into the Treasury, but we must wait for a depression, when tax revenues fall, to cut taxes. Whoever wrote this tax-veto message would have a tough time getting a passing mark in a course in freshman economics."

c. "Inflation, by definition, is a situation in which prices are rising, which is to say that the purchasing power of the dollar is falling. Since the value of each dollar is being reduced, it is in the interest of each person to retain command over as many of his dollars as possible; and thus it is appropriate in a period of inflation to cut taxes."

2. Following are seven separate problems pertaining to fiscal policy—i.e., adjustments (increase or decrease) in G (government spending) and in r (marginal and average tax rate). In *each* of the seven cases, assume the following initial situation:

C	S	I	G	Y	T	D
700	100	100	200	1,000	200	800

In each case, assume $c = \Delta C/\Delta D = .9$. There are no induced changes in G and none in I except in the last case.

Now, your job is to compute the *final equilibrium* rows (periods) for each case—with one or two or three of the figures already filled in.

a. Adjust G; r constant.

C	S	I	G	Y	T	D
		100		1,250		

b. G constant; adjust r.

C	S	I	G	Y	T	D
		100	200	1,250		

c. $G = 250$; adjust r.

C	S	I	G	Y	T	D
		100	250	1,000		

d. $G = 250$; adjust r.

C	S	I	G	Y	T	D
		100	250	900		

e. Adjust G; adjust r.

C	S	I	G	Y	T	D
		100	250	1,250		

f. Consumption initially falls autonomously by 50; adjust G; r constant.

C	S	I	G	Y	T	D
		100		1,250		

g. Adjust G; r constant; $i = \Delta I/\Delta Y = .05$.

C	S	I	G	Y	T	D
				1,250		

3. Assume the following equilibrium values:

$$Y = 1600 \qquad I = 380$$
$$C = 1000 \qquad G = 220$$
$$S = 310 \qquad T = \ ?$$

Assume further that investment remains constant at 380 throughout the analysis; finally, assume that *MPC* (with respect to disposable income) is .8.

a. What is the level of government tax collections?

b. Is the government running a surplus or a deficit? Of how much?

c. What is the level of disposable income (D)?

d. What is the numerical value of the multiplier?

e. Suppose that the government now balances the budget by adjusting its *expenditures* while still collecting the same number of dollars in taxes.

What will then be the new equilibrium values of: Y, D, C, S, I, and G? Now, go back to the original data (i.e., $Y = 1{,}600$, etc.). Suppose that the government again balances the budget, this time by adjusting the amount of *taxes collected* while leaving its expenditures unchanged.

f. The change in tax collections initially (i.e., autonomously) changes D by how much and in what direction?

g. As a result of this change in D, the initial change in C is how much and in what direction?

h. As a result of this initial change in C, the change in Y eventually (when the multiplier has fully worked itself out) is how much?

i. What will be the new equilibrium values of Y, D, C, S, I, and T?

4. a. Begin with the situation depicted below; it is assumed that $MPC = .8$ and $MPS = .2$ with respect to disposable income. Is income at an equilibrium level? Is the government budget balanced? Is there a necessary connection between the answers of those two questions?

C	S	I	G	Y	T	D
720	180	100	180	1,000	100	900

Initially, the average and marginal tax rates are both .1. Now, suppose that the objective is (a) to increase national income to an equilibrium level of 1,200, (b) by means of a cut in the *average* tax rate, leaving the marginal rate unchanged, (c) with the government budget balanced at a level of 100 in the new income equilibrium. Let there be a marginal propensity to invest (defined as $\Delta I/\Delta Y$) of appropriate size. Fill in the table for the first several periods and for the new equilibrium values. What is the relation between the numerical values of the marginal propensity to save and the marginal propensity to invest?

b. Next, alter the initial situation, with tax collections smaller than before and saving and disposable income correspondingly larger.

C	S	I	G	Y	T	D
720	190	100	180	1,000	90	910

The objective—raising income to 1,200 with a reduced average tax rate and with an ultimately balanced budget at 100—remains the same. Again fill in the table. And now what is the relation between *MPS* and *MPI*?

c. Finally, go back and fill in the tables again for each of the two alternative initial situations, keeping the objective unchanged, but let there be one difference from the earlier cases: while there is to be a cut in the average tax rate in period 2, as before, there is also an autonomous increase in investment in period 3 equal to 9 (i.e., an increase of 9—5 percent of the original level—throughout the investment schedule). Again, in these two new solutions, what is the relation between *MPS* and *MPI*?

5. **a.** In Route VI, we raised income to 1,200 by increasing both G and r, with a budget surplus in the new (higher) equilibrium. Can you work out an analogous case, beginning with the same initial situation, in which equilibrium income is *lowered* to 950 by *decreasing* both G and r, with a budget surplus in the new equilibrium?

b. In Route VII, G and r are reduced, and a deficit obtains in the new (higher) equilibrium. Can you *lower* income to 950 by *increasing* G and r in such fashion that a deficit exists in the new equilibrium?

35

MONEY, WEALTH, AND INCOME

Money

Everyone knows that money is what you use to buy things and pay debts. But we can usefully consider that nature and the functions of money and the consequences of changes in the total supply of money in some detail—consequences which pertain to shifting resources among products and consumption over time, the levels of the aggregate price index and of national income, and the amount of employment.

The basic functions of money are two: (a) money is a "standard of value," or "unit of account"; (b) money is a "medium of exchange" or, more prosaically, a "means of payment."[1] Life would go on, even if less opulently, without money, but money is so obviously useful that it is found in any society far enough advanced to spend most of its time out of the trees.

We earlier illustrated the great advantage of having a "monetary unit of account" in which to express and compare exchange values. To perform this function, money could be wholly intangible; that is, the unit of account itself could be simply a nonmaterial mode of expression. Transactions could be carried on entirely by bookkeeping shifts of "generalized" claims on goods and services, the unit of measurement of claims being called the "dollar" (or "mark" or "peso" or "purple blob"). Everyone could have a bank checking account, with payments made and revenues received solely by subtracting from or adding to one's account and with no specific, concrete items—such as engraved paper, stamped pieces of gold, or beads—being handled. In practice, however, an abstract unit of account

[1] It is permissible to review pp. 59–60 on the role of money.

is supplemented by concrete means of payment, which facilitate small transactions. It is more convenient to buy a local bus ride by paying a coin or two than by writing a check; and, for many somewhat larger deals, people often prefer to peel a paper bill from their wad to writing a check. So real monetary systems are characterized not only by abstract units of account but also by physical media of exchange.[2]

When you sell something, why are you willing to receive "money" in return? Do not try to account for the general acceptability of money with the old wives' tale that money is "backed" by, or convertible into, gold. Gold coins have not circulated in the United States since 1933, when private ownership of gold was prohibited and made a government monopoly. And although there still is a gold-reserve requirement for the bulk of paper currency (Federal Reserve notes), that reserve is only 25 percent; and, as has happened before, it could be made still smaller (all the way to zero) by Congress. Gold, then, does not give the dollar its value; however, notions of the value of gold are not based solely on mysticism. People have sought for good reason to own gold and use it widely as money. It is portable, easily recognizable, readily divisible, and storable. In a world ridden with unstable governments and threats of confiscation of wealth or expulsion from a country, people find gold a relatively attractive form in which to own wealth. (Consider the problems of hiding and secretly transporting peanuts, cotton, leather, steel, or land.)

You are willing to accept money in exchange for valuable things only because you are confident that you, in turn, can pass on the money to others in payment of what you wish to buy. The first essential quality of money is confidence in its *shiftability* to another holder. But anything possessing market value, by the meaning of the term, has value in respect to other assets. If every asset can "command" other objects in marketplace exchange, how does money differ from other assets?

There are *degrees* of shiftability. We follow most monetary analysts in most problems by designating "money" as (a) currency in the hands of the non-bank public—i.e., currency outside the monetary authorities (the Federal Reserve and the Treasury) and outside commercial banks; and (b) the public's demand, or "checking," deposits in commercial banks. Demand deposits are assets on the personal books of the depositors and liabilities to the banks in which the deposits are held: the customer of a bank owns a demand, or sight, asset which can be used to meet financial obligations and the dimensions of which are stated in a fixed number of dollars. A $1,000 demand deposit and $1,000 in cash can be

[2] It is commonly said that money performs two additional functions: (a) money is a "standard of deferred payments" (i.e., contracts calling for payments in the future can be written in monetary terms); (b) money is a "store of value" (i.e., wealth can be held in the form of monetary assets). But the first of these supplemental roles is subsumed under money as a unit of account, and the second is directly implied by money as a means of payment, for the means of payment at any given moment are being held (stored) by someone.

readily converted into each other at any time, whereas a nonmonetary asset with a market value of $1,000, when sold to one person today, may be worth more or less than $1,000 to someone else tomorrow. Although it is useful, and thus wholly appropriate, to consider demand deposits along with currency as money, the two assets differ slightly in their degrees of moneyness, for deposits are a bit less conveniently shifted and thus are somewhat less "generalized" in their purchasing power: before you can leave a store with merchandise by writing a check, you may have to identify yourself; whereas you do not have to show your driver's license in order to pay cash.

Why not include time or savings deposits in the money category? These deposits, too, are commercial-bank liabilities of fixed amounts of money and are owned by the bank's customers. However, checks cannot be written directly on time deposits. Indeed, legally, they cannot be converted immediately into currency or demand deposits so that they can be spent, for the bank can demand a warning period—although, in practice, they can generally be withdrawn "on demand." We might label time deposits as a "near money," for the basic spending and saving decisions of most people seem generally to be about the same whether they have a certain number of dollars wholly in a demand account or, say, split half and half between demand and time accounts. The demand for money apparently is no more accurately predictable when "money" is defined to include time deposits than when it is confined to currency plus demand deposits.

In January 1964, the money supply, thus defined, was some $158,000,000,000, of which over $32,000,000,000 was currency and almost $126,000,000,000 was demand deposits. Thus, nearly 80 percent of the money is in the form of demand deposits. The currency included $3,000,000,000 in metallic coins and about $30,000,000,000 in paper money, more than nine tenths of which was Federal Reserve notes.[3]

Demand for Money

Common experience suggests that a person is likely to spend more if he has more rather than less money. The most convenient amount of money to have depends in part on his income or wealth. If he has more than that amount of money, he will spend money at a higher rate until his stock of money is adjusted to the most appropriate amount. And if he has less money than that amount, he will reduce his spending until he accumulates a larger money balance. For ex-

[3] There are several other kinds of paper currency, which are quantitatively trivial and interesting mainly as historical curiosities. The only exception has been silver certificates, issued by the Treasury against silver bullion—primarily because several Western states have both silver and senators—and totaling close to $2,000,000,000. But, on the basis of legislation in 1963, silver certificates are to be gradually eliminated.

ample, a person with a $100-a-week income and total wealth of $5,000, of which $4,000 is in cash, would probably spend more than his current income as he exchanged (spent) some of his money for other kinds of goods. On the other hand, if he had only $10 in cash, he would reduce his expenditure rate relative to his income until he had accumulated enough cash to facilitate his normal purchase activities. The intended expenditure will depend in part upon the amount of money a person has. And this is true for the aggregate of all people. Whatever is the amount of money in existence in the community, a larger stock of money would be associated with a larger rate of expenditure.

In terms of the consumption and investment functions used in the earlier chapters to determine national income, the quantity of money affects the position of the consumption and the investment functions, and hence national income. If changes in the quantity of money are large enough and continue long enough, they can cause serious fluctuations in national income, employment, and production. In fact, they do. In this and the next three chapters, we shall investigate this connection between fluctuations in the quantity of money and employment, income and output in some detail.

The preceding propositions about the effects of changes in the quantity of money depend upon the demand for money; therefore, it is desirable to characterize that demand more precisely. People hold money because it permits them to economize on costs of exchange, for exchange by means of money is normally easier, quicker, and more flexible (that is, more efficient or economical) than barter exchange. Consider how you would have to rearrange your normal activities if you could not use any money in your daily life. Yet having a bank balance or a stock of cash—called in general "holding" money—involves a cost. To hold money, a person must sacrifice some interim consumption of goods or growth of wealth he could otherwise have obtained if he spent all his money immediately upon receipt. He could have more goods for consumption, or he could lend the money and get interest. But, if he did, he would sacrifice some conveniences of holding some money and thereby being able to buy goods at moments other than when he receives his income. A person will adjust his average money balances in accordance with the returns available from owning goods or lending money for interest.

Clearly, the greater the marginal gains from owning more of other types of goods (than money) or of lending money, the less will be the desired size of his money holdings, relative to his current money income and wealth. The alternative uses of money are (a) to hold it, which reduces future transactions costs, and (b) to spend it on goods, which adds to his utility, and (c) to lend or invest it, which gives him a growth in wealth equal to the rate of interest. Each of these can be increased at the expense of less of the other two. In equilibrium, that is, at a maximum utility position for a person, he will have adjusted his holdings of each so that the marginal return for a dollar more in each is equal in all three activities. Since that return is the rate of interest for loans, we know it is that same rate in all the other forms of wealth—in equilibrium.

In this analysis we are treating money as a special kind of good, but it is not special in the sense of being "sterile." It performs valuable services even when it is held in anticipation of eventual conjectural purchases. This deserves emphasis because of the long-standing myth (as far back as Aristotle) that money is sterile, that it has no inherent value in and of itself, and that it yields nothing to the person who holds it. These are myths because they overlook the services of money in avoiding the higher transactions costs of barter in a world in which it is impossible to foresee the future with perfect accuracy and complete confidence. This is the same general kind of service, as we saw earlier (pp. 550–552) provided by a fire extinguisher, stretcher, or eraser. While they stand "unused" and available for potential "use," would you say they were yielding no service, were of no inherent value, and were contributing nothing to one's utility? You would only if you believe that people have perfect foresight.

Preview of Effects of Changes in Quantity of Money

What are the implications of this demand for money? Consider the response to a reduction in the quantity of money. (Never mind now how the available quantity of money could decrease. Simply suppose that everyone lost 30 percent of his *money* in a fire or that the government taxes everyone 30 percent of his *money* and then destroys the money.) Everyone now has less wealth, but since the whole reduction in wealth was in money, the proportion of money to wealth and income has fallen. Given that people formerly held the desired amounts of money, and given their remaining wealth, income, and interests rates, they now have less money than they want at the lower wealth. They will attempt to recoup money balances by *spending less* of their income or by selling some of their other wealth. They will be buying less of current output and trying to sell some of their stocks, bonds, or other inventories in order to restore their money balances. But not *everyone* can do this, because people buy and sell to each other. Instead, as market demand falls, prices and, with them, income and wealth fall.

But not so fast! The adjustment in prices will not occur immediately with all existing goods and services being instantly and fully adjusted to the new situation. As we know from Chapter 31, if information about various market opportunities were instantly available, the decline in general demand would be accompanied by an immediate downward adjustment in prices, with no effect on real output or employment. Unemployment of labor and goods will increase during this episode of decreasing demand. And as long as the demand is falling, as it will if the money stock is steadily reduced, the rate of unemployment will stay high and the price level will decline.

These effects can be traced with the Keynesian analytic functions of the preceding chapters. Referring back to Figure 33–3, we can see that when the investment and the consumption functions are shifted downward, in response to reduced money balances, a lower level of income is implied. What is now being added to the earlier analysis is *explicit* recognition that *the positions of these functions are affected by changes in the quantity of money.*

An *increase* in the stock of money leads to the opposite shifts and effects. Suppose the government printed some new money and one night sprinkled it from the skies. Or suppose that mysteriously every bank account were increased by 30 percent. Finding himself with more money, everyone would keep his discovery a deep, dark secret. But with more money and no less of any other goods, everyone has more money than he wants (given his amount of other wealth and income). With more money, he decides he can buy some furniture, take a vacation, invest in stocks, or otherwise live it up. He will increase his spendings, though not by the full amount of his money increase. (Indeed, the increase in spending will be smaller for this presumably transient or temporary augmentation of rate of receipts than for an equivalent increase in the rate of income.) The consumption and the investment functions will shift upward. With everyone doing this, sales increase, inventories decrease, and manufacturers are asked to produce more. They seek more workers and resources. They have more "unfilled" jobs. Materials become "scarcer." If you recall the earlier discussion of the price of meat in Chapter 8, you will remember how an increased demand operates only gradually to raise prices in some markets. Furthermore, as we saw in Chapter 31, employers don't offer whatever wages are necessary to get new employees immediately, regardless of costs of moving or of finding appropriate workers.

But income, wealth, and employment soon do increase until at these higher levels people now find they have as much money as they find it most convenient to hold, given the *higher* levels of wealth and income. Then the expansion in income and wealth stops, as the new equilibrium level is achieved.

The Quantity Equation

The relationship between the money stock, the physical output, and the price level is usually summarized in a simple form by an equation,

$$Mk = PQ,$$

where M denotes the amount of money in the community, P is the general price level, and Q is an index of the quantity of output, so that PQ is a measure of the annual national income (expressed as the quantity of physical goods and services, Q, multiplied by their prices, P). The term k is the ratio of national income to money. This ratio is not an autonomous, institutionally fixed ratio. It depends upon several factors (for example, costs of holding and using money, the rate of interest, expectations about the rate of change of the price level). In the United States the gross national income is currently about $630,000,000,000 per year, while the money stock is about $160,000,000,000: therefore the ratio, k, is close to 4. The usefulness of the simple form of the equation $Mk = PQ$, as a means of describing the effects of a change in quantity of money, depends heavily on the presumption that k is relatively unresponsive to changes in M or that changes in M do not induce unpredictable changes in k.

In fact k is not constant. As we have already seen in Chapter 32, variations in the quantity of money are not in exact proportions to variations in the national income. Nevertheless, the changes are highly correlated both in direction and in relative size; we can therefore conclude that k is not a variable induced to adapt as a counterbalance or as an offset to changes in the quantity of money. Historically, the ratio k has varied from about 2.5 to 4 in slow swings in the past several decades, and has not been highly responsive to changes in the quantity of money.

Now *if* k is relatively constant when changes in M occur, we can by means of this equation express the proposition that a substantial increase in the quantity of money will induce a change in the same direction and in roughly the same proportion in gross national income. In using the qualifying adjective "substantial" in reference to changes in the quantity of money, we are not seeking to clothe a vacuous proposition with an aura of content. Instead, this is a way of recognizing that relatively small changes in the stock of money (say, under 3 percent a year) will produce effects that are hard to detect above the random noise of all the other contemporaneous factors. If, however, the quantity of money should increase by, say, 10 percent or more in one year, the impact should be unmistakably detected above the effect of all of the other contemporary factors.

Still to be settled is the question of how much of the change in national income is a change in P and how much a change in Q. Is the rise all in prices or in rate of output? This equation will not tell. Nor, for that matter, will the Keynesian analytical model used in earlier chapters. We have to have some new propositions or theorems to answer this. And, not surprisingly, one can be derived from the considerations presented in Chapter 31 on unemployment. In any event, more advanced analysis and substantial empirical evidence support the proposition that the higher the rate of unemployment, the less of a change in national income (induced by an increase in the money stock) that will be in the form of higher prices and the more in increased output. And the lower the rate of unemployment, the more of the increase in national income that will be simply higher prices (in response to an increase in the stock of money). In the extreme, if unemployment is less than about 2–4 percent, called full employment, an increase in the stock of money (beyond the rate required to match the secular growth in population and output) will be almost entirely in the form of an increase in prices.

For example, from 1933 to 1939, a period starting with heavy unemployment, an 80 percent increase in the money stock was associated with an increase in real output of about 50 percent, while the price level rose approximately 10 percent. On the other hand, 1943 through 1948 was a period of full employment. The money stock increased by about 75 percent, real output increased about 10 percent, and the price level rose about 50 percent. In both these periods the money stock rose at an average of about 10 percent *a year*.

For other periods when the money stock rose by a smaller rate—say, only 2–4 percent *a year*—the correlation was not detectable. For example, in the interval 1923 through 1929, a period of full employment, the money stock rose by about 20 percent with real output rising 33 percent and prices remaining almost constant (instead of falling, as would be implied if k were strictly constant). Again, in the interval 1954–60, a period of full employment, the money stock rose a little over 10 percent while real output rose about 20 percent and the price level rose about 15 percent (instead of falling). These increases in output are about equal to the secular growth of population and productivity.[4]

Clearly, the correlation between changes in the money stock and the changes in national income is not perfect; that is, the demand to hold money will shift around for reasons not made explicit in our present analysis. Nevertheless, the variations in the demand for money caused by the various other unspecified factors are sufficiently small that changes in the supply of money of about 10 percent a year yield observable effects on the real output and price level, even without attempts to correct for or adjust for the other concomitant factors. Furthermore, the cited periods illustrate the general proposition that money stock changes have a relatively greater effect on output than on prices in periods of unemployment.

Our purpose in noting again that an increase in national income can be composed of an increase in real output and in prices is to make clear that an increase in the quantity of money does not necessarily lead to only a price rise, on the one hand, nor to only an output increase without a price rise, on the other. Up to the present stage of our analysis, we have investigated how an increase in the quantity of money leads to higher income and wealth—regardless of whether it be in larger output or in higher prices—leaving it to the unemployment rate to be the index of whether the increase will be primarily in output (from low employment levels) or primarily in price increases (at high employment levels).

We must be careful to avoid a possible misinterpretation. Rising prices are not necessary to maintain full employment. We associate rising prices with full

[4] In Chapter 38, where inflation is discussed in detail, Figure 38–4 and the related discussion (pp. 730–732) provide more evidence.

employment because we usually achieve full employment by *restoring* it after a prior period of unemployment. But once full employment is restored, it is often sufficient merely to prevent *declines* in the per capita stock of money. If that can be done, the advancing technology will result in lower costs of output and prices to consumers, with increased production. That kind of decrease in price—in response to lower costs and larger output—does not induce increases in the rate of unemployment. In United States history, there have been episodes when prices fell slowly while employment stayed high. In the 1880s and early 1890s technology advanced, output grew, employment was high, and prices fell by about the amount that the advancing technology would imply. Again in the 1920s, output grew, employment was high, and prices were stable or slightly falling. Similar intervals exist. But if during those periods the money stock had increased more rapidly, prices would have fallen less or risen.

If changes in the money stock did not occur, then, despite their potential importance, we could conveniently ignore them. However, changes have been frequent and of large proportions, with traumatic effect on output, employment, and price levels.

Changes in the stock of money occur for several reasons. For one thing, they occur in response to individual actions of people and the operation of the commercial banks, as we shall see in the following chapter. The quantity of money is also influenced by the government's, and governmentally dominated agencies', attempts to control the quantity of money, with the avowed purpose of maintaining conditions conducive to full employment. In the next two chapters, we shall investigate these procedures and performances. Finally, the quantity of money is affected by the government's attempts to utilize changes in the quantity of money as a means of obtaining command over more of the community's wealth so as to direct its use more in accord with politically determined purposes—e.g., wars or transfers of wealth to politically powerful groups. Usually this third source of change in the money stock is manifested by what is typically called inflation—a phenomenon we shall investigate in Chapter 38.

Questions

1. Which of the following could not serve as money: tobacco, sugar, salt, cattle, nails, copper, grain, beads, tea, cowrie shell, fish hooks, chocolate, cigarettes, feathers, silver, gold, printed paper, stones, promissory notes, debt?

2. "Money is a medium of exchange. It is a common denominator or measure of value. It is a store of value. The first two are relatively unique to money, whereas the latter is not." Explain what is meant by each sentence.

3. What are some desirable physical attributes for a commodity if it is to serve as

money? For example, is its usefulness as money affected by its recognizability, portability, divisibility, durability, producibility? Why?

4. What is legal tender? A $10 Federal Reserve Note says, "This note is legal tender for all debts, public and private, and is redeemable in lawful money at the United States Treasury or at any Federal Reserve Bank." If you ask the Treasury to redeem that note for lawful money, what will you be given?

5. Does the value of money depend upon what it is made of or upon its quantity?

6. **a.** If the price of potatoes is 10 cents a pound, and a pound of butter is 50 cents, what is the "price of getting a dollar"?

b. If the interest rate is 6 percent per year, what is the cost of holding money? (Hint: Your answer should be consistent, in principle, with the answers to the following two analogous questions: What is the cost of obtaining ownership of a house whose price is $20,000? What is the cost of owning a house?)

7. "I never have too much money."

a. Are economic principles consistent with that assertion?

b. In what sense is that assertion incorrect?

8. Indicate whether the following have any effect on the demand for money and in what direction:

a. Total wealth.

b. Interest rate available on loans.

c. General price level.

d. Day of the month (after payday).

e. Month of year.

f. Net wealth (total assets minus liabilities).

g. Sex.

h. Number of people in one's family.

i. Age.

j. Occupation.

k. In residence or traveling.

l. Possession of a credit card.

m. Number of people to whom you are known in your community.

n. Fees for having less than a prescribed minimum balance in a checking account.

o. Proportion of other assets held in stocks and bonds instead of in consumers' goods and business equipment.

p. Rate at which you expect general price level to be rising (or falling).

q. Level of academic education.

r. Race.

s. Religion.

t. Kind of government.

u. Cost of convertibility to money of other types or nations.

v. Predictability of expenditure patterns in the near future.

w. One's credit standing in the community.

9. Estimate your average amount of money held during last September. Estimate your earnings during the year. Form the ratio of the latter to the former; that is, put the annual earnings in the numerator. This is your personal k. Does your k have a seasonal pattern of variation? Why?

10. The ratio of the amount of coins, paper money, and checking-account money in the United States is about 1:10:50, or 1.6 percent coins, 16 percent paper, and 83 percent checking accounts.

a. Count your amounts of each; if your ratios differ, why are you so abnormal?

b. Which people do you think would have higher ratios of coins? Who have higher ratios of paper money? Who would have higher ratios of checking-account money? Explain.

11. a. Do you think bus and subway tokens should be counted in the money supply? Why?

b. Would you consider time deposits or savings accounts to be money? Why?

c. Travelers checks?

12. Do you think the amount of money you would hold on the average would increase as much in response to a gift to you of $100 in wealth as for an increase in your wages of $10 per week. (Hint: What is the present value of an increase in wages of $10 per week? How does it compare with a gain of $100 in wealth?)

13. a. Would you like to have twice as large a house as you do now? Would you object if other people were also so lucky as to have twice as large a house?

b. Then why should you be happy to wake up and find you have twice as much money, but not if other people also have that lucky experience?

c. Would you behave differently if you were the only one who luckily doubled his money stock than if everyone else also got twice as much overnight? Why?

14. Describe your behavior in terms of shifts in the Keynesian consumption and investment functions—in response to the following charges:

a. You wake up some morning and find that your income and wealth are the same, but that someone has taken your car and left you ample cash payment in an envelope.

b. You wake up some morning and find the money in the envelope, but with nothing else changed.

36

MONEY AND COMMERCIAL BANKS

We have seen that the bulk of the money supply, as conventionally defined, consists of demand deposits, which are "sight" liabilities of commercial banks. The next step, then, in our study of money is consideration of the activities of commercial banks—with emphasis on those bank activities (and the limits and the control of those activities) that affect the quantity of money. And the simplest approach to understanding what banks do and can do is to organize and operate our own hypothetical bank, recording a variety of typical transactions in double-entry account books, commonly called "T accounts."

Commercial Bank Transactions

1. Our first transaction is simply to pass the hat among us would-be owners (i.e. stockholders) and obtain cash with which t start business. (Despite the modest protests o Alchian and Allen, the rest of you stockholders insist on naming our institution the A-and A Bank.) We may sell 10,000 shares of stoc at $100 per share, total proceeds being $1,000,000. From the standpoint of the ban itself (rather than the owners of the bank) the cash thus acquired from the sale of stoc is an asset, and, on the liability side of th bank's accounts, we may enter the same valu as "capital stock." (From an owner's view point, recorded in his personal balance shee one asset—cash—is reduced, and anothe asset—ownership claims in the bank, i.e., stoc —is increased.) The bank's balance sheet i thus:

Assets		Liabilities	
Cash	$1,000,000	Capital stock	$1,000,000

In all transactions, we shall designate with * the entries currently affected.

2. We have acquired cash. Now, we must have a place of public business. So we construct a building and appropriately furnish it. Just as confidence is the sine qua non of the monetary system generally, so it is for our individual bank. To prompt people to entrust their money to us, we try to engender confidence by using much marble on the building, perhaps with Grecian columns outside, heavy grills on the windows, and a massive vault (even if the door seems always to be wide open). Suppose that the building, fixtures, and equipment—designated "property," for short—cost $250,000 and that we pay for it with cash, so the cash asset is reduced and the property asset increased by the same amount:

Assets		Liabilities	
Cash	$750,000 *	Capital stock	$1,000,000
Property	250,000 *		

3. Dressed in our most conservative, confidence-inspiring garb, we deprecatingly open the doors of the bank to a public eager to "deposit" money with us. Suppose our customers thrust $400,000 in cash upon our tellers; of this total, $300,000 is placed in "demand" accounts and $100,000 in "time" (savings) accounts. How shall we record this in the bank's books? We dump the $400,000 in our gleaming vault, along with the other $750,000, and accordingly increase the cash item on the asset side. But our customers did not make us a gift of this cash; they have a claim on us for the whole amount. Indeed, as the word indicates, they can at any moment exercise that claim which is held as "demand" deposits; legally, the bank can require several days' notice before "time" deposits are withdrawn, although in practice we will not require such warning—because the competitor bank across the street does not. We are legally prohibited from paying interest to our customers on their demand deposits (indeed, we shall impose some "service charges" on them), but we will pay interest on the time accounts (the maximum rate being specified by law). Then why don't depositors put all of the money in time accounts? As we have seen, checks cannot be directly written on time accounts—they must first be transferred into demand deposits, and this nuisance makes time deposits somewhat less convenient for payment purposes than demand deposits. People are willing to forego some interest to obtain some additional convenience. The balance sheet is now:

Assets		Liabilities	
Cash	$1,150,000 *	Demand deposits	$ 300,000 *
Property	250,000	Time deposits	100,000 *
		Capital stock	1,000,000

4. Whatever may have been the motivations of the rest of you stockholders, Alchian and Allen are in this business to get rich. And as of now, although the bank has total assets of $1,400,000, we have no "earning" assets; except for the service charges we collect from our depositors, we are making no money. So let us invest some of our cash. We are legally restricted in the kinds of permissible investments, but a highly acceptable outlet for our funds is government bonds; so suppose we buy $1,000,000 worth. Thus:

Assets		Liabilities	
Cash	$ 150,000 *	Demand deposits	$ 300,000
Government securities	1,000,000 *	Time deposits	100,000
Property	250,000	Capital stock	1,000,000

5. Suppose that our bank is a member of the Federal Reserve System. (Of approximately 13,500 commercial banks in the United States, about 6,100—a little less than half—belong to the System. However, these member banks own 83 percent of all commercial banks' loans and investments and hold a like percentage of total demand deposits.) The Federal Reserve System is the American "central bank"; along with the Treasury, it is the "monetary authority," with various methods at its disposal (which we shall investigate later) to influence the money supply. The System includes twelve regional Federal Reserve banks (and a number of branches), which have substantial autonomy, particularly in their more routine activities, but which are supervised and coordinated by the Board of Governors in Washington, D.C. Despite the regional arrangement of the System, we shall be justified in generally discussing it as a monolithic institution under the direction of the Board of Governors.

Since our bank is a member of the System, it is required to hold at least a minimum of "reserves," the minimum being specified by the Board (within limits set by Congress). Two types of bank assets are counted as legal reserves: demand deposits of the commercial bank held in its Federal Reserve bank and cash held in the bank's own vault.[1] We shall later discuss reserve requirements and their connection with the Fed's monetary policies. For the moment, our attention is directed to the role of member-bank deposits in the Fed in the more mundane, but highly useful, function of clearing checks. (Many non-member banks also maintain a demand deposit in the Fed for check-clearing purposes.)

Without pausing here to calculate the current minimum reserve requirement for our bank, let us simply up and establish a $110,000 deposit in our regional Federal Reserve bank. Just as our customers brought cash to us and opened a demand deposit in our bank, so the bank can deposit cash in a demand account

[1] The Federal Reserve Act was passed in 1913, and the System was organized in 1914. During most of the history of the System—from 1917 to late 1959—member-bank deposits in the Fed were the only form of legal reserves. During 1959–1960, the definition of reserves was modified to include vault cash.

in the Fed: the Federal Reserve banks are banks for banks. After we deposit $110,000 in the Fed, the bank's balance sheet is:

Assets		Liabilities	
Cash	$ 40,000 *	Demand deposits	$ 300,000
Deposit in FR	110,000 *	Time deposits	100,000
Government securities	1,000,000	Capital stock	1,000,000
Property	250,000		

6. Now, one of our customers with a demand deposit has to pay a bill of $5,000, and the person to be paid does his banking with the outfit across the street. Our customer is entitled to draw out $5,000 in cash. But he is unlikely to want to come to the bank to draw out the money and then walk down the street with $5,000 in cash in his pocket. It is easier and safer to pay his bill by writing a check: his demand deposit is not only a sight claim on the bank, but also a checking account. A check is an *order to pay,* with the writer of the check ordering the bank to make payment to the beneficiary. The person receiving the check takes it to his own bank, the Bloated Trust Company, and deposits it in his demand account. The Trust Company, in turn, wants to collect on the check deposited in it; instead of the check's being sent directly to the A-and-A Bank, on which it was written, it will be sent to the Fed, at which both banks have deposits. The Federal Reserve bank "clears" the check by adding its amount to the account of the Trust Company and deducting it from the account of the A-and-A Bank.

The net result is that demand deposits and the deposit in the Fed fall by $5,000 for the A-and-A Bank, and demand deposits and the deposit in the Fed on the books of the Trust Company rise:

A-and-A Bank

Assets		Liabilities	
Deposit in FR	—$5,000	Demand deposits	—$5,000

Bloated Trust Company

Assets		Liabilities	
Deposit in FR	+$5,000	Demand deposits	+$5,000

Federal Reserve Bank

Assets		Liabilities	
		Demand deposit of A-and-A	—$5,000
		Demand deposit of Trust	+ 5,000

And the complete balance sheet of our bank is now:

Assets		Liabilities	
Cash	$ 40,000	Demand deposits	$ 295,000 *
Deposit in FR	105,000 *	Time deposits	100,000
Government securities	1,000,000	Capital stock	1,000,000
Property	250,000		

If one of our customers writes another check, but this time the beneficiary of the check also is a customer of this bank, the aggregate balance sheet would not change, assuming that the beneficiary deposits the check he receives. To be sure, the writer of the check has his bank balance reduced, but the deposit of the beneficiary increases by the same amount, so total deposits are unaffected. Since the check does not leave the bank, there are no clearings, either adverse (a loss of reserves) or favorable (an increase of reserves).

7. The public's demand for currency is a function of many variables, including interest rates, levels of income, prices, and employment, and anticipated directions and rates of change in such variables. Here, suppose we consider a seasonal change in demand: the Christmas period is approaching; retail sales presumably will rise; and, consequently, we expect that our customers will soon start withdrawing some cash. It would be downright embarrassing to run out of cash, so let's increase our vault holdings. Just as customers of the A-and-A Bank can withdraw cash and thereby reduce their demand deposits, so the bank can draw down its deposit in the Fed by taking out cash. The acquisition of, say, $10,000 in cash makes the balance sheet:

Assets		Liabilities	
Cash	$ 50,000 *	Demand deposits	$ 295,000
Deposit in FR	95,000 *	Time deposits	100,000
Government securities	1,000,000	Capital stock	1,000,000
Property	250,000		

The Federal Reserve bank has paid out cash in the form of Federal Reserve notes, which is an increase in a Federal Reserve liability, and has reduced the deposit of the A-and-A Bank, another liability.

Before taking up another transaction, let us calculate reserves. We are concerned with three reserve measures: actual reserves, required reserves, and excess reserves. So-called *actual* reserves are the assets owned by the A-and-A Bank which are legally designated as "reserves"; and, as we have seen, actual (i.e., legal) reserves consist of cash plus deposit in the Fed—in this case, $50,000 + $95,000 = $145,000. *Required* reserves are calculated as a percentage of deposit liabilities; more specifically, the bank is required to hold actual reserves equal at least to a specified percentage of the demand deposits in the bank plus a (smaller) specified percentage of time deposits, the percentages being specified by the Board of Governors.[2] *Excess* reserves are simply the difference, if any, between the dollar volume of actual reserves and the dollar volume of required reserves. Normally, actual reserves are larger than required, but excess reserves can be and sometimes are negative.

Suppose, quite realistically, that the designated reserve percentage against demand deposits is 20 percent and that for time deposits it is 5 percent. Required reserves (RR) are thus: (\$295,000 × .2) + (\$100,000 × .05) = \$64,000; we have seen that actual reserve (AR) possessed by the bank are \$145,000; excess reserves (ER) = $AR - RR$ = \$145,000 − \$64,000 = \$81,000.

8. Our expectations of "cash drain" prove correct: our customers with demand deposits withdraw \$15,000 in currency. The balance sheet then becomes:

Assets		Liabilities	
Cash	\$ 35,000 *	Demand deposits	\$ 280,000 *
Deposit in FR	95,000	Time deposits	100,000
Government securities	1,000,000	Capital stock	1,000,000
Property	250,000		

What does the withdrawal of cash do to the bank's reserve situation—in particular, to excess reserves? Before we calculate the exact numerical answers, note the *direction* of change in the reserve measures. Actual reserves fall, for cash is a component of actual reserves, and the other component, deposit in the Fed, is unaffected. Required reserves fall, for the required-reserve ratios are unchanged while the (demand) liabilities against which reserves must be held are now smaller. Although both actual and required reserves are smaller, actual reserves fall by the full amount of the cash drain, while required reserves fall by only 20 percent of the drain; consequently, excess reserves are diminished. Putting the data into the equation $AR - RR = ER$, we have, 130,000 − 61,000 = 69,000. Excess reserves thus are reduced by \$12,000—i.e., from \$81,000 to \$69,000, equal to 80 percent of the cash outflow.

9. Customers who own time deposits in our bank anticipate writing checks; so they shift \$50,000 from their time accounts into demand deposits:

Assets		Liabilities	
Cash	\$ 35,000	Demand deposits	\$ 330,000 *
Deposit in FR	95,000	Time deposits	50,000 *
Government securities	1,000,000	Capital stock	1,000,000
Property	250,000		

[2] Until recently, there were three sets of required-reserve ratios, the set applicable to any given bank depending on whether the bank was in the classification of "central-reserve city" (generally only New York and Chicago), "reserve city," or "other" (commonly called "country"). The percentage requirements have been highest for the first classification and lowest for the third. In 1962, the central-reserve-city classification was abolished.

Actual reserves are unchanged, but required reserves rise as deposit liabilities are moved from a relatively low reserve-requirement category to a relatively high reserve-requirement category; consequently, excess reserves are reduced. Specifically, excess reserves = 130,000 − 68,500 = 61,500.

10. Our calculations of required and excess reserves have been made with the required-reserve ratio against demand deposits (r_d) being 20 percent and the time-deposit ratio (r_t) being 5 percent. Of course, with a given balance sheet, required and excess reserves would have been different if the Fed had specified either higher or lower required ratios. The following figures illustrate reserve calculations for the current balance sheet, with alternative demand ratios (although the time-deposit ratio also could be varied):

I: $r_d = .2; r_t = .05$	II: $r_d = .25; r_t = .05$	III: $r_d = .15; r_t = .05$
$AR =$ 130,000	$AR =$ 130,000	$AR =$ 130,000
$RR =$ 68,500	$RR =$ 85,000	$RR =$ 52,000
$ER =$ 61,500	$ER =$ 45,000	$ER =$ 78,000

11. Finally, suppose that someone comes to the bank in quest of a loan of $20,000. Along with making investments (e.g., in government securities), granting loans is our major way of making money.[3] If the loan applicant is obviously enough a supplicant, we will presume to reach deep into our resources and our mercy and—after extracting from the customer a detailed personal financial statement and possibly collateral consisting of his every available asset—give him the loan. Just what does this involve? In all probability, the granting of the loan consists simply of two entries in the bank's *T* account: "loans" now appear on the asset side (for the bank now owns an I.O.U. from the borrower), and demand deposits on the liability side increase (for the proceeds of the loan are taken in the form of a checking account). The balance sheet now is: [4]

The granting of the loan has not affected actual reserves, but required reserves have gone up $4,000 (equal to 20 percent of the increase in deposits); excess reserves fall by the same amount, to a total of $57,500.

[3] We shall quickly see that the reference to "making money" by granting loans has a double meaning.

[4] For bookkeeping simplicity, but certainly unrealistically, we have ignored interest on the loan. If the amount actually loaned is the full $20,000 and interest of, say, $250, is to be collected at the end of the loan period, the balance sheet is as shown in the text; when the loan is ultimately repaid and the interest is simultaneously paid (by a check on this same bank), then the loan item in the balance sheet falls $20,000, and demand deposits fall $20,250, with "undivided profits," on the liability side, increasing $250. Alternatively, if the bank gives a "discounted" loan, the $20,000 loan entry will be matched by an increase in demand deposits of only $19,750 plus "interest collected but not earned" of $250; when the loan is repaid, the loan and the demand-deposit items both fall by $20,000, while a decrease in interest-collected-but-not-earned is offset by an increase in undivided profits of $250. You see, it really *is* simpler to assume zero interest.

Assets		Liabilities	
Cash	$ 35,000	Demand deposits	$ 350,000 *
Deposit in FR	95,000	Time deposits	50,000
Government securities	1,000,000	Capital stock	1,000,000
Loans	20,000 *		
Property	250,000		

In addition to noting the repercussion of the loan on the reserve situation, take a good look at what has happened to the money supply. Our customer, in getting the loan, obtains a checking account of $20,000. Does that mean that he now has $20,000 more in "real" money? We defined money in terms of what it can do or be used for, *viz.*, buy things; our customer can now buy $20,000 worth of things which he could not buy before. Certainly, demand deposits are money, and demand deposits have been increased by the bank granting a loan. Where did this new, additional money come from? Physically, it consists simply of notations in the accounts of the bank; so it came out of a fountain pen. Ignoring the grubby physical aspects, we can say more ethereally that it came out of thin air—and air is a free good.

Bankers often deny—sometimes with both embarrassment and indignation—that banks actually can "create money out of thin air." One objection is that the bank has done nothing more than "monetize" some nonmonetary asset of the customer; for, after all, the customer did give an I.O.U. (and possibly pledged collateral) to obtain the loan. True. But even though the borrower has legally committed himself to pay back the money, he *did* borrow money in the first place; he did have more money when he walked out of the bank than when he walked in. But, someone may ask, since he now has more money, doesn't someone else have less—with the aggregate money supply thus remaining constant? Who has less money now? Money consists of currency in circulation plus demand deposits in commercial banks, and no person or institution in the community now has less cash or smaller deposits than before the loan. Well, then, the trick must be that, while the public immediately obtains money because of the loan, what is now loaned by the bank is simply what it had earlier collected from the public through selling stock; and so we can scarcely say that the bank has "created" money. Sorry, that objection doesn't hold, either. Our bank did, indeed, pick up $1,000,000 in cash initially. But we now have only $35,000 in cash, and the loan could well have been more than that; in addition, no actual cash is involved in granting the loan, presumably it also will be repaid by check, and the borrower may never touch cash in connection with it during the life of the loan; indeed, in principle there need be no cash any place at all in the monetary system. No, the bank lending involves no trick, no hand-is-quicker-than-the-eye shuffling of old, already existing money: by lending, the bank brings into existence (creates) brand new money. Finally, it may be contended that, even if the loan at first increases the money supply, repaying the loan in due course reduces the money supply; so, in some sense, it all cancels out and doesn't really count. But isn't it better to say that bank lending creates money and repaying bank loans destroys money than just to ignore the whole business?

Table 36–1 summarizes the direction of change in reserve and monetary variables for most of the transactions already discussed, and the reader will do well to extend the table to include further transactions as they are brought up. The table, it must be noted, refers to the effects of the respective transactions on the *entire* group or system of commercial banks, not to the effects on the A-and-A Bank alone.

Expansion of the Single Bank and the Banking System

EXPANSION OF THE SINGLE BANK

The A-and-A Bank, let it not be forgotten, was organized and is operated in order to make profits. How does the bank earn income? It picks up a little through service charges, calculated in some esoteric way wholly incomprehensible to people not working for the bank. But the bulk of the income stems from two sources: dividends and interest on *investments* (e.g., government securities) and interest on *loans*. Our concern here is with the latter.

Since the bank's income is earned largely on loans, it would appear that the more loans, the better. Indeed, why not grant more and more loans without limit? A loan at any rate of interest which will yield revenue in excess of the variable administrative expenses involved will enhance profits. And since the money to lend can be created by the bank out of thin air, it would seem that a bank is in a position to earn unlimited profits. But there are limits to how far a bank can go in granting net additional loans. The limits, institutional in nature, are imposed mainly by the Federal Reserve. As we have seen, a bank possesses a certain amount of actual reserves, it can calculate the amount of its excess reserves at any given time, and normally the minimum allowable value of excess reserves (i.e., actual minus required reserves) is zero. The bank may "expand" (i.e., grant additional loans and thereby create additional demand deposits) as long as it has excess reserves; presumably, it will expand no further when excess reserves have fallen to zero.

Single-bank expansion: special assumptions. Given some initial amount of excess reserves, how big a loan can the bank make and still end up, after all checks are written and cleared, with exactly zero excess reserves?

If $r_d = .2$ and $r_t = .05$, with the balance sheet of Table 36–2, excess reserves equal $2,100 − $1,100 = $1,000. Faced with this situation, a banker may claim that the maximum loan he can safely make is $1,000—that is, he can lend just the amount of his excess reserves. Let's see if that is a reasonable rule of thumb.

Table 36–1

BANK TRANSACTIONS, RESERVES, AND MONEY SUPPLY

Transactions	Actual Reserves of Commercial Banks	Required Reserves of Commercial Banks	Excess Reserves of Commercial Banks	Demand Deposits in Commercial Banks	Currency in Hands of Public	Money Supply
1. One bank buys government securities from other banks, financed by shifting the banks' deposits in the FR.	0	0	0	0	0	0
2. A bank buys government securities from a private dealer, financed by the dealer's accepting a check, which he deposits in a demand deposit.	0	+	−	+	0	+
3. Check is written on an account in a reserve city bank and deposited in a demand account in another reserve city bank, the check being cleared through the FR.	0	0	0	0	0	0
4. Check is written on an account in a reserve city bank and deposited in a demand account in a country bank, the check being cleared through the FR.	0	−	+	0	0	0
5. A bank increases its vault cash by withdrawing cash from its account in the FR.	0	0	0	0	0	0
6. Public withdraws cash from demand deposits.	−	−	−	−	+	0
7. Owners of time deposits shift their deposits into demand accounts.	0	+	−	+	0	+
8. Minimum reserve ratio required against demand deposits is increased.	0	+	−	0	0	0
9. Individual obtains a loan from a bank, proceeds of which are taken in the form of a demand deposit.	0	+	−	+	0	+

Table 36–2

INITIAL SITUATION

Assets		Liabilities	
Cash	$ 200	Demand deposits	$5,000
Deposit in FR	1,900	Time deposits	2,000
Investments	2,000	Capital	1,000
Loans	3,000		
Property	900		
	$8,000		$8,000

We can usefully break down the entire analysis into two stages, the granting of the loan by the bank and the spending of the loan by the borrower. In each step, excess reserves are reduced.

Table 36–3 gives the balance sheet after the loan is made but before it is used. Actual reserves are unchanged ($2,100), but required reserves have increased (from $1,100 to $1,300), for liabilities against which reserves must be held have increased; therefore, excess reserves have fallen (from $1,000 to $800). Evidently, even if borrowers never spend the proceeds of their loans—or if any checks which are written go to people in the same bank—there still would be a limit to how far the bank could go in granting additional loans: demand deposits could be increased so much by loans that required reserves would become as large as actual reserves.

Table 36–3

STAGE I: LOAN IS GRANTED

Assets		Liabilities	
Cash	$ 200	Demand deposits	$6,000 *
Deposit in FR	1,900	Time deposits	2,000
Investments	2,000	Capital	1,000
Loans	4,000 *		
Property	900		
	$9,000		$9,000

But this is only half of the analysis, for presumably the borrower *will* write checks on his newly created demand deposit; and at least some of those checks *will* go to people who hold their deposits in other banks. More specifically, let us assume for the moment that *all* of the loan has checks written on it and that *all* of the checks go outside this bank. In that case, we end up with the balance sheet of Table 36–4.

Table 36–4

STAGE II: CHECKS ARE WRITTEN AND CLEARED

Assets		Liabilities	
Cash	$ 200	Demand deposits	$5,000 *
Deposit in FR	900 *	Time deposits	2,000
Investments	2,000	Capital	1,000
Loans	4,000		
Property	900		
	$8,000		$8,000

Naturally, demand deposits fall back to $5,000 when the loan money is spent, and when the checks are cleared the deposit in the Fed falls by $1,000. Required reserves are now back to their initial value ($1,100), and actual reserves are reduced to $1,100; therefore, excess reserves are zero. The net results for our bank are, then, that demand (and time) liabilities are unchanged, while actual reserves are reduced to the point where there are no excess reserves. The banker was right, on the assumptions we have employed: he could lend exactly the amount of his initial excess reserves.

Single-bank expansion: more general assumptions. We have concluded, as a first approximation, that the single bank can grant new loans equal, at most, to the value of its excess reserves. But this conclusion rests on two rather severe assumptions: (a) that all of the new loans are utilized (i.e., checks equal in value to the loans are written) and (b) that all of these checks go outside the bank (i.e., they are written to the orders of depositors holding accounts in other banks).[5] If we relax either assumption, or both, the bank can lend something more than its initial excess reserves without ending up, when all checks have been cleared, with negative excess reserves.

[5] Still another assumption is that the bank's customers are not, on balance, withdrawing cash. This matter of "cash drain" will be incorporated in our later analysis of expansion by the entire banking system.

Consider a deposit of $1,250, which increases "demand deposit of depositor" and "deposit in Federal Reserve" both by that amount. If the required-reserve ratio is 20 percent, excess reserves increase by $1,000; suppose that a new loan of $1,000 is made by the bank, thereby increasing "loans" and "demand deposit of borrower." Table 36–5 gives the changes in the balance sheet at this point.

Table 36–5

INITIAL SITUATION: DEPOSIT AND LOAN

Deposit in FR		$1,250	Demand deposit of depositor	$1,250
Required reserves	$ 250		Demand deposit of borrower	1,000
Excess reserves	1,000			
Loans		1,000		

Next, as reflected in Table 36–6a, a check of $1,000 is written, and the beneficiary of the check has his account in another bank. After the check is cleared, the deposit of the borrower and the bank's deposit in the Fed are reduced, and excess reserves again are zero. Up to this point, the analysis is an old story.

Now, consider an alternative. In Table 36–6b the assumptions are changed: only 90 percent of the loan is spent, and only 80 percent of the expenditure goes outside the bank. That is, checks totaling $900 are written; $720 (i.e., 80 percent of $900) in checks represents an adverse clearing for our bank, with the remaining $180 going into the accounts of other depositors in this same bank. In this case, excess reserves have been reduced only to $224, not to zero. The bank could then grant another loan equal to its excess reserves (i.e., $224), and, after the checks are written and cleared, excess reserves would still be greater than zero (maintaining our assumptions of 90 and 80 percent, how much greater than zero?). We could thus have a succession of loans, each equal to the excess re-

Table 36–6a

ALL OF LOAN USED; ALL CHECKS GO OUTSIDE BANK

Deposit in FR		$ 250	Demand deposit of depositor	$1,250
Required reserves	$250			
Excess reserves	0			
Loans		1,000		

Table 36–6b

SINGLE LOAN EQUAL TO EXCESS RESERVES:
90 PERCENT OF LOAN USED; 80 PERCENT OF CHECKS GO OUTSIDE BANK

Deposit in FR		$ 530	Demand deposit of depositor	$1,250
Required reserves	$306		Demand deposit of borrower	100
Excess reserves	224		Demand deposit of others	180
Loans		1,000		

serves of the moment, with excess reserves rapidly becoming smaller and approaching zero as a limit. Obviously, the sum of all these loans would be greater than $1,000, for the first loan itself is that large. Loans of $1,000 plus $224 plus the others add up to how much? Or, to put the problem a bit differently, instead of envisaging a *succession* of loans, we may ask, just how large could a *single* loan be, given all of our data (including the percentage of the loans used and the percentage of checks going outside the bank), so that we would end up with exactly zero excess reserves?

The problem is easily manageable with a bit of algebraic notation and manipulation. We may first identify our variables:

$E =$ initial excess reserves
$L =$ new loans
$r =$ reserve ratio required against demand deposits
$c =$ percentage of new loans (L) against which checks are drawn
$d =$ percentage of checks (cL) deposited in other banks

We start with actual reserves of $1,250, $250 of which are required against the $1,250 "deposit of the depositor" (see Table 36–5). This deposit and the corresponding required reserves remain constant throughout the analysis. But excess reserves are $1,000 initially and fall to zero by the end of the analysis: E is reduced from $1,000 to zero primarily through *loss of actual reserves*, as new loans are granted and checks are written and flow to other banks, and partly through *increase in required reserves*, for some of the deposits created by the loan stay on the books of this bank. The loss of actual reserves and the increase in required reserves together "absorb" all of the initial excess reserves of $1,000.

We can put this symbolically. The reserve outflow is equal to the percentage of new loans leaving the bank (cd) multiplied by those loans (L): Lcd; the increase in required reserves is equal to the percentage of new loans staying in the bank $(1 - cd)$ multiplied by the loans, all multiplied by the required-reserve ratio (r): $L(1 - cd)r$. Thus, $Lcd + L(1 - cd)r = E$. We may segregate L, stating it in terms of the other variables:

$$L[cd + (1 - cd)r] = E$$

$$L = \frac{E}{cd + (1 - cd)r}$$

$$= \frac{E}{cd(1 - r) + r}$$

Since c and d appear in the equation only together, as a product, we can simplify the appearance of the equation by substituting k for cd. With k representing the proportion of new loans leaving the bank through adverse clearings, we have:

$$L = \frac{E}{k + (1 - k)r}$$

$$= \frac{E}{k(1 - r) + r}$$

If both c and d equal unity, and therefore k also is unity—i.e., if all of the loan is spent and all of the checks leave the bank, as we had earlier assumed—then the denominator on the right side is unity, and $L = E$. But if, as in our current example, $c = .9$ and $d = .8$, and thus $k = .72$, then $L = 1{,}288.66$.

So if a banker is privy to a mysterious source of information, available presumably only to money changers, which accurately assures him that $k = .72$, he may lend a maximum of \$1,288.66, and the bank would ultimately be left with zero excess reserves. The resulting balance sheet is given in Table 36–7. Of course, if the source of information is anything less than infallible, the banker would be somewhat reckless in lending that much. To be sure, he could lend even more if it turns out that k is smaller than .72, but excess reserves will wind up with a negative value if k is larger than .72. He might feel, for example, that prudence befitting a banker calls for a working assumption that $c = .95$ and $d = .9$, so that $k = .855$. On that assumption, the maximum new loan, L, is calculated to be only \$1,131.22.

EXPANSION OF THE BANKING SYSTEM

We have seen that, as a rule of thumb, the *individual* bank, which is a member of a banking system, can grant a new loan no larger than its excess

Table 36–7

MAXIMUM SINGLE LOAN:
90 PERCENT OF LOAN USED; 80 PERCENT OF CHECKS GO OUTSIDE BANK

Deposit in FR		$ 322.17	Demand deposit of depositor	$1,250.00
Required reserves	$322.17		Demand deposit of borrower	128.87
Excess reserves	0		Demand deposit of others	231.96
Loans		1,288.66		

reserves. But what of the multi-member *banking system* itself? If the system is simply the single bank writ large, then presumably the maximum expansion of the system is equal to the total excess reserves of the system. This is an easy and obvious conclusion. It is also wrong.

If we confine ourselves to a "closed" economy (i.e., one with no trade and financial transactions with the rest of the world), it becomes immediately apparent that at least the mechanism of expansion is different for the system than for the single bank. Within an individual bank some customers will write checks that go to other banks, and, when these checks are cleared, reserves are lost; but other customers are depositing checks written on other banks, and clearing these checks increases reserves. A bank that grants loans readily, at a more rapid rate than the other banks, is likely to find that on balance its clearings are adverse; it thereby feels pressure to curtail its pace of expansion and to "get in step" with the average of other banks. However, the reserves lost by one bank are gained by another: *the banking system has no adverse* (or, indeed, favorable) *clearings.* Thus, the major constraint on expansion by the single bank does not exist for the system.

If the system does not experience adverse clearings, what *are* the factors determining the limit to expansion of all banks together? First, there remains, for the system as for the single bank, the constraint consisting of an increase in required reserves as demand deposits rise through additional loans. Second, we may incorporate the possibility of cash withdrawal from the banks as deposits increase.[6]

[6] Although cash drain was alluded to in connection with the single-bank expansion (n. 5), it could then be conveniently put aside. In the context of single-bank expansion, a drain of cash may be represented simply as a greater value of k, the proportion of new loans leaving the bank. Since the banking system has no such loss (i.e., no adverse clearings), the cash drain here must be analyzed separately.

Expansion of the system with no cash drain. At first, let us assume that the cash drain will be zero and concentrate solely on the first factor, the increase in required reserves.

Table 36–8

ADVERSE AND FAVORABLE CLEARINGS

Bank A

Cash		$1,250	Demand deposit of depositor	$1,250
Required reserves	$ 250			
Excess reserves	1,000 *		Demand deposit of borrower	1,000 *
Loans		1,000		

Bank B

Deposit in FR		$1,000	Demand deposit of depositor	$1,000
Required reserves	$200			
Excess reserves	800 *		Demand deposit of borrower	800 *
Loans		800		

We begin with a deposit of $1,250 in Bank A. Suppose that cash, rather than a check drawn on another bank, is deposited, so that the increase in Bank A's reserves need not represent an adverse clearing for another bank. With a required-reserve ratio of 20 percent, Bank A now has $1,000 in excess reserves (assume that the bank had zero excess reserves initially and also that no other bank in the system has excess reserves). On the basis of our conservative rule of thumb, Bank A now grants a maximum loan equal to its excess reserves; and, sure enough, the entire loan is spent by the borrower, and all of the checks go outside the bank. Thus, the items marked * in Bank A's balance sheet—i.e., the borrower's deposit and reserves of $1,000 (which was the value of excess reserves before the loan was made)—disappear from the books of Bank A.

If the borrower from Bank A wrote more than one check, the checks may be deposited now in more than one bank. But suppose that all of the borrower's expenditures are deposited in Bank B. As indicated in Table 36–8, Bank B thereby obtains $800 in excess reserves; assume that it lends $800 and that all of the loan is spent and leaves the bank. But, again, the deposits and reserves lost by one bank are gained by another, call it Bank C. Bank C thus has $640 in excess reserves, lends that much, and loses that much in deposits and reserves to Bank D. And so it goes, each bank in turn lending by the amount of its excess reserves; that amount, however, becomes progressively smaller as the action moves from bank to bank.

Table 36–9

EXPANSION OF THE BANKING SYSTEM

Bank	Reserves and Deposits Gained	Required Reserves	Excess Reserves	Loans: Deposits Created	Reserves Lost and Deposits Reduced
(1)	(2)	(3)	(4)	(5)	(6)
A			$1,000	$1,000	$1,000
B	$1,000	$ 200	800	800	800
C	800	160	640	640	640
D	640	128	512	512	512
E	512	—	—	—	—
—	—	—	—	—	—
	$5,000	$1,000		$5,000	$5,000

It may help to review this bank-by-bank expansion process with the aid of Table 36–9. The table picks up the story at the point where Bank A has excess reserves of $1,000 (recorded in column 4). Bank A then increases deposits by $1,000 through lending (column 5) and promptly loses both reserves and deposits of $1,000 (column 6). But the $1,000 lost in column 6 for Bank A pops up in column 2 for Bank B.

Table 36–9 carries the story through only a few rounds. How far does all this go? It is indicated in column 5 (and will be defended a little later) that the sum 1,000 + 800 + 640 + 512 + . . . = 5,000. A shrewd reader may deny, however, that this sum indicates that the banking system can create a total of $5,000 in deposits, *all* of which are in existence at the *end* of the process; for what is created in column 5 at every step along the way is lost in column 6. But a still shrewder reader will note that what is lost (out of a given bank) in column 6 is found (in another bank) in column 2. That is, the entries in column 2 are *still on the books* of the respective banks. While Bank B, for example, loses $800 in deposits (i.e., owes $800 less in the form of demand deposits) that is *not* a reduction of the initial $1,000 deposit in Bank B. Of course, the bank does lose $800 of the $1,000 in reserves that it initially picked up from Bank A, leaving

$200 of these acquired reserves to serve as "required" against the $1,000 deposit still in the bank. The original $1,000 deposit still owed by Bank B plus the $800 deposit still owed by Bank C plus all the other still existing deposits listed in column 2 add up to $5,000.

Just as it is legitimate and instructive to add the entries in columns 2, 5, and 6, all of which measure the loans granted and the deposits created, so we may total the figures in column 3. The column of "required reserves" lists the actually existing reserves in the respective banks which must be held by them against the actually existing deposits listed in column 2. It is to be noted that the sum of these required reserves, $1,000, equals the magnitude of the initial excess reserves of Bank A, which started the entire analysis and furnished the basis of the system's expansion. That is, the initial excess reserves of Bank A may be considered to be the only excess reserves in existence any place in the system at the beginning of the analysis; this $1,000 of *excess* reserves is gradually "absorbed" into the *required* category; when required reserves finally total $1,000 (column 3), no bank in the system has any excess reserves, and expansion has reached its limit.

Let us make the point again in slightly different words. On the basis of its excess reserves of $1,000, Bank A lends and creates deposits of $1,000. Although both the reserves and the deposits leave Bank A, they do not leave the system; they wind up in Bank B. Now, Bank B likewise lends and creates deposits equal to its excess reserves; but the excess reserves of Bank B are only $800: $200 of the initial excess reserves, while still some place in the system, has shifted from "excess" to "required" status. Thus it goes, each bank lending by the amount of its excess reserves, with the size of the excess reserves being progressively whittled down, bank by bank, to a level of zero. By that time, the lending activities of all these banks together have resulted in $5,000 in deposits, which do exist now but which were not in existence at the outset of the analysis.

It is now apparent that the system can grant loans in the aggregate which are several times greater than the initial excess reserves, although each single bank, in its turn, lends only the amount of its own excess reserves. But how large is the expansion coefficient? In our illustration, the new loans ($5,000) are five times the initial excess reserves ($1,000). One's jungle instinct suggests that the ratio 5:1, or its reciprocal, 1:5, is determined by the proportionate reserve requirement (20 percent).

In this case, instinct is confirmed simply by noting certain basic definitional relations. Let:

D = maximum amount of deposits in the system
A = amount of actual reserves available to the system
r = required (minimum) ratio of reserves to deposits

Given these definitions, it follows that $Dr = A$, and $D = A/r$. In our illustration, $r = .2$. And we may let A be equal to \$1,000, thus making $D =$ \$5,000. The student may feel uneasy about assigning the value of \$1,000 to *actual* reserves (A) when our previous analysis was couched in terms of *excess* reserves (E). We can easily make the reconciliation by noting that the value of actual reserves which is relevant for our analysis, the total of column 3 in Table 36–2, is equal to the initial excess reserves, held by Bank A; in short, $A = E$.

Or consider the matter as the maximum *change* in deposits (ΔD) associated with a given *change* in reserves (ΔA) and a given required-reserve ratio. Then: $\Delta D = \Delta A/r$. But if we suppose that each bank in the system initially has zero excess reserves, then an increase in the actual reserves of Bank A, in the absence of a concomitant increase in deposits, will mean an equal increase in excess reserves: $\Delta A = \Delta E$. So, if one prefers, he may write: $\Delta D = \Delta E/r = \$1{,}000/.2 = \$5{,}000$.

Actual reserves *can* increase without an accompanying increase in deposits. For example, the bank might sell some bonds and add the proceeds to its reserves: one asset decreases and another increases, with no change in deposits. But suppose that the increase in reserves *is* associated with an increase in deposits. To revert to our early illustration, perhaps the analysis begins not with \$1,000 in excess reserves in Bank A already somehow in existence, but with a deposit made into Bank A of \$1,250. Then, in Table 36–9, for Bank A, column 2 would have an entry of \$1,250, and column 3 would have \$250; the rest of the table would remain unchanged—except, of course, that the total for column 2 would be \$6,250, and column 3's total would be \$1,250. With this version of the analysis, obviously ΔA (\$1,250) is no longer equal to ΔE (\$1,000). But we can write: $\Delta D_g = \Delta A/r$, and $\Delta D_n = \Delta E/r$, where ΔD_n is the "net" increase in deposits from *lending* activities; i.e., the increase in deposits directly associated with the utilization of excess reserves, while ΔD_g is the "gross" increase in deposits, including not only the increase from lending but also the increase from the originating *deposit*.

Expansion of the system with cash drain. We have concluded that the banking system has a potential expansion of deposits equal to $1/r$ for each \$1 of excess reserves—assuming that there is no withdrawal of cash.[7] We may now modify the assumption. The amount of currency in circulation does change over time, and, unsurprisingly, it strongly tends to rise as the total money supply increases.

Table 36–10 is an elaboration of Table 36–9. The process begins as before, with Bank A possessing \$1,000 of excess reserves and granting loans of that amount. Then, in column 6, it is assumed that the bank's customers, including

[7] Another assumption has been that r is a ratio common to all the banks in question. This is a simplification; for, it will be recalled, in actuality there are two (and have been three) classes, or categories, of banks, each with its own reserve requirement.

Table 36–10

EXPANSION OF THE BANKING SYSTEM: CASH DRAIN

Bank	Reserves and Deposits Gained	Required Reserves	Excess Reserves	Loans: Gross Deposits (L_g)	Cash Drain (C)	Net Deposits (L_n)	Reserves Lost and Deposits Reduced
(1)	(2)	(3)	(4)	(5)	(6)	(7)	(8)
A			$1,000	$1,000	$150	$ 850	$ 850
B	$ 850	$170	680	680	102	578	578
C	578	115.6	462.4	462.4	69.32	393.08	393.08
D	393.08	78.62	314.46	314.46	47.17	267.29	267.29
E	267.29	—	—	—	—	—	—
—	—	—	—	—	—	—	—
	$2,656.25	$531.25		$3,125.00	$468.75	$2,656.25	$2,656.25

the borrower, draw out cash equal to 15 percent of the new loans.[8] The "gross" deposits (L_g) of $1,000 created by the loan are thus reduced to "net" deposits (L_n) of $850 by the cash drain ($C$) of $150; i.e., $L_g - C = L_n$. The remaining $850 of net deposits then are wholly spent, and all checks go outside the bank; i.e., to Bank B. The procedure is followed, bank by bank, with the cash-drain ratio, $c = C/L_g$, remaining a constant 15 percent.

How does the introduction of cash drain, or the cash-drain ratio, affect the maximum lending of the system? As before, the system can expand further only as long as excess reserves in the system are greater than zero. Or, to reverse the matter, potential expansion stops when excess reserves are exhausted. What happens to the initial excess reserves? They are "absorbed," or "dissipated," in two ways. First, some of the original excess reserves wind up in the *required* category, for demand deposits are created and remain in creation; specifically, required reserves (column 3) must be held against the new (net) deposits (column 2). The amount of required reserves equals the amount of net deposits multiplied by the required-reserve ratio ($L_n r$). Second, some reserves are lost by the banking system through the cash drain (C). Thus, the original excess reserves are reduced to zero, partly through an increase in required reserves and partly through a reduction in actual reserves: $E = L_n r + C$.

We have the following relations:

$$E = L_n r + C,$$
$$L_n = L_g - C,$$
$$C = cL_g.$$

With a little manipulation, we may now solve for L_g (the maximum loans of the system) in terms of E (the initial excess reserves) and c and r (the cash-drain and required-reserve ratios):

$$\begin{aligned} E &= (L_g - C)r + cL_g, \\ &= (L_g - cL_g)r + cL_g, \\ &= L_g(r - cr + c), \\ L_g &= \frac{E}{r - cr + c}, \\ &= \frac{E}{r(1 - c) + c}, \end{aligned}$$

[8] For the last dozen or so years, the ratio of total currency to the total money supply (i.e., currency plus demand deposits) has fluctuated between 19 and 20 percent. Of course, this "average" ratio of currency in circulation to all money is not necessarily equal to the "marginal" ratio—i.e., *change* in currency divided by *change* in money supply. The choice of 15 percent for the cash-drain ratio, while not obviously unreasonable, is thus largely arbitrary; it is assumed not to be 20 percent in order to avoid duplication of the value of the required-reserve ratio.

$$= \frac{E}{r - c(r-1)},$$
$$= 3{,}125.$$

And, of course, net loans (or, rather, net deposits), L_n—the value of which is found in columns 2, 7, and 8—are:

$$L_n = L_g(1 - c) = \frac{E(1-c)}{r(1-c)+c},$$
$$= \frac{E}{r + \dfrac{c}{1-c}},$$
$$= 2{,}656.25.$$

Thus, as reflected in Table 36–10, the initial \$1,000 of excess reserves is wholly accounted for by the loss in actual reserves (equal to the cash drain) of \$468.75 and the increase in required reserves (equal to 20 percent of the increase in net deposits) of \$531.25.

Obviously, the introduction of cash drain has made a substantial difference in the maximum expansion of the system. If the cash-drain ratio (c) were zero, we would have $L_n = L_g = E/r = 5{,}000$. But with $c = .15$, loans are only about three fifths of that value, and net deposits are just over one half.

Questions

1. We have spoken of the functions of money and the advantages of a monetary-exchange system over barter. But does money perform its functions perfectly? In particular, how well does money serve as a "store of value"? Can value be stored in the form of *non*monetary assets? Would you ever prefer storing value in nonmonetary form?

2. "Money is, of course, a useful device—but only in a very restricted way. It does only one thing: it facilitates exchange. It may be compared to oil, which allows machinery to operate with less friction. But while making exchange in the marketplace more convenient, money is also an analytical 'veil,' which tends to obscure the 'real' workings of the economy. Economic well being depends on production of actual goods and services and their distribution and exchange; analysis should be directed to such fundamental things, but in fact it tends to be diverted to wholly superficial phenomena such as changes in the money supply." Do you agree?

3. What is meant by "the demand for money"? Money itself is not eaten, worn, or otherwise consumed; so, except for the miserly joy of running through it in one's bare feet, what gains can there be in *not* spending all money on consumption as soon as it is received?

4. How do we decide what to count as part of the money supply—i.e., whether a given asset should rank as money? Choose the best criterion from the following and defend your choice:

(1) Does it have full gold backing—i.e., is it convertible by the government into gold upon demand of an individual?

(2) Is it recognized by the community at large as spendable—i.e., can it be freely and generally used to satisfy financial obligations?

(3) Is it a coin or paper currency (for in the last analysis these are the only things that can count as genuine money)?

(4) Has it been issued as lawful money by the federal government?

5. We have discussed "two complementary (and possibly competing) explanations for major fluctuations in rates of use of resources"—namely, the Keynesian and the quantity-of-money approaches. How, or in what senses, are these explanations complementary or competing? Is it possible that they are both?

6. Quarterly data since World War II show the following "peaks" and "troughs" for fluctuations in the money supply and in *GNP* (in billions of dollars).

MONEY SUPPLY

Peak:	1947—IV	110.667	
			− 1.9%
Trough:	1949—IV	108.500	
			+16.3%
	1953—II	126.167	
			+ .5%
	1954—II	126.800	
			+ 6.2%
Peak:	1957—I	134.667	
			− .8%
Trough:	1958—I	133.567	
			+ 5.5%
Peak:	1959—III	140.966	
			− 1.8%
Trough:	1960—II	138.300	
			+ 9.0%
	1963—III	150.700	

GROSS NATIONAL PRODUCT

Peak:	1948—IV	265.9	
			− 3.3%
Trough:	1949—IV	257.0	
			+43.5%
Peak:	1953—II	368.8	
			− 2.7%
Trough:	1954—II	358.9	
			+24.9%
Peak:	1957—III	448.3	
			− 3.4%
Trough:	1958—I	432.9	
			+16.4%
Peak:	1960—II	504.1	
			− .7%
Trough:	1961—I	500.4	
			+17.6%
	1963—III	588.7	

From these figures, suggest possible generalizations concerning the correlation of money and income—relating, for example, to directions of changes, relative magnitudes of changes, and timing or sequence of changes of the two variables.

7. The Federal Reserve gold reserve required against Federal Reserve notes and commercial bank deposits in the Fed is 25 percent; the requirement of legal reserves against demand deposits in commercial banks is about 20 percent. If both Federal Reserve banks and commercial banks were expanded to their limits, the gold "backing" of each dollar in the money supply (i.e., the value of gold as a proportion of the money supply) would be about what percentage?

8. "Along with making investments (e.g., in government securities), granting loans is a bank's major way of making money." Explain that the reference to "making money" by granting loans is a clever *double entendre*.

9. "A bank, through granting loans, can create money out of thin air. And air is a free good. Therefore, a bank can create loans (and thereby earn profits) without limit." Something is surely wrong in the quoted statement; straighten it out.

10. "Consider a single bank (one of many in the banking system); suppose that the required reserve ratio against demand deposits is 10 percent, and no excess reserves exist initially. Now, a customer adds to his demand deposit by depositing $1,000 in cash from his sugar bowl. As a result, with our first-approximation assumptions concerning adverse clearings, the bank is *not* in a position to grant loans and thereby create deposits equal to ten times its (excess) reserves; rather, if it expands to the limit, it reduces reserves to one tenth the initial deposit." With the aid of T accounts, indicate step by step *what* happens and *why*.

11. An initial balance sheet for a commercial bank is given in column 1. The balance sheets in columns 2 through 7 will be entirely *separate* from each other; each will be a modification of the *initial* balance sheet in column 1. In other words, this is *not* a cumulative problem: begin with the initial balance sheet in recording each transaction.

In calculating required and excess reserves at the bottom of the balance sheets, assume a required reserve ratio against demand deposits of 25 percent. Finally, calculate the maximum new loans that can be granted by (a) the individual bank in a banking system and (b) the system as a whole, assuming that excess reserves initially are zero in all the other banks.

	(1)	(2)	(3)	(4)	(5)	(6)	(7)
ASSETS							
Cash	100	____	____	____	____	____	____
Deposit in FR	200	____	____	____	____	____	____
Loans	500	____	____	____	____	____	____
Government bonds	200	____	____	____	____	____	____
LIABILITIES							
Demand deposits	900	____	____	____	____	____	____
Capital	100	____	____	____	____	____	____
Required reserves	____	____	____	____	____	____	____
Excess reserves	____	____	____	____	____	____	____
New loans: single bank	____	____	____	____	____	____	____
New loans: entire system	____	____	____	____	____	____	____

(1) Complete column 1.

(2) A check for $50 is drawn by one of the bank's depositors, given to a person who deposits it in another bank, and the check is cleared through the Fed. (Record the new balance sheet in column 2.)

(3) A depositor withdraws $20 in cash from the bank, and the bank restores its vault cash by withdrawing cash from the Fed. (Record in column 3.)

(4) A check for $60 drawn on another bank is deposited in this bank and cleared through the Fed. (Record in column 4.)

(5) The bank sells $100 in government bonds to a bond dealer who pays with a check drawn on another bank. (Record in column 5.)

(6) The bank makes a loan of $10, the proceeds of which are taken in the form of a demand deposit. (Record in column 6.)

(7) The required-reserve ratio against demand deposits is lowered to 20 percent. (Record in column 7.)

12. "The banking system is made up of individual banks; the former is simply the sum of the latter. Therefore, it can scarcely be possible for the system to expand demand deposits by a multiple of initial excess reserves when any given bank can expand by (approximately) only the amount of its excess reserves." How could anyone disagree?

13. The banking system can expand as long as excess reserves exist; expansion stops when excess reserves are zero. But the banking system (as opposed to a single bank) does not lose reserves—assuming a closed economy and no cash drain. So where can the excess reserves go? Do we properly conclude that the system does not lose excess reserves and that consequently the system can expand without limit?

14. The balance sheet of a single bank in a banking system is given. The legally required reserve ratio against demand deposits is 20 percent. Suppose that experience indicates that when a new loan is made, 70 percent of it will be spent by the depositor writing checks; further, 90 percent of these checks will go to people with accounts in other banks.

Cash	50	Demand deposits	5,000
Deposit in FR	1,000	Capital	1,100
Investments	2,050		
Loans	3,000		

a. As a conservative approximation, on the basis of the most severe assumptions we have used concerning adverse clearing balances, what is the maximum amount by which the bank can safely expand its loans?

b. Alternatively, on the basis of the assumptions indicated by experience (noted above), what is the maximum expansion of the bank?

c. How will the balance sheet appear some days after the loans in question (b) have been granted; that is, after all checks have been written and cleared?

d. Assuming no cash drain and no excess reserves in other banks at the outset of the problem, by how much can the system (including the bank that initiated the loan expansion) increase loans and deposits?

e. As an alternative to question (d), suppose that there is a cash drain, with the cash-drain ratio being 10 percent of (gross) new loans. Then, what is the maximum loan expansion of the banking system?

37

THE FEDERAL RESERVE AND MONETARY POLICY

We have seen that (a) the great bulk of the money supply consists of demand deposits in commercial banks, (b) these demand deposits change primarily with the lending activities of banks, and (c) these lending activities are constrained by the reserve positions of banks. The next appropriate topic is the control and determinants of bank reserves.[1]

The potential new lending (and thus money creating) by a bank or a banking system is limited by the amount of excess reserves; excess reserves are the residual of actual reserves minus required reserves; therefore, given the magnitude of deposit liabilities, excess reserves are determined by the absolute (i.e., dollar) *amount* of actual reserves and the required-reserve *ratio*. This review of familiar material suggests the basic rationale of requiring banks to hold reserves: minimum-reserve requirements and possible changes in such requirements provide the monetary authorities with a means of "credit control." The Fed's credit controls operate, directly or indirectly, mainly on reserves and to a minor extent directly on the money supply. The purpose of affecting reserves, of course, is to induce banks to follow desired lending (money-creating) activities. And control of the money supply is desired in the interests of promoting "aggregate stabilization," otherwise widely interpreted as "full employment with a stable price level."

It has not always been appreciated, even by economists, that reserve requirements constitute essentially a tool of monetary manage-

[1] There is reason to believe that Federal Reserve policy decisions are made with respect not to actual reserves or to excess reserves, but to excess reserves *minus* member-bank borrowings from the Fed (which equals "free reserves" if excess reserves are larger than borrowings and "net borrowed reserves" if borrowings are larger than reserves).

ment. Commonly, it has been suggested that banks are required to hold reserves equal at least to calculable minima in order to assure bank "liquidity" sufficient to protect the banks' depositors. Since depositors wish from time to time to withdraw cash, so the argument goes, banks should be required to hold a certain minimum amount of assets in the form of reserves.

Several remarks can be directed to the notion that required reserves are a direct device for protecting customers: (a) As mentioned earlier, from 1917 to 1959 legal reserves consisted solely of member-bank deposits in the Fed and not at all of cash, which could be readily paid out to customers. (b) Even now, as prior to 1959, vault cash typically is equal to only 2 or 3 or 4 percent of demand deposits; and, indeed, all reserves, including deposits in the Fed, generally are no more than 20 to 25 percent of deposits in the bank, so that only a small portion of deposits could be simultaneously covered by cash taken out of reserves. (c) It would be a bit awkward—to put the matter gently—to maintain required reserves while also paying out reserve funds to customers; for as soon as enough cash is withdrawn from a bank to reduce the bank's excess reserves to zero, any further drawing on reserves will result in negative excess reserves. (d) The real protection of depositors is not (inadequate) reserves stashed away by the bank for a rainy day, but the prevention of massive customer demands for cash in the first place; and such panic-inspired "bank runs" will scarcely materialize if the customers are confident that their deposits are safe, one method of generating such confidence being deposit insurance.[2]

Federal Reserve Controls

The Fed, then, may determine the required-reserve *percentage* and strongly affect the dollar *quantity* of reserves. Because the Fed can to a considerable extent directly control the *reserve position* of member banks, it wishes indirectly to affect the money supply and aggregate spending and thus national income, prices, employment, and output. We can easily indicate the nature of these Federal Reserve credit controls; then we shall examine briefly the record of use of the controls.

[2] Depositors will not wish simultaneously to exercise their claims on banks unless they begin to fear that it would not be feasible to get their money if they did decide to withdraw it. If the word begins to get around that little of the money really is available, the typical person will think it prudent to dash to the bank in order to get his before the bank runs out of cash. And after only a small proportion of deposits has been cashed in, the rumor is confirmed: sure enough, most of the money is not available! If the panic-inspired demand for cash continues, the bank may well be forced to close its doors. But the Banking Act of 1933 established the Federal Deposit Insurance Corporation (F.D.I.C.), which guarantees payment on all deposits up to a certain amount, now $10,000. All members of the Fed plus some non-member banks are covered by the F.D.I.C. With payment on deposits guaranteed, come what may, it would seem that a giant, and perhaps wholly decisive, step has been taken to preclude massive and widespread runs on the banks.

RESERVE-REQUIREMENT PERCENTAGE

In the initial Federal Reserve legislation of 1913, the percentage requirements against demand and time deposits in the different categories of banks were specified. In 1933 (temporarily) and 1935 ("permanently"), Congress gave the Board of Governors of the Fed authority to vary these requirements within a range. Table 37–1 gives the current range and the requirements in effect in the spring of 1964.

Table 37–1

REQUIRED-RESERVE RATIOS

	DEMAND DEPOSITS		TIME DEPOSITS	
	Reserve City Banks	**Country Banks**	**Reserve City Banks**	**Country Banks**
Range of legal requirements (%):				
Minimum	10	7	3	3
Maximum	22	14	6	6
In effect April 1, 1964	16.5	12	4	4

Our earlier discussion of bank expansion makes clear the effect of a change in the reserve-requirement ratio on potential lending. From the standpoint of a *single* bank, reducing (or increasing) the ratio, with other things remaining the same, directly increases (decreases) the *volume* of excess reserves. With a stroke of the pen, a change in the ratio changes required reserves; and, with a given value of actual reserves, a change in required reserves will change excess reserves. From the standpoint of the banking *system*, altering the ratio has a double effect: not only is the *volume* of excess reserves affected, but, in addition, the *expansion coefficient* (i.e., the multiple by which a dollar of excess reserves may give rise to, or support, new deposits) is changed. Thus, if the Federal Reserve authorities diagnose the current situation as one of "recession" and determine upon an expansionary policy, they can (within the prescribed limits) cut the required-reserve ratio, thereby (a) creating more dollars of excess reserves and (b) permitting a larger potential expansion of lending per dollar of excess reserves.

It would appear that changes in the reserve ratio can be a powerful tool.

(Currently in reserve city banks, demand deposits subject to reserve requirements total nearly $70,000,000,000; a 1 percent change in the required-reserve ratio would thus change excess reserves by $700,000,000—compared to excess reserves now in reserve city banks of only some $50,000,000 and of $400,000,000 for all member banks.) In practice, this tool has been used very gingerly. Changes in the ratio generally have been made only infrequently and by small amounts. To illustrate, consider the required-reserve ratio for demand deposits in reserve city banks. The original Federal Reserve law set this ratio at 10 percent. In 1936, it was raised to 15 percent; except for two changes of 2½ percent in 1937 and 1938 and one of 2 percent in 1948, all subsequent changes have been either 1 or ½ percent. In thirty years, there have been only 19 changes in the ratio, with the ratio varying between 15 and 22 percent from 1936 to 1964. Furthermore, most of these changes have come in several flurries; e.g., six successive decreases—from 22 percent to 18 percent—during four months in 1949.

Obviously, the reserve ratio is not used as a fine instrument, delicately modified from day to day or week to week. (Indeed, it is necessarily an uneven instrument, for a change in the ratio for any given classification of banks will apply to all banks in that group, regardless of different reserve positions. An increase in the ratio which will simply reduce very large excess reserves for one bank will create negative excess reserves for another bank.) Typically years go by between changes: the ratio was constant for 3½ years from early 1938 to late 1941, for almost 7 years from 1941 to 1948, for 2½ years from 1951 to mid-1953, for 3½ years from mid-1954 to early 1958, and for nearly 6 years as of the beginning of 1964.

REDISCOUNT RATE

While changes in the required-reserve percentage directly change the quantity of *required* reserves, changes in the "rediscount" rate may change the quantity of *actual* reserves.

The rediscount rate is the interest rate charged by the Federal Reserve banks on their loans to member banks. Just as a customer of a commercial bank is charged interest on his borrowing from the bank, so is the bank when it borrows from the Fed. And just as a bank's customer will make his decision regarding how much, if anything, he wishes to borrow partly in light of the interest rate, so the bank will be more inclined to borrow, or be inclined to borrow more, from the Fed at a lower rediscount rate than at a higher rate.

The setting of the rate is done at the discretion of the Fed. If the member banks respond to a lowering of the rate by borrowing more, then member-bank reserves increase, for the proceeds of the borrowing are taken in the form of a (larger) demand deposit in the Fed. On the books of the borrowing bank, we would enter the (larger) "deposit in Federal Reserve" on the asset side and "rediscounts and bills payable" with liabilities.[3] Of course, paying off the loan involves canceling "rediscounts and bills payable" and correspondingly reducing "deposit in Federal Reserve." And if the Fed wishes to pursue a more contractionary policy, in order to combat inflation, it can increase the rediscount rate—thereby presumably inducing banks to borrow less than they otherwise would have borrowed and thus prevent reserves from being increased as much. (For both expansionary and contractionary policies, in addition to changing the numerical *rate,* the Fed may change the *quality of collateral* required for a loan to a bank.)

At the beginning of the Federal Reserve System, the Reserve banks were expected to engage regularly and heavily in short-term rediscounting, and changes in the rediscount rate were to be *the* tool of credit control. Through the 1920s, this was the case; authority to change the required-reserve ratio did not yet exist, and use of "open-market operations," discussed below, was slight. By the end of 1929, the rediscount rate of the Federal Reserve Bank of New York had been altered thirty times, within a range of 3 to 7 percent. It was changed another fifteen times from the beginning of 1930 to the spring of 1934, the range being 1 to 4 percent. But there was only one change during the next fourteen years, and except for the period 1955–60, when there were eighteen changes, the rediscount rate has not been a very actively used measure for about thirty years.

Along with the relatively frequent changes in the rediscount rate in the 1920s, the volume of member borrowing from the Fed was relatively heavy; borrowings at the Fed were virtually zero from 1934 through 1943; during the past dozen years, average outstanding borrowings have approximated the volume of the mid-1920s—namely, around $500,000,000; but this equaled something like one quarter of actual reserves in the 1920s, and it is only 2 or 3 percent of reserves now. Indeed, since the early years of the Fed, there has developed a tradition which disfavors regular and substantial borrowing by banks from the Fed.[4]

[3] Typically, when a customer borrows $1,000 from a bank for one year (supposedly) at 5 percent, he does *not* receive $1,000 now and repay $1,050 a year later; rather, his I.O.U. is "discounted," and he receives $950 now and repays the face value of his note—i.e., $1,000—a year later. (Appreciate the infinite shrewdness of the banker: whereas 50/1,000 yields an interest rate of 5 percent, the actual rate is 50/950 = 5.051 percent.) Now, the bank can use the I.O.U., known more grandly as "commercial paper," as collateral for a loan from the Fed, and the Fed lends by discounting; since the same note is thus discounted a second time, it is rediscounted. However, the term "rediscount" rate applies also to the more common mode of bank borrowing from the Fed, in which the bank submits not already discounted commercial paper but a promissory note drawn on itself, with collateral generally but not always in the form of government securities.

[4] "The Federal Reserve policy of emphasizing to member banks that the use of its discount facilities should be temporary is reinforced in practice by a well-established tradition among this country's banks against operating on the basis of borrowed reserves—at least, for any extended period. This tradition does not mean that member banks feel reluctant to rely on Federal Reserve lending facilities to meet temporary or unusual cash drains. But it does mean that under normal conditions member banks manage their affairs so that they do not

OPEN-MARKET OPERATIONS

In general, the most important method of credit control by the Fed is open-market operations; that is, the Fed's buying and selling of securities, almost all of which are United States government securities. (Decisions to buy and sell securities are made for the entire Federal Reserve system by the Federal Open Market Committee—established in 1933 and reconstituted in 1935—which consists of all seven members of the Board of Governors plus five representatives elected by the reserve banks.) The actual transactions are conducted with a rather small number of dealers who specialize in such activities. The dealers hold an inventory of government securities. If they sell to the Fed, they receive checks, which they deposit in commercial banks; the deposits in and the reserves of these banks thus rise. If the dealers buy from the Fed, deposits in and reserves of banks fall.[5] The dealers can replenish or reduce inventories by buying from or selling to other people and institutions in the market. And the dealers, instead of buying or selling for their own account, can be middlemen for others in dealing with the Fed.

How do open-market operations compare with changes in the required-reserve ratio and in the rediscount rate? For one thing, open-market operations go on almost continuously, although not always on a massive scale and not with frequently occurring large net changes in the Fed's holdings of government securities; on the other hand, we know, the other tools of control are employed only occasionally and may be unemployed for prolonged periods.

Next, there is a certainty of effect of the Fed's actions with respect to open-market operations which is characteristic also of changes in the required-reserve ratio but not of changes in the rediscount rate. When the Fed buys or sells in the government-securities market, bank reserves—actual, required, and excess—will be affected as soon as the buyer's check is cleared; and when the Fed raises or lowers the required-reserve ratio, required reserves simultaneously increase or de-

---

need to resort to Reserve Bank borrowing . . . and so that, once in debt, they seek to repay such debt promptly." *The Federal Reserve System—Purposes and Functions* (Washington, D.C.: Board of Governors of the Federal Reserve System, 1961), pp. 44–45.

[5] Of course, buying and selling activities, with the associated shifts in supply and demand, can change the prices of government securities. If, for example, the Fed is combatting recession by heavy purchasing of bonds, this increased demand for securities will tend to raise their prices. And an *increase in price* of a bond will tend to *reduce the interest rate.* Indeed, for a bond paying an absolute dollar amount of interest, the reduction in the interest rate is not merely a tendency but an inevitable matter of arithmetic. If a bond pays $50 per year, the *rate* of interest is 5 percent if the price is $1,000 and 4.55 percent if the price is $1,100. Now, would such a decrease in the interest rate (if accompanied by a fall in rates generally) be supplemental to, or tend to offset, the basic anti-recession policy? If the general level of interest rates falls, one would suppose that the volume of borrowing would tend to increase; and thus the money supply and the amount of consumer and investment expenditures would be more than they otherwise would have been, which was what the expansionary open-market policy was trying to achieve.

crease (and excess reserves thus decrease or increase). But when the rediscount rate is changed, there may or may not be a discernible reaction on the part of banks; and, even if there is, the extent of the reaction is not mechanically determined.

Finally, there is another element of immediacy of effect of open-market operations which is not shared with either of the other two tools of control. Buying and selling in the open market not only affect banks' reserves, but also directly increase or decrease the money supply (i.e., demand deposits) by the amount of the transaction, whereas the other tools at best affect only reserves in the first instance; and any repercussion on the money supply involves a later lending reaction by the banks to the Fed's activity.

As suggested above, open-market operations were not dramatically consequential during the first part of the Fed's history. Throughout the 1920s, the Fed's holdings of government securities averaged around $200,000,000 or $300,000,000, never rising above $600,000,000 and remaining less than Fed lending to banks until 1930; from 1929 to 1933, holdings of securities rose to about $2,500,000,000 and stayed there until 1942. The financing of World War II is largely reflected in a tenfold increase to $25,000,000,000; and, after a dip in the early postwar period, security holdings of the Fed have been between $25,000,000,000 and $30,000,000,000 for a dozen years.

MORAL SUASION

The foregoing tools of credit control are tangible, and their implementation can be directly recorded. Less obvious is so-called "moral suasion," a genteel label for "arm-twisting." The influence of the Fed is not simply physical and mechanical; it partakes also of a more subtle mother-hen aspect. Does the Fed believe that the economy is becoming a bit too exuberant and that a little more monetary restraint (i.e., reduction in the money supply or smaller rate of increase) is in order? It may not yet wish to do much by means of the obvious tools, but still something should be done. So the Fed, without employing the "physical" controls over reserves, can tell the commercial banks that they might, in the light of the current situation, be just a bit more cautious in granting and extending loans. This word can be spread to the boys in the financial fraternity by such means as speeches and statements to Congressional committees by the chairman of the Board of Governors of the Fed; in addition, the numerous bank examiners can begin to get a little stickier on the quality of collateral the banks are accepting when making loans. And when the word thus gets out, the boys may well fall into step, following the cadence of the Fed.

The Record of the Federal Reserve

A split-second survey of the use of the three major credit controls since World War I suggests the following picture. The heyday of the rediscount rate was the 1920s (and into the early 1930s), when changes in the rate were more frequent and bank borrowing from the Fed was relatively heavier than in later periods; open-market operations appear to dominate the 1950s and 1960s, with the Fed holdings of government securities having risen to impressive levels and subject to appreciable changes in short periods of time, although in the middle and late 1950s there was a small flurry of activity with the rediscount rate; there has been no substantial period when manipulation of the required-reserve ratio was conspicuous; and from the early 1930s to the early 1950s all of the tools were generally unused—except for the Fed's acquisition of securities during World War II, and that inflationary mode of war financing is scarcely to be commended.

Although the Fed has not employed its tools of monetary control with great vigor and, indeed, has tended most of the time to be essentially passive and quiescent, it is appropriate to conclude this survey by asking about the "quality" of the Fed's actions. Have the tools, insofar as they have been used at all, been used at the right times and in the right directions? (One could ask also whether they have been used in appropriate volume and magnitude, but this is even more difficult to answer than the questions on timing and direction.)

In order to have some standard of reference in evaluating Federal Reserve policies, consider first an idealized "business cycle" and the timing and direction of the Fed's actions in order to dampen the cycle.[6] We may envisage a cycle of economic activity (measured, perhaps, by some appropriate conglomerate index of variables), fluctuating above and below a rising trend, and we assume that the Fed wishes to restrain both the inflationary upswings and the recessionary downswings. As contractionary, anti-inflation moves, the Fed would (a) raise the required-reserve ratio, (b) raise the rediscount rate, and (c) sell government securities; and expansionary, anti-recession policies would be the opposite. Thus, the required-reserve ratio and the rediscount rate would move in the same direction and opposite to holdings of government securities. How closely did Fed activity resemble this pattern in the periods 1929–41 and 1946–62?

Figures 37–1 and 37–2 will serve our simple, summary purposes. They pre-

[6] Despite the books, articles, and college courses devoted to "business cycles," there is reason to use the label with caution, or at least with quotation marks. Presumably, the idea of a "cycle" embodies notions of "automaticity," "regularity," and "self-generation": the "system" or "mechanism" is such that swings in economic activity will lead with some precision to a turning point which reverses the direction of the swing. That there have been *fluctuations* in the numerous indices of economic activity is apparent; that these fluctuations have been sufficiently neat and coherent, generated by an automatic mechanism, to warrant the label of "cycle" is not so apparent.

sent three indicators of the "level of economic activity": consumer prices, industrial production, and national income in current dollars. Quarterly data are presented for all three measures. The *magnitudes* of the fluctuations in these curves are not to be compared; for two of the measures (prices and production) are indices while the other (income) is in absolute dollar amounts, and the two indices are plotted on different scales. Our main concern here is with the *turning points*, and the three measures move together quite closely, generally changing (up or down) in the same direction.

These indicators point to the fourth quarter of 1929 as the beginning of what came to be known as the Great Depression, which hit bottom around the first quarter of 1933. What was the response of the Fed? As is evident in Figure 37–1, for 1929 to 1941, the required-reserve ratio remained constant by statutory provision; there was no significant change in holdings of government securities until mid-1932, and, even then, the increase seems very modest in light of the magnitude of the problem, however bold it might have appeared by historical standards. More attention was given to the rediscount rate.[7] After a full percentage-point increase in July 1929, it was progressively lowered until late 1931, when (for balance-of-international-payments purposes rather than domestic policy) it was sharply increased long before the depression reached its lower turning point, and then, after some backing and filling for two years, it settled down at a level maintained until well after World War II.

Do not pass over this experience lightly. From 1929 to 1933, the stock of money was reduced 25 percent, the major part of this reduction coming in the first two years. (Once before, in 1920–21, the money stock fell at an even greater rate—over 12 percent in one year.) Such enormous decreases in the money supply are bound to have severe effects on the state of general demand, prices, and employment. What was responsible? Several factors, but one fact stands out in embarrassing boldness. The Federal Reserve, an institution designed to stabilize the quantity of money, failed in a primary mission. While the money supply was falling and while banks were failing because of runs on them, the Fed persisted in looking primarily at interest rates and in largely eschewing open-market purchases of government bonds and private debt in order to prevent the demand-deposit contraction. It failed—not because its administrators were evil, but because they did not comprehend their primary function: to control the total quantity of money and not to act like private bankers. Had they acted more strongly within the limits of the Fed's powers, the decrease in the money supply would have been greatly ameliorated and the depression reduced in severity and length. Possibly they did not believe that changes in the quantity of money had anything to do with the level of unemployment, or they may have thought that only

[7] Each of the twelve Federal Reserve banks has its own rediscount rate. They do not always move quite simultaneously, and they do not always all settle at precisely the same level; but the changes and the levels do not greatly diverge. For expositional convenience, we here consider the rate of only the Federal Reserve Bank of New York.

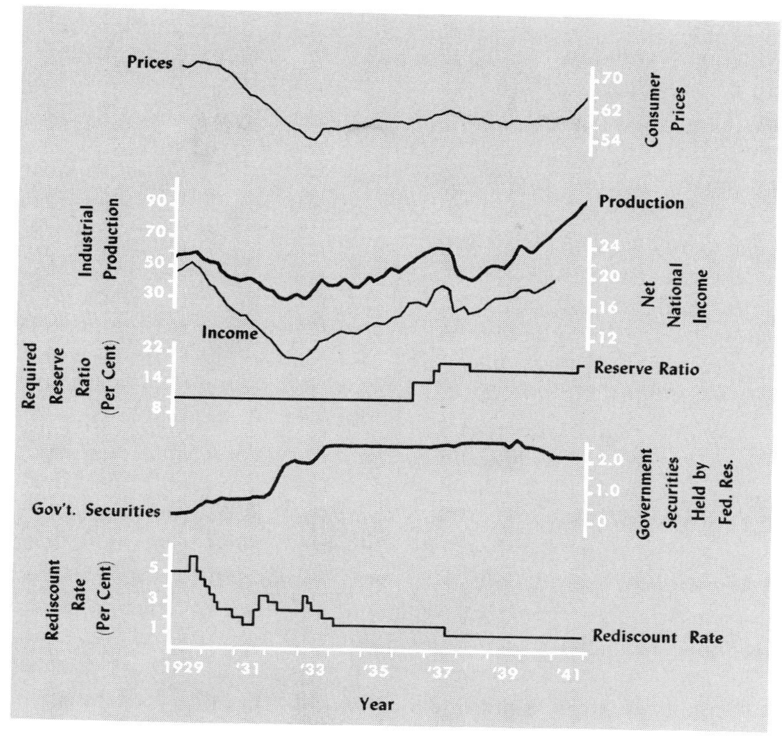

FIGURE 37–1. Prices, production, and income related to Federal Reserve actions, 1929–41. Source: Federal Reserve, *Monthly Bulletin.*

the interest rate counted or that the money supply was always automatically adjusted to the "needs" of business.

From about the beginning of 1934, open-market operations and the rediscount rate were virtually moribund, and the required-reserve ratio was doubled from 10 percent to 20 percent for reserve city banks[8] in 1936–37—just in time for the severe recession of 1937–38.

However well the charitable observer may account for these actions, it seems reasonable to drop the hint that, with the possible exception of handling the rediscount rate from late 1929 to late 1931, the record of the Fed in the 1930s is, at best, one of too little and too late, and in part even of dubious decisions as to direction of action.

Is its record after World War II more impressive? Look at Figure 37–2. Whereas in our "ideal" policy the required-reserve ratio and holdings of govern-

[8] As with rediscount rates, we choose one of several reserve-requirement ratios as representative, there being three (central reserve city, reserve city, and country) until mid-1962, when the central-reserve-city classification was dropped.

ment securities would be changed in opposite directions, they tended—if there is a tendency—to move together through 1957; and whereas the required-reserve ratio and the rediscount rate were to move together, there was actually almost no cyclical correlation—with the trends diverging—until early 1958, when both the ratio and the rate were belatedly reduced.

If one considers the counter-cyclical policies in the recessions of 1948–49, 1953–54, 1957–58, and 1960–61, the record is no better than mixed; and on balance it is not conducive to great confidence. To illustrate, take the first postwar recession, although the story would be similar for any of the others. We may date the beginning of the downturn as the fourth quarter of 1948 and the beginning of the upturn as the first quarter of 1950. What happened to the three credit controls? (a) The required-reserve ratio was raised in September 1948 and held constant until May 1949, although the index of industrial production fell steadily beginning in September 1948. Then, in the second half of the downturn, the ratio was lowered several times. (b) The rediscount rate was raised twice (January and August 1948) shortly before the upper turning point and then held constant all through the downswing. (c) The holdings of government securities followed, rather than ran counter to, the level of economic activity; after increasing in the fourth quarter of 1948, they fell precipitously through the second quarter of 1950. The proponents of counter-cyclical policy may feel, in the light of such experience, that, with friends like the Fed, who needs enemies?

This early postwar episode took place during a most peculiar period of Federal Reserve history. Through both world wars, the Fed followed the policy of standing ready to purchase *any quantity* of government securities from the market *at par,* thus making them virtually indistinguishable from money. The policy was intended to ensure purchase of all the bonds issued by the government in financing the wars. The public, notably including commercial banks, was encouraged to buy government bonds (i.e., lend to the government), for it knew that the bonds could be converted into money at a guaranteed price at any time; furthermore, the Fed bought directly from the Treasury nearly a third of the bonds issued by the government during World War II. The Treasury, in turn, found it expedient to issue bonds (i.e., borrow) in order to fill the gap between governmental expenditures and governmental tax collections. But this process of financing the government's spending by borrowing, directly or indirectly, from either commercial banks or the Fed resulted in increasing the money supply; the wars were financed in very large measure by creating new money. Indeed, the ultimate expansion of the money supply could be a multiple of the value of the government bonds, for the process tended to increase reserves of commercial banks. If the bonds were sold to commercial banks, they could be resold to the Fed, thereby increasing commercial-bank reserves; if the bonds were sold directly to the Fed, the newly created (i.e., enlarged) deposit of the Treasury would be spent, and the money would quickly find its way into the commercial banks and increase reserves; and if the bonds were sold to, say, insurance com-

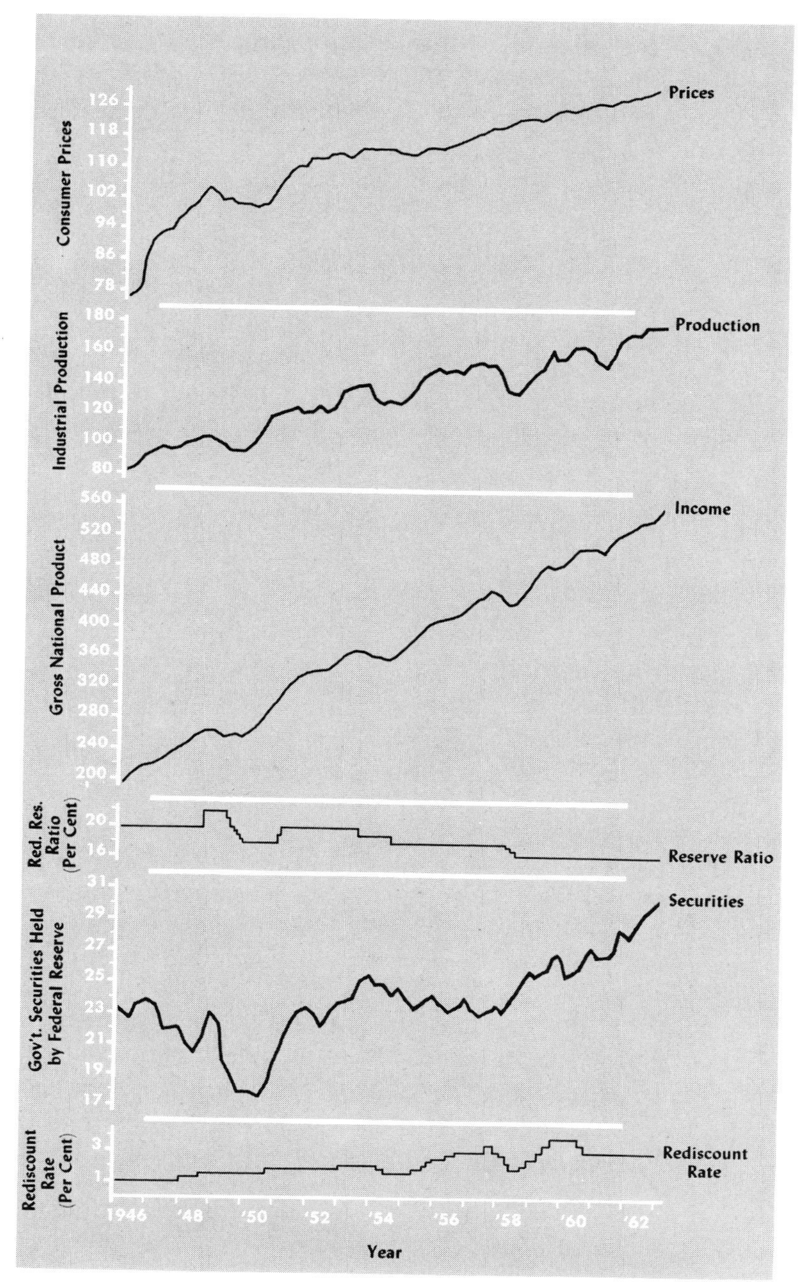

FIGURE 37–2. Prices, production, and income related to Federal Reserve actions, 1945–62. Source: Federal Reserve, *Monthly Bulletin*.

panies, they could be liquidated at the Fed, with the proceeds then deposited in commercial banks.

With the Fed thus acting as a willing "buyer of last resort" at a pegged price, the government-bond market was "stabilized" and made "orderly"; and, because the Fed supported bond prices, interest rates were kept from rising, which pleased the Treasury because borrowing costs were thereby kept low. The Fed continued its bond-support policy for another half-dozen years after the war. One effect of the policy was largely to nullify the effectiveness of the Fed's credit controls, during a period characterized for the most part (1945–48 and 1950–51, to mention only the postwar years) by strong inflationary pressures. The policy removed most of the discretionary power of the Fed over open-market operations: whenever bonds were presented to the Fed, they were bought, even if such purchases were undesirable—and sales might be in order—on the criterion of promoting full employment with a stable price level. Furthermore, the other credit controls lost much of their effectiveness, for if a bank found its reserve position growing tight, because of Fed action or other causes, it could simply sell some of its government bonds (in late 1945, at the end of the war, commercial banks had accumulated a total of over $90,000,000,000 in bonds), liquidating them into additional reserves. The quasi-abdication of its powers by the Fed was ended—or at least considerably modified—by a Fed-Treasury accord in early 1951.

Monetizing of the public debt by the Federal Reserve is, indeed, one of its essential tasks. But there is conflict between the two missions of central banks—namely, to control the quantity of money in the interest of full employment and a steady price level and to be ready to create money for the government at such times as the government decides. One can judge the behavior of the Fed appropriately only by considering which of these missions is most significant at any given time. During the war, the Fed had to fulfill its money-creation function, and it did that effectively at the sacrifice of the other mission. But when at other times it was free to accomplish the other mission, that of controlling the money supply as a means of avoiding cyclical fluctuations in prices and employment, its performance has been far less impressive.

It is in order, finally, to review the more conspicuous difficulties of conducting discretionary stabilization policy. There is, first, the problem of accurately diagnosing the problem in time to take some action before it goes away and is replaced by a different situation. There is a second lag: not only is there a question of time for the diagnosis to be made, but also it takes time for the prescribed medicine to take effect, and in a cycle swing of moderate length, we could very well find anti-recession policies becoming effective at about the time the upswing begins and anti-inflation policies taking hold at about the beginning of a downswing. Third, there are the matters of choosing which of the alternative tools to employ, if not all of them; the degree or vigor with which the various tools should be employed (should $250 million worth of securities be sold in the open market

—if, indeed, they should be sold rather than bought—or should the magnitude be more like $412.8 million?); and, at least for aesthetic purposes, the proper coordination of tools, so that one sort of action does not cancel out another. Just to list some of the more obvious problems of discretionary stabilization policy excites sympathy for the policy-maker—and fear of the possible consequences of his efforts. At any rate, if the gentle reader feels that we have not considered the Federal Reserve with sufficient awe, let it be observed that, in light of having survived for half a century and still being seemingly robust, the institution surely can shrug off a little disenchanted treatment from us.

Financing a Budget Deficit

In the discussion of fiscal policy (Chapter 34), we reviewed seven types of "routes to full employment." In five of those routes (I, II, III, V, VII), the budget was in deficit when the new income equilibrium was attained. We did not indicate how the governmental deficit might be financed. There are alternative financing methods, and some are more "expansionary" than others; that is, some means of financing would supplement and reenforce the basic fiscal policy more than would other means.

While a budget deficit may be financed up to some point by the Treasury drawing on previously accumulated bank balances, let us suppose that the first step is for the Treasury to obtain money by selling securities. But these government bonds may be bought by (a) Federal Reserve banks or (b) commercial banks or (c) the public. And just who the buyer is makes a difference with respect to (a) the money supply (currency in the hands of the public plus demand deposits of the public—not the Treasury—in commerical banks) and (b) the excess reserve position of the commercial banks. Consider the alternatives, in each case recording the steps of the financing procedure in the T accounts of the Treasury, the Federal Reserve, and the commercial banks.

1. Suppose the deficit is financed with funds obtained by the Treasury selling bonds to *Federal Reserve* banks. First, the bonds are sold to the Fed, which increases the Treasury's demand deposit in the Fed:

TREASURY		FEDERAL RESERVE	
Assets	**Liabilities**	**Assets**	**Liabilities**
Deposits in FR +	Bonds in FR +	Bonds +	Treasury deposits +

Second, the Treasury spends the proceeds of the borrowing, drawing on its account in the Fed, with the recipients of the spending (i.e., the public) then depositing the Treasury checks in commercial banks, which clear the checks through the Fed:

TREASURY		FEDERAL RESERVE	
Assets	**Liabilities**	**Assets**	**Liabilities**
Deposits in FR — Other +			Commercial bank deposits + Treasury deposits —

COMMERCIAL BANKS	
Assets	**Liabilities**
Deposits in FR +	Public deposits +

The first step, the sale of bonds by the Treasury to the Fed, did not affect either the money supply or excess reserves of the commercial banks. The second step, Treasury spending, increased both the money supply and excess reserves. The *actual* increase in the money supply plus the *potential* increase on the basis of the new excess reserves equals the value of the initial bond transaction multiplied by the expansion coefficient, $1/r$, with r being the required reserve ratio.

2. Now, let the Treasury sell bonds to *commercial* banks:

TREASURY		COMMERCIAL BANKS	
Assets	**Liabilities**	**Assets**	**Liabilities**
Deposits in commercial banks +	Bonds in commercial banks +	Bonds +	Treasury deposits +

While the Treasury keeps the great bulk of its operating balances in commercial banks, it does not spend directly out of such balances. Rather, the Treasury first transfers these funds to its accounts in the Fed and then writes checks on its Fed deposit. Thus, funds are shifted from commercial banks to the Fed:

TREASURY		FEDERAL RESERVE	
Assets	**Liabilities**	**Assets**	**Liabilities**
Deposits in commercial banks — Deposits in FR +			Commercial bank deposits — Treasury deposits +

COMMERCIAL BANKS

Assets	Liabilities
Deposits in FR —	Treasury deposits —

Finally, the Treasury spends out of its deposit in the Fed:

TREASURY

Assets	Liabilities
Deposits in FR —	
Other +	

FEDERAL RESERVE

Assets	Liabilities
	Treasury deposits —
	Commercial bank deposits +

COMMERCIAL BANKS

Assets	Liabilities
Deposits in FR +	Public deposits +

Neither of the first two steps (i.e., selling of bonds by the Treasury to the commercial banks and shifting Treasury deposits from commercial banks to the Fed) directly affects the money supply; but commercial bank excess reserves first fall (because required reserves increase) and then fall some more (as required reserves decrease less than do actual reserves). Indeed, the Treasury sometimes engages in "monetary policy" simply by switching funds from commercial banks to the Fed (thereby decreasing excess reserves) or from the Fed to commercial banks (which increases excess reserves). In the final step, in which the Treasury finances purchases from the public by drawing on its deposit in the Fed, both the money supply and excess reserves of commercial banks increase.

The net result of all this is that the money supply has increased and excess reserves are reduced (demand liabilities of commercial banks have increased, and actual reserves are unchanged). The *potential* contraction of the money supply because of smaller excess reserves equals the *actual* initial increase.

3. Finally, suppose that the Treasury bonds are sold to the *public*, thereby reducing the public's deposit and increasing the Treasury's deposit in commercial banks:

TREASURY

Assets	Liabilities
Deposits in commercial banks +	Bonds held by public +

COMMERCIAL BANKS

Assets	Liabilities
	Treasury deposits +
	Public deposits —

Again, the Treasury transfers funds from commercial banks to the Fed:

TREASURY		FEDERAL RESERVE	
Assets	**Liabilities**	**Assets**	**Liabilities**
Deposits in FR + Deposits in commercial banks −			Treasury deposits + Commercial bank deposits −

COMMERCIAL BANKS	
Assets	**Liabilities**
Deposits in FR −	Treasury deposits −

And, as before, the Treasury spends the funds out of its Federal Reserve account:

TREASURY		FEDERAL RESERVE	
Assets	**Liabilities**	**Assets**	**Liabilities**
Deposits in FR − Other +			Commercial bank deposits + Treasury deposits −

COMMERCIAL BANKS	
Assets	**Liabilities**
Deposits in FR +	Public deposits +

When the smoke clears away, we find that the money supply has not changed (the public's deposit in commercial banks first fell and then rose), and excess reserves also have not changed (required reserves and actual reserves both first fell and then rose).

We have surveyed three alternative ways of financing a government deficit. In each instance, the financing involved first providing the Treasury with revenue by selling government bonds, but the alternative differed with respect to the purchasers of the bonds. The significance of these differences has been indicated by two criteria: direct effects on the money supply and indirect (i.e., potential) effects on the money supply. Which of the alternatives is preferable? (a) If—as we have supposed—the general situation is one of "recession" and an expansionary policy is desired, then the bonds should be sold to the Federal Reserve. Selling to the Fed will reinforce the expansionary effects of the budget deficit itself. (b) But suppose that expansion is not desired: the deficit is the result of something—poor predictions, faulty planning, unexpected expenditures, lack of political courage—other than deliberate income-stabilization policy. If the problem is to finance the deficit in the least expansionary manner, obviously the bonds should not be sold to the Fed. Does it matter whether the purchaser is commercial banks or the public? *If* changes in excess reserves have their full potential repercussion in the second case (selling bonds to commercial banks), then the second and third cases are essentially identical, with zero effects on the money supply and excess reserves. But since the full potential may not be realized, there is some basis for perferring bond sales to the public, which will ensure zero effects.

Member-Bank Reserves: Determinants and Effects

Our concentration in this and the preceding chapters has been on the *money supply*. First, we noted the composition of the money supply: (a) coins and currency (mainly Federal Reserve notes and, to a lesser extent, silver certificates) held by the public and (b) demand deposits of the public held in commercial banks. Second, since demand deposits make up about 80 percent of the total money supply and since these deposits are liabilities of commercial banks, we considered typical transactions of such banks, with emphasis on lending (i.e., deposit-creating) activity. Third, we reviewed the several means available to the Federal Reserve to affect the limits of commercial-bank lending. The feasibility of new commercial-bank lending and the maximum magnitude of new lending—or the pressure to reduce the current level of deposits—rests upon bank reserves, including both the absolute volume of reserves and the required-reserve ratio. With specification of the required-reserve ratio in the hands of the Fed (subject to limits imposed by Congress), our next task is systematically to consider the various monetary factors that directly determine the magnitude of (member-bank) reserves.

Member-bank reserves themselves (i.e., vault cash plus deposits in the Federal Reserve), along with the immediate determinants of the reserves, are all entries in the monetary statements of the monetary authorities of the government—namely, the Federal Reserve and the Treasury. We may take the combined balance sheet for the twelve Federal Reserve banks and consolidate it with a "monetary account" of the Treasury prepared for this purpose; the cash and the deposits in the Fed of member banks will be liability entries in this consolidated Federal Reserve-Treasury account; thus, we may state member-bank reserves as the algebraic sum of all of the other entries in the account. It will be seen that only two or three of the remaining entries (determinants of reserves) dominate the picture.

Table 37–2 presents a consolidated balance sheet for the Federal Reserve banks. The balance sheet is somewhat incomplete and quite undetailed, but it presents the categories that are most important for our purposes. (Also here and in the following two tables, we cheat just a little with the numbers; for the data —all from the Federal Reserve *Bulletin*—are not always provided in the most convenient form.)

Table 37–2

FEDERAL RESERVE BANKS: CONSOLIDATED BALANCE SHEET, JUNE 1962
(Billions of Dollars)

Assets		Liabilities	
Federal Reserve bank credit	31.3	Federal Reserve notes held by:	
Gold certificates	16.2	public, member banks, non-member banks	28.5
Treasury currency	.4		
	47.9	Demand deposits of:	
		member banks	17.2
		others (non-member banks, Treasury, foreign institutions)	1.2
		Other (net)	1.0
			47.9

Although we have not previously used the term "Federal Reserve bank credit," in actuality we have discussed it—in connection with open-market operations of the Fed and with rediscount-rate changes. Federal Reserve bank credit subsumes several components, but it consists overwhelmingly of U.S. government securities; such securities held by the Fed made up nearly $30,000,000,000 of the $31,300,000,000 total. A very small proportion of the total—amounting to about $150,000,000—consisted of "discounts and advances" to commercial banks.

Although Federal Reserve bank credit is clearly the largest Federal Reserve asset, gold certificates are substantial. Gold certificates, issued by the Treasury, are "warehouse receipts" representing gold bullion bought by the Treasury. In contrast to silver certificates, gold certificates do not circulate in the hands of the public, but are issued only for purposes of Treasury deposit in the Fed.

The Treasury is committed to buy for $35 per ounce all gold brought to it. No one may keep gold in bulk; the law requires it to be sold to the U.S. government. The Treasury pays for gold by writing a check on its deposit in the Federal

Reserve. The seller of the gold then deposits the check from the Treasury in his account in a commercial bank; the bank clears the check with the Fed—i.e., the check is sent to the Fed, which adds the amount to the bank's deposit in the Fed and correspondingly reduces the Treasury deposit. Finally, the Treasury almost always replenishes its deposit in the Fed by issuing certificates with a face value equal to the value of the recently purchased gold and depositing the certificates in the Fed. The balance sheets of the commercial bank and of the Federal Reserve record the net results of these transactions: (a) Demand deposits (of the seller of the gold) in the commercial bank are increased. (b) The commercial-bank deposit in the Federal Reserve (i.e., the bank's reserve) is increased. (c) The Treasury deposit in the Federal Reserve first decreased (when the gold was bought) and then increased (when certificates were deposited in the Fed), ultimately being unchanged. (d) Federal Reserve assets in the form of gold certificates are increased. A gold sale by the Treasury results in changing the same balance-sheet entries, with opposite signs.

The other entries in the Fed's balance sheet are generally familiar from previous discussions.

The Treasury currency held by the Federal Reserve was only a small part of the total ($400,000,000 out of $5,600,000,000). Over three fourths of this modest amount consisted of silver certificates. The Federal Reserve notes held outside the Treasury and the Fed (i.e., held by the public and by commercial banks), totaled $28,500,000,000. We have had frequent occasion to refer to member-bank deposits in the Federal Reserve, since they make up nearly 90 percent of total reserves. The balance sheet indicates additional deposits in the Fed—held by non-member banks (about $300,000,000), the Treasury ($600,000,000) and foreign institutions ($300,000,000); but they are relatively insignificant.

The preceding is straightforward: there *is* a consolidated balance sheet—complete with assets and liabilities (including capital items)—for the Federal Reserve banks. But the monetary institutional arrangements are based upon the Treasury along with the Fed. And the Treasury engages in what may be termed money-holding, or fiscal, activities, as well as money-issuing, or money-creating, activities. Our present subject being the money supply, we are here interested in only the latter activities. Therefore, we want to utilize not an actual balance sheet for the Treasury, but only certain monetary categories. We shall arrange these relevant data into a "monetary account." The Treasury monetary account is not an actual balance sheet; there are no capital, or net worth, entries, and an accountant would be forgiven for blanching a little at the use of the terms "assets" and "liabilities." The so-called Treasury monetary account is an artifice, an organizational device for the useful presentation of appropriate data—and different analysts may have somewhat different notions of just *what* data to include and even of precisely *how* to present them. (Say to yourself twelve times each day: it is the validity of the *conclusions* of analysis—i.e., the validity of the derived implications of analysis giving a better comprehension of the world—which provides the pay-off and constitutes the acid test of a theory, not the descriptive "realism" of assumptions or the conventionality—i.e., the seeming lack of arbitrariness—of the devices and constructs of analysis.)

Table 37–3

TREASURY MONETARY ACCOUNT, JUNE 1962
(Billions of Dollars)

Assets		**Liabilities**	
Gold	16.4	Gold certificates held by Federal Reserve	16.2
Treasury currency outstanding	5.6	Treasury currency held by:	
		public, member banks, non-member banks	5.2
	22.0	Federal Reserve banks	.4
		Other (net)	.2
			22.0

The nation's monetary gold stock is held by the Treasury, and the gold certificates issued by the Treasury are held by the Federal Reserve. The gold stock is slightly larger than the aggregate value of the certificates, the excess representing partly a reserve against two obscure types of currency (United States notes and Treasury notes of 1890) and partly the "general fund" in gold. This small excess of gold over certificates makes up over half of a category known as "Treasury cash"—a category sufficiently small (about $400,000,000 in June 1962) and stable that we need pay no further attention to it here.

Treasury currency outstanding is held in small amount by the Fed (and in minute amount by the Treasury itself), but the bulk of it is in the hands of the public and of commercial banks. Treasury currency may be thought of as *silver* money. Silver certificates, which were mentioned in an earlier chapter, represented $2,300,000,000, and subsidiary silver coins amounted to another $1,700,000,000; among the remaining Treasury currency, other minor coins were $600,000,000, and silver dollars were $500,000,000.

Now, let us consolidate the Federal Reserve and the Treasury statements into one account. Two sets of items thereby cancel out: gold certificates held by the Federal Reserve and Treasury currency held by the Federal Reserve, both of which are Fed assets and Treasury liabilities. We are left with the account in Table 37–4.

Table 37–4

FEDERAL RESERVE AND TREASURY: CONSOLIDATED STATEMENT, JUNE 1962
(Billions of Dollars)

Assets		Liabilities	
Federal Reserve bank credit (F)	31.3	Federal Reserve notes and Treasury currency held by:	
Gold (G)	16.4	public (C_p)	30.3
Treasury currency outstanding (T)	5.6	member banks (C_m)	2.7
		non-member banks (C_n)	.7
	53.3	Demand deposits in Federal Reserve of:	
		member banks (D_m)	17.2
		others (D_o)	1.2
		Other (net) (O)	1.2
			53.3

We know that actual member-bank reserves (A) consist of vault cash in member banks plus member-bank deposits in the Federal Reserve:

$$
\begin{aligned}
A &= C_m + D_m \\
19.9 &= 2.7 + 17.2
\end{aligned}
$$

Since total assets ($F + G + T$) equal total liabilities ($C_p + C_m + C_n + D_m + D_o + O$) in the consolidated account, we can express member-bank reserves by the remaining entries:

$$
\begin{aligned}
A &= F + G + T - (C_p + C_n + D_o + O) \\
19.9 &= 31.3 + 16.4 + 5.6 - (30.3 + .7 + 1.2 + 1.2)
\end{aligned}
$$

Finally, we may segregate member-bank reserves held *in the Fed* (A_f). We saw earlier that, until late 1959, *only* member-bank deposits in the Federal Reserve constituted legal reserves; and they still make up the bulk of the total.

$$
\begin{aligned}
A_f &= D_m \\
17.2 &= 17.2 \\
&= F + G + T - (C + D_o + O) \\
&= 31.3 + 16.4 + 5.6 + (33.7 - 1.2 + 1.2)
\end{aligned}
$$

where $C = C_p + C_m + C_n$.

Thus, member-bank reserves held in the Fed at any *given* moment are equal to the sum of Federal Reserve bank credit, gold, and Treasury currency minus money in circulation and other deposits in the Fed (along with the residual item, O). It is conventional to call the first items (F, G, and T) "*sources* of (potential) reserves" and the latter items (C and D_o) "(alternative) *uses* of reserve funds." That is, were it not for C and D_o (and O), reserves would be equal to $F + G + T$; but, in actuality, a portion of these potential or would-be reserves is "absorbed" by, or diverted into, C and D_o. Reserves necessarily are equal to the total sources minus the alternative uses of potential reserve funds.

In addition to the "sources-uses" terminology, we may speak of "factors of increase" and "factors of decrease." Over a *period* of time, the *change* in reserves accompanies an equal net *change* in the other items. An *increase* in F or G or T tends to *increase* reserves (and a decrease in these tends to decrease reserves); F, G, and T, then, are known as "factors of increase." Conversely, a *decrease* in C or D_o tends to *increase* reserves held at the Fed (and an increase tends to decrease reserves); C and D_o are so-called "factors of decrease."

Table 37–5

MEMBER-BANK RESERVES, SELECTED SOURCES AND USES, DEMAND DEPOSITS, AND MONEY SUPPLY, 1917–63
(Billions of Dollars)

	A	A_f	$F + G - C$	$F + G$	D	M
1917		1.4	0	4.1	13.5	15.8
1918		1.6	.4	5.4	14.8	18.1
1919		1.8	.8	5.9	17.6	21.2
1920		1.8	.6	6.0	19.6	23.7
1921		1.7	.5	4.9	17.1	20.8
1922		1.8	.5	5.0	18.0	21.4
1923		1.9	.4	5.2	19.1	22.9
1924		2.2	.7	5.4	20.9	24.6
1925		2.2	.8	5.6	22.3	26.1
1926		2.2	.8	5.6	21.7	25.5
1927		2.4	.9	5.7	22.7	26.4
1928		2.4	1.0	5.7	23.1	26.7
1929		2.4	.9	5.6	22.8	26.4
1930		2.4	1.1	5.6	21.0	24.6
1931		2.1	.9	6.2	17.4	21.9
1932		2.4	.9	6.3	15.7	20.4
1933		2.6	1.2	6.7	15.0	19.8

Table 37-5—Continued

MEMBER-BANK RESERVES, SELECTED SOURCES AND USES, DEMAND DEPOSITS, AND MONEY SUPPLY, 1917–63
(Billions of Dollars)

	A	A_f	$F+G-C$	$F+G$	D	M
1934		4.0	5.1	10.7	18.5	23.1
1935		5.7	6.7	12.6	22.1	27.0
1936		6.7	7.1	13.7	25.5	31.0
1937		6.9	8.8	15.4	24.0	29.6
1938		8.7	10.1	17.0	26.0	31.8
1939		11.5	12.5	20.1	29.8	36.2
1940		14.0	15.5	24.2	34.9	42.3
1941		12.8	14.2	25.2	39.0	48.6
1942		13.2	13.6	28.7	48.9	62.9
1943		12.7	13.7	33.9	60.8	79.6
1944		14.2	15.1	40.3	66.9	90.4
1945		16.0	16.2	44.7	75.9	102.3
1946		16.5	16.2	45.2	83.3	110.0
1947		17.3	16.7	45.6	87.1	113.6
1948		20.0	19.8	48.2	85.5	111.6
1949		16.3	15.8	43.5	85.8	111.2
1950		17.4	16.7	44.5	92.3	117.7
1951		20.3	16.8	47.9	98.2	124.5
1952		21.2	20.1	50.6	101.5	129.0
1953		19.9	18.1	49.1	102.5	130.5
1954		19.3	17.3	48.0	106.6	135.6
1955		19.2	17.3	48.6	110.2	138.6
1956		19.5	17.3	49.1	111.5	140.3
1957		19.4	17.1	49.0	110.4	139.3
1958		18.9	16.5	49.0	115.5	144.7
1959	18.9	18.6	16.1	48.9	116.1	145.6
1960	19.3	16.7	14.1	47.1	115.2	144.7
1961	20.1	17.3	14.2	48.1	119.2	149.4
1962	20.0	16.9	13.9	49.2	120.4	151.6
1963	20.7	17.3	14.6	52.2	124.3	157.4

SOURCES: *Banking and Monetary Statistics* (Washington, D.C.: Board of Governors, Federal Reserve System, 1943); Federal Reserve *Bulletin*, various issues.

Note: Data for 1923–63 are December values; data for 1917–22 are June values.

Although our formulations of the A and A_f equations already are a bit simplified compared to data presented in the Federal Reserve *Bulletin* (the explicit formulation in the *Bulletin* is only for A_f), we can simplify still further. In the A_f equation, D_o and O are relatively small, and T is only moderately large; furthermore, $D_o + O$ approximates the value of T. The remaining three variables—F, G, and C—account for most of A_f. As Table 37–5 indicates, $F + G - C$ generally provides quite a good approximation of A_f, particularly from the mid-1930s through the early 1950s.

At least equally striking is the close relation between *changes* in $F + G - C$, on the one hand, and reserves, on the other. (It may be noted that while Treasury currency, T, is scarcely trivial—around \$5,000,000,000 since World War II—its changes from year to year typically are very small. Rarely is the annual change in T larger than \$100,000,000, and since 1917 the average is less than that.) In Table 37–5, there are 46 year-to-year changes over the period 1917–63. In ten of these cases, one of the two variables (i.e., either $F + G - C$ or A_f) was constant. In the 36 cases in which both variables changed (or, in one instance, the change in each was zero), they moved in the *same direction* 33 times, and in only three instances did they move in opposite directions: historically, an increase (decrease) in $F + G - C$ is typically accompanied by an increase (decrease) in reserves. Furthermore, the *magnitudes* of the changes in these two variables correspond closely. From 1917–18 through 1934–35, except for one instance (1933–34, when the dollar price of gold was drastically changed), the difference in the year-to-year changes in $F + G - C$ and in A_f was never larger than \$300,000,000, and it averaged only a little over \$100,000,000. Beginning in 1935–36, the discrepancy in the two annual changes has tended to be larger; but in 19 times out of 28, it has been no larger than \$500,000,000, in only four instances has it been \$1,000,000,000 or larger, and the average has been less than \$600,000,000.

With respect to year-to-year *changes*, the correlation of only $F + G$ with A_f is about as impressive as that of $F + G - C$ with A_f. (Of course, at any *given* time, $F + G$ is much larger than A_f.) Of the 46 annual changes (1917–63), in four instances either $F + G$ or A_f was unchanged; of the other 42 observations, in 37 cases (including three in which neither variable changed) the two variables moved together, and only five times did they move inversely. As for comparative magnitudes of the changes, in the general years of World War II (i.e., 1939–40 through 1944–45) there were substantial discrepancies in the changes in $F + G$ compared to the changes in A_f. But for the rest of the period (i.e., 1917–39 and 1946–63) the average annual discrepancy in the changes was well under \$500,000,000.

Figure 37–3 provides a visual comparison of the values over time of A_f, $F + G - C$, and $F + G$.

It is apparent, then, that historically member-bank reserves have approximately equaled the sum of Federal Reserve bank credit and monetary gold

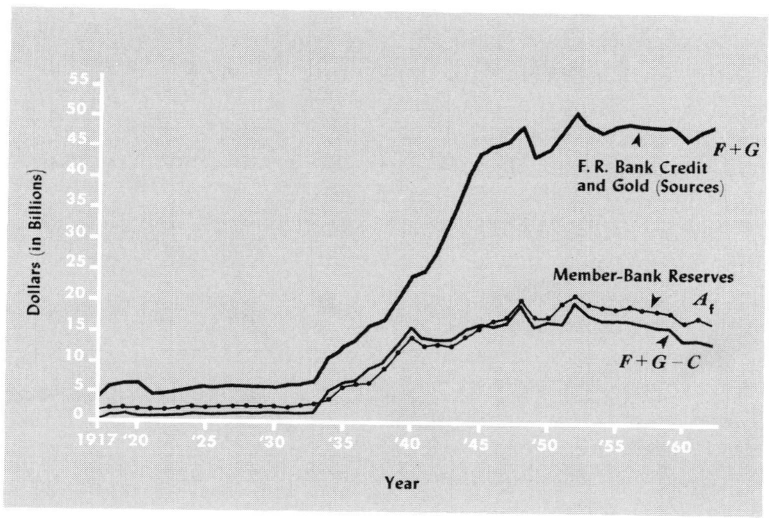

FIGURE 37–3. Member-bank reserves, sources, and uses, 1917–62 (A_f, $F + G - C$, and $F + G$). Source: Federal Reserve, *Monthly Bulletin.*

("sources," or "factors of increase") minus currency in circulation ("use," or "factor of decrease"). And changes in A_f have approximately equaled the net change in $F + G - C$. But over different periods, F, G, and C have differed in the relative importance of their respective changes. Table 37–6 breaks down the period 1934–63 into four sub-periods; for each sub-period, the *approximate* change in member-bank reserves in the Fed (ΔA_f^*) is derived from changes in the three major sources and uses (ΔF, ΔG, and ΔC), and the *actual* change in reserves (ΔA_f) also is given.

Table 37–6

RESERVES, SOURCES, AND USES, 1934–63
(Billions of Dollars)

	ΔF	+	ΔG	−	ΔC	=	ΔA_f^*	ΔA_f
1934–40	—.2		13.7		3.1		10.4	10.0
1940–45	22.4		—1.9		19.8		.7	2.0
1945–52	2.6		3.3		2.0		3.9	5.2
1952–63	9.3		—7.7		7.1		—5.5	—3.9

It is apparent that the major influence on reserves in the latter part of the Great Depression was the tremendous increase in gold, the gold flowing in mainly from Europe as World War II approached; Federal Reserve bank credit was virtually unchanged, and the reserve-increasing rise in the gold stock was only partially offset by the absorption of potential reserves through an increase in money in circulation.

During World War II, gold decreased a little; but war financing resulted in a great increase in the holdings of government securities by the Fed (i.e., Federal Reserve bank credit); reserves increased only moderately, largely because the increase in money in circulation counterbalanced most of the increase in Federal Reserve bank credit.

In the two postwar periods (with 1952 chosen for the dividing point simply because member-bank reserves were then at their peak), the absolute changes in the three sources and uses were of similar magnitude.

It would seem, then, that to know the value of $F + G - C$ is to have a good idea of the value of A_f; and to know $\Delta(F + G - C)$—or even just $\Delta(F + G)$—is generally to know quite closely the value of ΔA_f.

Before we proceed with additional relationships, we may ask to what extent the Federal Reserve can determine or change the magnitude of member-bank reserves. Gold and currency in circulation are not under the immediate control of the Fed, and only Federal Reserve bank credit can be determined "purely" on the initiative of the Fed. Many forces impinge upon the movement over time of G and C: interest rates and other prices both here and abroad; changes in technology and shifts in investment; international-exchange rates and barriers to foreign trade and capital movements; the price of gold; anticipations of consumers, investors, and speculators. Some of these factors themselves are shaped by actions of the Fed, but the influence of the Fed on G and C is not direct, immediate, and mechanical; rather, it is at least one step removed.

The influence of the Fed on F is mainly direct, since F consists overwhelmingly of government securities held by the Federal Reserve, and the Federal Reserve makes its own decisions whether to buy or to sell such securities. Of course, in making its open-market decisions, the Fed does have some constraints; indeed, Fed officials may sometimes feel that they cannot utilize open-market operations in a sufficiently aggressive and massive manner to juggle member-bank reserves precisely. But, in principle, the Fed can (and typically probably does) utilize such operations to keep member-bank reserves very close to the level it desires. Although there is not a very close linkage between the Fed and G and C, it is sufficient that there *is* a close linkage between the Fed and *one* of the major determinants of reserves, F. For F can be used either to supplement or to counteract changes in G and C in such manner as to generate the size of A which the Fed (whether or not wisely) desires.

Suppose that the Fed were to utilize its close linkage to F so as to control member-bank reserves within very narrow limits. What would Federal Reserve determination of reserves accomplish? After all, reserves in themselves are scarcely a matter of ultimate concern. They are important only to the extent that they influence other variables. The most obvious variables next in line are demand deposits of the public in commercial banks and the total money supply. The ratio of demand deposits to money supply rarely (although occasionally) changes appreciably from year to year and has shown only a slight downward trend since World War I. (In the 1920s, demand deposits made up about 85 percent of the money supply; in the 1930s, a little over 80 percent; and since World War II, slightly under 80 percent.) Our next question, therefore, is: How closely do demand deposits change with reserves?

Confining our attention to member-bank reserves in the Fed (A_f), we may first review:

$$A_f = R + E;$$

i.e., actual reserves equal required reserves plus excess reserves (in accordance with the pre-1959 regulations, when only deposits in the Fed were counted as reserves). Second, we may break down R into its components; that is, reserves required against demand deposits (r_dD) and reserves required against time deposits (r_tT):

$$A_f = r_dD + r_tT + E.$$

It is apparent that the linkage between changes in A_f and in D is by no means definite or purely mechanical, for three reasons. First, changes in A_f, on the left side of the equation, may be accompanied by a direct and equal change in E, on the right side, leaving D (and the money supply) wholly unaffected. Second, a change in A_f may be accompanied by an equivalent change in the reserves required against time deposits—the latter change, in turn, being determined by a change in either T or r_t, or both. Third, even if a change in A_f is matched by a change in the reserves required against demand deposits, the latter change may stem wholly from a change in r_d and not at all in D. Changes in r_d and in r_t are made by the Fed itself, but changes in T and E stem essentially from decisions by the banks and the public. In light of all this, we should scarcely expect to find reserves and demand deposits invariably moving together.

In the 42 year-to-year changes over the 1917–59 period, on six occasions either A_f or D did not change; in the 36 remaining observations, A_f and D moved in the same direction 24 times and in opposite directions 12 times.

In summary, we have seen (a) that changes in member-bank reserves can be accounted for, or are accompanied by, changes in several other monetary variables, the most important of which are Federal Reserve bank credit, gold, and currency in circulation, with the close control by the Fed over the first of these variables being sufficient to give the Fed generally effective control over reserves; and (b) that changes in member-bank reserves are associated only loosely, not invariably directly, with changes in demand deposits in member banks and in the money supply. Since the linkage between changes in reserves and changes in the money supply involves preferences and responses by the public and the banks—with respect to holding currency, demand deposits, and time deposits and to borrowing and lending—and since these preferences and responses can considerably shift over time, we cannot safely say that at any given moment the Fed has precise control over the money supply.

Questions

1. "From the standpoint of the banking *system,* altering the required-reserve ratio has a double effect: not only is the *volume* of excess reserves affected, but, in addition, the *expansion coefficient* (i.e., the multiple by which a dollar of excess reserves may give rise to, or support, new deposits) is changed."

a. Explain this "double effect" for the banking system.

b. How is the effect of changing the required-reserve ratio different for a single bank?

2. "To rely upon a reserve requirement for the meeting of cash-withdrawal demands of banks' customers is analogous to trying to protect a community from fire by requiring that a large water tank be kept full at *all* times: the water is useless in case of emergency if it cannot be drawn from the tank." Is the analogy a useful one? Is it wholly and perfectly applicable?

3. Why is the rediscount rate called the "rediscount" rate?

4. Compare—in both principle and historical practice—open-market operations with changes in the required-reserve ratios and changes in the rediscount rate.

5. Following are the consolidated balance sheets of the Federal Reserve banks and the member banks. (The data are rough approximations of the actual figures.)

FEDERAL RESERVE BANKS

Gold certificates	$ 15 billion	Federal Reserve notes	$ 31 billion
Government securities	32	Demand deposits	19
Other assets	5	Capital accounts	2
	52		52

MEMBER BANKS

Cash	$ 3 billion	Demand deposits	$108 billion
Deposit in Fed	17	Time deposits	80
Investments	75	Capital accounts	20
Loans	120	Other liabilities	7
	215		215

a. If the required-reserve ratios for all member banks are 15 percent for demand deposits and 4 percent for time deposits, what is the numerical value of actual reserves? Required reserves? Excess reserves?

b. How much would the member banks have to borrow from the Fed in order to have excess reserves of $2 billion?

c. If the member banks were to borrow enough from the Fed to have excess reserves of $2 billion, what would be the maximum expansion of demand deposits (assuming that time deposits remain at $80 billion)?

d. If the member banks were to borrow enough to have excess reserves of $2 billion, what would be the maximum expansion of time deposits (assuming that demand deposits remain at $108 billion)?

e. Suppose member banks have previously borrowed from the Fed (with "discounts and advances" included in "other assets" of the Fed, and "rediscounts and bills payable" included in "other liabilities" of member banks). How large a repayment could member banks make without reducing excess reserves below zero?

f. The Open Market Committee orders the Federal Reserve banks to buy $2 billion worth of government securities; the securities are sold by bond dealers out of inventories which are left depleted by the full amount of the transaction. Then what are actual reserves? Required reserves? Excess reserves?

g. To continue the preceding problem, suppose that the bond dealers replenish their inventories by buying $2 billion worth of securities from member banks. Then what are actual reserves? Required reserves? Excess reserves?

h. Reverting again to the original balance sheets, would the Fed buy or sell in the open market in order to make excess reserves equal to zero? Buy or sell how much (assuming that the security dealers do not make a second transaction in order to offset the initial change in their inventories)?

i. If the Board of Governors lowers the required-reserve ratio against demand deposits to 10 percent, holding the time-deposit ratio at 4 percent, what is the value of actual reserves? Required reserves? Excess reserves?

j. If the required-reserve ratio against time deposits is 4 percent, how high would the required-reserve ratio against demand deposits have to be in order to wipe out all excess reserves?

k. If the required-reserve ratio against demand deposits is 15 percent, how high would the time-deposit ratio have to be in order to eliminate excess reserves?

6. The Federal Reserve is the designated primary agency for the determination and conduct of monetary policy. On its record, indict the Fed for poor performance. Conversely, defend the Fed. Do you think it unjustified or in any relevant sense unfair to charge that "in 1930 and 1931, the Fed exercised its responsibility for monetary policy so ineptly as to convert what otherwise would have been a moderate contraction into a major catastrophe"?

7. We have considered alternative means of financing a government budget deficit, noting in each instance the effect of the financing on (i) the money supply and (ii) excess reserves of commercial banks. Now, suppose that we have a budget surplus, with tax receipts greater than expenditures; suppose further that the surplus is to be used to reduce the government debt—i.e., the Treasury is to use the surplus tax collections to buy back (retire) government bonds. The first step is the collecting of taxes from the

public, which reduces the public's demand deposits and increases the Treasury's demand deposits in commercial banks.

a. Analyze the use of the Treasury's deposit, after it has been transferred to the Fed, to buy bonds alternatively from (i) the Federal Reserve, (ii) commercial banks, and (iii) the public; record these alternative transactions in the T accounts of the Treasury, the Fed, and the commercial banks.

b. In each of the alternative bond purchases, note the effect on the money supply and on excess reserves; and determine the best seller of bonds if the purpose of the Treasury is to reduce the debt in an expansionary (or at least noncontractionary) manner or, alternatively, in a contractionary (or non-expansionary) manner with respect to the money supply and excess reserves.

8. One monetary specialist emphasizes the importance of active monetary policy. "Walter Bagehot said, 'Money will not manage itself.' If there must be management, there is need for machinery and operators who will manage it adequately and effectively" (E. A. Goldenweiser, *Monetary Management,* New York: McGraw-Hill Book Co., Inc., 1949, p. 6).

Another has little confidence in the monetary managers. "Both history and an examination of human nature suggest that we cannot rely upon men vested with discretionary monetary powers to act promptly and wisely. The undue anxiety of central bankers about the future and their tenacious and misguided hope that they can predict developments lead them to ignore present difficulties much too often. . . . We need not weapons to combat developed booms or depressions but stable monetary conditions maintained in accordance with some one, announced rule of action" (Lloyd W. Mints, "Monetary Policy and Stabilization," *American Economic Review,* XLI, May 1951, 191, 193).

A third suggests a rule stated "in terms of the behavior of the stock of money . . . a legislated rule instructing the monetary authority to achieve a specified rate of growth in the stock of money . . . an annual rate of X percent, where X is some number between 3 and 5. . . . While this rule would drastically curtail the discretionary power of the monetary authorities, it would still leave an undesirable amount of discretion in the hands of Federal Reserve and Treasury authorities with respect to how to achieve the specified rate of growth in the money stock, debt management, banking supervision, and the like" (Milton Friedman, *Capitalism and Freedom,* Chicago: University of Chicago Press, 1962, p. 54).

Compare these three positions with one another. To what extent can they be reconciled with each other? Do they necessarily conflict at all? On the basis of your assiduous study of income and monetary theory, what is your reaction to the Friedman statement?

9. Over a period of time, the following monetary and financial categories increased (+) or decreased (−):

Treasury currency outstanding	+ .7
Currency held by public	+1.5
Currency held by member banks	−1.0
Federal Reserve bank credit	+3.0
Member bank deposits held in Fed	+ .5
Non-member bank deposits in Fed	+ .5
Gold	−2.5
Treasury deposits in member banks	+2.0
Treasury deposit in Fed	− .3

a. "Federal Reserve bank credit" consists of several things. What is the major component?

b. In the period covered by the table, what was the change in "factors of increase"?

c. What was the change in member-bank reserves?

d. Over most periods, especially from the mid-1930s through the early 1950s, member-bank reserves have been closely approximated by the (algebraic) sum of three "sources" and "uses." What are these three variables?

10. Below is approximate data (in millions of dollars) on the three major variables supplying and absorbing member-bank-reserve funds.

	JUNE 1929	JUNE 1932	JUNE 1941	JUNE 1945	JUNE 1963
Reserve bank credit	1,300	2,300	2,300	22,300	33,500
Gold	4,000	3,700	22,600	20,300	15,800
Currency in circulation	4,400	5,200	9,400	26,600	35,300

a. From 1929 to 1932, did the change in currency in circulation add to, or subtract from, member-bank reserves?

b. From 1929 to 1932, did the change in gold add to, or subtract from, member-bank reserves?

c. From 1929 to 1932, on the basis of the data given, what was the change in member-bank reserves (plus or minus how much)?

d. From 1932 to 1941, what was the change in member-bank reserves?

e. From 1932 to 1941, did the change in gold add to, or subtract from, member-bank reserves?

f. From 1932 to 1941, the major change was in which variable? From 1941 to 1945, the major change was in which variable?

g. From 1941 to 1945, did the change in Reserve bank credit add to, or subtract from, member-bank reserves?

h. From 1945 to 1963, was the major change in the variables expansionary or contractionary?

i. What was the total of member-bank reserves in 1963? Were reserves in 1963 more or less than in 1945?

j. Normally, over which of these three variables do the monetary authorities have the greatest power of direct manipulation?

k. Is currency in circulation a "factor of increase" or a "factor of decrease"?

11. "The 'linkage' between member-bank reserves and demand deposits in member banks is not definite and purely mechanical. Thus it is not surprising that reserves of member banks and deposits in member banks do not always move closely together." Explain the nature of the "linkage" and how it permits the relation between reserves and deposits to be loose.

38

INFLATION

What Is Inflation?

Inflation is a rise in the general level of prices. However, if the prices of eggs, butter, and shoes rise, while those of clothing, gasoline, and fruits fall, it may be uncertain whether the general level of prices has risen, since the lower prices of one set of goods can offset the rise of the others. The question of the occurrence of inflation can be answered only if it is asked more rigorously. Economics poses the question as follows: "Can people purchase the same level of utility—not necessarily the same pattern of goods and services—at the same total cost?" If the cost has risen, there has been inflation.

We must know whether the new pattern gives the same utility, and this is almost always an impossible empirical task. When relative prices change, people use more of the relatively lower-priced good and less of the other good. But we don't actually know just how much substitution of cheaper items for more expensive items is required to leave people as well off as before. Hence, we can't compute the costs of the unknown combinations.

There is the further complication of changes in quality. If people switch from black and white to color television at three times the price, has the cost of living risen? Quality changes have been so extensive that what appears to be a rising price level may in fact be a rising utility level, with a *falling* price level for the *old* level of utility.

Can we never know, then, whether inflation has really occurred? Some evidence is provided if we observe the costs of fixed patterns of consumption from month to month, on the assumption that changes in quality or relative prices have been relatively insignificant. The U.S. Bureau of Labor Statistics each month publishes a Consumer Price Index as an approximation to the cost of living of the ordinary middle-income family. The course of that index over the past 140 years is shown in Figure 38–1. Because of sampling, quality changes, purchase-pattern shifts, to

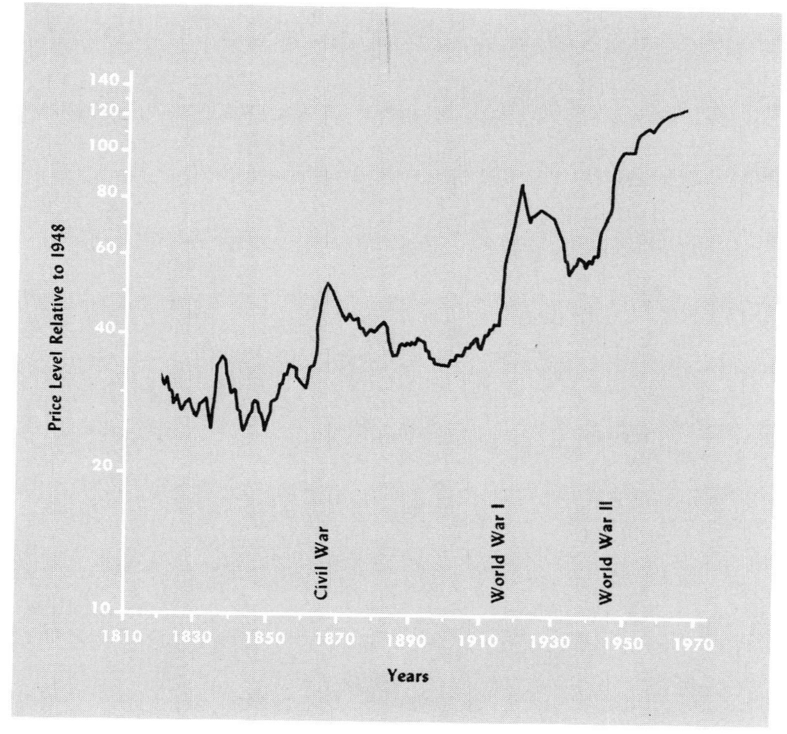

FIGURE 38–1. Consumer goods price index, 1820–1963. Source: U.S. Department of Labor, *Monthly Bulletin.*

name a few factors, the index is an approximation. Yet a change of over 2 to 4 percent in one year in that index could occur only if there really were a change in the general cost of living; this leeway of 2 or 3 percent reflects the margin of error or range of effects of fluctuations of the other pertinent elements. A change of some 90 percent within a few years, as happened from 1941 to 1947 in the United States, certainly is not the result of sampling deviations, changes in quality, or changes in purchase patterns. The major swings in that index are taken to be a reliable indicator of inflation or deflation.[1]

[1] Other indices of prices to consumers computed and published by other agencies would do about as well. Even wholesale-price indices would indicate inflations or deflations, although they would probably overstate the extent of the fluctuation. The major inflations and deflations have been great enough that their dates can be fairly well noted by any of several closely related measures of price levels.

More pronounced, spectacular, and faster have been the inflations in several other countries. For example, in the period since World War II the experiences of several countries show the rises graphed in Figure 38–2. That graph is plotted

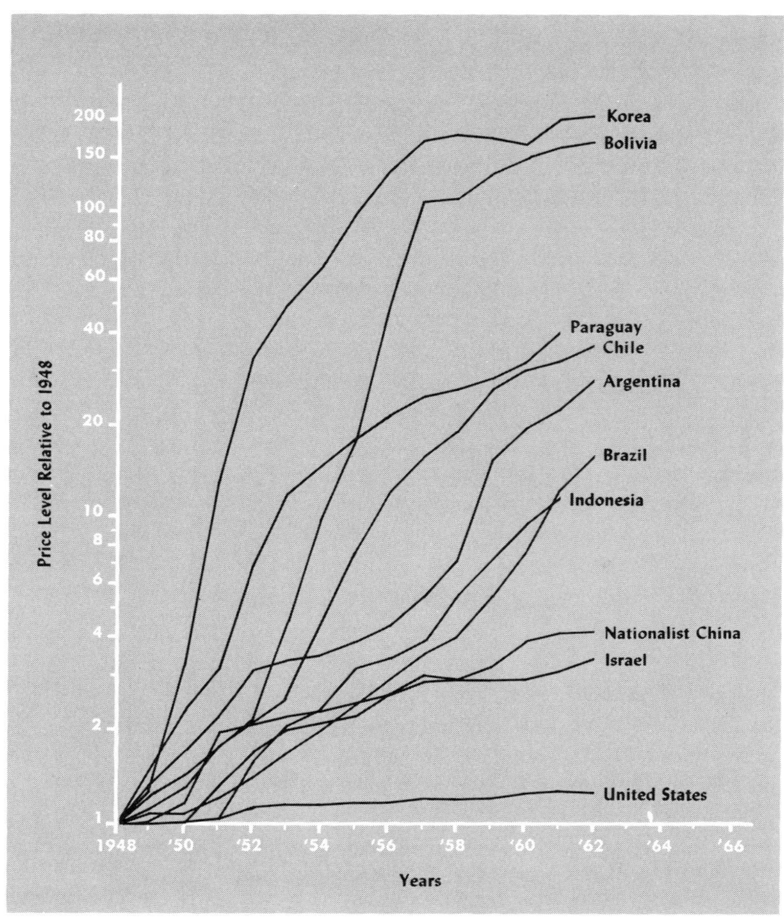

FIGURE 38–2. Recent inflations. Source: United Nations Bulletin of International Financial Statistics.

on a ratio scale for the vertical scale, so that constant upward slope shows a constant percentage rate of rise. (The price level for the United States in the same period is plotted for reference.) Just why these inflations have occurred is something we shall discuss later in this chapter.

The Meaning of the Effects of Inflation

Inflation, like fire, can be *caused* in several ways. But the *effects* of fire are always present. Similarly, regardless of the reasons for inflation, there are known, verified effects of the rise in the general level of prices.[2] There is a wealth loss to holders of money. And it is tempting to add that inflation always implies a transfer of wealth from creditors to debtors. That, however, is *not* logically implied for all types of inflations. To see why, a distinction is necessary between two different kinds of inflations.

It has become popular to give names to inflation: creeping, galloping, runaway, hyper, repressed, wage-push, and demand-pull. Some of these designate inflations by causes; some designate the kind of responsive action taken by the government; and some define the rate or extent of inflation. None of these is relevant for identification of effects. Instead, the critical distinction is between *unanticipated* and *anticipated* inflation.

Anticipated inflations are those in which people foresee accurately the timing and extent of the inflation, and they plan and act accordingly. If there is going to be a rise in the general price level of, say, 10 percent during the coming six months, and if people know or believe this is going to happen, their market actions will be different, immediately and during that six-month period, than if they had not foreseen the impending inflation. An anticipated inflation can be at a slow rate of, say, 2 percent a year or a hyper-inflation of 2,000,000 percent per year. And the same is true for unanticipated inflations. Inflations in which people underestimate the extent of the inflation are unanticipated inflations.

Wealth-Transfer Effects of Unanticipated Inflation

During *un*anticipated inflation wealth is transferred from owners of monetary assets to those who have monetary liabilities.

TWO TYPES OF ASSETS

The economic logic which implies that debtors gain from *un*anticipated inflation, but not from a correctly anticipated one, rests on the fact that there are two types of assets—monetary and real. Monetary assets are legal claims or rights to fixed amounts of money now or in the future (and usually carrying an explicit interest if they are claims to future amounts). The amount of the money claim

[2] We make no reference to the employment effects, since these were discussed more extensively in Chapter 31.

in any contractual right is independent of subsequent changes in prices of other commodities or services; it is therefore independent of inflation or deflation.[3]

Examples of monetary assets are money, time deposits, mortgages, bonds, promissory notes, and accounts receivable. On the opposite side of these contractual relationships is the debtor against whom these claims exist. Money is comprised, in the United States, of currency (primarily the non-interest-bearing debt of the Federal Reserve System) and the "demand-deposit" debts of the commercial banks. Time deposits are debts of commercial banks. Mortgages and bonds and promissory notes are monetary liabilities of the debtor. Accounts receivable are monetary assets to the person to whom they are owed and monetary liabilities of the debtor. To every monetary asset there is a monetary liability—the two sides of the same contractual relations.

"Real"—or nonmonetary—assets are assets that are not claims to fixed amounts of money. The thing claimed—house, car, pair of shoes, hour of labor—can change in money value. A real liability is an obligation to deliver some good, whose money value can change.

NET MONETARY DEBTOR STATUS AND INFLATION

To cut straight to the heart of the wealth-transfer process, start with the definition of equity or net wealth:

$$\text{(1) Equity} = \text{Assets} - \text{Liabilities.}$$

Classify assets and liabilities into real and monetary items:

$$\begin{aligned}\text{(2) Equity} &= (\text{real assets} + \text{monetary assets}) - \\ &\quad (\text{real liabilities} + \text{monetary liabilities}) \\ &= (\text{real assets} - \text{real liabilities}) + \\ &\quad (\text{monetary assets} - \text{monetary liabilities}) \\ &= \text{net real assets} + \text{net monetary assets.}\end{aligned}$$

If the price level rises by a ratio P, real assets and liabilities rise by P; so we have:

$$\text{(3) New equity} = P\,(\text{net real assets}) + (\text{net monetary assets}).^4$$

For equity to rise at all, as P rises, there must be net real assets. For it to rise as much as the price level, net monetary assets must be zero. For it to rise more, there must be net monetary liabilities.

[3] We do not assert that the current *price* of a monetary asset cannot change. The *price*, which is not the amount of the claim, of a bond, can change; but the bond is still a monetary asset.

[4] $P = 2$ if the price level doubles.

If there are net monetary assets, equity will rise less than in proportion to the rise in prices unless the monetary assets bear a rate of interest sufficient to compensate for the rising prices.

The relevance of the distinction between unanticipated and anticipated inflation can now be made clear. Anticipated inflations are those in which the rise in prices is foreseen, so that borrowers and lenders will have made loans with sufficient adjustments in interest rates, or amount to be repaid, to allow for the depreciation in the value of the unit of money. Unanticipated inflations are those which are not perfectly foreseen and for which such advance adjustments were not made. If net real assets exceed equity, an unanticipated inflation will increase equity more than in proportion to the rise in the price level, because net real assets can exceed equity only if net monetary assets are *negative*—which is to say that the monetary liabilities exceed the monetary assets. A rise in prices will reduce the "real" or "price-level-adjusted" value of one's liabilities. The principle can be summarized: An unanticipated inflation transfers wealth from monetary creditors to monetary debtors. On net, a person will gain wealth (in price-level-adjusted units) from unanticipated inflation if he is a net monetary debtor and will lose if he is a net monetary creditor.

Prior to applications of the principle, we give a few illustrative examples of the arithmetic. Before inflation, the balance sheet of an economic unit may be:

BEFORE UNANTICIPATED INFLATION

Assets		**Liabilities**	
Cash	$10	Debt	$ 6
Inventory	4	Equity	8
	$14		$14

If the price level doubles, the result is:

AFTER UNANTICIPATED INFLATION

Assets		**Liabilities**	
Cash	$10	Debt	$ 6
Inventory	8	Equity	12
	$18		$18

This economic entity is a net monetary creditor to the extent of $4; its monetary assets ($10) exceed its monetary liabilities ($6). Equity has increased only 50 percent, whereas the price level has increased by 100 percent. And "real" wealth is lost when prices rise by 100 percent while equity rises only 50 percent. Wealth is reduced from $8 to $12/2 = $6 (in pre-inflation prices).

Notice how this example is consistent with equation (3) on page 716. Thus:

$$\text{New equity} = P\,(\text{net real assets}) + (\text{net monetary assets}).$$
$$\$12 \quad = 2 \quad (\$4) \quad + \quad (\$10 - \$4).$$

The increase in prices, P, increases equity (assuming net real assets are positive) in money terms, but if the ratio of new equity to initial equity is less than P (as it will be if net monetary assets are positive), the real value of new equity is less than that of initial equity.

In the following example, the entity is neutral; that is, its monetary assets equal its monetary liabilities.

BEFORE INFLATION

Assets		**Liabilities**	
Cash	$ 6	Debt	$ 6
Inventory	4	Equity	4
	$10		$10

After an unanticipated doubling of prices, we have:

AFTER INFLATION

Assets		**Liabilities**	
Cash	$ 6	Debt	$ 6
Inventory	8	Equity	8
	$14		$14

Equity doubles to $8 when the price level doubles. Evidently, equity can increase proportionally to the general level of prices only if equity is equal to net real assets (i.e., if there are *zero net monetary* assets). The only way the entity can experience a rise in equity by a proportion greater than the rise in the price level is by being a net monetary debtor—that is, by owing more money than it has or than is owed to it.

For example, if our economic entity owes $6 and has $4 in money, it is a net monetary debtor to the extent of $2. The following balance sheets show the situation:

BEFORE UNANTICIPATED INFLATION

Assets		**Liabilities**	
Cash	$ 4	Debt	$ 6
Inventory	10	Equity	8
	$14		$14

AFTER A DOUBLING OF PRICES

Assets		Liabilities	
Cash	\$ 4	Debt	\$ 6
Inventory	20	Equity	18
	\$24		\$24

Equity has more than doubled, from \$8 to \$18.

One can obtain an increase of equity greater than the percentage change in the price level only by being in a *net monetary liability status.* Merely holding monetary debts is not sufficient. The entity must at the same time not have monetary assets in excess of his monetary debts. In the example, it was a net monetary *debtor* to the extent of \$2 (cash of \$4 minus monetary debt of \$6 = —\$2 net monetary assets).[5]

These examples illustrate that the source of the gain in equity which is proportionately greater than the rise in prices is a result *not* of holding real goods, but of owing more monetary assets (say money) than is owed to one.

[5] Let R and M be net real and net monetary assets, respectively, and E, the initial equity. Thus:

$$E = R + M.$$

If E' is the new equity when prices rise by proportion P, then:

$$E' = PR + M.$$

Finally, let Q be the proportionate increase in the money value of the equity:

$$Q = E'/E.$$

Now, substituting and rearranging:

$$\begin{aligned} Q &= \frac{PR + M}{E} \\ &= P\left(\frac{R}{E}\right) + \frac{M}{E} \\ &= P\left(\frac{E - M}{E}\right) + \frac{M}{E} \\ &= P - (P - 1)\frac{M}{E}. \end{aligned}$$

For example, in the third illustration, $Q = 2 - (2 - 1)\frac{-2}{8} = 2\frac{1}{4}$; and, to be sure, $18/8 = 2\frac{1}{4}$.

Whether Q is larger than, equal to, or smaller than P (assumed bigger than 1) is determined by whether $(P - 1)(M/E)$ is smaller than, equal to, or larger than zero; and that, in turn, hinges on whether M is negative, zero, or positive. In our first illustration, M was positive $(10 - 6 = 4)$, so Q was smaller than P $(1\frac{1}{2} < 2)$; in the second, M was zero, so Q equaled P; and in the third, M was negative, so Q was larger than P.

Holding real goods—which is the case in all three examples—will avail one no *gain* relative to the price level. He must be a net monetary debtor.

One of the commonest ways to be a net monetary debtor is to buy a house with a large mortgage. If a person can buy a $20,000 house and offset it with a monetary debt of $20,000, the two balance sheets show his equity before and after an unanticipated doubling of the price level.

BEFORE INFLATION

Assets		**Liabilities**	
Cash	$ 100	Debt	$20,000
House	20,000	Equity	100
	$20,100		$20,100

AFTER INFLATION (DOUBLING OF PRICE LEVEL)

Assets		**Liabilities**	
Cash	$ 100	Debt	$20,000
House	40,000	Equity	20,100
	$40,100		$40,100

His equity increased from $100 to $20,100, giving him an increase in wealth of $9,950 (in pre-inflation price-level units).

As of the present time, there are no reliable data to indicate whether a person's net monetary status depends on or is in any way related to age, wealth, or occupation. Folklore that old people suffer as a result of inflation must presume that they are all net monetary creditors. No evidence exists to verify this, although everyone can give examples of old people who are net monetary creditors—and of some who are net monetary debtors. Categorizing economic units according to such characteristics as age, sex, occupation, marital status, or degree of wealth seems to serve no valid purpose in detecting who gains or loses from the wealth transfer effect from inflation. Only the net monetary status is relevant.

Having derived, stated, and illustrated the principle, we can now investigate a few of the more important applications.

TAX ON MONEY

Money is an important form of monetary assets; furthermore, it rarely bears interest. Inflation will therefore impose a loss of wealth on its holder, this loss being the gain to the economic agent whose debts or promises constitute the money. As we saw earlier the economy's money stock is composed principally of (1) demand deposits, which are debts of the commercial banks, and (2) legal-tender money issued by the government and Federal Reserve banks.

Unanticipated inflation imposes a wealth loss on commercial banks because they are invariably net monetary creditors. A typical balance sheet is presented in Table 38–1. It is readily noticed that of its assets almost all are monetary. These exceed its monetary liabilities by the amount of $5,838. If the price level were to double it would lose half the real value of that net monetary credit.

Table 38–1

CITY NATIONAL BANK
(DECEMBER 31, 1963)

Assets	$ (000)	
Cash and due from banks	$ 17,360	Monetary Assets = $96,278
U.S. government bonds	15,957	
State and municipal banks	7,259	
Private bonds and notes	55,290	
Federal Reserve bank stock	412	
Bank premises and equipment	6,641	
	$102,919	

Liabilities	$ (000)	
Deposits	$ 88,240	Monetary Liabilities
Other liabilities	2,200	
	$ 90,440	

Ownership	$ (000)
Capital stock	3,820
Surplus	8,659
	$102,919

This means that the commercial banks are, in effect, intermediaries in a wealth-transfer process. During an unanticipated inflation, they obtain gains in wealth from the people to whom they owe the demand deposits (as the real value of those deposits decline), but they lose even more to the people who are indebted to the bank. In this way, the inflation imposes a "private tax," or an extra cost, on holders of money and monetary assets. The tax is not a government tax since it is not collected by the government—except insofar as the bank's assets are government bonds.

The second biggest item of money in the United States is currency and coins issued by the government or the Federal Reserve banks. Federal Reserve money is a debt of the Federal Reserve banks (which are owned by the government and the commercial banks). An inflation imposes a loss on holders of this money. The gains of the Federal Reserve banks are distributed to those who owe them money (their monetary debtors). The primary debtor of the Reserve banks is the U.S. government, for the Reserve banks hold primarily U.S. Government Bonds.

Inflation imposes a tax on money holders in proportion to the amount of money (not general wealth) that they hold, with the gains going to those whose debts constitute that money. A major beneficiary of unanticipated inflation, therefore, is the government, since it is typically a net monetary debtor to the rest of the community. It gains from its monetary liabilities, which serve as money, and also from its monetary debts (bonds and notes), which are held by the public.

What is meant by saying that the "government" gains wealth? The government is not *a* person; everyone is somehow involved. Strictly speaking, the government is part of the wealth structure of every person. People gain from inflation to the extent that their taxes are smaller and that they are beneficiaries of however the government uses the increase in its wealth. Even though no one may include his latent tax obligations in a balance sheet of his wealth, an inflation reduces the "real" value of the amount of future taxes that must be collected to pay interest on existing bonds; to that extent it benefits taxpayers.

GENERAL APPLICATIONS AND ILLUSTRATIONS OF INFLATION-INDUCED WEALTH REDISTRIBUTION

Many monetary assets (and liabilities) consist of more than money. Some are bonds, notes, accounts receivable, life-insurance policies, retirement pensions, and long-term leases. Substantial evidence has been collected from inflations of the past fifty years in the United States to establish that the inflations were unanticipated or incompletely anticipated, so that a transfer of wealth occurred from net monetary creditors to net monetary debtors. Strong evidence is provided by the experience of business firms whose stocks are owned by the public. Their annual financial balance-sheet reports show which business firms are net monetary creditors and which are net monetary debtors. The former have a larger total of cash and accounts receivable than they owe in accounts payable and bonds (to mention only the major monetary assets and liabilities), while the latter have the opposite balance.

An example of a net monetary debtor is Reynolds Metals Corporation. Its annual report, issued in 1963, showed that as of December 31, 1962, it possessed monetary assets totaling approximately $220,000,000 (consisting of cash, government securities, and loans to others); and it owed in monetary liabilities approximately $616,000,000 (consisting of accounts payable, bonds, and preferred stock). On net, Reynolds was a net monetary debtor of approximately $396,000,000. There were at that time about 100,000,000 shares of common stock. Each share bore almost $4 of the net monetary debt. You could buy a share of common stock in 1963 for about $35, thus becoming a debtor to the extent of about $4, or over 10 percent of your investment.

An example of a net monetary creditor is Amerada Petroleum, which reported that as of December 31, 1962, it owned monetary assets totaling about $63,000,000 (composed of cash, U.S. Government Bonds, and accounts receivable), while it owed about $15,000,000 in debts. The rest of its assets were in nonmonetary form. Each of the 7,400,000 common shares outstanding represented a claim to ($63 − $15)/7.4 = $6.5, which—at its price in 1963 of about $70 per share—is almost 10 percent. Thus, each dollar invested in ownership of Amerada Petroleum got its owner a claim to wealth consisting of 10 percent of net monetary assets.

An inflation will redistribute wealth to stockholders in Reynolds Metals, by virtue of net-monetary-debtor status of each share in that corporation; and inflation will transfer wealth away from Amerada Petroleum stockholders, because each share of ownership makes them net monetary creditors. During an inflation, as well as any other time, a host of factors affect the fortunes of every business firm—new products, changes in demands, new management, fires, inventions, etc. Nevertheless, one steady differentiating factor contributing to a gain for all the net-monetary-debtor firms relative to the net monetary creditors is the wealth-redistribution process just outlined. Therefore, on the average, the price of a share of common stock (share of ownership in the equity of the corporation) in firms that are net monetary debtors should, because of this wealth-transfer effect, rise *relatively* to those of net monetary creditors during unanticipated or incompletely anticipated inflations.

Since almost half of the business firms on the major stock exchanges are net monetary creditors while the other half are net monetary debtors, we can test for that wealth-transfer effect. Data of stock prices and assets and liabilities for thousands of firms over the period 1914–52 have been collected and bear out the analysis. Figure 38–3 presents the evidence. In every instance, net monetary debtors did better than net monetary creditors, as can be seen in the upper portion of that figure. Reversing the analysis, the opposite effect should be observed during deflations; the middle portion of Figure 38–3 shows the experience during two major deflations in the United States (1919–20, 1928–32); and during those episodes the predicted reverse relationship held. The equity value of net monetary creditors fell less than that of net monetary debtors. Finally, as is implied by

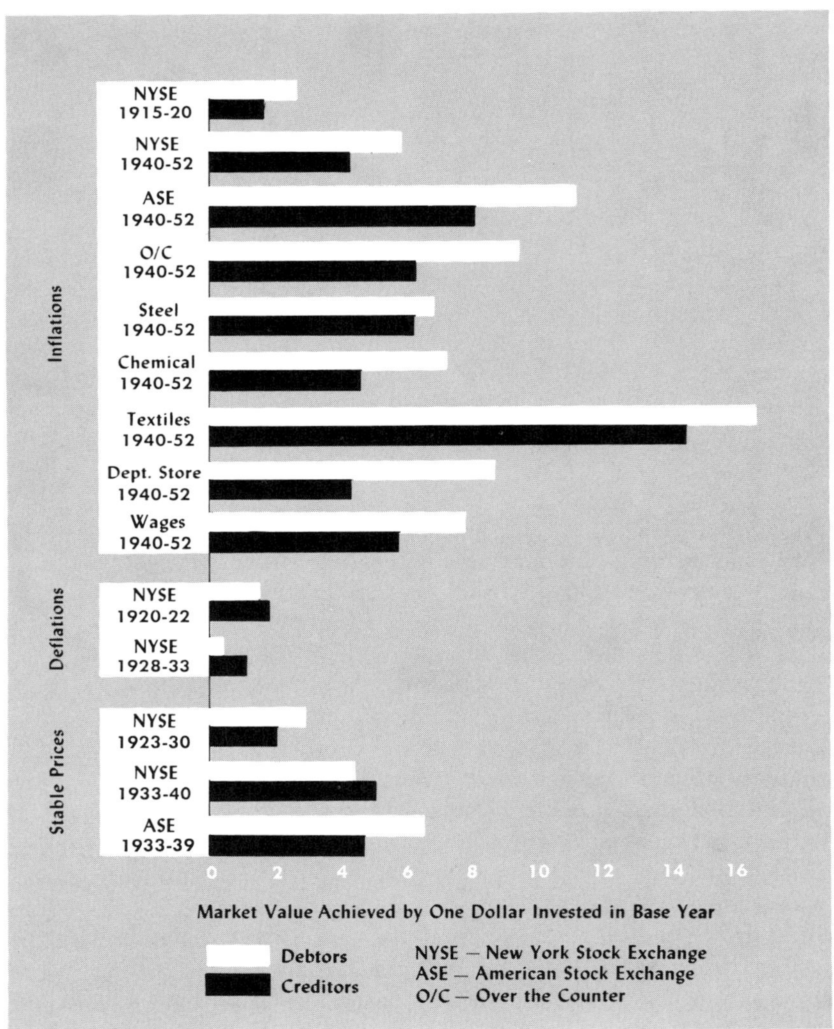

FIGURE 38–3. Market value of equity for debtors compared to creditors (per dollar of base-year common-stock value). Source: A. Alchian and R. Kessel, "Redistribution of Wealth through Inflation," *Science,* 130, No. 3375 (September 4, 1959), 538.

economic theory, during the episodes of stable prices, there was no significant difference between the two classes.

The Wage-Lag Doctrine: An Exercise in Debunking

One of the most common fallacies about inflation is that wage rates typically, if not always, lag behind prices. Exhaustive examination of available and cited historical evidence lends no support to that contention. During some inflations there was indeed a fall in "real" wages (money wages adjusted for price-level changes), but there were also times when they rose. There is no correlation of real wages with inflation.

What explains the persistent and erroneous belief that wages lag behind prices during inflations? First, anyone whose wages do not rise as much as other people's—whatever the reason—will seek some scapegoat. If there is concurrently an inflation, there is the excuse. (During that same time, people whose wages are rising more rapidly will attribute the rise not to inflation but to their own superiority.)

Second, everyone—whether he is selling labor, pencils, or automobiles—will imagine that the price of what he sells lags behind the level of other prices most of the time. His prices change sporadically, whereas the *average* of all other prices, being an average of a host of sporadically changing prices, will change more smoothly and steadily. Although his price is not rising, the average is rising. Of course, at the moment his is adjusted, it "leads" the general rise. This appearance of lead and lag is only a statistical artifact, in which a lag or lead is created because a more smoothly moving index is compared with a single less *smoothly* or intermittently moving price.

Third, inflations often occur in response to attempts to shift demand—for example, from peacetime goods to armaments or from consumer goods to space vehicles. The shift in demand toward certain goods will increase prices and wages of those goods (armaments and wages of armament workers) relative to other prices and wages. These are the normal responses to shifts in relative demands. Yet, if demand shifts are accompanied by the creation of money, inflation also will occur. Now, as demand shifts away from retail clerks, teachers, etc., to welders, machinists, and associated armament producers, it is easy to see why the relative decline in wages of teachers could be considered a result of inflation rather than of the revised demand. The government embarked on a policy of inflation during the last two world wars exactly to accomplish that revision in demand by creating new money to spend for the newly desired goods.

Fourth, although wage rates in a given job may not change much, workers will change jobs in response to revised demands. Even if there were no change in explicit wage rates in each job, relocation of employees from lower- to higher-paying jobs would mean an increase in *realized* wages. Concentration of attention on particular wage rates rather than the earning of employees can mislead one into thinking wages lag behind prices.

Fifth, because wages are paid for production of goods, which are sold later, it is often believed that a rise in the demand for some good will affect the wages of the producers only after the price of the product has increased. This error is based on the assumption that the economy is a simple sequence of production steps from raw materials to final products. In fact, some goods are inputs for earlier and for later stages, with feedbacks so that one cannot tell whether some good is at an earlier or later stage in a production process. Furthermore, even in a simple one-directional flow of services, the price response is not necessarily from consumer goods to labor-input wages. If you recall the example of the rise of the price of meat to consumers in response to demand increases (in Chapter 8), you will remember that a demand increase does not necessarily invoke a series of price rises starting at the *consumers'* end of the distribution process.

Sixth, the wage-lag belief has been fostered in part by naïve economic reasoning. Inflation increases the resources at the command of the government or the agency creating the new money. Given that they obtain more wealth, it follows that there is less left for the remaining segments of the economy. Someone must lose what the government or "business profiteers" gain. But the remaining segments are also experiencing increases of money incomes. If they are to consume less, and they must since there is less for them, the prices at which they buy must rise relative to their incomes. This is a decrease in the ratio of their money incomes relative to the cost of living. Where is the flaw in this analysis? It ignores the net-monetary-status principle of wealth transfer. The net monetary creditors will lose *wealth* and therefore will consume less; their *incomes* from earnings do not lag. For example, if a thief stole half the wealth of the public, the public would have to consume less. But this would not mean that its income from wages must fall relative to prices of goods it buys. Instead, it means solely that their wealth has decreased. Money-wage incomes rise with the price level, but the wealth value of resources owned by the net monetary creditors falls relative to the total wealth of the community. Inflation is a wealth transfer from monetary assets, *not* a tax on wage income.

An adjunct of the wage-lag doctrine is the "forced-savings" doctrine. This widely asserted doctrine contends that the "lost income" from the alleged "wage lag" goes to profit receivers in businesses, who invest it in new equipment. People have gone so far as to contend that it brought about the industrial revolution of Western Europe. During World Wars I and II this doctrine was so strongly believed, or at least espoused, that it served as a justification for special taxes on business profits in the belief that they represented unwarranted gains from "forced savings" imposed on their employees by a lag of wages behind prices during inflation. Yet, neither economic analysis nor empirical evidence supports such a notion. On the contrary, it is denied by the available evidence.

The Causes of Inflation

Deliberately, the causes of inflation have been ignored in order to isolate the effects. This is important, because the causes of inflation often have effects in addition to inflation, and these are easily confused with the effects of inflation itself.

To seek the cause of inflation is like asking why a fire truck is going so fast. Many causes can be adduced. First, more gasoline is being fed into the engine, with the result that the greater generated power is overcoming the resistance to its motion. This is a kind of "fundamental" reason. Second, the fire truck is going down a hill and would be going slower if it were going uphill. Third, the driver has opened the gasoline throttle wide. Fourth, the firemen want to reach a fire quickly. Fifth, the owner of the building on fire wants to curtail the fire damage. Silly as these "causes" may seem, they are on a par with many popular statements about the causes of inflation.

Examination of the "cause" of inflation can center on the following causes: (a) the *fact* of an increase in the supply of money relative to demand; (b) an explanation of the *ways* in which the quantity of money was increased relative to other economic goods, or the demand for it reduced; (c) an explanation of *why* the quantity of money was increased or why the demand for it was reduced. Each qualifies in strict logic as an answer to a reasonable interpretation of the "cause" of inflation. We shall discuss each.

The inflation occurred because the supply of money increased *relative* to the amount of money that people want to hold, given their existing wealth and income. If each of us awoke and found we had twice as much money as on the previous day and no less of any other goods or services, we would prefer to spend some of the money and reduce the proportion of our wealth in money. But not *everyone* can reduce his holdings of money by spending it, since that merely transfers it from person to person. As a result, the increased desire for other goods relative to money constitutes an increase in demand for other goods; and their prices are driven up. Everyone finds himself getting wealthier in dollar terms, some at a faster rate than others (depending upon his net-monetary-asset status). Prices will rise until every person's wealth and income is so large that he will *want* to hold as much money as he *has*. On the average, people will hold bank balances and pocket money aggregating to twice the amount formerly held, while prices, wealth, and income are about twice as high.

Very often it is not the quantity of money that changes but the physical stock of other goods. In a predominantly agricultural society, if the annual harvest is unusually small, prices of goods will be higher than usual. A historically significant case occurred during the Black Death in England in the fourteenth century. The outbreak of typhus fever killed a substantial fraction of the population, with no corresponding decrease in money. Wage rates rose spectacularly; the prices of other goods also rose, but not nearly so much, since their supply had not decreased as much relative to money. Money wages rose more than the price level, so that the survivors experienced a substantial increase in real income. This change in wages relative to other prices was a result of the change in relative amounts of labor and other goods—not of the inflation.

In the first of the two preceding examples, the population experienced a *decrease* of real wealth and income because it had a smaller agricultural crop to eat. It also experienced an inflation. Which is the cause? Which the effect? Common sense would suggest that the reduced crop (without a corresponding decline in money) induced the inflation of prices. But exactly this kind of situation has been carelessly called an example of an *inflation's* effect in reducing the real income of the community. In the other example, the inflation associated with the relative decrease in population relative to the money stock was accompanied by a *rise* in living standards for the survivors. This kind of situation has misled some people to deduce that inflation leads to increases in wealth.

Aside from changes in the stock of non-money goods, which were exogenous changes that changed the demand for money, the absolute quantity of money may change. But why would the quantity of money increase? If the money system enables people to increase the quantity of money by printing more or by issuing short-weighted gold and silver coins, then the temptation to print and issue "light-weight" money is overwhelmingly strong. The motives for increasing the supply of money by printing new money are always "patriotic." The government authorities, regardless of the form of the government, under pressures from various people, find it expedient to print money, rather than levy *explicit* taxes, to exert claims to a greater share of the wealth in the nation. This may be done to prosecute a war; to reach the moon; to give aid to the poorer people, to farmers, to businessmen, to education; to prevent or reduce unemployment; or to aid the politically powerful people directly. Short of collecting wealth by explicit taxes, the government embarks on a policy of money creation as a means of acquiring wealth and accomplishing its objectives.

If the government spends more than it receives from taxes or loans from the public, it can finance the remainder of its deficit by printing new money. Some governments simply start the printing presses, while others use more complicated procedures. In the United States, the federal government may "persuade" the Federal Reserve banks to buy U.S. Bonds. According to current law, a Federal Reserve bank can print new money or "reserves" if it has an equivalent of U.S. Bonds and some gold in its possession as "backing" for that new money. Bluntly put, this is known as monetizing the public debt; it is a roundabout way of creating money, but the result is the same. New money is created by a "central bank" instead of by the government's treasury itself. Thus deficit financing, *if* it is accompanied by money creation, becomes a "source" of inflation.

Currently, in every country experiencing substantial inflation, the cause is the government's creation of new money to finance its activities—which in no way implies that the government should not be undertaking those activities or engaging in inflationary finance. That depends upon the alternatives.

You will at one time or another undoubtedly hear that foreign aid, agricultural-support program, social security, and our space, military, education, or unemployment-relief programs are inflationary. All of these activities involve expenditures. Whether or not they will "cause" inflation depends upon how they are financed, in particular whether or not it is done by increasing the quantity of money. Whether the program itself or the increase in the quantity of money with which the program is financed is to be called the cause of the inflation depends upon how one chooses to construe the meaning of "cause."

Especially current in public discussion is the contention that action by the government to maintain full employment is resulting in a "wage-push" or "administered" price inflation. The argument contends that some wages and prices are arbitrarily increased because of some "market power" in the hands of "key" people and that all other people must adjust to these key or "bellwether" prices. Steel prices or union wage rates are often cited as examples. In fact and in theory, there are no key commodities to whose prices the prices of other goods adjust. It is easy to *say* that if the price of steel or wages of some group increase, then other prices must rise to reflect the costs of these components. However, even though an imposed rise in the price of steel will raise the costs of products using steel, it will also reduce the rate of output. Resources will be released to other goods, whose prices will fall as their supply is increased. The *average* price of all output remains unchanged. No inflation occurs; there is only a rise in the price of some goods and a fall in others.

Inflation *will* occur if the released (unemployed) resources consequent to the higher imposed price are able to induce the community to engage in a policy of inflation by increasing the quantity of money. The unemployed resources might succeed in persuading the political authorities to create new money with which to increase the demand for the products of the unemployed in their old jobs. The way in which the new money is spent will affect relative prices momentarily, but soon the increased quantity of money will raise all prices. Prices will rise to the former levels they had *relative* to the prices of the good whose prices were arbitrarily raised. This inflation restores the former relative price structure.

If in the process of creating new money and spending it, the bulk of it is first spent for the particular commodity whose price was arbitrarily raised, the situation is one with both a transient increase in the relative demand for "steel" and then an inflation. But underlying the development has been the policy of resorting to creation of new money with a resultant inflation in order to restore employment to producers of goods whose prices were arbitrarily raised above the free-market level.

This situation can be summarized as one in which inflation occurs because of an increase in the quantity of money; the political authorities adopt that policy of increasing money to obtain wealth with which to finance the increased demand for the resources whose prices were arbitrarily raised above open-market levels.

The *technique* of causing an inflation by the increase in the quantity of money must be kept distinct from the *motivation* for the increased quantity of money. In our example, the motive was to permit an increase in demand for particular goods to restore employment to certain resources in their *former* activities at the new higher imposed prices. If the government keeps its eye on the rate of unemployment in the steel industry, it is easy to see that steel could be called a "key" industry. If the government keeps its eye on some other industry or block of employees, they, too, could be called the "key" group—regardless of whether they be teachers, janitors, actors, or steel-industry employees.

Quantity of Money and Inflation: Some Historical Episodes

In measuring the amount of inflation, we can use either the rate of inflation (e.g., some percentage rate of rise of prices per month), or we can refer to the relative amount of rise over some long episode. In the first case a low rate may continue for a long period and thereby yield a large change over several years. Or a high rate may last for only a few months; for instance, 15 percent per month for three months gives a total rise of about 52 percent in three months. In some countries inflations have continued at a rate of only a few percent a month for several decades. In other countries there have been short, violent, spectacular rates of inflation.

Explosive inflations have occurred during episodes of catastrophes (e.g., invasions, revolutions). During such events normal productive activity is obstructed; also, the government finds its normal administrative taxing power diminished by these invasions and threatened revolutions. Sometimes a new government has seized power and has not arranged its administrative procedures. Creating more money remains as one easy means of financing government activity. The government always hopes that the abnormal physical or social or political conditions will be overcome before the inflation has proceeded far or the government toppled.

The proposition that larger quantities of money, relative to other goods, implies inflation does not say that a 1 percent increase in the stock of money relative to goods will increase the price level 1 percent. But it does say that the greater the increase in the stock of money, the greater the increase in the price level. Many other factors, besides a change in the stock of money, affect the price level. Changes in demand for money may occur, for example. But usually these changes in other factors are rarely big enough to induce a change in the price level of more than a few percent. Exactly how much change in money stocks must occur in, say, one month or six months in order to raise prices in general is not specifiable; however, in almost every instance of a change of money of, say, 5 percent within a month, a change in the price level is detectable. And certainly a 20 or 50 percent increase will be accompanied by a rise in the price level, frequently of that same order of magnitude.

For example, Figure 38–4 shows the correlation between the average annual rate of increase in the quantity of money and in prices for each of sixty-five countries for the period 1948–62. The relationship is striking.

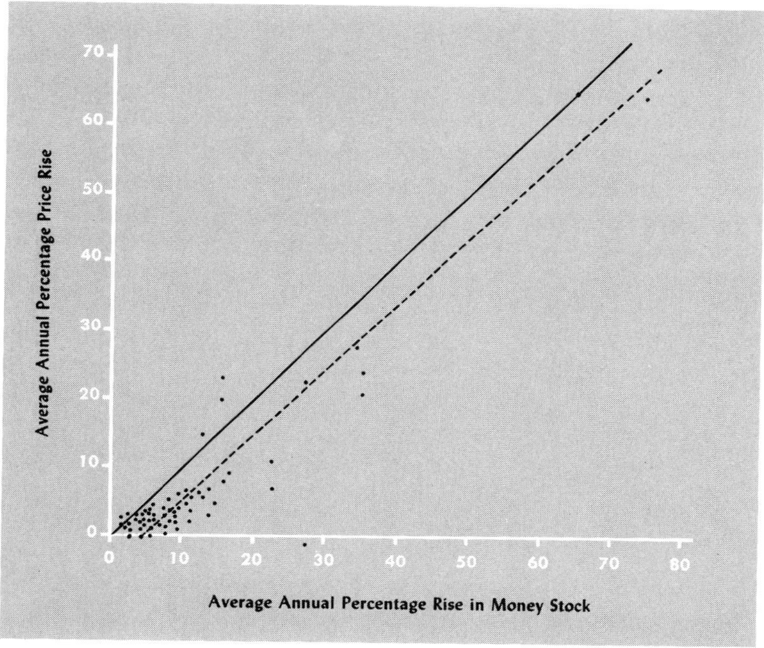

FIGURE 38–4. Money-supply increase and price-level rise (average annual percentage) for sixty-four countries, 1948–62. Source: *International Financial Statistics,* 1963–64 Supplement, International Monetary Fund, 1963. The general correlation between increases in money and the rise in the price level is vividly illustrated by this chart. The straight-dashed slanting line is the line of equal proportional changes in prices and quantity of money after allowance for a 4 percent annual growth of physical stock of goods. (Notice the unbelievable reported price fall for one country—Tunisia—despite a 28 percent per year increase of money. This is probably an index based on "legal" controlled prices only.)

The picture would be even more spectacular if it also showed experiences from extreme inflations such as occurred in Germany in 1923, when prices rose by about a factor of 100,000,000,000 in one year, while the amount of money increased by a factor of 10,000,000,000. This is equivalent to a doubling of prices every two weeks. Similar episodes occurred in Greece in 1944, in Poland in 1923, in Russia in 1921–23, and in Hungary in 1923 and again in 1946, to mention only a few. The Hungarian inflation of 1946 saw prices doubling on the average every two or three days to a factor of about 10 with 26 zeros after it, in about one year. Plotting these experiences on the graph would require an enormous graph, but, as expected, the plotted points would be in the far upper right.

Inspection of Figure 38–4 shows that, on the average, prices do not rise in proportion to the increase in the amount of money. If they did, the points would cluster around a 45-degree line out of lower left corner. Instead, most points lie below it. If, however, we experience a growth of population and non-money goods of about 3 or 4 percent a year, the price level will rise about 3 or 4 percent a year less than the rate of change in the amount of money. This implies that the points should lie around the dashed line drawn on the figure, and they do.

Demand for Money during Anticipated Inflation

Each person's demand for money balances, given his wealth and income, depends upon his beliefs about future price levels. If he expects prices to be higher tomorrow, he will seek to spend more of his money today. His demand for money to hold will fall. (If he expects prices to fall tomorrow, his demand for money will increase, and he will defer spending.) If people suspect that a rise in prices will be supported by appropriate increases in the quantity of money (whatever the objective sought in the creation of the new money or the higher price level), they will seek to adjust their holdings of money, because money will be more expensive to hold. Formerly, with anticipations of stable prices, the cost of holding money was the forsaken use derivable from other goods that could have been owned instead. Now, with money *known in advance* to be more expensive to hold, people will strive to hold less money in order to avoid some of those increased costs, just as they would with any good that has become more expensive.

People will not abandon the use of the money, for that would impose an even greater cost than holding some of the deteriorating money. The gains from holding and using money as a medium of exchange are so great that people will continue to use some money even though they expect the price level to rise at, say, a rate of 25 percent per week (which is equivalent to a loss of value of money of 20 percent per week). Of course, an anticipated rise of 25 percent per week will induce people to try to hold much less money. But not *everyone* can do this, since the money is transferred from person to person. Instead prices will rise to even higher levels, i.e., more than in proportion to the increase in nominal money. This is often expressed as a reduction in the "real" stock of money—despite an increasing nominal amount of money. This fall in the real value of money balances is a result of the efforts of people to economize on the use of resources expected to become dearer.

One means of economizing on the use of money is to hold a smaller proportion of one's wealth as money, with the attendant greater inconvenience of using the market. Specialization is facilitated by an efficient, low-cost market; and anticipated inflation increases the costs of using the market so that firms and people will shift more to barter and to non-market arrangements; therefore, the anticipated inflation will result in reduced output consequent to less efficient specialization. The higher costs of circumventing the market with a smaller amount of "real" money are willingly borne in order to avoid the still higher costs of holding larger amounts of deteriorating money.

In sum, anticipated inflation, depending upon its rate, imposes a cost in the form of a "destruction" of part of the money capital of the community. An analogy is illuminating. A tax on windows would collect wealth for the taxing agency, but at the cost of people's shifting to houses with smaller or fewer windows; thus, the cost of the tax is not merely the pecuniary wealth transferred to the taxing agency but also the reduced level of well-ventilated or lighted houses. And so it is with anticipated inflation; aside from the wealth transfer, the total level of wealth or income obtained is reduced by the loss of efficiency of the money-exchange system.

The greater inconveniences are described as a "shortage" of money. Yet, as we have seen, the reduced amount of "real" money is the result of each person's response to more costly money. The way to reduce that cost is to stop the inflation and thus remove the anticipation of further inflation. Strangely enough, some people contend that the way to alleviate the "shortage" of money is to print money even more rapidly—which would, of course, increase the rate of anticipated inflation and increase the shortage even more. The way to eliminate the shortage of money is to stop increasing the nominal amount of money—a solution that is paradoxical only to those who forget the difference between relative and absolute amounts of money.

Personal Protection from Inflation

You can take some steps to protect yourself from some of the effects of general price changes. You can avoid the wealth transfer by being neither a *net* monetary creditor nor debtor: hold assets of such form that your total monetary assets are equal to your total monetary liabilities. If you want to bet that inflation will occur and want to gain from it, be a net monetary debtor. If you want to gamble that there will be deflation, then be a net monetary creditor. But if you want to avoid that gamble, be a net monetary "neutral." One relatively easy way to do this is by appropriate investment in common stocks. The ownership of common stock in a corporation, while representing ownership in the corporation, also affects one's monetary wealth structure. If the corporation in which common stock is purchased is a net monetary debtor, then the stockholder is a monetary debtor. For example, a purchase of one hundred shares of Reynolds Metals would increase one's monetary indebtedness by about $350 (see pp. 722–723). On the other hand, a purchase of common stock in Amerada Petroleum Corporation would change his monetary-debtor status toward a net monetary neutral or creditor. Appropriate purchase of common stocks can alter substantially one's net-monetary-asset or liability status.

Remember, however, there is no assurance that the fortunes of Reynolds Metals, or whatever common stock one finds appropriate to balance his situation, will move along exactly with the price level; but then this is true for all forms of wealth. No one can attain complete certainty about the future value of any goods. Even holding only money exposes one to the risks of inflation. The only thing a person can do is own a mixture of goods or stocks, so that on the average the gains and losses come close to balancing or so that he bears risks in selected goods.

This averaging of risks of holding various types of goods explains part of the advantage of the corporate form of ownership. Several people can share in ownership, thereby enabling one person to distribute his wealth among several enterprises. Even though one firm may experience idiosyncratic gains and losses, a person distributing his wealth among several corporations in various lines of production can achieve a relatively well-balanced portfolio of risks.

Repressed Inflation

An almost automatic political response to inflation is an imposition of price controls (i.e., maximum permissible prices)—usually in an attempt to repress the inflation. This response usually comes, if we may hazard a conjecture, because the agents responsible for, and benefiting from, the inflation mistakenly attribute the inflation to greedy businessmen, landlords, and unions seeking to get higher prices and wages.

As a result of restrictions on prices at which exchanges may legally be negotiated, the market-exchange system loses some effectiveness as a transmitter of information about values of uses of resources and about the available supplies of resources. It also loses effectiveness in directing resources to various uses. Other allocative criteria and techniques of communication acquire greater relevance—along the lines presented in Chapters 9 and 12. More expensive means of communication and exchange are used. Instead of buying in an organized market, consumers trek to the producers to get goods. Consumers perform more distribution and transportation services themselves, because of reduced incentives and rewards to sellers to specialize in exchange-facilitating activities. Specialization is reduced, with the consequent loss of potential output, in accord with the fundamental principles of gains from specialization discussed in Chapters 16 and 17.

Clear examples of the effectiveness of the market system in transmitting information, directing resources, and providing incentives are found in experiences after World War II. In Germany, three years after the war, price controls were removed; and the economy responded with great increases in production of income. Japan and Italy had similar experiences. These were not such as to be attributed to recovery from war damage, but instead were sufficiently isolated and abrupt to reveal that market-price constraints reduce the economic efficiency of the market as an informative, allocative, incentive system.

Once the stock of money has increased relative to the stock of goods and services, *nothing* can be done to prevent a wealth transfer—unless everyone is a net monetary neutral. And for this to happen, the money must be entirely debt money or commodity money—with no legal-tender money issued by the government. With everyone neutral, the effect is merely to raise prices with no net effect on anyone's wealth, since everyone's assets and liabilities rise by the same proportion. In fact, it is probably never true that everyone is exactly a neutral. Hence, an increase in the relative stock of money will mean a wealth redistribution (from those who are net monetary creditors to the net monetary debtors).

Only four policies are available, once the money stock has increased. (1) Attempts to suppress prices will mean that people can't spend their money and get what they want at existing prices. Money as a medium of exchange of rights to goods will lose some of its competitive rationing power. Other systems of competition will be relied upon more for rationing. This means that money holders will suffer a loss of wealth claims. (2) If prices are allowed to rise freely in response to increased money supplies, the higher prices will reduce the real wealth value of the money, again imposing the wealth loss on money holders. But the relative role of exchange competition, *vis-à-vis* other forms of competition in rationing goods is not changed. Instead, the interpersonal weighting of money claims is changed. (3) A third alternative is to engage in a monetary "reform," a euphemism for the situation in which a portion of the money is simply canceled. (4) The fourth alternative is to impose a special tax on non-money wealth with which to buy up and cancel some of the money. This would avoid the inflation wealth loss of money holders. But, then, if this kind of tax could have been imposed, it would probably have been used instead of creating money. History records no instances of a special tax being imposed for this purpose. Thus, in the three relevant cases (i.e., whether prices are allowed to rise freely, or are suppressed, or the money supply is arbitrarily cut) the money holders lose wealth.

We are now in a position to see why inflation is often regarded as an evil —by net monetary creditors. They experience a loss of wealth, but the net monetary debtors gain. More spectacular inflations, in which prices rise at a rate of over 30 percent a year, are usually anticipated to some extent. The consequent reduction in efficiency of the market-exchange process reduces real national income—depending upon the rate of the inflation and the degree to which it is anticipated. What we should remember is that almost all taxes involve a redistribution of wealth and that inflation is a special kind of tax—one on money. Therefore, it is not the redistribution of wealth *per se* that is unusual about an inflation, but, instead, the particular classes between whom wealth is transferred. Similarly, many taxes also have an efficiency effect; a very high tax on the use of the market would bring about the same kind of reduction of specialization and output that is induced by anticipated inflation. Given these consequences of unanticipated and of anticipated inflation, the question of whether inflation is good or bad cannot be answered simply by looking at those consequences. Also relevant is the situation that otherwise would have existed had the inflation method of financing activity not been pursued. Since these alternatives are idiosyncratic to each special situation, they cannot be subjected here to general analysis.

Questions

1. If every price rises, can you be sure there has been an inflation? (Hint: What about changes in quality of goods?)

2. You spend one fourth of your income on good *A* at $1 per unit. And you spend three fourths on *B* at $1 per unit. Now the price of *B* doubles while the price of *A* falls to 80 cents. If these are the only two goods available, has there been a rise in the price level (counting money as a third good)?

3. The reported indices of price levels have an upward bias in their measure of the change in the price level. Thus, a reported rise of 3 percent in one year may be consistent with an actual decrease in the cost of obtaining a former level of utility—not to mention improved quality of goods. Almost all consumer price indices for the U.S. report a rise of about 5 to 10 percent over the price level of about ten years ago.

   a. To test your belief in that, would you rather—given an annual income of, say, $5,000—do all your purchasing from a 1955 Sears (or Ward's) mail-order catalogue or from a current one? (If you are tempted to pick the current one because of changes in styles of clothes, suppose the styles were to be altered at no cost.) Which year's catalogue would you choose?

   b. Remember, if you choose the current one, you are expressing disbelief in all the measures of the cost of living! How do you reconcile your position—if you choose the current one?

4. Is a monetary asset one whose price is fixed or is it one that represents a claim to a fixed value in money terms? Give an example of a good that satisfies the latter condition but not the former.

5. **a.** Is a one-year lease on an apartment a monetary or nonmonetary asset of the tenant?

b. Is it a monetary or a nonmonetary liability of the apartment owner?

c. Is a life-insurance policy a monetary or a nonmonetary asset?

6. Which of the following are monetary? Are they assets or liabilities?

a. Money: checking accounts.

b. Charge account at department store.

c. Prepaid subscription to *New York Times*.

d. Long-term lease for land.

e. Rental arrangement whereby tenant pays 1 percent of monthly sales as rental to the building owner.

f. U.S. Bonds.

g. A share of General Motors common stock.

h. House.

i. Social-security benefit rights.

j. Pension rights in a retirement fund.

k. Teacher's salary.

7. If, during an inflation, you held all your wealth in the form of cash, would you gain or lose wealth relative to the change in the price level? (Hint: Not sufficient information.)

8. If, during an inflation, you held all your wealth in the form of real goods would you gain or lose wealth relative to the price level? (Hint: What else must you know?)

9. Is there any evidence that schoolteachers are net monetary creditors as a class?

10. Explain how bank owners as a class suffer from inflation.

11. Refer back to page 638. Show how an inflation that doubles the price level will bring to the government more than twice as much in income taxes. (Hint: Estimate the taxes for a person earning $4,000 a year before the inflation and $8,000 after the inflation.)

12. "Inflation is an unmitigated evil that bleeds wealth and income from the poor unorganized wage earners, public employees, widows, orphans, and retired people." Aside from whether or not it is a mitigated or unmitigated evil, does inflation have the effects mentioned in that common assertion?

13. Today schoolteachers compare 1964 income status after taxes with the 1940 status after taxes. Because taxes have increased substantially more than in proportion to income, the teachers can show that their real income after taxes is smaller. As a legislator, tell why you would not shed tears for the plight of the teachers using this argument.

14.

THE AZ COMPANY
Balance Sheet of June 30, 1964

ASSETS		
Cash	$ 20,000	
U.S. bonds	50,000	
Accounts receivable	30,000	
Inventories	100,000	
Building and equipment	90,000	
Goodwill	100	
	$290,100	
LIABILITIES		
Current		
Accounts payable	$ 25,000	
Notes payable	80,000	
Prepaid orders	5,000	
Accrued taxes	4,000	
		$114,000
Long-term		
Notes	$ 40,000	
Bonds	100,000	
		140,000
Equity		
Common stock		30,000
Surplus		6,100
		$290,100

Is the AZ Company a net monetary creditor or debtor? By how much? If each of the 30,000 shares of common stock has *market* value of $40 (despite the initial value of $1 per share recorded in the balance sheet), and if you buy one share for $40, how many dollars of net monetary debtor or creditor status will you acquire?

15. a. In your college library, refer to Moody's *Industrials* as a source of balance sheets for American industrial corporations. Record the latest balance sheet for United Nuclear Corporation and indicate whether it is a net monetary debtor or net monetary creditor. An alternative source is Standard and Poor's *Statistical Reports*. The librarian should be able to guide you to these volumes.

b. Try to find a corporation that is a net monetary creditor. Check on the following, which were net monetary creditors as of 1963:

(1) Standard Oil Company (New Jersey).
(2) Ford Motor Company.
(3) International Resistance Company.
(4) New Park Mining Company.

(5) Tokheim Company.
(6) Piper Aircraft Company.
(7) American Greeting Card Company.
(8) McCloud River Lumber Company.
(9) Fenestra Company.
(10) Laboratory for Electronics, Inc.

16. To test whether average wages lag behind prices, someone examines the record for thirty years of price-level increases. He finds that half the time the wage rates rose less than the price level, while in the other half they rose more. He concludes that the wage-lag effect was present half the time. What would you have concluded? (Hint: If someone said a roulette wheel gave odd rather than even numbers and then on 100 trials he found that half the numbers were odd, would you say his assertion was correct half the time or that his assertion was simply wrong? Is this comparable to the wage-lag assertion?)

17. "Wages must lag behind prices simply because demand first affects selling prices and then filters down to the prices of productive inputs." Evaluate.

18. "If government increases its share of national income, there simply has to be less left for the private sector. With a smaller real income available to the private sector, and with the same wages, real wages must be smaller simply because available real income is smaller." Even if it is true that the real income left for the private economy is smaller, there is an error in that reasoning. What is it? Who loses the income obtained by the government?

19. If you were asked for the cause of the inflation in Brazil, how would you revise the question?

20. a. If you knew that every price was going to rise at the rate of 10 percent a week, would you try to hold larger or smaller amounts of money relative to your wealth and income?

b. Would you abandon the use of money and resort solely to barter to save 10 percent of your money wealth every week?

c. In 52 weeks how much higher would the price level be? (Use tables from Chapter 15 to compute the answer.) Are you now therefore not surprised to see why people will still use money even when they know the price level will rise by that amount in one year?

d. Are you convinced that even at an anticipated 100 percent per *week* rise in prices, people would still use money?

e. If people reduce their money balances relative to their wealth and income from say one fourth of their annual income to one tenth (in order to avoid so large a loss of wealth from decreasing the value of the money), approximately how much would prices jump?

21. Young movie stars under the age of 21 are ordered by judges to save a fraction of their weekly earnings and buy U.S. government bonds. They are not allowed to invest that savings in stocks.

a. If you were a young movie star, would you regard that as good advice?

b. If you were a judge, would you regard that advice as good?

c. Can you give any reasons why jurists and the legal system are prone to advise investments in U.S. government bonds?

22. a. If you were drawing up your will and were arranging for advice to your widow in investing or living off your life insurance, would you recommend that the funds be invested in bonds or in stocks?

b. How do the risks differ in each case?

23. In some countries in which the money supply has increased while wages and prices were subjected to legal controls, an attempt is made to prevent all wages and prices from rising by "reforming" the money system. This means that a portion of the money stocks are simply canceled out by government decree; thereby prices are kept from rising. Does that tactic avoid a wealth redistribution? Explain.

24. Suppose that all college teachers succeed in forcing the colleges to pay a minimum salary to professors of $25,000 per year in order to preserve the dignity of professors. Many professors will soon find themselves without jobs. Being of great influence in government, the professors tell the politicians that their demands are reasonable and that the basic trouble is insufficient demand. To increase demand the government can increase its expenditures to colleges to enable them to hire all the professors at $25,000. If it finances this by taxes, demand will fall elsewhere and unemployment will result until wages and prices there fall to keep resources employed. The fall in prices elsewhere simply offsets the rise in professors' wages. Or the government could have embarked on a program of general-demand expansion by spending more and taxing less, and meeting the deficit with money creation. If the government assures college professors that they will have full-employment demand conditions without wage cuts and without causing unemployment elsewhere, is inflation the inevitable policy? Why?

25. You are trying to compute a price index. The price of some good is reported as $100. However, the amount available in the shops is less than the amount demanded.

a. Do you think $100 is a meaningful price?

b. Suppose I offered to sell you a 1964 Cadillac for $1,000 when I have one in stock. I don't have one available now, nor is it likely I shall ever have one. Would you record that price as a relevant price?

c. How does this differ from the preceding case of the $100 good?

d. Suppose that apartments are subjected to rent controls and, at present rents, twice as many people want more housing as can get it at that price. How relevant is the controlled price as a measure of the rental costs?

26. Suppose the musicians' union raises the wages of musicians by 50 percent, and as a result one third of the musicians cannot get jobs as musicians.

a. Would you count their wage rates at the new level or as zero while they were not working?

b. If everyone insisted on twice his current salary, would that mean the average level of wages had doubled? (Hint: What about the relevant wages of those who can't find employment at that higher wage rate?)

c. Would you count as prices only those at which the resource is actually sold? What would you consider to be the prices of unsold or unemployed goods?

27. Emperor Julian exhorted the merchants of Antioch to practice self-restraint in pricing their wares. Today government leaders exhort businessmen and labor leaders to exercise statesmenlike self-restraint. Tomorrow the story will be the same. Why is such exhortation worse than useless?

28. "The progressive deteroriation in the value of money throughout history is not an accident, and has behind it two great driving forces—the impecuniosity of governments and the superior political influence of the debtor class. . . . The power of taxation by currency depreciation is one which has been inherent in the State. . . . The creation of legal tender has been and is a government's ultimate reserve; and no state or government is likely to decree its own downfall, so long as this instrument still lies at hand unused" (J. M. Keynes, *A Tract on Monetary Reform*, London: Macmillan and Co., Ltd., 1923, p. 9). Explain in more detail what Keynes meant.

29. "Price-level stability, assurance of full employment by government, and open markets are incompatible." Present the reasoning that appears to underlie that proposition.

30. "A mild and unanticipated inflation of about 3 to 5 percent a year is conducive to a faster rate of growth of wealth, because it avoids massive frictional unemployment." Explain the reasoning underlying that statement. Does anyone lose in order to facilitate that policy, if it is followed?

31. "Inflation causes price distortions because not all prices are equally responsive to changes in demand. Therefore, a period of rapid inflation causes inefficiencies in the economic system. Evidence of the distortion is evident if one looks at the fact that, during inflations, relative prices change." Would you consider that as evidence for the proposition that inflation causes a change in relative prices? Is there some other reason why you would expect the beginning of an inflation to be associated with greater relative changes in prices more than during the subsequent inflation or during periods when price levels are constant? (Hint: Why did the inflation occur? That is, what events caused the increase in money stock relative to demand for money?)

39

PRIVATE AND GOVERNMENTAL ECONOMIC ACTIVITY

Our society does not rely exclusively on a private-property, market-directed system for resolving economic problems. Governments are active also. In the first place, they are necessary for a private-property system since they enforce legal rights. In the second place, they often revise those rights, transferring legal rights from one person to another in an attempt to change behavior or redistribute wealth. In the third place, they act in economic matters in lieu of the private-property market system—either because that system is not conveniently enforceable or because some of its consequences are deemed undesirable. We pass over the first two reasons and concentrate on the third, wherein the government acts to supplement or supplant the private-property system. But as preparation we should know what we mean by a private-property system (and what is necessary for its operation).

Characteristics of Private Property

In a system of private property, roughly speaking, it is illegal for anyone to use goods in ways that have undesired physical effects on other people's goods. Less roughly, private-property rights in goods constitute the exclusive rights of the owners to use their goods, and only their goods, in any way they see fit, and to transfer these rights to other people. I cannot throw my hammer through your glass window, because that violates your right to use your window as you decide. If, in using my goods, I affect the physical or technological attributes of your goods, then I am violating some of your private-property rights. However, I can legally throw a rock through your window, or tear down your house and occupy your land, if and only if I obtain your permission or buy the rights from you. Like it or not (and this is not a study in what is good or bad, but what is and what is not), exclusivity of control constitutes a basic component of the private-property economic system. Finally, we emphasize: property rights are *not* rights of *property;* they are *rights of people* to use goods. In sum, two basic elements of private property are *definite exclusivity* of right of use and *voluntary transferability* or exchangeability of that right.

EXCLUSIVITY

A person has private-property rights to uses of goods if decisions as to those physical uses are not made by other people. The person who controls *all* physical attributes or uses of goods is called the owner—if he can exclude other people from use of the goods. If I own a house, you cannot paint it, burn it, or otherwise affect its technological or physical characteristics without my permission, under the laws characterizing a private-property economy.

Physical or technological attributes are mentioned to distinguish them from pecuniary or exchange-value effects, because private property, as generally defined, does not protect market values even though a drop in value can be as disastrous as a fire. If you build a better house and undersell me, or if you change other people's tastes by persuading them to buy something other than my product, so that the exchange value of my good is affected, I have no recourse under private-property rights. Values are the result of agreement between two people. For one person to prevent a second person from attracting the first person's customer would be a denial of the "right" (sometimes called "freedom") of the second party and also of the customer to make whatever exchanges they can negotiate to their mutual satisfaction.

If all the physical effects or uses of a good are determined solely by the owner, then all these consequences are borne by him. This is often expressed as an equality between private and social costs; he does not inflict some of the cost on the rest of society. In fact, however, rights to control every physical attribute of goods are not always clearly assigned to particular people or owners. Some uses of goods are not reserved to specified "owners." If I burn refuse or operate a factory so as to emit smoke, ashes, smells, soot, and airborne acids on and over your land, I am using my goods in ways that harmfully change the physical attributes of "your" goods without requiring your permission. When a neighbor walks his dog for its nightly relief, my property is damaged. When I drive my scooter with a blaring exhaust that sends sound vibrations across his property, I momentarily change its physical attributes for the worse, in his opinion. These are examples of actions that change the physical characteristics of the goods that other people are said to own—except that the owner does not "own" all physical-attribute rights.

TRANSFERABILITY

Transferability is the right to exchange property rights with other people at mutually agreeable terms. In the strong sense, transferability means exchangeability at terms that only the buyer and seller need approve. No third party can impose the terms. In a weaker sense, transferability could exist even if exchanges were permitted only at prices set by a third party.

A series of United States Supreme Court decisions reveals vacillation as to whether private property is to mean strong or weak transferability. Early in the nineteenth century imposition of legal limits on market prices was declared not to be a denial of private-property rights, but about fifty years later the decision was reversed and a legally imposed price was declared an invasion of private-property rights. Subsequently the justices of the Supreme Court again reversed the rule, and declared that price controls are not invasions of constitutionally defined private-property rights.

Costs of Private-Property System

Heretofore, we assumed that the definitional problems of an extensive and general system of property rights were well perceived, solved, and enforced. If, however, they are not, or if the implications of a system of private property are not well understood, or if they are deemed undesirable, the sanctioned property system will be less private. In any event, defining and sanctioning private-property rights for some goods with respect to some physical effects may be more costly than it is worth, even to those who would get the rights. For example, the cost of protecting a person's rights to property from all noise produced by other people may exceed the costs imposed on the people whose "rights" are attenuated by the noise. Similarly, the costs of disposing of old leaves by other than burning may be so high that people may prefer to burn them and contaminate each other's property. The costs of subduing some "nuisances," as the law calls these denials of private rights to exclusivity of use, may be greater than the damage done. For example, the costs of eliminating smog-creating exhausts or preventing smog from polluting other people's air is greater than the costs imposed by smog itself.

If property rights are cheap enough to define and enforce, we agree to compensate other people for any invasion of their property. The payment must, of course, be less than the cost we otherwise would incur. For example, I would be willing to pay a neighbor $50 for the right to dump refuse on his property, rather than pay $200 to cart it elsewhere. If I build a shopping center near your house and change the physical attributes (via noise and bright lights) of your property so that you cannot enjoy it as formerly, I could pay you $100 a year for the right to do so, if you prefer $100 to no such "nuisance." But if the courts are sufficiently inept in defining or understanding private-property rights, I can create the "nuisance" without paying you anything.

Land-use rights are enforced because we can survey the land, detect violators, and apprehend and punish them at a sufficiently small cost to make that worthwhile. On the other hand, it is claimed, we cannot, when property is despoiled, detect dogs and identify their owners at a sufficiently low cost to make it worthwhile.

Private-property rights in water are defined weakly, probably because of the problems of surveying and monitoring the water (underground reservoirs, for example). More extensive private-property rights in the more valuable commodity oil, however, have been defined, with more expensive methods of surveying, monitoring, and enforcing rights.

If an airport were to be used by noisy jet planes, the jet planes' owners could compensate the nearby landowners for the noise nuisance, so that the landowners would in effect be selling rights to particular uses of their land. It is interesting to note that this procedure is only rarely followed near airports. Instead, one of the following extremes is taken: (1) There is no compensation for the noise damage. (2) The planes are prohibited. (3) The neighboring land is bought and left empty as people are prohibited from living there—even though many would prefer to live there despite the noise, *if* they could buy the land at a low enough price and thereby be compensated for the noise. These extreme policies are based on an incorrect impression that it is impossible to buy the rights to "dump" noise on neighboring land.

A much more difficult problem arises from smog-producing chemical processes. Internal-combustion engines have smog-producing exhaust gases. To eliminate smog completely would require prohibition of gasoline engines; and the cost of that is higher than the gain from smog elimination. The other extreme is to permit unrestricted smog pollution by anyone. In between is some degree of legal restriction and incurring of costs to reduce smog. As yet, however, no one knows of a cheap enough, definable, and enforceable system of exchangeable private-property rights in clean air that would enable individuals to be protected from involuntary pollution of their air.

A capitalist system presupposes transferability and exclusivity of rights to physical use of human and nonhuman goods. When these rights do not prevail, the exchange system operates differently. Some other form of competition for determining uses of goods dominates. Examples are plentiful. (1) The Western states fight each other in the courts over use of water from various watersheds, but they don't fight about the use of forest timber, oil, iron ore, coal, or other "natural" resources—because rights to water are not transferable as they are for oil and lumber. Government agencies allocate water, whereas no agencies are required for wood or oil. (2) Traffic conditions on the public highways and behavior on public beaches are examples of "rights-claiming" competitive behavior with "fleeting, insecure, nonexchangeable" rights to land. (3) Sewage provides another example of unusual competition: cities upstream dump sewage, and cities downstream bear the consequences; so each city is tempted to build a pipeline farther upstream nearer the source to catch purer water. (4) Radio and television rights of use cannot be transferred at will by the "owner" of the station —even though he is protected by law from interferences of other radiation. This is a result not of the difficulty or cost of defining transferable property rights, but of a legislative or judical policy not to permit sale in the same way in which land can be sold. The Federal Communications Commission must authorize every proposed transfer of radio rights from one user to another, much as if an imaginary Federal Land Use Commission had to approve every sale of land to make sure the land was used in the "public" interest. Land, like television, would also be used in "strange" ways if it could not be rented or sold to other people for their different uses. In television, the station owner cannot sell his program to the *viewer*, but he can sell his program to an advertiser. This is purely a consequence of our laws, not of technology. The viewer cannot compete by exchange of private-property rights (i.e., market exchange) for what he would like to see, but the advertisers can compete about programs to be shown.

Consider how housing would be used if a similar situation were to exist there; one can imagine that an apartment-house owner would give away a jerry-built apartment house with small rooms whose wallpaper consisted of advertisements—not because he is commercially motivated or because advertisers have bad taste, but because alternative demands for the use of the good, whether it be land, houses, or television radiation, are *excluded* from competition. If some landowner were authorized to use his land for agricultural purpose and if it had a higher market value in urban uses, the existing landowner (if he were bound in the same way the television-station operator is by the Federal Communications Commission) could not sell or rent the land for urban uses. He would use the land in ways that the advertisers and regulatory board could determine. And if he were tempted to use the land in the "wrong" way (e.g., for growing watermelon, cantaloupes, raspberries, and other frivolous, low-nutrition goods), he would be threatened (like the television station that showed "too many" Westerns) with loss of his "license." Someone else who would promise to use the land in the "right" way would be given the license.

The more strongly exclusivity and transferability are enforced, the greater is the realizable market value of the good. The more surely a person can count on capturing the value of a good, the more surely he will use it in ways that reckon with its usefulness to other people who might buy the good from him. Definiteness of exclusivity and transferability of ownership provide incentives to use goods in ways that will take account of the highest use value and thereby enhance their marketable value. A good will have a higher market value if rights to its use are more exclusively centered in a definite owner rather than being left open to an indefinite set of users. The owner can control its uses so as to exclude from access to the good those who would use it in less valuable ways. But to do this he must have the right and incentive to respond to the highest bid value of competing uses.

The higher market value attaching to goods with strong ownership rights has provided an incentive for individuals to seek courts and laws that would strengthen or restructure use rights toward private-property rights. To do this, individuals have had to rely on the governments. However, not all jurists and politicians have viewed with uniform sympathy the tendency to seek private-property rights. To the extent that rights to uses of goods are reshaped into private-property rights, the power of the governments to control uses of goods decreases; for a major alternative to private property is public or government control of uses of goods. History is a long story of fluctuations and variations in this development. At times, private-property rights have become stronger; and at others they have been weakened and replaced by socialism, government ownership, or communal tribal ownership. We know of no provable generalizations suggesting that one form or the other will eventually dominate.

One confusion about the meaning and operation of a private-property system has arisen from the ways in which private-property rights are sometimes *created.* The way in which private-property rights are *created* is different from the way that system *operates* once it is in existence. An excellent example is provided by the Enclosure Movement in England about 500 years ago. Farmers had rights to *use* particular portions of land in common with other people. But no one had the right to sell (transfer) his right. If the rights had been legally salable, it would have paid a person to sell his use rights to the person who could make the most valuable use of the land. One would think that the law would have been modified, so that each holder of a right to use could be identified and allowed to sell his right to someone. If transferability by sale were authorized, all the former use-right holders would have been compensated for their rights. However, the common-use-right holders were not allowed to sell their rights; they simply were denied their use rights, and some lucky (politically powerful) person was declared to be in control of use and the salability of that right. This method of *creating* private property, of course, has no bearing on how the system will operate thereafter, but to the people of the time, the *operation* of a system of private property (capitalism) was identified with this particular method of *creation* of a system of property rights—expropriation of common-use rights. Tenants who lost their use rights regarded private property as theft.

Imagine how you as a student would feel if your rights to attend the university you now attend were simply revoked and given to new students, who in turn could resell those rights. You would feel cheated. But if your current "rights" to attend your university were converted to a "private-property" right that *you* could sell to other people, you would not lose anything. (Of course, the university administration would lose part of its rights to decide who came to school.

Hence, they are not likely to institute a system of "private-property admission rights.")

A more recent example of a similar process of shaping of private-property rights occurred in Ireland in the nineteenth century. A large number of Irish land tenants, with customary rights to use land but, again, without the right to sell those rights, were relieved of those rights without compensation. The rights were made salable thereafter by the owners. Little wonder that Irish land tenants regarded private property as evil.

A similar episode occurred in India after the English occupied the area. Seeking to establish a system of law along the lines of private property (in fact, thinking it already existed), the English sought to identify the owners of the various parcels of land. But after a few years they realized there were no owners in the private-property sense. In each area of land a host of people had various joint rights to use that land, and none of the rights were salable. Indian jurisprudence simply hadn't recognized the concept of private property in land. Unaware of this, the English, upon identifying the person with the principal rights in a piece of land, made him the owner in the sense of private property—to the consternation and resentment of the other people, whose use rights were extinguished. The creation of a system of private property had been attempted without compensation to those whose nontransferable use rights had been extinguished.

Currently in many of the less developed countries, land rights are being revised and redistributed in what are called land reforms. This usually means a new assignment of existing use rights to other people (but without rights to sell the newly acquired rights). This amounts to a reshuffling or redistribution of the existing use rights, rather than a reform of the structure of the property system. Recently in Iran, land-use rights were redistributed from big landholders to those with no land-use rights; but the *system* of property rights was left unchanged. Rights remained nontransferable by sale. In fact, they couldn't even be rented out. Mexico has also instituted what it calls land reform, and this has in many instances meant only a reassignment of *non*transferable rights. It has not involved a change to a new system of property ownership—i.e., private-property rights. In all these cases, holders of rights had these rights expropriated without compensation.

There was and is no necessity for those acquiring the private-property rights to have done so without compensating those whose rights were taken. Holders of preexisting customary rights could have been identified and paid for the loss of their rights. A restructuring of property rights, whether toward private property or socialism, does not require confiscation or injustice. Nevertheless, since the power to institute a new property system rests on political police power, the temptation to use that power to revise the property system without having to compensate former right holders is often overwhelming.

Most Americans are so accustomed to the idea of private property that we do not realize its rarity. Yet few places outside of Western Europe and the former English dominions have private-property rights in land as we know them in the United States.

External Benefits as Inducements to Use of Private Property

The term *private* property suggests that only private benefits to the owner of a good have any influence on his decisions about the use of privately owned goods. It is said that people act or use their goods with an eye to the benefits they get, not to benefits to other people. Yet, the way we use our resources very generally results in benefits for other people—called external benefits.

When you wear clean, good-looking clothes, or cultivate a pretty garden, or even read the kinds of books that I think you ought to read, my utility is increased. This kind of interdependence or external benefit was not ruled out in the preceding chapters; nor is it inconsistent with that analysis. Exchange, which is a use of goods, provides, as we saw, benefits to the other person, too. Still, there are actions you can take that would benefit other people, but which you do not take because they cannot or do not offer adequate inducements to you to take those actions.

Beneficial effects for other people that are *uninduced* by those beneficiaries are called non-induced external benefits. A non-induced external effect is one in which the owner of the good in question does not obtain a private benefit (i.e., increase in utility) as an incentive to produce that external benefit.

All exchange yields a benefit to some other "external" person, for one party obtains a private incentive (payment) to give up goods to the other party. The gains from exchange and specialization are induced "external" effects that have been induced by the reward of the quid-pro-quo exchange—a reward that is nothing more nor less than the market value of the service provided. The ability to sell or transfer the goods or their services means that other people can influence the use of goods, no matter who owns them. Potential external effects are not all left without influence on the decision about how goods shall be used. Every home owner takes into account the effect of his uses of his house on the sale value of the house. No man is an island; the use of his own marketable goods depends on the preferences and desires of other people. He can use the goods as he wishes, but he must reckon with the gains he otherwise could have. Sometimes this inducement feedback is called "internalizing the external effect." In essence, much of economic theory concerns the allocation of the uses of economic goods by internalizing external effects. However, it is relatively difficult to make the use of some kinds of goods respond to external effects.

The consequence of non-inducing external effects is not hard to discern.

Less of that kind of service or beneficial use of resources will occur than if somehow the owner could be induced by payments that reflected the value of benefits to other people.

OBSTACLES TO INDUCEMENT OF EXTERNAL BENEFITS

Why are some uses not inducible by ordinary market transactions?

Non-ownership. The services or goods may not be private property. Then no one has the authority to use resources in response to marketable inducements from other potential beneficiaries. We have already examined some examples: water, roads, national defense, and television programming. Why are private-property rights not sanctioned? Again, as suggested for some of these cases, the costs of enforcing exclusivity and transferability may be too high.

Public goods: nonexcludable beneficiaries. A technological feature of some goods sometimes adduced as a reason for not using private-property rights is *commonality of use* by several users at the same time, wherein the resources used to provide service for one beneficiary automatically provide services for other beneficiaries. For example, a public fireworks display at a Fourth of July celebration would benefit many viewers. An extra dollar's cost of display provides possibly 90 cents more utility to two persons, 80 cents more to another, and 40 cents more to another. The extra cost is $1; yet the sum of the independent marginal values is $3.[1]

The extra dollar of use is not worth that much to any one person; yet, because it provides utility to several people simultaneously the sum of the marginal values over all the beneficiaries exceeds the extra $1 of cost. Still, no one will offer to pay the $1, nor can any nonpaying beneficiary be excluded from benefit—if the service is provided.

Such at least is the case where the individual consumer is but one among many, and any contribution he may render covers only a small part of the total cost. Consider, for instance, such items as a flood control project, the more general benefits of which accrue to an entire region; a sanitary campaign that raises the general level of health throughout an area; expenditures for the judiciary system that secure internal safety and enforce contractual obligations; or protection against foreign aggression. All these contribute to the welfare of the whole community. The benefits resulting from such services accrue to all who live in the particular place or society where the services are rendered. Some may benefit more than others, but everyone knows that his benefit will be independent of his particular contribution. Hence, he cannot be relied upon to make a voluntary contribution. The government must step in, and compulsion is called for.[2]

[1] That $1 could be spent more in accord with one person's utility preferences and less in accord with another's. How the particular amount of resources should be used still poses a competitive problem of allocation, but the problem emphasized here is a different one.

[2] Richard A. Musgrave, *The Theory of Public Finance* (New York: McGraw-Hill Book Co., Inc., 1959), pp. 9–10.

We must, however, be careful. The single fact that several people benefit is not crucial. Nor, as we shall see, is government compulsion necessarily called for. At a theater, everyone pays; his contribution is only a small part of the total cost of the performance. Jointness of beneficiaries does not upset the ability of market exchange to get desired services performed to the extent desired. Clearly, commonality of benefits is not crucial. Flood-control projects, national defense, sanitary campaigns—all are identical with theatrical presentations and football games insofar as *commonality and simultaneity* of benefit is concerned. The crucial element is in the possibility (or costs) of *exclusion of nonpayers* from the right to receive the services. For some goods and services, they are "naturally" excluded; consumption of food by one person "naturally" excludes other people from consuming and thus eliminates the problem of nonpaying beneficiaries. For some kinds of goods the cost of excluding nonpayers is prohibitively expensive. If the costs of *collecting* individual admissions to a theater or football game were more than the value of the service to any spectator, there would be no economical way through voluntary arrangements to provide sufficient inducement for the service. Barring the possibility of economically collecting payments, as a condition of enjoying the services, the service will either not be provided in "optimal" amounts or will be free for some.

Examine the classic example—a lighthouse. All ships benefit from its existence. If the lighthouse builder were able to control the light rays so that any nonpaying shipowner could not see the light, beneficiaries could induce him to provide as much more of the service as it was worth. Barring this possibility, some shipowners will not voluntarily cooperate to pay for their value of service received. If they joined, they would have to pay a pro-rated share (say, $100) of the light they otherwise would get free (plus an amount—say, $10—to cover the cost of a larger light that they each might prefer). They would have to share payment for all the light ($110), but the worth of the additional light they get by cooperating is only the marginal increment ($10). As far as any one user is concerned, the choice is between paying the pro-rata share of the total cost of $110 to get a $10 marginal gain in value of light, or paying nothing and still getting some (or hoping others will provide) lighthouse services. Obviously, it will benefit him not to pay at all rather than pay $110 for $10 more light. And almost everyone will hope to get a "free ride"—which is better than paying the full cost of still better service. Normatively speaking, too few lighthouses would be built too late. The consequence arises from the "unwillingness" of the nonexcludable beneficiaries to induce the provider of the service to provide more.

The landlubber counterpart is television. If all who wanted the program were to pay the station, the program would be available, but no one person is willing to bear the full cost of an "optimum" amount of service if he can get some viewing for nothing. No one has to pay as a condition of getting the service. Each person holds back in the hope that someone else will act. In general, less of such "public-good" services will be made available the higher are the costs of getting the beneficiaries together, and of excluding nonpaying beneficiaries.

INCREASING THE INDUCEMENTS OF EXTERNAL BENEFITS

If there were a cheap way to exclude people from enjoyment of the service unless they paid—that is, if there were some way to identify the benefits of use by individuals—the external effects would be "internalized." As we have noted, it may not be desirable to internalize the benefits if the costs of doing so exceed the value of service. But there are some techniques for internalizing the effects without imposing excessive costs.

For example, a golf course may provide benefits to the neighboring property owners, who benefit without paying. A golf-course builder could handle this problem by buying enough land to build a course as well as the surrounding houses. Then when he sells the surrounding property, he captures the higher value stemming from proximity to the golf course. Those external benefits have been "internalized" as inducements to build the golf course.

Another example is provided by the apartment-house owner who includes maintenance of the gardens and exterior appearance of each apartment in the rental price, rather than having the tenant provide it. Similarly, the purchase price of a cemetery plot usually includes the costs of maintaining the cemetery rather than permitting each owner to choose the degree of maintenance—again, because of the neighborhood external effect.

A most important institution to "internalize or induce" external benefits is the partnership or corporation. These enable larger ventures to be undertaken so that more of the benefited resources can be owned by those who produce the benefits. If all the land of a suburban shopping center is owned by one enterprise, there can be a more complete response to the total effect of the shopping center on neighboring land values. A department store with all the departments in one building owned by one firm is another example of how the neighborhood effects of each department is "internalized" upon the others.

We can see that the extent of so-called "non-inducing" external benefits is not determined by "technological" conditions alone. The scope of uncaptured or non-inducing benefits is affected by the ownership arrangements, which are often adapted and modified so as to capture previously uncaptured benefits. People are ingenious. They invent decoders for television signals so that only those who pay can get a picture, or they use wire transmission so that only those who pay will get a picture. Fences are built around athletic arenas and high walls around theaters. Colleges keep out students by instructing professors to exclude nonpaying students. "Descramblers" for lighthouses, or fireworks displays, or for national defense, however, seem not to be economically feasible.

There remains still a normative issue of whether costs *should* be incurred to exclude potential beneficiaries. The issue can be explained with the example of pay television. *Once a signal is transmitted*, no one sees less if someone else also receives the signal. Excluding some potential viewers unless they pay can provoke under-utilization and waste of the provided service. However, if the television producer could charge each viewer a *different* fee for viewing rights and adjust that fee to each viewer's demand so that no potential viewers were excluded, no one would go without the right to receive the signal.

In defense of his "varying or discriminating fee" this pay-television owner could allege that he had a social conscience, because he was providing an "optimal" solution in that no one was being kept from viewing the shows—and no one, no matter how poor, "should" be refused the service, since *once the program is emitted* no one has to see less if someone else sees more.

Still another alternative to formal government exclusion of nonpayers is voluntary group action. The church is a prime example. In the United States, churches are not supported by taxes, although they are in some other countries (e.g., Scandinavia). In Scandinavian countries, the number of churches per person is lower than in areas with voluntary contributions to church support. Are there too many in one system or too few in the other? We cannot tell.

A business firm that relocates in a new area knows that it will provide a benefit to other firms that spring up in its neighborhood. Presumably, the initial firm would have to expect to capture the value of external benefits to other people in order for its decision to be influenced by those external effects. Yet, the owner may instead "bet" that while his action provides external benefits to other firms that locate near him, he will get reciprocal external effects from the new firms that spring up in the new location. An anticipated exchange of external effects is an inducement, even though a formal contractual exchange agreement is not involved.

Shopping districts spring up without formal advance contractual agreements among all who eventually open a business. Each businessman gambles on the mutual-benefit effect. A factory owner, when relocating his factory, "bets" that others will open nearby restaurants, apartments, housing tracts, and appurtenant services. House owners who cultivate gardens to beautify their homes "bet" that others will also do so with mutual external benefits. "Keeping up with the Joneses" is not always a silly social code.

Government Provision of Services

Government determination of provision of services, by tax and subsidy, sometimes reduces "contracting" costs by reducing costs of devices to exclude nonpayers. The cost of a descrambler or a high fence can be avoided if all beneficiaries are forced to pay; the police force performs the function of a descrambler or a fence, presumably at less cost. A major portion of governmental activity is exactly this kind of activity in which the external effects are expensive to capture as inducements under a private-property market system. Defense, highways, and education typically are considered to be in this class; and as can be seen from Tables 39–1 and 39–2, these constitute a major portion of government

Table 39–1

FEDERAL EXPENDITURES, TOTAL AND PER CAPITA, 1963

Purpose		Total (Billions)	Per Capita
National defense		$ 53	$280
Personnel	$13		
Operations	12		
Procurement	17		
Research and development	6		
Foreign military assistance	2		
Atomic energy	3		
Health, labor, welfare		26	140
OASDI	22		
Public assistance	3		
Other	1		
Interest		7	37
Agriculture		7	37
Veterans		6	31
Commerce and transportation		6	31
Space		3	16
Natural resources		2	10
International aid		2	10
General government		2	10
Education		1	5
Adjustments		—1	—
		$114	$607

SOURCE: U.S. Government Budget Message of President, January 1963.

expenditures at the federal, state, and local levels. National defense is primarily administered by the federal government while education and roads are primarily provided by the state and local governments. Per capita expenditures help give a sense of absolute magnitudes and are shown in Tables 39–1 and 39–2. State

Table 39–2

STATE AND LOCAL GOVERNMENT EXPENDITURES BY PURPOSES, 1962

Purpose	Total (Billions)	Per Capita
Education	$21.9	$117.0
Roads	10.3	55.6
Public assistance	5.1	27.4
Hospitals	3.7	20.0
Health	.7	3.7
Police	2.1	11.3
Fire	1.1	5.9
Sewage, sanitation	2.0	10.4
Parks, recreation	.9	4.7
Natural resources	1.4	7.4
Housing	1.1	5.9
Airports	.4	2.0
Water transportation	.2	1.5
Penal	.8	4.3
Libraries	.3	1.9
Employment assistance	.4	2.2
Administration	2.3	12.4
Interest	2.0	10.8
Liquor	1.0	5.4
Unemployment compensation	2.8	15.1
Utility expenditure	4.5	24.3
Other	3.0	16.0
	$68	$365

SOURCE: U.S. Department of Commerce, Bureau of Census, *Governmental Finances*, 1962.

and local expenditures are not uniform among the states; some states have per capita (state plus local) expenditures about twice as high as the overall average for all states, while some run to about half that level. Of course, the high state in any one category is not also the high state in every other category, although there is a strong consistency in relative ranking above or below the average.

GOVERNMENT RECEIPTS

Some summary information about taxes is shown in Tables 39–3 and 39–4. Table 39–3 presents the tax sources for the federal government, whose prime reliance is on the personal and corporation income tax, social security payroll taxes, and commodity and service taxes (called excise taxes).

Table 39–3

TOTAL FEDERAL TAX RECEIPTS, 1963
(In Billions of Dollars)

Source		Receipts
Personal income tax		$ 48.0
Corporation tax		22.0
Social security (OASDI)		18.0
Excises		14.7
Alcohol	3.5	
Gasoline, oil, diesel fuel	2.8	
Tobacco	2.1	
Auto and accessories	2.4	
Tariffs on imports	1.3	
Telephone	.9	
House appliances	.1	
Radio and television sets	.2	
Photographic equipment, Sporting goods, Firearms, Pens and pencils, Matches, electric light bulbs, Business equipment	.2	
Jewelry, Furs, Toilet preparations, Leather goods	.4	
Transportation tax	.2	
Sugar	.1	
Miscellaneous (all other)	.4	
Inheritance and gift tax		2.0
All other		4.5
	Total	$110.2

SOURCE: U.S. Government Budget Message of President, January 1964.

Table 39–4 shows, for the federal personal income tax, the total taxable income and income taxes paid in various income classes, along with the percentage of the taxable income that is taxed. The total taxable personal income shown at the bottom is about half of personal national income. The difference is explained by the fact that, in arriving at taxable income, personal national income is reduced by social security payments, income in kind and nonpecuniary imputed income, capital gains reported as income but not taxable, nonreporting of taxable income, income of nontaxable individuals, allowable deductions (e.g., contributions), personal exemptions, and miscellaneous minor items. Nearly two thirds of the difference is accounted for by personal exemptions, allowable deductions, nonreporting, and transfer payments. As seen from the percentage-of-income-taxed column, the percentage rises with income. The marginal tax rate—that is, the tax on each successive increment of taxable income—rises even more rapidly.

Table 39–4

DISTRIBUTION OF TAXABLE INCOME AND TAX BY TAXABLE INCOME CLASSES, 1963

(In Billions of Dollars)

Taxable Income Class	Total		Tax as Percent of Taxable Income	Cumulated from Bottom Class		
	Taxable Income	Tax		Taxable Income	Taxes	Percent of Total Tax
0 to $1,000	$ 76.7	$15.3	.20	$ 76.7	$15.3	.32
$1,000 to $2,000	52.7	10.5	.20	129.3	25.9	.54
$2,000 to $4,000	42.2	9.3	.22	171.6	35.2	.73
$4,000 to $6,000	13.2	3.4	.26	184.8	38.6	.81
$6,000 to $8,000	6.9	2.1	.30	191.7	40.7	.85
$8,000 to $10,000	3.9	1.3	.34	195.6	42.0	.88
$10,000 to $12,000	2.5	1.0	.38	198.2	43.0	.90
$12,000 to $14,000	1.9	.8	.43	200.0	43.8	.92
$14,000 to $16,000	1.4	.7	.47	201.5	44.5	.925
$16,000 to $18,000	1.1	.6	.50	202.6	45.0	.94
$18,000 to $20,000	.7	.4	.53	203.3	45.4	.95
$20,000 to $50,000	2.9	1.8	.62	206.2	47.2	.985
$50,000 to $100,000	.55	.44	.80	206.8	47.6	.995
$100,000 and over	.34	.31	.91	207.1	47.9	1.00
	$207.1	$47.9				

Thus, on the first $2,000 of taxable income, a person pays 20 percent in income taxes. Of the *next* $2,000 he pays 22 percent (plus the $400 he paid on the first $2,000). Of the $2,000 between $4,000 and $6,000 of taxable income he pays 26 percent (plus the $840 he must pay on the first $4,000). Table 39–4, taken from the 1963 income tax return form, shows the total amounts due and percentages on the successive income brackets for a single taxpayer.

The right side of Table 39–4 shows how much of the total federal income tax comes from the various income classes. Despite the rapidly increasing tax rate at higher incomes, only about 10 percent comes from people with more than $15,000 per person in taxable income (or $30,000 for married couples). If *all* the income of people receiving more than $30,000 per married couple were taxed, the total tax receipts would increase only about $3 billions, or about 6 percent more than is collected now (ignoring the inevitable effect on incentive to obtain income). If the minimum tax rate of 20 percent were raised to about 23 percent and kept constant over all income classes, the same amount of income tax would be collected (again ignoring incentive effects).

The corporation tax is 30 percent on the first $25,000 of net income and 52 percent on income over that amount.[3] Dividends paid are taxable under the personal income tax.

Payroll taxes of about $15 billions are collected under the Old Age, Survivors, and Disability Insurance system (OASDI). This tax rate is now about 8 percent (4 percent obtained from employer and 4 percent withheld from employee) of salary under $4,800 per year. By 1968 the total rate will be close to 10 percent.

Table 39–5 lists the primary tax sources of state and local governments by amounts. Variation among the state and local governments is substantial. Some states have no income taxes, while others have heavy ones. Similar variations exist for sales taxes. All, however, use the property tax extensively. The same generalization holds for local governments. Furthermore, both types of government are moving steadily toward greater reliance on income taxes, usually collected by the state and distributed to local governments.

To complete this analysis of government expenditures and receipts one should be able to show that taxes are levied consistently with the provision of services involving non-inducible external effects. But there is no known way to check this proposition. In the first place, taxes are not earmarked for the service they are to finance—except in rare cases. And if every tax were so identified, there would still be room for argument about whether the benefits received by each individual were in excess of the taxes paid for that activity. Claims and counterclaims about the benefits of more of each governmental activity certainly cannot be evaluated accurately enough to justify all expenditures. Finally, even if all of those obstacles could be overcome, there would still remain the fact

[3] See page 303 for some indication of the impact of this tax.

Table 39–5

STATE AND LOCAL GOVERNMENT RECEIPTS BY SOURCES, 1962

(In Billions of Dollars)

Source	Total
Individual income tax	$ 3.0
Corporation income	1.3
Sales taxes	13.5
Property tax	19.1
Fees, licenses	8.8
Utility revenue	4.1
Liquor store revenue	1.3
Unemployment compensation	2.8
Other, miscellaneous	5.1
Transfers from federal government	8.0
Increase in debt	6.0
	$73

SOURCE: U.S. Department of Commerce, Bureau of Census, *Governmental Finances*, October 1963.

that much government activity is not intended to provide non-induced external effects. Some is designed to serve a control function and some is designed to redistribute wealth.

Access to political power for influencing taxes, expenditures, and laws is not "ideal" or "perfect." In fact it is impossible even to define what is meant by an ideal system. Thus, we run the risk of confusing effects with purposes when we attempt to rationalize government activity on the grounds that government exists to provide uninduced external effects, to maintain law and order, to regulate the economic activity of people, and to redistribute the wealth.

It is about as meaningless to attempt to prescribe the proper scope of government activity as it is to prescribe proper mix of goods and activities provided by the capitalist system. In the case of government activity, we can only say what happens under different systems of competition for access to use of political power. And it isn't justifiable to say that the result is "right" (or, for that matter, "wrong") just because it is produced by the government or by the capitalist system.

EFFICIENCY OF GOVERNMENT SERVICES

Although the government can use its powers to ensure that more of certain services are provided, it cannot solve the problem of efficient production of those services. Socialists may have no qualms in decreeing how much of some good they think ought to be provided for society, but they have not solved the problem of devising an *incentive, reward, and control* system to induce public administrators to direct production efficiently. Under government ownership, the administrator does not lose wealth equivalent to the higher costs of more wasteful techniques nor is he responsible to any agent who does bear them. No system yet devised is as effective as private property in inducing the administrator to act in accord with those costs. This problem of making decisions respond to costs in the absence of private property is similar to the problem of converting external benefits into inducements guiding production in private-property sectors. Just as some external effects in a private-property economy are not fully reflected as inducements to direct resource uses, some external costs in socialist systems are not fully effective as inducements on the administrator.

In government operation, efficiency is not the sole criterion; capitalists who complain of inefficiency are using capitalistic standards in inappropriate places. Worrying about efficiency has been humorously compared with worrying about the cost of a plane ticket without first thinking about where one is going. Such comparisons are more misleading and obfuscating than informative. And it is equally obstructive to contend that those who deprecate the efficiency argument are interested only in the announced destination rather than in whether and how they will get there. However, we ought to undertand that all our choices between "this or that" depend upon *both* what the good is and upon how much it costs.

Redistribution of Wealth and Other Government Activities

Another important objective of government activity is a redistribution of wealth—usually imagined to be a redistribution from the richer to the poorer. Examples of redistributional activities are poor relief, unemployment payments, social security, farm subsidies and crop price supports, free public parks, public works, and free college education. Insofar as these activities are financed by taxing a higher proportion of larger incomes (progressive income taxes), they redistribute wealth from those who are earning more to those who are earning less. However, farm subsidies and crop price supports, free college education, free public parks, and government subsidies of the arts may in fact represent aid to the richer people. A strong argument can be made that government activity has redistributed wealth more to the rich than to the poor, particularly if one considers government restrictions on entry to many markets—the effect of which is to maintain higher prices for consumers and monopoly (type 1) rents for the favored groups. It is not incorrect to say that a major function of governments has been to redistribute wealth, especially to those with more access to political power from those with less. It is incorrect to say that government redistributive activity yields a more "equitable" distribution of wealth. It is not clear what is meant by more equitable, nor is it clear what the net effect of the redistributive activity has been.

Another role of government activity is that of preventing the use of the marketplace for providing certain kinds of services that consumers and producers could get in the market: gambling, drunkenness, prostitution, certain drugs, and low-quality foods. Any good that a majority deems it improper to obtain in the market may be banned—if the courts will interpret "immoral" broadly enough, as in other times and in some other countries.

Control of the money system and of some conditions pertinent to the level of employment are also objectives of much government action, as we have seen in Chapters 32–37.

These, then, are some of the actual roles of government: enforcement of a particular set of rules of competition for use of scarce resources; protection of selected groups from open-market competition; wealth redistribution among people; restriction of certain types of services that would otherwise be provided in an open market to willing consumers by willing producers; national defense; education and highways; and, more recently, exploration of space. Literally, there is no list of "proper" government activities. There is only a list of actual government activities. In the same way, there is no list of goods or activities that should properly be encompassed and controlled by private property.

In this chapter we have studied some reasons advanced for government provision of services akin to other services available in the market, and for government provision of services not available in that market system. Other economic facets of government activity, especially in a regulative capacity, have been investigated in other chapters; for example, we have already explored the creation of monopolies and restriction of sale of certain kinds of services. The role of government in controlling the money stock and in attempting to maintain high levels of employment was investigated in earlier chapters. Here we have presented a general rationalization of government activity in providing economic services. Conspicuously absent has been any extensive discussion of the proper kind of taxes that ought to be levied to support government activity (other than for external benefit). That would be like trying to tell people to spend more (or less) money on liquor, music, highways, clothing, or literature. There simply are no economic criteria of good or bad types of taxes—other than that the tax should not be expensive to administer, should not have unintended effects, should be equitable, and similar platitudes.

Questions

1. What is meant by an equality between private and social costs?

2. "Privately owned goods are those which a person has the right to use however he wishes." Explain why it is not necessary to add the clause "subject to not destroying other people's property." Explain why that first statement does not give an owner the right to hit you on the head with his hammer, or to dump his garbage on your property, or to disturb your home with loud noises.

3. The city of Palm Springs prohibits anyone from erecting a building whose shadow will fall on some other person's land between 9 A.M. and 3 P.M. Is that a restriction of private property or a strengthening of it? Explain.

4. A city passed a zoning ordinance prohibiting the owner of a large parcel of land from constructing homes on it because of a fear that the noise of a nearby airport owned by the city would be so disturbing to the new tenants that airport operations would have to be curtailed.

a. Whose rights were being curtailed by the zoning ordinance?

b. Under the definition of private-property rights, were the landowner's rights being taken from him?

c. Can you suggest some other solution to the problem?

d. If you were a taxpayer in that town and did not live near the airport, what solution would you have voted for?

e. If you owned vacant land near the airport, what solution would you advocate? If your vote is different in each case, do you think you are denying the morality of decisions by voting? Why?

5. "The city of Los Angeles is a classic example of the problem of balance between public and privately provided services. Magnificent factories and lavish numbers of automobiles—coupled with the absence of a municipal trash-collection service, which forced the use of home incinerators—made the air noxious." This close paraphrase of a writer on economic affairs is factually erroneous in that there was no absence of trash-collection services—just of a municipally owned one. Would that explain the use of incinerators by each household to burn trash?

6. "When property rights interfere with human rights, property rights have to give in." This statement is reported to have been made by a lieutenant governor of California. What do you think it means?

7. Shopping centers often provide free parking spaces. In effect, the shopping-center merchants provide free parking spaces for some nonshoppers so that their customers will find adequate space. Some observers allege that the number of parking spaces is excessive (that is, more resources go into the provision of parking space than should) where the space that "should" be available is the amount that would clear the market when a charge is levied to cover the construction and maintenance cost of the parking space. However, we should remember that policing "pay" parking spaces involves a cost of estimating charges, collecting fees, and prosecuting violators. Does the fact of that cost mean that it might be "better" to provide "too much" parking space than to provide the "right" amount with a price rationing system? Explain.

8. "National defense is shared by everyone. More of it for one person does not mean less for someone else. Therefore, it is a public good and should be provided via government taxes and operation."

a. Does greater anti-missile defense for New York City mean greater defense for Houston, Texas?

b. In a public concert, do more concerts on the west side of town mean more on the east side?

c. Does it follow that public goods—those that give benefits to several people without less to anyone else—really do not exist?

d. Do external benefits mean that more than one person benefits, or that a non-owner benefits, or that those who benefit do so without any less of the service to someone else?

9. If I don't reciprocate in social invitations with my friends, I find they stop inviting me to their social functions. If I am impolite to other people, they are impolite to me. Much of our social etiquette is a matter of formal, though nonmarket, exchange, with the exception that when I host a party I do not obtain a contract from my guests promising to invite me as a guest to one of their parties. Would it thereby follow that there are too few parties and too few guests invited? Why?

10. Are there any privately owned cities in the United States?

11. a. "Police activity is one kind that must be operated by the government." Do you agree? If so, how do you explain the fact that there are thousands of private policemen in London, and that many residential areas have private police service?

b. "Judicial activity is one kind of activity that must be handled by the government." Do you agree? If so, how do you explain the existence of private arbitration for adjudicating contract-term disputes between employees and employers?

c. "Lawmaking activity is one kind of activity that must be handled by the government." Do you agree? If so, then how do you explain the creation of labor and employee relations law by contract negotiation, custom and common-law development from precedents of arbitration, and social custom and enforcement via ostracism?

d. "Defense of the community is one kind of activity that must be handled by the government." Do you agree? If so, then how do you explain the existence of private armies in past history—armies used to defend cities and paid for by private citizens? How do you explain the papal army prior to the time of the papal state?

e. "There is no function that must be exclusively reserved to the government." Do you agree? If so, why? If not, which function refutes the assertion?

12. "The imbalance between governmentally and privately provided services is evidenced by the fact that the family that vacations in its air-conditioned, power-braked,

power-steered car passes through cities over dirty, badly paved congested streets, not to mention the billboards obstructing the beauties of the countryside. When the family picnics with excellent food provided by private business they must sit by a polluted stream and then spend the night in a public park that is a menace to health and morals and littered with decaying refuse. Private abundance and public poverty is a fact that assails every observant person. A plentiful supply of privately produced goods and a shortage of publicly provided services is inescapable testimony to the lack of a social balance between private and governmentally provided services."

Without trying to prove that there ought to be less or ought to be more governmentally provided services, tell why the arguments in the above close paraphrase taken from a popular book advocating more governmentally provided services are faulty and do not indicate anything at all about whether there is too little of governmentally provided services. (Hint: Note the use of the term "shortage"; what does it suggest? How are governmentally provided services rationed?)

13. "The fact that some airplanes collide is evidence that there is too little public provision of air traffic control." Evaluate. (Hint: What would it cost to avoid all risk of air collision?)

14. a. Non-inducible externalities are one reason for government economic activity. Free libraries are often justified on that ground. Look up the history of free libraries to see how they were started.

b. Subsidized education is also justified on that ground. Look up the early stages of subsidized or free education to see how it started.

c. Religion is not financed by government activity. Is that because it has no non-inducible external effects? Is there too little wealth devoted to religion? What evidence can you cite?

d. Name the top ten universities or colleges. How many of them are "private"? How do you explain that?

e. Do the preceding four problems imply that government does too much or too little in these areas?

15. "Social ostracism is a form of social control and is often a substitute for some government action." Evaluate.

16. If you use the proportion of government expenditures as a guide to the significance of government economic activity, you can be seriously misled. What types of government activity have a far greater impact than indicated by the costs of such activity?

17. If, in your state, it is proposed to make pay TV illegal, how would your wealth be affected if you were:

a. A movie-theater owner.

b. An advertising specialist.

c. A newspaper owner.

d. A retired person who watches television a lot?

e. In each case how would you vote?

f. Did you vote simply in accord with its effects on your wealth?

18. You are a judge in a court case in which Joe Sleepy is suing Bill Sellem for damages. Sellem has opened a supermarket next to Sleepy's house, and the bright lights and noise of cars on the adjacent parking lot are an annoyance to Sleepy.

a. Would you award damages to Sleepy?

b. Why?

19. A restaurant opens near an apartment. The cooking smells annoy the apartment tenants. The apartment owner sues for invasion of property rights.

a. You are on the jury. Would you find in favor of the restaurant or the apartment owner?

b. Would your decision depend upon whether or not the apartment owner lived in the affected apartments?

c. Do you know what decisions have actually been rendered in similar cases?

20. *A* owns a hillside lot with a beautiful view. *B*, owner of the lot just below, plants trees that grow up to 50 feet in height and block *A*'s view. *A* asks him to trim the tops. *B* refuses. *A* offers to pay for the trimming. *B* refuses. *A* offers $300 in addition. *B* refuses; *B* asks for $2,000. *A* sues for $5,000 damages to the marketable value of his property.

a. As the judge, how would you rule?

b. If, earlier, *A* had sued to force the person to trim the trees, how would you have ruled?

c. What will our courts really decide today in such suits?

21. *A* owns a home with a beautiful view of a park. The park owner announces he is going to convert it to a shopping plaza. *A* sues to prevent his doing so on the grounds it will destroy the view and reduce the value of *A*'s property. As the judge, how would you rule? Why?

22. *A* owns and lives in a home near an area in which it is announced a series of 20-story apartments will be built. This will have only trivial effect on a view, since the land is all flat. *A* sues to prevent the construction on the contention that it will create extra traffic hazards and congestion. In court, *A* proves to the judge's satisfaction that his allegation is correct. As the judge, how would you rule? Why?

23. In Mexico, landless people are invading large farms and settling on the land as "squatters." The government has not acted to maintain the property rights of existing owners. The new occupants are not claiming the right to sell the land to others. They claim only the right to the use and fruits of the land, called usufruct rights, which at law is the right to enjoy all the benefits of a thing without the right to sell it. Rights of usufruct often pass by inheritance or by occupancy.

a. What effect will this development have on the sale value of the land?

b. What effect will it have on the willingness of the owner to invest in the land?

c. If the usufruct rights and sale rights were assigned (owned) by the land owner, would that increase or decrease the incentive to invest in the land, as compared to separating those rights? Explain why.

24. You are asked by the government officials of a new "emerging" nation whether they should have private-property rights in land or whether only usufruct rights should be given to the occupants.

a. What would you recommend? Why?

b. You are then asked whether occupants should have the right to mortgage the land; some concern is expressed that the occupants might borrow against the land and then simply let the creditor have the land. What do you recommend and why?

c. Would you permit tenant farming—whereby the land is rented from the owner by a farmer? (If so, you are permitting absentee ownership, which is widely held in disrepute.)

25. "Property taxes are taxes on physical goods, but income taxes are taxes on people." Evaluate.

26. To subsidize the cultural arts, new taxes are proposed. It is proposed to levy taxes according to ability to pay. One group proposes to levy heavier taxes on rich people in an absolute sense, but to make the proportion of wealth taxed increase for the wealthier. Another group argues that such progressive or graduated rates is more than in accord with ability to pay, and advocates instead a constant proportional tax. Another group argues that even a constant proportion is too much and that it is more in accord with ability if the rich person just pays a greater absolute amount, although possibly a smaller proportion of his wealth. Another argues that old people should be taxed more heavily since they haven't so long to live and have more ability to pay taxes. What do you think is the meaning of ability to pay?

27. You are just married and you earn, let us happily imagine, $30,000 a year. You plan to build a $20,000 house.

a. Should you finance it out of this year's income as the house is built or should you borrow?

b. On the basis of what considerations did you decide to borrow, if that is what you decided?

c. Would that impose a burden on your children, who may have to pay off that debt if you die in the meantime?

d. Suppose a city wants some more roads. Should it borrow or pay for the roads out of currently collected taxes? Does this differ from question (a)?

e. If the city borrows, does this pass the cost on to the future generations?

f. Are future generations saddled with a burden they would not have if the taxes had been levied now?

28. The following is orthodox Chinese Communist (Marxist) economic doctrine: "The goal of socialist production is not profit but the satisfaction of social needs. Goods must be produced as long as they are needed by society, even if a loss is incurred. Not profits, but the calculation of assigned target goals and their fulfillment is the most important consideration. This follows from the Marxist-Leninist tenet that, contrary to capitalism

which seeks maximum profits, the objective of socialism is the maximum satisfaction of the material and cultural requirements of society. This fact gives the Communist Party, as representative of society, the right to determine society's requirements and what the economy should produce." However, in 1962 the Chinese Communists permitted some Chinese economists to publish the following ideas: "Profits should not be set against the goal of satisfying social needs. The profit level is the best measure of the effectiveness of management. This would mean that no enterprise would operate at a loss because the output would be curtailed unless the state valued its product sufficiently to raise its prices, and no enterprise would try to exceed the output plan at the expense of profits. There would be less need for political participation in enterprise management decisions, if prices were more realistic, in reflecting either market values or costs. The capitalist evil connotations of profits are not present in socialism, because under socialism profit takes on an entirely different character, where it is a good thing."

But still later in 1962, the Communist Party authorities reaffirmed their orthodox doctrine and did so both directly and by indirection with an attack on "revisionist" ideas as exemplified by Yugoslavia which has recently engaged in what the Chinese Communists regard as backsliding policies like adopting price reforms (i.e., permitting more prices to be set in the open market, decentralizing state enterprises and permitting more private property in farming and handicraft activities). In reaffirming their orthodox Marxist tenets, the Chinese Communists directed factory managers to adopt political and economic means to raise labor productivity and to overfulfill specified targets of gross value of outputs whenever possible.

In order to understand why the issues of "proper" pricing, the use of the market, and kinds of incentives are so crucial to the Communists, it is pertinent to understand the effects on the power position of the Communist Party politicians if the economists' 1962 proposal were adopted. What would those effects be? Explain why.

40

IMPORTS AND THE "GAIN FROM TRADE"

A large part of the first section of this book was devoted to the *bases* (or *prerequisites*) of mutually beneficial exchange, the *pattern* (or *direction*) of the trade, the *terms* on which the trade was conducted, and the *gain* from the trade. The discussion was couched in terms of *individuals*—the Cuban and the Hungarian. But to a very large extent, what was said about trade among individuals can be said also about trade among whole regions and nations.

Individuals, we concluded, can trade to their mutual advantage if they differ from each other in their (marginal) valuations of two or more commodities; each person gives (exports) articles which he values less than he values the things he acquires (imports); the terms of trade (the price of exports relative to the price of imports) will lie within limits, and the limits consist of the initial (pre-trade) respective personal (marginal) valuations of the two traders. Each person sacrifices the things he exports, but each values still higher the things he imports; so trade has allowed each person to move to a preferred consumption situation.

If we were to replace the names "Cuban" and "Hungarian" with "Cuba" and "Hungary" or "England" and "America," the same conclusions would hold. To be sure, some *additional* things should be said about international trade. Trade between *multi*-person economies presents issues of distribution of gains and costs not found in trade between *single*-person "economies": people in one country use the same monetary unit, whereas two currencies are involved in English-American trade; uncoordinated policies of autonomous governments, different financial institutions, different customs and laws all add complications to international trade. But basically the gains from productive specialization and from subsequent exchange are to be found in foreign trade as well as domestic. The gain from trade is the gain from trade, whether or not the traders reside in the same country. Only in an Alice-in-Wonderland world would one expect the principles of economics to be turned completely on its head at the national boundary; the boundary line does not in itself mysteriously vitiate the gain from trade, converting an activity which is useful and rational when conducted domestically into one which is hurtful and senseless when conducted internationally.

And yet, the community in general applauds domestic commerce but holds foreign trade suspect. At least, *imports* are suspect, if not condemned outright; *exports*, it is typically felt, are permissible and probably even to be encouraged; for they relieve the economy of "burdensome surpluses" and perhaps bring in gold. And, of course, nothing else is really quite as good as gold.[1]

Does the "gain from trade" really emanate most directly from *exports*? Is economic welfare actually enhanced if the outward flow of goods and services to the rest of the world is increased and the inward flow reduced? Economic well-being rests on the consumable and investable things that are possessed and can be utilized. One of our fundamental axioms has been that *more* (of desirable things) is *better* than less. How does foreign trade enable a community to obtain the most for its own use? Scarcely by giving to foreigners as much as possible of the fruits of domestic production and taking nothing in return. *Exports are a cost,* draining domestically produced output from the country; *the gain from trade stems from imports,* which add to the domestically available supply of goods and services.

If this is so, why export at all? Aside from sheer ignorance, on what ground can England, for example, adopt the slogan "Export or Die"? England bears the cost of exports in order to obtain imports—just as an individual is willing to hand over (export) a $10 bill in order to obtain (import) a sack of groceries, because he values the meat and potatoes more than the $10. But note that the gain from the transaction does not lie in paying out the $10; it lies in getting the merchandise. If the same sack of merchandise could be obtained for less than $10 or if $10 would fetch a bigger bundle of goods—that is, if the *price* of groceries were lower (or the "*terms of trade*" were better)—the gain from the transaction would be even greater.

The lower the price of things one buys, the better. A zero price—making

[1] Whatever the typical American attitudes toward international trade, (a) the United States—with exports and imports of goods and services at annual levels of around $30,000,000,000 and $25,000,000,000, respectively—is absolutely the biggest world trader by a large margin; and (b) foreign commerce represents a relatively modest proportion of its national income. Total United States trade (exports plus imports) approaches twice that of England and of West Germany, and it is roughly three times that of France and of Canada. However, the United States' average propensity to import (i.e., commodity imports relative to national income) is about .04, while it is .2 or greater (sometimes much greater) for many major commercial countries (e.g., Australia, Canada, Netherlands, Sweden, United Kingdom).

the "purchase" a "gift"—is best (assuming that we rule out negative prices, with the seller paying the buyer to take the stuff). But since the price of imports normally will be greater than zero, there is a limit to the amount of imports a country can "conveniently" *accept*—even if there is no limit in sight to the amount it *desires*. An individual can live too high off the hog and run into financial embarrassment; so can a country. As we shall see in more detail later, a nation that persists in "living far beyond its currently earned means" is courting a "balance-of-payments crisis."

Because imports normally are not free, we should modify our initial conclusion that imports are good, and the more imports the better: *imports are good and the more the better—to the extent that they can be "conveniently" financed.*

The Gold Bug, Foreign Aid, and National Income

A rather long period some centuries ago—from about 1500 to 1800—has been labeled the age of "mercantilism." Mercantilists, generally businessmen and government officials, were concerned with economic policies that might enhance the wealth and power of their respective emerging national states. Much of their attention was focused on foreign-trade policy, and they were motivated by fear of most imports and generally a passion for exports; for if the exports of goods and services exceeded the imports, the balance would be received in gold.

Despite their great attention to international commerce, the mercantilists failed to comprehend the economic rationale of international specialization of production and of free exchange. In short, they did not appreciate the real nature of the gain from trade, which was first clearly delineated by the "classical" economists, notably by David Ricardo in the early nineteenth century. However, many of them were not fools; and, in light of various conditions existing in their time, it is not strange that they came to their conclusions.

Especially conspicuous among the doctrines of modern (and ancient) mercantilists is the following: Foreign trade is suspect unless a country has an export surplus, and the major reason for an export surplus is to stimulate national income and employment. This was the most conspicuous and pervasive Congressional argument presented in support of the Reciprocal Trade Agreements Act in 1934 (and in the debates on the periodic extensions of the act); it has bulked large in debates on other measures of foreign economic policy, including the Marshall Plan in the late 1940s and the Trade Expansion Act of 1962, the successor of the Trade Agreements Act.[2]

[2] The Trade Agreements Act instituted a program of bilateral executive commercial agreements to achieve reciprocal reductions in tariff duties and amelioration of other trade restrictions. It was enacted "for the purpose of expanding foreign markets for the products of the United States," mainly in the interests of combating "the present economic depression." In order "that foreign markets will be made available," it was deemed necessary to afford

In order to put into reasonable perspective the mercantilistic proclivity for export balances in the interest of supporting national income, imagine that there evolved an unusual insect, which we shall call the gold bug. The gold bug has the ability and the desire to burrow into the vaults of Fort Knox, grasp a piece of gold, tunnel beneath the Atlantic Ocean, and leave the gold where it will be found by some European peasant.

The peasant is overjoyed, for he can get domestic currency—marks, francs, liras—from his monetary authorities in exchange for the gold.

The foreign monetary authorities are elated, for with gold they can acquire dollars from the United States Treasury, and with dollars they can buy American merchandise.

The Treasury presumably is delighted, for it has long stood ready to buy unlimited quantities of gold at a fixed price—and then put the gold into Fort Knox.

Finally, the American producers (and their employees) who now get purchase orders from abroad—orders which are paid in dollars—are highly pleased.

It appears that the antics of the gold bug have started a sequence of events in which everyone is happy. (Apparently no one pauses to wonder how a nation is enriched by transactions which, in the aggregate, involve giving up more goods and services than the nation receives in return.) There is, in fact, a circular flow of gold; but, since the gold bug's activity goes unnoted, there *seems* to be only a movement of gold into the United States, matched by United States exports of merchandise. No mercantilist could ask for anything more.

This supposedly happy process could continue indefinitely, as long as no one took an inventory at Fort Knox. Of course, if some snoop did check up (and people have been elected to Congress partly on the promise that they would audit our gold holdings) and find that the gold stock was not increasing as it should, there likely would be immediate and unbounded consternation in the United States—some of the nation's "wealth" had evaporated (or been stolen by the opposition party)!

If this gold-bug theory seems too farfetched to be enlightening, note that

---

"corresponding market opportunities for foreign products in the United States," but "the admission of foreign goods . . . [must be] in accordance with the characteristics and needs of various branches of American production."

The Trade Expansion Act broadens still further the authority of the President to enter into trade agreements, increasing the allowable percentage reductions in tariffs and permitting negotiated reductions by broad categories of goods rather than being restricted to item-by-item alterations. The act was largely a response to the European Common Market (the European Economic Community), which became effective January 1, 1958, and is intended progressively to eliminate trade barriers among the members (France, West Germany, Italy, Belgium, the Netherlands, and Luxembourg), while maintaining a common tariff vis-à-vis the rest of the world. In submitting the bill to Congress, President Kennedy contended: "Our bargaining authority" must be "increased in both flexibility and extent" in order "to empower our negotiators with sufficient authority to induce the EEC to grant wider access to our goods. . . ."

foreign aid achieves substantially the same results. With an American foreign-aid program, instead of obtaining dollars from selling gold-bug gold to the Treasury, foreign governments receive the dollars as a gift from the United States government—which can create as many dollars as it pleases (and sometimes more than is desirable). The American producers are just as happy to get these dollars for their merchandise as they were in the gold-bug case.

But while we all like to see American producers busy, for this maintains national income and employment, some are dubious about giving goods to foreigners. Perhaps we could have the best of all possible worlds (i.e., promote exports that foreigners never receive) if (1) the government, as under a foreign-aid program, creates dollars; (2) the government spends the dollars to buy domestically produced goods; (3) the goods, as before, are put on ships and set sail; and (4) the Air Force sinks the ships in mid-ocean. Not only can this achieve the economic objective of stimulating domestic employment, but in addition the Air Force gets some bombing practice.

However, eventually even some of the mercantilists may perceive that this is rather expensive target practice. Instead of "exporting" merchandise to the kingdom of Davy Jones, why not have it distributed in some way to American consumers? This does, indeed, appear reasonable. We thereby continue to maintain employment, but we avoid the waste of destroying goods.

Thus, *we have maintained employment without exports.* Full employment can be achieved through domestic (i.e., monetary and fiscal) measures, as we have previously discussed in some detail; we need not rely on foreign aid and trade policy to achieve that goal. Therefore, foreign economic policy well can, and clearly should, be determined on criteria other than probable repercussions (which in themselves might or might not be welcome) on domestic income and employment. In any case, foreign commercial policy as a means of attaining domestic, or internal, objectives is likely to be relatively ineffective; for some countries, including notably the United States, foreign transactions are a relatively small component of GNP and, by their nature, are not under the unilateral control of any one of the participating countries. Also, such use of commercial policy may well be disruptive of cordial international relations; attempts by one country to grab a bigger share of the current world-trade total by subsidizing exports and curtailing imports may inspire retaliation and then counter-retaliation. That foreign economic policy should be determined in its own right rather than employed as a tool of domestic income stabilization is the positive conclusion of our line of thought.

On the other hand, we should emphasize two points that are *not* implied by our analysis. First, we are not implying that foreign economic aid is inevitably useless or undesirable. To pass judgment on this issue requires consideration of many elements not included in this discussion. But we do conclude that the aid program is unnecessary for the specific purpose of keeping United States income high. Second, and even more fundamental, we certainly are not suggesting that there are no gains to be derived from international trade. But, contrary to the mercantilists, dead and alive, the gains from trade do not stem from a persistent export surplus.

International Payments and Exchange Arbitrage

The purpose of including here a brief discussion of some mechanics of "international finance" is not to explain how to run the foreign-exchange department of a New York bank. Rather, surveying in general how international payments are made and how rates of exchange are "equalized" through arbitrage will help understanding of other important matters: the determination of exchange rates, the balance of payments, and even international-trade theory.

MAKING INTERNATIONAL PAYMENTS

The most conspicuous problem associated with making international payments stems from the existence of more than one currency. When an American sells goods to an Englishman, the American normally wishes to receive payment in the form of dollars, while it serves the convenience of the Englishman to make payment in pounds sterling. It is feasible for the buyer to pay one currency and the seller to obtain another through the intermediary of foreign-exchange dealers —banks holding inventories of foreign monies, who are willing to buy and sell one kind of currency against another. The "conversion of currencies" is the primary function of the foreign-exchange market.

Foreign-exchange dealers simultaneously provide a "credit" function. Not only does the exporter in an international transaction wish to receive payment in a currency different from that in which the importer wishes to remit, but he may want the payment immediately, while the importer may want to delay at least until the goods are received and sometimes for several additional months. Both parties can be satisfied if a foreign-exchange dealer takes over the exporter's claim on the importer, reimbursing the former right away and extending a loan to—and receiving interest from—the latter.

Suppose that International Harvester, an American firm, contracts to sell a tractor to an Englishman for $2,100, and suppose further that International Harvester prefers to receive immediate payment while the buyer desires ninety-day credit. The exporter wants *dollars immediately*, and the importer wants to pay *pounds later*. We can trace the financing procedure with the help of Figure 40–1.

The exporter sends the tractor to a shipping firm. Among the various documents involved is a *bill of lading* (B/L), drawn by the shipping company and given to International Harvester as a receipt and serving also as a claim to the tractor when presented by a *bona fide* holder (step 1). As the goods are sent on their way, International Harvester draws a "draft" on the importer. The draft—otherwise known as a *bill of exchange* (B/E)—is a written order by International Harvester, directing the importer to pay a certain sum (in pounds) in ninety days to an appropriate third party. (An ordinary check used in domestic commerce, also being an order to pay, is a form of bill of exchange.) The number of pounds equivalent to $2,100 is determined by the rate of exchange, or exchange rate. An *exchange rate* is the price of one currency in terms of another. If, for example, $3 = £1 (or £.333 = $1), then $2,100 is equal to £700. The face value of the draft includes the interest to be paid on the ninety-day loan.

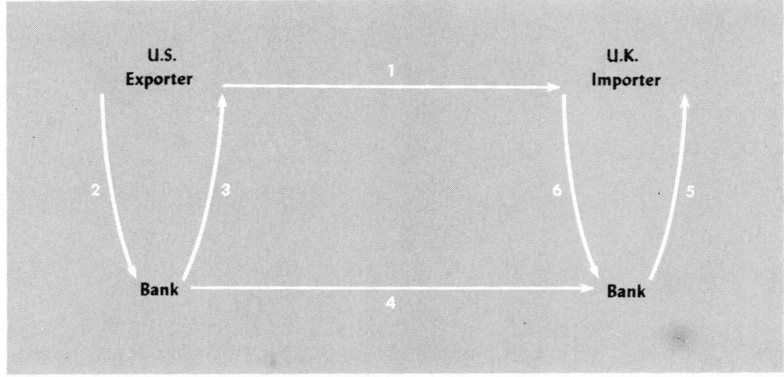

FIGURE 40–1. Financing an export.

International Harvester does not send the "order to pay" directly to the Englishman. Instead, it takes the B/E, along with the B/L and other attached documents, to a New York bank (step 2). International Harvester "discounts" the B/E at the bank; that is, it sells the draft to the bank for the face value minus the interest to be accumulated. The draft itself is denominated in pounds, but International Harvester receives dollars (step 3). In the normal course of events, this is the end of the transaction for International Harvester: it has produced, sold, and shipped a tractor and received immediate payment in dollars.

The U.S. bank that purchased the draft on the Englishman does not collect from him directly. Instead, it works through an English bank, which may be a branch of the U.S. institution or a "correspondent" bank with which the American bank has a working arrangement. The draft and documents are sent to the U.K. bank (step 4), which presents the B/L to the importer after the importer "accepts" the draft—that is, acknowledges his indebtedness by signing the draft (step 5). With the B/L thus acquired, the importer can go to the dock and claim the tractor. At the time of maturity of the draft, the importer pays pounds to the U.K. bank (step 6).

The pounds paid by the importer belong to the U.S. bank, which owned the draft on the importer, and are put in a demand deposit held by the U.S. bank in the English institution. The U.S. economy (through International Harvester) *supplied* a tractor to the rest of the world (and International Harvester was rewarded with dollars); the U.S. economy (through the New York bank) *received* a checking account in an English bank. Thus, the U.S. has *exported merchandise* and *imported a claim* on foreign goods and services.

The tractor transaction could be financed in an alternative manner. Instead of International Harvester's drawing a sterling draft and discounting it with a U.S. bank, the draft could be drawn in dollars and sent directly to the importer. The importer then must acquire dollars in order to meet his obligation. He does so by buying dollars from a U.K. bank holding a demand deposit in a U.S. bank. The importer pays pounds to his bank and acquires command of dollars; these dollars are then paid to International Harvester; and, of course, the U.K.-owned demand deposit in the U.S. bank is thereby reduced. In this case, the *U.S. merchandise export* is paid for—not by the U.S.'s importing a claim on England, but by *reduction of a U.K. claim on the U.S.*

Whether the U.S. export is financed by increasing U.S. claims on foreigners or by decreasing foreign claims on the U.S., the U.S. has supplied merchandise "on credit." The U.S. has *not* received goods and services or gold in return, nor has the U.S. given away the merchandise; the economy per se (not International Harvester) must, therefore, have granted a loan; that is, there was a "capital movement" from the U.S. to the U.K.

EXCHANGE ARBITRAGE

In the foregoing illustration, International Harvester received dollars, and the importer paid pounds. With two currencies involved, obviously a "link" or an "equivalence" must exist between them—namely, the rate of exchange. We assumed that $3 = £1. Is this the ratio of exchange between dollars and pounds in the New York or the London foreign-exchange market? Both. As a result of a market procedure or operation known as "arbitrage," the New York dollar price of the pound becomes 3, and simultaneously the London pound price of the dollar is ⅓. As the expression goes, the New York and London rates on the respective foreign currencies are "consistent"; that is, 3 and ⅓ are reciprocals.

Suppose that in fact there is a discrepancy in the rates, as indicated:

In New York: $3.00 = £1 or $1.00 = £.333
In London: $2.97 = £1 or $1.00 = £.337

With two prices existing for the same article, your instinct tells you that there surely must be a way to cash in, if you are not legally prevented from buying and selling as you please in foreign-exchange markets. But what to buy and what to sell?

Perhaps you do not require a college course in economics to appreciate the profit-making possibilities of buying low and selling high. An American arbitrageur may think: the New York dollar price of the pound is greater than the London price; put a bit differently, *given* the fact that the actual price of $1 in London is £.337, the dollar price of the pound *should* be $2.97, but actually in New York it is $3. However recognized, the fact is that the *New York dollar price of the pound is too high.* Also, *given* the fact that $1 = £.333 in New York, the price of the pound in London *should* be $3; so the actual *London dollar price of the pound* ($2.97) *is too low.*

Similarly, an Englishman investigating the domestic-currency (pound) price of foreign money (dollars) concludes that the *London pound price of the dollar is too high* (£.337 instead of £.333), and the *New York pound price of the dollar is too low* (£.333 instead of £.337).

Both the American and the Englishman capitalize on the inconsistent rates by *selling pounds and buying dollars in New York* and simultaneously *buying pounds and selling dollars in London.* The American, starting with dollars, can buy £1,000 in London for an outlay of $2,970 while selling £1,000 in New York for receipts of $3,000, netting a profit of $30. The Englishman, with pounds at his disposal, can pay £1,000 for $3,000 in New York while selling $3,000 in London for £1,010.1, yielding a gain of £10.1.

But the arbitrage activity itself tends to alter exchange rates in such fashion as to eliminate the basis of further arbitrage. In New York, the increased supply of pounds (demand for dollars) lowers (raises) the price of pounds (dollars) in terms of dollars (pounds); and in London, the increased supply of dollars lowers the value of the dollar, and the increased demand for pounds raises the value of the pound. With high prices falling and low prices rising, the price discrepancies are eliminated. The final result might be about $2.99 = £1 (or $1 = £.334) in both New York and London.

Arbitrage can involve more than two currencies. We can introduce the French franc. If $2.99 = £1 and, say, $.20 = fr1 (or $1 = fr5), then the equivalent, or consistent, cross rate between the pound and the franc is £.334 = fr5 (i.e., £1 = fr14.97 or £.0668 = fr1), for both £.334 and fr5 equal $1. If, for example, the actual rate were £1 = fr16 (instead of £1 = fr14.97), the pound would be at a "premium" in terms of francs, and the franc would be at a "discount" relative to pounds—opening the possibility of an American's using dollars first to acquire pounds and then sell the pounds against francs and, finally, convert the francs into dollars, ending with more than the original number of dollars.

As in the two-currency case, the triangular movement out of dollars into pounds, then into francs, and finally back into dollars tends to bring all three rates into alignment with each other. The increased supply of dollars against pounds (i.e., the increased dollar demand for pounds) operates to raise the dollar price of the pound (lower the pound price of the dollar); similarly, the pound price of the franc rises (the franc price of the pound falls), and the franc price of the dollar rises (the dollar price of the franc falls).

With *consistent* cross rates, then, \$1 multiplied by the pound price of the dollars (i.e., the number of pounds per dollar, which we can indicate by £/\$) yields the quantity of pounds attainable for \$1; that quantity of pounds multiplied by the franc price of the pound (fr/£) gives the quantity of francs attainable; and that quantity of francs multiplied by the dollar price of the franc gives the quantity of dollars—in this case, \$1—attainable, which is also the quantity of dollars with which we started. Thus:

$$\$1 \times £/\$ \times fr/£ \times \$/fr = \$1.$$

We can summarize in another way, using the consistent cross rates of an earlier illustration:

$$\$1 = £.334$$
$$£1 = fr14.97$$
$$fr1 = \$.20$$

Since these cross rates are consistent, the product of the three right-hand terms is unity:

$$.334 \times 14.97 \times .2 = 1.$$

Questions

1. On the basis of the analysis of this chapter, evaluate and compare the following statements on the immediate source of the "gain from trade" by an eighteenth-century economist and by a nineteenth-century economist:

". . . foreign trade . . . carries out that surplus part of the produce of their land and labour for which there is no demand among them, and brings back in return for it something else for which there is a demand. It gives a value to their superfluities, by exchanging them for something else, which may satisfy a part of their wants, and increase their enjoyments."—Adam Smith, *An Inquiry into the Nature and Causes of the Wealth of Nations* (1776), ed. E. Cannan (New York: Random House, Inc., 1937), p. 415.

"The only direct advantage of foreign commerce consists in the imports. A country obtains things which it either could not have produced at all, or which it must have produced at a greater expense. . . . Adam Smith's theory . . . was that it afforded an outlet for the surplus produce of a country. . . . The expression, surplus produce, seems to imply that a country is under some kind of necessity of producing the corn or cloth which it exports; so that the portion which it does not itself consume, if not wanted and consumed elsewhere, would either be produced in sheer waste, or if it were not produced, the corresponding portion of capital would remain idle. . . . Exportation ceasing, importation to an equal value would cease also, and all that part of the income of the country which had been expended in imported commodities, would be ready to expend itself on the same things produced at home, or on others instead of them."—John Stuart Mill, *Principles of Political Economy* (1848), ed. W. J. Ashley (London and New York: Longmans, Green & Co., 1929), p. 578.

2. "If imports are really desirable and exports are really a cost, it would seem ideal to have a situation in which we exported nothing at all and the rest of the world flooded us with their own goods and services." Do you accept this?

3. "The theory of international trade tells us that *imports* are good and the more the better. But typical international financial and commercial policy consists in trying to promote *exports* and perhaps discourage imports. Obviously, since we cannot have an import balance and an export balance at the same time, trade theory and economic foreign policy are in conflict. Perhaps the theory is bad or perhaps the policy makers have not taken a course in economics." On the basis of your study thus far, do you agree that there exists an irreconcilable dichotomy between theory and policy?

4. "Exports are an 'injection' into the domestic income stream, along with investment and government spending. Imports are a 'leakage' out of the income stream, along with saving and taxes. Since a bigger national income is preferable to a smaller, it follows that exports should be larger than imports." Right?

5. Review how "the foreign-exchange market" makes the following possible.

   a. An international seller of merchandise is paid in one currency while the buyer makes payment in a different currency.

   b. The seller receives payment immediately while the buyer makes payment at the end of a credit period.

6. Suppose that the rate of exchange between currencies X and Y is $1X = 2Y$, and between currencies X and Z it is $.25X = 1Z$.

   a. What is the consistent cross rate between Y and Z?

   b. Suppose that you own some of currency X and that the actual cross rate is now $1Y = 3Z$. As an arbitrageur, what currencies would you buy and sell in sequence?

   c. In light of arbitrage activity, specify carefully what happens to the demand for and supply of each currency.

   d. In what directions do the three sets of exchange rates move?

41

INTERNATIONAL TRADE THEORY: COMPARATIVE ADVANTAGE

Two Countries and Two Commodities

Suppose that the world contains only two countries, the U.S. and the U.K., and only two commodities, hats and coats. Each country has its own monetary unit in terms of which prices are stated: the dollar and the pound sterling in the U.S. and the U.K., respectively.

"EQUAL" ADVANTAGE

Consider the prices of the two commodities in the two countries, as given in Table 41–1. Given this price information, our initial question is: Does the situation present a basis for *mutually beneficial, two-way* trade? Is it feasible for the U.S. to undersell the U.K. in one commodity (and thus be able to export it) and for the U.K. to undersell the U.S. in the other?

Table 41–1

EQUAL PRICE RATIOS

	U.S.	U.K.
Hats	\$ 5	£2
Coats	\$10	£4

Is a price of \$5 for a hat more or less than a price of £2? Obviously, we must have a rate of exchange between the two currencies, so that we can convert the U.K. pound price of hats into dollar terms—or convert the U.S. dollar price of hats into pounds. If the exchange rate is \$2.50 = £1, the dollar equivalent of £2 is \$5, and hats would be of the same price in both countries. At any higher dollar price of the pound (e.g., \$3 =

£1), the U.K. price of hats would be the equivalent of more than $5; and, in the absence of trade barriers, the U.S. could export hats to the U.K. And if the rate on the pound is less than $2.50, the U.K. could undersell the U.S. in hats.

It happens—since the ratio 5/2 equals the ratio 10/4—that we have precisely the same results with respect to coats: the U.S. will export coats if the dollar price of the pound is more than 2.5, and it will import coats if the price is less.

It follows that the total situation of Table 41–1 does not allow *two*-way trade. For any exchange rate that allows the U.S. to export hats (e.g., $3 = £1 or $1 = £.333) will also allow the U.S. to export coats; and any rate leading the U.S. to import either commodity (e.g., $2 = £1 or $1 = £.5) will mean importing the other as well.

Now, *one*-way trade, with one country exporting both commodities and the other importing both, is possible. If, for example, the U.S. is the exporting country, U.S. banks (exchange dealers) can build up demand deposits in English banks or U.K. deposits in American banks can be depleted, as we illustrated earlier in discussing the making of international payments. But as U.S. banks continue to pile up their inventory of pounds in English banks, they will be willing to buy still more pounds only at a lower price; that is, they will give fewer dollars to U.S. exporters for a given pound draft; the exchange rate thus changes, with the dollar price of the pound falling. And as the dollar inventory of U.K. banks is persistently reduced, they will charge U.K. importers higher and higher pound prices for a dollar. Pressure on the exchange rate will continue until the rate reaches $2.50 = £1 (i.e., $1 = £.4). But at that rate, hats will be equally priced in both countries, as will coats; then there is no basis for even one-way trade. Similarly, if initially the dollar price of the pound is less than 2.5, the U.S. will import both commodities, and the dollar rate on the pound will be bid up to 2.5.

We may conclude that *when the price ratios are equal*—5/2 = 10/4 or, alternatively, 5/10 = 2/4—*there is no basis for two-way trade* or even, in a foreign-exchange market in which rates are free to move, for prolonged one-way trade. Any exchange rate which permits any trade will induce *one*-way trade, and such trade puts pressure on the exchange rate, tending to move it to a value which eliminates the basis of all trade.[1]

[1] The foregoing discussion assumes that the rate is free to move. But the pressure on the rate through changes in exchange dealers' inventories may be obviated for a time through gold movements and other pegging devices. Under either the "classic" (pre-1914) gold standard or the post-World War II International Monetary Fund, a "par" rate of exchange is defined on the basis of the prices of gold in the respective currencies.

If, for example, the dollar price of gold is $30 per ounce and the pound price is £10 per ounce, then $30 = £10, or $3 = £1. It might cost 2 cents to ship between the U.S. and the U.K. the amount of gold that sells for £1 (i.e., 1/10 ounce). Therefore, if the rate in the foreign-exchange market moves to $2.98 = £1, an English importer is indifferent between buying dollars directly, obtaining $2.98 for £1, and buying gold for £1 in the U.K., selling it for $3 in the U.S., and paying 2 cents in shipping costs. The dollar price of the pound

"COMPARATIVE" ADVANTAGE

In Table 41–2, the U.K. price of coats is £8, rather than £4, as in Table 41–1. The *ratios* now are *different*—$5/2 \neq 10/8$, and $5/10 \neq 2/8$; consequently, there should exist the possibility of *two-way trade to the advantage of each country*. This is directly analogous to saying, in earlier discussions, that there is a basis for mutually beneficial exchange between the Cuban and the Hungarian when their subjective valuations between hats and coats differ.

Table 41–2

UNEQUAL PRICE RATIOS

	U.S.	U.K.
Hats	$ 5	£2
Coats	$10	£8

As before, we must have an exchange rate in order to make the U.S. and U.K. prices comparable. If the rate is $5 = £2 (i.e., $2.5 = £1), neither country can undersell the other in hats; if the rate is $10 = £8 (i.e., $1.25 = £1), coats will have the same price in both countries. These two rates—$2.5 = £1 and $1.25 = £1—are the outside limits; if the actual rate falls within these limits (i.e., if the dollar price of the pound is less than 2.5 and more than 1.25), we can have two-way trade. For illustration, suppose that the rate is $2 = £1 (or $1 = £.5). We can then convert all prices of Table 41–2 into either dollars or pounds, as seen in Table 41–3. Stated in terms of either currency, hats are cheaper in the U.K., and coats are cheaper in the U.S. Therefore, the U.S. will

---

would not fall below 2.98, for, with the option of shipping gold to the U.S., the Englishman (or anyone with pounds) would not accept less than $2.98 for £1. Thus $2.98 = £1 is the U.K. "gold export point" (and the U.S. gold import point); similarly, $3.02 = £1 is the upper dollar price of the pound and is known as the U.K. gold import, or U.S. gold export, point.

The situation is analogous under the I.M.F., except that gold may (and does) flow before the market exchange rate hits the specified limits. If, in our illustration of a U.K. import balance from the U.S., English exchange dealers begin to run short of dollars, they can replenish their inventories by buying dollars with pounds from the Bank of England. If the Bank, in turn, is short of dollars, it can purchase more with gold sold in the U.S. Finally, if the Bank runs short of both dollars and gold, it may be able to purchase (borrow) dollars with pounds at the I.M.F.

While the exchange rate may be pegged for a time at a level which allows the trade imbalance to persist, there are limits on the necessary "ammunition"—foreign exchange, gold, and borrowing power. As we shall see later, if the ammunition lasts long enough, the trade imbalance may be eliminated by means other than a change in the exchange rate.

produce coats, consume some of them, and export the remainder in return for some English hats; and the U.K. will specialize in hats, export some of its output, and import U.S. coats.

Table 41–3

COMPARABLE DOLLAR AND POUND PRICES

	Dollar Prices		Pound Prices	
	U.S.	U.K.	U.S.	U.K.
Hats	$ 5	$ 4	£2.5	£2
Coats	$10	$16	£5	£8

In what sense are both the U.S. and the U.K. better off as a result of the specialization and exchange? The most obvious answer is that buyers prefer a lower price to a higher price: Americans prefer to buy hats at $4 (the U.K. price) to buying at $5 (the U.S. price), and Englishmen prefer paying only £5 for a coat (the U.S. price) to £8 (the U.K. price).

In the U.S., before foreign trade with the U.K. began, both hats and coats were produced, because there was a demand to consume both. What was the market-exchange ratio between hats and coats? With hats priced at $5 and coats at $10, two hats had the same market value as one coat: $2h = 1c$. Similarly, in the U.K., four hats at £2 equaled one coat at £8: $4h = 1c$.

Money may always be used in the buying and selling of hats and coats, rather than bartering hats directly against coats, but the purchase of a coat in, say, the U.S. requires an expenditure which, as an alternative, could have bought two hats. The consumer has foregone the potential buying of two hats in order to acquire the coat. Thus, even in a money economy, it is meaningful to say that the hat price of a coat was 2, and the coat price of a hat was .5.

Now, an American can say: I would be better off if, with foreign trade, I could buy a coat for anything less than the equivalent of two hats or sell a coat for more than two hats, or if I could buy a hat at a price of less than .5 coats or sell a hat at more than .5 coats. And an Englishman would be pleased to be able to buy a coat for a sacrifice of less than four hats or give up a coat in exchange for more than four hats, or buy a hat at less than .25 coats or sell a hat at more than .25 coats. These alternatives, in terms of hat prices of coats, are summarized in Table 41–4.

Asterisks indicate the feasible foreign-trade combination: the U.S. wishes to import hats and export coats if the terms of trade are anything *more* than *two* hats for one coat, and the U.K. is willing to export hats for coats if the terms

Table 41–4

INTERNATIONAL BUYING AND SELLING PRICES

	U.S.	U.K.
Domestically (in the absence of foreign trade):	$2h = 1c$	$4h = 1c$
With foreign trade, import hats and export coats if:	$(2+)h = 1c$*	$(4+)h = 1c$
With foreign trade, import coats and export hats if:	$(2-)h = 1c$	$(4-)h = 1c$*

are such that she must yield anything *less* than *four* hats in exchange for a coat.

An individual, then, gains from foreign trade, for with foreign trade he can acquire the import commodity at a lower price (in terms of the export commodity), or sell the export commodity at a higher price (in terms of the import commodity) than would be possible with only domestic trade. In short, with appropriate international production specialization, the terms of international trade are better for residents of both countries than the respective domestic exchange ratios before foreign trade commenced.

We can put the matter in terms of the economy per se. The $2h = 1c$ domestic *exchange* ratio in the U.S. prior to foreign trade is a reflection, we may suppose, of a $2h = 1c$ (marginal) *production* ratio. That is, a given bundle of resources could produce $2h$ *or* $1c$. The economy can produce an additional $2h$ by putting a minimum additional quantity of resources into the hat industry. Assuming full employment of resources, these additional resources would have to be transferred out of the coat industry. And, in this illustration, the amount of resources required to expand hat output by two units would have produced one unit of coats. The coat *cost* of $2h$ is 1, just as is the coat *price* of $2h$.[2]

[2] Strictly, we should say that the *exchange* ratio equals the *production* (or *physical transformation*) ratio in *long-run, competitive equilibrium.* To envisage the market mechanism by which the exchange ratio is equated with the production ratio, suppose initially that the trading ratio differs from the technological ratio of $2h = 1c$: perhaps in the marketplace, trades are taking place at a ratio of $3h = 1c$. In such a case, what wise entrepreneur would use his resources to produce hats? The market is "undervaluing" hats and "overvaluing" coats; the enterpreneur can devote himself to producing coats (at a cost of foregoing *two* hats for each coat produced) and then swapping the coats for hats (obtaining *three* hats for each coat sold). But as this realization spreads through the economy, more and more resources are drawn out of the hat industry into the coat industry, and the ever growing supply of coats and demand for hats reduces the hat price of coats (raises the coat price of hats) until the equilibrium rate of $2h = 1c$ is attained.

Suppose that the terms of international trade are $3.5h = 1c$. Therefore, the U.S. can sacrifice (export) $1c$ and obtain (import) $3.5h$, whereas without foreign trade the sacrifice of $1c$ (by shifting resources from coat production to hat production) would have yielded only $2h$. The U.S. thus can obtain hats more cheaply in real terms by specializing her production in coats and then trading some coats for hats than by producing hats directly with her own resources. Similarly, the U.K. can import $1c$ by exporting only $3.5h$, whereas by domestic production alone one more coat would have meant a cost of $4h$.

With foreign trade, each country obtains more for a given cost, or, alternatively, each obtains a given bundle of commodities for a smaller cost. As long as aggregate resources of an economy are constant and employment is full, the maximum "production possibilities" are unchanged, and, in the absence of foreign trade, the "consumption boundary" is the same as the "production boundary"; but the introduction of foreign trade, in a situation of comparative advantage, extends the consumption boundary. With given resources, more goods and services are available with foreign trade than without foreign trade. That is the "gain from trade."

A bit more should be said about the *terms* of trade. We have seen that the terms of international trade must (if there is to be two-way trade) lie within the limits consisting of the respective domestic-exchange ratios: $2h = 1c$ (the U.S. ratio), and $4h = 1c$ (the U.K. ratio). Also, we have seen that the rate of exchange must lie within limits consisting of the ratios of dollar and pound prices of the respective commodities: \$2.5 = £1 (the hat ratio), and \$1.25 = £1 (the coat ratio). We can relate the terms of trade and the exchange rate, since knowledge (or assumption) of one value implies a necessary value of the other.

Assume arbitrarily, as we did before, that the exchange rate is \$2 = £1. As seen in Table 41–3, the equivalent dollar price of U.K. hats is \$4. How many hats at \$4 each are required to equal in value one coat at \$10? Answer: $2\frac{1}{2}h = 1c$—which, of course, falls within the limits of the terms of trade.

Alternatively, given the terms of trade, we can deduce the exchange rate. If the terms of trade are $2\frac{1}{2}h = 1c$ and if the price of a coat is \$10, it follows that the hat price is \$4, for \$4 × 2½ = \$10; and if the price of hats in the U.K. is £2, then the exchange rate is \$4 = £2, or \$2 = £1.

Finally, we may underscore the meaning of such a statement as "The U.S. specializes its production in, and exports, coats, because it is more efficient in coat production, and similarly the U.K. is better in hat production." How are we to interpret "efficient" and "better"? In physical (technological) input-output terms, is the U.S. "absolutely" superior to the U.K. in producing coats? That is, with given real inputs (labor and other resources), can the U.S. produce more coats than can the U.K.? With just the information given, we cannot tell. Table 41–3 gives only the *money* prices of outputs. We can tell the exchange ratio in the U.S. in the absence of foreign trade; for example, the *hat* price of one coat is 2. But neither the *money* price of a coat nor the *hat* price of a coat tells us whether the *input* price of a U.S. coat is more or less than the quantity of resources required to produce a coat in the U.K.

The U.S. may be physically superior in producing both commodities; it may be inferior in both; it may be superior in coat production and inferior in hat production.[3] It does not matter for present purposes. For two-way, mutually beneficial trade, it is necessary only that domestic exchange ratios in the countries be different. *Comparative,* not *absolute,* advantage is the great principle.

Three Countries and Three Commodities

Obviously, a two-country, two-commodity model is a very simple schema. The world economy consists actually of dozens of countries and hundreds of commodities. We can illustrate this more involved case by introducing a third country and a third commodity, the price data being given in Table 41–5. However, although the expanded model adds to the complexity and cumbersomeness of manipulation, the same sort of analysis as in the foregoing discussion is useful, and the basic results are essentially the same.

Table 41–5

THREE COUNTRIES AND THREE COMMODITIES

	U.S.	U.K.	France
Hats	$ 5	£2	fr30
Coats	$10	£8	fr90
Shoes	$15	£10	fr120

The money-price ratios differ and imply the differing exchange ratios:

in the U.S.:

$$1h = .5c = .333s$$
$$1c = 2h = .667s$$
$$1s = 3h = 1.5c$$

in the U.K.:

$$1h = .25c = .2s$$
$$1c = 4h = .8s$$
$$1s = 5h = 1.25c$$

in France:

$$1h = .333c = .25s$$
$$1c = 3h = .75s$$
$$1s = 4h = 1.333c$$

[3] But it may *not* be inferior in coat production and superior in hat production.

As we have seen, if *the* ratios (expressed as either price ratios or exchange ratios) differ, there is a basis for trade. But who trades what?

The U.S. is the cheapest producer of coats *in terms of the other two commodities;* i.e., both the hat price and the shoe price of a coat are lower in the U.S. than in the U.K. or in France. Similarly, the U.K. is cheapest in hats. However, with these data, we cannot say that France is cheapest in shoes: the French hat price of shoes is lower than in the U.K. but higher than in the U.S., and the French coat price of shoes is lower than in the U.S. but higher than in the U.K. Still, it is possible to have triangular trade, with the U.S. exporting coats, the U.K. exporting hats, and France exporting shoes.

Whether such a trade pattern develops and what the terms of such trade would be will depend upon the set of exchange rates relating the dollar, the pound, and the franc. As in our simpler case, there are limits within which the rate between any two currencies must lie. These limits are equal to the ratios of respective domestic prices for different goods. We want *two* limits—upper and lower; but there are *three* commodities. Between the dollar and the pound, we have the ratios 5/2 ($2.5 = £1), 10/8 ($1.25 = £1), and 15/10 ($1.5 = £1). Which two constitute the limits? We can eliminate the last, for shoes will not be traded between the U.S. and the U.K.: both countries are importers of shoes from France. Therefore, the dollar-pound rate must fall within the limits

$2.50 = £1 or $1 = £.4
$1.25 = £1 or $1 = £.8

Similarly, the dollar-franc rate is limited by the price ratios for coats and shoes, which are traded between the two countries—not by the price ratio of hats, which are imported by both from a third country. The limits, then, are

$.111 = fr1 or $1 = fr9
$.125 = fr1 or $1 = fr8

And the pound-franc limits, determined by the hat and shoe relative prices, are

fr15 = £1 or fr1 = £.067
fr12 = £1 or fr1 = £.083

In our earlier discussion of exchange arbitrage, it was concluded that we can arrange exchange rates in the form

$1 = £?
£1 = fr?
fr1 = $?

and, with consistent cross rates, the product of the three right-hand terms is unity. To insert the limits deduced in the present illustration:

$1 = £.4–.8
£1 = fr12–15
fr1 = $.111–.125

Therefore, in equilibrium, we must (a) have a pound price of the dollar between .4 and .8, a franc price of the pound between 12 and 15, and a dollar price of the franc between .111 and .125, such that (b) multiplying the three prices together will yield unity. If both conditions are met, each country will export one commodity.[4]

One possible set of exchange rates is:

$1 = £.65
£1 = fr13
fr1 = $.118

All three rates fall within the acceptable limits, and, furthermore, .65 × 13 × .118 = 1. Therefore, we should have triangular trade, with the U.S. exporting coats, the U.K. exporting hats, and France exporting shoes. This is confirmed when we put all prices in terms of dollars, as in Table 41–6. The pattern of trade is illustrated in Figure 41–1.

Table 41–6

DOLLAR EQUIVALENT PRICES

	U.S.	U.K.	France
Hats	$ 5	$ 3.08	$ 3.54
Coats	$10	$12.31	$10.62
Shoes	$15	$15.38	$14.16

[4] A word of caution: Sometimes condition (b) can be met without satisfying condition (a). To illustrate, suppose that we assume two exchange rates, $1 = £.7 and £1 = fr14, both of which are within the indicated limits. The consistent cross rate between the franc and the dollar is readily calculated: .7 × 14 × $/fr = 1, and, therefore, $\$/\text{fr} = \frac{1}{.7 \times 14} = .102$; that is, fr1 = $.102. However, fr1 = $.102 lies outside the limits: this dollar price of the franc is too low, for (.7 × 14) is too large. The consequence of this consistent but too low dollar price of the franc is that France will undersell the U.S. in coats as well as export shoes, the dollar-equivalent prices of the various commodities in the three countries being:

	U.S.	U.K.	France
Hats	$5	$2.86	$3.06
Coats	$10	$11.43	$9.18
Shoes	$15	$14.29	$12.24

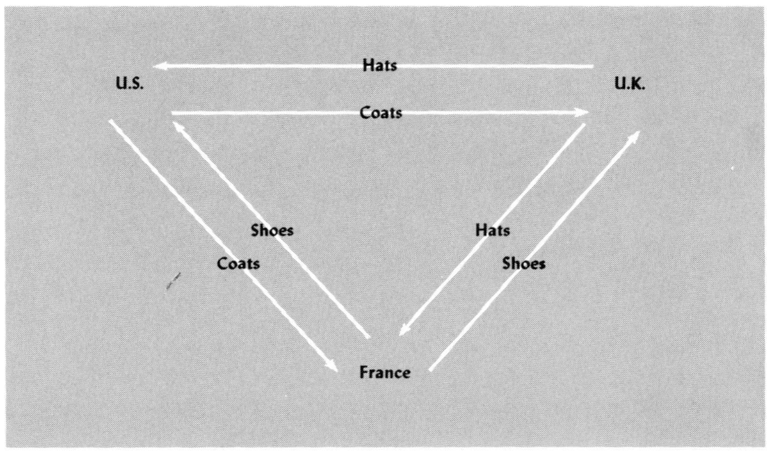

FIGURE 41–1. Triangular trade.

Each country, then, can import two of the three commodities more cheaply than those commodities could be purchased at home. For example, the U.S. can buy hats from the U.K. at \$3.08, compared to a domestic price of \$5; and the U.S. can buy shoes from France at \$14.16, compared to \$15 at home. This is tantamount to saying that the terms of international trade for these goods are better than the domestic exchange ratios. Domestically, the U.S. would obtain only two hats for the sacrifice of one coat, but through foreign trade the U.S. can import 3.24 ($= 10/3.08$) hats for each coat exported; and whereas in domestic trade $1c = .67s$, internationally, $1c = .71s$. As the reader can readily verify with his own calculations, the U.K. and France gain in similar fashion.

Questions

1. Assume the following price data in the U.S. and the U.K. in their respective domestic currencies:

	U.K.	U.S.
Shoes	£5	\$15
Coats	£4	\$ 6

a. In general terms, what is the evidence that there exists a basis for mutually beneficial, two-way trade?

b. The U.S. has a comparative advantage in which commodity? Which commodity will the U.K. export?

c. Define "rate of exchange." In this example, what are the limits to the possible rates of exchange which would provide a basis for long-run trade?

d. Define "terms of trade." What are the limits to the possible terms of trade in this illustration?

e. What relation do the terms of trade have to the concept of "opportunity (or alternative) cost"? What is the opportunity (alternative) cost of imports?

f. If the exchange rate is \$2 = £1, what are the terms of trade?

g. If the terms of trade are $2c = 1s$, what is the exchange rate?

2. You are given the following price information:

	U.S.	U.K.	France
Hats	\$ 6	£4	fr80
Coats	\$ 8	£8	fr120
Shoes	\$12	£16	fr200

a. What are the limits of the dollar-franc, dollar-pound, and franc-pound exchange rates?

b. If \$1.25 = £1, give a possible set of dollar-franc and franc-pound rates which are consistent and will permit each country to export one commodity.

c. Given the foregoing data and your calculations, what commodity does the U.S. export? What commodity does the U.K. export? Does the U.S. "gain" from its foreign trade? In what sense? What is your evidence?

3. We have discussed situations of two-countries-and-two-commodities and three-countries-and-three-commodities. Now consider the case of more commodities than countries, with the set of prices being:

	U.S.	U.K.
Hats	\$ 5	£2
Coats	\$10	£8
Shoes	\$15	£10

a. In the absence of foreign trade, what are the equilibrium hat-coat, hat-shoe, and coat-shoe exchange values (ratios) in the U.S.? In the U.K.?

b. Measuring the cost (price) of one commodity in terms of the others, which country is the cheapest producer of coats? Of hats? Of shoes?

c. If now foreign trade is introduced—with each country exporting at least one commodity and importing at least one—what is the pattern of trade (i.e., what does each country import and export)? Is there more than one possible pattern of trade?

d. In order that each country export at least one commodity, what are the upper and lower limits to the dollar-pound exchange rate? In order that each export only one commodity (thereby omitting the third commodity from international trade), what must be the exchange rate?

e. If the exchange rate is \$2 = £1, what are the hat-coat, hat-shoe, and coat-shoe terms of trade?

f. If the hat-coat terms of trade is $3.6h = 1c$ (or $1h = .278c$), what is the exchange rate?

4. "Nothing useful can be deduced about patterns of production specialization and exchange or the gains from trade or the terms of trade from only price data—especially price data expressed in different national currencies. Money prices are not sufficient. We must have information on *physical* input-output relations." If that statement is correct, this chapter has been a big mistake. Salvage the chapter.

42

RECIPROCAL DEMAND, THE TARIFF, AND RESOURCE ALLOCATION

We have seen that both the exchange rate and the terms of trade must lie within limits if two-way trade is to prevail. We have seen further that if either the exchange rate or the terms of trade are given, the other is implied. But we have not yet discussed the actual determination of these ratios. *Why* are the exchange rate and the terms of trade what they are? What is the *equilibrium* exchange rate, and the corresponding terms of trade?

Reciprocal Demand

With the aid of a particular assumption, our answer to these questions centers on "reciprocal demand." The assumption is that nothing enters into the (two-way) trade other than hats and coats: there are no transactions in other commodities or in services or in gold or in I.O.U.'s (capital movements); and there are no international gifts (unilateral transfers). In such a case, the value of U.S. coat exports equals the value of U.K. hat exports; that is, each country has "balanced" trade.

To continue the illustration of the preceding chapter, the U.S. and the U.K. prices for hats and coats are given in Table 42–1:

Table 42–1

UNEQUAL PRICE RATIOS

	U.S.	U.K.
Hats	\$ 5	£2
Coats	\$10	£8

Since these prices are given without reference to quantities produced or sold, it is implied that they hold for all quantities. Since, for example, the price of a U.S. coat is \$10 irrespective of quantity, the *supply* curve of U.S. coats would be a horizontal line at a price level of $10.

But Table 42–1 gives no information on the U.S. and U.K. *demand* schedules for hats and coats. Since we are analyzing international trade, and since the U.S. is importing hats and the U.K. is importing coats, we wish to know the U.S. demand for hats and the U.K. demand for coats. Assume that they are as given in Tables 42–2a and 42–2b:

Table 42–2a

U.S. HAT DEMAND

Dollar Price	U.S. Quantity Demanded
6	0
5	1,000
4	2,000
3	3,000
2	4,000
1	5,000
0	6,000

Table 42–2b

U.K. COAT DEMAND

Pound Price	U.K. Quantity Demanded
10	0
9	200
8	400
7	600
6	800
5	1,000
4	1,200
3	1,400
2	1,600
1	1,800
0	2,000

In the absence of foreign trade, the U.S. price of hats is $5, at which price 1,000 hats are bought and sold; in the U.K., 400 coats at £8 are exchanged. The U.S. will import British hats at a price of less than $5, and the U.K. will import American coats at a price below £8. As we have seen, the dollar equivalent of the U.K. £2 price of hats is $5 if the exchange rate is $2.50 = £1, and the hat price will be less than $5 if the dollar rate on the pound is less than 2.5. If $2 = £1, the price to Americans of U.K. hats is $4; if $1.50 = £1, the price of hats is $3. Similarly, U.S. coats will have a pound-equivalent price of £8 if $1.25 = £1, and the price will be less than £8 if the dollar price of the pound is more than $1.25.

This is illustrated in Figures 42–1a and 42–1b. In Figure 42–1a, the commodity, quantities of which are measured horizontally, is hats; the price per unit, measured vertically, is in dollars; the U.S. demand schedule of Table 42–2a is plotted, with the segment between the limiting exchange rates of $2.50 = £1 and $1.25 = £1 being an *import* demand schedule; and selected alternative U.K. supply curves are drawn, each reflecting a unique exchange rate. Figure 42–1b is similarly constructed, the commodity being coats, the prices expressed in pounds, with the U.K. demand and alternative U.S. supplies at different exchange rates.

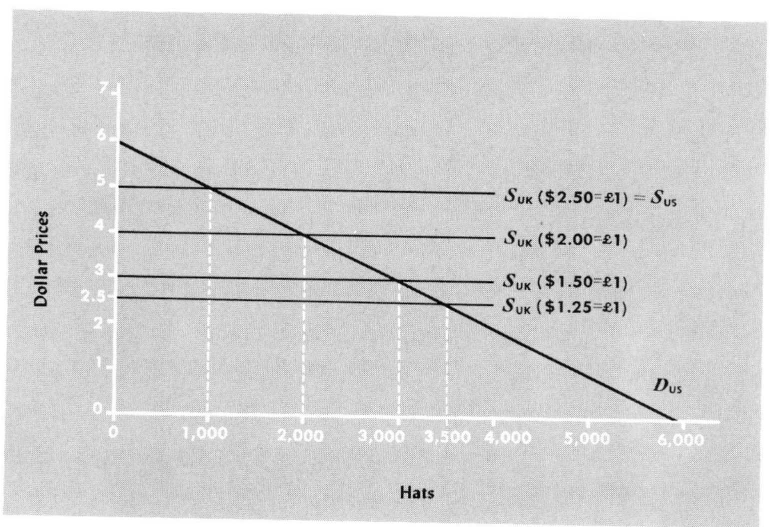

FIGURE 42–1a. Hats: U.S. demand and U.K. supply.

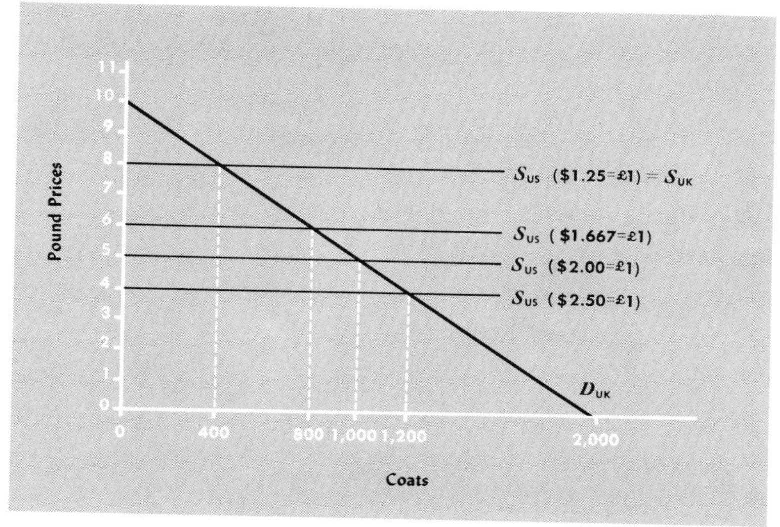

FIGURE 42–1b. Coats: U.K. demand and U.S. supply.

Consider now the calculations in Tables 42–3a and 42–3b. Each country is both a supplier and a demander internationally: the U.S. demands (imports) hats and supplies (exports) coats, and the U.K. demands coats and supplies hats. Columns 1 and 2 of Table 42–3a repeat the U.S. demand schedule from Table 42–2a. Column 3 is simply price multiplied by quantity (i.e., column 1 times column 2); the total expenditure (as well as data in columns 4, 6, 7, and 8) is calculated only for prices \$5 through \$2.50, for this is the import-price range delimited by the set of possible exchange rates. The dollar price of the pound (column 4) is the dollar price of hats divided by 2, the pound price of hats; for example, since hats sell in the U.K. for £2, the equivalent dollar price can be \$5 only if \$2.50 = £1. So much for U.S. hat demand, giving quantities demanded and dollar expenditure at alternative dollar prices of hats and corresponding exchange rates.

The U.S. supply price for coats is \$10 per unit for any number of units (column 5). Since we have assumed that import value always equals export value, column 6 (dollar receipts from export of hats) is identical with column 3. Column 7 is calculated from columns 5 and 6; e.g., if receipts total \$5,000 and the price per unit is \$10, then 5,000/10 = 500 units must have been sold. Finally, we have the terms of trade (column 8) expressed as hat quantity (column 2) divided by coat quantity (column 7).

Table 42–3b is prepared in exactly the same manner. Only column 4 calls for comment: we know that the U.S. price of coats is \$10; if the U.K. price is, say, £8, it follows that the exchange rate is 10/8 = \$1.25 per pound.

At the equilibrium terms of trade, the market is cleared: quantity demanded equals quantity supplied. Quantities of what? We can express the analysis in terms of hats or in terms of coats. As indicated by single asterisks in Tables 42–3a and 42–3b (for the moment, ignore the double asterisk in Table 42–3a), the equilibrium terms of trade are 2.823 hats = 1 coat: at those terms, the quantity of coats (870.6) demanded by the U.K. equals the quantity supplied by the U.S., and the quantity of hats (2,458) demanded by the U.S. equals the quantity supplied by the U.K.

It is useful to present the tabular data of Tables 42–3a and 42–3b in a diagram. In Figure 42–2, we have plotted the arithmetic data. Note that *quantities of commodities* are measured on the axes: hats (the U.K. export and U.S. import commodity) are measured vertically, and coats (the U.S. export and U.K. import commodity) are measured horizontally. Exchange ratios between the commodities thus are indicated by the slope of a line drawn through the origin: the steeper the slope, the greater the ratio of hats to coats (and the smaller the ratio of coats to hats). The two dotted lines radiating out of the origin are the limits to the hat-coat ratio: $4h = 1c$ and $2h = 1c$; the terms of international trade must lie within those respective domestic-exchange ratios. The U.S. reciprocal-demand curve (which is the U.S. demand for hats and also supply of coats) at first follows the U.S. domestic-ratio line of $2h = 1c$ and then bends upward and

Table 42–3a

U.S. HAT DEMAND, COAT SUPPLY, THE EXCHANGE RATE, AND THE TERMS OF TRADE

HATS				COATS			
U.S. $ Demand Price	Quantity Demanded	U.S. $ Import Expenditure: (1) × (2)	Exchange Rate: $\frac{\$}{£} = \frac{\$\text{ Demand Price}}{2}$	U.S. $ Supply Price	U.S. $ Export Receipts	Quantity Exported: (6) ÷ (5)	Terms of Trade: Hats/Coats: (2) ÷ (7)
(1)	(2)	(3)	(4)	(5)	(6)	(7)	(8)
6	0	—	—	10	—	—	—
5.5	500	—	—	10	—	—	—
5	1,000	5,000	2.500	10	5,000	500	2.000
4.5	1,500	6,750	2.250	10	6,750	675	2.222
4.2475	1,752.5	7,443.744	2.124	10	7,443.744	744.374	2.354**
4	2,000	8,000	2.000	10	8,000	800	2.500
3.542	2,458	8,706.236	1.771	10	8,706.236	870.624	2.823*
3.5	2,500	8,750	1.750	10	8,750	875	2.857
3	3,000	9,000	1.500	10	9,000	900	3.333
2.5	3,500	8,750	1.250	10	8,750	875	4.000
2	4,000	—	—	10	—	—	—
1.5	4,500	—	—	10	—	—	—
1	5,000	—	—	10	—	—	—
.5	5,500	—	—	10	—	—	—
0	6,000	—	—	10	—	—	—

Table 42–3b

U.K. COAT DEMAND, HAT SUPPLY, THE EXCHANGE RATE, AND THE TERMS OF TRADE

COATS				HATS			
U.K. £ Demand Price	Quantity Demanded	U.S. £ Import Expenditure: (1) × (2)	Exchange Rate: $\frac{\$}{£} = \frac{10}{£\text{ Demand Price}}$	U.K. £ Supply Price	U.K. £ Export Receipts	Quantity Exported: (6) ÷ (5)	Terms of Trade: Hats/Coats: (7) ÷ (2)
(1)	(2)	(3)	(4)	(5)	(6)	(7)	(8)
10	0	—	—	2	—	—	—
9	200	—	—	2	—	—	—
8	400	3,200	1.250	2	3,200	1,600	4.000
7	600	4,200	1.429	2	4,200	2,100	3.500
6	800	4,800	1.667	2	4,800	2,400	3.000
5.6469	870.62	4,916.304	1.771	2	4,916.304	2,458.152	2.823*
5	1,000	5,000	2.000	2	5,000	2,500	2.500
4	1,200	4,800	2.500	2	4,800	2,400	2.000
3	1,400	—	—	2	—	—	—
2	1,600	—	—	2	—	—	—
1	1,800	—	—	2	—	—	—
0	2,000	—	—	2	—	—	—

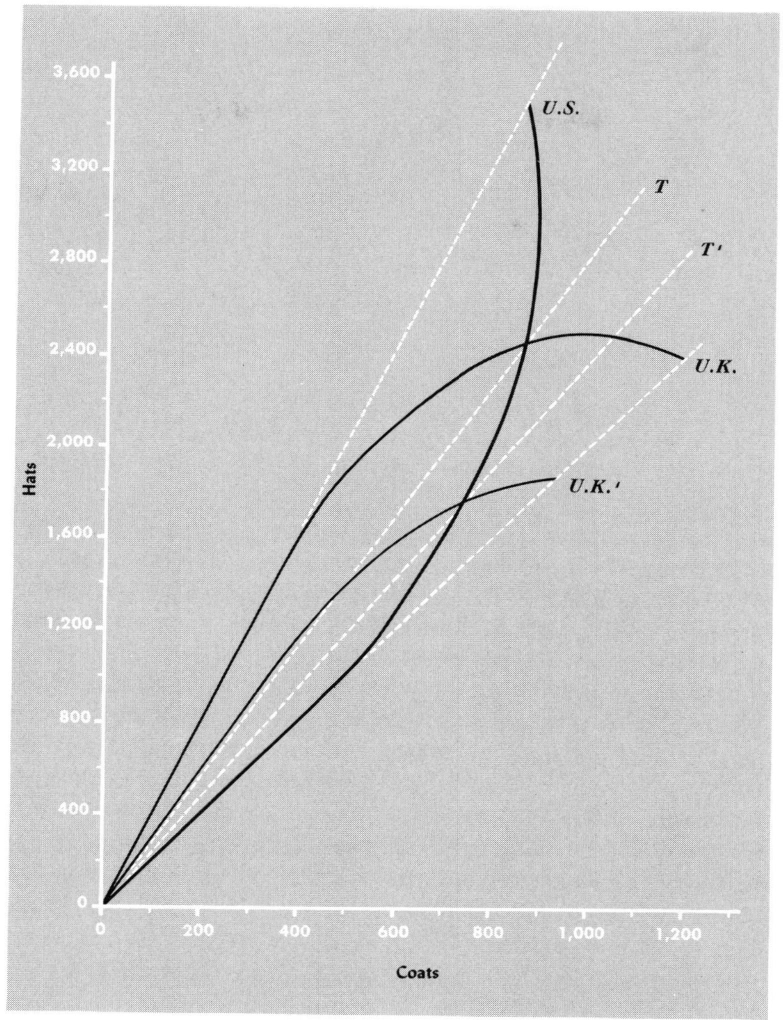

FIGURE 42–2. Reciprocal demand and the terms of trade.

finally back toward the left; that is, as the coat price of hats falls, the quantity of hats demanded increases, and the coat expenditure on hats first increases and then decreases. (Can you translate this into terms of *elasticity*?) The U.K. curve (U.K. demand for coats and supply of hats) sweeps upward and then down to the right in an inverted U-shape. Where the two curves cross, the terms-of-trade line ($0T$) has a slope of 2.823—i.e., $2.823h = 1c$; and quantity demanded equals quantity supplied of both hats and coats.

Suppose that one of the reciprocal-demand curves shifts—for instance, the

U.K. curve "falls" to U.K.′ With curve U.K.′, at any given terms of trade, England is demanding fewer coats and supplying fewer hats than she was with the original U.K. curve. The point of intersection of U.S. and U.K.′ determines a new terms-of-trade line (OT'). Compared to the steeper OT, OT' represents fewer hats per coat (or more coats per hat). Since the U.K. is buying coats and selling hats, she is pleased to have a lower hat price of coats (and a higher coat price of hats): the terms of trade have improved from the U.K. point of view. And, correspondingly, the terms from the U.S. point of view have worsened.

Note that a change in the *terms* of trade is one criterion for determining the welfare effects of the shift in the U.K. reciprocal demand, but there are other criteria—notably, change in the *volume* of trade. At the new equilibrium, the U.K. is suffering a smaller drain of exports, but she is also enjoying fewer imports. But suppose that the U.K. curve were to intersect the U.S. curve in the range where the latter is "bending backward." Then, as Figure 42–3 illustrates,

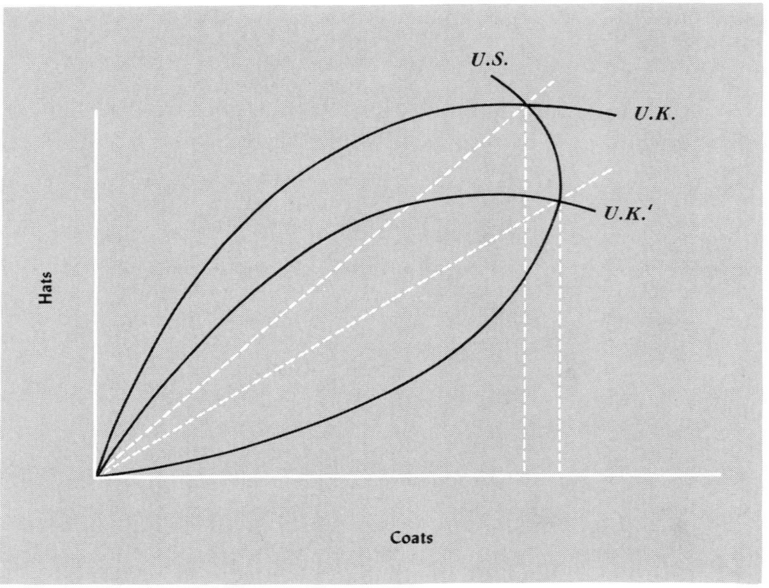

FIGURE 42–3. The terms of trade and the volume of trade.

not only would the terms of trade improve for England, but also the quantity of U.K. imports would rise.

Why, or how, would the U.K. curve shift to U.K.′? One possibility is a fall in English national income, which reduces English demand for coats; for example, in Table 42–3b, if the figures in column 2 (quantity demanded) were reduced, the calculated reciprocal-demand schedule would shift from the U.K. curve toward the U.K.′ curve. There would be the same sort of shift if the U.K.

supply of hats were reduced; for example, if in column 5 of Table 42–3b the pound supply price were 3 instead of 2.

Tariffs and Trade

Let us pursue in more detail a particularly interesting case of reducing the U.K. reciprocal demand: the imposition of a tariff on imports into England. Suppose that the British government levies a tariff on coat imports equal to 25 percent of the "gross" price, inclusive of the tariff (i.e., 33⅓ percent of the "net" price, exclusive of the tariff). In itself, the imposition of the tariff does not affect the U.K. demand schedule *as seen by residents of the U.K.* For example, before the tariff was imposed, people in the U.K. demanded 400 coats if the price was £8; and after the tariff is levied, they are *still* willing to buy 400 at £8 each. Thus, in Table 42–4, columns 1 and 4 are the same as columns 1 and 2 in Table 42–3b. However, if the price *paid* by the U.K. consumer is £8, the price *received* by the U.S. seller is only £6; for the U.K. government collects £2 as tax (£2 being 25 percent of the "gross" price and 33⅓ percent of the "net" price). To put it a bit differently, the U.K. buyer is confronted by a "domestic" price of £8; and it is a matter of indifference to him that part of his outlay goes to the government, leaving the "world" price received by the U.S. exporter at only £6.

In Table 42–4, column 2 is 25 percent of column 1, and column 3 is column 1 minus column 2. Column 5 is "world" expenditure—expenditure received by the U.S. exporter and not including the U.K. government tax collection; it is calculated by multiplying columns 3 and 4. As indicated in the column heading, the exchange rate (column 6) is calculated on the basis of *net* import price. Column 7 is given data; and, since trade is always balanced, column 8 is equal to column 5. Column 9 is equal to column 8 divided by column 7. And the terms of trade (column 10) are deduced by dividing column 9 by column 4.

Plotting columns 9 and 4 gives curve U.K.′ in Figure 42–2. The intersection of U.K.′ with the unchanged U.S. curve determines new terms of trade; the double asterisks in Tables 42–3a and 42–4 indicate terms of trade of $2.354h = 1c$, with approximately 1,752.5 hats exchanging for 744.4 coats.

Thus, the U.K. definitely improves her terms of trade by imposing a tariff, and U.K. imports may decrease or increase, depending on whether the U.K. and U.K.′ curves cross the U.S. curve where the latter is sloping up to the *right* (as in our text illustration) or up to the *left*.[1] But these effects of the tariff imposed

[1] What should be *desired* with respect to import volume? It depends upon one's criteria or perspective. We have earlier concluded that the "gain from trade" lies in the imports, to the extent that they can be conveniently financed; so, from the viewpoint of the economy as a whole, more imports are presumably desirable. But perhaps the immediate motivation for the tariff was, for good or ill, to protect U.K. coat manufacturers from foreign competition. If so, it would be unamusing and perhaps a bit confusing for a tariff to *increase* coat imports.

Table 42–4

U.K. RECIPROCAL DEMAND WITH A TARIFF

COATS						HATS			
U.K. Gross £ Demand Price (1)	Tariff: 25% of Gross (2)	U.K. Net £ Demand Price: (1) — (2) (3)	Quantity Demanded (4)	U.K. £ Import Expenditure: (3) × (4) (5)	Exchange Rate: $\frac{\$/£ = 10}{\text{Net £ Demand Price}}$ (6)	U.K. £ Supply Price (7)	U.K. £ Export Receipts (8)	Quantity Exported: (8) ÷ (7) (9)	Terms of Trade: Hats/Coats: (9) ÷ (4) (10)
10	—	—	0	—	—	2	—	—	—
9	—	—	200	—	—	2	—	—	—
8	2	6	400	2,400	1.667	2	2,400	1,200	3.000
7	1.75	5.25	600	3,150	1.905	2	3,150	1,575	2.625
6.278	1.5695	4.7085	744.4	3,505.007	2.124	2	3,505.007	1,752.504	2.354**
6	1.5	4.5	800	3,600	2.222	2	3,600	1,800	2.250
5.333	1.333	4	933.33	3,733.333	2.500	2	3,733.333	1,866.67	2.000
5	—	—	1,000	—	—	2	—	—	—
4	—	—	1,200	—	—	2	—	—	—
3	—	—	1,400	—	—	2	—	—	—
2	—	—	1,600	—	—	2	—	—	—
1	—	—	1,800	—	—	2	—	—	—
0	—	—	2,000	—	—	2	—	—	—

by England are contingent on an absence of foreign retaliation. In Figure 42–4, we begin with initial reciprocal-demand curves, U.S.$_1$ and U.K.$_1$, which intersect at point 1. Now England levies a tariff, moving her reciprocal demand to

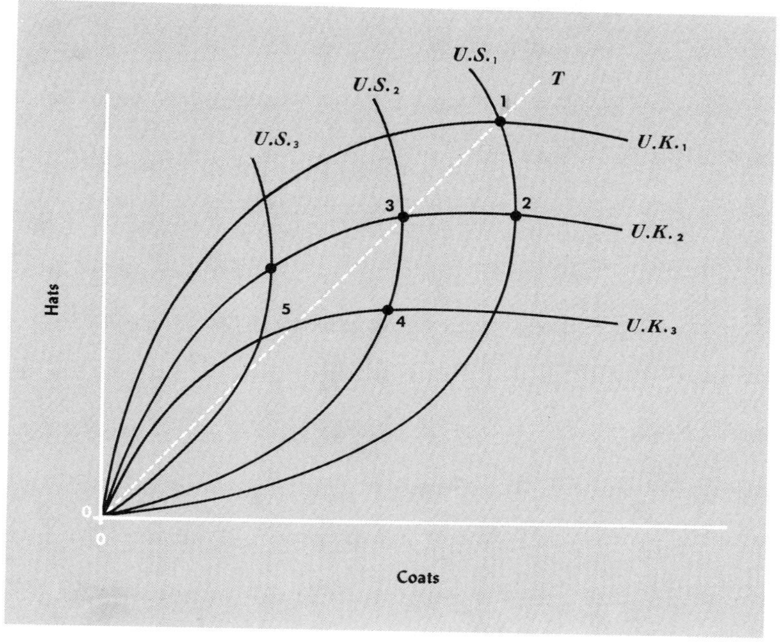

FIGURE 42–4. Tariff retaliation and counter-retaliation.

U.K.$_2$ and the intersection to point 2. This position represents an improvement in the U.K.'s terms of trade: U.K. exports fall, and U.K. imports rise. But suppose that the U.S. retaliates with her own tariff, moving her reciprocal demand to U.S.$_2$; in the move from intersection point 2 to point 3, the terms are worsened for the U.K. (improved for the U.S.), and exports fall for both countries. Then England can counter-retaliate with a higher tariff (U.K.$_3$), followed again by the U.S. (U.S.$_3$), etc. The result of this terribly imaginative (but, unhappily, not historically imaginary), red-blooded tariff warfare is that, on balance, when the smoke has cleared away, the terms of trade probably will not have been greatly changed from the original $0T$, but almost certainly both countries will have suffered a great decline in the volume of trade.

To summarize: in the absence of retaliation, imposition of a tariff

(a) improves the terms of trade for the tariff-levying country;

(b) reduces exports of the tariff-levying country, which

(i) is good from the aggregate standpoint of decreasing the drain of goods and services out of the country;

(ii) is bad from the aggregate standpoint of decreasing earnings of foreign money which can be used to pay for imports;

(iii) is bad from the standpoint of individual firms and industries whose sales are heavily oriented to foreign markets;

(iv) tends to reduce money national income—which is good or bad, depending on whether the general setting is one of inflation or deflation;

(c) may increase, decrease, or leave unchanged the volume of imports, an increase being desirable from the aggregate standpoint of increasing the total of goods and services available to the community but being undesirable from the view of individual firms and industries competing with those foreign-made products, and a decrease being oppositely evaluated.

If there is retaliation, and especially if there is initiated a process of counter-retaliation, the terms of trade can either worsen or improve, but may change very little, for a given country; and both imports and exports probably will be reduced, perhaps very greatly.

This discussion scarcely exhausts the subject of tariffs. But enough has been said to indicate that various criteria may (should) be used in evaluating such a policy as tariffs and that a given policy may well be "good" according to some criteria and "bad" according to others. We have suggested that one can envisage circumstances in which a policy of interference in the market can be helpful, say, from the viewpoint of the entire economy as a unit (as when a tariff both improves the terms of trade and increases imports while reducing exports) but hurtful from the viewpoint of components of the whole (as with domestic producers of goods being imported in increasing volume). The world, in short, is a complicated place.

Trade and Resource Allocation

In the first part of the chapter, on the basis of indicated assumptions and given data, we deduced the U.S. and the U.K. reciprocal-demand schedules. With these schedules, we then could determine the equilibrium terms of trade and the quantities of hats and of coats traded internationally. Specifically, we discovered that the U.S. would export (and the U.K. would import) 870.6 coats, and the U.S. would import (the U.K. would export) 2,458 hats, the terms of trade being $2.823h = 1c$. Furthermore, the relative commodity prices in the two countries before foreign trade opened reflected the (marginal) production ratios: in the U.S. the production-exchange ratio is $2h = 1c$, and in the U.K. the commodities can be substituted for each other in either production or exchange at the rate of $4h = 1c$.

The foregoing covers a good deal of ground, but additional relevant questions remain. Before foreign trade, what were the total quantities of hats and coats produced and consumed in the respective countries? With foreign trade, what is the world production pattern, and how much of the two commodities is being consumed by the U.S. and the U.K.? And with appropriate additional information, we can answer still other questions relating to the allocation of resources and to shifts in the allocation as foreign trade is conducted.

Consider first the *general* situation of the U.S. in Figure 42–5. Let us suppose that the U.S. has available at present a fixed quantity of resources, which, for convenience, we shall call "labor." If *all* of the labor produced nothing but

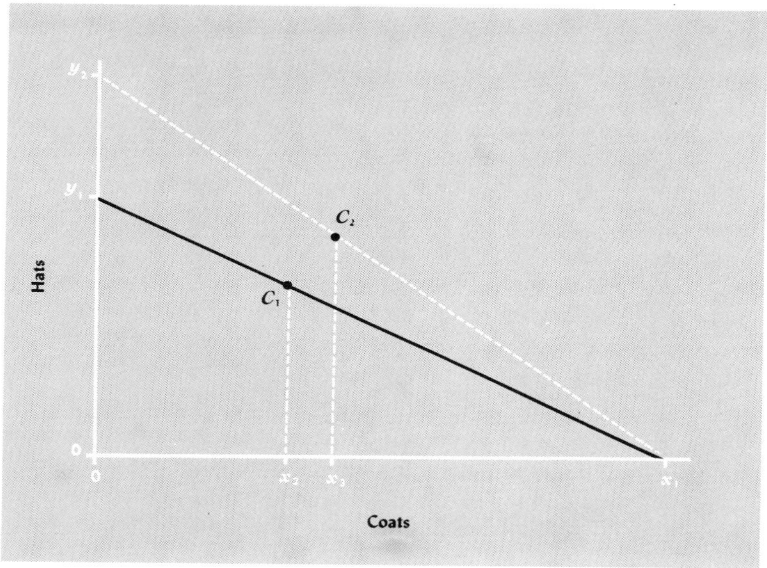

FIGURE 42–5. Production and consumption boundaries.

hats, the maximum hat output per time period would be Oy_1; if the U.S. specialized completely in coats, Ox_1 coats could be produced; if some of both commodities are to be produced, it is feasible to produce any combination of hats and coats indicated by the straight line y_1x_1. Since line y_1x_1—which includes the end points, y_1 and x_1—gives us the infinite possible combinations of hats and coats, it may be labeled the *production-possibility* curve. Moving down the curve to the right indicates that it is possible to produce more and more coats at the (alternative) cost of foregoing production of more and more hats; and moving up the curve to the left shows the coat cost of producing more hats. The *straightness* of the curve manifests the *constancy* of marginal cost: no matter where we start on the curve, the cost of producing one more coat is two hats, and the cost of one more hat is one half a coat. Before the introduction of foreign trade, the U.S. will presumably wish to consume some of both commodities and therefore will produce some of both: C_1 could be the consumption-production point, with the combination of $0x_2$ coats and x_2C_1 hats.

Before trade, then, line y_1x_1 is the "production boundary," and, since the isolated economy cannot consume more than it produces, y_1x_1 is also the "consumption boundary."

Now, trade opens with the U.K. Suppose that the U.S. has a comparative advantage in coats. It is reasonable (although not literally necessary) to suppose in that case that the U.S. will concentrate her production wholly on coats: the U.S. will produce $0x_1$ coats and no hats, the *production* point then being x_1. The *consumption* point is to be found on the terms-of-trade line. From the production point, x_1, we trace out a straight line, the slope of which measures the terms of international trade. On this terms-of-trade line, suppose that C_2 is the consumption point.

To summarize: *Before* trade, the U.S. both produces and consumes at C_1; and *with* trade, she produces at x_1 and consumes at C_2. If the U.S. is now producing $0x_1$ coats and consuming only $0x_3$, the remainder, x_3x_1, is *exported;* and if she is consuming x_3C_2 hats while producing none, she is *importing* x_3C_2.

Now, let us insert such numbers as we can into a diagram analogous to Figure 42–5. We know the following: x_3C_2 (2,458), x_3x_1 (870.62), x_2C_1 (1,000), the slope of y_1x_1 (2), and the slope of y_2x_1 (2.823). Figure 42–6 is constructed on the basis of such data. There is one bit of arbitrariness in Figure 42–6a: the location of the production point at 1,500 coats. (All we can say about the volume of coat production, on the basis of previously available data, is that it must be at least 870.62, the volume of exports.) Having selected 1,500 for the production point, we can draw the production-possibility and the terms-of-trade lines at their proper slopes. Then we can locate C_1, because we know the volume of hat consumption before trade; and we can locate C_2, on the basis either of hat imports or of coat exports.

Similarly, Figure 42–6b is constructed for the U.K., incorporating known data and the arbitrary placing of the production point at 4,000 hats.

In Figure 42–5, consumption point C_2 represents more of *both* commodities than does C_1, whereas in Figure 42–6 (a and b), the introduction of foreign trade results in a country's consuming more of one commodity but less of the other. Either case is possible, depending on demand-elasticity conditions.[2] But in either case, the terms-of-trade line (i.e., the consumption boundary) lies beyond the production-possibility line (i.e., the production boundary). In Figure 42–6a, the U.S. at point C_2 (with foreign trade) consumes more hats but fewer coats than at point C_1 (before foreign trade). But the point on the more ex-

[2] Specifically, the before-trade equilibrium point on the U.S. demand for hats, as on the U.K. demand for coats, is a point of *elastic* demand. If the before-trade equilibrium point had been one of *inelastic* demand, we would have the same sort of situation as depicted in Figure 42–5.

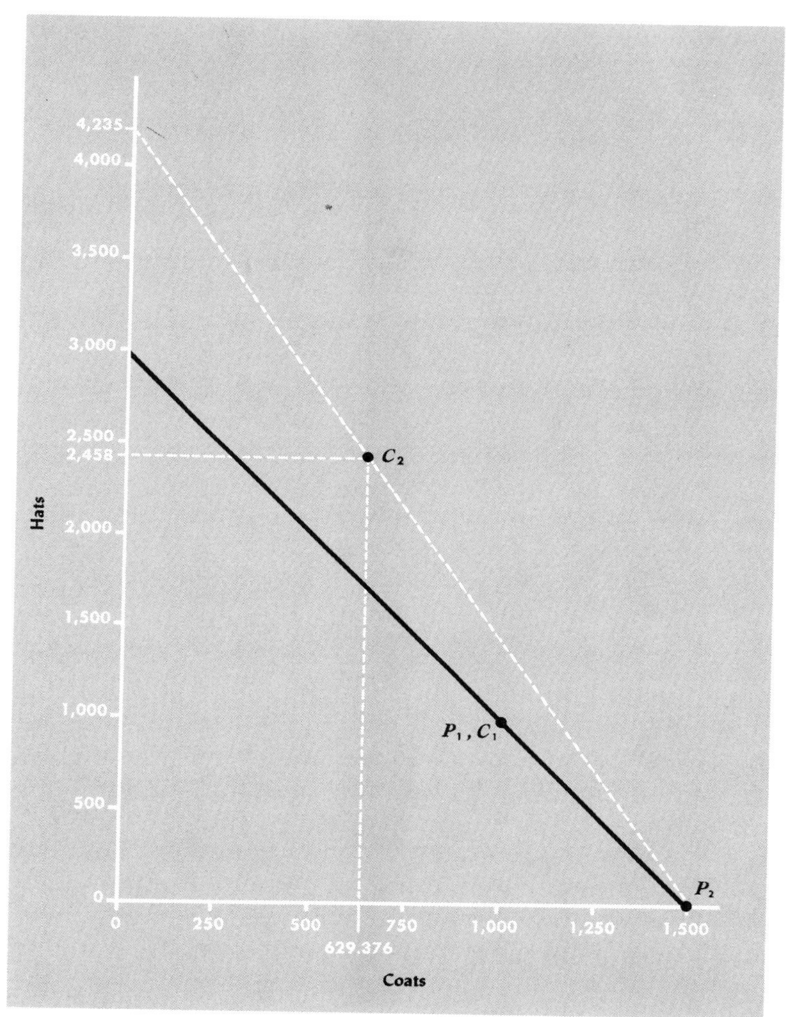

FIGURE 42–6a. United States production, consumption, and trade.

tended boundary is preferred to that on the initial, inner boundary: if C_1 were preferred to C_2, the U.S. could stay at C_1 simply by not trading.

Having shown diagrammatically for each country the shift in production from P_1 to P_2, the shift in consumption from C_1 to C_2, and the amounts of imports and of exports, we approach the matter arithmetically.

In the upper, "before-foreign-trade" half of Table 42–5, the commodity prices in column 2 continue our old illustration, and the quantities (both pro-

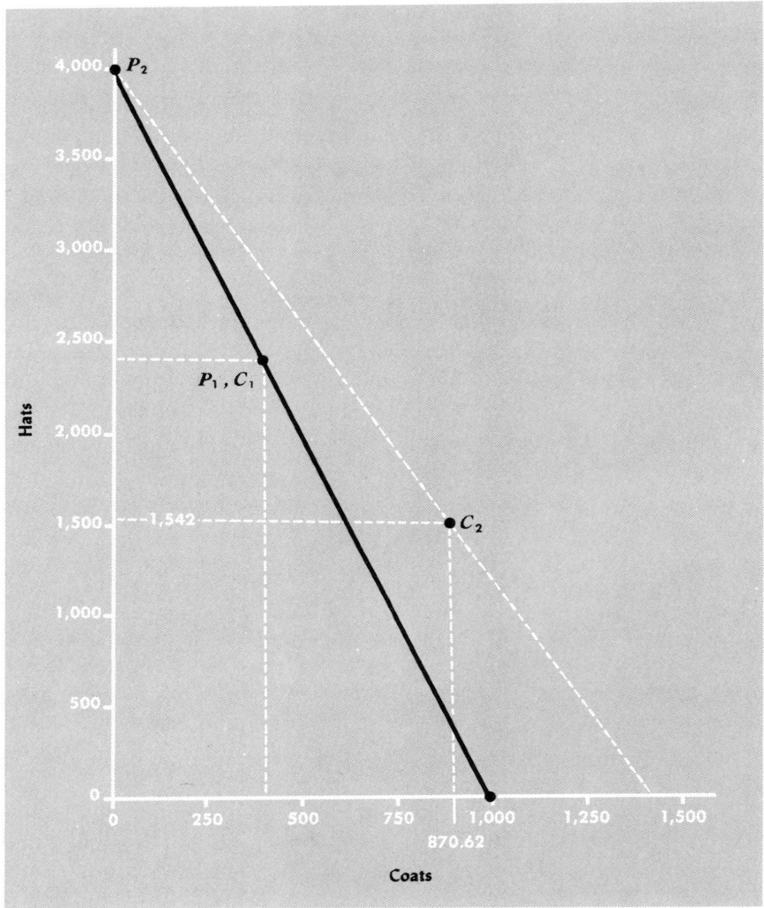

FIGURE 42–6b. United Kingdom production, consumption, and trade.

duced and consumed) in column 3 are taken from Figure 42–6. The *absolute* values of the numbers in column 4 are arbitrary, but the *ratios* of 5/2.5 and 10/2.5 reflect the respective relative commodity prices in column 2. *Given* column 4, we can calculate the number of workers required in the industries: column 5 = column 3/column 4. Since we have assumed labor to be the only input, all receipts are disbursed as wages: column 6 = column 2 × column 3. And column 7 = column 6/column 5.

Now, let foreign trade open between the U.S. and the U.K.; the consequences are summarized in the lower half of Table 42–5. These data continue to follow the earlier illustration. The U.S. specializes production completely in coats, and the U.K. produces only hats. With an exchange rate of $1.771 = £1,

Table 42–5

BEFORE FOREIGN TRADE

Commodity	Price	Quantity	Output/ Worker	No. of Workers	Total Wages	Wages/ Worker
(1)	(2)	(3)	(4)	(5)	(6)	(7)
			U.S.			
Hats	$ 5	1,000	5	200	$ 5,000	$25
Coats	$10	1,000	2.5	400	$10,000	$25
				600	$15,000	
			U.K.			
Hats	£2	2,400	10	240	£4,800	£20
Coats	£8	400	2.5	160	£3,200	£20
				400	£8,000	

WITH FOREIGN TRADE ($1.771 = £1)

Commodity	Price	Quantity	Output/ Worker	No. of Workers	Total Wages	Wages/ Worker
			U.S.			
Hats	[$ 3.542	2,458]	—	—	—	—
Coats	$10	629.38 + 870.62 = 1,500	2.5	600	$15,000	$25
			U.K.			
Hats	£2	1,542 + 2,458 = 4,000	10	400	£8,000	£20
Coats	[£5.647	870.62]	—	—	—	—

the U.K. hat export price of £2 is the equivalent of $3.542; the U.S. hat demand schedule (see Table 42–3a) then indicates U.S. imports of 2,458. These import figures are given in brackets in Table 42–5.

Similarly, the $10 coat price is £5.647, at which price the U.K. imports 870.62, as given in brackets.

Since the U.S. produces 1,500 coats and exports 870.62, then 629.38 are available for home consumption. There are alternative ways of calculating this volume of home consumption. For example, when the U.S. imports 2,458 hats at a price of $3.542 per unit, total expenditure on imports is $8,706.24. But total income is $15,000. And $15,000 — $8,706.24 = $6,293.76. At $10 per coat, the expenditure of $6,293.76 buys 629.38 coats.

Or note that the U.S. income of $15,000 stems wholly from expenditure on coats. The U.S. exports 870.62 coats at $10 per unit, giving an export value (equal to import value) of $8,706.20. This leaves domestic expenditure on coats of $15,000 — $8,706.20 = $6,293.80, the equivalent of 629.38 coats. Notice that the price of coats is still $10, as it was before foreign trade. At the pre-trade price, why is not the quantity demanded still 1,000 rather than 629.38? To conclude that quantity demanded has changed at a *given* price is to say that demand has changed. But we did *not* assume that the *hat* demand had changed: we simply moved down the original schedule in Table 42–3a until we reached a price of $3.542. Is it quite cricket to hold the U.S. hat demand constant while shifting the U.S. coat demand?

Recall that a demand schedule remains constant while certain other things—income, prices of other goods, and preferences—remain constant. Here we do hold income constant (at $15,000), and we assume no change in preference patterns. Moreover, when we consider hat demand, prices of other goods (i.e., the price of coats) remain constant; therefore, the demand for hats has not shifted. But when we consider coat demand, prices of other things *do* change—specifically, the price of hats to U.S. consumers (from $5 to $3.542); therefore, the demand for coats can change (in this case, from 1,000 to 629.38). At the constant coat price of $10, more coats, fewer coats, or the same number of coats may be demanded with foreign trade, depending on whether the lowered price of hats leads to less expenditure, more expenditure, or unchanged expenditure on hats. In this instance, the fall in the price of hats to U.S. buyers induced a greater expenditure on hats; thus, expenditure on coats was reduced, and, at an unchanged coat price, the number of coats bought also was reduced.

If foreign trade results in a country's consuming more of *both* commodities, the country, considered as an economic entity, is apparently better off. But is the U.S. (or the U.K.) clearly benefited when, as in our illustration, it ends up with *less* of one commodity, even though it has more of the other? We earlier indicated one answer to that question: The terms-of-trade line is the "consumption boundary," and foreign trade has pushed out this boundary, making larger the alternative consumption combinations which now are potentially feasible. Furthermore, we suggested that a nation is presumably not obliged to trade—if it prefers a consumption point on the production-possibility curve to the point on the terms-of-trade line which is consistent with trade equilibrium, it will not trade; therefore, the existence of trade must reflect some gain.

With the aid of selected data from Table 42–5 and some additional calculations, which appear in Table 42–6, we can present a quantified answer to the question of whether there is a gain from trade. The first part of Table 42–6 repeats the U.S. "before-trade" and "with-trade" consumption and price information. Also, it indicates that before-trade quantities multiplied (weighted) by

Table 42–6

MEASUREMENT OF THE GAIN FROM TRADE

	BEFORE TRADE	WITH TRADE
Consumption		
Hats	1,000	2,458
Coats	1,000	629.38
Prices		
Hats	$ 5	$ 3.542
Coats	$10	$10
Consumption Values at Current Prices		
Hats	1,000 @ $5 = $5,000	2,458 @ $3.542 = $8,706.2
Coats	1,000 @ $10 = $10,000	629.38 @ $10 = $6,293.8
Total	$15,000	$15,000.04
Consumption Values at before-Trade Prices		
Hats	1,000 @ $5 = $5,000	2,458 @ $5 = $12,290
Coats	1,000 @ $10 = $15,000	629.38 @ $10 = $6,293.8
Total	$15,000	$18,583.8 (increase 23.89%)
Consumption Values at with-Trade Prices		
Hats	1,000 @ $3.542 = $3,542	2,458 @ $3.542 = $8,706.2
Coats	1,000 @ $10 = $10,000	629.38 @ $10 = $6,293.8
Total	$13,542	$15,000.04 (increase 10.77%)

before-trade prices give a total money value of consumption equal to $15,000, as do with-trade quantities weighted by with-trade prices. But while the money value of total consumption of hats and coats is unchanged by trade, the composition of consumption and the price of one of the commodities are different. How can we compare one basket of goods valued at one set of prices with a different basket valued at other prices?

We can compare the different baskets if each combination of goods is weighted by the *same* set of prices. And the set of prices used may be either the original (before-trade) prices or the new (with-trade) prices. Thus, at the original prices, the before-trade combination of goods is valued at $15,000; *if* both prices remain unchanged, the with-trade combination is valued at $18,584, an increase of almost 24 percent. By contrast, *if* both baskets are weighted by the new prices, the value of the new combination will be about 11 percent greater than that of the original ($15,000 compared to $13,542). The magnitude of the change in value will depend on which set of prices is used as the weight; but in both cases the value of the consumption basket with trade is greater than that of the before-trade basket.

Tariffs and Wages

One other matter should be noted in connection with Table 42–5. While we have taken pains to indicate that the U.S. (and similarly the U.K.) is better off with trade than without trade, what can be said about U.S. per capita income relative to U.K. per capita income with trade?

Table 42–5 indicates that with trade, as before trade, U.S. wages are $25 and U.K. wages are £20. With an exchange rate of $1.771 = £1, the dollar equivalent of U.K. wages of £20 is $35.42. Since both countries face the same commodity prices, the higher *money* wage in the U.K. reflects a greater *real* wage. But how can the U.K. engage in two-way trade, exporting as well as importing, if her wages are substantially higher? Some people believe that a country with absolutely higher wages cannot compete with (i.e., export to) countries with lower wages—unless a tariff is levied by the high-wage country to offset the "unfair advantage" of the "pauper-labor" country. But actually, in the analysis summarized in Table 42–5, no use was made of a tariff, and the U.K. still was able to undersell the U.S. in hats.[3]

[3] The would-be and erstwhile U.K. coat manufacturers may complain that tariff protection is appropriate in light of lower U.S. wages. To be sure, they assure anyone who will listen (and they *are* constituents of members of Parliament) that they desire no unfair advantage for themselves. No, all that is appropriate is a tariff rate that is "scientifically" determined. And, obviously, a "scientific" tariff is one that just "equalizes costs of production." If the tariff "equalizes" costs of producing coats in the two countries, then producers in the U.K. and the U.S. can start the race for survival at the same place, so to speak, and may the better man win this fair competition.

Even the American hat producers can agitate for such a scientific tariff. U.S. wages are, indeed, lower than those in the U.K. But *somehow* the U.K. costs of hat production still are lower—and this is unfair.

So, still assuming that average total cost per unit equals price, it follows that the British should levy an import tax on each coat of £8 − £5.647 = £2.353, and the American tariff on hats should be $5 − $3.542 = $1.458. These tariffs equalize costs and prices, *and they eliminate the basis of trade.*

It is not difficult to discover that the basis of U.K. higher wages (and higher real income) is greater per capita productivity. The output per worker is the same in both countries in coat production; so in coats the lower U.S. money wage results in a lower cost (and price) in the U.S. But in hats, the U.K. output per worker is greater than the U.S. productivity; more specifically, the U.K. superiority in productivity (2:1, or 200 percent) is greater than the U.K. superiority in wage rate (approximately 7:5, or 140 percent). That is, the excess of U.K. wages over U.S. wages is *more than offset* by the excess U.K. productivity in hats over U.S. productivity, thereby resulting in a lower cost per unit (price) of hats.

Not only is it *possible*, in this case, to have two-way trade when U.K. wages are higher, it is *necessary* that they be higher. For if both countries had the same wage rate, they would have the same cost (price) of coats; and there would be no incentive for the U.K. to import American coats. If the U.S. is to export coats, U.K. wages must be somewhat higher: this is the lower limit of the ratio U.K. wages/U.S. wages. There is also an upper limit of the ratio: U.K. wages must be somewhat less than twice U.S. wages, in order for the U.K. to be able to export hats.

Similarly, suppose that the U.K. output per worker were greater in *both* commodities. For example:

	Hats	Coats
U.S.	5	2.5
U.K.	10	3

The upper limit of the ratio U.K. wages/U.S. wages, determined by the productivity ratio in the U.K. specialty (hats), would still be 2:1; but the lower limit would be 3:2.5, or 6:5, based on the productivity ratio in the U.S. specialty (coats). That is, if two-way trade is to prevail, the U.K. wage *must* be something more than 20 percent higher than the U.S. wage—and less than twice as high.

Finally, consider a somewhat different situation—one in which *each* country is absolutely more productive in *one* commodity (and, therefore, less productive in the other). For example:

	Hats	Coats
U.S.	5	2.5
U.K.	10	2

The "true," "scientific" tariff criterion of cost equalization was advocated in the Republican platform first in 1904; the Democratic platform did not explicitly reflect this degree of enlightenment until 1928, but many Democrats joined Republicans in their support prior to World War I. The notion is embodied in the Tariff Act of 1922 and is retained in the Smoot-Hawley Act of 1930.

The upper limit of the ratio U.K. wages/U.S. wages is still 2:1 (based on hat outputs per worker). But in the lower limit, U.K. wages can no longer be higher than, or even equal to, U.S. wages. For the U.S., in this case, can export coats even if U.S. wages are higher; specifically, U.S. wages can be greater by anything up to 25 percent more than U.K. wages (based on coat outputs). That is, the lower limit of the U.K.:U.S. wage ratio is 2:2.5, or 1:1.25.

Questions

1. Explain why, or in what sense, a "reciprocal-demand curve" is *both* a demand curve and a supply curve.

2. At any given point on a reciprocal-demand curve, we can measure a desired quantity of imports demanded, the maximum quantity of exports which will be supplied for those imports, and the corresponding export price of imports (i.e., the terms of trade); the import and export quantities are measured by *distances* along the vertical and horizontal axes, and the terms of trade are indicated by the *slope* of a line through the origin. Now, could you plot this same information—imports, exports, price—in the sort of diagram used earlier in the book, in which quantity demanded is measured horizontally, price is measured vertically, and the demand curve slopes downward to the right?

3. A reciprocal-demand curve can "bend backward." For example, in Figure 42–2, the U.S. curve first rises from left to right, then becomes vertical, and finally rises with a negative slope. This means that as the export price of imports falls, the quantity of imports demanded increases—which reflects the basic law of demand; but it means also that the total quantity of exports offered first reaches a maximum and then diminishes. Doesn't it seem a little odd that, beyond a certain terms of trade, a country can import a larger and larger quantity while giving up less and less exports? Is this a manifestation of any concept discussed earlier in the book?

4. "A tariff normally improves the terms of trade of the tariff-levying country. A tariff may increase or decrease the quantity of imports. The improvement in the terms will be greater, the smaller is the decrease or the larger is the increase in imports. Speaking generally, a large improvement in the terms is accompanied by a large increase in imports." Demonstrate the foregoing geometrically. Is it "good" and "desirable" that the greater the improvement in the terms, the greater the value of imports? From what perspective: the economy "as a whole," or domestic producers competing with imports? Is it good from the viewpoint of a nation trying to protect domestic "infant" industries?

5. A common sophomore complaint runs something like this: "Economics is so frustratingly inconclusive. Take the matter of tariffs. Surely the economist should be in a position to pass final judgment. Are tariffs good or are they not? Instead, he agonizingly (a) spells out *various* criteria in judging tariffs and (b) points out that, with respect to a *given* criterion, tariffs may be either good or bad, depending on one's objective or perspective. We have run into similar inconclusiveness in other areas (e.g., in comparing alternative expansionary fiscal policies). Such subtleties may amuse the economists, but red-blooded youths want *answers*. And in many other social science courses,

we *do* get answers: by the end of the semester we are sure that we *know* things; and the questions in these other, non-economics courses are every bit as vital and grandiose as the topics in this course." Come to the defense of the beleaguered economics teacher. What reply can he reasonably give to the complaining student?

6. "If the introduction of foreign trade increases the domestic consumption of *both* commodities (in a two-commodity case), we can reasonably say that trade is beneficial to that country. But it is entirely possible that the with-trade consumption combination will include *less* of one of the commodities than in the before-trade combination; and in that situation it is quite ambiguous as to whether there is a gain from the trade, and we can say nothing about the matter." Can't we say *anything* about the possible gain in this situation?

7. "Suspicious as we may well be of dealing with foreigners, there may be some sense in buying things abroad when they can be produced there absolutely more efficiently (i.e., with greater output per unit of input). But it can make no sense at all to spend good dollars to buy an article abroad when it can be produced more efficiently (i.e., with fewer resources) here." Right?

8. "Unfettered world trade would tend powerfully to reduce all workers (and other resource owners) to the world's lowest level. For a nation with lower wages—and all nations do have wages lower than those in the U.S.—could then undersell us, not only in 'third' markets, but right here in our own country. Thus, American producers would be ruined; or, in order for us to be able to sell and thus to survive, our wages would have to be cut to the lowest level of our competitors. It would be ridiculous to expose our high standard of living to the ruinous competition of the poorer rest of the world." Surely no nonsubversive could dispute this. Could you? How?

9. What is the so-called "scientific" tariff? Naturally, you support it, for who would want a *non*scientific tariff?

10. Assume that labor is the only input. In Abyssinia, five units of labor produce either 20 bushels of wheat or 20 yards of linen; in Bechuanaland, five units of labor produce either 30 bushels of wheat or 45 yards of linen.

a. In the absence of foreign trade, what would be the equilibrium ratio of exchange between wheat and linen in Bechuanaland?

b. If trade opens between the two countries (and neither trades with any third nation), which nation will export wheat?

c. The terms of trade must lie between what ratios of linen and wheat, assuming two-way trade?

d. Explain how, or in what sense, each nation gains from trade if the terms of trade are 10 wheat = 13 linen.

e. In order to allow mutually beneficial, two-way trade, must the wage rate be higher in one country or may it be higher in either? What are the limits of the ratio of the two wage rates?

f. If the Bechuanalandian wage rate were 10.7 times as large as that in Abyssinia, could there be any foreign trade between the two countries? If so, what would be the pattern of trade? Would there be any economic forces tending to change the ratio of wages?

11. In country *A*, one laborer can produce two units of *Y* or two of *X*; in country *B*, one laborer can produce two of *Y* or six of *X*. Each country has 100 laborers. After trade opens, each country specializes production completely in one commodity.

a. If *A* produces nothing but *X*, how many units can it produce? If *A* produces nothing but *Y*, how many units can it produce?

b. *A* has a comparative advantage in which commodity?

c. Assume terms of trade of $2X = 1Y$. If *A* now consumes 100 units of *X*, it will consume how much *Y*?

d. If *A* consumes $100X$, how much *Y* will *B* consume?

e. How many units of *X* will *B* consume?

f. Suppose that *before* trade began, *A* was producing and consuming $100X$. How much *Y* was it producing and consuming?

g. Suppose that *before* trade, *B* was producing and consuming $100Y$. How much *X*?

h. Therefore, *before* trade, *A* and *B* together were producing and consuming a total of how many units of *X* and how many of *Y*? *After* trade begins, they produce and consume how much *X* and how much *Y*?

12. Reinterpret the analysis of Chapter 16 in terms of international trade, with *A* and *B* being two countries. What was the exchange ratio between *A*'s money and *B*'s money? Then answer questions analogous to those given in Question 10 above.

43

THE BALANCE OF PAYMENTS AND ITS INTERPRETATION

The "gain" from trade, we have seen, lies most immediately in imports, not exports. Therefore, the more imports, the better—*to the extent that they can be "conveniently" financed.* A nation or any other economic unit living beyond its currently earned means is faced with a balance-of-payments problem. It is time to take a look at the balance of *international* payments, our interest being not in the sheer bookkeeping mechanics of the statement but in the use that may be made of this accounting record in evaluating the international financial situation of an economy.

The balance of payments of a nation is an accounting statement, compiled in double-entry bookkeeping fashion, of the country's international economic transactions over a period of time, commonly a year. Here is recorded the values of goods, services, investment income (i.e., dividends and interest), claims, gold, and gifts exchanged between the residents of the country in question and the residents of the rest of the world.

There are two sides of the balance, generally labeled "credits" and "debits," or "receipts" and "payments," or simply "plus" and "minus." The credits or receipts or plus side is basically the *export* side. Listed there, in terms of money value, are the country's exports of merchandise, services, claims, and gold—i.e., sales or transfers of things to foreigners: sales are "credited," and sales establish a claim to "receipts." And the debits or payments or minus side is to be considered the *import* side: purchases are "debited" and give rise to "payments."

Consider a series of international transactions of the U.S. and how they are recorded in the U.S. balance of payments.

1. A U.S. firm sells a tractor to an Englishman for $2,100, the sale being financed by

an increase in U.S.-owned demand deposits held in a London bank. The value of the tractor *export* is listed on the *credit* side in the *merchandise* account. The increase in the demand deposit held abroad constitutes an *import* of a claim (for demand deposits are money, and money is generalized command over goods and services) and is listed on the *debit* side under *short-term capital*.[1]

2. The preceding transaction was financed by a "time" bill of exchange, giving the importer ninety days in which to pay, the interest charged the importer being the pound equivalent of $10. The receipt of the interest by the U.S. bank is listed as *investment income* on the *credit* side. The interest payment of $10 by the importer is entered under the *short-term capital* account on the *debit* side.

3. In accordance with the contract between the exporter and the importer, the exporter pays for shipping the tractor. A French ship is used, and payment of $150 is made in dollars, which the Frenchman leaves on deposit in a U.S. bank. The increase of foreign claims on the U.S. is a *credit* in the *short-term capital* account. And the U.S. has bought (i.e., imported) shipping services, the value of which is listed as a *debit* in the *services* account.

4. American residents purchase British linen for $450, paying for it by drawing down the U.S.-held demand deposits in the U.K., which were accumulated in earlier transactions. The reduction in these U.S. claims is a *short-term capital* entry on the *credit* side; the *merchandise* import is a *debit*.

5. American investors spend $600 for Canadian twenty-year bonds, making payment by drawing down previously accumulated balances in Canadian banks. The reduction of U.S. demand deposits held abroad is a *credit* in the *short-term capital* account; the import of the bonds is a *debit* of *long-term capital*.

6. The American government gives $700 worth of wheat to Pakistan. The wheat export, like the tractor export in the first transaction, is a *credit* in the *merchandise* account. But how is it financed; that is, what does the U.S. receive that can be listed on the debit side? Since the wheat is a gift, nothing is received. But the books are kept in balance by insertion among the *debits* of an account called *unilateral transfers*, "unilateral" denoting the one-way aspect of the transaction as opposed to the normal commercial two-way exchange. Inclusion of the unilateral-transfer account not only keeps the double-entry books in balance (to

[1] On the basis of the conventional time criterion, the dividing line between short-term and long-term capital is one year. Since demand deposits are payable on demand, they are clearly short-term claims.

Remember that an increase in U.S. claims on foreigners (or a reduction of foreign claims on the U.S.) is the form of what actually amounts to "giving credit" by the U.S. or to "granting a loan" by the U.S. or to "investment" by the U.S. Or, as the expression generally goes, it constitutes a "capital movement" from the U.S. to the U.K. This may be a confusing expression, for this capital "export" or "outflow" is listed on the debit (i.e., import) side of the balance of payments. But a so-called "capital export" refers to an import of a claim (either an initial import of a foreign I.O.U.—e.g., increasing U.S. demand deposits held abroad—or a repatriation of an old American I.O.U. held by foreigners—e.g., decreasing foreign-held demand deposits in the U.S.), and imports of claims against foreigners are debits, just as are imports of goods and services.

humor the accountants); it also gives explicit notice that some of the period's transactions were gifts and not sales or purchases.

7. The Bank of England uses $300 previously accumulated in the Federal Reserve Bank of New York to buy gold from the U.S. Treasury.[2] The export of gold is a *credit* in the *gold* account, and the reduction of foreign demand deposits in the U.S. is a *debit* under *short-term capital.*

Now, let us list all seven transactions together in the U.S. balance of payments:

	Credits	Debits
Merchandise	2,100 + 700 = 2,800	450
Services		150
Investment income	10	
Unilateral transfers		700
Long-term capital		600
Short-term capital	150 + 450 + 600 = 1,200	2,100 + 10 + 300 = 2,410
Gold	300	
	4,310	4,310

Of course, the balance of payments balances: total credits equal total debits. This *aggregate* balance is inevitable; for each *individual* transaction, recorded in double-entry manner, balanced.[3] But since the aggregate balance is inevitable regardless of the international financial position of the country, it is not analytically interesting.

In order to make use of the balance of payments, we must concentrate not on the certain aggregate balance but on the balances (or imbalances) of appropriately chosen sub-categories or groups within the total statement. One such group is the *current account,* comprising the merchandise, services, and investment-income entries.[4] In our illustration, the current account balance is (2,800 + 10) − (450 + 150) = 2,210. This is variously known as a "surplus" balance, an "export" balance, a "positive" balance, a "favorable" balance, or an "active" balance (where balance clearly means "difference," not "equality").

It is common, also, to group all entries constituting change in international claims (i.e., a change in the international creditor-debtor status of a country) into a *capital account.* For some purposes, it is advisable to segregate long-term

[2] Only foreign monetary authorities—central banks and treasuries, not private persons and business firms—may buy gold from the Treasury.

[3] The balance of payments *must* balance, not only in principle but also in practice. To ensure balance, the statisticians insert, if need be, an entry of appropriate size on the appropriate side of the statement; the entry is called "errors and omissions."

[4] We may call the balance of merchandise alone the "balance of trade," here equal to 2,800 − 450 = 2,350. The balance of trade is thus part of the balance on current account.

from short-term capital, but the total account in our illustration is 1,200 — (600 + 2,410) = —1,810. The minus value indicates a net outward flow of capital—a net increase in the U.S. creditor (or decrease in the U.S. debtor) position.

While we must divide the total statement into at least these two accounts—current and capital—it is useful to make the division still more detailed. For present purposes, we note two more accounts: gold and unilateral transfers. The *gold account* is generally segregated, for gold is a means of international payment; i.e., it is an asset constituting "money" in the world economy. As indicated earlier, the *unilateral-transfer account* reflects "one-way" transactions: normally, a country gives up something in payment when it receives something else; if it sells an asset, it obtains payment; but when a gift is made or received, there is no counter-movement.

Now that we have mastered the basic mechanics of how to record transactions in the balance of payments and to group the entire statement into a number of categories (anyone who has not mastered it should review the foregoing until he has), what do we do with the information? Let it be conceded that analysis of the record of past transactions can be instructive only within limits. The problem even of how best to *define* "balance-of-payments equilibrium," much less the problem of actually how to *measure* "disequilibrium," is still a topic of discussion—sometimes heated, sometimes subtle, never conclusive. Indeed, in a fine show of humility, analysts frequently avoid the terms "equilibrium" and "disequilibrium" and speak instead simply of "shortage" or "gap" or "deficit" or "imbalance."

It may be interesting to review two approaches to balance-of-payments analysis, illustrated by two recent periods in U.S. data: 1946–49 and 1958–62.

Table 43–1

U.S. BALANCE OF PAYMENTS, 1946–49
(Net Annual Averages in Millions of Dollars)

Current account		8,140
Goods and services	7,255	
Investment income	885	
Unilateral transfers		—4,073
Long-term capital		—3,650
Short-term capital		— 55
Gold		—1,120
Errors and omissions		758

Table 43–1 covers the four-year period after World War II, a period characterized by so-called "dollar shortage," or "dollar gap." Many a fine-spun theory

was advanced—in terms of different international rates of growth of productivity, different rates of inflation, peculiar combinations of various marginal propensities, etc.—to explain *why* the dollar shortage existed. We shall not get entangled with them. Our problem is to determine *what* was the dollar shortage, measurable in terms of the balance of payments.

Table 43–1 tells us that the U.S. had a net export balance on current account financed by net gifts, net long-term capital outflow (i.e., U.S. investment abroad and foreign disinvestment in the U.S.), net short-term capital outflow (to a very minor extent), and net import of gold. Of course, the aggregate financing (net debits) balanced the current U.S. surplus (net credits). But was it a matter of insignificance *how* the financing was done? If one kind of financing by the rest of the world of its net current purchases from the U.S. was just as good as any other, there was no balance-of-payments problem. But, in fact, the so-called "dollar shortage" was one of the most crucial problems of public policy, with significant implications for domestic economies as well as for international relations.

If one is to detect a dollar shortage in Table 43–1, it is either (a) because there is *no* way to finance the current account surplus (i.e., U.S. export balance) which can be deemed commercially "proper" or "legitimate" or "acceptable" or "normal"—i.e., the *total* imbalance of the current account must equal the dollar shortage; or (b) *some* ways of financing are "proper," but some are not—i.e., the dollar shortage is equal to that *part* of the current account imbalance that is not covered by "proper" forms of financing.

Consider the net debit ("financing") entries individually. To the extent that the rest of the world depends upon gifts to "settle" its net imports on current account from the U.S., it is relying upon "abnormal" means; the persistent and conspicuous presence of unilateral transfers in the accounts may be considered a signal that all is not well. It is straining the concept to say that a balance of payments is in "equilibrium" when it contains a large volume of unilateral transfers—however wise, under the existing circumstances, the giving or receiving of the gifts may be. Presumably, the U.S. made net annual gifts in excess of $4 billion precisely because it was believed that the rest of the world (or a large part of it) was not in a healthy financial position and that, in the absence of the gifts, the rest of the world would be undesirably (from America's point of view) "short" of dollars.

Heavy and persistent reliance on short-term capital and gold also may be taken as an indication of international financial trouble. Short-term claims on foreigners and gold together make up the "international reserves," or "liquidity," of a country. Within ill-defined limits, a nation may draw upon its reserves, as an individual may spend some of his cash, without a balance-of-payments crisis obtaining. But a financing procedure which is appropriate in small, occasional doses is cause for alarm if pressed too far—for either a country or an individual. The gold holdings of the rest of the world could eventually be drained away entirely, as could previously accumulated foreign balances in U.S. banks; there is no such obvious physical limit on foreign short-term borrowing from the U.S. (which, like the reduction of foreign-held balances in the U.S., is a debit in the U.S. balance of payments), but monetary officials abroad may well wonder how far, and on what terms, they can go on borrowing in the U.S.

Large U.S. debit balances on unilateral transfers, short-term capital, and gold, then, suggest that the rest of the world has bought too much (relative to how much it has sold) on current account and has thus been forced to fall back excessively on means of financing which are non-sustainable or otherwise indicative of market imbalance. If there is any appropriate way for the rest of the world to pay for its current purchases other than through current sales (thus not requiring a zero balance on current account), it appears to be by U.S. purchases of long-term foreign securities. It may well be that the residents of a nation can prudently obtain financing for their international purchases by selling long-term bonds and stocks to foreigners. In the nineteenth century, for example, U.S. railroads were built with considerable assistance in the form of British capital; and few would suggest that this long-term capital inflow into the U.S. was evidence of a decades-long balance-of-payments crisis. Long-term loans are not necessarily wise, for either lender or borrower, just because they are long-term; but such financing is not likely to reflect the immediate financial pressures and panic associated with a forced scramble to scrape up large amounts of "international cash" (short-term capital and gold). Long-term financing may make feasible the initiation of well-planned investment activity over a substantial future period; massive reliance on short-term capital and gold is likely to be the consequence of past and current disasters and imprudence.

According to this line of thought, the dollar shortage is the absolute (arithmetic) difference between the U.S. current-account surplus and the U.S. long-term capital outflow—i.e., 8,140 − 3,650 = 4,490. But since total credits equal total debits, the imbalance of these two categories must be matched by an equal-sized imbalance (of opposite sign) of all the other categories. Thus, we can measure the absolute size of the dollar shortage alternatively: 4,073 + 55 + 1,120 − 758 = 4,490.[5]

A major warning is in order. Do not suppose that *first* the "shortage" sprang full grown out of nowhere and *now* the existing "shortage" must be financed, or the "gap" must be filled. The $4,490 imbalance of the current and long-term capital accounts could exist only because net financing of $4,490 in the aggregate was available. With less financing available, the shortage would have been smaller. Indeed, if the U.S. had made no net gifts and no short-term loans and if the rest of the world had not drawn down short-term claims on the U.S. or

[5] As one might suppose, a number of variations of this approach have been suggested. One obvious possibility is to include errors and omissions with the current and long-term capital accounts, thus making the shortage 8,140 − 3,650 + 758 = 5,248 = 4,073 + 55 + 1,120. However, it is a common presumption that most of the errors and omissions are unrecorded short-term capital movements.

shipped gold to the U.S.—in short, if the financing had been zero—there could have been no shortage.

This point is of particular interest with respect to unilateral transfers, which closely approached the size of the shortage. Some have suggested that the role of U.S. gifts was to fill a balance-of-payments deficit which already had come into existence, and that a bigger gap would have "required" still more aid. What would have happened to the balance of payments if unilateral transfers had been eliminated? At least in principle, the dollar shortage could have remained the same, with larger gold and short-term capital movements taking up all the slack: a given shortage does not "necessitate" a given amount of aid or, indeed, any aid at all. At the other extreme, as a consequence of eliminating U.S. gifts, foreign purchases on current account in the U.S. might be equally reduced—dollar for dollar. But if all the balance of payments other than the unilateral transfers and current account remained the same, then the dollar shortage would be reduced by the amount of the decrease in U.S. gifts. In actuality, probably the U.S. current-account surplus would have fallen somewhat if unilateral transfers had been eliminated, but by a lesser amount. It thus appears that, instead of the size of U.S. gifts being "dictated" by the size of an existing gap, the gap is itself a function of the magnitude of the gifts. The greater or smaller the amount of U.S. aid, the greater or smaller the dollar shortage.

According to the foregoing approach, then, based on comparing the current and the long-term capital accounts, in 1946–49, the rest of the world had a "dollar shortage"—that is, the U.S. balance of payments was in *surplus* disequilibrium—of about $4,500,000,000 on a yearly average. The situation has been rather different in recent years, especially since 1957. Now, the U.S. balance of payments, it is widely concluded, shows an average annual *deficit* of almost $3,200,000,000. However, the commonly used measure of the recent deficit is not the previously used measure of the surplus. (Table 43–2 indicates that, according to the old measure, the U.S. still had a surplus of over $2,500,000,000 in 1958–62.)

This new measure of the imbalance is used because of the great change in "liquid" international assets held by U.S. monetary authorities and in "liquid" international liabilities (actual and potential) of U.S. monetary authorities. The assets in question consist primarily of gold, and the liabilities consist of short-term claims on the U.S. held by foreigners—claims which, directly or indirectly, can be converted into U.S. gold.[6]

According to Table 43–1, the "dollar shortage" of the early postwar period was accompanied by an annual average inflow of gold equal to over $1,100,000,000 and a small short-term capital outflow (increase in U.S. claims on foreigners and decrease in foreign claims on the U.S.). But, according to Table 43–2, since

[6] As mentioned earlier, only foreign central banks and treasuries can buy U.S. monetary gold. But private foreigners can sell their dollar assets to their monetary authorities, who then can demand U.S. gold.

Table 43–2

U.S. BALANCE OF PAYMENTS, 1958–62
(Net Annual Averages in Millions of Dollars)

Current account		4,999
Goods and services	2,465	
Investment income	2,534	
Unilateral transfers		—4,333
Long-term capital (other than foreign purchases of U.S. government securities)		—2,499
U.S. short-term capital		—1,076
Foreign short-term capital (including foreign purchases of U.S. government securities)		1,900
Gold		1,268
Errors and omissions		—259

1957, the gold movement has reversed and has flowed outward at an annual rate of almost $1,300,000,000, and foreign short-term claims on the U.S.[7] have risen at the rate of $1,900,000,000.[8]

Especially since World War II, the dollar has been very widely used as a medium of international payment. Many nations have looked upon the dollar as the equivalent of gold in computing and managing their "international reserves," and the dollar is thus a "reserve currency." And as the major commercial

[7] These foreign short-term claims, otherwise known as liquid dollar assets, include foreign purchases of U.S. government securities of all maturities.

[8] In Table 43–2, the short-term capital account has been divided into two components: foreign investments in the U.S. and American investments abroad. The *net* short-term capital inflow was 1,900 — 1,076 = 824. In the measure of the deficit, only the change in foreign short-term claims on the U.S., rather than the net figure, is used. This measure is to reflect the "international liquidity" position of the country *from the viewpoint of the U.S. monetary authorities:* whereas these foreign claims can be used, directly or indirectly, to buy American gold, the private U.S. claims on foreigners are not at the disposal of the monetary authorities.

One consequence of using only the foreign component of the short-term capital account in measuring the deficit is a certain asymmetry of effect on the deficit from alternative ways of financing a given transaction. Suppose the U.S. imports an article from England. It may be financed, as we have seen, either by (a) reducing U.S. deposits in an English bank or (b) increasing an English deposit in an American bank. In either case, we credit the over-all short-term capital account. But under alternative (a), which involves a movement of U.S. capital out of England, the balance-of-payments deficit is not affected, whereas under alternative (b), which is a movement of foreign capital into the U.S., the deficit is increased.

nations gained in financial strength in the 1950s, they were happy to build up their liquid dollar assets. As long as the world considers the dollar "as good as gold," there is little likelihood of a "run on the dollar"—i.e., a general move by foreigners to cash in their dollar assets for gold. However, if the feeling developed that the U.S. was on the verge of curtailing the freedom of foreign monetary authorities to buy gold or that the dollar was soon to be devalued (i.e., the dollar price of gold raised), then there would be a scramble for U.S. gold.

Thus far, there have been only a few, short-lived signs of a panicky demand for U.S. gold. Of the total "deficit," above 60 percent has taken the form of increased foreign holdings of liquid dollar claims. Still, the remaining 40 percent has represented a substantial gold outflow. Most or all of the gold outflow thus far—reducing the U.S. monetary gold stock from $24,600,000,000 at the end of 1949 (about 70 percent of the world total, with the exception of Russia and China) to under $16,000,000,000 at the end of 1963 (about 40 percent of the total) —may have been a desirable world redistribution. But a prolonged continuance of such a large gold outflow would drain the coffers dry. To denude the U.S. of most of its international liquidity would be worse than embarrassing. It would cramp American foreign trade and investment, and it would unsettle much of the world's commerce—based, as it is, on the dollar as the major "reserve currency" and with exchange rates held essentially stable.

The gold outflow would be reduced if the total "deficit" were reduced and if the 60–40 ratio of foreign short-term capital and gold were maintained. Probably, if the total "deficit" were substantially reduced (and thus confidence in the dollar enhanced), even the proportion of the deficit represented by gold would fall: the gold output would be a smaller part of a smaller total. Put in these terms, the solution to the U.S. liquidity (gold) problem is to "adjust" the balance of payments so as to reduce or eliminate the "deficit." And, in very large measure, "balance-of-payments adjustment" centers on modification of the current account. Our next task is to review the major methods of balance-of-payments adjustment.

Questions

1. The credits (or receipts) side of the balance of payments is the *export* side; for example, the export of merchandise is recorded on the credits side. But we also put *capital imports* (or *inflows*) on the credit side. Aside from utter confusion on the part of the compilers of the international records, on what basis can you account for this inconsistency?

2. "The U.S. balance of payments always shows some unilateral transfers (otherwise known as donations), and beginning in 1941 they have bulked very large. But the balance of payments is compiled on a *double*-entry basis; that is, each transaction involves

both a credit entry (in general, what we export) and a debit entry (what we import). And since we import nothing when we make a gift and export nothing when we receive a gift (a unilateral transfer is a *one*-way 'transaction'), the recording of unilateral transfers necessarily unbalances the international accounts, leaving total credits not equal to total debits." Really?

3. Suppose we were to have zero unilateral transfers and zero gold movements, so that the balance of payments would consist solely of the current account and the capital account. On the basis of what criterion may we distinguish between the current and capital accounts; that is, what is the basis on which a given entry is included in one account instead of the other?

4. Following are the balances of payments of four countries:

	I		II		III		IV	
	CREDITS	DEBITS	CREDITS	DEBITS	CREDITS	DEBITS	CREDITS	DEBITS
A. Merchandise	900	1100	2000	1770	1930	1210	1000	1700
B. Services	100	350	230	300	195	190	100	150
C. Interest	200	275	390	190	75	40	250	125
D. Unilateral	10	0	30	375	10	440	50	50
E. Short capital	550	150	200	185	125	150	70	60
F. Long capital	90	120	170	350	150	300	690	150
G. Gold	195	50	305	155	20	175	125	50

a. What is the magnitude of the balance of trade of Country I?

b. What is the balance of trade of Country II?

c. Is the balance of trade of Country III an import or an export balance?

d. What is the balance of payments on current account of Country III?

e. What is the balance of payments on current account of Country IV?

f. Does Country I have a "favorable" or an "unfavorable" balance on current account?

g. On balance, is Country II selling or buying services?

h. Is Country IV receiving net interest payments from abroad or making payments?

i. Is Country II receiving or making net unilateral transfers?

j. Is Country II exporting or importing net long-term capital?

k. Is Country I experiencing a gold inflow or a gold outflow?

l. In its general configuration, which country best represents the U.S. in the late 1940s? Explain.

m. In its general configuration, which best represents the U.S. since 1957?

n. Of the remaining two countries, one seems more nearly in long-run "equilibrium" than the other. Which one? What is your evidence?

5. Person *A* claims: "The only straightforward way to consider the status of the balance of payments is to concentrate on the current account. There is no really 'satisfac-

tory' way to finance an imbalance in the current account. Something is wrong, and it is a sign of financial misfortune or weakness to have to use any capital movements—long or short—or gold movements or gifts to balance the current account." Person *B* contends: "It is ridiculous to identify financial health with a balanced current account. Net capital movements (i.e., borrowing and lending) on either long or short term are as reasonable (and as inevitable) for a nation as for the individuals and businesses who largely make up the nation. There is only one thing to worry about: gold movements. To evaluate the status of the balance of payments, we need concern ourselves only with the gold account." Defend each of these persons in turn. Rebut each in turn. Which do you think has the stronger position? Do you fully accept either argument?

6. "The size of the so-called 'dollar gap' or 'shortage' in the late 1940s was, in large measure, a function of United States aid. Odd as it may seem, the 'dollar gap' would have been smaller with less aid and larger with more aid." Explain the line of thought behind that statement.

7. Since 1957, the U.S., it is said, has "suffered" a large balance-of-payments "deficit." How has this "deficit" been measured? Why has it been measured that way (what is the rationale of the measure)? Who cares about the "deficit" (who is worse off and in what sense is he worse off because of the "deficit")? What would be the nature of the cost, if any, if the "deficit" were to double in size?

8. The chapter discussed two approaches to balance-of-payments interpretation, two ways of measuring deficits and surpluses. The method commonly used to measure the U.S. deficit of recent years—i.e., U.S. gold outflow plus inflow of foreign short-term capital—is defended by Walther Lederer, chief of the Balance of Payments Division of the Department of Commerce: "The definition of surplus or deficit is a matter of analysis, and analysis may vary with the purpose for which it is made. . . . The analysis which I believe to be [most] useful is designed to meet essentially a practical purpose: to measure the changes in our capability to defend the exchange value of the dollar. This defense is the responsibility of our monetary authorities, and their capability depends upon their liquid resources and the liquid claims which can be exercised against these resources" ("Measuring the Balance of Payments," in *Factors Affecting the United States Balance of Payments* [Joint Economic Committee, 87th Congress, 2nd session, 1962], 81–82). Lederer suggests alternative purposes and types of analyses. Can you suggest others? Must the emphasis of balance-of-payments interpretation be on the provision of guides and indicators to monetary authorities? How about the approach we applied to the data of the late 1940s; does it have any relevance for today's analysis?

44

BALANCE-OF-PAYMENTS ADJUSTMENT

While there is broad room for discussion on both the conceptual *meaning* of balance-of-payments disequilibrium and particularly the best manner of empirical *measurement* of balance-of-payments disequilibrium, no one denies that balance-of-payments problems and strains can and do exist. How are such problems solved or such strains eased? To express the question more formally, what are the "balance-of-payments adjustment mechanisms" *provided by the market?*

The focal point of an adjustment mechanism is the current account. To be sure, gold and especially capital movements also will be affected *directly* by those variables—interest rate, exchange rate, commodity prices, national income—that impinge upon the current account. But our emphasis is on the *indirect* effects of such market variables on international reserves (consisting mainly of gold and short-term international assets) through altering the current account. The basic objective, then, is to induce the current account into such a balance that there is no net movement of international reserves.[1]

Some direct, discretionary balance-of-payments policies may, in principle, not impinge upon the current account at all. For example, to meet the post-1957 U.S. problem, the government might drastically reduce unilateral transfers. Although, as we noted in the preceding chapter, a great reduction in foreign aid presumably would be partially matched by a fall in U.S. exports, we can schematically envisage the current account's

[1] An attempt to specify the meaning of "balance-of-payments adjustment mechanism" in terms of the "objective" of adjustment again raises questions of defining balance-of-payments balance or equilibrium. For example, assuming that long-term assets are not considered part of international reserves, the condi-

remaining unchanged, the entire counterpart to the cut in aid being a reduction in the U.S. gold outflow and in the build-up of liquid dollar claims by foreigners. But such a discretionary policy, however reasonable it may be, is not an example of a *market*-induced and *market*-directed adjustment.

Even more decidedly to be excluded from the group of *market*-adjustment mechanisms are the various direct interferences with trade and payments. Such interferences affect the current account generally by reducing the *volume* of trade, by altering the commodity *composition* of trade, and by redirecting the geographic *pattern* of trade. They include tariffs, import quotas, export subsidies, and foreign-exchange rationing schemes. All such devices, particularly so-called "quantitative restrictions" and "exchange controls," are discriminatory in some sense to some degree—often deliberately so.

To illustrate, a country faced by the problem of a dwindling gold supply and exhaustion of previously accumulated foreign-exchange holdings may curtail the purchase of foreign goods, services, and securities by use of a system of licenses. A would-be importer seeking foreign exchange must not only spend domestic money to acquire it; he must also obtain an import license from the government. By limiting the number of licenses, the government can limit the value of imports. The government may be relatively liberal in granting licenses for the purchase of foreign tractors but permit the importation of few Cadillacs—perhaps just enough to supply the government officials. And the tractor-import licenses may—for economic or political-military reasons—permit purchase of tractors from Country *A* but not from Country *B*. With discretionary decisions required from the bureaucratic Mt. Olympus on *how much* of *which* goods from *what* countries will be imported by *whom*, the possibilities of economic inefficiency (however reasonably defined)—not to mention the sordid possibilities of moral corruption—are awe-inspiring.

Leaving aside, then, both administration of the government components of the balance of payments (i.e., foreign aid, military expenditures, government capital movements) and government direct controls over other trade and payments, what are the *market* variables which, if allowed to be effective, constitute an adjustment mechanism?

---

tion of zero net movement of reserves does not require a zero net balance on current account: a surplus or a deficit could be accompanied by an equal-sized long-term capital outflow or inflow, respectively. This, as we have indicated earlier, has sometimes been used as the characteristic of balance-of-payments "equilibrium." But suppose that the current account imbalance is matched by unilateral transfers; there would still be no movement of reserves, but this could scarcely be called a situation of "equilibrium." Or suppose that the current account is balanced (or that the imbalance is matched by long-term capital); despite this seeming "equilibrium," there could be a drain (or gain) of reserves because of granting (or receiving) unilateral transfers.

Adjustment and Absorption

What an economy *produces* in a year and what it has available for *domestic use* (i.e., *absorbs*) may be different magnitudes, as we have noted previously (pp. 575–577). Our earlier emphasis was on the "closed" economy and on the fact that "capital consumption" and inventory reductions give rise to a difference between output and absorption. Here, we are concerned with the "open" economy, one with international trade relations.

As before, let Y represent income (the measure of output), and let A represent absorption of goods and services by the domestic economy. Not all of the domestically produced output is available for use in the home economy, for some of it is exported to other countries; and some things which are available in the home economy were not produced there, for they were imported. If the money value of exports equaled the money value of imports, then (with Y being gross national product and assuming no net reduction in inventories) there would be no discrepancy between Y and A. (Does it follow that there is necessarily no gain from trade which is "balanced"—i.e., $X = M$? Anyone who answers "yes" must write "comparative advantage" 578 times.)

The nation's standard of living rests on the goods and services actually available, rather than on output as such. Some output is drained away in the form of exports, whereas imports contribute to absorption. With a given Y, A becomes larger as X decreases and M increases. We can write: $A = Y - X + M$, and $Y - A = X - M$: the difference between income and absorption is equal to the current account balance. And it follows that $A > Y$ if $M > X$, and the trade balance can be improved (i.e., X increased relative to M) only if Y is increased relative to A.[2]

The relation of Y and A is relevant to the matter of balance-of-payments adjustment, to the extent that adjustment involves altering X and M (i.e., the current account). In light of the U.S. loss of gold and the increase in foreign-owned liquid dollar assets, some urge that U.S. *exports* be *increased:* if foreigners spend more of their purchasing power in this country on goods and services, they will have less to spend on gold and liquid assets. Others urge that U.S. *imports* be *reduced:* curtailed purchases abroad by Americans will supply less purchasing power to foreigners, and they will thus find it expedient to cut back on acquiring

[2] M is one component of A. What are the others? We have:

$$A = Y - X + M,$$

and

$$Y = C + I + G + X.$$

Therefore, by substituting:

$$A = (C + I + G + X) - X + M$$
$$= C + I + G + M.$$

U.S. gold and liquid assets. The first method tends to reduce absorption by draining away additional domestic production, leaving less of a given Y for C, I, and G; the second method reduces absorption directly by reducing one of its components.

Thus with a *given* income, balance-of-payments adjustment hurts, for it involves a cut in absorption. Adjustment is feasible with unchanged absorption *if* income rises and exports rise (or imports fall) equally; but this—producing more but absorbing no more—hurts, too.[3]

The Adjustment Alternatives

THE PRICE-SPECIE-FLOW MECHANISM

In the mid-eighteenth century, building on the writings of numerous predecessors, David Hume formulated a theory of balance-of-payments adjustment based on gold flows and price changes. The essence of Hume's theory is simple: if Country *A* has an export balance, it will be financed by an inflow of gold, which raises domestic prices and lowers foreign prices (and, incidentally, raises the foreign-currency price of domestic currency), thereby reducing *A*'s exports and increasing *A*'s imports; similarly, an import balance generates a gold outflow, which alters relative domestic price levels in such fashion as to eliminate the imbalance.

As a first approximation, this is useful. However, a number of elaborations are in order. For one thing, the development of fractional-reserve banking and the expanding role of central bank action complicate the monetary mechanics, sometimes intensifying the basic process envisaged by Hume and sometimes dampening it. Also, Hume's model can be well supplemented by modern income theory, and his meager reference to exchange rates should be expanded.

THE MONEY SUPPLY

We have previously discussed determinants of the money supply and relations between the money supply and the price level. We shall not pursue the second topic further, but it is desirable to look a bit more closely at the effects of various international transactions on the money supply.

In our investigation of the balance of payments, seven illustrative transactions were specified (pp. 815–817). Table 44–1 lists these transactions and notes

[3] In discussing the relation between absorption and reduction of the trade balance, we have measured the various variables in *money* units. Although the *money* value of absorption necessarily falls when balance-of-payments adjustment is attained with a given income, "anything" is possible with respect to *real* values (i.e., physical magnitudes) unless all prices are held constant.

whether they increase (+), decrease (−), or leave unchanged (0) the U.S. money supply and excess reserves of U.S. commercial banks. The money supply is here defined to include demand deposits in commercial banks and currency in the hands of the public (although these transactions presumably will not directly affect currency holdings). And we distinguish between deposits held by domestic residents and those owned by foreigners.

Table 44–1

INTERNATIONAL TRANSACTION, THE MONEY SUPPLY, AND RESERVES

	Money Supply			Commercial Bank
	Domestically Held	Foreign Held	Total	Commercial Bank Excess Reserves
1. U.S. export of merchandise, financed by increase in U.S. deposits held abroad	+	0	+	−
2. Receipt of interest by U.S. bank in form of deposit held abroad	0	0	0	0
3. U.S. import of services, financed by increase in foreign deposits in U.S.	−	+	0	0
4. U.S. import of merchandise, financed by decrease in U.S. deposits held abroad	−	0	−	+
5. U.S. import of bonds, financed by decrease in U.S. deposits held abroad	−	0	−	+
6. U.S. gift of merchandise	0	0	0	0
7. U.S. export of gold, financed by decrease in foreign deposits in Federal Reserve	0	0	0	0

In four of the seven transactions, neither the money supply nor excess reserves are changed. Transaction 6 is a unilateral transfer of merchandise, and no monetary variables are involved. In transaction 2, the U.S. bank presents its bill of exchange, including interest charged as well as principal, and receives a U.K.

demand deposit: the bank gives up one asset and gains another, but neither deposits in U.S. banks nor excess reserves of U.S. banks are affected. Transaction 3 is a case of shifting ownership of deposits in U.S. banks from domestic ownership to foreign, but total deposits remain the same; therefore, excess reserves also are unchanged. Transaction 7 may be surprising, for here a gold outflow has no monetary effects, in contrast to the gold movements discussed earlier (pp. 698 ff.). But whereas before we had assumed that the purchaser of gold from the U.S. Treasury paid for it with a deposit in a *commercial* bank, here payment is made from a deposit in a *Federal Reserve* bank.[4]

In transaction 1, it is implied that the U.S. exporter drew a draft on the importer and sold it to a domestic bank, and the bank, in turn, collected pounds from the U.K. importer. The balance sheet of the U.S. bank shows an increase in domestically held demand deposits (liability) and an increase in demand claims on foreigners (asset). With increased demand liabilities and no change in reserves, excess reserves are lower.

Transactions 4 and 5 are similar. An American importer (of merchandise or of securities) meets his obligation by buying, with dollars, foreign currency owned by a U.S. bank. This reduction in demand deposits, with no change in actual reserves, increases excess reserves.

These sample transactions are sufficient to indicate that there is considerable slippage in the linkage between international transactions, on the one hand, and the money supply, on the other. Exports do not always increase the money supply; imports do not always reduce the money supply; even gold movements do not necessarily affect the money supply.

It should be added that, even if there were normally an *automatic* relation between foreign trade and the money supply à la Hume, the connection could be affected by *discretionary* action by the monetary authorities. The central bank might follow "the rules of the game" by supporting and intensifying the normal effects on the money supply—e.g., raising the rediscount rate when a balance-of-payments deficit appears; this was international financial protocol under the pre-1914 gold standard. But it is possible also that, in the interests of stability of the domestic economy, the central bank will deliberately try to counterbalance the foreign-trade effects on the money supply, particularly when a balance-of-payments deficit exists and the money supply may therefore normally tend to fall.

NATIONAL INCOME

We have seen earlier (p. 578) that "exports" (X) and "imports" (M)—the current account of the balance of payments—can be incorporated into the

[4] In terms of sources and uses of member-bank reserve funds (see Chapter 00), a decrease in a "factor of increase" (gold) is offset by a decrease in a "factor of decrease" (other—i.e., foreign—deposits in the Fed), with the Treasury deposit in the Fed (another "factor of decrease") first rising with the proceeds of the gold sale, and then falling as gold certificates are retired.

basic income equations. Exports, representing expenditure on domestic output, are a variable in the income-creation equation:

$$Y = C + I + G + X.$$

Imports also represent spending—but on foreign, not domestic, output; imports are, therefore, a form of income disposal:

$$Y = C + S + T + M.$$

Imports, like consumption and saving, are a function of disposable income, and we can refer to the marginal propensity to import—defined, analogously to other marginal propensities, as $m = \Delta M/\Delta D$. The income received in one period is disposed of in the following period as consumption, saving, and imports; therefore, in our expanded model, $c + s + m = 1$.

For illustration, suppose that investment and government spending remain unchanged ($\Delta I = 0$ and $\Delta G = 0$) while the initial income equilibrium is upset by an autonomous increase in exports, perhaps because foreigners reduced their tariffs on American goods. Table 44–2 is an elaboration of the tables employed in Chapter 34, to include columns for imports, exports, and the trade balance $(X - M)$; the marginal propensities are indicated.

Table 44–2

FOREIGN TRADE AND INCOME WITH AUTONOMOUS INCREASE IN EXPORTS

$c = .6; s = .3; m = .1; r = .1$

C	*S*	*M*	*G*	*I*	*X*	*X—M*	*Y*	*T*	*D*
700	150	50	100	150	50	0	1,000	100	900
700	150	50	100	150	70	20	1,020	102	918
710.8	155.4	51.8	100	150	70	18.2	1,030.8	103.08	927.72
716.632	158.316	52.772	100	150	70	17.228	1,036.632	103.663	932.969
719.781	159.261	53.705	100	150	70	16.195	1,039.781	103.978	935.803
.	.	.	.	.	.	.	.	.	.
.	.	.	.	.	.	.	.	.	.
.	.	.	.	.	.	.	.	.	.
723.478	161.739	53.913	100	150	70	16.087	1,043.478	104.348	939.130

In the first period, there is an equilibrium level of income (as well as a zero trade balance), evidenced by the fact that total leakages $(S + T + M)$ equal total injections $(I + G + X)$. In the second period, exports rise autonomously by 20 and stay at that new level. This, in itself, constitutes an increase in income and gives rise to an increase in disposable income in that same period, the increase in disposable income inducing increases in consumption, saving, and imports in the following period $(D_1 = C_2 + S_2 + M_2)$. And the sum of spending on domestic output in any period creates income in that period $(Y_1 = C_1 + I_1 + G_1 + X_1)$. Income rises at a decreasing rate and ultimately levels out at a new equilibrium value.[5] Of course, in the new income equilibrium, total leakages again equal total injections. And in the process of reaching the new equilibrium, the export balance is reduced from 20 to a bit over 16: the rise in income has induced additional imports and thereby reduced, but not eliminated, the foreign-trade surplus.

For further illustration of the relation of national income and the trade balance, consider the problem posed in the first period of Table 44–3. Income equilibrium obtains, but there is an import balance of 10. Suppose that the objective is to reduce the balance-of-payments deficit to zero by *cutting government spending* sufficiently to reduce imports—assuming that exports remain constant—through a fall in disposable income. Instead of asking about the effect of autonomous changes in trade on national income, we here analyze the problem of the effect of autonomous changes in income components on trade. What must be the (reduced) value of G such that D will be just the value required to induce exactly the amount of M which will equate M with the unchanged X?

The table illustrates that the new G must be 48.889. We can calculate that in the following way. In the equilibrium row of the table, we can immediately insert the values for I and for X, for they are assumed to be unchanged. Also, we know that $M = 50$, for that is the assumed objective, and thus $(X - M) = 0$. But if $\Delta M = -10$ and if $m = .1$, it follows that $\Delta D = -100$, and thus $D = 800$. Knowing that $\Delta D = -100$ and the values of c and of s, we can easily calculate the new equilibrium values of C and of S. Also, since $\Delta D = (1 - r)\Delta Y$ and $\frac{\Delta D}{1 - r} = \Delta Y$, it is apparent that $\Delta Y = -100/.9 = -111.111$, and $Y = 888.889$.

[5] We can derive a ΔY equation in the same manner used in footnote 1, p. 625, except that here the autonomous change in spending is ΔX instead of ΔG:

$$\Delta Y = \frac{\Delta X}{1 - c + cr},$$

$$= \frac{20}{1 - .6 + (.6)(.1)} = 43.478.$$

Table 44–3

FOREIGN TRADE AND INCOME WITH AUTONOMOUS FALL IN GOVERNMENT SPENDING

$c = .6; s = .3; m = .1; r = .1$

C	S	M	G	I	X	$X-M$	Y	T	D
700	140	60	100	150	50	−10	1,000	100	900
700	140	60	48.889	150	50	−10	948.889	94.889	854
672.4	126.2	55.4	48.889	150	50	− 5.4	921.129	92.129	829.16
657.496	118.748	52.916	48.889	150	50	− 2.916	906.379	90.638	815.741
649.445	114.722	51.574	48.889	150	50	− 1.574	898.334	89.833	809.501
.	.	.	.	.	.	.	.	.	.
.	.	.	.	.	.	.	.	.	.
.	.	.	.	.	.	.	.	.	.
640	110	50	48.889	150	50	0	888.889	88.889	800

Finally, since $Y = C + I + G + X$, and we now know all these values except G, it follows that $G = 48.889$.[6]

THE EXCHANGE RATE

Consider once again a two-country case, with each country exporting one commodity to the other. Suppose that we are given the U.S. demand for U.K. goods and the U.S. (perfectly elastic) supply of goods to the U.K., both the U.S. demand and supply prices stated in dollars; also, we know the U.K. demand

[6] Somewhat more elegantly, we can calculate ΔG by means of equations. We have seen earlier that $\Delta Y = \dfrac{\Delta G}{1 - c + cr}$. Since $\Delta D = (1 - r)\Delta Y$ and $\Delta M = m\Delta D$, we can write:

$$\Delta D = \frac{(1-r)\Delta G}{1 - c + cr},$$

$$\Delta M = \frac{m(1-r)\Delta G}{1 - c + cr},$$

and thus:

$$\Delta G = \frac{\Delta M(1 - c + cr)}{m(1-r)},$$

$$= \frac{-10(1 - .6 + .06)}{.1(1 - .1)} = -51.111.$$

for imports from the U.S. and the U.K. (perfectly elastic) supply of exports, with prices stated in pounds. Of course, we can convert the dollar prices into pounds and the pound prices into dollars by means of the exchange rate. Assume that initially the rate of exchange is $4 = £1, and then the pound is devalued (i.e., the dollar is appreciated) to $3.20 = £1. The given and the derived data are presented in Table 44–4 and plotted in Figure 44–1.

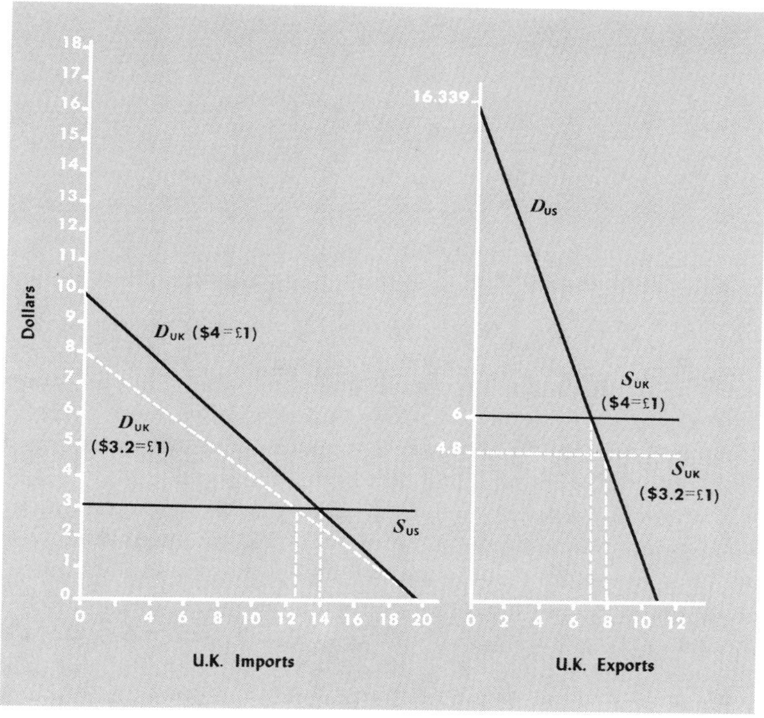

FIGURE 44–1a. Balance-of-payments adjustment: prices in terms of dollars.

All of the supply and demand schedules of the two countries remain unchanged in terms of "domestic" currency. That is, the *U.S.* curves are constant in *dollar* prices, and the *U.K.* curves are constant in *pound* prices. But when the pound is devalued with respect to the dollar, the *U.K.* curves measured in *dollar* prices *fall* at every quantity by the proportion of devaluation; and when the dollar is appreciated with respect to the pound, the *U.S.* curves measured in *pound* prices *rise* at every quantity by the proportion of appreciation.

As a result of the change in the exchange rate, what happens to the balance of payments of, say, the U.K.? In *quantity* terms, clearly U.K. imports are reduced, and U.K. exports are increased. But in balance-of-payments analysis, we

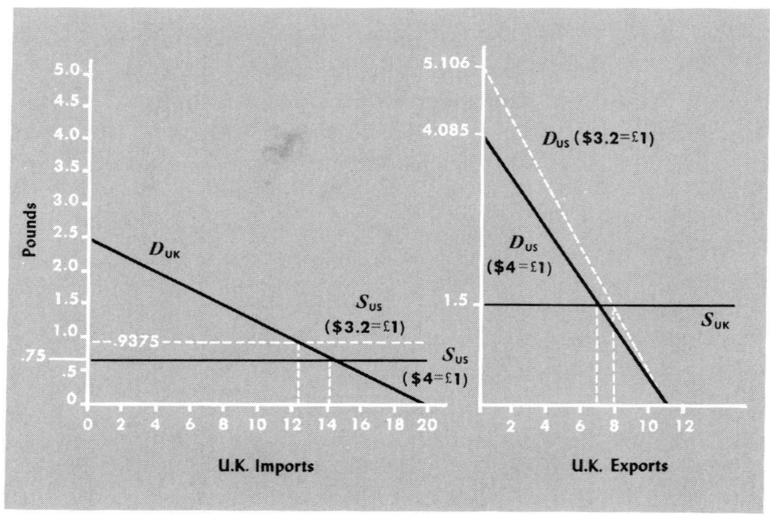

FIGURE 44–1b. Balance-of-payments adjustment: prices in terms of pounds.

are interested in the change in the *value* of exports relative to imports; and if the focus of the analysis is the international (rather than domestic) situation of the country, we would do well to make our measurements in foreign currency (i.e., the dollar, from England's point of view).

U.K. import value in dollars definitely falls: a smaller quantity is imported (12.5 units compared to the original 14) at an unchanged price. What happens to U.K. export value is not so obvious: a greater quantity is exported (7.8125 compared to 7), but price is lower ($4.8 compared to $6). In this case, export value is reduced; for in the price range of $4.8 to $6, U.S. demand is inelastic.

We can summarize the effects of pound devaluation as follows:

	U. K. Imports					**U.K. Exports**					**Trade Balance**				
	Price	×	quantity	=	value	Price	×	quantity	=	value	*X*	−	*M*	=	Balance
Initially	$3	×	14	=	$42	$6	×	7	=	$42	$42	−	$42	=	0
Devaluated	$3	×	12.5	=	$37.5	$4.8	×	7.8125	=	$37.5	$37.5	−	$37.5	=	0

We began with balanced trade, and after devaluation trade is still balanced. (Although the *balance* of trade is unaffected, the *volume*—i.e., *quantity*—of trade has changed, with fewer imports and more exports. Is that good or bad?) An unchanged balance is not a general result. In other circumstances, devaluation could raise export value relative to import value (even if export value absolutely fell); and export value could fall more than import value, thus creating an import balance of trade. In this case of horizontal supply curves, the crucial consideration—determining whether devaluation leaves the trade balance

Table 44–4

SUPPLIES AND DEMANDS WITH ALTERNATIVE EXCHANGE RATES

U.S. DEMAND FOR IMPORTS FROM U.K.

Quantity	Given Dollar Price	Derived ($4 = £1) Pound Price	Derived ($3.2 = £1) Pound Price
0	$16.339	£4.085	£5.106
1.58	14	3.5	4.375
2.94	12	3	3.750
4.29	10	2.5	3.125
5.65	8	2	2.500
7	6	1.5	1.875
8.35	4	1	1.250
9.71	2	.5	.625
11.06	0	0	.000

U.S. SUPPLY OF EXPORTS TO U.K.

Quantity	Given Dollar Price	Derived ($4 = £1) Pound Price	Derived ($3.2 = £1) Pound Price
All amounts	$3	£.75	£.9375

U.K. DEMAND FOR IMPORTS FROM U.S.

Quantity	Given Pound Price	Derived ($4 = £1) Dollar Price	Derived ($3.2 = £1) Dollar Price
0	£2.5	$10	$8
4	2	8	6.4
8	1.5	6	4.8
12	1	4	3.2
16	.5	2	1.6
20	0	0	0

U.K. SUPPLY OF EXPORTS TO U.S.

Quantity	Given Pound Price	Derived ($4 = £1) Dollar Price	Derived ($3.2 = £1) Dollar Price
All amounts	£1.5	$6	$4.8

unchanged at zero or creates an export balance or an import balance—is the *sum of the elasticities* of U.S. and U.K. *demand.*

Elasticity at a point can be measured by OP/PT, where O is the origin, P is the price, and T is the vertical-axis intercept.[7] Thus, at a price of $3, the elasticity of the initial (pre-devaluation) U.K. demand is $OP/PT = 3/7 = .4286$; and, at the same price, the elasticity of the new (post-devaluation) schedule is $3/5 = .6$. We shall take the average, $\frac{.4286 + .6}{2} = .5143$, as *the* elasticity. Similarly, the elasticity of U.S. demand at $6 is $6/10.339 = .5803$, and at $4.8 it is $4.8/11.539 = .4160$, the average being .4982. The sum of these averages is $.5143 + .4982 = 1.0125$; for most practical purposes, we may say that the sum is *unity.*

We conclude that in a situation of (a) horizontal supply curves and (b) initially balanced trade, *devaluation does not change the trade balance if the sum of the demand elasticities of the two countries is unity.* But if either demand curve were flatter, still going through the point of initial intersection with the supply curve, the elasticity of the demand curve in question would be greater at any price; and the value of imports would fall more, or the value of exports would fall less (or even increase): *When the sum of demand elasticities is greater than unity, devaluation improves the trade balance.* And if either demand curve were steeper than in Figure 44–1, still going through the same initial equilibrium point, then import value would be reduced less by devaluation, or export value would fall more: *If the sum of demand elasticities is less than unity, devaluation worsens the balance of payments.*

The foregoing focuses on the balance of payments in dollars, the foreign currency. But what of the effects of devaluation on national income in domestic currency? The income effects are important not only for their own sake, but also because of possible repercussions of income changes on the balance of payments. Indeed, some observers feel that devaluation is unlikely to have an appreciable (and nontemporary) beneficial effect on the balance of payments; for if devaluation does stimulate exports, income will rise, thereby inducing additional imports and also hurting exports through greater domestic absorption and higher domestic prices.

It appears in Figure 44–1b that the value of U.K. exports expressed in pounds definitely rises: more physical units of exports are sold at an unchanged pound price. U.K. import value may rise, fall, or remain the same, depending on the elasticity of U.K. demand in the price range of £.75 to £.9375. Is it possible in these circumstances to keep U.K. money income unchanged?

[7] It will be recalled that elasticity measures the proportionate change in quantity divided by the corresponding proportionate change in price; it may be designated $e = \frac{\Delta Q/Q}{\Delta P/P}$. Thus elasticity of demand curve TT' at point P' is equal to $\frac{MM'}{OM} \div \frac{RP'}{MP'}$. By substituting and rearranging, we have: $e = \frac{RP''}{PP'} \cdot \frac{OP}{RP'} = \frac{RP'}{RP''} \cdot \frac{OP}{PT} = \frac{PP'}{PP'} \cdot \frac{OP}{PP'} = \frac{OP}{PT}$.

Recall our income-creation and income-disposal equations:

$$Y = C + I + G + X,$$
$$Y = C + S + T + M.$$

If X rises, Y will remain unchanged only if $C + I + G$ falls by the amount of the increase in X. If M also rises, we might expect some reduction in C, for at least some of the increased expenditure on imports might represent a shift of spending away from domestic goods; and if C falls, the requisite decrease in $I + G$ is that much smaller. But if C should rise, perhaps in part because of a fall in M, then $I + G$ must fall enough to offset the greater C as well as the greater X. Finally, if devaluation is successful in creating an export balance,[8] and if income is to be held constant, then absorption $(C + I + G + M)$ must be reduced: $C + I + G$ falls by the amount that X rises; and M, if it rises at all, cannot rise as much as does X.

PEGGED VERSUS FREELY FLUCTUATING RATES

We have been analyzing the consequences of a change in the exchange rate. What immediately accounts for the change? If the rate is permitted freely to fluctuate, it will be determined by market forces of supply and demand. For example, envisage an increase in English demand for American goods: U.K. imports (and U.S. exports) rise, while U.K. exports (U.S. imports) remain unchanged. The U.K. trade deficit is financed, we may suppose, by a combination of reducing U.K.-owned demand deposits in New York and of increasing U.S.-owned demand

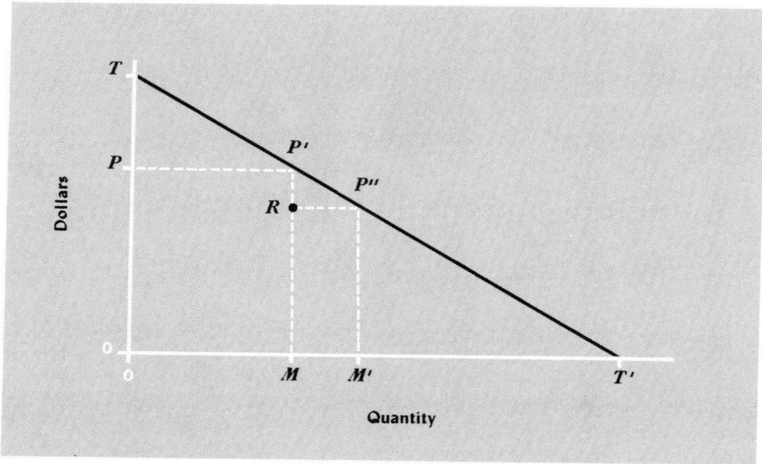

[8] Starting with balanced trade, the creation of an export balance stated in dollars must mean also the creation of an export balance stated in pounds.

deposits in London. The increase in demand for dollars and supply of pounds, resulting in lowering the dollar inventories and increasing the pound inventories of foreign exchange dealers, will bid up the pound price of the dollar and bid down the dollar price of the pound.

By contrast, the institutional arrangement may be such, as under the International Monetary Fund, that the rate is maintained ("pegged") within narrow limits for indefinitely long periods (see p. 780, n. 1). A change beyond the limits will involve a discretionary act by monetary authorities.

Supposedly expert opinion is not unanimous on the question of whether a system of freely fluctuating exchange rates or an I.M.F. system of pegged but infrequently adjustable rates is preferable. The case for flexible rates includes the following considerations. (a) If the exchange rate is held constant for prolonged periods, the balance of payments must be adjusted through other means. These alternative methods of adjustment—essentially, variations in domestic incomes and prices—require unsettling the internal economy, which is too high a price to pay to avoid movements in the exchange rate. And if neither the exchange rate nor the domestic income and price levels are to be allowed to induce balance-of-payments adjustment, reliance must be placed eventually on trade-reducing and trade-distorting direct controls over foreign commerce and payments. (b) If there is to be neither a process of continuous adjusting nor suppression of certain manifestations of disequilibrium through the exercise of direct controls, very large international reserves must be available. Indefinitely to preclude adjustment in an otherwise free market is to run the risk of having to finance a balance-of-payments deficit for an indefinite period. Even if it be anticipated that the fat years of surplus (that is, financially fat, but with a net drain from the economy of goods and services) ultimately will balance the lean years of deficit, the deficits can greatly strain or exhaust a country's reserves of international liquidity. (c) Even if a rate is pegged at what is initially an equilibrium level, as circumstances change, the equilibrium value of the rate is likely to diverge further and further from the actual value. As the balance-of-payments strain accumulates, policy decisions must be made. When should the rate be changed? In which direction? By how much? In anticipation of the alteration of the rate, speculation will be encouraged,[9] and, when the change finally is made, it very probably will be sizable. By contrast, a freely fluctuating rate would provide a constant adjustment procedure, avoiding the piling up of a problem, characterized by a reserve crisis

[9] For example, suppose a rumor begins to circulate that the pound is likely to be devalued vis-à-vis the dollar. Then those with pounds will begin to sell them for dollars at, say, $4 = £1, in the hope of being able later to repurchase pounds at less than $4 per £1. If the rumor proves false, nothing will have been lost (unless the interest return in the U.S. money market is substantially lower than the rate in the U.K.); if the rumor is well founded, a gain of perhaps 30 or 40 percent will be obtained. And even if the rumor initially was not well founded, the act of speculation tends to be self-fulfilling, for a large movement out of pounds into dollars will tend to bring about (or to aggravate) a drain of foreign-exchange reserves and gold, which will make devaluation more likely.

and unsettling speculation, which eventuates in forcing a largely arbitrary and uncertain act of discretion by the monetary authorities.

Powerful as the case for freely fluctuating rates appears to be, many find it less than wholly convincing. If the rate is perfectly free to move, it will move, and the movements create problems. The swings in the rate may be very wide, it is feared, because of cumulative speculation. If, for example, it is thought that the dollar price of the pound is likely to rise, dollars are spent in demand for pounds; and if there is no institutional ceiling on the dollar price of the pound, the sky supposedly is the limit.

Even modest movements in the exchange rate can be disturbing to foreign trade and investment. Unless the transaction is hedged against adverse changes in the rate, an American exporter selling a tractor for £1,000 will be chagrined to convert his proceeds into dollars at $2 = £1 when he had anticipated a rate of $2.50 = £1, and an American importer will be discouraged to find that he must pay $2.50 = £1 when the rate was $2 = £1 at the time he ordered the English linen. However, it is possible to hedge transactions in major currencies for periods of several months through the facilities of the "forward" foreign-exchange market.[10] If the U.S. exporter contracts with the Englishman to deliver a tractor in three months at a price of £1,000, he can protect himself against a fall in the dollar price of the pound (but also will forego any windfall gain from an appreciation of the pound) by entering into a second contract. This additional contract is with a foreign-exchange dealer, calling for the dealer *three months from now* to supply dollars against the exporter's pounds at an exchange rate agreed upon *now*. This future, or forward, rate may not be the same as the current, or "spot," rate of $2.50 = £1, but it will not deviate far. Similarly, the U.S. importer, who contracts to pay £1,000 in, say, six months, can contract *now* with an exchange dealer to acquire the pounds for dollars at that *future* time.

Even if forward facilities are available to hedge all trading and some investing transactions,[11] there still might be undesirable consequences from constant fluctuations in the exchange rate. For a substantial change in the rate could induce a shift in resource allocation, encouraging the expansion (or initial creation) of this industry and leading to the curtailment (or elimination) of that industry; then, once production plans were changed and perhaps were being implemented in their new form, the rate might change in the opposite direction, upsetting all schemes again.

[10] Perhaps the resources and the ingenuity now being directed to expansion and possible elaborate modification of the I.M.F. might better be devoted to broadening the currency coverage and the time scope of the forward market.

[11] While the facilities of the forward market do not provide protection from rate fluctuations for long-term investment, the risk for the investor may be no greater under a system of freely moving rates than under the I.M.F. system. For it is apparent that over periods of five or ten or twenty years, rates can be moved under the I.M.F., and presumably it is a matter of indifference to the investor whether they move continuously and gradually or by big jumps at irregular intervals.

Neither abstract analysis nor economic history gives clear indication that freedom of the exchange rate to move typically would have such unhappy consequences. What *is* clear from both analysis and history is that there must inevitably be *some* method of balance-of-payments adjustment or means to make balance-of-payments disequilibrium sustainable. Either adjustment or the camouflaging of disequilibrium will be costly. The question is: Are the costs increased or reduced by heavy reliance on movements in the rate of exchange?

Adjustment and the I.M.F.

We have several times referred to the International Monetary Fund, a post-World War II institution, which (a) provides the bulk of the non-Communist world with a system of pegged exchange rates and (b) can supply member nations with short-term (say, three- to five-year) loans to help finance temporary balance-of-payments deficits. But merely *financing* deficits is not necessarily to *eliminate* them; indeed, too ready financing of an essentially nontemporary deficit (and who can reasonably say at the outset just how temporary an incipient deficit will turn out to be?) can undesirably increase and prolong the deficit by delaying the application of necessary correctives. Presumably, the major role of the I.M.F. is to contribute to balance-of-payments adjustments. Does the Fund furnish an "automatic mechanism" of adjustment?

One potential adjustment variable, as we have discussed, is the rate of exchange, which, under the Fund arrangement, is free to move only within very narrow limits. The Fund has vigorously defended its system of indefinitely pegged rates. It asserts, quite correctly, that "stability" of rates over substantial periods need not and should not mean absolute "rigidity" of rates throughout all eternity.[12] Rates are to be "realistic" as well as stabilized, and they may be altered if they "have lost touch with economic realities."[13] But the condemnation of fluctuating rates is so strong and the Fund's attitude toward the possibility of occasional rate changes is so cautious and restricted as to suggest something of a "fetish" (denied by the Fund) for exchange stability.[14] *If*, for good or ill, a system of stable rates is to prevail, perhaps they should be very firmly stable.

[12] International Monetary Fund, *Annual Report, 1949*, p. 21.

[13] *Annual Report, 1948*, p. 21.

[14] The Fund agrees that a change in the rate *may* be preferable to the alternatives of a violent contraction in domestic economic activity and of direct controls. "A fixed exchange rate is desirable as long as a country is able to adjust its economy to changes in its real international economic position. But when the adjustments needed in face of a *radical* change in a country's international economic position cannot be made through home prices and costs, it *may* be necessary to change the exchange rate. . . . It *may* be preferable for a country to change an unsuitable exchange rate . . . rather than to subject its economy to the risks of *serious* deflation and unemployment or to impose restrictions that keep imports so low as to *endanger its well-being and efficiency*." *Annual Report, 1949*, pp. 21–22 (emphases added).

But the Fund sometimes may wrongly conceive that arguments for infrequent and grudging changes in pegged rates are also arguments for a system of pegged rates in the first place.

Devaluation is inevitable, the Fund feels, in the "exceptional circumstances" of persistent and strong inflation.[15] But the Fund—considering devaluation a *cause,* as well as a *consequence,* of inflation—believes it must be handled very gingerly. To be effective, it is emphasized, devaluation must be supported by restrictive domestic policies—policies which, the Fund seems to suggest, come close to being a *substitute* for devaluation.

Direct trade and exchange controls are possible means of achieving nominal payments equilibrium. But the Fund is intended to promote nondiscrimination and multilateralism. Its support of these objectives, often powerfully stated, has been tempered by a reasonable (and sometimes perhaps unreasonable) regard for the difficulties in making haste in dismantling controls adopted in the 1930s and 1940s.

The Fund apparently relies heavily on two remaining adjustment possibilities. First, simply wait—perhaps with the aid of borrowed Fund resources—and hope that the trouble will go away. Second, if the balance-of-payments deficit is too persistent, then domestic measures are in order. While inflation is strongly condemned, little suggestion has been made that a country actually deflate. All this is scarcely a neat answer—running in terms of a discernible and quasi-automatic market mechanism—to the question of which domestic variables are to alter, to what degree, within what limits, in which direction, and in response to what proximate stimuli. However, the Fund has established close consultative relations with member nations, based on analyses and advice of broad scope and backed by considerable, although not massive, resources. This emphasis on domestic policies suggests the gold-standard mechanism, but the discipline of the gold standard has been considerably modified.

The Fund may be establishing itself as a considerable force in behalf of "responsible" domestic and foreign-exchange policies and international financial cooperation. Still, aside from the limited provision of additional exchange resources, the prospect of occasional rate adjustments in accordance with uncertain criteria, and the urging by the Fund of "proper" economic behavior, it is not apparent that the Fund provides, or can provide, a perceptible *mechanism* for either cyclical adjustments or more basic and long-term corrections.

Questions

1. "Correction of a balance-of-payments deficit is perfectly simple—if only we deal with it directly and straightforwardly. A deficit means that we are spending more than

[15] *Annual Report, 1948,* p. 26.

we are receiving, buying more than we are selling. Well, then, if we are serious about eliminating the deficit, why pussy-foot around trying to *induce* people to buy less by juggling interest rates, tax rates, exchange rates, and the like? Why not just *forbid* buying too much? Go right to the heart of the problem: a little judicious exchange control will effectively ration our foreign spending to keep payments down to receipts. Such imposed restrictions (determined and administered by public servants in the national interest) are quick and certain, and we practical people like that." Are you, too, a practical person?

2. The "absorption" approach to analysis of balance-of-payments adjustment tells us that elimination of an import balance requires that the economy must pull in its belt and absorb fewer goods and services. Correct?

3. In an essay of 1752, David Hume wrote: "Suppose four-fifths of all the money in Great Britain to be annihilated in one night, . . . what would be the consequence? Must not the price of all labour and commodities sink in proportion . . . ? What nation could then dispute with us in any foreign market, or pretend to navigate or to sell manufactures at the same price, which to us would afford sufficient profit? In how little time, therefore, must this bring back the money which we had lost, and raise us to the level of all the neighbouring nations? Where, after we have arrived, we immediately lose the advantage of the cheapness of labour and commodities; and the farther flowing in of money is stopped by our fulness and repletion.

"Again, suppose that all the money of Great Britain were multiplied fivefold in a night, must not the contrary effect follow? Must not all labour and commodities rise to such an exorbitant height, that no neighbouring nations could afford to buy from us; while their commodities, on the other hand, became comparatively so cheap, that, in spite of all the laws which could be formed, they would be run in upon us, and our money flow out; till we fall to a level with foreigners, and lose that great superiority of riches, which had laid us under such disadvantages?"

Does this theory of balance-of-payments adjustment have any applicability to today's world? Is it at all deficient? If it can be salvaged but still requires modification or elaboration, what changes would you make in it?

4. With the introduction of foreign trade (or, more specifically, the current account) into the income model, the condition of equilibrium is that in a given period total injections—I, G, and X—equal total leakages—S, T, and M. So we concluded. But how or why do we include exports among the injections, and imports among the leakages? Is there no difference between X, on the one hand, and I and G, on the other; and between M and S and T? In particular, we earlier spoke of S and T as forms of non-consumption, but M certainly may (and does) consist largely of consumption goods.

5. The income-creation and income-disposal equations have expanded to:

$$Y = C + I + G + X,$$

$$Y = C + S + T + M.$$

Now, suppose that (a) $M > X$—i.e., we have an import balance; (b) Y is stipulated to remain constant, perhaps because we already have "full employment" and we wish to avoid inflation; and (c) the "adjustment" policy is to reduce M to the level of X by direct controls. When M is thus reduced, what are the repercussions on C, S, T, I, and G? Does the imposition of direct controls over imports obviate the use of fiscal and monetary policies?

6. In the text, we discussed eliminating an import balance by an autonomous decrease in government spending, which reduced disposable income and thereby induced a fall in imports. Now, starting again with the first period and the marginal propensities in Table 44–3, reduce the current-account deficit to zero by autonomously changing the tax-collection schedule, holding G (along with I and X) constant at the initial level.

7. Explain whether you agree or disagree with the following summary statement: "With normally shaped export and import supply-and-demand schedules, devaluation of its currency by a country will increase the volume (i.e., quantity) of its exports and decrease the volume of its imports, and thus it must improve the balance of payments."

8. Demonstrate with the aid of diagrams the following proposition: It is sufficient, for devaluation to improve the balance of payments, that *either* one (and not necessarily both) of the export supply curves be vertical—assuming that the import demand curves are not vertical.

9. We have noted that, starting with balanced trade and devaluing the pound from, say, $3 = £1 to $2 = £1, the creation of an export balance measured in dollars ($B_\$$) will create an export balance expressed also in pounds ($B_£$). For example:

EXCHANGE RATE	$X_\$ - M_\$ =$	$B_\$$	$X_£ - M_£ =$	$B_£$
$3 = £1	90 − 90 =	0	30 − 30 =	0
$2 = £1	80 − 50 =	30	40 − 25 =	15

What generalizations can you make from the following cases of pound devaluation with an initial dollar deficit?

	EXCHANGE RATE	$X_\$ - M_\$ =$	$B_\$$	$X_£ - M_£ =$	$B_£$
(1)	$3 = £1	60 − 90 =	−30	20 − 30 =	−10
	$2 = £1	60 − 60 =	0	30 − 30 =	0
(2)	$3 = £1	60 − 90 =	−30	20 − 30 =	−10
	$2 = £1	74 − 64 =	10	37 − 32 =	5
(3)	$3 = £1	60 − 90 =	−30	20 − 30 =	−10
	$2 = £1	42 − 58 =	−16	21 − 29 =	− 8
(4)	$3 = £1	60 − 90 =	−30	20 − 30 =	−10
	$2 = £1	56 − 76 =	−20	28 − 38 =	−10
(5)	$3 = £1	60 − 90 =	−30	20 − 30 =	−10
	$2 = £1	42 − 68 =	−26	21 − 34 =	−13
(6)	$3 = £1	60 − 90 =	−30	20 − 30 =	−10
	$2 = £1	50 − 80 =	−30	21 − 34 =	−13

10. A good deal of the debate on pegged versus freely fluctuating exchange rates has turned on the issue of "speculation." The proponents of each of the alternative systems of rates have urged that their system would minimize the problem of speculation. What is the problem of speculation? Indeed, what is exchange-rate speculation itself?

11. What is the "balance-of-payments adjustment mechanism" under the International Monetary Fund?

45

SAVING, FOREIGN AID, AND GROWTH

Economic "development" or "growth" has become a quite pervasive shibboleth. Many people believe that the economist and the policy maker are not sufficiently alert to the basis of their own economy's well-being or sensitive to the plight of their poorer brothers abroad unless their major attention is given explicitly to so-called "growth." The "growth race" has become a facet of the cold war. We may supplement the preceding several chapters on international trade and finance with a review of the growth difficulties and potentialities of the less wealthy nations and the possible role of foreign aid in that growth. Just as the subject of foreign trade did not call for a brand-new theory, basically distinguishable from the analysis of the first part of the book, so also "economic development" is to be considered with our now familiar constructs and techniques.

There are difficulties both in defining and in measuring economic development. But presumably the crux of economic development is a "substantial" and "persistent" rate of increase in per capita income, perhaps with allowance for valuation of leisure (if you receive $100 for forty hours of work and I receive $100 for fifty hours, do we have equal incomes?) and perhaps also with the proviso that the increased output of the community be "reasonably" widely dispersed.

The ever enlarging flow of goods and services which provides economic betterment is not manna from heaven, nor is it produced with an unlimited supply of resources. The overriding economic fact of scarcity thus calls for productive efficiency. And efficiency, in turn, calls for the devoting of some resources to capital goods: factories, equipment, dams, harbors, roads, schools.

Assistance from abroad may be intended

to help in the accumulation of capital. Capital accumulation doubtlessly is a *necessary* condition of economic development, but it is not a *sufficient* condition. And foreign aid is neither necessary nor sufficient for an appreciable degree of capital accumulation—a degree which, however, many will deem inadequate on various grounds. The value of American aid to underdeveloped countries, while scarcely negligible, is basically limited, because (a) growth requires more than capital, and (b) "saving" must be done by the growing country itself.

We shall not pursue far the point of growth prerequisites other than capital. Suffice it to note that such prerequisites are "social" and "political" as well as narrowly "economic."

Are there enough literate and energetic workers? Are there enough experienced and imaginative entrepreneurs? Is there a favorable ratio of working force to other means of production? Are there adequate incentives for efficient work—and appropriate penalties for inefficiency? Is the government sufficiently stable, consistent, and honest to maintain economic, political, and civil order, to generate confidence in a future for which plans may be made, and probably to undertake certain production projects not attractive enough commercially to engage private enterprises? Are the mores and philosophy of the community cordial to "growth" activities? Are the people sufficiently flexible and mobile, geographically and occupationally? Can population increase be kept under control?

Note the words of a man who was for fourteen years in the "development business," first as a vice-president of the International Bank for Reconstruction and Development and then as president of the International Finance Corporation:

> Let us briefly examine some of the frequently cited causes of underdevelopment.
>
> It is often claimed that geography and natural resources are determining. They are of course important. . . . But resources lie inert and have no economic worth except as people bring them into use. It is easy to attribute the progress of the United States to its wide expanse and abundant physical resources. However, other areas—in Latin America, Africa, Asia—have comparable natural wealth, but most of it is still untouched. On the other hand, there are countries in Western Europe with limited fertile land and meager mineral deposits, yet they have achieved high levels of economic life. . . .
>
> Perhaps most often lack of capital is blamed. . . . In the first place, there is in most developing countries more potential capital than is admitted. But large amounts are kept outside, because of political instability and depreciating currency at home. Or it is invested in often unproductive land, low priority buildings, or otherwise hoarded. . . . Over the postwar period immense sums have been made available to the developing areas. Some of these funds have been well applied and have produced sound results, others have not. . . . If [money] is applied to uneconomic purposes, or if good projects are poorly planned and executed, the results will be minus, not plus. The effective spending of large funds requires experience, competence, honesty and organization. Lacking any of these factors, large injections of capital into developing countries can cause more harm than good. The test of how much additional capital is required for

development is how much a country can effectively apply with any given period, not how much others are willing to supply.

It is popular in many quarters to charge colonialism with lack of development in territories which have been dependent. This argument seems less persuasive when we observe that a number of countries which have been their own masters for long periods are no further advanced.

I am, therefore, forced to the conclusion that economic development or lack of it is primarily due to differences in people—in their attitudes, customs, traditions and the consequent differences in their political, social and religious institutions.[1]

Having thus suggested that the world is a complicated place, we will emphasize here the second reason that American aid cannot by itself ensure foreign growth: The would-be growers must, in a real sense, do their own saving.

Sources of Capital

If, for the moment, we ignore receipts of foreign gifts and investments, an economy can accumulate capital only if it saves. There are two basic internal sources of capital: (1) Some resources that are now producing for current consumption may shift into production of capital goods. (2) The total output of the economy may be increased, with the additional output (or some of it) being channeled into capital production. In either case, total output is greater than consumption; the excess requires an act of saving and constitutes investment.

Capital accumulation, then, involves currently producing more than is currently consumed. Current production in excess of current consumption makes feasible the devoting of output to capital goods. If there is an excess of production over consumption, the gap involves saving. For *saving*, as we have seen before, is usually defined as *income currently received* (earned in current production) and *not currently consumed.*

But suppose that country Alpha consumes all of her own output. Could she not then build up her capital with gifts from abroad or with borrowing? Under the definition of saving given above, the answer is yes. But a modified definition will clarify matters. Let us now define saving as the gap between consumption and the *whole* of the community's available resources, including those supplied by foreigners through gifts and loans as well as those stemming from domestic production. Then American aid will not contribute to Alphian capital accumulation if Alpha fails to save and instead uses the foreign resources simply for more current consumption.

[1] Robert L. Garner, International Finance Corporation, *Summary Proceedings, 1961 Annual Meeting of the Board of Governors*, September 21, 1961, pp. 4–6.

Robinson Crusoe and Friday

Consider the case of Robinson Crusoe. He catches fish by hand, fishing eight hours per day, catching one fish per hour. He may decide that fishing with a net would be more efficient. Building the net is a process of investment and results in capital accumulation. How shall the process be carried out? What is the source of the capital?

There are alternatives. First, Crusoe may continue to catch eight fish per day, but he might eat only six and store two. After gathering enough fish to feed himself for the necessary time, he could then stop fishing long enough to construct the net.

There is a more likely variation (particularly in light of the problems in storing fish) of this first possibility. Instead of doing nothing but catch fish for a while and then nothing but build the net, Crusoe might cut his fishing to six hours and devote the remaining two hours to working on the net. In either variation, current consumption (of fish) is reduced so that resources can be directed to accumulating capital (in the form of a net). In full-employment economies in time of war, this substitution of one kind of output for another can take the familiar alternative-cost form of "guns versus butter."

The second basic alternative involves a greater total output. For Crusoe, this means reducing leisure, working perhaps ten hours per day. He could then continue to catch and consume eight fish per day while devoting two hours to making the net. Total current consumption (of fish, but not of leisure) remains unchanged. For economies in depression, this alternative may take the form of accumulating capital, not by cutting consumption, but through using hitherto idle resources and thereby expanding aggregate production.[2]

Both of these basic alternatives have one crucial point in common: consumption must be less than total output. Whether we accumulate capital through holding total output constant and cutting consumption, or through holding consumption constant and increasing output, there must be a gap between the two. The creation of this gap involves saving; and saving frees resources for capital accumulation. Saving makes "productive" investment possible. Whether the resources are wisely used is another matter. Crusoe might devote his investment not to producing a net but to constructing a totem pole. In either case, the first step is saving.

[2] For some underdeveloped countries, the second alternative may be realized by shifting into investment industries resources which are now being wasted in agriculture. It is widely, whether or not correctly, believed that frequently a large part of the labor force in agriculture in underdeveloped countries is actually producing little or nothing; that is, the marginal productivity of labor is near or at zero. Shifting this labor into capital production would not reduce agricultural output, and consumption could be maintained while capital is accumulated.

Thus far we have assumed that Crusoe is isolated. If he is to acquire a net, he must construct it with his own resources. The resources may have been diverted from catching fish for a time or may have come from working longer hours. Now perhaps Mr. Friday appears. With two economic units in the picture, there is the possibility of starting "international" flows of trade, loans, and gifts between them. Under these circumstances, what is the relation between saving and capital accumulation? Does international trade, investment, or aid enable a country to develop economically without being subject to the discipline of saving?

Crusoe and Friday might engage in balanced trade; that is, the money value of Crusoe's exports equals the money value of his imports. In money terms, Crusoe gives up as much as he gets. He is presumably better off in "welfare" or "satisfaction"—why else would he have bothered to trade? But is balanced trade a source of capital accumulation?

With trade (and the presumed production specialization in accordance with comparative advantage on which it is based), Crusoe—and Friday, too—will have available more commodities than if there had been no trade. Trade makes possible a more efficient use of resources, so that a greater output can be obtained from given inputs. But whether there will be capital accumulation depends on whether Crusoe devotes some of this additional income to investment or whether it all goes into consumption. Actual capital goods need not be imported; consumer goods may be bought abroad and substituted for domestic goods—thereby allowing domestic resources to be shifted to investment projects.

Again we arrive at the conclusion that saving means foregoing consumption out of current production and income, and saving releases resources for capital accumulation.

Consider another situation. Instead of exporting valuable goods in order to obtain desired items from Friday, suppose that Crusoe gets a loan or a gift from Friday. Here, one might suppose, is an easy, burdenless way to achieve economic growth. Instead of Crusoe's having to suffer the pains of saving, he will accumulate capital with foreign resources.

If Crusoe wants to be technical, he may claim that now he can accumulate without saving, according to the usual definition of foregoing some consumption of current production; for Crusoe is not, of course, producing the goods he receives from Friday as a gift or a loan. Assuming that his own production remains constant, Crusoe can maintain his old level of consumption—thus no additional saving, according to the conventional definition—and still accumulate. But in a fundamental sense, Crusoe would be kidding himself. If he gets a loan or a gift from Friday, he now has at his disposal additional commodities. This, in itself, neither constitutes nor guarantees capital accumulation. The problem obviously is what Crusoe does with his acquired command over foreign resources. Does he import tractors or solid gold Cadillacs?

It may be objected that if Friday has granted the gift or loan in order to aid economic development by Crusoe, he could specify, as a condition of the aid, that Crusoe buy tractors. But can Friday really thereby direct Crusoe to save instead of consume? Not if Crusoe is already doing some saving. Unless Crusoe has been consuming all of his output, he could now import tractors, according to the order of Friday, and simply increase consumption of his own output. Thus "foreign saving" (i.e., using the foreign loan or aid for investment in tractors instead of in consumption of Cadillacs) is offset by reduced domestic saving (i.e., increased consumption of domestic output).[3]

Saving, Population, and Per Capita Income

Loans and gifts from abroad make *possible* capital accumulation without curtailing consumption. Also they make possible additional consumption. It is essential that consumption rise by less than the amount of the foreign aid. The moral is clear: Although assistance from abroad can help a country grow economically, such assistance does not excuse that country from the onerous chore of saving. Outside aid can supplement domestic saving but cannot supplant it.

In general, the underdeveloped countries save relatively small percentages of relatively small incomes; and they usually have, or threaten to have, relatively high rates of population growth, thus preventing the rate of *per capita* accumulation from rising much, if any, above zero.

The "natural increase" of population equals the birth rate minus the death rate. Population grows relatively slowly if (1) both birth and death rates are low or (2) both rates are high. The first possibility is one of "low growth potential," on the assumption that the birth rate is unlikely to rise greatly and the death rate has little possibility of falling still further. In this category are most of Western Europe, North America, and Japan, where annual birth rates are generally around 17 to 25 per 1,000 population and death rates are around 8 to 12, giving a rate of population increase of about 5 to 15 per 1,000—i.e., an average of about 1 percent. (The U.S. rate of population increase is approximately 1.5 percent.)

[3] Cf. pp. 28–29. "The earmarking of particular foreign loans or grants to specific investment projects may do something to ensure the productive use of funds, but is not by any means a basic remedy. Only where there is no domestic saving at all to start with can such earmarking be fully effective. . . . The Austrian government, so the story goes, asked for the release of counterpart funds to reconstruct the Vienna opera. The E.C.A. [Economic Cooperation Administration, directing the Marshall Plan for postwar European reconstruction] is said to have replied that this would not be a productive investment and that the release could not be granted for this purpose. Then the Austrian government remembered that it was itself financing the construction of an electric power plant in the mountains. It went back to the E.C.A. and asked for a release of counterpart funds to pay for this piece of construction, to which the E.C.A. agreed. So all that happened was a switch: the wily Austrians, having got the E.C.A to take over the financing of the power plant, now financed the reconstruction of the opera from their own resources." Ragnar Nurkse, *Problems of Capital Formation in Underdeveloped Countries* (Oxford: Basil Blackwell, 1953), pp. 95–96.

The second possibility, with both birth and death rates large, is one of "high growth potential," for the death rate may well fall sooner and faster than the birth rate. The Far East and Asia (excluding Japan), Africa, and the Near East generally represent this sort of situation, with birth rates of 35 to 45 and death rates of 25 to 35, the rate of increase thus being in the neighborhood typically of 1 percent. (India's rate is about 1.8 percent.)

There is a third general category, a "transitional" group which continues to have high birth rates but has attained a lowered death rate, giving rise to relatively rapid population growth. In this classification, including Eastern Europe, Russia, and Latin America, birth rates are, say, 30 to 45 and death rates are generally from 10 to 20, giving a rate of population growth of perhaps 2 percent, with a few rates as high as 3.5 to 4 percent.

The rate of change in national income ($\Delta Y/Y$) minus the rate of population change ($\Delta P/P$) approximately equals the rate of change in per capita income $\left(\frac{\Delta(Y/P)}{Y/P}\right)$. Obviously, if national income increases at only 1 or even 2 percent per year, per capita income can hardly increase much, and it may even fall. Compare the U.S. and Mexico, the latter having a rate of population increase of about 3.3 percent. If per capita income is to grow at 1 percent, U.S. income must grow by $1.0 + 1.5 = 2.5$ percent; but in Mexico the required income growth is $1.0 + 3.3 = 4.3$ percent. Or, to reverse the problem, if national income grows at 4 percent in both countries, U.S. per capita income grows at $4.0 - 1.5 = 2.5$ percent, while in Mexico it grows at only $4.0 - 3.3 = .7$ percent.

Americans, who are fabulously wealthy compared to most of the world's residents, should recognize that saving may be more irksome for the poor of the globe—for two reasons: (a) When income is desperately low, consumption cannot easily be cut; and if income is raised a bit, there is tremendous temptation to consume, rather than save, the increase. (b) The fact of income and consumption disparities in the world, while possibly inspiring the poor to save in order to "catch up," seems more likely to lead the poor to emulate the wealthy as much as possible in their consumption. (With per capita income some ten or more times that of two thirds of the world's people and a net saving rate of around 10 percent of national income, the average American saves each year an amount greater than the annual income of most of the inhabitants of the world.)

The Dismal Mathematics of Growth

Suppose that the discipline of saving is maintained and the costs are borne, perhaps with aid from the world's wealthy supplementing the resources of the poor. What can we reasonably expect to be the results?

An objective sometimes indicated, explicitly or implicitly, is that the tremendous gap between per capita national incomes of advanced and underdeveloped countries should at least not increase and, indeed, should soon begin appreciably to decrease. One gathers that some time prior to Armageddon, the gap will be eliminated.

"The world looks" for "an early solution," Pakistan representatives have warned, to the problem of "the slums of the world, which are otherwise called backward areas." "A stable world order cannot be achieved with a growing disparity between the productivity and living standards of the underdeveloped and advanced countries." [4] And Eugene R. Black, while president of the World Bank, agreed that we must not "be content to sit by and watch the gap widen between the standards of living. . . . Surely, if such a wide gap between standards of living . . . did not exist today—if during the last hundred years greater effort had been devoted towards improving conditions in the less developed areas of the world . . . —we might not today be witnessing so much social unrest. . . ." [5]

No one knows what tomorrow—much less the next century or two—holds. But it is suggestive to investigate the consequences of certain alternative and comparative reasonable rates of growth in per capita income. And the mathematics of income growth are not very comforting.

For the sake of our illustrative calculations, take per capita annual income of the U.S. to be $2,500 (in 1961, gross national product per capita was approximately $2,800 and national income about $2,300) and the income per person in country Alpha to be $250. This is a ratio of 10:1, which is not exaggerated: a ratio of 15:1 or even 20:1 appears appropriate for the U.S. vis-à-vis many poor countries.[6]

Suppose we consider alternative U.S. annual growth rates for per capita in-

[4] Ghulam Mohammed, International Monetary Fund, *Summary Proceedings, Fifth Annual Meeting,* 1950, p. 115; Mohamad Ali, International Bank of Reconstruction and Development, *Summary Proceedings, Annual Meeting of the Board of Governors,* Washington, D.C., 1953, p. 3. ". . . the gap between the two groups tends to widen rather than to narrow . . . making industrialized countries richer and richer, and the developing countries poorer and poorer, comparatively speaking. It is clear, therefore, that our primary problem is to seek ways and means which would not only enable the developing countries to telescope into one generation what has taken the industrialized countries many decades and even centuries of economic endeavor to achieve but also to arrest the growing disparity between them." Tan Siew Sin, Minister of Finance, Malaya, I.B.R.D., *Annual Meeting,* Washington, D.C., September 27, 1960, press release.

[5] I.B.R.D., *Summary Proceedings, Annual Meeting of the Board of Governors,* 1950, p. 9. Black also has stated: "I have noticed a tendency at times for development to be regarded as something which is due, as of right, from the more advanced nations to those less well developed. Whatever the rights and obligations of different nations may be, development is not something which can be imported from abroad. It is something which can only be won internally by acceptance of responsibility, hard work and sacrifice." *Ibid.,* p. 11.

[6] The 1961 GNP per head has been estimated to be $70 for India, $84 for Nigeria, $120 for Iran, $188 for the Philippines, $240 for Portugal, and $268 for Brazil. It is generally agreed, however, that such estimates substantially understate the incomes of other countries relative to that of the U.S.—the lower the income, typically, the greater the degree of understatement; a more accurate picture might be obtained by increasing the foregoing figures by some 50 to 100 percent. But even such large adjustments leave it obvious that the international income disparities are very great.

come, and ask what must be the corresponding rates of income growth in Alpha in order just to maintain the initial *absolute gap* of $2,250 (= $2,500–$250). As illustrated in Table 45–1, the answer varies with the time period in question, the required rate of growth in Alpha being smaller the longer is the time horizon. For example, if the U.S. per capita income grows at 2 percent, the income of $2,500 would rise to $2,550 after one year, an increase of $50. To maintain the absolute gap, Alpha's income must rise also by $50, but for Alpha $50 is a 20 percent increase. However, the absolute gap will be unchanged after ten years if Alpha grows at 12.30 percent; if we take a time period of 100 years, the required Alphian growth rate is 4.24 percent.

Table 45–1

REQUIRED PERCENTAGE RATES OF FOREIGN GROWTH TO MAINTAIN ABSOLUTE GAP OF $2,250
(U.S. Initial Income: $2,500; Alpha Initial Income: $250)

		Years				
		1	10	25	50	100
Alternative	1%	10	7.42	5.51	4.10	2.93
U.S. Growth	2%	20	12.30	8.34	5.94	4.24
Rates	3%	30	16.07	10.43	7.36	5.35

A bit of elaboration is in order. We have just noted that if the U.S. grows at 2 percent and Alpha at 4.24 percent, the absolute gap will be $2,250 at the end of 100 years, as it was initially. But this does not mean that the gap will be constant through all those years. On the contrary, at these constant respective rates of growth, the gap will grow larger for a time; at the end of 50 years, it will be more than doubled, reaching a maximum of $5,440 after 72 years. It will then fall back to $2,250 by the end of the hundredth year. (See Table 45–2.) Thus, even if Alpha maintains the very impressive rate of 4.24 percent for a century, while the U.S. grows at 2 percent, at the end of 100 years the absolute gap will be as large as it was initially; and during most of that period, the gap will be much larger.[7]

[7] Two considerations modify the gloominess of these calculations. First, the initial 100 (or 72) years are the hardest; and, beginning with the second century, the absolute gap becomes smaller than $2,250. Indeed, ultimately—after only six more years—Alpha's income will catch that of the U.S. and then become greater. Second, the *ratio* of Alphian income to American income rises continuously, from the original 10 percent to almost 88 percent after 100 years.

It is not generally anticipated that the Alphas of the world will grow indefinitely at between 4 and 5 percent; by historical standards, such a growth rate over a prolonged period would be remarkable. Growth anticipations and objectives for per capita income very often are stated at around 2 or 2.5 percent. Obviously, if both the U.S. and Alpha grow at 2 percent, the gap between their incomes will become ever larger. Even if U.S. per capita income does not grow at all and Alpha grows at 2 percent, it would take 116 years for the gap to be eliminated; and if the U.S. grows at a modest 1 percent, it would take 232 years for Alpha to catch up.

Table 45–2

U.S. AND ALPHA INCOMES
(U.S. Grows at 2 Percent; Alpha Grows at 4.237 Percent)

	Years						
	0	1	10	25	50	72	100
U.S. income	2,500	2,550	3,047.49	4,101.51	6,728.97	10,402.50	18,111.62
Alpha income	250	260.69	378.58	705.47	1,990.77	4,962.08	15,861.62
U.S. — Alpha	2,250	2,289.41	2,668.91	3,396.04	4,738.20	5,440.42	2,250

Concluding Meditations

Over the past quarter of a century, America has given economic assistance to the rest of the world in a manner and on a scale unique in history. The aid was vital in repulsing the legions of the Axis in the early 1940s; it may have been instrumental in keeping the Russian flag from the British Channel and the Mediterranean in the later 1940s. The aid has continued—not to help win a war or to clear the rubble after a war, but in large measure to alleviate the misery of appalling poverty, which afflicts most of the world's people.[8] We need not be

[8] The following table gives some details of United States foreign aid (in millions of dollars) since World War II:

Fiscal Years	Economic Aid [a] Grants [b]	Loans [c]	Total	Military Aid [d]	Total
1946–48	$ 6,331	$ 7,724	$14,055	$ 481	$14,536
1949–52	16,223	3,127	19,351	2,839	22,190
1953	2,159	454	2,613	4,272	6,885
1954	2,268	152	2,419	3,412	5,831
1955	2,013	674	2,686	2,509	5,195
1956	1,885	735	2,620	2,979	5,598
1957	2,017	1,270	3,287	2,134	5,421

reluctant to say forthrightly that the basic objective and the ultimate test of American aid, or of any public use of our resources, is American survival and general well-being. But in a world in which progressing and prospering allies are an asset, this objective and test has seemed to many to be consistent with our motivations of compassion and generosity.

The main resources and the main effort for growth must come from the growing nations themselves. American aid can usefully complement, but can never replace, their own means and endeavors. Indeed, gifts and loans are not the major contribution we can make to economic growth abroad. More important, in all probability, is that we maintain a fully and efficiently employed and expanding economy of our own and that we maintain free access to this economy by the rest of the world. Neither in good sense nor in good conscience can we expend our resources on foreign aid while at the same time leaving clogged the channels of foreign trade and investment.

Finally, we must appreciate that the world is a complicated place. In important respects, it is far more complicated and discouraging for today's economically underdeveloped countries than it was for the underdeveloped nations, including the U.S., of 150 or 200 years ago. In America, the cultural background; the supply of acquired skills of workers and of experienced investors and managers; the legal, religious, and economic institutions; the climate; the endowment of natural resources; the ratio of population to other resources—all were favorable to growth and, by and large, remain favorable to continued growth. Not all areas of the world are so blessed. And even if they were, the living standard of this part of the world is now far higher than that of most regions; and the size of the gap very likely will grow much larger during the next several decades, if not indefinitely.

The economic development of poor countries is not easy, and, with or without considerable aid from the rest of the world, it probably will not be rapid.

1958	1,728	1,239	2,967	2,404	5,371
1959	1,730	1,845	3,574	2,160	5,735
1960	1,955	1,417	3,372	1,845	5,217
1961	2,202	2,224	4,426	1,454	5,880
1962	2,248	2,836	5,084	1,526	6,611
Total	42,760	23,695	66,455	30,678	97,133

[a] Data are on an obligation or loan-authorization basis.

[b] Includes grants by the Agency for International Development and its predecessors; P.L. 480 programs (sales of surplus farm products for local currencies, etc.); and capital subscriptions to the World Bank, the International Development Association, the International Finance Corporation, and the Inter-American Development Bank.

[c] Includes loans by the Agency for International Development and its predecessors; Export-Import Bank long-term loans; and the $3,750,000,000 loan of 1946 to the United Kingdom.

[d] Primarily grants of military equipment, supplies, and services; annual data are net deliveries, while the total represents amounts programmed; all annual figures prior to 1956 are grants, with loans from 1956–62 totaling $244 million.

SOURCES: Agency for International Development, *U.S. Foreign Assistance, July 1, 1945–June 30, 1962* (April 1963), p. 1; footnotes mainly from summary in First National City Bank, *Monthly Economic Letter* (July 1963), p. 78.

Without hope nothing will be accomplished. And there is a basis for hope, for *something* generally can be accomplished. It may be a condition of our survival that *much* be accomplished. But wishing will not make it so—nor will fervent expressions of exaggerated expectations or insistence on unrealistic demands.

And that, gentle readers and young scholars, is the end of the book. What did you expect? A pot of gold?

Questions

1. What is an "underdeveloped country," and what constitutes "economic development"? Evaluate the following statements by Jacob Viner, *International Trade and Economic Development* (Glencoe: The Free Press, 1952).

(a) An underdeveloped country is one "which has good potential prospects for using more capital or more labor or more available natural resources, or all of these, to support its present population on a higher level of living, or, if its per capita income level is already fairly high, to support a larger population on a not lower level of living. . . . On the basis of this definition, a country may be underdeveloped whether it is densely or sparsely populated, whether it is a capital-rich or a capital-poor country, whether it is a high-income per capita or low-income per capita country, or whether it is an industralized or an agricultural country. . . . This definition, I am aware, would . . . be objectionable to those who want 'economic development' even at the cost of a lowering of per capita income levels provided it brings the filling up of empty spaces, or urbanization, or industrialization. Patriotic citizens may want their national economies to grow in size of aggregate income or of aggregate output because of prestige considerations or strategic considerations even if this involves a lowering of average living standards. To others, living standards may be a weighty consideration, but in terms of the living standards . . . of a particular class or a particular regional category of the population . . . A colonial power may be interested in the economic development of a possession as an incident to its becoming an enlarged market for the mother country's export products or an enlarged source of supply . . . without regard to the economic welfare of the colonial population" (pp. 125–126).

(b) "Let us suppose . . . that a country which has embarked on a program of economic development engages in periodic stock-taking of its progress, and finds not only that aggregate wealth, aggregate income, total population, total production, are all increasing, but that per capita wealth, income, production, are also increasing. All of these are favorable indices, but even in combination do they suffice to show that there has been 'economic progress,' an increase in economic 'welfare,' rather than retrogression? Suppose that someone should argue that the one great economic evil is the prevalence of a great mass of crushing poverty, and that it is a paradox to claim that a country is achieving economic progress as long as the absolute extent of such poverty prevailing in that country has not lessened or has even increased? Such a country, nevertheless, might be able to meet all the tests of economic development which I have just enumerated. If its population has undergone substantial increase, the numbers of those living at the margin of subsistence or below, illiterate, diseased, undernourished, may have grown steadily consistently with a rise in the average income of the population as a whole. Not only this, but if immigration is a significant factor, these statistical tests are consistent with no native having undergone an improvement in his economic status . . . Were I to insist, however, that the reduction of mass poverty be made a crucial test of the realization of economic development, I would be separating myself from the whole body of literature in this field" (pp. 126–127).

2. What is the connection between "saving," as usually defined, and "capital accumulation"? How is the connection altered by introducing the possibility of receiving foreign loans or gifts?

3. The "source" of capital may be internal (domestic) or external (when the economy is "open"). Furthermore, we can distinguish more than one internal source and more than one external source. Review the various sources of capital.

4. "Saving equals investment, ex post. Investment is necessary for capital accumulation. Capital is necessary for maximum production. Production is the basis of economic welfare. Therefore, the necessary and sufficient condition for increasing welfare (i.e., for economic development) is saving; and the larger is the rate of saving, the faster (proportionately) will be development." What do you think of that as a recipe for economic growth?

5. "A wealthy nation can do the saving for a poor nation: a nation receiving (sufficient) foreign aid can finance its economic development without itself doing any saving." Is this statement all right? Is it all wrong?

6. Very wealthy nations (e.g., the United States) and very poor nations (e.g., India) typically have relatively low rates of population increase (say, 2 percent or less); nations of "intermediate" wealth (e.g., Mexico, Venezuela) quite typically have high rates of population increase (3 percent or more). Isn't this a curious pattern? Why isn't there a better correlation between wealth and population increase—with, e.g., wealthy nations having a low rate of population increase, moderately wealthy a higher population rate, and poor the highest rate?

7. Recently India proposed to build a steel mill, and she asked the United States government to finance the project. In defense of her request, an economist serving as American ambassador to India wrote: "Although it would be a large mill, there is no doubt that the steel is needed. While the plant would be costly, it would soon pay for itself in the imports that it would save. To import a million tons of steel products would cost the Indians about $200 million. The proposed mill with an annual capacity of 1 million tons would cost $513 million to build. Three years of operations would thus recover the dollar cost of the mill and more. Since India combines her pressing need for steel with an equally acute shortage of dollars, the economic attraction is obvious. She could not, in fact, afford to import the steel that the mill could supply." Explain why every sentence of that quotation—except the third and fourth—is wrong, nonsensical, or irrelevant.

8. We have discussed the growth rates of Alpha, which would be required to raise Alphian per capita income to the U.S. level after alternative periods of time and with alternative U.S. growth rates, when per capita income is $2,500 in the U.S. and $250 in Alpha. Now, let us change the problem a bit. Again, let the initial incomes be $2,500 and $250. If U.S. income grows at 1 percent and Alphian income at 2 percent per year, how many years would be required for income in Alpha to equal *one half* the U.S. income at the end of the period? How many years if the U.S. and Alpha grow at 2 and 2.5 percent, respectively? Or 2 and 4 percent? (A table of common logarithms will be helpful.)

Answers

Chapter 1

1. We don't care what you think now. Wait till you finish the book. Then answer the question again.

2. The statement is false. It is because people act reasonably in accord with their interest that there are economic problems and wars.

3. a. You can think what you wish.

   b. We don't know what "socially preferred" means: e.g., that some prefer it; that a majority prefers it; that everyone prefers it; or that the speaker prefers it.

5. Maximizing the welfare of the maximum number is impossible unless you have an infinite supply of sources of welfare at your disposal. This common expression about the maximum good for the maximum number is an empty emotional piece of music or poetry.

8. Compare your answer with the definition in Chapter 16 when you get to that chapter.

16. a. Lowest tenth gets 1 percent; fifth group gets 8 percent; highest tenth gets 30 percent. Effect of graduated income tax is to reduce share in top two tenths and increase share for all lower tenths.

    b. Higher-income spending units have a larger number of individuals in the unit; spending units are defined as groups of "all persons living in the same dwelling and belonging to the same family, who pool their incomes to meet their major expenses."

Chapter 2

1. The first statement does not imply that people are rational; it could apply to atoms, whereas the second statement does not. Neither statement has any implications about free will or interpersonal dependencies.

3. Individuals, not abstract things called "colleges," make decisions.

4. The first statement means that more of one goal is achieved at the cost of having less of another. The second statement means that both goals are desirable.

11. a. It is.

b. No. I might insist on making the choice, but would toss a coin to decide, rather than let you make the choice. But if I did this, you might think I was odd.

13. **a.** Let X be measured on the horizontal and Y on the vertical axis.

c. Postulates 4 and 2 together.

d. Yes.

e. Postulate 4.

f. Postulate 5.

17. **a.** Economics does not use concept of satisfaction. It refers only to choices among available options. Remember "utility" is merely a name for an index for ordering choices.

b. Ditto.

c. We do not compare value of one good with another any place in this analysis. We use, as a measure of value, ratios between increments and decrements of goods that people would accept in exchange.

18. By drawing another curve above this one (or to the right of it) with the same general properties (slope and curvature).

20. **a.** Yes.

b. We don't know.

c. This question often kills a discussion of some topic.

25. Because we use maximizing principle in our theory as a logical apparatus for deriving observable implications.

28. *No* to all questions.

29. Because habits are chosen and not acquired haphazardly.

Chapter 3

1. **a.** Yes.

b. We know of no institution with dominant power of coercive violence that is not the government in any country. Government is an institution for enforcing certain admissible rules and procedures for resolving interpersonal conflicts of interest. The making and enforcement of laws and the judicial settlement of disputes are events that support the propositions. (Note that the statements say that government is *an* agency, not the only agency. For example, many social disputes are resolved by social ostracism, and by agreement to use an arbitrator.)

2. G. Washington; D. Eisenhower; John Adams.

4. **a.** We would first want to know the behavioral consequences of each kind. More than that, we can't say now.

b. The only kind of competition made illegal by a price ceiling is that of offering more money (and all that can be bought with it) than the legal limit as means of offsetting weaknesses in other attributes in competing for goods.

Fair-employment laws (prohibiting choice of employees by color, creed, or age) prohibit competition in terms of offering employer the personal attributes he may prefer. Pure Food and Drug Laws prohibit offers of inferior food at lower prices or of new and possibly better but untested (according to government tests) foods and drugs. Private-property rights prohibit competition by violence and involuntary dispossession of goods deemed to be private property. Socialism prohibits competition in terms of offers of types of services and goods that individuals privately prefer, without having to obtain authorization of government officials for propriety of producing the services. These are merely examples of types of competition that are ruled out—not a complete chronicle, and certainly not an evaluation of the desirability of the various types.

7. **a.** Promises to raise or lower taxes (affect other people's wealth) in order to benefit those who vote for you. Can't offer to sell services as a businessman can.

b. Will letters of recommendation help you get a better grade in this course? Does your past record influence the teacher of this course in making grades? Does wealth of parents?

c. Employees can offer to work for lower salary to get a job with favored employer in preferred town. Will this work in fraternities? How about candidate's ability to increase wealth of fraternity?

10. **a.** Yes—because these all involve social, interpersonal interactions. As such, one person's behavior with respect to these characteristics or attributes will affect other people, and their response to his behavior will vary accordingly. Their response and their ability to influence his actions will depend upon whether or not there is private property—for reasons we shall see as we progress through the book.

b. Nothing like asking this question to kill a discussion! (Remember, evidence does not consist of one's own idiosyncratic memories or *ad hoc* examples.)

11. All societies use force and compulsion. The capitalist system forces thieves into jail. The pertinent issue is what kinds of coercion and force do various economic, political, and social systems use. The capitalist system uses the compulsive force of self-interest; it is coldly impersonal in its market effects; it is a severe and unforgiving taskmaster. He who produces at a loss is forced out of business, perhaps more severely and with less compassion than under a socialist dictator, who could spread the loss over other people. More relevant than the question of which system uses less force is the question of the effects of the various kinds of forces, incentives, rewards, signals, orders, and penalties—in terms of the resultant effects on the economic, cultural, and political behavior. For example, how is freedom of speech, job mobility, social fluidity, individual dignity, religious worship, search for the truth, etc., affected? The effects on all the various goals of a person must be considered.

Not even reference to the use of the rule of law versus the rule of arbitrary dictators is a basis for ultimate judgment. Here too the question is what law and what rules will be enforced by the ruling law: the rule of private-property rights or the rule of socialism or of still some other variant?

Differences are implied about the kinds of opportunities or "freedoms" provided to individuals living under each system. The implications of the analysis are that under an open-market system individuals have a greater range of variety of consumption mixes or patterns or goods from which to choose. Whether it is "good" that individuals should have such a greater range of options to explore is a question that economic theory cannot answer. Whether it is "good" to let people exploit that greater variety of consumption and more easily display their idiosyncrasies may depend upon your ideas as to whether they should make the same preferences or choices that you would. A greater range of choice can be regarded as a greater range of temptation, risk, error, regret, and deviant behavior. Just as a parent restrains his children's choices for their own good, we may prefer to restrain the choices of adults simply because everyone, even though over 21, still retains some childlike impulses.

Whether you wish to regard one system or the other as giving more freedom depends upon your meaning of "freedom." In one sense, freedom can include protection from the costs of resisting temptation and from making unfortunate choices; and, in another sense, freedom might include the right to bear those costs and to make those choices and explore tempting alternatives. Whatever the interpretation you give to "freedom" and whichever situation you prefer, the implications derived from economic theory about the factual consequences of different allocative systems will be helpful in forming a judgment.

Chapter 4

1. **a.** Between .25 and .33 meat for one unit of vegetable. Or, saying the same thing in reverse, between 3 and 4 vegetables for one unit of meat.

   c. Linus values vegetables higher in terms of meat than does Charlie. But Charlie values meat in terms of vegetables more than does Linus. So we could say that Linus, instead of valuing vegetables higher, values meat less than does Charlie. Implication is that values of any one good are expressed and measured in terms of some other good. Hence, both are involved in valuation, and we cannot tell which *one* is being valued; each is being valued in terms of the other.

   f. Consumption-substitution ratios must differ between two people, at their present situations, if exchange is to be mutually acceptable.

3. No. They do not imply what is good, bad, better, or worse. They imply what will be observed in the real world.

4. No. They say only that when a person trades or makes an exchange choice, he, at the moment of choice, "prefers" it. Whether or not he will later regret it and want to trade back or change his choice is irrelevant.

8. **a.** It is nonsense. It might be supposed to mean that one area had more of some good than it wanted (could possibly use at all?). In that case the statement is dead wrong. We call it nonsense because we doubt it means that. And we can't think of anything else it might mean.

   b. As an alternative we propose that the relative supplies were different so that relative values were different—leading to the possibility of mutually preferred exchange and re-allocation of goods among Mediterranean and Baltic people, à la Charlie and Linus.

11. No, it does not. It is the theory and its structure that conform to laws of logic and rationality. The predictable regularities of response of people to changes in their environment do not require they be "rational" any more than the response of water to the slope of hill requires rationality by each molecule of water.

Chapter 5

1. a. Yes. It is true for all goods.
   b. We have yet to find one.
   c. Nonsense question.

5. Middlemen facilitate exchange and specialization, while "do-it-yourself" is a reduction of specialization and exchange.

6. It assumes that the middleman performs no service to consumers or producers in facilitating exchange and that therefore he can be eliminated without someone else's having to perform the service in which he specialized. Eliminating the middleman is a form of do-it-yourself and as such is not necessarily more economical.

9. All are denials of open markets.

12. Read section titled "Constraints on Open Markets."

Chapter 6

1. Borrow one pair of shoes; sell the pair for four shirts; sell the four shirts for eight pairs of socks; then sell the six pairs of socks for one pair of shoes—leaving you with two pairs of socks. Repeat the operation, each time picking up a net gain of two pairs of socks.

2. *Exchange rates* among goods are prices, whether or not money be one of the pairs of goods in the exchange. Prices are not bids or offers that are unaccepted by the other party.

4. Recognizability, portability, storability, divisibility—all of which go to make the price of the good relative to any other goods less susceptible to variation among people. Possibility of producibility would induce production until value of one unit of the money would equal cost of production—unless quantity is limited by law or controlled by government.

6. Rate of 1,825 gallons a year.

8. 70 gallons, because he will have consumed 140 gallons in the week rather than 70 gallons.

10. It is a fall in the price of candy in ice-cream units. Candy is cheaper relative to ice cream than formerly.

12. a. No.
    b. The negative functional relationships between price and amount de-

manded. The explicit numbers serve merely to illustrate explicitly the meaning of the negative relationship.

16. **a.** Incorrect. Ratio (ignoring the algebraic sign) is greater than one.

b. Correct.

c. It is conventional to call this an increase in amount demanded, not an increase in demand—which refers to a shift in the whole demand relationship.

20. He who purchases seven per week, for that is the same as a rate of 365 per year, and he does it at a higher price.

25. **a.** Economic theory says they would. Compare cars in countries with higher gasoline prices. How about extent to which automatic transmissions would be used?

b. Increases gas use.

c. Effects would be more extensive in three years than in three months.

26. All except last one. (Why?)

27. Nonsense expressions. These terms mean only that someone wants more of something than he now has.

28. **a.** No such thing as basic need. We could use more and we could also get by with less security. It's a matter of what price we are willing to pay.

b. We "need" more of everything that is not free. The amount of any economic good we choose to have is a function of its price. To say our children need more schools ignores what we propose to give up to get more schools.

c. It depends upon the price, whether it is good enough to have at the price. If this says simply that more is better than less, o.k. Otherwise, it seems to deny relevance of alternatives.

33. If this happened with *equal* prices for slums and for high-quality spacious apartments, we would be stumped. In fact, however, we find that the prices of the high-quality dwellings are higher, which reduces the amount of the high-quality apartments demanded. Given the law of demand, we see that with a higher price of higher quality apartments, it is possible to reduce the amount people want or demand so that it does not exceed the amount available. Just why the price of slums should be so low as to induce more slums to be wanted than are available is something we shall take up later. For the moment we are interested in showing the implications of the law of demand.

Chapter 7

1. **a.** 0, 1, 2, 4, 6, 8, 9, 11, 13, 15 for prices from 10 through 1.

b. 4 to *A* and 2 to *B*.

c. Shortage.

d. Surplus.

e. All depends upon where price is.

3. a. Shortage if price is held by law at old level. If open-market pricing, then no shortage; instead, price will be higher—enabling re-allocation of X with B selling $1X$ to A at price of $7, the new equilibrium price.

   b. Impose a price of $8 (or more) as the legal price of cars.

4. b. No. He values a sixth one at $5.

6. True.

7. True.

9. First is rate; second and third are stocks.

13. What does invaluable mean? We are reminded of a caption seen in *Life* Magazine describing a pearl necklace: "This priceless four-strand necklace is now in the possession of Mrs. Lovely who bought it for $85,000." Rarely do we find such an incongruous juxtaposition of obvious inconsistencies. However, in fairness to those who often use the term "priceless," we suspect they usually mean that the priceless good is not reproducible. Thus, a Grecian urn or original Dufy cannot be replaced and is sometimes called priceless to indicate that there is no price that can be paid to get it replaced if destroyed. At the same time, one should be careful not to think it can't be bought at a finite price, or that a non-reproducible item is necessarily valuable.

Chapter 8

1. If individual demands for housing should shift, then those who want more housing than they now have will become purchasers, while those whose demands have fallen will become sellers.

4. Disagree. A higher price permits a re-allocation of existing goods—a re-allocation that would not occur in the absence of higher prices. Immorality is a gratuitous judgment. That the profits to those who own the goods when prices rise is "unwarranted" is also a gratuitous judgment. If government takes over, the higher price means an enrichment to government. Difficult to see why that makes it "warranted." The point of question is to note that higher prices do have a consequence not mentioned in question—re-allocation—and that a personal judgment about "unwarranted" or "unjust" gains should not blind one to that fact.

Chapter 9

1. Both. The act of choice is an act of discrimination.

2. All.

3. True.

5. Price controls do not increase probability that lower-income groups will get more housing than otherwise. They may get less (and over time with effect on production of housing, housing quality and quantity will deteriorate). Outcome

depends more upon possession of nonpecuniary attributes that now play a greater weight in allocative decision.

8. Open-market prices would encourage (force) consumers to use other good. Restaurant customers will take other foods, of course; but then this means households use more rice than if they too had to pay higher price. Greater revision in food habits occurs for those who eat in restaurants rather than at home. Continues apparition of "shortage."

9. Yes, for it does advance the argument (analysis?) to grasp the meaning of scarcity and to understand that economics says nothing about which goods ought to be allocated via the exchange market form of competition or other kinds of competition. We leave it to you to try to figure out why the "degree of scarcity" should affect the form of competition that should determine how a scarce resource is allocated among alternative uses and users. We can't.

10. The belief that money or market-exchange value is the sole criterion of allocation is so widespread, deeply ingrained, and incorrect that it is worth spending some time in examining it. Money is not the only criterion; that much has already been established with our analysis. (That it ought to be, if it were not, or that it ought not to be, if it were, is not the issue.)

When I dine in a restaurant, I select my dinner according not only to prices but also according to what the item is. I never tell the waitress to bring me the cheapest items only. The taste, nutrition, and looks of the item are considered. Similarly, when buying a suit, I take into account the style, feel, looks, and fit, as well as the price. For national security, we don't buy the cheapest weapon regardless of what it will do, nor the most modern, expensive weapon simply because it is the most expensive or modern—but not as effective as three units of a cheaper weapon (e.g., one B-70 as compared to three missiles).

Only if the options are equivalent in *all* other respects do money costs become the *sole* criterion, simply because cost is the only one that, in this case, makes any difference. On the other hand, if money costs were equal, then only the other attributes would be relevant.

Suppose that I own some land next door to where I live. Of two people who apply to buy the land—one, an ordinary man who offers $1,000; the other, a beautiful woman who offers at most only $995—I will sell to the woman. Her presence as a neighbor is worth more than $5 to me. The man could overcome his handicap if he offered $100 more. Money (i.e., exchange value) does count, but it is not the sole nor even the dominant (whatever that means) criterion.

A related criticism of the capitalist system says it relies on *market*-revealed money demands rather than intrinsic or humanitarian needs. By now there is no "need" to discuss the nonsense of "needs." But why do *market* demands count so much? The reason market demands are so effective is simply that exchange is a way to increase utility. Every person is free to reject the market demand and to exchange his wealth with "more deserving" people who offer less attractive market bids. But the market demand for exchange is heeded because people prefer to gain by exchange—not because they are perverted by capitalism or a desire for money.

If private-property rights did not exist, people would not be able to make such extensive market offers, because they would have nothing legally to buy or sell. In a university, the faculty does not have private-property rights in offices and classrooms; therefore, there is no marketplace where classrooms and offices are so easily exchanged. In a socialist system, market money demands are less effective simply because there is relatively less exchangeable property.

11. According to this criticism, a person is so influenced by his interest in his economic wealth that other criteria are dominated. However, the exchanging of goods does not make it difficult for anyone to be influenced by the artistic, social, humanitarian, or cultural uses to which he can put his goods and services.

Playwrights complain that the financial "backer" invokes his crass monetary standards. Artists complain that businessmen want mere display copy, not true art. The architect complains because builders do not want the artistic designs he proposes. What they really are objecting to are other peoples' tastes and preferences. But the issue is rarely put in so embarrassing a way.

Saying that only lowbrow products sell well seems to suggest that this is a result of the money-value system. But that system effectively reveals and enforces the "lowbrow" tastes and desires of the public. The actors and writers wish the public valued such quality more than it in fact does. Hence, actors and artists are frustrated because other people don't want as much "quality" as the artists would like to provide at the prices they would like to get. Or putting it "selfishly," the artists must admit that the income they can get from "low-quality" work is so high that they prefer to produce low-quality plays and get a big income rather than produce high-quality plays and live with a lower income. In this case, it is also the artists' and actors' own tastes for more wealth, not merely that of the public's, that precludes quality.

Chapter 10

1. At $2 per bushel, I could not affect price by withholding my stocks of wheat. Best price I could get is the market price of $2, whether I sell 1 or 1,000 bushels.

2. a. No.
   b. Horizontal straight line.

5. Yes, although in strict terms we assume that there is no rise in price as a result of withholding one's offers. This analytical classification yields implications that are for all practical purposes equivalent to those of a less extreme, discrete classification. For example, in this instance, it would not pay anyone to reduce sales for a higher price. The trivial effects are, for all intents and purposes, equivalent to no effects at all. Hence, in all the discussion it must be understood that we are using an extreme assumption simply because it makes the analysis so much easier without changing any of the pertinent implications.

7. Yes. Because higher rate of sales is available without a lower price, hence increase in revenue for each higher rate is equal to the price of the unit of the higher rate.

8. Constant.

Chapter 11

1. a. Data for blanks appear on p. 868.

PRICE	QUANTITY	REVENUE: TOTAL	REVENUE: MARGINAL	REVENUE: AVERAGE
20	2	40		20
			17	
19	3	57		19
			15	
18	4	72		18
			13	
17	5	85		17
			11	
16	6	96		16
			9	
15	7	105		15
			7	
14	8	112		14
			5	
13	9	117		13
			3	
12	10	120		12
			1	
11	11	121		11
			−1	
10	12	120		10
			−3	
9	13	117		9

c. Six units.

d. $16.

e. Yes.

f. See (g).

g. Have smaller profits than if price were set at $16.

2. **a.** He is searching for the wealth-maximizing price.

b. He is likely to find himself losing money as others enter business and reduce the price-cost spread.

4. **a.** Marginal revenue is $3.50 for a price cut from $13 to $12; and $5.20 for a price cut from $11 to $10.

b. From the increased receipts of extra units sold, there must be subtracted reduction in price on number formerly sold.

5. **a.** Either $5 or $6.

b. $7.

c. None. It is the wealth-maximizing price.

7. **a.** Yes.

b. Two more, for a total of eight trees.

c. No. Remember, an eighth tree is worth at most $3. What you paid for "earlier" trees is irrelevant except insofar as it affects your remaining income and thus your demand for everything else. But this effect is spread over all your purchases, and we assume here it is a trivial amount compared to your total income.

d. Eight.

e. Yes.

f. Marginal price is same under each circumstance, and we adjust to price of extra units.

Chapter 12

1. Law of demand relates purchase rate to price. Law of demand and supply states price is at intersection of supply and demand. The former holds in general. The latter does not.

2. False.

4. First come, first served is displaced by market offers. For example, in some airline waiting terminals, seats with views of the runways are rationed by a coin-operated turnstile. Similarly, binoculars are available on coin-controlled stands, thus preventing children from "monopolizing" them.

5. Seats are allocated first come, first served, rather than sold to worshipers—except in some churches, where a person donates a large sum and is given a special pew as a token of appreciation.

7. False.

9. a. Camp sites are not privately owned.

b. Less space per person.

13. As many as people want to use or create. No other objective test of the right number.

15. Depends upon extent to which you want to give parents authority to determine allocation of funds to family members.

17. Building and non-faculty purposes gain and faculty also gains to extent faculty salaries are raised more than they otherwise would have been raised. Money that would be spent for faculty salary increases can be spent for other purposes.

20. a. $200 release of money for other purposes, plus a better education, which you deem worth $300 more than the one you otherwise would have purchased.

b. Parents gain a cash release of $200 (and you get an education worth $300 more to you).

30. a. Price of stock fell.

c. National and Eastern gained wealth value of the airline route. Taxpayers lost the value of those rights, which otherwise could have been kept by government when it sold those rights—as it sells timber and gas-prospecting rights on federal lands.

33. Tendency to price public parks and services at less than a market-clearing price is explanation. Motels are priced higher than facilities in parks, thus relying on the law of demand to keep amount demanded in line with facilities available.

34. The market-exchange system characteristic of private property (capitalism) has been the dominant institutional context of the preceding chapters. The economic theory used in the analysis is applicable to any system of competition (capitalist, communist, or what have you) for resolving conflicts of interest among people arising from the fact of scarcity. In fact, the analysis of allocation with prices at less than the free-market price is an application of economics to a socialist society in which free-market prices are not used. Think of the actual money price as being zero, or at some level below the free-market price. Then how will goods be allocated among the competing claimants? (Review Chapter 9.) The relatively greater non-pecuniary "discrimination" should come as no surprise.

Many communist systems rely on money prices and private property to ration existing stocks of some consumers' goods. In Russia, many goods are sold for money, and individuals get money income from wages and salaries—*but not* from ownership of productive physical capital goods and instruments and land. Given a person's money income, he is allowed to choose among a variety of consumption patterns by voluntary exchanges with other people via controlled (as distinct from open) market prices.

The postulates are not idiosyncratic to capitalist systems. They hold for all known societies. The laws of demand and production hold also, whether or not exchange of resources *via* a private-property exchange system is used. We illustrated the use of these laws under non-capitalist situations in Chapter 12 and in other portions where private property and open markets were not the ruling institutions for the particular goods and services investigated.

What we are striving to emphasize is that a distinction be carefully kept in mind between economic theory and analysis on the one hand and, on the other hand, the institutional (legal and political) circumstances or conditions to which it is applied as a means of increasing our understanding of how different economies and societies behave.

Chapter 13

1. **a.** Advise only other wives to join.

b. Those who don't strike.

c. None except a frustrating sense of self-satisfaction.

3. **a.** No.

b. To some degree, among California colleges only.

c. Illegal.

d. No.

e. Not privately owned for profit businesses—is our guess.

f. Yes. Less incentive to cheat—because less possibility of capturing gains for one's own personal wealth.

9. **a.** Must keep neighbors from secretly offering more to get all the milk they want.

b. Yes.

10. Yes. And estimates of present value (at entry to college) for medical students suggests this is very likely what the facts are. In effect, medics live poorly while young and then far above average when old, whereas the rest of us do not have to wait so long.

11. All-Americans.

Chapter 14

1. a. May through September.

   b. May price is lower than March price, suggesting new crop is appearing. Lower prices for July suggest new crop is still being harvested and stocks are increasing, permitting higher consumption rates at lower prices.

   c. One or two cents a bushel—estimated by differences between futures prices during interval when no wheat is being added to stocks.

2. Primarily for profit.

3. Perishable. Increase in new supplies will be greater relative to carryovers, enabling greater increase in rate of consumption and lower prices. High storage costs (high perishability) implies lower future supplies (and larger present consumption).

5. False.

6. False.

7. Spot.

11. Can't tell. Do not know who has greater range of possible future positions nor what their relative probabilities are.

12. In the sense of having a greater range of potential future positions with greater probability of having a different wealth than now, I have the greater risk.

16. a. I bet on Mets and you bet on Dodgers.

    b. We have shared some risk and reduced range of our resultant wealths; in that sense we have reduced risk. I buy some (half) rights to your parking lot and you buy (half) rights to mine for the World Series days. Neither of us expects actually to help the other operate the parking lot. Instead, we just buy out the contracts later. He who lives in the winning team's town simply pays half his parking revenue (zero, since there are no games in his town). Each gets half the receipts regardless of which team wins the playoff game.

18. If we assume the price of the futures contracts falls by the same amount as the spot price, he will be able to buy back his futures contract at 35 cents per 100 pounds less than the price at which he sold it. The profit on his futures contract (ignoring contracting costs of about $30) is $175 (i.e., 35 cents per 100 pounds for 50,000). This will offset his loss on the processed soybeans—if the two prices move together by exactly the same amount.

20. It usually protects against large losses, but not at the cost of giving up rights to large gains.

24. No. Speculation also exists where future is uncertain. Futures markets permit re-allocation of speculative burden.

25. Disagree. Open futures markets reveal information for all at a lower cost.

Those with superior knowledge could benefit from abolition of futures markets because they could then more readily keep their information secret.

28. Ask those who consider it immoral. Some people say "Selling what you haven't already got is immoral." A contractor who bids on a building at a fixed price sells what he doesn't yet have. He has sold a promise or commitment. Short sellers do the same thing.

29. **a.** We couldn't think of any method. Can you?

30. To \$50.

32. Open-market exchange system via private property; in other words, the capitalistic market system.

34. **a.** No. It means there is less exchange and re-allocation of risks.

b. Processors, growers, middlemen, and some consumers.

Chapter 15

1. $\frac{(\$370 - \$350)}{\$350} = .057.$

2. $\$250(1 + .07)^3 = 306.25.$

3. Refer to Table 15–1, present value of \$1. At 10 percent the present value of \$1 deferred one year is now \$.9091. Therefore, the present value of \$220 deferred one year is $\$220 \times .9091 = \$200.$

7. $5.075 \times \$50 - \$253.75.$

9. \$5,000.

11. \$1,000 and it will stay at that value.

14. Nothing will happen to your wealth now. And in one year it will be the same as it is now.

15. Annuity of five years with present value of \$1,000 at 6 percent rate of interest is $\$1{,}000/4.2124 = \$242.48.$

17. **a.** They fall relative to costs.

b. Reduce profitability.

19. Yes. With higher rate of interest you still buy other resources equivalent to your house, but with fire you can buy only half a house or equivalent type of resource. In both cases you do suffer a loss relative to some other resources, but loss is more general in case of fire.

Chapter 16

1. **a.** Usually production is used to refer only to activity that is not illegal. We wish we knew of a better answer. The question helps to reveal the hidden normative content of concepts which at first seem to be objective and free of ethical presuppositions.

2. a. 7 and .6; 6 and .8; 5 and 1; etc.

b. 5 bushels of oats per soybeans.

c. .2 bushels soybeans for 1 bushel of oats.

d. Yes.

h. Meaningless question. Does it refer to weight, volume, value, calories? Without some conversion rule for converting to equivalent common units, there is no way to assign meaning to question. As it is now, one has more soybeans, the other more oats.

3. f. Nonsense question. (i) is 6.5 oats and 4.5 soybeans while (ii) is 2.67 of each.

g. Still meaningless.

h. No, for reasons we shall see later.

4. b. Different set.

5. a. Smith grows oats and Black grows soybeans.

b. Switch to soybeans.

c. If the price of oats is less than five times the price of a bushel of soybeans, Smith should switch to soybeans.

6. (1) Production is efficient if the output of one of the possible products is maximized for stated amounts of the other products. (2) Production is efficient if a further increase in output of one of the products can be achieved only by reducing the output of some other product.

10. Private property with open markets and observance of contracts.

11. a. Large.

b. Greater variety of relative talents and training so that differences between people's relative abilities are smaller. Further, the larger market enables a person to sell more of his special output at profitable prices.

c. Greater concentration of time on same repeated subtasks. For example, hair-shearing for poodles only; specialists in color-TV only; architects specializing only in certain types of buildings; greater number of specialty shops.

14. Suggests I shall be poorer and engage in more "do-it-yourself." Reduced opportunity to trade limits extent to which gains from trade can be achieved.

Chapter 17

1. Costs are not undesirable consequences of an act; they are the highest valued of the forsaken output—the opportunity forsaken.

3. a. Highest valued.

b. Expressed in a common denominator or measure of value.

c. In general, answer is No. Not if more than one thing could have been produced—including leisure.

4. Disagree. Lower cost is measure of substitution ratios between outputs, not a measure of the maximum amount of a good that can be produced.

5. The slope is the ratio of the change in output of one good to the implied change in the other, along an efficient possibility curve. This ratio of substitution in production possibilities is called marginal costs.

8. **a.** *B*.

b. *A*.

9. **a.** *C* and *E* produce *Y*; *A* and *D* produce *X*. *B* can produce either.

b. Yes.

c. All except *A* produce *Y*.

d. Yes.

10. **a.** Output of *Y* would increase to eight units.

b. Appears here as increased demand for *Y*. But relatively there is no difference.

11. **a.** Rates of output, say per day—not measures of total output of *X* and *Y* over time.

b. No. It means that if demand changed at noon, 7.5 units would have been produced that morning at a rate of 15 per day.

c. 60*Y* and 85*X* in five days.

14. *A*, *C*, *D* lose compared to what they would have been able to purchase with their income had *C* been able to produce *Y* and sell to *A*, *C*, and *D*. *E* gains in wealth compared to what he would have had with open access to markets. *C* loses wealth also. That *C* lives on an island across the Pacific rather than on the American continent does not change effects.

18. No. It merely assumes that existing knowledge can be used and subjected to performance tests. Assumes no restrictions on rights to purchase or exchange knowledge. Knowledge is a valuable (economic) resource. To assume it is free is, for example, to deny that schools exist and that teachers perform a useful desired service, and we can't deny that! A substantial fraction of our wealth is devoted to gathering information of one kind or another. Do not assume that ignorance is irrational, ridiculous, or the result of inefficiency or wastefulness or deliberate lying.

20. **a.**

GOODS			
X		*Y*	
8	and	0	
7	"	1.5	*A* produces 1.5
6	"	2.9	*A* produces 2.9
5	"	3.9	*B* produces 1*Y*; *A* produces 2.9*Y* (and 3*X*)
4	"	4.9	*B* produces 2*Y*; *A* produces 2.9*Y* (and 3*X*)
3	"	5.9	*B* produces 3*Y*; *A* produces 2.9*Y* (and 3*X*)
2	"	6.8	*B* produces 3*Y*; *A* produces 3.8*Y*
1	"	7.5	*B* produces 3*Y*; *A* produces 4.5*Y*
0	"	8	*B* produces 3*Y*; *A* produces 5*Y*

Increments of Y per successive units of X sacrificed are 1.5, 1.4, 1, 1, 1, .9, .7, .5. These diminishing increments of Y for unit sacrifices of X mean that marginal costs of Y increase for higher rates of output of Y. Thus, marginal costs of Y increase from $.67X$, to $.71X$, to $1X$ and on to $2X$, and then to infinite costs, since no more than $8Y$ can be produced per day.

b. Mr. *A* would be first; Mr. *B* would be last.

c. Mr. *A* would be first.

21. a. Yes.

b. We have assumed independent additive outputs from each person, as if they were lifting boxes separately. If they work jointly, two might do more than twice the work of each. We should then denote a team of workers as *A*, and another team as *B*. Similarly we could denote a team as a business firm, and then same principles would be applicable to firms. Joint interdependencies or "external" effects do not affect allocative principle but do instead make the exposition and analysis much more complicated. At the present level of exposition, the simplification employed here is permissible.

Chapter 18

4. Yes. Also salable without permission of other owners.

5. Convenient way to assemble capital. No one owner has to put all his wealth in one company in order for company to be large. Easy salability of ownership also enhances attraction of investment. In other words, it is an efficient form of property risk bearing.

6. No to all questions.

7. Depends upon what you mean by "very few." Annually many corporations show decreases in the value of their common stock. Approximately 30 to 40 percent of all corporations reporting to the Internal Revenue Collector report losses for the year, although the firms reporting losses are not always the same. Since 1916 the percentage has always been above 20 percent and has been over 50 percent in several years. For all reporting corporations the aggregate reported earnings (after taxes) normally run about 5 times that of the losses. For more details consult *Statistics of Income:* U.S. Treasury, issued annually.

9. The "boss" is able to tell people what to do because he pays them. Turning it around, the employee tells the boss what to do—that is, to pay the employee some money. Obviously, neither tells the other what to do. Each agrees to do something if the other will do something. If it be said an employer can fire an employee, so can an employee fire his boss by changing jobs.

12. a. No. In "ordinary circumstances" we would expect stability.

b. Should the typical voter or minority groups be able to turn out the governor of their state? It is precisely in order to prevent every single owner from making his own will count that voting systems are utilized.

c. Yes. It means a majority controls through the medium of a minority of the stockholders to whom a majority gives its votes, as the Congress represents a minority of the American public, being only some 537 people representing nearly 200,000,000.

13. a. Wealth constraints are different in the two classes of cases.

b. The former, since reduced possibility of personally capturing capitalized value of improvements of new management—as can be done in private-property corporations via purchase and sale of common stock.

Chapter 19

1. Yes. By definition.

2. Because they include future foreseeable sacrifices of present actions.

4. a. \$3,000 (to nearest dollar).

b. \$3,682.

d. Two-year annuity with present value of \$3,682 is \$2,122 per year.

f. \$971 per year.

5. a. $\$5{,}000 - (\$3{,}000 \times .909) = \$2{,}273$.

c. \$2,000.

e. $(\$6{,}000 \times .909)$ plus $\$2{,}273 = \$7{,}727$.

f. $(\$6{,}000 \times .909)$ plus $(\$6{,}000 \times .909^2)$ plus $\$3{,}761 = \$14{,}171$.

g. $f - e = \$6{,}444$.

h. \$1,000.

6. a. Present value of receipts is \$19,662. Subtracting present value of costs of two-year ownership and operation (from question 5f), \$14,191, the difference \$5,491 is the imputed profit.

10. The renter of the car pays for the depreciation as part of his rental charges. He avoids tying up capital funds only in the sense that the leasing company is lending him the car and charging him for its rental, whereas he could have borrowed money, bought a car, and then paid rental on the borrowed money (as interest). The rise of leasing services is primarily a consequence of business tax laws too detailed to go into here. But the point is that renting or borrowing money or paying out of your already accumulated wealth doesn't change the costs at all—aside from idiosyncracies of the business tax laws.

11. Old firms are not burdened by old equipment. They too can switch to new goods. That they don't simply means they can compete by using old equipment, whose value is recapitalized to whatever level will enable it to continue to be used—unless its value must be zero, in which case it will certainly be retired. Second sentence is a non sequitur since first sentence is fallacious. First sentence is typical of a very common error—an error that ignores market's valuation process of existing goods.

Chapter 20

2. Sentence is correct. By selective purchase of assets of personal wealth holdings, people can vary their mixtures to suit their risk-bearing preferences.

3. Socialism does not permit selective, discretionary, optional selection of wealth holdings by each individual. Profits and losses are borne in accord with taxes, rights to use government resources, and powers of political office.

4. Former facilitates or permits the latter to be revised in accord with personal preferences.

8. Can't ask this question too often. Some students will miss it again even after being told answer to same type of question in Chapter 11 (question 3).

10. Both—you first had a profit of $50; then, by continuing to hold that wealth, you incurred a loss of $25 during the second month. Whether or not you convert it to cash has nothing whatever to do with the fact of your change in wealth—i.e., of profits or losses. Only the income-tax people use the conversion to money principle for computing taxes—but do not be misled by their procedural rules.

15. A loss was realized when the stock price fell. If the price rises, the old loss is now fortunately offset by a new profit. You can't hide from losses by burying your head in the sand or by not converting your wealth from one form to another. You merely throw away options with that kind of reasoning. Don't make the logical and economic error of thinking you can escape a loss by not selling while the price is lower than it used to be, or even lower than what you paid for it. That kind of thinking does not engender strong survival traits for your wealth.

17. a. All. Some by patent rights, some by licensing which limits entry, some by limiting access to open markets for competitors, and one (Sinatra) by natural superiority.

19. They perform selective risk-bearing function, whether they know it or not. In prospecting for oil, some will lose and some may win. And some of us do not have to commit our wealth to that risky venture. Still, if we want more oil, the "lucky" investors who bear the risks relieve us of that risk. For that function they are allowed, under private-property system, to obtain profits. As for taxing them away, that depends upon your desire to have risks borne selectively, voluntarily, upon your willingness not to renege on general agreement to let lucky ones keep wealth, and upon attitudes toward differences in wealth among people.

Chapter 21

1. Rate and the total amount planned for production.

3. 4,000,000 units.

4. Cost increases less than in proportion to volume. (What did you assume about rate of output?)

6. Decreases.

8. Decreases.

10. Yes.

13. Public prefers lower cost more than greater variety of models.

16. Price will be greater for quick delivery of completed product.

19. The latter—regardless of the relationship between output and cost.

23. Usually to large volumes.

24. It is not because of lower costs of bigger outputs that selling price is lower, but because of negative demand function. The word "therefore" is the defect in the second sentence.

26. a. None. That they will not far exceed it for long is a result of open markets.
 b. None.

27. a. Impossible to divide costs between these two uses.
 b. Not answerable. Can divide it half and half if you wish. But what difference does it make for any real problem? None.

29. Less effective control of rates and entry internationally than intranationally.

Chapter 22

1. No.

2. Output program is 15 if price is $1.50; $6.20 profit; output program, if price is $5, is 24.

4. a. To produce more would involve costs that exceed the value of the extra amount produced. Resources could be used elsewhere in higher valued uses—as reflected in their costs.

7. b. $1.40.

 c. 1,400 per year.

 f. Buyers or sellers who want to buy or sell more than they can at the existing price.

 m. Under our assumption that all firms are identical, yes; all would survive up until total output reached 2,100. If more enter, losses will occur and some will have to leave or continue to lose wealth.

 o. Profits will be capitalized into costs; and costs, recognizing value of all the resources used by the firm, will equal revenue.

9. Marginal costs along with marginal revenue indicate maximum wealth output, while average costs in relation to price indicate whether the profits are positive or negative.

10. Suppose only president of company knew secret and also owned some shares. He would be less willing to sell at old price and would be willing to buy more shares. In other words, his demand to hold shares increases and thus affects market demand. Certainly several people in company knew the secret and several also

owned stock in the company. Price would rise because their own demand to hold the stock had increased in the light of the secret developments.

11. **a.** Reduce the output.

b. At first, if output is not reduced but taxes are paid, the wealth of peanut growers will fall. Higher marginal costs indicate a lower output as the new wealth-maximizing output. Or some who formerly made profit or broke even will now have a loss and be induced to abandon or reduce peanut production.

c. Reduced supply, shown by shift of supply curve to left, implies higher price.

d. Land will fall in value only to extent it was worth more for peanut growing than for next-best use.

h. Peanut consumers.

14. Resources will be increased in production of *X* until extra value of output of *X* falls to $5.

15. Not "consumer sovereignty" but "individual sovereignty" is more accurate. Individuals make choices as consumers (buyers) and as producers (sellers). An individual expresses choices about working conditions as much as about consumption goods. If mining is unpleasant compared to cutting timber, so that individuals are more willing to work at the latter rather than the former, the amount of lumber will be larger relative to coal than if individual preferences as producers had been reversed.

Because there are so many other people, each of us is usually powerless to affect output or market demand in a significant way. This does not mean we cannot choose among alternative purchases or products to produce. Nevertheless, because we cannot significantly change the range of offers made to us, each open-market producer thinks the consumer (a personification of the market) is sovereign, while the consumer erroneously thinks that producers (personification of supply) decide what consumers can have.

Chapter 23

2. Demand curve is horizontal at highest price at which seller can sell any of his product, while in price-searchers' market his demand curve is a negatively sloped function.

6. Yes, because extent of exchange and specialization is reduced, with consequent smaller wealth.

8. **a.**

PRICE	QUANTITY	REVENUE	
		TOTAL	MARGINAL
$4.00	0	0	0
3.90	0	0	0
3.80	0	0	0
3.70	0	0	0
3.60	0	0	0
3.50	0	0	0

PRICE	QUANTITY	REVENUE TOTAL	REVENUE MARGINAL
3.40	1	3.40	3.40
3.30	2	6.60	3.20
3.20	3	9.60	3.00
3.10	4	12.40	2.80
3.00	5	15.00	2.60
2.90	6	17.40	2.40
2.80	7	19.60	2.20
2.70	8	21.60	2.00
2.60	9	23.40	1.80
2.50	10	25.00	1.60

b. Output is 18.

9. **a.** Same as before.

10. **a.** Raise it.

11. **a.** Price-searcher—i.e., a type-2 monopolist.

12. **a.** Yes.

13. Price that maximizes their wealth depends on demand, not on their own desire for more wealth. Prices three times as high would, in opinion of sellers, yield smaller wealth or profits.

17. Sales price, if goods were available at that price at time of sale. Price means exchange prices, not hoped-for price.

19. Disagree. Advertising gives information about new locations of banks. Banks are not identical even though they are guaranteed and regulated. Personal terms of service, location, facilities differ. If advertising were prohibited, some people would be less informed about other alternative opportunities. To say it does *no* good is a pretty strong statement that is easily disproved.

21. **b.** Yes.

c. It is, when I do it. How about you?

23. **a.** Yes.

b. The government is not a monolithic agency of just one person. It often does conflicting things at the same time, in response to different pressures.

Chapter 24

1. **a.** Slightly more than 10 cents. We shall call it 10 cents for subsequent computations.

b. Between 65 and 67 cents. Call it 67 cents for subsequent computations.

c. Each would sell ten units at 67 cents each, for \$6.70 daily.

d. Formerly received (10 cents × 20 units) \$2 daily. Now gets \$4.70 more.

2. **a.** Each will want the other to absorb most of reduction.

b. New firm has growth expectations and won't want to be tied to former small output.

5. Government agencies enforcing laws against collusions concentrate on collusions against government. Second, government uses system of sealed bid, publicly opened and with identification of each bidder's bid and specifications. This provides an ideal publicity method for preventing secret price cutting or evasion of collusion of colluding firms.

6. a. Your guess is as good as ours.

b. Newspapers are privately owned and use privately owned resources. Their right to publish is not controlled by government agency.

8. Embarrassing question. We conjecture answer is that they are state owned.

10. Collusion connotes elements of deception in seeking to negotiate exchanges in the pretense that the sellers are acting as independent competitors. Buyers are misled into presuming sellers are acting as independently owned enterprises. If buyers knew sellers were in agreement, buyers would be alerted to incentive of each seller not to bid as he otherwise would. Without element of secrecy, buyers are aware of lack of inter-seller conflict of interest—as, for example, among the two salesmen of the same firm. The pretense of competing with respect to prices and quality is designed to induce buyer to think he is already obtaining advantages of inter-seller competition.

With open collusion, such as mergers, there is no pretense. Buyers are not deceived and can then obtain offers from other sellers whose interests are not merged with those of other sellers. Open agreements not to compete are not deceptive and consequently are much less effective in open markets. Partnerships being open are not deceptive, hence do not connote elements of collusion. Element of deception is undesirable.

Competition connotes elements of method of resolving who will get what of existing resources, while cooperation connotes joint action to increase total stock of wealth to be distributed. Some actions do both at the same time. Thus, exchange with specialization is both competitive and cooperative in increasing wealth as well as in allocating it.

Chapter 25

4. Don't answer until discovering the effects of each system. Unfortunately not a great deal is known, except that rental system of patented item enables discrimination among renters, which gives patent holder more wealth (and less to renter) than if purchase were allowed. No way to tell whether that is good or bad. Rental with bigger wealth for patentee serves as bigger inducement for new innovations. But then how much reward should they be given relative to unpatentable innovations? Unanswerable question!

5. b. Yes, because it permits discrimination among customers according to their demand.

8. Each can judge what is best for himself, we suppose. As for us, we would prefer formal exchanges not to shut off trading in particular securities, thereby reducing exchange opportunities. Under present system, presumption is built up

that stock-exchange officials are good judges of what price changes are justified or what news ought not to be allowed to affect decisions of individual investors —a presumption which not even the stock-exchange officials will defend. Rationale for restrictive practice is that wide swings as a result of news that turns out to be incomplete or exaggerated are often blamed on the stock market, with suggestion that stock-market officials were responsible or that they ought to have prevented such unjustified (with hindsight) swings. In fact, these wide swings are the result of incomplete information, which no one can improve on at the time. On the other hand, if the stock exchange closes trading at such uncertain times, and if the news is verified and does bring a persisting change in demand and supply conditions, the exchange can say that the new price truly reflects the situation. What this ignores is that stopping trading during those times locks existing owners into continuing ownership even though they would prefer to shed the uncertainty by selling to others who are more willing to bear it. Bad news thereby is made more damaging for existing holders in that they cannot sell out as early at the suggestion of worsening conditions. Consequently, it is not correct to say that closing down the exchanges at the arrival of big news (assassination of president, outbreak of war), or suspension of trading in particular stocks, is a good thing.

9. **a.** Owners of high-cost stations and stations already in existence. Low-cost stations and those who might enter business are hurt.

b. Your guess is as good as ours. How about men with prettiest wives?

10. **b.** As any of these groups, we would oppose the development proposed. Would you?

12. **a.** We, for what our opinion is worth, think students can discriminate as ably as any other group you would suggest. To the argument that students are prone to take snap, popular, "theatrical" courses, we ask, "What is bad about popular, theatrical courses if the course is nevertheless good?" To say that students select snap courses (meaning courses that are easy—not because teaching is good but because course content is trivial) is to provoke question as to why students do that. To say they are lazy is to presume that they should not be lazy or that only hard-working students should attend a class—a rather presumptive judgment. More germane is question of why students who are able and motivated to go to college should nevertheless sacrifice "good" courses for sake of an easy grade. Does it suggest something about the criteria imposed on the students by the college administrators? What?

15. **a.** The best—by definition, since the students can select from the entire world, rather than just within one state.

16. **a.** We asked for *your* explanation.

17. **a.** No. We know only of more economical goods driving out less economical goods. Ignoring price or costs, we can cite examples in each direction—a sort of irrelevant exercise.

19. Ask them. Do you believe they will have given you the real reason that advertising is not viable in that area?

21. **a.** Students living near campus will have first priority, after those receiving special scholarships from campus of their first choice. In other words, residential districting will be employed for most students.

d. Send your answer to the Regents of the University of California.

e. Send your answer to your state legislative representative. Do you think it will have any effect?

22. **a.** Longer-run consequences are, insofar as foreseen, discounted into present capital value of the enterprise and are hence borne by the present owner.

b. If he did not have salable rights, these effects would be borne by those who come along later. He would be more concerned with the immediate effects than if salable and hence capitalized values of assets under his control were his to bear; for these current values would more fully reflect long-run effects.

23. That capitalist money-seeking activity cultivates deceitful advertising, false claims, and dishonesty is so serenely believed by some people that it's a shame to waken them. The fact is that dishonesty and deceit often do pay. Therefore, it is sometimes said that free and open competition in the market gives a seller an incentive to lie in order to get customers from his competitors. Yet politicians also lie and don't tell the whole truth when campaigning or making speeches. They are not more honest than commercial advertisers. The socialist governments are not distinguished for their devotion to the truth. Surely there are good grounds for doubting that capitalism is more conducive to dishonesty than other systems. Nevertheless, it is worth considering the questions "Does capitalism reward one more for cheating than does any alternative system? Is the cheater likely to be discovered in the capitalist system and punished as effectively as in a different system? Is the public more likely to be deceived?"

That everyone has an incentive to lie and cheat is not denied. But is the ability to get away with it affected by the ease of competitors' making counter-claims? The question has only to be posed to be answered. A newspaper will be more careful with the truth if it knows that other news media can challenge its veracity. Politicians are more cautious if they know opponents can challenge their statements. A witness in court is more careful with the statements of facts if he knows he is going to be cross examined by the opposition. The easier it is for all to enter the market of ideas, the more counterclaims and different interpretations of events will be offered. In open-market capitalism, the incentives to disprove the claims and to submit counterclaims are increased.

What is not found is some authority to whom appeals can be made as to what the truth is about every matter in which one may be interested. If truth were a monolithic thing that an expert could readily detect, and this expert would never have any incentive to tell less than the whole truth, we could have some confidence in authorities who were supposed to permit publication of only truthful statements. But neither presumption is valid. The truth is not so readily definitive, nor is anyone free of reasons for his own "mellowing" of the truth. That is why it is a good rule to talk to a Ford salesman if you want to detect the truth about Chevrolets, and conversely.

In a capitalistic society, the probability of detecting falsehood is higher; therefore, more of it will be noticed, but less of it will be effective. One could contend that the more liars and cheaters we discover, the better that system is as a means of reducing such behavior. The city with the highest record of arrests is not necessarily the most crime ridden. Only the naïve contend that capitalism is more conducive to dishonesty or that censors supposed to certify the truthfulness of advertising will give us less deceit and dishonesty.

Chapter 26

1. There are many alternative ways of doing something, all of which can be technically efficient. But, of these, only one minimizes the value of forsaken opportunities; that is the economically efficient one.

3. Can't tell from that information. Don't know costs.

6. Can't tell. This tells us nothing about cost. We presume new method is technologically or technically efficient, in that no more could be obtained as output for given amount of specified inputs. But this doesn't tell us output is worth the input.

8. **b.** To include exchange efficiency. Values of outputs are being included as judged by what people will pay in an exchange system. Thus, efficiency is broadened to include deciding what to produce, rather than merely the cheapest way to produce an arbitrary output.

10. **a.** Suppose you had one piece of paper and were told to maximize your use of that paper. What would you do? Is it clear now that the expression has no meaning or that it means anything you want it to mean? Usage is not something you maximize; for usage is not measurable in a single-dimensional sense. In international radio-communications conferences, the statement sounded good to many radio and electronic engineers working for the Federal Communications Commission and for the State Department—precisely because it lets them interpret radio uses however they wish to. It's like having your parents tell you to maximize the use of your time at college.

12. **a.** All now twice as large.

    b. Increases them proportionally to rise in price.

13. **a.** Three labor and 4 capital, but if we interpolate we can do still better by using a little less than 4 capital and a little more than 3 labor—but not as much as 4 labor and 3 capital, which costs more than using 3 labor and 4 capital.

    b. 2 capital and 5 labor.

    c. Same one is cheaper. Relative prices of inputs did not change.

14. In the law of diminishing marginal returns, delete the word marginal.

17. Jobs of workers on railroad engines and jobs the displaced workers will accept elsewhere; also, jobs of workers on railroad engines and jobs of workers making equipment that will be used if railroads can revise their work rules and assignments.

19. **a.** Yes. Equipment on the bus for a laborer on the bus.

    b. Yes. Labor off the bus for labor on the bus.

    c. Yes. Total labor is re-allocated in its tasks. No labor is released from work force, since that labor is used to produce more of other goods—except to the extent that some now choose a bit more leisure (as total output is larger).

21. Unlimited number of jobs available; only those are filled which are highest-value jobs, given present knowledge and resources. New inventions induce labor to move to other unfilled jobs. Each time the labor moves to a less valuable job, relative to old job. But at the same time the total wealth of the community is increased. The displaced person, as explained in the text, has no assurance of realizing a net gain from the particular innovation which displaces his most profitable job opportunities; but he does gain from most other innovations that do not displace his job.

23. a. Increase the amount of that resource used relative to other resources.

24. a. Fixity of ratios of kinds of inputs in the final product says absolutely nothing about the ratios in which those inputs will be used to produce the good.

27. Explained in text on pages 441–443.

28. See text, pages 441–443.

29. The desire for greater wealth, and competition among actual and potential employers for those resources to be used in ways that give greater rather than less wealth.

31. a. Same as before: maximize utility. But, now less profit or net value of output can be retained or taken out by the owner; hence, less attention to profits as a source of utility.

c. Possibly some, but not as strongly as if enterprise privately owned. Would let it depart from ratio if thereby obtained more utility from other uses of resources rather than for profits or higher pecuniary exchange value. Recall discussions, Chapter 12.

34. b. Invest in personal intellectual skills, since these are not as easy as physical wealth for the state to appropriate.

Chapter 27

3. Both can be correct—as explained in text.

4. Depends upon infant mortality rate. If half of all children died in first year, and .2 survived to age 10, and if desire for children reflects desire for "grown-up" children, and if these mortality rates were lower for higher wealth and education of parents, we would expect higher number of births for poorer parents and fewer for richer; but in number of children in family at age 10, we could find more for richer than for poorer. The point is that in comparing countries, if one uses the same definition of "children," he can be misled about effects of wealth and education and population growth.

7. People differ in their productive abilities, and there is a cost of acquiring skills. The cost of acquiring skills (costs referring to all factors that restrain one person's ability to duplicate that of another) are such that differentials can exist; these differentials will be smaller than the costs of acquiring skills so as to enable lower-paid workers to do work of higher-paid people. Except for fortuitous matching of demands and supplies at wages that just happen to be equal in all tasks, differences in wages will persist to the extent that they are less than costs of acquiring skills of higher-paying jobs, or less than any other (or the total of such) transfer costs.

8. An unlimited number of jobs are available in a world of scarcity. If productivity in those jobs or tasks that people can perform in Arizona is not as great as elsewhere, population increase will decrease as people move elsewhere.

10. It means that 300,000 workers in jobs now refuse to cut wages enough to compete with new techniques in present jobs and prefer to accept jobs elsewhere at not so great a cut in wages. Of course, they prefer not to shift to a new job at all at a wage cut. What automation is doing is revising the relative demands for labor on various jobs, lowering some and raising some. Only those that are lowered are noticed in this statement that is being evaluated. (We do not hold out the number 300,000 as a valid number, other than for purposes of discussion.)

13. An infinite number of "unskilled jobs" exist. Most pay less than people are willing to accept, because they can get more money elsewhere. Whatever the reason for the unemployed, it is not that there are fewer unskilled jobs than unskilled workers. (We discuss some reasons for unemployed later—in Chapters 28 and 31.)

15. Movie producers do believe that receipts from picture will be at least that much larger if they have Taylor rather than Hepburn. In other words, last sentence of quoted statement is challenged. Whether or not she is worth that much more in the picture is part of judgment that producer has to make; and his actions reveal that if Hepburn could have been obtained for only $1,000,000, the marginal product of Taylor is, in his opinion, greater by at least $4,000,000.

Marginal product in demand for resources is reflected in estimates of what marginal product will be when the resources are employed. On what basis would you as an employer estimate and make judgments about marginal product of various resources to you as an employer? Would you ignore past record of various people? Would you as a football coach pay no attention to high school athletic performance when recruiting athletes, or would you look only at their physical appearance? Undoubtedly there are many talented people who could do just as well—if you only knew who they were. Marginal-productivity theory does not say that marginal product of every person in every possible job is known to all people. It says instead that demand for any resources is based on employer's estimates of marginal product of any given resource to him. It also says demand is a negative function of price of resource. Whether the theory is useless or false depends upon how well its implications agree with facts of economic life (compared to how well other theories do). On that score it is far and away the best available theory of the demand for productive resources.

18. A person should be able to get a job at a salary close to his last salary without a significant cost of finding such a job.

21. **a.** Because it is illegal. Induced higher rate of immigration. Perhaps labor already in U.S. wanted to restrict entry of new laborers from Europe. Ask your history teacher. (Note that today you can import a foreigner if you will guarantee him a job or guarantee that he will not be a public-welfare recipient for a year.)

22. We don't know.

24. No. He chooses not to accept best alternative job he has so far discovered and is instead looking at more jobs—which is not to say that he is lazy or deserves to be poorer.

Chapter 28

3. All the statements are empty, wrong, or irrelevant. This question is designed not as a device to evaluate unions but rather as a device to evaluate sentences written about unions. That many sentences written about unions are empty, wrong, or irrelevant in no way implies that unions are useless, wrong, or misunderstood.

4. **a.** Ask the judge.

b. Ditto.

6. Decreased. Union will set wages higher to keep only full-time employees at work, with less interest in casual, seasonal laborers.

9. Correct. Those who cannot provide services worth as much as the minimum-wage rate will have to work as self-employed or commission-basis employees. Thus, in saying that a higher minimum wage reduces employment, we meant employment for wages—not productive work as self-employed or commission-basis employees.

11. **a.** It will aid people who already are employed and who are going to have heart attacks and who either do not plan to shift to new jobs or who appear not prone to heart attacks.

b. It will make job shifting more difficult. Will hurt those who reveal a higher probability of heart attacks insofar as they want to change jobs. Will help them as long as they stay with *current* employer (i.e., with employer at time of passage of law).

c. All new employees will bear some of costs since heart attack is not perfectly predictable. People with record of attack will bear heaviest cost, since they will not be able to get jobs at as high a wage as formerly.

14. Increase. Self-employment is a way of evading wage regulation.

16. **a.** Doesn't differ except in degree to which it reveals implications of what is said.

b. At $5, reduction in number of employees would be too great. Self-employed do not join unions. Meany depends upon unions.

19. True, but not necessarily bad.

21. Those people who would be willing to work at open-market wages and who do not belong to unions. You explain why.

23. Too embarrassing for us to answer.

24. Yes, except for important fact that union is type-1 monopoly and U.S. Steel is type-2 monopoly. (With respect to world open markets, both are type-1 monopolists as a result of immigration laws and tariff and taxes on imports.)

27. Self-employed have less access to unemployment compensation; hence, less incentive to affect unemployment record. Concept of unemployment is narrower for self-employed people. Real-estate agents, for instance, do not call themselves unemployed during months in which they sell no houses.

30. Some employers will still be producing even after substantial increases in costs. Some may even be better off in that they are more vulnerable to lower-quality service. For example, some service stations that hire high-quality attendants and give superior service hire higher-wage employees. If the union could eliminate low-wage employees hired by lower-quality service stations, it would succeed in eliminating some competitors of high-quality service stations. Now apply same reasoning to orchestras, actors, retail stores, etc.

31. We asked the question first. You answer it.

Chapter 29

1. Personal human capital. Less subject to expropriation. If I were absolutely sure there would be no expropriation, I would invest in nonpersonal capital; for the buyer of the services of such goods does not associate them with the owner's personal characteristics as much as he would if buying personal services.

5. It increases the marketable pecuniary value of wealth because it increases the future available consumption.

6. **a.** Yes. A fall in the rate of interest.

b. Increases the profitability.

c. Reduce the ratio of the price of raisins to grapes. Raise it back toward earlier level.

7. **a.** $50 per year.

c. $10 per year.

e. Increases from $5 to $6 per year.

10. False. Remember, only the more productive roundabout methods are employed. Those that are less productive are shunned. Important thing is to get right kind of capital goods—not *any* capital goods.

12. **a.** $115.60.

b. Three years.

13. Soon as someone thinks an apple is ripe enough to eat with more satisfaction than not eating one at all (contrasted to eating it when it is riper and better). Apples will be eaten before they get as ripe as if privately owned.

Chapter 30

1. **a.** Correct.

b. A different definition than that given in this question is used. (See next question.)

2. Investment is defined as that rate of conversion to wealth (of present income) which can be profitable. The function relating these rates to the rate of interest is the investment demand function. Saving is defined as that rate of conversion of present income to wealth that the community wants to engage in. This desired rate, or rate at which the community is willing to divert income from current income to wealth accumulation, is a function of the rate of interest (among other things); and this relationship between the saving rate and rate of interest is the supply of savings function.

5. a. No.

b. In the sense that he could have even more wealth if he used his wealth differently. To say the interest rate is 10 percent means he could have used his wealth so as to have $110 at the end of one year. If he actually made it grow to $110 (regardless of what he then consumed) he did do the best expected. If instead he managed to have it grow only to $105, his poor management has cost him $5 in consumption. We can say his poor management is equivalent to a $5 consumption activity, except that we doubt he regarded the joys of poor management as a sort of consumption activity. But then again, who knows; maybe he did—by hiring pretty girls as congenial employees rather than pecuniarily efficient ones.

6. a. About 200,000 rabbits.

9. Higher rate of investment means a higher rate of production of some goods, and this implies a higher cost per unit of those goods.

11. It said that the payment of brokerage fees raises costs of business and threatens safety of deposits. Western banks contend that the *real* reason was that Eastern banks objected to this competition. (Can you spot a weakness in Home Loan agency's argument?)

15. Ignoring the effects arising from the adjustments of the person from whom you got the money, and looking at only your own impact, the effect of the sequence of actions would be to push down interest rates in the bond market as you purchased bonds—but later to be reversed as we sell the bonds preparatory to purchase of other goods. If we assume the money received was new money issued by the government, then, in addition to the above transient effect, the general price level would be pushed up as the demand for goods experiences a net increase. (Admittedly, $10,000 is a drop in the bucket for the whole economy, but even drops have their ripples; and sensitive enough measuring devices can measure fractions of drops.)

Chapter 31

2. Does not make any reference to wages he is asking, and therefore can be a question-begging definition—even though it is a very widely used definition. As is usual, you must use the one that is pertinent for the particular phenomenon you are interested in understanding.

3. False. There are jobs paying what many would regard as ridiculously low wages—which, of course, forces us to face the issue of what wage rate is not ridiculous, and how do we know?

4. Because I know others like me are getting more than $1.50 at other jobs and I believe I can find such a job myself with less loss of wealth than taking a wage cut. Taking a wage cut and working while also looking for a job is not as efficient

as spending full time looking for a job; else I would take the cut and then quit when I found the better job I prefer.

7. a. Yes.

b. Yes, and it pays not to cut rental in order to get an immediate occupant (because the cost of his moving quickly for the short period of time is greater than wage cut would be worth).

c. No.

12. a. No. The sum of a random variable, summed over trials (one for each firm), will still be a random variable. Random deviations do not cancel each other exactly.

b. Almost certainly. Very rare that every firm would have bigger sales on following day.

c. Almost certainly. Very rare that every firm would experience a decrease in sales from one day to the next.

Chapter 32

2. *All* transactions include exchanges of "intermediate" products and of previously produced assets; they give a total value, for which many types of output are counted more than once. *Final* transactions yield Gross National Product, which counts each item of current output only once and thus gives a better measure of the economy's production. The total of final transactions equals the total of values added by all the producing units.

3. a. False. The value of "the total amounts" sold by individual units of the economy is much greater than the values added by the respective units, for these values "double-count" input, or intermediate, products produced by other units.

b. False. While a negative value of inventory has no meaning, we can speak of a negative *change* (i.e., *decrease*) in inventory—which is so-called "disinvestment."

c. False. Only payments for *currently* produced *final* outputs produced *domestically* form a part of Gross National Product.

d. False. Value equals price times quantity. The dollar value of *GNP* in *current* prices may rise while real output increases, decreases, or remains constant. Calculation of *GNP* in *constant* prices is intended to obviate the effects of price changes.

7. The change in real output can be measured by the change in GNP_{con}. This involves calculating 1930 *GNP* in constant dollars, using 1929 as the base. $GNP_{cur}/P = GNP_{con}$, and we find in Table 32–1 that in 1930 $P = .96$. Therefore, $GNP_{con30} = 91.1/.96 = 95.1$. The fall in GNP_{con} from 1929 to 1930 is thus from 104.4 to 95.1—a fall of about 9 percent. The fall in GNP_{cur} is from 104.4 to 91.1—some 13 percent. Thus, the fall in price is approximately $13 - 9 = 4$ percent. More briefly, we can see in Table 32–1 that prices fell 4 percent (from 1.00 to .96), and since the fall in GNP_{cur} is 13 percent, the fall in GNP_{con} must be about 9 percent.

Chapter 33

1. There is no circular reasoning involved here. Rather, it is a case of mutual determination of income and consumption. In the income-creation equation, C in a *given* period is a *determinant* of income in that *same* period; in the income-disposal equation, C in a *given* period is a *function* of income created.

3. An autonomous change is a *shift* in an entire schedule. For example, consumption expenditure is now different from initial values at all income levels; or quantity demanded of a good is now different at each alternative price. An induced change involves moving *along* a constant schedule. As the term is used in the present context, the movement along the curve is induced by a change in income, which is analogous to moving along a demand curve as a result of a change in price.

5. a. The saving schedule is a straight line with a -150 intercept on the vertical axis and a 300 intercept on the horizontal axis.

   b. $S = -150 + .5Y$.

   c. $C = 150 + .5Y$.

   d. $MPC = \Delta C/\Delta Y$; MPC is the ratio of the absolute change in consumption expenditure associated with a given absolute change in income.

   e. .5.

   f. $Y = 400$; $C = 350$; $S = 50$.

   g. Autonomous.

   h. $Y = 300$; $C = 300$; $S = 0$.

   i. $k = \Delta Y/(\text{autonomous change in spending})$; k is the change in the equilibrium level of income resulting from an autonomous injection (or disinjection) of spending.

   j. 2.

   k. $MPI = \Delta I/\Delta Y$; MPI is the ratio of the absolute change in investment expenditure associated with a given absolute change in income.

   l. .167.

   m. $Y = 450$; $C = 375$; $S = 75$.

   n. $Y = 300$; $C = 300$; $S = 0$.

7. Starting with an equilibrium level of income, an autonomous increase in saving will, indeed, upset the equilibrium, and equilibrium will not be re-established until again $S = I$. But what closes the gap of S over I? Unless we conveniently assume an autonomous increase in I to match that in S, then S will be equated to I by a *fall* in income. Income will fall enough to induce the community to save no more per period than is being invested.

8. The fact that $MPC + MPS = 1$ derives from the income-*disposal* equation: since $\Delta Y = \Delta C + \Delta S$, then $\Delta Y/\Delta Y = \Delta C/\Delta Y + \Delta S/\Delta S$, or $1 = MPC + MPS$. All this has nothing to do with investment, which is a variable in the income-*creation* equation.

9.

C	S	I	Y
900	100	100	1,000
800	200	100	900
720	180	75	795
636	159	48.75	684.75
547.8	136.95	21.187	568.987

C	S	I	Y
900	100	100	1,000
1,000	0	100	1,100
1,080	20	125	1,205
1,164	41	151.25	1,315.25
1,252.2	63.05	178.813	1,431.013

It appears that when the marginal propensity to spend ($MPC + MPI$) is greater than unity, an autonomous change which disturbs the initial equilibrium will trigger a multiplier mechanism which is "explosive" (i.e., income decreases or increases at an increasing rate, rather than leveling out at a new equilibrium).

13.

YEAR	SHOE DEMAND	SHOES PER MACHINE	NO. MACHINES	DEPRECIATION RATE (10 YR.; 10%)	REPLACEMENT DEMAND	EXPANSION DEMAND	TOTAL DEMAND
(1)	(2)	(3)	(4)	(5)	(6)	(7)	(8)
20	100,000	5,000	20	4	4	0	4
21	110,000	5,000	22	4	4	2	6
22	130,000	5,000	26	4	4	4	8
23	150,000	5,000	30	4	4	4	8
24	155,000	5,000	31	4	4	1	5
25	155,000	5,000	31	4	4	0	4
26	145,000	5,000	29	6	4	0	4
27	140,000	5,000	28	8	7	0	7
28	140,000	5,000	28	8	8	0	8

YEAR	SHOE DEMAND	SHOES PER MACHINE	NO. MACHINES	DEPRECIATION RATE (20 YR.; 5%)	REPLACEMENT DEMAND	EXPANSION DEMAND	TOTAL DEMAND
(1)	(2)	(3)	(4)	(5)	(6)	(7)	(8)
20	100,000	5,000	20	1	1	0	1
21	110,000	5,000	22	1	1	2	3
22	130,000	5,000	26	1	1	4	5
23	150,000	5,000	30	1	1	4	5
24	155,000	5,000	31	1	1	1	2
25	155,000	5,000	31	1	1	0	1
26	145,000	5,000	29	1	0	0	0
27	140,000	5,000	28	1	0	0	0
28	140,000	5,000	28	1	0	0	0

The point to be emphasized here is that the more durable is the machine (i.e., the lower the depreciation), the greater is the degree (percentage) of fluctuation in total machinery demand: the increase in column 8 from one machine to five is a greater proportionate change than the increase from four to eight.

In addition, the tables contain other complications. In the first table, note the larger depreciation figures (column 5) in years 26–28, reflecting a five-year lag behind acquisitions in years 21–23. In the second table, replacement demand (column 6) in years 26–28 reflects the creation of excess productive capacity (because machine requirements fell faster than machines wore out) in year 26.

Chapter 34

1. a. *If* tax collections had to rise by the amount of government spending, we would be confined to the balanced-budget "route to full employment," which has a government-spending multiplier of only unity. But the government can (and, of course, does) obtain money by borrowing as well as by taxing.

   b. If the government wishes to follow a "counter-cyclical," rather than perennially balanced-budget, policy, it is appropriate to increase tax receipts relative to expenditures in boom periods and to reduce tax receipts relative to expenditures in recessions.

   c. At any given moment, it appears beneficial to any given person to have his taxes cut. But when taxes for the whole community are cut in a period of inflation, there is a strong tendency for the inflation to be further promoted. And if employment is already essentially "full," inflation will not induce an increase in real output.

2.

	C	S	I	G	Y	T	D
a.	880	120	100	270	1,250	250	1,000
b.	950	127.778	100	200	1,250	172.222	1,077.778
c.	650	94.444	100	250	1,000	255.556	744.444
d.	550	83.333	100	250	900	266.667	633.333
e.	900	122.222	100	250	1,250	227.778	1,022.222
f.	830	170	100	320	1,250	250	1,000
g.	880	120	112.5	257.5	1,250	250	1,000

3. a. 290.

   b. Surplus of 70.

   c. 1,310.

   d. 5.

   e. $Y = 1{,}950$; $D = 1{,}660$; $C = 1{,}280$; $S = 380$; $I = 380$; $G = 290$.

   f. Increase 70.

   g. Increase 56.

   h. 280.

   i. $Y = 1{,}880$; $D = 1{,}660$; $C = 1{,}280$; $S = 380$; $I = 380$; $T = 220$.

4. a. Income is at an equilibrium level, for total injections $(G + I)$ equal total leakages $(S + T)$. It happens that the budget is balanced (i.e., $G = T$). There is no necessary connection between the two: it can be the case that $G + I = S + T$ whether or not $G = T$.

C	S	G	I	Y	T	D
720	180	100	180	1,000	100	900
720	180	100	180	1,000	80	920
736	184	100	180	1,016	81.6	934.4
747.52	186.88	100	183.2	1,030.72	83.072	947.648
*880	220	100	220	1,200	100	1,100

$MPS = .2 = MPI$. Since $G = T$ in both the initial equilibrium and the new equilibrium, then $\Delta S = \Delta I$. And since in this illustration $\Delta Y = \Delta D$, it follows that $\Delta S/\Delta D = \Delta I/\Delta Y$.

b.

C	S	G	I	Y	T	D
720	190	100	180	1,000	90	910
720	190	100	180	1,000	80	920
728	192	100	180	1,008	80.8	927.2
733.76	193.44	100	181.92	1,015.68	81.568	934.112
*872	228	100	228	1,200	100	1,100

$.2 = MPS < MPI = 48/200 = .24$.

c.

C	S	G	I	Y	T	D
720	180	100	180	1,000	100	900
720	180	100	180	1,000	80	920
736	184	100	189	1,025	82.5	942.5
754	188.5	100	192.875	1,046.875	84.688	962.187
*880	220	100	220	1,200	100	1,100

$.2 = MPS > MPI = 31/200 = .155$.

C	S	G	I	Y	T	D
720	190	100	180	1,000	90	910
720	190	100	180	1,000	80	920
728	192	100	189	1,017	81.7	935.3
740.24	195.06	100	192.315	1,032.555	83.256	949.299
*872	228	100	228	1,200	100	1,100

$.2 = MPS > MPI = 39/200 = .195$.

5. **a.** We can lower equilibrium income by decreasing G and r with any type of budget: balanced, surplus, or deficit—which are analogues of Routes IV, V, and VI. In the surplus case, reduce G by anything less than 50 (i.e., the fall in income). One possibility is:

C	S	G	I	Y	T	D
720	180	100	180	1,000	100	900
710	177.5	60	180	950	62.5	887.5

b. As in Route VII, in which there must be a deficit if income is to rise with decreases in G and r, there can be only a surplus if income is to fall with increases in G and r.

Chapter 35

1. All have served as money at one time or another in various countries.

2. Most exchanges involve money as one of the goods, and the exchange rates are expressed in terms of money. But many goods have value that persists over time.

6. a. Ten pounds of potatoes or 2 pounds of butter.

b. The cost of holding a dollar of money (aside from the costs of keeping it secure) is 6 percent per year, just as it is for any other good.

11. a. No. They are used only for exchange for a particular good. They are receipts for prepayment for a special kind of service to be rendered you.

b. We would not, because they are not used generally for purchases; instead, they are first converted to currency or checking accounts. But they are so readily transferred to money that for some problems it may prove more useful to consider them as money.

c. Yes.

12. More for the increase in wages.

Chapter 36

1. Money is hardly perfect, even as a medium of exchange (try giving a $10 bill to a bus driver at rush hour). The deficiencies of money stem most fundamentally from the variability of the price level—i.e., inflation and deflation. A dollar is always a dollar, but a dollar does not forever and always equal the same purchasing power over goods and services. There is an infinite variety of nonmonetary assets, and value can be "stored" by holding many assets. Indeed, holding wealth in the form of nonmonetary assets can scarcely be avoided, for goods are durable to some degree—e.g., clothing is not consumed entirely in the instant of purchase. In addition to the convenience of holding some nonmoney goods, inventories of nonmoney wealth may rise—as well as fall—over time in terms of money.

2. There is some justification for the quoted remark. Money does indeed facilitate exchange. Also doubtlessly money has on occasion acted as an obscuring veil and a diversion to individual analysts. Still, money *is* more than just oil in the machinery. Changes in the money supply can affect the levels of prices and of output and the distribution income. In short, money—and changes in the money stock—has significant "real" effects on the operation of the economy.

4. Question (2) is the most fundamental one. However important gold and government decree may be *institutionally*, the key characteristic of the *nature* of money is its general acceptability in discharge of obligations. Whether only coin and currency should be included in the money supply or whether money subsumes also demand deposits or time deposits or still other assets is a pragmatic matter of usefulness in empirical research. Most analysts include demand deposits, along with currency, under "money."

5. Historically—particularly in the 1940s and into the 1950s—the Keynesian "income-expenditure" approach and the "quantity of money" approach have quite

typically been considered alternative ways to elucidate and predict the economy's aggregative behavior. In their simplest forms, the two approaches often have been made to appear almost wholly unique and distinct from each other. The "income" theory is then couched in terms of expenditure and leakage schedules, with fiscal measures dominating policy proposals, with money and monetary processes entering the picture only marginally, if at all, and with little or no attention given to the level of prices. And the "money" theory places emphasis well nigh solely on the money stock and its variations, relating the money source to bank activity and to actions of monetary authorities. Fiscal activities are of interest primarily only in the way that the government budget is financed and the government debt is managed; attention is directed at least as strongly to the general price level as it is to the national income level. Without denying—or necessarily decrying—that the "income" theory and the "money" theory provide, or encourage, somewhat different orientations and emphases, we have indicated that the analyst is better equipped with both approaches than with either one alone.

In simplest summary, the various schedules of the 45-degree diagram and their slopes and shiftings provide a highly convenient expository framework in which to consider the determination of equilibrium income, but the analysis is much fuller and more complete if the position or shift in a spending or leakage schedule is related to the quantity, and changes in the quantity, of money. In a significant sense, the quantity of money "lies behind" and largely determines the configuration in the 45-degree diagram; for example, consumption is better considered a function of income *and* of money supply, rather than of income alone. The consumption curve is plotted higher (i.e., consumption is larger at any given income level), the greater the increase in the money stock. And with both approaches at our disposal, we more naturally and readily incorporate income *and* prices, fiscal *and* monetary policy, in our analysis.

7. $.20 \times .25 = .05$—i.e., 5 percent.

9. Of course, there are legal limits to loan expansion. The limits take the form of minimum reserve requirements. But even in the absence of legal limits, there would still be the constraining influence of adverse clearing balances for a given bank that expands much more rapidly than banks in general. If all banks were to expand together, with no substantial problem of adverse clearings, they could expand farther—but they still would be subject to cash drain to the public.

10. (1) The cash is deposited:

Cash		1,000	Demand deposit of depositor	1,000
Required reserves	100			
Excess reserves	900			

(2) A loan equal to initial excess reserves is granted:

Cash		1,000	Demand deposit of depositor	1,000
Required reserves	190		Demand deposit of borrower	900
Excess reserves	810			
Loans		900		

(3) The loan is spent, and all checks go outside the bank:

Cash		1,000	Demand deposit of depositor	1,000
Deposit in Fed		−900		
Required reserves	100			
Excess reserves	0			
Loans		900		

Thus, the loan is equal just to the excess reserves (not ten times those reserves) existing at the time. But, on our assumptions, there is an adverse clearing equal to the loan, which reduces actual reserves by that amount, thereby eliminating excess reserves.

11. Blanks should be filled in as follows:

	(1)	(2)	(3)	(4)	(5)	(6)	(7)
Cash	100	100	100	100	100	100	100
Deposit in FR	200	150	180	260	300	200	200
Loans	500	500	500	500	500	510	500
Government bonds	200	200	200	200	100	200	200
Demand deposits	900	850	880	960	900	910	900
Capital	100	100	100	100	100	100	100
Required reserves	225	212.5	220	240	225	227.5	180
Excess reserves	75	37.5	60	120	175	72.5	120
New loans: single bank	75	37.5	60	120	175	72.5	120
New loans: entire system	300	150	240	480	700	290	480

13. The reserves that were initially "excess" do not "go" any place. But they do shift from the "excess" category to "required" as the banks' demand liabilities increase—and when all of the actual reserves are required, expansion is halted.

14. **a.** 50.

b. $\dfrac{50}{.63(1-.2)+.2} = 71.02.$

c.

Cash	50	Demand deposits	5,026.28
Deposit in FR	955.26	Capital	1,100
Investments	2,050		
Loans	3,071.02		

d. 250.

e. $\dfrac{50}{.2-.1(.2-1)} = 178.57.$

Chapter 37

1. **a.** Excess reserves = actual reserves − required reserves. Lowering the required-reserve ratio reduces required reserves and thereby increases excess reserves; raising the ratio decreases excess reserves. The change in excess reserves divided by the required-reserve proportion gives the possible or necessary change in deposits; the lower (higher) is the reserve ratio, the larger (smaller) is deposit expansion.

b. Changing the ratio changes the volume of excess reserves for each bank. But the expansion of a given bank will still be (approximately) confined to whatever excess reserves are: the expansion coefficient for the single bank is still (approximately) unity.

3. The rediscount rate is the interest rate charged by the Fed on loans to commercial banks. The collateral for those loans may be I.O.U.'s the banks have already discounted in making loans to their own customers. If now these I.O.U.'s are discounted a second time, we can speak of the rate of "rediscount." (But, more commonly, the collateral for loans from the Fed are new I.O.U.'s drawn by banks on themselves.)

5. **a.** Actual reserves = 20; required reserves = 19.4; excess reserves = .6.
   b. 1.4.
   c. 13.333.
   d. 50.
   e. .6.
   f. Actual reserves = 22; required reserves = 19.7; excess reserves = 2.3.
   g. Actual reserves = 22; required reserves = 19.4; excess reserves = 2.6.
   h. Sell .706.
   i. Actual reserves = 20; required reserves = 14; excess reserves = 6.
   j. 15.556.
   k. 4.75.

7. **a.** (i) The Treasury buys bonds from the Fed:

TREASURY		FEDERAL RESERVE	
Deposits in FR	decrease	Bonds	decrease
Bonds in FR	decrease	Treasury deposits	decrease

(ii) The Treasury buys from commercial banks:

TREASURY		FEDERAL RESERVE	
Deposits in FR	decrease	Treasury deposits	decrease
Bonds in commercial banks	decrease	Commercial bank deposits	increase

COMMERCIAL BANKS			
Bonds	decrease	Deposits in FR	increase

(iii) The Treasury buys from the public:

TREASURY		FEDERAL RESERVE	
Deposit in FR	decrease	Treasury deposits	decrease
Bonds held by public	decrease	Commercial bank deposits	increase

COMMERCIAL BANKS			
Deposits in FR	increase	Public deposits	increase

b. In (i), neither the money supply nor excess reserves are affected; in (ii), the money supply is again unchanged, but excess reserves rise; in (iii), both the money supply and excess reserves increase. If expansion is desired, the Treasury should buy bonds from the public; if contraction, or non-expansion, is desired, the Treasury should buy from the Fed.

9. **a.** Government securities owned by the Fed—which amounted to \$33.7 billion out of total Federal Reserve bank credit of \$36.6 in December 1963 (see Board of Governors, *Federal Reserve Bulletin*, January 1964, p. 48).

b. $.7 + 3.0 - 2.5 = 1.2$.

c. $(.7 + 3.0 - 2.5) - (1.5 + .5 - .3) = -.5 = (-1 + .5)$.

d. Federal Reserve bank credit, gold, and currency in circulation.

10. a. Subtract.

b. Subtract.

c. -100.

d. 14,700.

e. Add.

f. 1932–41: gold. 1941–45: Reserve-bank credit.

g. Add.

h. Expansionary.

i. 14,000. Less.

j. Reserve-bank credit.

k. Factor of decrease.

Chapter 38

2. The average price has risen from \$1 to (\$2 + \$.80)/2 = \$1.40. On the other hand, you will rightly contend that we should weight them by their importance—i.e., weighting the price of good *A* by ¼ and that of *B* by ¾. Then the average is $(\frac{1}{4} \times 2.00 + \frac{3}{4} \times .80)/1 = .50 + .60 = 1.10$, indicating a rise of 10 percent. But, on second thought, you will remember the law of demand and take account of the fact that people will now choose to buy more of the relatively cheaper good. Therefore, suppose that, after the price change, the proportion of one's income spent on good *A* falls to .1, while that on good *B* rises to .9. Now new prices weighted by the new proportions give $(.1 \times 2.00) + (.9 \times .80) = .92$. Clearly, we can't tell whether or not there has been an inflation. Some prices have risen and some have fallen, and the average depends upon which prices we consider more important (the weight we assign to each).

5. a. A lease is a real asset to the leaseholder, the lessee; he has a claim to use of the building.

b. The owner of the building, the lessor, has a monetary asset—a claim to a fixed series of money receipts.

c. Life insurance is a monetary asset.

7. Must know what my liabilities are. If I owe more monetary liabilities than I hold as money, I would gain from an inflation.

9. No.

10. They are net monetary creditors. Part of their equity or net wealth, represented by this amount of net monetary assets, does not rise in proportion to the price level.

12. All the evidence is that it does not. Net monetary creditors lose wealth—and

none of the people listed in that assertion are necessarily or even more likely as a class to be net monetary creditors.

16. The wage-lag assertion usually refers to a systematic force and not to random events, so lag should be apparent more than half the time. All evidence refutes the existence of a lag.

18. Acquisition of a greater share of resources and services is a wealth acquisition. Rest of economy is poorer, and this effect is a wealth effect—revealed and made effective by the reduced value of money—not by a decrease in the real wages. Suppose a thief stole half of your money and gave it to the government; your income from wages would be no smaller, although your total income would be smaller simply because you have lost wealth, not because prices at which you buy have increased relative to prices (wages) at which you sell your services.

21. **a.** I would not.

b. Yes, because legal ethics and principles are concerned only with the nominal absolute value of the funds and not with their real value (relative to price-level changes).

c. Our legal system seems to be premised on non-inflation as a fact of life—so that nominal value of investment is all that has to be protected by a prudent trustee of your investments.

23. No. See text discussion on p. 735.

24. Yes. Reason detailed in body of question shows why inflation is the only method of fulfilling that assurance.

27. Directs attention away from source of inflation and will restrain extent of trade—which you may consider undesirable.

31. The desire to revise the pattern of demand is often a reason for resorting to a policy of money creation. The inflation does not therefore cause the revised price pattern; instead, the revised demand brought about by the new money causes the relative price changes. At least this interpretation is consistent with facts about sources of inflations and observed changes in relative price patterns. The statement that inflation in and of itself causes a dispersion of prices because of price rigidities is not entirely false if regard is given to prices that are fixed by law and can be changed only by appeal to a regulatory agency (as with public-utility prices). But assertion usually is made in a more sweeping context, and for that there is no supporting evidence.

Chapter 39

1. All costs of a decision are borne by the decision maker.

3. If you define access to sunlight as an aspect of land ownership, then it is a strengthening of private-property rights.

6. Nonsense. Property rights are the rights of people to do things with goods and services. They are human rights. Usually objection is made to the way a person uses his property, which means that the conflict usually is between one set of human rights and another set of human rights—not between human rights and property rights.

7. Yes. Using a price or exchange system for rationing involves a cost, and this should not be ignored.

10. Yes.

14. e. Nothing is implied about that.

16. The laws and regulations have an impact far beyond any measure of cost of implementing them. For example, restricting use of markets to all but those with licenses can be considered a greater role than building a dam, which may cost more.

19. a. The apartment owner.

b. No, it would not.

c. In some cases damages have been awarded, but this is rarer.

22. *A* is suing for property rights to uncongested streets. Under current law this kind of right seems not to be recognized. Presume we would rule against him. What do you say?

25. Property taxes are usually based on a person's physical wealth, while income taxes are based on his income from personal services as well as income from non-human wealth. The taxes, whatever serves as a basis for the amount to be paid, are taxes levied against people.

Chapter 40

3. Whether or not policy is typically formulated with conscious attention to, and desire to act consistently with, formal theory, it is not necessarily irrational or naïve for policy makers to be concerned with maintaining or promoting exports. Exports in general provide the wherewithal to finance imports. While the gains from trade derive immediately from imports, imports will not be obtainable without exports.

5. The essence of the matter is that a foreign-exchange dealer, or bank, acts as a third party, or intermediary, between the importer and the exporter.

a. The dealer pays off the exporter in one currency and collects payment from the importer in the other currency.

b. The paying of the exporter and the collecting from the importer need not occur simultaneously; i.e., a credit period may elapse before the importer meets his obligation.

6. a. $1X = 2Y$, and $1X = 4Z$; therefore, $2Y = 4Z$ or $1Y = 2Z$.

b. Since Y is overvalued in terms of Z (and Z is undervalued in terms of Y), use X to buy Y, then use Y to buy Z, and finally use Z to buy X.

c. The X demand for Y (i.e., the supply of X in exchange for Y) increases, and the Y demand for X (supply of Y for X) decreases; the Y demand for Z (supply of Y for Z) increases, and the Z demand for Y (supply of Z for Y) decreases; and the Z demand for X (supply of Z for X) increases, and the X demand for Z (supply of X for Z) decreases.

d. The X price of Y, the Y price of Z, and the Z price of X all go up—which is to say that the Y price of X, the Z price of Y, and the X price of Z all go down.

Chapter 41

1. **a.** The price ratios differ: $15/6 = 5/4$.

   b. U.S. has comparative advantage in coats. U.K. exports shoes.

   c. Rate of exchange: price of one currency in terms of another. Limits: \$3 = £1 and \$1.5 = £1.

   d. Terms of trade: international-exchange ratio, the price of exports in terms of imports. Limits: $2.5c = 1s$ and $1.25c = 1s$.

   e. The terms of trade indicate the export cost of imports. The most immediate opportunity cost of imports is the exports with which the imports are purchased.

   f. $1.67c = 1s$.

   g. \$2.4 = £1.

2. **a.** \$1 = fr15 (i.e., \$.067 = fr1) and \$1 = fr16.67 (i.e., \$.06 = fr1); \$1.5 = £1 (i.e., \$.67 = £1) and \$1 = £.75 (i.e., \$1.33 = £1); £.25 = fr1 (i.e., £1 = fr20) and £.067 = fr1 (i.e., £1 = fr15).

   b. £1 = \$1.25; \$1 = fr15 − 16.67; fr1 = £.05 − .067. One possible set is \$1 = fr15.5 and fr1 = £.052.

   c. The U.S. exports shoes. The U.K. exports hats. U.S. residents can now buy hats at \$5 from the U.K. (compared to \$6 at home) and coats at \$7.74 from France (compared to \$8 at home).

3. **a.** In the U.S.:

$$1h = .5c = .333s$$
$$1c = 2h = .667s$$
$$1s = 3h = 1.5c$$

   In the U.K.:

$$1h = .25c = .2s$$
$$1c = 4h = .8s$$
$$1s = 5h = 1.25c$$

   b. The U.K. is cheapest in hats; the U.S. is cheapest in coats; the U.K. is cheapest in shoes with respect to the coat price, but the U.S. is cheapest in shoes with respect to the hat price.

   c. The U.K. exports at least hats, and the U.S. exports at least coats. If \$1.5 = £1, shoes do not enter foreign trade; at higher dollar prices of the pound, the U.S. exports shoes; at lower rates, the U.K. exports shoes.

   d. \$5 = £2 (i.e., \$2.5 = £1), and \$10 = £8 (i.e., \$1.25 = £1).

   e. $2.5h = 1c$; $3.75h = 1s$; $1.5c = 1s$.

   f. \$1.39 = £1.

Chapter 42

2. The same type of information is found in each sort of diagram. (a) The reciprocal-demand diagram presents the quantity demanded (i.e., imported) as a distance along an axis, as does the usual diagram. (b) The reciprocal-demand diagram presents the quantity supplied of the exported good (i.e., expenditure) as a distance along the other axis; in the usual diagram, expenditure (in the form of money rather than of another commodity) is an area of price times quantity. (c) In the reciprocal-demand diagram, price (i.e., terms of trade) is indicated by the slope of a line through the origin; in the usual diagram, price is a distance along an axis.

3. The question relates to elasticity of demand. Where elasticity is arithmetically greater than 1 (i.e., the schedule is elastic), a fall in price yields an increase in total expenditure by the buyer; expenditure reaches a maximum at the price where elasticity is unity; and in a range of demand where elasticity is less than 1 (inelastic), a lower price is accompanied by smaller expenditure. In the reciprocal-demand case, expenditure takes the form of exports. Thus changes in export expenditure, as the terms of trade change, reflect varying elasticity along the reciprocal-demand schedule.

6. Without foreign trade, the "consumption" point is the same as the "production" point, and, with full and efficient employment, that point is some place on the production-possibility curve. With foreign trade, the production point will still be on the production-possibility curve (generally at an axis intercept, reflecting complete production specialization), but the consumption point will be on the terms-of-trade line, which lies beyond the production boundary. Thus (a) the consumption boundary has been extended outward, and (b) the terms of international trade imply a lower price of the imported commodity than would prevail in the absence of foreign trade. But the consumption point, while presumably indicating greater consumption of what is now the *imported* commodity, may well reflect smaller consumption of what is now the *exported* commodity. For as we sweep out alternative terms-of-trade lines, rotating around the production point and showing lower and lower export prices of imports, the quantity of imports demanded will increase; but the quantity of export expenditure also will increase within a range—specifically, the range of elastic demand for imports—and thereby leave less of domestic production of that good for domestic use.

7. Except for such people who believe that they obtain status from importing just because the imports are foreign-made, it would make no sense to buy things abroad at a *money* price higher than that charged domestically. But an article may have a lower *money* price abroad although its *input* price (cost) is higher there than domestically. And if the foreign money price is lower, it is sensible to buy the commodity there regardless of the relative international physical input-output efficiencies.

10. a. 1.5 linen = 1 wheat.
   b. Bechuanaland.
   c. 1 linen = 1 wheat and 1.5 linen = 1 wheat.
   d. Abyssinia obtains (imports) 1.3 linen for each 1 wheat given up (ex-

ported) rather than only 1 linen for 1 wheat without foreign trade; Bechuanaland must give up only 1.3 linen to obtain 1 wheat rather than 1.5 linen.

e. The wage rate must be higher in Bechuanaland, which has an absolute productive superiority in both commodities; the limits of the wage-rate ratio are 1.5/1 and 2.25/1.

f. There would be only *one*-way trade, with both commodities moving from Abyssinia to Bechuanaland and being financed by either gold or I.O.U.'s moving in the opposite direction. The great demand for goods of Abyssinia and the zero demand for goods of Bechuanaland would increase wages in the former country relative to wages in the latter.

11. **a.** 200*X*; 200*Y*.

b. *Y*.

c. 150.

d. 50.

e. 500.

f. 100.

g. 300.

h. Before trade: 400*X* and 200*Y*; after trade: 600*X* and 200*Y*.

Chapter 43

1. There is no "inconsistency" when the chosen phraseology puts emphasis on the direction of movement of the *asset* rather than on the direction of the *financing* of the transaction. This is the convention when the asset in question is merchandise or services. But when the asset is an I.O.U. (e.g., a bond or a bank account), it is customary to emphasize the movement of the financing rather than of the asset itself. Thus, if the U.S. *exports* a bond (i.e., a foreigner buys a U.S. bond), the value of the bond sale is listed on the *credit* side of the U.S. balance of payments—as would be the export of merchandise. But the commonly used phraseology labels this I.O.U. export a "capital import," which does indicate the direction of the international investment—i.e., from the rest of the world to the U.S.

4. **a.** −200.

b. 230.

c. Export.

d. 760.

e. −625.

f. "Unfavorable."

g. Buying.

h. Receiving.

i. Making.

j. Exporting.

k. Outflow.

l. Country III. Large current-account surplus is financed primarily by making unilateral transfers, exporting long-term capital, and importing gold.

m. Country II. Still sizable current-account surplus and debit balances on unilateral transfer and long-term capital accounts, but with a large gold outflow.

n. Country IV would seem to be in the better position. Both countries, I and IV, have import balances on current account. But the current deficit is financed primarily by long-term-capital inflow by country IV and by short-term-capital inflow by country I. Also country I has a greater gold outflow, and long-term capital adds to—rather than helping to finance—country I's deficit.

6. We may refer to the "dollar gap" as the excess of net foreign purchases from the U.S. on current account over net inflow of U.S. long-term capital into the rest of the world. The excess had to be "financed" somehow; the necessity of "financing" is reflected in the inevitable equality of total U.S. credits and debits. One form of "financing" was by U.S. gifts. By giving dollars and goods to the rest of the world, the U.S. made feasible a larger net credit balance on current account; and a larger current surplus with a given long-term-capital outflow constitutes a larger "dollar gap."

Chapter 44

2. Elimination of an import balance does not necessarily require an *absolute* fall in absorption. Rather, it requires a fall in absorption *relative* to income. If income rises, reduction of an import balance is consistent with an *increase* in absorption. Since $Y - A = X - M$, an increase in X relative to M is accompanied by an increase in Y relative to A, but the size of A itself may increase or remain unchanged (if Y increases) as well as decrease.

4. Certainly there are differences between X, on the one hand, and I and G, on the other; indeed, there are differences between I and G. It is hardly a matter of indifference in all respects whether production goes into goods and services bought by foreigners, by private investors, or by government. But X, I, and G have one thing in common: each represents a portion of currently produced, final, domestic output; and spending on these components of output—whether the buyers are foreigners or domestic residents—contributes to money national income.

Similarly, M, S, and T differ in various ways, but each is a disposition of income that does not constitute spending on domestic output. Imports consist largely of (foreign) consumption goods, but imports—like saving and taxes—do not involve consumption of domestic goods.

5. If M is autonomously reduced while Y is held constant, then $C + S + T$ must rise by the amount that M falls. If C remains constant—so that $S + T$ alone offsets the change in M—the income-creation equation is not affected. If monetary and fiscal policies do not succeed in channeling all of the increase into S and T, then C rises—in both equations. In the income-creation equation, a larger C requires a smaller $I + G + X$: If we hold X constant (in order to retain a zero trade balance), then $I + G$ alone must offset C; and a reduction of I and G again calls for monetary and fiscal policies.

6.

C	S	M	G	I	X	$X-M$	Y	T	D
700	140	60	100	150	50	−10	1,000	100	900
700	140	60	100	150	50	−10	1,000	146	854
672.4	126.2	55.4	100	150	50	− 5.4	972.4	143.24	829.16
640	110	50	100	150	50	0	940	140	800

9. Case 1: If a dollar deficit is eliminated, the pound deficit is eliminated.

Case 2: If a dollar deficit is converted into a surplus, the pound deficit becomes a surplus.

Cases 3, 4, 5: If a dollar deficit is reduced but not eliminated, the accompanying pound deficit may decrease, remain constant, or increase.

Case 6: If a dollar deficit is not reduced, the pound deficit rises.

Chapter 45

4. One can hardly quarrel with the contention that saving (in some relevant sense) is a *necessary* condition for development, but it is clear also that saving is not a *sufficient* condition. Saving makes resources available for production and accumulation of "productive" capital. But much investment contributes little to output-increasing capacity and instead finds its way, for example, into private accumulations of gold and deposits in foreign banks and into industrial monuments (e.g., steel mills and airlines) for which there is no comparative advantage.

6. Natural population change is a function of both the birth rate and the death rate. Population does not rise rapidly if the birth rate is only a little greater than the death rate, whether both rates are large (India) or small (U.S.). Typically, in the early stages of economic development, the death rate falls sooner and faster than the birth rate, giving rise to a rapid increase in population.

8. Let U.S. income grow at an annual rate of 1 percent, beginning at a level of \$2,500, and Alpha's income grows at 2 percent, beginning at \$250. At the end of t years, the U.S. income is to be twice as large as Alpha's. That is:

$$\begin{aligned} 2{,}500(1.01)^t &= 2(250)(1.02)^t \\ 5(1.01)^t &= 1.02^t \\ 5 &= (1.02/1.01)^t \\ \log 5 &= t(\log 1.02 - \log 1.01) \\ .69897 &= t(.00860 - .00432) \\ t &= 163 \end{aligned}$$

If the growth rates are 2 and 2.5 percent, $t = 329$; if the rates are 2 and 4 percent, $t = 83$.

INDEX